The Handbook of Clinical Adult Psychology
Third edition

This third edition of *The Handbook of Clinical Adult Psychology* has been thoroughly updated throughout to take account of recent research. As well as updating existing sections, the editors have added sections on problems which are only now showing promise of being amenable to psychological treatment, such as post-traumatic stress disorder, the psychoses and cyclical emotional disorders.

Following the same format as previous editions, the book describes causes, influences and corresponding investigation for each of the main problems that face clinical psychologists, before outlining approaches to evidence-based treatment. Practical guidance is provided on treatments for disorders including depression, sexual dysfunction, psychosis, substance misuse disorders, social phobia and personality disorder.

This comprehensive and thoroughly up-to-date account of current best practice will be invaluable for both trainee and qualified clinical psychologists, psychiatrists, counsellors and social workers.

Stan Lindsay is a senior lecturer at the Institute of Psychiatry, where he has pursued research on anxiety disorders, behavioural medicine and dentistry.

Graham Powell is in independent professional practice in London, specialising in neuropsychology and forensic psychology and in the design and development of psychological services.

Contributors: Brendan Bradley, Niall Broomfield, Tony Canavan, Paul Chadwick, Padmal de Silva, Amanda C. de C. Williams, Catherine Dooley, Colin Espie, Michael Gossop, Nick Grey, Gisli Gudjonsson, Peter Hayward, Colette Hirsch, Jane Hutton, Louise Johns, Elizabeth Kuipers, Nick Lake, Dominic Lam, Tony Lavender, Stan Lindsay, Yvonne Linney, Warren Mansell, Freda McManus, Stephen Morley, Emmanuelle Peters, Graham Powell, Jane Ridley, Julian Walker, Jane Wardle, Edward Watkins, Matt Wild, Barbara Wilson, Bob Woods, Lidia Yágüez.

The Handbook of Clinical Adult Psychology

Third edition

Edited by Stan Lindsay and Graham Powell

Routledge
Taylor & Francis Group

LONDON AND NEW YORK

First edition published 1987
by Gower Publishing Company Ltd

Second edition first published 1994 by Routledge
11 New Fetter Lane, London, EC4P 4EE

Reprinted 1995, 1997, 1999, 2002

Third edition published 2007 by Routledge
27 Church Road, Hove, East Sussex BN3 2FA

Simultaneously published in the USA and Canada
by Routledge
270 Madison Ave, New York, NY 10016

Routledge is an imprint of the Taylor & Francis Group, an Informa business

Typeset in Times by RefineCatch Limited, Bungay, Suffolk
Printed and bound in Great Britain by T J International Ltd, Padstow,
Cornwall
Paperback cover design by Sandra Heath

British Library Cataloguing in Publication Data
A catalogue record for this book is available from the British Library

Library of Congress Cataloging-in-Publication Data
The handbook of clinical adult psychology / edited by Stan Lindsay and
Graham Powell. – 3rd ed.
     p. cm.
   Includes bibliographical references and index.
    ISBN 1-58391-865-5 (hbk) – ISBN 1-58391-866-3 (pbk) 1. Clinical
psychology – Handbooks, manuals, etc. I. Lindsay, S. J. E. II. Powell,
Graham E.
   RC467.2.H355 2007
   616.89 – dc22   2006027414

ISBN: 978-1-58391-865-4 (hbk)
ISBN: 978-1-58391-866-1 (pbk)

Contents

Figures

Tables

Contributors

Brendan Bradley, University of Southampton

Niall Broomfield, University of Glasgow

Tony Canavan (deceased), Institute of Psychiatry, London

Paul Chadwick, University College London

Padmal de Silva, Institute of Psychiatry, London

Amanda C. de C. Williams, University College London

Catherine Dooley, South West London and St. Georges Mental Health NHS Trust

Colin Espie, University of Glasgow

Michael Gossop, Institute of Psychiatry, London

Nick Grey, South London and Maudsley Mental Health NHS Trust

Gisli Gudjonsson, Institute of Psychiatry, London

Peter Hayward, South London and Maudsley Mental Health NHS Trust

Colette Hirsch, Institute of Psychiatry, London

Jane Hutton, South London and Maudsley Mental Health NHS Trust

Louise Johns, Institute of Psychiatry, London

Elizabeth Kuipers, Institute of Psychiatry, London

Nick Lake, Salamons, Canterbury Christ Church University

Dominic Lam, University of Hull

Tony Lavender, Salamons, Canterbury Christ Church University

Stan Lindsay, Institute of Psychiatry, London

Yvonne Linney, Hammersmith and Fulham West London NHS Trust

Warren Mansell, University of Manchester

Freda McManus, Oxford Cognitive Therapy Centre

Stephen Morley, University of Leeds

Emmanuelle Peters, Institute of Psychiatry, London

Graham Powell, Powell Campbell Edelmann, London

Jane Ridley, Richmond Centre, Richmond, Surrey

Julian Walker, Fromeside Clinic Bristol

Jane Wardle, University College London

Edward Watkins, University of Exeter

Matt Wild, University of Glasgow

Barbara Wilson, MRC Cognition and Brain Sciences Unit, Cambridge

Bob Woods, University of Wales, Bangor

Lidia Yágüez, Institute of Psychiatry, London

Foreword

The first edition of this Handbook was so authoritative and comprehensive that it made an extraordinary contribution to clinical psychology. Remarkably for an academic book, the first and second editions were repeatedly reprinted and sold over 7000 copies. Acknowledging the contribution of the Handbook, this introduction provides an opportunity to notice some important changes that have taken place in clinical psychology since the first edition was published.

The idea that clinical psychologists should be scientist practitioners was promoted by academic clinicians in the UK in the 1950s, and was the foundation on which the early training courses were based. A leading role was played by the psychologists in the Department of Psychology at the Institute of Psychiatry of London University, and the training model became known as the 'Maudsley' model because most of the clinical training took place at the Maudsley Hospital, which had been established as a research and training hospital. Nowadays, this idea is so widely accepted that it is seldom discussed, but it was not always so. The Maudsley model, for example, was heavily criticised and some potential students were discouraged from attending such misguided training courses. However, many gifted students turned to the Institute precisely because of its high aspirations and rigorous standards. Most of the contributors to the first and second editions of this Handbook studied at the Institute, or comparable courses at other universities, and I believe that the excellence and value of the book validates their talent and reflects the rigorous standards of their training as scientist practitioners.

It was argued that clinicians – practitioners – should strive to provide scientific justification for their assessment and treatment procedures and, as a result, numerous randomised controlled trials were carried out. In the early days, most of these were designed to test the efficacy of behaviour therapy, the only substantial therapy available at that time. Over the years, the design and standards of the trials improved significantly, and they eventually became the gold standard. Repeated demonstrations that it is possible to carry out rigorous evaluations of treatment and assessment in turn validated the idea that clinical psychology can and should be based on a firmly scientific basis. An important manifestation of this recognition is the growing insistence that psychological treatments should be 'evidence based' and, in the UK and US at least, regulatory and other official bodies rely heavily on the results of randomised controlled trials, and other evidence, in making their recommendations.

Recently, I described to a senior engineer the shift towards the adoption of evidence-based psychological treatments. He listened attentively, thought about it and then said, 'But what did you do before? If it wasn't based on evidence, what was it based on?' It is disarming to recall that it has taken over 40 years to reach the adoption of evidence-based treatment, and troubling that the acceptance of this standard still meets occasional opposition.

Another important change that has taken place since the first edition is the infusion of cognitive concepts and theories into the prevailing behavioural models, and the expansion into cognitive-behaviour therapy is an exciting and productive development, fully covered in the present edition. Thus far, most progress has been made in fashioning and testing cognitive-behavioural treatments for anxiety disorders and eating disorders but, as is evident from this book, extremely promising work on mood disorders and delusional disorders has been completed.

I hope and expect that the present book will be as successful as the earlier editions and congratulate the editors, and the contributors, for the continuing excellence of this Handbook.

Prof. S.J. Rachman
Vancouver 2006

Editors' introduction

Clinicians in publicly funded practice are now strongly encouraged to adopt treatment that has been supported in randomised controlled trials (RCTs). There are bodies, such as the National Institute for Health and Clinical Excellence (NICE), and publications, such as *What Works For Whom?* (Roth and Fonagy, 2005) and *A Guide to Treatments that Work* (Nathan and Gorman, 2002) that are either sponsored by government health departments or have grown in response to recommendations by professional organisations, such as the American Psychological and American Psychiatric Associations. This has probably influenced privately funded practice also; witness the decline in popularity of psychoanalysis and the growth in enthusiasm for cognitive-behaviour therapy (CBT). This Handbook, throughout its three editions, has sought, therefore, to recommend clinical practice based on evidence from published research. However, such evidence is not always available to prescribe remedies neatly for every single person whom we seek to help.

As in previous editions, the book therefore describes aetiology and corresponding investigation for each of a number of problems before outlining approaches to treatment. That is because we believe that careful investigation is the cornerstone of effective intervention. That depends on a careful diagnostic formulation for each person: identification of the problem and its causes together with factors that influence its persistence. We note other approaches to this: notably formulations based on therapeutic models. For the latter, formulations based on CBT are emphasised in this book. However, diagnostic formulations must come first and these have adopted some of the terminology of diagnostic manuals such as the DSM-IV. So, in a diagnostic formulation a client might be described as depressed; causal and maintaining influences such as being unemployed and drinking excessive alcohol might be identified. Then a CBT-based formulation following several interviews might identify other influences, such as a persistent belief in the client that he is unattractive to women or that he needs to achieve a certain standard in his work that proves to be unobtainable. Approaches to other problems may concentrate diagnostic formulations on a symptom such as a delusion and influences therein (diagnostic categories in DSM-IV such as schizophrenia having fallen out of favour with psychologists).

Although CBT-based formulations are widely recommended, there being several books on the subject, research has yet to show that different clinicians agree well with one another in identifying cognitive influences in clients. This can present problems in supervision of trainee clinicians and in peer review of one clinician by another. Who is right and does disagreement matter? Some commentators have suggested that accurate formulations are not important and so agreement is not necessary. Be that as it may, we make the assumption that constructive approaches to clients must depend on the careful collection of data and corresponding diagnostic formulation.

For example, we have seen inexperienced trainee clinicians suggesting to clients with a panic disorder that, as a behavioural experiment, they undertake to walk round a supermarket, where they have been afraid to go, at a quiet time. However, a more careful investigation might have identified excessive alcohol consumption as an influence on anxiety in the client, and thus the diagnostic formulation would have suggested a different priority. On further enquiry, a CBT-based formulation might then have suggested a demonstration of the effects of hyperventilation as a more apt way of challenging the client's belief that she would succumb to breathing difficulties in a panic attack. Thus we seek to avoid a decision resembling the mad Queen's recommendation in Alice in Wonderland, 'Sentence first – verdict afterwards'.

Careful investigation and corresponding formulations are also necessary to decide on priorities for intervention. As the popularity of psychological treatment has increased, so the demand has exceeded the supply of clinicians. Decisions have to be made about who needs treatment and who, with what level of expertise, could provide that.

Clinical psychologists are often asked to provide information that could influence the treatment of clients by others, such as courts of law, neurologists and neurosurgeons. Therefore, there is an additional reason for having separate chapters on investigation and treatment in this book. Neuropsychology is probably the discipline that is most prominently engaged in providing evidence to other professionals in, for example, assessing the level of impairment in a client in order to determine the amount of compensation to be awarded for a head injury. However, we must guard against neuropsychology's being seen as a discipline apart from others in clinical psychology. For example, neuropsychology might help to provide quantitative assessments of the cognitive impairment suffered by psychotic clients against which improvement with treatment could be assessed. At the same time, however, we should guard against the long out-dated practice of routine neuropsychological testing, which fails the test: would anything different be done for the client if neuropsychological testing was to provide data?

At all times we have to be prepared for the unexpected and the following striking illustration demonstrates a useful collaboration between neuropsychology and other disciplines. A young man with a long history of difficulty at work, including poor time-keeping, was referred for treatment of depression. As a way of testing the hypothesis that he was unable to concentrate or enjoy anything, he agreed to develop his interest in learning Spanish. This led to his enrolling in Spanish classes, which required him to attend a college on three days a week. He became less depressed. However, shortly afterwards, a routine inspection of his rented accommodation discovered that a gas fire was leaking carbon monoxide and had been doing so since its installation 20 years previously. The client had lived there with his mother and brother throughout that time. He had complained of memory problems. Psychometric testing confirmed that he had probably undergone a cognitive deterioration, including in the capacity for learning new material. This suggested that his poor performance at work and his difficulty in rising in the morning for work was probably the result of carbon monoxide poisoning. The improvement in his depression might have occurred in part because his being away from home more frequently reduced his exposure to carbon monoxide. This evidence thus contributed to his claim for compensation from his landlord.

We hope that this illustrates the importance of clinical investigation as a basis for intervention and points to the need for vigilance in watching for the unexpected. We trust that the chapters of this book, which have been written by international experts in research and the treatment of psychological problems, will help clinicians to be prepared for most eventualities.

References

Nathan, P. E. and Gorman, J. M. (eds) (2002) *Treatments That Work* (2nd edition). New York: Oxford University Press.

Roth, A. and Fonagy, P. (2005) *What Works for Whom? A Critical Review of Psychotherapy Research*. New York: Guilford Press.

Chapter 1

Practical issues of investigation in clinical psychology

Stan Lindsay and Graham Powell

INTRODUCTION

Clinical psychologists who consider clients for treatment will always have to conduct a preliminary investigation. As psychologists also provide opinions to others, such as law courts and neurologists, this chapter reviews practical issues in psychological investigation to promote the effective delivery of all sources of help to clients. Accordingly, it is recognised that the clinician frequently has to answer the question: 'What treatment, by whom, is most effective for this individual with the specific problem, under which set of circumstances and how does it come about' (Paul, 1969)?

For its first Axis, the *Diagnostic and Statistical Manual of Mental Disorders IV – Text Revision* (DSM-IV-TR; American Psychiatric Association (APA), 2000) gives rules for the classification of patients into categories such as major depression. Axis 2 presents disorders of personality and development; Axis 3 is physical illness. Two other axes are identified to describe, 4, 'the severity of psychosocial stressors' consisting of environmental influences and life crises, and 5, 'global assessment of functioning'. The latter takes into account the client's occupational functioning, the use of leisure time and social relationships as well as severity of symptoms. Formal diagnosis according to DSM-IV involves interviews of proven reliability for Axis-1 disorders: the Diagnostic Interview Schedule (DIS; Robins and Helzer, 2000) and the Structured Clinical Interview (SCID; Spitzer et al., 1996). It must be recognised that the validity of Axis-1 concepts in DSM-IV has been strenuously disputed, especially in their application to psychological treatment (Bentall, 2003) However, such formal diagnosis by DSM-IV and other codices is not often necessary in clinical practice, except for the requirements of law courts and other medical legal practice.

THE FIRST INTERVIEW

Comprehensive guidelines are available (e.g. Goldberg and Murray, 2002) but what follows summarises what should be sought (Table 1.1). Some information may be of little or no relevance to some clients and so the clinician has to be selective. Exhaustive, over-inclusive interviewing may antagonise clients, especially when they are in considerable distress. To avoid repetitive and redundant questioning, and for other reasons of efficiency, clinicians should record their observations as they are made. With some very distressed clients, however, the first interview might have to be spent in getting to know them with very little recording.

Table 1.1 Summary of information to be sought

- Reason for referral
- Client's own description of difficulties
- Why help sought; why now?
- Chronological history of difficulties.
- Client's situation: marital, living where and with whom?
- Client's opinion of the impairments produced by the difficulties in occupation, recreation, relationships and mood
- Client's biological functioning as affected by difficulties (eating, sleeping, sexual activity, maintenance of body weight)
- How has the client coped with the difficulties; how have others coped with these; what professional treatment received?
- Prevailing mood; the mood at its worst
- Abnormal sensory experiences as hallucinations (e.g. voices from external sources not visible)
- Abnormal experiences of the environment, body or self, e.g. feelings of being controlled by outside agency or believing television broadcasts are about him or her as ideas of references
- The client's beliefs as delusions or as normal: how abnormal in the culture, how easily challenged, how rational is the supporting argument?
- Degree of intrusiveness and distress caused by those beliefs
- Client's appearance and behaviour, including manner of speaking, during interview
- Client's orientation in time and place and memory for recent information
- Client's attitudes to difficulties (e.g. blaming others or condemning self)
- Developmental, educational and occupational, sexual and marital history
- History of serious medical illnesses
- Current intake of drugs, alcohol, etc.
- Close relatives and partner: their experience of psychological problems
- *Provisional formulation*: what is the most disturbing difficulty for the client; what were the causes and what maintains this difficulty; what effects does the difficulty have (or would have if it remained untreated); do those effects warrant intervention; what further data by more interviewing, tests, record-keeping or observations are necessary to test these hypotheses; what intervention would be necessary?

For some it will be necessary to seek information from others who know the difficulties of the client well: parents, partner, social workers, occupational therapists and care staff. This will be essential for clients with some learning difficulties and for disturbed elderly or psychotic clients who may be unable to communicate reliably. In addition, people in the client's environment may influence the clients' problems, influence or be affected by them and may have to participate in therapy. The services of an interpreter would be advisable for those whose first language is not the same as the clinician. Wherever possible, the client's full approval should be obtained before the clinician consults others.

In most cases, *the reason for the referral* will have been given in an introductory note from the referring agent or will have been communicated at a clinical team meeting. Nevertheless, it will be highly desirable to hear clients describe the main difficulties in their own words, if only to encourage co-operation in obtaining further information and in implementing treatment.

Most frequently, it will be valuable first to enquire why help has been sought and how long the main complaint has persisted. It will often be important at this point, if possible, to reassure the client, or whoever is most concerned, that the complaint is not exceptional or outrageous in the clinician's experience and that it should be possible to offer some help. The clinician should explain that, to understand the client's difficulties it will be necessary to obtain as much information about the problem as possible.

A brief chronological history of the complaint follows. When did the problem first occur and how did the client and others react to it? What was the client's situation at its outset and at times during its subsequent development – occupation, marital status, living with parents, at school? What attempts have been made to treat the problem or help the client in other ways?

The impairments that have been produced by the client's difficulties: how has the client's relationships with his or her family, work colleagues or other patients changed with the problem? How have performance and interest at work or in recreation changed? How has the client's biological functioning altered – in sleeping, sexual activity, eating and maintenance of body weight? Have there been any difficulties in coping with responsibilities, such as managing household budgets and in taking decisions?

For many clients, the concept of a change or onset of the problem may not be appropriate or may not be easy to pinpoint. Many problems, such as difficulties in meeting and speaking to other people, may have been present to some extent throughout the client's life and have only recently become of critical concern. This can arise when such a client applies for a job for the first time.

How have the client and others coped with the problem: drinking alcohol to excess, smoking heavily, taking tranquillisers, withdrawing to a bedroom for long periods, having friends and relatives take on the client's tasks, seeking reassurance? Safety behaviours such as practising relaxation to try and curtail panic attacks may fall into this category.

The clinician should also investigate a number of variables that may not be the substance of the main referred complaint. What is the client's *prevailing mood* or what emotional state does the client experience at certain times and circumstances: fear, anxiety, anger, frustration, sadness, irritation?

Sometimes the client will have difficulty in reporting any such mood. Some clients may not experience strong emotions even when these would be expected (a condition known as flatness of affect). Sudden mood swings may also occur. The clinician will have to rely on the client or other informants reporting these changes because, for example, clients in a panic attack may not be visibly anxious during the interview.

The content of the client's reported thoughts will also be of interest – troublesome intrusive thoughts or preoccupations, especially as these relate to changes in emotion; plans and ambitions, realistic or otherwise. What does the client think will happen at times when he or she is in greatest distress?

Abnormal experiences in all sensory modalities should be noted: the external environment (such as voices as hallucinations from no visible source, or feelings of unreality or *dèja vu*), in the body (such as feelings of numbness or tingling sensations in extremities in anxiety disorders) or in the self (such as depersonalisation or awareness of disturbances in thinking).

The client's reported beliefs and interpretations of events will often be of significance. Are there abnormal beliefs as delusions (Leeser and Donohue, 1999) about the environment, including broadcast media and the behaviour and attitudes of other people? How easily can these be challenged? Are they abnormal even in the client's community or culture? Does the client have unrealistic beliefs about his or her physical attributes or functioning? Facial appearance or body size may be of abnormal concern. Inappropriate persistent beliefs about the client's worth are frequently held to be unrealistic sources of distress. Clients may believe that certain experiences, such as intrusive thoughts, mean that they are going insane or that such experiences are unique to them. Do the clients believe that they have no control over events? What does the client think about the difficulties that have been presented?

The client's appearance and behaviour during the interview should also be recorded – characteristic unusual movements and posture; abnormalities of speech, such as being inaudible or very loud, speaking fast or slowly, requiring prompting or being difficult to interrupt, answering questions directly or as in thought disorder, sudden changes in topic, using made-up words or using the same words or phrases repeatedly. Is the client attending to the interviewer or to something else in the environment that is either evident or not apparent to the interviewer?

The client's attitude to his or her difficulties could be instructive: whether they are considered trivial or life-threatening, common-place or unusual; whether the client is resigned to them as hopeless; what hypotheses the client has formulated for them.

Cognitive functioning: is the client working, thinking and concentrating as efficiently as would be expected from his or her level of education or employment? Does the client or informant believe that the client has difficulty in remembering information? Can the client report his or her name, age, other biographical information, present orientation in time and place, together with a brief account of current news events?

Background information such as the client's occupations, illnesses and especially psychiatric history should be noted. In particular, are there precedents for the client's own difficulties in other family members or close peers? What family crises have occurred, such as deaths, sudden changes in income, marital difficulties in the parents? How did these affect the client?

Early developmental history should be investigated, especially if the client is still young. What sort of school did the client go to? Did the client go to school at the normal age and how did he or she cope with schooling? Behavioural difficulties at school will be of interest in young adults. Were there any conduct problems, such as truancy or school refusal, stealing, fighting, difficulty in making friends? To understand the impairment produced by current complaints, it will often be essential to determine the client's academic attainments at school and after. Difficulties in attaining goals at school or matching achievements with other children may have contributed to the occurrence of behavioural and emotional problems. How well can the client read?

The client's experience of adolescence may often indicate the onset of social and sexual difficulties. Hence that stage in development may be investigated for problems in relating to other adolescents: how did the client cope with the standards set by peers for sexual and social behaviour? Were there any notable periods of unhappiness, extreme and prolonged withdrawal?

Occupational and educational history: what did the client attain at school and after? Have the client's jobs matched the educational history? Has the client had long periods out of work, frequent changes of occupation or been continually dissatisfied with work? Again occupational history, when compared with current occupational data, may indicate the client's current level of difficulty. Occupational difficulties may contribute to, or be the product of, behavioural and other problems of interest to the clinician.

Sexual history will be of interest certainly where marital, sexual or other relationship problems have been pinpointed.

Intimate relationships: how have these related to the development of the main difficulties? For example, how has the client's partner coped with the client? Have there been frequent quarrels, threats of, or actual, separation? Are there any children? How are they? Do they have any notable difficulties at home or in school?

What previous psychiatric, psychological or medical help has been given to the client? What medication, if any, is the client taking? The success or failure of any such interventions, especially as the client sees them, should be ascertained because that will probably influence the client's expectations about forthcoming treatment.

Medical history will be of more direct concern where the client complains of and has been referred for physical symptoms, such as headaches or dizzy spells. These should be the subject of a physical examination, if this has not already been carried out. There might also be physical symptoms, which may be related to the behaviour that is of direct concern to the clinician but which may not themselves be target variables in treatment. The symptoms of drug and alcohol withdrawal are in this category, as are the signs of more permanent neurological damage with drug and alcohol addiction. It should be made clear to the client at the outset that the responsibility for any medical condition or treatment remains with the the client's own physician.

RISK OF HARM TO SELF AND OTHERS

The ability to assess and cater for the danger that clients present to themselves and others is an essential characteristic of a responsible clinical service and must be an important focus at the first interview. The risk of suicide and less severe self harm (Clark and Fawcett, 1992) is greatest in people who show signs of severe mental illness, excessive use of alcohol, have planned for and have the means for self harm, are isolated and lack social support, and who have had previous occurrences of self harm. The absence of any suicide thoughts can be misleading because more than half of suicide victims have expressed no such thoughts hitherto. The presence of a mental illness must be addressed by diagnosis and should not be assumed only by the presence of low mood. The Beck Hopelessness Scale has cut-off points for detecting suicide risk (Beck et al., 1974).

Danger to others (Norko and Baranoski, 2005) is probably greatest in those who abuse alcohol and other drugs, who are young, male and of low socio-economic status. Mental illness has a lesser influence and a history of violence is a less significant predictor than commonly supposed (Farrington, 2001). Among those who have a severe mental illness, personality disorders and substance abuse increase the risk of violence (Monahan, 2001). Actuarial methods such as the Hare Psychopathy Checklist probably have a greater part to play in the prediction of causing harm to others than to oneself (Norko and Baranoski, 2005).

THE STATISTICAL REQUIREMENTS OF PSYCHOLOGICAL INVESTIGATION

To be worth using, questionnaire scales, tests and interviews should have a number of statistical properties as follows (Kaplan and Sacuzzo, 2005).

They should thus minimise the biases that can arise from gender and socio-cultural differences between client and clinician and from expectations about clients such as may be generated by their having a history of mental illness (Garb, 1998).

Reliability

When a client produces a score on an inventory, test or rating scale, that score is subject to sampling error. The 'true' score will lie somewhere within a certain range of the obtained score determined by the *standard error of the obtained score*, which is equal to $\sigma_t \sqrt{1 - r_{tt}}$, where σ_t is the standard deviation of the distribution of obtained scores and r_{tt} is the reliability coefficient for the scale. If it were possible to sample the subject's score repeatedly, 95% of those scores would lie within the range ± two standard errors of the obtained score: the 95% level of confidence. Hence one measure of a scale's capacity for giving true scores with minimum error is the scale's *internal consistency reliability* measured, for example, by Cronbach's alpha statistic. A method that can be applied to variables for which temporal stability is an important property is the *test–retest reliability*, which is estimated by the correlation between scores obtained on the same scale completed on different occasions.

Such correlation analyses are only estimates of reliability. The standard error of, for example, a product-moment correlation coefficient decreases with the size of the obtained correlation and the number of observations on which that correlation is based.

Validity

Does the procedure detect and measure the variable that it purports to identify? First, does it represent all the different aspects that are held to describe the variable of interest, that is, does the measurement procedure have acceptable *content validity*?

Note: it will often be necessary to use measures in several different modalities to ensure content validity. Questionnaire measures are often not sufficient. Daily records and observations of behaviour and emotions are often necessary in addition.

Does the measure have high *convergent validity*? That is, does it correlate highly with another variable, a test or questionnaire scale, which is closely related to the variable of interest? The correlation statistic must, however, be able to take account of systematic discrepancies between variables. For example, the time to stage 2 of an EEG sleep record is often positively correlated with the time to fall asleep reported by subjects themselves, the longer the time to sleep onset according to an EEG, the greater is the delay estimated by the subjects. Nevertheless, the latter is often longer than that measured by the EEG: a systematic discrepancy.

Correlations with other measures can present problems. For example, measures of social anxiety can be spuriously correlated with measures of depression, which can inhibit social activity; measures of depression can be inflated in physical illness because both can be characterised by fatigue. The Social Phobia and Anxiety Inventory (Beidel et al., 1993) and the Hospital Anxiety and Depression Scale (Zigmond and Snaith, 1983) seek to avoid these confusions.

Does the scale have *construct validity* in measuring a variable that might not be evident on inspection but which is identified by a statistical procedure such as factor analysis?

Sometimes there can be conflict in ensuring the validity and reliability of a measure. For example, to increase the content validity of a scale it may be necessary also to increase the number of different attributes sampled, thus decreasing the internal consistency of the test. The result may have to be a compromise between the content validity and the measurement reliability, especially if attempts to ensure that both are high result in a long and clumsy investigative procedure.

It should also be possible to determine the sensitivity of a given measure for detecting change reliably with treatment, evidence of *discriminant capacity*. However, even for scales designed to measure change, this information is usually not readily available.

COPYRIGHT OF TESTS AND QUESTIONNAIRES

The authors of tests and questionnaires hold the copyright of their works (Jacob et al., 2003). Often this right is transferred to the publishers of a test or the publishers of the journal where the work is described. Therefore, clinicians should not copy tests and questionnaires without the copyright-holder's permission. Most of the tests and questionnaires described in this book have their own websites, which give information about the copyright holders. Comprehensive libraries of scales can be bought from the American Psychiatric Association (APA; Rush et al., 2000) and NFER-Nelson, who have published *A Mental Health Portfolio* (Milne, 1992) and the *Measures in Health Psychology Portfolio* (Wright et al., 1997). Purchase of these entitles clinicians to use the scales freely without seeking permission for use of each scale.

PSYCHOMETRIC SCREENING

Inventories completed by clients can limit the workload of the clinician in detecting significant distress and in measuring progress in treatment. The following, which are currently in print, are the most widely used and are well supported by tests of reliability and validity. Other scales described in the section 'Comprehensive measures' can also be used.

The General Health Questionnaire

The General Health Questionnaire (GHQ; Goldberg and Williams, 1988) can be 60, 30, 28 or 12 items long. It screens for the presence of psychiatric distress, determined by cut-off scores, which is verified by a psychiatric interview. The GHQ is probably best designed to detect distress of recent onset, all the questions being prefaced by the phrase 'Have you recently . . .?' Patients with chronic serious difficulties, such as generalised anxiety, can fail to acknowledge symptoms with the answer, 'No, I have always felt like this'. Other questionnaires, such as the BSI (see below), are more suitable for detecting prolonged difficulties.

The Symptom Checklist-90-Revised (SCL-90-R)

The Brief Symptom Inventory has 50 questions (BSI; Derogatis and Melisaratos, 1983) each with five multiple choice answers, and is designed to measure nine constructs of psychopathology as determined by factor analyses: somatisation (such as 'trouble in getting your breath') obsessive-compulsive difficulties, interpersonal sensitivity (such as 'feeling inferior to others'), depression, anxiety, anger-hostility, phobic anxiety, paranoid ideation and psychoticism (such as 'having thoughts that are not your own'). The original reference provides normative data for clinical and normal samples. Unfortunately, only four of the nine dimensions identified in the original reference for a longer version have been reproduced in later independent research (Cyr et al., 1988). Moreover, there have been no satisfactory attempts to determine convergent validity based on a comparison with, for example, DSM-IV, and so the total score for the questionnaire – the Global Severity Index – is probably the most valid measure. It has a cut-off score to indicate when clients would be in need of more detailed enquiry. Norms include those for a large sample of the adult population in the United Kingdom (Francis et al., 1990). Unfortunately, the response rate in that survey was so poor that the sample could not be said to be representative of the population.

PROBLEM FORMULATION

Diagnostic formulation

The information gathered in the first interview is used to determine hypotheses about causes and maintaining influences: the diagnostic formulation of the client's difficulties (see Table 1.1). Consider, for example, a client who is depressed, being frequently in tears and with thoughts of ending her life. She complains of panic attacks and uses alcohol to excess. She also has to live in unsatisfactory housing. What are the causal relationships among these behaviours and circumstances? For example, are the panic attacks the cause or effect of her alcohol consumption? Does her depression stem from her problems in accommodation or does depression make it difficult for her to remedy the situation? Clarification is often necessary before intervention can proceed. The following two additional approaches can be applied to enable cognitive and behaviour therapy to be conducted.

Functional analysis

This approach (Sturmey, 1996) is now most often applied to observable behaviour, especially in children and adults with learning difficulties, but it can provide a useful approach to behaviour under environmental control in, for example, wards for acutely ill clients. By functional analysis the clinician seeks to identify the discriminative stimuli and reinforcements that are associated with the occurrence of the behaviour of clinical interest. The setting conditions are also identified. For this, the occurrence of the chosen behaviour is recorded on charts as it is observed, together with the antecedent stimuli and the consequences of that behaviour (Haynes and O'Brien, 1990), over a period of, say, a week. The preceding stimuli may include what other people were doing or the arrival of certain people. The consequences may include a material object given to or acquired by the client or a social event, such as a cigarette, praise or laughter by others. For example, a client who suffers from a chronic pain disorder, such as low back pain, may, on seeing what she perceives as anger in her husband, complain that she is in discomfort. As a result, the husband looks less irritated, offers to make his wife a cup of tea or is solicitous in other ways. Behaviour analysis of this kind has also drawn attention to the influence of setting events, prolonged ongoing activity or situations. For example, the foregoing sequence might occur only when no other people were present.

Such analysis depends on the adequate collection of data. Clinicians can be tempted into making functional analyses based on memory of events, which can be prone to bias and spurious correlation (Garb, 1998). In addition, relationships can be perceived among variables but will turn out to be spurious on careful examination of data carefully collected. It is also unwise to assume that certain events, such as praise, act as reinforcement for all clients. Praise may be encouraging for some but belittling and patronising for others. Unfortunately, little work has been done to test the reliability and validity of decision-making in functional analysis (Haynes and O'Brien, 1990; Garb, 1998).

Formulations for cognitive behaviour therapy

Cognitive behaviour therapy (CBT) reduces distress in clients by helping them to challenge the beliefs that maintain that distress. For example, successfully challenging the belief that panic attacks could have fatal consequences can help to reduce their frequency, severity and the distress which they cause.

A valid formulation for a client's difficulties (e.g. Needleman, 2003) is assumed to be necessary for effective CBT (Bruch and Bond, 1998; Morrison et al., 2004; Kuyken et al., 2005). Nevertheless, in spite of the evidence that CBT has been shown to be effective for many problems, Kuyken et al. (2005) have shown that over half of the CBT formulations constructed by 115 qualified practitioners for depictions of clients were rated as 'poor' or 'very poor', although the quality of formulations was 'good enough' in 63% of the practitioners who were accredited by the British Association of Cognitive and Behavioural Psychotherapy. The formulations had to include the identification of, and causal relationships among, the clients' early experiences, beliefs, compensatory strategies, automatic thoughts and emotions.

Percentage agreement among the clinicians about each aspect of the formulations varied considerably. For example, agreement about core beliefs varied from 73% to 37%; agreement about conditional assumptions ranged from 62% to 11%. Persons and Bertagnolli (1999) have shown similar low levels of agreement among clinicians making formulations for depictions of people with depression.

Nevertheless, Wilson (1997) has noted that, in outcome studies, standard treatment packages used for all clients have been no less beneficial than treatments designed according to formulations unique to each client. However, such outcome studies have excluded clients who have additional problems, such as excessive use of alcohol, when the target problem has been a panic disorder. Furthermore, people with a minimal education are also unlikely to be recruited for outcome studies (see Chapters 13 and 14).

Therefore, despite the low reliability of problem formulation, it will be necessary to adapt treatment according to some formulation of clients' difficulties. As examples, it may not be practicable to use copious written records and instruction manuals for clients who have difficulties in reading; it may be desirable to reduce alcohol dependence at the outset if that has a causal influence on a client's panic attacks.

QUALITY OF LIFE

It has been evident that clients with a mental illness are often unable to sustain close personal relationships, pursue a higher education or hold down paid employment. As a result, they lack many material benefits and they may be less happy about their quality of life than people who are in normal health. In recent years, therefore, measures of the quality of life have been used to assess not only distress and corresponding behaviour but also the impact of mental illness and its treatment. However, there is a plethora of meanings and lack of agreement about the content validity of measures for quality of life (Holloway and Carson, 2002).

Nevertheless, decisions about whether to treat a disorder in clients is often based, in part, on formulations in which the quality of life is important. For example, there are people who endure psychotic experiences but who are so little impaired in their daily lives that they are not deemed in need of treatment (Bak et al., 2005). The client whose handicap consists, because of a panic disorder, in being unable to travel abroad on holiday might not be seen with the same urgency as a client who is unable to travel to work and whose income and marriage may consequently be in trouble.

A few scales purport to measure some aspects of the quality of life (*sic*), such as the Quality of Life Index for Mental Health (Becker et al., 1993). However, to attain high content validity, several measures probably need to be used. This chapter reviews comprehensive measures of distress, behaviour, disability and the concept of clinical significance (Gladis et al., 1999; Kazdin, 1999), which could be subsumed by the title 'quality of life related to mental health'.

COMPREHENSIVE MEASURES

HONOS: a clinician-rated instrument

The Health of the Nation Outcome Scales (HONOS; Wing et al., 1998) has 12 items, each rated on a five-point scale by the clinician; the items cover aggression, self-harm, drug and alcohol abuse, cognitive problems, physical illness and disability, hallucinations and delusions, depression, other symptoms, relationships, activities of daily living, residential environment and daytime activities. The five-point rating scales range from 0: 'no problems' to 4: 'severe to very severe problem'. All but the last item have shown good interobserver agreement. However, clinicians from different disciplines have given different ratings, social workers giving less favourable scores than psychiatrists (Wing et al., 1998).

In a special issue of the *British Journal of Psychiatry* devoted to HONOS, Bebbington et al. (1999) found that clinicians gave only 'minor' or 'mild' ratings to describe severely ill patients on most items: an underestimate. This suggests that the rating scales are not sufficiently well anchored to give valid absolute assessment to help determine what action, such as involuntary detention, should be taken for clients. Does HONOS give valid relative judgements to determine if clients have improved with treatment? Change scores in the HONOS from before to after treatment were most often not significantly correlated with change scores on well-established criterion scales such as the Social Behaviour Schedule when the assessment was done by a key worker. Bebbington et al. (1999) concluded that key workers would have to be highly trained in the use of HONOS to make valid assessments.

The CORE-OM: a client-rated instrument

Barkham et al. (2001) have developed a questionnaire, Clinical Outcomes in Routine Evaluation (CORE-OM) consisting of 34 items, each rated on a five-point scale from 'not at all' to 'most of the time'. It provides a total score and four subscale scores, subjective well-being, problems or symptoms, functioning and risk. The CORE is probably unique among comprehensive scales in including items on risk.

However, the CORE risk scale includes items describing threat to oneself such as, 'I have thought it would be better if I were dead' as well as danger to others, for example, 'I have been physically violent to others'. The authors intended that the risk scale should be used separately from the remaining items, which provide their own total. There are four items describing risk of self harm but only two for risk to others, so that the scale is not equally sensitive to these two problems. The validity of the total risk scale remains unclear, therefore. Additional means of risk assessment will be necessary in practice because risk to self and others often require very different treatments.

Cut-off scores are provided for each of the scales but these and other psychometric data have been based on samples, the selection of which is not clearly described in the source articles (Evans et al., 2002). The CORE may therefore be regarded best as under development.

Global Assessment of Functioning: a clinician-rated instrument

The Global Assessment of Functioning Scale (GAF; APA, 2000) is designed to be administered by clinicians to give ratings based on accounts of symptoms and social and occupational functioning. Ratings from 0 to 100 are made with descriptors for ten intervals on the scale. These range from 9 'Superior functioning in a wide range of activities, life's problems never seem to get out of hand . . .' to 'persistent danger of severely hurting self or other or persistent inability to maintain minimal personal hygiene or. . . .' The scale thus provides a total score for functioning.

Jones et al. (1995) and Startup et al. (2002) recorded moderate to high interobserver reliability correlations for total scores at different stages of severe mental illness in clients. However, it is not clear if observers would agree about absolute ratings. Some observers may give higher ratings than others.

The Sickness Impact Profile: a clinician-rated instrument

The Sickness Impact Profile (SIP; Bergner et al., 1981) assesses the disability produced by illness. It has 190 questions and was developed especially to measure physical disability, such as occurs with low back pain, and includes items about the ability to dress oneself. It includes items about social functioning. A short form is available (Roland and Morris, 1983).

Work and Social Adjustment Scale: a client-rated instrument

Mundt et al. (2002) and Mataix-Cols et al. (2005) have produced a questionnaire of five items, each rated by the client on a nine-point scale, to describe impairment of work, leisure, home management and relationships. The scale has shown high internal consistency and a single construct, disability, according to factor analysis in a sample of phobic patients.

SOCIAL SUPPORT

The Significant Others Scale

Lack of social support is frequently believed to contribute to the seeking of professional help by people in distress. The presence of effective support from friends and relatives may help people to recover from, or cope with, serious distress without professional help.

The Significant Others Scale (SOS; Power et al., 1988; reproduced by Milne, 1992) is designed to measure emotional and practical support, both actual and ideal. The latter is the amount of which the client 'thinks things should be, if . . . things worked out exactly as you hoped . . .'. The clients are asked to provide the names of up to six people known to them and are asked to rate on a seven-point scale ('never' to 'always') how often they can (actual support) or should (ideal support) rely on the support of each of those people in a number of activities. For example, clients are asked to describe how often they receive support from X to 'lean on and turn to in times of difficulty'.

Although the SOS has been widely used, more data are needed to testify to its validity and reliability. It is difficult, moreover, to predict what level of social support would be desirable. The authors suggest that the discrepancy between ideal and actual support should be minimal. Indeed, experiencing much less support than their ideal would be a source of distress for some clients. However, some clients could argue that, the less support they should have, the more satisfactory is their position. Indeed, elderly people appear to tend to this view (Lam and Power, 1991). Often, however, it will be necessary to decide if that support is helpful or is likely to continue as long as the client's difficulties persist. Many patients with chronic difficulties lose or exhaust the support upon which they rely.

COGNITIVE FUNCTIONING

The most well-established global test of cognitive functioning, notably the Wechsler Adult Intelligence Scales and related tests, was designed to make predictions about performance in education (Deary, 2005) and about other aspects of cognitive functioning, such as memory. However, clinical psychologists are even now sometimes asked to provide opinions about clients in order to make predictions about, say, capacity for independent living, or to shed some light on clients who are difficult to understand. Such predictions are probably crude and prone to error based on idiosyncratic formulations by the clinicians (Garb, 1998).

The Mini-Mental State Examination

The Mini-Mental State Examination (MMSE; Folstien et al., 1975; reproduced by Goldberg and Murray, 2002) is composed of 11 questions that the clinician, with a little training, can ask the client. Items include the request to the client to repeat, 'No ifs, and or buts'. It has high reliability according to test–retest and integrated measures. The MMSE has been translated into many language as a screening instrument to detect cognitive impairment, such as dementia, although it assesses only current cognitive functioning not extent of deterioration. It probably puts clients with minimal education or a low socio-economic status at a disadvantage, giving a higher false-positive detection rate for dementia in these groups (Malloy et al., 1997).

The Wechsler Adult Intelligence Scales and related measurers

The Wechsler Adult Intelligence Scales, now in its third edition (WAIS-III; Wechsler, 1997a, 1999) provides verbal, performance and full-scale intelligence quotients (IQs). These are presented as estimates within 90% and 95% statistical confidence limits. The whole test can take more than 2 hours to administer and so a short version, the Wechsler Adult Scale of Intelligence (WASI) is available.

The Wechsler Test of Adult Reading (WTAR; Wechsler, 2001) is designed to estimate pre-morbid IQs based on the client's capacity to read accurately a list of 20 words. More accurate estimates are provided by including the level of the client's educational attainment. Tables provide pre-morbid estimates of the client's performance on the Wechsler Memory Scales (Wechsler, 1997b).

Raven's Progressive Matrices

This test (Raven, 1998), having gone through three editions, presents a series of geometric figures that the client has to complete by choosing from a number of alternatives. The test is designed to measure eductive ability and, because no linguistic skills are required, is minimally sensitive to linguistic or cultural bias (Raven, 2000). It is sold with a vocabulary scale to assess verbal ability.

AD HOC SCALES

Sometimes it will be necessary to devise a scale to measure change in a variable that has been identified for a given client as of central importance and for which no suitable scale is available for recording. A single symptom, such as a certain pain, may be reported by the client. The occurrence of behaviour, such as crying, can be observed by the client's family, the clinician and others. Such behaviour can vary in frequency, intensity and duration. The behaviour should be defined as specifically as possible – 'crying' rather than 'appearing unhappy', or 'striking another patient' rather than 'being aggressive'. The occurrence of these events can then be recorded against a timescale on a checklist to determine their frequency over a given period.

The intensity of symptoms and other complex variables, however, may require the construction of a rating scale. See, for example, the items of the GAF and the WSAS described above. The number of descriptors for the anchor points can be two or more but it is probably not necessary to use more than five or six anchoring points for reliable and discriminating measurement (McKelvie, 1980).

CLINICAL SIGNIFICANCE: IMPROVEMENT OR DETERIORATION

This is the final consideration that can be subsumed by 'quality of life' to determine whether treatment should be implemented or completed. 'Clinical significance' has been reserved for statistical criteria applied to measures reflecting current state or change, improvement or deterioration in cognitive functioning (Massen, 2001). Jacobson and Truax (1991) have had the greatest influence, having presented two approaches as follows.

Present status

This can describe the position of a client before and after treatment on a measure such as the BSI. A client is deemed to be in need of no further intervention if his or her score (illustrated in Figure 39.4, p. 838):

- is better by at least two standard deviations than the mean of normative data for untreated psychiatric patients, *or*
- falls within two standard deviations of the mean of normal subjects, *or*
- is closer to the mean of normal subjects than the mean of psychiatric patients.

Jacobson and Truax (1991) suggest that the last measure is least arbitrary. However, if the client had a score before treatment in the lower range of a measure, such as the BDI, for depressed subjects, very little improvement would be necessary to attain the third criterion. Therefore, it can be desirable to calculate the clinical significance of the improvement in a client's score in order to determine the success of treatment.

Improvement or deterioration in status

Jacobson and Truax (1991) present a Reliable Change Index (RCI) as:

$$\frac{x_2 - x_1}{s_{diff}}$$

where x_1 is the client's score at time 1, say, before treatment, and x_2 is the score afterwards and:

$$s_{diff} = \sqrt{2 \text{ (standard error of measurement)}^2}$$

where the standard error of measurement

$$= s_1\sqrt{1 - r_{xx}}$$

s_1 being the standard deviation for a normal sample of subjects on the measure and r_{xx} being the test–retest reliability coefficient available from the source article or manual for the measure. For example, see Ch. 39.

An RCI greater than 1.96 would show ($P < 0.05$), according to convention, that the change score is greater than would be expected by chance alone. The RCI can also be applied to detect significant deterioration in, for example, cognitive functioning as shown by the Wechsler Adult Intelligence Scales.

INVESTIGATION IS A CONTINUOUS PROCESS

When a client is seen several times for treatment, cognitions and behaviour will change and this will often have to be recorded as described above. In addition, clients can produce fresh memories and beliefs. For example, clients may acknowledge that they consume more alcohol or cannabis than previously admitted, which might explain their continuing distrust. Another might remember, prompted by progress in treatment, that his first panic attack had occurred after rushing to work having consumed only black coffee. Hence formulations, corresponding treatment and data collection will have to be adapted continually.

REFERENCES

American Psychiatric Association (APA) (2000) *Diagnostic and Statistical Manual of Mental Disorders, 4th edn, text revision (DSM-IV-TR)*. Washington, DC: APA.

Bak, M., Inez, M-G., Delespaul, P., Vollebergh, W., de Graaf, R. and van Os, J. (2005) Do different psychotic experiences differentially predict need for care in the general population? *Comprehensive Psychiatry*, 46, 192–199.

Barkham, M., Margison, F., Leach, C., Lucock, M., Mellor-Clark, J., Evans, C. et al. (2001) Service profiling and outcomes benchmarking using the CORE-OM: Toward practice-based evidence in the psychological therapies. *Journal of Consulting and Clinical Psychology*, 69, 184–196.

Bebbington, P., Brugha, T., Hill, T., Marsden, L. and Window, S. (1999) Validation of the Health of the Nation Outcome Scales. *British Journal of Psychiatry*, 174, 389–394.

Beck, A. T., Weissman, A. W., Lester, D. and Trexler, L. (1974) The assessment of pessimism: The Hopelessness Scale. *Journal of Consulting and Clinical Psychology*, 42, 861–865.

Becker, M., Diamond, R. and Sainfort, F. (1993) A new patient-focused index for measuring quality of life in persons with severe and persistent mental illness. *Quality of Life Research*, 2, 239–251.

Beidel, D. C., Turner, S. M. and Cooley, M. R. (1993) Assessing reliable and clinically significant change in social phobia: Validity of the Social Phobia and Anxiety Inventory. *Behaviour Research and Therapy*, 31, 331–337.

Bentall, R. (2003) *Madness Explained. Psychosis and Human Nature*. London: Penguin Books.

Bergner, M., Bobitt, R., Carter, W. B. and Gilson, B. S. (1981) *Sickness Impact Profile* Waltham, UK: The Medical Outcomes Trust.

Bruch, M. X. and Bond, F. W. (eds) (1998) *Beyond Diagnosis. Case Formulation Approaches in CBT*. Chichester: John Wiley.

Clark, D. C. and Fawcett, J. (1992) Review of empirical risk factors for evaluation of the suicidal patient. In: Bongar, B. (ed) *Suicide. Guidelines for Assessment, Management and Treatment*. New York: Oxford University Press.

Cyr, J. J., Doxey, N. and Vigna, C. M. (1988) Factorial composition of the SCL-90-R. *Journal of Social Behaviour Personality*, 3, 245–252.

Deary, I. J. (2005) Intelligence, health and death. *The Psychologist*, 18, 610–613.

Derogatis, L. R. and Melisaratos, N. (1983) The Brief Symptom Inventory: An introductory report. *Psychological Medicine*, 13, 595–605.

Evans, C., Connell, J., Barkham, M., Margison, F., McGrath, G., Mellor-Clark, J. and

Audin, K. (2002) Towards a standardised brief outcome measure: Psychometric properties and utility. *British Journal of Psychiatry*, 180, 51–60.

Farrington, D. P. (2001) Predicting adult official and self-reported violence. In: G. F. Pinard and L. Pagani (eds) *Clinical Assessment of Dangerousness: Empirical Contributions*. Cambridge: Cambridge University Press.

Folstein, M. F., Folstein, S. E. and McHugh, P. R. (1975) Mini-Mental state: A practical method for grading the cognitive state of patients for the clinician. *Journal of Psychiatric Research*, 12, 189–198.

Francis, V. M., Rajan, P. and Turner, N. (1990) British community norms for the Brief Symptom Inventory. *British Journal of Clinical Psychology*, 29, 115–116.

Garb, H. N. (1998) *Studying the Clinician*. Washington, DC: American Psychological Association.

Gladis, M. M., Gosch, E. A., Dishuk, N. M. and Crits-Christopher, P. (1999) Quality of Life: Expanding the concept of significance. *Journal of Consulting and Clinical Psychology*, 67, 320–331.

Goldberg, D. and Murray, R. (2002) *The Maudsley Handbook of Practical Psychiatry*. Oxford: Oxford University Press.

Goldberg, D. and Williams, P. (1988) *A User's Guide to the General Health Questionnaire*. Windsor, UK: NFER-Nelson.

Haynes, S. N. and O'Brien W. H. (1990) Functional analysis in behaviour therapy. *Clinical Psychology Review*, 10, 649–668.

Holloway, F. and Carson, J. (2002) Quality of life in severe mental illness. *International Review of Psychiatry*, 14, 175–184.

Jacob, R., Alexander, D. and Lane, L. (2003) *A Guide to Intellectual Property: Patents, Trade Marks, Copyright and Designs*. London: Sweet and Maxwell.

Jacobson, N. S. and Truax, P. (1991) Clinical significance: A statistical approach to defining meaningful change in psychotherapy research. *Journal of Consulting and Clinical Psychology*, 59, 12–19.

Jones, S. H., Thornicroft, G., Coffey, M. and Dunn, G. (1995) A brief mental health outcome scale. Reliability and validity of the Global Assessment of Functioning, *British Journal of Psychiatry*, 166, 654–659.

Kaplan, R. M. and Sacuzzo, D. P. (2005) *Psychological Testing. Principles, Applications and Issues*, 6th edn. Belmont, CA: Thomson Wadsworth.

Kazdin, A. E. (1999) The meaning and measurement of clinical significance. *Journal of Consulting and Clinical Psychology*, 67, 332–339.

Kuyken, W., Fothergill, C. D., Musa, M. and Chadwick, P. (2005) The reliability and quality of cognitive case formulation. *Behaviour Research and Therapy*, 43, 1187–1201.

Lam, D. and Power, M. (1991) Social support in a general practice elderly sample. *International Journal of Geriatric Psychiatry*, 6, 89–93.

Leeser, J. and O'Donohue, W. (1999) What is a delusion? Epistemiological dimensioms. *Journal of Abnormal Psychology*, 108, 687–694.

Malloy, P. F., Cummings, J. L., Coffey, C. E., Duffy, J., Fink, M., Lauterback, E. et al. (1997) Cognitive screening instruments in neuropsychiatry: a report of the Committee on Research of the American Psychiatric Association. *Journal of Neuropsychiatry and Clinical Neurosciences*, 9, 189–197.

Massen, G. H. (2001) The unreliable change of reliable change indices. *Behaviour Research and Therapy*, 39, 495–498.

Mataix-Cols, D., Cowley, A. J., Hankins, M., Schneider, A., Bachofen, M., Kenwright, M. et al. (2005) Reliability and validity of the Work and Social Adjustment Scale in phobic disorders. *Comprehensive Psychiatry*, 46, 223–228.

McKelvie, S. J. (1980) Graphic rating-scales: How many categories? *British Journal of Psychology*, 69, 185–202.

Milne, D. (1992) *A Mental Health Portfolio*. Windsor, UK: NFER-Nelson.

Monahan, J. (2001) Major mental disorder and violence: Epidemiology and risk assessment. In: Pinard, G. F. and Pagani, L. (eds) *Clinical Assessment of Dangerousness: Empirical Contributions*. Cambridge: Cambridge University Press.

Morrison, A. P., Ronton, J. C., Dunn, H., Williams, S. and Bentall, R. F. (2004) *CBT for Psychosis. A Formulation-Based Approach*. Hove, UK: Brunner-Routledge.

Mundt, J. C., Marks, I. M., Shear, M. K. and Greist, J. M. (2002) The Work and Social Adjustment Scale: A simple measure of impairment in functioning. *British Journal of Psychiatry*, 180, 461–464.

Needleman, L. D. (2003) Case conceptualization in preventing and responding to therapeutic difficulties. In Leahy, R. L. (ed) *Roadblocks in CBT*. New York: Guilford Press.

Norko, M. A. and Baranoski, M. V. (2005) The state of contemporary risk assessment research. *Canadian Journal of Psychiatry*, 50, 18–26.

Paul, G. L. (1969) Behavior modification research: Design and tactics. In: Franks, C. M. (ed) *Behavior Therapy: Appraisal and Status*. New York: McGraw-Hill.

Persons, J. B. and Bertagnolli, A. (1999) Inter-rater reliability of cognitive-behavioral case formulations of depression: A replication. *Cognitive Therapy and Research*, 23, 271–283.

Power, M. J., Champion, L. A. and Aris, S. J. (1988) The development of a measure of social support: The Significant Others Scale (SOS). *British Journal of Clinical Psychology*, 27, 349–358.

Raven, J. (1998) *Raven's Progressive Matrices and Vocabulary Scales*. London: Harcourt Assessment.

Raven, J. (2000) The Raven's Progressive Matrices: Change and stability over culture and time. *Cognitive Psychology*, 41, 1–48.

Robins, L. N. and Helzer, J. E. (2000) *Diagnostic Interview Schedule – IV*. St Louis: Washington University School of Medicine.

Roland, M. and Morris, R. (1983) A study of the natural history of back pain. I: Development of a reliable and sensitive measure of disability in low-back pain. *Spine*, 8, 141–144.

Rush, A. et al. (2000) *Handbook of Psychiatric Measures*. Washington, DC: American Psychiatric Association.

Startup, M., Jackson, M. C. and Bendix, S. (2002) The concurrent validity of the Global Assessment of Functioning (GAF). *British Journal of Clinical Psychology*, 41, 417–422.

Spitzer, M. B., Spitzer, R. L., Gibbon, M. and Williams, J. B. W. (1996) *Structured Clinical Interview for DSM-IV Axis I Disorders, Clinician Version* (SCID-CV). Washington, DC: American Psychiatric Press.

Sturmey, P. (1996) *Functional Analysis in Clinical Psychology*. Chichester: John Wiley.

Wechsler, D. (1997a) *The Wechsler Intelligence Scale for Adults-III (WAIS-III)*. New York: Psychological Corporation.

Wechsler, D. (1997b) *WMS. Wechsler Memory Scale for Adults – III*. San Antonio, TX: The Psychological Corporation.

Wechsler, D. (1999) *WMS Wechsler Intelligence Scale for Adults – III*. London: The Psychological Corporation.

Wechsler, D. (2001) *WTAR. Wechsler Test of Adult Reading*. San Antonio, TX: The Psychological Corporation.

Wilson, G. T. (1997) Treatment manuals in clinical practice. *Behaviour Research and Therapy*, 35, 205–210.

Wing, J. K., Beevor, A. S., Curtis, R. H., Park, S. B. G., Hadden, S. and Burns, A. (1998) Health of the Nation Outcome Scales (HoNOS). Research and Development. *British Journal of Psychiatry*, 172, 11–18.

Wright, S., Johnston, M. and Weinman, J. (1997) *Measures in Health Psychology Portfolio*. Windsor, UK: NFER-Nelson.

Zigmond, A. S. and Snaith, R. P. (1983) The Hospital Anxiety and Depression Scale. *Acta Psychiatrica Scandinavica*, 67, 361–370.

Chapter 2

An introduction to treatment

Stan Lindsay and Graham Powell

INTRODUCTION

Since the second edition, in 1994, of *A Handbook of Clinical Adult Psychology* there has been an enormous increase in the popularity of psychological treatment. This has been evident in the output of research reports and the reviews of treatment effectiveness by government organisations such as the United Kingdom Institute for Health and Clinical Excellence (NICE). Public attention is drawn to psychological treatment at times of disasters, such as the Asian tsunami of 2004, reports of which described the need for counsellors ready to help. Very striking, however, has been the growth in the number of websites on the internet. Most prominent is the number of sites devoted to cognitive behaviour therapy (CBT): 1,180,000 at the time of writing this book. This exceeds the 483,000 sites devoted to psychoanalysis, which has been the most influential psychotherapy in the USA.

Many independent practitioners offer CBT and so distressed members of the public stand to be perplexed by the deluge of opportunities for treatment. Equally bewildering is the huge array of courses and teaching materials, ranging from books and videos costing a few dollars to year-long programmes costing thousands. Cursory examination of websites will show that the promise of CBT is sometimes even used to attract the public to courses on something else.

Accompanying this confusing growth in the popularity of CBT, practitioners have organised themselves into professional associations promoting therapy. These include, in the USA, the International Association of Cognitive Psychotherapy, the American Institute of Cognitive Therapy, the Academy of Cognitive Therapy and the National Association of Cognitive Behavioural Therapists. In Europe they include the British Association for Behavioural and Cognitive Psychotherapy (BABCP) and the European Association for Behavioural and Cognitive Therapy, to which organisations from 39 countries contribute. Nevertheless, because training of therapists in CBT is highly variable, from brief to prolonged and intensive, from being evidence-based to being founded more on clinical experience, therapy itself will vary in effectiveness. There have been attempts to address this by BABCP, which offers accreditation to therapists who have undergone an approved training. Membership of national professional organisations, such as the British Psychological Society and the American Psychological Association, also offers registration or its equivalent, which can be withdrawn from registrants if they do not meet certain professional standards. However, membership of a professional organisation is not necessary to permit therapists to practise CBT.

Given the proliferation of training courses and teaching materials, how can prospective therapists select suitable training? Given the corresponding numbers and variety of therapists, how can publicly funded health-care organisations employ responsible, effective therapists; how can medical insurance companies approve courses of treatment?

Guidance has been forthcoming from organisations that have considered the evidence base for the treatment of psychological problems and psychiatric illness: NICE in the UK and the American Psychiatric Association (APA) in the USA. They have shown that CBT can provide effective therapy for several problems and they recommend, although with less clarity, how CBT in such cases should be delivered.

This book takes a similar perspective in considering investigations and treatments for a wide range of problems. This chapter endeavours to outline the requirements for evidence and conditions supportive of effective therapy and the corresponding training of therapists. The following chapters accordingly consider and recommend the most appropriate investigations and interventions for a wide range of problems.

PRINCIPLES OF EVIDENCE FOR EVIDENCE-BASED TREATMENT

Randomised controlled trials (RCTs) have become the source of evidence to support treatments in medicine and have become accepted as the test for psychological therapies. See for example the reviews, *What Works for Whom?* (Roth and Fonagy, 1996) and *A Guide to Treatments That Work* (Nathan and Gorman, 2002).

In RCTs, a sample of clients with a given problem, say major depression, is selected at random from a larger group, usually clients who are attending a clinic for treatment. The clients are then selected at random for a non-established treatment, say cognitive therapy, or another procedure as a control such as an established treatment, say, a selective serotonin re-uptake inhibitor (SSRI) antidepressant medication. The trial seeks to determine whether the new treatment, cognitive therapy, is more efficacious than the well-established treatment, the SSRI antidepressant. Measures with proven reliability and validity (see Chapter 1) are used before the onset of the treatments and during their administration to test this. In this way, CBT for depression and anxiety disorders has been compared with control treatments such as supportive counselling, medication, pharmacological placebos and other psychological therapies. See, for an outstanding example, the multicentre trial for the treatment of depression (Elkin, 1994).

The CONSORT guidelines

Recently, more rigorous standards, the CONSORT guidelines (available at: http://www.consort-statement.org) have been devised for RCTs and have been adopted by the most prestigious professional journals.

The CONSORT guidelines require authors of RCTs to have met adequate standards for: (1) how the trial's participants were allocated to the interventions (treatment or control); (2) the scientific background and the rationale of the study; (3) the criteria by which the participants were chosen for the study (usually the diagnostic criteria); (4) descriptions of the interventions and their method of administration; (5) the objectives and hypotheses for the trial; (6) measures of outcome; (7) determination of the sample sizes so that the trial would have had a sufficient number of participants, to test hypotheses adequately; (8), (9) and (10) the methods of random allocation to the interventions; (11) keeping the participants and those conducting the interventions unaware ('blind') of the allocation of the participants and descriptions of how, if applicable, the concealment was effected; (12) the statistical tests used to analyse the outcome data. Further criteria are described for the results of the trial.

Because the CONSORT guidelines have been adapted only within the last few years, and only by a few psychology journals, most RCTs of psychological treatment would not have met all the CONSORT standards. Some standards would be very difficult to meet, most notably the double-blind concealment of the nature of the treatment being undergone by the participants. That requirement has been adopted from trials of pharmacological therapies in which a new medication with putative active properties is compared with another, well-established, treatment or with a placebo with no active properties. The placebo, if it does produce some benefit, does so because the participants have understood that it will be effective and it is their expectations alone that have produced the beneficial outcome for the placebo.

The need for comparison with a placebo

CBT in RCTs has been compared with keeping clients on a waiting list or with a pharmacological placebo or with a well-established psychological therapy (Butler et al., 2006). Few trials have been conducted with a placebo psychological treatment as the comparison (Butler et al., 2006). Placebo comparisons have been well exploited in trials of pharmacological treatment where the placebo resembles the active medicine in appearance and taste but the clients are unaware of the difference between the two medications. However, as noted in pharmacological RCTs, it is often impossible to conceal from participants and the clinicians the fact that one group has received a placebo and the other has had an active medicine (Margraf et al., 1991). The occurrence of side effects and changes in symptoms betrays the concealment. The nature of psychological treatments in RCTs has made the double-blind concealment for most comparisons almost impossible, as noted in the reviews by NICE of treatments for anxiety and depression. Most participants would be able to guess, for example, that the treatment they were receiving, say cognitive therapy, differed from the treatment that others were receiving, say, antidepressant medication.

The need to conceal from participants the nature of psychological interventions as a means of controlling or eliminating the effect of expectations in RCTs has been neglected. There have been no published RCTs in which a psychological intervention has been designed as a placebo so that it closely resembles CBT, so would generate the same expectations as the CBT and has been shown to have been accepted as a treatment as effective as the CBT under investigation (see the review of reviews by Butler et al., 2006). There have been a few RCTs in which CBT has been compared with 'non-specific' treatment, such as supportive counselling or reflective listening and symptom monitoring for panic disorders and depression (Elkin, 1994; Taylor, 2000; Westen and Morrison 2001; Butler et al., 2006) but few could be shown to have met the CONSORT criteria for concealment of the nature of treatment differences from participants. For example, Shear et al. (1998) did find that a cognitive behavioural treatment package and a 'non-prescriptive' intervention, consisting of 'reflective listening' were both effective in producing a high reduction in numbers of panic attacks. However, there appears to have been no attempt to design the comparison therapy, the 'non-prescriptive' intervention, so that it would have been indistinguishable from the CBT. Furthermore, there is no evidence that the clients were blind to the fact that they were receiving different treatments.

More recently, Orbach et al. (2007) have shown that a placebo programme that was designed to resemble a CBT programme delivered over the internet was successful in reducing test anxiety. The CBT package gave instruction *inter alia* in relaxation and in recording and challenging negative automatic thoughts. The placebo programme asked clients to record their thoughts and, without detailed instruction, to practise relaxation. The CBT procedure was more efficacious than the placebo programme but it is not clear if the participants assigned to the latter were sufficiently unaware that they had been allocated to a placebo procedure. Nevertheless, the study does point to the possibility that a well-designed placebo therapy, resembling CBT, could be as effective as orthodox CBT.

It remains to be seen, therefore, whether well-designed placebo procedures, adequately concealed as such from participants, would be as efficacious as orthodox CBT or other treatment. In the early days of behaviour therapy there were several controlled trials in which a placebo procedure designed to resemble relaxation and desensitisation was sometimes shown to be beneficial (Grissom, 1996). Perhaps the greater complexity of cognitive therapy makes the design of placebo treatments more difficult in trials of CBT. In addition, CBT has become so well established that clinicians can consider it unethical to offer placebo CBT to clients in research trials.

What is really necessary for effective treatment?

CBT has been developed under the influence *inter alia* of client-centred therapy. The pioneers of CBT have assumed that it is necessary for the therapist to show to the client evidence of 'empathy, understanding, genuine respect and non-possessive positive regard' (Sanders and Wills, 2005). These have been regarded as the 'non-specific' aspects of psychotherapy (Lambert and Ogles, 2004). Research on CBT for depression (Oei and Shuttlewood, 1996) suggests that non-specific factors are certainly not sufficient to explain recovery from depression in CBT. On the contrary, the process of CBT, including the challenging of a negative thinking, allows non-specific-factors to influence recovery. Oei and Shuttlewood (1996) used their own unpublished scales for non-specific factors to show this.

Castonguay et al. (1996) have reported that the 'therapeutic alliance' (that is, the quality of the relationship between clinicians and clients) as well as the clients' 'emotional involvement', did predict recovery from depression. However, it is not clear if the apparent affect of the non-specific factors was the cause or the result of the improvement in depression. It would be easy to understand that clients who became less depressed because of the techniques of cognitive therapy then came to feel more confident about the therapist and so the relationship between them improved. The clients then became more ready to express negative and positive emotions in therapy.

These authors did also show a negative influence of CBT procedures on specific factors in recovery. They report that the extent of the therapist's focus on the role of negative thinking in depression had a negative relationship with recovery: the more the therapists concentrated on the influence of the clients' negative thinking, a crucial aspect of cognitive therapy, the less likely were the clients to recover. The authors suggest that this occurred because the therapists increased their attention to cognitive therapy procedures only to compensate for difficulties in the therapeutic relationship, thus imposing some more strain on this and so impairing the influence of non-specific factors. Lambert and Ogles (2004) suggest that adherence to treatment manuals is not sufficient to implement successful treatment and may even impede it if non-specific factors are neglected.

Conclusions

The proliferation of courses and training materials, which vary considerably in depth and length, suggests that many clinicians offer CBT of a kind that does not match the treatment delivered in RCTs. It is ironic that the pioneers of CBT, who have been associated with RCTs and have been prolific in writing instructive and popularising material, could have contributed to such an adulteration of CBT. There is even a possibility that some clinicians therefore conduct placebo CBT. The efficacy of placebo CBT has not been tested. It is, therefore, difficult to say how efficacious CBT is in the wide world. Nevertheless, until trials of placebo CBT have been conducted and compared with orthodox CBT to answer the question 'What is really necessary for effective CBT?', it would be advisable to follow the treatment in manuals that have been used in RCTs. These approaches have been exemplified in the specialist chapters of this book. It would also be advisable to conduct CBT in accordance with the assumptions of empathy, sincerity, understanding and non-possessive positive regard, the non-specific factors in CBT.

HOW EFFECTIVE CAN CBT BE IN THE WIDE WORLD?

Treatment in randomised controlled trials is now conducted according to manuals describing the treatment procedure. The CONSORT guidelines make that mandatory. Furthermore, NICE has recommended that, in clinical practice, treatment should follow those manuals (see the NICE *Guidelines for Anxiety, Depression and for Panic Disorder*, which are available from the NICE website: http://www.nice.org.uk).

Clinicians often distrust the results of RCTs, complaining that they do not have the same success with their clients even when they have attended training courses and have followed the recommended treatment procedures. In part this may occur because RCTs have almost always been conducted on samples of clients selected to be free from other psychiatric difficulties and complicating social problems. Having sought treatment voluntarily, they are often probably from higher socio-economic and better educated groups. RCTs have thus assessed CBT under ideal conditions: efficacy has been demonstrated. The value of CBT in clinical practice in the wide world, its effectiveness, has been less widely examined.

To challenge this disquiet, Wade et al. (1998) examined the outcome of treatment for 110 clients who had a primary diagnosis panic disorder with or without agoraphobia. They conducted their treatment in a community mental health centre and thus not in a centre where RCTs had been undertaken. Treatment was conducted according to a protocol in a self-help manual that had been published by pioneers of CBT (Barlow and Craske, 1994). Details were recorded of the clients' demographic characteristics: gender, age, marital status and level of education. None had an additional psychiatric disorder other than depression or other anxiety disorders. There was no record of disorders on axes other than Axis 1 of DSM-IV. Over 80% of the clients after treatment reported anxiety and numbers of panic attacks within the range reported by normal subjects, a significant improvement of around 60%.

The numbers of panic attacks post-treatment were very similar to those reported in two clinical trials, one of which had been conducted by the authors of the treatment protocol used by Wade et al. (1998). The study offers further encouragement in that the clients were substantially less well educated than those in the comparison study for which educational data were available. Nearly a third of Wade's clients had completed a college education compared with nearly 50% in the comparison study. Therefore, treatment of panic disorder, conducted according to a published manual, can be as effective as that exemplified in a controlled research trial. However, the clinicians in Wade's study may have been aware that they were participating in an examination of this treatment and so this outcome may not be typical of routine practice with such a manual. Similar conclusions may be drawn about the treatment of depression in another study by the same team (Merrill et al., 2003).

More typical of routine clinical practice is the study by Westbrook and Kirk (2005) of 1,200 adult patients who completed treatment between 1987 and 1998 in the Oxford Clinical Psychology Department in the UK. This department is close to the Oxford University department that pioneered CBT and which has influenced the clinical department. The clients presented non-psychotic disorders as the primary problem. Data about co-morbid problems, common in such practices, were not reported and the only demographic characteristics noted are gender and age.

Following treatment, mainly CBT, around half the sample showed a reliable improvement on Jacobson's Statistical Index of Clinical Significance (see Chapter 1) in the outcome measures, which were the Beck Depression and Anxiety Inventories. About two-thirds of that improved group had recovered to within normal limits. The effect sizes of improvement, a measure of the discrepancy between pre- and post-treatment scores expressed as function of the sampling error in the data (Kirk, 1995), suggest that the average improvement in all diagnostic categories was high. However, there was no account of medication that might have been prescribed for the clients and so the extent of the improvement due to psychological intervention is not clear. The degree of improvement might have been greater if less specific measures, such as the Brief Symptom Inventory (see Chapter 1) had been used.

Thus, as represented, the number of clients showing improvement in this study was quite modest and somewhat less by the authors' own estimates than has been recorded in controlled treatment trials and despite the presence of an eminent research and teaching department nearby. Nevertheless, a substantial number of clients did improve, so CBT is clearly a worthwhile intervention outside research and teaching departments.

DOES PSYCHOLOGICAL TREATMENT REACH ALL WHO COULD BENEFIT?

Non-attendance and dropping out of treatment

Many studies have shown that the failure by clients to attend initial and subsequent appointments in clinical psychology and counselling services is substantial, around 32% of referrals on average (Addison, 2006). This figure may be higher among populations of ethnic minorities but this remains to be investigated (Beutler et al., 2004). Therefore, from the perspective of clients accepting treatment, CBT and other psychological treatment may not be effectively delivered. However, it must be noted that there is little information about clients who do not attend. An indeterminate number may not need treatment.

Remedies

There have been many attempts to increase attendance, such as sending leaflets to clients advising them of the nature of the service (Keen et al., 1996) (this has not been very effective), sending reminders of appointments, telephone prompting, giving clients choice of appointment times (Kenwright and Marks, 2003) and even monetary incentives or penalties (Stark, 1992; Kazdin 1994). However, studies have concentrated on comparing these interventions with standard arrangements for invitations to appointments. There has been no comparison among these methods to show which is the most effective. Furthermore, it is not clear what is necessary to increase attendance because no study has used a control group to test the effect of the extra attention that these interventions give to clients. Perhaps these interventions have been effective because the extra attention suggests to clients that the service is a more caring one.

Theoretical perspectives

Little attention has been paid to theoretical perspectives that could identify causes of non-attendance and which could recommend more effective ways of encouraging attendance. However, there is a substantial literature on acceptance of recommendations for medical treatment and this has stimulated the development of social-cognitive models of the beliefs that clients can hold about therapy.

The earliest theory, the Health Belief Model (Becker and Maiman, 1975), suggested that clients would tend to accept and persevere with treatment according to the severity of the threat they believed that their condition posed. The condition could be an illness such as high blood pressure. Their beliefs about susceptibility to illness would be a related consideration; for example, ideas about their susceptibility to cancer as the result of smoking. Clients also entertain beliefs about the efficacy of the behaviour that has been recommended, such as ceasing smoking or taking medication for high blood pressure. Clients may, for example, point to the evidence that the majority of people who smoke do not die of lung cancer, thus ignoring the risk of other smoking-related illness, and so they persist in smoking.

Clients' beliefs about the cost of accepting treatment or changing their health-care behaviour, also noted by the Health Belief Model, can refer not only to monetary burdens but to the time and trouble that clients believe could be involved in, for example, taking time off work to attend a counselling service. Some employers attempt to reduce the cost to them and their employees by arranging for health checks of their staff on work premises.

However, the Health Belief Model has not been very successful in predicting health-care behaviour, explaining at best 4% of the variance of outcome variables (Harrison et al., 1992). Other theories have therefore been developed, such as the Theory of Reasoned Action (Fishbein and Ajzen, 1975; Abraham and Sheeran, 1997), which emphasises the development of clients' intentions about health-care behaviours and the opinions of others about the behaviour.

Most recently, and currently most influential, has been the Self-Regulation Model or the Common Sense Model of Self-Regulation (CSMSR; Horne, 2000). This covers clients' beliefs about their need for treatment, their concerns about the treatment, such as its perceived costs, side effects, disruption to daily living, the risk of dependence on the treatment and the treatment's effectiveness. The perceived consequences of the illness and the timeline, which is the duration of the illness and its treatment, are also subsumed by the CSMSR. Also important are the client's beliefs in his or her ability to carry out the health-care behaviour, such as taking daily blood samples. The model also accommodates the role of fear and, perhaps most important of all, the observation that clients' beliefs in all these respects can change and influence beliefs and behaviour: hence the term 'self-regulation'.

In the delivery of psychological treatment, many of the clients' beliefs about the illness and therapy would be impossible to address adequately until the clinician has seen the client for assessment. Of course, clients would have been subject beforehand to information from all sources, including, for many, the internet, and could therefore have formed an opinion about their difficulties and treatment. These may be erroneous. Many clients come to psychologists with a request for 'counselling'. Their ideas about this may include expecting the clinician to provide all the solutions while they remain passive, expecting to talk at length about anything that arises *ad lib* or expecting to be able to see the clinician for either of these activities indefinitely. Leaflets distributed in primary health care clinics or sent to referred clients have addressed some of these expectations but with little success in encouraging attendance (Keen et al., 1996).

Costs of treatment have been addressed by providing psychology services within primary care clinics, which can be closer than hospital departments to clients' homes but which may be at some distance from their places of work. There has been no evidence that this affects attendance, although clients often express a preference for services in primary care because of the stigma attached to visiting places for the severely mentally ill where many psychology departments are based. At present, the Department of Health in the UK aims to provide more accessible primary care services. This has included, most recently, a recommendation that primary care clinics should remain open during the evenings, i.e. after most people have left work. It remains to be seen whether such an arrangement would increase the attendance of clients for psychological treatment.

The effects of clients' following recommended treatment procedures: 'compliance'

The efficacy of CBT can be impaired if clients fail to carry out homework, as shown by Schmidt and Woolaway-Bickel (2000) in a study of clients with panic disorder. In this study, the clients and their therapist compiled ratings of the compliance with advice given during treatment. There were significant negative correlations between the therapists' ratings of the clients' compliance and measures of improvement and the client's responses to questionnaires. That is, the more diligently the clients followed the therapist's advice, the better was the outcome. However, there is no evidence that the therapist was blind to the client's panic frequency or intensity and other signs of progress so that the therapist's ratings of compliance may have been influenced by changes in the panic disorder. This conclusion is reinforced by the observation that the client's ratings of compliance ratings showed no relationship with improvement. Therefore, there is no clear evidence from this study or others (Schimidt and Woolaway-Bickel, 2000) that non-compliance, within moderate limits, is destructive of progress. The extent of such non-compliance, apart from drop-out from treatment is not clear but evidence from objective measures throughout medicine shows that it is widespread. In psychological treatment, Hoelscher et al. (1984) have shown that the practice of relaxation was conducted much less frequently, as shown by electronic monitoring of their clients' use of a tape recorder, than the clients had reported.

AN OUTLINE OF CBT

This section describe treatments, mainly CBT, for a wide range of problems as supported by published research. The following is an outline of the practice of CBT so that some of the broader issues in treatment are not lost in the detail of the specialist chapters that follow. More comprehensive general introductions are available in the books by Sanders and Wills (2005) and Beck (1995).

Discussion throughout treatment is collaborative, the therapist welcoming the client's opinions and suggestions. Open-ended questions starting with why, how, where or what encourage this. For example, 'What do you think of my suggestion that the fact that you now watch for the signs of panic brings on some of the symptoms'?

This discussion of the cognitive model (see especially Chapters 11 and 12, and 13 and 14) is illustrated with examples that show the client's circular relationship, in which negative thoughts provoke emotions that in turn result in more negative thoughts. More general background issues, such as a belief in the client, which seems to underlie all the client's thinking and which occurs again and again, can be illustrated: a core belief. These are generally best discovered well into therapy if they are seen to be obstructing progress.

Emotions versus negative automatic thoughts

At first there is a need to clarify the distinction between emotions, which can be described in one word such as 'anger', 'sadness', 'hopelessness', 'depression' and so on, and negative automatic thoughts that do not contain such words but are statements that express the client's beliefs, such as, 'I looked stupid' or 'I was going to collapse and die'.

Agenda setting

The first step in any session is an agreement about the topics to be discussed so that all issues for the day are adequately covered. Items will usually include a discussion of the client's thought records completed since the previous visit. They may also include reflections on the last interview.

Recording emotions, negative automatic thoughts and strength of beliefs

Written record keeping plays an important part in cognitive therapy. The client keeps records, as homework from day to day, of negative emotions and corresponding negative automatic thoughts as they occur, together with challenges to those thoughts. The records may also include a note of the circumstances in which the emotions occurred. It is desirable to keep written records in this way because thoughts and emotions can easily be forgotten or distorted in recall. The need for this can be illustrated in a first interview by asking the client to describe, for example, his or her most recent angry outburst. Instead of describing an event in the past tense the client is asked to use the present tense to describe a general or typical impression. Written records can also help to clarify the distinction between negative automatic thoughts and emotions, and to prevent a confused verbal outpouring of emotions and thoughts. This can often be seen in an assessment interview when the client rushes headlong from one concern to another without pausing for breath or taking stock of what has been said.

Rating the client's belief in the validity of each negative thought is also an important part of the record. The aim is to find challenges to each negative thought, which reduces the strength of that belief.

The recording of negative thoughts in this way requires practice and discussion and it is important to encourage clients to see this, or they can be quickly discouraged. The first session should usually be used to demonstrate the effectiveness of such record-keeping based on a recent episode of distress. However, many clients have difficulty in keeping written records because they are not used to writing or because they have difficulties reading. In such cases it can be better to use a simplified form without belief ratings. Change in the strength of beliefs can instead be elicited in a discussion of the thought record. Others may not be able to keep written records at all and so each session may have to consist, in part, in the therapist's writing down the client's negative thoughts and challenges as they describe them.

Clarifying and challenging negative automatic thoughts

During each session the client's negative automatic thoughts, as recorded, are clarified and then discussed to develop effective challenges. Open-ended questions that start with 'how', or 'what' or 'why' open the discussion to this possibility. See also Table 6.2, p.105. For example:

... what evidence do have for believing that?
... what will happen if you continue to stay indoors?
... what else could you do?
... why do you think that should help?
... last week you said that . . . now you say . . ., how do you come to believe differently?
... how would you view that in somebody else?
... what action could you take to change things?

Closed questions can draw attention to negatively biased thinking, for example:

... are you being selective, emphasising your flaws and ignoring your strengths?
... are you thinking in all-or-none terms, how would you feel if (therapist suggests an intermediate point of view)?
... could you just accept this and start afresh?

A downward arrow technique, also known as peeling an onion or vertical descent, can be used to identify a core belief underlying the client's thinking. The crucial question is, 'so if that is true (or that did happen) what would that mean to you?' For example, a client who was afraid that she would become incontinent during her panic attacks on a crowded train on her way to work was asked as follows:

Therapist: So if you did become incontinent, what would happen?
Client: I would have to rush to the toilet.
Therapist: What would be so bad about that?
Client: Everybody would look up and watch me?
Therapist: What would that mean for you?
Client: They would think I was stupid?
Therapist: So what would be wrong with that?
Client: That's the story of my life, people do think me stupid.

The therapist can then help the client challenge this belief through further challenging.

Behavioural experiments

The impact of safety behaviours

Clients often come to therapy having practised certain activities that they believe keep undesirable events from happening. For example, an agoraphobic client took her car to the local supermarket and, if she felt nervous, told the security staff that she was ill and asked them to bring her shopping to her. She believed that if she did not do that, she could collapse with possible fatal consequences. Another client, socially phobic, remained silent in group meetings at work because she believed that if she spoke, she would blush and the others would think that she was stupid.

Practical behavioural experiments

Having established through a discussion what the client's beliefs are under these circumstances, the therapist can suggest an experiment in which the safety behaviours are dropped, or at least curtailed, so that the client sees that the hitherto anticipated outcome does not happen.

For example, the agoraphobic client may agree to venture into the supermarket at a quiet time with a companion. The experiment may show to the client that, despite becoming anxious, she did not faint. The socially phobic client could agree to hold a discussion with the therapist's colleagues and have this recorded on video. The client, seeing the video as an objective observer, could then see that signs of disinterest, which she had expected from her audience, were not evident and so change her belief that her audience would think her stupid.

Behavioural experiments such as these are now regarded as the most powerful tools in cognitive therapy (Bennett-Levy et al., 2004). They are designed to change strength in belief of cognitions elicited in prior discussions with the therapist.

Other behavioural experiments

Rouf et al. (2004) describe other behavioural experiments. Through therapist modelling and the client's observation, the therapist may demonstrate that the outcome feared by the client does not materialise. For example, the client who was afraid that she would attract much attention if she rushed to the toilet in a crowded train, could observe that almost nobody looked up when the therapist demonstrated this behaviour.

Clients can also be encouraged, as homework, to seek evidence to challenge their beliefs. For example, to challenge the belief that panic attacks are uncommon, they could seek estimates on the internet of their prevalence. A client who had abnormal cells in the lining of his oesophagus was told by a junior surgeon that he had a tenfold greater risk than normal of contracting cancer. This terrified him so that he had panic attacks daily and was afraid to leave the sight of his wife. He was encouraged to look for information about the absolute risk, rather than the relative risk already presented to him, of having oesophageal cancer. The absolute risk of contracting cancer of the oesophagus was around 1 in 100,000 and so the client's belief that he would get cancer was reduced.

CONCLUDING REMARKS

This chapter has attempted to give an outline of CBT and a critical appraisal of its contribution to the care of distressed people. No therapy can be effective with everybody and so clinicians must not be afraid to refer clients on to other sources of help, such as centres of excellence in CBT or multidisciplinary psychiatric care. Clinicians have to be careful that they do not offer help beyond their competence. This has been the most common misdemeanour requiring disciplinary action of members by the British Psychological Society.

Although there are books that demonstrate techniques for eliciting and challenging negative thinking (e.g. Leahy, 2003) and give examples of behavioural experiments (Bennett-Levy et al., 2004), therapists often have to use their ingenuity in devising fresh challenges for idiosyncratic beliefs and safety behaviours presented by their clients.

Our opening remarks indicate that there is an enormous and growing demand for psychological therapies. Health services are struggling to cope with this demand and recommend, for example, that clients with minor difficulties should be treated in primary care by clinicians with only a summary training in CBT. More seriously distressed clients will require the attention of more thoroughly trained clinicians and the most disturbed and complex clients will require the attention of multidisciplinary teams.

There have been many attempts to develop computer-aided CBT to reduce the demand for face-to-face therapy. At the time of writing, however, the effectiveness of this in primary care had yet to be confirmed by NICE in the UK. Books and leaflets are plentiful and can reduce clinicians' workload by telling clients about different psychiatric problems and the contribution which CBT can make. The most notable series are those published by the Oxford Cognitive Psychology Centre (http://www.octc.co.uk) and the *Overcoming . . .* series of books by Robinson Publishing Ltd.

REFERENCES

Abraham, C. and Sheeran, P. (1997) Cognitive representations and preventive health behaviour: A review. In: K. J. Petrie and J. A. Weinman (eds) *Perceptions of Health and Illness*. Amsterdam: Harwood

Addison, S. (2006) *Reducing Non-attendance Rates for Clinical Psychology Sessions Appointment in a Primary Care Setting*. London: Institute of Psychiatry.

Barlow, D. H. and Craske, M. G. (1994) *Mastery of your Anxiety and Panic II*. Albany, NY: Graywind.

Beck, J. S. (1995) *Cognitive Therapy Basics and Beyond*. New York: Guilford Press.

Becker, M. H. and Maiman, L. A. (1975) Sociobehavioral determinants of compliance with health and medical care recommendations. *Medical Care*, 13, 10–24.

Bennett-Levy, J., Westbrook, D., Fennell, M., Cooper, M., Rouf, K. and Hackman, A. (2004) Behavioural experiments: Historical and conceptual underpinnings. In: J. Bennett-Levy, G. Butler, M. Fennell, A. Hackmann, M. Mueller, M. and D. Westbrook (eds) *Oxford Guide to Behavioural Experiments*. Oxford: Oxford University Press.

Beutler, L. E., Malik, M., Alimohamed, S., Harwood, T. M., Talebi, H., Noble, S. and Wong, E. (2004). Therapist variables. In: M. J. Lambert (ed) *Bergen and Garfield's Handbook of Psychotherapy and Behaviour Change*. New York: John Wiley & Sons.

Butler, A. C., Chapman, J. E., Forman, E. M. and Beck, A. T. (2006) The empirical status of cognitive-behavioral therapy: A review of meta-analyses. *Clinical Psychology Review*, 26, 17–31.

Castonguay, L. G., Goldfried, M. R., Wiser, S., Reue, P. J. and Hayes, A. M. (1996) Predicting the effect of cognitive therapy for depression: A study of unique and common factors. *Journal of Consulting and Clinical Psychology*, 64, 497–504.

Elkin, I. (1994) The NIMH treatment of depression collaborative research program: Where we began and where we are. In: A. E. Bergin and S. L. Garfield (eds) *Handbook of Psychotherapy and Behaviour Change*. New York: John Wiley.

Fishbein, M. and Ajzen, I. (1975) *Belief, Attitude, Intention and Behaviour: An Introduction to Theory and Research*. Reading, MA: Addison-Wesley.

Grissom, R. J. (1996) The magical number 0.7 ± 0.2 meta-meta-analysis of the probability of superior outcome in comparisons involving therapy, placebo and control. *Journal of Consulting and Clinical Psychology*, 64, 973–982.

Harrison, J. A., Mullen, P. D. and Green, L. W. (1992) A meta-analysis of studies of the Health Belief Model with adults. *Health Education Research*, 7, 107–116.

Hoelscher, T. J., Lichstein, K. L. and Rosenthel, T. L. (1984) Objective vs. subjective assessment of relaxation compliance among anxious individuals. *Behaviour Research and Therapy*, 22, 184–194.

Horne, R. (2000) Treatment perceptions and self-regulation. In: L. D. Cameron and H. Leventhal (eds) *The Self-Regulation of Health and Illness Behaviour*. London: Routledge.

Kazdin, A. E. (1994) Methodology, design and evaluation in psychotherapy research. In: A. E. Bergin and S. L. Garfield (eds) *Handbook of Psychotherapy and Behaviour Change*. New York: John Wiley.

Keen, A., Blakey, R. and Peaker, A. (1996) The effects on non-attendance of enclosing an information leaflet to prospective clients for clinical psychology. *Clinical Psychology Forum*, October, 33–35.

Kenwright, M. and Marks, I. M. (2003) Improving first attendance for cognitive behaviour therapy by a partial booking appointment method: Two randomised controlled trials. *Journal of Mental Health*, 12, 385–392.

Kirk, R. E. (1995) *Experimental Design: Procedures for the Behavioural Sciences*. Pacific Grove, CA: Brooks-Cole.

Lambert, M. J. and Ogles, B. M. (2004) The efficacy and effectiveness of psychotherapy. In: M. J. Lambert (ed) *Bergin and Garfield's Handbook of Psychotherapy and Behaviour Change, 5th edn*. New York: John Wiley.

Leahy, R. L. (2003) *Cognitive Therapy Techniques. A Practitioner's Guide*. New York: Guilford Press.

Margraf, J., Ehlers, A., Roth, W. T., Clark, D. B., Sheikh, J., Agras, W. S. et al. (1991) How blind are double blind studies? *Journal of Consulting and Clinical Psychology*, 59, 184–187.

Merrill, K. A., Tolbert, V. E. and Wade, W. A. (2003) Effectiveness of cognitive therapy for depression in a community mental health centre: A benchmarking study. *Journal of Consulting and Clinical Psychology*, 711, 404–409.

Nathan, P. E. and Gorman, J. M. (eds) (2002) *A Guide to Treatments That Work, 2nd edn*. New York: Oxford University Press.

Oei, T. P. S. and Shuttlewood, G. J. (1996) Specific and non-specific factors in psychotherapy: A case of cognitive therapy for depression. *Clinical Psychology Review*, 16, 83–104.

Orbach, G., Lindsay, S. and Grey, S. (2007) A randomised placebo-controlled trial of a self-help Internet-based intervention for test anxiety. *Behaviour Research and Therapy*, 45, 483–496.

Roth, K. and Fonagy, P. (1996) *What Works for Whom? A Critical Review of Psychotherapy Research*. New York: Guilford Press.

Rouf, K., Fennell, M., Westbrook, D., Coper, M. and Bennett-Levy, J. (2004) Devising effective behavioural experiments. In: J. Bennett-Levy, G. Butler, M. Fennell, A. Hackmann, M. Mueller and D. Westbrook (eds) *Oxford Guide to Behavioural Experiments*. Oxford: Oxford University Press.

Sanders, D. and Wills, F. (2005) *Cognitive Therapy. An Introduction*, 2nd edn. London: Sage.

Schmidt, N. B. and Woolaway-Bickel, K. (2000). The effects of treatment compliance on outcome in cognitive-behavioural therapy for panic disorder: Quality versus quantity. *Journal of Consulting and Clinical Psychology*, 68, 13–18.

Shear, M. K., Pilkonis, P. A., Cloitre, M. and Leon, A. C. (1998) Cognitive behavioural treatment compared with nonprescriptive treatment of panic disorder. *Archives of General Psychiatry*, 51, 395–401.

Stark, M. J. (1992) Dropping out of substance abuse treatment: A clinically oriented review. *Clinical Psychology Review*, 12, 93–116.

Taylor, S. (2000) *Understanding and Treating Panic Disorder*. New York: John Wiley.

Wade, W. A., Treat, T. A. and Stuart, G. L. (1998) Transporting an empirically supported treatment for panic disorder to service clinical setting: A benchmarking strategy. *Journal of Consulting and Clinical Psychology*, 66, 231–230.

Westen, D. and Morrison, K. (2001) A multidimensional meta-analysis of treatments for depression, panic and generalised anxiety disorder: An empirical examination of the status of empirically supported therapies. *Journal of Consulting and Clinical Psychology*, 69, 875–893.

Westbrook, D. and Kirk, J. (2005) The clinical effectiveness of cognitive behaviour therapy: Outcome for a large sample of adults treated in routine practice. *Behaviour Research and Therapy*, 43, 1243–1262.

Chapter 3

Obsessions and compulsions

Investigation

Padmal de Silva

INTRODUCTION

Obsessions and compulsions come under the term 'obsessive-compulsive disorder' in traditional psychiatric classifications. Obsessive-compulsive disorder is one of several anxiety disorders. Epidemiological studies show that the disorder is much more common than previously thought. A lifetime prevalence of up to 3% in the general population has been reported (Robins et al., 1984; Karno et al., 1988; see Krochmalik and Menzies, 2003, for review). The phenomena of obsessive-compulsive disorder are so striking that they are very well described and recognised (Rachman and Hodgson, 1980; de Silva, 2003; de Silva and Rachman, 2004).

Before examination of the definition of obsessions and compulsions as they occur in patients described as suffering from obsessive-compulsive disorder, a point should be made on obsessional personality. Traits such as excessive cleanliness, meticulousness, perfectionism, a strong need for order, rigidity, and indecisiveness, which are loosely called 'obsessional', do of course occur in normal persons and, when some of these features appear as a strong cluster in someone, the terms 'obsessional personality' and 'anankastic personality' are used. Those with an obsessional personality do not necessarily develop obsessive-compulsive disorder, nor do obsessive-compulsive patients necessarily have a pre-morbid personality of this type, although there is some overlap between the two categories (Rachman and Hodgson, 1980; Pollack, 1987).

DEFINING FEATURES OF OBSESSIVE-COMPULSIVE DISORDER

The criteria widely used for the diagnosis of obsessive-compulsive disorder are given below (cf. American Psychiatric Association (APA), 1994; World Health Organization (WHO), 1992):

1   The essential features are recurrent obsessions or compulsions. For a diagnosis, the person must have either obsessions, or compulsions, or both.
2   Obsessions are recurrent, persistent thoughts, images or impulses that intrude into consciousness. They are not experienced as voluntarily produced, although the person recognises them as his or her own thoughts. They are seen as inappropriate, and they cause anxiety or discomfort. They are generally resisted and attempts are made to ignore or suppress them, or to neutralise them with some other thought or action.
3   Compulsions are repetitive behaviours or mental acts that the person feels driven to perform in response to an obsession or according to rules that must be applied rigidly. These behaviours or mental acts are aimed at preventing or reducing distress, or preventing some dreadful event or situation. However, they are not connected in a realistic way with what they are designed to prevent, or are clearly excessive.
4   The obsessions or compulsions cause considerable distress, and/or impair the person's functioning.
5   The obsessions or compulsions are not due to any other disorder.

Obsessions

Obsessions are unwanted and intrusive thoughts, impulses or images, or a combination of them, which are generally resisted. They are also recognised to be of internal origin. Some clinical examples follow:

*   A young woman had the recurrent intrusive thought that her husband would die in a car crash. She also had vivid visual imagery accompanying this thought.
*   A man had the recurrent intrusive doubt that he may have knocked someone down while they were crossing the road.
*   A young woman had the recurrent intrusive thought that she was contaminated by dirt and germs from strangers.
*   A young married woman had a recurrent intrusive impulse to strangle children and animals. This would be followed by the thought/doubt that she may actually have done this.
*   A man had the recurrent intrusive impulse to shout obscenities in public or on solemn occasions.
*   A young man had recurrent intrusive images of himself violently attacking, with an axe, his elderly parents. He also had the thought that he might actually commit this act. This experience included images of the victims, of blood flowing and of injuries caused.
*   A young woman had the recurrent intrusive thought that she might offend people by touching them in an inappropriate manner.

The content of obsessions is usually associated with contamination, violence and aggression, harm, disease, orderliness, sex and religion, and with pervasive doubting, although obsessions that relate to unusual and seemingly trivial matters can also occur (Rasmussen and Tsuang, 1986; Khanna and Channabasavanna, 1988; de Silva, 2003; Rachman, 2003). It is also worth pointing out that most normal people also experience such unwanted, intrusive obsessions, but they are less intense and less frequent, and neither disabling nor unduly distressing (Rachman and de Silva, 1978; Salkovskis and Harrison, 1984).

Compulsions

Compulsions are repetitive and seemingly purposeful overt behaviours or mental acts, preceded or accompanied by a subjective sense of compulsion and generally resisted by the person. They are performed according to certain rules or in a stereotyped fashion. Despite the resistance, these behaviours are actively carried out by the person.

Common compulsions are ritualistic behaviours involving checking and washing/cleaning. Other compulsive behaviours include doing things in a stereotyped way, ordering inanimate things and doing things in a strictly rigid sequence. Sometimes a certain special number is involved, in that the behaviour has to be carried out that number of times. Some examples of compulsions are as follows:

- A young woman repeatedly and extensively washed her hands to get rid of contamination by germs. The washing was done in an elaborate ritual six times without soap and six times with soap, on each occasion.
- A young man checked door handles, gas taps and electric switches every time he went past them.
- A 15-year-old girl cleaned and washed the area around her bed, including the wall, every night before going to bed to rid it of germs and dirt.
- A man opened letters he had written and sealed, to make sure that he had written the correct things. He would rip open the envelope, reread the letter and put it into a new one several times before posting it.
- A woman in her forties complained that every time she entered a room she had to touch the four corners of it, starting from the left.
- A young man had the compulsion to touch with the left hand anything he had touched with the right hand, and vice versa.
- A young man had the compulsion to empty his bladder before each meal. Even if he had urinated a short while before, he would go and empty his bladder prior to sitting down to the meal. He felt that otherwise he would not be able to enjoy his meal.

The above are all of overt compulsive behaviours, which are observable by others; they involve motor actions. As noted above, compulsions can also take the form of mental acts or covert behaviours. Consider these examples:

- A man had the compulsion to say silently a string of words whenever he heard or read of any disaster or accident.
- A middle-aged woman, who was distressed by the intensive repetitive appearance in her consciousness of obscene words, carried out a compulsive ritual each time this happened. This consisted of changing these words into similar but acceptable ones – for example, 'well' for 'hell', and saying them silently four times.
- A middle-aged man had the compulsion to visualise everything that was said in conversation to him, and what he was going to say in reply. He would not reply until he had obtained these visual images. Often this would take time, leading to long silences that were puzzling to others.

Relationship of obsessions and compulsions

It must not be assumed that every obsession leads to a compulsion, or that every compulsive behaviour is preceded by a clear and distinct obsession. In order to examine the relationship between the two sets of phenomena, it will be useful to consider the events that may be present in an episode of obsessive-compulsive experience and their relationships. Table 3.1 attempts to present such a sequence.

Thus an obsession may arise with or without a trigger, which can be external (e.g. sight of knife: doubt, 'Did I stab someone?') or internal (e.g. remembering a meeting with someone: thought, 'I am taller than him, am I not?'). The obsession can take the form of a thought, image, impulse or combination of these. The obsession usually leads to discomfort/anxiety/distress. This could lead to an urge to engage in a certain compulsive behaviour or ritual, and this behaviour could be either overt (e.g. washing) or covert (such as counting backwards in silence; conjuring-up a particular mental image). Carrying out this compulsion would normally lead to a reduction of discomfort, though there can be exceptions.

A compulsive behaviour can sometimes arise without a preceding obsession. Consider a man who accidentally touches a part of the wall of a public

Table 3.1 Possible sequence of events in an obsessive-compulsive experience

Trigger	External/internal/none
Obsession	Thought/doubt/image/impulse/none
Discomfort	+
Compulsive urge	+/−
Compulsive behaviour	Overt/covert/none
Discomfort reduction	+/?

toilet and immediately rushes into a washing ritual. It can be argued, of course, that the touching of the wall in this case led to a fleeting obsession ('I am contaminated', 'I am dirty'), which was directly responsible for the compulsive behaviour, but it is doubtful whether the postulation of such a step is of any value. To all intents and purposes, it was the trigger (touching the wall) that led to discomfort and then to an urge to carry out the ritualistic behaviour. This pattern is fairly common with long-standing compulsive behaviours that have, over the years, acquired a habit-like quality.

Thus, obsessions and compulsions can take place in the absence of each other, although in practice they are commonly found to occur together. In clinical practice, one often comes across patients described as having obsessions only ('obsessional thoughts', 'obsession ideas', and so on) and the relatively high frequency of such descriptions may lead one to assume that obsessions without compulsions are quite frequent. However, many of the patients described in this way in fact have covert compulsive behaviours, the details of which one has to elicit by careful enquiry.

Other major features

Avoidance

Avoidance can be a significant feature in the clinical picture, although it is not part of the obsessive-compulsive experience itself. The avoidance behaviour commonly concerns stimuli and situations that, potentially, can trigger the obsession or the compulsion. For example, those with obsessions about contamination by dirt or germs and associated washing or cleaning rituals usually strive to avoid what they believe to be dirty or contaminating; and those with checking rituals may avoid situations that demand checking. Some patients with severe and excessive fears of contamination confine themselves to their bedrooms; the rest of the world is seen as not clean and has to be avoided. A woman who had the obsessional thoughts that she might stab her children went to great lengths to avoid contact with knives, scissors and other sharp objects. A young man who feared that he might catch venereal disease totally avoided certain areas of the city he lived in. Sometimes it is not places or things that are avoided, but behaviour. A patient may not wash in the morning, or at all, for several days because this behaviour requires a long and complicated ritual. An example of the avoidance of both objects and behaviour is given by de Silva and Rachman (2004):

> A married woman in her late 20s had the obsessional thought that she had cancer. After several years of checking for cancer symptoms, she began to avoid any situation where she might discover she had signs of cancer. Thus, she could not make her bed in the morning, or look at her used underwear, for fear of discovering bloodstains which, to her, would

be a sign of the dreaded illness. She even stopped looking at herself in the mirror or at her own body. She began to wear blouses and jumpers with long sleeves so that she could not see her arms, and trousers to that she could not see her legs. She stopped washing herself properly, as she feared that she would discover lumps and suchlike on her body.

In some cases, certain numbers are avoided because the patient feels that such avoidance is needed to avoid some disaster, usually to a loved one. An illustration of this is found in the following example, again from de Silva and Rachman (2004):

> A young married woman began to avoid the number four. Her husband's birthday was on the fourth day of a month and her obsessional logic dictated that if she did not avoid the number, she would cause some great harm to him. She went to great lengths to achieve this; for instance, she would skip the fourth page of books and magazines she was reading, would never write the number four, never eat four of anything (e.g. potatoes or slices of toast) and so on. Life became impossible when this gradually extended to all numbers beginning or ending with four, multiples of four, those that were adjacent to four and so on, at which point she sought help.

Fears of disaster

These are found frequently. The patient feels that a certain disaster will happen unless he or she wards it off by engaging in his or her compulsive behaviour. For example, an elderly man had the very strong fear that, if he did not check the gas taps in his house a certain number of times, the house would explode and go up in flames. The relationship between the specific disaster feared by the patient and the compulsive behaviour is of course, not always logical; a young man felt that his hand-washing rituals protected his mother from accidents when she was flying in aircrafts. Similarly, patients who are troubled by obsessive fears, such as that of developing cancer, may wash excessively, even though they know that washing one's hands is irrelevant and ineffective as a precaution against cancer.

Resistance

It has been noted by many authorities that both the obsession and compulsion may be resisted by the sufferer. In his much-quoted paper, Sir Aubrey Lewis (1936) argued that the central and indeed essential feature of obsessive-compulsive disorder was the strong resistance that the patient had. More recent studies (e.g. Stern and Cobb, 1978; Rachman and Hodgson, 1980) have shown that, although resistance is very common, it is not found invariably. It is possible that in the early stages a patient may resist his or her obsessions and/or compulsive urges strenuously but, after repeated failures over a period of time, may begin to show much less resistance. There are chronic obsessive-compulsive patients in whom resistance to symptoms is quite low (Rasmussen and Tsuang, 1986).

Reassurance seeking

Many obsessive-compulsive patients resort to seeking reassurance from others, usually members of their families. Often, obsessional thoughts such as 'Will I go insane?', 'Did I do it properly?' and 'Do I need to check the taps again?' lead to the patient asking for reassurance. When reassurance is received, the patient feels some relief from his or her discomfort. Reassurance seeking is often done repeatedly, much to the exasperation of friends and family. At best, provision of such reassurance provides only brief relief. Sometimes reassurance seeking is an undisguised attempt to enlist someone else to help in one's checking (Rachman and Shafran, 1998).

Disruption

An obsessive-compulsive patient who is engaged in his or her compulsive behaviour needs to carry it out precisely as he or she feels it has to be done. For many, if the behaviour is disrupted in any way it is invalidated and needs to be restarted. For long and complicated rituals this can be extremely time consuming and exhausting. The events that can act as disruptors vary from noise and other external disturbances to certain classes of experience and thought (e.g. seeing something 'dirty', such as a dustbin; a 'sinful' thought; an image of a disaster; a thought of death).

The need to form a safe or suitable thought before carrying out a compulsive or other act is also common. If the action is disturbed or disrupted by an unacceptable thought, the compulsive sequence has to be repeated in full.

In some instances, the person feels impelled to remove all other thoughts before attempting to carry out the compulsive activity, for example, removing distracting thoughts all the better to concentrate on making sure that one has checked gas taps correctly.

Inflated responsibility

Many patients experience an inflated sense of responsibility, even for events over which they have no control whatever. Indeed, some authorities consider an exaggerated sense of responsibility to be a cardinal feature of the disorder (e.g. Salkovskis, 1985). Salkovskis (1999) stresses that obsessive-compulsive patients also feel responsibility for not preventing, or not trying to prevent, harm to others or self – in other words, responsibility for inaction. Clinical observation shows that an inflated sense of responsibility is particularly common among those whose main problem is excessive checking. The inflated responsibility also tends to generate intense guilt.

Ruminations

A rumination is a somewhat complex phenomenon sometimes found in obsessive-compulsive disorder. The patient attempts to think through a question or topic, such as 'Is there a life after death?' or 'Am I genetically abnormal?' and this thinking is inconclusive, prolonged and frustrating. The patient does this compulsively, and the compulsion is often triggered by the appearance of the relevant obsessional thought.

CLINICAL PRESENTATIONS

It is now necessary to look at the common clinical presentation of obsessive-compulsive patients. Typically, an individual comes for help suffering from a disability arising from one major aspect of the disorder, which is the predominant problem for that individual. Thus, on initial clinical presentation, patients fall into a few conveniently defined categories, which are listed below. It is important to bear in mind, however, that this is a classification based only on the predominant feature of the presenting problem. A full assessment of the individual case is needed before a proper description of the patient, let alone therapy, can begin.

Main categories

1   Those with washing/cleaning compulsions as the prominent problem.
2   Those with checking-type compulsions as the prominent problem.
3   Those with other kinds of overt compulsions as the prominent problem.
4   Those whose obsessive-compulsive problems do not include overt compulsions.
5   Those with primary obsessional slowness.
6   Those with compulsive hoarding.

Primary slowness

A word of explanation is necessary about the patients described as 'primarily obsessionally slow'. Rachman (1974) has described a small number of obsessional patients whose main problem is excessive slowness. Most patients with obsessive-compulsive disorder would be slow anyway but their slowness is secondary to their repetitive compulsive behaviour, which can be time consuming. These patients, on the other hand, are *primarily* slow: their slowness is not a secondary consequence of other difficulties. Simple tasks take up a great deal of time in their lives. They do things correctly and meticulously. They are very concerned about the manner in which they do things, and the main area where this affects them is self-care. Rachman (1974, 2003) has shown that they are profitably treated as a distinctive subgroup of obsessive-compulsive patients, and independent reports confirm this (e.g. Takeuchi et al., 1997).

Compulsive hoarding

The main problem here consists of collection and retention of large numbers of articles that are useless or are of limited value. This can result in the accumulation of piles of objects that occupy a steadily increasing amount of living space, often causing fire and health hazards. Sometimes the house is so cluttered with items that the person – and the family – have to navigate through them with great difficulty. Hoarders tend to fear that they may throw away something that may become needed in the future. They find it very hard to decide what to discard and what to retain. A detailed discussion of this phenomenon is given by Frost and Hartl (2003).

Exclusions

A note on certain other behavioural problems that are given the descriptive term 'compulsive' but which do not come under the disorder in question is warranted. These are certain addictive behaviours (such as compulsive drinking, compulsive gambling) and habit disorders (such as compulsive nail biting, compulsive hair pulling). Despite the loosely used term 'compulsive', these problems are different from obsessions and compulsions as defined above, and will not be dealt with here.

ASSESSMENT

Introduction

The clinical assessment of obsessive-compulsive disorder is in principle no different from the assessment of other disorders. The aim is to obtain as full a picture of the problem as possible, using a variety of data-collection techniques. The nature of the difficulty, its extent and severity, the degree of disability it has caused and the factors that may be relevant to its possible modification all have to be examined. Where possible, quantifiable data should be obtained. The assessment approach should be comprehensive and can profitably include a behavioural analysis as described by, among others, Kanfer and Saslow (1969).

Clinical interview

The clinical interview is the main data source in the assessment. Obsessive-compulsive patients are usually cooperative and will give a good account of the difficulties as they see them. One problem is that, unlike many other groups of patients, they may talk too much and give too many details, so that the main thrust of the interview can get affected and the whole process delayed. Some tend to take a very long time giving answers because of their own doubts about what to say; others check with the interviewer repeatedly about previous answers, to make sure they did not give wrong details. The inability to give an exact answer often distresses the patient. It is therefore important for the assessor to be sympathetic but also to maintain control of the interview and follow a loose but clear structure. Acknowledging the patient's difficulty is also helpful. Additional details may be discouraged when clearly irrelevant, at least in the initial interview. Detailed discussions of interviews with obsessive-compulsive patients are found in, among others, Clark (2004).

Areas of enquiry during clinical interview

The interview should aim to get information about what the main problems are, when and where they occur, how they affect patient's life and work, how the patient's family are affected, and of course the history. The sequence of events suggested in Table 3.1 would be a useful basis to make specific enquiries about the phenomena themselves with regard to each problem area. For compulsive behaviour, the time taken for the rituals and the number of times they are repeated must be enquired into. The degree of disability has to be assessed in different areas of life, such as work, leisure, family and sex. The role of anxiety/discomfort is an important aspect that will have a bearing on therapy. What brings on anxiety/discomfort? What compulsive activity, if there is any, brings it down? Are there other ways in which the patient can reduce anxiety, such as getting someone else to do some of the checking? The nature and the extent of avoidance needs to be gone into fully, as does the presence or absence of identifiable triggers. An assessment of mood, using a standard depression scale (see Chapter 5), should be undertaken. The effects of mood on the obsession/compulsion, and *vice versa*, should be examined (see p. 55).

The stimuli/situations that cause problems or are avoided have to be explored in detail. A list of such situations should be constructed, graded in terms of how much discomfort they arouse as estimated by the patient (see p. 54). This is broadly similar to a fear hierarchy used with phobic patients in desensitisation (Wolpe, 1958, 1991) – that is, it will include diverse situations that have a basic discomfort-arousing quality (e.g. contamination) in common, rather than a series of finely graded events different in the degree of closeness to the main problem stimulus in space or time.

It will often be found in clinical assessment interviews that the patient has not looked at the problem closely, or in terms of what would be valuable clinical data, and thus may not volunteer details unless asked. So careful questioning and prompting will be needed. Sometimes the patient may have to be asked keep a daily record (see pp. 50–51) in order to be able to provide some of the required details.

Particular attention needs to be paid to the cognitive aspects of the problem (see Rachman and Shafran, 1998). The patient's beliefs related to the obsessions and compulsions should be explored carefully. What does the obsession signify to the person? What does he or she think it can lead to? Is the occurrence of a thought or image about doing something unacceptable as bad as actually doing it? Does having such a thought increase the chances of bad things actually happening? Exploring the patient's beliefs about obsessions covering these areas gives valuable information. Rachman (2003) has provided excellent guidelines for such enquiry. The patient's beliefs about compulsions are equally important. What does he or she believe will happen if the compulsion is not carried out? Does the patient feel responsible for ensuring the safety of others and therefore that the compulsive behaviour *has* to be carried out? Some of these issues are well discussed by Clark (2004).

Diagnostic interviews

There are two currently used diagnostic interview schedules that can help in the assessment. One is the Standard Clinical Interview for DSM, Axis I (SCD-1; First et al., 1995); this is intended to be administered by trained clinicians. The second is the Anxiety Disorders Interview Schedule (ADIS; Di Nardo et al., 1994), which provides an assessment of anxiety disorders, common co-morbid conditions and those disorders that are commonly assessed to screen participants for research trials. This is also designed for use by trained clinicians.

Differentiation from other disorders

Patients who are referred to clinical psychologists for assessment for their disorder are generally assumed to have been screened previously. It is not, however, entirely unusual to have as referrals people whose obsession-like or compulsive-like features may in fact reflect a different condition. It is worth remembering, therefore, some distinguishing features of apparently similar phenomena as they occur in other conditions. Following Rachman and Hodgson (1980), these may be summarised as follows:

- In schizophrenia, intrusive ideas and so on are attributed to external sources, are not necessarily ego-dystonic, are not regarded as senseless and are not generally resisted.
- In organic impairments, repetitive ideas or acts lack intellectual content, lack intentionality and have a mechanical and/or primitive quality.

The stereotyped behaviours in severe mental retardation and the repetitive responses in Gilles de la Tourette syndrome should hardly ever present a problem of differential diagnosis. A good discussion of the problems of differential diagnosis is available in Rasmussen and Eisen (1992).

Key informants

An interview with a key person in the patient's life, usually parent or spouse, will help in getting a valuable complementary account of the problem in question. The time taken by compulsive rituals, the number of times a ritual is performed per day, the specific situations and stimuli that provoke problem behaviours, the extent of avoidance, reassurance seeking and the degree to which the immediate family has been drawn into, and affected by, the patient's obsessive-compulsive problems can usually be elucidated by such informants. Equally important, perhaps, is the role of the family in maintaining and fostering the patient's problems. A somewhat extreme, but instructive, clinical example will illustrate this point:

> A 17-year-old female patient was referred with severe contamination fears and related cleaning and washing rituals. Her main focus as a contamination source was the boyfriend of her older sister. She became upset if she came in contact with anything he had touched, and had to engage in extensive washing. The parents did not approve of the boyfriend for various reasons but would not express their disapproval to the daughter as they felt – and said – the girls were old enough to make their own decisions, and were free to bring home anyone they wished. The patient's inability to tolerate her sister's boyfriend coming to stay for weekends was, however, a great relief to the parents, who used it as a reason to keep the young man away.

Daily records/diaries

A fairly simple assessment technique is to ask the patient to keep a daily diary of relevant cognitions and behaviours, with details of time, circumstances, and so on. This is particularly valuable as a source of baseline data. Many obsessive-compulsive patients keep meticulous and detailed diaries when asked to. To avoid being flooded with hundreds of pages, the clinician may supply a structured format, concentrating on a few relevant headings. An example of a daily record sheet used for this purpose is given in Figure 3.1. A simple counter to keep frequency tallies can be a useful addition.

Date:_____ Target[1]:_____

Time	Frequency[2]	Highest discomfort[3]	Highest compulsive urge[4]	Details and comments[5]
Before 7 a.m.				
7–10 a.m.				
10 a.m.–1 p.m.				
1–4 p.m.				
4–7 p.m.				
7–10 p.m.				
After 10 p.m.				

[1] The particular obsession or compulsion monitored.
[2] How many times it happened in each time period.
[3,4] Rated on a 0–100 scale; give the highest felt during the time period.
[5] Details of what happened; when, where, what was the trigger, how long taken, number of repetitions, and so on, of the worst episode.

Figure 3.1 An example of a daily record sheet.

Questionnaires, inventories and rating scales

Several questionnaires and inventories are available to assess these patients. These are not intended to be a substitute for clinical assessment. They supplement interview assessment and also provide quantified scores.

One difficulty with the use of self-report measures is that, like in the interview, some obsessive-compulsive patients may have problems in deciding which response option to use for each item. This is because they need to be absolutely sure that they have given the correct response. This can slow them down considerably, and the clinician needs to be patient and use gentle encouragement. Asking the patient to complete the measure/s on his or her own, and not during the consultation, saves time.

Compulsive Activity Checklist

This instrument is used both for self-rating by the patient and for rating by the therapist (Marks et al., 1977). It consists of items related to 38 specific activities (e.g. having a bath or shower, touching door handles). Each activity is rated on a four-point scale of severity. A total score is obtained by adding the individual score items. What is more important, however, is the identification of the activities that cause real difficulty for the patient. A shorter version of this instrument has also been reported (Steketee and Freund, 1993).

Maudsley Obsessional-Compulsive Inventory

The Maudsley Obsessional-Compulsive Inventory (MOCI) is easy and quick to administer, being made up of 30 items with 'true'/'false' answers (Hodgson and Rachman, 1977; Rachman and Hodgson, 1980). In addition to a global score, it gives four subscores: checking, washing/cleaning, slowness/repetitiveness and doubting/conscientiousness. Unfortunately, the inventory has only two items covering thoughts (obsessions). Nor does it assess degree of disability and severity as opposed to the extent of the problem. However, it does differentiate between obsessive-compulsive patients and those with other anxiety disorders. On the whole, the MOCI is a useful and easy-to-use instrument, and can be easily included in the routine assessment procedure. It is particularly useful for monitoring change with therapy. A revised version of this instrument is currently being developed.

Padua Inventory

The Padua Inventory was developed in Italy (Sanavio, 1988). It consists of 60 items, using five-point ratings, and is designed to evaluate a range of clinical obsessions and compulsions. It has four subscales: contamination, checking, impaired control of mental activities, and urges and worries over losing control of motor behaviour. It can be used to determine the severity of the problems and to monitor response to treatment.

Obsessive-Compulsive Inventory

The Obsessive-Compulsive Inventory (OCI) was developed by Foa and colleagues (Foa et al., 1998) and consists of 42 items. It contains seven subscales: washing, checking, doubting, ordering, obsessing, hoarding and mental neutralising. For each item, a four-point rating scale is used for frequency and for distress. A shorter version of this scale has also been developed (Foa et al., 2002); this has 18 items.

Yale–Brown Obsessive-Compulsive Scale

The Yale–Brown Obsessive-Compulsive Scale (Y-BOCS) is a comprehensive clinician-administered instrument that is widely used in the United States (Goodman et al., 1989). It allows the clinician to estimate the severity of the disorder, particularly the extent to which disorder affects the person's life. It is useful as a screening instrument for obsessive-compulsive disorder and as an aid to monitor progress in treatment. Self-report versions, both paper-and-pencil (Steketee et al., 1996) and computerised (Rosenfeld et al., 1992), are also available.

Clark–Beck Obsessive-Compulsive Inventory

The newly developed Clark–Beck Obsessive Compulsive Inventory (CBOCI; Clark and Beck, 2002) is a self-report screening measure consisting of 25 items. Each item is scored from 0 to 3, as in Beck's depression and anxiety inventories, alongside which this instrument is recommended to be used. The CBOCI yields a total score, an obsession subscale score and a compulsion subscale score.

Psychophysiological assessment

Psychophysiological measures – heart rate, pulse rate and skin conductance – have been used in a few studies of obsessive-compulsive phenomena (e.g. Boulougouris et al., 1977; Grayson et al., 1980; Kozak et al., 1988) but there is insufficient evidence to recommend the use of these measures in routine clinical assessment. It has also been argued that caution is needed in the use and interpretation of these measures (Salkovskis, 1990).

Behavioural tests

Behavioural performance tests are perhaps the most useful and most direct assessment method available. Simple behavioural tests can be carried out in a clinical interview setting – for example, asking patients to touch a 'contaminating' object, observing the reaction and degree of avoidance, and getting a self-rated measure of discomfort and of urge to wash (see below). This should be done for selected target problems – usually the ones that cause greatest difficulty to the patient. More structured and better planned behavioural tests will attempt to sample the relevant problems more fully. Such a planned assessment will ideally include systematic manipulation of several variables, including presence or absence of family, and so on. It must be remembered, however, that the degree of obsessive-compulsive problems is likely to be temporarily lessened in a new environment. Thus, in the first few days of hospitalisation, even a severely affected patient may not demonstrate the phenomena he or she has reported.

Behavioural tests carried out in the home environment by the patient can also be used and provide valuable information.

Naturalistic observation

Observation of the patient in the natural environment can throw useful light on the nature of the problems, but this is usually difficult in practice. However, if there are problems in specific situations (such as excessive checking at work, avoidance of any contact with people in public transport), direct observation by the clinician in the target situations should be seriously considered. In assessing compulsive hoarding, this is particularly important.

Self-ratings

In behavioural tests, as indeed in interview assessment and diary keeping, the patient is asked to rate his or her subjective reactions (de Silva and Rachman, 2004). A 0–100 scale, similar to a 'fear thermometer', is relatively easy to use for these purposes. The patient will rate his or her 'discomfort' (a more natural term than 'anxiety'), and – where relevant – the strength of the urge to engage in compulsive behaviour. Despite problems of reliability and validity, these simple self-rating measures are easy for patients to learn to use and add a useful dimension to purely verbal self-reports. The discomfort ratings are particularly useful in preparing hierarchies of difficult situations (see p. 63).

Special problems

Absence of overt phenomena

In cases where the predominant problem presents as cognitive phenomena, that is, with no external manifestations, special care has to be taken in assessing the problem. While the basic techniques and tools described above are all generally relevant, particular enquiry must be made about covert rituals. The performance task for the patient in such cases would include producing the obsession upon instruction and then recording the reactions in terms of discomfort, urge to ritualize and so on. A verbatim report of the obsession and covert compulsions should be recorded. The actual form the obsession takes, that is, whether it is a thought, image or an impulse, is also important to record (de Silva, 1986). A semi-structured interview for the assessment of obsessions has been produced by Rachman (2003).

Primary slowness

Where the problem is primary slowness, particular attention has to be paid to the time taken for various day-to-day activities, mainly the patient's self-care. The order of behaviour sequences also need to be elicited and observed. Behavioural tests will involve the patient carrying out specific self-care or other relevant activities.

Depression

It was noted earlier that the patient's mood needs to be assessed. This is because there is a relationship between depression and obsessive-compulsive disorder. Obsessive-compulsive disorder can lead to the development of a secondary depressive disorder (Demal et al., 1993). It is well known that when the patient is significantly depressed, obsessions and compulsions can get worse (Rachman and Hodgson, 1980). A further relevant consideration is that obsessive-compulsive patients are less likely to respond to cognitive-behavioural treatment when they are significantly depressed (Abramowitz and Foa, 2000). Given the interrelationship between obsessive-compulsive disorder and depression, careful enquiry into mood is an essential aspect in the investigation of patients presenting with obsessive-compulsive symptoms. Routine assessment of depression with a suitable instrument is recommended.

Biological and neuropsychological aspects

Several investigators have looked for a biological basis for obsessive-compulsive disorder, and many claims have been made. Some have suggested, citing evidence from brain-imaging techniques, that abnormalities in the frontal lobe and the basal ganglia may be involved (Malloy, 1987; Wise and Rapoport, 1989). The current evidence on the role of these in the genesis of compulsive obsessive-compulsive disorder is, at best, unclear (see Frampton, 2003, for a review). There is limited relevance of these considerations for the clinical assessment of this disorder at the present time. In recent years, strong claims have been made that a neurotransmitter, serotonin, may be involved in the disorder. Certain drugs that act on serotonin have been shown to have some effect in patients with this disorder (e.g. McDonough, 2003). However, the current evidence for a direct causal role for serotonin, or any other substance, in obsessive-compulsive disorder is not persuasive. More light will no doubt be thrown on these issues by further research.

CONCLUDING COMMENTS

The assessment package a psychologist uses for any individual patient will depend on the nature of presenting problems and circumstances. This chapter has attempted to indicate the main types of measure that are available in the assessment of obsessions and compulsions. A comprehensive assessment will include a full clinical interview, key informant interviews and behavioural assessments, self-report and other instruments, and data from the patient's natural environment. More emphasis will be placed on types of data particularly relevant to the specific problems and on data that have a direct bearing

on the therapeutic strategy to be used. Assessment will also aim at eliciting
data that will allow for measuring change.

REFERENCES

Abramowitz, J. S. and Foa, E. B. (2000) Does comorbid major depression influence
    outcome of exposure and response prevention for OCD? *Behavior Therapy*, 31,
    795–800.
American Psychiatric Association (APA) (1994) *Diagnostic and Statistical Manual of
    Mental Disorders*. Washington, DC: APA.
Boulougouris, J. C., Rabavilas, A. D. and Stefanis, C. (1977) Psychophysiological
    responses in obsessive-compulsive patients. *Behaviour Research and Therapy*, 15,
    211–230.
Clark, D. A. (2004) *Cognitive-Behavioral Therapy for OCD*. New York: Guilford
    Press.
Clark, D. A. and Beck, A. T. (2002) *Manual for the Clark–Beck Obsessive-Compulsive
    Inventory*, San Antonio, TX: Psychological Corporation.
Demal, U., Lenz, G., Mayrhofer, A., Zapotoczky, H. G. and Zitterl, W. (1993)
    Obsessive-compulsive disorder and depression: A retrospective study on course
    and interaction. *Psychopathology*, 26, 145–150.
de Silva, P. (1986) Obsessional-compulsive imagery. *Behaviour Research and Therapy*,
    24, 333–350.
de Silva, P. (2003) The phenomenology of OCD. In: R. G. Menzies and P. de Silva
    (eds) *Obsessive-Compulsive Disorder: Theory, Research and Treatment*. Chichester:
    John Wiley.
de Silva, P. and Rachman, S. (2004) *Obsessive-Compulsive Disorder: The Facts, 3rd edn*.
    Oxford: Oxford University Press.
Di Nardo, P., Brown, T. A. and Barlow, D. H. (1994) *Anxiety Disorders Interview
    Schedule for DSM-IV (ADIS-IV)*. Albany, NY: Graywind.
First, M. B., Spitzer, R. L., Gibbon, M. and Williams, J. B. W. (1995) *Structured
    Clinical Interview for DSM-IV Axis I Disorders – Patient Edition (SCID–I/P,
    Version 20)*. New York: Biometrics Research Department, New York State Psychi-
    atric Institute.
Foa, E. B., Kozak, M. J., Salkovskis, P. M., Coles, M. E. and Amir, N. (1998)
    The validation of a new obsessive-compulsive disorder scale: The Obsessive-
    Compulsive Inventory. *Psychological Assessment*, 10, 206–214.
Foa, E. B., Hupert, J. D., Leiberg, S., Langner, R., Kichik, R., Hajack, G. and
    Salkovskis, P. M. (2002) The Obsessive-Compulsive Inventory: Development and
    validation of a short version. *Psychological Assessment*, 14, 485–496.
Frampton, I. (2003) Neuropsychological models of OCD. In: R. G. Menzies and
    P. de Silva (eds) *Obsessive-Compulsive Disorder: Theory, Research and Treatment*.
    Chichester: John Wiley.
Frost, R. O. and Hartl, T. L. (2003) Compulsive hoarding. In: R. G. Menzies and
    P. de Silva (eds) *Obsessive-Compulsive Disorder: Theory, Research and Treatment*.
    Chichester: John Wiley.
Goodman, W. K., Price, L. H., Rasmussen, S. A., Mazure, C., Fleischmann, R. L.,

Hill, C. L. et al. (1989) Yale–Brown Obsessive-Compulsive Scale (Y-BOCS). Part 1: Development use and reliability. *Archives of General Psychiatry*, 46, 1006–1011.

Grayson, J. B., Nutter, G. and Mavissakalian, M. (1980) Psychological assessment of imagery in obsessive-compulsives: A pilot study. *Behaviour Research and Therapy*, 18, 580–593.

Hodgson, R. J. and Rachman, S. (1977) Obsessive-compulsive complaints. *Behaviour Research and Therapy*, 15, 389–395.

Kanfer, R. H. and Saslow, G. (1969) Behavioral diagnosis. In: C. M. Franks (ed) *Behavior Therapy: Appraisal and Status*. New York: McGraw-Hill.

Karno, M., Golding, M. J., Sorenson, S. B. and Burnham, A. (1988) The epidemiology of obsessive-compulsive disorder in five US communities. *Archives of General Psychiatry*, 45, 1094–1099.

Khanna, S. and Channabasavanna, S. M. (1988) Phenomenology of obsessions in obsessive-compulsive disorder. *Psychopathology*, 21, 12–18.

Kozak, M. J., Foa, E. B. and Steketee, G. S. (1988) Process and outcome of exposure treatment with obsessive-compulsives: Psychophysiological indicators of emotional processing. *Behavior Therapy*, 19, 157–169.

Krochmalik, A. and Menzies, R. G. (2003) The classification and diagnosis of OCD. In: R. G. Menzies and P. de Silva (eds) *Obsessive-Compulsive Disorder: Theory, Research and Treatment*. Chichester: John Wiley.

Lewis, A. J. (1936) Problems of obsessional illness. *Proceedings of the Royal Society of Medicine*, 29, 325–336.

Malloy, P. (1987) Frontal lobe dysfunction in obsessive-compulsive disorder. In: E. Perecman (ed.) *The Frontal Lobe Revisited*. New York: IRBN Press.

Marks, I. M., Hallam, R. S., Connolly, J. and Philpott, R. (1977) *Nursing in Behavioural Psychotherapy*. London: Royal College of Nursing.

Pollack, J. M. (1987) Relationship of obsessive-compulsive personality to obsessive-compulsive disorder: A review of the literature. *Journal of Psychology*, 121, 137–148.

Rachman, S. (1974) Primary obsessional slowness. *Behaviour Research and Therapy*, 11, 463–471.

Rachman, S. (2003) *The Treatment of Obsessions*. Oxford: Oxford University Press.

Rachman, S. and de Silva, P. (1978) Abnormal and normal obsessions. *Behaviour Research and Therapy*, 16, 233–248.

Rachman, S. and Hodgson, R. J. (1980) *Obsessions and Compulsions*. Englewood Cliffs, NJ: Prentice-Hall.

Rachman, S. and Shafran, R. (1998) Cognitive and behavioral features of obsessive-compulsive disorder. In: R. P. Swinson, M. M. Antony, S. Rachman and M. A. Richter (eds) *Obsessive-Compulsive Disorder: Theory, Research, and Treatment*. New York: Guilford Press.

Rasmussen, S. A. and Eisen, J. L. (1992) The epidemiology and differential diagnosis of obsessive-compulsive disorder. *Journal of Clinical Psychiatry*, 53(4), suppl: 4–10.

Rasmussen, S. A. and Tsuang, M. T. (1986) Clinical characteristics and family history in DSM-III obsessive-compulsive disorders. *American Journal of Psychiatry*, 143, 317–322.

Robins, L. N., Helzer, J. E., Weissman, M. M., Orvaschel, H., Greenberg, E., Burke, J.

D. Jr and Regier, D. A. (1984) Lifetime prevalence of specific psychiatric disorders at three sites. *Archives of General Psychiatry*, 41, 949–958.

Rosenfeld, R., Dar, R., Anderson, D., Kobak, K. A. and Greist, J. H. (1992) A computer-administered version of the Yale–Brown Obsessive-Compulsive Scale. *Psychological Assessment*, 4, 329–332.

Salkovskis, P. M. (1985) Obsessional-compulsive problems: A cognitive-behavioural analysis. *Behaviour Research and Therapy*, 23, 571–583.

Salkovskis, P. M. (1990) Obsessions, compulsions and intrusive cognitions. In: D. F. Peck and C. M. Shapiro (eds) *Measuring Human Problems: A Practical Guide.* Chichester: John Wiley.

Salkovskis, P. M. (1999) Understanding and treating obsessive-compulsive disorder. *Behaviour Research and Therapy*, 37, S29–S52.

Salkovskis, P. M. and Harrison, J. (1984) Abnormal and normal obsessions: A replication. *Behaviour Research and Therapy*, 22, 549–552.

Sanavio, E. (1988) Obsessions and compulsions: The Padua Inventory. *Behaviour Research and Therapy*, 26, 169–177.

Steketee, G. S. and Freund, B. (1993) Compulsive Activity Checklist (CAC): Further psychometric analysis and revision. *Behavioural Psychotherapy*, 21, 13–25.

Steketee, G. S., Frost, R. and Bogart, K. (1996) The Yale–Brown Obsessive-Compulsive Scale: Interview versus self-report. *Behaviour Research and Therapy*, 34, 675–684.

Stern, R. S. and Cobb, J. (1978) Phenomenology of obsessive-compulsive neurosis. *British Journal of Psychiatry*, 132, 233–239.

Takeuchi, T., Nakagawa, A., Harai, H., Nakatani, E., Fujikawa, S., Yoshizato, C. and Yamagami, T. (1997) Primary obsessional slowness: Long-term findings. *Behaviour Research and Therapy*, 35, 445–449.

Wise, S. P. and Rapoport, J. L. (1989) Obsessive-compulsive disorder: Is it a basal ganglia dysfunction? In: J. L. Rapoport (ed) *Obsessive-Compulsive Disorder in Children and Adolescents.* Washington, DC: American Psychiatric Press.

Wolpe, J. R. (1958) *Psychotherapy by Reciprocal Inhibition.* Stanford, CA: Stanford University Press.

Wolpe, J. R. (1991) *The Practice of Behavior Therapy, 4th edn.* New York: Pergamon Press.

World Health Organization (WHO) (1992) *The International Classification of Diseases, 10th edn.* Geneva: WHO.

Chapter 4

Obsessions and compulsions
Treatment

Padmal de Silva

INTRODUCTION

The treatment of obsessions and compulsions has witnessed considerable progress in recent decades. The almost resigned acceptance seen very commonly even in the 1960s (e.g. Slater and Roth, 1969) of the poor outcome of therapy has given way to an attitude of optimism (e.g. Clark, 2004). Psychologists have been developing and using increasingly effective and refined cognitive-behavioural intervention techniques for these disorders, and it is common practice today for obsessive-compulsive patients be referred to clinical psychologists for treatment.

Before we look in some details at these techniques, brief reference must be made to non-psychological forms of therapy.

NON-PSYCHOLOGICAL TREATMENTS

Drug treatments

Many psychiatrists believe that pharmacological treatment is of considerable value in obsessive-compulsive disorder, and there is evidence that some types of medication are effective.

Sometimes patients are given anxiolytic benzodiazepine drugs, such as chlordiazepoxide or diazepam. Usually, these give temporary relief from the feelings of anxiety or tension, but tend to have little effect on the obsessions and compulsions themselves. These drugs can also be habit-forming. Phenothiazines, such as chlorpromazine, are also occasionally prescribed but there is seldom real benefit from them.

Antidepressant drugs are often prescribed, with varying degrees of success. In cases where the obsessive-compulsive disorder is compounded by depression, direct treatment of the depression is often needed. In some, the successful treatment of the depression is followed by alleviation of the obsessive-compulsive problems, and additional treatment may not be necessary. In the majority, reduction of the depression leaves the obsessions and compulsions weakened, but still disabling and distressing. Additional treatment is then required.

The alleviation of depression that accompanies obsessive-compulsive disorder can be achieved by standard antidepressant medication. Strong claims have been made that the tricyclic antidepressant clomipramine is of particular value in the treatment of obsessive-compulsive patients. While it may be particularly efficacious in reducing depression in these patients, whether it also has a specific effect on obsessive-compulsive disorder is a matter for debate. A major study carried out in London in the 1970s, with the support of the Medical Research Council, observed that clomipramine did reduce both depression and obsessive-compulsive problems in a group of patients who suffered from both. However, in those patients who had little depression, clomipramine failed to produce significant improvement. The results of more recent studies do not provide a consistent picture. On balance, the evidence points to the conclusion that clomipramine is an effective treatment, especially when depression is also present, but the improvements are seldom complete and a significant minority of patients do not benefit from the drug. Recent research also suggests that the initial response to clomipramine is not a good predictor of the longer-term effects of this medication. Patients tend to relapse when they stop taking the drug.

Of the other antidepressant drugs tested in recent years, encouraging results have been achieved with fluoxetine and fluvoxamine. These belong to the group of drugs called selective serotonin re-uptake inhibitors (SSRIs). Other drugs in this group include paroxetine, sertraline and citalopram.

The overall, long-term value of these drugs in the treatment of obsessive-compulsive disorder is still to be determined. On current evidence, long-term benefit depends on the continuation of medication. There is a high chance of relapse when the drug is withdrawn. McDonough (2003) and Simos (2002) have provided useful reviews of this area.

Some psychiatrists recommend the use of these drugs along with psychological treatment. For those obsessive-compulsive patients who find it difficult to accept a cognitive behavioural treatment programme, initial treatment with suitable medication can help. Additional cognitive-behavioural treatment will help to maintain the treatment gains. Such combined treatment programmes need to be carefully planned and monitored.

Neurosurgery

Another form of treatment that has been used for these disorders is psychosurgery. It is worth noting that what goes on as psychosurgery is not one uniform procedure, but several different ones, including standard leucotomy, modified leucotomy and stereotactic limbic surgery.

It has been pointed out (Rachman, 1980; Rachman and Hodgson, 1980) that no logical explanation has been given as to why brain surgery should be expected to help these patients. As for empirical data, reviews of psychosurgical treatment for obsessive-compulsive patients indicate that it is essentially a treatment of last resort (Jenike et al., 1998) and, even in this role, caution is advocated (see McDonough, 2003, for a brief review).

COGNITIVE BEHAVIOURAL TREATMENT

The treatment of choice for obsessive-compulsive patients is cognitive behavioural therapy. The early work of Wolpe (1958) and of Meyer (1966) led to the development of behavioural techniques that have been used with considerable success and shown to be more effective than the treatments used until their advent (Rachman and Hodgson, 1980). In more recent years, cognitive interventions have been used, often in an integrated cognitive behavioural framework (McLean and Woody, 2001; Clark, 2004).

In clinical practice, the specific treatment strategy to be used for a given patient will be determined by the nature of the main or predominant problem. As Chapter 3 shows, the events comprising an obsessive-compulsive experience are many and they may occur in different combinations. The decision as to what specific treatment strategy is to be used depends largely on which of these events predominate and how they interfere with the individual's functioning.

Exposure and response prevention for those with overt compulsions

In the mid-1960s a psychologist in London, Victor Meyer, began to treat patients who had compulsive rituals with what he called 'apotrepic therapy'. This consisted of two elements: placing the patient in real-life situations that generated anxiety or discomfort and provoked his compulsive urges (*in vivo* exposure); and preventing the patient from carrying out the compulsive behaviour (response prevention). This combination of *in vivo* – or real life – exposure plus response prevention was further developed by Rachman and colleagues (see Rachman and Hodgson, 1980) and soon became well established as a technique for treating patients with overt compulsive behaviour. Research in the UK, the USA and the Netherlands further developed and refined this treatment and provided convincing evidence of its efficacy. It remains the treatment of choice for these patients today (Kyrios, 2003).

Rationale

Before describing the details of this form of treatment, the rationale behind it needs to be noted. Typically, an obsessive-compulsive patient with overt behavioural compulsions experiences discomfort and a strong urge to ritual-ise when provoked by the occurrence of the obsession, or by exposure to the trigger stimulus or situation. When the patient engages in the compulsive behaviour (say, hand-washing) the level of discomfort and the compulsive urge go down. What would happen if the discomfort and the urge to engage in the compulsive behaviour were provoked, but the patient then refrained from carrying out the compulsion? Several studies have shown that, in this situation, the level of discomfort and the strength of compulsive urges still go down, but much more slowly (Rachman et al., 1976). When this is done in repeated sessions, there is a cumulative effect leading to the patient feeling progressively lower levels of discomfort and weaker urges to engage in the compulsive behaviour. Also, the urges and discomfort decline progressively more quickly as treatment progresses.

The role of modelling

In the practice of therapy, modelling is often added as a third element in the treatment package: the therapist carryes out the action that he instructs the patient to do – touching door handles, for example – in the presence of the patient, by way of demonstration. The therapist does this in a calm and controlled way, with no sign of anxiety or discomfort, and also models cop-ing with this exposure by not needing to wash and clean. Modelling facilitates therapy and often is needed to encourage a fearful or hesitant patient to carry out certain behaviour needed in treatment. It is, however, not an essential ingredient. The essentials are exposure and response prevention.

Imaginal exposure

In some cases, imaginal exposure is used. This may be done for situations that it is not practical to expose the patient to in real life, and also as an initial step to prepare the patient for *in vivo* exposure to a situation. Some research suggests that, for patients who fear that disasters may occur in the future if they do not engage in their compulsions, imaginal exposure to these disasters may be a useful additional element in therapy. A patient may be asked, for example, to imagine vividly and clearly, a bloody accident or air crash involv-ing a loved one – the feared disaster. Such imaginal exposure is claimed to improve the long-term results of therapy, when used in addition to *in vivo* exposure and response prevention.

Therapy in practice: washing/cleaning compulsions

How is the treatment done? It is important to stress that different therapists will set about their task in different ways, although the same principles are involved. So, the account given below should not be taken as a definitive account of what all therapists do, but rather as an example that highlights the general principles and issues.

In the following paragraphs we shall focus on the treatment of washing/cleaning compulsions. The general principles, however, apply to the treatment of all overt compulsive problems using exposure and response prevention.

In the assessment (Chapter 3), the therapist obtains detailed information from the patient about the full range of difficulties; the rationale for the treatment is also discussed in detail. The therapist and the patient then discuss the priorities and decide which compulsion, or set of compulsions, will be treated first. For each selected target, the therapist asks the patient for a full account of the objects or situations that trigger the obsession and/or lead to the compulsive rituals. A list is constructed, indicating how difficult these triggers or cues are for the patient to face. This is usually done by asking the patient to estimate a rating of discomfort that he or she will experience in each of these situations, usually on a scale of 0–100 (where 0 means 'no anxiety or discomfort' and 100 means 'extremely severe anxiety or discomfort'). Similar ratings may also be obtained for the strength of the compulsive urge, with 0 indicating 'no urge' and 100 indicating 'extremely high, irresistible urge'. An example of such a list, or hierarchy, is given in Table 4.1.

The therapist and the patient then agree on where in this list, or hierarchy, exposure should begin. Ideally, it is best to tackle a high point, even the highest, early on, but in practice many patients are reluctant to agree to this. The starting point is often the highest item that the patient is willing to try despite discomfort, provided it is not too low in terms of discomfort and compulsive urge. The patient is then exposed to this in an active, even exaggerated, way. Exposure to several related items may be tackled together. For example, if the concern is with dirt and germs on the floor, door handles, and

Table 4.1 An example of a hierarchy of problem situations of an obsessive-compulsive patient

Items	Discomfort 0–100	Compulsive urge[1] 0–100
Using a public toilet	100	100
Touching the inside of the kitchen waste bin	95	90
Touching the toilet seat at home	80	85
Touching the outside of the kitchen waste bin	70	75
Picking up something from the kitchen floor	70	70
Shaking hands with a stranger	65	55
Using a public telephone	60	50
Touching door handles in a public place	55	45
Bumping into a stranger	55	50
Touching money given by a cashier in a supermarket	50	35

[1] The strength of the urge to engage in strenuous hand-washing after the activity concerned.

so on, the patient is asked to touch very thoroughly, with the therapist usually first modelling the actions, several door handles, the floor, the rim of the dustbin and so on. The 'contamination' may then be spread to the patient's arms and clothes by the patient rubbing his or her hands on them. This exposure is followed by a period of response prevention. The patient refrains from washing or engaging in any other cleaning ritual. The therapist usually stays with the patient during this time. It is extremely rare for a patient to need to be actually physically restrained from engaging in the compulsive behaviour. In fact, most therapists agree that this should never be done, because the patient needs to be sufficiently motivated to comply with the response prevention instructions. If this is not the case, no amount of coercive work will be useful.

The therapist needs to be sympathetic about the patient's discomfort, and help to make it easier for him or her, for example, by distraction, conversation and so on. The response prevention period with the therapist may last for 2 hours or so; by this time, the patient's discomfort arising from the exposure, and the related compulsive urge, will normally have diminished considerably. If they are still high, the session should be continued until there is a significant reduction, particularly in discomfort. The patient is advised not to engage in the ritual even after this time period. Normal washing is allowed, as needed for reasons of hygiene, but the patient must not ritualise or exceed the set limit.

Another important requirement in this therapy is to withhold reassurance. The patient may ask for reassurance from the therapist or, at home, from a family member. These requests should not be complied with. Family members are instructed not to give any reassurance. If, for example, the patient asks 'Are you sure nothing will happen?' or 'Are you sure it is all right?', the family is asked to respond with something like 'We agreed not to talk about that, didn't we?' or 'Remember, your therapist told me not to answer such questions'.

It sometimes happens that a patient, out of his or her great unease during the response prevention period, engages in brief, unnoticeable rituals or even mental rituals as a temporary substitute for the real ones. These possibilities are usually discussed with the patient in advance, to ensure that he or she tries not to resort to such means, which can only frustrate the therapy. Equally, in the exposure part of the treatment, a patient may touch the contaminating object very briefly and/or just with the tips of the fingers or the back of the hand. This does not help, as the resultant discomfort and the compulsive urge may then not be very high. Again, the therapist usually explains that proper exposure is needed, and makes sure that this happens.

It is possible to expose the patient continuously, for hours or even days, to the discomfort-arousing stimuli. For example, if animal fur is the major source of discomfort, the patient may be asked to carry around a small packet of dog hair all the time; a patient with obsessions about the colour black may be instructed to wear black underwear and to sleep on a pillow with a black pillowcase.

Sessions are held quite frequently in the early stages of treatment. Numerous stimuli or situations are used from the hierarchy, or from several hierarchies. The patient is told at the outset about the need for a good deal of time to be set apart for therapy. Because of the time factor, the therapist may also use others as co-therapists, or helping therapists. These people need to be fully familiar with the patient's problems and the details of the treatment programme.

It is preferable for the patient not to be taking anxiolytic medication at the time of treatment. Those who have been taking medication, such as diazepam, should be taken off it, or have the dosage reduced, because the anti-anxiety effects of the drug may impede the effects of exposure and response prevention treatment. As mentioned above, the rationale for this type of approach is that the anxiety or discomfort must be provoked, and then extinguished by allowing it to dissipate spontaneously. So any drug, including alcohol, that blocks or reduces the anxiety will hinder this effort.

The details of the programme always depend on the individual patient's problems and how the therapist plans to deal with them after joint discussion. No two patients are alike and the therapist has to develop a suitable programme for every case. When the therapy is done on an out-patient basis, which happens in the vast majority of cases, a family member may be enlisted as a co-therapist to help with supervision, or even extra sessions, at home. Patients are given specific homework sessions to supplement the work in the clinic. If an in-patient programme is used, either because of the severity of the problems or practical difficulties in implementing therapy on an out-patient basis, attempts will be made to carry out most of the sessions away from hospital and in the home situation as soon as it is practicable. A family member may be invited to participate in some of the therapy, even in hospital.

The following case example illustrates the exposure and response prevention therapy package. It is taken from de Silva (1978).

A 22-year-old male undergraduate was referred with extensive washing rituals related to obsessions he had about being contaminated by dogs. Specifically, he feared that he might catch rabies (although he knew that the chances of this were slim) or some other serious infection. He engaged in repeated and time-consuming washing rituals every time he felt he was contaminated; this would happen if he passed a dog or saw dog faeces on the road, if someone who had been with a dog came near him, or if he happened to touch or brush against anything to do with dogs, like a discarded collar or lead, or a feeding bowl. He also had a great deal of avoidance behaviour. He would cross the road to avoid having to pass a dog. He began to avoid friends and others whom he knew had dogs (in the end, he stopped going to classes). He would throw away any item of clothing he happened to be wearing when he went past or got anywhere near a dog. His life became very restricted as a result of this. He had no other obsessive-compulsive behaviour except some minor checking rituals that were not causing any problems.

Initial cognitive exploration showed that the patient recognised the irrationality of his behaviour but that he did not feel confident about this. The rationale of the treatment was explained to him, which he was able to accept. He was treated with exposure and response prevention, with modelling. A list of situations that caused him anxiety was prepared on the basis of his ratings on a 0–100 scale. He was willing to accept exposure to the highest four items in this list. These were: touching a dog with both hands (anxiety 100); touching a bowl from which a dog had eaten (anxiety 90); touching a piece of cloth that had come in contact with a dog (anxiety 80) and walking barefoot on the ground where dogs had previously been (anxiety 75). The exposure to the first three items involved him having to touch the item very thoroughly and then rubbing his hands on his clothes and arms. He had agreed not to wash his hands or take a bath, nor to change the affected clothes, for a period of 3 hours after each session. He had three or four treatment session a day. He had to keep with him, all the time, a piece of cloth that had been rubbed on a dog in his presence, even keeping this under his pillow when he slept to ensure continuous exposure.

Despite being anxious to begin with, he cooperated well with the programme and, within a few days, was very much improved. The lower items in the original list (for example, holding the hand of someone feeding a dog; anxiety 50) did not prove too difficult when he was later asked to do them. He began to display fewer and fewer avoidance behaviours and began to move freely and use public transport.

The patient maintained his gains well. At one stage, several months later, when he noticed some signs of the problem returning, he treated himself, as he now knew what the principles of therapy were, and quickly brought the problem under control.

Therapy for other overt compulsions

The principles of exposure and response prevention described above are applicable to all overt compulsive rituals. For checking compulsions, the patient is asked to engage in behaviour that provokes checking (e.g. leaving the house, closing drawers, putting things into envelopes and sealing them, switching off electrical appliances and so on), and then to desist from carrying out the checking. An effort is made to ensure that no reassurance is given.

Those with compulsions to do certain things in bizarre or highly ritualised ways are asked to engage in this behaviour in other, more normal, ways. For example, a patient who does not leave a room without touching the four walls will be taken into and persuaded to leave rooms, but with no touching. Someone who has to have her table and wardrobe arranged in a very rigid way will be asked to disarrange the things on the table and in the wardrobe, and discouraged from putting them back in her compulsive fashion. In short, any overt compulsions can be treated by this approach.

Reduction of avoidance

All these programmes need to have built into them the reduction of avoidance behaviour. Even after successful therapy focused on difficult target situations, a patient may still avoid many other situations, partly out of habit and partly because of residual worries. Patients are therefore encouraged to go out of their way to face all sorts of situations that can provoke rituals, not just those to which they have been exposed in the therapy sessions.

In cases where the major problem is compulsive avoidance, the main therapeutic strategy is to expose the patient extensively to the avoided situations or stimuli. Let us illustrate this with an example (de Silva and Rachman 2004).

A female patient had obsessions about cancer. She had extensive avoidance behaviour at the time of referral and was admitted to hospital. She avoided anything she feared might lead her to discover signs of cancer. Her treatment programme consisted of getting her to engage in all the behaviour that she avoided, initially with supervision and help. For example, she was regularly made to look at herself in a full-length mirror, to wash and bathe herself, to make her bed in the morning, to wash her underwear without looking away, to palpate her breasts and so on. She had long sessions with the nurse during which she carried out these activities, very thoroughly. This treatment programme led to considerable improvement within a short period of time. At 5 years' follow-up she was still free of the problem and leading a normal life.

Cognitive strategies

The description given above of exposure and response-prevention therapy concentrated on behavioural techniques. The approach was initially developed as a behavioural one, and largely remains so. However, there is a role for cognitive techniques, and in many programmes today these are used as integral elements. In the initial assessment, the patient's beliefs, attitudes and other cognitions related to the problems are fully explored. Dysfunctional cognitions elicited this way will need to be worked on. Often, these patients have an unfounded or vastly exaggerated estimation of the consequences of actions. These have to be dealt with in therapy. A patient's belief that cancer may be contracted by touching, for example, will be challenged and correct information given. Many patients, especially those with checking compulsions, have a vastly inflated sense of responsibility, which is a major factor maintaining their rituals. These cognitions need to be re-structured, using cognitive techniques (Ladouceur et al., 1996; Salkovskis, 1999). Several useful discussions of these additional elements are available in the literature (e.g. McLean and Woody, 2001; Marks, 2003; Clark, 2004).

Treatment of obsessions

The progress made around 30 years ago in treating compulsive behaviour, notably compulsive cleaning and compulsive checking, was not accompanied by comparable advances in dealing with obsessions. However, considerable progress has been accomplished in recent years, mainly by changes in our understanding of the nature of these unwanted, repugnant intrusive thoughts. As noted in Chapter 3, it seems likely that these intrusive thoughts, which are experienced by almost everyone at one time or another, can become transformed into obsessions if and when the person interprets them to be of great personal significance. The thoughts are interpreted by the person as being revealing, and as signifying that he or she is immoral, evil, dangerous, insane or a combination of these qualities. The person might also believe that the thoughts will lead to catastrophic consequences and fear that he or she might lose control. These thoughts are extremely distressing and can give rise to attempts to put matters right, to neutralise or conceal or suppress the thoughts, and also to avoid places or people that might trigger the thoughts.

As a result of this new analysis of obsessions (Rachman 1997, 1998), the primary aim of treatment has shifted away from the earlier methods and now focuses on the patient's interpretation of the thoughts. The therapist aims to assist the patient in making more realistic and accurate interpretations of the significance of the unwanted, intrusive thoughts. This involves an analysis of the thoughts and the meaning that the patient places on them. Equally important, it is pointed out that the occurrence of intrusive thoughts is a normal experience of most people. A range of cognitive strategies are used to achieve the designed changes (see Freeston and Ladouceur, 1998; Rachman, 2003b).

The earlier methods of treatment included thought stopping, distraction, repeated exposure to the intrusive thought (by encouraging the patient repeatedly to form the thoughts to instruction), re-shaping the intrusive images by deliberate exercise and discouraging the avoidance of situations in which the person was inclined to re-experience the intrusive thought. These methods continue to have their uses but are no longer the core treatment.

For over 30 years, thought stopping was used by therapists in an attempt to help the patient achieve control over the unwanted and usually uncontrollable thoughts (Wolpe, 1958). The therapist asks the patient to relax and close his or her eyes. The patient is then asked to verbalise the obsession and, when he or she does so, the therapist shouts 'Stop!' loudly. The procedure is repeated several times and in the second stage the patient is asked simply to form the thought, and to indicate to the therapist with a pre-arranged signal when he or she has accomplished the formation. At this point the therapist interrupts the thought by shouting 'Stop'. This too is repeated several times. In the next stage, the patient shouts the word 'Stop' and, after some training, will move on to the final stage, in which he or she makes the stop command silently. There are variants of thought stopping, which include thought switching or thought substitution. They all share the purpose of helping the patient acquire the ability to dismiss the unwanted thought and think another thought, usually a pre-selected pleasant one, in its place. Another variant uses a mildly aversive stimulus, for example a rubber band worn on the wrist, which the patient pulls and releases against the wrist while giving him- or herself the silent 'Stop' command. Thought stopping can be helpful but is seldom sufficient and nowadays plays a subsidiary part in treatment at best.

Another approach is to get the patient deliberately to form the thought when instructed; in some ways this is the opposite of thought stopping (Rachman, 1976). It is sometimes referred to as 'habituation training' and the aim is to get the patient to become accustomed to the unwanted thought. As a result of repeated and/or prolonged exposure, the thought gradually becomes less and less upsetting and eventually should no longer arouse anxiety or discomfort. In this application the patient is asked to get the thought and keep it focused in his or her attention, dwelling on it without losing it. In this way the patient can be exposed to the thought for up to an hour at a time. In practice, most people are unable to retain a specific thought for longer than a few minutes at time. During treatment they are asked repeatedly to re-form the thought to ensure prolonged exposure. An alternative way of ensuring prolonged exposure is to ask the patient to write out the thought repeatedly. Another variant is to ask the person to make a tape recording of a description of the obsession and then to listen to the audiotape repeatedly (Salkovskis, 1983). An advantage of this method is that the exposure can be continued at the patient's wish and is not confined to sessions at the clinic.

In all types of treatment, whether the early methods or new variants, an essential component is to encourage the person to avoid avoiding, that is, to reduce and hopefully eliminate all avoidance behaviour that is designed to keep the person away from situations in which he or she might experience the obsessions. This kind of strong and persistent avoidance behaviour may help avoid discomfort temporarily but ultimately fails to control the anxiety, and it is best eliminated. Avoidance behaviour may even reinforce the obsessions.

The main shift in emphasis that has been taking place during the past few years can be described as a movement away from helping the patient to cope with the unwanted and uncontrollable thoughts to actively undermining their occurrence by substituting more realistic and accurate interpretations of the significance of the intrusive thoughts themselves.

Dealing with covert compulsions

In the treatment of obsessions, the patient's covert compulsive behaviour or neutralising cognitions are also dealt with (Rachman, 2003b). The patient may be asked to carry out little behavioural experiments to demonstrate that refraining from the neutralising compulsions after getting the intrusive thought does not, in fact, result in the consequences he or she fears. For example, if the patient believes that thoughts can kill unless they are neutralised, he or she may be asked to 'kill' a house plant with the thoughts, then a goldfish and so on (McLean and Woody, 2001). Where necessary, elaborate covert rituals carried out in response to an obsession or a trigger may also be dealt with using the standard exposure and response prevention paradigm (de Silva et al., 2003).

The problem of images

In some cases, the obsession takes the form of mental imagery. When the patient's main problem is an intrusive image, special techniques have been used (de Silva, 1986). With some practice one can learn to manipulate and 'play about' with one's mental images. In experiments, normal subjects have been shown to be able to rotate, expand, shrink and otherwise manipulate their visual images. This facility can be improved with practice. An obsessive-compulsive patient who complains of distressing images might be instructed to deal with the image by modifying it in various ways. For example, a patient whose unwanted, intrusive image was of dog faeces was trained to shrink the image smaller and smaller, until it became just an innocuous dot; another patient who complained of distressing images of a violent scene was trained to focus on a marginal detail of the image and 'zoom in' on this part. In this way it was possible to make this part of the image, which did not arouse discomfort, larger and larger, so that the discomfort-arousing part of the image 'overflowed' from the image space. The image thus became less upsetting. Techniques such as these for manipulating one's unwanted images are probably effective because of the sense control the patient gets by successfully manipulating them. After all, one of the reasons why obsessions are a problem is that they intrude despite one's resistance and are hard to dismiss. If, therefore, the patient achieves some control over the image, that makes it less of a problem.

Although useful, these image-manipulation techniques are not the main treatment for intrusive images. The new cognitive approach used for intrusive thoughts and described above, is equally applicable to images. Like thoughts, the images are distressing because the person attaches undue significance to them, and so helping the person to interpret them in a different way is the core treatment.

Treatment of compulsive hoarding

In cases of compulsive hoarding, treatment is usually difficult because of fears, especially fears that arise from the threat of other people touching, re-arranging or discarding the collection. Until recently, most therapists took the view that the best that could be done was to help hoarders adopt procedures for reducing or limiting their collection in order to make their everyday life more tolerable. This was a steady, gradual process, marked by occasional purges. The patient would be persuaded to let a therapist help with the disposal of agreed items, and when this was the case better and speedier results were achieved.

Recent publications (Hartl and Frost, 1999; Frost and Hartl, 2003) show that a comprehensive cognitive behavioural treatment approach can be effective with these patients. Such a programme would include education/information about hoarding, help with organisational and decision-making skills, re-structuring of cognitions related to hoarding, and actual behavioural work. The behavioural work focuses not only on discarding collected items but also on refraining from acquiring new items to hoard. This comprehensive approach appears to be a promising development in the treatment of hoarding.

Therapy for primary obsessional slowness

For those patients whose problem is primary obsessional slowness, a therapy involving pacing, prompting and shaping is used (Rachman, 1974, 2003a; Takeuchi et al., 1997). The patient's behaviour is paced, with repeated urging to speed up. Time limits are set for selected behaviours and the patient is helped to keep to these time targets. The therapist assists by prompting the patient. Some modelling may be used as well: the therapist may demonstrate, for example, how to comb one's hair in just 2 minutes, and get the patient to do likewise. The patient is also given feedback on how well he or she is doing, and praised for completing a behaviour quickly. A selected target behaviour may be 'shaped', in the sense that the time allowed for it in each session is gradually shortened.

This kind of treatment is very time consuming and requires a great deal of input by the therapist. Some of these patients require hospital-based treatment initially and, after the in-patient phase, much home-based therapy is also needed. These patients improve only gradually and may not retain their improvement unless further help is given by booster sessions. Fortunately, patients in this category are few in number. An example illustrating the treatment of primary obsessional slowness is given below (de Silva and Rachman, 2004).

A 38-year-old man with chronic and severe obsessive-compulsive disorder was referred for treatment. The main feature of his disorder was excessive slowness – he took roughly 3 hours to prepare himself for work each morning. He bathed infrequently because he needed up to 5 hours to complete the process. By the time he was referred for help he was in danger of losing his job because he was regularly quite late for work.

The treatment programme covered a wide range of self-care behaviour; only the management of brushing his teeth is cited here, as an example.

Initially, he was advised and instructed on how to brush his teeth in a reasonable length of time. This produced a small impact; soon a plateau was reached beyond which no improvement took place – a typical feature with these patients. Then, the patient was asked to carry out the brushing in the presence of the therapist for a few occasions; it was clear that the slowness resulted from his wish to brush each tooth in turn, in a particular sequence, and in a meticulous manner. He was then given a demonstration of brushing teeth at normal speed, and he was asked to imitate the therapist. Some improvement was obtained immediately. In the next stage of therapy, he was instructed to brush his teeth on a number of occasions during which the therapist set up a speeded-up goal and provided time checks every 30 seconds. This produced further improvement, although the patient found it difficult to break the 5-minute barrier, which was the agreed goal.

Following this approach in dealing with all of his problems, a significant overall improvement in bathing, washing, teeth-cleaning and dressing was achieved. He gradually learned to complete his daily self-care chores in an acceptable manner and within an acceptable time period. The improvements ensured that he was able to retain his job.

Other behavioural techniques

Various other behavioural treatments have also been used with obsessive-compulsive patients. One is systematic desensitisation, in which the patient imagines problem situations in a graded series of steps while under relaxation. This was a common treatment of phobias in the early days of behaviour therapy (see Wolpe, 1958) and is still used in some cases. Sometimes this also includes real-life exposure to situations. In this procedure, anxiety or discomfort is kept to a minimum, in contrast to the exposure and response prevention approach, where discomfort is provoked.

Contingency management is an approach that manipulates the consequences of a behaviour. For example, if a patient's rituals receive a lot of positive attention and sympathy, an attempt may be made to ensure that rituals cease to produce favourable results. Instead, alternative behaviour is rewarded. Sometimes, aversive procedures are used, for example, a mild electric shock or the use of a rubber or elastic band for obsessions. These techniques have been shown to have only a limited effect.

The use of contingency management has a role as an additional element in therapy, in some cases. If it is clear that the patient's obsessive-compulsive behaviour has become very rewarding then the results of any exposure and response prevention programme may be lessened by this factor. For example, a rather shy and timid young man who had severe obsessive-compulsive problems, including excessive avoidance of going out, was treated with standard therapy but the results were short lived. It quickly became clear that the disabilities caused by the problems (inability to go out, wash his own clothes, do any outdoor work and so on) had the effect of his mother doing everything for him and waiting upon him. It was necessary to break this pattern of events through counselling sessions, in which the mother was fully involved, before the young man's problems could be brought under control effectively. This is a somewhat atypical example but the general principle that it illustrates is clear. Do the obsessive-compulsive symptoms bring any 'benefit' (such as attention, endearing words or work being done for him) for the patient? Therapists will normally look into this in their analysis of the problems. If such a functional analysis, which looks closely into a problem behaviour and its triggers or antecedents on the one hand, and its consequences on the other, shows that the symptoms do lead to such 'benefit' for the patient, some work will need to be undertaken to change this pattern, in addition to the main treatment techniques used.

Sometimes, these patients are taught muscle relaxation. This is a fairly simple procedure in which all the major muscle groups in the body are relaxed in a series of exercises. Some early therapists using thought stopping had the patient in a relaxed state for this procedure, although this was not seen by many as an essential ingredient. Training in relaxation can help obsessive-compulsive patients in an indirect way; stress and tension tend to make one's obsessions and compulsions worse. Sometimes, the problem reappears after a relatively clear period of time, in the wake of stressful experiences. Therefore, if one learns to relax oneself as a means of coping with stress and of reducing tension, it can be of considerable use later.

OUTCOME OF THERAPY

If the therapy is carried out properly and consistently, the outcome of cognitive behaviour therapy, including exposure and response prevention, can be quite impressive. There may be initial distress and some patients might even want to give up therapy but, once this stage has passed, it becomes easier. The therapist needs to be supportive but firm, and to have a good relationship with the patient. A substantial amount of therapy time may be needed: dozens of sessions rather than two or three, and each session needs to be long, at least initially. As patients who repeatedly experience reductions in discomfort and in their compulsive urges, despite being exposed to whatever they are worried about, they gain in confidence. The new freedom they begin to feel as their problem gradually comes under control is very rewarding. One patient said 'I can go anywhere now. I can do so many things which I couldn't even imagine myself doing. This is wonderful.'

This freedom, paradoxically, can be a problem. Patients who have been severely affected for several years may have had a very limited life, socially and otherwise. The family, too, is likely to have developed a lifestyle revolving around the patient's problems and demands, and the patient's improvement now gives everyone a good deal of freedom and free time. New activities, or restarting of old ones, is needed. In short, patients and their families have to re-adjust to normal life. Most therapists nowadays will make it a point to help patients and relatives by counselling them in these matters.

PROBLEMS IN THERAPY

Effects of depression

It is known that the chances of obsessive-compulsive patients benefiting from cognitive behaviour therapy are reduced if they are very depressed (Foa, 1979) These patients are best treated after their depression has been relieved by other means, psychological or pharmacological.

Motivation and compliance

Some patients find the demands of a cognitive behavioural treatment pro-gramme prohibitive. They may either refuse to accept the therapy offered or show poor co-operation and tend to drop out (Steketee et al., 1982). Therapists usually make an effort to persuade a reluctant patient to accept the treatment offered, by answering his or her queries in detail and pointing out that the chances of improvement are high. A reluctant or doubting patient may be helped by the opportunity to talk with a successfully treated patient. In the end, however, the patient must decide for him- or herself whether to accept therapy. Careful cognitive therapy at the preliminary stages often facilitates treatment acceptance and co-operation. It is important to ensure that the patient is well-motivated. A patient with low motivation to change is unlikely to benefit much from treatment and is unlikely to adhere fully to the instructions of a treatment programme. Cases in which patients are pressured into therapy by family members tend to have poor results unless the patients themselves see the need to comply. Therapist should carefully assess a patient's motivation to accept therapy, before undertaking to treat him or her.

GROUP APPROACHES

Although group therapy is commonly used in many psychiatric disorders, it has been of limited popularity among clinicians treating obsessive-compulsive patients. There is some evidence that a group approach may be beneficial, both for obsessive-compulsive patients and their families, as an adjunct to individual treatment (Tynes et al., 1992). Steketee et al. (2000) have shown the value of group work with patients with compulsive hoarding.

SELF-ADMINISTERED THERAPY

It has been argued that much of the behavioural treatment of obsessive-compulsive disorder can be undertaken by patients, with little involvement of the therapist (e.g. Hoogduin and Hoogduin, 1984). In many therapy programmes, clinic-based treatment is augmented by self-administered therapy sessions, sometimes with the help of a family member. However, the problems need to be carefully assessed by an experienced therapist, and the treatment well supervised. Except in mild cases, unsupervised self-treatment is not advisable.

PSYCHODYNAMIC PSYCHOTHERAPY

In psychodynamic theory, obsessions and compulsions are seen as symptoms of underlying psychic conflicts and other repressed material (Jakes, 1996). The individual finds a relatively safe way of giving expression to repressed thoughts, feelings and so on, through his or her obsessions and/or compulsions. The individual's experiences during the so-called anal stage of development are considered to be particularly important in causing these symptoms in later life (see, for example, Fenichel, 1946). Psychotherapy would aim at exploring the patient's unconscious phenomena in order to unravel the hidden conflicts and anxieties. The results of such therapy, which is time consuming, have not been established to be satisfactory for any disorder (Eysenck, 1952). The problems in evaluating the outcome of psychotherapy are many, and these have been discussed fully in the literature (Rachman and Wilson, 1981). One of the problems is whether a treatment produces better results than the improvement rate that occurs spontaneously. This makes it particularly difficult to evaluate therapies that are carried out over a long period of time. The results of psychotherapy for obsessive-compulsive problems are not encouraging.

REFERENCES

Clark, D. A. (2004) *Cognitive-Behavioral Therapy for OCD*. New York: Guilford Press.
de Silva, D. (1978) Behaviour therapy for obsessional neurosis. *Nursing Mirror*, 146, 15–17.
de Silva, P. (1986) Obsessional-compulsive imagery. *Behaviour Research and Therapy*, 24, 333–350.
de Silva, P. and Rachman, S. (2004) *Obsessive-Compulsive Disorder: The Facts, 3rd edn.* Oxford: Oxford University Press.
de Silva, P., Menzies, R. G. and Shafran, S. (2003) Spontaneous decay of compulsive urges: The case of covert compulsions. *Behaviour Research and Therapy*, 41, 129–137.
Eysenck, H. J. (1952) The effects of psychotherapy: An evaluation. *Journal of Consulting Psychology*, 16, 319–324.
Fenichel, O. (1946) *The Psychoanalytic Theory of Neurosis*. London: Kegan Paul.
Foa, E. B. (1979) Failure in treating obsessive-compulsives. *Behaviour Research and Therapy*, 17, 169–176.
Freeston, M. and Ladouceur, R. (1998) The cognitive-behavioural treatment of obsessions. In: V. E. Caballo (ed) *International Handbook of Cognitive and Behavioural Treatment for Psychological Disorders*. Oxford: Pergamon.
Frost, R. O. and Hartl, T. L. (2003) Compulsive hoarding. In: R. G. Menzies and P. de Silva (eds) *Obsessive-Compulsive Disorder: Theory, Research and Treatment*. Chichester: John Wiley.
Hartl, T. L. and Frost, R. O. (1999) Cognitive-behavioural treatment of compulsive hoarding: A multiple baseline experimental case study. *Behaviour Research and Therapy*, 37, 451–461.
Hoogduin, A. and Hoogduin, W. A. (1984) The out-patient treatment of patients with obsessive-compulsive disorder. *Behaviour Research and Therapy*, 22, 455–459.
Jakes, I. (1996) *Theoretical Approaches to Obsessive-Compulsive Disorder*. Cambridge: Cambridge University Press.

Jenike, M. A., Rauch, S. L., Baer, L. and Rasmussen, S. A. (1998) Neurosurgical treatment of obsessive-compulsive disorder. In: M. A. Jenike, L. Baer and W. E. Minichiello (eds) *Obsessive-Compulsive Disorder: Practical Mangement, 3rd edn.* Chicago: Mosby.

Kyrios, M. (2003) Exposure and response prevention for OCD. In: R. G. Menzies and P. de Silva (eds) *Obsessive-Compulsive Disorder: Theory Research and Treatment.* Chichester: John Wiley.

Ladouceur, R., Leger, E., Rheaume, J. and Dube, D. (1996) Correction of inflated responsibility in the treatment of obsessive-compulsive disorder. *Behaviour Research and Therapy*, 34, 767–774.

Marks, M. (2003) Cognitive therapy for OCD. In: R. G. Menzies and P. de Silva (eds) *Obsessive-Compulsive Disorder: Theory, Research and Treatment.* Chichester: John Wiley.

McDonough, M. (2003) Pharmacological and neurosurgical treatment of OCD. In: R. G. Menzies and P. de Silva (eds) *Obsessive-Compulsive Disorder: Theory, Research and Treatment.* Chichester: John Wiley.

McLean, P. and Woody, S. R. (2001) *Anxiety Disorders in Adults: An Evidence-Based Approach to Psychological Treatment.* Oxford: Oxford University Press.

Meyer, V. (1966) Modification of expectations in cases with obsessional rituals. *Behaviour Research and Therapy*, 4, 273–280.

Rachman, S. (1974) Primary obsessional slowness. *Behaviour Research and Therapy*, 12, 9–18.

Rachman, S. (1976) The modification of obsessions: A new formulation. *Behaviour Research and Therapy*, 14, 437–443.

Rachman, S. (1980) Psycho-surgical treatment of obsessive-compulsive disorders. In: E. S. Valenstein (ed) *The Psychosurgery Debate.* San Francisco: W. H. Freeman.

Rachman, S. (1997) A cognitive theory of obsessions. *Behaviour Research and Therapy*, 35, 793–802.

Rachman, S. (1998) A cognitive theory of obsessions: Elaborations. *Behaviour Research and Therapy*, 36, 385–401.

Rachman, S. (2003a) Primary obsessional slowness. In: R. G. Menzies and P. de Silva (eds) *Obsessive-Compulsive Disorder: Theory, Research and Treatment.* Chichester: John Wiley.

Rachman, S. (2003b) *The Treatment of Obsessions.* Oxford: Oxford University Press.

Rachman, S. and Hodgson, R. (1980) *Obsessions and Compulsions.* Englewood Cliffs, NJ: Prentice-Hall.

Rachman, S. and Wilson, G. T. (1981) *The Effects of Psychological Therapy.* New York: Pergamon.

Rachman, S., de Silva, P. and Roper, G. (1976) The spontaneous decay of compulsive urges. *Behaviour Research and Therapy*, 14, 445–453.

Salkovskis, P. M. (1983) Treatment of an obsessional patient using habituation to audiotape ruminations. *British Journal of Clinical Psychology*, 22, 311–313.

Salkovskis, P. M. (1999) Understanding and treating obsessive-compulsive disorder. *Behaviour Research and Therapy*, 37, S29–S52.

Simos, G. (2002) Medication effects on obsessions and compulsions. In: R. O. Frost and G. Steketee (eds) *Cognitive Approaches to Obsessions and Compulsions: Theory, Assessment, and Treatment.* Amsterdam: Pergamon.

Slater, E. and Roth, M. (1969) *Clinical Psychiatry*, 3rd edn of W. Meyer-Gross,

E. Slater and M. Roth's *Clinical Psychiatry*. London: Ballière, Tindall and Cassell.

Steketee, G., Foa, E. B. and Grayson, J. B. (1982) Recent advances in the behavioral treatment of obsessive-compulsives. *Archives of General Psychiatry*, 39, 1365–1371.

Steketee, G., Frost, R. O., Wincze, J., Greene, K. A. I. and Douglass, H. (2000) Group and individual treatment of compulsive hoarding: A pilot study. *Behavioural and Cognitive Psychotherapy*, 28, 259–268.

Takeuchi, T., Nakagawa, A., Harai, H., Nakatani, E., Fujikawa, S., Yoshizato, C. and Yamagami, T. (1997) Primary obsessional slowness: Long-term findings. *Behaviour Research and Therapy*, 35, 445–449.

Tynes, L. L., Salins, C., Skiba, W. and Winstead, D. K. (1992) A psycho-educational and support group for obsessive-compulsive disorder patients and their significant others. *Comprehensive Psychiatry*, 33, 197–201.

Wolpe, J. (1958) *Psychotherapy by Reciprocal Inhibition*. Stanford, CA: Stanford University Press.

Wolpe, J. (1991) *The Practice of Behavior Therapy, 4th edn*. New York: Pergamon.

Chapter 5

Depression

Investigation

Edward Watkins

INTRODUCTION

Although depression is a broad and heterogeneous diagnostic grouping, the central elements common to all depressions are depressed mood and/or loss of pleasure in most activities. This chapter will consider the diagnoses and symptoms of unipolar major depression and dysthymia (described comprehensively in the *Diagnostic and Statistical Manual of Psychiatric Disorders*, 4th edition; American Psychiatric Association (APA), 1994). Unipolar major depression refers to an episode in which mood is seriously compromised (e.g. at least 2 weeks of continuous depressed mood or loss of interest/anhedonia, most of the day, nearly every day) and there are at least four additional depressive symptoms from: loss of energy, low self-worth, guilt, suicidal ideation, sleep disturbance and appetite disturbance. Dysthymia refers to at least 2 years of depressed mood more days than not, accompanied by additional depressive symptoms that do not meet the threshold for major depression.

A broader view of depression is adopted out of practical considerations: in clinic settings, a patient may still experience considerable distress and benefit from treatment even if he or she does not meet diagnostic criteria. Furthermore, research indicates that milder syndromes of depression (e.g. minor depression, defined as three or four symptoms of major depression, including depressed mood or anhedonia for at least 4 weeks, or residual depression, defined as partial remission from major depression following treatment) are often precursors to more severe episodes and relapse (Fava et al., 1998a, 1998b; Judd et al., 1999; Rapaport et al., 2002).

Depression is one of the most common and most disabling psychological conditions: at any one time approximately 5% of the population meet criteria for major depression (point prevalence; Blazer et al., 1994), with 10–20% of people suffering from major depression within their lifetime (Blazer et al., 1994). The World Health Organization (WHO) ranked depression as the number one cause of disability in the world and as fourth in disease burden among all medical and psychiatric disorders (Murray and Lopez, 1996). Depression is associated with increased mortality: approximately 10–15% of people with severe depression commit suicide and depression seems to triple the risk of fatal heart disease (Carney et al., 1995, 1997; Penninx et al., 2001; Carney and Freedland, 2003). Depression is a chronic and recurrent disorder: 50–85% of people who have had depression will have it again (Keller et al., 1984), with the risk for repeated episodes greater than 80% (Judd, 1997). Following recovery, rates of relapse and recurrence are high: 30% relapse within 6 months and 40% recurrence within 1 year (Belsher and Costello, 1988).

THE FUNCTIONS OF INVESTIGATION AND ASSESSMENT FOR DEPRESSION

There are a number of distinct approaches to investigating depression: standardised and structured interviews, more open unstructured clinical interviews, observation, diary records and psychometric measures. Each approach has different advantages and disadvantages, depending on the context and function of the assessment. The rest of this chapter focuses on the four principal functions for investigation and assessment in depression.

The first function is *to determine diagnosis*, that is, whether a client meets criteria for major depression and/or other psychiatric disorders. The main approach to assessing diagnosis is through structured diagnostic interviews such as the Structured Clinical Interview for DSM-IV (SCID); Spitzer et al., 1996). Whilst determining whether a client presenting with depressive symptoms meets diagnostic criteria is clearly of value for research, it might be considered less helpful in a therapeutic setting, given that psychological interventions for depression are fairly similar whatever the severity of the depression. Nonetheless, assessing diagnosis in a more formal way is important for considering co-morbidity, for formulating causal relationships between diagnoses and for ruling out differential diagnoses. In planning treatment, it is essential to determine which disorder is the principal difficulty, and/or the cause of the other difficulties and/or the main obstacle to recovery. For example, in a patient with alcohol dependence and depression, are the depressive symptoms a consequence of the drinking, or is the drinking a response to the depression?

The symptoms characteristic of unipolar major depression overlap with a number of other disorders and it is important to check these alternative diagnoses, particularly when referrals are brief and note only that the client suffers from depressed mood and anxiety. Specific questions asking about manic symptoms are necessary to establish whether a client presents with unipolar or bipolar depression; unless currently florid, manic symptoms can be easily missed unless specifically investigated. Other psychiatric disorders that are co-morbid with depression and that have overlapping symptoms are generalised anxiety disorder (GAD), body dysmorphic disorder (BDD), substance and alcohol abuse/dependence and chronic fatigue. Identifying and differentiating between these diagnoses will be relevant to planning treatment as the approach to therapy may differ for each disorder. For example, investigating whether clients have extreme long-lasting preoccupations about aspects of their physical appearance would distinguish between BDD and depression.

Another relevant aspect of assessing diagnosis is screening for depression. Despite the common presentation of depression, it often goes undetected and untreated in primary and secondary care settings (at levels of up to 50%; Goldberg, 1998). The recent National Institute for Health and Clinical Excellence (NICE) guidelines for the management of depression recommend the use of two questions to screen for depression: 'During the last month, have you often been bothered by feeling down, depressed or hopeless?' and 'During the last month, have you been bothered by little interest or pleasure in doing things?' (NICE, 2004). A positive answer to either question should initiate a full check for depression.

The second major function of investigation is *determining the nature and severity of the depressive symptoms*, which is key for establishing which problems to focus on with a patient (e.g. is poor concentration or poor sleep something to work on?). Furthermore it provides a baseline from which to monitor and evaluate the progress of therapy. Regular (often weekly) measures of severity can help establish whether therapeutic approaches are being effective and, thereby, guide therapy. Measures of severity include observer-rated instruments (e.g. the Hamilton Rating Scale for Depression, the Inventory for Depressive Symptomatology) and self-report questionnaires (e.g. the Beck Depression Inventory, the Hospital Anxiety and Depression Scale). Such measures can be used to determine how and when to finish therapy. Given that residual symptoms of depression predict increased risk for future relapse (Fava et al., 1998), the final sessions of therapy need to pay close attention to any remaining symptoms.

The third main function of investigation is *to determine the cognitive, affective, physiological, situational, interpersonal, behavioural and contextual factors contributing to the onset and maintenance of the depression*, that is, to establish potential mediators and moderators of the depression. Such assessment is critical to developing an idiosyncratic formulation of each individual's depression so as to guide the focus and strategies of therapy and, indeed, to select between different psychological treatment options. This chapter emphasises the value of adopting a biopsychosocial model of depression in assessment: whichever treatment orientation is favoured, it is useful to be aware of the full range of factors that can influence a client's depression. This form of investigation typically involves more open-ended exploratory clinical interviews. To provide an overview of such functional assessment, this chapter will review assessment approaches from cognitive behavioural therapy (CBT) and interpersonal therapy (IPT), two empirically validated effective treatments for depression. Critically, assessment is more than just information gatheing: it plays a vital role in the therapeutic process by providing patients with a rationale and socialisation into the treatment approach. Skilful assessment can provide clients with initial hope and help to normalise, clarify and explain their problems.

The final function of assessment is *to determine prognostic and prescriptive factors*. Both prognostic (predicts how well the client will respond to therapy) and prescriptive (predicts which therapy will be more helpful for the client) factors are more important as the resources available for treatment need to be delivered more effectively and efficiently. Ideally, patients should be matched to the most useful therapy and expensive therapy resources only used for those patients who will benefit.

THE INVESTIGATION AND ASSESSMENT OF DIAGNOSIS

The principal standardised assessment measures for diagnosis are semi-structured and structured diagnostic interviews, such as the SCID (Spitzer et al., 1992, 1996; Williams et al., 1992), the Schedule for Affective Disorders and Schizophrenia (SADS; Endicott and Spitzer, 1978), the National Institute for Mental Health's Diagnostic Interview Schedule (DIS; Robins et al., 1981) and the Composite International Diagnostic Interview (CIDI; Robins et al., 1988; Wittchen et al., 1991). These interviews are typically used for research and follow a standardised format, producing greater validity and reliability of diagnosis (Wittchen et al., 1991), although they can be time consuming. In normal clinical practice, it is more efficient to ask about the key diagnostic criteria (low mood, loss of interest/pleasure, energy, sleep, appetite, libido, concentration, worthlessness and suicidal thoughts) and to only use standardised interviews for complex cases or where there are concerns about co-morbidity (e.g. asking about elevated mood or irritability to check on mania).

THE INVESTIGATION OF SEVERITY OF DEPRESSION

A range of observer and self-report measures is used to investigate severity of depression. When using these measures, we need to consider the degree to which they specifically address symptoms of depression compared to other psychopathology, their reliability and validity, and sensitivity to change in symptoms following treatment for depression. The measures reviewed here are relatively successful at satisfying these criteria, except where noted. The choice of the particular measure used will depend, among other things, on the nature of the problem presented by the patient, on the population from which the patient comes and on the assessor's aims in doing the assessment.

Care must be taken with interpreting scores on psychometric measures.

The particular meaning of a scale depends on the purpose and theoretical construct underlying the development of the scale. For example, the Beck Depression Inventory (BDI) has a large number of cognitive items, reflecting the cognitive model's concern with patterns of negative thinking. Both global scores and particular sub-item scores should be examined, especially as two very differently presenting patients can obtain the same overall score if one patient has many symptoms at a mild level and the other patient has a few symptoms at a severe level. Particular care needs to be taken in interpreting somatic items in patient groups who are likely to have high levels of symptoms for non-psychiatric reasons, e.g., in the physically ill, pregnant women or the elderly. None of the measures of severity is suitable for determining a diagnosis of depression.

OBSERVER RATING SCALES

Observer rating scales can include specifically designed idiosyncratic measures, for example, behavioural observation of relevant depression-related behaviour, such as time spent in bed, number of times observed crying, or levels of activity. Such measures can help to establish the severity of symptoms as well as the consequences and functions of these symptoms for patients. Observations by the interviewer are also an important source of information. During the interview, the clinician can look out for and record depressive behaviours and see how they relate to particular contexts. Paying attention for signs of agitation and retardation (slowing of speech or movements) and emotional lability (shifts in facial expression, verbal tone, tearfulness) can help the clinician to identify the reactivity/rigidity of the depression, to spot interpersonal and cognitive factors that may trigger shifts in mood and to gauge the impact of the depressed person's behaviour on others.

Hamilton Rating Scale

The original Hamilton Rating Scale for Depression (HRSD; Hamilton, 1960) had 21 items [including depressed mood, guilt, interest in sex, suicidal tendencies, insomnia (early, middle and late), work and interests, energy level, anxiety and irritability, somatic symptoms of anxiety, hypochondriasis, appetite, loss of weight, insight, retardation, agitation, diurnal variation, depersonalisation, paranoid and obsessional symptoms], which were rated independently by two raters on 0–2 or 0–4 scales, depending on item, with the final score the sum of the two raters. This approach had good inter-rater reliability (correlation of +0.90; Hamilton, 1960) and high correlations with other measures of depression, such as the Beck Depression Inventory. More recently, the HRSD has been adapted to be used by a single rater and a 17-item version has been produced (dropping diurnal variation, depersonalisation, paranoid and obsessional symptoms). For the 17-item version, a total score of 0–7 indicates no depression, 8–17 mild depression, 18–25 moderate depression and scores of 26+ severe depression (guidelines for the HRSD have been produced by Williams, 1998). The HRSD has been found to be sensitive to treatment effects in numerous trials of CBT and antidepressant medication and it has high reliability, validity and international acceptance. On the minus side, the HRSD can be slow to administer, it is less sensitive for discriminating between moderate and severe depression and many of its items do not specifically discriminate for depression.

Inventory for Depressive Symptomatology – clinician and self-report versions

The Inventory for Depressive Symptomatology (IDS; Rush et al., 1986) is a 30-item measure of depressive signs and symptoms, and can be administered either in an interview by a clinician or completed in a self-report format by clients. It focuses on items assessing 'mood', 'anxiety', 'weight', 'sleep' and 'atypical features', and covers a similar range of symptoms as the HRSD. Both versions have high internal consistency and validity. The IDS can be repeatedly photocopied by purchasers of the *Mental Health Portfolio* (Milne, 1992).

SELF-RATING SCALES

Beck Depression Inventory

There are three forms of the Beck Depression Inventory (BDI; Beck et al., 1961, 1988): the original 21-item BDI-I, a shortened 13-item version of the BDI-I for research and clinical screening purposes (Beck and Beck, 1972) and a revised 21-item BDI-II, with each item scored on a 0–3 scale. All versions measure the severity of depression in adults and adolescents, indexing somatic, cognitive and behavioural aspects of depression. The original BDI-I is completed for how the patient has been feeling for the past week, including today. Good reliability and validity is reported (Beck et al., 1988). For the original 21-item version, the criteria for scores were: 0–9 no depression, 10–18 mild–moderate depression, 19–29 moderate–severe depression, 29+ extremely severe depression.

The original BDI was criticised for being overly focused on cognitive/self-evaluation items such that it is very sensitive to negative thinking. It may also be susceptible to subjective biases when completed: scores on the BDI are typically higher than scores on observer measures such as the HRSD in out-patient groups (Enns et al., 2000). Enns et al. (2000) found that higher BDI scores relative to HRSD scores were predicted by younger age; higher educational attainment; an atypical, non-melancholic subtype of depression; high neuroticism; low extraversion and low agreeableness, suggesting that the BDI may tap into constructs other than depressive symptoms, such as low self-esteem and personality effects on symptom reporting.

The new BDI-II was created to make the questionnaire more relevant to the determination of the diagnosis of major depression (Beck et al., 1996a, 1996b). To this end, the time frame for endorsing the items was expanded to the last 2 weeks, including today (to match DSM-IV criteria) and the specific diagnostic criteria of agitation, worthlessness, concentration difficulty and loss of energy replaced the items of weight loss, body image change, somatic preoccupation and work difficulties. The items on appetite and sleep were adapted so that patients could report oversleeping and overeating as well as insomnia and loss of appetite (the only options in BDI-I), in order to capture this atypical presentation of depression. The BDI-II appears to have better internal consistency and reliability than the BDI-I (Beck et al., 1996a, 1996b). For the BDI-II, scores of 0–13 indicate no depression, 14–19 mild depression, 20–28 moderate depression and scores of 29–63 severe depression.

Centre for Epidemiological Studies – Depression Scale

The Centre for Epidemiological Studies – Depression Scale (CES-D) is a 20-item (each scored 0–3) self-report measure of the key depressive symptoms during the past week. The measure shows good consistency and ability to discriminate depressed patients from both psychiatric and normal controls (Radloff, 1977; Weissman et al., 1977).

Hospital Anxiety and Depression Scale

The Hospital Anxiety and Depression Scale (HADS; Zigmond and Snaith, 1983) is a self-report scale that is useful for examining depression symptoms in the physically ill; it has a reduced number of somatic items. The HADS (Zigmond and Snaith, 1983; Snaith and Zigmond, 1986) has seven depression items and seven anxiety items (each item rated from 0 to 3), which are designed to assess the severity of depression and anxiety in general hospital out-patient departments. The HADS is brief, making it a good screening measure in primary care, and has few somatic items, making it useful for examining symptoms in the physically ill. However, it is not a precise measure of major depression given the absence of many of the core symptoms of depression. Scores on the total scale are interpreted as follows: 0–7 no significant anxiety or depression, 8–10 doubtful or mild cases, 11–21 likely to be definite cases.

Two other scales that are useful within populations who experience somatic difficulties are the Geriatric Depression Scale designed for elderly patients

(GDS; Yesavage et al., 1983; Yesavage, 1991) and the Edinburgh Post-Natal Rating Scale for Depression (Cox et al., 1987), designed initially for pregnant women. Both of these scales focus on less somatic symptoms of depression. The EPDS is a 10-item measure used to assess depression following childbirth, each symptom scored on a scale from 0–3. Scores greater than 13–14 are considered to indicate depression.

ASSESSMENT FOR DEVISING A CASE FORMULATION AND PLANNING TREATMENT

This section reviews some key principles and assumptions relevant to how assessment can aid the selection and planning of psychological treatments. Such assessments will primarily depend on an open-ended interview to determine the context, background, onset and maintaining factors in the depression, as well as the specific symptoms and problems that the client wishes to resolve. To provide a description of a broad and thorough assessment within a wider biopsychosocial framework, both CBT and IPT approaches to assessment are reviewed. The ease with which a client's presentation is relevant to any particular treatment model is a useful heuristic for treatment selection: the more the client's problems make sense within a model, the more workable that treatment approach will be to the therapist and the more meaningful the approach will be for the client. Research suggests that when the rationale for the treatment intervention does not match the reasons for the depression held by patients, the treatment is less effective, e.g. when the patient believes the reasons for the depression are relationship oriented there is poorer response to CBT (Addis and Jacobson, 1996).

When assessing depression, the following principles are valuable. First, the clinician needs to ascertain the extent and nature of the problems that cause the client to present for help, whether those problems are related to depression or not. Rather than relying on referral information, it is best to ask the client an open-ended question such as 'Can you briefly tell me what is difficult for you?', and to then follow-up on the response. It is useful to check the full range of depressive symptoms, as well as asking about practical problems (e.g. finance, housing, unemployment, health), interpersonal problems (e.g. difficult relationships, divorce, isolation) and intrapersonal problems (e.g. low self-esteem, alcohol/substance abuse). Many patients with depression will have some or many actual difficulties. In such situations, it is useful to normalise the depression, noting that it is entirely understandable that the patient may be despondent and down given the circumstances. Nonetheless, there is an important distinction between experiencing a chronically stressful event and being clinically depressed: many people cope despite extreme adversity, such that depression is not a foregone conclusion after severe difficulties. Thus, the assessment should focus on which behavioural, cognitive, environmental or social factors contribute to depressed mood becoming prolonged clinical depression.

Second, the clinician needs to determine which problems the client is actively seeking help for, and which the client is motivated to work on. Patients can be referred for very different problems from those that they personally view as most important. Patients may also not directly discuss their major concerns or difficulties, perhaps because of shame and embarrassment, or hopelessness and passivity secondary to the depression, or past negative reactions. Clients may need some time to develop a sense of safety and trust before they can fully discuss difficulties. Sensitively acknowledging that shame or hopelessness may make it hard to discuss problems and normalising these feelings, as well as providing the patient with information and options that indicate some understanding of his or her experience can facilitate openness.

Third, the clinician needs to investigate the course of the depression. When and under what circumstances did the depression start? For first episodes of depression, there are often salient loss or defeat events, e.g. bereavements, loss of employment, end of a relationship (Brown and Harris, 1978; Shrout et al., 1989). For subsequent recurrences, the trigger events may become less obvious. The relationship between stressful life events and onset of major depression decreases as the number of previous depressive episodes increases (Kendler et al., 2000, 2001, 2004). When there are no objectively salient life events, the clinician will have to explore events preceding the depression, trying to ascertain their subjective meaning for the client. Assessing the onset and development of the depression – 'Has it worsened with time or stayed relatively stable?', 'Was the onset rapid or gradual?', 'What changed as the depression worsened?' – guides treatment planning and relapse prevention. Determining relapse signatures for patients and focusing on situational stressors and warning signs (e.g. reduced activity, irritability, tension) that precede an onset of depression can be very useful for devising future coping plans.

Fourth, it is useful to get a picture of the client, his or her strengths and weaknesses and his or her past history and family background. Key areas to ask about include schooling, childhood, family set-up, occupation, any major life changes, relationships, previous psychiatric problems and previous treatment. It is particularly useful to get a feel for the exclusiveness of the depression and the interpersonal functioning of the client. Clients can present with episodes of depression against a background of remission to an euthymic state where they function well and have a positive sense of themselves: therapy with such clients, within whatever orientation, would focus on re-activating and consolidating the healthy sense of self. Alternatively, depressed patients can report finding it difficult to recall times when they functioned well and can have very little positive sense of themselves: typically these clients have more neglected, abusive or traumatic early life experience, present with dysthymia and show patterns of disturbed inter-personal behaviour. For such patients, therapy may involve building-up a more positive sense of self – from the start, therapy with such clients is likely to be more involved and prolonged.

Fifth, it is useful explicitly to investigate issues of abuse in patients present-ing with depression. High levels of physical, sexual and emotional abuse are found in patients presenting with depression. Depression is often associated with a past history of abuse or experience of trauma (Hill, 2003). Half of all women seeking help for domestic violence had significant levels of depressive symptoms (Cascardi et al., 1999) and depression is elevated in women in violent relationships (Andrews and Brown, 1988). Similarly, humiliation events, such as the discovery of a partner's infidelity, are found to greatly increase the risk of depression (Brown et al., 1986; Christian-Herman et al., 2001). Awareness of these issues is important because it may influence the focus of treatment, e.g. work on coping with shame and trauma or specific adaptations of CBT for working with adult victims of child sexual abuse (Jehu, 1988). Recent evidence suggests that CBT adapted for people with chronic depression and a history of early abuse is efficacious and superior to pharmacotherapy alone (Nemeroff et al., 2003). More immediately, for a minority of patients, escape from an abusive relationship may be a necessary first step for their physical and psychological well-being.

A final area always to consider is hopelessness and suicide risk. All clients should be asked if they have had any suicidal thoughts or impulses in the last week and, if yes, to check whether they have made any plans and what has stopped them from acting on them. Past attempts at suicide, impulsiveness, hopelessness, poor problem solving, substance abuse and easy access to fatal means (e.g. a store of pills, shotguns in farming communities) all increase the risk of suicide. If the risk of suicide seems high, then all assessment and treatment energies should be focused here.

Hopelessness can be routinely screened with the Beck Hopelessness Scale (BHS; Beck and Steer, 1988). This 20-item scale measures pessimism and hopelessness about the future. Patients who report a greater sense of hope-lessness (seeing that they are trapped, there is no way out, things cannot improve, unable to see anything positive in the future) are more likely to commit suicide (Beck et al., 1990). The BHS has been found to be a good predictor of long-term outcome with the following interpretations suggested for the scores: 0–3 no suicide risk; 4–8 mild risk; 9–14 moderate risk, requir-ing monitoring; 15+ severe, definite suicide risk. For the moderate risk and above groups, the clinician should explore thoughts about suicide, suicidal ideation and intention, previous attempts at suicide and whether the client has any plans for suicide. Endorsements of 2 or greater on item 9 on the BDI can also usefully prompt this more intensive questioning.

Assessment and intervention during therapy is an ongoing process. Whereas initial sessions are usually predominantly devoted to assessment, further information gathering will occur within the context of clinical sessions, and initial hypotheses and formulations will need to be revised in the light of new data.

ASSESSMENT FOR DEPRESSION WITHIN A COGNITIVE BEHAVIOURAL FRAMEWORK

Within CBT for depression, the assessment is focused on understanding the patient and his or her problems, establishing rapport, defining the goals of the therapy, detecting negative cognitions and unhelpful behaviours, engaging the patient in the therapy and instilling hope and optimism to counteract pessimism. Three key approaches to achieving these goals within the early sessions are: (1) problem definition; (2) investigating the cognitive triad; and (3) providing a treatment rationale.

During problem definition, the therapist and the patient work together to identify a list of specific problems that the patient wishes to tackle during therapy. These problems are then prioritised on the basis of how important each problem is, how central it is to the patient's distress and how amenable it may be to change. Specific goals within each problem area are determined collaboratively, with the successful outcome of the goal operationalised as concretely as possible, for example by questions like 'How would you like things to be different in this area?', 'How would you act differently if this goal was achieved?'. Problem definition and goal setting provide a focus for therapy, help patients feel listened to and, often, make difficulties seem less overwhelming.

Within CBT, a core focus of treatment is the identification and challenging of negative automatic thoughts. The initial assessment focuses on identifying some prototypical negative thoughts in order to start formulating the client's beliefs and to illustrate the role of cognition in his or her symptoms. Therapists look for thoughts reflecting the cognitive triad: negative thoughts about the self (e.g. 'I am a failure'), negative thoughts about the future (e.g. 'I will never get better') and negative thoughts about the world (e.g. 'No one cares about me'). Such thoughts are elicited by asking questions like 'What went through your mind just then?' when clients report negative feelings, recall a recent upsetting event or are observed to experience shifts in emotion during the session.

CBT approaches to depression also emphasise looking at behaviour, and in particular assessing changes in behaviour, asking clients if there are any activities they have stopped, reduced or started during the onset and development of the depression. Most patients report a reduction in occupational and leisure activities, exercise and sports, and social contact. Initial steps in activity scheduling to improve mood will usefully build back up whatever activities each patient has reduced. In the same light, a detailed functional analysis of antecedents, consequences and modulators of depressed symptoms is an important part of the investigation, for example, asking 'When/where/how/who with/doing what do you feel better/worse?' (for further details on functional analysis, see Chapter 1).

Recent developments in behavioural approaches to depression, e.g. behavioural activation (see Jacobson et al., 1996; for full details see Martell et al., 2001), emphasise the assessment of secondary avoidant behaviours when treating depression. The behavioural activation approach proposes that unhelpful secondary coping responses lead to the maintenance of depression. Typically, these unhelpful responses involve attempts to escape from an aversive environment (e.g. arguments, confrontations, reminders of loss) or to avoid aversive situations or emotional states (risk of failure or embarrassment). Avoidance behaviours include being passive, withdrawal, rumination, complaining or avoiding new activities. Because these behaviours reduce exposure to aversive situations they are negatively reinforced and become more prevalent, reducing the frequency and narrowing the range of other behaviours, which in turn reduces contact with positive reinforcers and increases the risk for depression. Within the behavioural activation approach, the assessment will explicitly ask about possible forms of avoidance, the context in which avoidance occurs (e.g. 'What is the situation where you have kept silent?', 'Under what conditions have you been active and under what conditions have you not been active?') and the functions of behaviours (e.g. 'What are the consequences of not saying anything?'). Identifying these aspects of avoidance leads into treatment plans.

To establish the rationale for CBT, patients are informed about the active, structured and collaborative nature of CBT and that it is a proven, effective treatment. The value and importance of completing homework assignments is emphasised. Through examining and feeding-back moment-by-moment changes in thoughts, feelings and behaviours as reported by the patient when discussing upsetting situations, the therapist can illustrate the reciprocal relationships between cognition, emotion and behaviour highlighted in the cognitive model. Drawing out these relationships can provide some understanding of why a patient is depressed and can be used to indicate how CBT explicitly targets different parts of the cycle to help recovery. Such examples can suggest the possibility of change by demonstrating how the patient can break out of the vicious circle by altering thoughts and behaviour. The use of the patient's own experiences makes the rationale more meaningful and convincing and can instil hope that the therapy may help him or her.

ASSESSMENT FOR DEPRESSION WITHIN AN INTERPERSONAL THERAPY FRAMEWORK

Interpersonal psychotherapy (IPT) treats depression by focusing on current relationship issues that contribute to the individual's difficulties. People with depression have difficulties in their interpersonal behaviour and often engender negative and rejecting responses from others (Coyne, 1976; Segrin, 2000). Furthermore, the onset of depression is often associated with interpersonal difficulties: marital difficulties or criticism from significant others predict subsequent depression (Weissman, 1987; Hooley and Teasdale, 1989; O'Leary et al., 1994; Fincham et al., 1997). The assessment phase of IPT explicitly focuses on the symptoms of depression and interpersonal functioning. Assessment within IPT concentrates on: (1) building a collaborative working alliance with the patient; and (2) identifying the interpersonal foci most relevant to the patient. Within IPT, depression is viewed as a consequence of a failure to work through the emotions linked to interpersonal difficulties and a failure to develop more adaptive interpersonal behaviours in response to these difficulties. The therapy focuses on a core interpersonal situation that is hypothesized to underpin the onset and maintenance of each client's depression. The four proposed foci are grief, interpersonal disputes, role transitions and interpersonal deficits (Klerman et al., 1984). Grief is chosen as a focus only when there has been the death of an actual person. Role disputes refer to unresolved arguments with significant others, whether explicit or covert. Transitions refer to changes in life roles resulting from life events, such as change in relationship status (e.g. marriage, divorce, parenthood) or changes in occupational status (e.g. promotion, redundancy, retirement). The changes can be positive, negative or neutral. Interpersonal deficit refers to reduced quality and quantity of interpersonal relationships, such that the client is isolated or lonely.

IPT directly explores whether each client has experienced any of the focal interpersonal situations by reviewing interpersonal changes from the 6 months before the onset of the depression onwards to the present day. The therapist will concentrate on building up a thorough interpersonal inventory of the client, summarising all the important people – past and present – in their life and the nature of these relationships. Patients are asked to describe their social support network, working through the people they have seen today, last week, last month, etc. The quality of these relationships is assessed. Are relationships intimate and confiding or superficial? Are relationships supportive and reciprocal? Many depressed patients report uneven relationships where they give a lot of time and energy to others without receiving much back, such that they feel 'taken for granted'. Do others provide any support? Is this emotional, instrumental or financial? Useful questions to ask include 'Is there anyone who would be willing to lend you £1000 in an emergency?', 'Is there anyone you could phone up in the middle of the night if you were distressed?'. It is useful to check for more negative relationships: there may be people in the social network who have a negative influence because they are abusive, critical or encourage unhelpful behaviour such as drug and alcohol use.

Any changes, disruptions or omissions in the social network also need to be determined. Life changes can change the quantity and quality of relationships, for example, a promotion may reduce contact with important people in the network or alter their attitude to the patient. Both past changes and upcoming changes are worth considering (e.g. a terminally ill parent, children about to leave home). Have potentially important people not been mentioned, such as partners, parents or any friends? Such omissions may indicate some degree of separation or conflict with that person.

Throughout the assessment, IPT explicitly links the symptoms of depression to the identified interpersonal focus (e.g. noting that the depression started following the bereavement, mood worsens when reminded of grief), to provide a rationale for the therapy. This approach also normalises the depression, making the depression understandable. Future therapy will then concentrate on helping patients work through both positive and negative feelings associated with this interpersonal focus and on developing more helpful interpersonal responses.

DETERMINING PROGNOSIS AND MAKING PRESCRIPTIVE JUDGEMENTS ABOUT THERAPY

Assessment measures can predict whether someone will respond to, say, CBT for depression (a prognostic indicator) and whether someone will respond better to CBT than to IPT (a prescriptive indicator). A number of patient variables predict poor outcome to all interventions (medication included), such as increased severity (particularly BDI > 30) and chronicity of the depression (longer than 6 months), inadequate response to previous treatment, two or more previous episodes and co-morbidity (for a review of specific predictors for CBT, see Hamilton and Dobson, 2002). Nonetheless, it is important to note that even patients with very severe depression can benefit from CBT and IPT if delivered skilfully and for sufficient duration, particularly in combination with antidepressant medication.

The ease with which a patient can identify and discuss cognitive, emotional, behavioural and interpersonal factors may indicate prognosis. Patients who are more psychologically minded and better able to recognise and differentiate thoughts, feelings and interpersonal responses may benefit more from CBT and IPT.

Are there predictors of superior response to different psychotherapies? Married patients appear to do better with CBT than single patients (Jarrett et al., 1991), whereas single patients do better in IPT than in CBT (Barber and Muenz, 1996). Patients with avoidant tendencies as determined by diagnostic criteria seem to respond better to CBT than to interpersonal therapies (Barber and Muenz, 1996, for avoidant personality disorder; Hardy et al., 1995, for avoidant, obsessive-compulsive or dependent personality disorder). However, in general there is little evidence for prescriptive discrimination between therapies.

CONCLUSION

Assessment and investigation of depression is a key step in planning and evaluating treatment. Successful assessment will use a convergent range of measures (self-report, record-keeping, interview, observation) to determine diagnosis, measure severity of symptoms and investigate the cognitive, behavioural, situational, emotional and interpersonal factors underpinning the depression. This information is crucial for formulating and guiding the therapy approach and in evaluating the progress of therapy. Assessment is an ongoing process throughout therapy for depression, which serves to inform the therapy, as well as to engage the patient.

REFERENCES

Addis, M. E. and Jacobson, N. S. (1996) Reasons for depression and the process and outcome of cognitive-behavioral psychotherapies. *Journal of Consulting and Clinical Psychology*, 64, 1417–1424.

Andrews, B. and Brown, G. W. (1988) Marital violence in the community – a biographical approach. *British Journal of Psychiatry*, 153, 305–312.

Barber, J. P. and Muenz, L. R. (1996) The role of avoidance and obsessiveness in matching patients to cognitive and interpersonal psychotherapy. Empirical findings from the treatment for depression collaborative research program. *Journal of Consulting and Clinical Psychology*, 64, 951–958.

Beck, A. T. and Beck, R. W. (1972) Screening depressed patients in family practice. A rapid technique. *Postgraduate Medicine*, 52, 81–85.

Beck, A. T., Brown, G., Berchick, R. J., Stewart, B. L. and Steer, R. A. (1990) Relationship between hopelessness and ultimate suicide: A replication with psychiatric outpatients. *American Journal of Psychiatry*, 147, 190–195.

Beck, A. T. and Steer, R. A. (1988) *Manual for the Beck Hoplessness Scale.* San Antonio, TX: Psychological Corporation.

Beck, A. T., Steer, R. A. and Brown, G. K. (1996a) *The Beck Depression Inventory – 2nd edn.* San Antonio, TX: Psychological Corporation.

Beck, A. T., Steer, R. A., Ball, R. and Ranieri, W. F. (1996b) Comparison of Beck Depression Inventories-IA and -II in psychiatric outpatients. *Journal of Personality Assessment*, 67, 588–597.

Beck, A. T., Steer, R. A. and Garbin, M. G. (1988) Psychometric properties of the Beck Depression Inventory – 25 years of evaluation. *Clinical Psychology Review*, 8, 77–100.

Beck, A. T., Ward, C. H., Mendelson, M., Mock, J. and Erbaugh, J. (1961) An inventory for measuring depression. *Archives of General Psychiatry*, 4, 561–574.

Belsher, G. and Costello, C. G. (1988) Relapse after recovery from unipolar depression – a critical review. *Psychological Bulletin*, 104, 84–96.

Blazer, D. G., Kessler, R. C., McGonagle, K. A. and Swartz, M. S. (1994) The prevalence and distribution of major depression in a national community sample – the National Comorbidity Survey. *American Journal of Psychiatry*, 151, 979–986.

Brown, G. W., Andrews, B., Harris, T., Adler, Z. and Bridge, L. (1986) Social support, self-esteem and depression. *Psychological Medicine*, 16, 813–831.

Brown, G. W. and Harris, T. (1978) *Social Origins of Depression*. London: Tavistock.

Carney, R. M. and Freedland, K. E. (2003) Depression, mortality, and medical morbidity in patients with coronary heart disease. *Biological Psychiatry*, 54, 241–247.

Carney, R. M., Freedland, K. E., Rich, M. W. and Jaffe, A. S. (1995) Depression as a risk factor for cardiac events in established coronary heart disease – a review of possible mechanisms. *Annals of Behavioral Medicine*, 17, 142–149.

Carney, R. M., Freedland, K. E., Sheline, Y. I. and Weiss, E. S. (1997) Depression and coronary heart disease: A review for cardiologists. *Clinical Cardiology*, 20, 196–200.

Cascardi, M., O'Leary, K. D. and Schlee, K. A. (1999) Co-occurrence and correlates of posttraumatic stress disorder and major depression in physically abused women. *Journal of Family Violence*, 14, 227–249.

Christian-Herman, J. L., O'Leary, K. D. and Avery-Leaf, S. (2001) The impact of severe negative events in marriage on depression. *Journal of Social and Clinical Psychology*, 20, 24–40.

Cox, J., Holden, J. M. and Sagovsky, R. (1987) Detection of postnatal depression – development of the 10-item Edinburgh Postnatal Depression Scale. *British Journal of Psychiatry*, 150, 782–786.

Coyne, J. C. (1976) Toward an interactional description of depression. *Psychiatry*, 39, 28–40.

Endicott, J. and Spitzer, R. L. (1978) A diagnostic interview: The schedule for affective disorders and schizophrenia. *Archives of General Psychiatry*, 35, 837–844.

Enns, M. W., Larsen, D. K. and Cox, B. J. (2000) Discrepancies between self and observer ratings of depression – the relationship to demographic, clinical and personality variables. *Journal of Affective Disorders*, 60, 33–41.

Fava, G., Rafaeli, C., Grandi, S., Conti, S. and Belluardo, P. (1998a) Prevention of recurrent depression in cognitive behavioural therapy: Preliminary findings. *Archives of General Psychiatry*, 55, 816–820.

Fava, G. A., Rafanelli, C., Grandi, S., Canestrari, R. and Morphy, M. A. (1998b) Six-year outcome for cognitive behavioral treatment of residual symptoms in major depression. *American Journal of Psychiatry*, 155, 1443–1445.

Fincham, F. D., Beach, S. R. H., Harold, G. T. and Osborne, L. N. (1997) Marital satisfaction and depression: Different causal relationships for men and women? *Psychological Science*, 8, 351–357.

Goldberg, D. (1998) Depression presenting at different levels of care. In: S. Checkley (ed) *The Management of Depression* (pp. 27–41). Oxford: Blackwell Science.

Hamilton, K. E. and Dobson, K. S. (2002) Cognitive therapy of depression: Pretreatment patient predictors of outcome. *Clinical Psychology Review*, 22, 875–893.

Hamilton, M. (1960) A rating scale for depression. *Journal of Neurology, Neurosurgery and Psychiatry*, 12, 52–62.

Hardy, G. E., Barkham, M., Shapiro, D. A., Rees, A., Stiles, W. B. and Reynolds, S. (1995) Impact of cluster-C personality disorders on outcomes of contrasting brief psychotherapies for depression. *Journal of Consulting and Clinical Psychology*, 63, 997–1004.

Hill, J. (2003) Childhood trauma and depression. *Current Opinion in Psychiatry*, 16, 3–6.

Hooley, J. M. and Teasdale, J. D. (1989) Predictors of relapse in unipolar depressives – expressed emotion, marital distress, and perceived criticism. *Journal of Abnormal Psychology*, 98, 229–235.

Jacobson, N. S., Dobson, K. S., Truax, P. A., Addis, M. E., Koerner, K., Gollan, J. K. et al. (1996) A component analysis of cognitive-behavioral treatment for depression. *Journal of Consulting and Clinical Psychology*, 64, 295–304.

Jarrett, R. B., Eaves, G. G., Grannemann, B. D. and Rush, A. J. (1991) Clinical, cognitive, and demographic predictors of response to cognitive therapy for depression – a preliminary report. *Psychiatry Research*, 37, 245–260.

Jehu, D. (1988) *Beyond Sexual Abuse: Therapy with Women who were Childhood Victims*. Chichester: John Wiley.

Judd, L. L., Paulus, M. P., Zeller, P., Fava, G. A., Rafanelli, C., Grandi, S. et al. (1999) The role of residual subthreshold depressive symptoms in early episode relapse in unipolar subthreshold depressive symptoms in early episode relapse in unipolar depressive disorder. *Archives of General Psychiatry*, 56, 764–765.

Judd, L. L. (1997) The clinical course of unipolar major depressive disorders. *Archives of General Psychiatry*, 54, 989–991.

Keller, M. B., Klerman, G. L., Lavori, P. W., Coryell, W., Endicott, J. and Taylor, J. (1984) Long-term outcome of episodes of major depression – clinical and public-health significance. *Journal of the American Medical Association*, 252, 788–792.

Kendler, K. S., Kuhn, J. and Prescott, C. A. (2004) The interrelationship of neuroticism, sex, and stressful life events in the prediction of episodes of major depression. *American Journal of Psychiatry*, 161, 631–636.

Kendler, K. S., Thornton, L. M. and Gardner, C. O. (2000) Stressful life events and previous episodes in the etiology of major depression in women: an evaluation of the kindling hypothesis. *American Journal of Psychiatry*, 157, 1243–1251.

Kendler, K. S., Thornton, L. M. and Gardner, C. O. (2001) Genetic risk, number of previous depressive episodes, and stressful life events in predicting onset of major depression. *American Journal of Psychiatry*, 158, 582–586.

Klerman, G. L., Weissman, M. M., Rounsaville, B. J. and Chevron, E. (1984) *Interpersonal Psychotherapy of Depression*. New York: Basic Books.

Martell, C. R., Addis, M. E. and Jacobson, N. S. (2001) *Depression in Context: Strategies for Guided Action*. New York: Norton.

Milne, D. (1992). *The Mental Health Portfolio*. Windsor, UK: NFER-Nelson.

Murray, C. J. L. and Lopez, A. D. (1996) Evidence-based health policy – Lessons from the global burden of disease study. *Science*, 274, 740–743.

Nemeroff, C. B., Heim, C. M., Thase, M. E., Klein, D. N., Rush, A. J., Schatzberg, A. F. et al. (2003) Differential responses to psychotherapy versus pharmacotherapy in patients with chronic forms of major depression and childhood trauma. *Proceedings of the National Academy of Sciences*, 2336126100.

O'Leary, K. D., Christian, J. L. and Mendell, N. R. (1994) A closer look at the link between marital discord and depressive symptomatology. *Journal of Social and Clinical Psychology*, 13, 33–41.

Penninx, B. W. J. H., Beekman, A. T. F., Honig, A., Deeg, D. J. H., Schoevers, R. A., van Eijk, J. T. M. et al. (2001) Depression and cardiac mortality – results from a community-based longitudinal study. *Archives of General Psychiatry*, 58, 221–227.

Rapaport, M. H., Judd, L. L., Schettler, P. J., Yonkers, K. A., Thase, M. E., Kupfer, D. J.

et al. (2002) A descriptive analysis of minor depression. *American Journal of Psychiatry*, 159, 637–643.

Robins, L. N., Helzer, J. E., Croughan, J. and Ratcliff, K. S. (1981) National Institute of Mental Health Diagnostic Interview Schedule – its history, characteristics, and validity. *Archives of General Psychiatry*, 38, 381–389.

Robins, L. N., Wing, J., Wittchen, H., Helzer, J. E., Babor, T. F., Burke, J. et al. (1988) The Composite International Diagnostic Interview – an epidemiologic instrument suitable for use in conjunction with different diagnostic systems and in different cultures. *Archives of General Psychiatry*, 45, 1069–1077.

Segrin, C. (2000) Social skills deficits associated with depression. *Clinical Psychology Review*, 20, 379–403.

Shrout, P., Link, B. G., Dohrenwend, B. P., Skodol, A. E., Stueve, A. and Mirotznik, J. (1989) Characterizing life events as risk factors for depression – the role of fateful loss events. *Journal of Abnormal Psychology*, 98, 460–467.

Snaith, R. P. and Zigmond, A. (1986) The Hospital Anxiety and Depression Scale. *British Medical Journal*, 292, 344.

Spitzer, R. L., Williams, J. B. W., Gibbon, M. and First, M. B. (1996) *Structured Clinical Interview for DSM-IV (SCID)*. Washington, DC: American Psychiatric Association.

Spitzer, R. L., Williams, J. B. W., Gibbon, M. and First, M. B. (1992) The Structured Clinical Interview for DSM-III-R (SCID). 1. History, rationale, and description. *Archives of General Psychiatry*, 49, 624–629.

Weissman, M. M. (1987) Advances in psychiatric epidemiology: Rates and risks for major depression. *American Journal of Public Health*, 77, 445–451.

Williams J. B. W. (1998) A structured clinical interview guide for the Hamilton Depression Rating Scale. *Archives of General Psychiatry*, 45, 742–747.

Williams, J. B. W., Gibbon, M., First, M. B. and Spitzer, R. L. (1992) The Structured Clinical Interview for the DSM-III-R (SCID). 2. Multisite test–retest reliability. *Archives of General Psychiatry*, 49, 630–636.

Wittchen, H., Robins, L. N., Cottler, L. B., Sartorius, N., Burke, J. D. and Regier, D. (1991) Cross-cultural feasibility, reliability and sources of variance of the Composite International Diagnostic Interview (CIDI). *British Journal of Psychiatry*, 159, 645–653.

Yesavage, J. (1991) Geriatric Depression Scale – consistency of depressive symptoms over time. *Perceptual and Motor Skills*, 73, 1032.

Yesavage, J., Brink, T. L., Rose, T. L., Lum, O., Huang, V., Adey, M. et al. (1983) Development and validation of a geriatric depression screening scale – a preliminary report. *Journal of Psychiatric Research*, 17, 37–49.

Zigmond, A. and Snaith, R. P. (1983) The Hospital Anxiety and Depression Scale. *Acta Psychiatrica Scandinavica*, 67, 361–370.

Chapter 6

Depression

Treatment

Edward Watkins and Brendan P. Bradley

INTRODUCTION

This chapter focuses only on those treatment approaches demonstrated to have been effective in treatment studies in randomised controlled trials (RCTs), where the therapy is compared with another effective treatment (e.g. medication) and/or with a control condition (e.g. placebo or waiting list control). This chapter considers both treatments for acute depression and more recent developments designed to prevent relapse and recurrence of depression.

EMPIRICALLY VALIDATED TREATMENTS FOR DEPRESSION

Effectiveness of cognitive-behavioural therapy for depression

Cognitive-behavioural therapy (CBT) has been demonstrated to be a generally effective treatment for acute depression across a large number of studies and settings (Dobson, 1989) including atypical depression (Jarrett et al., 1999), chronic depression (using an adaptation of CBT, the Cognitive-Behavioral Analysis System of Psychotherapy; Keller et al., 2000) and in-patient settings (Thase and Wright, 1991; Stuart et al., 1997; Wright, 2003). CBT has been found to be as effective as pharmacotherapy for depression, even in better-controlled studies that utilise experienced pharmacologists and monitor compliance and plasma medication (e.g. Murphy et al., 1984; Hollon et al., 1992; but see Parker et al., 2003 for recent critique). A recent large-scale, well-controlled study found that CBT was better than pill placebo and as effective as antidepressant medication at treating moderate-to-severe depression (DeRubeis et al., 2005).

Preventing relapse and recurrence

One potential benefit of CBT for depression is that it reduces relapse/ recurrence to a greater extent than antidepressant medication. Given that recurrence is a major problem for patients with major depression (Judd, 1997), treatments that reduce relapse/recurrence are urgently needed. After 1- or 2-year follow-up, relapse rates following treatment with CBT are lower than for patients treated with pharmacotherapy, when both treatments are stopped at termination (Kovacs et al., 1981; Simons et al., 1986; Thase et al., 1991; Evans et al., 1992; Shea et al., 1992; Gortner et al., 1998) (see also the meta-analysis by Gloaguen et al., 1998), although some of these studies used Beck Depression Inventory (BDI) scores greater than 16 and 'treatment re-entry for depression' as the relapse criteria, rather than a diagnosis of major depression. An important comparison group is antidepressant continuation; patients maintained on antidepressants appear to do as well as patients who received CBT (Evans et al., 1992). In a recent study designed to investigate these issues more stringently, patients withdrawn from CBT had significantly fewer relapses than patients withdrawn from antidepressant medication and did not differ significantly from patients maintained on antidepressant medication, with relapse defined in terms of meeting criteria for depression (Hollon et al., 2005). Blackburn and Moore (1997) found that maintenance CBT was as effective at preventing the recurrence of depression as continued antidepressant medication.

Fava and colleagues have developed CBT that focuses on the residual symptoms remaining after successful treatment of an acute episode by pharmacotherapy (Fava et al., 1994, 1996, 1998). RCTs found that CBT for residual depression results in significantly less relapse/recurrence over 2 years (25%) than standard clinical management in the absence of antidepressant medication (80%; Fava et al., 1998). Paykel and colleagues (Paykel et al., 1999) further demonstrated that, compared to clinical management alone, clinical management plus CBT reduced relapse in patients with recent major depression that had partially remitted with antidepressant treatment.

An alternative approach to preventing relapse/recurrence has specifically targeted people with a history of recurrent depression who are currently in remission. Based on the hypothesis that these people tend to be caught up in ruminative depressive processing at times of potential relapse/recurrence, it was proposed that using mindfulness meditation, which fosters a relationship to thoughts and feelings antithetical to such rumination, might prevent future episodes of depression (Teasdale et al., 1995). Elements of a mindfulness-based stress-reduction programme (Kabat-Zinn, 1990) were incorporated into CBT to create Mindfulness-Based Cognitive Therapy (MBCT). MBCT is delivered in weekly group training sessions, in which participants practise and develop a moment-by-moment, non-judgemental awareness of sensations, thoughts and feelings through the use of formal and informal meditation exercises. These awareness exercises are further practised during homework (see Segal et al., 2002). For people with a history of three or more episodes of major depression, MBCT significantly reduced risk of relapse/recurrence over 1 year compared to treatment as usual in two RCTs (Teasdale et al., 2000; Ma & Teasdale, 2004).

Effectiveness of interpersonal therapy for depression

Interpersonal therapy (IPT) has been found to be equally effective as antidepressant medication in treating acute unipolar depression (Elkin et al., 1989). IPT has also been studied as a continuation or maintenance treatment, where it is provided following remission of the acute episode in order to prevent relapse or recurrence. Frank et al. (1990) compared monthly maintenance sessions of IPT alone, monthly IPT with antidepressant, monthly IPT with placebo, antidepressant (imipramine) or placebo following successful treatment of the acute episode by combined imipramine and IPT in recurrently depressed patients. Monthly IPT substantially reduced risk of relapse compared to placebo, although it was not as effective as continued medication in reducing relapse (Frank et al., 1990).

Comparisons between psychotherapies

There have been a few direct comparisons of the different psychotherapy approaches, most notably, the large multi-site National Institute of Mental Health (NIMH) Treatment of Depression Collaborative Research Program trial (Elkin et al., 1989), which compared CBT, interpersonal psychotherapy, imipramine and a placebo control in 250 moderate to severely depressed out-patients across three different treatment sites. Although there were few significant differences between treatments at end of treatment, for more severe patients, pharmacotherapy (imipramine) and interpersonal therapy did better than CBT, with CBT only doing as well as placebo control on several outcome measures. This result has been much debated, with questions about differences in the quality of CBT across sites (Jacobson and Hollon, 1996).

An important RCT demonstrated that just one aspect of CBT – behavioural activation (BA), which focuses on monitoring of daily activities, assessment of pleasure and mastery, graded task assignment, cognitive rehearsal and problem-solving and social skills training – was as effective as BA plus modification of automatic thoughts (AT) and the full CBT treatment at completion of treatment, 6-month follow-up (Jacobson et al., 1996) or 2-year follow-up (Gortner et al., 1998). Behavioural activation has been elaborated into a full treatment, focusing on understanding the context in which depression occurs and targeting avoidance behaviours in depression (Martell et al., 2001).

In general, CBT, IPT and BA all appear to be effective treatments for depression, with more recent comparisons of treatments finding them of equal potency. Indeed, a recent comprehensive meta-analysis of therapies for depression, which controlled for therapist training, quality of therapies and other methodological problems, found that all brief therapies were equally effective (Wampold et al., 2002), contrary to Dobson's (1989) review, which favoured CBT.

COGNITIVE THERAPY

Beck's theory of depression proposes that depressed affect results from negative thoughts and negatively biased perception (Beck, 1976; Beck et al., 1979). Indeed, depression is associated with increased levels of negative thinking, and increasing negative thinking can increase depressed mood, whilst reducing negative thinking can reduce depressed mood (see Clark et al., 1999 for a comprehensive review). Likewise, depressed patients are typically pessimistic and show defined distortions in their thinking, such as making over-generalisations (i.e. inferring a general characterological fault from a single mistake), thinking in black and white terms ('If it is not perfect, it is a failure') and focusing on the negative while ignoring the positive.

The cognitive theory emphasises negative automatic thoughts (NATs), which are negative judgements and interpretations that automatically and involuntarily pop into people's minds, as central features in the onset and maintenance of depression. These thoughts are considered to contribute to the different symptoms of depression: the cognitive model proposes a reciprocal interaction such that negative thoughts exacerbate symptoms, which in turn exacerbate negative thinking. NATs are typically seen as part of a negative cognitive triad, consisting of negative thoughts about the self, the world and the future. The self is regarded as defective or inadequate in a psychological, moral or physical sense, leading to feelings of low mood and worthlessness. The world is seen as unhelpful and difficult, and life is viewed as a struggle. The negative view of the future leads to pessimistic expectations, anticipating failure. In turn, these pessimistic expectations are presumed to reduce motivation and produce inactivity and inertia. As the pessimistic thoughts become more extreme, the patient becomes hopeless and suicidal.

The cognitive model proposes that these negative thought processes depend on the activation of underlying structures, such as negative schemas or dysfunctional attitudes. These underlying schemas often focus on extreme and unrealistic beliefs concerned with acceptance, approval, competence, control and achievement, e.g. beliefs like 'I need to do everything perfectly'. These maladaptive beliefs are proposed to develop through formative early experiences, modelled from key adults or derived implicitly in response to patterns of reward and punishment. For example, a child who is only praised when she does extremely well and ignored at other times may develop schemas about excellence being necessary for acceptance. These schemas may be verbalised conscious beliefs, although, more commonly, patients act *as if* they have learnt a rule.

The model proposes that these maladaptive beliefs lie dormant and are activated only when precipitated by resonant situations, such as a loss or a failure. It is hypothesised that once these precipitating situations occur, the underlying schema activates NATs. In turn, these negative processes and associated emotions influence future behaviour by reducing activity and increasing social withdrawal, in such a way as to maintain the depressed mood.

The application of CBT

CBT is a treatment package derived from cognitive theory, the aims of which are to identify and challenge negative thoughts, to develop alternative, more accurate and more functional thoughts, and to promote more useful behavioural responses. CBT for depression is a structured, problem-focused, brief, and active therapy grounded in 'collaborative empiricism'. Collaborative empiricism means that the patient and therapist work together to examine and test out the usefulness of the way the patient is thinking and behaving in order to achieve therapeutic goals. Core to this approach is the notion of setting-up each negative thought or schema as a hypothesis to be tested, and the use of a guided discovery process to explore the evidence for and against the hypothesis. This typically involves the therapist using carefully selected Socratic questioning to help patients reflect on their own experience, as well as the designing of behavioural experiments to test out hypotheses in the real world. Feedback is provided regularly and sought by the therapist to ensure that therapist and patient share a common understanding of what is happening in therapy and to consolidate what is learnt. This approach is less likely to be perceived as criticism or further evidence of failure by depressed patients than more confrontational or didactic methods. Furthermore, the framing of thoughts as hypotheses begins to help patients step back from their negative view of the world and consider that their NATs may only be 'mental events' rather than facts.

CBT focuses on identifying and agreeing core problems and goals to be worked on together in therapy (see Chapter 5). An agenda of items is set at the beginning of each session, covering the points to be discussed within that session. The therapy emphasises the importance of the patient actively working on his or her problems in their real-world environment. Therefore, each week, plans are agreed for the tasks the patient will attempt between sessions ('homework'). The implementation of these plans, and any associated successes and difficulties, are reviewed at the beginning of the next session.

Typically, therapy occurs weekly for sessions lasting 50–60 minutes, over a course of between 6 and 20 sessions. A trial of 5–8 sessions is often the best way of determining whether the therapy is appropriate for a client. The majority of clients who benefit from therapy will have shown some improvement in symptoms during this period (Fennell and Teasdale, 1987).

For unipolar depression, CBT typically works through a structured sequence of phases (see Beck et al., 1979, for seminal account; Moore & Garland, 2003, for adaptation for chronic and recurrent depression).

CBT: the initial stage

The initial sessions focus on assessment, establishing rapport, socialisation to the therapy and increasing hope (see Chapter 5). The cognitive model is illustrated by considering the relationship between thoughts and feelings. A common example consists of asking what thoughts and feelings would result if, in the middle of the night whilst sleeping in an unfamiliar house, the patient heard the crash of breaking glass. Feelings of alarm and fear, and the thought of a burglary might be elicited. The therapist could then ask the patient to question that thought and think of alternative explanations, such as, 'Maybe the cat has knocked something over'. What would the patient then feel – relief?

The early sessions continue by working on the prioritised and agreed target problems. CBT for depression starts by using behavioural techniques to reduce target problems such as inactivity, withdrawal and loss of pleasure. Patients record the activities and feelings for each hour of the day on a Weekly Activity Schedule (WAS) form, which identifies how time is spent, and when and during which activities patients tend to feel better or worse. This activity monitoring can then lead into specific activity scheduling in which plans are agreed for patients to increase the more helpful activities. For more depressed patients, plans to establish a daily routine, increase physical exercise and re-establish some social contact are particularly useful. For example, if the patient is very inactive, spending many hours lying in bed passively, it would be useful to build up simple, not-too-demanding activities, e.g. phoning a friend, going for a short walk. To increase success, plans need to be operationalised at a very concrete level, considering when, where, how and with whom the plans will be implemented, as well as potential obstacles and how to overcome them.

The use of graded task assignment, in which activities are broken down into smaller steps is useful for surmounting the initial hurdle of getting patients started on an activity. For example, a patient who avoided cleaning her flat was asked to outline the various tasks and rooms involved. She revealed that, when she thought of the cleaning, she thought of all the tasks that needed to be done, such as dusting the furniture in four rooms, vacuum-cleaning all the floor area, and so on. Questioning revealed that the living area was seen as most urgently needing cleaning and that 10 minutes of vacuum-cleaning would make a significant difference, so this was set as the first task to be done. By breaking tasks down like this, patients with depression can be helped to make headway with tasks that had seemed overwhelming and impossible. These behavioural techniques are used within the 'collaborative empiricism' approach, such that before plans are implemented, thoughts and beliefs relevant to the activity (e.g. 'It is pointless to try') can be set out as hypotheses to be tested.

Behavioural approaches to depression within CBT have been further developed and elaborated within behavioural activation (BA: Martell et al., 2001), which focuses on the context and functions of thoughts and behaviours rather than their form or content, concentrating on variability and situatedness in feelings and behaviours. BA emphasises identifying avoidance patterns and coaching clients to develop alternative coping. To reduce passive coping, clients are coached to act in line with their goals rather than their feelings. For example, for the goal of better self-esteem, behaviour associated with better self-esteem would be determined in detail, e.g. assertiveness, more eye contact, more erect and dignified posture, and plans made for the client to enact these behaviours as if they had better self-esteem. The rationale is that it is easier and faster to change actions, over which clients have direct control, which may in turn influence their feelings (to change from the 'outside-in'), than to change their feelings in order to act differently (e.g. acting when it feels right, i.e., from the 'inside-out'). Clients are encouraged to divorce action from their mood state and to learn that they, rather than the mood, can control their actions by acting even when they don't feel like it.

Specific cognitive techniques can be used to address target problems, in particular the identification and challenging of NATs. Within sessions, therapists will help patients to learn how to identify NATs by eliciting negative thoughts, either asking what went through the patient's mind in response to specific situations or when shifts in mood are observed in the session. When NATs are not obviously available to the patient, it can be useful to ask what the meaning of an upsetting situation might be. Once patients have grasped how to identify NATs, they are shown how to record their thoughts, the situations in which they occur, and accompanying emotions, on a Daily Record of Dysfunctional Thoughts (Beck et al., 1979; see Table 6.1). This exercise is designed to help patients become more aware of their negative thoughts.

Useful approaches to challenging NATs include listing evidence from past experience that supports and refutes each hypothesis, generating alternative explanations, checking whether a thought may reflect a cognitive error and re-attributing negative events to factors other than the patients' personal inadequacy (Table 6.2). For example, if the negative thought were 'I am useless at everything', the patient could be encouraged to recall specific

Table 6.1 Example of recording alternative thoughts

Date	Emotion (0–100)	Situation	Negative thought belief (0–100)	Alternative thought	(1) Belief in negative thought (2) Emotion (3) What can you do now?
7 Dec.	Depressed (70)	Arrived home from work	I didn't do a thing right today (90)	That's not true, I made five phone calls and cleared my desk	(1) 50 (2) 40 (3) Plan to do one satisfying activity at work tomorrow
7 Dec.	Fed up (80)	Argument with husband	I'm always in the wrong (90)	We're both contributing to this/I don't usually argue	(1) 20 (2) 40 (3) We can sit down and discuss this issue when we're not tired

success experiences, and a homework task could be devised where the depressed individual predicts failure but where past performance suggests that success is likely.

When testing NATs, it is useful to clarify exactly what a patient means, such that a clear test of the hypothesis can be designed. For example, when a patient says that she is 'horrible', it is necessary to define precisely what this means to her before it can be challenged. Like identifying NATs, challenging NATs is first practised in the session and then becomes a homework exercise using the Daily Thoughts Record.

What is the evidence?

John, a 39-year-old actor, indicated that he was a 'has been' who had no future on the stage. On being asked what evidence backed this up, he said that he had not received an offer of a job for the previous few weeks. Further discussion revealed that this was not uncommon among actors and, in any case, he had tended to avoid chasing up offers that had been made to him in the past, disliking the idea of 'selling himself'. Following the discussion, he realised that the evidence that he had used did not in fact support his original conclusion. When asked to provide evidence against his negative thoughts, John revealed that he had recently acted in a well-received play, he had broadened his acting style and had, a few months previously, been approached by two leading agents.

Table 6.2 Guidelines on questioning negative thoughts

Looking for alternative perspectives

1. *What is the evidence?*
   What evidence do I have to support my thoughts?
   What evidence do I have against them?

2. *What alternative views are there?*
   How would someone else view this situation?
   How would I have viewed it before I got depressed?
   What evidence do I have to back these alternatives?

3. *What is the effect of thinking the way I do?*
   Does it help me, or hinder me from getting what I want? How?
   What would be the effect of looking at things less negatively?

4. *What are the biases in my thinking?*
   Am I thinking in all-or-nothing terms?
   Am I condemning myself as a total person on the basis of a single event?
   Am I concentrating on my weaknesses and forgetting my strengths?
   Am I blaming myself for something that is not my fault?
   Am I taking something personally that was little or nothing to do with me?
   Am I expecting myself to be perfect?
   Am I using a double standard – how would I view someone else in my situation?
   Am I paying attention only to the down side of things?
   Am I over-estimating the chances of disaster?
   Am I exaggerating the importance of events?
   Am I fretting about the ways things ought to be instead of accepting and dealing with them as they come?
   Am I assuming I can do nothing to change my situation?
   Am I predicting the future instead of experimenting with it?

5. *What action can I take?*
   What can I do to change my situation?
   Am I overlooking solutions to problems on the assumption they won't work?
   What can I do to test the validity of my rational answers?

Source: Adapted by M. Fennell (unpublished) from Emery (1981) and reproduced here with permission from M. Fennell, gratefully acknowledged.

What are the alternatives?

John attributed his failure to receive any offer of work in the previous few weeks to an internal and stable factor, that he was a 'has-been'. But he was able to produce two plausible alternatives:

1. 'Not receiving an offer of a job for a few weeks is relatively common in my business and this has happened to me and to others many times before and was always followed by work.'
2. 'I fail to get work because I do not let people know I want work.'

Jill, a 30-year-old secretary, believed that her work colleagues did not want to talk to her. She was unable to provide evidence of this and she generated the alternative thought that if she made more effort to talk to them, then they would be friendlier and would talk to her more. Her rating of strength of belief in this thought was 50%, and she agreed to test out her thoughts in a behavioural experiment. Initially in homework, she noted what the other secretaries talked about. She found out that one of them, a woman she particularly wanted to get to know, was interested in tennis. In a therapy session she role-played what to say. At work she managed to choose an appropriate moment to say a few words. Her colleague smiled and followed up on Jill's remarks. The conversation lasted about 5–10 minutes. Jill reported back that her belief in the alternative thought was now 90% and her belief in the negative thought had reduced from 100% to 30%.

CBT: the later sessions

The next phase of therapy focuses on working on the underlying beliefs and dysfunctional assumptions. Dysfunctional assumptions are hypothesised for each patient on the basis of the recurring themes in his or her reported thoughts, behaviours and past experience. For example, with a patient who constantly experiences self-critical thoughts about not being good enough, works excessively hard on projects and who reports a background of only being praised when he or she did very well, one might hypothesise a perfectionistic schema. A further way to draw out underlying assumptions is via the downward arrow technique, where the meaning of a negative automatic thought is explored, through a question like 'Supposing that thought were true, what would it mean about you?' This question is repeated in turn to each response to uncover the underlying concerns of the patient.

Thought challenging and behavioural experiments are used to challenge these assumptions. The advantages and disadvantages of the assumptions are explored and the possibility of adopting more functional, alternative rules is discussed. Early life events that may have led to the adoption of these rules are explored and can be challenged, for example by using imagery to relive the event coupled with guided discovery to introduce new perspectives. Behavioural plans designed to act against assumptions are perhaps the most powerful way to change assumptions, by providing personal experience that counters the assumption e.g. a perfectionist deliberately seeking out situations where he is likely to make mistakes, to discover that failure is not catastrophic.

For patients with core negative beliefs about themselves, other approaches that may be helpful include: (1) using a positive data-log where the client deliberately records his or her positive qualities, positive interactions and positive achievements every day, to counter-balance their negative bias; (2) reviewing evidence for and against the negative view of the self, through behavioural experiments and a detailed life review in which periods of the client's past are examined to see if there is any evidence against the negative view of him- or herself, or alternative interpretations for negative events that previously supported the sense of worthlessness. Such interventions often require experiential approaches, including imagery and role-play, and sessions need to be organised to ensure there is sufficient time for intense emotions to settle before the session finishes; (3) helping clients to focus on being compassionate and forgiving towards themselves. Experiential approaches in which clients use imagery to generate feelings of warmth and compassion towards themselves and others can be quite powerful (Gilbert & Irons, 2004). Further details on changing dysfunctional assumptions and core beliefs have been developed in the context of schema-focused therapy (Young, 1990, 1999; Padesky, 1994; Young et al., 2003), although proper evaluation of the effectiveness of this approach within a RCT design has not yet been reported.

The final sessions of therapy focus on consolidating what has been learnt and working on preventing future relapse. Patients are encouraged to summarise the skills they have gained and to draw-up a contingency plan for the future, identifying potentially risky situations and warning signs of depression and specifying the cognitive and behavioural strategies they would use in response to these cues. To consolidate progress, future goals and plans for the next 6–12 months can be drawn up, providing the patient with a framework to continue to practise their skills once therapy finishes.

INTERPERSONAL THERAPY

IPT, like CBT, is a brief structured and active therapy, based on the scientific literature indicating the importance of interpersonal relationships in depression (see Chapter 5).

IPT: the initial sessions (1–4)

The focus of the initial sessions in IPT is the establishment of a working collaborative relationship and identification of the interpersonal focus best representing the patient's reported interpersonal relationships (for further details, see Chapter 5). The therapist diagnoses the symptoms of depression as a medical illness and educates patients about depression, explaining its symptoms and how it can impair work and social functioning. Information that depression is common and treatable is essential in normalising the symptoms and providing a sense of optimism. The full range of symptoms is reviewed so that patients can learn that many of their difficulties are secondary to the illness. The other main early intervention is giving the patient the sick role. Patients are encouraged to recognise that they have a serious illness and, as with any serious illness, that they need to be easier on themselves and to give themselves a chance to recover. Patients are excused from being depressed and encouraged to reduce their expectations of themselves, as well as burdensome activities, obligations and responsibilities, until they recover. A useful analogy is to ask patients whether they would expect themselves to run a marathon with a broken leg.

The therapist will then link the depression and its symptoms to the identified focus, for example with statements like 'It seems to me that your depression started when your father died' or 'Your mood seems to be worse when you are having arguments at home'. Linking the symptoms with the interpersonal focus indicates a positive way forward, for example with statements like 'My sense is that if you can do something to resolve this problem, it'll not only help your relationships but relieve your depression'

IPT: the middle sessions (4–12)

For all foci, there are similar core tasks undertaken within and across sessions. First, the therapist reviews the patient's symptoms and links them to the focus area. At the beginning of each session, the therapist inquires about mood, e.g. 'How have things been since we last met?', 'What happened that might have contributed to your feelings?'. During each session, the therapist looks for examples of how symptoms have been linked to interpersonal events and reflects this back to the client via bridging statements such as:

'Your symptoms seem to fluctuate depending on how your settling into your new job is going'. Likewise, the therapist reviews any changes or developments in the chosen interpersonal focus.

Second, the therapist aims to encourage full expression of all feelings, both positive and negative, related to the chosen focus, to allow the patient to come to terms with any interpersonal changes or difficulties. Thus, when the focus is grief, the strategy is to reconstruct in detail the relationship, how the patient got on with the dead person, examine the sequence of events leading up to the death and the sequence of events associated with mourning (e.g. funeral, sorting through will, etc.) as a means of eliciting affect. The patient is encouraged to express both positive and negative feelings about the relationship, e.g. 'What do you miss about the person?', 'What was not so good about the relationship?'. Similarly, when the focus is a transition, the aim is to help the patient mourn the loss of the old role and accept the new role, again by detailed exploration of the positive and negative aspects of the new and old roles. The therapist may have to specifically probe for emotions, asking how the patient felt in each situation and checking for unmentioned feelings that might seem appropriate to a situation. The validation of feelings is important, with empathic expressions encouraging further openness about emotions.

Education about how feelings are normal and adaptive in response to difficult events and not evidence of weakness can be useful. Encouraging patients to stay with an emotion and let it develop can help coming to terms with interpersonal events.

Third, the therapist and patient work together to develop new relationships and new interpersonal behaviours to reduce the difficulties highlighted in the interpersonal focus. The therapist acts as a coach, encouraging the patient to explore different options and alternatives, rather than assuming that there is no other way of dealing with things. An active problem-solving approach is taken, asking questions like 'What can you do to repair your situation?', 'What would you like to happen?', 'What would help you to feel better?'. When possible options are identified, the therapist does not make an explicit homework plan but encourages the patient to try things out, e.g. 'Can you try that this week?'.

For interpersonal disputes, this stage will focus on clarifying the nature of the dispute, the style of communication and the client's expectations about relationships. Attempts are made to encourage re-negotiation of the dispute, if at all possible, with the acknowledgement that this may increase negative affect at first, if the dispute is an unacknowledged one or is deeply buried. Detailed moment-by-moment analysis of communication between the client and the other protagonists is essential to understand what contributes to the maintenance of the problem. Patients may have very little direct communication, using lots of indirect or non-verbal messages, which they expect the other party to 'mind-read', or there may be overly aggressive and hostile verbal and non-verbal communications. Encouraging direct expression of wants can be helpful, e.g. 'Why not try to have a conversation with him about that?'. The expectations, values and goals of the patient need to be explored to determine whether they are matched by the other person – different sets of expectations may contribute to the problem and may require open negotiation. Useful questions include 'What would you have wanted him to do?', 'What do you expect from her?', 'How did you feel when he did that?', 'Let's look at your expectations about how others will react if you do that'. It can be particularly useful to point out contrasts between how patients envision their role and how they behave. Direct role-playing of interactions in the session can be very informative.

When the focus is on interpersonal deficits, the treatment concentrates on building-up a social support network. Where there are few current relationships to review and learn from, the therapist considers past relationships or the therapeutic relationship itself as a source of information. Patterns from past relationships are reviewed to see how the patient may be acting in ways that maintain a sense of isolation.

IPT: the final sessions

The final sessions involve discussion and acknowledgement that the end of therapy and the end of a supportive therapeutic relationship may be a time of loss and sadness. This allows an opportunity for the patient to learn how to cope with feelings about loss – to recognise that such feelings can be normal and healthy, and that, when worked through properly, do not lead to further depression. The therapist also explicitly tells the patient that he or she has graduated from the sick role, offering congratulation for all the hard work and progress. The work of the therapy is reviewed, reminding patients of the main principles of the therapy, what strategies they have learnt and what progress they have made. A contingency plan linking early warning signs and a coping plan is also drawn up. If IPT has not helped, it is important to blame the failure on the therapy ('it is not perfect – does not work for everyone') and not the patient.

PROBLEMS AND DIFFICULTIES

Suicide and hopelessness

Suicidal thoughts, intentions and attempts are common in depression. The single best predictor of suicide is a previous suicide attempt. Therapists need to be alert for suicidal thoughts and plans, and for the concomitant hopelessness and sense of being trapped that often develops into suicidal thinking. Expressions suggestive of suicidal intent like 'I can't take it any more', changes in affect, such as increased calmness and resignation, and changes in behaviour, such as increased secretiveness, should be explored. Suicidal intent and plans need to be explicitly discussed with the patient. The first step in dealing with suicidal intent is to minimise the immediate risk of a suicide attempt.

Reducing the risk involves understanding the motives for wanting to attempt suicide. Typical motives include wanting to escape a situation that is perceived as intolerable and inescapable and/or attempting to engineer some interpersonal response, whether it be a 'cry for help' or an impulsive attempt to spite others. Once the therapist and patient are able to discuss the possible reasons for wanting to attempt suicide, it is then possible to explore whether the situation is as intolerable and unchangeable as perceived. Socratic questioning can be used to instil hope by helping patients to see that there might be alternative interpretations of their situation and that they have alternative options to deal with the problem. Drawing out both reasons for dying and reasons for living, including the advantages and disadvantages of each option, can help to produce a more objective view of the situation.

The most practical step is to work on reducing access to the means of suicide (e.g. pills). As many suicidal attempts are impulsive, the simple expedient of removing the means significantly increases survival rates. A close analysis of previous attempts at suicide can reveal the series of events that escalate into a suicide attempt, and help to identify the decision points and key contingencies that behavioural plans can modify to reduce risk. For example, for many clients, the decision to try to reduce negative feelings through drugs or alcohol can be a critical step towards suicidal behaviour. The therapeutic relationship is also an important tool, with therapists trying to keep patients involved in the process of therapy.

Once there is progress in helping patients to consider alternative views of their difficult situation, the next step is to facilitate problem solving to reduce the crisis or difficulties that contribute to the hopelessness. Problem solving is typically impaired in suicidal and depressed patients, and explicit attempts to define problems in specific detail and to work on generating alternative responses can be very powerful for these patients.

Patient does not respond to therapy

For IPT and CBT, therapists need to monitor their patient's progress; if, after 4–8 sessions, there seems to be no improvement in the patient, a comprehensive review is necessary. First, the patient may not be convinced by the rationale and techniques of the therapy. It is critical to check whether patients do experience any changes in belief or emotion following each intervention. If there is no change during CBT, the therapist needs to explore what is maintaining the patient's negative beliefs and what doubts the patient has about alternative interpretations or disconfirming evidence. In both IPT and CBT, it is important to check that the exploration of difficulties and evidence both activates emotions and draws richly on the patient's own personal experience rather than on dry abstractions.

Second, it is possible that the therapist is not being flexible enough and not adapting or selecting the approaches that best match the patient's idiosyncratic concerns and approaches.

Third, therapy may not work if it is not focused on the core problem. The main thrust of therapy could be misplaced and thus having a trivial impact. For example, therapy may be focused on the goal of returning a patient to employment when the main problem is the patient's marital relationship. Careful assessment and formulation can help to avoid this difficulty and can remedy such an impasse when it occurs. Depressed patients may be avoidant and find it difficult to share important information with a therapist because they find it shaming. Explicit acknowledgement of this reluctance is helpful, as is the acceptance that sometimes critical information is only shared by the patient after a good therapeutic relationship has developed. Finally, not every therapy (or therapist) suits every patient, so if collaborative attempts to refocus CBT or IPT are still not successful, then referrals to alternative treatments should be considered.

Relapse and recurrence

Preventing relapse and recurrence is a priority for the development of therapeutic approaches to depression. Once acute symptoms are reduced, it is important to target remaining symptoms, such as rumination, worry, anxiety and irritability. Therapy can then focus on enhancing well-being (rather than just reducing depression) by modifying thoughts and behaviours associated with the maintenance or termination of positive experience. New developments focusing on mindfulness meditation are useful for currently remitted patients with a history of three or more previous episodes of recurrent depression, although less useful in patients with fewer previous episodes (for treatment details, see Segal et al., 2002). Finally, for patients with a history of chronic or recurrent depression, monthly IPT or CBT 'booster' sessions seem to reduce relapse.

TRAINING

The effectiveness of both IPT and CBT depend on the skilfulness of the therapist. Extensive training and practice is necessary for either therapy to be delivered well. There are now numerous training courses for CBT in the US and UK (for details, see the British Association of Behavioural and Cognitive Psychotherapy website: http://www.babcp.org). Training in IPT is widespread in the USA and provided at several sites in the UK (for details, see: http://www.interpersonalpsychotherapy.org.uk).

CONCLUSIONS

Cognitive, behavioural and interpersonal approaches have all been found to be effective treatments for depression. Despite being a severe and recurrent illness, depression is treatable, and a persistent, optimistic and skilful therapist can provide significant help to a patient with depression. The provision of an optimistic rationale, the establishment of a clear focus and structure in therapy, a focus on new action and alternative perspectives rather than passive repetition of past themes, the use of plans that build up in small increments, and active engagement by the therapist are key elements in the treatment of depression. Therapists need to retain a sense of hopefulness and not become caught up in the depressive world view of their patients. Both CBT approaches (challenging the therapist's negative thoughts) and IPT approaches (suitable expression of feelings within an empathic support network for the therapist) can help to keep therapists motivated and positive. A key area for consideration is how to prevent future relapse and recurrence, through the development of contingency plans, treatment of residual symptoms and by planning maintenance therapy.

REFERENCES

Beck, A. T. (1976) *Cognitive Therapy and Emotional Disorders*. New York: International Universities Press.

Beck, A. T., Rush, A. J., Shaw, B. F. and Emery, G. (1979) *Cognitive Therapy of Depression*. New York: Guilford Press.

Clark, D. A., Beck, A. T. and Alford, B. A. (1999) *Scientific Foundations of Cognitive Theory and Therapy of Depression*. New York: John Wiley.

DeRubeis, R. J., Hollon, S. D., Amsterdam, J. D., Shelton, R. C., Young, P. R., Salomon, R. M. et al. (2005) Cognitive therapy vs medications in the treatment of moderate to severe depression. *Archives of General Psychiatry*, 62, 409–416.

Elkin, I., Shea, M. T., Watkins, J. T., Imber, S. D., Sotsky, S. M., Collins, J. F. et al. (1989) National Institute of Mental Health treatment of depression collaborative research program – general effectiveness of treatments. *Archives of General Psychiatry*, 46, 971–982.

Evans, M. D., Hollon, S. D., DeRubeis, R. J., Piasecki, J. M., Grove, W. M., Garvey, M. J. et al. (1992) Differential relapse following cognitive therapy and pharmacotherapy for depression. *Archives of General Psychiatry*, 49, 802–808.

Fava, G. A., Grandi, S., Zielezny, M., Canestrari, R. and Morphy, M. A. (1994) Cognitive-behavioral treatment of residual symptoms in primary major depressive disorder. *American Journal of Psychiatry*, 151, 1295–1299.

Fava, G. A., Grandi, S., Zielezny, M., Rafanelli, C. and Canestrari, R. (1996) Four-year outcome for cognitive behavioral treatment of residual symptoms in major depression. *American Journal of Psychiatry*, 153, 945–947.

Fava, G. A., Rafanelli, C., Grandi, S., Canestrari, R. and Morphy, M. A. (1998) Six-year outcome for cognitive behavioral treatment of residual symptoms in major depression. *American Journal of Psychiatry*, 155, 1443–1445.

Fennell, M. J. V. and Teasdale, J. D. (1987) Cognitive therapy for depression – individual differences and the process of change. *Cognitive Therapy and Research*, 11, 253–271.

Frank, E., Kupfer, D. J., Perel, J. M., Cornes, C., Jarrett, D. B., Mallinger, A. G. et al. (1990) 3-year outcomes for maintenance therapies in recurrent depression. *Archives of General Psychiatry*, 47, 1093–1099.

Gilbert, P. and Irons, C. (2004) A pilot exploration of the use of compassionate images in a group of self-critical people. *Memory*, 12, 507–516.

Gloaguen, V., Cottraux, J., Cucherat, M. and Blackburn, I. M. (1998) A meta-analysis of the effects of cognitive therapy in depressed patients. *Journal of Affective Disorders*, 49, 59–72.

Gortner, E. T., Gollan, J. K., Dobson, K. S. and Jacobson, N. S. (1998) Cognitive-behavioral treatment for depression: Relapse prevention. *Journal of Consulting and Clinical Psychology*, 66, 377–384.

Hollon, S. D., DeRubeis, R. J., Evans, M. D., Wiemer, M. J., Garvey, M. J., Grove, W. M. et al. (1992) Cognitive therapy and pharmacotherapy for depression – singly and in combination. *Archives of General Psychiatry*, 49, 774–781.

Hollon, S. D., DeRubeis, R. J., Shelton, R. C., Amsterdam, J. D., Salomon, R. M., O'Reardon, J. P. et al. (2005) Prevention of relapse following cognitive therapy vs medications in moderate to severe depression. *Archives of General Psychiatry*, 62, 417–422.

Jacobson, N. S. and Hollon, S. D. (1996) Cognitive-behavior therapy versus pharmacotherapy: Now that the jury's returned its verdict, it's time to present the rest of the evidence. *Journal of Consulting and Clinical Psychology*, 64, 74–80.

Jacobson, N. S., Dobson, K. S., Truax, P. A., Addis, M. E., Koerner, K., Gollan, J. K. et al. (1996) A component analysis of cognitive-behavioral treatment for depression. *Journal of Consulting and Clinical Psychology*, 64, 295–304.

Jarrett, R. B., Schaffer, M., McIntire, D., Witt-Browder, A., Kraft, D. and Risser, R. C. (1999) Treatment of atypical depression with cognitive therapy or phenelzine – a double-blind, placebo-controlled trial. *Archives of General Psychiatry*, 56, 431–437.

Judd, L. L. (1997) The clinical course of unipolar major depressive disorders. *Archives of General Psychiatry*, 54, 989–991.

Kabat-Zinn, J. (1990) *Full Catastrophe Living: How to Cope with Stress, Pain and Illness Using Mindfulness Meditation*. New York: Delacorte.

Keller, M. B., McCullough, J. P., Klein, D. N., Arnow, B., Dunner, D. L., Gelenberg, A. J. et al. (2000) A comparison of nefazodone, the cognitive-behavioral analysis system of psychotherapy, and their combination for the treatment of chronic depression. *New England Journal of Medicine*, 342, 1462–1470.

Kovacs, M., Rush, A. J., Beck, A. T. and Hollon, S. D. (1981) Depressed outpatients treated with cognitive therapy or pharmacotherapy – a one-year follow-up. *Archives of General Psychiatry*, 38, 33–39.

Ma, S. H. and Teasdale, J. D. (2004) Mindfulness-based cognitive therapy for depression: Replication and exploration of differential relapse prevention effects. *Journal of Consulting and Clinical Psychology*, 72, 31–40.

Martell, C. R., Addis, M. E. and Jacobson, N. S. (2001) *Depression in Context: Strategies for Guided Action*. New York: Norton.

Moore, R. G. and Garland, A. (2003) *Cognitive Therapy for Chronic and Persistent Depression*. Chichester: John Wiley.

Murphy, G. E., Simons, A. D., Wetzel, R. D. and Lustman, P. J. (1984) Cognitive therapy and pharmacotherapy – singly and together in the treatment of depression. *Archives of General Psychiatry*, 41, 33–41.

Padesky, C. A. (1994) Schema change processes in cognitive therapy. *Clinical Psychology & Psychotherapy*, 1, 267–278.

Parker, G., Roy, K. and Eyers, K. (2003) Cognitive behavior therapy for depression? Choose horses for courses. *American Journal of Psychiatry*, 160, 825–834.

Paykel, E. S., Scott, J., Teasdale, J. D., Johnson, A. L., Garland, A., Moore, R. et al. (1999) Prevention of relapse in residual depression by cognitive therapy – A controlled trial. *Archives of General Psychiatry*, 56, 829–835.

Segal, Z. V., Williams, J. M. G. and Teasdale, J. D. (2002) *Mindfulness-based Cognitive Therapy for Depression: A New Approach to Preventing Relapse*. New York: Guilford Press.

Shea, M. T., Elkin, I., Imber, S. D., Sotsky, S. M., Watkins, J. T., Collins, J. F. et al. (1992) Course of depressive symptoms over follow-up – findings from the National

Institute of Mental Health treatment of depression collaborative research program. *Archives of General Psychiatry*, 49, 782–787.

Simons, A. D., Murphy, G. E., Levine, J. L. and Wetzel, R. D. (1986) Cognitive therapy and pharmacotherapy for depression: Sustained improvement over one year. *Archives of General Psychiatry*, 3, 43–48.

Stuart, S., Wright, J. H., Thase, M. E. and Beck, A. T. (1997) Cognitive therapy with inpatients. *General Hospital Psychiatry*, 19, 42–50.

Teasdale, J. D., Segal, Z. and Williams, J. M. G. (1995) How does cognitive therapy prevent depressive relapse and why should attentional control (mindfulness) training help. *Behaviour Research and Therapy*, 33, 25–39.

Teasdale, J. D., Segal, Z. V., Williams, J. M. G., Ridgeway, V. A., Soulsby, J. M. and Lau, M. A. (2000) Prevention of relapse/recurrence in major depression by mindfulness-based cognitive therapy. *Journal of Consulting and Clinical Psychology*, 68, 615–623.

Thase, M. E. and Wright, J. H. (1991) Cognitive behavior therapy manual for depressed inpatients – a treatment protocol outline. *Behavior Therapy*, 22, 579–595.

Thase, M. E., Simons, A. D., Cahalane, J., McGeary, J. and Harden, T. (1991) Severity of depression and response to cognitive behavior therapy. *American Journal of Psychiatry*, 148, 784–789.

Wampold, B. E., Minami, T., Baskin, T. W. and Tierney, S. C. (2002) A meta-(re)analysis of the effects of cognitive therapy versus 'other therapies' for depression. *Journal of Affective Disorders*, 68, 159–165.

Wright, J. H. (2003) Cognitive-behavior therapy for chronic depression. *Psychiatric Annals*, 33, 777–784.

Young, J. E. (1990) *Cognitive Therapy for Personality Disorders: A Schema-focused Approach* (revised edn). Sarasota, FL: Professional Resource Exchange.

Young, J. E. (1999) *Cognitive Therapy for Personality Disorders: A Schema-focused Approach*, (3rd edn.) Sarasota, FL: Professional Resource Press.

Young, J. E., Klosko, J. and Weishaar, M. E. (2003) *Schema Therapy: A Practitioner's Guide*. New York: Guilford Press.

Chapter 7

Bipolar disorder

Investigation

Dominic Lam and Warren Mansell

INTRODUCTION

Epidemiology

Bipolar disorder affects around 1–1.5% of the adult population (Robins et al., 1984; Weissman et al., 1988; Bebbington and Ramana, 1995). Pooled data from 22 studies were used to estimate that the mean age of onset is 28 years (Goodwin and Jamison, 1990) and that the peak frequency of onset appeared to be between 15 and 19 years, with similar levels in the 20 to 24-years range. Clearly, therefore, this indicates a disorder that usually develops within early adulthood and can present in the teenage years.

Bipolar disorder typically runs a course of frequent relapses. Winokur et al. (1969) estimated that 80% of individuals with an initial diagnosis of mania would go on to have further episodes, whilst Tohen et al. (1990), having followed up 75 bipolar patients from an index mood episode, reported that, by 5 years, approximately 90% had experienced at least one relapse. Even when compliance with mood stabilisers is high, recurrences are experienced by up to 60% of patients within 2 years of an acute episode (Coryell et al., 1989; Gelenberg et al., 1989; Markar and Mander, 1989; Shapiro et al., 1989; Harrow et al., 1990; Miklowitz, 1992; Gitlin et al., 1995). Angst et al. (2003) followed-up a sample of 220 bipolar patients every 5 years from 1965 to 1985 and established that the recurrent risk of a bipolar episode was about double that of major depression. A 10-year prospective study of 173 bipolar patients (Lavori et al., 1996) reported a persistent risk of well and ill transitions in this patient group. Interestingly, the recurrent risk remained constant over the life span and there was no clear gender difference in the rate of recurrence. In another study, a systematic shortening of the duration of the illness episode only occurred between cycles 1 and 2, later there was no clear trend (Turvey et al., 1999; Angst and Sellaro, 2000).

Subsyndromal and persisting symptoms

Many patients suffer from subsyndromal symptoms between episodes (Keller et al., 1992; Fava, 1999). These symptoms, although not reaching the severity of an acute episode, can cause significant distress and disruption. Gitlin et al. (1995) reported that over an average follow-up of 4.3 years, 46% of patients who did not relapse continued to report significant levels of affective symptomatology. Goldberg et al. (1995) found that approximately 50–60% of bipolar patients taking lithium had subsyndromal symptoms and moderately impaired social functioning. A prospective study of 146 bipolar I patients (see later for definitions of the distinction between bipolar I and II) over an average of 12.8 years after discharge found that patients showed depressive symptoms 31.9% of the weeks, manic or hypomanic symptoms 8.9% of weeks and 5.9% of the weeks were spent cycling or with mixed symptoms (Judd et al., 2002). The subsyndromal symptoms were nearly three times as frequent as full-blown bipolar episodes. In a similar design, 86 bipolar II patients had depressive symptoms during 50.3% of the follow-up weeks, 1.3% of the weeks with hypomanic symptoms and 2.3% of the weeks with cycling or mixed symptoms, and again subsyndromal symptoms were around three times more common than episodes of major depression (Judd et al., 2003). The presence of such subsyndromal symptoms, as well as causing distress and impairment in social function in its own right, also predisposes patients to greater risk of full relapse (Goldberg et al., 1995).

Suicide risk

Risk of suicide and suicide attempts is high. The lifetime suicide risk of bipolar sufferers is thought to be as high as 19% (Isometsae, 1993). However, the rates of suicide attempts could be higher. Angst et al. (2003) reported a 12-fold increase in successful suicide attempts compared to the general population in their 34- to 38-year follow-up study. Estimates for rates of suicide attempts have varied across studies. Goodwin and Jamison (1990) reviewed 30 studies and found suicide rates of bipolar patients ranged from 9 to 60%. Within the Stanley Bipolar Research Network, 34% of patients were found to have a history of suicide attempts (Leverich et al., 2003).

Social functioning

Patients suffering from bipolar illness can have multiple impairments across many areas of psychosocial functioning in the education, employment and interpersonal domains. Even the ability to live alone or to enjoy and profit from non-work activity can be impaired in some patients. Romans and McPherson (1992) found that bipolar patients had smaller and less adequate networks than a randomly selected community sample. These reductions in social support were associated with the length of the illness and recurrent manic episodes in particular. Another study implicated concern about other peoples' stigmatisation of the disorder as leading to avoidance of people outside the family (Perlick et al., 2001). Bauwens et al. (1991) compared the social adjustment of unipolar patients and bipolar patients with a community sample matched for sex and age. It was found that both patient groups showed worse overall adjustment than controls in terms of social and leisure activities, with diminished contact with friends the most prominent feature for bipolar patients. In the bipolar sample, the current level of residual symptoms was associated with social adjustment deficits. In terms of work, Gitlin et al. (1995) reported good occupational outcome in only 28% of subjects in their longitudinal study of 82 bipolar patients over a mean period of 4 years. Prien and Potter (1990) reported on a US Department of Health, Education and Welfare study that estimated that an average woman experiencing bipolar disorder with onset at 25 years might expect to lose 14 years of major effective activity (which would relate to both work and family responsibilities).

DSM criteria for bipolar disorder

According to the *Diagnostic and Statistical Manual of Mental Disorders*, 4th edition Revised (DSM-IV-TR; American Psychiatric Association (APA), 2000), bipolar disorder is characterised by both major depressive episodes (MDE) and either manic, hypomanic or mixed episodes. The criteria for major depressive episodes, mania, hypomania and mixed episode according to DSM-IV-TR are described below.

The diagnostic criteria for an MDE include five (or more) characteristic symptoms of depression during the same 2-week period: depressed mood; marked diminished interest or pleasure in activities; weight loss when not dieting, or weight gain, or decease or increase in appetite; insomnia or hypersomnia; psychomotor agitation or retardation; loss of energy; feelings of worthlessness or excessive guilt; impaired concentration or indecisiveness; recurrent thoughts of death or recurrent suicidal ideation. At least one of the symptoms must be either depressed mood or marked diminished interest or pleasure in activities that were previously enjoyed. These symptoms have to be present most of the day and nearly every day during the 2-week period.

The criteria for mania are a distinct period of abnormally and persistently elevated, expansive or irritable mood, lasting for 1 week. In addition, during the period of mood disturbance, at least three of the following symptoms have to be present to a significant degree: inflated self-esteem or grandiosity; decreased need for sleep, e.g. feeling rested after only 3 hours of sleep; more talkative than usual or pressure of speech; flight of ideas or subjective experience that thoughts are racing; distractibility; increase in goal-directed activity or psychomotor agitation; and excessive involvement in pleasurable activities that have a high potential for painful consequences. If irritability is the persistent mood, then four other symptoms have to be present.

For hypomanic episodes, the criteria are similar to a manic episode but the duration is 4 days. If it is the same duration as mania, the episode cannot be severe enough to cause marked impairment in social or occupational functioning. If there are psychotic features, or the episode leads to hospitalisation, a diagnosis of mania, rather than hypomania, is made.

Mixed bipolar episodes, as defined by DSM-IV-TR, are rare. For mixed episodes, the criteria for both a manic episode and for a major depressive episode have to be fulfilled nearly every day for at least a 2-week period. 'Mixed states' involve the presence of significant depressive symptoms during mania or significant manic symptoms during depression and have been variously termed 'depressed mania', 'dysphoric mania' and 'mixed mania'. They are not currently defined using diagnostic criteria and for this reason remain contentious and range widely in estimated rates from 5% to 70% (Dayer et al., 2000). However, they may be clinically important, with evidence suggesting that they are associated with higher suicidal risks than 'pure' mania (Dilsaver et al., 1994; Strakowski et al., 1996; Goldberg et al., 1998), longer episodes duration and a worse outcome (Dilsaver et al., 1993; Swann et al., 1997). Consequently, there has been a call for the development of diagnostic criteria to define mixed states (Dayer et al., 2000). Rapid cycling refers to at least four episodes of a mood disturbance in the previous 12 months that meet criteria for a major depression, manic, mixed or hypomanic episode.

DSM-IV-TR acknowledges two subtypes of bipolar illness. Bipolar I disorder refers to least one manic episode or mixed episode and one major depressive episode. Bipolar II disorder is more common and refers to at least one hypomanic episode and one major depressive episode but no manic or mixed episodes. It is worth emphasising that, according to DSM-IV-TR, there must be a change from previous functioning in addition to the presence of symptoms before a diagnosis of bipolar episode can be made.

Co-morbidity

Bipolar disorder is highly co-morbid with many other psychological disorders (for a review, see Strakowski et al., 1994). For example, there is a close association with certain impulse-control disorders (e.g. pathological gambling, kleptomania; McElroy et al., 1992). Anxiety disorders are the most common co-morbid diagnosis in bipolar disorder, estimated at between 33% and 92.9% (Kessler et al., 1997; Cosoff and Hafner, 1998; Cassano et al., 1999; Perugi et al., 1999). The rates of co-morbidity in bipolar disorder are generally higher than rates within unipolar depression (Regier et al., 1990; Chen and Dilsaver, 1995). The presence of co-morbidity is associated with greater severity of illness. For example, Young et al. (1993) found that, compared to patients with low levels of anxiety, patients with high levels of anxiety were more likely to make suicide attempts, to have suffered from alcohol abuse and to be less responsive to lithium.

Substance abuse

Substance abuse is common in bipolar disorder. Regier et al. (1990) reported that more than 60% of bipolar I and 50% of bipolar II patients had a lifetime substance abuse history. Goodwin and Jamison (1990) estimated an overall rate of alcohol abuse and alcoholism of 35% in people with bipolar disorder, based on their review of 20 studies. The rate of alcohol abuse was between 3 and 15% in the general population. Rates for cocaine use in bipolar patients ranges from 58% (Estroff et al., 1985) to 10% (Miller et al., 1989), as compared to a general population rates of around 5%. Patients with co-morbid lifetime substance abuse tend to have more hospitalisations (Cassidy et al., 2001) and a poorer long-term outcome (Tohen et al., 1990). Regier et al. (1990) report that most affective disorder predated substance abuse. This possibility of affective state preceding substance use coincides with clinical descriptions of self-medication. It is common for bipolar patients to use alcohol to try to control their depression and anxiety or fuel their mania. Likewise, the use of stimulant drugs can be a means of sustaining hypomanic states or indeed of intensifying the effects of elevated mood states. In these cases then, the substance use would be more accurately described as a symptom of manic or depressed behaviour.

ASSESSMENT

Bipolar disorder is a complex condition and requires a comprehensive assessment prior to therapy. The information drawn together through a proper assessment will provide patients with their first opportunity to understand the relationships between experiences, emotions and behaviour, often previously recalled as separate events. This process itself can be therapeutic, as well as enhancing engagement with therapy.

It is worth pointing out that assessment and therapy are an integral process. During therapy, the therapist will unveil new information, which may lead to further assessment of areas that need to be explored more thoroughly than before. Here, for the sake of clarity, assessment and treatment are separated into two chapters. In this chapter, assessment is referred to as the initial assessment.

Family and individual history

Many people with bipolar disorder have other family members who suffer from unipolar depression or bipolar disorder. Goodwin and Jamison (1990) reviewed ten studies and concluded that consistent across studies, the most frequent affective disorder in first-degree relatives is unipolar depression. Bipolar disorder is the next most frequent affective illness. Where there has been affective disorder among patients' parents this can clearly have caused disruption during their development. It affects how the individual has come to his or her own particular beliefs about the world, self and others. For example, if both parents were engrossed in coping with the illness of a sick parent, the patient might have felt lonely and isolated. Losing support from a parent who was frequently ill may make the patient feel that seeking support from others causes unnecessary burden to them. Sometimes a depressed parent can appear to be distant, undemonstrative and critical. Under these circumstances, it may be hard for the patient to feel 'unconditional love' from significant others. The perceived parenting and interaction with significant figures in early life may affect a patient's perception of the 'self' as less than lovable and 'others' as being unsupportive or unsympathetic. Sometimes parents suffering an affective disorder can have perfectionistic standards for themselves and their offspring. This can be internalised by patients, who in turn become unrelenting achievers. Sometimes patients' siblings can also suffer from the illness before they become ill. Therapists should enquire about this. The affected sibling may be very disabled and cause substantial anxiety in patients about becoming like their chronically ill siblings. This may contribute to denial of having the illness themselves.

Illness history

Many patients will already have had similar interviews with their psychiatrists and may not immediately see the relevance of reviewing this area. However, in the psychological assessment, apart from hearing his or her history of the illness, emphasis is placed on the patient's own perception and explanation of mood and illness fluctuations. It is helpful to build this information into a life chart (Figure 7.1) in which they are laid out chronologically. Such a life chart would also include information about previous bipolar episodes, life events, medication, occupation/school and intimate relationships. It is important to assess the patient's occupation/education history in relation to the illness. The advantage of having these important domains in the life chart is that patients may not feel it is all about medication and relapses. It gives the message that intimate relationship and occupational attainment are also important aspects of the patient's life. For many patients it is very helpful to draw up all the information on a sheet of paper and then try to make sense of their illness.

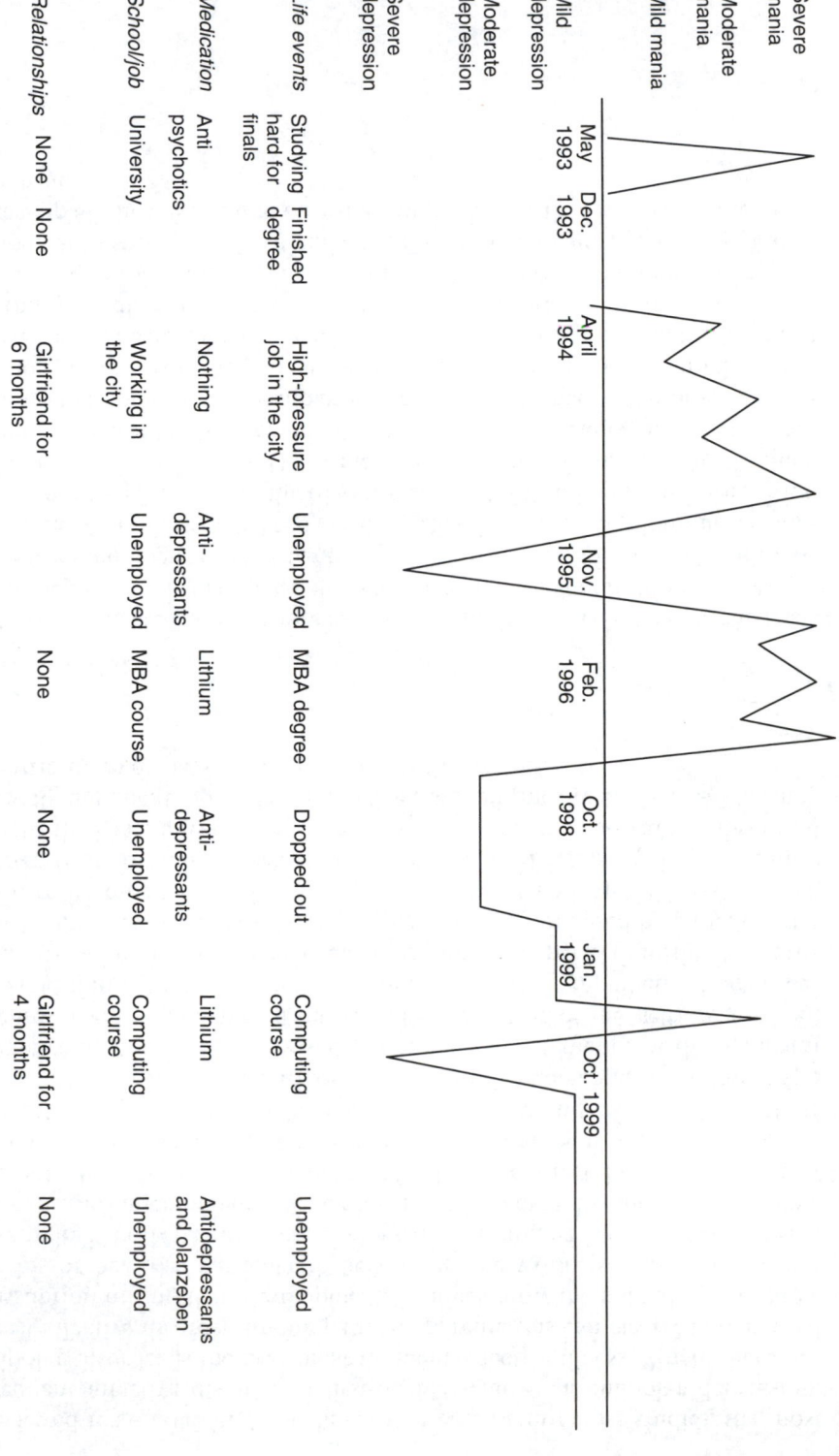

Figure 7.1 John's life chart.

Figure 7.1 depicts the life chart of a patient, John, who came from an Asian family of high achievers. He was the only son. His family had high aspirations for him to achieve academically and then had hopes of a lucrative professional job. John did well at school and went to study economics in a prestigious university. He performed well and was expected to get a degree with first-class honours. He already had a job offer from a prestigious city bank during the university milk round and he was determined to get a first-class degree. He described how he studied round the clock before his finals. There were days when he did not leave his room to eat. He had a 'manic' breakdown in May 1993 and was prescribed antipsychotics. In the end, he obtained an upper-second-class degree. Because he remained relatively unstable throughout the summer, he postponed starting working in the bank until the following spring. From April 1994 to November 1995, John worked in a high-pressure city job. His mood was unstable and he experienced several mild to moderately severe manic episodes. John described this 'manic' energy as giving him the edge over his peers in the bank. He was able to trade shares successfully. Then finally he had a severe manic breakdown and lost his job. He was unemployed and unsuccessful in getting a job despite repeated applications. John became depressed from November 1995 until September 1996, when he decided to do a masters degree in business studies. During his studies for his masters degree, again he developed a manic episode. Looking back, he admitted that he was trying to prove to himself and other people that he was well by studying hard and also doing some part-time projects. His mood was very unstable. He had a severe manic episode during which he jumped in front of a car. The episode led him to abandon his studies. From June 1997 to January 1999, John was depressed but struggling at home and tried voluntary work. In September, he enrolled on a computing course. John described how he used to get up at 7 a.m. and do a 2-hour workout at home before going to college or studying at home from 9 a.m. until 9 p.m. He admitted to again trying to prove to himself that he was able. He had another manic breakdown at the end of October and, since then, he had been unemployed at home.

Life charts serve several functions. They provide evidence of which types of medication have been helpful or counterproductive. As referred to in the treatment chapter, mood stabilisers fail to protect a significant proportion of bipolar patients. Therapists should have an open mind and examine the effect of drugs based on evidence in the life chart. Hopefully, it will provide evidence that stability of mood can also enable patients to make long term commitments in work and social areas.

> In John's case, medication such as lithium did not seem to have much impact in preventing manic episodes. He complained that lithium affected his memory and made him lose his concentration. He appeared to be doing better with a combination of antidepressants and olanzepan.

A life chart can also provide valuable evidence of how the patient copes with the condition. The completed life chart, drawn up collaboratively with the patient, then forms a shared document, which indicates the interrelationship between mood and other important factors. This information also serves to illustrate that often mood changes and recurrences of the illness can occur within a context, rather than being events, which are outside the patients control.

> John's case is a good illustration of how some bipolar patients, who place a lot of sense of self worth in achievement, try to 'catch up for lost time' due to the illness. He had more manic episodes linked to ambitious goals and loss of sleep and routine. John made several attempts to regain his confidence by pushing himself too hard and perhaps too soon. He also tried several times to return to studies after losing his job in the city. Whenever he returned to studying, John set very punitive schedules and studied until the small hours of the morning. Currently John was unemployed but he maintained a strict routine and spent most of his days studying computing on his own. Interestingly, he only had two brief relationships since his illness started. However, John was not bothered by this because he was focused on trying to succeed in his studies and career.

Patients' perception of the illness and medication compliance

Assessing patients' perception of the illness and their views of taking long-term medication is the beginning of a collaborative therapeutic process. Therapists should be empathic and non-judgemental. The whole emphasis is to have an open and honest discussion, respecting the patient's view.

Therapists should be open-minded and prepared for patients to differ in their view of their diagnosis. Some patients feel initially that having an identified illness for which there is a treatment is a relief in comparison with a previous fear of undefined 'madness'. By contrast, many patients believe that the diagnosis is a label, which they do not accept. Exploring the patient's perception of the causes and consequences of the illness, and his or her perceived control over it, also forms part of the assessment process. It is not uncommon for patients to have mixed feelings about their diagnosis. In any case, awareness of the patient's ambivalence will be key to the development of shared therapy goals and overcoming obstacles within therapy.

Likewise, many patients have similar views about medication. Many drugs used for bipolar disorders have side effects. Being told to take mood stabilisers for their rest of their life can cause a lot of anxiety. And the meaning of long-term medication in terms of loss of 'healthy self' and being an ill person needs to be explored sympathetically. Again, it is important that therapists have an open mind about the effectiveness of medication and acknowledge that not every patient benefits from the same medication and that there are pros and cons of taking medication. Considering this in relation to the life chart as described above can prove a useful introduction to later sessions where adherence issues are discussed. A good and empathic assessment of patients' perception of their illness and medication taking can form a basis for a good therapeutic alliance, which enables the therapist to lay the foundations for future work.

Life events

Life events have been associated with both the onset and recurrence of affective disorders (Bebbington et al., 1993). In bipolar disorder, there is evidence that life events that disrupt sleep–wake routines play an important role prior to the onset of a manic episode. Malkoff-Schwartz et al. (1998) found that, in the 8 weeks prior to manic episodes, a significantly greater proportion of patients had social rhythm disruption events than the 8-week episode-free control period. Bipolar patients are also known to relapse after long-distance travelling or jet lag (Jauhar and Weller, 1982). Hence, lack of sleep seems an important element in the aetiology of mania (Wehr et al., 1987). Therapists should examine not just life events prior to this current episode, but also check on the life chart if there were similar life events prior to previous episodes as well. It is not uncommon for therapists to unearth life events of sleeplessness due to patients' attempts to 'catch up for lost time' as a way of coping with the illness. Typically, this happens at an early stage of the illness with some highly driven patients. They may rush back to work immediately after an episode. The way they coped with 'lost time' due to the illness was to take on a lot more work, and sometimes not just in terms of quantity but also in terms of the difficulty of tasks, deliberately to over-compensate their bruised self-esteem in an attempt to prove to themselves and others that they are well and able.

Alcohol and street drugs

An important area to assess is risky behaviour or situations that can lead to relapses. These include the use of street drugs and excessive alcohol. Both can be associated with poor routine and fuel subsyndromal symptoms into a full-blown episode. For example, alcohol is a short-term hypnotic. Patients who use it as a hypnotic tend to wake up after a couple of hours and cannot get back to sleep. Patients should be asked about the use of alcohol or street drugs and the functions of such use as a matter of routine.

Dysfunctional attitudes

Dysfunctional attitudes were found to be elevated in a group of individuals with remitted bipolar disorder as compared to a group of non-affectively disordered individuals (Scott et al., 2000) and elevated differentially in remitted, hypomanic and depressed bipolar patients (Scott and Pope, 2003). Certain dysfunctional beliefs may be specific vulnerability factors in bipolar disorder. Dysfunctional attitude levels have been found to interact with the presence of negative life events to predict not only increases in depressive symptoms but also increases in manic symptoms in bipolar individuals (Reilly-Harrington et al., 1999). Euthymic bipolar patients scored significantly higher on the goal-attainment subscale in the Dysfunctional Attitudes Scale (DAS) than euthymic unipolar patients (Lam et al., 2004). The goal-attainment score correlated with the number of past hospitalisations due to manic episodes and to bipolar episodes as a whole. The DAS high-goal attainment subscale consists of items such as 'If I try hard enough I should be able to excel at anything I attempt', 'I should be happy all the time' and 'I should be able to solve problems quickly and without a great deal of effort'. Individuals who believe in their own ability to excel at anything they attempt, or in their ability to solve problems quickly and effortlessly, would value being creative, productive, optimistic and dynamic. The initial assessment of dysfunctional attitudes can be done by means of the DAS. This gives some general ideas of patients' beliefs. Another scale, the HAPPI (p. 131) is also helpful.

The patient's sense of self

Clinically, it is observed that some bipolar patients like being in a state of constant high arousal, positive mood and being behaviourally active. They perceive themselves as possessing personal attributes associated with being mildly 'high' and value these attributes as desirable, examples being: persuasive, creative, dynamic, entertaining and outgoing. These attributes were assessed by the Sense of Hyper-Positive Self Scale (SHPSS; Lam et al., 2005). These patients often aspire to achieve the qualities described in the SHPSS. This state of mild hypomania, although not reaching the severity of clinical hypomania or mania, often leads to chaotic routine and highly driven behaviour (Lam et al., 1999, 2005). Hence this outlook on life is contrary to the relapse-prevention goals of regulating mood and behaviour within a narrower range of intensity. These characteristics of outlook and behaviour can lead to sleeplessness and to a chaotic and irregular lifestyle, which in turn can lead to frequent episodes. Lam et al. (2005) reported that goal-attainment dysfunctional beliefs contribute to the 'sense of hyper-positive self' independent of current mood measures of both depression and mania. It was hypothesised that these patients with high levels of 'sense of hyper-positive self' would not respond well to therapy and will continue to have frequent relapses. In their cognitive therapy for bipolar disorder study, Lam et al. (2005) indeed found that patients who scored high on the SHPSS did not respond to cognitive therapy. It was thought that more intensive and focused cognitive methods to explore and address patients' affinity with these qualities may be necessary at a much earlier stage of therapy. Hence, it may prove important for therapists to ask patients to fill out an SHPSS to get a sense of their usual and ideal state. Similarly, positive beliefs about the symptoms of hypomania should be assessed early on and before commencing relapse-prevention techniques.

The symptom profile

Patients with a diagnosis of bipolar disorder can often find it difficult to distinguish between when they are well and when they are unwell. The patient and his or her family and friends may come to equate the patient's personality or their emotional reactions with the illness. For example, brief assertive displays of anger during euthymic states may be perceived as a relapse or an indication that the patient is still mentally ill. The symptom profile provides a method to help distinguish between 'normal' mood states and personality traits, on the one hand, and symptoms of depression, hypomania or mania, on the other. The therapist produces three columns: depression, remission (or 'normal') and mania. The therapist and patient work together to identify which specific symptoms were present during the patient's previous episodes and place them in the appropriate columns. They complete the remission column with items such as personality traits (intellectual, sociable, conscientious), normal moods (happy, contented, angry, sad) and behaviours (planning my diary, relaxing with friends). Some patients who have had a history of prolonged unstable mood may find it difficult to complete this column from their experience, but may complete it later in therapy as they identify qualities and mood states if they experience them outside an episode. The symptom profile provides psychoeducation about the symptoms of bipolar disorder, helps to make the distinction between remission and illness episodes, and can be used early on in therapy to identify a possible relapse. It also leads on to the assessment of prodromes as described below.

Ability to detect and cope with bipolar prodromes

Clinically, it is observed that mania can fuel itself and depression can spiral down (Lam et al., 1999; Mansell and Lam, 2003). For example, during an early stage of mania, patients may not be totally aware that increases in goal-related activities, re-emergence of feelings of being sociable and confident, and decreased need for sleep are part of the early stages of mania. Some patients may be tempted at this stage to seek more social stimulation, leading to further disruption in sleep and routine. Likewise, lack of motivation and loss of interest in people may be an early stage of depression. Patients at this early stage may feel guilty for being lazy or not being able to function properly and hence become 'depressed about being depressed'. These early stages are also known as prodromal stages.

Studies have found that bipolar patients can report prodromes of relapses reliably (see Lam and Wong, 2005, for a review). In particular, they are better at reporting mania prodromes than depression prodromes. The patterns of prodromes are different for different patients. Common prodromal symptoms of mania are: decreased need for sleep, increased activities, being more sociable, racing thoughts and sharper senses. Common depression prodromal symptoms are: loss of interest, not being able to put worries aside and interrupted sleep. There is evidence that adaptive coping with prodromes, particularly mania prodromes, predicted patients' current level of functioning (Lam and Wong 1997) and also predicted relapses during an 18-month follow-up study (Lam et al., 2001). As patients' pattern of prodromes can be very idiosyncratic, it is best to construct patients' own 'relapse signature' by an open-ended interview. An open-ended interview approach is advocated also because it accesses patients' recall of the most prominent prodromes for them. The technique involved is described in Chapter 8.

Social functioning

As stated above, bipolar patients often have impaired social functioning. There is evidence that social functioning, particularly functioning at work, could predict shorter times to relapse (Gitlin et al., 1995). Hence it is important to target areas of low social functioning in therapy. A number of measures of social functioning can be used, including the Social Performance Schedule (Hurry et al., 1983), a semi-structured interview approach, which is the most commonly used instrument for studies of psychological intervention for bipolar disorder.

Patients' current mood state: observer and self-reported instruments

As stated above, many bipolar patients suffer from residual symptoms left from a previous episode. The presence of such residual symptoms can predispose patients to greater risk of full relapses during their illness course. Hence, it is important to enquire about such residual symptoms within the assessment interview. In addition, it is helpful to combine this with some standardised self-report and observer measures to provide a comprehensive picture. Useful measures are considered below.

SUMMARY OF USEFUL INSTRUMENTS

Self-report mood measures include:

- *Beck Depression Inventory* (BDI; Beck and Steer, 1987): this 21-item self-report measure is applicable to both adults and adolescents. It enquires into the physical, behavioural and cognitive features of depression in the previous week. Each item is rated on a three-point scale. Score ranges are: 0–9 asymptomatic, 10–18 mild–moderate depression, 19–29 moderate-severe depression, > 29 extremely severe depression.
- *Beck Hopelessness Scale* (BHS; Beck and Steer, 1988): this is a 20-item self-report measure. Score ranges are: 0–3 normal, 4–8 mild, 9–14 moderate, >14 severe.
- *Internal States Scale* (Bauer et al., 1991): this consists of 16 self-report 100-mm visual analogue items to assess the severity of manic and depressive symptoms. The scale has four subscales: activation, well-being, perceived conflict and depression index; there is also a global bipolar scale. The construct validity of the scale was supported by significant relationships between activation scores and clinicians' ratings of mania, and between the depression index scores and clinical ratings of depression. Figure 7.2 depicts the Internal State Scale. A recent paper (Glick et al., 2003) reported the use of Likert-based format, which makes it less labour intensive to score.

Observer-rated mood measures include:

- *Mania Rating Scale* (MRS; Bech et al., 1978): this consists of 11 items that map into patients' motor activity, visual activity, flight of thoughts, voice/noise level, hostility/destructiveness, mood level (feeling of well-being), self-esteem, contact (intrusiveness), sleep (average of the past three nights), sexual interest and decreased work ability. Each item is rated on a five-point scale (0 not present, 1 mild, 2 moderate, 3 marked and 4 severe or extreme). The total scores are interpreted as: 0–5 no mania, 6–9 hypomania (mild), 10–14 probable mania, 15 or more definite mania. The scale has good inter-rater reliability and construct validity.

For each of the following statements, please mark an 'X' at the point on the line that best describes the way you have felt over the past 24 hours. While there may have been some change during that time, try to give a single summary rating for each item.

	Not at all/ Rarely	Very much so/ Much of the time
1. Today my mood is changeable		
2. Today I feel irritable		
3. Today I feel like a capable person		
4. Today I feel like people are out to get me		
5. Today I actually feel great inside		
6. Today I feel impulsive		
7. Today I feel depressed		
8. Today my thoughts are going fast		
9. Today it seems like nothing will ever work out for me		
10. Today I feel overactive		
11. Today I feel as if the world is against me		
12. Today I feel 'sped up' inside		
13. Today I feel restless		
14. Today I feel argumentative		
15. Today I feel energised		

Right now I feel:	Depressed/ Down	Normal	Manic/ High

Figure 7.2 Internal state scale.

- *Hamilton Rating Scale for Depression* (HRSD; Hamilton, 1960): this is a 17-item observer-rated scale assessing physical, cognitive and behavioural features of depression. Compared to the Beck Depression Inventory, this scale places more emphasis on the physical symptoms. Score ranges are: 0–7 no/minimal depression, 8–17 mild, 18–25 moderate, > 26 severe depression.

Other useful scales are:

- *Medication Compliance Questionnaire* (Lam et al., 2000): this is a report of compliance of any prescribed mood stabilisers. Respondents have a choice of whether patients in the past month have: never missed taking their medication, missed taking it once or twice, missed taking it between 3 to 7 times, missed taking it more than 7 times or stopped taking it altogether. This gives more detailed information about whether patients have been taking their medication.
- *Short Version of Dysfunctional Attitude Scale* (DAS-SV; Power et al., 1994): this is a 24-item self-report inventory designed to measure maladaptive attitudes. Similar to the original DAS (Weissman and Beck, 1978), the items are rated on a seven-point scale ranging from 'totally agree' through 'neutral' to 'totally disagree'. The shortened version is derived from a factor analytic study of the original DAS Form A and Form B. Further principal component analyses with a pure bipolar sample on the 24-item DAS were reported by Lam et al. (2004).
- *The Hypomanic Attitides and Positive Predictions Inventory* (HAPPI) by Mansell (2006) is a 50-item self-report scale designed to specifically target the cognitions for therapy that distinguish between individuals with bipolar disorder and healthy controls. A brief version is also available (Mansell and Jones, 2006). The scale has five subscales that are described in Mansell (2006). Example items include: 'When I feel more active I realise that I am a very important person', 'When I feel really good, people don't understand me' and 'When I feel agitated and restless it means that I am about to have a breakdown'. Each statement is rated from 0% (not at all) to 100% (completely).
- *MRC Social Performance Schedule* (SPS; Hurry et al., 1983): this is a semi-structured interview that provides a quantitative assessment of social performance in the last month. The informant is the patient. The interview is directed towards actual behaviour and performance in each area and is rated on a four-point scale: 0 fair to good performance, 2 serious problems on occasions but can sometimes manage quite well, 3 serious problems most of the time, 4 not able to cope at all. The schedule covers eight areas of social performance and an overall score is obtained by totalling the scores.
- Several scales are available to assess cognitive processes that are thought to maintain a range of psychological disorders ('transdiagnostic' processes; for references to these scales, see Harvey et al., 2004). Measures of symptoms of co-morbid psychological disorders can be found in the relevant chapter for each disorder.

REFERENCES

American Psychiatric Association (APA) (2000) *Diagnostic and Statistical Manual of Mental Disorders, 4th edn. Text revision.* Washington, DC: APA.

Angst, J. and Sellaro, R. (2000) Historical perspectives and natural history of bipolar disorder. *Biological Psychiatry*, 48, 445–457.

Angst, J., Gamma, A., Sellaro, R., Lavori, P. W. and Zhang, H. (2003) Recurrence of bipolar disorders and major depression: A life-long perspective. *European Archives of Psychiatry and Clinical Neuroscience*, 253, 236–240.

Bauer, M. S., Crits-Christoph, P., Ball, W. A., Dewees, E. et al. (1991) Independent assessment of manic and depressive symptoms by self-rating: Scale characteristics and implications for the study of mania. *Archives of General Psychiatry*, 48, 807–812.

Bauwens, F., Tracy, A., Pardoen, D., Vander Elst, M. and Mandlewicz, J. (1991) Social adjustment of remitted bipolar and unipolar out-patients: A comparison with age- and sex-matched controls. *British Journal of Psychiatry*, 159, 239–244.

Bebbington, P. and Ramana, R. (1995) The epidemiology of bipolar affective disorder. *Social Psychiatry and Psychiatric Epidemiology*, 30, 279–292.

Bebbington, P., Wilkins, S., Jones, P. B., Foerster, A., Murray, R. M. et al. (1993) Life events and psychosis: Initial results from the Camberwell Collaborative Psychosis Study. *British Journal of Psychiatry*, 162, 72–79.

Bech P., Rafaelsen, O. J., Kramp, P. and Bolwig, T. G. (1978) The Mania Rating Scale: Scale construct and inter-observer agreement. *Neuropharmacology*, 17, 430–431.

Beck, A. T. and Steer, R. A. (1987) *Beck Depression Inventory.* San Antonio, TX: Psychological Corporation.

Beck, A. T. and Steer, R. A. (1988) *Beck Hopelessness Scale.* San Antonio, TX: Psychological Corporation.

Cassano, G. B., Pini, S., Saettoni, M. and Dell'Osso, L. (1999) Multiple anxiety disorder comorbidity in patients with mood spectrum disorders with psychotic features. *American Journal of Psychiatry*, 156, 474–476.

Cassidy, F., Ahearn, E. P. and Carroll, B. J. (2001) Substance abuse in bipolar disorder. *Bipolar Disorders*, 3, 181–188.

Chen, Y. W. and Dilsaver, S. (1995) Comorbidity of panic disorder in bipolar illness: evidence from the Epidemiologic Catchment Area Survey. *American Journal of Psychiatry*, 152, 280–282.

Coryell, W., Endicott, J., Keller, M., Andreasen, N. et al. (1989) Bipolar affective disorder and high achievement. A familial association. *American Journal of Psychiatry*, 146, 983–988.

Cosoff, S. J. and Hafner, R. J. (1998) The prevalence of comorbid anxiety in schizophrenia, schizoaffective disorder and bipolar disorder. *Australian and New Zealand Journal of Psychiatry*, 32, 67–72.

Dayer, A., Aubry, J-M., Roth, L., Ducrey, S. and Bertschy, G. (2000) A theoretical reappraisal of mixed states: Dysphoria as a third dimension. *Bipolar Disorders*, 2, 316–324.

Dilsaver, S. C., Swann, A. C., Shoaib, A. M., Bowers, T. C. and Halle, A. T. (1993) Depressive mania associated with nonresponse to antimanic agents. *American Journal of Psychiatry*, 150, 1548–1551.

Dilsaver, S. C., Chen, Y. W., Swann, A. C., Shoaib, A. M. and Krajewski, K. J. (1994) Suicidality in patients with pure and depressive mania. *American Journal of Psychiatry*, 151, 1312–1315.

Estroff, T. W., Dackis, C. A., Gold, M. S. and Pottash, A. L. C. (1985) Drug abuse and bipolar disorders. *International Journal of Psychiatry in Medicine*, 15, 37–40.

Fava, G. A. (1999) Subclinical symptoms in mood disorders. *Psychological Medicine*, 29, 47–61.

Gelenberg, A., Kane, J., Keller, M., Lavori, P., Rosenbaum, J., Cole, K. and Lavelle, J. (1989) Comparison of standard and low serum levels of lithium for maintenance treatment of bipolar disorders. *New England Journal of Medicine*, 321, 1489–1493.

Gitlin M., Swendsen, J., Heller, T. and Hammen, C. (1995) Relapse and impairment in bipolar disorder. *American Journal of Psychiatry*, 152, 1635–1640.

Glick H. A., McBride, L. and Bauer, M. S. (2003) A manic-depressive symptom self-report in optical scanable format. *Bipolar Disorders*, 5, 366–369.

Goldberg, J. F., Harrow, M. and Grossman, L. S. (1995) Course and outcome in bipolar affective disorder: A longitudinal follow-up study. *American Journal of Psychiatry*, 152, 379–384.

Goldberg, J. F., Garno, J. L., Leon, A. C., Kocsis, J. H. and Portera, L. (1998) Association of recurrent suicidal ideation with non remission from acute mixed mania. *American Journal of Psychiatry*, 155, 1753–1755.

Goodwin, F. K. and Jamison, K. (1990) *Manic-Depressive Illness*. New York: Oxford University Press.

Hamilton, M. (1960) A rating scale for depression. *Journal of Neurology, Neurosurgery and Psychiatry*, 23, 56–62.

Harrow, M., Goldberg, J., Grossman, L. and Meltzer, H. (1990) Outcome in manic disorders: A naturalistic follow-up study. *Archives of General Psychiatry*, 47, 665–671.

Harvey, A. G., Watkins, E. R., Mansell, W. and Shafran, R. (2004) *Cognitive Behavioural Processes Across Psychological Disorders: A Transdiagnostic Approach to Research and Treatment*. Oxford: Oxford University Press.

Hurry, J., Sturt, E., Bebbington, P. and Tennant, C. (1983) Socio-demographic associations with social disablement in a community sample. *Social Psychiatry*, 18, 113–121.

Isometsae, E. T. (1993) Course, outcome and suicide risk in bipolar disorder: A review. *Psychiatric Fennica*, 24, 113–124.

Jauhar, P. and Weller, M. P. I. (1982) Psychiatric morbidity and time zone changes: A study of patients from Heathrow Airport. *British Journal of Psychiatry*, 140, 231–235.

Judd, L. L., Akiskal, H. S., Schettler, P. J., Endicott, J., Maser, J., Solomon, D. A. et al. (2002) The long term natural history of the weekly symptomatic status of bipolar I disorder. *Archives of General Psychiatry*, 59, 530–537.

Judd, L. L., Akiskal, H. S., Schettler, P. J., Coryell, W., Endicott, J., Maser, J., Solomon, D. A. et al. (2003) A prospective investigation of the natural history of the long-term weekly symptomatic status of bipolar II disorder. *Archives of General Psychiatry*, 60, 261–269.

Keller, M. B., Lavori, P. W., Kane, J. M., Gelenberger, A. J. et al. (1992) Subsyndromal symptoms in bipolar disorder: A comparison of standard and low serum levels of lithium. *Archives of General Psychiatry*, 49, 371–376.

Kessler, R. C., Rubniow, D. R., Holmes, C. et al. (1997) The epidemiology of DSM-III-R bipolar I disorder in a general population survey. *Psychological Medicine*, 27, 1079–1089.

Lam, D. H. and Wong, G. (1997) Prodromes, coping strategies, insight and social functioning in bipolar affective disorders. *Psychological Medicine*, 27, 1091–1100.

Lam, D. H. and Wong, G. (2005) Prodromes and coping strategies in bipolar disorders: A review. *Clinical Psychology Review*, 25, 1028–1042.

Lam, D. H., Jones, S., Hayward, P. and Bright, J. (1999) *Cognitive Therapy for Bipolar Disorder: A Practician's Guide to the Theory, Practice and Therapy*. Chichester: John Wiley.

Lam, D. H., Bright, J., Jones, S., Hayward, P., Schuck, N., Chisholm, D. and Sham, P. (2000) Cognitive therapy for bipolar illness: A pilot study of relapse prevention. *Cognitive Therapy and Research*, 24, 503–520.

Lam, D. H., Wong, G. and Sham, P. (2001) Prodromes, coping strategies and course of illness in bipolar affective disorders – a naturalistic study. *Psychological Medicine*, 31, 1397–1402.

Lam, D., Wright, K. and Smith, N. (2004) Dysfunctional assumptions in bipolar disorder. *Journal of Affective Disorders*, 79, 193–199.

Lam, D., Wright, K. and Sham, P. (2005) Sense of hyper-positive self and response to cognitive therapy for bipolar disorder. *Psychological Medicine*, 35, 69–77.

Lavori, P. W., Dawson, R., Mueller, T. I., Warshaw, M., Swartz, A. and Leon, A. (1996) Analysis of course of psychopathology: Transitions among states of health and illness. *International Journal of Methods in Psychiatric Research*, 6, 321–334.

Leverich, G. S., Altshuler, L. L. et al. (2003) Factors associated with suicide attempts in 648 patients with bipolar disorder in the Stanley Foundation Bipolar Network. *Journal of Clinical Psychiatry*, 64, 506–515.

Malkoff-Schwartz, S., Frank, E., Anderson, B., Sherrill, J. T., Siegel, L., Patterson, D. and Kupfer, D. J. (1998) Stressful life events and social rhythm disruption in the onset of manic and depressive bipolar episodes. *Archives of General Psychiatry*, 55, 702–707.

Mansell, W. (2006) The Hypomanic Attitudes and Positive Predictions Inventory (HAPPI): A pilot study to identify items that are elevated in individuals with bipolar affective disorder compared to non-clinical controls. *Behavioural and Cognitive Psychotherapy*, 34, 467–476.

Mansell, W. and Jones, S. H. (2006) The HAPPI: A questionnaire to assess cognitions that distinguish between individuals with a diagnosis of bipolar disorder and non-clinical controls. *Journal of Affective Disorders*, 93, 29–34.

Mansell, W. and Lam, D. (2003) Conceptualising a cycle of ascent into mania: A case report. *Behavioural and Cognitive Psychotherapy*, 31, 363–367.

Markar, H. and Mander, A. (1989) Efficacy of lithium prophylaxis in clinical practice. *British Journal of Psychiatry*, 155, 496–500.

McElroy, S. L., Hudson, J. I., Pope, H. G. Jr and Aizley, H. G. (1992) The DSM-III-R impulse control disorders not elsewhere classified: Clinical characteristics and relationship to other psychiatric disorders. *American Journal of Psychiatry*, 149, 318–327.

Miklowitz, D. J. (1992) Longitudinal outcome and medication noncompliance among manic patients with and without mood-incongruent psychotic features. *Journal of Nervous and Mental Disease*, 180, 703–711.

Miller, F. T., Busch, F. and Tanebaum, J. H. (1989) Drug abuse in schizophrenia and bipolar disorder. *American Journal of Drug and Alcohol Abuse*, 15, 291–295.

Perlick, D., Rosenbeck, R. A., Clarkin, J. F., Sirey, J. A., Salahi, J., Struening, E. L. and Link, B. G. (2001) Adverse effects of perceived stigma on social adaptation of persons diagnosed with bipolar affective disorder. *Psychiatric Services*, 52, 1627–1632.

Perugi, G., Akiskal, H. S., Ramacciotti, S., Nassini, S., Toni, C., Milanfranchi, A. and Musetti, L. (1999) Depressive comporbidity of panic, social phobic and obsessive-compulsive disorders re-examined: Is there a bipolar II connection? *Journal of Psychiatric Research*, 33, 53–61.

Power, M. J., Katz, R., McGuffin, P., Duggan, C. F., Lam, D. and Beck, A. T. (1994) The dysfunctional attitude scale (DAS): A comparison of forms A and B and proposal for a new sub-scaled version. *Journal of Research into Personality*, 28, 263–276.

Prien, R. F. and Potter, W. Z. (1990) NIMH workshop report on treatment of bipolar disorder. *Psychopharmacology Bulletin*, 26, 409–427.

Regier, D. A., Farmer, M. E., Rea, D. S., Locke, B. Z., Judd, L. L. and Goodwin, F. K. (1990) Comorbidity of mental disorders with alcohol and other drug abuse – results from the epidemiologic catchment area study. *Journal of American Medical Association*, 264, 2511–2518.

Reilly-Harrington, N. A., Alloy, L. B., Fresco, D. M. and Whitehouse, W. G. (1999) Cognitive styles and life events interact to predict bipolar and unipolar symptomatology. *Journal of Abnormal Psychology*, 108, 567–578.

Robins, L. N., Hezler, J. E., Weissman, M. M., Orvaschel, H. et al. (1984) Lifetime prevalence of specific psychiatric disorders in three sites. *Archives of General Psychiatry*, 41, 949–958.

Romans, S. E. and McPherson, H. M. (1992) The social networks of bipolar affective disorder patients. *Journal of Affective Disorders*, 25, 221–228.

Scott, J. and Pope, M. (2003) Cognitive styles in individuals with bipolar disorders. *Psychological Medicine*, 33, 1081–1088.

Scott, J., Stanton, B., Garland, A. and Ferrier, I. N. (2000) Cognitive vulnerability in patients with bipolar disorder. *Psychological Medicine*, 30, 467–472.

Shapiro, D., Quitkin, F. and Fleiss, J. (1989) Response to maintenance therapy in bipolar illness. *Archives of General Psychiatry*, 46, 401–405.

Strakowski, S. M., McElroy, S. L., Keck, P. W. and West, S. A. (1994) The co-occurrence of mania with medical and other psychiatric disorders. *International Journal of Psychiatry in Medicine*, 24, 305–328.

Strakowski, S. M., McElroy, S. L., Keck, P. E. and West, S. A. (1996) Suicidality among patients with mixed and manic bipolar disorder. *American Journal of Psychiatry*, 153, 674–676.

Swann, A. C., Bowden, C. L., Morris, D., Calabrese, J. R., Petty, F., Small, J. et al. (1997) Depression during mania: Treatment response to lithium or divalproex. *Archives of General Psychiatry*, 54, 37–42.

Tohen, M., Waternaux, C. M. and Tsuang, M. T. (1990) Outcome in mania: A 4-year prospective follow-up of 75 patients utilizing survival analysis. *Archives of General Psychiatry*, 47, 1106–1111.

Turvey, C. L., Coryell, W. H., Solomon, D. A., Leon, A. C., Erdicott, J., Keller, M. B. and Akiskal, H. S. (1999) Long-term prognosis of bipolar disorder. *Acta Psychiatrica Scandinavica*, 99, 110–119.

Wehr, T. A., Sack, D. A. and Rosenthal, N. E. (1987) Sleep reduction as a final common pathway in the genesis of mania. *American Journal of Psychiatry*, 144, 201–204.

Weissman, A. and Beck, A. T. (1978) *Development and validation of the Dysfunctional Attitude Scale: A preliminary investigation*. Paper presented at the annual meeting of the American Educational Research Association.

Weissman, M. M., Leaf, P. J. et al. (1988) Affective disorders in five United States communities. *Psychology Medicine*, 18, 141–153.

Winokur, G., Clayton, P. J. and Reich, T. (1969) *Manic Depressive Illness*. St Louis: CV Mosby.

Wong, G. and Lam, D. (1999) The development and validation of the coping inventory for prodromes of mania. *Journal of Affective Disorders*, 53, 57–65.

Young, L. T., Cooke, R. G., Robb, J. C., Levitt, A. J. and Joffe, R. T. (1993) Anxious and non-anxious bipolar disorder. *Journal of Affective Disorders*, 29, 49–52.

Chapter 8

Bipolar disorder

Treatment

Warren Mansell and Dominic Lam

INTRODUCTION

Bipolar disorder is typically treated with pharmacotherapy, yet several different psychological treatments are becoming increasingly available, nearly always as a supplement to medication. A wide range of pharmaceutical treatments is used. Most patients are prescribed a mood stabiliser for its prophylactic effects. The most common and long-standing mood stabiliser is lithium, although carbomazipine and sodium valproate are also widely used. Patients who experience more regular or severe depressions are also likely to be subscribed an antidepressant, most often a selective serotonin re-uptake inhibitor (SSRI). More recently, new antipsychotic drugs, such as olanzepine, have been used as prophylactics, and lamotrigine is being used as a long-term prophylactic against depression. During acute episodes of mania, antipsychotics or valporate are typically used. Many patients with high levels of agitation or overactivity may also be prescribed benzodiazepines to promote sleep in the short term.

The psychological treatments for bipolar disorder have a history dating back to early psychoanalytical approaches, but they now encompass a range of evidence-based approaches including family-focused therapy (FFT), cognitive behavioural therapy (CBT) and psychoeducation. Interpersonal social rhythm therapy (IPSRT) is also an approach under investigation, but its efficacy is not yet known. CBT has also been used to enhance medication adherence. For the sake of clarity and coherence, only CBT will be described in detail in this chapter. It is the most extensively validated psychological therapy in bipolar disorder and shares several features with other psychological approaches.

THE PLACE OF PSYCHOLOGICAL METHODS IN THE TREATMENT OF BIPOLAR DISORDER

Patients with bipolar disorder have traditionally been viewed as poor candidates for psychological therapy. However, since the 1990s, the efficacy of psychological treatments for this patient group has become more evident. There are several reasons for considering a psychological intervention. First, a large number of patients relapse despite taking appropriate medication. For example, some studies indicate that around 50% of patients on lithium relapse within 2 years (Solomon et al., 1995; Goodwin, 2003). Thus, medication is not a sufficient treatment for many patients. Second, there is increasing evidence to suggest that psychosocial factors are associated with increased risk of relapse in bipolar disorder and/or increased symptoms. Specific factors that have been identified include high levels of hostility and criticism from family members (Miklowitz et al., 1988), stressful life events (Ellicott et al., 1990), events relating to personal goal attainment (Johnson et al., 1999) and events that disrupt routine and the sleep–wake cycle (Malkoff-Schwartz et al., 1998). Third, considerable evidence suggests that patients with bipolar disorder show dysfunctional cognitive styles and processes that are equivalent to those found in other forms of psychopathology, even during periods of apparent remission. Examples include elevated levels of dysfunctional attitudes (Scott et al., 2000; Scott and Pope, 2003; Lam et al., 2004), over-general memory (Scott et al., 2000; Mansell and Lam, 2004), poor problem solving (Scott et al., 2000) and recurrent distressing memories (Mansell and Lam, 2004).

EFFECTIVENESS OF CBT

CBT for bipolar disorder targets both current symptoms and attempts to reduce relapse rates. Research trials have assessed the effectiveness of CBT in both domains. Zeretsky et al. (1999) evaluated 20 sessions of CBT for current depression in two groups of patients: bipolar and unipolar. They showed equivalent reductions in depression symptoms in both groups. Scott et al. (2001) showed that 25 sessions of cognitive therapy led to greater reductions in symptoms of mania and depression and greater improvement in global functioning over 6 months relative to a waiting-list control group. Lam et al. (2000) compared 12–20 sessions of CBT to treatment as usual, and demonstrated fewer bipolar episodes, fewer mood fluctuations and higher social functioning over 6 months. To date, only one randomised controlled trial of CBT in bipolar disorder has been published (Lam et al., 2003), although several others await completion or publication (e.g. Sachs et al., 2003). In the published study, cognitive therapy led to fewer bipolar episodes, fewer days in a bipolar episode, fewer bipolar admissions and higher levels of social functioning relative to treatment as usual assessed at 12 months. The cognitive therapy group also had lower levels of depression at 6 months. One recent study has shed some light on the mechanism of change in CBT: Wright et al. (2005) found that patients with bipolar disorder who had received CBT showed a smaller increase in dysfunctional attitudes following a negative mood induction. Thus, one may speculate that CBT partly serves to reduce the activation of dysfunctional thinking styles during depressed mood states.

COGNITIVE THERAPY FOR BIPOLAR DISORDER: OVERVIEW

CBT for bipolar disorder shares many of the elements of CBT for other psychological disorders. The therapeutic relationship is based on collaborative empiricism. Sessions are structured using an agenda and patients are expected to carry out 'homework' in between sessions. The individualised formulation for treatment draws on the patient's experiences and involves the reciprocal links between mood, thought, behaviour, physiology and the environment that are thought to maintain and exacerbate symptoms.

Therapists need to bear in mind the biopsychosocial findings of bipolar disorders when working with bipolar patients. In fact, it is crucial that therapists should be familiar with the disorder and not treat it as CBT for unipolar depression with the mania side added on. CBT for bipolar disorder has several features that differentiate it from CBT for unipolar depression, and these have an impact on the approach and the techniques used. First, attitudes towards bipolar disorder itself need to be considered. Patients with bipolar disorder may have specific difficulties in coming to terms with their diagnosis, taking their medication, understanding the causes of their condition and dealing with stigmatisation from others. The therapist therefore needs to be familiar with the facts of bipolar illness and common medication use. Second, as many patients come for treatment when they are outside a full-blown episode, the therapy pays particular attention to developing strategies that may help prevent a future episode. Third, the therapy draws on psychosocial findings such as life events (Malkoff-Schwartz et al., 1998; Johnson et al., 1999) and cognitive theories concerning the idiosyncratic biases in cognition and behaviour that are associated with the symptoms of mania and hypomania (Beck, 1967; Healy and Williams, 1989, Lam et al., 2004). It is proposed that biological factors, past experiences and family environment contribute to the formation of dysfunctional beliefs and schemata that bias the processing of, and reactions to, current experience. In bipolar disorder, the high goal-attainment and high-achieving cognitions are particularly relevant in driving the behaviour that may lead to vulnerability to further episodes. Fourth, the interpersonal style of patients with bipolar disorder often has consequences for the therapeutic relationship that need to be taken into consideration. Owing to these extra factors, CBT typically averages around 15 to 25 sessions.

CBT: Early sessions

The early sessions may involve certain elements of assessment that need to be extended, such as the life chart (see Chapter 7). In addition, the following elements are involved.

Psychoeducation

Every type of short-term, focused therapy has a psychoeducation component that provides a common framework for both the therapist and the patient to work within. In cognitive therapy for bipolar disorder, psychoeducation usually consists of the following topics. First, it is explained that the diathesis–stress model states that there is thought to be a genetic or physical basis of bipolar disorder but that the environment, including stressors, can trigger the onset of the condition and subsequent episodes. The rationale of combined medication and psychotherapy is based on the diathesis–stress model. Second, the importance of routine and sleep is spelled out. Third, the importance of targeting unhealthy or dysfunctional beliefs is stressed. Fourth, a brief summary of the nature of cognitive therapy is given. Therapy can reduce or prevent stress and patients are taught cognitive behavioural skills to tackle stress and cope with the condition. This involves monitoring and regulating mood and behaviour. The importance of medication to tackle the diathesis side should be emphasised. The use of an information sheet can be helpful (see Lam et al., 1999). In addition to discussing these topics, the summary generally gives an account of the common experience of bipolar patients so that patients feel their experience is echoed and that the therapist has some idea what it is like to live with the illness. The information sheet is usually given to patients during the first or second session to take home and read. They are told to mark and comment on the pamphlet, which serves as a platform for discussion. In the next session, patients are asked what they found to be useful or interesting in the leaflet, and what aspects of it they found difficult to apply to themselves.

The aim of psychoeducation is not simply to present the model in a didactic manner. Patients often come to therapy with strong views about their illness and some may have read widely and are already well informed. It is important to acknowledge that patients' experiences may be different from that described in the leaflet. They do not have to accept everything in the leaflet either. Some patients may deny the illness and may resent the medical model. They may feel the medical diagnosis is unhelpful and stigmatising. For them, the limitations and problems which they perceive as being associated with their illness may seem very painful and learning to accept the illness can highlight these problems. The therapist should be empathic and show willingness to listen and understand. In some cases, the patient and the therapist might agree that certain aspects of the medical model may be unhelpful.

However, with a great deal of sensitivity from the therapist, most patients can choose to be pragmatic and set some goals for therapy so that they could put themselves on 'the road of normal living'.

The other extreme is that some patients may be excessively reliant on the medical model. They may feel that, because bipolar disorder is an 'illness', the only possible treatment must be medication. A discussion of the false dichotomy between the physical and psychological may prove helpful for these patients. There are numerous examples of how lifestyle and behaviour can affect physical illness, e.g. diabetes and high blood pressure. However, therapists should be prepared for patients to regard bipolar disorder very differently from physical illnesses. Psychoeducation therefore provides a good platform for the patient and therapist to begin a collaborative relationship. Most patients can choose to experiment with coping with their illness differently.

Problem list and goal setting

Within the first few sessions, the patient and therapist draw up a problem list. This may include any of a range of issues including understanding the illness and preventing future episodes, identifying risky situations and behaviours, identifying triggers, learning to detect prodromes and cope with them, stabilising mood, problems with medication, interpersonal issues, concerns about the future symptoms including depression, anxiety and hypomania. Discussion of the issues raised in the educational pamphlet can often help to identify therapy goals.

The patient and the therapist need to agree on which of the problems can be addressed within the time-limited course of therapy and set a list of realistic goals. The list should emphasise the element of relapse prevention (see later). Some patients, often those who have waited months or years for therapy, may have a particularly long list of problems that they wish to address. The extreme is patients who have not given much thought about psychological help or are not very insightful about how their high goal-attainment beliefs and highly driven beliefs may impact on the course of the illness. Therapists need to be patient and use Socratic questioning and guided discovery techniques to help patients to identify these areas as problematic and set goals to tackle them. For patients who have a long list of goals, prioritisation is crucial, and will vary greatly depending on the patient and on his or her history, level of acceptance of the problems and the current phase of illness. Usually, once the therapist states that prioritisation is necessary, therapist and patient can work together to identify the most important goals. It helps if the first goal addresses a current problem and has a strong likelihood of success.

Symptoms of depression are often the target for patients who are currently depressed or have subclinical symptoms. Many patients report excessive anxiety and worry about a future relapse, involving concerns such as poor sleep and difficult social situations. Patients who have a long history of illness but are currently well will often want to review their life and understand their previous episodes. Many patients are in relationships in which they are highly dependent on certain family members and this may provide a focus of intervention. Current symptoms of hypomania often need to be targeted immediately because of their potential dangers (see later).

For some bipolar patients with high goal-attainment beliefs, therapy can be part of their achievement goals in regaining total control of life. Typically, these patients set a long list of goals and are eager to learn as many techniques as possible while not necessarily engaging in emotional processing of their experiences (Rachman, 1980). They may take on the educational and technique elements of therapy at an intellectual rather than emotional level. Some even take copious notes in therapy sessions as if they have been given an academic tutorial. Issues and techniques may be discussed without much personal meaning to them. Their way of coping with the illness is often to be completely in control. This may relate to their being trapped in the vicious cycle of 'catching up with lost time', learning the techniques so that they can rush back into 'normal life'. Therapists should be aware of this and share their conceptualisation with the patients. Slowing down and taking stock in therapy on how to learn to live with the illness can be as therapeutic as any techniques.

Monitoring and regulating

Monitoring and regulating are crucial aspects of cognitive behavioural therapy for relapse prevention in bipolar disorders. The patient is encouraged to carry out monitoring in the early stages of therapy. This not only provides the data for testing the patient's beliefs but it also encourages a reflective stance to his or her experiences. The reflective stance involves monitoring, emotional engagement and problem solving, and it contrasts with the modes of thinking involved in depression and mania. The mode of thinking in depression is typically ruminative, focused on details and over-analytical, whereas the mode of thinking in mania and hypomania is typically focused on holistic meanings and results in impulsive responding (see Barnard, 2003, for further discussion of modes of processing).

The Mood and Activity Schedule provides an ideal tool for monitoring. It is adapted from the measures traditionally employed in depression. First, the schedule covers 24 hours, which enables the therapist to gain an overall picture of the patient's sleep and wake routine. Second, a daily mood rating ranging from −10 extreme depression to +10 extreme elation is used. The rationale of the mood rating is to help patients to learn and identify normal mood fluctuation from abnormal mood fluctuations. Some patients can become fearful of any mood variations and so discriminating normal from abnormal mood swings can allow patients to begin to accept normal mood states. In a −10 to +10 scale, '0' would represent a 'neutral' mood. Mood ratings between −5 to +5 are typically seen as within normal mood fluctuations, particularly if the mood fluctuations can be related to events or activities in the schedule and there are no prodromal warnings. This linking of mood to activities can also serve as a good educational process of the cognitive model that behaviour and mood can affect each other. However, anything beyond the normal range may serve as a warning sign, particularly if the pattern of the mood increase or decrease is continuing without any obvious reason. Ratings of pleasure and mastery in the activities are used so that patients can learn about these concepts. However, therapists should use their clinical acumen to introduce these concepts gradually so that patients are not too overwhelmed. In addition, the activity schedule gives a good indication of patient's routine. From the schedule, some patients evidently have very disorganised routines, others in contrast have very rigid and demanding routines. Some may be avoiding certain activities owing to severe anxiety about experiencing a relapse. Often, they can be encouraged to introduce planned activities into their routines in a graded manner.

Some patients are trapped in a vicious cycle to 'catch up for lost time'. Typically, they see the period of having just emerged from an episode of illness as a crucial time to make up for the time they have lost in their career or study. Instead of having a planned and gradual return to study or work routine, they may immediately throw themselves into a frenzy of working all their waking hours, delaying sleep or having no leisure time at all. It is not unknown for bipolar patients to overcompensate at work after a period of absence by taking on many new projects to prove to themselves and other people that the illness is over and that they are their old competent self again. An activity schedule often can detect these patterns very early. It also forms a basis for the discussion of alternative routines, which, although they might involve shorter periods of work, may actually be likely to be more productive in the longer term due to a reduced chance of interruption through relapse and hospital admission.

Some bipolar patients have quite variable sleep habits even when well; some have jobs that do not inherently provide a structured routine of nine-to-five work hours. For example, they may be drawn to more creative and artistic jobs such as painting, pottery or acting. When the demands from external factors become more intrusive or frequent then changes to sleep routines can become excessive, raising the risk of relapse. Once the 'risky' pattern of sleep has been identified from the monitoring sheets, session time can be devoted to identifying realistic routine targets. Patients may perceive routine to be excessively limiting and controlling. However, they can be guided to test out the benefits of adopting a healthy routine. Sleep-management techniques are deployed if necessary. Behavioural experiments can be set up to test the idea of having regular routine and examine the effect of feeling less tired on work output. A significant number of patients may be excessively anxious about poor sleep (Harvey et al., 2005) and therefore interventions may instead be directed at normalising minor sleep disruptions and challenging beliefs about sleep.

An example of an activity schedule completed by 'Josephine' at the beginning of therapy is presented in Figure 8.1.

This activity schedule was very revealing. First, it revealed that Josephine had very little routine during the day. She sometimes procrastinated when she had to do any serious work. She also got distracted very easily and was not task focused, as exemplified by spending 3 hours going to the building society. On closer questioning, she was distracted into going into shops and spent about 2 hours in a bookshop. Second, her sleep routine appeared very poor. Josephine recognised that she was very tired and lacking in energy during the week because her sleep routine was particularly disrupted over the weekend. Third, it also provided evidence that if she drank too much in the evening, she often had a bad night. Alcohol helped her to fall asleep initially but she would often wake up at the early hours of the morning and could not go back to sleep. Going to clubs was also was a risky situation for her as she often got drunk over the weekend. This left her tired for a couple of days at the beginning of the week. The tiredness and poor sleep routine made her unable to plan and commit herself, which in turn left her very anxious and depressed about not able to get on with life. Therapy consisted of monitoring and reducing drinking, a graded approach of going to bed earlier and limiting her time in the club during Saturday. Josephine quickly felt the benefit of having a better sleep routine and reducing her alcohol intake. She felt less tired and was able to plan her week. An added bonus was that her friends told her that she was more pleasant to be with as she did not get drunk and did not become loud and volatile.

Making these apparently simple changes in sleep and routine can be difficult for some patients. Therapists need to be sensitive to reasons for resistance to such changes and listen to the patient's point of view. Some bipolar patients have strong views about having to press on with life despite the illness and some may dislike routine and having to conform. A collaborative working relationship enables patients to weigh up the pros and cons and make an informed decision. Compromises may well need to be made in terms of other external demands on the patient. However, as long as this allows the patient to sustain a regular routine and reasonable sleep pattern it will be an important contribution to maintaining psychological health.

Another way to use activity schedules is to help patients to plan their routines better. This may include making time for pleasurable activities that do not involve a drive to perform well. Examples include reading, walking, watching television and having a quiet chat with a friend. Patients with chronic residual depression symptoms can come to believe that they can have no influence over their mood ('I have no control over whether I go high or low'). Information from the mood and behaviour records can demonstrate

WEEKLY ACTIVITY SCHEDULE   Week beginning: _____   Name: _Josephine_____

Please describe in a few words what you are doing for each hour of the day. For activities that give you a sense of achievement, please mark an A, with a score from 1 to 10, where 1 = very little and 10 = as much as possible. For activities that give you a sense of pleasure please mark a P, again with a score from 1 to 10.

Time	Monday	Tuesday	Wednesday	Thursday	Friday	Saturday	Sunday
6–7 a.m.	Bed	Bed	Bed	Bed	Bed	Club	Club
7–8 a.m.	Up and breakfast	Up and practice on the computer	Bed	Bed	Bed	Club	Club
8–9 a.m.	Course work on the computer	Practice on computer	Bed	Up and leisurely breakfast	Bed	Bed	Club
9–10 a.m.	Ditto	Computer course	Last-minute prepare for course	Leave for course	Up and breakfast	Bed	Club
10–11 a.m.	Ditto	Ditto	Computing course	Computing course	House chores	Bed	Club
11 a.m.–12 p.m.	Ditto	Ditto	Course	Ditto	Shopping	Bed	Bed
12–1 p.m.	Building society	Ditto	Course	Ditto	Library	Bed	Bed
1–2 p.m.	Building society	Phone calls and correspondence	Practice computing	Went home	Leave for Maudsley	Bed	Bed
2–3 p.m.	Building society	Ditto	Studying	Course work	Maudsley	Bed	Bed
3–4 p.m.	Course work	Coffee with a friend	Studying	Course work	Home	Tidy up flat	Bed
4–5 p.m.	Course work	Coffee with a friend	Studying	Course work	Tidy up flat	Tidy up flat	Bed

Figure 8.1 An example of an activity schedule.

Continued

Time	Monday	Tuesday	Wednesday	Thursday	Friday	Saturday	Sunday
5–6 p.m.	Procrastinating	Home	TV	Frantic cleaning of flat	Course work	Gym	Bed
6–7 p.m.	Procrastinating	TV	TV	Ditto	Ditto	Gym	Bed
7–8 p.m.	TV and dinner	Radio and dinner	Cooked dinner	TV	Course work	Gym	TV
8–9 p.m.	Tidy up flat	TV	TV	TV	Read	Gym	TV
9–10 p.m.	TV	Letter writing	TV	Procrastinating	Club	Meet a friend in pub	TV
10–11 p.m.	TV and phone calls	TV	Start more course work	Soho meal on my own	Club	Pub	TV
11 p.m.–12 a.m.	TV	Ditto	Ditto	Pub	Club	Pub	Ring mother
12–1 a.m.	Reading in bed	Ditto	Ditto	Pub	Club	Club	Bed
1–2 a.m.	Reading in bed	Ditto	Ditto	Bed	Club	Club	Bed
2–3 a.m.	Bed	Ditto till 2.30 a.m.	Bed (2.30 a.m.)	Bed	Club	Club	Bed
3–4 a.m.	Bed	Bed	Bed	Bed	Club	Club	Bed
4–5 a.m.	Bed	Bed	Bed	Bed	Club	Club	Bed
5–6 a.m.	Bed	Bed	Bed	Bed	Club	Club	Bed

Figure 8.1 continued.

that even during low periods they can affect the extent of low mood. They can experiment by developing a repertoire of mood enhancing activities during their periods of low mood and monitoring the effects. Through these exercises patients can come to learn that they can have some control over their mood, but also that having complete control over one's mood may not be possible.

Patients who are becoming 'high' can use the activity schedule to set targets to moderate the temptations of excess activity, such as taking on more and more tasks at work or staying at work for longer and longer, and build in calming activities and regular and sufficient rests to stop the mood from going higher. Potential difficulties at work and in the interpersonal domain can be avoided by patients not exposing themselves to risky situations.

Attitudes towards hypomanic symptoms and their effects on behaviour

Patients' attitudes towards their hypomanic symptoms ranges from extreme positive enthusiasm to crippling anxiety, panic attacks and avoidance. The symptoms may be perceived as a way to pursue their long-held goals or as a herald of an imminent relapse involving hospitalisation, humiliation and further stigmatisation. Indeed, some patients may hold both beliefs. CBT can help patients articulate, understand and modify their strong and ambivalent attitudes towards hypomania.

The pros and cons table is a classic tool in cognitive therapy and provides a structured way to explore patients' attitudes towards their hypomanic symptoms. An example is provided in Table 8.1. First, the patient and therapist work to identify the main symptoms of hypomania for the patient, for example increased energy and creativity. The patient is first asked to list the positive features of these symptoms, and then the negative features. Therapists must be genuine and respectful – patients are encouraged to express both the pros and cons and not simply to focus on the negative side. Once the table is produced it provides an immediate forum for discussing any the

Table 8.1 Example of a pros and cons table for hypomania

Advantages of hypomania	Disadvantages of hypomania
I feel better about myself	If I go to hospital I may get treated badly
People like me more	If I go to hospital I may receive nasty medications
I can get more things done	I may do something that upsets people or that I regret
Other people will look after me	I don't want to be a 'career patient'
It is a way out when there is no other way to deal with my problems	

ambivalence, allowing the therapist to empathise with the patient that the symptoms are indeed a double-edged sword and that this conflict must lead to serious problems for the patient. It allows the patient to realise that the therapist is not trying to remove these experiences from the patient's life and is willing to acknowledge the positive elements. Patients may be left to consider this table in between sessions to gradually come to a more considered appraisal of the hypomanic symptoms. A more direct method can involve asking the patient whether it is possible that the positive consequences of hypomania can be attained through other, less risky, means. For example, one patient felt that she was liked by other people more when she was 'high', but could acknowledge that there may be other ways to be liked by other people, such as being considerate and listening to them. The pros and cons table therefore provides a good starting point to start to set up behavioural experiments. Before the next session, this patient made a point of listening more to her friends' problems and felt closer and more appreciated by her friends as a consequence.

Several key patient beliefs can form the target for behavioural experiments (Mansell, 2006). We cited above a test of the belief that one needs to respond to social situations by being active and energetic in contrast to being quiet and considerate. Patients can also experiment by comparing their common tendency to act immediately in response to a challenging situation with delaying their reaction until the next day. Often they find that they are more able to consider more perspectives if they wait, leading to a better solution. Typically, patients are tempted to seek more stimulation when they feel 'high', for example going out later or drinking more alcohol or caffeinated drinks. They may have strongly held beliefs that they need to do this to enjoy themselves or perform effectively. Again, behavioural experiments can be constructed to test out these beliefs in practice, by substituting relaxing experiences for stimulating activities and monitoring the effects. Dent et al. (2004) provide further explanations of how to structure behavioural experiments in bipolar disorder.

CBT: Later sessions

Prodromes, coping and relapse prevention

The prodromal period is defined as the period from the time of the first appearance of symptoms to the time when a full-blown episode is evident. The concept of prodromes is more complex in psychiatric or psychological problems as the presentation of these first symptoms can be more idiosyncratic and is probably a complex mixture of biology, psychology and environmental factors. The term 'prodromes' is used as a shorthand for the early warnings that patients may notice at the early stages of an episode. The early detection of these warnings and early interventions may help prevent full-blown episodes, as indicated by several studies (Perry et al., 1999; Lam et al., 2001; Colom et al., 2003).

To define the individual's pattern of prodromes, patients are simply asked from their experience what sort of things in their behaviour, thinking or mood may lead them to think they are going into either a manic or a depressive episode. It is important to bear in mind that the symptoms have to be specific and easily detectable. Often, it is helpful to ask patients to anchor their prodromes in a social context, for example in their social interaction with others and comments from other people.

Each individual prodromal symptom is written on a piece of paper. Patients are encouraged to sort the pile of paper into three groups: the early, middle and late stages. Most patients find it useful to sort the pile of paper first into early and late stages and the rest go into the middle stage. The therapist and the patient then further fine-tune the pattern of prodromes to make sure there is no ambiguity in wording. Mood states are difficult to gauge. Hence, they are often carefully defined and anchored in the patients' social context if possible. The behaviour linked to the mood state should also be mapped out. Often behaviour is easier to monitor. For example, if irritability is a prodromal symptom, therapists can ask how the irritability shows itself. One patient was able to say that he is usually irritable with his wife and picks on her at the very early stage of an episode. As the episode unfolds he is usually irritable with his daughter and, at the final stage, he is irritable with almost anyone. In practice, the last stage of the prodromal phase is almost a full-blown stage for most patients. However, it is important to distinguish it from the full-blown episode. Sometimes patients find the transition into the full-blown stage quite blurry and usually move from the late stage of mania prodromes to a full-blown episode within a day.

The prodromal symptoms of these three stages are copied onto a prodromes form. Next, patients are asked to estimate the time intervals they have before the very early stage becomes the middle stage and the middle stage becomes the late stage. The therapist then discusses with the patient ways of coping with bipolar prodromes, using cognitive and behavioural techniques. Some examples of coping strategies of mania prodromes are: avoiding stimulation, engaging in calming activities, resisting the temptation to engage in further goal-directed behaviour and prioritising tasks. Cognitive behavioural techniques of routine, prioritising, making time for pleasurable and mastery activities and challenging of negative thoughts play an important part in coping with depression prodromes. During the depression prodromal stage, activating the patient's social network for support is important. Social companionship and shared activities can prevent patients from ruminating about their depression and thus increasing their depression symptoms (Nolen-Hoeksema, 1991; Lam et al., 2003). Most patients find it helpful to discuss unrealistic worries with a close other. An empathic confidant can inject some reality into patients' overwhelming and unrealistic worries.

Medical appointments and self-medication can also be seen as coping strategies. It is often helpful for patients to show their key workers or prescribing doctors their record of 'coping with prodromes' form. It is a good practice to enclose this record in the discharge report. How early professionals should be called upon to help depends on the patients' resources as well as how long the prodromal stages last. Genuine examples of early, middle and late prodromes and coping strategies are provided in Table 8.2.

There are several considerations to bear in mind when eliciting prodromes. First, the decision of where the prodromal phases end and a full-blown illness begins can be difficult when onset is more gradual. The onset of mania can be

Table 8.2 Examples of prodromal warning signs and coping strategies identified by a patient

Time period	Prodromal warning signs		Coping strategies
Early	1.	Feelings of being energised in the early morning or late at night	Use energy during the day, both physically and mentally. Stay in
	2.	The thought 'I will do what I want' in every-day things	bed until normal getting up time. Ask partner to remind me about
	3.	Regularly drinking the equivalent of more than one bottle of wine per night	my responsibilities and joint needs. Negotiate issues in a reasonable way. Check desire to
	4.	Progressively and consistently wanting to stay up later	drink more. Remind myself that going to bed before 12 a.m. is better for me and partner
Middle	5.	Enjoy memories of early manic experiences	Note down unusual thoughts in diary and challenge them.
	6.	Saying to myself 'I'll never get depressed again'	Become aware that these signs are serious, so challenge and
	7.	Feeling compelled to seek situations so as to flirt and meet other women	stop the behaviours and discuss them with my partner and psychiatrist. Avoid going to clubs
	8.	Buying unusual things when I don't need them, e.g. flamboyant clothes	and bars on my own and behaving as if single
	9.	Contacting people I have known when high	
Late	10.	Sleeping less than 4 to 5 hours every night	Allow partner to take control of income. Talk to partner and
	11.	Thinking 'I have a right to spend my own money' without considering debts to others	psychiatrist about pharmaceutical methods to help reduce the energy. Bring in the
	12.	Behaving cruelly and thoughtlessly towards partner	contract with partner and friends so that they decide the
	13.	Decide to leave relationship and home	appropriate action to be taken
	14.	Verbally aggressive, confrontational, emoting, slamming doors, etc.	

more acute and is less of a problem, but a depressive episode may gradually become worse over several weeks or months. Second, it is not unusual for patients to suffer from residual symptoms, which may be similar to the prodromal symptoms. When this is the case it is even harder to define when residual symptoms change to a prodromal stage. As mentioned above, some patients find it hard to detect prodromes spontaneously, particularly for depression. Consistent with the ethos of monitoring and regulating, therapists should take every opportunity to map out the details of individual patterns of prodromes whenever patients are in a prodromal stage and to help patients to practise a more adaptive way of coping. For patients who truly cannot list prodromes spontaneously, it is often helpful to suggest that they should discuss them with close others. As a last resort, a list of common prodromes can be presented to help patients to identify those that are applicable to them (Wong and Lam, 1999; see Jackson et al., 2003, for a review). Great care should be taken that the prodromes identified are then elaborated and anchored in the idiosyncratic context. Finally, bipolar patients can sometimes exhibit frightening psychotic symptoms at an early stage; as the episode deepens, these psychotic experiences can become increasingly bizarre. Patients often find it helpful to discuss these frightening experiences with someone who is treating them with empathy and understanding. These experiences can be very 'lonely' if patients cannot share them even with their intimate partners or close friends.

When working out coping strategies, it is often advisable to build on the patients' own resources and ideas. Therapists should rely on Socratic questioning and guided discovery rather than prescribing coping strategies. If therapists rely on persuasion or prescribing coping strategies, patients may find their sense of autonomy offended and hence reject therapist's suggestions. In any case, different patients' circumstances are often different. Techniques prescribed routinely without taking patients' experience and circumstances into consideration are unlikely to work.

It is not unusual for bipolar patients to like the early stages of mania. They find it enjoyable to feel more confident, energetic and sociable. They might also want to pursue certain risky behaviours to get the best out of their high levels of energy. The temptation is understandable, particularly when patients usually suffer from depressive residual symptoms. Therapists should respect the patients' opinions but discuss the pros and cons of certain coping strategies to guide patients to come to a conclusion about whether these strategies are dysfunctional. It often works better if patients can see the pros and cons and then decide on the most appropriate coping strategies.

Moderating risky behaviour and avoiding risky situations

A particularly important component of cognitive therapy is to examine risky behaviour or situations that may have led to relapses in the past. They are often very idiosyncratic and this process is best done by going through the life chart. It may include situations, such as the use of street drugs, excessive alcohol, examinations and work situations, when the patient may switch into a disorganised routine or a state of sleep deprivation. Work may involve long hours and extensive travel requirements that can be associated with an onset of prodromal symptoms. With some very driven patients, returning to studying or work after an illness episode could be a dangerous time when they might try to 'prove' to themselves and others that they are now well by working extremely hard to over-compensate. It is therefore important that the individual acts to moderate these areas as far as is possible. For example, the patient and therapist could explore whether a balanced lifestyle that involves regular and consistent work hours in fact might actually enhance work output and performance in the long run.

Moving forward after therapy

As in other psychological disorders, the end of CBT involves reviewing what the patient has learned from previous sessions, acknowledging the patient's and therapist's feelings about ending therapy, and identifying future goals and plans including returning to work. The warning signs and coping strategies are reviewed. Many patients may want help in identifying realistic goals for returning to work in a gradual fashion. Problem-solving techniques can be used to address the potential obstacles. Given the potentially chronic nature of the condition, patients may have plans to link up with other sources of support in their mental health team and they may want to join a user group.

KEY ISSUES DURING THERAPY

Medication compliance

As mentioned earlier, many patients do not take their medication as prescribed. It is worth bearing in mind that bipolar disorder is not unique in this respect; many patients with physical illnesses, as well as other psychiatric problems, also show poor compliance. The reasons for poor compliance are manifold. For some, there are practical difficulties of remembering and organising themselves. For many, the medication provides a daily reminder of their illness. They may also be experiencing side effects or fear experiencing them. When they are feeling better they may feel that they no longer need their medication. The therapist can explore the patient's own reasons and discuss interventions accordingly. For example, practical difficulties can be addressed through providing labelled pill boxes or planning specific times of the day to take the medication. A pros and cons table can allow patients to articulate their ambivalent attitudes towards the medication and form a more balanced view. Reviewing the life chart can often help, as patients may be reminded that their previous relapses were preceded with reductions in medication. Of course, it is sometimes necessary for the patient to experiment with a new regimen of treatment sanctioned by the prescribing psychiatrist, which is monitored and evaluated.

For women of reproductive age, the issue of adverse medication effects in pregnancy often comes up in therapy, even though the majority of psychotherapists are not the prescribing psychiatrists. Goodwin (2003) summarised the risks of congenital malformations. The risk of major congenital malformation is about 2–4% in the general population; this risk is increased to 4–12% in lithium-exposed babies (Cohen et al., 1994), 11% in valproate-exposed babies (Kaneko et al., 1999) and 6% in carbamazepine-exposed babies (Rosa, 1991). However, the risk of congenital abnormalities is increased with the number of anti-epileptic agents taken by the mother (Samren et al., 1999). Most of the danger for organ development is in the first 2 months of pregnancy. Obviously, female patients of reproductive age should be educated about the risks of unplanned pregnancy when taking long-term medication and should be advised to consult the prescribing pharmacotherapist when planning a pregnancy. The potential risk to the baby against the protective effects of medication should be carefully weighed and an informed decision should be arrived at with support from other health professionals.

Perfectionism and fear of failure

Individuals with bipolar disorder report levels of perfectionism that are at least as high as those in unipolar depression (Scott and Pope, 2003). They often set high standards for their own behaviour and the behaviour of people around them. Patients may try hard to please the therapist, offering to take on large amounts of homework and reading. While this can often benefit therapy, the therapist needs to be aware of overloading the patient and should be more attentive to the quality of work that is done between sessions rather than the quantity. One well-considered behavioural experiment may be more effective than ten sessions of neatly completed thought diaries that the therapist has no time to go through in detail and discuss with the patient. The patient may also become irritated with apparent criticism from the therapist. The therapist may need to raise this concern and apologise for his other role in any genuine misunderstanding. The patient's appraisal of the therapist's apparent criticism can then be challenged gently with alternative interpretations.

Minimisation and denial

During hypomania and mania, negative experiences or emotions may not be explicitly acknowledged. In particular, certain patients may become convinced that they will not relapse this time. Unfortunately, a firm belief of this kind may lead them to neglect their use of relapse prevention techniques. Some patients may also display a degree of minimisation of their problems when outside an episode. The therapist needs to be aware that the patient may 'gloss over' what might sound like major problems and not give them due emphasis. With the permission of the patient, the therapist may obtain information from other people as to their perception of the problem, and these alternative viewpoints can be shared with the patient. For example, a woman experiencing hypomania felt that all her negative experiences could be eliminated by 'thinking positive' and by using a technique from an alternative therapy book that involved writing all her negative thoughts down on a sheet of paper and then ripping the paper up and replacing it with a list of positive thoughts. Her husband had a different view but he did not share it with her. He was becoming increasingly upset because she could not easily empathise with his current stress at work. The therapist pointed to the observation that they each had different views on how to deal with negative experiences, and they agreed to try to spend some time in the evening to talk about the husband's stressful work situation. Although the patient found that this made her feel worse initially, she felt better afterwards and they later had a more enjoyable evening.

Hypomanic and manic states

Occasionally, a patient will come to therapy during hypomania or mania. It is typically impossible to follow the plans made during the previous session. Instead it may be better for the therapist to focus on dealing with the hypomania *in situ*, while keeping open the option of postponing the session another day if the patient finds it difficult to concentrate and is easily frustrated. Therapists must avoid getting into an argument and jeopardising the therapeutic relationship. Normally, the session is spent in activating plans for patients to avoid further stimulation, as they might have ideas and plans that may lead to further stimulating behaviour. A pros and cons table can provide a useful tool to explore the consequences of the patients acting on their ideas when they leave the session. The patient is encouraged to list the positive consequences first, and then the negative consequences. When patients observe the completed table, they can sometimes display a better consideration of the negative consequences of acting on their ideas, and may be gently encouraged to try to postpone their plans. If the patient shows increased irritability during the session, it may indicate that they do not feel that they are being understood or that they perceive that the therapist is trying to thwart their plans. The therapists can respond by trying to listen to the patient's ideas without necessarily having to agree with them.

A related intervention is the time delay rule (e.g. Newman et al., 2002). This is based on the clinical observation that impulsive decisions can be damaging when the patient is in a manic phase. Examples are particular plans involving business ventures, impulse buying or flirtatious or unwelcomed sexual approaches. Time delay rules can therefore be very useful, particularly if these have been set up early in therapy. The therapist can empathise with the idea in theory, but not necessarily identify with the way that the patient aims to pursue the idea, i.e. impulsively without considering other peoples' views. A verbal agreement can be arrived at in which the patient promises to hold off from implementing such ideas for at least 48 hours. The idea is that if the idea is as good as the patient suggests, it will still be good after the time delay, but if it is not any good, limitations to the idea will have been given time to surface. There is therefore 'nothing to lose'.

In the early stages of mania, people tend to become increasingly active in both their behaviour and cognition. They may experience increasing numbers and frequency of ideas, often in association with increased verbosity, making listening to others and partaking in the turn-taking aspects of conversation very difficult. Agreement can be made that when patients are tempted to engage in excessive goal-directed behaviour, they can experiment with sitting down and using the energy to focus on activities that may have a calming effect. The patient may discover that this method can be helpful in reducing the escalation of overactivity and the fragmentation of social rhythms. Ideally, patients getting into a hypomanic state will have a clear plan of avoiding further activity or stimulation for the next couple of days. They should be encouraged to go home to a quiet and calming environment. It is always advisable to enquire from patients' past experience how the 'high' might develop. Such states of escalating mania should always be treated seriously as a manic episode can develop very quickly and result in serious social, occupational and financial damage. Sometimes the first sight of mania can be very subtle and idiosyncratic. It is well worth knowing about these signs early in therapy so that therapist can detect them. Often, it is necessary to agree that the patient rings the therapist the next day to enable the therapist to check the patient's mood and reaffirm the agreed plans and actions to preventing mood escalating further. For patients who get into a manic state very quickly, it may be necessary to alert the mental health team and organise an early medical appointment. However, it is unlikely that these self-control measures are feasible when patients are in a full-blown mania. Hence early detection is again a priority. In case of a near full-blown mania, therapists should use their rapport with patients and aim at getting the medical team involved.

Family, friends and wider sources of support

It is important to understand the patient's social network. Family and friends can have both positive and negative impacts on the patient's well-being. For example, evidence shows that patients living with families who show lower levels of hostility and criticism have lower levels of relapse (Miklowitz et al., 1988). The patient may wish a family member or friend to attend at least one session, and they can usually provide very useful information. Most patients are happy for their warning signs and coping strategies to be shared with at least one family member, and they can act as effective monitors of symptoms when the patients themselves are not aware of them. Many family members find that identifying objective signs can help them worry less about the patient relapsing and be less oversensitive to day-to-day fluctuations in mood.

Dealing with stigma

Stigmatisation is a real issue for patients with bipolar disorder and it is important that therapists acknowledge this with patients. Wider society shows a poor understanding of mental illness and discrimination is the norm rather than the exception. As patients understand their own condition better, they often gain in confidence and can explain to people close to them about the condition. However, the disclosure of the diagnosis to acquaintances, prospective partners, work colleagues, employers and many friends is a difficult issue. The therapist can try to help the patient weigh up the pros and cons of telling these people. Some patients may unfortunately experience explicit humiliation or traumatisation as a consequence of other people's perceptions of their illness and this may be associated with a co-morbid anxiety disorder. For these patients, the direct treatment of their anxiety disorder using existing models may form a focus of treatment (see later). For example, one patient's parents had a poor understanding of how to deal the patient's manic episodes and resorted to constraining her by tying her to a post. Along with several other traumas, this incident contributed to post-traumatic stress disorder. In addition, the parents had attempted to hide the patient away to prevent her meeting other people for fear that the whole family would be stigmatised by their daughter's illness. Avoidance of social contact outside the family is a common consequence of bipolar disorder (Perlick et al., 2001).

Suicidal thoughts and behaviour

Suicidal thoughts, threats or attempts are treated in a similar way to unipolar depression. The therapist should be proactive in identifying the extent of a client's plans, his or her current level of risk and his or her existing coping strategies, including alternative ways of dealing with stress, identifying positive reasons for living and having the contact number for the emergency clinic. Newman et al. (2002) provide an excellent protocol on dealing with suicidal bipolar patients that addresses the multiple beliefs that may underlie suicidal behaviour (e.g. 'It will solve all my problems', 'It is the only way to escape my distress').

PREDICTORS OF RESPONSE

There is little systematic research on predictors of response to CBT for bipolar disorder. Generally, patients with co-morbidity, such as a personality disorder diagnosis, do not respond so well to pharmacotherapy. However, it is not so clear in psychosocial intevention. In fact, Colom et al. (2004) reported that patients with a personality disorder diagnosis benefited equally well from psychoeducation.

In a hypothesis-led study, Lam et al. (2005a) developed the Sense of Hyper-positive Self Scale (SHPSS), which predicts patients' response to therapy. This was designed to try to capture the attributes associated with a state of mild hypomania (e.g. dynamic, optimistic and creative) that many patients may strive to maintain. The authors predicted that patients scoring high on this scale before entering therapy may respond less well to CBT when it focuses on trying to prevent future episodes. The study confirmed this prediction, finding that this group showed higher rates of relapse in the 6 months following the CBT intervention of Lam et al. (2005b). In addition, patients who scored higher on goal-attainment subscales of the Dysfunctional Attitudes Scale (DAS; Lam et al., 2004) showed higher drop-out rates. Thus, a tentative conclusion is that a good response to therapy is predicted by less hyper-positive sense of self and lower levels of dysfunctional goal-attainment beliefs.

TRAINING AND DELIVERY OF TREATMENT

CBT for bipolar disorders requires a high level of skill. Therapists need to be prepared to use CBT flexibly. Equally important to CBT skills, therapists should know about bipolar disorders in order to adapt CBT to the disorder. Many bipolar patients are intelligent and know a great deal about the nature of the disorder and its medical treatment. CBT therapists do not usually prescribe the pharmacological treatment but need to be up-to-date with the treatment for bipolar disorder so as to gain credibility. There are several pharmacotherapy treatment guidelines therapists can refer to. These include: *American Psychiatric Association Practice Guideline for the Treatment of Patients with Bipolar Disorder*, 2nd edition (American Psychiatric Association (APA), 2002), the World Federation of Societies of Biological Psychiatry (WFSBP) *Guidelines for Biological Treatment of Bipolar Disorders, Part 1: Treatment of Bipolar Depression* (Grunze et al., 2002) and the *Evidence-based Guideline for Treating Bipolar Disorder: Recommendations from the British Association for Psychopharmacology* (Goodwin, 2003).

A clinical psychologist carrying out CBT with bipolar patients needs existing experience with CBT in addition to a working knowledge of bipolar disorder itself. Alternatively, they may be relatively inexperienced in these specific areas but receive close, weekly supervision by a clinical psychologist who has the relevant experience. Some of the centres interested in the training of CBT for bipolar disorder in the UK are the Institute of Psychiatry, the University of Manchester and the Royal Edinburgh Hospital. In addition, there are experienced clinical psychologists based at the Oxford Cognitive Therapy Centre and Norfolk Mental Health Care Trust. International centres include the University of Philadelphia Cognitive Therapy Centre, University of Texas Southwestern Medical School, and University of Toronto Department of Psychiatry.

It is worth remembering that, for most patients with bipolar disorder, the clinical psychologist is only one of many health professionals and support providers. Most health professionals know the patient before the clinical psychologist arrives on the scene and will know the patient for long after CBT has ended. It is important for the psychologist to be aware of this and to make contacts in order to find out about previous treatments or interventions and work out how the current psychological intervention might be integrated. The clinical psychologist can also potentially play a role in providing psychoeducation and training for other health professionals within a multi-disciplinary team.

Owing to the very recent development of CBT for bipolar disorder, the dissemination of treatment remains at the early stages and demand for psychological intervention greatly outstrips supply. Therefore, avenues other than one-to-one CBT need to be considered at the service level. The encouraging results of a recent trial suggest that group psychoeducation should be considered (Colom et al., 2003). In addition, certain patients may benefit from reading self-help manuals (Jones et al., 2003; Scott, 2001) and from attending local service user meetings, which often involve the sharing of experiences and coping strategies (Manic Depression Fellowship, 2004).

NEW DEVELOPMENTS

CBT for bipolar disorder is new. The first randomised controlled study was published in 2003 (Lam et al., 2003). A 2-year post-therapy study (Lam et al., 2005b) reported that the effect of CBT lasted even though the strength of the treatment effect was in the first year of treatment. A health economy study (Lam et al., 2005b) also reported that the CBT group used fewer health services than the treatment-as-usual group during the 30-month study period. The cost of CBT was offset by fewer in-patient and community resources in the CBT group. However, not all bipolar patients benefited from CBT. Lam et al. (2005a) identified a subgroup of bipolar patients who liked being high and aspired to being high (this group scored higher on the Sense of Hypersensitive Self Scale; see earlier) and who did not respond so well to their current treatment manual. Patients who received CBT were rated as coping consistently better than the control group at 6-monthly intervals in coping with manic prodromes by raters blind to patient group status at the time of the interview. However, the effect of CBT was stronger in preventing depression than mania relapses. The authors suggested that one of the problems was the lack of a psychological model for mania. Hence, there are two obvious candidates for refining CBT for bipolar disorders further. First, it is important to investigate the characteristics of patients who score high on the Sense of Hypersensitive Self Scale in order to understand their way of coping with the illness, which may include routine and structure, level of ambivalence and coping skills. Second, there is an urgent need to develop a CBT model of mania. This would include how cognitive processes can lead to the ascent into mania (cf. Mansell and Lam, 2003), how bipolar patients respond to social feedback (Mansell and Lam, 2006), other cognitive variables including whether dysfunctional beliefs may be activated further by mood (Wright et al., 2004), and the sense of self being an active agent to bring about success.

Bipolar disorder is also highly co-morbid with other psychological disorders, including impulse control disorders, substance abuse disorder, personality disorders and, most commonly, anxiety disorders (see Strakowski et al., 1994, for a review). The levels of co-morbidity have tend to be higher than those found in unipolar depression (Regier et al., 1990; Chen and Dilsaver, 1995), although it is wise to be cautious about diagnosing personality disorder in bipolar patients (Goodwin, 2003). Many unstable bipolar patients tend to be misdiagnosed as personality disorder. However, for some patients outside an episode of depression or mania, an anxiety disorder may be the current presenting problem. There is very little systematic research into the reasons for the high levels of co-morbidity in bipolar disorder but it is very likely that the co-morbid disorders overlap in symptoms and cognitive processes. One published case study has described a formulation of social phobia, post-traumatic stress symptoms and mania in one patient (Mansell and Lam, 2003). For example, disrupted sleep, elevated arousal and excessive drinking are elevated in anxiety disorders and are also risk factors for a relapse of mania. Avoidance of fear-provoking situations can often decrease social reinforcement and provoke depression. In addition, dysfunctional cognitive processes such as rumination, recurrent distressing memories and worry appear to be shared across psychological disorders (Harvey et al., 2004) and therefore they are also likely to be implicated in maintaining symptoms in bipolar disorder (Mansell and Lam, 2004). No studies have evaluated the treatment of co-morbid psychological disorders in patients with bipolar disorder. Clinicians are recommended to follow the treatment guidelines for the co-morbid disorder in question while paying close attention to how it can relate within the formulation to the bipolar disorder and the risk of relapse.

GUIDELINES

• CBT for bipolar disorder is based on the standard format but the content reflects the idiosyncratic features of bipolar disorder.
• Psychoeducation provides a common framework for the therapy. It sets the stage for discussing the patient's model of his or her illness and to begin to form a collaborative understanding.
• The goals for therapy vary widely according to the phase of illness and it is important to set priorities from multiple goals.
• The monitoring of mood and activity provides data for testing beliefs about mood change and routines. It also sets the stage for generating methods to regulate mood and activity.
• Ambivalent attitudes towards hypomanic symptoms can be explored using a pros and cons table; beliefs about symptoms can be tested using behavioural experiments.
• Relapse prevention involves identifying early, middle and late prodromes that are anchored in the patient's daily life, and build on the patient's resources and ideas to generate personally effective coping strategies.
• Medication compliance is typically addressed by identifying attitudes towards medication and weighing up the pros and cons.
• Barriers to the therapeutic relationship that may need particular attention include perfectionism, minimisation of problems and current hypomanic symptoms.
• Family, friends and the wider social network provide an important potential source of support for bipolar patients and they are often involved in elements of the therapy, such as relapse prevention.
• The stigmatisation of bipolar patients is a very real phenomenon and needs to be addressed sensitively and proactively.
• Future developments in CBT for bipolar disorder include wider dissemination and training, refining the existing CBT packages to target patients who value the attributes of being high, developing a CBT model for mania and developing methods to treat co-morbid psychological disorders.

REFERENCES

American Psychiatric Association (APA) (2002) *American Psychiatric Association Practice Guideline for the Treatment of Patients with Bipolar Disorder*. Washington, DC: APA.
Barnard, P. (2003) Asynchrony, implicational meaning and the experience of self in schizophrenia. In: A. David and T. Kircher (eds) *The Self in Neuroscience and Psychiatry*. Cambridge: Cambridge University Press.
Beck, A. T. (1967) *Depression: Clinical, Experimental, and Theoretical Aspects*. New York: Harper & Row.

Chen, Y. W. and Dilsaver, S. (1995) Comorbidity of panic disorder in bipolar illness: Evidence from the Epidemiologic Catchment Area Survey. *American Journal of Psychiatry*, 152, 280–282.

Cohen, L. S., Friedman, J. M., Jefferson, J. W., Johnson, E. M. and Weiner, M. L. (1994) A reevaluation of risk of in utero exposure to lithium. *Journal of the American Medical Association*, 271, 146–150.

Colom, F., Vieta, E., Martinez-Aran, A., Reinares, M, Goikolea, J. M., Benabarre, A. et al. (2003) A randomised trial on the efficacy of group psychoeducation in the prophylaxis of recurrences in bipolar patients whose disease is in remission. *Archives of General Psychiatry*, 60, 402–407.

Colom, F., Vieta, E., Sanchez-Moreno, J., Martinez-Aran, A., Torrent, C., Reinares, M. et al. (2004) Psychoeducation in bipolar patients with comorbid personality disorders. *Bipolar Disorders*, 6, 294–298.

Dent, J., Close, H. and Ryder, J. (2004) Bipolar affective disorders. In: J. Bennett-Levy et al. (eds) *Oxford Guide to Behavioural Experiments in Cognitive Therapy*. Oxford: Oxford University Press.

Ellicott, A., Hammen, C., Gitlin, M., Brown, G. and Jamison, K. (1990) Life events and the course of bipolar disorder. *American Journal of Psychiatry*, 147, 1194–1198.

Goodwin, G. M. (2003) Evidence-based guidelines for treating bipolar disorder: Recommendations from the British Association for Psychopharmacology. *Journal of Psychopharmacology*, 17, 149–173.

Grunze, H., Kasper, S., Goodwin, G., Bowden, C., Baldwin, D., Licht, R. et al. (2002) World Federation of Societies of Biological Psychiatry (WFSBP) guidelines for biological treatment of bipolar disorders. Part I: Treatment of bipolar depression. *World Journal of Biological Psychiatry*, 3, 115–124.

Harvey, A., Watkins, E., Mansell, W. and Shafran, R. (2004) *Cognitive Behavioural Processes across Psychological Disorders: A Transdiagnostic Approach to Research and Treatment*. Oxford: Oxford University Press.

Harvey, A. G., Schmidt, D. A., Scarna, A., Neitzert Semler, C. and Goodwin, G. (2005) Sleep-related functioning in eurythmic patients with bi-polar disorder, patients with insomnia and subjects without sleep problems. *American Journal of Psychiatry*, 162, 50–57.

Healy, D. and Williams, J. M. G. (1989) Moods, misattributions and mania: An interaction of biological and psychological factors in the pathogenesis of mania. *Psychiatric Developments*, 1, 49–70.

Jackson, A., Cavanagh, J. and Scott, J. (2003) A systematic review of manic and depressive prodromes. *Journal of Affective Disorders*, 74, 209–217.

Johnson, S., Sandrow, D., Meyer, B., Winters, R., Miller, I., Solomon, D. and Keitner, G. (1999) Increases in manic symptoms after life events involving goal attainment. *Journal of Abnormal Psychology*, 109, 721–727.

Jones, S., Hayward, P. and Lam, D. (2003) *Coping with Bipolar Disorder*. Oxford: Oneworld Publications.

Kaneko, S., Battino, D., Andermann, E., Wada, K., Kan, R., Takeda, A. et al. (1999) Congenital malformations due to antiepileptic drugs. *Epilepsy Research*, 33, 145–158.

Lam, D. H., Jones, S., Hayward, P. and Bright, J. (1999) *Cognitive Therapy for Bipolar Disorder: A Therapist's Guide to the Concept, Methods and Practice*. Chichester: John Wiley.

Lam, D. H., Bright, J., Jones, S., Hayward, P., Schuck, N., Chisholm, D. and Sham, P. (2000) Cognitive therapy for bipolar illness – a pilot study of relapse prevention. *Cognitive Therapy and Research*, 24, 503–520.

Lam, D. H., Wong, G. and Sham, P. (2001) Prodromes, coping strategies and course of illness in bipolar affective disorder – a naturalistic study. *Psychological Medicine*, 31, 1397–1402.

Lam, D. H., Watkins, E., Hayward, P., Bright, J., Wright, K., Kerr, N. et al. (2003) A randomised controlled study of cognitive therapy of relapse prevention for bipolar affective disorder – outcome of the first year. *Archives of General Psychiatry*, 60, 145–152.

Lam, D., Wright, K. and Smith, N. (2004) Dysfunctional attitudes: Extreme goal-attainment beliefs in remitted bipolar patients. *Journal of Affective Disorders*, 79, 193–199.

Lam, D., Wright, K. and Sham, P. (2005a) Sense of hyper-positive self and response to cognitive therapy for bipolar disorder. *Psychological Medicine*, 35, 69–77.

Lam, D., Hayward, P., Watkins, E., Wright, K. and Sham, P. (2005b) Outcome of a two-year follow-up of a cognitive therapy of relapse prevention in bipolar disorder. *American Journal of Psychiatry*, 162, 324–329.

Malkoff-Schwartz, S., Frank, E., Anderson, B., Sherrill, J. T., Siegel, L., Patterson, D. and Kupfer, D. J. (1998) Stressful life events and social rhythm disruption in the onset of manic and depressive bipolar episodes. *Archives of General Psychiatry*, 55, 702–707.

Manic Depression Fellowship (2004) Online. Available: http://www.mdf.org.uk

Mansell, W. (2006) The Hypomanic Attitudes and Positive Predictions Inventory: a pilot study. *Behavioural and Cognitive Psychotherapy*, 34, 467–476.

Mansell, W. and Lam, D. (2003) Conceptualising a cycle of ascent into mania: A case report. *Behavioural and Cognitive Psychotherapy*, 31, 363–367.

Mansell, W. and Lam, D. (2004) A preliminary study of autobiographical memory in remitted bipolar disorder and the role of imagery in memory specificity. *Memory*, 12, 437–446.

Mansell, W. and Lam, D. (2006). I won't do what you tell me! Elevated mood and the computer-based assessment of advice-taking in euthymic bipolar affective disorder. *Behaviour Research and Therapy*, 44, 1787–1801.

Miklowitz, D. J., Goldstein, M. J., Nuechterlein, K. H., Snyder, K. S. and Mintz, J. (1988) Family factors and the course of bipolar affective disorder. *Archives of General Psychiatry*, 45, 225–231.

Newman, C. F., Leahy, R. L., Beck, A. T., Reilly-Harrington, N. A. and Gyulai, L. (2002) *Bipolar Disorder: A Cognitive Therapy Approach.* Washington, DC: American Psychological Association.

Nolen-Hoeksema, S. (1991) Responses to depression and their effects on the duration of depressive episodes. *Journal of Abnormal Psychology*, 100, 569–582.

Perlick, D., Rosenbeck, R. A., Clarkin, J. F., Sirey, J. A., Salahi, J., Struening, E. L. and Link, B. G. (2001) Adverse effects of perceived stigma on social adaptation of persons diagnosed with bipolar affective disorder. *Psychiatric Services*, 52, 1627–1632.

Perry, A., Tarier, N., Morriss, R. et al. (1988) Randomised controlled trial of efficacy of teaching patients with bipolar disorder to identify early symptoms of relapse and obtain treatment. *British Medical Journal*, 318, 138–153.

Rachman, S. (1980) Emotional processing. *Behaviour Research and Therapy*, 18, 51–60.

Regier, D. A., Farmer, M. E., Rae, D. S., Locke, B. Z., Keith, S. J., Judd, L. L. and Goodwin, R. K. (1990) Comorbidity of mental disorders with alcohol and other drug abuse: Results from the Epidemiological Catchment Area (ECA) Study. *Journal of the American Medical Association*, 264, 2511–2518.

Rosa, F. W. (1991) Spina bifida in infants of women treated with carbamazepine during pregnancy. *New England Journal of Medicine*, 324, 674–677.

Sachs, G. S., Thase, M. E., Otto, M. W., Bauer, M., Miklowitz, D., Wisniewski, S. R. et al. (2003) Rationale, design, and methods of the systematic treatment enhancement program for bipolar disorder (STEP-BD). *Biological Psychiatry*, 53, 1028–1042.

Samren, E. B., van Duijn, C. M., Christiaens, G. C., Hofman, A. and Lindhout, D. (1999) Antiepileptic drug regimens and major congenital abnormalities in the offspring. *Annals of Neurology*, 46, 739–746.

Scott, J. (2001) *Overcoming Mood Swings: A Self-help Guide to Using Cognitive Behavioural Techniques*. London: Robinson.

Scott, J. and Pope, M. (2003) Cognitive styles in individuals with bipolar disorders. *Psychological Medicine*, 33, 1081–1088.

Scott, J., Stanton, B., Garland, A. and Ferrier, I. N. (2000) Cognitive vulnerability in patients with bipolar disorder. *Psychological Medicine*, 30, 467–472.

Scott, J., Garland, A. and Moorhead, S. (2001) A pilot study of cognitive therapy in bipolar disorder. *Psychological Medicine*, 31, 459–467.

Solomon, D. A., Keitner, G. I., Miller, I. W., Shea, M. T. and Keller, M. B. (1995) Course of illness and maintenance treatments for patients with bipolar disorders. *Journal of Clinical Psychiatry*, 56, 5–13.

Strakowski, S. M., McElroy, S. L., Keck, P. W. and West, S. A. (1994) The co-occurrence of mania with medical and other psychiatric disorders. *International Journal of Psychiatry in Medicine*, 24, 305–328.

Wong, G. and Lam, D. H. (1999) The development and validation of the coping inventory for prodromes of mania. *Journal of Affective Disorders*, 53, 57–65.

Wright, K., Lam, D. H. and Strachan, I. (2005) Attitudes and induced mood in bipolar disorder. *Journal of Abnormal Psychology*, 114(4), 689–696.

Zaretsky, A. E., Segal, Z. V. and Gemar, M. (1999) Cognitive therapy for bipolar depression: A pilot study. *Canadian Journal of Psychiatry*, 44, 491–494.

Chapter 9

Post-traumatic stress disorder

Investigation

Nick Grey

INTRODUCTION

This chapter describes the nature of post-traumatic stress disorder (PTSD) and associated reactions to traumatic events. It provides the formal diagnostic criteria, an overview of the epidemiology of PTSD and a description of the different biopsychosocial factors that lead to the development and maintenance of PTSD. While the focus is on PTSD following single or a small number of traumatic events in adulthood, there is some discussion of other reactions to traumatic events. The assessment of PTSD is discussed in detail, including structured clinical interviews, self-report questionnaires and the assessment of cognitive themes and maintaining processes that can be addressed in treatment, based on Ehlers and Clark's (2000) cognitive model.

HISTORY

It has long been evident that experiencing a traumatic event can cause psychological problems. Perhaps the first mention of traumatic stress symptoms, following deaths in battle, comes from Sumerian cuneiform tablets dating from 2100 BCE (Ben Ezra, 2001). Various names have been used to refer to traumatic stress symptoms, including 'shell-shock' and 'concentration camp syndrome'. Initially, it was thought that such problems had an organic cause or were due to pre-existing psychological difficulties. PTSD is a relatively recent addition to psychiatric classification. It was first included in the *Diagnostic and Statistical Manual of Mental Disorders* (DSM) in 1980 (American Psychiatric Association (APA), 1980). One important factor was heavy lobbying in the US from Veterans' Associations following the war in Vietnam. At this stage it was formally recognised that traumatic events, including combat, natural disasters, accidents and physical and sexual assaults, give rise to a characteristic pattern of symptoms. The study of post-traumatic stress symptoms has often been a controversial area, subject to scientific, political and legal influences (Brewin, 2003).

DIAGNOSIS

The formal diagnostic criteria have changed as the understanding of PTSD has increased. A key question is 'what makes an event traumatic?'. DSM-III-R required the stressor be 'outside the range of usual human experience' and that it 'would be markedly distressing to anyone' (APA, 1987). However, PTSD is also caused by events that are actually very common, such as road traffic accidents and assaults.

DSM-IV is now more specific. It requires that the individual 'experienced, witnessed, or was confronted with an event or events that involved actual or threatened death or serious injury, or a threat to the physical integrity of self or others' and that the person's 'response involved intense fear, help-lessness, or horror'. The full current diagnostic criteria are given below (APA, 2000):

DSM-IV Criteria for PTSD

A. The person has been exposed to a traumatic event in which both of the following have been present:

(1) the person experienced, witnessed, or was confronted with an event or events that involved actual or threatened death or serious injury, or a threat to the physical integrity of self or others (2) the person's response involved intense fear, helplessness, or horror.

B. The traumatic event is persistently reexperienced in one (or more) of the following ways:

(1) recurrent and intrusive distressing recollections of the event, including images, thoughts, or perceptions.

(2) recurrent distressing dreams of the event.

(3) acting or feeling as if the traumatic event were recurring (includes a sense of reliving the experience, illusions, hallucinations, and dissociative flashback episodes, including those that occur upon awakening or when intoxicated).

(4) intense psychological distress at exposure to internal or external cues that symbolize or resemble an aspect of the traumatic event.

(5) physiological reactivity on exposure to internal or external cues that symbolize or resemble an aspect of the traumatic event.

C. Persistent avoidance of stimuli associated with the trauma and numbing of general responsiveness (not present before the trauma), as indicated by three (or more) of the following:

(1) efforts to avoid thoughts, feelings, or conversations associated with the trauma

(2) efforts to avoid activities, places, or people that arouse recollections of the trauma

(3) inability to recall an important aspect of the trauma

(4) markedly diminished interest or participation in significant activities

(5) feeling of detachment or estrangement from others

(6) restricted range of affect (e.g., unable to have loving feelings)

(7) sense of a foreshortened future (e.g., does not expect to have a career, marriage, children, or a normal life span)

D. Persistent symptoms of increased arousal (not present before the trauma), as indicated by two (or more) of the following:

(1) difficulty falling or staying asleep

(2) irritability or outbursts of anger

(3) difficulty concentrating

(4) hypervigilance

(5) exaggerated startle response

E. Duration of the disturbance (symptoms in Criteria B, C, and D) is more than one month.

F. The disturbance causes clinically significant distress or impairment in social, occupational, or other important areas of functioning.

> *Diagnostic and Statistical Manual of Mental Disorders,*
> *Fourth Edition, Text Revision* (Copyright 2000). (Reprinted with
> permission from the American Psychiatric Association)

Similar criteria are also given by the World Health Organization (WHO) in the *International Statistical Classification of Diseases and Related Health Problems* (ICD; WHO, 1992). However, these are perhaps less widely used in the literature on PTSD, mainly due to the preponderance of US-based research in this area. Ehlers (2000) provides a comparison of the classification schemes. Of note is that PTSD is classified as an anxiety disorder in DSM whereas in ICD it is classified under reactions to severe stress and adjustment disorders. Furthermore, factor analyses of traumatic stress symptoms have indicated that a four-factor structure (re-experiencing, avoidance, numbing and hyperarousal) is a better fit to the available data than a three-factor structure (with avoidance and numbing combined together, as in DSM-IV; Foa et al., 1995). Those studies that examine psychological health following traumatic events in non-Western populations have tended to adopt Western psychiatric classifications, although this approach has been criticised (Summerfield, 2001).

EPIDEMIOLOGY

It is normal to experience symptoms such as nightmares and flashbacks in the aftermath of traumatic events. However, it is inaccurate to say that meeting diagnostic criteria for PTSD is 'a normal reaction to an abnormal event'. In fact, most people recover from the early appearance of traumatic stress symptoms without any formal intervention and it is a subgroup that goes on to develop chronic PTSD. For example, Rothbaum et al. (1992) found that 94% of women who had been raped experienced traumatic stress symptoms 1 week after the event. This dropped to 65% at 1 month and 47% at 3 months. Furthermore, rates of PTSD following rape are higher than that following other events.

Methodological differences between studies provide differing estimates of frequency of traumatic events, conditional risk of developing PTSD and prevalence of PTSD (Ehlers, 2000; Lee and Young, 2001). These factors include the diagnostic criteria used, the method of inquiry, the population studied, the nature of the traumatic stressor and the country in which the research is conducted. Most research is from the US and research from developing nations is under-represented.

How often do traumatic events occur?

The estimates of lifetime rates of exposure to traumatic events in Western societies vary between 25% for men and 18% for women (Perkonigg et al., 2000) to 92% for men and 87% for women (Breslau et al., 1998). The largest sample, from the US National Comorbidity Survey, found rates of 61% in men and 51% in women (Kessler et al., 1995). Rates of exposure in some non-Western societies are higher due to greater exposure to natural disasters and warfare.

What is the risk of developing PTSD in response to a traumatic event?

Kessler et al. (1995) found the risk for men is 8% and for women 20%. In a young, urban population, Breslau et al. (1998) found the risk for men to be 13% and for women 30%. Research from outside the US has not fully replicated this sex difference (Creamer et al., 2001). PTSD rates also depend on the type of traumatic event. Events such as rape and torture are associated with the highest rates of PTSD and events such as accidents and natural disasters have lower rates (Kessler et al., 1995). Further risk factors are discussed later.

How prevalent is PTSD?

Lifetime prevalence rates in Western community samples are usually around 5–10%. Kessler et al. (1995) found a lifetime prevalence in women of 10.4% and in men of 5.0%. In a valuable epidemiological study in survivors of war or mass violence who were randomly selected from community populations, de Jong et al. (2001) found prevalence rates of PTSD of 37% in Algeria, 28% in Cambodia, 16% in Ethiopia and 18% in Gaza. Higher rates of PTSD are found in refugees and asylum seekers who have fled from their country of origin. Turner et al. (2003) examined a large group of Kosovan Albanian refugees in the UK and found that 49% met criteria for PTSD.

Co-morbidity

Between 75 and 90% of people with PTSD also meet criteria for a co-morbid psychiatric diagnosis (Kessler et al., 1995; Creamer et al., 2001). The most common co-morbid conditions are affective disorders, substance-use disorders and other anxiety disorders. It is unsurprising that there is high co-morbidity as many symptoms overlap with other diagnoses. In most cases of co-morbid depression or substance-use disorders, the PTSD was primary (Breslau et al., 1997; Chilcoat and Breslau, 1998). In a review of co-morbidity profiles, Deering et al. (1996) found that they differ according to the type of trauma experienced and the population studied. For example, the rates of substance-use disorders among combat veterans with PTSD is higher than those with PTSD from other traumatic events, and trauma involving physical suffering may be more likely to lead to somatisation in PTSD.

OTHER TRAUMATIC STRESS REACTIONS

PTSD can only be formally diagnosed 1 month after the traumatic event. Within the first month, individuals may meet diagnostic criteria for acute stress disorder (ASD) if they have the requisite number of symptoms, similar to those in PTSD but also specifically requiring the presence of three dissociative symptoms. Although the diagnosis of ASD was introduced to help identify those people who were more likely to go on to meet criteria for PTSD, the utility of the diagnosis ASD has been questioned (Harvey and Bryant, 2002).

If an individual has symptoms characteristic of PTSD without meeting criterion A for the traumatic stressor, DSM would currently classify this as an adjustment disorder. A common example is the reaction to relationship break-ups or work-place bullying in which no criterion A event has occurred but intrusive memories and nightmares relating to these events occur. There is relatively little research in this area and into the best available treatment strategies. Recent theorising about other PTSD-like presentations has focused on emotions such as sadness (e.g. grief reaction) and anger (Dalgleish and Power, 2004).

The PTSD literature often differentiates between type I trauma and type II trauma. Type I trauma is essentially a one-off traumatic event, such as a road traffic accident, assault or natural disaster; type II trauma refers to prolonged, repeated traumatic events such as repeated abuse or torture. Such circumstances may lead to more complex traumatic stress presentations. Herman (1992) refers to this as 'complex trauma'. This is characterised by poor affect and impulse regulation, dissociation, somatisation and patho-logical patterns of relationships. Following some debate, DSM-IV chose not to include the category 'disorders of extreme stress not otherwise specified' (DESNOS) to address such cases.

ICD-10 attempts to cover these presentations with the diagnosis 'enduring personality change following catastrophic experience' (EPC; WHO, 1992). The criteria include: a permanently hostile or distrustful attitude to the world; social withdrawal; a constant feeling of emptiness or hopelessness; an enduring feeling of feeling 'on edge', including hypervigilance and irrit-ability; and a permanent feeling of being changed or different from others. Such difficulties may be seen clinically in some refugees and asylum seekers, who may have experienced multiple and prolonged traumatic events, in their country of origin, during flight and in the new 'safe' country.

It has also been suggested that Borderline Personality Disorder (BPD) is better conceptualised as a complex trauma reaction. Certainly, there are similarities in the criteria for BPD and the specified symptoms given above for EPC and 'complex trauma'. Furthermore, those people who could be diagnosed with BPD also often experience traumatic stress symptoms. How-ever, epidemiological studies demonstrate that many individuals meet criteria for BPD without meeting criteria for PTSD, and that they are more likely to also meet criteria for a mood disorder, particularly depression, rather than PTSD (Zanarini et al., 1998). Similarly, people who present with dissociative disorders often have a long history of traumatic experiences. Psychological explanations of the controversial diagnosis 'dissociative identity disorder' have some focus on the reaction to traumatic events, usually in early childhood (Allen, 2001).

The utility of terms such as 'complex trauma' or the further specific diag-nostic categories is currently unclear. The term 'complex trauma' is used in differing ways, all of which try to describe some sense of difficulty or pro-found impact on the client not captured by PTSD. It is preferable to describe the actual problems or symptoms an individual may have and to use an idiosyncratic psychological formulation. Models of depression, PTSD and other anxiety disorders may be helpful in planning treatment approaches. Allen (2001) provides further descriptions and discussion of such presentations, particularly with respect to 'traumatic relationships' both in childhood and adulthood.

BIOLOGICAL PROCESSES

There has been considerable work investigating whether there are biological markers for PTSD (Yehuda, 2001). Urinary and plasma cortisol levels are considerably lower in PTSD patients than in non-PTSD trauma survivors and normal controls. People with PTSD tend to exhibit hyper-suppression of cortisol when given a low dose of dexamethasone, thus showing a different pattern of hypothalamic–pituitary–adrenal (HPA) response from those with depression. The HPA axis in PTSD is characterised by enhanced negative feedback, which is secondary to an increased sensitivity of glucocorticoid receptors in target tissues. The sensitisation of the HPA axis is consistent with the clinical picture of hyper-reactivity and hyper-responsiveness in PTSD. While this has raised the prospect that a biological test for PTSD could be found, no such test currently has sufficient sensitivity or specificity.

Several neurotransmitter systems are dysregulated in PTSD. Subgroups of PTSD patients exhibit sensitisation of noradrenergic and serotonergic systems, respectively (Southwick et al., 1997). Increased levels of noradrenaline can cause symptoms of hyper-arousal and re-experiencing. Serotonin depletion is associated with inability to modulate arousal. Overall, it appears that there may be numerous neurobiological mediators of stress-resilience and risk to development of PTSD (Southwick et al., 2003). The overall effect of these biological factors is that they may make people with PTSD hyper-responsive to stressful stimuli, especially stimuli that are reminiscent of the trauma (Van der Kolk, 1996; Ehlers, 2000).

In addition, magnetic resonance imaging studies have detected smaller hippocampal volumes in people with PTSD. However, a twin study and a prospective longitudinal investigation have demonstrated that smaller hippocampal volume is a risk factor for PTSD, rather than PTSD 'shrinking' the hippocampus (Bonne et al., 2002; Gilbertson et al., 2002).

PSYCHOSOCIAL RISK FACTORS FOR PTSD

Two thorough meta-analyses have provided strong evidence for particular risk factors for the development of PTSD (Brewin et al., 2000; Ozer et al., 2003). Female sex, younger age and membership of a minority ethnic group predicted PTSD in some populations but not others. Low education, previous trauma and general childhood adversity predicted PTSD more consistently but still varying by population and study. Psychiatric history, reported childhood abuse and family psychiatric history had more uniform predictive effects. Importantly, stronger predictors of PTSD than prior characteristics were post-trauma support and life stress, and peri-traumatic psychological processes. Peri-traumatic processes are those happening during the traumatic event, encompassing both dissociation and indices of trauma severity. Interpersonal events such as rape and torture are more likely to lead to the development of PTSD than natural disasters or accidents. For example, refugees who have experienced torture are more likely to exhibit PTSD than those refugees who have experienced traumatic events that do not include torture (Holtz, 1998). Many prospective studies have demonstrated that peri-traumatic dissociation is a good predictor of later PTSD (Murray et al., 2002).

It may be that peri-traumatic responses to the trauma mediate pre-trauma factors, or that there is an interaction of pre-trauma factors with both trauma severity or trauma responses to increase the risk of PTSD (Brewin et al., 2000). Recent studies also indicate the role of post-traumatic cognitions as important predictors of the development of PTSD following road traffic accidents and assaults (e.g. Ehlers et al., 1998).

Experimental psychology studies are investigating possible risk factors for the development of intrusive memories. In non-clinical samples, increased intrusions after viewing a distressing film are associated with higher levels of schizotypy (Holmes and Steel, 2004) and performing a verbal distraction task as opposed to a visuo-spatial task at encoding (Holmes et al., 2004). It is yet to be established whether such results hold in clinical populations.

PSYCHOLOGICAL MODELS

The most effective psychological treatments for PTSD are cognitive-behavioural (Foa et al., 2000) and it is these models that are used as the basis for assessment approaches in this chapter. Brewin and Holmes (2003) provide a valuable summary of psychological models of PTSD. They briefly review a number of earlier approaches including social-cognitive, conditioning, information processing and anxious apprehension models of PTSD. While many of these have been influential in the field (e.g. Horowitz, 1986; Janoff-Bulman, 1992) they have essentially been superseded by more recent developments. Brewin and Holmes (2003) go on to compare Emotional Processing Theory (Foa and Rothbaum, 1998), Dual Representation Theory (Brewin et al., 1996; Brewin, 2001, 2003) and Ehlers and Clark's (2000) cognitive model. Each of these models addresses key elements of PTSD, including alterations in memory functioning and specific appraisals during and following the traumatic events. The models are not mutually exclusive but have differing emphases. Dual Representation Theory focuses more on the manner in which trauma memories are represented. Ehlers and Clark (2000) focus more on the cognitive appraisals that help to maintain PTSD. It is beyond the scope of this chapter to describe these in detail.

Ehlers and Clark's (2000) model offers the clearest guidelines for therapy and also has increasing empirical evidence to support it (Ehlers et al., 2005). They propose that PTSD arises when individuals process traumatic information in a way that produces a sense of current threat, whether this is physical or psychological. The three mechanisms that produce and maintain this are the fragmented, relatively un-integrated nature of the trauma memory, negative appraisals of the trauma and/or its sequelae, and coping strategies that do not allow changes in these two areas (such as avoidance). This is described in more detail in Chapter 10.

Like other anxiety disorders, PTSD is associated with various cognitive biases. These include selective attention to external threat, explicit memory bias for trauma-related words, over-general memory, threatening interpretive biases and elevated expectancies for negative events (see Harvey et al., 2004, for a review).

PTSD ASSESSMENT

The most common aims of assessment are clinical assessment prior to possible treatment, assessment for research purposes and assessment for specific report writing, such as an expert witness report for court proceedings. The methods used for each are essentially the same but different elements will be emphasised in each. A number of texts provide considerable detail on the assessment of traumatic stress reactions and their many facets (e.g. Wilson and Keane, 1997). The main focus here is on general clinical assessment. This includes specific questions to identify emotional, cognitive and behavioural processes that are important in treatment, as derived from the cognitive model of Ehlers and Clark (2000). The areas covered are: structured interviews, self-report questionnaires, 'open' interview assessment, assessment of cognitive themes and assessment of possible maintaining factors.

Assessment is also an ongoing process throughout treatment. The person's reaction to particular treatment strategies will identify other issues, blocks to progress and problems that will need to be addressed. Such an approach is particularly necessary in complicated cases such as where there is fluctuating substance use or risk of suicide (Kimble et al., 1998).

A structured clinical interview is the most reliable and valid way of establishing whether someone meets the diagnostic criteria for PTSD. A common interview is the Structured Clinical Interview for DSM (SCID; First et al., 1996). However, probably the nearest thing that there is to a 'gold standard' for

PTSD assessment is the Clinician Administered PTSD Scale (CAPS; Blake et al., 1990), which is used extensively in current PTSD research. This covers the diagnostic criteria, with helpful follow-up questions and qualifiers to establish both frequency and severity of symptoms, and further associated features such as guilt and dissociation. It can sometimes be lengthy to complete (at least 45 minutes) but is very thorough and can provide lots of clinically useful information. It is in an easily accessible form, together with some self-report measures in a specialised assessment pack (Turner and Lee, 1998).

Self-report questionnaires are very useful instruments for efficiently obtaining a lot of information both at assessment and during the course of treatment. There are a number of well-established general symptom measures with good psychometric properties. The most widely used is the Impact of Event Scale (Horowitz et al., 1979). The better, revised version comprises 22 items asking about each of the symptom clusters of: intrusions, avoidance and hyperarousal (IES-R; Weiss and Marmar, 1997). A good alternative scale is the 17-item Posttraumatic Diagnostic Scale (Foa et al., 1997), which more carefully follows the DSM-IV criteria for PTSD. Other trauma-specific scales are also available.

These scales cannot provide a diagnosis of PTSD. Rather, they provide additional information that can corroborate and lend weight to a clinical assessment. Furthermore, it is sensible to enquire further about the answers provided on the self-report questionnaires. An individual may indicate that he or she regularly has 'intrusive memories' but this would not necessarily distinguish between flashbacks of the event or later rumination. Such distinctions have important treatment implications. You should ask what exactly the answer is referring to. If the person has experienced multiple traumatic events it is important to know with respect to which event or events the questionnaire has been completed.

There are also useful self-report questionnaires that ask about other aspects of traumatic stress reactions. The Posttraumatic Cognitions Inventory (PTCI; Foa et al., 1999) helps identify many cognitive themes, which help formulation and treatment.

For screening 3–4 weeks post-trauma, a recent 10-item scale that covers the re-experiencing and hyperarousal symptoms of PTSD can be used (Brewin et al., 2002).

General clinical assessment

The pre-requisites for an accurate clinical assessment, such as an ability to establish rapport and general counselling skills, are assumed. Assessing for PTSD can elicit high levels of affect. The emotional memories of the traumatic event are likely to enter the person's mind when asked about his or her experiences. An ability to acknowledge this difficulty and empathise with the person while still managing to elicit sufficient information can be a difficult art. In particular, it can be reassuring for people to know that they will not have to go into details any more than they feel comfortable with in the first appointment. It is sensible to allow at least 90 minutes for an assessment of PTSD. It is uncertain in how much detail the person will be able to describe the traumatic events and how distressing it will be. It may be necessary to have more than one pre-treatment assessment session.

Although a large number of possible questions are provided below, it is not expected that you will need to ask every single question, nor that these are entirely comprehensive. The usual general assessment questions about family history, medication taken, etc. should also be asked. Where the words 'trauma' or 'the event' is used, whatever words the person themselves uses to describe their experience ('accident', 'attack', 'incident' etc.) should be used.

Current problems and symptoms

'What are the main the problems you are having at the moment?'
'Any other problems?'
'Which of these is the worst problem/most important problem?'

Description of event

'I only know a little about what actually happened'.
'It would be helpful if you could describe to me what you experienced.'
'Only do it in as much detail as you feel comfortable at the moment.'
During this description you continue to assess by careful observation of how the person describes the event. In particular, you should note emotional reactions, or a lack of them, and at what point these occur. This may include crying, becoming very quiet, skipping over parts more briefly than others, or spacing out/dissociating. You may also be able to observe how fragmented or coherent the memory is by how disorganised the account is or by how much trouble the person has putting it in chronological order. After this description, ask how the person felt describing it and whether that was how he or she felt at the time. This may elicit particular emotional or cognitive themes. In particular, it may help clarify, if necessary, whether the person experienced fear, helplessness or horror during the event, which is a requirement of criterion A for a formal diagnosis of PTSD to be made. During this first description of the event it is probably better to allow people to simply tell their story as they want to and then come back to ask questions about it afterwards if necessary.

'Have you told this story to many other people?'
'Did you do it like you did just here?'
Sometimes people have had to describe the event to many people such as

police, solicitors and assessors for legal reports and they have an 'agreed version' that they just tell without emotion as if it happened to someone else.

'Have you told anyone else in detail what has happened?'

'Had you been using alcohol or any other drugs at the time of the event?'
'Did you experience any blows to the head during the event?'
'Did you lose consciousness?'
'For how long do you think?'
'What bits can't you remember?'
'Did you have a scan at the hospital?'
'What did they tell you at the hospital?'
'Did anyone mention a head injury?'
'Have you had any treatment for this since?'

The possibility of a neuropsychological assessment should be considered, particularly if the person was unconscious, had a post-traumatic amnesia of more than a few minutes or has noticed other cognitive changes other than poorer concentration and memory for new material. It is important to try to distinguish organic from psychogenic amnesia.

Impact on life

'What impact have these problems had?'
'How have they affected your relationships with family?'
'With friends?'
'How have they affected work?'
'How have they affected social and leisure activities?'
'Are there things that you used to do that you no longer do?'

Co-morbidity

'Are there any other problems?'
'How much are you drinking?'
'Do you use recreational/street drugs?'
'How is your mood?'
'Have you been feeling down or depressed?'
'Any thoughts of harming yourself or killing yourself?'

Assessment of risk is important, especially as there is an increased risk of suicide in people with PTSD (Tarrier and Gregg, 2004).

Reactions of others

'How did other people react to you during this?'
'After this?'

'Now?'
'Who have you had support from?'
'How has that been?'
'Who are you closest to now?'
'Is that different from before?'
'Have you had any unhelpful reactions from others?'
'What?'
'What did you make of that?'

Current circumstances

'Are you receiving any other treatment as a result of the trauma?'
'Any ongoing medical treatment or physiotherapy?'
'Is there any ongoing legal action as a result of the trauma?'
'What is the situation with that?'
'What has your solicitor/the police told you about it?'
'How long is it likely to take?'

It may be necessary to have a discussion with the person prior to treatment being offered about the likely effect of treatment on legal action, such as a final settlement being lower if the person improves, what his or her motivation is to improve and whether he or she wishes to proceed. If the person is a witness in criminal proceedings it is wise to check with the solicitor that starting treatment now is acceptable, and not seen as 'coaching' of the story.

Prior trauma

'Have you ever experienced similar events before in your life?'
'Have you ever experienced other types of traumatic, life-threatening or very frightening events before in your life?'
'How about when you were a child?'
'How did you cope with them then?'
'Did you ever have intrusive memories or bad dreams following these events?'
'How did you cope with that?'
'How well did that work?'

Even if this is the first traumatic event a person has experienced, ask *'How have you coped with other stressful times in your life?'* and *'What sort of things do you usually do to cope with stress?'*

Goals

'What do you want to get out of treatment?'
'What would you most like to be different?'
'How would you know that you have improved?'

'What do you want to be doing again?'
'What don't you want to be doing any more?'

Assessment of cognitive themes

Intrusions

'What are the main intrusive memories you have?'
'Which come most often?'
'Which are the most emotional?'
'What emotions?'
'What is the "main" intrusive memory?'
'What were you thinking at that moment during the event?'
Care should be taken to distinguish intrusive memories of what actually happened at the time of the traumatic event from post-traumatic ruminative thoughts and images of the consequences and sequelae. Intrusive memories are also seen in disorders such as depression, and following bereavement. Reynolds and Brewin (1999) found no significant difference in the number of people with depression and PTSD who described their intrusive memories as involving 'reliving'. The subjective understanding of the 'reliving' nature of involuntary memories needs to be researched, particularly with respect to the possible uniqueness or otherwise of reliving to PTSD. However, there is some evidence that flashbacks have different features to ordinary autobiographical memories of trauma. Passages of trauma narratives written while experiencing flashbacks are characterised by greater use of detail, particularly perceptual detail, more mentions of death, fear, helplessness and horror and use of present tense than ordinary memory periods (Hellawell and Brewin, 2004). This can also potentially be observed during assessment.

Worst moments during the trauma (or 'hotspots')

'What were the worst moments during the event itself?'
'What were you feeling and thinking at that moment?'
There is more detail on the assessment of these hotspots in Chapter 10 (see also Grey et al., 2002). Further identification of hotspots may be guided by the intrusive memories, as most are also hotspots (Holmes et al., 2005).

Post-trauma and pre-trauma beliefs

In addition to the use of the PTCI, ask:
'What have been the most difficult things since the trauma?'
'How has this event changed how you see: yourself as a person; other people; the world; the future?'

Assessment of possible maintaining factors

Fragmentation of memory

Some sense of this can be gained from the observation of the description of event as described earlier. Also ask:

'*How much does it feel that the memory is all one narrative, or does it feel disjointed?*'
'*Is it unclear it what order some things happened?*'
'*Are there any gaps in important parts of what happened?*'

Rumination

'*Do you ever dwell on what happened?*'
'*What aspects?*'
'*Do you ever think about how it could have been avoided, or of things that you could have done differently?*'
'*How long do you dwell for?*'

Avoidance

'*Are there things you avoid now, such as people, places, reminders, thoughts, feelings?*'
'*Why is that?*'
'*What do you think would happen if you didn't avoid these things?*'

Thought suppression

'*When you have intrusive memories or thoughts about what happened what do you do?*'
'*Do you ever push these out of your mind?*'
'*Do you try to suppress thoughts and feelings related to the trauma?*'
'*Why do you do that?*'
'*What do you think would happen if you didn't do that?*'

Safety behaviours

'*Do you ever take extra precautions now?*'
'*Are there particular things that you do to try to keep yourself safe?*'
'*Are there things you always make sure you have with you when you go out?*'

Numbing

'Do you ever feel like you have no feelings at all?'
'Do you ever do anything to try to make this happen or take unpleasant feelings away?'
'Do you try to numb out?'
'Do you use alcohol and/or drugs to take these feelings away?'

Misinterpretation of symptoms

'What do you make of these symptoms that you are experiencing?'
'Do you have any particular concerns about what these symptoms mean?'
'Do you ever think that these symptoms mean you are going mad or "losing it"?'

Sense of permanent change

'Do you ever think that things are never going to change?'
'What things do you think will never change?'
'Are there things that have permanently changed since the trauma?'
'Any permanent physical changes?'
'What have the doctors told you?'
'Any things that you have lost due to the trauma? Work, home, friends?'
'Do you think that this is permanent?'

At the end of assessment you should explain that following an assessment it is common and normal for people to experience an increase in traumatic stress symptoms, especially intrusive memories and bad dreams. Additionally, people often feel very tired after an assessment and you should ask where the person is going next, e.g. work or home, and if there is anyone in particular there who he or she can ask for support if necessary.

Legal assessments and other reports

At some stage you will be asked to provide written reports on your clients with PTSD. This may range from a standard form to complete for the Criminal Injury Compensation Authority to a request from a solicitor for an expert witness report. It is important that the roles of treating clinician and expert witness are not combined or confused. If an expert witness report is needed on your client, an independent assessor should perform this, usually having asked for a copy of all your clinical notes. However, as the treating clinician you can provide a report in that specific capacity. While solicitors are usually aware of this distinction and the associated issues, this may not always be the case. When providing an expert witness report you are looking to combine information from all possible sources: structured interview, self-report questionnaires, observation of reactions in the assessment session and other reports and notes made available. A key issue is to clearly separate facts and opinion. Facts can include what you observe in the session while performing the assessment (such as signs of distress when describing the trauma or an exaggerated startle response). It is the convergence of facts that lead to the strength of your opinion. Currently there is no specific test to detect malingering in people who claim to have PTSD (see Guriel and Fremouw, 2003, for a review).

CONCLUSION

Most people experience some traumatic stress symptoms, such as intrusive memories or nightmares, in the immediate aftermath of a traumatic event. Post-traumatic stress disorder develops in a subset of these people, with life-time prevalence in Western community populations of about 5–10%. Vulnerability is mediated by both neurophysiological and psychological factors, with the current evidence suggesting that peri-traumatic responses and post-trauma stressors, support and appraisals are more important than pre-trauma factors. People who have experienced multiple or prolonged traumatic events may present with difficulties more profound than the term PTSD fully captures. Assessment of PTSD should include a combination of standardised interview (the gold standard being the CAPS), self-report questionnaires and a general clinical interview tailored to the needs of the specific assessment. Assessment is an ongoing process throughout treatment, particularly in more complicated cases.

ACKNOWLEDGMENTS

Many thanks to Ben Smith, Blake Stobie and Kerry Young.

INTERNET RESOURCES

UK Trauma Group: http://www.uktrauma.org.uk
This includes listings of specialist UK trauma services.

David Baldwin's Trauma Information Pages: http://www.trauma-pages.com
Probably the longest established website on traumatic stress.

International Society for Traumatic Stress Studies: http://www.istss.org
The largest professional organisation focused on traumatic stress.

National Center for PTSD: http://www.ncptsd.org
This is a programme of the US Department of Veteran Affairs. Recent clinical
and research updates are available, *Clinical Quarterly* and *Research Quarterly*,
which can be downloaded for free. The Center also maintains the free-access
Published International Literature on Traumatic Stress (PILOTS) database,
which is the best place to start looking for trauma references.

National Institute of Health and Clinical Excellence: http://www.nice.org.uk
The recently published NICE report on PTSD is the current definitive
summary of PTSD assessment, treatment, and service provision within the
NHS. All clinicians will benefit from reading these guidelines.

REFERENCES

Allen, J. G. (2001) *Traumatic Relationships and Serious Mental Disorders*. Chichester:
John Wiley.
American Psychiatric Association (APA) (1980) *Diagnostic and Statistical Manual of
Mental Disorders*, 3rd edn. Washington, DC: APA.
American Psychiatric Association (APA) (1987) *Diagnostic and Statistical Manual
of Mental Disorders*, 3rd edn revised. Washington, DC: APA.
American Psychiatric Association (APA) (2000) *Diagnostic and Statistical Manual of
Mental Disorders*, 4th edn Text-Revision (TR). Washington, DC: APA.
Ben Ezra, M. (2001) Earliest evidence of post-traumatic stress? *British Journal
of Psychiatry*, 179, 467.
Blake, D., Weathers, F., Nagy, L., Kaloupek, D., Klauminzer, G., Charney, D. and
Keane, T. (1990) *Clinician Administered PTSD Scale (CAPS)*. Boston: National
Center for PTSD, Behavioural Sciences Division.
Bonne, O., Brandes, D., Gilboa, A., Gomori, J. N., Shenton, M. E., Pitman, R. K. and
Shalev, A. Y. (2002) Longitudinal MRI study of hippocampal volume in trauma
survivors with PTSD. *American Journal of Psychiatry*, 158, 1248–1251.
Breslau, N., Davis, G. C., Andreski, P., Peterson, E. L. and Schultz, L. R. (1997) Sex
differences in post-traumatic stress disorder. *Archives of General Psychiatry*, 54,
1044–1048.
Breslau, N., Kessler, R. C., Chilcoat, H. D., Schultz, L. R., Davis, G. C. and Andreski,
P. (1998) Trauma and posttraumatic stress disorder in the community: The
1996 Detroit Area Survey of Trauma. *Archives of General Psychiatry*, 55, 626–
632.
Brewin, C. R. (2001) A cognitive neuroscience account of posttraumatic stress
disorder. *Behaviour Research and Therapy*, 39, 373–393.
Brewin, C. R. (2003) *Posttraumatic Stress Disorder: Malady or Myth?* New Haven,
CT: Yale University Press.
Brewin, C. R. and Holmes, E. A. (2003) Psychological theories of posttraumatic stress
disorder. *Clinical Psychology Review*, 23, 339–376.
Brewin, C. R., Dalgleish, T. and Joseph, S. (1996) A dual representation theory of
post-traumatic stress disorder. *Psychological Review*, 103, 670–686.
Brewin, C. R., Andrews, B. and Valentine, J. D. (2000) Meta-analysis of risk factors

for posttraumatic stress disorder in trauma-exposed adults. *Journal of Consulting and Clinical Psychology*, 68, 748–766.

Brewin, C. R., Rose, S., Andrews, B., Green, J., Tata, P., McEvedy, C. et al. (2002) A brief screening instrument for posttraumatic stress disorder. *British Journal of Psychiatry*, 181, 158–162.

Chilcoat, H. D. and Breslau, N. (1998) Post-traumatic stress disorder and drug disorders. *Archives of General Psychiatry*, 55, 913–917.

Creamer, M., Burgess, P. and McFarlane, A. C. (2001) Posttraumatic stress disorder: Findings from the Australian National Survey of Mental Well-being. *Psychological Medicine*, 31, 1237–1247.

Dalgleish, T. and Power, M. J. (2004) Emotion-specific and emotion-non-specific components of posttraumatic stress disorder: Implications for a taxonomy of related psychopathology. *Behaviour Research and Therapy*, 42, 1069–1088.

Deering, C. G., Glover, S. G., Ready, D., Eddleman, H. C. and Alarcon, R. D. (1996) Unique patterns of comorbidity in posttraumatic stress disorder from different sources of trauma. *Comprehensive Psychiatry*, 37, 336–346.

De Jong, J. T. V. M., Komproe, I. H., Van Ommeren, M., El Masri, M., Araya, M., Khaled, N. et al. (2001) Lifetime events and posttraumatic stress disorder in 4 post conflict settings. *Journal of the American Medical Association*, 286, 555–562.

Ehlers, A. (2000) Posttraumatic stress disorder. In: M. G. Gelder, J. J. Lopez-Ibor and N. Andreason (eds) *New Oxford Textbook of Psychiatry*. Oxford: Oxford University Press.

Ehlers, A. and Clark, D. M. (2000) A cognitive model of posttraumatic stress disorder. *Behaviour Research and Therapy*, 38, 319–345.

Ehlers, A., Mayou, R. A. and Bryant, B. (1998) Psychological predictors of chronic posttraumatic stress disorder after motor vehicle accidents. *Journal of Abnormal Psychology*, 107, 508–519.

Ehlers, A., Clark, D. M., Hackmann, A., McManus, F. and Fennell, M. (2005) Cognitive therapy for PTSD: Development and evaluation. *Behaviour Research and Therapy*, 43, 413–431.

First, M. B., Spitzer, R. L., Gibbon, M. and Williams, J. B. (1996) *Structured Clinical Interview for DSM-IV Axis I Disorders, Clinician Version*. Washington, DC: American Psychiatric Press.

Foa, E. B. and Rothbaum, B. O. (1998) *Treating the Trauma of Rape: Cognitive Behavioural Therapy for PTSD*. New York: Guilford Press.

Foa, E. B., Riggs, D. S. and Gershuny, B. S. (1995) Arousal, numbing, and intrusion: Symptom structure of PTSD following assault. *American Journal of Psychiatry*, 152, 116–120.

Foa, E. B., Cashman, L., Jaycox, L. and Perry, K. (1997) The validation of a self-report measure of posttraumatic stress disorder: The posttraumatic diagnostic scale. *Psychological Assessment*, 9, 445–451.

Foa, E. B., Ehlers, A., Clark, D. M., Tolin, D. F. and Orsillo, S. M. (1999) The Post Traumatic Cognitions Inventory (PTCI): Development and validation. *Psychological Assessment*, 11, 303–314.

Foa, E. B., Keane, T. M. and Friedman, M. J. (eds) (2000) *Effective Treatments for Posttraumatic Stress Disorder: Practice Guidelines from the International Society for Traumatic Stress Studies*. New York: Guilford Press.

Gilbertson, M. W., Shenton, M. E., Ciszewski, A., Kasai, K., Lasko, N., Orr, S. P.

and Pitman, R. K. (2002) Smaller hippocampal volume predicts pathologic vulnerability to psychological trauma. *Nature Neuroscience*, 5, 1242–1247.

Grey, N., Young, K. and Holmes, E. (2002) Cognitive restructuring within reliving: A treatment for peritraumatic emotional hotspots in PTSD. *Behavioural and Cognitive Psychotherapy*, 30, 63–82.

Guriel, J. and Fremouw, W. (2003) Assessing malingered posttraumatic stress disorder: A critical review. *Clinical Psychology Review*, 23, 881–904.

Harvey, A. G. and Bryant, R. A. (2002) Acute stress disorder: A synthesis and critique. *Psychological Bulletin*, 128, 886–902.

Harvey, A., Watkins, E., Mansell, W. and Shafran, R. (2004) *Cognitive Behavioural Processes Across Psychological Disorders: A Transdiagnostic Approach to Research and Treatment*. Oxford: Oxford University Press.

Hellawell, S. J. and Brewin, C. R. (2004) A comparison of flashbacks and ordinary autobiographical memories of trauma: Content and language. *Behaviour Research and Therapy*, 42, 1–12.

Herman, J. L. (1992) *Trauma and Recovery: From Domestic Abuse to Political Terror*. London: Pandora.

Holmes, E. A. and Steel, C. (2004) Schizotypy: A vulnerability factor for traumatic intrusions. *Journal of Nervous and Mental Disease*, 192, 28–34.

Holmes, E. A., Brewin, C. R. and Hennessy, R. G. (2004) Trauma films, information processing, and intrusive memory development. *Journal of Experimental Psychology: General*, 133, 3–22.

Holmes, E. A., Grey, N. and Young, K. A. D. (2005) Intrusive images and 'hotspots' of trauma memories in posttraumatic stress disorder: An exploratory investigation of emotions and cognitive themes. *Journal of Behaviour Therapy and Experimental Psychiatry*, 36, 3–17.

Holtz, T. H. (1998) Refugee trauma versus torture trauma: A retrospective controlled cohort study of Tibetan refugees. *Journal of Nervous and Mental Disease*, 186, 24–34.

Horowitz, M. J. (1986) *Stress Response Syndromes*, 2nd edn. Northvale, NJ: Jason Aronson.

Horowitz, M. J., Wilner, N. J. and Alvarez, W. (1979) The Impact of Event Scale: A measure of subjective stress. *Psychosomatic Medicine*, 41, 209–218.

Janoff-Bulman, R. (1992) *Shattered Assumptions: A New Psychology of Trauma*. New York: The Free Press.

Kessler, R. C., Sonnega, A., Bromet, E., Hughes, M. and Nelson, C. B. (1995) Post-traumatic stress disorder in the National Comorbidity Survey. *Archives of General Psychiatry*, 52, 1048–1060.

Kimble, M. O., Riggs, D. S. and Keane, T. M. (1998) Cognitive behavioural treatment for complicated cases of post-traumatic stress disorder. In: N. Tarrier, A. Wells and G. Haddock (eds) *Treating Complex Cases: The Cognitive Behavioural Therapy Approach*. Chichester: John Wiley.

Lee, D. and Young, K. (2001) Post-traumatic stress disorder: Diagnostic issues and epidemiology in adult survivors of traumatic events. *International Review of Psychiatry*, 13, 150–158.

Murray, J., Ehlers, A. and Mayou, R. (2002) Dissociation and posttraumatic stress disorder: Two prospective studies of motor vehicle accident survivors. *British Journal of Psychiatry*, 180, 363–368.

Ozer, E. J., Best, S. R., Lipsey, T. L. and Weiss, D. S. (2003) Predictors of posttraumatic stress disorder and symptoms in adults: A meta-analysis. *Psychological Bulletin*, 129, 52–73.

Perkonigg, A., Kessler, R. C., Stortz, S. and Wittchen, H-U. (2000) Traumatic events and post-traumatic stress disorder in the community: Prevalence, risk factors, and comorbidity. *Acta Psychiatrica Scandinavica*, 101, 46–59.

Reynolds, M. and Brewin, C. R. (1999) Intrusive memories in depression and post-traumatic stress disorder. *Behaviour Research and Therapy*, 37, 201–215.

Rothbaum, B. O., Foa, E. B., Riggs, D. S., Murdock, T. and Walsh, W. (1992) A prospective examination of posttraumatic stress disorder in rape victims. *Journal of Traumatic Stress*, 5, 455–476.

Southwick, S. M., Krystal, J. H., Bremner, J. D., Morgan, C. A., Nicolaou, A. L., Nagy, L. M. et al. (1997) Noradrenergic and serotonergic function in posttraumatic stress disorder. *Archives of General Psychiatry*, 54, 749–758.

Southwick, S. M., Morgan, C. A., Vythilingam, M., Krystal, J. H. and Charney, D. S. (2003) Emerging neurobiological factors in stress resilience. *PTSD Research Quarterly*, 14(4), 1–7.

Summerfield, D. (2001) Asylum seekers, refugees and mental health services in the UK. *Psychiatric Bulletin*, 25, 161–163.

Tarrier, N. and Gregg, L. (2004) Suicide risk in civilian PTSD patients: Predictors of suicidal ideation, planning and attempts. *Social Psychiatry and Psychiatric Epidemiology*, 39, 655–661.

Turner, S. and Lee, D. (1998) *Measures in Post Traumatic Stress Disorder: a Practitioner's Guide*. Windsor, UK: NFER-Nelson.

Turner, S. W., Bowie, C., Dunn, G., Shapo, L. and Yule, W. (2003) Mental health of Kosovan Albanian refugees in the UK. *British Journal of Psychiatry*, 182, 444–448.

Van der Kolk, B. (1996) The body keeps the score. Approaches to the psychobiology of posttraumatic stress disorder. In: B. Van der Kolk, A. McFarlane and L. Weisaeth (eds) *Traumatic Stress: The Effects of Overwhelming Experience on Mind, Body and Society*. New York: Guilford Press.

Weiss, D. and Marmar, C. (1997) The impact of event scale – revised. In: J. Wilson and T. Keane (eds) *Assessing Psychological Trauma and PTSD*. New York: Guilford Press.

Wilson, J. and Keane, T. (1997) *Assessing Psychological Trauma and PTSD*. New York: Guilford Press.

World Health Organization (WHO) (1992) *International Statistical Classification of Diseases and Related Health Problems, 10th revision*. Geneva: WHO.

Yehuda, R. (2001) Biology of posttraumatic stress disorder. *Journal of Clinical Psychiatry*, 62 (suppl.), 41–46.

Zanarini, M. C., Frankenburg, F. R., Dubo, E. D., Sickel, A. E., Trikha, A., Levin, A. and Reynolds, V. (1998) Axis I comorbidity of borderline personality disorder. *American Journal of Psychiatry*, 155, 1733–1739.

Chapter 10

Post-traumatic stress disorder

Treatment

Nick Grey

INTRODUCTION

In this chapter, the evidence for the treatment of post-traumatic stress disorder (PTSD) following traumatic experiences in adulthood is briefly reviewed. The further aim is to provide clinicians with an introduction to practical strategies to treat people with PTSD following trauma as an adult. Ehlers and Clark's (2000) cognitive model of PTSD and the treatment derived from this are detailed. This includes the role of exposure/reliving and cognitive therapy for negative appraisals. The focus will be on those techniques that are most particular to PTSD, rather than on more general cognitive therapy strategies. Complicating factors in the treatment of PTSD are also considered.

WHAT TO DO SOON AFTER A TRAUMATIC EVENT

For many years clinicians have provided immediate treatment for people who have experienced traumatic events. The general term commonly used is 'debriefing'. This is taken to refer to asking the individual to recount in great detail what occurred during the trauma as soon as possible afterwards. It was seen as promoting emotional processing of the event. However, there is increasing evidence that individual debriefing in the immediate aftermath of a traumatic event is at best of no benefit or at worst positively harmful (Rose and Bisson, 1998; Mayou et al., 2000). The original conceptualisation of debriefing was for ready-formed groups of people who had all experienced the same event, such as emergency service personnel. There are no studies of group debriefing that provide firm evidence whether it is in fact beneficial or harmful.

The current accepted clinical wisdom is to provide advice and support after a traumatic event. People should be encouraged to access their usual supports and to look after themselves physically and psychologically. This includes regular eating and sleeping, maintaining valued activities and limiting alcohol and drug use. In addition, specific information about reactions to traumatic events should be provided, both verbally and in written form. This aims to normalise common early reactions, such as intrusive memories, nightmares, hyper-vigilance and numbness. Formal treatment should not be provided until at least about 4 weeks post-trauma.

PHARMACOLOGICAL TREATMENT OF PTSD

There are a limited number of controlled trials of medication for PTSD and no controlled trials that examine a combination of medication and psychotherapy (Nagy and Marshall, 2002). Selective serotonin re-uptake inhibitors (SSRIs) are currently the only medication with data to support an indication for PTSD. Paroxetine and sertraline are the only ones licensed in the UK. They should be given in similar dosages as used for depression and response is gradual. Improvements may be seen at 3–4 weeks and continue over 8–12 weeks. Improvement is usually partial and there are no data guiding the length of treatment (Nagy and Marshall, 2002).

PSYCHOLOGICAL TREATMENT OF PTSD

Exposure-based treatments are the most effective for PTSD (Foa et al., 2000; National Institute for Health and Clinical Excellence (NICE), 2005). These involve discussing the details of the traumatic event, usually many times, and often listening to the audiotapes of such sessions, or writing a narrative of the experience. There are a number of different versions of such treatment. The traditional explanation for their effectiveness is due to 'emotional processing' of the memory and habituation to the anxiety associated with it.

In addition, there are brand-named treatments, which are also exposure based, such as Eye Movement Desensitisation and Reprocessing (EMDR; Shapiro, 1995). EMDR is a well-structured treatment that includes therapist-directed saccadic eye movements while the client holds images of the traumatic event in mind. Practically, the therapist moves his or her fingers or some other cue back and forth in front of the client to direct the eye movements. However, 'EMDR appears to be no more effective than other exposure techniques, and evidence suggests that the eye movements integral to the treatment, and to its name, are unnecessary' (Davidson and Parker, 2001). Adherents of EMDR would refute such findings. EMDR and other novel trauma treatments are sometimes referred to collectively as 'power therapies', as they make claims to cure PTSD in a single session or very few sessions. There is little evidence that these treatments are more effective than existing exposure-based treatments and the effects seen may be explained due to the exposure components of the protocol (Lohr et al., 2003).

Studies have investigated the role of cognitive restructuring in the treatment of PTSD, as excessively negative appraisals of threat are a feature of PTSD. Two found no differences between exposure, cognitive restructuring and a combination of the two (Marks et al., 1998; Tarrier et al., 1999). These studies show that cognitive therapy alone, without explicit exposure instructions, can be an effective treatment for PTSD. A further study indicates that cognitive restructuring in combination with imaginal exposure may enhance treatment gains (Bryant et al., 2003).

More recently, Ehlers and Clark (2000) have proposed a newly synthesised cognitive model, described below, which provides specific treatment implications. Their treatment approach results in the largest treatment effect sizes seen in the field (Ehlers et al., 2003, 2005). Importantly, their approach has also been disseminated to frontline health service therapists without any reduction in effectiveness (Gillespie et al., 2002).

The studies above focused on the experience of a single, or a few, traumatic event(s). Far fewer studies have examined the treatment of multiple or prolonged traumatisation. Those that exist investigate the use of exposure-based treatments for refugees and asylum seekers, and suggest that these treatments can successfully be used in such populations (Paunovic and Ost, 2001)

COGNITIVE THERAPY FOR PTSD

Harvey et al. (2003) provide a general review of cognitive behaviour therapy for PTSD. This chapter focuses on the Ehlers and Clark's (2000) model, as the treatment derived from it is highly effective, as noted above. An alternative, but similar, cognitive model is Brewin's Dual Representation Theory (Brewin et al., 1996; Brewin, 2001, 2003) and is directly compared to Ehlers and Clark's (2000) model in Brewin and Holmes (2003).

Ehlers and Clark (2000) suggested that PTSD becomes persistent when traumatic information is processed in a way that leads to a sense of serious *current* threat. This can be a physical threat and/or a psychological threat to one's view of oneself (Figure 10.1).

Due to high levels of arousal at the time of the trauma, the trauma memory is poorly elaborated and poorly integrated with other autobiographical memories, and can be unintentionally triggered by a wide range of low-level cues. In particular, there is no 'time-code' on the memory that tells the individual that the event occurred in the past. Thus, when the memory intrudes, it feels as if the event is actually happening again to some degree.

The persistence of the sense of current threat, and hence PTSD, arises from not only the nature of the trauma memory but also the negative interpretations of the symptoms experienced (e.g. 'I'm going mad'), the event itself (e.g. 'It's my fault'), and sequelae (e.g. 'I should have got over it by now',

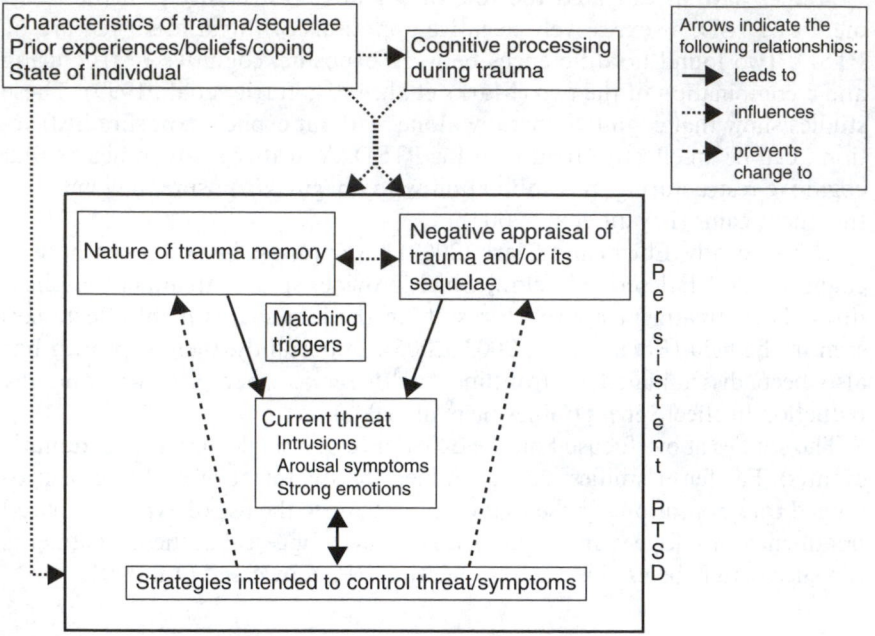

Figure 10.1 Cognitive model of post-traumatic stress disorder (PTSD).

Reprinted from Ehlers and Clark (2000), with permission from Elsevier.

'Others don't care about me'). Change in these appraisals and the nature of the trauma memory is prevented by a variety of cognitive and behavioural strategies, such as avoiding thoughts and feelings, places or other reminders of the event, suppression of intrusive memories, rumination about certain aspects of the event or sequelae, and other avoidant/numbing strategies such as alcohol and drug use.

The aim of treatment derived from Ehlers and Clark (2000) is therefore threefold:

1   To reduce re-experiencing by elaboration of the trauma memory and discrimination of triggers, and integration of the memory within existing autobiographical memory.
2   To address the negative appraisals of the event and its sequelae.
3   To change the avoidant/numbing strategies that prevent processing of the memory and reassessment of appraisals.

A wide range of both general and PTSD-specific cognitive-behavioural interventions can be used to achieve such changes (Ehlers and Clark, 2000; Ehlers et al., 2005; Mueller et al., 2004).

Overall structure and therapy context

The therapeutic relationship is of utmost importance when working with people who have experienced traumatic events. The provision of a safe environment, both physically and psychologically, is paramount. This includes factors such as client choice of therapist gender. The therapist must clearly demonstrate empathy and be comfortable with hearing about traumatic experiences in some detail (the effects of which are discussed later). Treatment sessions should be 90 minutes long, as talking about the trauma may take some time and the client may become very distressed. All sessions are audio-taped for the benefit of the client, who listens to them for homework in order to consolidate discussions from within the session. Other exposure-based treatments also audio-tape the detailed discussion of the trauma in order for the client to repeatedly listen to it.

In the Ehlers and Clark group, after initial assessment, clients are offered 12 weekly 90-minute sessions followed by three sessions on a monthly basis. Following assessment, the first one or two sessions cover normalisation of symptoms, starting 'reclaiming your life' and the formulation and rationale for reliving. The next session will include reliving of the trauma and identification of hotspots and peri-traumatic cognitive themes. Following this there is an interleaving of work on the trauma memory directly, such as reliving, use of a written narrative, discrimination of triggers and *in vivo* exposure, and work on changing excessively negative post- and peri-traumatic appraisals using cognitive therapy techniques.

Initial interventions

Providing information

The first intervention for PTSD is to provide information about the disorder and the symptoms experienced both verbally and in written form. This helps normalise the symptoms experienced, address particular misinterpretations of symptoms such as 'I must be going mad' and validate the client's experience.

A general treatment rationale is provided for the patient based on the cognitive model outlined above. This is individualised to the particular symptoms that are most prevalent and distressing for the client, and covers each of the three main areas of the model: differences in memory, negative appraisals and unhelpful coping strategies. This can be done partly in the form of metaphor as described below. For some people it can be helpful to more fully describe the potential differing memory systems in PTSD and processes underlying the phenomena (Ehlers and Clark, 2000; Brewin, 2001).

Reclaiming your life

Following traumatic events, people often withdraw from activities they previously enjoyed and/or valued. This results in a loss of pleasure and may also contribute to a sense of being 'in limbo' or 'stuck' in their lives. It is helpful to identify any areas of the person's life that have changed, such as relationships with friends and family, work, exercise and other leisure activities, and to restart some activities as soon as possible, such as spending some time playing with the children, going for a run, going back to bingo with friends. 'Blocking' cognitions such as 'I won't enjoy it', 'It won't be like it used to be', 'They won't want me there' can be tested in the form of a behavioural experiment (Mueller et al., 2004).

Thought suppression

An important early intervention is to discus the role of thought suppression. This is best done experientially (from Ehlers and Clark, 2000):

Therapist: Let's look at the effect of deliberately pushing thoughts out of your mind. For the next couple of minutes I want you to think about whatever you want except one thing. I want you to make sure that you don't think about a green rabbit sitting on my head [or some idiosyncratically meaningful memorable image]. Now make sure you're not thinking about it . . . still don't think about it . . .

Invariably, people have the image come into their mind. This leads into a discussion that active suppression increases intrusions and decreases perceived control. Further discussion should identify that this strategy does not allow the memory to be more fully processed and that it will be important to allow the memory to pass through one's mind. An analogy can be drawn between the intrusive thoughts and memories with a train passing through a station. Rather than standing on the tracks trying to push the train back to prevent it coming into the station the person should be like a detached observer on the platform noticing the train pass in and pass out of the station (their mind). Such a mindful approach should be encouraged from the start of treatment. The train analogy can be extended to rumination, which is akin to jumping on the train and closely examining all the parts (and hence thoughts about the trauma).

Elaboration/processing of the trauma memory

A number of strategies can help elaborate and process the trauma memory. The most used is prolonged exposure, also known as reliving. Other complementary approaches are constructing a written narrative, *in vivo* exposure and working on the discrimination of triggers.

Reliving/exposure

This has a number of functions, which may be seen as 'processing' the memory. Overall, it allows for reconstruction of fragments and elaboration of the memory. Within a cognitive framework it allows access to meanings that are contained within the trauma memory and that may not be ordinarily accessed during more general discussion.

Although exposure/reliving is a very successful treatment for PTSD, it is a frightening prospect for people and a clear rationale must be provided. The first stage of this is to use the person's individual circumstances and information concerning all of the possible maintaining factors, fitting within the model as discussed above. This should lead to some understanding as to why talking about the trauma may be helpful. Socratically presented metaphors are also useful to explain this and can be elaborated to account for the particular circumstances of each client (Richards and Lovell, 1999; Ehlers and Clark, 2000). Two examples are provided below:

Therapist: The memory can be compared to a duvet cover that has just been stuffed into a linen cupboard and it keeps making the door pop open. What needs to happen is for you to take out the duvet, fold it up properly, make space for it in the cupboard and then put the duvet back in so that the door doesn't pop open.

Therapist: Processing the memory is like it going down a conveyor belt before being stored away with normal memories in a filing cabinet. Those memories in the filing cabinet you have more control over and can bring them out when you want to. At the moment every time the memory comes back onto the conveyor belt, when it pops into your mind, you just push it off not allowing it to be fully processed.

Before starting reliving, the moment that the event started or 'became traumatic' for the client should be ascertained, and also when he or she felt safer again. It may have continued to be traumatic during time in hospital or getting to a place of safety. The person is asked to describe the event from shortly before the agreed start in as realistic a way as possible. Clients are asked to close their eyes, imagine the events clearly and to talk in the first person and present tense. They are encouraged to provide information on all senses and also the emotions and thoughts experienced (Foa and Rothbaum, 1998).

During the first reliving it is usually best to allow the patient to describe the whole event without much questioning or interruption, while still being attentive, supportive and encouraging. If people do not give much detail, cue in information with occasional questions: 'What can you see, hear, smell?', 'What are you feeling?' They can be helped to remain in the present tense by repeating any statements in the past tense again in the present tense: 'I was walking down the street' to 'So, you *are* walking down the street'.

During or after the reliving, ratings (0–100%) of distress and vividness of the imagery should be taken as a guide. After the reliving, a number of questions should be asked:

'How did you find that?'
'How did it compare to how you predicted?'
'Were there any changes or differences to how you remembered it before?'
'Did anything surprising come up?'
'Were you holding back at all?'
'What were the worst moments?'

For homework, the person is asked to listen to the tape of the reliving each day if possible, rating the distress each time, and any other information he or she thinks is significant.

A number of authors have highlighted the need to focus on the moments of highest emotion experienced during the traumatic event, referred to as 'hotspots' (Foa and Rothbaum, 1998; Richards and Lovell, 1999; Ehlers and Clark, 2000; Grey et al., 2002). Treatment failures with the use of reliving alone may be as a result of not directly addressing peri-traumatic (within-trauma) appraisals. Equally, cognitive therapy in a non-reliving session is very helpful for post-traumatic negative appraisals but it is unlikely to affect the emotions and cognitions experienced peri-traumatically, as these structures are accessed only during reliving. Thus there is a need to explicitly address the meanings attached to these hotspots and use this information to 'update' the traumatic memory during reliving, including the information that the event occurred in the past – providing a 'time-tag' for the memory (Ehlers and Clark, 2000).

The cognitive restructuring of these hotspots follows the outline given below:

- Initial reliving.
- Identify peri-traumatic hotspots during reliving: ask what were the worst moments and observe any indicators of affect change and ask about those moments.
- Identify the associated cognitions/meanings ('What was going through your mind at that moment?', 'What does that mean to you?').
- Outside of reliving, discuss these meanings and use cognitive restructuring to address distortions in the appraisals. This may take some sessions in the case of particular self-evaluations, such as 'I'm weak' and 'I'm to blame'.
- Discuss that these new meanings are needed to help update the trauma

memory (see Grey et al., 2002) and rehearse the specific cognitive reappraisals and at which points they will be introduced.

- Begin reliving again, either of the whole event or focusing only on a particular hotspot.
- Ask the client to hold the hotspot vividly in mind and prompt the person to bring in the 'new' (and rehearsed) information into their mind in order to update the previous meaning. This can be done either verbally or with an image that conveys the new meaning.

Mark had been raped and presented with classic PTSD symptoms, including nightmares each night. During the first reliving he went very quiet at one point and looked downwards for a few moments before continuing his narrative. After completing the reliving I asked him what had been going through his mind at the moment that he had gone quiet. He looked downwards again and remained silent. I said that it was very common for men who are raped to get an erection themselves and asked whether this had happened to him. Mark looked up, appearing surprised. He said that that was what had happened to him at that moment. The particular meaning for him was that it must have meant that he wanted it to happen and that it must mean he is gay. I gave him further information about physiological responses to sexual assault. After this he said that he no longer believed that he had wanted it to happen or that it meant that he was gay. He listened to the tape of the session for homework. However, at the next session he reported that he had continued to have his nightmares and that it was always of that moment during the rape when he had an erection. In his nightmares, and when he had flashbacks to it, he still believed that he must have wanted it to happen. A theoretical understanding of this is that although the discussion about normal physiological responses to rape had affected his beliefs in his normal autobiographical memory they had not affected the meaning held in the differently stored and processed trauma memory. Thus it was necessary to explicitly update this traumatic memory in order to change the meaning of this hotspot. A table was drawn up of all the hotspots experienced together with updates of what he knew now in reality, which followed from discussion and cognitive restructuring outside of reliving (Table 10.1).

Mark then began the reliving again and at each hotspot he was guided to bring in the new updated (and rehearsed) information by asking at the appropriate moment in the narrative 'And in reality what is the case' 'What do you know now?':

Table 10.1 Mark's hotspots

Situation	Cognition	Emotion	Update ('What I know now')
At gunpoint	They're going to shoot me and kill me	Terrified	They don't shoot me. I don't die
Get an erection when penetrated	I must have wanted this to happen. I must be gay	Ashamed	It's a normal physiological response. It doesn't mean I wanted it to happen. It doesn't mean I'm gay
Left on floor at end	I should've known this would happen. It's my fault	Guilty	It's not my fault. I couldn't've known what was going to happen. [They] are to blame. They are bad people

Therapist: What is happening now?

Mark: They are standing next to me. I can see the gun pointing at my head. I'm shaking. I'm really afraid they are going to kill me.

Therapist: And in reality what is the case?

Mark: They don't shoot me ... I don't get killed ... [with some surprise evident in his voice] ...
Later ...

Therapist: What is happening now?

Mark: I am being penetrated. I am getting an erection. [looks downwards]

Therapist: Holding this image clearly in your mind, how do you feel right now?

Mark: Really bad.

Therapist: What do think this means?

Mark: I must have wanted it to happen. I must be gay.

Therapist: And in reality what is the case?

Mark: It's common to get an erection if you are raped. It doesn't mean I'm gay. I didn't want it to happen.

Therapist: That's right ... and now what is happening?
And so on ...

> Following this reliving, Mark reported that he felt strongly relieved at the moment he brought this new information about the erection into his mind. He listened to the tape with this 'updated reliving' for homework. The following session he reported a decrease in the frequency and severity of the nightmares and flashbacks. Grey et al. (2002) give a number of further examples of this procedure with therapy transcripts.

Caution should be used with reliving when there is an objective ongoing threat and when the person is unable to effectively process information. Some established sense of safety is a requirement to allow the memory to be 'put in the past'. If people are still in a situation in which they are at genuinely high objective risk of further traumatic events, such as in ongoing abusive situations, practical safety should be ensured first. An inability to effectively process information during the session may occur for various reasons. One common reason is alcohol or drug abuse and/or dependence. Second, if the client dissociates very easily then no effective processing can occur and grounding strategies will be important (see below). Third, if the person is extremely depressed it may be necessary to lift his or her mood at least somewhat before using reliving techniques.

Written narrative

It can also be helpful for the client to write a narrative account of the trauma (Resick and Schnicke, 1993). This may be particularly helpful in those with prolonged duration of trauma or with a very confused or fragmented memory of the trauma. It can be done either for homework or together with the therapist in the session. Ideally, the narrative should be in the present tense. Commonly, clients will also include their thoughts about the consequences of the trauma or questions and issues that they dwell and ruminate on. It is important to help the client identify which parts of the narrative are ruminative (i.e. post-traumatic) and which are truly peri-traumatic. The points at which they became most emotional when writing the account can identify hotspots. The narrative at these points can then be expanded with further details, in particular the emotions and thoughts and meanings. Discussion and cognitive restructuring of these meanings can then be later added to the narrative. To make it clearer these sections can be written in different colour ink or a different font used on a word processor. For example:

> They are holding me down and one of them penetrates me. I can feel pain. I get an erection. I feel really bad and think that this must mean that I am gay and want this to happen. But I know now in reality that this is a

normal physiological response and it does not mean that I am gay or wanted it to happen. They continue . . .

Restructuring images

This chapter cannot do this topic justice. Images can contain a wealth of meanings not easily verbalised and changing images or introducing new images has the aim of changing meanings (Hackmann, 1998). Imagery can be used to update a trauma memory in a similar fashion to verbal restructuring and updating. For example, individuals who feared during the traumatic event that they would never see their children again can bring into their mind an image of their children as they are now at that point of the reliving. Another use of imagery is to try to gain a new perspective on the event. If someone is inappropriately guilty about what they did or didn't do, it can be helpful if he or she runs through the event from an observer's perspective in imagery, and then be asked whether or not that person could have done anything different and who is truly responsible? Actions *not* taken can be explored in imagery. For example, a man who thought he should have fought back against his attackers vividly imagined in the session what would have occurred if he had. He realised that things would have probably been very much worse for him if the level of violence had escalated.

Discrimination of triggers

Trauma memories, which feel as if they are being relived, often appear to come out of the blue. However, careful questioning may identify triggers. These may be a match of sensory information or emotions experienced at the time of the trauma. It is helpful for the client to keep a diary of flashbacks and intrusions in order to identify the possible triggers. This can increase the sense of control over the re-experiencing symptoms.

For example, Dawn, a pedestrian, was hit by a car that mounted the pavement on a dark and cool evening. Her main intrusive memory was seeing the headlights of the car. One day she had a severe flashback when she opened her fridge door. This was initially inexplicable to her and she was frightened that she was 'losing it'. On discussion, she realised that unusually on this occasion her fridge had been empty and hence she could see the light at the back of the fridge very clearly. This, together with the blast of cold air, was enough to trigger the memory of her accident. This understanding eliminated her belief that this showed she was 'losing it'. We explicitly wrote out the similarities and differences of these situations as in Table 10.2.

The homework following this session was deliberately to open her empty fridge and, if the memory was triggered, explicitly remind herself of all the differences to the accident. This allowed her to gain control and not experience further flashbacks in this situation.

Table 10.2 Discriminating triggers: 'then' versus 'now'

Then	Now
Cold air	Cold air
Light in front of me	Light in front of me
Car coming towards me	Just the fridge
Outside on the pavement	In my kitchen
In danger	Safe

This approach can be used in a wide range of situations that may act as reminders and helps to update the memory with a 'time-code' that it is happening in the past rather than again right now. The overall procedure is:

- Identify the trigger and the similarities between this situation and/or object and the traumatic event.
- Identify explicitly all the differences between the traumatic situation and the current situation in which the memory is triggered. In particular, focus on the fact that the current situation is safe.
- Deliberately trigger the exact bit of the trauma memory. A variety of cues can be used, such as visual cues, sounds or even physical posture.
- When the memory is triggered, the person should explicitly remind him- or herself of what is different now, both verbally and physically, by acting in ways that he or she was unable to at the time. For example, if the person was trapped during the event, he or she can stand up and move around when the memory is triggered.

Revisiting the site of the event

If it is practically possible, it can be very helpful to accompany the client back to the site of the traumatic event, even if reliving and other memory-focused techniques have been successfully used. Commonly, this will occur in the second half of a 12-session treatment programme.

Clients often report that the site does not appear the same as it is in their memory, and they are often surprised at changes that may be present (such as changes to road layout, or simply different weather). Identifying these differences can be useful to help the discrimination between what was happening *then* versus what is happening *now*. New memories or further aspects of the trauma may also return. The procedure can be set up as a behavioural experiment, first identifying the beliefs about what would happen if they do re-visit the site (such as 'I'll go mad' or 'I'll be attacked again', etc.).

It can also help clarify confusion and to work out how an event may have occurred. For example:

> John was attacked after he had been drinking. He had a very patchy memory of what occurred, with many gaps, and much confusion about both chronological order and how events unfolded. Prior even to reliving we visited the area where the attack occurred. Whilst very distressing, it allowed John to recall a couple of further fragments, and for us to piece together a possible account of events, given the geography of the area. He continued to have gaps in memory but felt relieved that he had a plausible narrative for the attack and he felt more in control of his symptoms.

Cognitive restructuring negative appraisals

The restructuring of negative appraisals in PTSD can proceed in the same manner as any other cognitive restructuring. Some specific reactions in PTSD are highlighted below.

Guilt

Guilt is common in PTSD. People may feel guilty about the fact that the event happened at all, the fact that they survived while others didn't, and most commonly about what they did or did not do during the event. Usually, people are displaying a hindsight bias, when knowledge about the outcome of the event biases or distorts beliefs about knowledge possessed before the outcomes were known. In addition they discount other explanations for events and any positive actions they may have done.

A large number of well-established cognitive therapy strategies can be used to address guilt, including the use of a pie chart to examine relative responsibility for the event. Socratic questioning is used to address the hindsight bias, violation of personal standards and emotional reasoning (Kubany, 1998).

Shame

People may feel shame about what actually happened, how they reacted at the time and about the development of symptoms. Clients rarely report the things that they are most ashamed of early in treatment. It is only with the establishment of an empathic, trusting relationship that shame can be addressed. However, there are some common reactions during trauma that people may feel ashamed of that can be helped with education and normalising. For example, people may wet themselves when very frightened, and may become aroused during a sexual assault. Shame may be spotted in a session through possible behavioural indicators, such as gaze aversion and silence. The underlying meaning of these moments needs to be addressed. Sometimes they may be linked to long-standing negative beliefs about the self such as 'I'm weak' or 'I'm unworthy'. Work by Gilbert is very helpful for working with shame (e.g. Gilbert, 1999). In addition Lee et al. (2001) provide helpful clinical models of shame-based and guilt-based PTSD.

Anger

People with PTSD are often angry at what others did or did not do, both during the experience and following it. In such situations it is important to first very clearly empathise with the person, without rushing in to challenge or change things (*'I'd be angry'*, *'I'm not surprised you're angry'*, *'It is unfair'*). The person should be allowed time to explain exactly who and what his or her anger is focused on. To aid this it can be helpful for the person to write a letter to those he or she is angry with, explaining the effects of the trauma. This letter need not be sent.

If the person is angry at the behaviour of others during and after trauma, explanations for a person's behaviour can be explored. *Distorted* assumptions, such as those about malicious intent, can be challenged *if appropriate* (such as 'they deliberately drove the car into me') once the whole context and information is taken into account. Rigid standards that lead to anger ('no one should ever make a mistake driving') can be addressed with traditional cognitive therapy. Anger may be masking shame or humiliation, particularly in interpersonal trauma.

A crucial approach is to challenge assumptions about letting anger go: *'If you weren't angry what would that mean to you?'*. Common beliefs are that the event will be forgotten or that the perpetrator will have 'got away with it'. Socratic questioning around these assumptions can follow the line *'And how does remaining angry stop this?'*. Finally, a functional approach can be taken: *'Who wins if you remain angry?'*. People can take a conscious decision to stop someone else controlling their life. Equally, it is understandable if people remain angry following a trauma – it is only if it continues to interfere with their life that it remains a concern (Chemtob and Novaco, 1998).

Overgeneralisation of danger

People with PTSD feel that further bad events could happen at any time. They overestimate risk in situations where the objective risk has not changed. Strategies include evaluating the actual risk using sequential probabilities *'How many times have you driven in the past?'*, *'How many accidents have you had?'*, etc. This can lead to developing behavioural experiments to test out their predictions. The aim is to help people make a fairer assessment of risk, and to learn to live with that. The role of deliberate hypervigilance can be highlighted by asking people to be hypervigilant in a non-trauma-related situation to investigate the effect of hypervigilance on their level of anxiety. For example, somebody who has been assaulted can be asked to stand by a roadside and look for any signs of road danger – this hypervigilance invariably leads to increased anxiety.

Common additional problems

Rumination

Rumination is common following trauma. The content of rumination is often addressed when addressing the cognitions underlying guilt, shame and anger. In addition, it is also important to address the process of rumination and the possible beliefs that underlie it by discussing the pros and cons of continuing to ruminate. 'Banning' rumination, using distraction or later 'worry' time, may be an initial intervention.

Dissociation

Broadly, dissociation is a sense of detachment or a compartmentalisation of experience. It includes experiences such as day-dreaming, spacing out, feeling unreal or dreamlike and out-of-body experiences. Flashbacks are truly dissociative when the person loses the sense of where they are in reality and act as if the traumatic event is actually happening again. In these cases, 'grounding' strategies should be developed to maintain an awareness of 'here and now'. This can include the use of grounding objects, images, smells and phrases (Kennerley, 1996). The work on discriminating triggers also will help in this regard. Wagner and Linehan (1998) provide further approaches to work with dissociative behaviour. If the client fully dissociates during reliving it precludes any processing of new information into the trauma memory. They should be 'grounded' by telling them repeatedly where they are in reality, what is happening, and they are safe. They should not be physically touched unless this has been discussed in advance. A more graduated approach to addressing the trauma memory such as using a written narrative and keeping the eyes open during reliving can be adopted.

Physical injuries

Physical injuries following a traumatic event are often associated with more persistent PTSD symptoms. Within treatment, the meaning of injury both now and in the future should be identified. Any *distorted* sense of permanent change can be addressed while empathising for the losses that the person has experienced, and the associated grief. For distorted appraisals regarding others' beliefs and reactions to scars, etc., social phobia treatment techniques can be employed (Clark and Wells, 1995).

Panic attacks and co-morbid panic disorder

Panic attacks occur only on exposure to trauma-related triggers, or else a separate panic disorder may be present. Specific treatment for the panic attacks may be necessary prior to, and concurrent with, PTSD treatment so that people are willing to tolerate raised affect during reliving and other procedures. This can be well integrated within the overall cognitive therapy approach (Falsetti and Resnick, 2000).

Substance misuse

It is important to help people see the maintaining role of the misuse of alcohol and other substances. Treatment will not work if people are not able to do the necessary cognitive and emotional processing. Usually, dependence on alcohol or drugs will require specific treatment prior to PTSD treatment (although see Najavits, 2002, for treatment of co-morbid PTSD and substance misuse).

Further information

It may be important to obtain further information to discuss with the client. For example, some people who initially are not cut out of their car in an accident by the first emergency services to arrive at the scene perceive this as others not caring, whereas in fact it may have been due to a fear of back or neck injury or waiting for the correct cutting equipment. Information about the nature and effects of alcohol and certain drugs, e.g. following drug-rape, may help make sense of memory gaps or confusion and disorientation at the time of the trauma. Some confusion or disorientation during hospitalisation may occur when given medication.

Court proceedings

Ongoing court proceedings are not a contra-indication for treatment but may be obstacle. It may be maintaining specific beliefs, particularly underlying anger. An open discussion about the effect of treatment on any financial settlement, and the pros and cons of delaying treatment, might be necessary. If the person is a witness in criminal proceedings, it is wise to check with the solicitor that starting treatment now is acceptable, and not seen as 'coaching' of the story.

PROLONGED AND MULTIPLE TRAUMATISATION

A detailed analysis of how to flexibly alter treatment in more complicated traumatic stress presentations is beyond the scope of this chapter. All treatment approaches for this group can be summarised by the framework presented by Herman (1992), which was initially developed to help adult survivors of childhood abuse. First, a sense of safety must be established. Second, work on recollecting and understanding the nature of the traumatic event, which includes any reliving work. Third, reconnection to people, communities and the world. Within this framework the specific techniques described above can be used. Kimble et al. (1998) present a phasic model of treatment for complicated PTSD that focuses on when to apply particular techniques. Possible treatment guidelines for refugee and asylum-seeker populations have been provided by Van der Veer (1998) and Young and Grey (2004).

EFFECTS ON AND EFFECTS OF THE THERAPIST

The therapist's reactions can be examined on a number of levels. First, the immediate counter-transference and assumptions evident in the session. Even many experienced therapists do not use exposure-based treatments much of the time, even though they are the best treatment for PTSD (Becker et al., 2004). Therapists may have concerns about their own skills and/or inaccurate beliefs, such as 'they'll be re-traumatised'. Second, there are the general effects on therapists of providing psychological therapy encompassed by terms such as 'emotional exhaustion', 'compassion fatigue' and 'burn-out'. These refer to a general sense of no longer being able to empathise with the client and not experiencing any personal accomplishment in one's work. Third, and more specific to working with people who have experienced traumatic events, there is the possibility of secondary PTSD or vicarious traumatisation. On hearing and discussing traumatic events it is common and normal for the therapist to experience intrusive memories or bad dreams related to the client's experience.

Like clients, therapists should not suppress such intrusions. More generally, it is important for therapists to look after themselves. In addition to formal supervision, it can be helpful to have a colleague that you can simply 'off-load' to straightaway after a difficult session. It is important that therapists not only receive training in treatments for PTSD but that they also receive ongoing supervision. This can address the problems that arise in applying such treatments and also the therapist's own concerns about what may occur. In addition the therapist's own emotional reaction should be a standard part of supervision.

ACKNOWLEDGMENTS

Many thanks to Ben Smith, Blake Stobie and Kerry Young.

REFERENCES

Chapter 9 contains a list of useful internet resources.

Becker, C. B., Zayfert, C. and Anderson, E. (2004) A survey of psychologists' attitudes and utilization of exposure therapy for PTSD. *Behaviour Research and Therapy*, 42, 277–292.

Brewin, C. R. (2001) A cognitive neuroscience account of posttraumatic stress disorder. *Behaviour Research and Therapy*, 39, 373–393.

Brewin, C. R. (2003) *Posttraumatic Stress Disorder: Malady or Myth?* New Haven, CT: Yale University Press.

Brewin, C. R. and Holmes, E. A. (2003) Psychological theories of posttraumatic stress disorder. *Clinical Psychology Review*, 23, 339–376.

Brewin, C. R., Dalgleish, T. and Joseph, S. (1996) A dual representation theory of post-traumatic stress disorder. *Psychological Review*, 103, 670–686.

Bryant, R. A., Moulds, M. L., Guthrie, R. M., Dang, S. T. and Nixon, R. D. V. (2003) Imaginal exposure alone and imaginal exposure with cognitive restructuring in treatment of posttraumatic stress disorder. *Journal of Consulting and Clinical Psychology*, 71, 706–712.

Chemtob, C. and Novaco, R. W. (1998) Anger. In: V. Folette, J. Ruzek and F. Abueg (eds) *Cognitive Behavioral Therapies for Trauma*. London: Guildford Press.

Clark, D. M. and Wells, A. (1995) A cognitive model of social phobia. In: R. Heimberg, M. Leibowitz, D. A. Hope and F. R. Schneier (eds) *Social Phobia: Diagnosis, Assessment and Treatment*. New York: Guilford Press.

Davidson, P. R. and Parker, K. C. H. (2001) Eye movement desensitization and reprocessing (EMDR): A meta-analysis. *Journal of Consulting and Clinical Psychology*, 69, 305–316.

Ehlers, A. and Clark, D. M. (2000) A cognitive model of post-traumatic stress disorder. *Behaviour Research and Therapy*, 38, 319–345.

Ehlers, A., Clark, D. M., Hackmann, A., McManus, F., Fennell, M., Herbert, C. and Mayou, R. (2003) A randomised controlled trial of cognitive therapy, self-help booklet, and repeated early assessment as early interventions for PTSD. *Archives of General Psychiatry*, 60, 1024–1032.

Ehlers, A., Clark, D. M., Hackmann, A., McManus, F. and Fennell, M. (2005) Cognitive therapy for PTSD: Development and evaluation. *Behaviour Research and Therapy*, 43, 413–431.

Falsetti, S. A. and Resnick, H. S. (2000) Cognitive behavioural treatment of PTSD with comorbid panic attacks. *Journal of Contemporary Psychotherapy*, 30, 163–179.

Foa, E. B. and Rothbaum, B. O. (1998) *Treating the Trauma of Rape: Cognitive Behavioural Therapy for PTSD*. New York: Guilford Press.

Foa, E. B., Keane, T. M. and Friedman, M. J. (eds) (2000) *Effective Treatments for Posttraumatic Stress Disorder: Practice Guidelines from the International Society for Traumatic Stress Studies.* New York: Guilford Press.

Gilbert, P. (1999) Shame and humiliation in complex cases. In: N. Tarrier, A. Wells and G. Haddock (eds) *Treating Complex Cases: The Cognitive Behavioural Therapy Approach.* Chichester: John Wiley.

Gillespie, K., Duffy, M., Hackmann, A. and Clark, D. M. (2002) Community based cognitive therapy in the treatment of post-traumatic stress disorder following the Omagh bomb. *Behaviour Research and Therapy*, 40, 345–357.

Grey, N., Young, K. and Holmes, E. (2002) Cognitive restructuring within reliving: A treatment for peritraumatic emotional hotspots in PTSD. *Behavioural and Cognitive Psychotherapy*, 30, 63–82.

Hackmann, A. (1998) Working with images in clinical psychology. In: P. Salkovskis (ed) *Comprehensive Clinical Psychology, Vol. 6: Adults: Clinical formulation and treatment.* Oxford: Pergamon/Elsevier.

Harvey, A. G., Bryant, R. A. and Tarrier, N. (2003) Cognitive behaviour therapy for posttraumatic stress disorder. *Clinical Psychology Review*, 23, 501–522.

Herman, J. L. (1992) *Trauma and Recovery: From Domestic Abuse to Political Terror.* London: Pandora.

Kennerley, H. (1996) Cognitive therapy of dissociative symptoms associated with trauma. *British Journal of Clinical Psychology*, 35, 325–340.

Kimble, M. O., Riggs, D. S. and Keane, T. M. (1998) Cognitive behavioural treatment for complicated cases of post-traumatic stress disorder. In: N. Tarrier, A. Wells and G. Haddock (eds) *Treating Complex Cases: The Cognitive Behavioural Therapy Approach.* Chichester: John Wiley.

Kubany, E. (1998). Trauma related guilt. In: V. Folette, J. Ruzek and F. Abueg (eds) *Cognitive Behavioral Therapies for Trauma.* London: Guildford Press.

Lee, D., Scragg, P. and Turner, S. (2001) The role of shame and guilt in traumatic events. A clinical model of shame-based and guilt-based PTSD. *British Journal of Medical Psychology*, 74, 451–466.

Lohr, J. M., Hooke, W., Gist, R. and Tolin, D. F. (2003) Novel and controversial treatments for trauma-related stress disorders. In: S. O. Lilienfeld, S. J. Lynn and J. M. Lohr (eds) *Science and Pseudoscience in Clinical Psychology.* New York: Guilford Press.

Marks, I., Lovell, K., Noshirvani, H., Livanou, M. and Thrasher, S. (1998) Treatment of posttraumatic stress disorder by exposure and/or cognitive restructuring – a controlled study. *Archives of General Psychiatry*, 55, 317–325.

Mayou, R. A., Ehlers, A. and Hobbs, M. (2000) Psychological debriefing for road traffic accident victims: Three-year follow-up of a randomised controlled trial. *British Journal of Psychiatry*, 176, 589–593.

Mueller, M., Hackmann, A. and Croft, A. (2004) Post-traumatic stress disorder. In: J. Bennett-Levy, G. Butler, M. Fennell, A. Hackmann, M. Mueller and D. Westbrook (eds) *Oxford Guide to Behavioural Experiments in Cognitive Therapy.* Oxford: Oxford University Press.

Nagy, L. and Marshall, R. (2002) PTSD: psychopharmacology basics for non-physicians and beginning psychiatrists. *PTSD Clinical Quarterly*, 11, 33–39.

Najavits, L. (2002) *Seeking Safety: A Treatment Manual for PTSD and Substance Abuse.* New York: Guilford Press.

National Institute for Health and Clinical Excellence (NICE) (2005) *Post-traumatic Stress Disorder: The Management of PTSD in Adults and Children in Primary and Secondary Care*. London: Gaskell and the British Psychological Society.

Paunovic, N. and Ost, L.-G. (2001) Cognitive-behaviour therapy vs. exposure therapy in the treatment of PTSD in refugees. *Behaviour Research and Therapy*, 39, 1183–1197.

Resick, P. and Schnicke, M. (1993) *Cognitive Processing Therapy for Rape Victims: A Treatment Manual*. London: Sage Publications.

Richards, D. A. and Lovell, K. (1999) CBT treatment for PTSD. In W. Yule (ed) *Post-traumatic Stress Disorders: Concepts and Therapy*. Chichester: John Wiley.

Rose, S. and Bisson, J. (1998) Brief early psychological interventions following trauma: A systematic review of the literature. *Journal of Traumatic Stress*, 11, 697–710.

Shapiro, F. (1995) *Eye Movement Desensitisation and Reprocessing*. New York: Guilford Press.

Tarrier, N., Pilgrim, H., Sommerfield, C., Faragher, B., Reynolds, M., Graham, E. and Barrowclough, C. (1999) A randomized controlled trial of cognitive therapy and exposure in the treatment of chronic posttraumatic stress disorder. *Journal of Consulting and Clinical Psychology*, 67, 13–18.

Van der Veer, G. (1998) *Counselling and Therapy with Refugees and Victims of Trauma: Psychological Problems of Victims of War, Torture and Repression, 2nd edn*. Chichester: John Wiley.

Wagner, A. W. and Linehan, M. M. (1998) Dissociative behavior. In: V. Folette, J. Ruzek and F. Abueg (eds) *Cognitive Behavioral Therapies for Trauma*. London: Guildford Press.

Young, K. A. D. and Grey, N. (2004) *Cognitive Behaviour Therapy for Traumatised Asylum Seekers and Refugees*. Workshop presented at European Association for Behaviour and Cognitive Therapy Conference, Manchester, UK, 8 September.

Chapter 11

Social phobia

Investigation

Freda McManus and Colette Hirsch

INTRODUCTION

The extent to which any individual experiences social anxiety lies on a continuum, from those who experience only occasional anxiety in the most difficult social performance situations, such as public speaking, to those who are debilitated by the fear of negative evaluation in almost all social situations. Socially anxious people believe that this negative evaluation will occur as a consequence of showing signs of anxiety, or behaving in manner that will embarrass or humiliate themselves in social situations, such as conversations with people they do not know well, writing or eating in public, or group situations. In its more extreme form, high social anxiety can result in a diagnosis of social phobia. Social phobia can be specific and affect only one situation such as signing your name in public, or it may be generalised, affecting a wide range of everyday social interactions. Social phobia is the third most prevalent psychiatric disorder, with onset often in childhood or early teens (Schneier et al., 1992) and with an estimated lifetime prevalence rate of 13.3% (Kessler et al., 1994). Although clinical observation suggests that people with social phobia rarely receive explicit negative feedback from other people, left untreated, social anxiety tends to persist throughout adult life (Reich et al., 1994), with distressing and disabling consequences for sufferers. Individuals with social phobia often underperform at work and find it difficult to develop and maintain close relationships (Turner et al., 1986). Furthermore, social phobia can lead to alcohol dependence, depression and suicide (Schneier et al., 1992).

DEFINING SOCIAL PHOBIA

Social phobia is differentiated from social anxiety by the degree of distress and impairment experienced, and by the extent of avoidance behaviour. The *Diagnostic and Statistical Manual of Mental Disorders*, 4th edition, revised (DSM-IV-TR; American Psychiatric Association (APA), 2000) outlines the following criteria for the diagnosis of social phobia:

- A marked or persistent fear of one or more social or performance situations in which the person is exposed to unfamiliar people or to possible scrutiny by others. The individual fears that he or she will act in a way that will be humiliating or embarrassing.
- Exposure to the feared social situation produces an immediate anxiety response, which may take the form of a panic attack.
- The person recognises that the fear is excessive or unreasonable.
- The feared social situations are avoided, or endured with intense anxiety or distress.
- The avoidance or anxiety interferes significantly with personal, social or academic functioning.
- If under 18 years of age, the duration is at least 6 months.
- The fear is not related to a general medical or psychological condition, such as Parkinson's disease or stuttering.

DIFFERENTIATING SOCIAL PHOBIA FROM OTHER DISORDERS

What differentiates social phobia from other anxiety disorders is the emphasis on concerns about evaluation by others. For example, an individual with social phobia would not normally fear experiencing an anxiety symptom, such as sweating, if nobody else were present, or if he or she was confident that the symptom could not be observed. By contrast, the client with agoraphobia who associates sweating with panic attacks in which he or she fears death, may fear sweating even more if unaccompanied because help would be less readily available. In differentiating social phobia from agoraphobia it is helpful to remember that while both types of client may fear the same symptom or situation, the client with agoraphobia is more concerned about the experience of the symptom, whereas the client with social phobia is more concerned about other people's evaluation of him or her experiencing the symptom.

We have found it useful to differentiate social phobia from more general low self-esteem. Some individuals with social phobia view themselves as basically acceptable people who give others the erroneous impression (usually through showing anxiety symptoms) that they are not acceptable. However, some people with social phobia view themselves as basically inadequate or unacceptable and fear that this 'true self' will be revealed. For the purposes of treatment, it is important to know whether clients have a negative view of themselves or not, as this will influence the target of intervention in treatment. For example, for social phobia clients with low self-esteem, more emphasis will be placed on changing their view of themselves. Whereas for social phobia clients who do not have low self-esteem but believe that their poor performance in social situations gives others an erroneous negative impression, more time will be spent on looking at how negative their performance is, and what impression others get from it.

CO-MORBIDITY

Diagnostic co-morbidity is the rule rather than the exception in social phobia (Schneier at al., 1992). Among the most common co-morbid diagnoses are depression, substance abuse and avoidant personality disorder. In the case of depression, it is important to check that the social phobia is not secondary to a primary depressive illness (i.e. that the person still has significant social anxiety even when they are not depressed). Frequently, depression occurs as a result of the life-limiting consequences of social phobia. Similarly, many socially anxious clients use alcohol to self-medicate in advance of, or during, social interactions. Finally, the relationship between social anxiety and avoidant personality disorder has been the subject of much debate (Widiger, 1992). Although there appears to be little empirical or theoretical justification for qualitative distinctions between the two categories, DSM-IV-TR (APA, 2000) considers them as separate diagnostic categories. In our experience, individuals with co-morbid avoidant personality disorder tend to have more severe levels of disability and impairment but are just as likely to respond to treatment. However, they may require more sessions to reach the same outcome as clients who do not have avoidant personality disorder because the problems of socially phobic clients with avoidant personality disorder may be more widespread and they are likely to start from a lower level of functioning.

CLARK AND WELLS' (1995) MODEL OF SOCIAL PHOBIA

A number of models have been put forward to explain social phobia. This chapter describes one of the current cognitive-behavioural models that has been shown to have experimental support and to form a useful model on which to base therapy.

Clark and Wells' (1995) cognitive model of social phobia, presented in Figure 11.1, focuses on the factors that maintain social phobia and attempts to explain why individuals with social phobia fail to benefit from the naturalistic exposure that is provided by their everyday interactions with other people. In this model, social phobia is seen as resulting from problematic beliefs about oneself and one's social world, which lead individuals to interpret social situations in an excessively negative fashion. These negative interpretations, also known as feared predictions or social fear beliefs, are then maintained by the following processes: (1) increased self-focused attention and a linked decrease in observation of other people and their responses; (2)

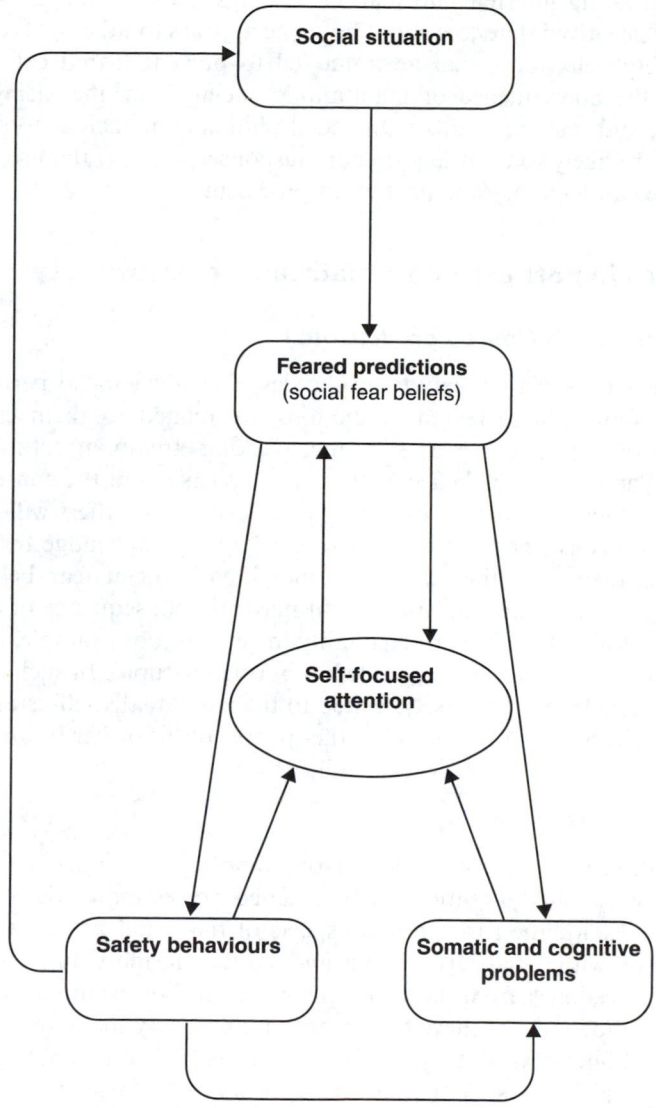

Figure 11.1 Clark and Wells' (1995) cognitive model of social phobia.

Adapted from R. Heimberg, M. Liebowitz, D. A. Hope and F. R. Schneier (eds) (1995) *Social Phobia: Diagnosis, Assessment and Treatment.*

use of misleading internal information (feelings and self-images) to make excessively negative inferences about how one appears to others; (3) extensive use of safety behaviours that are intended to prevent feared catastrophes that have the consequence of maintaining social fears, increasing feared symptoms, and making clients with social phobia come across to others in ways that are likely to elicit less friendly responses; and (4) the use of negatively biased anticipatory and post-event processing.

Processes hypothesised to maintain social anxiety

Social fear beliefs (feared predictions)

Individuals with social anxiety typically view their own social performance negatively. Often, these feared predictions are related to them exhibiting symptoms of anxiety, such as sweating, shaking, trembling, stuttering or blushing. The fear is usually accompanied by beliefs about the consequences of revealing such symptoms. For example, believing that others will interpret such symptoms as signs of weakness or inadequacy, and judge the sufferer harshly for them. In other cases, the individual's social fear beliefs may not relate to their anxiety symptoms but may be a consequence of concerns he or she has about his or her personality in general. For example, the client may fear that he or she will be revealed as boring or stupid. In such cases, the social fear beliefs may be closely related to the individual's self-esteem, or to global beliefs about him- or herself, other people or his or her future.

Self-focused attention

Preoccupation with how well the person comes across in social situations results in self-focused attention, or heightened processing of the social self, which reduces attention to external aspects of the social situation. In turn, this interferes with social performance and reduces the individual's awareness of objective feedback from the social environment. For example, individuals with social phobia may believe that people are bored by them, or that others have noticed how anxious they are, but they rarely check this out by observing other people or by soliciting feedback from others. Instead, persons with social phobia focus on a self-generated image or impression of how they are coming across to others, and mistakenly assume that this impression accurately reflects how others perceive them. This image or impression is a negatively distorted view of how they come across (e.g. looking much redder than they really look) and is often based on an aversive social experience in the client's past. Unfortunately, clients do not make an association between the earlier event and their current impression, instead believing the image to be an accurate reflection of how they currently appear.

Safety behaviours and avoidance

One mechanism by which people with social phobia attempt to prevent their fears from becoming realised is by using avoidance or safety behaviours. Safety behaviours are overt or covert behaviours or strategies that are engaged in with the goal of preventing the individual's feared outcomes (being evaluated negatively) from occurring (Salkovskis, 1991). Examples of safety behaviours are mentally rehearsing sentences to reduce the chance of stumbling over words, avoiding eye contact to prevent an anxious expression from being seen by others, or gripping glasses tightly to prevent shaking. Although people with social phobia engage in safety behaviours and avoidance in an attempt to reduce anxiety, these behaviours often have the paradoxical effect of perpetuating their negative predictions about how other people will perceive them and thus, in turn, contribute to the maintenance of the person's anxiety. This can happen in a number of ways. Avoidance of the situation will mean that individuals continue to feel anxious about a situation because they have not learned that they would have been OK anyway. Even if they enter the feared social situation, using safety behaviours will result in them attributing the fact that the feared prediction did not come about to the safety behaviours, rather than to the fact that the feared prediction would not have happened anyway. Most safety behaviours increase self-monitoring and self-consciousness and hence make people more likely to experience anxiety in the situation. Performing safety behaviours (including monitoring how one is coming across) takes up attention, which results in individuals with social phobia seeming rather distant and uninterested in other people. Unfortunately, other people are likely to interpret this as a sign that the individual does not like them and they are then likely to be less friendly in return (Curtis and Miller, 1986; Alden and Bieling, 1998). In this way, safety behaviours contaminate the social interaction, paradoxically making it less successful and thereby perpetuating anxiety about future social interactions. Finally, safety behaviours may also directly increase the likelihood of feared predictions occurring (e.g. mentally rehearsing sentences may make it more likely that you will stumble over your words, and gripping glasses tightly may make it more likely that your hands will tremble) and this maintains anxiety about future interactions.

Anticipatory and post-event processing

Anticipatory and post-event processing have also been highlighted as maintaining processes. In anticipation of problematic social situations, the individual with social phobia tends to worry about the situation. This anticipatory processing may involve reviewing perceived failures in past social interactions and planning and rehearsing conversation and behaviour to avoid such failures recurring. This strategy often serves to increase anxiety. On leaving the social situation, exposure to the negative aspects of the encounter does not end. People with social phobia are prone to ruminate about aspects of the situation and their behaviour that they were not happy with. This is typically about how they felt and how they believe they came across, because the individual with social phobia is typically self-focused during the situation and thus is more likely to remember such internal information, rather than external information. This post-event processing contributes to an overemphasis on negative aspects of the encounter.

ASSESSING SOCIAL PHOBIA

Structured assessment interviews for diagnosis

The diagnostic criteria of social phobia can be assessed by the use of structured diagnostic interviews or by a thorough clinical interview. The most commonly used structured interviews for social phobia are the Anxiety Disorders Interview Schedule for DSM-IV (ADIS-IV; Brown et al., 1994) and the Structured Clinical Interview for DSM-IV (SCID-I; First et al., 1994). Both aim to generate specific diagnoses for a problem, or combination of problems, that are compatible with DSM-IV (APA, 1994). Although the ADIS takes longer to administer than the SCID, it does provide more information. For example, it requires ratings of the degree of fear and avoidance felt in response to a given list of situations. This can be especially useful as a baseline against which to measure change during therapy; some clients may benefit greatly from treatment but still meet diagnostic criteria at the end of treatment, and so being able to assess the degree of change along a continuum, as opposed to just assessing diagnostic status, can be helpful.

Both the SCID and the ADIS require training to ensure proper administration and interpretation. Given adequate training, several studies report high levels of test–retest and inter-rater reliability for the SCID (Skre et al., 1991; Ventura et al., 1998) and the ADIS (Di Nardo et al., 1993).

Questionnaires

Self-report measures are extremely useful in the assessment of social anxiety. On a practical level, questionnaires are efficient, requiring little therapist time to collect large amounts of information. They can be repeated to assess the impact of therapeutic interventions and to assess which areas remain problematic. They also allow the clinician to place a particular client along a continuum of severity for the assessed symptom, or phenomenon. Furthermore, they eliminate the need for the therapist to interpret clients' responses, thereby reducing one source of bias.

The Fear of Negative Evaluation scale (FNE; Watson and Friend, 1969) is a 30-item true–false measure developed specifically to measure one aspect of the authors' understanding of the constructs underlying social anxiety – the fear of negative evaluation by others. As one of the earliest measures of social anxiety, the FNE has become one of the most frequently used and has been demonstrated to have good levels of reliability and validity (Watson and Friend, 1969). However, it has been criticised for being relatively insensitive to changes in social phobia symptoms following treatment due to its focus on only one aspect of social phobia and its true–false format. Leary (1983) developed a brief (12-item) version of the FNE, using a five-point Likert scale rather than the original true–false format, which correlates highly with the original FNE. This has acceptable levels of reliability and validity. The brief FNE may be especially suitable for evaluating the effects of treatment due to its Likert response scale and to its brevity facilitating repeated administration.

The Social Phobia Anxiety Inventory (SPAI; Turner et al., 1989) is a comprehensive, 45-item scale that was empirically derived to assess the symptoms of social phobia, including avoidance and distress, across a range of potentially distressing situations. Responses are given on a seven-point Likert scale, with higher scores indicating more symptoms, distress and impairment. Thirty-two of the items address social phobia and 13 assess agoraphobia. A social phobia difference score can be calculated by subtracting the agoraphobia subscale score from the social phobia subscale score. Beidel and Turner (1992) recommend using the difference score to assess the severity of social phobia symptoms specifically. However, other authors prefer to use the social phobia subscale score and have cautioned that using the difference score may produce false negatives (i.e. when a person is said to not have social phobia when in fact he or she does) for people who have both social phobia and agoraphobia (Herbert et al., 1991). The SPAI has been shown to have good levels of reliability and validity, and to be sensitive to the effects of treatment (Taylor et al., 1997; Turner et al., 1989).

The Social Interaction Anxiety Scale (SIAS) and the Social Phobia Scale (SPS) were developed by Mattick and Clark (1998) to assess social anxiety and are based on the conceptualisation that social anxiety occurs in two types of situation: those involving interaction with others and those involving being observed or scrutinised by others. As yet, the support for this distinction is unclear; hence, it may be more useful for the clinician to treat the SIAS and SPS as subscales of the same measure. Both have been demonstrated to have good levels of internal consistency, reliability and validity (Heimberg et al., 1992; Mattick and Clark, 1998) and are sensitive to changes following treatment (Mattick and Peters, 1988; Mattick et al., 1989). Both scales have 20 items, which are rated on a five-point Likert scale.

The Liebowitz Social Phobia Scale (LSPS; Liebowitz, 1987) was originally developed as an interviewer-rated scale for assessing the severity of social phobia symptoms, but has more recently become commonly used as a self-report measure. It lists 24 situations, which are rated for the degree of fear and avoidance that the client feels in relation to each one. The items are classified as either social-interaction or performance situations. However, the clinical validity for this classification is not clear so the scale is usually used to generate a total score, or to generate separate fear and avoidance scores. Despite this limitation it can be clinically useful for getting a feel for the types and range of situations that the client fears and avoids.

Two unpublished scales, developed by Clark and colleagues, may also be clinically useful in assessing and tracking change in social phobia. The Social Phobia Weekly Summary Scale (SPWSS; Clark et al., 2003; reproduced in McManus, 2004) was developed to measure the processes hypothesised to underlie the maintenance of social phobia in Clark and Wells' (1995) cognitive model of social phobia. Respondents rate the following variables on an eight-point Likert-type scale: severity of social anxiety, social avoidance, self-focused attention, anticipatory processing and post-event processing. Although the psychometric properties of the SPWSS are yet to be evaluated, it is very brief and directly related to the variables hypothesised to maintain social phobia in Clark and Wells' (1995) model. Hence, it can be used to track change in these variables on a session-by-session basis. Similarly, the Social Cognitions Questionnaire (SCQ; Wells et al., unpublished) is not yet validated but is a useful measure of the frequency and degree of belief in the thoughts that are typical of socially phobic patients. It lists a wide range of negative self-appraisals, fear of negative evaluation by others and negative beliefs typical of social phobia and asks respondents to rate the frequency with which they have had that thought, and how much they believed it, in the last week (see Wells, 1997, for further description and preliminary validation data).

Clinical interview

In contrast to structured diagnostic interviews, the clinical assessment interview is a more general, semi-structured interview that does not necessarily aim to generate a specific diagnostic label for a presenting complaint, but to generate a clinically useful formulation of the client's difficulties as a starting point for treatment.

Style of interview

The assessment is usually the individual's first face-to-face contact with the therapist or service and thus provides the opportunity to put the client at ease and begin to build a good working rapport. The nature of social anxiety presents particular challenges for both the therapist and client at the initial assessment interview. It is important that the client feels as at ease as possible during the interview and does not feel scrutinised, interrogated or that he or she is not giving the right answers. Typically, the more anxious the clients become during the interview, the more they feel that their mind is going blank and the more difficult they find it to answer questions. Clients with social phobia may not be able to fully answer all of the questions without having a chance to think about them, so the opportunity to answer in their own time is especially useful. Similarly, if they feel scrutinised or disapproved of in any way it will be even more difficult for them to be open about the difficulties that they are experiencing. It is critical that the therapist gives feedback that the client is giving the right kind of information and that the therapist understands their difficulties. We have found it helpful to be guided by the client on how much eye contact should be made during the interview, since for some clients eye contact is threatening. The seating should be configured such that the client has a choice about whether they wish to maintain eye contact, with chairs at right angles to each other rather than the client and therapist facing each other directly. Furthermore, due to the high levels of self-consciousness and self-focused attention, it is particularly helpful to write down the important information on a whiteboard so the client and therapist can have a shared focus of attention on the board itself, rather than by looking at each other.

For the client, challenges that are inherent in the assessment process may include having to overcome extreme anxiety about attending the meeting and discussing their difficulties for the first time. People with social phobia are often very embarrassed about their difficulties and rarely realise how common social anxiety is. In addition, it is the nature of their condition that they fear being judged negatively and are vigilant for signs of disapproval. Given the chronic and unremitting nature of social phobia, and the fact that the symptoms have usually been present since childhood, clients have often formed the view that these difficulties are simply part of their personality, and thus may experience a strong sense of shame in discussing them and have difficulty in recognising the ways in which their life has been impacted by the disorder. For example, they may see their lack of a social life and paucity of relationships as a reflection of their personality ('It's just the way I am') and not as part of an anxiety disorder. Moreover, they may not miss these potential aspects of life if they have never experienced or enjoyed them.

The challenge for the therapist is to put clients at ease enough for them to be able to discuss their difficulties in an open and frank way. Although open-ended questions are generally preferred for assessment interviews, these tend to work less well in the initial stages with individuals with social phobia. It may be preferable to begin the interview with more directive conversation or with easy-to-answer questions, such as asking for demographic information. If clients are feeling anxious during the assessment and are self-focused it can be difficult for them to generate answers to open-ended questions. If this happens, it may be appropriate for the therapist to provide a range of possible answer, or types of answer, from which clients can form the basis of their answer. For example, the therapist may say 'Some people I have worked with get anxious in a wide range of social situations, whereas others get anxious only in one or two situations, such as when talking to someone in authority or when they fear they might look anxious. How does your anxiety affect you? Does it happen in a variety of situations? Or just one or two?'. After the client responds, the therapist can ask for further detail with questions such as 'Which situations are most difficult for you?'. Providing those who are struggling to answer with some structuring information can facilitate their confidence that the therapist is familiar with these types of issues and has met other people with similar problems.

Areas to cover in a clinical interview

There is considerable heterogeneity among those with social phobia, which is reflected in patterns of symptoms, the course of the disorder, the degree and areas of impairment and in the types of situations that elicit anxiety. A good clinical interview will cover each of these areas to form a comprehensive picture of the individual's difficulties. Clinical interviews often begin by asking the client for a detailed description of the presenting problem(s) and its history. The history will cover how the problem began and its course. One of the main aims of a historical assessment of the problem is to elicit information that may contribute to a formulation of the problem and its modulating factors. It is important to get an understanding of the client's view of his or her problem and understanding of its ebbs and flows, and what he or she has found helpful in coping with it in the past. The assessor would also want to know about the ways in which these difficulties impact the client's life, and perhaps use this information to begin to think about what the client's goals for treatment are, and how he or she thinks these goals might be achieved.

In assessing the current status of the problem, the assessor would be looking for a detailed description of the main affective, physiological, cognitive and behavioural symptoms, as well as a detailed description of the range of situations that elicit anxiety. To establish a baseline against which to measure change, the assessor needs to get a clear picture of the current frequency and severity of anxiety and related symptoms. This will include not only the experiential symptoms of anxiety itself, but also avoidance symptoms and safety behaviours.

In assessing the cognitive aspects of the problem, the assessor will be attempting to identify the client's fears, because these are hypothesised to underlie the anxiety symptoms. The assessor is seeking to discover exactly what it is that the client fears could happen in anxiety-provoking social situations. This may involve several levels. For example, when questioned about what they fear, clients may initially reply that they fear getting anxious. However, it is important to continue to probe for further explanation until the 'bottom line' (Fennell, 1999) is reached:

> Josh initially stated that he feared getting anxious. It was thus important to ask what was the worst thing about getting anxious. He replied that he feared that others would notice his anxiety and conclude that he was an anxious person.

Again, it is important to understand the idiosyncratic meaning of this for the client, so it is important to continue asking what would be the worst thing if others did conclude that he was an anxious person. In this instance:

> Josh believed that if other people saw him as an 'anxious person' they would view him as weak and not have any respect for him, and he would then be unable to respect himself. The 'bottom line' was that he would end up alone and seeing himself as worthless.

The 'bottom line' varies enormously and often reflects underlying low self-esteem. Each of the different levels (that he will become anxious, that his anxiety will be visible to others, that others will notice his anxiety, that they will conclude that he is an anxious person, that they will lose respect for him, and that he will end up alone and unable to respect himself) can be a target for intervention in treatment.

A good clinical interview should also cover co-morbid problems, especially those that are known to commonly be co-morbid with social phobia, such as substance abuse and depression. Furthermore, it is important to be aware of any associated personality psychopathology such as avoidant or other personality disorders.

Behavioural assessment, self-monitoring and observation

Both symptom diaries and the assessor's observations during the interview or during a behavioural task can yield useful information for the assessment. Symptom diaries, in which clients record what anxiety symptoms (and beliefs and behaviours) they have experienced in different situations, can identify useful information about the current frequency and severity of symptoms, as well as being an *aide memoire* for a fine-grained analysis of the factors involved in maintaining the problem. Asking the client to carry out a behavioural task can enable the therapist to gain a moment-by-moment understanding of what happens for the client in a socially anxious situation. A behavioural task may be particularly informative if the client has not con-fronted the source of anxiety for many years and thus does not accurately recall the details of what it is he or she fears and the exact sequence of events in anxiety-provoking situations. Asking the client to go some way towards confronting the feared situation in the session can reactivate such fears. For example, asking a client with social phobia to have a conversation with a stranger might make it easier for the client to identify what predictions he or she is making about what could go wrong. Observing a client in a social-anxiety-provoking situation may also help the therapist to identify aspects of the problem that the client is not aware of, such as subtle avoidance behaviours that have become habitual (e.g. avoiding eye contact or not talking about oneself). Furthermore, it can be useful for the therapist to get an objective picture of how the client is functioning in anxiety-provoking situations. For example, it is helpful for the therapist to know if the client really *does* comes across as badly as he or she thinks (although in our experience this is rarely the case, as clients usually have an overly negative impression of how they come across), and the likely causes of this, before deciding which direction treatment should take. For example, if the client is carrying out extensive safety behaviours that *do* make him or her come across less well, then it would be sensible to focus on modifying the use of these strategies before moving on to reducing situational avoidance and soliciting objective feedback from others.

ASSESSMENT FOR FORMULATION

A comprehensive assessment will often conclude with a formulation of the problem that outlines the possible maintaining factors. The remainder of this chapter discusses how a formulation based on Clark and Wells' (1995) model of social phobia can be derived.

Eliciting the information required for formulation

Clark and Wells' (1995) cognitive model of social phobia has been annotated in Figure 11.2 to outline the types of questions that we have found useful in eliciting the information required for each of the relevant areas. The numbers indicate the rough order in which we have found it easiest to elicit this information. However, it is always more important to be responsive to the client in discussing the various areas of difficulty, rather than to follow a predetermined order that makes sense for the therapist. The process of drawing out the information required to formulate an individual's social anxiety according to this model is described in more detail below.

1. Information about the situation

For the purposes of drawing out the model, it is useful to begin by asking the

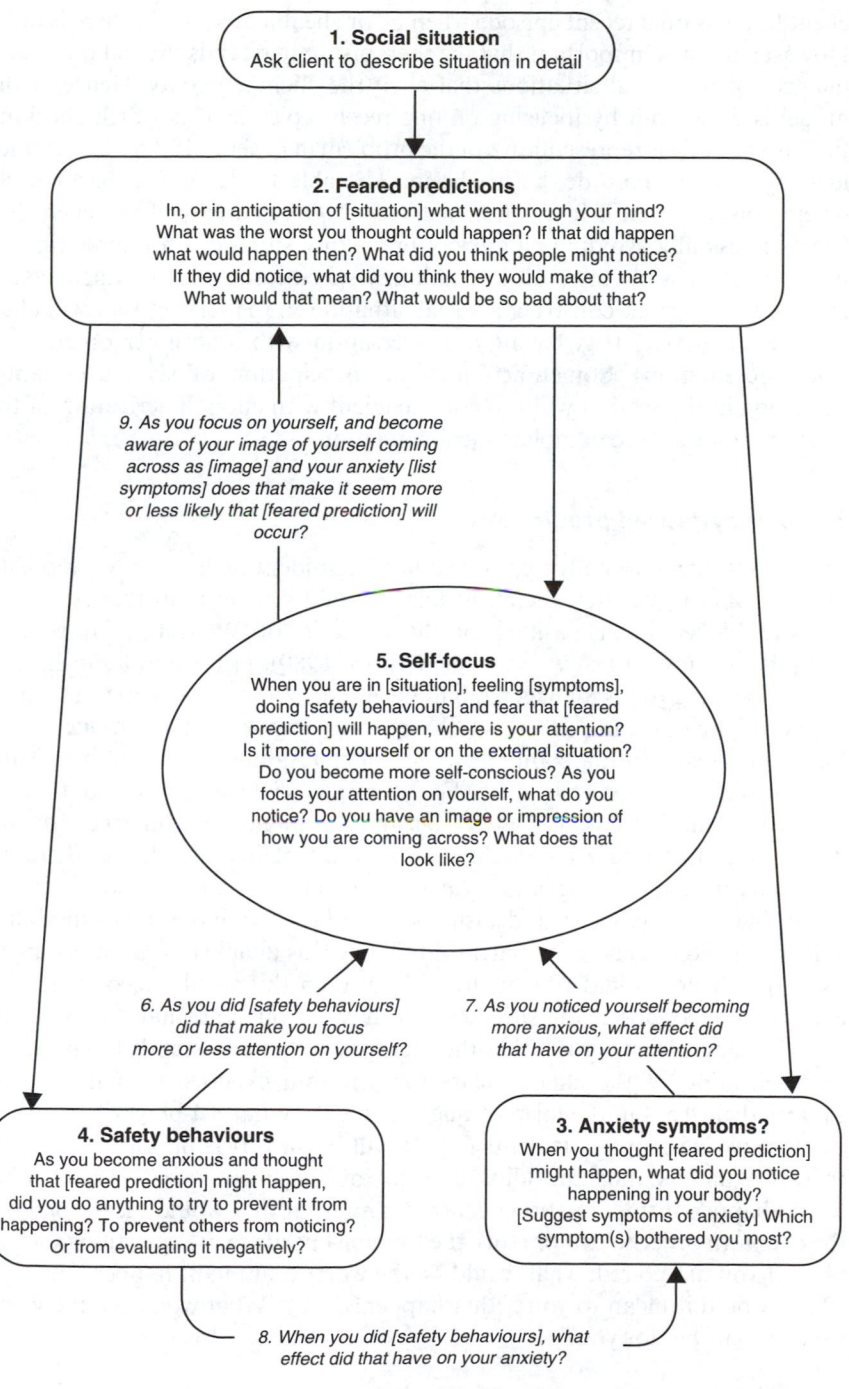

Figure 11.2 Clark and Wells' (1995) cognitive model of social phobia annotated to aid assessment.

client to focus on a recent episode when he or she felt anxious (if there is one). However, it is also important that the therapist understands the full range and nuances of the social situations that elicit the client's anxiety. Hence, if the model is drawn out by focusing on one recent episode, it is worth checking that this episode is representative of the problem in general. If the client cannot identify a recent episode, he or she may be able to describe a particularly severe episode, even if it was not that recent. Occasionally, if the client has been successfully avoiding all anxiety-provoking situations for some time, it may not be possible to recall in detail any specific episode, in which case it may be necessary to construct a social situation in the session that will elicit the client's anxiety (e.g. having a conversation with a stranger or giving a brief presentation). Sometimes, just the anticipation of such a situation occurring in the session will provide the client with enough activation of the problem to be able to complete the formulation.

2. Eliciting feared predictions

Once a specific episode (or episodes) has been identified, the next step is to identify what it was that the client feared could go wrong in that situation. Usually this will involve asking the client a series of 'What if . . .' questions, as in the downward arrow technique (Burns, 1980). For example, Josh, who feared speaking to his manager, might be asked, 'What is the worst that could happen if you did?'. In using this technique, it is important to continue asking for further fears until a comprehensive understanding of the severity of the client's difficulties is arrived at. For example, if Josh responded that he avoided asking his boss for advice because he might get embarrassed, this does not seem to be a comprehensive account of his fear. If the therapist followed this up by asking 'and if you did get embarrassed, what would be the worst that could happen?' and Josh responded by saying that he would blush a deep red and then be so embarrassed that he was unable to face returning to work and hence would risk his livelihood, then this would account for his extreme anxiety about the situation. In drawing out information about the client's fears it is important that the therapist fully understands the meaning or implication of the client's fears or symptom experiences. Clients may express their fears in the form of questions (e.g. 'What if I blush?') that need to be re-worded into statements (e.g. 'I will blush'). It is important that the therapist understands the idiosyncrasies of the client's fears about what would happen if this situation occurred, and what that would mean to/about the client. In order to explore this, the therapist needs to ask questions such as 'And if you did go red, what would be the worst that might happen then?' or 'What would it mean to you if that happened?' or 'What would be the worst thing about that for you?'

3. Information about anxiety symptoms

The therapist aims to get a comprehensive picture of the anxiety symptoms that the client experiences in social situations, and to identify which symptoms the client fears most. Once the client has had an opportunity to list the symptoms, it can be useful for the therapist to suggest symptoms of anxiety that the client might have experienced (e.g. 'Were you sweating? Did your heart race? Did you feel yourself going red? Did you feel as if you were shaking? What about your voice – was that affected?'). This can act as an *aide memoire* and can also help to normalise the symptoms. It is important to be as specific as possible, so if the client responds that he or she was shaking, it is useful to know where in the body the shaking was, how severe it was, and even to ask the client to show the therapist what it looked like. In this way, the therapist can begin to formulate ideas about how severe the client's physical symptoms are and whether the client's impression of these symptoms is distorted. It is also important to know which symptoms the client fears most (these are usually the ones perceived to be most visible to others).

4. Identifying safety behaviours

To orient the person and facilitate memory, it can help to reflect back what he or she has already told you, i.e. that the client was in [describe situation], feeling increasingly anxious and experiencing symptoms such as [list symptoms], and fearing that [feared predictions] would happen, and then ask whether the client did anything to help him- or herself in that situation [safety behaviours]. For the formulation to be useful for therapeutic purposes, it is important that the full range of safety behaviours is elicited. This is best done by asking whether the client did anything to: (1) prevent the feared prediction from occurring; (2) prevent it from being noticed by others; or (3) prevent it from being evaluated negatively by others. This sequence of questions is then repeated for each feared prediction.

5. Identifying the content and focus of attention

Again, it may be useful to orient clients by reminding them of what they have already told you before asking about where their attention was focused, e.g. 'When you are in [client's specified situation], and fear that [client's feared predictions] will happen, and you are doing [list safety behaviours], where is your attention? Is it more focused on yourself, or on the external situation? Do you find yourself concentrating more on what is going on inside your own body, or on what is actually happening in the external situation?'. Usually, clients report that their focus of attention is much more internal than external, that is to say, their attention is largely taken up with monitoring their anxiety symptoms and carrying out safety behaviours, leaving relatively little attention for actually processing what is going on in the situation. Once an internal focus of attention has been established, the next step is to identify whether clients have an image or impression of themselves while in the social situation. If they do report having an image/impression, then they are asked to describe in as much detail as possible what this image or impression looks and sounds like. It is also useful to ask them whether the image relates to a memory of an earlier social event, as images are often based on earlier aversive social experiences.

6. Establishing links between components

It is clinically important that clients understand how the different components of their anxiety affect each other and work together to create a vicious circle in which their anxiety is maintained. Some questions for establishing the links are outlined in Figure 11.2. To establish the link between safety behaviours and self-focus, it is useful to list the individual's safety behaviours and ask whether they focus more or less on themselves as they do those safety behaviours. Any safety behaviours that involve self-monitoring or internal processing (e.g. rehearsing what to say, monitoring physical symptoms of anxiety) will cause the individual to become more internally focused. Similarly, the more anxiety symptoms people are experiencing, the more self-conscious they are likely to feel and the more they will think they need to monitor their internal states (for example, to check how red they are going or how much they are shaking). Drawing out this formulation is also a useful opportunity to begin to educate people about the nature of their social anxiety. For example, Socratic questioning can help the client understand that safety behaviours may directly increase their anxiety symptoms, prevent them from discovering that their fears were not going to happen anyway, and contaminate the social interaction. It may be useful to demonstrate these points by the use of role plays (e.g. showing that holding something very tightly to try to stop shaking actually causes shaking).

The final link to establish is the one between self-focused attention and an increased belief in social fears. This link can often be established by asking 'as you focus on yourself, and become aware of your impression of yourself coming across as [client's image] and your [anxiety symptoms], does that make it seem more or less likely that [client's feared prediction] will occur?' Clients usually report that this self-focused attention makes it seem more likely that their fears will be realised. An example of this type of formulation for Josh is shown in Figure 11.3.

Sharing the formulation with the client

We have found it most useful to draw out the formulation collaboratively with the client on a white board. Not only does working on a white board

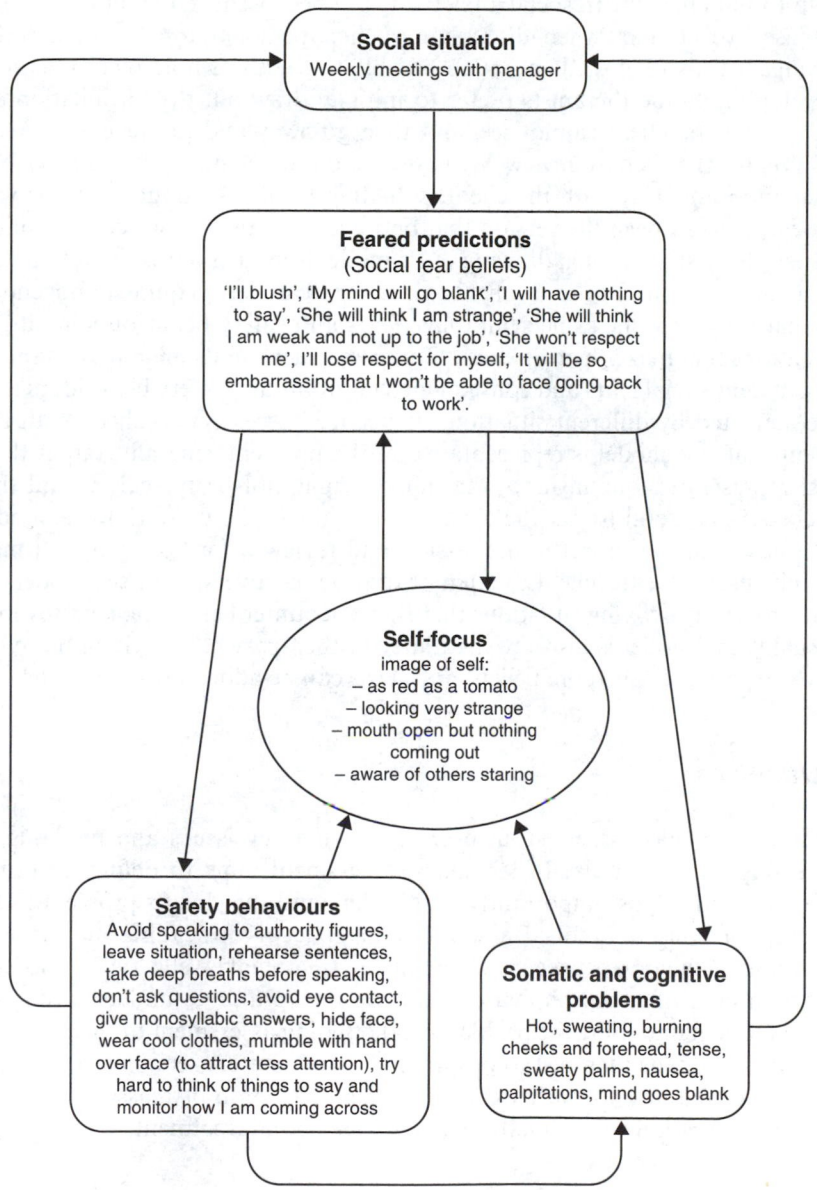

Figure 11.3 Formulation of Josh's social phobia according to Clark and Wells' (1995) cognitive model of social phobia.

help to put clients with social anxiety at ease because it reduces the need for intense eye contact when discussing such a personal topic with a near-stranger, it also helps the client to be able to see the whole picture as it is developing. Some therapists prefer to initially draw out the formulation on paper that the client cannot see, and then go away and produce a 'correct' version for the client to review. We have found it much more effective to work contemporaneously with the client, soliciting feedback about the fit as you proceed, to establish the version that best accounts for his or her difficulties. Often, the first attempt at drawing out a model is used as a draft that is added to in later sessions. For some clients, their social anxiety is quite homogenous in that they have the same symptoms, fears and safety behaviours in all the situations that make them anxious. However, other clients might have a range of different social fears and consequent symptoms and safety behaviours that are activated by different situations, hence it is necessary to check with the client that this model is representative of the problem generally, rather than just representing one instance that may or may not be typical. To aid this process, it is useful to ask the client to copy down the version of the model that has been drawn out in the session and review it for homework. It may also be useful for the client to attempt to produce a version of the model for any anxiety-provoking situations that they encounter before the next session. Usually, the model is also revisited later in therapy when working more on early experiences and core beliefs, and these can be added into the model.

SUMMARY

This chapter has presented an overview of the key issues and methods in assessing social phobia. In summary, assessment aims to define, describe, measure and – most importantly – to understand the client's problems. The concept of a once-and-for-all assessment in anxiety is misleading and can lead to a false distinction between assessment and treatment (Wells, 1997). Successful treatment of social phobia depends on an up-to-date understanding of the factors maintaining the problem, and ongoing assessment of these factors is required for the therapist to be aware of which factors remain as treatment progresses. Failure to meet treatment goals may prompt reassessment and hence, any session will be mixture of assessment and treatment.

ACKNOWLEDGMENTS

The assessment procedures described in this chapter have been developed from the work of the Oxford Anxiety Disorders Group which included David M. Clark, Anke Ehlers, Ann Hackmann, Freda McManus, Melanie Fennell, Adrian Wells, and Gillian Butler.

REFERENCES

Alden, L. E. and Bieling, P. (1998) Interpersonal consequences of the pursuit of safety. *Behaviour Research and Therapy*, 36, 53–64.

American Psychiatric Association (APA) (1994) *Diagnostic and Statistical Manual of Mental Disorders*, 4th edn. Washington, DC: APA.

American Psychiatric Association (APA) (2000) *Diagnostic and Statistical Manual of Mental Disorders, 4th edn*. Text revised. Washington, DC: APA.

Beidel, D. C. and Turner, S. M. (1992) Scoring the Social Phobia and Anxiety Inventory: Comments on Herbert et al. (1991). *Journal of Psychopathology and Behavioural Assessment*, 14, 377–379.

Brown, T. A., DiNardo, P. A. and Barlow, D. H. (1994) *Anxiety Disorders Interview Schedule for DSM-IV (ADIS-IV)*. Albany, NY: Graywind.

Burns, D. (1980) *Feeling Good*. New York: New American Library.

Clark, D. M. and Wells, A. (1995) A cognitive model of social phobia. In: R. Heimberg, M. Liebowitz, D. A. Hope and F. R. Schneier (eds) *Social Phobia: Diagnosis, Assessment and Treatment* (pp. 69–93). New York: Guilford Press.

Clark, D. M., Ehlers, A., McManus, F., Hackmann, A., Fennell, M. J. V., Campbell, H. et al. (2003) Cognitive therapy vs. fluoxetine in generalized social phobia: A randomized controlled trial. *Journal of Consulting and Clinical Psychology*, 71, 1058–1067.

Curtis, R. C. and Miller, K. (1986). Believing another likes or dislikes you: Behaviors making the belief come true. *Journal of Personality and Social Psychology*, 51, 284–290.

Di Nardo, P. A., Moras, K., Barlow, D. H., Rapee, R. M. and Brown, T. A. (1993) Reliability of DSM-III-R anxiety disorder categories using the Anxiety Disorders Interview Schedule – Revised (ADIS-R). *Archives of General Psychiatry*, 40, 251–256.

Fennell, M. J. V. (1999) *Overcoming Low Self-esteem: Self-help Guide Using Cognitive Behavioural Techniques*. London: Constable and Robinson.

First, B. M., Spitzer, R. L., Gibbon, M. and Williams, J. B. (1994) *Structured Clinical Interview for Axis I DSM-IV Disorders – Patient Edition*. New York: New York State Psychiatric Institute, Biometrics Research Department.

Heimberg, R., Liebowitz, M., Hope, D. A. and Schneier, F. R. (eds) (1995) *Social Phobia: Diagnosis, Assessment and Treatment*. New York: Guilford Press.

Heimberg, R. G., Mueller, G. P., Holt, C. S., Hope, D. A. and Liebowitz, M. R. (1992) Assessment of anxiety on social interaction and being observed by others: The Social Interaction Anxiety Scale and the Social Phobia Scale. *Behaviour Therapy*, 23, 53–73.

Herbert, J. D., Bellack, A. S. and Hope, D. A. (1991) Concurrent validity of the Social Phobia and Anxiety Inventory. *Journal of Psychopathology and Behavioural Assessment*, 13, 357–369.

Kessler, R. C., McGonagle, K. A., Zhao, S., Nelson, C. B., Hughes, M., Eshleman, S. et al. (1994) Lifetime and 12-month prevalence of DSM-III-R psychiatric disorders in the United States; results from the National Comorbidity Survey. *Archives of General Psychiatry*, 51, 8–19.

Leary, M. R. (1983) A brief version of the Fear of Negative Evaluation Scale. *Personality and Social Psychology Bulletin*, 9, 371–375.

Liebowitz, M. R. (1987) Social phobia. *Modern Problems in Pharmacopsychiatry*, 22, 141–173.

Mattick, R. P. and Clarke, J. C. (1998) Development and validation of measures of social phobia scrutiny fear and social interaction anxiety. *Behaviour Research and Therapy*, 36, 455–470.

Mattick, R. P. and Peters, L. (1988) Treatment of severe social phobia: Effects of guided exposure with and without cognitive restructuring. *Journal of Consulting and Clinical Psychology*, 56, 251–260.

Mattick, R. P., Peters, L. and Clarke, J. C. (1989) Exposure and cognitive restructuring for social phobia: A controlled study. *Behaviour Therapy*, 20, 3–23.

McManus, F. (2004) Assessment of anxiety. *Psychiatry*, 4, 16–21.

Reich, J., Goldenberg, I., Vasile, R., Goisman, R. and Keller, M. (1994) A prospective follow-along study of the course of social phobia. *Psychiatry Research*, 54, 249–258.

Salkovskis, P. M. (1991) The importance of behaviour in the maintenance of anxiety and panic: A cognitive account. *Behavioural Psychotherapy*, 19, 6–19.

Schneier, F. R., Johnson, J., Hornig, C. D., Leibowitz, M. R. and Weissman, M. M. (1992) Social phobia: Comorbidity and morbidity in an epidemiological sample. *Archives of General Psychiatry*, 49, 282–288.

Skre, I., Onstand, S., Torgersen, S. and Kringlen, E. (1991) High inter-rater reliability for the Structured Clinical Interview for DSM-III-R Axis I (SCID-I). *Acta Psychiatrica Scandinavica*, 84, 167–173.

Taylor, S., Woody, S., McLean, P. D. and Koch, W. J. (1997) Sensitivity of outcome measures for treatments of generalised social phobia. *Assessment*, 4, 181–191.

Turner, S. M., Beidel, D. C., Dancu, C. V. and Keys, D. J. (1986) Psychopathology of social phobia and comparison to avoidant personality disorder. *Journal of Abnormal Psychology*, 95, 389–394.

Turner, S. M., Beidel, D. C., Dancu, C. V. and Stanley, M. A. (1989) An empirically derived inventory to measure social fears and anxiety: The Social Phobia and Anxiety Inventory. *Psychological Assessment*, 1, 35–40.

Ventura, J., Liberman, R. P., Green, M. F., Shaner, A. and Mintz, J. (1998) Training and quality assurance with the Structured Clinical Interview for DSM-IV (SCID-I/P). *Psychiatry Research*, 79, 163–173.

Watson, J. and Friend, R. (1969) Measurement of social evaluative anxiety. *Journal of Consulting and Clinical Psychology*, 33, 448–457.

Wells, A. (1997) *Cognitive Therapy of Anxiety Disorders: A Practice Manual and Conceptual Guide*. Chichester: John Wiley.

Widiger, T. A. (1992) Generalised social phobia versus avoidant personality disorder: A commentary on three studies. *Journal of Abnormal Psychology*, 101, 340–343

Chapter 12

Social phobia

Treatment

Colette Hirsch and Freda McManus

BACKGROUND

Traditionally, psychological treatments of social phobia have had statistically significant but clinically limited effects (Taylor, 1996). In line with developments in the treatment of anxiety generally, recent research into the treatment of social phobia has concentrated on the development of cognitive behavioural treatments with promising results. Several different forms of cognitive behaviour therapy for social phobia have been developed (e.g. Heimberg et al., 1998). Due to space limitations, the current chapter describes only the form of cognitive therapy for social phobia that has arisen from Clark and Wells' (1995) cognitive model of social phobia.

Clark and Wells and their colleagues have developed and refined a 14-session treatment for social phobia that has been demonstrated to be effective in three randomised controlled trials. In the first trial, Clark et al., (2003) compared cognitive therapy alone with: (1) a selective serotonin re-uptake inhibitor (fluoxetine) plus self-exposure instructions; and (2) placebo medication plus self-exposure instructions. All three treatments were associated with significant improvements, but cognitive therapy was associated with a greater treatment gain than the other interventions. In the second trial, Stangier et al. (2003) compared individual cognitive therapy with group cognitive therapy and a waiting-list control condition. Both versions of cognitive therapy were superior to the waiting list. On a number of measures, the individual treatment was superior to the group treatment. In a third trial Clark et al. (2006) demonstrated that individual cognitive therapy was superior to exposure with applied relaxation, and that both treatments were superior to a waiting-list control. This chapter outlines individual treatment for social phobia.

AIMS AND SEQUENCING OF THERAPY

The aim of this form of cognitive therapy for social phobia is to reverse the hypothesised maintaining processes in Clark and Wells' (1995) cognitive model of social phobia that is outlined in Chapter 11. Typically, this is done in a certain order. During the assessment, or first session, the therapist and client will collaboratively draw out an idiosyncratic version of the cognitive model that relates to this individual's social anxiety (see Chapter 11 for how this is done). This begins to socialise the client into the idea that certain processes, such as beliefs, are involved in the maintenance of his or her anxiety. One of the first stages in treatment is to demonstrate the unhelpful effects of using safety behaviours and self-focused attention (see the section Self-focused attention and safety behaviours experiment, below). This usually has the effect of demonstrating that using safety behaviours and self-focusing makes the person feel more anxious and come across less well. Understanding the detrimental role of safety behaviours, clients are able to reduce their use of safety behaviours, which helps them to discover that they can change things to help themselves feel better in social situations. It is important to tackle the use of safety behaviours and avoidance early on in treatment, as otherwise they will prevent belief change from occurring (because, when feared outcomes do not occur, clients often erroneously attribute this to the use of safety behaviours or avoidance).

Video feedback from the self-focused attention and safety behaviours experiment is then used to demonstrate several important points (such as that clients do not come across as badly as they think they do) that help clients feel able to move on the next stage of therapy, which involves testing out their social fears referred to as feared predictions. When working on testing-out feared predictions we have found it helpful to follow the rough order of:

1   Establishing whether the feared symptoms occur as frequently/severely as the client is predicting.
2   When the feared symptom does occur, establishing whether it is as noticeable/visible as the client predicts.
3   When the feared symptom does occur and is visible, establishing whether it is as noticed by others as the client predicts.
4   When the feared symptom does occur, and is visible, and is noticed by others, establishing whether they evaluate it as negatively as the client predicts.

Before therapy ends, it is important that the client has tested out the consequences at all four of these levels. For example, it is not satisfactory for clients to end treatment being convinced that they do not blush as often as they think and people don't notice blushing as much as the client thinks, without the client also knowing what would happen if someone did notice. In this case we would hypothesise that the client may still have catastrophic beliefs relating to what would happen if someone did notice his or her blushing, and thus would be vulnerable to relapse. Hence, in the later stages of treatment the client is encouraged to 'widen the bandwidth of acceptable behaviour' and carry out experiments to discover what would happen in the 'worst case scenario'. Whilst working on testing out the client's specific feared predictions, it is important that the role of cognitive processes that contribute to the maintenance of social anxiety, such as self-focused attention and pre- and post-event processing, is not neglected. Interventions aimed at changing these processes are outlined below. Finally, in the middle and later stages of treatment clients are also encouraged to work on constructing a 'veridical self image' (i.e. a more realistic and less negative image of how they come across to others).

SPECIFIC INTERVENTIONS

Self-focus attention and safety behaviours experiment

After a shared conceptualisation has been derived (see Chapter 11), the next task in therapy is the safety behaviours and self-focused attention experiment. As outlined above, it is thought that both self-focused attention and the use of safety behaviours contribute to the maintenance of social anxiety. To explore the effects of safety behaviours and self-focused attention, the client is asked to take part in two social interactions during the session. Collaboratively, the client and therapist identify a social situation that would elicit a moderate level of anxiety for the client, and that he or she would be prepared to enter into during the session. This typically involves a conversation with someone he or she has not met before, who is a colleague of the therapist (a stooge), but if this is not anxiety provoking enough, then the task could involve taking part in a group discussion, or giving a short speech. Alternatively, if speaking with a stranger seems too anxiety provoking, then it could simply be having a conversation with the therapist. It is important that this social situation is videotaped for later video feedback.

Once a relevant situation has been identified, the therapist elicits the client's feared predictions by asking what he or she is worried could go wrong in this situation, what is the absolute worst that could happen, and what it would mean if those things did happen. For example, Josh, described in Chapter 11, fears that when he speaks to people in authority he will blush and they will think he is weak. The situation he took part in for the experiment was having a conversation with someone in authority (in this case a professor in the department). The therapist identified that Josh was predicting 'I will blush', 'I will have nothing to say', 'she will think I'm weak'. The client is asked to rate each of his or her feared predictions on a 0–100 scale. The anchors on the scale can be modified to suit the particular belief, for example, they may reflect how often something will happen (0 'none of the time' to 100 'all of the time') or how severe it will be if it does happen (e.g. 0 'not weak at all' to 100 'completely weak all the time'; 0 'not blushing at all' to 100 'as red as a tomato'). The therapist then identifies the client's safety behaviours by asking what he or she does to prevent the feared predictions from happening, or from being noticed by others or from being evaluated negatively by others. For Josh, these included putting his hand over his face (to hide his blush), rehearsing in his mind what he is about to say before he says it (to check he has something to say) and monitoring how he is coming across.

Once all the safety behaviours have been identified, the client is asked to engage in the social situation for a few minutes. In this first interaction, the client is asked to do his or her safety behaviours and monitor how they are coming across as much as possible. To facilitate comparison of the two interactions, the client is asked to rate the extent to which he or she engaged in safety behaviours, how anxious he or she felt, how anxious he or she thinks he or she looked and the extent to which the feared catastrophes occurred (from 0 'not at all' to 100 'totally'). The client is also asked to rate how well he or she performed (from 0 'not at all well' to 100 'extremely well'). The client also rates the extent to which his or her attention is focused externally (i.e. on the situation or other people), or internally (i.e. on him- or herself). This can be assessed on a −3 'totally self-focused' to +3 'totally externally focused' scale.

After making the ratings, the client is asked to repeat the interaction but this time to try not to engage in any safety behaviours and to focus his or her attention externally, on the situation and other people, and away from him- or herself. This instruction is intended to help the client switch off the self-focused attention and monitoring. The client is asked to become absorbed in the conversation and not to think about what he or she is saying or how he or she is coming across. The aim is to get clients to just let themselves come across as they would naturally. It is often necessary to practise dropping safety behaviours and self-focus with the therapist before trying to do it during the social interaction with the stooge. Once they have practised dropping their safety behaviours and self-focus, clients then engage in a second social interaction with the stooge and make ratings as before (without referring back to their earlier ratings).

Sometimes, clients believe that the second interaction was better just because they had met the person/people before. If there is any suggestion that they have thought this, then ask them to engage in a third interaction, this time using their safety behaviours again and make ratings as before, so that they can see that it is not merely a practice effect. Another problem that may occur is that even with practice sometimes clients are unable to drop their safety behaviours in the second interaction. If this happens, then clients are asked to engage in a third interaction, and this time do their safety behaviours as much as possible. Ratings from the third interaction (where they used their safety behaviours and self-focus a lot) can then be compared to the second inter-action (where the safety behaviours and self-focus will be used relatively less). This will enable clients to see what effect using safety behaviours and self-focus excessively has on how they feel and how they believe that they come across.

When the final interaction has been completed and ratings taken, the client and therapist review the client's ratings of the different interactions. This can lead to useful insights. Often, the feared predictions do not happen as much as clients expected. Furthermore, clients learn that they feel less anxious, and their feared predictions happen less, when they do not use safety behaviours and self-focus. From this they can conclude that they do not need to use safety behaviours to prevent feared predictions from happening, and that they feel less anxious and come across better when they are focusing externally and not using safety behaviours. These conclusions can be further developed by seeking feedback from the conversation partner or 'stooge'.

After the final conversation with the client, the stooge is asked to complete a feedback sheet for each of the interactions. The stooge is asked to complete the feedback sheet as if they had met the person in a non-therapy context. To avoid orienting the stooge to the client's concerns, it is best to have an open-ended question on the first side of the piece of paper, such as 'What did you think of Josh?' and then more specific questions relating to the clients concerns on the other side, e.g. 'Did you notice that Josh was anxious? If so, how anxious (0–100)?', 'If you did notice that he was anxious, what did you make of it?', 'How much did he blush (0–100)?', 'What did you make of him blushing?', 'Did you think that Josh was weak? If so, how weak (0–100)?'

Examining the stooge feedback enables clients to learn about how they come across to other people and how others view any signs of anxiety that were actually exhibited. This provides clients with the insight that, even if they believed a feared prediction occurred to some extent, that it was not noticed as much (if at all) by the stooge and that the stooge did not judge the client negatively. They will also learn that other people do not base their view of the client on the same concepts as the client had expected (e.g. if the stooge noticed any blushing, it was not the only piece of information he or she used to form their opinion of the client). This is where questions enquiring about what the stooge noticed and, if any anxiety symptoms were noticed, what he or she made of them, can be very helpful.

The conclusions from this experiment lead into the homework of practis-ing focusing externally and not using safety behaviours in social situations. This exercise encourages clients to process what is really going on in the social situation, rather than judging it from their own impressions, which are usu-ally based on their anxious feelings. Usually, the feedback from the stooge will have been a pleasant surprise for the clients and this can be presented as a rationale for attending to the environment to determine how others are responding to them. This will enable them to get more objective feedback on whether or not their social fears are being realised. They may also realise that focusing on themselves has the effect of them not being able to fully engage in the conversation, and this in turn can have adverse consequences for how they come across.

A typical homework exercise might be to practise shifting attention onto different stimuli (see Wells & Papageourgiou, 2001, for more details). This is first practised in non-social situations so that clients can master the skill before having to use it in difficult social interactions. This might involve listening to music and focusing in on a particular instrument, letting each sound fill their attention for a while before moving onto the next instrument. Alternatively, practice can involve listening to the sounds in the close environment (e.g. the room), the near environment (e.g. the rest of the house) and in the more distant environment (e.g. outside). Clients are then asked to attend to different modalities (visual, tactile, etc.) and to practise switching their attention between them. Clients may also find it helpful to practise switching their attention between self-focus and external focus in non-social situations. Once they are able to do this, they can begin to apply this to social situations, where they are encouraged to shift from their natural tendency to focus on themselves to a more external focus of attention, particularly in the context of anxiety-provoking social interactions. Clients who find this difficult can work towards focusing on the social situation by initially focusing their attention on aspects of the immediate environment (e.g. the physical surroundings) and then shifting their attention onto the conversation and the people involved in it. Even once clients have managed to be able to direct their attention to the social situation they often find that their attention shifts back internally, especially when they become anxious. Hence, clients should be encouraged to make efforts to focus externally every time they find that their focus of attention has come back to themselves.

A second homework exercise arising from the self-focused attention and safety behaviours exercise is to ask clients to refrain from using safety behaviours in social situations. Usually, clients will have concluded from the experiment that using safety behaviours makes them feel more anxious in the situation, increases self-focus and does not enhance (and may even detract from) their social performance. Thus, dropping safety behaviours is one thing that clients can do that will have an immediate effect of reducing their anxiety in social situations. It is important that clients are encouraged to drop all safety behaviours, as even if only one or two remain this can undermine belief change. For example, if Josh entered a difficult social situation and did not blush he may attribute this to the use of safety behaviours such as avoiding talking to people in authority and wearing cool clothing. Hence, it is important that he engages in such situations without using any safety behaviours, and focuses on how others are responding to him, so he can conclude that either he didn't blush, or if he did blush, that the response from others was not as negative as he feared.

Video feedback

Video feedback is an extremely useful tool for achieving belief change and to help clients develop a more realistic image of how they come across. It is normally carried out several times in the course of treatment, the first time usually being during the session after the safety behaviours and self-focus experiment. As discussed in Chapter 11, individuals with social phobia have an overly negative impression of how they are coming across in social situations and they often generate images of themselves performing poorly when in social situations. This negative imagery has a detrimental impact and video feedback is a potentially powerful way to help clients to discover that their self-images are overly negative.

Prior to video feedback, clients are asked to recall the social interactions that they engaged in during the safety behaviours and self-focus attention experiment. They are asked to think about each interaction in turn and to picture how they came across. The therapist reminds the clients of what they feared would go wrong in anticipation of entering the situation (i.e. feared predictions) and what they thought had gone badly after the interactions. Clients are asked to visualise and describe in detail how they came across in each interaction and rate the extent to which each of their feared predictions occurred. It is important that the therapist also asks clients whether any new concerns about their performance have arisen since the last session. All possible fears should be rated on an appropriate scale (e.g. how anxious the client was from 0 to 100, how red they went from 0 to 100, how much their hands were shaking from 0 to 100). Next, clients watch the video recording of the interactions. They are asked to watch the videotape as though they were watching a stranger, paying particular attention to what is actually evident on the videotape, rather than on how they were feeling at the time. Referring to the person on videotape in the third person can enhance this. After watching each interaction, clients are asked to re-rate how anxious they looked, how well they came across (their overall performance) and the extent to which each of their feared predictions was evident on the videotape. The next stage is for therapist and client to compare the ratings of what the client predicted would be seen with what was actually was apparent on the videotape. In this way clients learn that, however anxious they felt in a social situation, they do not appear as anxious as they predicted or perform as poorly as they felt they did. By contrasting ratings from the safety behaviour and self-focus interaction with the ratings from the no safety behaviours and external-focus interaction, clients can also see that they do not benefit from focusing on themselves or using safety behaviours. Furthermore, if clients think that they came across poorly in the safety behaviours and self-focus interaction, then it can be pointed out that this was because they were using a deliberate strategy (safety behaviours and self-focus). Given that clients choose to engage in safety behaviours, it can be pointed out that they can learn to not use such strategies, and this will improve their social performance and reduce their social anxiety. Video feedback also emphasises the fact that they should not base their judgements of how they come across on how they feel, their negative image or other internal information, because this leads to an overly negative impression of how they come across. By contrast, clients benefit from attending to the environment and not using safety behaviours because this provides them with more objective information about whether their social fears occur and the impact they have on others.

Therapists who have not used video feedback before may be reluctant to show clients the video of their interactions because, in the therapist's opinion, the client did appear anxious or came across badly. In our experience it is still better to show the client the video because clients tend to have an even more negative impression of how they came across than can be seen on the video and so they will still discover that they did not come across as badly as they felt they did. Furthermore, if clients do come across badly, this is often due to the use of safety behaviours impairing their performance. For example, one client was so concerned about generating interesting and intelligent things to say that he became completely tongue-tied and was unable to say almost anything in the whole interaction. After viewing the video he was able to conclude that his safety behaviour was impairing his performance and he noticed that the things other people said were not always interesting and intelligent, but that nobody seemed to mind. He concluded that he was more likely to be able to make an interesting contribution to conversations if he changed strategy and focused on the conversation and just said whatever came into his head.

In cases where aspects of a client's anxiety or social performance are likely to be observed by others and evaluated negatively, there is little point in saving the client from seeing this on the video, as he or she will be getting feedback from the real world indicating this anyway. For example, there is no point in the therapist trying to convince patients that they do not blush visibly if their blushing is so obvious that it is likely to elicit comments from others. Such an experience would undermine the client's trust in the therapist. We have found it much more effective to work on whether the blushing is as bad as the client perceives it to be, whether it is as noticeable as the client perceives it to be and whether others are evaluating it as negatively as the client believes.

Another potential problem in using video feedback effectively is when clients are unable to separate how they felt in the situation from what they see on the video. In this instance, client and therapist will disagree about what can be seen on the video – the client will view the video much more negatively than the therapist. To resolve this discrepancy the therapist can ask clients how they could find out what 'the average person' (or the people whose evaluation the client is most concerned about) would think if they viewed the video. This next step is to get a group of the target audience to view the video and give feedback to the client. For example:

Annalise was convinced that her hands were shaking very visibly when she watched the video of her interactions. The therapist could not see her hands shaking at all on the video. When this difference of opinion was discussed, it became clear that Annalise felt that the therapist could not see the shaking because she was a nice person who was trained not to be critical of others. Annalise felt that her peers would be much more critical and would notice the shaking and view it negatively. The result of this discussion was to carry out an experiment in which a group of Annalise's peers viewed the video and rated how much she was shaking and what they made of it. Annalise was surprised to discover that none of the other people who saw the video noticed any shaking. This helped her to realise that she was still processing her feelings rather than what was actually visible to other people.

It can be useful for clients to watch the videotape repeatedly for homework. It is important that they watch it objectively, as if watching a stranger. This helps them develop a more realistic image of themselves in social situations. Another clinically useful technique involves asking clients to recall and hold in mind the realistic image of themselves (i.e. what they saw on videotape) when they are in subsequent social situations, because this more accurate 'video image' can counteract the aversive impact of the negative image that they will have been generating repeatedly for many years.

Usually in therapy for social anxiety, video feedback would be carried out a number of times, in different situations. Hence, it is useful to video all behavioural experiments. Indeed, it is useful to video all treatment sessions as things may come up unexpectedly (e.g. a severe episode of the feared symptom) that can be useful to review in video feedback.

Behavioural experiments

The main purpose of behavioural experiments in cognitive therapy for social phobia is to test the validity of clients' social fears. This will involve clients going into a range of social situations that they find anxiety provoking to find out whether their feared catastrophes do indeed occur. To discover whether their feared catastrophes happen, clients will need to focus on the social situation and refrain from using safety behaviours. To gain the most from behavioural experiments, it is important that they are well thought through and set up carefully using a behavioural experiment record sheet (Figure 12.1). This provides a structure for clients to learn to set up behavioural experiments themselves in order to systematically test out their predictions in social situations. Having patients keep a file of the completed experiment

Date	Situation	Prediction	Experiment	Outcome	What I learned
		What do you think will happen? How much do you believe it will, 0–100? How would you know if it had?	What can you do to test the prediction?	What actually happened? Was the prediction correct?	Is there a more balanced view? How much do you believe your first prediction will happen in future, 0–100?
2/11	At a team meeting with my boss	I will go bright red 100% I will not have anything to say 80% My mind will go blank 60% They will think I am weak 80% They will make critical comments 60%	Ask a question at the meeting and do not use my safety behaviours. Try to get interested in the meeting and absorbed in it so that I can gather more information about how others respond	I went bright red 20% I did not have anything to say 0% My mind went blank 0% They thought I am weak 20% They made critical comments 0%	My feared predictions did not occur nearly as much as I predicted and although people might have thought my question was not very good they did not seem bothered by it and did not seem to view me negatively. I need to do more behavioural experiments to test this out within a public speaking situation

Figure 12.1 Behavioural experiment record sheet.

sheets also provides them with a good source of information to challenge any tendency to dismiss positive outcomes of experiments as being chance occurrences.

An example, the behavioural experiment record sheet shown in Figure 12.1 has been completed in relation to an experiment that Josh carried out. The date is entered in the first column and a brief description of the situation in the second column. In the third column the client makes predictions about what he or she thinks will happen in the social interaction. These predictions need to be as specific as possible (e.g. 'I will go red', 'I will sweat', 'People will laugh at me'). Often, clients generate predictions in the form of questions, e.g. 'What if they think I am weak?'. When this happens, the question needs to be changed into a prediction that can be tested. In this example, the prediction would be 'They will think I am weak'. If the predictions involve judgements by others, then it is important to identify how they will be able to tell if that judgement has been made. In this example, if the prediction is that others will find him weak, the client needs to operationalise how he could tell if others found him weak, and what percentage of people will find him weak (e.g. that 70% of people will find him weak and will show this by making critical comments). It is important that clients make specific predictions in advance since otherwise their fears may appear to be confirmed by the experiment. For example, Annalise thought that she could tell if people had noticed her shaking by the fact that they looked at her. This non-specific prediction (people looking at her) undermined the effects of behavioural experiments because in any situation, sooner or later, someone would look at her. In order to fully test out her fears, Annalise needed to compare whether people looked at her *more often* than they looked at someone else. Hence, the therapist helped her to carry out a series of experiments in which they compared how often people looked at Annalise with how often they looked at the therapist. She concluded that people did not look at her any more often than they looked at the therapist and hence their looking at her was unlikely to be a sign that they had noticed her shaking. Thus it is important to make the predictions as specific as possible and to rate them on the appropriate '0 to 100' scale.

The next column specifies the 'experiment' column. This is where clients summarise what they plan to do in the social situation in order to test out their feared predictions. Behavioural experiments often involve clients entering a feared social situation and not using their safety behaviours but instead focusing externally to gather information about other peoples' reactions to them. Hence, a summary of this experiment is to 'Ask a question at the meeting and do not use my safety behaviours. Try to get interested in the meeting and absorbed in it so that I can gather more information about how others respond'. As therapy progresses and clients learn that they come across better then they thought, and that if they do exhibit symptoms or perform poorly then this is not judged negatively by others, they will be more willing to go into the situations that are most likely to bring on their anxiety symptoms. These situations give the client the opportunity to focus on the situation, not use safety behaviours, and gather information about other people's reactions to them while exhibiting the feared symptom or behaviour. In later experiments the behavioural experiment record sheet can be used to test out what happens if clients deliberately exhibit a symptom of anxiety to a greater extent than they would normally (see the section Widening the bandwidth, below). After the experiment has been set up, the behavioural experiment record sheet is put to one side until the experiment has been undertaken. At this point, the remaining columns of the sheet are completed.

In the next column, clients rate whether each of the feared predictions identified in column 3 did actually happen, from 0 'not at all' to 100 'totally'. In the final column clients summarise what they have learnt from the experiment, including any conclusions drawn from the comparison of predicted and actual outcomes. It is useful to get clients to give as much detail as possible about the effect of dropping safety behaviours, the way others behaved and what the client made of that. They can also write down how they could build on the experiment, and the extent to which they believe their feared predictions will happen in the future. If clients have any remaining belief that their feared predictions will occur in future social situations then it is important to explore their evidence for this, and to set up further behavioural experiments to test this out. For example, Josh carried out another behavioural experiment to see if a member of the management team would notice his blushing in a 5-minute conversation. Even though she did not show any signs of noticing his blushing, Josh's belief that people would notice his blushing in future social situations only reduced from 50% to 30%. When asked about this remaining 30%, Josh explained that although he was confident that this person had not noticed his blushing, he was not sure that the same would be true for other people in authority because: (1) they might be more observant than this woman was; and (2) he may blush more severely. When asked what he needed to do to be confident that people would not notice his blushing, Josh decided that he needed to repeat the experiment with other people in authority and in front of an audience (as this would make him blush).

As therapy progresses, clients are encouraged to set up and carry out behavioural experiments for homework, reviewing the outcome and setting up further experiments with the therapist in session. Ideally, clients will carry out at least one behavioural experiment a day, recording the outcome on a behavioural experiment record sheet as soon as possible after they leave the situation. If it is not possible to carry the behavioural experiment sheets with them, then they can fill it in at the end of the day, but it is better to do it as soon as possible after the experiment because they will remember more information immediately after the situation and this will minimise any adverse effects of post-event processing (see below). A further useful source for information on behavioural experiments in cognitive therapy is Bennett-Levy et al. (2004).

Sometimes, clients will find themselves unexpectedly in anxiety-provoking situations that have not been set up as a behavioural experiment beforehand. In this situation it can be useful for them to have a default experiment to do. For example, they could be asked to drop their safety behaviours, focus on the social situation and get data about how other people respond to them. In this way clients can still have a basic experimental aim to carry out in any social situation that they find anxiety provoking. This can also facilitate a reduction in avoidance by making all situations where the client has social fears such as 'I will blush' as a trigger for a behavioural experiment. This can be encapsulated into the idea that every time they have the thought 'I won't speak up', then 'I won't do that', will become a trigger for them to do an experiment. Similarly, clients may report situations that were not experiments but which provided useful information in relation to their feared predictions. For these unplanned experiments, a behavioural experiment record sheet written retrospectively can be a very useful way of reflecting on what they have learnt, its impacts on their beliefs and how best to take the issue forward.

As therapy progresses, clients will have collected a number of completed behavioural experiment record sheets. It is useful for clients to go through them and summarise what they have learnt over the course of the experiments. This process consolidates learning and also gives clients a chance to reflect on how many times their predictions were overly negative and realise that their feared predictions were based on how they felt in the social situations, rather than how they actually came across. Furthermore, the weight of evidence can challenge any thought that a given situation went well only by chance.

Surveys

It is helpful for clients to learn that experiencing some amount of social anxiety is the norm rather than the exception, and to learn that even if they did exhibit their feared symptoms or perform poorly, that people would not necessarily interpret this as critically as they fear. This can be done through the use of surveys where other people are asked a series of questions assessing what they think about a person exhibiting a given symptom of anxiety (e.g. blushing), whether their opinion of the person would change in a negative way, and if they would remember noticing the symptom of anxiety in the long term. To do this, the client and therapist construct a survey to address the client's idiosyncratic concerns about their feared symptoms. For Josh, his survey included questions like 'Have you ever blushed?' 'Do you ever notice other people blush?', 'What did you make of that?', 'Did you think they were weak? If so how much (0–100)?', 'Do you remember them blushing a day/month/year later?'. The survey can be carried out by either the client or the therapist, in person via e-mail or audiotaped responses that can be played to the client. It may be necessary to target the survey at a particular population that the client believes will be most likely to respond negatively. The aim is for the client to learn that most people experience anxiety, and that the majority of people do not judge others critically or reject them for showing symptoms of anxiety or performing poorly. Clients should also learn that people do not form their judgements of others solely on the basis of whether they appear anxious or how they perform in social situations. Indeed, people often comment that they like someone more if they show some anxiety because it makes the person seem more human and easy to relate to.

WIDENING THE BANDWIDTH OF ACCEPTABLE BEHAVIOUR

As therapy progresses, clients will learn that they do not exhibit their feared symptoms of anxiety or poor performance to the extent they previously had thought. Furthermore, their symptoms may be less evident as their social anxiety diminishes. It is therapeutically important, however, for clients to learn that even if they did exhibit their anxiety symptoms or perform poorly, this would still not be as catastrophic as they fear. One of the most effective ways of demonstrating this point is for the therapist to model being in a real social situation (e.g. local shops or cafes) whilst exhibiting an exaggerated form of the client's feared symptom (e.g. using cosmetics to make the therapist's face redder than is physically possible to blush). It is important that the symptoms are more evident than the client believes they could actually ever exhibit, because otherwise they will dismiss the experiment by saying 'Yes, but I might go even redder than that'. A behavioural experiment sheet is set up to assess other people's reactions to the therapist when they are exhibiting the exaggerated feared symptom. The client observes others' reactions to the therapist. It is a surprise to the client (and sometimes to the therapist) that people do not seem to notice the exaggerated form of the symptom and, if they do notice, they do not react in a negative way. Then clients repeat this exercise themselves, completing another behavioural experiment record sheet and monitoring others' reactions to them very closely. If the therapist has access to a camcorder this can record others' reactions to the client, so that they can look at it later. This experiment provides data that others either do not notice symptoms that are perfectly visible, or that they do not react critically (if at all) to them. It also enables clients to realise that being in a social situation whilst exhibiting an extreme version of the symptom is tolerable and that they could cope if the worst happened. In another experiment, clients can deliberately draw people's attention to the fact that they are showing symptoms of anxiety. This can be done by the client and therapist talking loudly about the feared symptom in a busy place (e.g. a bus), or by mentioning to people that they are blushing or sweating ('I've got so embarrassed and I can feel myself going red'), or by discussing their social anxiety with people. Again the behavioural experiment record sheet is completed to record whether or not people are interested in the fact that they are blushing, sweating, etc. and, if so, how they respond to it.

Clients may be concerned that they will be unable to cope if someone responds in a hostile way to the client's feared behaviours or symptoms of anxiety. If clients report this concern, then role-playing an assertive response to the criticism can be very helpful. Initially, the client role-plays being the hostile person making critical comments and the therapist takes the role of client responding to these criticisms. Then, in a second role-play, the client practises defending him- or herself from such an onslaught. This helps the client to see that if this unlikely to event were to occur, he or she could cope and it would reflect far more negatively on the other person than on the client.

Looking at numbers

Another useful technique further into therapy is calculating the number of times the feared outcome has actually occurred when clients thought that they were showing anxiety symptoms. This can be calculated by asking clients how many times a day they have had the thought that they are showing their feared symptom (for Annalise this was three) then multiplying this by 365 days (i.e. 1095) and then by the number of years that they have had their fear (in her case 10 years, which means 10,950 times she believed the blush was evident). The client is then asked to think of the number of times someone has commented on the symptom, or seemed to notice it. Typically, this is very rarely and then the client can thus begin to see how the symptom is either not noticed or not deemed to be important most of the time they thought it has been present. The client can then be asked how many times the other person's reaction was negative. For Annalise it was commented on only twice in 10 years and both times it was not negative. So her feared outcome occurred 0 times in the 10,950 times she had believed that she blushed.

Anticipatory processing

Another cognitive process that needs to be addressed in therapy is anticipatory processing. Asking clients to list its costs and benefits enables them to conclude that it is not helpful, as it is not possible to predict and plan for what may go wrong in a social interaction and it increases anxiety. Clients will have learned from earlier behavioural experiments that things usually do not go as badly as they anticipate, demonstrating that they overestimate danger prior to social events. Clients are encouraged to generate behavioural experiments that encapsulate their worries in the form of feared predictions, and then test the validity of the predictions after the event. Once the behavioural experiment has been set up there is no need for clients to engage in any further anticipatory processing. It is acknowledged that thoughts may well come into their mind about impending situations, but once they notice that this has happened, clients are asked to stop anticipatory processing and refocus their attention on the current situation. It may be necessary for clients to remind themselves that anticipatory processing is not useful, and that it is more effective to go into the situation and treat it as a behavioural experiment. If clients continue to have difficulty stopping anticipatory processing, then strategies used in the treatment of worry may be helpful (see Wells, 1997).

Post-event processing

After clients with social phobia leave the anxiety-provoking social situation they often think about how they came across in detail, focusing on any perceived poor performance. To address this, clients should list the advantages and disadvantages of engaging in post-event processing. Then the advantages can be re-examined to determine if there are other ways of finding out this information, without embarking on post-event processing. For example, if clients were externally focused they could gauge how others are responding to them at the time and so would not need to engage in post-event processing to determine what others thought of them. Clients are asked to complete the outcome and conclusion columns of the behavioural experiment record sheet as a way of assessing the situation in a confined time period rather than engaging in lengthy post-event processing. Clients are then encouraged to not engage in post-event processing because it does not help and only makes them feel worse.

Blueprint

Over the course of therapy clients will have accumulated lots of information relating to their social anxiety in the form of behavioural experiment record sheets, surveys, etc. Towards the end of therapy it is useful to get the client to reflect on what they have learnt about their social anxiety and generate a summary in the form of a blueprint. This is a few pages that detail the client's understanding of why the social anxiety developed and what maintained it, information on what the client has learned from behavioural experiments, video feedback and surveys, as well as key challenges to his or her negative thoughts. The blueprint should include a plan of what the client needs to do in the next year to address the social anxiety further, and what to do if he or she has a set back.

CONCLUSIONS

Cognitive therapy for social phobia involves using specific interventions designed to address the cognitive and behavioural processes hypothesised to maintain the disorder. The standard techniques and sequence of therapy have been described above. It is, however, important to remember that there is much variation and co-morbidity amongst clients with social phobia. Hence, treatment within the context of a good therapeutic relationship will be formulation driven and therapists may need to call on techniques from the broader field of cognitive therapy, or from other disciplines to achieve optimal results. For example, for many clients with social phobia their difficulties also relate to low self-esteem, unassertiveness, interpersonal difficulties or perfectionism. For such clients, the individually tailored formulations will the guide the therapist in incorporating additional strands to the treatment to address these issues.

ACKNOWLEDGMENTS

The therapeutic procedures described in this chapter have been developed from the work of the Oxford Anxiety Disorders Group which included David M. Clark, Anke Ehlers, Ann Hackmann, Freda McManus, Melanie Fennell, Adrian Wells and Gillian Butler.

REFERENCES

Bennett-Levy, J., Butler, G., Fennell, M., Hackman, A., Muller, M. and Westbrook, D. (2004) *Oxford Guide to Behavioural Experiments in Cognitive Therapy*. New York: Oxford University Press.

Clark, D. M. and Wells, A. (1995) A cognitive model of social phobia. In: R. G. Heimberg, M. Liebowitz, D. Hope and F. Schneier (eds) *Social Phobia: Diagnosis, Assessment and Treatment* (pp. 69–93). New York: Guilford Press.

Clark, D. M., Ehlers, A., McManus, F., Hackmann, A., Fennell, M., Campbell, H. et al. (2003) Cognitive therapy vs. fluoxetine in generalised social phobia: A randomised control trial. *Journal of Consulting and Clinical Psychology*, 71, 1058–1067.

Clark, D. M., Ehlers, A., Hackman, A., McManus, F., Fennell, M., Grey, N. et al. (2006) Cognitive therapy versus exposure and applied relaxation in social phobia: A randomized, controlled trial. *Journal of Consulting and Clinical Psychology*, 74, 568–578.

Heimberg, R. G., Liebowitz, M. R., Hope, D. A., Schneier, F. R., Holt, C. S., Welkowitz, L. A. et al. (1998) Cognitive behavioral group therapy vs phenelzine therapy for social phobia: 12-week outcome. *Archives of General Psychiatry*, 55, 1133–1141.

Stangier, U., Heidenriech, T., Peitz, M., Lauterbach, W. and Clark, D. M. (2003) Cognitive therapy for social phobia: Individual versus group treatment. *Behaviour Research and Therapy*, 41, 991–1007.

Taylor, S. (1996) Meta-analysis of cognitive-behavioral treatment for social phobia. *Journal of Behavior Therapy and Experimental Psychiatry*, 27, 1–9.

Wells, A. (1997) *Cognitive Therapy of Anxiety Disorders: A Practice Manual and Conceptual Guide*. Chichester: John Wiley.

Wells, A. and Papageourgiou, C. (2001) Brief cognitive therapy for social phobia: A case series. *Behaviour Research and Therapy*, 39, 713–720.

Chapter 13

Panic disorders

Investigation

Stan Lindsay

THE SYMPTOMS OF PANIC DISORDERS

The *Diagnostic and Statistical Manual of Mental Disorders*, 4th edition (DSM-IV; American Psychiatric Association (APA), 2000) lists symptoms that can occur in panic attacks. These 'include' in descending frequency of their occurrence as reported by subjects (Rapee et al., 1990), the following: palpitations (a trembling or fluttering sensation in the chest or throat), fear of losing control, feeling dizzy or unsteady or light-headed or faint, trembling or shaking, sweating, shortness of breath or feelings of suffocation, discomfort or pain in the chest, de-personalisation or de-realisation, chills or hot flushes, a fear of dying, paraesthesias (numbness, pins and needles or tingling sensations in the extremities), nausea or abdominal discomfort and choking. Other symptoms can include a feeling of losing control of one's bowels and going crazy. To define a panic attack according to DSM-IV, at least four of these symptoms must occur and reach a peak within 10 minutes.

According to the DSM-IV, panic disorder is diagnosed if the panics are unexpected, i.e. come out of the blue with no evident precipitant, internal or external. These are followed by a continual fear of having more panic attacks or fear of the significance of a panic such as a threat to one's life or mental health. Panic disorder may also include a substantial alteration to one's life such, as frequent visits to the doctor or hospital for re-assurance or calling for an ambulance. Panic disorder is diagnosed if the panics are not caused by substances, such as caffeine, or a medical problem, such as mitral valve prolapse.

Agoraphobia, which often accompanies panic disorder, occurs when a person is intensely afraid of, and may avoid, places from which escape to safety is difficult. These situations may include open parkland, underground trains, crowded supermarkets or sitting in a hairdresser's or dentist's chair. Hallam and Haffner (1978), in a factor analysis, included fear of enclosed spaces in the same category as agoraphobia. Thus claustrophobia is often associated with agoraphobia.

Because people with panic disorder can be afraid of many bodily sensations, other symptoms may provoke fear even though they are not considered as typical (APA, 2000) of a panic. For example, an elderly lady with a long history of generalised anxiety had been treated for several years with trifluoperazine, a major tranquilliser more frequently used for treating psychosis. Following the death of her husband, she developed nocturnal and diurnal panics with agoraphobia. In her panic attacks she experienced dizziness, shakiness and hot and cold flushes. She also was afraid of burning sensations on her skin at these times and more continually. The latter were attributed by her doctor to her anxiety. However, a literature review suggested that these were early symptoms of Parkinson's disease, of which she showed other signs, such as stiffness of gait; these had been attributed to rheumatism. However, within a year, a diagnosis of Parkinson's disease, possibly the result of prolonged treatment with neuroleptics, had been confirmed. This illustrates the care that is needed to avoid attributing all feared symptoms in panics to panic disorders. It also emphasises the need for careful medical screening of subjects who present panic symptoms.

Several medical conditions (Taylor, 2000) – hyperthyroidism, cardiovascular disorders, seizure disorders, asthma, vestibular disorders, mitral valve prolapse and illnesses such as phaechromocytoma affecting the endocrine systems – can all produce or contribute to some of the symptoms of panic attacks. Moreover, clients who have illnesses such as ventricular fibrillation, leading to fast, irregular heart beats, can develop a panic disorder because of fear. The DSM-IV definitions of panic disorder and agoraphobia have been applied for all the research studies quoted in this review and in Chapter 14. However, patients can present with less than four symptoms, lasting for less than 10 minutes, which can create much alarm for them. The level of distress and disability may warrant treatment.

Panic attacks are to be found not only in panic disorder and agoraphobia. They occur in most fears, including social phobia, and in specific fears, as of spiders and medical and dental treatment. In agreement with Barlow et al. (1985), who examined very small samples of subjects, Starcevit and Bogojevic (1997) estimated that over 65% of people with other fears experienced panic attacks. However, it is the significance of panic to the subjects that is probably most important in distinguishing among these different fears. Panics can be sources of embarrassment to those with social phobia but they can be signs of serious illness to those with panic disorder. This, and Chapter 14, will discuss only panic disorder and agoraphobia.

SAFETY BEHAVIOURS AND SAFETY SIGNALS

Many people learn to identify ways of preventing and coping with panic attacks. For agoraphobics, these include avoidance of open spaces and public places, but they can also include more ingenious activities that can only be observed when they are exposed to situations that alarm them. These include holding on to a trusted companion or taking a route that passes hospitals, cab ranks, medical clinics and pharmacists. One agoraphobic lady, in addition to consuming tranquillisers before going to an unfamiliar destination, had bought a house close to a hospital. When she felt that a panic attack was imminent, she went for a walk down the main hospital corridor. Other safety behaviours include taking a cab instead of walking, calling for an ambulance when a panic attack occurs, doing deep breathing and relaxation exercises and insisting on complete medical investigations. All such behaviours need to be noted and dealt with if treatment is to be completely successful.

PREVALENCE OF PANIC DISORDERS AND ACCESS TO TREATMENT

Panic disorder with or without agoraphobia can be found at any given time in 4–7% of the population. Up to 35% of students have had at least one panic attack in the previous year (Norton et al., 1992). Taylor (2000; quoting Rice and Miller, 1993), notes that anxiety disorders, among which panic is common, account for 32% of the economic costs of psychiatric disorders. That is more than for schizophrenia and mood disorders in the USA. Furthermore, panic disorders account for more cost than other anxiety disorders such as social phobia.

However, although panic disorders account for a large proportion of visits to emergency departments in hospital (Goodwin and Anderson, 2002; Weisman, 1991) only a minority of people with panic disorder do seek professional help (Goodman and Anderson, 2002). Being married, handicapped by agoraphobia or being dependent on alcohol or other substances predicts the seeking of treatment (Goodwin and Anderson, 2002) according to multivariate analysis. Univariate analysis, however, showed that being female, having a higher education and being Caucasian favoured access to professional help for panic disorders (Goodwin and Anderson, 2002).

NOCTURNAL PANICS AND RELAXATION-INDUCED PANICS

Between 18 and 45% of people with panic disorder suffer from panic attacks at night while in bed (Craske el al., 2002). That is, just before sleeping or as they wake in mid-sleep they experience panic attacks. That is probably not surprising because several times during sleep normal subjects awaken briefly. Moreover, around those times subjects have been dreaming, as shown by their rapid eye movements. Furthermore, muscle atonia occurs then so that body movement is curtailed. Waking from a dream under these conditions could be alarming. In addition, in the state between light sleep and waking it can be difficult to distinguish between dreaming and reality and so hypnagogic imagery can be vivid and frightening. On the other hand, in a state of maximum relaxation, as occurs in sleep, it would be expected that with physical activity at very low levels, symptoms of panic would occur only in those people who are especially tense and vigilant, those with a severe form of panic disorder.

However, Craske et al. (2002) found no evidence that people who endure nocturnal panics have a more severe panic disorder than those who do not. Nor was there any evidence that they differed in sleep mentation. However, there was no report in the study of the frequency of nocturnal panic attacks during the period of the study. Hence it is not clear if those possible influences on nocturnal panic were adequately addressed.

Schredl et al. (2001) did find a moderate correlation in panic disorder patients between the frequency of nightmares and the number of panic attacks at night. There was no significant correlation with dreaming. It would be tempting to conclude that nightmares caused the panics. However, it is possible that panics occurred and contributed to the nightmares in a manner similar to the incorporation of exteroceptive stimuli in dreams. Because nightmares occur in rapid eye movement sleep (Kahn et al., 1991) and because brief awakenings can occur during light sleep at that time, both those explanations are plausible,

In an earlier study, Craske and colleagues (2001) compared nocturnal panickers with normal controls and people who had only daytime panics. They underwent voluntary hyperventilation, 'meditative relaxation' and a task in which they had to count their heartbeats. Only during relaxation did the nocturnal panickers experience more anxiety and more symptoms than the group who reported only daytime panics. The authors concluded that people with nocturnal panics have a need to be continuously vigilant. Relaxation can reduce vigilance even to the extent of promoting sleep and so nocturnal panickers become distressed. This is consistent with earlier studies which have shown that some people become – paradoxically – more anxious and aroused during progressive muscular relaxation, a procedure designed to make them less nervous (Heide and Borkovec, 1983, 1984; Knott et al., 1997). Therefore, treatment is directed at relaxation – induced anxiety may reduce the distress produced by nocturnal panics. Because relaxation has played a part in the treatment of panic disorders (see Chapter 14), it would be appropriate to assess subjects' tolerance of muscular relaxation before, if it is to be used in therapy.

HOW DANGEROUS ARE PANIC ATTACKS AND PANIC DISORDERS?

Many people believe that they could die of a cardiac arrest or a stroke during panics. They can also believe that panics are signs of serious illness, such as a brain tumour. Furthermore, some believe that panics could have a cumulative damaging effect and so could hasten their deaths. Nevertheless, they are always reassured that panics are harmless. However, two longitudinal prospective studies may challenge this. Haines et al. (1987) examined a sample of adults drawn from the adult population and found that those who had acknowledged phobias in response to the Crown–Crisp screening questionnaire were more likely to have major cardiovascular disease and die from that in the following 6 years. The authors had made allowance for risk factors, notably smoking and obesity. They believed that hyperventilation, which can occur in panic disorders and which can cause transient reduction in blood flow in the coronary arteries of the heart, may have been the crucial factor. However, their screening instrument is now little used and has been superceded by other measures. Bowen et al. (2000), using DSM diagnostic criteria for anxiety disorders, found a higher risk of subsequent cardiovascular disease in a sample of 15-year-olds followed over 10 years. These authors did not take account of other risk factors but their anxious subjects would have been more likely to smoke (Bergen and Caporaso, 1999), and so would be at greater risk of cardiovascular disease. Nevertheless, these studies suggest that the risks to health from anxiety disorders are small.

Other surveys have noted that people with panic disorders are associated with an increased risk of suicide, probably because they are more likely than others to suffer from other psychiatric disorders (Warshaw et al., 2000). Many people become depressed because of the restrictions imposed by their panic disorder, which can thus become an indirect cause of self-harm.

How dangerous are panic disorders to others? The performance of skills in the laboratory can be impaired if subjects are confronted with stimuli which remind them of their fears. For example, Kroeze and Van den Hout. (2000) showed that subjects with panic disorder, when shown a trace of an electrocardiogram, presumably a reminder of danger, were slowed on their performance of a dot and probe reaction time task. However, it is not clear if similar impairment would occur during the performance of real-life tasks such as driving. Moreover, there appears to be no epidemiological evidence to test the possibility that, during panic attacks, there is an increased risk of mishaps in tasks such as driving. Nevertheless, pilots who have developed panic disorders have been taken off flying duties as a precaution (Bohnker et al., 1991; Schultz et al., 2003).

That people with panic disorders, and their employers, believe that panic attacks can contribute to serious accidents is illustrated by the following.

> Simon was an interior decorator who shared his work with his girl-friend. His main symptoms in panic attacks were awareness of a racing heart and dizziness and he was afraid that the demand on his heart was so great that it would suddenly stop. Because his symptoms increased when he was climbing ladders, he had to leave all high work to his girlfriend.

Many authors believe that respiratory hyperventilation – breathing in excess of metabolic needs – plays a prominent part in panic attacks. As a result, blood vessels in the heart and the brain can become constricted (Agadzhanyan and Terkhin, 2002) and this can lead to angina in people with cardiovascular disease and to cognitive impairment. However, naturally occurring hyperventilation may not happen often during panic attacks, as noted below in 'Hyperventilation: cause or effect . . .'. Nevertheless, panic attacks and hyperventilation may not be benign in people with cardiovascular disease and so patients should be screened medically before treatment.

WHAT COMPLEXITIES BESET PEOPLE WITH PANIC DISORDERS?

Only in recent years have investigators taken account of other problems present in people with panic disorders. Surveys of co-morbidity (Boyd et al., 1990; Agosti et al., 2002) have shown that they are more likely to be depressed or dependent on alcohol or cannabis or have psychotic illnesses or personality disorders.

However, less commonly discussed are the causal relationships between, say, depression and panic disorders. It may be constructive in clinical practice to determine whether depression is the result of a prolonged panic disorder or contributes to its influence. For example, it would be understandable if a person who could not do household shopping because of panics, and who became dependent on a partner for this, became depressed. This indirect relationship has been shown for other chronic disorders (Rudy et al., 1988). It would be plausible also to expect that a person who was already depressed would become less willing to venture into public places. Hence opportunities would be lost as a means of challenging a belief that panics were inevitable and could be less intense than expected. So psychological treatment would be directed at the panic disorder for the former whereas, for the latter, depression would be a target. For example:

> Simon, the interior decorator who had to rely on his girlfriend to climb ladders and whose panic disorder was a constant distraction, found that their relationship was under strain. He had become depressed as a result. Pharmacological treatment for panic disorder is probably best delivered by antidepressants (Roy-Byrne and Cowley, 2002) which could thus be of benefit to the depression.

More neglected in studies of co-morbidity in panic disorder is the role of social problems such as difficulties in housing or problems with the neighbours. Nevertheless, studies of the onset of panic disorder have noted the high incidence of environmental stresses, social problems among them, around that time (Pollard et al., 1989). For example:

> A young girl who had been sexually assaulted by a boyfriend developed panic attacks when she met another man to whom she became engaged. Her anxiety about sustaining this more rewarding relationship probably contributed to the panics. That was treated successfully. However, she developed a recurrence of this panic disorder when she felt that her mother-in-law was excessively critical of her.

As noted by several authors, anxiety about such matters and the development of panic disorders can be correlated.

WHAT IS THE NATURAL COURSE OF PANIC DISORDERS?

Ehlers (1995) observed a sample of 39 patients with panic disorder with or without agoraphobia over a period of 1 year and compared them to others who had specific phobias, to a sample who had infrequent panics, to a group who had had a panic disorder but were in remission and to others who had no psychiatric illness. Ninety-two per cent of the panic-disorder patients experienced panic attacks in the following year; 41% of those in remission had panic attacks compared with 50% in the infrequent panic group and only 2% in the normal control group. There was a small correlation with the occurrence of co-morbid disorders such as depression and agoraphobia. That is, those who were most avoidant of outside activity were more likely to be depressed and have other psychiatric problems, although there was no relationship between co-morbidity and panic frequency. However, the causal relationship between co-morbidity and agoraphobia was not described. Because most people with panic disorder either do not seek or are not referred for professional help, the persistence of panics is likely to be commonplace. Ehlers also observed that persistence and recurrence of panic disorder was greater in those subjects with a strong fear of panic symptoms.

In a retrospective survey conducted over a much longer period, Franklin (1987) observed that agoraphobics had first developed panic disorders in which they became afraid of bodily sensations such as a racing pulse and restricted breathing. Then their fears of venturing out of doors and into crowded places became more common and so they became agoraphobic. However, not all people with panic disorder develop agoraphobia (Langs et al., 2000). Those who were most likely to do so were those whose panic disorder occurred when they were young, or had been ill for a long time or had intense fears of losing control.

INFLUENCES ON PANIC

Many people who drink alcohol to excess suffer from anxiety disorders (Kushner et al., 2000). It is probably not surprising that people with panic disorders, who are afraid of experiencing depersonalisation, become anxious when intoxicated. Withdrawal from alcohol can also produce physical symptoms, which are alarming for people with anxiety disorders.

Paradoxically, anxious people can use alcohol to reduce anxiety, especially in social situations, and so the incidence of excessive alcohol use is probably greater in social phobia than other anxiety disorders (Boyd et al., 1990). There can, therefore, be a complex two-way relationship between the use of alcohol and the development and course of panic disorders (Kushner et al., 2000).

The consumption of caffeine in coffee, tea, cola and other carbonated drinks is probably higher in psychiatric patients than in the general population (James, 1997), although this may not always be a cause of anxiety but may be rather a source of comfort to anxious people. Caffeine has been associated with a higher level of somatic symptoms in such groups and agoraphobic patients have claimed that caffeine exacerbates their anxiety symptoms (James, 1997). A controlled trial distinguished cause and effect in the relationship between caffeine and symptoms of anxiety and panic. Therefore, Charney et al. (1985) examined the effects of a standard weight-related dose of caffeine in 17 normal subjects and 21 with panic disorder with or without agoraphobia. There were significantly greater increases in subject-rated anxiety, nervousness, fear, nausea, palpitations and tremors in the panic subjects than in the others. Nearly three-quarters of the former said that the symptoms were similar to those experienced in their panic attacks. There was no placebo for comparison and so it is not clear if expectations in the subjects influenced reports of their symptoms. Moreover, because there is a positive correlation between anxiety and the occurrence of panic (Bouton et al., 2001) it is not clear if pre-existing anxiety contributed to the panic symptoms attributed to the caffeine. Could the experimental procedure alone have induced an increase in symptoms? Finally, James (1997) has noted that it is not clear if people can develop tolerance of caffeine so that its anxiety-inducing effects can be reduced with use.

CAUSES OF PANIC DISORDER

Pete was a mountaineer who was concerned that he was overweight. One morning he set out from a valley in the Swiss Alps to walk strenuously for 2 hours uphill to reach the hut at the foot of the mountain. He had set off without eating breakfast and was exhausted when he arrived at the hut. He took off his sweater and sat in front of the fire to recover but, as he did so, his breathing became fast and shallow, he experienced tingling sensations and then numbness in his fingers. He felt his face and lips stiffening and his fingers curled up as if in a grasp. He thought he was losing consciousness. His friends, like Pete himself, were highly alarmed at this and so they called out the emergency services. As the helicopter arrived, they had to struggle to straighten his hands to put on his sweater and jacket. By the time he reached hospital he had recovered and all investigations were normal. Back home in England he developed panic attacks, especially when he had to meet senior colleagues and visitors at work. Thus an episode of acute hyperventilation, leading to neuromuscular tetany, appeared to have been a learning experience for the production of a panic disorder.

Other people with panic disorders can remember their first panic attack occurring whilst suffering a hangover after a night of a heavy intake of alcohol. Others can recall their first panic having occurred as they sat on the train to work, having rushed from home with only black coffee for breakfast. Nevertheless, many people are unable to recall a trigger experience that could account for their first panic. Be that as it may, why do panic attacks occur and persist?

Anxiety sensitivity

Early theories emphasised biological mechanisms for the occurrence of panic (Margraf et al., 1986). For example, Klein (1993) has postulated a 'suffocation monitor', which is sensitive to an increase of carbon dioxide and lactate, a product of anaerobic (oxygen-free) respiration in the blood. Hyperventilation follows to reduce carbon dioxide. Such theories were responsible in the 1980s for a spate of experiments on 'biological challenges' in which subjects were infused with lactate or were asked to inhale high concentrations of carbon dioxide.

These procedures rarely produce panic in normal subjects (Margraf et al., 1986; Holloway and McNally, 1987; Stein and Rapee, 1999). Furthermore, not all people with panic disorders exhibit panic under these conditions. Therefore, additional influences have been sought. The fear provoked by sensations of panic and similar experiences, measured by the Anxiety Sensitivity Index (ASI; Peterson and Plehn, 1999; Reiss et al., 1986), have been investigated for this. For example, normal subjects high in ASI become more anxious during inhalation of high concentrations of carbon dioxide than do those low in ASI. However, the amount of variance in anxiety explained by anxiety sensitivity has been very low (Stein and Rapee, 1999). As reviewed by Stein and Rapee (1999), anxiety sensitivity has not been very successful in predicting anxiety during sundry biological challenges even in people with panic disorder. These authors note that although anxiety sensitivity is higher in people with panic disorder than those without, the variance of the ASI within that group is so narrow that it is difficult to test the relationship between the ASI and panic.

Schmidt (1999) reviewed longitudinal prospective studies of anxiety sensitivity in people who do not have a panic disorder at the outset. Studies show that high anxiety sensitivity at that time is associated with the later development of panic disorders but that the relationship is not high and the low prevalence of panic disorder makes it difficult to test. In addition, the occurrence of a panic disorder probably increases anxiety sensitivity. Therefore, it has not been possible to conclude that anxiety sensitivity plays a major part in the occurrence of panic attacks and so other cognitive influences have been postulated. See the section on 'The influence of attention, perception and beliefs', below.

Learning theory

Bouton et al. (2001) have reviewed contemporary learning theory and corresponding evidence, which suggests how a major panic could lead to further panics. Superficially, the first panic resembles the unconditioned response and the subsequent panics are the conditioned responses. However, explanations based on the conditioning model have had difficulty in identifying the unconditioned stimulus. Sometimes, the first panic has been described as the unconditioned stimulus as well as the unconditioned response. More realistically, a biological event such as hyperventilation has been identified as the unconditioned stimulus.

In addition, there have been difficulties in identifying the neutral stimulus, the conditioned stimulus, which comes to provoke subsequent panics. Bouton et al. (2001) suggest that internal 'interoceptive' sensations are the conditioned stimuli. Alternatively, they suggest that early symptoms in a panic attack are the conditioned stimuli for the fully developed panic. As noted by the DSM-IV definition of panics, symptoms increase in severity as the panic attack progresses. Bouton et al. (2001) also distinguish between anxiety and panic so that the first panic could be the unconditioned stimulus, which provokes anxiety, the unconditioned response. This becomes associated with the conditioned stimuli, and so on.

Another major difficulty in conditioning theory lies in the selective nature of the conditioned stimuli. Why do people not develop panics in response to any stimulus which has been present in the environment at the time of the first panic? Why did Pete, the mountaineer, not produce panics at the sight of coal fires resembling that in front of which he had his first panic in a mountain hut? Conditioning theory has had to acknowledge the influence of expectation and beliefs about conditioned and unconditioned stimuli in human subjects (Davey, 1997). Therefore, anxiety sensitivity and beliefs about the physical sensations of a panic, such as breathing difficulties signifying danger (Hibbert, 1984), may contribute to the ease with which certain stimuli, such as restricted breathing, come to provoke panics following a major panic attack.

Hyperventilation: cause or effect of panic attacks or rare phenomenon?

In the 1980s, hyperventilation, defined as breathing in excess of metabolic needs, was very popular as an explanation of panic attacks. Voluntary hyperventilation can be demonstrated in the laboratory by asking subjects to breathe deeply and in excess of the 15–18 breaths per minute of normal breathing. Subjects may then feel some of the symptoms of a panic, such as dizziness and feelings of unreality. These are the result of alkalaemia in arterial blood, over-breathing having blown off carbon dioxide. Receptors that are sensitive to carbon dioxide are important for the regulation of breathing. Therefore, when arterial carbon dioxide is reduced to critical levels (hypocapnia), breathing slows down or stops altogether (apnoea). This continues until oxygen, of which there is abundance in the blood, can be used to form more carbon dioxide to trigger breathing again. Apnoea produced in this way resembles the difficulty in drawing enough breath about which panic-stricken subjects often complain. Levels of carbon dioxide can be chronically low in some subjects so only a small and imperceptible change in breathing would be necessary to reduce carbon dioxide to critical levels (Sinha et al., 2000) and so produce panics.

Hypocapnia would be of further interest because it can be responsible for vasoconstriction in the coronary arteries around the heart and the blood vessels in serving the brain. Hence chest pain can occur in patients with angina during hyperventilation. Cognitive impairment can also occur. Hyperventilation was thus seen as the unexpected cause of panic attacks, including the first, in people with a panic disorder. So prominent an explanation did it become that 'hyperventilation syndrome' became synonymous with panic disorder. Attractive though this hypothesis has been, it has been radically challenged; diametrically opposed opinions remain: 'There is a substantial body of literature demonstrating that hyperventilation is a common event in panic disorder patients during panic attack episodes (Sinha et al., 2000). However, Bass (1997) has described hyperventilation syndrome as a 'chimera' and Hornsveld and Garssen (1997) have concluded that it is a 'scientifically untenable concept'.

Two studies have reinforced this by testing transcutaneous measures of carbon dioxide. Hibbert and Pilsbury (1989) monitored 15 patients with panic disorder as they went for walks outside the laboratory. All experienced a panic attack according to written logs kept by them. Only seven showed critical reductions in carbon dioxide during their attacks. Moreover, these appeared to follow the onset of the panics rather than precede them. They appeared, therefore, to be the effect rather than the cause of the panics. Garssen et al. (1996) observed a reduction in carbon dioxide in only one of 24 panic attacks in 28 patients. Although these two studies used only small samples, they are clearly inconsistent with one another.

Gardner (1994) has noted that transcutaneous measures of carbon dioxide have a slow response time and so observations of carbon dioxide may not be well synchronised with panic attacks. Therefore, the panic attacks in Hibbert and Pilsbury's (1989) study may have been the result of hyperventilation after all. However, Gardner (1994) made his criticisms of trancutaneous monitoring without reference to relevant evidence. Nevertheless, no objection has been brought to the possibility that hyperventilation may have been the cause of the first panic in a panic disorder.

The hyperventilation provocation test has been used to determine if a typical panic attack has been the result of overbreathing. In this test subjects are asked to over-breathe for up to 3 minutes to reduce arterial carbon dioxide. Hornsveld and Garssen (1996) have compared this procedure with a placebo in which subjects over-breathed in an atmosphere of carbon dioxide so that their arterial levels did not diminish. Although many people said that their symptoms during the real hyperventilation test resembled those of a typical panic, many also recognised these symptoms under the placebo. The authors concluded that hyperventilation has a negligible influence on symptoms. However, this test often provokes much anxiety in people with panic disorder.

Furthermore, many symptoms that are, said to be the result of hyperventilation (Grossman and Deswart, 1984) resemble those of anxiety which, of course, arises in panic attacks and which could occur in panic disorder patients under a placebo. Therefore, it may be difficult to distinguish between the effects of hyperventilation and anxiety provoked by such comparisons.

Therefore, the main value of the hyperventilation provocation test lies in its ability to provoke anxiety in people with panic disorder. The time for which they can tolerate this procedure can thus be one of the behavioural tests in panic disorder.

The influence of attention, perception and beliefs in panic disorders

Cognitive theories place less emphasis on the development of panic disorders (Clark, 1988). Instead, they postulate that people with panic disorder have come by indeterminate means to be vigilant for internal sensations such as chest pain or laboured breathing and to interpret them as signs of danger (Clark et al., 1997). Experimental studies have shown that people with panic disorder are prone to perceptual biases, which may influence the occurrence of panic attacks (Harvey et al., 2004). Furthermore, clinical experiments have shown that recalling panics can produce the symptoms of a panic attack (Bass et al., 1989) but neither approach, as with the study of anxiety sensitivity noted above, has been shown to be sufficient to account for the occurrence of panic disorders or even of panic attacks. The following, however illustrates how vigilance and interpretation can occur in people with a panic disorder.

Simon, the interior decorator described above, frequently checked his pulse for the onset of a panic attack because he believed that his heart beat so fast during panics that it would suddenly stop, exhausted and he would die.

Cognitive theories also postulate a trigger that provokes these sensations, although this often cannot be clearly identified in clinical practice. The notion of a trigger is somewhat paradoxical for unprovoked panic attacks in panic disorder described by DSM-IV. Furthermore, almost all studies of panic disorder have selected their subjects according to DSM criteria. Bouton et al. (2001) have suggested that subjects may be unconscious of the trigger stimuli, the conditioned stimuli, which provoke panic. Nevertheless, people with panic disorders say that they are highly aware of sensations of pulse rate (Ehlers and Breuer, 1992), more so than for other sensations. They are thus unlike patients with other anxiety disorders. Schmidt et al. (1997) also have noted that panic disorder patients are highly vigilant for 'internal bodily sensations'.

Ehlers et al. (1988) have recorded that panic-disorder patients become more anxious when they see a display showing that their heart rate has increased abruptly. However, Van der Does et al. (2000), in a review, concluded that although subjects are not very accurate in estimating their own heart rates, those with panic disorders are more accurate than people without. There is no evidence, therefore, that panic patients overestimate their heart rates and so become anxious. Furthermore, as noted earlier in this chapter, pulse rates are not highly correlated with the occurrence of panic attacks (Turner et al., 1988).

The most useful measure in this context, therefore, in the treatment of panic disorders is the Body Sensations Interpretations Questionnaire (Clark et al., 1997), although Austin and Richards (2001) have claimed that the measure does not adequately cover the beliefs about symptoms that can be presented by people with panic disorder.

MEASURES OF PANIC

Panic attacks can be characterised by their frequency, numbers of symptoms, their severity and duration as well as the degree of avoidance of situations that provoke the panic as in agoraphobia. Fear associated with their occurrence and recurrence is also important. The following published questionnaires address some or all of these aspects.

The Panic Disorder Severity Scale (PDSS; Shear et al., 1997; Rush et al., 2000) has seven items, each rated by the interviewing clinician on a five-point scale, to describe frequency of panic, fear of future panics, distress during panics, avoidance of internal sensations reminiscent of panic attacks, avoidance of situations that could provoke a panic, interference with social functioning and interference with work. This has been shown to have high inter-rater reliability and moderate internal consistency.

The Panic Attack Symptoms Questionnaire, which has high internal consistency (PASQ; Clum et al., 1990), has 30 items for assessing the duration of panic symptoms rated by the subjects themselves during a typical panic attack.

The Panic Rating Scale (Clark et al., 1994) contains three items completed by clients themselves or their clinicians to measure frequency of panics, disability or disturbance generally caused by them. A third item, the frequency with which situations are avoided because of the panics, was added later. The authors report for the first two items that there were significant differences between treatments (Clark et al., 1994, 1999) but they report no other psychometric data, such as measures of agreement between patients and clinicians.

BEHAVIOURAL TESTS AND RECORD KEEPING

Beurs et al. (1992) asked panic-disorder patients to estimate retrospectively the number of panics they had experienced in the previous 7 days. They were also instructed in recording panic attacks as they were experienced. Retrospection over-estimated the number of panics which had occurred. Therefore, only diary-keeping by subjects of their panics as they happen can provide valid estimates of their occurrence. These records need to be supplemented by a diary recording those activities and situations that the subject recognises as provoking panic. This is necessary because progress in treatment may appear spuriously successful if patients avoid situations that they believe have provoked panic attacks. Behavioural tests can be used to estimate subjects' tolerance of the experiences that safety behaviours are used to avoid or bring comfort.

Tolerance of open spaces and public places in agoraphobics can be estimated by the time they can spend, or the distance they can travel, in open parkland or a busy street. A certain situation can be used repeatedly for such tests to determine progress in treatment. It is always important, however, to watch subjects during theses tests to see if they fortuitously or deliberately encounter places of safety or use safety behaviours which could compromise the test. For example, an agoraphobic man, on the second repetition of his walk in the centre of the park, spotted a bench to which he accelerated his pace. An agoraphobic woman saw a pharmacist's shop which she recognised as a place of safety in her progress down a busy street.

Time spent doing a number of repetitions of the following (Anthony et al., unpublished (quoted by Taylor, 2000); Clark and Salkovskis, 1987) can also provide behavioural tests:

- For numbness and tingling sensations, place the head between the knees and then move to an upright position.
- For trembling or shaking, tense as many muscles as possible simultaneously throughout the body.
- For dizziness, faintness or depersonalisation, spin in a standing position (breath-holding and hyperventilation can also provoke this.)

A racing pulse and pounding heart can be produced by running on the spot or up and down stairs; breathlessness can be provoked by breathing through a straw with the nose pinched shut.

SUMMARY OF ASSESSMENT IN PANIC DISORDERS

Influences such as the consumption of caffeine, alcohol, cannabis and benzodiazepines, as well as co-morbid disorders, need to be treated first if they have a causal influence on a panic disorder. Clients may need to be convinced of their significance and so record-keeping and corresponding experiments can help to clarify this. For example, Cook et al. (1990) showed that women who believed that their panics occurred more often around menstruation were

Table 13.1 Summary of data collection in panic disorders

Variable	Measure
Frequency, severity and duration of panic attacks	Panic Disorder Severity Scale (Shear et al., 1997; Rush et al., 2000) *and* daily panic diary
Stimuli and activities that provoke panic attacks	Behavioural testing to measure time for which certain activities, such as hyperventilation or walking down a busy street, can be tolerated
Fear of bodily sensations	Anxiety Sensitivity Index (Reiss et al., 1986)
Beliefs about internal sensations	Body Sensations Questionnaire (Clark et al., 1997)
Fear and avoidance in agoraphobia	The Agoraphobia Scale (Öst, 1990)

shown to be incorrect. Others can be shown by record-keeping of alcohol intake that panics are less frequent during prolonged abstinence than during alcohol consumption. Table 13.1 shows measures which are commonly of value for showing levels of distress and disability before, during and at the conclusion of treatment.

REFERENCES

Agadzhanyan, N. A. and Terekhin, P. I. (2002) Physiological mechanisms of respiratory phenomena in anxiety and depressive disorders. *Human Physiology*, 28, 351–361.

Agosti, V., Nunes, E. and Levin, F. (2002) Rates of psychiatric comorbidity among US residents with lifetime cannabis dependence. *American Journal of Drug and Alcohol Abuse*, 28, 643–652.

American Psychiatric Association (APA) (2000) *Diagnostic and Statistical Manual of Mental Disorders*, 3rd edn (text revision). Washington, DC: APA.

Austin, D. W. and Richards, J. C. (2001) The catastrophic misinterpretation model of panic disorder. *Behaviour Research and Therapy*, 39, 1277–1292.

Barlow, D. H., Vermilyea, J., Blanchard, E. B., Vermilyea, B. B., DiNardo, P. A. and Cerny, J. A. (1985) The phenomenon of panic. *Journal of Abnormal Psychology*, 94, 320–328.

Bass, C. (1997) Hyperventilation syndrome: A chimera? *Journal of Psychosomatic Research*, 42, 421–426.

Bass, C., Lelliott, P. and Marks, I. (1989) Fear talk versus voluntary hyperventilation in agoraphobics and normals, a controlled study. *Psychological Medicine*, 19, 669–676.

Bergen, A. W. and Caporaso, N. (1999) Cigarette smoking. *Journal of the National Cancer Institute*, 91, 1365–1375.

Beurs, E. de, Lange, A. and Van Dyck, R. (1992) Self-monitoring of panic attacks and retrospective estimates of panic: discordant findings. *Behaviour Research and Therapy*, 30, 411–413.

Bohnker, B., Fraser, J., Baggett, J. and Hayes, G. (1991) In flight anxiety conditioned presenting with 'break-off' symptoms. *Aviation and Space Environmental Medicine*, 62, 342–345.

Bouton, M. E., Mineka, S. and Barlow, D. H. (2001). A modern learning theory perspective on the etiology of panic disorder. *Psychological Review*, 108, 4–32.

Bowen, R. C., Senthilsetvan, A. and Barale, A. (2000) Physical illness as an outcome of chronic anxiety disorders. *Canadian Journal of Psychiatry*, 45, 459–464.

Boyd, J. H., Rae, D. S., Thompson, S. W., Burns B. S., Bordon, K., Locke, B. Z. and Regier, D. A. (1990) Phobia: Prevalence and risk factors. *Social Psychiatry and Psychiatric Epidemiology*, 25, 14–23.

Charney, D. S., Heninger, J. and Jatlow, P. (1985) Increased anxiogenic effects of caffeine in panic disorders. *Archives of General Psychiatry*, 42, 233–243.

Clark, D. M., Salkovskis, P. M., Öst, L-G., Breitholtz, E., Koehler, K. A., Westling, B. E. et al. (1997) Misinterpretation of body sensations in panic disorder. *Journal of Consulting and Clinical Psychology*, 65, 203–213.

Clark, D. M., Salkovskis, P. M., Hackman, A., Wells, A., Ludgare, J. and Gelder, M. (1999) Brief cognitive therapy for panic disorder: A standardised controlled trial. *Journal of Consulting and Clinical Psychology*, 67, 583–589.

Clark, D. M. (1988) A cognitive model of panic attacks. In: Rachman, S. and Maser, J. D. (eds) *Panic: Psychological Perspectives*. New York: Wiley.

Clark, D. M. and Salkovskis, P. M. (1987) *Cognitive Therapy for Panic Attacks: Therapist's Manual*. Oxford: Department of Psychiatry, University of Oxford.

Clark, D. M., Salkovskis, P. M., Hackmann, A. and Middleton, H. et al. (1994) A comparison of cognitive therapy, applied relaxation and imipramine in the treatment of panic disorder. *British Journal of Psychiatry*, 164, 759–769.

Clum, G. A., Broyles, S., Borden, J. and Watkins, P. L. (1990) Validity and reliability of the Panic Attack Symptoms and Cognitions Questionnaire. *Journal of Psychopathology and Behavioral Assessment*, 12, 233–245.

Cook, B. L., Noyes, R., Garvey, M. J. and Beach, V. (1990) Anxiety and the menstrual cycle in panic disorder. *Journal of Affective Disorders*, 19, 221–226.

Craske, M. G., Lang, A., Tsao, J. C. I., Mystkowski, J. L. and Rowe, M. K. (2001) Reactivity to interoceptive cues in nocturnal panic. *Journal of Behaviour Therapy and Experimental Psychiatry*, 32, 173–190.

Craske, M. G., Lang, A. J., Mystokowski, J. L., Zacker, B. G., Bystintsky, A. and Yan-go, F. (2002) Does nocturnal panic represent a more severe form of panic disorder? *Journal of Nervous and Mental Disease*, 190, 611–618.

Davey, G. C. L. (1997) A conditioning model of phobias. In: G. C. L. Davey (ed) *Phobias. A Handbook of Theory Research and Treatment*. Chichester: John Wiley.

Ehlers, A. (1995) A 1-year prospective study of panic attacks: Clinical course and factors associated with maintenance. *Journal of Abnormal Psychology*, 104, 164–172.

Ehlers, A., and Breuer, P. (1992) Increased cardiac awareness in panic disorder. *Journal of Abnormal Psychology*, 101, 371–382.

Ehlers, A., Margraf, J., Roth, W. T., Taylor, C. B. and Birnbauer, N. (1988) Anxiety induced by false heart rate feedback in patients with panic disorder. *Behaviour Research and Therapy* 26, 1–11.

Franklin, J. A. (1987) The changing nature of agoraphobic fears. *British Journal of Clinical Psychology*, 26, 127–133.

Gardner, W. N. (1994) Diagnosis and organic causes of symptomatic hyperventilation. In: B. H. Timmons and R. Ley (eds) *Behavioural and Psychological Approaches to Breathing Disorders*. New York: Plenum Press.

Garssen, B., Buikhuisen, D. and Van Dyck, R. (1996) Hyperventilation and panic attacks. *American Journal of Psychiatry*, 153, 513–518.

Goodwin, R. and Anderson, R. M. (2002) Use of the Behavioural Model of Health Care Use to identify correlates of use of treatment for panic attacks in the community. *Social Psychiatry and Psychiatric Epidemiology*, 37, 212–219.

Grossman, P. and Deswart, J. C. G. De (1984) Diagnosis of hyperventilation syndrome on the basis of reported complaints. *Journal of Psychosomatic Research*, 28, 97–104.

Haines, A. P., Imeson, J. D. and Meade, T. W. (1987) Phobic anxiety and ischaemic heart disease. *British Medical Journal*, 295, 297–299.

Hallam, R. S. and Haffner, R. J. (1978) Fear of phobia patients: factor analyses of self-report data. *Behaviour Research and Therapy*, 16, 1–6.

Harvey, A., Watkins, E., Mansell, W. and Shafran, R. (2004) *Cognitive Behavioural Processes Across Psychological Disorders*. Oxford: Oxford University Press.

Heide, F. J. and Borkovec, T. D. (1983) Relaxation-induced anxiety: Paradoxical anxiety enhancement due to relaxation training. *Journal of Consulting and Clinical Psychology*, 51, 171–182.

Heide, F. J. and Borkovec, T. D. (1984) Relaxation-induced anxiety: Mechanisms and theoretical implications. *Behaviour Research and Therapy*, 22, 1–12.

Hibbert, G. A. (1984) Ideational components of anxiety: their origin and content. *British Journal of Psychiatry*, 144, 618–624.

Hibbert, G. and Pilsbury, D. (1989) Hyperventilation: Is it a cause of panic attacks? *British Journal of Psychiatry*, 155, 805–809.

Holloway, W. and McNally, R. J. (1987) Effects of anxiety sensitivity on the response to hyperventilation. *Journal of Abnormal Psychology*, 96, 330–334.

Hornsveld, H. and Garssen, B. (1996) The low specificity of the hyperventilation provocation test. *Journal of Psychosomatic Research*, 41, 435–449.

Hornsveld, H. and Garssen, B. (1997) Hyperventilation syndrome: An elegant but scientifically untenable concept. *Netherlands Journal of Medicine*, 50, 13–20.

James, J. E. (1997) *Understanding Caffeine. A Biobehavioral Analysis*. Thousand Oaks, CA: Sage Publications.

Kahn, E., Fisher, C. and Edwards, A. (1991) Night terrors and anxiety dreams. In: S. J. Ellman and J. S. Antrobus (eds) *The Mind in Sleep. Psychology and Psychophysiology*. New York: John Wiley.

Klein, D. F. (1993) False suffocation alarms, spontaneous panics and related conditions: An integrative hypothesis. *Archives of General Psychiatry*, 50, 306–317.

Knott, V. J., Bakish, D., Lusk, S. and Barkely, J. (1997) Relaxation-induced EEG alterations in panic disorder patients. *Journal of Anxiety Disorders*, 11, 365–376.

Kroeze, S. and Van den Hout, M. A. (2000) Selective attention for cardiac information in panic patients. *Behaviour Research and Therapy*, 38, 63–72.

Kushner, M. G., Abrams, K. and Butchadt, C. (2000) The relationship between anxiety disorders and alcohol use disorders: A review of major perspectives and findings. *Clinical Psychology Review*, 20, 149–171.

Langs, G., Guehenberger, F., Fabish, K., Khug, G., Fabisch, H. and Zapotoczky, H. G. (2000) The development of agoraphobia in panic disorder: A predictable process? *Journal of Affective Disorders*, 58, 43–50.

Margraf, J., Ehlers, A. and Roth, W. T. (1986) Biological models of panic disorder and agoraphobia – a review. *Behaviour Research and Therapy*, 24, 553–567.

Norton, C. R., Cox, B. J. and Malan, J. (1992) Non-clinical panickers: A critical review. *Clinical Psychology Review*, 12, 121–139.

Öst, L.-G. (1990) The Agoraphobia Scale: An evaluation of its validity and reliability. *Behaviour Research and Therapy*, 28, 323–330.

Peterson, R. A. and Plehn, K. (1999) Measuring anxiety sensitivity. In: S. Taylor (ed) *Anxiety Sensitivity. Theory, Research and Treatment of the Fear of Anxiety*. Mahwah, NJ: Lawrence Erlbaum Associates, Inc.

Pollard, C. A., Pollard, H. J. and Corn, K. J. (1989) Panic onset and major events in the lives of agoraphobics: A test of contiguity. *Journal of Abnormal Psychology*, 98, 318–321.

Rapee, R. M., Craske, M. G. and Barlow, D. H. (1990) Subject-described features of panic attacks using self-monitoring. *Journal of Anxiety Disorders*, 4, 171–181.

Reiss, S., Peterson, R. A., Garsky, D. M. and McNally, R. J. (1986) Anxiety sensitivity, anxiety frequency and the prediction of fearfulness. *Behaviour Research and Therapy*, 24, 1–8.

Rice, D. P. and Miller, L. S. (1993) The economic burden of mental disorders. *Advances in Health Economics and Health Services Research*, 14, 37–53.

Roy-Byrne, P. P. and Cowley, D. S. (2002) Pharmacological treatments for panic disorder, generalised anxiety disorder, specific phobia and social anxiety disorder. In: P. E. Nathan and J. M. Gorman (eds) *A Guide to Treatments That Work*, 2nd edn. New York: Oxford University Press.

Rudy, T. E., Kerns, R. D. and Turk, D. C. (1988) Chronic pain and depression: toward a cognitive-behavioral mediation model. *Pain*, 35, 129–140.

Rush, A. et al. (2000) *Handbook of Psychiatric Measures*. Washington, DC: American Psychiatric Association.

Schmidt, N. B. (1999) Prospective evaluations of anxiety sensitivity. In: S. Taylor (ed) *Anxiety Sensitivity: Theory, Research and Treatment of the Fear of Anxiety*. Mahwah, NJ: Lawrence Erlbaum Associates, Inc.

Schmidt, N. B., Lerew, D. R. and Trakowski, J. H. (1997) Body vigilance in panic disorder: evaluating attention to bodily perturbations. *Journal of Consulting and Clinical Psychology*, 65, 214–220.

Schredl, M., Kronenberg, G., Nonnell, P. and Heuser, I. (2001) Dream recall, nightmare frequency and nocturnal panic attacks in patients with panic disorder. *Journal of Nervous and Mental Disease*, 189, 559–562.

Schulz, J. J., Jones, D. R., Marsh, R. W. and Drummond, F. E. (2003) You're the flight surgeon. Anxiety. *Aviation and Environmental Medicine*, 74, 894–895.

Shear, M. K., Brown, T. A., Barlow, D. H., Money, R., Sholoomskas, D. E., Woods, S. W. et al. (1997) Multicenter Collaborative Panic Disorder Severity Scale. *American Journal of Psychiatry*, 154, 1571–1575.

Sinha, S., Papp, L. and Gormon, J. M. (2000) How study of respiratory physiology aided our understanding of abnormal brain function in panic disorder. *Journal of Affective Disorders*, 61, 191–200.

Starvevic, V. and Bogojevic, G. (1997) Comorbidity of panic disorder with agoraphobia and specific phobia: Relationship with the subtypes of specific phobia. *Comprehensive Psychiatry*, 38, 315–320.

Stein, M. B. and Rapee, R. M. (1999) Biological aspects of anxiety sensitivity: Is it all in the head? In: S. Taylor (ed) *Anxiety Sensitivity: Theory, Research and Treatment of the Fear of Anxiety*. Mahwah, NJ: Lawrence Erlbaum Associates, Inc.

Taylor, S. (2000) *Understanding and Treating Panic Disorder. Cognitive-behavioural Approaches*. Chichester: John Wiley.

Turner, S. M., Beidel, D. C. and Jacob, R. G. (1988) Assessment of panic. In: Rachman, S. and Maser, J. D. *Panic: Psychological Perspectives*. New York: John Wiley.

Van der Does, W., Antony, M., Ehlers, A. and Barsky, A. J. (2000) Heartbeat perception in panic disorder: A reanalysis. *Behaviour Research and Therapy*, 38, 47–62.

Warshaw, M. G., Dolan, R. and Keller, M. (2000) Suicidal behaviour in patients with current or past panic disorder: Five years of prospective data from the Harvard/Brown anxiety research program. *American Journal of Psychiatry*, 157, 1876–1878.

Weisman, M. M. (1991) Panic disorder: impact on quality of life. *Journal of Clinical Psychiatry*, 52, 6–9.

Chapter 14

Panic disorders

Treatment

Stan Lindsay

INTRODUCTION

Two major recent reviews of contemporary treatment for panic disorders (Barlow et al., 2002; McIntosh et al., 2004) have considered, among others, the two most influential approaches to treatment in recent years. One of these approaches was originated in the USA by David Barlow and colleagues (Barlow and Craske, 1994; Craske and Barlow, 2001); the other was developed in the UK by David Clark and associates (Clark, 1989).

The guidelines produced by the National Institute for Health and Clinical Excellence (NICE; McIntosh et al., 2004) for the treatment of panic disorders in primary care advocate cognitive-behaviour therapy (CBT), by which term they appear to include exposure and cognitive therapy. They also recommend the use of selective serotonin re-uptake inhibitors (SSRIs), i.e. antidepressant/anxiolytic medication. Barlow et al. (2002) recommend the package developed by Craske and Barlow (2001) – 'panic control treatment' – as well as cognitive therapy alone; they also say that applied relaxation deserves consideration. The programme by Barlow and colleagues (2002) consists of education about panics, cognitive re-structuring, breathing retraining, applied relaxation, exposure to the internal bodily sensations that can be experienced in panics (interoceptive exposure) and exposure to the external stimuli that have provoked the victim's fears. However, breathing retraining probably adds little to the other components (Schmidt et al., 2000). Applied relaxation has been controversial in that its author (Öst, 1987) has found more favourable results when comparing the technique with cognitive therapy than have the protagonists for cognitive therapy (Clark et al., 1994). Arntz and Van den Hout (1996), being independent of those parties, found that cognitive therapy was superior to applied relaxation in reducing the frequency of panic attacks and in some questionnaire measures. Applied relaxation was, however, more successful than keeping clients on a waiting list but only 12 weeks after the start of treatment. Beck and colleagues (Beck et al., 1994) compared progressive tension-release relaxation with minimal telephone contact and with cognitive therapy, which was designed to avoid exposure. They concluded that both treatments were more successful on several measures of panic than the 'minimal contact'. There were no unambiguous differences between relaxation and cognitive therapy.

Could relaxation add anything to the several interventions in a multi-component package (Barlow and Craske, 1994; Craske and Barlow, 2001)? Could relaxation enhance or reduce the impact of cognitive therapy and other treatments? There appears to be no evidence to test this. Nevertheless, the theory underlying cognitive therapy (Clark, 1988) would suggest that relaxation could be a safety behaviour that could undermine the impact of cognitive therapy. Clients who prefer relaxation, and who may have attempted to use that before seeking professional help, may avoid the opportunity in treatment to disconfirm their beliefs that panic attacks are harmful.

The present review, therefore, describes exposure and cognitive therapy as the main approaches to treatment. Relaxation, breathing retraining medication and other measures are then described, with a suggestion for their more limited use.

Early treatment of panic disorder with agoraphobia (Matthews et al., 1981) sought to minimise the occurrence of severe anxiety during treatment. This was done by exposing clients to graded hierarchies of situations, which varied in the degree of the anxiety they provoked. However, other programmes, such as flooding, made no attempt to reduce the anxiety experienced by clients in treatment. The principle underlying treatment has been described as follows: '... the patient endures the fear-provoking situation until the discomfort subsides. Exposure therapy resembles the way in which repeated presentation of the relevant stimuli habituate and extinguish normal innate and acquired fear' (Marks, 1987, p 457). However, further explanations of exposure include extinction of conditioned responses and cognitive restructuring (Tryon, 2005).

There has been no agreement about how much fear should occur to bring about a good outcome for exposure (Matthews et al., 1981; Marks, 1987). Conversely, cognitive therapy, which is based on a different principle, could even require that clients in treatment should experience panic attacks of maximum severity. This would amount to a behavioural experiment challenging the belief held by clients that panic attacks can be fatal. However, it can be difficult to encourage people to undergo experiences in therapy that could provoke high anxiety. Simply telling clients that their anxiety will decline with exposure is often implausible to them. Around a third of people with agoraphobia reject the offer of exposure treatments and fear of treatment is a prominent reason (Emmelkamp and Van der Hout, 1983). Recent studies (e.g. Murphy et al., 1998; Arntz, 2002) give too little information to determine the influence of anxiety about treatment on drop-out or refusal of therapy. Nevertheless, therapists of any persuasion have to be careful to avoid frightening their clients away from treatment. It must be remembered, all the same, that the principle of informed consent requires that clients are advised about the nature and effects of treatment.

TREATING CO-MORBID PROBLEMS

If clients have acknowledged dependence on alcohol or cannabis – these are common problems often associated with panic disorders – it may be helpful to advise or help them to abstain from that intake before treatment of their panic disorder. This may be presented to a client as a behavioural experiment; for example, 'You say that alcohol helps to make you less anxious. It can be difficult to know if alcohol makes a panic disorder worse or makes it more bearable or helps to make you less anxious. If you are able to do without alcohol, it should help us to find out how alcohol affects your panics'. Clinical experience suggests that sometimes this is sufficient to treat panic disorders successfully. Therefore, it can be constructive to arrive at a formulation about the role of alcohol or cannabis in a panic before embarking on cognitive therapy (Taylor, 2000). It may be necessary to advise a client to seek specialist help to reduce their use of alcohol or cannabis if it appears to have a contributory effect on panic disorder.

Similar arguments could be applied to depression, also commonly associated with panic disorders. However, Tsao et al. (2002) showed that the frequency and severity of depression, generalised anxiety disorder and specific phobia declined significantly following CBT for panic disorders, with or without agoraphobia. Moreover, the presence of co-morbid depression and anxiety did not adversely affect treatment outcome for the panic disorders. This would be expected if the clients had become depressed or anxious because of their panic disorder. However, there is insufficient information about the causal relationship between the panic disorders and the other problems in that study to establish the nature of the effect of treatment on the latter. This is disappointing because almost all the influential studies of treatment outcome in panic disorder exclude or do not mention the occurrence of other disorders in their participants. Therefore, it is often advisable to attempt to formulate the role of co-morbid problems when embarking on the treatment of panic disorders.

The following illustrates this difficulty:

A client had a panic disorder in which a fear of losing control of her bowels was prominent. Some years previously, she had been engaged to be married but that relationship foundered, causing her great distress. When she developed a new, rewarding relationship to a man whom she wished to marry, she became very afraid that attachment would also end. She became very depressed at this. However, the distress and uncertainty about her relationship was successfully treated and the panic disorder improved significantly without direct intervention. The formulation, aided by data collection, suggested that the panic disorder was the secondary problem. Nevertheless, the panic disorder returned a year later when the client had more interpersonal difficulties. Should the panic disorder have been treated more directly during the first presentation?

PRELIMINARY EDUCATION ABOUT PANIC DISORDERS AND TREATMENT

Chapter 13 reviewed the nature of panic disorders, relevant influences and effects and that information can be discussed with clients. However, it is probably important not to tell clients everything the therapist thinks they ought to know. Rather, the emphasis should be on eliciting the clients' own beliefs and corresponding behaviours. Nevertheless, some information may be useful as an introduction. Having heard an outline of the client's experiences, it can be helpful for the therapist to give a diagnosis, namely that the client is probably suffering from a panic disorder. It can be reassuring to tell clients that they are not alone in this, and so giving them a rough estimate of the prevalence of panic disorders could be the next step. It is often important to disabuse clients of the idea that there is 'nothing wrong', which they will have heard from doctors who have found no abnormalities in tests such as electrocardiograms. Clearly there *is* something wrong: a panic disorder.

Next, the symptoms of anxiety, such as accelerating heart rate and fast breathing, excessive perspiration associated with feeling hot or cold, should be described. Of course, it is important to encourage clients to describe their own symptoms of anxiety to see how far their symptoms match that picture. Then, regardless of whether the therapist's plan is to base treatment on the exposure principle or on cognitive therapy, the cognitive model outlined in the previous chapter (see Figure 14.1, p. 274) could be used to describe how thoughts about anxiety symptoms can intensify them. Again, clients are asked how far this resembles their own experiences. They are then asked: 'After the panic attack subsided, did you think it would happen again?'. If clients agree, they could be asked about being vigilant for the start of symptoms suggesting that another attack was on its way. The therapist may suggest that changes in bodily activities occur all the time, such as with a cup of coffee or exercise, and that these can be misinterpreted by people who have had a panic attack. Avoidance of activities such as running up stairs, which the client believes can bring on frightening symptoms, can illustrate this.

If the client complains of shortness of breath during panics, it may be helpful to describe the role of carbon dioxide in the body. It is important for stimulating breathing. If a client over-breathes, carbon dioxide will be expelled on each exhalation. As a result, the breathing will be slowed by an internal reflex so that carbon dioxide is allowed to accumulate so as to stimulate normal breathing again. When carbon dioxide is at a low level, symptoms such as dizziness and feelings of unreality will occur. However, the role of carbon dioxide is controlled by reflexes, so the client will not lose consciousness. In cognitive therapy (discussed below), the client can be encouraged to practise voluntary hyperventilation as a behavioural experiment to demonstrate the truth of this.

Clients may be afraid that they could faint in an attack. However, they should be told that fainting occurs as the result of a large drop in blood pressure but that in anxiety, which occurs in panic, blood pressure rises so that fainting is unlikely in a panic attack. Clients, however, sometimes complain that they have lost consciousness. It would be advisable for the therapist to accept this because sometimes some loss of consciousness through a medical emergency can trigger a panic disorder although subsequent attacks are panics in which consciousness is not lost.

Before seeking professional help, clients will often have read books or have searched the internet for reassurance and solutions. Some of these sources contain valid information that could reinforce the above accounts but others have a commercial interest at stake, which may prejudice their advice. An exhaustive review of these is well beyond the scope of this chapter because there are over 50 books and over 600,000 websites devoted to panic disorders. The following books are the most prominent in searches and provide some reliable accounts.

Panic Attacks (Ingham, 2000) gives a thorough account of influences on panic but presents an uncritical account of treatment. The section on pharmacotherapy does not mention SSRIs. As much attention, albeit less than a page, is paid to psychodynamic treatment as to cognitive therapy, which is inconsistent with current evidence. For that, compare the encyclopaedic review of cognitive behavioural treatment (Taylor, 2000) with the most recent attempt to apply psychodynamic therapy (Milrod et al., 2000).

Overcoming Panic (Silove and Manicavasagar, 2001) tells readers how to treat their panic disorder themselves, although it does describe the use of medication for which medical advice and supervision are necessary. It attributes a prominent part to hyperventilation as a cause of panics and recommends corresponding treatment, such as slow breathing and re-breathing from a paper bag to replenish carbon dioxide. This emphasis on hyperventilation is, therefore, somewhat out of date (see Chapter 13). This book describes how one may expose oneself to frightening symptoms such as dizziness and rapid heart rate. Dizziness is provoked by spinning around slowly with the eyes open. However, the authors do not mention voluntary hyperventilation as an exposure exercise in spite of the part that over-breathing is said by them to play in panic attacks. There is a section on how to challenge frightening beliefs about symptoms. Readers are asked to look for evidence to question the beliefs, to think of other less alarming explanations for the symptoms or to ask other people for their interpretations. Progressive muscular relaxation is described as a technique for changing one's lifestyle. *Overcoming Panic*, therefore, is somewhat out of date and inconsistent with evidence about panic disorders.

Panic Disorder: the facts (Rachman and de Silva, 2004) presents a thorough review of research-based evidence about the theories of panic and influences on its occurrence. It describes exposure mainly as a treatment of avoidance in agoraphobia. Cognitive therapy, including behavioural experiments, is extensively described. Perhaps more attention is paid to hyperventilation and breathing training than current research would recommend. Relaxation, instructions for which are included in an appendix, is described in association with exposure and desensitisation. A section on pharmacotherapy pays most attention to benzodiazepine tranquillisers and tricyclic antidepressants and less to the SSRIs, even though these are more commonly prescribed because they are less toxic or addictive. In conclusion, *Panic Disorder: the facts* is probably the most helpful book for the lay reader on the market.

Such books can assist the therapist in presenting an account of panic disorders and their treatments, and possibly convey a greater authority and conviction than orally delivered information. They may be sufficient to reduce fear of panic attacks significantly but the evidence for this is not clear. Febbraro et al. (1999) found that reading a treatment manual was no more effective than being kept on a waiting list in reducing panic attacks and symptoms. The manual presented treatment similar to the symptom control package of Barlow and others (Barlow and Craske, 1994). The participants had not been selected to meet diagnostic criteria for panic disorder and so may not have had clinically significant panic disorders. Furthermore, the sample may not have been large enough to detect any difference between the waiting list group and the treatment groups, the largest having only ten participants. Therefore, used alone without the intervention of a therapist, treatment manuals may have only a weak therapeutic effect. Nevertheless, they can be useful aids in introducing patients to treatment.

Professional associations have websites on the internet and present leaflet summaries of panic disorders. These are provided by the American Psychological Association (http://www.apa.org), the American Psychiatric Association (http://www.psych.org), which includes advice about breathing, and the National Institute of Mental Health (http://www.nlm.nih.gov).

EXPOSURE

Exposure to feared situations has long been the recommended treatment for agoraphobia with panic attacks. The rationale for exposure has to be explained to the client: fear, including panic, normally subsides within half an hour, although this period can vary from individual to individual. It is important to allow this to happen by not leaving the shop, going home or calling for a cab. In other words, the client should endure the situation for as long as it takes for the anxiety to subside. Otherwise the opportunity to show this reduction could be lost.

Matthews et al. (1981) describe graded programmes for visiting super-markets, travelling by bus and taking walks out of doors. The supermarket programme, for example, starts with the therapist and client going to the shop at a quiet time. Next, it suggests going in together but splitting up inside for a while. Further steps include the therapist staying outside the shop, and so on, until the client visits the shop with the therapist at busy times and then at such times alone. Care has to be taken to ensure that the client does not engage in safety behaviours, such as shopping near the exits or looking for security personnel or staff who have been reassuring in the past. Rushing around the supermarket without pausing to select goods carefully may also be a safety behaviour.

There is no clear agreement about how frequently, whether practised massed or spaced, within a given period of, say, 2 weeks, these exercises should be done (Barlow et al., 2002). Probably, however, several exercises within a week are desirable. Kent (1989) has shown how memories of a benign experience of a hitherto frightening event can change for the worse. Therefore, if clients visit a supermarket and find that it was not as distressing as expected, after 2 or 3 weeks without further practice, they might come to remember it as more distressing than it had been. Clients can justify this by claiming that the benign experience had not been typical but rather was a chance aberration. There is a possibility that, if treatment is not conducted frequently, clients will construct an unrealistic memory of a suc-cessful exposure based on a conglomerate memory of previous distressing experiences.

The duration of each exercise is probably important. Long exposures, say, 20 minutes, are probably more effective than brief exposures, although precise guidelines about this have not been established (Marks, 1987).

There have been attempts to enhance the outcome of exposure in agora-phobic clients by using cognitive therapy. The most recent (Öst et al., 2004) used the programme of Clark et al. (1995) to include exposure, as a behavioural experiment, suggested in cognitive therapy with the clients. This was compared with clients kept on a waiting list and with graded exposure similar to that described above. On almost all measures, both active treat-ments produced a greater improvement than was evident in those clients on the waiting list. However, there were no differences between the two treatment groups on the numbers of panic attacks or on fear and the performance of behaviour tests. Furthermore, there were no consistent differences to suggest that testing more participants would show significant differences between the two treatments. It would appear, therefore, that the most recently developed cognitive therapy added no benefits to treatment by exposure. However, this may have occurred because the treatments were insufficiently different, both groups undergoing exposure. The authors provide no details about exposure in the cognitive therapy group to test this.

However, interoceptive exposure may be used to treat agoraphobia when situational exposure is unsuitable. Experiencing symptoms simulating those of a panic attack may be a more direct and efficient means of doing that. Several authors have listed ways of exposing clients to the symptoms of a panic attack (Clark and Salkovskis, 1987; Anthony et al., unpublished (quoted by Taylor, 2000); Hackman, 2004; Taylor, 2000). These are shown in Table 14.1 and need to be practised as frequently and for as long as situational exposure in the treatment of agoraphobia, as noted above. Therefore, homework and records of this will be important.

How accurately do symptoms of panic need to be simulated in this way? As noted in Chapter 13, the over-breathing test does not reproduce the symptoms of panic reliably. Furthermore, there are no studies of the other procedures in the accuracy with which they can simulate panic symptoms. However, the array of procedures for interoceptive exposure in Table 14.1 suggests that no single exercise would be sufficient to replicate all symptoms in every person who experiences panic attacks. Nevertheless, it is unclear what degree of resemblance between panics and interoceptive exposure is necessary for successful treatment. Some clients, for example, can say that feelings of unreality in provocation tests do not match their experience of unreality in panic. Nevertheless, sometimes exposure to such tests can diminish their anxiety.

Table 14.1 Provocation tests that may simulate interoceptive sensations of panic

Sensation	Procedure
Dizziness or feelings of unreality	Spinning in a standing position Over-breathing for 30 breaths/minute while seated
Shaking or trembling	Tense the muscles in the forearm and hold that for several minutes
Feelings of unreality	Stare at a grid or a spot on the wall.
Restricted breathing	Hold breath for 30 seconds or breathe through the mouth with a straw
Racing pulse or heart beat or breathlessness	Run on the spot or up stairs or do press-ups as long as fitness allows
Chest pain	Inhale deeply while holding the muscles of the upper chest tightly for around 2 minutes

COGNITIVE THERAPY

Exposure to feared situations may not produce a satisfactory outcome in some cases (Fava et el., 2001). In addition, some patients can be highly distressed at the prospect or occurrence of panic attacks but show minimal avoidance of situations where they have occurred. Therefore, it can be necessary to use cognitive therapy to treat the panic attacks. Cognitive therapy (Clark, 1989; Clark and Salkovskis 1987; Clark et al., 1999) elicits clients' hypotheses about their symptoms, especially about the triggers for their onset and about their causes and possible outcome. Clients' safety behaviours have to be identified: how the clients have coped with the panics. This is clarified in a discussion about the most recent panic, or the most alarming one, which is usually the first (Figure 14.1). Under what circumstances did it happen? How did symptoms develop? It is important to obtain an account of all of these. Sometimes it is necessary to prompt the client with a list because clients will often describe the most frightening one and forget the rest. Next, it is important to ask clients what they did immediately and what they have done as a consequence since: the safety behaviours. They may describe attempting to take deep breaths, feeling their pulse, sit down and rest, slow their breathing, attempt to relax or make up a shopping list or rush to the toilet. Subsequently, they may have visited their doctors, planned routes that passed places of safety, such as pharmacists and hospitals, sat next to toilets or attempted to increase their physical fitness by visiting an aerobics classes or avoided strenuous exercise altogether. What did they think was happening to them? Some will say the symptoms meant that they were about to have a heart attack; others may acknowledge that they had a panic attack, especially if they have been advised by their doctors or emergency ambulance crews. However, they may believe that panic attacks can cause serious damage such as heart failure.

The escalation of panic and the development of a panic disorder: a flow diagram

With the client, all these experiences should be written in a flow diagram (see Figure 14.1) as a model for the escalation of panic: the circumstances and what could have been the trigger for the panic, the symptoms and how they developed, the client's beliefs about what was happening, the development of the client's anxiety; then what happened to the symptoms, what the client did next, how much more vigilant and attentive to symptoms and so on. The circular nature of these influences can be illustrated in the diagram, which shows how, at each of these points, the symptoms and anxiety grows worse. At this juncture, the client's behaviours afterwards to prevent panics recurring or escalating could be discussed with a series of questions and observations. 'What do you think would happen if you didn't . . .?', 'Doing . . . hasn't

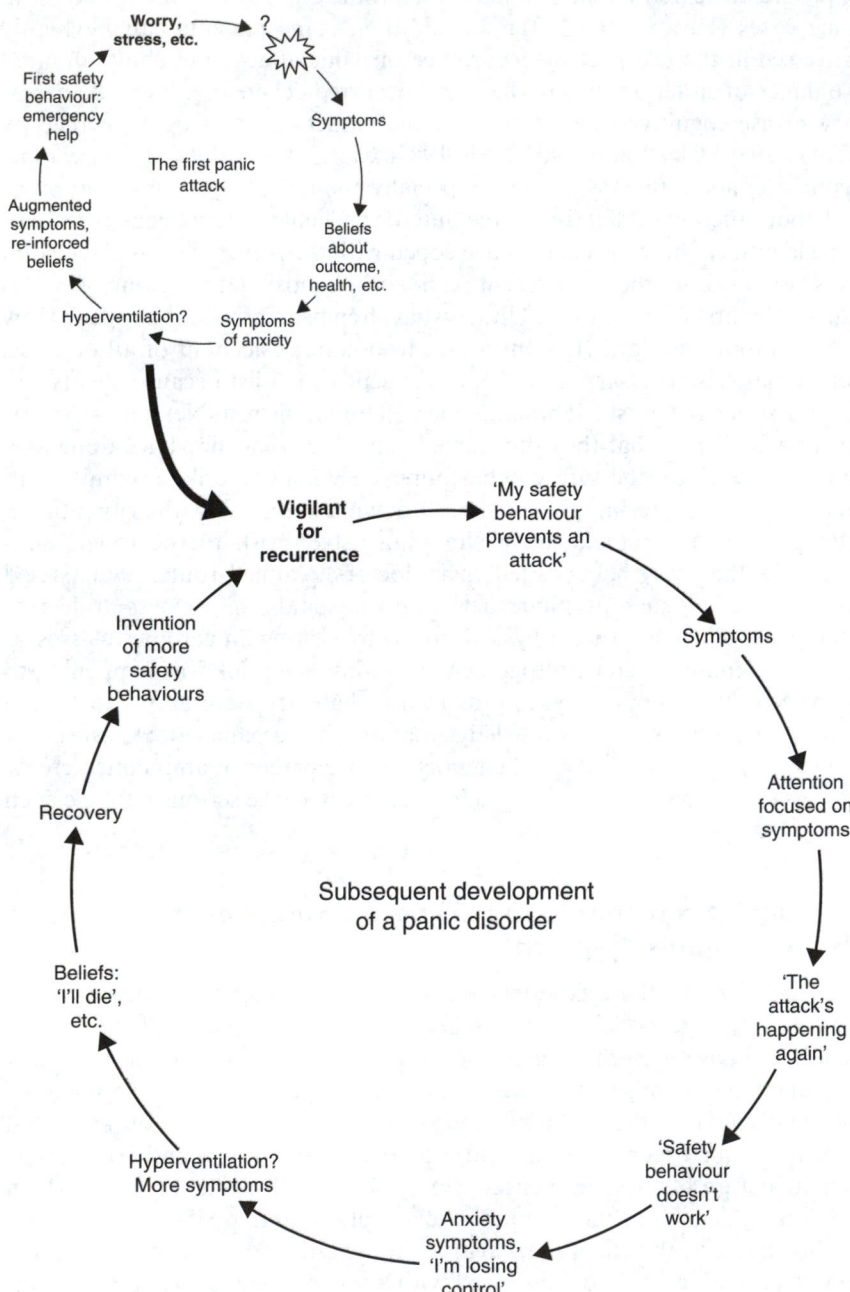

Figure 14.1 The origins and development of a panic disorder.

stopped you having panics', 'If the panics were really harmless, what effect do you think doing . . . would have?'

HYPOTHESIS TESTING AND CHALLENGING: USING BEHAVIOURAL EXPERIMENTS

A client who attributes symptoms to anxiety

A client experienced abdominal discomfort as one of the first symptoms of a panic attack on her daily journey to work. She acknowledged that her abdominal discomfort was a symptom of anxiety. She believed that her discomfort meant that she would lose control of her bowels, which would make her rush to the toilet; many people would look up and notice her discomfort or even that she was soiling herself. This belief made her more anxious, which led to greater abdominal discomfort but as long as she remained near the toilet she believed that her anxiety would not be so great that she would lose control of her bowels. As an additional measure she ate nothing for breakfast and did not have a coffee as she did when she did not have to go to work. She agreed that in this way she would not form a realistic belief about the likelihood that she would lose control of her bowel movements in public. Rating on a ten-point scale, she believed that she had no control over her bowel movements.

The client agreed to drop the safety behaviour of eating no breakfast and avoiding coffee. She was accompanied on her journey to work by a therapist, who sat at some distance from her to check that the client was not using safety behaviours that had not been disclosed.

Having repeated this for a week, the client acknowledged that the strength of her belief in having no control had diminished with the experiment. However, she attributed this to the presence of the therapist: she believed that she felt less apprehensive because of that and was less likely to become so anxious that she would become incontinent. Therefore, she agreed to sit alone in a carriage on the train and to be met by the therapist at her destination. Again, her belief about the likelihood of incontinence diminished over a week as her anxiety did not lead to that outcome. In the next behavioural experiment she agreed to sit in a carriage where she was not near any toilet and she had not checked to see where the toilet was. At this point her belief about incontinence had diminished consistently to near zero levels and she continued to take the train to work.

Other experiments had been considered to disconfirm her belief that fellow passengers would watch her if she had to go to the toilet abruptly and so would notice if she soiled herself. The strength of her belief in the validity of this could have been challenged by the therapist acting as a model while the client watched the reactions of others. The client could then act this out herself as further disconfirmation.

In practice, a single behavioural experiment is often not sufficient to tackle a panic disorder. A series of experiments, even repeating the same one, is often necessary to challenge clients' new hypotheses.

A client who attributes symptoms to suffocation

A client had to travel to the South of France from London by rail whenever she visited her parents. This entailed passing through the tunnel under the English Channel for about 20 minutes. During this time on her last journey she had experienced a panic attack, and believed that this would occur on subsequent trips. In the panic attack she had difficulty in breathing. She thought that she would use up the available air so she would suffocate. When asked what was happening to her that led her to use the air, she said that her anxiety about going through the tunnel made her breathe fast. That was probably correct because anxiety can accelerate breathing. The therapist asked if the other passengers would also be using up the available air and so would also suffocate. The client responded by saying that they would not be so anxious and so would not be breathing so fast. When it was suggested to her that she would be using up their air also, the strength of her belief that she would suffocate, unlike them, did not diminish.

The client's most notable safety behaviour was to take a diazepam before entering the train and again shortly before it entered the tunnel, or even earlier if she began to experience breathing difficulties. She agreed, however, that despite the diazepam she believed that she could still get a panic attack. The therapist then confirmed that people do breathe more rapidly during anxiety and that this probably means that they need more air. Anxiety requires the body to use more energy and it needs more oxygen for that. The therapist then said that there are reflexes in the body to prevent one passing out in these circumstances. This was explained without reference to the carbon dioxide explanation of hyperventilation (see Chapter 13). With some people who might readily understand it, a description of the role of carbon dioxide in stimulating specialised receptors to trigger breaking can be helpful.

However, therapists should avoid relying on giving clients explanations as these, from doctors and others, will not have provided sufficient reassurance before. Instead, the therapist in this case suggested a behavioural experiment, 'I wonder if we could show you what happens to you when you become anxious so that we can show you that you would not pass out'.

The therapist then arranged to use a small testing cubicle, which had enough space to accommodate the therapist, an assistant and the client. It had no windows and had a heavy sound-proof door. The client would not allow the therapist to take her there using the elevator in the building so they had to use the staircase. Then she would not allow the therapist to close the door of the cubicle. However, after 10 minutes rest, she allowed this.

To demonstrate that fast breathing could cause some of the symptoms that she had experienced on the train, but would not cause her to collapse, the therapist and then the assistant modelled over-breathing. After over-breathing at 30 breaths per minute for 3 minutes they described their symptoms. These were mainly dizziness, sensations of unreality and breathlessness on stopping. The client did not believe strongly that the demonstration had exhausted the air in the cubicle but she was asked to rate her belief that if she were to over-breathe, she could collapse. The therapist then followed the same procedure, which had involved calling out 'breath in, breath out' at 2-second intervals, so that the client could practise over-breathing. The strength of her belief about collapsing did reduce with this exercise. She agreed that she had been breathing far faster than she had remembered doing in the train. The therapist then arranged with the client to repeat the exercise a week later, the client having agreed not to take any diazepam before the test.

Other, similar experiments could be devised by using the other provocation tests listed above for exposure treatment. The success of both of these examples can be explained by the exposure principle, which suggests that exposure to the anxiety provoked by curtailing visits to the toilet (in the first case) and undergoing hyperventilation (in the second) would allow fear to peak and then diminish. Indeed, exposure is often part of cognitive therapy (Clark et al., 1995; Marks et al., 1995). However, the explanation given to clients is different and the immediate measure of outcome also differs. In cognitive therapy it is the strength of belief in the client's hypothesis that is recorded; in exposure therapy, the client's anxiety at each exposure is noted.

In cognitive therapy, as with exposure noted above, there can be some difficulty in finding a provocation test (see Table 14.1) that can reproduce the symptoms of a panic attack. Nevertheless, almost any interoceptive sensation in some clients can provoke the belief that such sensations are dangerous and so an exact match may not be necessary to challenge this.

Safety behaviours can be counter-productive

Some safety behaviours not only prevent the client's testing hypotheses but also can make the symptoms worse. Behavioural experiments can be arranged to demonstrate this to clients, as shown in the following example.

> A client experienced panic attacks, especially during the onset of sleep, brought on by a feeling of flatulence in his abdomen. He believed that his panic attacks were symptoms of anxiety brought about by his belief that his abdominal discomfort was a sign of cancer. To reduce this feeling, he would attempt to expel air by belching repeatedly. It was possible that this induced him to swallow air, which led to increased flatulence shortly after. His doctor had referred him with a note that he probably suffered from 'aerophagia'. To test this, the client was asked to record the strength of his belief that his discomfort meant that he had cancer. He also recorded his level of anxiety about this, as well as a rating to describe his flatulence. He then made these ratings every evening, having agreed not to attempt to expel air for 2 weeks. Within this period, his anxiety, belief and abdominal discomfort had diminished substantially.

Similar paradoxical effects have been noted in clients who take deep breaths when they feel that a panic attack is imminent. That can amount to over-breathing, which could augment the symptoms of panic. This is common in agoraphobic clients: they avoid exercise, which brings on feared symptoms of exertion, so they become less physically fit so that alarming symptoms such as breathlessness become more frequent.

Demonstration that thoughts can start symptoms of panic

For some subjects, describing in great detail the occurrence of their worst panic can produce symptoms of panic (Bass et al., 1989). In the demonstrations by Bass et al. several of patients had low resting levels of carbon dioxide and so may have been experiencing mild panic symptoms already. Clark et al.

(1988) describe a task in which clients read their symptoms paired with a word denoting a distressing outcome. For example, 'unreality' is accompanied by 'insane'. In their study of a small sample, the authors noted that the majority of their patients experienced symptoms similar to those of the onset of panic.

Demonstrations that vigilance can increase symptoms

To demonstrate that heightened vigilance in the cognitive model can make symptoms noticeable, asking clients to focus attention on an activity such as their breathing, can demonstrate how easily symptoms, normally out of consciousness, can be detected. Conversely, distracting them by, say, asking them to name all the objects in the room beginning with a certain letter can make current symptoms less noticeable. This may help to convince clients that vigilance can play a part in escalation of symptoms. However, that may then encourage clients to use distraction as a safety behaviour.

PHARMACOLOGICAL TREATMENT

The NICE guidelines (McIntosh et al., 2004) recommend the antidepressant SSRIs paroxetine, sertraline, fluvoxamine, fluoxetine and citalopram as the first-line pharmacological treatment for panic disorders. However, most studies of SSRIs do not study participants after they have been withdrawn from the medication. Studies that do conduct follow-up trials after the pharmacological treatment of the acute phase of a panic disorder show that between 30 and 50% of patients relapse (Roy-Byrne and Cowley, 2002). The NICE guidelines advise against the use of anxiolytic tranquilliser benzodiazepines, such as diazepam and lorazepam, because of their long-term adverse effects (Petursson and Lader, 1984) and the rapidity with which they lose their clinical effectiveness. Tricyclic antidepressants, notably imipramine and clomipramine, which are not licensed for panic disorders in the UK, may be used if SSRIs are not sufficiently effective. The most notable study of combined psychological and pharmacological treatment (Barlow et al., 2000) has shown that imipramine plus cognitive therapy is more effective than cognitive therapy alone during the acute phase of the illness. However, when the medication was withdrawn, the group who had the combined treatment was more distressed than the patients who had received only cognitive therapy. Moreover, the combined group was no better than the patients who had been given imipramine alone.

Therefore, imipramine can accelerate recovery with cognitive therapy during the early stages of panic disorder but can be counter-productive during the later stages of the illness when it is withdrawn. This may occur because the use of imipramine in active treatment detracts from clients' using the approaches practised in cognitive therapy. In addition, it can be difficult to persuade clients to give up medication that appears to have helped them. This study appears to suggest that imipramine should not be withdrawn after the acute phase and so this regime would confirm clients' beliefs. Therefore, the consequences of indefinite use or difficulties in persuading patients to give up the medication need to be weighed against the advantages in treating the early stages of a panic disorder.

OTHER TREATMENTS

Relaxation

Some clients can present with medical complications, such as asthma and coronary artery disease, which might restrict the use of some of the procedures (see Table 14.1) for exposure and behavioural experiments noted above. Some of the following may be helpful but should be discussed with the client's physician before being used.

In progressive muscular relaxation, clients are asked to tense each muscle group in turn and then relax them. For example, 'Clench your fists, hold that until count to ten, 1 . . . 7, 8, 9, 10; now relax' and so on. Progressive muscular relaxation has a long history as a treatment for anxiety disorders, despite discouraging evidence (Lichstein, 1988) that it has little immediate effect on subjects' reports and physiological signs of anxiety. However, as noted earlier in this chapter, one study (Beck et al., 1994) has shown that progressive relaxation was as effective as cognitive therapy, although the study results are confusing. Both treatments were better than 'minimal contact' with a therapist in the number of panic symptoms reported at the end of treatment. However, only in the clients who had cognitive therapy was there a significant decline in the number of symptoms. This was because they presented more symptoms at the outset. The cognitive therapy was an early version of the symptom control package of Barlow and others (Barlow and Cerny, 1994). It is not clear, therefore, if relaxation would be as effective in comparison with other disciplines of cognitive therapy (e.g. Clark, 1989).

Applied relaxation (Öst, 1987) trains clients in progressive muscular relaxation and recognition of early signs of anxiety before giving practice in relaxation to brief prompts in tension-provoking situations. However, the only study independent of Öst and his colleagues provided little support for applied relaxation as a treatment for panic disorder.

Breathing training

Because some clients inhale without expanding their diaphragms (the muscles underlying the chest), their intake of air is much less than need be. They probably breathe fast to compensate, with some risk of over-breathing. Barlow and Cerny (1994) encouraged clients to raise the abdomen under the chest while keeping the upper chest still as they breathed in. Then the clients were asked to slow their breathing until they take 8 seconds for each inhalation–exhalation cycle.

Cappo and Holmes (1984) made use of a reflex during exhalation that slows heart rate. They instructed their clients, who were not selected for panic disorder, to breathe slowly at a rate of 6 cycles per minute, inhaling for 2 seconds and breathing out for 8. The clients' reports and physiological measures, when they were told to anticipate electric shocks, showed reduced arousal. Electric shocks were not, however, given.

Sartory and Olajide (1988) used another procedure to slow heart rate, which they describe as follows, 'pressing on one eye during expiration, secondly massaging the carotid (artery) and thereby stimulating baroreceptors and, finally, Valsalva. This consists in increasing the pressure in the chest by means of tensing abdominal and intercostal muscles after a deep inhalation' (p. 432). This, together with relaxation and practice in abdominal breathing, showed some benefits in reducing the impact of panic attacks in nine patients.

Computer delivery of cognitive behaviour therapy

Many studies of CBT have been delivered to clients by computer with material stored in compact discs or on the internet. However, a recent NICE technical report has concluded that the evidence is not strong enough to recommend this source of treatment (Kaltenhaller et al., 2002).

CONCLUDING REMARKS

The common occurrence of other problems with panic disorders has been noted on several occasions in these chapters. Depression is probably the most common co-morbid affliction. However, almost all outcome studies ignore this. Nevertheless, as noted earlier, depression may benefit from successful treatment of co-existing panic disorder (Tsao et al., 2002). Moreover, depression has not impeded the success of CBT in treating panic disorder in one study (McLean et al., 1998). This would be expected if the panic disorder had led to the depression by restricting the clients' quality of life. There is no formulation in this paper to suggest how the successful treatment of the panic disorder affected depression.

What is the clinical significance of the outcome of CBT for panic disorders? Studies that have followed clients for up to 15 months after treatment suggest that average beneficial effects are retained, although around a third still have panics (Clark et al., 1994, 1999).

How uniform are the effects of treatment across settings and therapists?

Stuart et al. (2000) observed that clients treated in a service setting, not a centre normally associated with clinical trials, were just as often free of panics as patients reported in controlled outcome studies. Nevertheless, it is not clear if the therapists were alerted to the fact that they were participating in a trial and so it is not clear if this outcome could be typical of a service setting. The study does not describe the participating therapists but another study (Huppert et al., 2001) has shown that therapists do differ in their effectiveness in conducting CBT for panic disorder even though they were trained and practised to a similar level of competence. Length of experience in conducting psychotherapy, but not in CBT, was influential.

Nevertheless, the NICE recommendations (McIntosh et al., 2004) say that treatment should be delivered according to standard and proven guidelines. However, clients may not follow therapists' recommendations; they may prefer their own safety behaviours. Evidence suggests that if clients do not follow the recommended procedures they are less likely to benefit (Schmidt and Woolaway-Bickel, 2000).

Do clients' educational backgrounds influence their response to treatment? Very few studies have addressed this. Moreover, most studies do not even describe the educational or social status of their participants. People with a higher education are more likely to seek treatment (Goodwin and Anderson, 2002) and so are more likely to be the participants in clinical trials (Stuart et al., 2000). However, the one outcome study that does describe the educational status of clients (Stuart et al., 2000) provides no data about the effect of educational status of clients on the effectiveness of CBT for panic disorders. This treatment therefore, is proven for literate, educated people but not for others. Accordingly, experience suggests that people who have minimal literacy skills should not be overburdened with written record-keeping and wordy treatment manuals and explanations.

REFERENCES

Arntz, A. (2002) Cognitive therapy v. interoceptive exposure as treatment of panic disorders without agoraphobia. *Behaviour Research and Therapy*, 40, 325–341.

Arntz, A. and Van den Hout, M. (1996) Psychological treatments of panic disorder without agoraphobia: Cognitive therapy versus applied relaxation. *Behaviour Research and Therapy*, 34, 113–121.

Barlow, D. H. and Cerny, J. A. (1994) *Psychological Treatment of Panic*. New York: Guilford Press.

Barlow, D. H. and Craske, M. G. (1994) *Mastery of your Anxiety and Panic – II*. San Antonio, TX: Psychological Corporation.

Barlow, D. H., Gorman, J. M., Shear, M. K. and Woods, S. W. (2000) Cognitive-behavioural therapy, imipramine or their combination for panic disorder. A randomised controlled trial. *Journal of the American Medical Association*, 283, 2529–2536. [erratum in *JAMA*, 2000, 284, 2450].

Barlow, D. H., Raffa, S. D. and Cohen, E. M. (2002) Psychosocial treatments for panic disorders, phobias and generalised anxiety disorder. In: P. E. Nathan and J. M. Gorman (eds) *A Guide to Treatments That Work*, 2nd edn. New York: Oxford University Press.

Bass, C., Lelliott, P. and Marks, I. (1989) Fear talk versus voluntary hyperventilation in agoraphobics and normals, a controlled study. *Psychological Medicine*, 19, 669–676.

Beck, J. G., Stanley, M. A., Baldwin, L. E., Deagle, E. A. et al. (1994) Comparison of cognitive therapy and relaxation training for panic disorders. *Journal of Consulting and Clinical Psychology*, 62, 818–826.

Cappo, B. M. and Holmes, D. S. (1984) The utility of prolonged respiratory exhalation for reducing physiological and psychological arousal in non-threatening and threatening situations. *Journal of Psychosomatic Research*, 28, 265–273.

Clark, D. M. (1988) A cognitive model of panic attacks. In: S. Rachman and J. D. Maser (eds) *Panic: Psychological Perspectives*. New York: John Wiley.

Clark, D. M. (1989) Anxiety states: Panic and generalised anxiety. In: K. Hawton, P. Salkovskis, J. Kirk et al. (eds) *Cognitive Behaviour Therapy for Psychiatric Problems: A Practical Guide*. Oxford: Oxford University Press.

Clark, D. M. and Salkovskis, P. (1987) *Cognitive Treatment for Panic Attacks: Therapist's Manual*. Oxford: Department of Psychiatry, University of Oxford.

Clark, D. M., Salkovskis, P., Gelder, M. G., Koehler, C., Martin, M., Anastasiades, P. et al. (1988) Tests of a cognitive theory of panic. In: I. Hand and H. Wittchen (eds) *Panic and Phobias 2*. Berlin: Springer-Verlag.

Clark, D. M., Salkovskis, P. M., Hackmann, A., Middleton, H. et al. (1994) A comparison of cognitive therapy, applied relaxation and imipramine in the treatment of panic disorder. *British Journal of Psychiatry*, 164, 759–769.

Clark, D. M., Salkovskis, P. M., Hackmann, A. and Middleton, H. (1995) Cognitive therapy for panic: Reply. *British Journal of Psychiatry*, 166, 542–543.

Clark, D. M., Salkovskis, P. M., Hackman, A., Wells, A., Ludgare, J. and Gelder, M. (1999) Brief cognitive therapy for panic disorder: A standardised controlled trial. *Journal of Consulting and Clinical Psychology*, 67, 583–589.

Craske, M. G. and Barlow, D. H. (2001) Panic disorder and agoraphobia. In: D. H. Barlow (ed) *A Clinical Handbook of Psychological Disorders: A Step-by-Step Treatment Manual, 3rd edn*. New York: Guilford Press.

Emmelkamp, P. N. G. and Van der Hout, A. (1983) Failure in treating agoraphobia. In: E. B. Foa and P. N. G. Emmelkamp (eds) *Failures in Behaviour Therapy*. New York: John Wiley.

Fava, G. A., Rafanelli, C., Grandi, S., Conti, S., Reini, C., Mangelli, L. and Belluardo, P. (2001) Long term outcome of panic disorder with agoraphobia treated by exposure. *Psychological Medicine*, 31, 891–898.

Febbraro, G. A. R., Clum, G. A., Roodman, A. A. and Wright, J. H. (1999) The limits of bibliotherapy: A study of the differential effectiveness of self-administered interventions in individuals with panic attacks. *Behaviour Therapy*, 30, 209–222.

Goodwin, R. and Anderson, R. M. (2002) Use of the Behavioural Model of Health Care Use to identify correlates of use of treatment for panic attacks in the community. *Social Psychiatry and Psychiatric Epidemiology*, 37, 212–219.

Hackman, A. (2004) Panic disorder and agoraphobia. In: J. Bennettt-Levy, G. Butler, M. Fennell, A. Hackman, M. Mueller and D. Westbrook (eds) *Oxford Guide to*

Behavioural Experiments in Cognitive Therapy. Oxford: Oxford University Press.

Huppert, J. D., Bulka, L. F., Barlow, D. H., Gormon, J. M., Slear, M. K. and Woods, S. W. (2001) Therapists, therapist variables and cognitive behavioural therapy outcome in a multicenter trial for panic disorder. *Journal of Consulting and Clinical Psychology*, 69, 747–755.

Ingham, C. (2000) *Panic Attacks*. London: Thorsons.

Kaltenhaler, E., Shackleg, P., Stevens, K., Deverley, C., Parry, G. and Chilcott, J. (2002) *Computerised Cognitive Behaviour Therapy for Depression and Anxiety*. London: National Institute for Health and Clinical Excellence.

Kent, G. (1985) Memory of dental pain. *Pain*, 21, 187–194.

Lichstein, K. L. (1988) *Clinical Relaxation Strategies*. New York: John Wiley.

Marks, I. (1987) *Fears, Phobias and Rituals*. Oxford: Oxford University Press.

Marks, I., Basoglu, M. and Noshirvani, H. (1995) Cognitive therapy for panic. *British Journal of Psychiatry*, 166, 541–542.

Matthews, A. M., Gelder, M. G. and Johnson, D. W. (1981) *Agoraphobia: Nature and Treatment*. London: Tavistock.

McIntosh, A., Cohen, A., Turnbull, N., Esmonde, L., Dennis, P., Eatock, J. et al. (2004) *Clinical Guidelines and Evidence Review for Panic Disorder and Generalised Anxiety Disorder*. Sheffield: University of Sheffield/London: National Collaborating Centre for Primary Care. (Available on the National Institute for Health and Clinical Excellence (NICE) website: http://www.nice.org.uk).

McLean, P. D., Woody, S., Taylor, S. and Koch, W. J. (1998) Comorbid panic disorder and major depression: implications for cognitive-behavioural therapy. *Journal of Consulting and Clinical Psychology*, 66, 240–247.

Milrod, B., Busch, F., Leon, A. C., Shapiro, T., Aronson, A., Raiphe, J. et al. (2000) Open trial of psychodynamic psychotherapy for panic disorder: a pilot study. *American Journal of Psychiatry*, 157, 1878–1880.

Murphy, M. T., Michelson, L. K., Marchione, K. et al. (1998) The role of self-directed in vivo exposure in combination with cognitive therapy, relaxation training or therapist-assisted exposure in the treatment of panic disorder with agoraphobia. *Journal of Anxiety Disorders*, 12, 117–138.

Öst, L-G. (1987) Applied relaxation: description of a coping technique and review of controlled studies. *Behaviour Research and Therapy*, 25, 397–409.

Öst, L-G., Thulin, U. and Ramnero, J. (2004) Cognitive behaviour therapy vs exposure in vivo in the treatment of panic disorder with agoraphobia. *Behaviour Research and Therapy*, 42, 1105–1128.

Petursson, H. and Lader, M. (1984) *Dependence on Tranquilisers*. Oxford: Oxford University Press.

Rachman, S. and de Silva, P. (2004) *Panic Disorder. The Facts*. Oxford: Oxford University Press.

Roy-Byrne, P. P. and Cowley, D. S. (2002) Pharmacological treatments for panic disorder, generalised anxiety disorder, specific phobia and social anxiety disorder. In: P. E. Nathan and J. M. Gorman (eds) *A Guide to Treatments That Work*, 2nd edn. New York: Oxford University Press.

Sartory, G. and Olajide, D. (1988) Vagal innervation techniques in the treatment of panic disorder. *Behaviour Research and Therapy*, 26, 431–434.

Schmidt, N. B. and Woolaway-Bickel, K. (2000). The effects of treatment compliance on outcome in cognitive-behavioural therapy for panic disorder: Quality versus quantity. *Journal of Consulting and Clinical Psychology*, 68, 13–18.

Schmidt, N. B., Woolaway-Bickel, K., Trakowski, J., Santiago, H., Storey, J., Koselka, M. and Cook, J. (2000) Dismantling cognitive-behavioral treatment for panic disorder: questioning the utility of breathing retraining. *Journal of Consulting and Clinical Psychology*, 68, 417–424.

Silove, D. and Manicavasagar, V. (2001) *Overcoming Panic*. New York: New York University Press.

Stuart, G. L., Wade, W. W. and Treat, T. A. (2000) Effectiveness of an empirically based treatment for panic disorder delivered in a service clinic setting: 1-year follow-up. *Journal of Consulting and Clinical Psychology*, 68, 506–512.

Taylor, S. (2000) *Understanding and Treating Panic Disorder. Cognitive-Behavioural Approaches*. Chichester: John Wiley.

Tryon, W. W. (2005) Possible mechanisms for why desensitisation and exposure therapy work. *Clinical Psychology Review*, 25, 67–96.

Tsao, J. C., Mystkowski, J. L., Tucker, B. G. and Gaske, M. G. (2002) Effects of cognitive behavioural therapy for panic disorder on comorbid conditions: Replication and extension. *Behaviour Therapy*, 33, 493–509.

Chapter 15

Sexual dysfunction

Investigation

Padmal de Silva

INTRODUCTION

Dysfunction and deviation

Sexual dysfunctions are persistent impairments or disturbances in sexual desire, arousal or orgasm. They are usually considered as a group of problems within 'normal' sexuality, different from sexual deviations, or paraphilias, and the two are treated as separate clinical categories. This is a convenient distinction, but it must be noted that there can be overlap between the two (de Silva, 1995; Metz and Sawyer, 2004). For example, a male presenting with erectile difficulties with his wife may, on close enquiry, show a history of paraphiliac sexual activity involving, say, leather and rubber garments, and the content of his sexual fantasies may be exclusively or predominantly geared to these activities. Clearly this would be a case of sexual dysfunction and sexual deviation co-existing and interrelated. Similarly, it is not uncommon to find patients whose presenting problems take the form of sexual deviation and who also have difficulties in normal sexual activity. Not infrequently, sex offenders with a history of sexual abuse against children report recurrent failure in their attempts at normal sexual activity with consenting adult partners. Thus the distinction between sexual dysfunction and sexual deviation should not be seen as a mutually exclusive and rigid one, but only as a convenient general grouping based on the nature of the presenting problem. In the assessment of patients presenting with sexual dysfunction, enquiry has to be made about paraphiliac activities, desires and fantasies, and the relationship of these factors to the dysfunction needs to be examined.

Degrees of dysfunction

Another point to be borne in mind is that sexual dysfunction cannot be considered as a discrete phenomenon qualitatively different from non-dysfunction. It is not the case that there are persons who have developed sexual dysfunction and those who have not, in an absolute sense. More often, functional and dysfunctional presentations are on the same continuum; there are, in other words, degrees of dysfunction, and – in one person or couple – areas of very satisfactory sexual activity alongside areas of difficulty. Also, what is seen as dysfunctional may vary from person to person, from couple to couple and from culture to culture (Bhugra and de Silva, 1993). It is worth noting that non-clinical populations – that is, individuals and couples who do not consider themselves to be sexually dysfunctional and who therefore do not attend clinics or go for other help – include among them a proportion whose sexual functioning is in some respect less than satisfactory. Frank et al. (1978) reported a study of 100 well-educated, happily married couples. Over 80% of the couples reported that their sexual and marital relations were happy and satisfactory. However, 40% of the men reported erectile or ejaculatory problems and over 60% of the women reported problems of arousal or orgasm.

CLASSIFICATION

With these constraints in mind, let us now look at the common categories of sexual dysfunction that present at clinics and other services for help. Many useful classifications have been proposed (Masters and Johnson, 1970; Hawton, 1985; World Health Organization (WHO), 1992; American Psychiatric Association (APA), 1994), although there are inherent problems in all these classificatory systems (Potts and Bhugra, 1995). The following section gives simple and clinically useful classifications of male and female dysfunctions.

It must be noted that all of these can either be lifelong (the problem has been there since the onset of sexual functioning) or acquired (the problem has developed only after a period of normal functioning). Another distinction that applies to all dysfunctions is that between generalised (the problem is present in any situation or with any partner) and situational (the problem is limited to some situations or partners, e.g. a man may have good erections when masturbating but not when he is with a partner).

Male disorders

Male sexual dysfunctions can be classified as follows. As can be seen, the categories are not necessarily mutually exclusive:

* low sexual interest/desire
* erectile dysfunction
* premature ejaculation
* orgasmic dysfunction

- dyspareunia
- sexual aversion.

Low sexual interest/desire is not uncommon (Kaplan, 1977, 1979; Weeks and Gambescia, 2002). The individual will not normally complain of this except in the context of a relationship when it becomes a problem for the couple or when there has been a marked or sudden reduction from a previous level.

Erectile dysfunction refers to erectile failure or difficulty. There may be an inability to get or to sustain an erection; or the problem may be lack of strong-enough erections for successful sexual activity (Masters and Johnson, 1970; Weeks and Gambescia, 2000) Erectile problems are quite common and are probably the most common complaint of males who seek help in sex therapy clinics (Simons and Carey, 2001).

Premature ejaculation refers to the reaching of sexual climax far too soon for satisfactory sexual activity for the couple. It is often cited as one of the most common sexual dysfunctions (e.g. Kaplan, 1974; Laumann et al., 1999). The typical complaint of the male who seeks help with this problem is that he arrives at orgasm 'too quickly'. What is 'too quick'? This obviously cannot be defined in terms of time or in terms of the questionable concept of voluntary control (Kaplan, 1979). The problem has to be assessed in terms of how much it interferes with the sexual activity and the enjoyment of the couple. For example, consistent ejaculation before or immediately after penetration will clearly be a problem, whereas occasional climaxing within a short time will not. It is perhaps worth noting the Kinsey Report finding that 75% of their sample of 6,000 American males reported that they reached a climax within 2 minutes of penetration (Kinsey et al., 1948).

Orgasmic dysfunction, previously commonly called 'retarded ejaculation', refers to the failure or delay in reaching a climax despite a good deal of stimulation (Masters and Johnson, 1970; Dow, 1981). This is far less common than erectile dysfunction or premature ejaculation. It is important to note that in some cases the male does reach an orgasm, but does not ejaculate. This is a different problem and does not come under orgasmic dysfunction. It is called 'retrograde ejaculation' as what happens is that seminal fluid travels backwards into the bladder. This may occur as a result of certain drugs, or due to certain physical causes.

Dyspareunia, or pain in intercourse, is rare in males (Bancroft, 1989) and usually has a physical cause.

Sexual aversion refers to a strong dislike of certain aspects of sex. For example, a man may dislike his penis being touched at all, whereas his sexual desire in general and ability to engage in satisfactory intercourse is not impaired. It is also possible for someone to have a more pervasive sexual aversion, despite there being no lack of sexual desire; thus he may have frequent and enjoyable masturbatory experiences but would avoid, or not enjoy, interpersonal sex (APA, 1987; WHO, 1992).

Female disorders

Female sexual dysfunction may similarly be classified into the following, not necessarily mutually exclusive, categories:

- low sexual interest/desire
- arousal dysfunction
- orgasmic dysfunction
- vaginismus
- dyspareunia
- sexual aversion.

Low sexual interest/desire is similar to that in males (Lief, 1977). This becomes a presenting problem usually only within the context of a relationship. It is the most common problem presented by females attending sex clinics (e.g. Bancroft, 1989; Simons and Carey, 2001).

Arousal dysfunction is the impairment of the physiological arousal, indicated by failure of vaginal lubrication and expansion of the vaginal canal (Kaplan, 1979; Read, 1995).

Orgasmic dysfunction, also commonly referred to as 'anorgasmia', is the inability to reach orgasm, and is a common clinical presentation (Bancroft, 1989; Simons and Carey, 2001).

Vaginismus refers to the involuntary spasm of the muscles of the outer third of the vagina so that penetration is almost impossible (Masters and Johnson, 1970; APA, 1994). Typically, the muscle spasms occur in anticipation of intercourse or when penetration is attempted (Lamont, 1978). Its presentation in cases of non-consummated marriage is well known (Duddle, 1977). Bancroft (1989) reported that 13% of females presenting at his clinic ($n = 577$) complained of vaginismus. Low-frequency rates have been reported in many survey studies (Simons and Carey, 2001).

Dyspareunia is pain associated with intercourse, and is commonly related to other problems, including physical ones (Masters and Johnson, 1970; Meana et al., 1997).

Sexual aversion in females is similar to that in males. It refers to dislike either of all aspects of sex or of some specific aspects. For example, a woman may complain of an intense dislike of being touched on the breasts, or being kissed on the mouth. Sometimes there will be aversion to sex with a partner, while self-stimulation is enjoyable (Kolodny et al., 1979).

Some related factors

The above account of the main categories of the sexual dysfunction did not refer to certain key variables, which may contribute to the problem concerned. These are briefly mentioned below.

Ignorance, i.e. lack of proper information about sexual functioning, can be a major problem in sexual dysfunction (Bancroft, 1989; d'Ardenne, 2000). Not infrequently, the presenting problem is the result of either ignorance of basic facts about the sexual response system or certain misconceptions about sex (Masters and Johnson, 1970; Zilbereld, 1978, 1992). Young men sometimes worry a great deal about what they see as the rapidity with which they reach a climax in sex and, believing that the norm is much longer than it actually is, get into a state of stress and worry, which in turn can contribute to the development and maintenance of erectile or ejaculatory problems. In females, lack of knowledge or misconceived ideas can lead to fears about sex – such as that sexual intercourse is necessarily painful – which can cause real difficulties. Certain cultural groups foster some beliefs that can lead to difficulties in sexual adjustment. Among some Asian communities, for example, loss of semen excessively, or in adolescence, is considered as a cause of major sexual and other pathology. This can lead to problems in men who believe that they have made themselves vulnerable to these illnesses (de Silva and Dissanayake, 1989; Bhugra and de Silva, 1993).

The quality of a patient's knowledge about sex, and associated beliefs, are therefore as important to explore as the nature of the presenting problem itself.

Attitudes and other cognitions about sex and sexual activity are related to knowledge and beliefs. A person who has been brought up with a strictly moralistic attitude to sex, that is, that sex is for procreation only and not to be enjoyed, may find himself or herself sexually inhibited (Masters and Johnson, 1970). Such a person may also find a more libertarian attitude in his or her partner to be a source of conflict. One partner's desire for experimenting with different types of foreplay, with different positions for intercourse, and so on, may be unacceptable to the other partner whose attitudes reflect a stricter background. Attitudinal problems can thus play a crucial part in generating and perpetuating sexual dysfunction. Long-standing attitudes do not change easily and need to be examined in assessing a person's or couple's sexual life. It is interesting to note that the prevalence of vaginismus is much higher among Irish women than in many other groups studied (O'Sullivan, 1979; Barnes, 1986a, 1986b). Recent developments in cognitive theory have led to several useful discussions of cognitive factors that may contribute to sexual dysfunction (e.g. Andersen and Cyranowski, 1994; Andersen et al., 1999).

Anxiety is a major factor associated with sexual dysfunction (Masters and Johnson, 1970; Bancroft, 1989; McConaghy, 1993). Some difficulties are caused, at least partially, by anxiety and many are maintained and perpetuated by it. Wolpe (1958) stated that anxiety could be conditioned to sexual activity by experiences at any stage of life. The effects of early traumatic experiences on later sexual functioning, mediated via conditioned anxiety, is well documented (e.g. de Silva, 2001; Baker, 2002). Such anxiety can also arise from adulthood experiences. Anxiety about failure is a common factor associated with sexual dysfunction. Consider the example of a young man who fails to get an erection in an attempt to have intercourse in circumstances far from favourable for relaxed, comfortable sex (for example, in the back of a car, or in a place where there is the possibility being observed or disturbed). This failure may lead to anxiety about possible failure on subsequent occasions where sexual intercourse is attempted or contemplated, and this anxiety can now lead to repeated failure, which – in turn – increases the person's anxiety. With females, traumatic or unpleasant sexual experiences, such as being sexually assaulted or abused, may lead to generalised sexual anxiety that contributes to a sexual aversion. Sometimes the problem takes the form of a full-blown phobia of sex, or of men or male genital organs. Current anxieties, such as fear of getting pregnant, can also cause sexual difficulties. McConaghy (1993) gives a detailed discussion of the role of anxiety in sexual problems.

'Spectatoring' is associated with anxiety (Masters and Johnson, 1970). This refers to the tendency in a person to watch himself or herself during sexual activity. Sexually anxious persons may get into this role out of fear of failure. Rather than enjoying the sexual activity fully, the person is partly playing the role of a spectator of his or her own activity and success or failure. This may then lead to inhibited sexual action and enjoyment or even true failure. It must be noted, however, that spectatoring is not necessarily an inhibiting factor. Many men and women find watching themselves and their sexual reactions quite stimulating. The problem is that, when spectatoring becomes a feature in the sexual activity of someone already anxious about sex, it can perpetuate and sometimes worsen the difficulty (Beck et al., 1983).

Relationship problems and the relevance of the quality of the relationship between a couple to their sexual problems are self-evident (Woody, 1992; Crowe and Ridley, 2000). Sexual difficulties can develop easily in the context of a poor marital relationship; jealousy, fears and worries about infidelity, constant conflicts in areas of life other than sex, all may contribute to, or be reflected by, a sexual problem. When one considers the continuous nature of satisfactory sexual functioning and dysfunction, it is easy to see how non-sexual relationship problems can emphasise and exacerbate whatever minor difficulties there may be in a couple's sex life. Sex sometimes becomes the main battleground for marital conflicts, such as those associated with dominance, jealousy and punitiveness. Equally, a frankly sexual problem can cause wider relationship difficulties and, when couples present with marital problems, it is not unusual for enquiry to reveal that they are suffering from focal sexual dysfunctions (Zimmer, 1987). The overlap and inter-relationship between the two types of problem can be significant. See Chapter 17 for a discussion of relationship problems.

Physical problems can cause, or be associated with, sexual problems. The relevance of such factors as prolonged alcoholism, diabetes, ageing, neurological disorders, drugs, and so on to sexual activity is well established

- The nature of the problem in as much detail as required to obtain a full picture of the difficulty and all its associated factors, including anxiety and situational variations. In men with erectile dysfunction, particular inquiry should be made about whether early morning erections are present or not, as their presence usually helps to rule out the possibility that the problem is organic.
- The history of the problem: its beginnings and course, and present sexual activity, including masturbation.
- Partner's reactions to the problem, both in the sexual situation and in general.
- The extent of the person's knowledge about sexual matters.
- Cognitions about sex and about the problem, and general beliefs and attitudes about sexual matters, including those determined by his or her religion and culture.
- The person's sexual likes, dislikes and preferences, including paraphiliac interests, and fantasies.
- Past sexual history, including relevant early experiences.
- Psychiatric and medical factors, including drugs, alcohol, etc.; current depression is particularly important to assess.
- Menstrual history and relation of problem to menstrual cycle.
- Contraception and past pregnancies, and attitude to possibility of conception.
- General relationship factors.
- Previous relationships.
- Background factors, such as job, income, accommodation, and so on, which can be sources of stress.
- Previous treatment, if any.

More details may be needed in some of the areas than in others in a given case, and this is a matter of clinical judgement as the interview proceeds. Needless to say, the clinician must be prepared to vary his or her enquiry to suit each patient, as needed. Most clinicians rely on a general checklist of topics to enquire about as a matter of routine. Examples of such checklists are available in, among others, Hawton (1985) and Spence (1991). In practice, while such detailed checklists are indeed useful, flexibility is needed in their use; such a list should serve as a general guide rather than as something to be rigidly followed.

Individual and couple interviews

One major issue in interviewing patients with sexual dysfunction is whether the partners – when a couple present themselves for help – should be interviewed together or not. Different viewpoints have been expressed about this (Masters and Johnson, 1970; Bancroft, 1989; Wincze and Carey, 2001).

In general, a good arrangement is to see the couple jointly to start with and then to conduct assessment interviews separately. If two therapists are available, this may be done in parallel sessions; if not, more time should be spent with the partner with the presenting problem, followed by a briefer interview with the other partner. For the final part of the assessment, the partners are brought together again.

Motivation and selection

Assessment of the motivation of the patient/couple for therapy is an important aspect of the interview, although this may not prove easy in one interview except perhaps to identify those who are clearly unwilling to accept the therapy offered. As for suitability for therapy, an assessment comprising two interviews at most is usually sufficient to identify those who are clearly not likely to benefit from the therapy that can be offered. For example, presence of clear psychiatric illness will often require treatment of that condition first; and, when physical factors seem to be involved, investigations of these, and a physical examination, will have to be arranged prior to acceptance for therapy.

Physical examination and investigations

Some clinicians believe that all patients presenting with sexual dysfunction should routinely be examined physically (Kolodny et al., 1979; Spence, 1991). This is unnecessary, but it is essential that the facilities to have this and relevant investigations done if required in a given case are available. Bancroft has given an extremely useful set of indications for physical examination (Bancroft, 1989). These are: complaints of pain or discomfort during sex; recent history of ill-health or physical symptoms other than the sexual problem; recent onset of loss of sex drive with no apparent cause; when the patient believes that a physical cause is most likely, or is concerned about the genitalia (e.g. a man complaining that his penis is too small or bent, or a woman suspecting that there is something abnormal about her sexual organs); history of abnormal puberty or other endocrine disorder; in men, age over 50; in women, being in the pre- or post-menopausal age group; and in women, history of marked menstrual irregularities or infertility.

Where appropriate, the medical practitioner carrying out the physical examination will also carry out, or arrange for, relevant laboratory investigations. Details of the common investigations may be found in Hawton (1985), Bancroft (1989), McConaghy (1993) and Wincze and Carey (2001).

Questionnaires and inventories

Data obtained from the clinical interview can profitably be supplemented by the use of questionnaires and inventories. These help to cover some important areas quickly but, more importantly, they provide quantitative data that are particularly useful in evaluating the efficacy of treatment.

Several useful instruments are available for measurement of sexual experiences, attitudes, dysfunctions and other related matters. Hoon et al. (1976a) provide an inventory for the assessment of female sexual arousal. Lo Piccolo and Steger (1974) have developed an inventory to assess sexual interaction and satisfaction of a couple. Lief and Reed (1972) provide a questionnaire to assess both sexual knowledge and sexual attitudes, while Wilson (1978) describes a useful fantasy questionnaire that measures fantasies, desires and actual behaviours. The Derogatis Sexual Functioning Index (Derogatis and Melisaratos, 1979) is a wide-ranging scale of sexual functioning covering ten domains (e.g. information, desire, attitudes). However, although its comprehensiveness is no doubt an asset, its prohibitive length (245 items) makes it somewhat unwieldy for routine clinical use.

A valuable and widely used instrument is the Golombok–Rust Inventory of Sexual Satisfaction (GRISS; Rust and Golombok, 1986). This 28-item questionnaire, which has male and female versions, is intended for use with heterosexual couples or individuals in a current heterosexual relationship, and yields an overall score of the quality of sexual functioning. In addition, the following subscores can also be obtained: impotence, premature ejaculation, anorgasmia, vaginismus, infrequency, poor communication, dissatisfaction, non-sensuality and avoidance. This instrument has good reliability and is easy to use. In view of the wide range of measures it yields, the GRISS is an economical instrument to use routinely. A parallel, and equally economical, instrument for the assessment of the overall relationship is the Golombok–Rust Inventory of Marital State (GRIMS; Rust et al., 1988).

A few recently developed instruments are also worth considering. The International Index of Erectile Function (IIEF; Rosen et al., 1997) is a 15-item self-report questionnaire that has been validated in several languages. In addition to erectile function, it also yields scores in the domains of orgasmic function, sexual desire, satisfaction with intercourse and overall satisfaction.

A parallel version for measuring female sexual function has also been developed; this is the Female Sexual Function Index (FSFI; Rosen et al., 2000). It consists of 19 items and yields scores on sexual desire, arousal, lubrication, orgasm, satisfaction and pain.

A new instrument developed by Nobre and Pinto-Gouveia (2003), the Sexual Modes Questionnaire (SMQ), is a measure of the interactions among cognitions, emotions and sexual responses. The male version of the SMQ has 30 items and the female version 33 items. The rationale for developing the instrument was the need for assessing cognitions and emotions, and their impact on sexual functioning. The authors used cognitive theory as their framework.

The Sexual Dysfunctional Beliefs Questionnaire (Nobre et al., 2003) is a measure of beliefs about sexuality that are considered to be related to the development of sexual problems. This has 40 items, and there are male and female versions. Each item is rated on a five-point Likert scale.

A comprehensive compendium of sexuality-related measures has been produced by Davis et al. (1998), and may be consulted for information and comments on a wide range of instruments that are available.

When depression is a relevant factor needing to be assessed, a depression inventory such as the Beck Depression Inventory (BDI; Beck et al., 1961) may be used for this purpose (see Chapter 5).

Subjective ratings

Self-rating numerical scales may be used as part of assessment of the major variables in question for a given patient. For example, anxiety in sex, desire and sexual arousal may be rated by the patient on a 0–100 scale indicating subjective estimates. Patients usually find these scales easy to use. Equally simple to use are diaries, recording the frequency of target behaviours on a daily basis. Associated cognitions and anxiety ratings can also be recorded. A pre-designed diary provided by the assessor/therapist, specifying the targets to be recorded, is an effective way of obtaining baseline data as well as of monitoring change. Conte (1986) and Spence (1991), among others, provide discussions of these.

Physiological measures

Psychological techniques have been used widely in the measurement of male sexual function following impetus from the work of Masters and Johnson (1966, 1970). Penile plethysmography for the assessment of erection is widely used in research and can be used in clinical practice where needed and practicable (Wincze et al., 1988). The measure may be of either penile volume or penile circumference changes. Penile plethysmography has also been used to assess nocturnal erections in an attempt to distinguish psychogenic from organic erectile problems (e.g. Bradley et al., 1985). Detailed discussions of these and other laboratory techniques for the assessment of erectile problems are provided by McConaghy (1993), Schiavi (1992) and Wiegel et al. (2002). Physiological measures for female sexual functioning are more limited. One example is the photoplethysmography technique (Hoon et al., 1976b), in which vasocongestion in the vaginal walls is measured with the help of a probe.

In a clinical setting, however, the use of physiological methods for routine assessment is not feasible. Also, interpretation of their results in the clinical context is not always clear-cut (see Conte, 1986; Bancroft, 1989).

Formulation

The data obtained in the assessment will enable the assessor to arrive at a formulation of the problem. In the formulation, information from all sources is brought together, providing a brief descriptive account and a tentative explanation of the presenting problem. Various authors have suggested different ways in which the formulation may be organised (Wincze and Carey, 2001; Wiegel et al., 2002). Many clinicians favour the use of a formulation that includes the following:

- description of the problem
- predisposing factors
- precipitating factors
- maintaining factors.

The formulation will provide the basis for therapy. It is useful to discuss the formulation with the patient/couple at the end of the assessment. It is presented not as a rigid statement but as a tentative account of the problem and the therapist's understanding of it, open to revision and refinement as and when relevant new information becomes available.

CONCLUDING COMMENTS

In clinical practice, assessment is necessarily multi-faceted. In the assessment of sexual dysfunction, the clinician has more constraints placed on him or her than in the assessment of most other disorders. Despite these constraints, the clinician still has a variety of techniques at his or her disposal. The clinical interview will be the main source of information. Other techniques will be used, both within the interview and without, for obtaining additional data and for improving the quality of information. Which of these additional methods are to be used will depend on the nature of the presenting problem, its circumstances and the context of service.

REFERENCES

American Psychiatric Association (APA) (1994) *Diagnostic and Statistical Manual of Mental Disorders, 4th edn*, Washington, DC: APA.
Andersen, B. L. and Cyranowski, J. M. (1994) Women's sexual self-schema. *Journal of Personality and Social Psychology*, 67, 1079–1100.
Andersen, B. L., Cyranowski, J. M. and Espindale, D. (1999) Men's sexual self-schema. *Journal of Personality and Social Psychology*, 76, 645–651.
Baker, C. D. (2002) *Female Survivors of Sexual Abuse*. Hove, UK: Brunner-Routledge.

Bancroft, J. (1989) *Human Sexuality and Its Problems, 2nd edn*. Edinburgh: Churchill Livingstone.

Barnes, J. (1986a) Primary vaginismus 1. Social and clinical features. *Irish Medical Journal*, 79, 59–62.

Barnes, J. (1986b) Primary vaginismus 11. Aetiological factors. *Irish Medical Journal*, 79, 62–65.

Beck, A. T., Ward, C. H., Mendelsohn, M., Mock, J. and Erbaugh, J. (1961) An inventory for measuring depression. *Archives of General Psychiatry*, 4, 561–571.

Beck, J. G., Barlow, D. H. and Sakheim, D. (1983) The effects of attentional focus and partner arousal on sexual responding in functional and dysfunctional men. *Behaviour Research and Therapy*, 21, 1–8.

Bhugra, D. and de Silva, P. (1993) Sexual dysfunction across cultures. *International Review of Psychiatry*, 5, 243–252.

Bradley, W. E., Timm, G. W., Gallagher, J. M. and Johnson, B. K. (1985) New method for continuous measurement of nocturnal penile tumescence and rigidity. *Urology*, 26, 4–9.

Conte, H. R. (1986) Multivariate assessment of sexual dysfunction. *Journal of Consulting and Clinical Psychology*, 54, 149–157.

Crowe, M. (2002) Sexual dysfunctions and sexual therapy. *Psychiatry*, 4, 60–63.

Crowe, M. J. and Ridley, J. (2000) *Therapy with Couples, 2nd edn*. Oxford: Blackwell.

Davis, C. M., Yarber, W. L., Bauserman, R., Schreer, G and Davis, S. L. (eds) (1998) *Handbook of Sexuality-Related Measures*. Thousand Oaks, CA: Sage.

d'Ardenne, P. (2000) Couple and sexual problems. In: L. Champion and M. Power (eds) *Adult Psychological Problems: An Introduction*, Hove, UK: Psychology Press.

Derogatis, L. R. and Melisaratos, N. (1979) The DFSI: A multidimensional measure of sexual functioning. *Journal of Sex and Marital Therapy*, 5, 244–281.

de Silva, P. (1995) Paraphilias and sexual dysfunction. *International Review of Psychiatry*, 7, 225–229.

de Silva, P. (2001) Impact of trauma on sexual functioning and sexual relationships. *Sexual and Relationship Therapy*, 16, 269–278.

de Silva, P. and Dissanayake, S. A. W. (1989) The loss of semen syndrome in Sri Lanka: A clinical study. *Sexual and Marital Therapy*, 4, 195–204.

Dow, S. (1981) Retarded ejaculation. *Journal of Sex and Marital Therapy*, 7, 49–53.

Duddle, M. (1977) Etiological factors in the unconsummated marriage. *Journal of Consulting and Clinical Psychology*, 54, 156–160.

Frank, E., Anderson, C. and Rubinstein, D. (1978) Frequency of sexual dysfunction in normal couples. *New England Journal of Medicine*, 299, 111–115.

Hawton, K. (1985) *Sex Therapy: A Practical Guide*. Oxford: Oxford University Press.

Hoon, E., Wincze, J. and Hoon, P. (1976a) The SAI: An inventory for the measurement of female sexual arousal. *Archives of Sexual Behavior*, 5, 291–300.

Hoon, E., Wincze, J. and Hoon, P. (1976b) Physiological assessment of sexual arousal in women. *Psychophysiology*, 13, 196–208.

Kanfer, F. H. and Saslow, G. (1969) Behavioral diagnosis. In: C. M. Franks (ed) *Behavior Therapy: Appraisal and Status*. New York: McGraw-Hill.

Kaplan, H. S. (1974) *The New Sex Therapy: Brief Treatment of Sexual Dysfunction*. New York: Brunner/Mazel.

Kaplan, H. S. (1977) Hypoactive sexual desire. *Journal of Sex and Marital Therapy*, 3, 3–9.

Kaplan, H. S. (1979) *Disorders of Sexual Desire*. New York: Brunner/Mazel.

Kinsey, A. C., Pomeroy, W. B. and Martin, C. G. (1948) *Sexual Behavior in the Human Male*. Philadelphia: Saunders.

Kolondy, R. C., Masters, W. H. and Johnson, V. (1979) *Textbook of Sexual Medicine*. Boston: Little Brown.

Lamont, J. A. (1978) Vaginismus. *American Journal of Obstetrics and Gynaecology*, 131, 632–636.

Laumann, E. O., Paik, A. and Rosen, R. C. (1999) Sexual dysfunction in the United States: Prevalence and predictions. *Journal of the American Medical Association*, 281, 537–544.

Lechtenberg, R. and Ohl, D. (1994) *Sexual Dysfunction: Neurologic, Urologic, and Gynaecologic Aspects*. Malvern, PA: Lea and Febiger.

Lief, H. I. (1977) Inhibited sexual desire. *Medical Aspects of Human Sexuality* 11(12), 51–57.

Lief, H. I. and Reed, D. M. (1972) *Sexual Knowledge and Attitude Test (SKAT)*, *2nd edn*. Centre for the Study of Sex Education in Medicine, University of Pennsylvania.

Lo Piccolo, J. and Steger, J. C. (1974) The Sexual Interaction Inventory: A new instrument for assessment of sexual dysfunction. *Archives of Sexual Behavior*, 3, 585–595.

Masters, W. H. and Johnson, V. E. (1966) *Human Sexual Response*. Boston: Little Brown.

Masters, W. H. and Johnson, V. E. (1970) *Human Sexual Inadequacy*. Boston: Little Brown.

McConaghy, N. (1993) *Sexual Behavior: Problems and Management*. New York: Plenum.

Meana, M., Binik, Y. M., Khalife, S. and Cohen, D. R. (1997) Biopsychosocial profile of women with dyspareunia. *Obstetrics and Gynaecology*, 90, 583–589.

Metz, M. E. and Sawyer, S. P. (2004) Treating sexual dysfunction in sex offenders: A case example. *Journal of Sex and Marital Therapy*, 30, 185–197.

Nobre, P. J. and Pinto-Gouveia, J. (2003) Sexual Modes Questionnaire: A measure to assess the interactions among cognitions, emotions, and sexual responses. *The Journal of Sex Research*, 40, 368–382.

Nobre, P. J., Pinto-Gouveia, J. and Gomes, F. A. (2003) Sexual Dysfunctional Beliefs Questionnaire: An instrument to assess sexual dysfunctional beliefs as vulnerability factors to sexual problems. *Sexual and Relationship Therapy*, 18, 171–204.

O'Sullivan, K. (1979) Observations on vaginismus in Irish Women. *Archives of General Psychiatry*, 36, 824–826.

Potts, S. and Bhugra, D. (1995) Classification of sexual disorders. *International Review of Psychiatry*, 7, 167–174.

Pryor, J. P. (2002) Orgasmic and ejaculatory dysfunction. *Sexual and Relationship Therapy*, 17, 87–95.

Read, J. (1995) Female sexual dysfunction. *International Review of Psychiatry*, 7, 175–182.

Rosen, R. C., Riley, A., Wagner, G., Osterloh, I. H., Kirkpatrick, J. and Mishra, A. (1997) The International Index of Erectile Function (IIEF): A multidimentional scale for assessment of erectile dysfunction. *Urology*, 49, 822–830.

Rosen, R. C., Brown, C., Heiman, J., Leiblum, S., Meston, C., Shabsig, R. et al. (2000)

The Female Sexual Function Index (FSFI): A multidimensional self-report instrument for the assessment of female sexual function. *Journal of Sex and Marital Therapy*, 26, 191–208.

Rust, J. and Golombok, S. (1986) *The Golombok–Rust Inventory of Sexual Satisfaction*. Windsor, UK: NFER-Nelson.

Rust, J., Bennun, I., Crowe, M. J. and Golombok, S. (1988) *The Golombok–Rust Inventory of Marital State*. Windsor, UK: NFER-Nelson.

Schiavi, R. C. (1992) Laboratory methods for evaluating erectile dysfunction. In: R. C. Rosen and S. R. Leiblum (eds) *Erectile Disorders: Assessment and Treatment*. New York: Guilford Press.

Simons, J. S. and Carey, M. P. (2001) Prevalence of sexual dysfunctions: Results from a decade of research. *Archives of Sexual Behavior*, 30, 177–219.

Spector, L. P. and Carey, M. P. (1990) Incidence and prevalence of the sexual dysfunctions: A critical review of the literature. *Archives of Sexual Behavior*, 19, 389–408.

Spence, S. H. (1991) *Psychosexual Therapy: A Cognitive-Behavioural Approach*. London: Chapman and Hall.

Weeks, G. R. and Gambesia, N. (2000) *Erectile Dysfunction: Integrating Couple Therapy, Sex Therapy and Medical Treatment*. New York: Norton.

Weeks, G. R. and Gambesia, N. (2002) *Hypoactive Sexual Desire: Integrating Sex and Couple Therapy*. New York: Norton.

Wiegel, M., Wincze, J. P. and Barlow, D. H. (2002) Sexual dysfunction. In: M. A. Antony and D. H. Barlow (eds) *Handbook of Assessment and Treatment Planning for Psychological Disorders*. New York: Guilford Press.

Wilson, G. D. (1978) *The Secrets of Sexual Fantasy*. London: Dent.

Wincze, J. P. and Carey, M. P. (2001) *Sexual Dysfunction: A Guide for Assessment and Treatment, 2nd edn*. New York: Guilford Press.

Wincze, J. P., Bansal, S., Malhotra, C., Balko, A., Susset, J. G. and Malamud, M. (1988) A comparison of nocturnal penile tumescence and penile response to erotic stimulation during waking states in comprehensively diagnosed groups of males experiencing erectile difficulties. *Archives of Sexual Behavior*, 17, 333–347.

Wolpe, J. R. (1958) *Psychotherapy by Reciprocal Inhibition*. Stanford, CA: Stanford University Press.

Woody, J. D. (1992) *Treating Sexual Distress: Integrative Systems Therapy*. Newbury Park, CA: Sage.

World Health Organization (WHO) (1992) *The ICD-10 Classification of Mental and Behavioural Disorders: Clinical Descriptions and Diagnostic Guidelines*. Geneva: WHO.

Zilbergeld, B. (1978) *Men and Sex*. Boston: Little Brown.

Zilbergeld, B. (1992) *The New Male Sexuality*. New York: Bantam Books.

Zimmer, D. (1987) Does marital therapy enhance the effectiveness of treatment for sexual dysfunction? *Journal of Sex and Marital Therapy*, 13, 193–209.

Chapter 16

Sexual dysfunction

Treatment

Padmal de Silva

INTRODUCTION

Interest in sexual dysfunction and its therapy has witnessed a phenomenal increase in the last three decades. The impetus provided by the work of Masters and Johnson (1970), and the pubic awareness of the availability of treatment for sexual problems, have contributed to the vast increase in those seeking and receiving help for these difficulties. In addition to the psychiatric and psychological services, marriage guidance organisations, counselling centres, family planning centres and general practitioner clinics have begun to include sexual dysfunction therapy among their services. There are also specialist training programmes in this field. In clinical psychology, this group of problems is now an integral part of the range of disorders with which a practitioner is expected to deal.

The therapies for sexual dysfunction used by clinical psychologists are, in the main, cognitive behavioural. The original behaviour-therapeutic approach to problems, as described by Wolpe (1958) and other pioneer behaviour therapists, has been applied to sexual dysfunction for over four decades (Wolpe, 1958; Lazarus, 1963). The approach of Masters and Johnson (1970), which contributed to the rapid growth of sex therapy as a specialist field, is itself largely behavioural although it includes elements that do not fall strictly within the spectrum of conventional behaviour therapy (cf. Murphy and Mikulas, 1974). In more recent years, cognitive elements have been added to this basic behavioural approach, reflecting the increasing influence of cognitive theory on the understanding and treatment of psychological problems (e.g. Spence, 1991; d'Ardenne, 2000; Weeks and Gambescia, 2000; Wincze and Carey, 2001).

Before discussing this approach, however, the alternative approaches need to be briefly mentioned.

NON-COGNITIVE-BEHAVIOURAL APPROACHES TO THERAPY

Psychotherapy

Psychotherapy based on psychodynamic principles has been used tradition-ally with sexual dysfunction cases (Rosen, 1977). The assumption is that the presenting problem is the result of an unconscious conflict or a repressed memory of a past experience, usually related to the Oedipal stage of devel-opment. The rationale, therefore, is to bring to surface the unconscious material by analysis. While orthodox analysts still use this form of psycho-therapy for patients with sexual dysfunction, there is a scarcity of evidence for the efficacy of this time-consuming and usually expensive approach (Killman and Auerbach, 1979).

Kaplan (1974, 1979) has advocated an approach combining focal problem-oriented therapy with a psychodynamic orientation. The interest here is in exploring and resolving psychological conflicts and other relationship factors as they arise in therapy. This is, thus, not an entirely psychotherapeutic approach, as the main emphasis is on dealing with specific problems and is best described as eclectic. Kaplan (1987) has also made clear that psycho-dynamic exploration is undertaken only in a proportion of cases, where a behavioural approach fails to progress beyond a certain point.

Hypnosis

The use of hypnosis in sexual dysfunction has been described by several writers (e.g. Beigel, 1971; Cheek, 1976). It has been employed to explore 'hidden' sexual fears and memories, to reduce tension and induce relaxation, to attempt to change responses by post-hypnotic suggestion, and as an adjunct to other forms of therapy (e.g. Fuchs et al., 1973). There is no con-vincing evidence of the efficacy of hypnosis as a therapeutic intervention in its own right for these problems.

Bio-feedback

Bio-feedback has been used to enhance erections in males with erectile prob-lems. The patient is usually shown erotic material to encourage arousal, and changes in penile circumference are amplified and immediately fed back to him, by visual and/or auditory means. While this has some potential as a therapeutic strategy, bio-feedback training with these patients is not yet estab-lished. While the value of bio-feedback in research is beyond doubt, its role in clinical practice is limited. A useful review of this area is found in Rosen and Beck (1988).

Hormone therapy and other pharmacological treatments

A common treatment used in medical settings for sexual problems is hormonal therapy. Although it is frequently used inappropriately, this form of therapy does have a role in the treatment of cases where there is a clear hormonal abnormality and, when used in this way, can be effective. Low sexual drive in males in whom the testosterone level is low may be corrected with testosterone supplementation (Davidson and Rosen, 1992). In post-menopausal women, in whom a fall in oestrogen levels can lead to impairment of arousal and/or loss of interest, oestrogen therapy is quite beneficial (Bancroft, 1989; Walling et al., 1990).

As was pointed out in Chapter 15, it is important to carry out the necessary physical examination and investigations to identify those patients whose problems may be amenable to hormonal and other physical treatments. When the problem is not due to or complicated by organic factors, these treatments are ineffective and can even be counterproductive.

The use of oral medication for erectile dysfunction has attracted considerable public interest with the advent of Viagra (sildenafil). Studies have found that many men with erectile problems find that this helps to achieve stronger erections, when taken 1 hour before intercourse. There are, however, contraindications, and careful medical assessment is needed before Viagra, or similar medications, are prescribed. Another oral medication used for this problem is yohimbine. Overall, however, these pharmacological preparations are not recommended as treatments on their own, as the patient and the partner often need psychological therapy/counselling along with the medication. The value of an integrated approach in such instances cannot be overemphasised (see McCarthy and Fucito, 2005).

Surgical methods

Physical methods of treatment include surgery. An overtight foreskin or a tough hymen, causing pain in intercourse and/or difficulty in penetration, can be corrected by minor surgery. For men with erectile problems that are considered organic, penile prostheses can be used. Solid or inflatable implants have been used with patients with some success (Wagner and Green, 1981). Other developments in this field include corrective surgery on arterial supply and on abnormal drainage problems where necessary (Wagner and Green, 1981; Melman and Tiefer, 1992).

Mechanical aids

Mechanical devices or aids are also used in the treatment of sexual dysfunction. The best known perhaps are the penile ring, an ebonite ring claimed to help in maintaining erections (Cooper, 1974), and the vibrator (Gillan, 1987). The use of the vibrator as an aid in treatment of both male and female dysfunction is well recognised. The proper use of the vibrator, however, is not as a sole therapeutic means but as part of a wider package. Vacuum devices are also used as an aid for men to obtain erections (Cooper, 1987). Several devices are currently in the market. The process, however, is found cumbersome by many couples (Crowe, 2002). A recent publication has reported the use of a desensitising ring as a treatment for premature ejaculation (Wise and Watson, 2000). Further work is needed to evaluate its efficacy.

Injections for inducing erections

The 1980s saw the advent of the use of injections of papaverine (a smooth muscle relaxant) into the corpus cavernosum of the penis to induce erections (Brindley, 1983, 1986). In recent years, prostaglandin E_1 has replaced papaverine (Crowe, 2002). The erections induced in this way may last from 1 to 4 hours and are in many cases adequate for satisfactory intercourse. The patient is taught to give these injections himself. The use of this method to help men with organically caused erectile problems, or those who have failed to respond to psychological or behavioural methods, is advocated by several authorities. There is, however, a need for further research, and the use of this approach needs caution (Crowe and Qureshi, 1991; Althof and Turner, 1992). Additional psychological counselling is also often needed.

BEHAVIOUR THERAPY: DESENSITISATION

The main standard behavioural treatment technique that has been used in this field is desensitisation. Where the problem is seen as primarily an anxiety-based one, reduction of anxiety by imaginal and *in vivo* desensitisation can be useful (Wolpe, 1958). The anxiety-arousing situations are elicited from the patient and arranged in a hierarchy of lowest anxiety to highest (see Chapter 13) and these are then presented to the patient to imagine, in graded fashion, under relaxation. The hierarchy typically involves non-sexual items at the lower end (for instance, looking at partner in a crowded room) and moves upwards towards explicitly sexual situations (such as being in bed with the partner, both nude). The desensitisation steps may of course be carried out *in vivo*, in a carefully graded way, or in a combination of imaginal and *in vivo* exposures (Wolpe, 1958, 1991; Obler, 1973). Successful desensitisation in group settings has also been reported (O'Gorman, 1978).

THE CONJOINT THERAPY APPROACH

While desensitisation represents an early technique of standard behaviour therapy for sexual dysfunction where suitable, the treatment package most widely used today is the conjoint therapy of Masters and Johnson (1970), modified in significant ways by subsequent writers and practitioners (Hawton, 1985; Gillan, 1987; Bancroft, 1989; Spence, 1991; Crowe and Ridley, 2000; Wincze and Carey, 2001). In present-day practice, a range of cognitive behavioural techniques is used. Where necessary, systemic strategies are also employed, to deal with relationship issues.

In the Masters and Johnson conjoint therapy approach, the presenting partner and his or her spouse are seen as a couple for therapy. In the original programme, each couple was seen by a male and female co-therapist team. The therapy was carried out on an intensive basis – daily sessions over a 2-week period (Masters and Johnson, 1970). Other researchers have found that the involvement of a second therapist adds little to the programme, and that the sessions do not need to be closely massed together (Crowe et al., 1982; Arentewicz and Schmidt, 1983; Bancroft, 1989).

Features of the conjoint therapy approach

The main elements of the conjoint therapy approach can be summarised as follows:

- *Treat the problem as a joint problem*: this helps to reduce worry and guilt in the presenting partner and also emphasises that the need is to learn, or re-learn, how to have satisfactory sex jointly.
- *Reduce anxiety*: this is achieved in several ways, including an agreement by the couple to refrain from any attempt at intercourse until instructed by the therapist at the appropriate stage of therapy. This removes the pressure to perform. Relaxation training may also be used as an extra help. Identifying and dealing with anxious cognitions is also used.
- *Set sexual tasks or assignments to be carried out at home*: these are specific behavioural tasks and involve touching, caressing and so on. The two main stages of this are 'non-genital sensate focus', where the touching excludes genitals and breasts, and 'genital sensate focus' where these are included. These basic tasks aim to help the couple to learn giving and receiving pleasure by touch, with no anxiety or performance demands, moving gradually from less sexual to more intimate interactions.
- *Educate the couple in sexual knowledge*, for example, anatomy, physiology, coital positions: many couples have inadequate knowledge and understanding in this area, and the provision of accurate data plays an important part in therapy. Correcting myths and misinformation, and related beliefs, is also part of this aspect of therapy.

- *Help the couple to develop sexual communication skills.*
- *Use specific techniques for specific dysfunctions*: while the above are common to all, there are specific interventions designed to deal with specific presenting problems. They are usually introduced after genital sensate focus.

This programme is primarily a cognitive-behavioural package. There is no attempt to interpret the presenting symptoms in terms of psychodynamic constructs. The degree to which strategies for unravelling conflicts and relationship problems is incorporated into this varies from therapist to therapist and case to case (e.g. Beck, 1992; Woody, 1992). Bancroft (1989), for example, describes a programme that, while basically close to the conjoint therapy format, emphasises these factors a great deal. It must be recognised that severe relationship problems could make the programme impossible for the couple to carry out successfully; and sometimes the relationship problems come to the forefront only when the couple have attempted some of the tasks. These problems need to be looked into where relevant (Crowe and Ridley, 2000). Specific strategies, including behavioural work on aspects of the couple relationship and systemic techniques, may be used (see Chapter 17).

The sensate focus assignments help a couple to learn to relax in each other's company and enjoy physical contact and interaction without worries of failure. In this relaxed, mutually pleasuring stage, they can acquire the confidence to move towards more intimate interactions. It is perhaps worth noting here that the progression from non-genital to genital sensate focus, and from there to more specific and more explicitly sexual acts, is similar in many ways to an *in vivo* desensitisation programme.

Self-exploration and self-stimulation may be incorporated into the programme where required. Communication, both verbal and non-verbal, on matters of pleasure, sensations and sexual responses is encouraged and taught (for example, how to indicate to the partner where and how to touch, and how to express pleasure at what the partner is doing). The verbal aspects of this kind of simple, but to many couples new, interaction may be role-played and rehearsed during sessions in the presence of the therapist.

The meetings with the therapist are crucial in discussing progress or otherwise of the assignments, and difficulties and problems are discussed fully. Not infrequently in these feedback discussions, relevant new material about the relationship emerges for the first time (Hawton, 1985; Bancroft, 1989).

Specific techniques used in conjoint therapy

The specific techniques that are incorporated into the general programme, usually after the initial stages are successfully completed, are summarised in the following sections.

Erectile dysfunction

In the genital sensate focus stage, 'teasing' is introduced; that is, periods of penile stimulation alternating with absence of stimulation. While erections may spontaneously occur, these are not considered the aim of therapy and the couple are encouraged to let the erection subside before re-stimulating. This helps in training them not to rush to intercourse once an erection is there, and also in demonstrating that erections, when lost, can re-appear.

The next stage is vaginal entry, in the female superior position but with no movement. In the following stage the female makes slow movements, eventually leading to the male participating in and/or initiating movement, and using different positions.

Premature ejaculation

There are two, closely similar, techniques used for premature ejaculation. Masters and Johnson (1970) recommended what is called the 'squeeze' technique. The couple are asked to practise this in the genital touching stage. The female stimulates the penis of her partner with her hand, and when the man feels he is about to reach a climax he indicates this to her with a pre-arranged signal. She then squeezes the penis hard for 2–3 seconds. For squeezing, the penis is held with the thumb on the frenulum and the first and the second fingers on the opposite surface, one on each side of the coronal ridge. The squeeze makes the man lose his urge to ejaculate, and also perhaps some of the erection. This process of stimulation and squeeze is repeated many times in a session. Several sessions of this leads to gradual increase in ejaculatory control, and the couple is then asked to effect vaginal entry, in the woman above position. At first, entry is not followed by movement. If the man feels he is about to ejaculate, he communicates this to his partner who then lifts herself off him lightly and applies the squeeze. Kolodny et al. (1979) have recommend a basilar squeeze technique at this stage so that the penis does not have to be completely disengaged. The penis is held at the base, anterior to posterior, and the pressure applied. Eventually the couple may revert to preferred positions.

The squeeze technique is, in fact, a variant of the start–stop method described in 1956 by Semans, and is used and recommended by many therapists (Kaplan, 1974, 1979; Crowe, 2002). This consists of stimulating the penis and stopping at the point of near climax, and repeating the process several times. Initially, the stimulation is with a dry hand; later a lubricant is used to increase sensitivity and make the sensations more like the experience of vaginal entry (Gillan, 1987). The rest of the programme consists of vaginal entry without movement, followed by movement in the woman above position.

The start–stop and the squeeze techniques, incorporated within a cognitive-behavioural framework, are considered the treatments of choice for this problem (St Lawrence and Madakasira, 1992).

Orgasmic dysfunction in the male

The aim is to work towards intra-vaginal ejaculation, in a series of steps gradually approaching this goal. Again the instructions are introduced at the genital stage. For those males who do not ejaculate easily in any situation, vigorous stimulation with the aid of a lubricant is recommended. The use of a vibrator may also be considered. Once orgasm can be achieved in this way, vaginal entry, after some initial manual stimulation, may be attempted. In those men whose problem is that they cannot reach orgasm in the vagina but can do so with manual stimulation, a graded programme in which orgasm is achieved by manual stimulation, with penis increasingly close to the vagina, is recommended. In the next stage vaginal entry is achieved, after stimulation by hand close to orgasm. Even then, some manual stimulation may be needed to achieve orgasm once the penis is in the vagina. Subsequently, vaginal stimulation alone will be sufficient for orgasm (Kaplan, 1987).

Vaginismus

This is treated by helping the patient to learn to relax and to explore her own genitals. Following this, a graded series of steps achieving penetration using her own fingers and dilators (or trainers) of increasing sizes is undertaken (Gillan, 1987; Wincze and Carey, 2001). This is done with the patient retaining control. The use of imaginal desensitisation using scenes of varying degrees of sexual closeness and penetration may also be used (Fuchs et al., 1973). As the patient becomes more comfortable with the insertion of fingers/dilators, the partner can be included in the procedure.

Orgasmic dysfunction in the female

For females with orgasmic dysfunction, the main additional element in the therapy package is a good deal of self-focusing and self-stimulation (Lo Piccolo and Lobitz, 1972; Barbach, 1980; Lo Piccolo and Stock, 1986; Gillan, 1987; Heiman and Lo Piccolo, 1988). This helps the patient to learn to enjoy the sexual sensations in a relaxed manner. These self-sessions, including stimulation until orgasm is achieved, can be built into the basic programme as parallel assignments. It has been shown that the use of vibrators can help these women to achieve orgasm; this may be done by the patient herself at first, and the partner may help her to achieve orgasm with the vibrator in later stages. The use of fantasy and erotic materials may also be recommended as an adjunct (Gillan 1987; Spence, 1991).

Exercises to achieve control over the pubococcygeus muscle and to strengthen its tone, usually referred to as 'Kegel exercises', have also been recommended as an aid to achieving orgasm (Kegel, 1952; Gillan, 1987).

For females who are unable to achieve orgasm with the partner but have no problem in masturbation, other elements may need to be added to the programme. For example, orgasmic reconditioning may be attempted, in which the patient is taught to pair the positive pleasurable aspects of self-stimulation or other sexual situations with images of the partner in a fantasy-based graded programme (Asirdas, and Beech, 1975; Gillan 1987).

Low sexual desire

Lack of, or low, interest usually begins to respond to the general treatment package if nothing more serious is underlying. Additional techniques are self-focusing, self-stimulation, use of vibrators, and stimulation with erotic material – pictures, videos, audiotapes, and so on (Gillan, 1987). It is important, however, that the kind of erotic material recommended or provided is not distasteful to the patients and so the choice is best left to them. Fantasy training is a related technique sometimes useful for those whose fantasies are minimal (Spence, 1991; Weeks and Gambescia, 2002). To encourage fantasies, published fantasy materials may be used, such as the volumes of fantasies published by Nancy Friday (Friday, 1976, 1991). The use of agreed timetables for sex is also found to be helpful (Crowe and Ridley, 2000). The therapist would negotiate with the couple a timetable for sex; for example, intercourse will take place on certain days of the week, or sex will be initiated by each partner on certain days only. This approach is often quite effective in cases where the partner with the low level of desire finds the demands made by the spouse too much, thus making the problem worse. The agreed timetable helps to establish an acceptable pattern or schedule, within which further progress can be made.

Some additional considerations on conjoint therapy

Needless to say, the above is only a brief, and perhaps over-simplified, account of conjoint therapy. Some general points about this treatment approach need to be made:

- The package in its basic form is for the use with all sexual dysfunctions, with the specific elements added to suit specific difficulties. There are, however, many instances where there is no need to apply the whole package, where perhaps sexual counselling giving basic education is all that is needed (Hawton, 1985; Kaplan, 1987). Needless to say, the therapist must have a flexible approach in applying the therapy package or parts of it.
- The programme is primarily intended for those whose problems have no

clear organic causes. On the other hand, there is no reason why the early stages of the programme should not be used even with those whose problems are not entirely psychologically determined, as a way of helping them to relax in their sexual activity and enhance their sexual experience. For example, in elderly men with erectile dysfunction who, due to ageing and other physical causes, may not be able to have erectile function restored, much can still be achieved by a programme aimed at enhancing their enjoyment of sexual activity, enabling them to accept that sex need not always mean vaginal intercourse (Gibson, 1992). (Note also that couples can be encouraged to have and enjoy intercourse with a limp or semi-flaccid penis. Couples can achieve this with the aid of a good lubricant and using a position that permits easy access to the female genitals.) It is also important to remember that the psychogenic-organic distinction is not always clear cut, and often there is overlap. A problem caused, or triggered, by a physical condition may often be aggravated or maintained by psychological factors such as anxiety, negative thoughts, invalidism and diminished self-esteem. In many cases, psychological help is needed in addition to a physical intervention, and this is best accomplished by using a well-planned integrated framework (McCarthy and Fucito, 2005).

- The programme is meant to be applied flexibly. The needs of each couple determine what changes to aim for, and the therapist must be prepared to alter the direction of a programme as and when required. For example, the basic problem for a couple presenting with premature ejaculation may turn out to be lack of arousal in the female. Some couples require a good deal of direct education; a shy patient may not be able to participate fully in therapy sessions until his or her embarrassment is overcome, and will need considerable time and effort to reach the point where therapy can proceed. The need for flexibility is well illustrated by Lobitz et al. (1976) and Winzce and Carey (2001).

- The programme can sometimes meet with resistance. A couple may not carry out the homework assignments, or do them only infrequently or cursorily. Their difficulties will need to be fully explored. Relationship problems may come to the surface at this stage, in which case the lack of progress with the assignments is entirely understandable and efforts should be directed towards resolving these (Bancroft, 1989; Crowe and Ridley, 2000).

- Additions to the basic programme need not be confined to the specific techniques mentioned above. Any suitable cognitive-behavioural technique for aspects of the problem may be incorporated as required. For example, when a strong phobic element is present, an intervention to deal with the phobia may be attempted; for a man whose dysfunction is bound up with deviant desires, additional treatment may be required (Metz and Sawyer, 2004).

The idea of functional analysis (e.g. Kanfer and Saslow, 1969) is still extremely useful in devising individualised treatment programmes. When the assessment shows clearly identifiable factors related to the problem behaviour, the systematic manipulation of these can achieve considerable results – usually as part of the main programme, but also sometimes as the main intervention itself (Lobitz et al., 1976).

Cognitive aspects

It was stated earlier that the approach advocated here is primarily a cognitive-behavioural one. As has been noted in the above paragraphs, maladaptive cognitions that may contribute to the problem(s) need to be elicited and modified. Common myths, attitudes and idiosyncratic beliefs often contribute to sexual difficulties (e.g Zilbergeld, 1978, 1992; Bishay, 1988; Nobre and Pinto-Gouveia, 2000). The use of cognitive techniques as part of the therapy package therefore often needs to be considered. Spence (1991) has provided a particularly helpful discussion of the use of cognitive strategies in the treatment of sexual difficulties. She includes fantasy training and attention-focusing skills as possible aspects of therapy. The major cognitive interventions, however, consist of identifying and restructuring the relevant cognitions. Several recent discussions of these are available (Carey, 1998; Wincze and Carey, 2001).

The relationship context

The importance of relationship factors was referred to in several previous paragraphs. In conjoint therapy, relationship factors are taken into account in varying degrees. Some practitioners, such as Woody (1992), take the view that dealing with these is an essential aspect of sex therapy, and she proposes an integrative systems approach. Relationship factors are sometimes a key element in the aetiology of sexual problems; more often, they have a role in their maintenance. Issues in the relationship, such as status, power and dominance, trust, jealousy and intimacy, sometimes have a crucial role in the clinical picture. When this is the case, conjoint therapy needs to pay due attention to these and deal with them as required. Useful discussions of these are available in Crowe and Ridley (2000), Leiblum and Rosen (1992) and Woody (1992). See also Chapter 17.

Maintaining gains

The improvement achieved during therapy may not be fully sustained in the long term. This is true of any problem, and therapists are increasingly mindful of the need to help patients with relapse prevention. For patients with sexual dysfunction, an excellent set of relapse prevention strategies has been proposed by McCarthy (1993). These include: encouraging patients to re-allocate therapy session time (i.e. the time that would have been taken by therapy sessions) for 'couple dates' after termination of treatment; establishing 6-monthly follow-up sessions up to 2 years; scheduling sensate focus sessions at least once a month; teaching the patients that, if and when a problem occurs, it is a lapse to learn from rather than an inevitable decline into relapse; and advising the couple on how to establish intimate and erotic ways to strengthen their sexual relationship, without limiting themselves to conventional roles.

Some practical issues

As was noted in a earlier paragraph, Masters and Johnson (1970) used a male and female team of co-therapists in their programme, but others have shown that a second therapist adds little to the programme effectiveness. However, in certain cases an additional therapist of the opposite sex to the main therapist can be an advantage, for example by making it easier for each of the partners to communicate about the problem and his or her feelings about it.

Giving written instructions, with illustrations, is a valuable addition to the therapy programme. While written instructions have been used with some success as the main mode of therapy (Lowe and Mikulus, 1975), they should be used as a supplement to verbal instructions. Equally useful is to recommend a well-written basic book on sex. There are many good books that may be recommended, for example – Barnes and Rodwell (1992) and Delvin (1974). Films, videos and slides may also be used (Gillan, 1987). Books for specific problems may be recommended; for example, Heiman and Lo Piccolo (1988) for women with difficulties achieving orgasm. When written materials are given or books/videos are recommended, it is important that the therapist is prepared to find the time to discuss them with the patients, as needed.

PATIENTS WITHOUT PARTNERS

When a patient comes to therapy without a partner, what help can be offered? If the patient has a steady partner who, though unwilling to come to the clinic, will co-operate with a therapy programme, a 'remote control' approach may be used, with the presenting partner also acting as communicator of instructions. The use of written material will be particularly useful in such cases. Clinical experience suggests that this is a less than ideal substitute for conjoint therapy, but should be considered in the right circumstances. If the refusal of the partner to attend clinic reflects a poor relationship and an attitude that it is all the other's problem, then clearly the chances of joint work being successfully carried out are slim. However, if the reluctance of the spouse to come is more the result shyness or embarrassment and co-operation at home is assured, the therapy has better prospects of succeeding.

A somewhat different problem arises when the patient has no partner available. Many young men with erectile or ejaculatory problems not only do not have a steady partner but also avoid, through fear of failure and rejection, developing relationships. Individual therapy is the only option available in such cases, unless group therapy is considered and facilities are available for it (see below; also Anson, 1995).

Basic principles of individual sex therapy are the same as for couples: education, counselling, anxiety reduction in various ways including relaxation, self-focusing, self-stimulation and fantasy training, and dealing with faulty or dysfunctional cognitions, are all possible and useful elements in such a programme. As for specific techniques, those with premature ejaculation will find the start–stop technique more feasible than the squeeze. Imaginal desensitisation may be used for fear of anxiety, while role-play and social skills training can be useful in some cases (McCarthy, 1992). The sexual re-education programme of Zilbergeld (1978, 1992) is particularly appropriate for males with sexual worries and associated dysfunctions. Zilbergeld considers it important to dispel some widespread 'myths' about sex (such as that sex always means intercourse, that the male must always take the active role, and so on) in helping these persons, and exploration – and correction – of the individual's misconceptions about sex will be a useful element in an individual sex therapy programme (Zilbergeld, 1992). For females, masturbatory exercises, Kegel exercises, vibrator use and other such techniques referred to in earlier paragraphs, which are possible for the individual to use without a partner, may profitably be used.

SURROGATES

The use of surrogate partners in the treatment of patients who come without partners has been tried and recommended by some therapists. Masters and Johnson used surrogates for some of their male patients but later gave up this practice. Several sex therapists in the USA still use surrogate therapy (Dauw, 1988; Noonan, 2004), while in the UK Cole (1988) has described surrogate therapy with 425 patients, 390 men and 35 women. Of these, 316 (74.4%) completed therapy; unfortunately, follow-up was possible in only 13.3% of these.

There are serious problems with the use of surrogate therapy, including obvious legal and ethical issues (see Anson, 1995; Noonan, 2004). For example, nearly a quarter of the Cole sample was married and in many cases the spouse was not even aware that the patient had come for therapy. A serious clinical question is whether someone who has been treated with a surrogate partner will be able to generalise his or her gains to other situations.

In view of these reservations it is difficult to recommend surrogate therapy as an option in the management of sexual dysfunction.

GROUP THERAPY

The group therapy format has also been used in the treatment of sexual dysfunction (Anson, 1995). There have been male groups, female groups, couple groups and mixed-single groups; and there have been groups for patients with similar problems and groups for heterogeneous problems (Zilbergeld, 1975; Auerbach and Killman, 1977; Barbach and Flaherty, 1980; Spence, 1985; Kayata and Szydlo, 1988). The groups have used a variety of techniques, including education, task-setting, relaxation, desensitisation, instructions to use masturbation and vibrators, and open discussion of problems. Particularly for young and sexually diffident persons, the experience of group therapy can have benefits (Bancroft, 1989) over and above the specific gains they make. There are, however, significant limitations to the group approach, which reduces the therapist's flexibility and thus the ability to provide tailor-made treatment for the patient or couple.

HELPING GAY COUPLES AND INDIVIDUALS

Gay couples, and single gay persons, increasingly present at clinics seeking help for sexual dysfunctions (Butler and Clarke, 1991; Simons, 1991). Their difficulties are largely similar to those of heterosexuals seeking help, and the principles outlined above should be used in treating them. However, they may also have different concerns, for example with regard to attitudes towards certain acts such as oral and anal sex (Reece, 1988; Spence, 1991). Worries about the sexual orientation itself may sometimes contribute to the problem, as may particular fears and concerns about safe sex. The therapist needs to elicit the patient's worries and concerns carefully and patiently, and deal with them as appropriate. Some of the special issues in the treatment of gay men are well discussed by Bhugra and Wright (1995) and Spitalnick and McNair (2005).

EFFICACY OF THERAPY

What about the efficacy of the various therapeutic approaches and techniques that have been discussed above? The very high success rates reported by Masters and Johnson (1970) and by Kolodny et al. (1979) have not been matched by later investigators (see Hawton, 1992), but there is, generally, evidence that the conjoint approach using cognitive-behavioural techniques referred to in this chapter are beneficial to many patients (Arentewicz and Schmidt, 1983; Hawton et al., 1986; Bancroft, 1989; Spence, 1991; Crowe, 2002). A thorough, critical evaluation of these is not very easy to undertake because of various factors: heterogeneity of samples, lack of uniformity in outcome measures, ambiguity of criteria of improvement, preponderance of single-case reports, poor descriptions of patient characteristics, absence of data on drop-outs and failures, and so on. Within these limitations, the available data are encouraging. While the conjoint therapy used within a cognitive-behavioural framework is the best option when it is feasible, it is up the individual clinician to use his or her ingenuity and judgement in choosing, for each case, those elements of therapy that are particularly suitable for the problems he or she is called upon to deal with.

REFERENCES

Althof, S. E. and Turner, L. A. (1992) Self-injection therapy and external vacuum devices in the treatment of erectile dysfunctions: Methods and outcome. In: R. C. Rosen and S. R. Leiblum (eds) *Erectile Disorders: Assessment and Treatment.* New York: Guilford Press.

Anson, M. (1995) Non-couple therapy for sexual dysfunction. *International Review of Psychiatry*, 7, 205–216.

Arentewicz, G. and Schmidt, G. (1983) *The Treatment of Sexual Disorder: Concepts and Techniques of Couple Therapy.* New York: Basic Books.

Asirdas, S. and Beech, H. R. (1975) The behavioural treatment of sexual inadequacy. *Journal of Psychosomatic Research*, 19, 345–353.

Auerbach, R. and Killman, P. R. (1977) The effects of group systematic desensitisation on secondary erectile failure. *Behavior Therapy*, 8, 330–339.

Bancroft, J. (1989) *Human Sexuality and Its Problems, 2nd edn.* Edinburgh: Churchill Livingstone.

Barbach, L. (1980) *Women Discover Orgasm.* New York: Free Press.

Barbach, L. G. and Flaherty, M. (1980) Group treatment of situationally anorgasmic women. *Journal of Sex and Marital Therapy*, 6, 19–29.

Barnes, T. and Rodwell, L. (1992) *A Woman's Guide to Loving Sex.* London: Boxtree.

Beigel, H. (1971) The hypnotherapeutic approach to male impotence. *Journal of Sex Research*, 7, 168–176.

Bhugra, D. and Wright, B. (1995) Sexual dysfunction in gay men: Diagnosis and management. *International Review of Psychiatry*, 7, 247–252.

Bishay, N. R. (1988) Cognitive therapy for sexual dysfunction: A preliminary report. *Journal of Sex and Marital Therapy*, 3, 83–90.

Brindley, G. S. (1983) Cavernosal alpha-blockade: A new technique for investigating and treating erectile impotence. *British Journal of Psychiatry*, 143, 332–337.

Brindley, G. S. (1986) Maintenance treatment of erectile impotence by cavernosal unstriated muscle relaxant injection. *British Journal of Psychiatry*, 149, 210–215.

Butler, M. and Clarke J. (1991) Couple therapy with homosexual men. In: D. Hooper and W. Dryden (eds) *Couple Therapy: A Handbook*. Buckingham, UK: Open University Press.

Carey, M. P. (1998) Cognitive-behavioural treatment of sexual dysfunctions. In: V. E. Caballo (ed) *International Handbook of Cognitive and Behavioural Treatments for Psychological Disorders*. Oxford: Elsevier.

Cheek, J. B. (1976) Short-term hypnotherapy for frigidity using exploration of early life attitudes. *American Journal of Clinical Hypnosis*, 19, 20–27.

Cole, M. (1988) Sex therapy for individuals. In: M. Cole and W. Dryden (eds) *Sex Therapy in Britain*. Buckingham, UK: Open University Press.

Cooper, S. J. (1974) A blind evaluation of a penile ring: A sex aid for impotent males. *British Journal of Psychiatry*, 124, 402–406.

Cooper, S. J. (1987) Preliminary experience with a vacuum tumescence device (VTD) as a treatment for impotence. *Journal of Psychosomatic Research*, 31, 413–418.

Crowe, M. (2002) Sexual dysfunctions and sexual therapy. *Psychiatry*, 4, 60–63.

Crowe, M. J. and Qureshi, M. J. H. (1991) Pharmacologically induced penile erections (PIPE) as a maintenance treatment of erectile impotence: A report of 41 cases. *Journal of Sexual and Marital Therapy*, 6, 273–285.

Crowe, M. J. and Ridley, J. (2000) *Therapy with Couples, 2nd edn*. Oxford: Blackwell.

Crowe, M. J., Gillan, P. and Golombok, S. (1982) Form and content in the conjoint treatment of sexual dysfunction: A controlled study. *Behaviour Research and Therapy*, 19, 47–54.

d'Ardenne, P. (2000) Couple and sexual problems. In: L. Champion and M. Power (eds) *Adult Psychological Problems: An Introduction*. Hove, UK: Psychology Press.

Dauw, D. C. (1988) Evaluating the effectiveness of the SECS surrogate-assisted sex therapy model. *Journal of Sex Research*, 24, 269–275.

Davidson, J. M. and Rosen, R. C. (1992) Hormonal determinants of erectile function. In: R. C. Rosen and S. R. Leiblum (eds) *Erectile Disorders: Assessment and Treatment*. New York: Guilford Press.

Delvin, D. (1974) *The Book of Love*. London: New English Library.

Friday, N. (1976) *My Secret Garden: Women's Sexual Fantasies*. London: Quartet.

Friday, N. (1991) *Women on Top*. London: Hutchinson.

Fuchs, K., Hoch, L., Paldi, E., Abramovici, H., Brandes, J., Timor-Tritisch, I. and Kleinhaus, M. (1973) Hypnodesensitization therapy of vaginismus, I. In vitro method; II. *In vivo* method. *International Journal of Clinical and Experimental Hypnosis*, 21, 144–156.

Gibson, N. B. (1992) *Love, Sex and Power in Later Life*. London: Freedom Press.

Gillan, P. (1979) Stimulation therapy for sexual dysfunction. *British Journal of Sexual Medicine*, 6 (June), 13–14.

Gillan, P. (1987) *Sex Therapy Manual*. Oxford: Blackwell.

Hawton, K. (1985) *Sex Therapy: A Practical Guide*. Oxford: Oxford University Press.

Hawton, K. (1992) Sex therapy research: Has it withered on the vine? *Annual Review of Sex Research*, 3, 49–72.

Hawton, K., Catalan, J., Martin, P. and Fagg, J. (1986) Long term outcome of sex therapy. *Behaviour Research and Therapy*, 24, 665–675.

Heiman, J. R. and Lo Piccolo, J. (1988) *Becoming Orgasmic*. Englewood Cliffs, NJ: Prentice Hall.

Kanfer, F. H. and Saslow, G. (1969) Behavioral diagnosis. In: C. M. Franks (ed.) *Behavior Therapy: Status and Appraisal*. New York: McGraw-Hill.

Kaplan, H. S. (1974) *The New Sex Therapy: Active Treatment of Sexual Dysfunction*. London: Baillière Tindall/New York: Brunner/Mazel.

Kaplan, H. S. (1979) *Disorders of Sexual Desire*. New York: Brunner/Mazel.

Kaplan, H. S. (1987) *The Illustrated Manual of Sex Therapy, 2nd edn*. New York: Brunner/Mazel.

Kayata, L. and Szydlo, D. (1988) Sex therapy in groups. In: M. Cole and W. Dryden (eds) *Sex Therapy in Britain*. Buckingham, UK: Open University Press.

Kegel, A. (1952) Sexual functions of the pubococcygeus muscle. *Western Journal of Surgery, Obstetrics and Gynaecology*, 60, 521–524.

Killman, P. R. and Auerbach, R. (1979) Treatment of premature ejaculation and psychogenic impotence: A critical view of the literature. *Archives of Sexual Behavior*, 8, 81–100.

Kolodny, R. C., Masters, W. H. and Johnson, V. E. (1979) *A Textbook of Sexual Medicine*. Boston: Little Brown.

Lazarus, A. A. (1963) The treatment of chronic frigidity by systematic desensitization. *Journal of Nervous and Mental Disease*, 136, 272–278.

Leiblum, S. R. and Rosen, R. C. (1992) Couples therapy for erectile disorders: Observations, obstacles and outcomes. In: R. C. Rosen, and S. R. Leiblum (eds) *Erectile Disorders: Assessment and Treatment*. New York: Guilford Press.

Lobitz, W. C., Lo Piccolo, J., Lobitz, G. K. and Brockway, J. (1976) A closer look at simplistic behaviour therapy for sexual dysfunction: Two case studies. In: H. J. Eysenck (ed) *Case Studies in Behaviour Therapy*. London: Routeledge & Kegan Paul.

Lo Piccolo, J. and Lobitz, W. C. (1972) The role of masturbation in the treatment of orgasmic dysfunction. *Archives of Sexual Behavior*, 2, 163–171.

Lo Piccolo, J. and Stock, W. (1986) Treatment of sexual dysfunction. *Journal of Consulting and Clinical Psychology*, 54, 158–167.

Lowe, J. C. and Mikulas, W. L. (1975) Use of written material in learning self-control of premature ejaculation. *Psychological Reports*, 37, 295–298.

Masters, W. H. and Johnson, V. E. (1970) *Human Sexual Inadequacy*. Boston: Little Brown.

McCarthy, B. W. (1992) Treatment of erectile dysfunction with single men. In: R. C. Rosen and R. S. Leiblum (eds) *Erectile Disorders: Assessment and Treatment*. New York: Guilford Press.

McCarthy, B. W. (1993) Relapse prevention strategies and techniques in sex therapy. *Journal of Sex and Marital Therapy*, 19, 142–146.

McCarthy, B. W. and Fucito, L. M. (2005) Integrating medication, realistic expectations, and therapeutic intervention in the treatment of male sexual dysfunctions. *Journal of Sex and Marital Therapy*, 31, 319–328.

Melman, A. and Tiefer, L. (1992) Surgery for erectile disorders: Operative procedures and psychological issues. In: R. C. Rosen and S. R. Leiblum (eds) *Erectile Disorders: Assessment and Treatment*. New York: Guilford Press.

Metz, M. E. and Sawyer, S. P. (2004) Treating sexual dysfunction in sex offenders: A case example. *Journal of Sex and Marital Therapy*, 30, 185–197.

Murphy, C. V. and Mikulus, W. L. (1974) Behavioral features and deficiencies of the Masters and Johnson programme. *Psychological Record*, 24, 221–227.

Nobre, P. and Pinto-Gouveia, J. (2000). Erectile dysfunction: An empirical approach based on Beck's cognitive theory. *Sexual and Relationship Therapy*, 15, 351–366.

Noonan, R. J. (2004) Sex surrogates: The continuing controversy [in the entry on the United States of America]. in: R. T. Francoeur and R. J. Noonan (eds) *The Continuum Complete International Encyclopedia of Sexuality*. New York: Continuum.

Obler, M. (1973) Systematic desensitization in sexual disorders. *Journal of Behavior Therapy and Experimental Psychiatry*, 4, 93–101.

O'Gorman, E. (1978) Treatment of frigidity: A comparative study of group and individual desensitization. *British Journal of Psychiatry*, 132, 580–584.

Reece, R. (1988) Special issues in the etiologies and treatments of sexual problems among gay men. *Journal of Homosexuality*, 15, 43–57.

Rosen, J. (1977) The psychoanalytic approach to individual therapy. In: J. Money and H. Musaph (eds) *Handbook of Sexology*. Amsterdam: Elsevier.

Rosen, R. C. and Beck, G. J. (1988) *Patterns of Sexual Arousal: Psychophysiological Processes and Clinical Applications*. New York: Guilford Press.

St Lawrence, J. S. and Madakasira, S. (1992) Evaluation and treatment of premature ejaculation: A critical review. *International Journal of Psychiatry in Medicine*, 22, 77–97.

Semans, J. H. (1956) Premature ejaculation: A new approach. *Southern Medical Journal*, 49, 353–358.

Simons, S. (1991) Couple therapy with lesbians. In: D. Cooper and W. Dryden (eds) *Couple Therapy: A Handbook*. Buckingham, UK: Open University Press.

Spence, S. H. (1985) Group versus individual treatment of primary and secondary orgasmic dysfunction. *Behaviour Research and Therapy*, 23, 539–548.

Spence, S. H. (1991) *Psychosexual Therapy: A Cognitive-Behavioural Approach*. London: Chapman and Hall.

Spitalwick, J. S. and McNair, L. D. (2005) Couple therapy with gay and lesbian clients: An analysis of important clinical issues. *Journal of Sex and Marital Therapy*, 31, 43–56.

Wagner, G. and Green, R. (1981) *Impotence: Physiological, Psychological, Surgical Diagnosis and Treatment*. New York: Plenum Press.

Walling, M., Anderson, B. L., and Johnson, S. R. (1990) Hormonal replacement therapy for post-menopausal women: A review of sexual outcomes and gynaecological effects. *Archives of Sexual Behavior*, 19, 119–137.

Weeks, G. R. and Gambescia, N. (2000) *Erectile Dysfunction: Integrating Couple Therapy, Sex Therapy, and Medical Treatment*. New York: Norton.

Weeks, G. R. and Gambescia, N. (2002) *Hypoactive Sexual Desire: Integrating Sex and Couple Therapy*. New York: Norton.

Wincze, J. P. and Carey, M. P. (2001) *Sexual Dysfunction: A Guide for Assessment and Treatment, 2nd edn*. New York: Guilford Press.

Wise, M. E. and Watson, J. P. (2000) A new treatment for premature ejaculation: A case series for a desensitizing band. *Sexual and Relationship Therapy*, 15, 345–350.

Wolpe, J. R. (1958) *Psychotherapy by Reciprocal Inhibition*. Stanford, CA: Stanford University Press.

Wolpe, J. R. (1991) *The Practice of Behavior Therapy, 4th edn*. New York: Pergamon.

Woody, J. D. (1992) *Treating Sexual Distress: Integrative Systems Therapy*. Newbury Park, CA: Sage.

Zilbergeld, B. (1975) Group treatment of sexual dysfunction in men without partners. *Journal of Sex and Marital Therapy*, 1, 204–214.

Zilbergeld, B. (1978) *Men and Sex*. Boston: Little Brown.

Zilbergeld, M. (1992) *The New Male Sexuality*. New York: Bantam Books.

Chapter 17

Relationship therapy

Investigation

Jane Ridley

INTRODUCTION

Marriage is no longer the only form of long-term relationship, it does not necessarily last, nor is it necessarily the relationship within which children are born and raised. Many children are born to cohabiting couples. In parallel with these changes is the rise in divorce and remarriage. This brings with it multi-dimensional relationships with past partners and issues about who finances whom, who is responsible for whom and who is allowed to discipline or decide on boundaries for which child. The term 'less-traditional' is used here to include the multiplicity of relationships that occur and which are not husband/wife and children of that marriage. Within a multi-cultural society, these changing patterns add pressure on more traditional cultural and religious values and practices.

Same-sex couples have gained a legal status for their relationship along with rights and responsibilities. This civil partnership is registered and there is a formal court-based process for its dissolution. This may make it easier for same-sex couples to seek help for their relationship. Although social attitudes to sexuality can be said to be more liberal, there is little evidence to suggest that attitudes to infidelity have changed. In an attitude survey throughout the European Union respondents, asked what they thought marriage meant today, said 'committing yourself to being faithful to your partner' (Eurostat, 1995). Therefore the clinician has to be open to new knowledge, current trends and to be prepared to learn from the couple.

In spite of the centrality of the sexual relationship (Crowe and Ridley, 2000) many assessments ignore this; the quality of the sexual relationship should become a routine part of an initial investigation. This is inhibited, first, because many couples find it difficult to discuss their sexual life; second, relationship therapy is often divided between services, one set of clinicians working with the 'relationship' and others working with the 'sexual relation-ship'. I suggest that a skilled clinician can be respectful of the couple's sensi-tivity regarding sexuality but include this aspect within early investigations. Where an individual is receiving treatment for depression or ongoing physical health problems, it would also be useful to include the partner in any investigation.

THE QUALITY OF THE RELATIONSHIP: A HEALTH DIMENSION

Relationship satisfaction is very strongly linked to mental health; depressed people are often less satisfied with their relationship (Kurdek, 1991, 1998). Depression and poor physical health in either the man or woman are often associated with reduced sexual desire (Porto, 2004). A poor or absent sexual relationship can lead to further discontent. Poor physical health can negatively affect relationship quality, although this can be moderated by the characteristics of the illness, income, attitudes and mutual activities (Burman and Margolin, 1992; Booth and Johnson, 1994). Diabetes, for example, may affect the man's erectile function; pain and restricted movement through arthritis or injury may affect the couple's sexual and sensual life. Marital status has long been identified as one of the social characteristics associated with heart disease and stroke (Bainton and Peterson, 1963; Carter and Glick, 1970; Medalie, 1972). Survival rates from cancer are particularly influenced by the individual's marital state (McAllister, 1995). 'Relationship breakdown is one of the major causes of suicide world wide' and 'all of the available evidence shows that those who are divorced and separated are more prone to deaths from accidents' (McAllister, 1995).

THE QUALITY OF THE RELATIONSHIP: LIFE EVENTS

In men, being unemployed can challenge the individual's sense of self and interpersonal security within a relationship. In women, hysterectomy, mastectomy, or loss of fertility through illness or the menopause can have a similar effect. Rape, of either the man or woman, is another event that can make the individual fearful of intimate contact and, unless acknowledged, can make it difficult for the clinician.

Life events that are seen as desirable, such as a house move, promotion or a new baby, may bring added stress that will affect the couple. Ross et al. (1991) conclude that, when children come along, the psychological well-being of parents does not increase. In some instances, mothers are actually more distressed than childless women.

Sexually transmitted diseases, such as trichomonas, chlamydia, candida and human immunodeficiency virus (HIV), often accompany an increase in sexual activity in the younger age groups and the effects on health and fertility can affect couples' sexual and inter-personal relationships.

It is becoming clearer that earlier sexual or physical abuse can severely affect the couple relationship. Where abuse has been disclosed, the impact on the couple is often unpredicted and traumatic. They experience anger at the earlier 'deception', overprotectiveness of the partner and anger against the perpetrator, who may be a family member. Many current relationships to be addressed are changed, therefore Douglas et al. (1989) suggest that knowledge of the initial abuse may be necessary for the clinician to be of best service to the client/couple. It may also be important to offer sessions to the non-abused partner. The sex of the clinician may be influential in this; some clients who have been abused by a man may request a female therapist. However, it is not clear whether it is therapeutically necessary to match the sex of the client and clinician. Research into this is urgently needed.

THE QUALITY OF THE RELATIONSHIP: AFFAIRS

Many clients seek help because of an affair by one partner; some having occurred during the client's first pregnancy. Secrecy surrounding affairs probably makes statistical accuracy difficult. Nevertheless, The Sexual Attitude and Lifestyles Survey (1994) found that infidelity in married men is greatest in the higher social classes but that in women, social class and educational differences do not seem to influence its occurrence. However, women who work away from home are nearly three times as likely as women in general to have had two or more concurrent sexual relationships during the past 5 years.

Most people still regard extra-marital sex with disapproval (Barlow et al., 2001). Men and women may vary, women being upset by the emotional aspect and men more by the sexual and physical aspect of infidelity. Clinical experience suggests that it is often extremely difficult for the 'betrayed' partner to forget or forgive the affair, especially if it occurs during a pregnancy. Issues of trust and rules governing the couple's commitment have all to be re-negotiated (Afifi et al., 2001). Those who engage in adultery are less likely to report happy marriages. Infidelity has also been linked to men's sexual dissatisfaction and to women's perception of inequity in the marriage (*Relationships Today*, 2004).

The disclosure of an affair, although traumatic, even similar to post-traumatic stress responses (Lusterman, 1995; Glass and Wright, 1997), does not necessarily herald the end of the relationship. One can hypothesise that an affair is a 'call for help' or a 'warning signal' that a relationship requires attention. Where the couple are determined to rebuild, it is often possible to do so, but unless the issues of trust and betrayal are addressed, the relationship is likely to deteriorate (*Relationships Today*, 2004).

THE QUALITY OF THE RELATIONSHIP: MULTI-CULTURAL ASPECTS

Religious beliefs and attitudes are also involved in defining a 'good enough' relationship. Butler-Schloss (2004) makes an eloquent appeal to recognise that 'arranged', as opposed to 'forced,' marriages are an important stabilising aspect of society. She notes the close parallels between Christianity, Judaism, Islam, Hinduism and Sikhism in their attitudes to the meaning and stability of marriage. Nevertheless, similarity in age, race, religious affiliation, education and social class has been seen as important for relationship satisfaction (Craddock, 1991).

To be culturally sensitive to different beliefs and attitudes, the clinician must learn from the individual or couple. There should be joint assessment and decision-making between the client and professional to overcome the barriers imposed by different belief systems. 'It is well known that for a certain group of men, sexual dysfunction is a form of communication, a way of signaling to themselves or to others that something needs attention in their personal or emotional lives' (Gann, 1995).

THE QUALITY OF THE RELATIONSHIP: SAME SEX AND BI-SEXUALITY

Investigating the difficulties faced by same-sex couples is currently compounded by ambivalent attitudes to being gay or lesbian, by both clients and clinicians. The attitude of clinicians is always important (see Chapter 18), and it may be significant for them to examine their own gender orientation and attitude to same-sex relationships before beginning an exploration of the couple's difficulties.

Gay men, even now, may feel uncertain or unhappy about their orientation. Society has been less punitive towards lesbians, possibly making it easier for women to be at ease with their gender orientation but insufficient evidence about this is available. In any case, it is important for clinicians to be comfortable with their own gender and attitudes.

A small number of couples encompass relationships in which one partner can accept or tolerate the bi-sexuality or sexual deviation of the other. These are outside the brief of this chapter but may need to be understood in any investigation for couple therapy. Casual one-night stands or regular attendance at prostitutes may be an understated aspect of couple relationships.

THE QUALITY OF THE RELATIONSHIP: DOMESTIC VIOLENCE AND SEXUAL COERCION

Minority women are less likely than others to report violence because of their discomfort with the power relations that they would have to negotiate were they to report (Davey, 2000). The Department of Health has recommended that professionals consider routine enquiries in women patients about domestic violence but Ramsay et al. (2002) have said there is insufficient evidence that subsequent interventions are effective. Where the topic has been raised, 60% have said that one or both partners had been violent to each other in the preceding years, as opposed to only 10% who report domestic violence spontaneously (Vetere, 2002). The most serious domestic violence is perpetrated by men against women, although O'Leary and Cascardi (1989) found that within 30 months of marriage there was little difference in rates of aggression between men and women. However, there is general agreement that the physical damage inflicted by men is greater than that by women.

Women often have better verbal skills than their male partner but they may be unaware of the powerful impact that their critical remarks may have on a man, particularly if directed at sexual prowess (Ridley, 1999). Men may resort to physical violence to win an argument when all else fails (Markman et al., 1994; Kurdeck, 1995).

THE QUALITY OF THE RELATIONSHIP: INFERTILITY TREATMENT, PREGNANCY AND CHILDBIRTH

Infertility treatment intrudes into the physical and sexual lives of the couple and may take several years before a successful outcome: 'Where *in vitro* fertilization (IVF) is required, or donor sperm is needed, or more unusually, another woman's womb is used (and she becomes the surrogate mother of another couple's child), it can be very difficult to predict the emotional or practical results' (Crowe and Ridley, 2000). Clinical experience suggests that even where the outcome is successful, the impact on the couple's relationship can be severe, especially on sexual life, which was interrupted during the treatment (Read, 1997).

Women's responses to first-trimester spontaneous abortion can be complex, ranging from grief to depression (Friedman, 2004). Other experiences, such as a difficult labour, a stillbirth, the birth of a disabled child or a child with a health problem, can also affect a relationship. Harrison (2004) has reported that 23% of couples thought that having a disabled child had brought them closer together but 13% said that it had caused major problems and 9% claimed that it had led to separation.

THE QUALITY OF THE RELATIONSHIP: GENDER ISSUES

Women may need to talk about feelings and go over the impact of emotionally arousing situations whereas men may often approach an emotionally arousing situation by trying to solve the problem. Tensions can arise because of these different approaches. Gender differences affect couples in how they communicate, the priority placed on penetrative sex, sharing of feelings, talking together and ways in which they express their aggression (Ridley, 1999). Ridley has developed a checklist to help clinicians notice when gender differences may interfere with a couple's relationship. She suggests that failure to understand the opposite gender's intimacy needs can contribute to relationship distress.

THE QUALITY OF THE RELATIONSHIP: THE CHANGING STRUCTURE

Unemployment, the need to take care of dependent children, the problems of financing a growing family, educational attainment, as well as the financial and interpersonal consequences of separation and divorce are complex influences. Following a divorce, the woman's economic situation declines sharply (Taylor et al., 1994) but men's economic circumstances are less adversely affected (Lillard and Waite, 1995).

Financial difficulties may be more severe for less traditional families: 'Frequently, money problems arise because of obligations left over from first marriages. Remarried husbands may end up financially responsible for children from their first marriages and step-children ... Some second wives also feel resentful about the proportion of the husband's income that goes to the first wife ... Or a second wife may feel guilty about the burden of support her own children place upon their step-father' (Lamanna and Reidman, 1997). Similar disagreements occur in cohabiting relationships.

Within less traditional relationships there are few clear guidelines for roles and responsibilities. When new relationships begin, the couple may carry with them links and responsibilities from previous relationships. The new partner may wish to assert his authority with the step-child, while the mother may see it as her responsibility (Kurdeck and Fine, 1991; Emery, 1994; Lamanna and Reidman, 1997). Members of the extended families may feel uncertain about their relationship with the new couple. Boundaries can become blurred and alliances, either covert or imagined, may undermine the couples relationship (Crowe and Ridley, 2000). Older couples who have begun a new relationship occasionally feel that 'it should be easier' this time, forgetting that they are in a 'young' relationship that has to be negotiated.

THE QUALITY OF THE RELATIONSHIP: THE INTERNET

Clinical experience suggests that excessive time spent 'on the computer', the downloading of pornography or use of the internet for relationships can cause controversy. Traeen et al. (2004) suggest that 'the internet as an arena for finding a partner seems more important to bi-sexuals than heterosexuals'. Whitty (2004) suggests that internet 'infidelity' has the same impact on the couple as a traditional 'offline' affair.

THE QUALITY OF THE RELATIONSHIP: AN INTER-PERSONAL DIMENSION

Falling in and out of love, 'stonewalling', poor eye contact, the need to be close or distant, longing for or fear of intimacy, dominance and submission, wanting to be listened to and having sufficient regular sex that is satisfying to both partners are among the many less obvious aspects of relationship that the clinician will want to investigate.

'Falling in love', as opposed to economic or social reasons, is often the reason for becoming an 'item' or marrying; equally, falling out of love, is presented as the reason why a relationship should end. Within psychoanalytic literature much is made of the adult need to re-create the 'state of sharing' experience between the mother and baby in the adult state of 'being in love' (Papousek and Papousek, 1974; Stern, 1983). Whether this is accurate or not, it is helpful in underlining the irrational nature of 'falling in' or 'out of love' described by some couples as most important.

Some authors think there is a movement towards egalitarian relationships based on mutual support and affection (Rampage, 1994); yet others consider that many are pragmatic, marrying because they are ready (Mansfield and Collard, 1988). In many parts of the world, marrying for love is not the basis for marriage and, according to Butler-Schloss (2004), many couples in Britain are still formed by family consultation. Reasons for cohabitating may be similar.

When couples divorce or separate, a high emotional cost is experienced by all, even if the end of the relationship is welcomed. A sense of a 'failed' relationship, of an ideal that could not be achieved, often accompanied by disputes over home, furniture, children and pets, may lead to a level of cynicism accompanying both partners into new relationships.

Positive and responsive facial expression, voice quality, touch and tenderness and, above all, eye contact have been identified as indicators of a good outcome for marital therapy (Hahlweg et al., 1984; Schaap and Jansen-Nawas, 1987; Gottman, 1991). Non-verbal aspects of relating are seen as crucial to a good long-term relationship. Gottman (1991) described a relationship in which a 'stonewalling' man is faced with a 'pursuing' woman. He would listen with an immobile face, little eye contact and few responses to demonstrate he was listening. The woman would increase her attempts to involve him by speaking more. Not surprisingly this would lead to discontent within the relationship.

Couples were more likely to separate (Gottman, 1991) if the woman's face showed 'disgust', 'contempt' or a 'miserable smile' or the husband's face showed 'fear' or a 'miserable smile'. Congruent with this, wives criticised and complained more; husbands disagreed more and both husbands and wives 'yes butted'. These important findings were recorded within a research setting with trained observers and set tasks for the participants. Nevertheless, the clinician should be aware of the central significance of non-verbal interaction.

THE QUALITY OF THE RELATIONSHIP: FIVE DIFFERENT APPROACHES

The psychoanalytic approach

The psychoanalytic approach views couple interaction from the perspective of the conscious and unconscious self. The adult transfers onto the partner unconscious wishes and fantasies, which often relate to unreconciled needs from early childhood, the hope being that the partner can satisfy these needs. There is a shared unconscious fantasy that the couple acts out. Where these fantasies are distorted, problems are likely to occur. Anxious-ambivalent attachment in childhood is believed to lead to relationship difficulties in adult life. Transference and counter-transference defence mechanisms as projections are also derived out of unconscious and conscious dilemmas and echoed within the couple relationship. This approach is still seen as of uncertain value because of the length of time that it would take, the difficulty in researching the underlying assumptions, as well as the difficulty of testing the outcome. However, it can be useful to include hypotheses derived from psychoanalytic thinking, giving meaning to 'repetitive negative interactions'.

The behavioural approach

In behaviour therapy and current extensions into cognitive therapy, there is a strong reliance on observed behaviour, or clearly acknowledged and observed cognitive structures. The observations are detailed: the eye contact, position in the chair, voice tone, use of language. Behaviour therapy is therefore more easily researched and useful strategies seen to be effective. For example, observation of negative and critical interaction has led to emphasis being on positive behaviour rather than coercion to improve relationships.

The behaviourist observing a couple sees relationships as a contract carrying with it rewards and costs; as the relationship develops when the costs outweigh the rewards, problems may occur. The observer has a detailed observational task but a simpler conceptual framework of the mutually beneficial exchange that may need adjusting by changing behaviours to those which are seen as more rewarding by the partner. This can be how tasks are negotiated or how the couple communicates.

The cognitive approach

Within cognitive therapy the clinician is listening for 'negative automatic thoughts' and the 'schema' underpinning them. Within couple therapy, negative thought patterns can be reinforced by the partner in repetitive cycles. The observer notes the minutiae of the language and the thought processes.

Rational emotive therapy

Rational emotive therapy (Dryden, 1985) draws on both the behavioural and psychoanalytic approaches and is in some way similar to systems thinking, which is developed further in Chapter 18. Distinctions are drawn between relationships where behavioural style negotiations can be used and relationships that are characterised by intense emotions. Work is then done to modify the thinking attached to these emotions; couples are encouraged to express desires as opposed to commands.

Systems thinking

When taken together, three concepts – circularity, rules that appear to govern repetitive sequences and the concept that there is a consistency over time – form the basis on which hypotheses are developed. Using a hypothesis enables the clinician to consider the couple interaction without blaming either partner. Labelling an individual as sick or bad is seen as a process arising out of the context of the total relationship rather than purely an individual illness or behaviour pattern. This is particularly helpful in relationships that seem very 'stuck' in behaviour that the individuals appear to wish to change. Rules that appear to govern the system and maintain a steady state can help to explain the apparent inability of couples to change. This has led to the development of a contentious intervention, the 'paradoxical message'. (see Chapter 18).

Closeness and distance

In this, an assumption is made that partners may need to keep each other at an acceptable emotional distance. For example, a couple whose sex life is improving may start arguing more vehemently than usual, thus helping the couple stay at a safe emotional distance. Individuals seek levels of closeness or intimacy but may also be somewhat fearful of that closeness (Feldman, 1979). This hypothesis can be extended to encompass the rules that seem to keep couples avoiding sexual intimacy or physical or non-verbal closeness, emotional intimacy or daily discussions of practical aspects of living together ('operational closeness'; Holmes, 1997; Crowe and Ridley, 2000).

At different stages in the life cycle, each partner may look for different elements of closeness or distance. The mother of a new baby may seek a greater degree of physical and non-verbal closeness. As a man is retiring, he may look forward to spending more time with his partner whereas she, now the children have left home, may be ready to spend more time out of the home. This keeps them at a safe emotional distance even if it also leads to discontent.

Avoidance of conflict

Another hypothesis that fits clinical experience is avoidance of conflict. Couples demonstrate different ways of avoiding issues that may cause conflict. A couple might be extremely polite to each other but their relationship has not been consummated, or the woman may find penetration painful or impossible and the man is gentle and attentive to her and is fearful of causing pain. Using a hypothesis enables the clinician to think about the couple interaction as having a positive benefit to them.

This is particularly useful when thinking about couples where one partner is depressed. Depression may protect the partner from showing painful feelings. Jealousy in one partner and pleas of faithfulness from the other partner may reassure couples where there is low self-esteem, anxiety about their attractiveness or an intense need to depend on the other. Sexual refusal by one partner may be part of a power struggle in which one partner dominates in the sexual area and the other dominates in the non-sexual aspect of the couple relationship. Difficulties experienced in older relationships can be hypothesised, depending on the circumstances, to keep adolescents at home, to avoid boredom or to avoid thinking about their old age together.

THE QUALITY OF THE RELATIONSHIP: CAN IT BE MEASURED?

Couples who seek therapy often do so because they have decided that 'something is wrong'. Common phrases used are: 'he doesn't listen to me' and 'she spends too much time with the children'. Can such distress and lack of satisfaction be measured?

Fredman and Sherman's (1987) handbook includes most of the useful measures. Measures such as those designed by Locke-Wallace (1959) and Spanier (1976) are reliable but they are standardised only within the USA. GRIMS, the Golombok-Rust Inventory of Marital Satisfaction (Rust et al., 1986) has a unidimensional score on marital satisfaction. GRISS, the Golombok–Rust Inventory of Sexual Satisfaction (Rust and Golombok, 1986) is also well validated (Rust and Golombok, 1985), but more complicated as it scores separately for male and female sexual satisfaction and for specific sexual dysfunctions. However, the GRIMS and the GRISS are standardised only in the UK. Moreover, it is not clear if such self-report questionnaires are effective, reliable and valid within a multi-cultural community or where literacy skills are low.

Couples complain that the questions of the the Golombok–Rust Inventory of Sexual Satisfaction are too intrusive and personal to answer in a formal written way. What may be more valuable is a semi-structured interview, which would use the skills of a sensitive clinician with an inventory such as GRISS to make it more possible for an assessment of the sexual relationship to be included effectively.

The Conflict Tactics Scale (Strauss, 1979) may be useful when dealing specifically with conflict resolution issues. Olsen et al. (1983) have developed FACES III, a complicated family rating scale with a couple version. It measures factors such as adaptability and cohesion and demonstrates that good communication is a facilitating aspect of good relationships. This uses a combination of self-report and therapist's assessment. Other measures use direct observation via a one-way screen and analysis of video-taped interaction scored under different categories (Hops et al., 1972; Hahlweg et al., 1984). A life history questionnaire and a sex history sheet (Crowe and Ridley, 2000) can help the initial investigation.

However, the clinician will need to develop a relationship with the couple, being sensitive to their concerns about disclosing sexual material, at the same time as helping the couple understand why it may be useful to include their sexual relationship. Where personal, religious or cultural reasons intervene, these must be respected.

THE QUALITY OF THE RELATIONSHIP AND THE QUALITY OF THE CLINICIAN

The behavioural-systems approach advocated here requires the clinician to be flexible, familiar with the wide spectrum of forces affecting a couple and to be prepared to learn from them. It also requires that the clinician is comfortable working within the sexual as well as the relationship aspect of a couple relationship. It asks the clinician to be respectful of cultural and religious beliefs that may be different to his or her own. Flexibility and the ability to move between different theoretical orientations according to the needs of the client is also important. Training, which is outside the remit of this chapter, must be seen as a priority to equip clinicians with these skills.

REFERENCES

Afifi, W. A., Falato, W. L. and Weiner, J. L. (2001) Identity concerns following a severe relational transgression: The role of discovery method for the relational outcomes of infidelity. *Journal of Social and Personal Relationships*, 18, 291–308.

Bainton, C. R. and Peterson, D. R. (1963) Deaths from coronary heart disease in persons fifty years and younger. *New England Journal of Medicine*, 268, 569–575.

Barlow, A., Duncan, S., James, G. and Park, A. (2001) Just a piece of paper? Marriage and cohabitation. In: A. Park, J. Curtice, K. Thomson, L. Jarvis and C. Bromley (eds) *British Social Attitudes: Public, Social Ties*. London: Sage.

Booth, A. and Johnson, D. R. (1994) Declining health and marital quality. *Journal of Marriage and the Family*, 56, 218–223.

Burman, B. and Margolin, G. (1992) Analysis of the association between marital relationships and health problems: an international perspective. *Psychological Bulletin*, 112, 36–63.

Butler-Schloss, D. (2004) *Rites of Passage. The Bulletin 8*. London: One Plus One.

Carter, H. and Glick, P. (1970) *Marriage and Divorce: A Social and Economic Study*. Cambridge, MA: Harvard University Press.

Craddock, A. E. (1991) Relationships between attitudinal similarity, couple structure and couple satisfaction within married and de facto couples. *Australian Journal of Psychology*, 43, 11–16.

Crowe, M. and Ridley, J. (2000) *Therapy with Couples: A Behavioural-Systems Approach to Relationship and Sexual Problems*. Oxford: Blackwell Science.

Davey, S. (ed) (2000) *Global Forum for Health Research: Mapping a Global Pandemic. Review of Current Literature on Rape, Sexual Assault and Sexual Harassment of Women*. Geneva: World Health Organization.

Douglas, A., Matson, I. C. and Hunter, S. (1989) Sex therapy for women incestuously abused as children. *Sexual and Marital Therapy*, 4, 143–160.

Dryden, W. (1985) Rational-emotive marital therapy. In: W. Dryden (ed) *Marital Therapy in Britain*. London: Harper and Row.

Emery, R. E. (1994) *Renegotiating Family Relationships: Divorce, Child Custody and Mediation*. New York: Guilford Press.

Eurostat (1995). *Women and Men in the European Union: A Statistical Portrait*. Luxembourg: Office for Official Publications of the European Communities.

Feldman, L. (1979) Marital conflict and marital intimacy. An integrative psychodynamic-behavioural-systemic model. *Family Process*, 18, 101–105.

Fredman, N. and Sherman, R. (1987) *Handbook of Measurements for Marriage and Family Therapy*. New York: Brunner Mazel.

Friedman, T. (2004) Emotional loss, miscarriages and the reasons to want to continue to conceive. *Sexual and Relationship Therapy*, 19, S77, abstract C423.

Gann, S. Y. (1995) *A Functional View of Erectile Insufficiency*. London: British Association of Sexual and Relationship Therapists.

Glass, S. P. and Wright, T. L. (1997) Reconstructing marriage after the trauma of infidelity. In: K. Halford and H. J. Markman (eds) *Clinical Handbook of Marriage and Couple Intervention*. New York: John Wiley.

Gottman, J. M. (1991) Predicting the longitudinal course of marriages. *Journal of Marital and Family Therapy*, 17, 3–7.

Hahlweg, K., Schindler, L., Revensdorf, D. and Brengelmann, C. (1984) The Munich Marital Therapy Study. In: K. Hahlweg and N. S. Jacobson (eds) *Marital Interaction*. New York: Guilford Press.

Harrison, J. (2004) *Support for Families with Disabled Children. The Bulletin, 8(2)*. London: One Plus One.

Holmes, J. (1997) Attachment, autonomy, intimacy: Some clinical implications of attachment theory. *British Journal of Medical Psychology*, 70, 231–248.

Hops, H., Wills, T. A., Patterson, G. R. and Weiss, R. L. (1972) *Marital Interaction Coding System*. Eugene, OR: University of Oregon Research Institute.

Kurdeck, L. A. (1991) Marital stability and changes in marital quality in newly wed couples. A test of the contextual model. *Journal of Social and Personal Relationships*, 8, 27–48.

Kurdeck, L. A. (1995) Predicting changes in marital satisfaction from husband's and wife's conflict resolution styles. *Journal of Marriage and Family*, 57, 153–164.

Kurdeck, L. A. (1998) The nature and predictors of the trajectory of change in marital quality over the first four years of marriage for first married husbands and wives. *Journal of Family Psychology*, 12, 494–510.

Kurdeck, L. A. and Fine, M. A. (1991) Cognitive correlates of satisfaction for mothers and step fathers in step-father families. *Journal of Marriage and the Family*, 53, 565–572.

Lamanna, M. A. and Reidman, A. (1997) *Marriages and Families*. Belmont, CA: Wadsworth.

Lillard, L. A. and Waite, L. J. (1995) Till death do us part: Marital disruption and mortality. *American Journal of Sociology*, 100, 1131–1156.

Locke, H. J. and Wallace, K. M. (1959) Short marital adjustment and prediction tests: Their reliability and validity. *Marriage and Family Living*, 21, 251–255.

Lusterman, D. (1995) Treating marital infidelity. In: R. H. Mikesell, D. Lusterman and S. H. McDaniels (eds) *Integrating Family Therapy: Handbook of Family Psychology and Systems Theory*. Washington, DC: American Psychological Association.

Mansfield, P. and Collard, J. (1998) *The Beginning of the Rest of Your Life*. London: Macmillan Press.

Markman, H. J., Stanley, S. and Blumber, S. (1994) *Fighting for Your Marriage*. San Francisco: Jossey Bass.

McAllister, F. (ed) (1995) *Marital Breakdown and the Health of the Nation*, 2nd edn. London: One Plus One.

Medalie, J. H. (1972) *Factors associated with the first myocardial infarction: Five years observation of 10,000 adult males*. Presented at the Symposium of Epidemiology and Prevention of Coronary Heart Disease, Helsinki.

Olsen, D. H., McCubbin, H. I., Barnes, H., Larsen, A., Muxen, M. and Wilson, M. (1983) *Families: What Makes Them Work*. Los Angeles: Sage.

O'Leary, K. D. and Cascardi, M. (1989) *Frequency of homicide in intimate relationships: a decade of FBI reporting*. Unpublished manuscript, Stony Brook, USA: Psychology Dept., University of New York.

Papousek, H. and Papousek, M. (1974) Mirror image and self recognition in young human infants: A new method of experimental analysis. *Developmental Psychology*, 7, 149–157.

Porto, R. (2004) Depression and sexuality. *Sexual and Relationship Therapy*, 19, S30, abstract A444.

Rampage, C. (1994) Power, gender and marital intimacy. *Journal of Family Therapy*, 19, 30.

Ramsay, J., Richardson, J., Carter, Y. H., Davidson, L. L. and Feder, G. (2002) Should health care professionals screen women for domestic violence? *British Medical Journal*, 325, 314–318.

Read, J. (1997) *Sexual Problems and Fertility*. London: BICA.

Relationships Today (2004) *Sexual Infidelity*. London: One Plus One.

Ridley J. (1999) *Intimacy in Crisis*. London: Whurr Publishing Company.

Ross, C. E., Mirkowsky, J. and Goldsteen, K. (1991) The impact of family on health. In: A. Booth (ed.) *Contemporary Families, Looking Forward, Looking Back*. Minneapolis, MN: NCFR.

Rust, J. and Golombok, S. (1985) The validation of the Golombok–Rust Inventory of Sexual Satisfaction. *British Journal of Clinical Psychology*, 24, 63–64.

Rust, J. and Golombok, S. (1986) The GRISS: A psychometric instrument for the assessment of sexual dysfunctionl. *Archives of Sexual Behaviour*, 15, 157–165.

Rust, J., Bennun, I., Crowe, M. and Golombok, S. (1986) A psychometric instrument for assessment of marital discord (GRIMS). *Sexual and Marital Therapy*, 1, 55–60.

Schaap, C. and Jansen-Nawas, C. (1987) Marital interaction, affect and conflict resolution. *Sexual and Marital Therapy*, 2, 35–51.

Spanier, G. (1976) Measuring dyadic adjustment. *Journal of Marriage and the Family*, 38, 15–28.

Stern, D. (1983) Self, other and self and other. In: J. D. Lichtenberg, and S. Kaplan (eds) *Reflections on Self Psychology*. Hillsdale, NJ: Analytic Press.

Strauss, M. (1979) Measuring intrafamilial conflict and violence: the Conflict Tactics (CT) Scales. *Journal of Marriage and the Family*, 41, 74–86.

Taylor, M., Keen, M., Buck, N. and Corti, L. (1994) Income welfare and consumption. In: J. Buck, D. Rose and J. Scott (eds) *The British Household Panel Survey, 1990–1992*. Colchester, UK: University of Essex: ESRC Research Centre on Micro-Social Change.

Traeen, B., Sorheim, T. and Stigum, H. (2004) Use of pornography and the internet as an arena for erotic chatting and finding a partner in Norway. *Sexual and Relationship Therapy*, 19, S21, abstract A427.

Vetere, A. (2002) Violence in the family: How do we talk about it? *The Psychologist*, 15, 515–516.

Wellings, K., Field, J., Johnson, A. M. and Wadsworth, J. (1994) *Sexual Behaviour in Britain, the National Survey of Sexual Attitudes and Lifestyles*. London: Penguin Books.

Whitty, M. (2004) Internet infidelity: Men's and women's understanding of cheating online. *Sexual and Relationship Therapy*, 19, S63, abstract C125.

Chapter 18

Relationship therapy

Treatment

Jane Ridley

INTRODUCTION

This chapter builds on the previous and considers alternative ways of treating couples. It should be clear that many complex issues affect the couple and the clinical work. The method described here is the behavioural-systems approach, detailed in Crowe and Ridley (2000). It offers a basic clinical guideline to enable the clinician to choose alternative interventions according to the flexibility or rigidity of the couple interaction and the presence of a symptom or symptoms in one partner.

Clients may be referred by general practitioners, consultants, courts, social workers, probation officers and other health-care professionals, or themselves choose to seek treatment. An important early decision is whether to offer treatment to one client only or to ask the partner to attend for treatment, even though the client may consider his or her difficulty to be solely individual. From a couples therapist's perspective, this is a central clinical issue. Much traditional treatment has focused on the clinician's offering individual support or counselling, supplemented by medication as appropriate. This chapter suggests that an alternative may be to include the partner in treatment where the 'presenting problem' may impact upon the couple relationship.

INITIAL INFORMATION GATHERING AND HYPOTHESISING

It is important to allow oneself freedom to think around what is happening for the couple. Before the couple is seen, questionnaires, records and the referral letter can be scrutinised for behavioural and systemic information (see Chapter 17). Questions such as, 'why now?' around what is happening now that makes this couple seek therapy; 'what for?' as a focus for considering what is being asked of therapy (Kraemer, 1986).

An initial hypothesis for the couple who are very polite, with a non-existent sex life, may be that they fear conflict and believe that good couples never argue. If this hypothesis is useful, therapy may help them experience arguments that enhance their relationship and their sex life. Hypotheses such as this are not held to be 'true' but are used as simple tools for the therapist. Where clinicians work with colleagues from different orientations, it is very creative to draw on these orientations when formulating initial hypotheses. Family or individual life-cycle experiences, life events, attachment issues and the reason for referral are all considered, as well as the richness of alternative orientations. A word of caution: clinicians can be enthusiastic when hypothesising and it is important to stay well grounded in simple and practical ideas. A further word of caution from clinical experience: the couple who walks through the door may be quite different from the descriptions provided. Some referrals are dominated by medical, psychiatric or behavioural problems and the basic humanity of the couple can be lost.

THE FIRST INTERVIEW: KEEPING THE MOMENTUM GOING

At the beginning of the session, agency and professional requirements may need to be raised. These include: introducing the setting and describing what will happen, explaining about one-way screen facilities if used, inviting the couple to meet the team behind the screen should they wish. When a session break is used, the couple should be told at the beginning of therapy and suggestions can be made about how they may use the break. A break is used to give the therapist time to think about the session and to formulate any message to be given.

Where a video or audio tape is used, written informed consent is required. Where material is used for teaching purposes, this too must be included in informed consent. In some settings, the professional organisation to which clinicians belong should be stated. Issues regarding confidentiality, legal requirements and access to complaint procedures may need to be made clear. This will take some time but is a requirement that demonstrates that the clinician is respectful of the couple's rights.

The behavioural-systems approach (Crowe and Ridley, 2000) was developed within a relationship and sex therapy clinic in a busy, publicly funded psychiatric hospital where it was clear that couples were anxious about whether anything could change. In the first interview, the process of change and hope can begin. It is not just a time to collect information, although that may be necessary if no social history is available before the couple is seen. Where possible, the therapist begins the work of finding one small behavioural task that the couple can achieve at home before the next session.

The behavioural-systems approach asks the therapist to work quickly with the current relationship of the couple as the focus for treatment. This requires high levels of empathy and an ability to engage quickly and to intervene in the couple's interaction. Many individually trained therapists find intervention difficult, especially if they are accustomed to a 'listening' rather than 'interactive' role. Experience suggests that couples gain confidence in their ability to change with a therapist who is comfortable with intervening gently but firm to encourage changes in the way they relate.

The first interview of necessity is unpredictable and the therapist will require considerable experience or good supervision to help therapy stay on track and to keep the momentum focussed on the present relationship of the couple. It is easy to get sidetracked into listening too long to one partner, hearing long descriptions of past experiences and explanations as to 'why' things have gone wrong or becoming sidetracked into medical matters and never quite concentrating on the couple's interaction in the session.

In the first and subsequent sessions, it is important that the therapist hears what both partners have to say, joins with each partner, pays attention and takes seriously their initial presentation, but stays in control to focus on the couple interaction.

Staying in control may mean interrupting monologues, asking one partner to ask the other how she or he sees the situation, interrupting descriptions of history to ask each partner to tell the other how the history affects their present relationship. To make these interventions, a recommended procedure for the early part of the first and ongoing sessions is for the therapist to 'decentre'.

Decentring

The therapist asks the couple to move their chairs to face each other. The therapist may then move his or her chair a little further apart. If a couple is hesitant, it may be necessary for the clinician to stand up and help move chairs. The aim is to help the couple communicate directly with each other and for the therapist's interventions to encourage the couple to talk to each other. Clients may try to pull the therapist in on their side. It is therefore important to pay attention to how the therapist sits and whether too much eye contact is made.

Where a partner asks the therapist, 'Do you think we can change?', an appropriate response would be to say, 'Ask your partner that question'. Similarly in response to, 'I think Jim doesn't want to be here', as another opportunity for the couple to talk to each other by the therapist says, 'Can you ask Jim if what you are saying is correct?'. By doing so the therapist encourages direct contact. It also encourages the couple to 'check it out' instead of mind reading.

Finding a reciprocal task for the couple to take home

For some couples, the first interview reveals such a range of difficulties that the therapist's task is to hear their story and to ensure that both partners participate in as balanced a way as possible, so it may not be appropriate to find a small task for the couple to take home. More frequently, even in the presence of severe difficulties, the couple can be asked to talk together and make small suggestions as to something that can be changed. This encourages the hope that change may be possible.

Using a behavioural model, the therapist tries to ensure that suggestions or requests are kept small, practical and achievable before the next session; they should be well balanced between the partners. Where the first interview reveals that the relationship is complicated and emotions are running high, it is still important to focus on a small, achievable task without ignoring the complexity of their situation. For example, where a disclosure of an affair has occurred, or one partner is contemplating separation, the therapist, at the end of a session, can acknowledge the depth of feeling being experienced but can suggest that a way forward may best be achieved by taking small steps.

Taking a session break and ending the session with a message

It is important to take a session break to think about a message that can be given at the end of the session. During training, with a one-way screen and a team, a session break is taken after 40–45 minutes. If the therapist works alone or without a one-way screen, it is still appropriate to take time for a session break to think about the session and formulate a message. Where possible, it is helpful to share thinking with a colleague as it is easy to be pulled in on one side or another, or to be caught up in the couple's despair.

A message to the couple can acknowledge that attending therapy is not easy and for many couples this is a new and unusual experience. For some this may be all that is necessary. When a simple behavioural task has been negotiated in the session, it should be spelled out in simple understandable language.

The next session's date and time should be given before the message. An example of a message after a turbulent first interview may go something like this:

> Thank you for coming. I am aware that this is the first time you have sought help together, which has not been easy. You have given a vivid description of the many problems you face as a couple, among these are arguments about finances, disagreements about Tom's attitude to Joan's daughter and the fact that Joan doesn't know if she can continue in this relationship. You spent time in this first session asking for the following small changes: Tom to bring Joan a cup of tea before he leaves for work in the morning; Joan will do the same for Tom on his return from work. I will find out from you, at the next session, how you got on with this small step forward.

As sometimes happens, the first session may be the only one the couple attends and any work done in the session should be done with that in mind.

THE BEHAVIOURAL-SYSTEMS APPROACH

The behavioural-systems approach offers a simple guideline, shown in Figure 18.1, which indicates how a therapist can select interventions that are appropriate to different levels of complexity and rigidity in a couple's interaction.

Therapist interventions: more need for therapist ingenuity; less reliance on couple's stated goals

Figure 18.1 suggests which level of intervention could be used, depending on key aspects of the presenting relationship. The vertical axis of the diagram represents the couple. As one ascends the hierarchy there is an increase in three areas: (1) the symptom; (2) individual focus; and (3) the rigidity of the system.

The horizontal axis represents the clinician and how she or he may choose to intervene according to the intensity of the symptom, the individual focus and the rigidity or flexibility of the system. As these increase in intensity so the therapist relies less on the stated goals of the couple and more on the ingenuity of the therapist to use the interventions higher up the hierarchy.

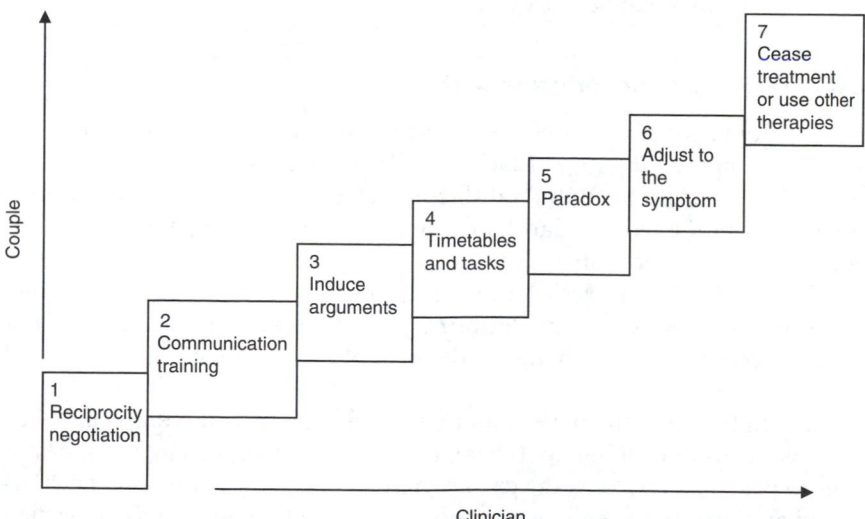

Figure 18.1 The levels of the intervention hierarchy in ascending order (for explanation, see text).

Reprinted from Crowe and Ridley (2000) with permission.

The hierarchy can be used very flexibly. Where couples are found to be rigid and difficult to change, interventions drawn from higher up the hierarchy are chosen. As couples improve, communication training or reciprocity negotiation from the lower levels can be used. From a purely practical perspective, a skilled clinician may use several approaches within one session doing some negotiating, encouraging some arguments and ending with a systemic or structural message or timetable.

When to use reciprocity negotiation

Many couples seek therapy because they believe the difficulties they experience originate within their relationship. Arguments, constant bickering and disputes over children, about extended family members or finances are often the source of tension and may be managed by using a simple reciprocity negotiation approach. Other couples seek help because one partner feels, 'something is wrong' and persuades the other that they should seek help. This more nebulous approach may be presented as 'We have stopped getting on but we still love each other', 'We don't talk', 'He's too busy at work and I'm unhappy', or general anxiety about the relationship.

Begin with reciprocity negotiation when couples present with:

- constant arguments
- general bickering
- 'something is wrong'
- constant complaints.

Using reciprocity negotiation with couples

Reciprocity negotiation is well researched and documented (Birchler et al., 1975; Gottman et al., 1977; Mackay, 1985; Crowe and Ridley, 2000). It is based on a belief that couples' satisfaction depends on high levels of positive reaction from the partner and that couples are usually prepared to 'give to get' what they need within a relationship. Complaining is thought to occur to enable an individual to get what he or she needs, when this does not occur, he or she complains harder. Reciprocity negotiation is a way to interrupt negative complaints by changing them into specific requests for a small change.

It is helpful if the therapist is aware of potential areas of complaints. For example, sharing washing up, tidying away dirty clothes, or moving shoes or bags to places preferred by the partner may sound simple, but a small achievable change can bring a glimmer of hope. If a couple cannot think of a small achievable change, the therapist may introduce ideas. This should be done with a light touch and a sense of humour. How the sink is left after washing up seems to cause wry smiles for many couples.

Stopping complaints is not sufficient on its own and should be followed up by reciprocal positive responses such as 'I noticed when you did . . . that was great'.

In the following example, Alan and Amy demonstrated their negative cycle of complaint/complaint:

Amy: You are late, as usual you missed bathing the twins, and it's too late to read to them.

Alan: You shouldn't have bathed them, you could have waited until I got home, you always undermine me in these ways.

Amy: That's rich, you could get in on time. Anyway, the boys don't want to be late for bed as they will be late for school in the morning.

Alan: Now you are using the boys against me, can't you see I try my best.

Amy: If you were trying you would get in on time, and I wouldn't be left to look after the twins on my own; you don't care about me or the boys.

Alan and Amy could carry this on indefinitely. Using reciprocity negotiation, the clinician asks them to think about one thing they could each ask of the other that would make things better:

Amy: (*carrying on complaining*) It would be better if he could occasionally help washing up or cook but of course he . . .

The therapist interrupts to say, 'Let's focus on what happens when Alan comes home. Can you ask Alan for what you would like?'

Amy: I know he won't do it.

Therapist: Try it out, what is it you would like to ask?

Amy: I would like him to come home in time to bath the boys.

Therapist: OK, try asking Alan now.

Amy: (*looking a bit grumpy*) Alan can you please come home every night by bath time?

The therapist then works with the couple to find out how often, what time, etc. and whether this would be practical for Alan. He agreed that on Monday, Wednesday and Friday he would be home by 6.45 p.m. but would be late on Tuesday and Thursday. This satisfied Amy.

To ensure that the requests are balanced and reciprocal, the therapist then asked Alan what he would like to ask of Amy. Alan asks to take the boys swimming on Saturdays without Amy present. He surprises Amy by making a request in a different area. He says that Amy has usually gone with them and 'spent her time sitting worrying about the boys' safety', but he would like time with them on his own. As Amy accepts his request, it seems sensible to try it out and see how it works. Where a request is very unbalanced, the therapist can intervene to try for a better balance. The clinician should ensure that the requests are simple, practical, reciprocal, well balanced between the partners and achievable before the next session.

In negotiating a reciprocal task, the therapist may work for a while with one partner's request but, to maintain a balance within the session, it may be necessary to switch to the other partner. Being flexible and having a sense of humour help to create a more positive atmosphere. Once negotiated, the details are restated in the message and checked at the next session. If the tasks have not been achieved, this is explored and a different task may be set. When tasks are not completed, this may indicate a more rigid system and it may be useful to think about moving up the hierarchy.

When to use communication training

When couples cannot solve problems together, it may be because of the way they communicate. It is useful to see if simple communication training may help. How a couple communicates verbally can be hindered by constant mind reading, where one partner speaks for the other; by the use of 'We always', which disables the couple from open disagreement, or by difficulty in using simple 'I' statements such as, 'I would like'. Statements that end with a sting in the tail are particularly destructive. A pattern easily missed is the 'over-verbal' couple who seem to use words as a way of not communicating.

Where a couple is reasonably flexible, focusing on communication may be sufficient to open up their relationship so that they can themselves find solutions or be helped to use reciprocity negotiation to change their relationship in a positive direction.

Use communication training where reciprocity negotiation is impeded by:

- mind reading
- one person speaks for both
- use of a sting in the tail
- few 'I' statements
- too many 'we' statements
- too much verbal interaction.

Using communication training with couples

'Communication training shares with reciprocity negotiation the rather naïve idea that both partners wish to have a good and peaceful relationship with logical and matter-of-fact communication' (Crowe, 1982). Ridley (1999) additionally suggests that gender issues can affect how men and women communicate. For example, a verbally articulate woman and a verbally slower man may have extra difficulties. Most therapists agree that good communication is usually part of a healthy functioning relationship, although there may be some disagreement as to whether 'blunt or brutal honesty' is always required (Stuart, 1980). Good communication usually requires that what is said by one partner is understood by the other, and vice versa.

> Positive communication skills include the following: sending clear and congruent messages, empathy, supportive statements and effective problem solving. Conversely, negative communication skills include the following: sending incongruent and disqualifying messages, lack of empathy, non-supportive (negative) statements, poor problem-solving, and paradoxical and double bind messages.
>
> (Olson et al., 1983)

How does the clinician encourage positive communication skills? First, couples are usually aware that their communication is problematic. Therefore, when a therapist suggests that she or he can help them change the way they communicate, the couple is usually appreciative. The clinician should be open and clear with a couple that she or he will focus on their communication. Second, within the session, good observation and clarity in giving feedback is required. Third, setting simple 10–15-minute tasks focusing on a different style of communication is useful. The structure of the session is similar to that of reciprocity negotiation. The therapist decentres early in the session, is vigilant in keeping the couple to the task, intervenes gently and firmly while keeping rapport and balance with both partners.

It is good to watch out for non-verbal interactions, which give clues to unstated feelings. If one partner sniffs and turns away while the other says, 'We can talk about everything', an intervention suggesting that the partner be asked if she or he agrees, may elicit a response. Consider, for example, 'When do we talk about the money you give to your ex-wife?' or 'Yes, everything but our non-existent sex life'. Both provide a basis for discussion.

Communication training will usually focus, by checking what the partner means, on helping the couple to stop mind reading. A simple intervention suggests that partner B restates what she or he thinks partner A has said and then checks with A if that is correct. This is then reversed. Encouraging 'I' statements, making positive requests, discouraging the 'sting in the tail' and helping couples check out the meaning given to non-verbal interaction all help a couple to talk more effectively to each other. Encouraging what we have called 'the mutual exchange of emotional messages' is also important, although complicated (Crowe and Ridley, 2000). Men and women may seek different levels of emotional sharing and each partner is likely to have individual capacities for sharing or keeping a distance emotionally. The aim would be that each learns to understand and respect each other's emotional needs.

Couples can express a limited range of emotions. For example, some couples can be angry with each other but not gentle; others can tease but not be serious. With these relationships the therapist can feed back this observation and suggest they try expressing another emotion, say, irritation or excitement. The over-emotional couple can be asked to have 'committee meetings' occasionally, or the couple who always communicate in a business-like manner can be encouraged to talk about feelings. In these ways, the therapist uses his or her ability to observe communication styles and develops interventions that make communication simpler, more empathic and more respectful of each other's style.

This is equally important where couples are separating, particularly where children are involved, as they will need to continue to communicate about the children after the separation about issues that are often hard to discuss: finances, family problems, celebrations or tragedies. Good communication, which can embrace a level of emotion, will be essential.

Set simple, short homework tasks such as: a talking/listening timetable where one partner talks for 5 minutes and the other listens, is empathic and does not make negative comments or explanations. This is then reversed and the second partner talks while the other listens. Communication tasks should again be set in a clear, well-structured manner. They are best timetabled, preferably at short, regular spaces. Couples can be encouraged to experiment and enjoy the homework. As before, where a couple does not engage in the tasks at home, or the communication style does not improve, it may be necessary to think of moving up the hierarchy and using a different approach.

Using reciprocity negotiation or communication training as an assessment tool

Detailed observation of the couple's interaction often highlights more rigid patterns, such as a dominant and a submissive partner (one speaking and one silent), or non-verbal interaction, suggesting that there are unstated resentments or anger. Where the couple relationship is more rigid, however skilled the therapist may be in using communication training, she or he may be puzzled by the lack of response of the couple and their apparent inability to change. For these couples, therapy may progress only by offering the next step up the hierarchy: that of inducing arguments.

Beginning therapy by offering reciprocity negotiation or communication training or a combination of both in the first session will help the clinician to assess the rigidity or flexibility of the couple, according to whether they are to modify their behaviour using these approaches. Simple behavioural tasks can be set, derived from the session, to be completed before the next session. Whether these tasks have been attempted or completed will help to indicate the flexibility or rigidity of their interaction.

Use reciprocity negotiation or communication training and behavioural tasks at the beginning of treatment to:

- assess the rigidity or flexibility of the couple
- do not move up the hierarchy too soon.

When to select encouraging arguments

Therapists may find this intervention bizarre because therapy can usually be understood as 'bringing peace' to warring couples. While practising reciprocity negotiation or communication training, the therapist also observes how the couple interacts. Who speaks first, who speaks for whom, is one partner silent, how do the couple interact non-verbally, what is the dynamic of the couple? Is there a dominant/submissive relationship, are there sulky silences, do you sense that there are unspoken resentments, is the couple very polite to each other but their sex life non-existent? In these ways, the clinician observes their interactions and thinks about areas that are not being presented by the couple. The less assertive partner may present mild depressive or anxiety symptoms or loss of sexual desire. Encouraging arguments can be used to prompt the less assertive partner to speak about some of the needs which are not being met and to enable the more assertive partner to respect this.

Use encouraging arguments when the relationship dynamics are

- dominant/submissive
- unstated resentments
- reduced sexual desire
- over politeness.

Encouraging arguments using a trivial issue as the focus

With practice, and used selectively, encouraging arguments can be very useful, particularly where there is a loss of sexual desire, a mild to moderately depressed partner, where there are unstated resentments, where one partner is submissive or where couples are excessively polite to each other. In this section, the examples focus on a female and male issue of loss of sexual desire or arousal. Encouraging arguments seems particularly suited to these couples. It can also be considered when one partner is in a dependent, submissive or depressed position within the couple.

Where one partner has lost interest in their sexual relationship, which was previously fine, a general aim would be to ask partner A, who is uninterested in sex, to think of one small and trivial thing that partner B does and which A would like to ask the partner to change. Where the female is reluctant to have sexual intercourse and is being pressurised, it may be helpful to begin by offering them a timetable for sex, perhaps once a week. For the rest of the week there should be no pressure and no sex (Crowe and Ridley, 1986).

Betty and Bob had had a good sex life, but within the last 8–9 months Betty had become increasingly upset by Bob's advances and was beginning to fear that she was 'frigid'. Bob, a tall, good-looking 34-year-old was baffled by her responses and continued to pressurise her and tease her. Betty, a somewhat shy but pretty 31-year-old felt it was all her fault as Bob was so good to her in every way.

The therapist asked Betty if there was anything about Bob that irritated her or she would like him to change:

Betty:	N . . . n . . . no, of course not, he's great.
Therapist:	I'm sure he is great, but nobody is perfect, try to think about one small thing he does that you would like him to change.
Betty:	No, really, it's fine the way it is. It's just me, I think I am a bit frigid.
Therapist:	You are being very hard on yourself, tell Bob now if there is one small thing he does that you would like him to change. Maybe he leaves his socks on the floor, or doesn't tidy the sink or . . .

Betty interrupted stammering a little: 'You mean like I wish he would have a shower before we go to bed':

Therapist:	Yes, that seems a good one to start with. Now ask Bob if he can do that.
Betty:	(*hesitantly in a soft voice*) Bob, would it be all right if you had a shower before you came to bed?
Bob:	(*smiling*) No way, you know I always have my shower in the morning.
Betty:	(*giving in*) OK, I just . . .
Therapist:	Betty, have you persuaded him?
Betty:	(*grimacing*) It doesn't matter.
Therapist:	(*persisting*) Go on, have a go and try again. Maybe you could use a louder voice.
Betty:	(*sitting up and speaking a little louder*) Bob, please, just for me, could you sometimes have a shower at night.
Bob:	Why, what's your problem?
Betty:	Well, if you really want to know, if you don't mind me saying, I just prefer you sweet smelling at night, is that all right?
Bob:	(*again smiling*) Why, do I smell? You don't mind a bit human sweat do you?
Betty:	(*holding her ground*) No, but it is nice to go to bed together after a shower.

At this point Bob gave in and Betty became more assertive.

Notice that the therapist was allying strongly with Betty to challenge a hypothesised rule that 'it is not possible to ask for what you want'. In further sessions, Betty was able to ask Bob to help more around the house and to be more available to spend time with the children. Side by side with these interventions they were using non-genital sensate focus exercises, in a sexual timetable once a week, and gradually their sex life improved. The theoretical basis for this is that there is an interconnection between what is happening within the relationship and the sexual aspect of the couple's world. The hypothesis was that when Betty could ask for and receive what she wanted in their social life, she would no longer need to say, 'No' sexually. This hypothesis often bears fruit within therapy.

A similar approach can be used where the man has erectile difficulties, with no physical causes, and sex had been fine. If the dynamics of the couple revolve around the woman being a great manager, mother, financial organiser and in many ways is 'perfect', or at least the male partner sees her that way, it is worth trying to encourage an argument. In this situation the man is asked to choose a trivial issue, which he persuades his female partner to change. Encouraging arguments over trivial issues can be used for many couple interactions stuck as described above.

When to use timetables and tasks

The clinician begins to think about moving up the hierarchy to use structural timetables and tasks as it becomes clear that a behavioural approach has no impact; the interaction of the couple is assessed as being more rigid and may be accompanied by symptoms presented as belonging to one partner. Symptoms as defined here are not necessarily medical or psychiatric but can be seen as chronic or repetitive interactions that affect the couple negatively. Perhaps the partners are a couple whose daily routine is full of work, children, caring for dependents, surfing the web, telephoning, being with friends or family and watching television, with no time to nurture the relationship. A task or timetable could be to ask the couple to find time to talk, or to 'do nothing together'. Other symptoms may be intractable arguments, loss of sexual desire, particularly in the female, couples where an affair is invariably the focus of conversations, mild to moderate depression or anxiety or non-psychotic cases of jealousy. Indeed, where there are rigid repetitive cycles, the setting of timetables or tasks may be useful.

Use timetable or tasks for couples whose symptom can be described as:

- always too busy
- intractable arguments
- loss of sexual desire
- an affair is the focus of conversations
- mild to moderate depression or anxiety
- non-psychotic jealousy
- repetitive rigid interaction.

Tasks and timetables, when used at this level, offer a simple way of 're-structuring' the daily interaction of a couple and bring a small degree of flexibility into an otherwise rigid system. Another reason for using tasks and timetables for these rigid and repetitive cycles is to bring apparently out-of-control behaviour under the control of the couple. Where a couple's communication focuses overwhelmingly on the partner's jealousy, the impact of the affair, the regular late night use of the computer, etc., this can be brought within the control of the couple by timetabling discussion of this behaviour. Outside the timetable, the couple are required not to raise these topics. This changes the structure of how the couple interact, thus allowing the possibility for further change.

Using tasks and timetables

Within the behavioural-systems approach, many tasks are carefully designed to be reciprocal and to improve the couple's communication so there is a constant cross-fertilisation between the behavioural and systems approach. Setting a task gives a framework and encourages the couple to work together to facilitate small changes. As many couples come into therapy when their relationship is fragile, achieving even a small task adds a degree of hope. Timetables are often an essential ingredient where couples have sexual difficulties.

Although a simple intervention, timetables can be thought of as containment for out-of-control behaviour or a play space for couples who have rarely experienced 'playing together'. Where work is anxiety provoking, a clearly identified time, place, structure and ending may provide a secure base for the gradual reinstatement of trust in a more intimate relationship. A timetable may offer legitimacy to pathological behaviour by encouraging its expression at some times and not at others, and may help to remove the labelling of behaviours over time. At a simple, practical level it may offer a better chance that tasks may be performed.

> However, we speculate that the modest timetable may contain within it many of the conditions necessary for the secure development of more pliant relationships in which sensitivity, intimacy, assertiveness, disagreements, intense emotion, playfulness and vulnerability can be experienced by couples as they develop greater security and expressiveness within these structures.
>
> (Crowe and Ridley, 2000)

When a timetable is set, regardless of its purpose, the day, time, length and how the couple will end should all be detailed in the session and not left to chance. This prevents arguments about when the activity should take place and makes it more likely that it will be used.

The timetable can be tailored to each couple's needs and many other options could be added to the following. For the couple that:

- is too busy: set aside time to do nothing together
- is very serious: time for some lightness and fun
- keeps going over the past: time together with no going over old ground or talk about the future not the past
- never argues: time to disagree (short 5–10 minutes)
- never goes out together: to do something together
- always goes out with the children: to go out without the children
- disagrees about what to do: one week do something he likes, the next do something she likes.

For the couple where:

- mother looks after the children but complains: father takes the children out while mother has time for herself
- sex is a problem: time to be together when no one asks for sex.

In the following timetables it is important to ensure that outside the time set aside these behaviours are discouraged and kept for the next timetabled session:

- where she or he is very jealous: times for the partner to take the jealousy seriously
- where she or he has had an affair: time to talk about the affair
- where a step-relationship is problematic: time to discuss these issues seriously
- where there are constant worries over finances: time to discuss these.

As already suggested, timetables should be tailored to each couple. The therapist may need to be creative in search for a suitable timetable or task and to remember the need to help couples use these times to play and experiment.

When to consider the use of the paradox or split-team message

The paradox and its uses are controversial for two main reasons: first, it is difficult to know whether, or why, it may work and so it is consequently impossible to research. Second, it can be used in a negative and punitive way with a couple if the therapist is frustrated by lack of progress. If used, this second aspect is to be avoided at all costs and should be an intervention of last choice (Perotta, 1986). However, used with care and empathy, the paradox can offer a way forward with couples where little else seems to facilitate the change they desire.

Where a clinician feels that a paradoxical intervention may be useful, an option is to use the split team message, an approach developed by the Maudsley Marital Therapy Clinic. A split team message is exactly as described, a message that contains two parts, a paradoxical and a non-paradoxical part. The couple is given a choice and the therapist can use the paradox without being punitive but the 'bite' of the message may of necessity be diminished.

The paradox or split team message can be used for couples where 'all else has failed'. Usually, this means that several sessions have elapsed using interventions from lower down the hierarchy. Couples have done neither tasks nor timetables and there is no change. For inexperienced clinicians it is preferable to use interventions only from lower down the hierarchy.

Alternatively, it may become clear in the initial interview that the severity of the difficulties suggests simple tasks and timetables are unlikely to be used. Usually this would imply a strong individual focus or preoccupation with a psychiatric symptom.

The advantage of the paradox on its own, used by experienced therapists, is that it may impact on couples where one partner is severely depressed or jealous, and for couples where one partner may exhibit neurotic symptoms, such as phobias, panic attacks or obsessional behaviour. Where the decision has been made to use the paradox it may be helpful to repeat the paradox in following sessions while reminding the couple not to give up on their past behaviour too quickly.

Using the paradox

A paradox is an intervention of last resort and requires training and good supervision before use. It is briefly included here but is only recommended with the above requirements. The elements of the paradox are: (1) a positive connotation of apparently negative reciprocal interactions; (2) reasons why these behaviours may be useful to the couple; (3) possible inclusion of the feared consequences of change; and (4) prescribing the symptom, which means telling the couple to carry on as they are, i.e. not to change. A paradox where one partner is depressed and the other a carer may go something like this as the therapist addresses the couple:

> Catherine, by being depressed, is helping Colin to be a strong and effective carer, and protects him from expressing feeling. Colin is showing Catherine how much he cares for her and protects her from taking more responsibility for herself and the family. You may both fear the consequences of Catherine becoming stronger as Colin would have to give up his role as carer and may then become depressed. For the moment,

you may prefer to stay the way you are, rather than take the risk of facing these changes.

Such a message would only be given if the therapist knows the couple well, has a strongly empathic relationship with them, and feels this is an accurate statement. A good paradox may not be paradoxical (Dell, 1986; Crowe and Ridley, 2000).

When to adjust to the symptom

Relationships that contain an individual with a recurrent psychotic illness flourish best when the relationship is low in critical comment and emotional arousal and is best approached using simple problem solving (Leff and Vaughan, 1985). This means helping the couple adjust to the symptom. With illnesses such as multiple sclerosis and Parkinson's disease, the courses of which are rarely predictable, the adjustment needs will change over time but the relationship aspect can be treated in the usual way.

When to cease treatment or use other therapies

The behavioural-systems approach does not claim to solve all relationship difficulties and many situations are best treated by other approaches. Where there is gambling, drug addiction or alcohol dependency, the couple can be referred to specialist agencies. Unless an agency is well equipped to ensure the safety of both the couple and therapist, working with domestic violence is not advocated. Where safety of the couple and therapist are ensured, this approach has many benefits. Reciprocal negotiation, arguments that are contained and effectively used tasks and timetables are often lacking with couples where domestic violence occurs. The behavioural-systems approach can encourage their use and thus contain an otherwise out of control relationship. Victims of sexual abuse or rape may require individual treatment in addition to couple work. Equally, with couples where the woman has vaginismus or pain on penetration, or the man has premature ejaculation, individual work may be used in addition to couple therapy.

In general, other approaches whether psychiatric, medical or individually oriented therapy is encouraged. However, where one partner is in long-term psychotherapy, the couple work may be impeded when material is taken to the individual psychotherapist rather than being available within couple therapy. This aside, the behavioural-systems approach is well able to work together with other approaches and treatments.

SYSTEMS THINKING

As one moves up the hierarchy and into systemic interventions, a shift is made in thinking. Instead of using the stated goals of the couple, the therapist now is more concerned with the repetitive and circular patterns of interaction. Minuchin (1974) describes this as a 'paradigm shift'. It requires a reformulation of conceptual thinking and way of working with the couple as well as the ability to simplify and observe the process and pattern of what is occurring rather than the small details of interactions (Sluzki, 1978). Individually oriented therapists often find this shift very difficult and some practice within training and supervision is necessary before making use of this way of working.

There are several key concepts underlying systems thinking, as follows. Circularity is a view that interactions are circular rather than linear, thus setting down the concept of linear causal thinking. There are interconnected concepts: (1) that there are rules that appear to govern repetitive sequences; and (2) that these are consistent over time (homeostasis). A further central concept is that the observed interaction (which often includes a symptom) is serving a function for the system, which can be hypothesised but not tested.

Further concepts include the idea that within the system there are likely to be alliances, boundaries and hierarchies, some of which are overt, some covert. A central alliance to be observed is that of the parental pair and how it operates. Finally, useful, but still little researched, is the concept of closeness and distance regulation as a way of thinking about much relationship behaviour.

Concurrent with this theoretical shift, the therapist has to make a shift in how she or he intervenes: instead of always keeping a balance between the two partners the therapist may ally more heavily with one partner to change the current system. The therapist now intervenes to challenge the assumptions being made, the patterns emerging within the session and the rules that appear to govern the system. When encouraging arguments, the therapist is challenging the rule that 'good couples never argue'. The aim of therapy within the session is to give the couple a new and good experience of a different way of relating. The aim of any message at the end of therapy is to continue this change by offering tasks that can be practised at home.

As with many theoretical approaches, systems thinking is imperfect. Whilst considering the function of a 'symptom' it also accepts the reality of physical illnesses. The developmental cycle that includes rapid change does not sit easily with systems thinking, nor does the individual's personal history or internal world seem congruent with systems thinking. Despite these reservations, systems thinking, used selectively, can offer a different perspective with more complex couples and may facilitate changes which otherwise would not have occurred (Crowe and Ridley, 2000).

CONCLUSION

The behavioural-systems approach has been described as simply as possible to demonstrate that it offers alternative interventions for a wide variety of couple interactions. It can be used to help a couple modify a very stuck or rigid relationship and some couples who may previously have been seen as impossible to help can now be included. It provides a flexibility that may not be available in other approaches. In general, couples can begin with small and trivial issues but, over time, can be helped to gain confidence in therapy to discuss difficult issues that they are afraid to broach at home. Homework and timetables encourage couples to continue at home the work that was begun in the session. The focus is the couple relationship and the aim is to offer the possibility of positive changes.

REFERENCES

Birchler, G. R., Weiss, R. L. and Vincent, J. P. (1975) A multi-method analysis of social reinforcement exchange between mentally distressed and nondistressed spouse and stranger dyads. *Journal of Personality and Social Psychology*, 31, 349–360.

Crowe, M. J. (1982) The treatment of marital and sexual problems, a behavioural Approach. In: A. Bentovim, G. G. Barnes and A. Cooklin (eds) *Family Therapy, 1*. London: Academic Press.

Crowe, M. J. and Ridley, J. (1986) The negotiated timetable, a new approach to marital conflicts involving male demands and female reluctance for sex. *Sexual and Marital Therapy*, 1, 157–173.

Crowe, M. J. and Ridley, J (2000) *Therapy with Couples: A Behavioural-Systems Approach to Relationship and Sexual Problems*. Oxford: Blackwell Science.

Dell, P. F. (1986) Why do we still call them paradoxes? *Family Process*, 20, 37–51.

Gottman, J., Markman, H. and Notarius, C. (1977) The topography of marital conflict: A sequential analysis of verbal and nonverbal behaviour. *Journal of Marriage and the Family*, 39, 461–477.

Kraemer, S. (1986) Why worry, why now, what for? *Tavistock Clinic Paper* 45. London: Tavistock Clinic.

Le H, J. and Vaughen, C. (1985) *Expressed Emotions in Families*. New York: Guilford Press.

Mackay, D. (1985) Marital therapy: The behavioural approach. In: W. Dryden (ed) *Marital Therapy in Britain*. London: Harper and Row.

Minuchin, S. (1974) *Families and Family Therapy*. London: Tavistock Publications.

Olson, D. H., McCubbin, H. I., Barnes, H., Larsen, A., Muxen, M. and Wilson, M. (1983) *Families, What Makes Them Work*. Los Angeles: Sage Publications.

Perrotta, P. (1986) Leaving home: Later stages of treatment. *Family Process*, 25, 461–474.

Ridley, J. (1999) *Intimacy in Crisis*. London: Whurr Publishing.

Sluzki, C. E. (1978) Marital Therapy from a Systems Perspective. In T. J. Paolins and B. S. McGrady (eds) *Marriage and Marital Therapy*. New York: Brunner Mazel.

Stuart, R. B. (1980) *Helping Couples Change*. New York: Guilford Press.

Chapter 19

Psychosis

Investigation

Emmanuelle Peters, Yvonne Linney,
Louise Johns and Elizabeth Kuipers

THE HISTORICAL ORIGINS OF SCHIZOPHRENIA AND THE PSYCHOSES

Psychosis refers to some loss of contact with reality. Psychotic disorders can be divided into affective psychoses (bipolar disorder, psychotic depression) and non-affective psychoses (schizophreniform disorder, schizophrenia, schizo-affective disorder, delusional disorder). In this chapter and the next, the term 'psychosis' refers to non-affective psychotic disorders, of which schizophrenia is the most common.

Emil Kraeplin (1896, 1913) first coined the term 'dementia praecox' to refer to a group of illnesses (catatonia, hebephrenia and the dementia paranoides) that were all associated with a poor outcome. The characteristics of dementia praecox included hallucinations, delusions, decreased interest in the outside world, thought disorder, lack of insight and judgement, emotional blunting and stereotyped behaviour. His classification of the illness was consistent with his belief that mental illnesses fall into a small number of discoverable types and that these can be identified by studying symptoms and (biological) aetiologies.

Eugene Bleuler (1911) proposed the term 'schizophrenia' to describe these illnesses, because he noticed that they did not occur only in young people (praecox) and were not always associated with a severe form of mental deterioration (dementia). Bleuler also believed the causes of this illness to be biological but he believed that four subtle (psychological) symptoms were fundamental to it and could be found in everyone with the disorder. These symptoms were: a loosening of the associations that link together stream of thought, ambivalence (the holding of conflicting feelings or emotions towards others), autism (withdrawal from the social world) and inappropriate affect (the display of emotions that are incongruent with the person's circumstances). Bleuler believed that symptoms such as hallucinations and delusions, which Kraeplin had described as fundamental to dementia praecox, were more appropriately viewed as psychological reactions to the disorder, which not everybody with the illness would exhibit. Unlike Kraeplin, Bleuler also believed that schizophrenia and manic depression were not distinct illnesses but instead ran on a continuum.

In attempting to address the difficulty in distinguishing schizophrenia from more general problems of personality, Kurt Schneider (1959) identified what he believed to be the first-rank symptoms of schizophrenia. These symptoms, which were chosen because of ease of recognition, were not proposed to be crucial to schizophrenia but instead were thought to be, more often than not, indicative of the illness. Schneider identified eleven such symptoms and, in contrast to Bleuler, all of these symptoms were forms of hallucinations, delusions or passivity experience. In addition, Schneider emphasised that it was the form of the experience, rather than the content of the experience, that was of utmost importance.

The main diagnostic classification systems that are currently in use are the *Diagnostic and Statistical Manual of Mental Disorders*, 4th edition (DSM-IV) (American Psychiatric Association (APA), 1994) and the *International Statistical Classification of Diseases and Related Health Problems*, 10th edition (ICD-10 World Health Organization (WHO), 1992). In DSM-IV, the diagnostic criteria for schizophrenia include a number of symptoms, two of which must be present for a period of at least a month. The symptoms are predominantly positive (i.e. abnormal by their presence: delusions, hallucinations, disorganised speech or behaviour), with negative symptoms (i.e. abnormal by their absence: avolition, alogia, blunted affect, anhedonia) listed collectively as a single item; however, only one symptom is considered necessary if hallucinations involve a running commentary on the person or two or more voices talking with each other, or if delusions are bizarre. The diagnostic criteria in ICD-10 are similar except that passivity phenomena (e.g. delusions of control) and experiences of thought interference (e.g. thought broadcast) are listed among those symptoms of which only one need be present for a diagnosis. Furthermore, both classification systems specify that there must be deterioration in functioning, and DSM-IV specifies that there must be continuous signs of deterioration for at least 6 months (whereby positive and/or negative symptoms are present). In addition, in DSM-IV, there are exclusions of manic or depressive illnesses, as well as disturbances due to organic disorder or substance abuse. Both ICD-10 and DSM-IV also specify a number of clinical subtypes, namely paranoid, catatonic and undifferentiated schizophrenia (both ICD-10 and DSM-IV), disorganised and residual schizophrenia (DSM-IV only) and hebephrenia (ICD-10 only).

THE SYMPTOM-ORIENTED APPROACH

The drawbacks of employing discrete diagnostic categories have been discussed in detail by Bentall, Boyle, van Os and others, who point to significant problems with the reliability and validity of such classification systems (Bentall, 1990a; 2003; van Os et al., 1999; Boyle, 2002).

Given what he considers to be a lack of persuasive evidence for the reliability and validity of schizophrenia, Bentall (2003) argues for abandoning psychiatric diagnoses altogether and advocates the alternative approach of attempting to understand and explain the actual behaviours and experiences of psychotic people. More specifically, he believes that mental health professionals and researchers should focus on the *symptoms* of psychosis, such as delusions, hallucinations, and thought disorder (which he refers to as 'complaints'), rather than diagnoses. Van Os and his colleagues have also demonstrated empirically that dimensions of psychosis are indeed more useful clinically than categorical representations (van Os et al., 1999).

Another topical issue is whether there is a qualitative difference between those who are considered mentally ill and those that are considered 'healthy', or whether psychosis can be conceptualised as being on a continuum of normal individual variation (Claridge, 1985, 1997). In recent years, a number of surveys investigating the prevalence of psychotic symptoms in non-clinical populations have accumulated. Indeed, one widely cited study reported that almost one-fifth (17.5%) of a general population sample of over 7000 participants had experienced positive psychotic symptoms, such as hallucinations or delusions (van Os et al., 2000). In support of these findings, a number of other studies have demonstrated the relatively widespread occurrence of positive psychotic symptoms in non-clinical populations (see Johns and van Os, 2001, for a review), thus providing substantial support for the notion that psychotic experiences run on a continuum with normality.

Nevertheless, the views that diagnoses should be abandoned in favour of symptoms, and that psychosis is part of normal individual variation, are far from accepted by all mental health professionals and, to date, remain controversial issues. Indeed, one argument against the view that diagnoses should be abandoned in favour of symptoms is that the various symptoms may be phenomenologically different between different diagnoses, so, for example, delusions in mania may differ from delusions in schizophrenia. Nevertheless, despite these concerns, there has been a substantial movement towards a symptom-oriented approach, particularly among psychologists. Indeed, the last decade has seen a plethora of studies investigating psychological aspects of specific psychotic symptoms, and this has particularly been the case for positive symptoms. Furthermore, in accordance with a continuity model of psychosis, much of this work has involved using normal psychological processes to understand symptoms such as delusions and hallucinations, which had previously been seen to be bizarre and senseless, and not easily understood from a psychological viewpoint.

SYMPTOMS OF PSYCHOSIS

The term 'psychosis' is used clinically as a generic term to refer to the positive symptoms of psychotic disorders, namely unusual beliefs (delusions) and anomalous experiences (hallucinations and other perceptual abnormalities), as well as disturbances of thought and language.

Delusions

Delusions are of particular interest because they are, in some respects, the *sine qua non* of psychosis, and were described by Jaspers (1913) as 'the basic characteristic of madness'. They have traditionally been classified in terms of the themes represented in their content. The most common are persecutory delusions, which have also generated the largest amount of research (Bentall et al., 2001; Freeman and Garety, 2004). However, themes in delusional thinking often overlap in a way that makes classification imperfect (Freeman and Garety, 2000). Nevertheless, DSM-IV (APA, 1994) describes the following types of delusion:

- *Bizarre delusion*: a delusion that involves a phenomenon that the person's culture would regard as totally implausible.
- *Delusional jealousy*: the delusion that one's sexual partner is unfaithful.
- *Erotomanic delusion*: a delusion that another person, usually of higher status, is in love with the individual.
- *Grandiose delusion*: a delusion of inflated worth, power, knowledge, identity or special relationship to a deity or famous person.
- *Delusion of being controlled:* a delusion in which feelings, impulses, thoughts or actions are experienced as being under the control of some external force rather than being under one's own control. The categorisation of these phenomena (as well as thought broadcasting and thought insertion; see below) as delusions is controversial, as they are equally well classified as passivity experiences.
- *Delusion of reference*: a delusion whose theme is that events, objects or other persons in one's immediate environment have a particular and unusual significance. They are usually of a negative or pejorative nature (with a substantial overlap with persecutory delusions), but may also be grandiose in content.
- *Persecutory delusion*: a delusion in which the central theme is that one (or someone to whom one is close) is being attacked, harassed, cheated, persecuted or conspired against.

- *Somatic delusion*: a delusion whose main content pertains to the appearance or functioning of one's body.
- *Thought broadcasting*: the delusion that one's thoughts are being broadcast out loud so that they can be perceived by others.
- *Thought insertion*: the delusion that certain of one's thoughts are not one's own, but rather inserted into one's mind.

Despite the fact that delusions are easily identifiable in the clinic (Wing et al., 1974), they are notoriously difficult to define (David, 1999). Psychiatric definitions ascribe three basic characteristics to delusions, namely: (1) being held with extraordinary conviction (certainty); (2) being impervious to other experiences and to compelling counter-argument (incorrigibility); (3) their content being impossible (falsity).

However, there are problems with each of these themes. Many delusions are not held with absolute conviction (Garety et al., 2005) and conviction in the same belief can wax and wane over time (Sharp et al., 1996). In any case, absolute conviction is not pathological in itself, as all beliefs that are personally significant tend to be held with absolute conviction, such as religious or scientific beliefs (Maher, 1988). Delusions are not necessarily impervious to experience and there is variation in how much deluded individuals accommodate new evidence into their existing delusions (Brett-Jones et al., 1987). There is also now ample evidence that delusions are open to modification through cognitive-behavioural techniques (see Chapter 20). Holding 'false beliefs' is a common occurrence (Cox and Cowling, 1989) and delusional themes commonly reflect beliefs held in the normal population (Peters et al., 1999b; Freeman et al., 2005). The links found in large community samples between discrimination and the development of paranoia (Janssen et al., 2003; Johns et al., 2004) also suggest that delusions can reflect personal histories.

Newer psychological definitions have tended to concentrate on more descriptive, operational criteria. Garety and Hemsley (1994) describe delusions as: (1) continuous rather than dichotomous; (2) multi-dimensional rather than uni-dimensional; (3) potentially responsive rather than fixed; (4) psychologically understandable; and (5) involving rational processes. Perhaps the most important recognition in these psychological definitions is the emphasis on delusions being neither dichotomous nor uni-dimensional, with the main dimensions consisting of conviction, preoccupation, distress and impact on functioning (Kendler et al., 1983; Garety and Hemsley, 1987; Harrow et al., 1988). Increasingly, emotional processes are recognised to form a key part of delusional maintenance and distress (Freeman et al., 2002; Freeman and Garety, 2003).

Hallucinations

Hallucinations are defined as perceptions that occur in the absence of a corresponding external stimulus. They may involve any of the perceptual senses: auditory, visual, tactile, olfactory or gustatory. They span a number of psychiatric and non-psychiatric diagnoses, and have been found to occur in association with a range of organic and emotional states (Asaad and Shapiro, 1986; Slade and Bentall, 1988). Hallucinations vary in their degree of structure and meaningfulness, and are relatively common in the general population (between 4% and 15%; Tien, 1991; Johns et al., 2002), with a wide cultural variation in attitudes towards them, arguing against an all-or-none approach to hallucinations.

Slade and Bentall (1988) proposed a working definition of hallucinations, namely:

> Any percept-like experience which (a) occurs in the absence of an appropriate stimulus, (b) has the full force or impact of the corresponding actual (real) perception, and (c) is not amenable to direct and voluntary control by the experiencer.

Auditory hallucinations (either verbal (voices) or non-verbal (noises, music)) are one of the most common symptoms of psychosis and were recorded in 74% of patients with schizophrenia in the International Pilot Study of Schizophrenia (Wing et al., 1974). The presumption that visual hallucinations are rare in psychosis, and usually indicate the presence of organic pathology, is not borne out by research, with the better-designed studies showing that over 50% of individuals with chronic psychosis experience visions (Bracha et al., 1989). However, to date, most of the research has concentrated on auditory hallucinations, with some notable exceptions (e.g. Gauntlett-Gilbert and Kuipers, 2003)

In a study examining in detail the phenomenology of auditory hallucinations in a large sample of psychotic patients, Nayani and David (1996) report that the most frequent form of voices were those that spoke directly to the person or gave instructions to the person (second-person hallucinations) and those that commented about the person (third-person hallucinations). The descriptions of hallucination content, in decreasing order of frequency, consisted of: commands, critical, abusive, frightening, neutral, arguing, pleasant, questioning, laughing/sarcastic and sad. The most common hallucinated utterances reported were simple terms of abuse.

A number of factors influence the occurrence of hallucinations, including stress, individual predisposing factors such as personality and suggestibility, environmental stimulation, and expectancy. In addition, various theories have been proposed to explain the mechanisms underlying hallucinations. The available evidence seems to indicate that some kind of reality discrimination or self-monitoring deficit underlies the generation of hallucinations, which results in patients misattributing their own internal events to an external source (Bentall, 1990b; Morrison et al., 1995; Cahill et al., 1996).

Recent psychological models of hallucinations have emphasised the importance of the appraisals held about voices (for instance, concerning their identity, cause, power or control over the person) in determining subsequent distress and their emotional and behavioural impact (Chadwick and Birchwood, 1994). The relationship the person holds with regards to their voices is also seen as a key factor in understanding voice maintenance, distress and compliance (Birchwood et al., 2000).

Passivity experiences

Passivity experiences can be centred on a person's thoughts, intentions, will, actions and emotions, and generally involve a disturbance in the experienced integrity of the self. As such, they are sometimes referred to as disturbances of ego boundary (Mullen, 1997). Different types of passivity experience include:

- *Thought insertion*: the essence of this symptom is the loss of the sense of possession of the thought. The idea of insertion is a secondary delusional elaboration, made likely by the oddity of the central experience.
- *Thought broadcast*: individuals experience their thoughts as being unbounded by their sense of their inner world. Individuals may then worry that their thoughts are available to other people, which is a delusional elaboration.
- *Thought block*: this symptom implies passivity, and is unlike the more common experience in states of anxiety or tiredness where the train of thought is lost. In thought block, the train of thought stops suddenly and then it resumes. There is no desperate searching for the lost thought content, and both the cessation and the resumption are passively experienced.
- *Thought withdrawal*: in some cases this can be regarded as present if an individual interprets thought block as due to the removal of thoughts by some other agent and, as such, it is a delusional explanation. However, in other people the withdrawal is described as actually felt or experienced.
- *Thought echo*: this experience has some cardinal features of an ordinary echo, where the original thought is owned but the individual lacks the sense of possession over the repetition of the thought. However, they share the same modality, i.e. thought, just as in an ordinary echo where the original and the repeat are both sounds.
- *Thought commentary*: with this experience the individual possesses one set of thoughts but lacks a sense of possession over a second stream

of thoughts that are essentially commentary on the first. This second element is experienced as thought, and not as a voice.

- *Gedankenlautwerden (loud thoughts)*: individuals experience their thoughts as having the quality of loudness. They have a sense of possession of the thoughts, and the thoughts are experienced as being within internal subjective reality.
- *Control of actions*: Simple actions or complex behaviour are experienced as being caused by an external force.
- *Control of feelings*: feelings are experienced as being imposed by an external agency.

Whether passivity phenomena can best be understood as beliefs or experiences is a debated issue (Frith, 1992; Mullen, 1997). Frith (1992) points out that these symptoms are not false beliefs as such but are, instead, reflections of abnormal experiences, whereby the person is no longer aware of the sense of effort or the prior intention that normally accompanies a deliberate act. Mullen (1997) describes how these phenomena are sometimes classified as beliefs (Spitzer and Endicott, 1978) but agrees that, for most individuals, they are direct experiences rather than beliefs, although they may give rise to delusional explanations. However, as mentioned above, such phenomena are often classified as delusions, and are incorporated in a number of delusional scales, as described below.

ASSESSMENT MEASURES IN PSYCHOSIS

See Kuipers et al. (2006) for more details.

Psychiatric measures

The main psychiatric assessments of psychosis tend to measure the severity and/or frequency of the main clinical features. They are invariably interview based rather than self-report, as lack of insight is traditionally seen to be central to the disorder (David, 1990). Most include both items rated from the information elicited from the respondent, and others rated on the basis of observation during the interview. Their administration can range from 20 minutes to several hours, depending on how symptomatic the individual is. The most widely used measures include the Present State Examination (PSE; Wing et al., 1974), now incorporated in the Schedules for Clinical Assessment in Neuropsychiatry (SCAN; WHO, 1992); the Brief Psychiatric Rating Scale (BPRS; Overall and Gorham, 1962); the Scales for the Assessment of Positive Symptoms (SAPS; Andreasen, 1984a) and for the Assessment of Negative Symptoms (SANS; Andreasen, 1984b); the Positive and Negative Symptom Scale (PANSS; Kay et al., 1987, 1988, 1989); the Krawiecka Scale (also known as the Manchester Scale and the KGV; Krawiecka et al., 1977; Hyde, 1989) and the Comprehensive Psychiatric Rating Scale (CPRS; Asberg et al., 1978; Jacobsson et al., 1978).

Each of these scales has advantages and disadvantages, and the appropriateness of their use will depend on the purpose of the assessment (see Barnes and Nelson, 1994). For instance, the PSE will enable a reliable classification of syndromes but is not useful to look at change over time. The BPRS is better for the detection of change but its reliability and validity are poorer. The PANSS is used extensively in research but the interview is not user-friendly for clinical purposes. The SAPS and SANS are the most thorough in terms of positive and negative symptoms but do not include other areas of clinically relevant psychopathology, such as disorganisation or emotional problems.

Symptom measures

The recent symptom approach has led to the emergence of a number of self-report scales and interviews concentrating on single symptom dimensions. The most widely used currently is the Psychotic Symptom Rating Scales (PSYRATS; Haddock et al., 1999), which is a semi-structured interview measuring psychological dimensions, rather than categorical types, of delusions and hallucinations. The Personal Questionnaires (PQs; Brett-Jones et al., 1987) also assess psychological dimensions such as conviction, preoccupation and distress for delusions, and frequency, intensity and distress for hallucinations. PQs differ from other questionnaire forms in that they are devised for each individual, using that person's words to describe his or her beliefs, experiences or feelings.

Other measures to assess delusions include the Maudsley Assessment of Delusions Schedule (MADS; Buchanan et al., 1993), the Delusions-Symptoms-States Inventory – Revised (DSSI-R; Foulds and Bedford, 1975), the Brown Assessment of Beliefs Scale (BABS; Eisen et al., 1998) and the Peters et al. Delusions Inventory (PDI; Peters et al., 1999b, 2004). Other measures to assess hallucinations include the Auditory Hallucinations Record Form (Slade, 1972) and Self-Report Form (Hustig and Hafner, 1990), the Mental Health Research Institute Unusual Perceptions Schedule (MUPS; Carter et al., 1995), the Structured Interview for Assessing Perceptual Anomalies (SIAPA; Bunney et al., 1999) and the Cardiff Anomalous Perceptions Scale (CAPS; Bell et al., 2006). An important dimension of hallucinations consists of the beliefs people hold about their voices (Chadwick and Birchwood, 1994), and the Beliefs about Voices Questionnaire – Revised (BAVQ-R; Chadwick et al., 2000), and the Cognitive Assessment of Voices Interview Schedule (Chadwick et al., 1996) assess this dimension specifically. Two further measures are worth mentioning, namely the La Trobe University 'Coping with Auditory Hallucinations' Interview Schedule (Farhall and

Gehrke, 1997) and the 'Interview with a Person who Hears Voices' (Romme and Escher, 2000).

Thought disorder has not received as much attention as delusions and hallucinations in the research literature, and this is reflected by the smaller number of scales available, namely the Scale for the Assessment of Thought, Language and Communication (Andreasen, 1986) and the Comprehensive Index of Positive Thought Disorder (Marengo et al., 1986). There are no scales available to assess passivity phenomena specifically, although they are often included in delusions scales.

Similarly, apart from the general psychiatric measures mentioned above such as the SANS and the PANSS, there are few specific negative symptoms scales. One notable exception includes the Subjective Experience of Negative Symptoms Scale (SENS; Selten et al., 1993), which is a self-rating scale based on the SANS items, and measures awareness of negative symptoms plus associated disruption and distress. Otherwise, clinical researchers have used assessment tools measuring social functioning and quality of life, both related to negative symptoms. Social functioning scales include the Social Behaviour Scale (Wykes and Sturt, 1986), the Social Functioning Scale (Birchwood et al., 1990), the Global Assessment of Functioning Scale (GAF (DSM-III-R); APA, 1987), and an adapted version of the GAF, the Social and Occupational Functioning Assessment Scale (SOFAS; Goldman et al., 1992). Quality-of-life scales are numerous but tend to be too lengthy for use with psychotic populations. Again, one exception is the Manchester Short Assessment of Quality of Life (MANSA; Priebe et al., 1999).

Assessing 'at-risk' mental states

There is an increasing emphasis on detecting psychosis early, to reduce the length of time individuals are left with an untreated psychosis (the so-called 'duration of untreated psychosis' or DUP) and to accelerate access to care (McGorry, 1998). As a result, a number of assessment tools have been devised to identify prodromal patients, or individuals with an 'at-risk mental state' (ARMS). The most well known include the Comprehensive Assessment of At Risk Mental States (CAARMS; Yung et al., 2004), the Structured Interview for Prodromal Syndromes (SIPS; Miller et al., 1999; 2002), the Bonn Scale for the Assessment of Basic Symptoms (Gross et al., 1987; Klosterkutter et al., 2001), and the Wisconsin Manual for Assessing Psychotic-like Experiences (Kwapil et al., 1999).

In addition, a couple of measures have been developed for use in epidemiological studies looking at the incidence of psychosis in the general population. The Psychosis Screening Questionnaire (PSQ; Bebbington and Nayani, 1995) is a very brief screening interview to ascertain the presence of hypomania, thought insertion, paranoia, strange experiences, and hallucinations. The Community Assessment of Psychic Experiences (CAPE; Stefanis et al.,

2002) is a 40-item self-report instrument based on the PDI (Peters et al., 1999b, 2004), but with added questions on hallucinations, negative symptoms and depression. Each item assesses both frequency of the experience and associated distress.

ASSESSMENTS FOR PSYCHOLOGICAL INTERVENTIONS

Family interventions

The importance of assessing carers' needs is increasingly becoming recognised, and is now a requirement of the National Service Framework (Standard 6). A number of formal assessment measures are available to assess these needs, such as the carer version of the Camberwell Assessment of Needs (CAN; Phelan et al., 1995) and the relatives' version of the Cardinal Needs Schedule (RCNS; Barrowclough et al., 1998). The Knowledge About Schizophrenia Interview (KASI; Barrowclough et al., 1987), the Modified Illness Perception Questionnaire – Schizophrenia Carers Version (IPQ-SCV; Barrowclough et al., 2001), and the Recovery Attitudes Questionnaire (RAQ; Borkin et al., 2000) can also be useful measures to assess relatives' understanding and perceptions of the disorder. Increasingly, a more sophisticated stress–appraisal–coping approach (Lazarus and Folkman, 1984) to understanding caregivers' experience of caring has been taken, and the Experience of Caregiving Inventory (ECI; Szmukler et al., 1996) can be used specifically to assess appraisals of both positive and negative experiences of caring for individuals with psychosis.

In addition to such measures, assessing levels of depression (e.g. with the Beck Depression Inventory; Beck et al., 1961) can be a useful step because depression is linked with poor coping and low self-esteem, and often with high expressed emotion and burden, thus requiring intervention in its own right. However, it should be remembered that during family interventions the therapist has a duty to balance everyone's needs, and formal assessments would therefore not take place in those sessions.

Cognitive-behaviour therapy for psychosis

The two most important areas to identify when working psychologically with psychotic individuals consist of what distressing experiences they bring to the therapy and what sense they make of them, that is, what 'model' or perspective they have about their experiences. From the start of the assessment it is vital to use the person's own terminology for the psychotic experiences, rather than using psychiatric jargon such as 'voices' or 'delusions': for instance, the person may not recognise that he or she is 'hearing voices' if what he or she hears is his or her father talking, or if he or she is hearing spirits accompanied by their visual appearance. Words such as 'schizo-phrenia' or 'mental illness' may be offensive to the person and should not be used unless the person is happy with a medical model explanation.

Throughout the assessment it is crucial to remember that the ultimate goal of the therapist is to try to understand, rather than to try to make the person change his or her mind by challenging the reality of the voices and delusions. Rather than challenging, empathy with the distress caused by the experiences is an important therapeutic tool in early stages of assessment and engagement.

The 'funnel' method of assessment is a useful model to follow. In the first instance, an overview assessment of distressing experiences is carried out, which might include positive symptoms, negative symptoms and emotional disorders. When specific problems have been identified, they can then be assessed in more depth.

For hallucinations, a useful place to start is by identifying the physical characteristics of the voices (although, as noted above, hallucinations in other modalities are also common). Important factors include the frequency of the voices, duration, loudness, number, location and type. The content of the voices should be identified, although some clients may not be ready to disclose this until trust in the therapist has been established, for instance if the content of the voices is shaming or dangerous. The PSYRATS (Haddock et al., 1999) or Romme and Escher (2000)'s 'Interview with a Person who Hears Voices' can be useful guides for this part of the assessment. An ABC assessment will also be helpful, that is, identifying antecedents or triggers, and consequences. Triggers can be both environmental (where, when, etc.) and internal or emotional (e.g. anxiety). Consequences to look out for should be both behavioural and emotional, as well as the general impact on function-ing. The extent to which people resist or comply with their voices, especially in the case of command hallucinations, is an important factor to identity. Voices diaries can be useful to identify the ABCs outside of the sessions.

It is also crucial to assess the beliefs people hold about their voices (Chadwick and Birchwood, 1994), as much of the psychological work will attempt to modify those beliefs to reduce emotional distress and enhance feelings of control, rather than reducing the frequency of hallucinations *per se*. Crucial dimensions include the identity ('Who are they?', 'Are they bene-ficial or harmful?'), the perceived cause ('What causes them?'), their power ('How powerful are they?') and control ('How much control does the person have over the voices?', 'How much control do the voices have over the per-son?'). The type of relationship the person has with his or her voices is also a key feature (Birchwood et al., 2000, 2004). Again, useful guides for the cognitive and interpersonal aspects of voices include Romme and Escher's (2000) 'Interview with a Person who Hears Voices' and the PSYRATS, as well as Chadwick et al.'s (1996) 'Cognitive Assessment of Voices' Interview Schedule.

As mentioned above, it is important to view delusions as lying on more than one dimension rather than being all-or-nothing false beliefs (Garety and Hemsley, 1987; Peters et al., 1999a). Once the content and number of delusions have been identified, the crucial dimensions to assess consist of conviction ('How much do they believe it?'), preoccupation ('How much time do they think about it?'), distress ('How upsetting are the beliefs?') and disability ('What impact does it have on their lives?'). The PSYRATS covers these dimensions. Alternatively, patients can be asked to rate conviction, preoccupation and distress on 0–100% or any kind of Likert scale on a session-by-session basis.

Like voices, delusions are often inextricably linked with emotional factors (Freeman and Garety, 2003) and potential maintaining factors, such as safety behaviours, should also be identified. Delusions, especially those of a persecutory or grandiose nature, can also be linked with self-esteem and such associations should be explored before attempting to reframe the beliefs. The links may either be direct (i.e. reflecting low self-esteem; Freeman et al., 1998) or indirect (i.e. protecting against low self-esteem; Bentall et al., 2001). Finally, it can be useful to assess cognitive flexibility about delusions (i.e. the extent to which the client is willing to entertain the idea that there may be an alternative explanation, even if alternative explanations are not actually available to the client), because there is some preliminary evidence that flexibility is associated with good outcome in cognitive behavioural therapy (CBT) (Garety et al., 1997).

In clinical practice, there are no clear-cut distinctions between engagement, assessment and intervention in psychological interventions for psychosis, with engagement and assessment remaining key therapeutic factors throughout therapy (Table 19.1). Interventions in psychosis are discussed in Chapter 20.

Table 19.1 Summary of areas of assessment for cognitive behavioural therapy for psychosis

Delusion-specific:
- Content
- Conviction, preoccupation, distress
- Behavioural impact
- Initial formation (e.g. life events)
- Day-to-day examples
- Triggers and consequences (ABCs)
- Coping strategies
- Clarify thoughts/beliefs/emotions/behaviours (within context of internal/external events, what is psychotic and what is normal)
- Maintenance factors (including other psychotic symptoms, emotional processes, safety behaviours, environment, drug and alcohol abuse)
- Change over time (including adaptation to symptoms)
- Meaning of belief (for self and others)
- View of self without delusions (e.g. being persecuted may be better than being mad)
- Develop hierarchy of distressing beliefs (if necessary)

Voice-specific:
- Triggers: environmental (where, when, etc.) and internal or emotional (e.g. anxiety)
- Consequences: behavioural and emotional, as well as general impact on functioning
- Frequency
- Content
- Number
- Location
- Type
- Resistance versus compliance with the voices
- Coping strategies
- Beliefs about voices:
- Identity (Who are they? Are they beneficial or harmful?)
- Cause/origin (What causes them? Where do they come from?)
- Power (How powerful are they?)
- Control (How much control does the person have over the voices?)

Psychosis-specific:
- Cognitive biases (jump-to-conclusions, theory-of-mind deficits), attributional biases (personal, externalising bias) but also normal biases in belief formation)
- Cognitive deficits (difficulties in concentration, memory, planning, ability to manage complex information)
- Illness model
- Attitude towards medication
- Risk (for instance, of complying with voices, of acting on delusions)

Person-specific:
- Personal beliefs (e.g. religion)
- Relationship with services
- Social support and social relationships
- Short- and long-term goals and plans
- Core beliefs, dysfunctional assumptions and schemas (sometimes)
- Life history (sometimes)
- Daily activities

Secondary disturbances:
- Other emotional problems (low mood, anxiety, worry, intrusive thoughts)
- Cognitive distortions (as found in depression and anxiety)
- Substance use

Look out for:
- Reaction to hypothetical contradiction (some flexibility about delusions potential predictor of good outcome)
- Accommodation (i.e. incorporation of experiences into delusion)
- Cognitive flexibility

REFERENCES

American Psychiatric Association (APA) (1987) *Diagnostic and Statistical Manual of Mental Disorders (DSM-III-R)*, 3rd edn, revised. Washington, DC: APA.
American Psychiatric Association (APA) (1994) *Diagnostic and Statistical Manual of Mental Disorders (DSM-IV)*, 4th edn, revised. Washington, DC: APA.

Andreasen, N. (1984a) *Scale for the Assessment of Positive Symptoms (SAPS)*. Iowa City, IA: Department of Psychiatry.

Andreasen, N. (1984b) *Scale for the Assessment of Negative Symptoms (SANS)*. Iowa City, IA: Department of Psychiatry.

Andreasen, N. (1986) Scale for the assessment of thought, language and communication. *Schizophrenia Bulletin*, 12, 473–482.

Asaad, G. and Shapiro, B. (1986) Hallucinations: Theoretical and clinical overview. *American Journal of Psychiatry*, 143, 1088–1097.

Asberg, M., Montgomery, S., Perris, C., Schalling, D. and Sedvall, G. (1978) The comprehensive psychopathological rating scale. *Acta Psychiatrica Scandinavica*, suppl 271, 5–27.

Barnes, T. R. E. and Nelson, H. (1994) *The Assessment of Psychoses. A Practical Handbook*. London: Chapman & Hall Medical.

Barrowclough, C., Tarrier, N., Watts, S., Vaughn, C., Bamrah, J. S. and Freeman, L. (1987) Assessing the functional value of relatives' knowledge about schizophrenia: A preliminary report. *British Journal of Psychiatry*, 151, 1–8.

Barrowclough, C., Marshall, M., Lockwood, A., Quin, J. and Sellwood, W. (1998) Assessing relatives' needs for psychosocial interventions in schizophrenia: A relative's version of the Cardinal Needs Schedule (RCNS). *Psychological Medicine*, 28(3), 531–542.

Barrowclough, C., Lobban, F., Hatton, C. and Quinn, J. (2001) An investigation of models of illness in carers of schizophrenia patients using the Illness Perception Questionnaire. *British Journal of Clinical Psychology*, 40, 371–386.

Bebbington, P. and Nayani, T. (1995) The Psychosis Screening Questionnaire. *International Journal of Methods in Psychiatric Research*, 5, 11–19.

Beck, A., Ward, C. H., Mendelson, M. et al. (1961) An inventory for measuring depression. *Archives of General Psychiatry*, 4, 561–571.

Bell, V., Ellis, H. and Halligan, P. W. (2006) The Cardiff Anomalous Perception Scale: A new validated measure of anomalous experience. *Schizophrenia Bulletin*, 32, 366–377.

Bentall, R. P. (1990a) The syndromes and symptoms of psychosis: Or why you can't play twenty questions with the concept of schizophrenia and hope to win. In: R. P. Bentall (ed) *Reconstructing Schizophrenia*. London: Routledge.

Bentall R. P. (1990b) The illusion of reality: A review and integration of psychological research on hallucinations. *Psychological Bulletin*, 107, 82–85.

Bentall, R. P. (2003) *Madness Explained*. Penguin: London.

Bentall, R. P., Corcoran, R., Howard, R., Blackwood, N. and Kinderman, P. (2001) Persecutory delusions: A review and theoretical integration. *Clinical Psychology Review*, 21, 1143–1192.

Birchwood, M., Smith, T., Cochrane, R. et al. (1990) The Social Functioning Scale. *British Journal of Psychiatry*, 157, 853–859.

Birchwood, M., Meaden, A., Trower, P., Gilbert, P. and Plaistow, J. (2000) The power and omnipotence of voices: Subordination and entrapment by voices and significant others. *Psychological Medicine*, 30, 337–344.

Birchwood, M., Gilbert, P., Gilbert, P., Gilbert, J., Trower, P., Meaden, A. et al. (2004) Interpersonal and role-related schema influence the relationship with the dominant 'voice' in schizophrenia: a comparison of three models. *Psychological Medicine*, 34, 1571–1580.

Bleuler, E. (1911) *Dementia Praecox or the Group of Schizophrenias*. Translated by J. Zinkin (1950) New York: International Universities Press, Inc.

Borkin, J. R., Steffen, J. J., Ensfield, L. B., Krzton, K., Wishnick, H., Wilder, K. and Yangarber, N. (2000) Recovery Attitudes Questionnaire: Development and evaluation. *Psychiatric Rehabilitation Journal*, 24(2), 95–102.

Boyle, M. (2002) *Schizophrenia: A Scientific Delusion?* 2nd edn. New York: Routledge.

Bracha, H. S., Wolkowitz, O. M., Lohr, J. B., Karson, C. N. and Bigelow, L. B. (1989) High prevalence of visual hallucinations in research participants with chronic schizophrenia. *American Journal of Psychiatry*, 146, 526–528.

Brett-Jones, J., Garety, P. A. and Hemsley, D. (1987) Measuring delusional experiences: a method and its application. *British Journal of Clinical Psychology*, 26, 257–265.

Buchanan, A., Reed, A., Wessely, S., Garety, P., Taylor, P., Grubin, D. and Dunn, G. (1993) Acting on delusions. II: The phenomenological correlates of acting on delusions. *British Journal of Psychiatry*, 163, 77–81.

Bunney, W., Hetrick, W., Bunney, B., Patterson, J., Jin, Y., Potkin, S. and Sandman, C. (1999) Structured Interview for Assessing Perceptual Anomalies (SIAPA). *Schizophrenia Bulletin*, 25, 577–592.

Cahill, C., Silbersweig, D. and Frith, C. (1996) Psychotic experiences induced in deluded patients using distorted auditory feedback. *Cognitive Neuropsychiatry*, 1, 201–211.

Carter, D., Mackinnon, A., Howard, S., Zeegers, T. and Copolov, D. L. (1995) The development and reliability of the Mental Health Research Institute unusual perceptions schedule (MUPS): An instrument to record auditory hallucinatory experience. *Schizophrenia Research*, 16, 157–165.

Chadwick, P. and Birchwood, M. (1994) The omnipotence of voices: A cognitive approach to auditory hallucinations. *British Journal of Psychiatry*, 164, 190–201.

Chadwick, P., Birchwood, M. and Trower, P. (1996) *Cognitive Therapy for Delusions, Voices and Paranoia*. Chichester: John Wiley.

Chadwick, P., Lees, S. and Birchwood, M. (2000) The revised Beliefs About Voices Questionnaire (BAVQ-R). *British Journal of Psychiatry*, 177, 229–232.

Claridge, G. S. (1985) *Origins of Mental Illness*. Oxford: Blackwell.

Claridge, G. S. (1997) *Schizotypy: Implications for Illness and Health*. Oxford: Oxford University Press.

Cox, D. and Cowling, P. (1989) *Are you normal?* London: Tower Press.

David, A. S. (1990) Insight and psychosis. *British Journal of Psychiatry*, 156, 798–808.

David, A. S. (1999) Commentary: On the impossibility of defining delusions. *Philosophy, Psychiatry and Psychology*, 6, 17–20.

Eisen, J., Phillips, K., Baer, L., Beer, D., Atala, K. and Rasmussen, S. (1998) The Brown Assessment of Beliefs Scale: Reliability and validity. *American Journal of Psychiatry*, 155, 102–108.

Farhall, J. and Gehrke, M. (1997) Coping with hallucinations: Exploring stress and coping framework. *British Journal of Clinical Psychology*, 36, 259–261.

Foulds, G. A. and Bedford, A. (1975) Hierarchy of classes of personal illness. *Psychological Medicine*, 5, 181–192.

Freeman, D. and Garety, P. A. (2000) Comments on the content of persecutory delusions: Does the definition need clarification? *British Journal of Clinical Psychology*, 39, 407–414.

Freeman, D. and Garety, P. A. (2003) Connecting neurosis and psychosis: The direct influence of emotion on delusions and hallucinations. *Behaviour Research and Therapy*, 41, 923–947.

Freeman, D. and Garety, P. A. (2004) *Paranoia: The Psychology of Persecutory Delusions. Maudsley Monographs*. Hove, UK: Psychology Press.

Freeman, D., Garety, P., Fowler, D., Kuipers, E., Dunn, G., Bebbington, P. and Hadley, C. (1998) The London–East-Anglia randomised controlled trial of cognitive-behaviour therapy for psychosis. IV: Self-esteem and persecutory delusions. *British Journal of Clinical Psychology*, 37, 415–430.

Freeman, D., Garety, P. A., Kuipers, E., Fowler, D. and Bebbington, P. E. (2002) A cognitive model of persecutory delusions. *British Journal of Clinical Psychology*, 41, 331–347

Freeman, D., Garety, P. A., Bebbington, P. E., Smith, B., Rollinson, R., Fowler, D. et al. (2005) Psychological investigation of the structure of paranoia in a non-clinical population. *British Journal of Psychiatry*, 186, 427–435.

Frith, C. D. (1992) *The Cognitive Neuropsychology of Schizophrenia*. Hove, UK: Lawrence Erlbaum Associates/Taylor & Francis.

Garety, P. A. and Hemsley, D. R. (1987) Characteristics of delusional experience. *European Archives of Psychiatry and Neurological Science*, 236, 294–298.

Garety, P. A. and Hemsley, D. R. (1994) *Delusions: Investigations into the Psychology of Delusional Reasoning. Maudsley Monographs 36*. Oxford: Oxford University Press.

Garety, P. A., Fowler, D., Kuipers, E., Freeman, D., Dunn, G., Bebbington, P. et al. (1997) The London–East-Anglia randomised controlled trial of cognitive-behavioural therapy for psychosis. II: Predictors of outcome. *British Journal of Psychiatry*, 171, 420–426.

Garety, P. A., Freeman, D., Jolley, S., Dunn, G., Bebbington, P. E., Fowler, D. G. et al. (2005) Reasoning, emotions and delusional conviction in psychosis. *Journal of Abnormal Psychology*, 114, 373–384.

Gauntlett-Gilbert, J. and Kuipers, E. (2003) Phenomenology of visual hallucinations in psychiatric conditions. *Journal of Nervous and Mental Disease*, 191, 203–205

Goldman, H. H., Skodol, A. E. and Lave, T. R. (1992) Revising Axis V for DSM-IV: A review of measures of social functioning. *American Journal of Psychiatry*, 149, 1148–1156.

Gross, G., Huber, G., Klosterkotter, J. and Linz, M. (1987) *Bonner Skala für die Beurteilung von Basissymptomen*. Berlin: Springer-Verlag.

Haddock, G., McCarron, J., Tarrier, N. and Faragher, E. B. (1999) Scales to measure dimensions of hallucinations and delusions: The Psychotic Symptom Rating Scales (PSYRATS). *Psychological Medicine*, 29, 879–889.

Harrow, M., Rattenbury, F. and Stoll, F. (1988) Schizophrenic delusions: An analysis of their persistence, of related premorbid ideas and three major dimensions. In: T. F. Oltmanns and B. A. Maher (eds) *Delusional Beliefs*. New York: John Wiley.

Hustig, H. H. and Hafner, R. J. (1990) Persistent auditory hallucinations and their relationship to delusions and mood. *Journal of Neurology and Mental Disorders*, 178, 264–267.

Hyde, C. (1989) The Manchester Scale: A Standardised Psychiatric Assessment for Rating Chronic Psychotic Patients. *British Journal of Psychiatry*, 155, suppl 7, 45–47.

Jacobsson, L., Von Knorring, L., Mattsson, B., Perris, C., Edenius, B., Kettner, B. et al. (1978) The comprehensive psychopathological rating scale – CPRS – in patients with schizophrenic symptoms. *Acta Psychiatrica Scandinavica* (suppl) 271, 39–44.

Janssen, I., Hanssen, M., Bak, M., Bijl, R. V., De Graaf, R., Vollebergh, W. et al. (2003) Discrimination and delusional ideation. *British Journal of Psychiatry*, 182, 71–76

Jaspers, K. (1913) *General Psychopathology*. Translated by J. Hoenig and M. W. Hamilton (1959). Manchester: Manchester University Press.

Johns, L. and van Os, J. (2001) The continuity of psychotic experiences in the general population. *Clinical Psychology Review*, 21, 1125–1141.

Johns, L., Nazroo, S., Bebbington, P. and Kuipers, E. (2002) Occurrence of hallucinatory experiences in a community sample and ethnic variations. *British Journal of Psychiatry*, 180, 174–178.

Johns, L., Cannon, M., Singleton, N., Murray, R. M., Farrell, M., Brugha, T. et al. (2004) Prevalence and correlates of self-reported psychotic symptoms in the British population. *British Journal of Psychiatry*, 185, 298–305.

Kay, S., Fiszbein, A. and Opler, L. (1987) The Positive and Negative Syndrome Scale (PANSS) for schizophrenia. *Schizophrenia Bulletin*, 13, 261–275.

Kay, S., Opler, L. and Lindenmayer, J-P. (1988) Reliability and validity of the Positive and Negative Syndrome Scale for schizophrenics. *Psychiatry Research*, 23, 99–110.

Kay, S., Opler, L. and Lindenmayer, J-P. (1989) The Positive and Negative Syndrome Scale (PANSS): Rationale and standardisation. *British Journal of Psychiatry*, 155, suppl 7, 59–65.

Kendler, K. S., Glazer, W. M. and Morgenstern, H. (1983) Dimensions of delusional experience. *American Journal of Psychiatry*, 140, 466–469.

Klosterkotter, J., Hellmich, M., Steinmeyer, E. M. and Schultze-Lutter, F. (2001) Diagnosing schizophrenia in the initial prodromal phase. *Archives of General Psychiatry*, 58, 158–164.

Kraepelin, E. (1896) *Psychiatrie*. Translated in part in J. C. Cutting and M. Shepherd (eds) (1986) *Schizophrenia: The Origin and Development of its Study in Europe*. Cambridge: Cambridge University Press.

Kraepelin, E. (1913) *Dementia Praecox and Paraphrenia*. Translated by R. M. Barclay (1919). Edinburgh: Livingstone.

Krawiecka, M., Goldberg, D. and Vaughan, M. (1977) A Standardised Psychiatric Assessment Scale for Rating Chronic Psychotic Patients. *Acta Psychiatrica Scandinavica*, 55, 299–308.

Kuipers, E., Peters, E. R. and Bebbington, P. (2006) Schizophrenia. In: A. Carr and M. McNulty (eds) *Handbook of Adult Clinical Psychology: An Evidence-Based Practice Approach*. London: Routledge.

Kwapil, T. R., Chapman, L. J. and Chapman, J. (1999) Validity and usefulness of the Wisconsin Manual for Assessing Psychotic-like Experiences. *Schizophrenia Bulletin*, 25, 363–375.

Lazarus, R. S. and Folkman, S. (1984) *Stress, Appraisal, and Coping*. New York: Springer.

McGorry, P. (1998) Preventive strategies in early psychosis: verging on reality. *British Journal of Psychiatry*, 172 (suppl 33) 1–2.

Maher, B. A. (1988) Delusions as the product of normal cognitions. In: T. F. Oltmanns and B. A. Maher (eds) *Delusional Beliefs*. Chichester: John Wiley.

Marengo, J., Harrow, M., Lanin-Kettering, I. and Wilson, A. (1986) Comprehensive Index of Thought Disorder. *Schizophrenia Bulletin*, 12, 497–509.

Miller, T. J., McGlashan, T. H., Woods, S. W., Stein, K., Driesen, N., Corcoran, C. M. et al. (1999) Symptom assessment in schizophrenic prodromal states. *Psychiatric Quarterly*, 70, 273–287.

Miller, T. J., McGlashan, T. H., Rosen, J. L., Somjee, L., Markovich, P. J., Stein, K. and Woods, S. W. (2002) Prospective diagnosis of the initial prodrome for schizophrenia based on the Structured Interview for Prodromal Syndromes: Preliminary evidence of inter-rater reliability and predictive validity. *American Journal of Psychiatry*, 159, 863–865.

Morrison, A. P., Haddock, G. and Tarrier, N. (1995) Intrusive thoughts and auditory hallucinations: A cognitive approach. *Behavioural and Cognitive Psychotherapy*, 23, 265–280.

Mullen, P. (1997) The mental state and states of mind. In: R. M. Murray, P. Hill and P. McGuffin (eds) *The Essentials of Postgraduate Psychiatry, 3rd edn*. Cambridge: Cambridge University Press.

Nayani, T. and David, A. S. (1996) The auditory hallucination: A phenomenological survey. *Psychological Medicine*, 26, 177–189

Overall, J. and Gorham, D. (1962) The brief psychiatric rating scale. *Psychological Reports*, 10, 799–808.

Peters, E. R., Day, S., McKenna, J. and Orbach, G. (1999a) The incidence of delusional ideation in religious and psychotic populations. *British Journal of Clinical Psychology*, 38, 83–96.

Peters, E. R., Joseph, S. and Garety, P. A. (1999b) The assessment of delusions in normal and psychotic populations: Introducing the PDI (Peters et al. Delusions Inventory). *Schizophrenia Bulletin*, 25, 553–576.

Peters, E. R., Joseph, S., Day, S. and Garety, P. A. (2004) Measuring delusional ideation: The 21-item PDI (Peters et al. Delusions Inventory). *Schizophrenia Bulletin*, 30, 1005–1022

Phelan, M., Slade, M., Thornicroft, G., Dunn, G., Holloway, F. and Wykes, T. et al. (1995) The Camberwell Assessment of Need: The validity and reliability of an instrument to assess the needs of people with severe mental illness. *British Journal of Psychiatry*, 167, 589–595.

Priebe, S., Huxley, P., Knight, S. and Evans, S. (1999) Application and results of the Manchester Short Assessment of Quality of Life (MANSA). *International Journal of Social Psychiatry*, 45, 7–12.

Romme, M. and Escher, S. (2000) *Making Sense of Voices. A Guide for Mental Health Professionals working with Voice-Hearers*. London: Mind Publications.

Schneider, K. (1959) *Clinical Psychopathology*. Translated by M. W. Hamilton. New York: Grune and Stratton.

Selten, J. P., Sijben, N. E., van den Bosch, R. J., Omloo-Visser, J. and Warmerdam, H. (1993) The subjective experience of negative symptoms: A self-rating scale. *Comprehensive Psychiatry*, 34(3), 192–197.

Sharp, H. M., Fear, C. F., Williams, J. M., Healy, D., Lowe, C. F., Yeadon, H. and Holden, R. (1996) Delusional phenomenology – dimensions of change. *Behaviour Research and Therapy*, 34, 123–142.

Slade, P. D. (1972) The effects of systematic desensitization on auditory hallucinations. *Behavioural Research Therapy*, 10, 85–91.

Slade, P. D. and Bentall, R. P. (1988) *Sensory Deception: Towards a Scientific Analysis of Hallucinations*. London: Croom Helm.

Spitzer, R. L. and Endicott, J. (1978) Medical and mental disorder: Proposed definition and criteria. In: *Critical Issues in Psychiatric Diagnosis* (pp. 15–39). New York: Raven Press.

Stefanis, N. C., Hanssen, M., Smirnis, N. K., Avramopoulos, D. A., Evdokimidis, I. K. and Stefanis, C. N. et al. (2002) Evidence that three dimensions of psychosis have a distribution in the general population. *Psychological Medicine*, 32, 347–358.

Szmukler, G. L., Burgess, P. and Herrman, H. (1996) Caring for relatives with serious mental illness: The development of the Experience of Caregiving Inventory. *Social Psychiatry and Psychiatric Epidemiology*, 31, 137–148.

Tien, A. Y. (1991) Distributions of hallucinations in the population. *Social Psychiatry and Psychiatric Epidemiology*, 26, 287–292.

van Os, J., Gilvarry, C., Bale, R., van Horn, E., Tattan, T., White, I. and Murray, R. (1999) A comparison of the utility of dimensional and categorical representations of psychosis. *Psychological Medicine*, 29, 595–606.

van Os, J., Hanssen, M., Bijl, R. and Ravelli, A (2000) Strauss (1969) revisited: Evidence for a psychosis continuum in the general population? *Schizophrenia Research*, 45, 11–20.

Wing, J. K., Cooper, J. E. and Sartorius, N. (1974) *Measurement and Classification of Psychiatric Symptoms*. Cambridge: Cambridge University Press.

World Health Organization (WHO) (1992) *ICD-10: International Statistical Classification of Diseases and Related Health Problems, 10th revised edn*. Geneva: WHO.

World Health Organization (WHO) (1992) *SCAN: Schedules for Clinical Assessment in Neuropsychiatry*. Geneva, WHO.

Wykes, T. and Sturt, E. (1986). The Social Behaviour Scale. *British Journal of Psychiatry*, 16.

Yung, A. R., Phillips, L. J. and McGorry, P. D. (2004) *Treating Schizophrenia in the Prodromal Phase*. London: Taylor and Francis.

Chapter 20

Psychosis

Treatment

*Louise Johns, Emmanuelle Peters
and Elizabeth Kuipers*

INTRODUCTION

The first line of treatment for psychosis is almost always antipsychotic medication, either typical (e.g. chlorpromazine, haloperidol) or atypical (e.g. risperidone, clozapine) neuroleptics. Anomalous dopamine function is central to the emergence of psychotic symptoms (Kapur, 2003) and these medications share a common action in reducing cortical dopamine transmission. However, psychotic symptoms do not always respond to antipsychotic medication (Curson et al., 1988), or patients may not take it because of intolerable side effects, beliefs about their symptoms or forgetfulness. Thus it is important that patients have access to additional, non-pharmacological, interventions. There has been considerable development in psychological interventions for psychosis over the last 15–20 years. These interventions include family therapy; social, cognitive and occupational rehabilitation; cognitive behaviour therapy (CBT) and early intervention (EI). They are not proposed as alternatives to medication but are used as adjunctive therapies. There is some evidence that relapse rates can be reduced by as much as 50% by adding psychosocial treatments (Hogarty and Ulrich, 1998).

Individuals with psychosis often have numerous and complex difficulties. These include understanding and coping with psychotic symptoms; attitudes towards illness and medication; relationships within their environmental and social networks; managing disabilities in the cognitive, occupational and social spheres; emotional disturbances of depression and anxiety; and other co-morbid problems, such as substance abuse. It is now recognised that improving the course of psychosis means going beyond symptom control and involves the psychosocial reintegration of patients in their communities (May, 2004). Recently, special emphasis has been given to implementing 'early intervention' services in an effort to prevent a deteriorating course following a first psychotic episode. In addition, primary carers often experience substantial burden of care that in turn has implications for the patient's own mental health.

FAMILY INTERVENTIONS

Background

Family interventions (FI) were one of the earliest psychological approaches to psychosis. They were driven by research, starting in the 1960s (Brown and Rutter, 1966), on the importance of family factors in predicting outcome for people with schizophrenia living with carers. The impact of caring for a severely mentally ill relative can be quite substantial (Fadden et al., 1987). Families do not cause schizophrenia or psychosis but the burden of care affects the quality of the relationship between carer and patient, which in turn impacts on the course of psychosis once developed.

Intervention

Various therapeutic elements are important in FI, including psychoeducation, problem solving, support, communication and skills training, emotional processing and cognitive reappraisal. The kinds of intervention found to be helpful for families have been discussed in several published manuals (Falloon et al., 1984; Anderson et al., 1986; Barrowclough and Tarrier, 1992; Kuipers et al., 2002). All are characterised, to a differing extent, by the following features:

* engaging with the family and improving listening and negotiating skills
* offering specific advice and information about diagnosis, medication and the problems that carers are likely to face
* a problem-solving approach to immediate difficulties that all family members have to cope with
* identifying, normalising and cognitively reappraising the emotional and behavioural impact of problems
* encouraging medication adherence in those with the diagnosis.

Practicalities

To carry out this kind of FI (Kuipers et al., 2002), the clinician needs to organise appropriate initial training, managerial support and access to supervision. It is suggested that any family work is done with pairs of professionals. Being able to balance competing demands from different family members is more feasible with co-therapists, who can also provide modelling in communication skills that may have been lost in the stress of the caregiving situation.

It is not clear how intense family sessions need to be. The evidence is best for longer-term interventions (> ten sessions, over 6 months or more; National Institute for Health and Clinical Excellence, (NICE), 2003). This suggests that fortnightly sessions, reducing to monthly, is a reasonable aim. Families may be difficult to engage at non-crisis times (Szmukler et al., 2003) and many of the research trials have focused more productively on interventions that begin at a time of crisis, such as an admission or shortly after a relapse. These times have the benefit of making it clear that there are indeed problems (which can otherwise be denied or minimised by someone in the family) and can be a catalyst for change. Initially, there will be issues about when, where and who is included. Visits based at home for about an hour with whoever is willing to attend usually allow more family members to engage, are less demanding of them and are more likely to be successful.

Not all patients live at home, and the relationships between patients and staff carers are subject to the same sorts of factors, despite the staff's ostensibly different roles to relatives (Herzog, 1992; Moore et al., 1992). This work suggests that mental health teams need to consider the training, supervision and support of their staff carers to reduce the potentially negative effects of the high demands being made of them, both in terms of staff burn-out and poorer patient outcomes.

Evidence for efficacy

Overall, there is good evidence that family interventions improve outcome, as measured by relapse rates (Penn and Mueser, 1996): typically, 9-months relapse rates decrease to less than 20%, compared with the 50% found in high-expressed-emotion families receiving standard care. This finding has been replicated by many research groups in a number of different cultures. Tarrier and Barrowclough (1995) found that positive effects were apparent even 8 years after the intervention. Nevertheless, there is evidence that a sizeable number of families either refuse intervention or drop out at an early stage. Family intervention has recently been endorsed by the NICE guidelines (2003) as effective, particularly for people with persistent positive symptoms and a relapsing course of illness. The meta-analysis evaluated 18 randomised controlled trials ($n = 1,458$) and found that FI improved outcome, particularly relapse rates, both during treatment and up to 15 months afterwards. The evidence was strongest for interventions that included the patient.

Attempts have been made to focus on the specific interventions that help families to change, but so far the results have been limited. Although psychoeducation alone does not seem to be helpful (NICE, 2003), NICE nevertheless recommends as good practice that easily accessible information should be available as part of an effective intervention. Information is likely to improve optimism and understanding of some terminology, but on its own will not change attitudes or behaviour.

Despite the demonstrated cost savings of family interventions (Tarrier et al., 1991), they have so far failed to be integrated routinely into clinical practice and remain an effective but underused intervention. The main reasons for limited service implementation are that FI is tremendously time consuming for staff and that resources are scarce. In addition, FI involves a shift in practitioners' thinking, from focusing on the individual patient to considering the wider social context.

REHABILITATION

The focus of rehabilitative therapies is on the social, cognitive and occupational disabilities exhibited by individuals with psychosis.

Social skills training

Social skills training (SST) aims to remediate the interpersonal deficits demonstrated by patients with psychosis, which militate against the ability to integrate into society and therefore contribute to poor long-term outcome. The evidence regarding the efficacy of SST is mixed, and variations in the form and length of interventions make it difficult to draw firm conclusions. SST that involves structured educational methods combining social reinforcement, modelling and role-play appears to be relatively successful (Liberman et al., 1986) and seems to be maintained for long periods (Wirshing et al., 1992). However, a meta-analytic review of 23 studies concluded that although SST was associated with improved interpersonal functioning and lower social anxiety in specific role-play tests, generalisation of skills and community functioning over a longer time span was less robust (Benton and Schroeder, 1990). SST is much less popular in the UK than in the USA, due to reservations regarding its effectiveness and the generalisation of acquired skills to novel situations. The meta-analysis from the NICE guidelines (2003) (nine randomised controlled trials, $n = 436$) confirmed the view that such skills do not tend to generalise for patients with schizophrenia. It found no evidence for the effectiveness of social skills training as a discrete intervention, and its clinical use is not currently recommended in the UK, in contrast to the USA (PORT: the Schizophrenia Patient Outcomes Research Team; Lehman et al., 2004). Nevertheless, the philosophy of improving social or interpersonal skills is often integrated into routine occupational therapy groups, even if not practised as stand-alone psychological interventions in the UK.

Cognitive Remediation Therapy

Many patients with psychosis have cognitive deficits, particularly in attention and working memory, and these deficits are associated with poor outcomes (Wykes, 1994). Therefore, reducing cognitive deficits via cognitive remediation therapy (CRT) has the potential to increase the patient's quality of life and reduce dependence on psychiatric care. Techniques such as errorless learning, scaffolding and verbalising instructions may be particularly useful in trying directly to 'remediate' or correct these cognitive processes (Wykes and Van der Gaag, 2001; Wykes and Reeder, 2005). CRT attempts to reduce deficits by training patients, either individually or in a group format, to improve their performance on various cognitive tasks or to practise specific cognitive abilities.

Although there is a clear rationale behind cognitive remediation and comprehensive programmes have been documented (Delahunty and Morice, 1993; Brenner et al., 1994; Wykes, 2000; Wykes and Reeder, 2005), the evidence for its efficacy is mixed (Bellack et al., 1999). While many studies (e.g. Spaulding et al., 1998) are effective in improving specific cognitive deficits, there is less evidence for generalisation to other cognitive skills or to the patient's social and occupational functioning. In one randomised controlled trial (RCT), however, Wykes et al. (1999b) found that cognition and self-esteem improved at outcome, as did social functioning if improvements in cognitive deficits reached a particular threshold. The improvements in cognition and social functioning, but not self-esteem, were still apparent at a 6-month follow-up (Wykes et al., 2003). More recent reviews do report evidence that cognitive rehabilitation can indeed improve task performance in patients with schizophrenia, and that this effect is apparent on tasks outside those practised during the training procedure (Krabbendam and Aleman, 2003). Overall, however, the NICE (2003) meta-analysis (7 RCTs, $n = 295$) found no consistent evidence that cognitive remediation improved outcomes in the targeted cognitive functions or core symptoms. This again stands in contrast to the American guidelines (PORT; Lehman et al., 2004), which have endorsed CRT. Nevertheless, despite some promising outcome data, the individualised and intensive approach required for such improvements has so far hindered the incorporation of CRT into standard clinical practice in the UK.

COGNITIVE BEHAVIOUR THERAPY

Background

The main assumption behind CBT is that the occurrence and maintenance of psychological difficulties are mediated by cognitive, behavioural and emotional factors (Beck et al., 1979). Therapy aims to break the vicious cycles between thoughts, feelings and behaviours by helping people to learn more adaptive ways of thinking and coping, which then leads to reduction in distress. In the 1980s and 1990s, research on single psychotic symptoms led to interventions that adapted the successful use of CBT for anxiety and depression to the more complex problems of psychosis.

Intervention

The aims of CBT for psychosis are to:

- increase understanding of psychosis and symptoms
- reduce distress and disability arising from psychotic symptoms
- promote coping and self-regulation of the disorder
- reduce hopelessness and counter negative appraisals (of self and illness).

Several books offer guides to CBT for psychosis: Fowler et al. (1995); Chadwick et al. (1996); Haddock and Slade (1996); Nelson (1997); Morrison (2002); Kingdon and Turkington (2002, 2005); Morrison et al. (2003); Byrne et al. (2005). A useful overview is provided by Fowler et al. (1998). CBT for psychosis is not based on a single psychological model and includes a combination of elements and therapeutic activities. The basic stages of therapy (adapted from Fowler et al., 1995) are as follows:

- engagement and assessment
- promoting self-regulation of psychotic symptoms (coping)
- developing a shared formulation of psychosis
- addressing delusions and beliefs about voices
- addressing dysfunctional assumptions about self and others
- addressing social disability and risk of relapse.

Not all stages are implemented with all patients, and therapy often consists of see-sawing between the various stages, rather than going through them sequentially as therapy progresses. For each patient, the intervention will depend on the presenting problems and case formulation. The NICE guidelines recommend at least 6 months and a minimum of ten sessions of CBT. The various components of CBT are discussed in more detail below.

Engagement

It is crucial that individuals are able to 'engage' in the therapy, and that the patient is able to maintain a therapeutic relationship with the therapist. Patients with psychosis may have particular difficulties in engaging in therapy. Positive symptoms can hinder engagement: patients may be distracted by voices during therapy or they may have paranoid ideas about the therapist. Individuals with psychosis are more likely to have small social networks and increased social isolation is associated with poor insight (White et al., 2000). Patients may also have problems of concentration and memory, plus selective attention to negative events, reasoning biases, and a tendency to attribute events externally (Garety et al., 2001).

Therapists need to be very sensitive to the impact of discussion of symptoms on the patient. It is important that sessions are not aversive, as this may increase the person's anxiety and trigger or exacerbate psychotic symptoms. Sessions may need to be short and activities varied (e.g. going for a walk mid-session, having a cigarette break). Therapists need to be very flexible and tolerant of rapid changes in the client's mental state. Unlike CBT for neurotic disorders, the therapist should be prepared to take more responsibility for the session, and to apologise and give reassurance if things are misinterpreted.

Coping strategy enhancement

Many psychotic patients already use some coping strategies for their experiences, but these may be sub-optimal. Improving coping responses is typically attempted during the initial assessment and engagement period. Coping strategy enhancement (CSE) (Tarrier et al., 1990; Tarrier, 2002) is a structured intervention that involves building on a patient's existing repertoire of coping strategies. Although coping may only provide short-term relief from symptoms, it can increase the patient's sense of control and foster therapeutic optimism, and coping methods can be integrated into work on patients' beliefs about the controllability of psychotic experiences. Some coping strategies used by patients can be conceptualised as safety behaviours within a cognitive model (Morrison, 2001), in that they give short-term relief but maintain delusional beliefs in the long term. Therefore, it is important to assess and formulate coping strategies thoroughly, particularly the purpose and consequences of these behaviours.

Sharing a formulation

The cognitive-behavioural therapist always intervenes according to a formulation. Although there is little empirical evidence for this (Chadwick et al., 2003), it can be useful to try to bring all the information together and to collaborate with the client in drawing out a model of factors that have led up to and maintain their current problems. Cognitive models (e.g. Morrison, 2001) provide useful templates for constructing an individualised formulation of the person's psychotic symptoms. A formulation is usually shared with the patient, although the amount of information shared varies depending on the impact of doing so, for example, how helpful, confusing or distressing it is for the patient. It is often useful to build up a case formulation over the course of therapy, starting with a simple model and gradually incorporating more factors (Kinderman and Lobban, 2000).

Cognitive behavioural interventions with positive symptoms

Cognitive models posit that it is the person's appraisal or interpretation of anomalous experiences, which in themselves are not necessarily problematic, that generates distressing psychotic symptoms. Garety et al. (2001) focus on the externalising nature of appraisals, whereas Morrison (2001) highlights the culturally unacceptable nature of psychotic appraisals. The focus on appraisal has been particularly useful in helping patients make sense of their unusual experiences, and react and cope with them differently in order to reduce distress. This body of work has concentrated on the positive symptoms of delusions and hallucinations.

Delusions

Current models of delusions emphasise the importance of unusual experiences in driving delusional explanations, the presence of reasoning biases ('jump-to-conclusions' reasoning style, externalising attributional bias), motivational aspects of delusions in defending against poor self-esteem, and the impact of a 'theory of mind' deficit in forming beliefs about the self and others (Garety and Freeman, 1999). The central role of emotions in influencing the formation and maintenance of delusions is also increasingly becoming recognized (Freeman et al., 2002; Freeman and Garety, 2003).

As delusions are viewed as attempts to make sense of events and experiences, the aim of therapy is *not* to challenge delusions head on, but to provide patients with an alternative, plausible and less distressing explanation of their experiences. Reframing delusions encourages patients to view their beliefs as hypotheses and uses verbal and behavioural strategies to re-evaluate these beliefs. These techniques include:

- Examining the evidence for and against a belief. This process involves considering impartially how the person uses the evidence for his or her beliefs, whether there are any inconsistencies, and whether there may be aspects that he or she has not considered beforehand. It is easiest to work initially with the evidence for a belief, rather than the belief itself, starting with the least strong piece of evidence for the least strongly held belief first, and gradually working up to more central ideas.
- Considering alternative explanations for the person's past and ongoing experiences, with evidence for and against each explanation. Patients with psychosis often have difficulty generating alternative explanations (Freeman et al., 2004) and therapists may need to suggest alternatives. Much care (and creativity) should be taken in providing alternatives that are compelling and plausible: for many patients 'having an illness' is simply not a plausible explanation of their powerful experiences.
- Considering the advantages and disadvantages of holding a particular belief. Helping the patient to examine these can aid engagement and motivation to change. If a delusion does have advantages (e.g. a grandiose delusion boosting self-esteem), these need to be addressed before working on the belief, exploring alternative sources of these benefits.

- Educating patients about normal psychological processes (cognitive biases, anxiety processes), which might otherwise be interpreted in a delusional way.
- Behavioural experiments or reality testing. Behavioural tests allow clients to test out the accuracy of a belief and provide the chance of obtaining disconfirmatory evidence. Before carrying out a reality test, care must be taken to consider the possible outcomes and the impact of these on the person; they should not be carried out just to prove the person wrong.

With some patients it is not possible (or desirable) to consider non-delusional explanations for experiences. In these cases, there is a need throughout the sessions to work within the delusional system. The aims of such intervention are to: reduce the distress associated with the delusion, increase coping with the consequences of delusions, learn to have greater control over the situation, find alternative ways of reacting and enhance coping strategies, reduce the influence of the delusions on activities and relationships, spend less time thinking or acting on the beliefs and reduce triggers of delusional thoughts.

Hallucinations

Interventions so far have concentrated on auditory hallucinations, while visual, olfactory and tactile hallucinations have received little attention. Psychological models of auditory verbal hallucinations (voices) are based on a number of clinical and experimental findings:

- Auditory verbal hallucinations are externally attributed thoughts (Frith, 1987; Bentall, 1990).
- Hallucinations tend to worsen under conditions of increased arousal (Margo et al., 1981).
- Interpretations of hallucinations account for at least some of the resulting distress (Chadwick and Birchwood, 1994).
- Increased self-focused attention is associated with hearing voices (Morrison and Renton, 2001).
- There seems to be a link between exposure to trauma and subsequent development of hallucinations (Romme and Escher, 1989; Read et al., 2005).
- Patients' relationships with their voices can be understood as part of social relationships in general (Birchwood et al., 2000a, 2002).

The types of intervention used differ in their emphasis on behavioural and/or cognitive techniques (see Haddock et al., 1998; Shergill et al., 1998; Morrison and Renton, 2001, for reviews), and on which psychological model they are based. There are a number of possible therapeutic techniques:

- reduce and manage triggers to voices
- develop new and enhance existing coping strategies
- place hallucinations within a wider formulation, making links with past experiences, especially traumatic ones
- modify beliefs about voices (as for delusions), such as beliefs about power, controllability, meta-cognitive beliefs and positive beliefs
- challenge the content of the voices (in a similar way to challenging negative automatic thoughts in anxiety and depression)
- conduct cost–benefit analyses of responding to voices
- modify attention to voices
- alter the relationship with voices.

It is recognised that medication-resistant hallucinations are difficult to reduce using psychological means. However, an increase in perceived control over the hallucinations or a reduction in associated distress can have an enormous effect on quality of life even if the frequency of hallucinations has not changed (Trower et al., 2004). Studies also suggest that a group therapy format may be advantageous in helping people with their hallucinations (Wykes et al., 1999a; Chadwick et al., 2000).

Working with negative symptoms

Negative symptoms are also amenable to CBT (Rector et al., 2003; Falzer et al., 2004), although they have received less attention than positive symptoms. Some of the cognitive techniques used for depression are helpful for negative symptoms. Some specific strategies include:

- identifying and questioning negative and self-defeating cognitions
- activity scheduling and monitoring, including both mastery and pleasure activities
- goal setting (small, achievable goals)
- problem solving, e.g. overcoming obstacles to doing things
- making activities more enjoyable.

Johns et al. (2002) piloted a group CBT intervention for negative symptoms, particularly targeting avolition/apathy. There was a reduction in patients' avolition following the group, and some reduction in distress.

Beliefs about self and others/self-esteem

Low self-esteem is common in psychosis (Freeman et al., 1998), as are rates of co-morbid depression and anxiety. Self-esteem can be improved using similar methods to those used for depression. Hall and Tarrier (2003, 2004) describe a self-esteem intervention that encourages clients to write down, and generate evidence for, positive qualities about themselves each week for 5 weeks. Chadwick (2003) discusses using a 'two-chair method' to enable the person to experience not just his or her usual negative self, but also a positive self in the other chair. Other cognitive techniques for schema change (Padesky, 1994) can be helpful.

Relapse prevention

Birchwood et al. (1989) pioneered work on helping individuals and carers identify 'relapse signatures' as an aid to understanding prodromal symptoms and preventing future relapses. A relapse signature is a set of general and idiosyncratic symptoms, occurring in a specific order, over a certain time period, that are early warning signs of relapse. For example, a feeling of unease and suspiciousness might be a precursor to more serious symptoms of paranoia. The Back in the Saddle (BITS) intervention (Plaistow and Birchwood, unpublished manual) involves helping individuals to identify their relapse signature and then developing a 'relapse drill' or action plan to prevent progression towards a full psychotic episode. This proactive approach can be empowering for clients.

The cognitive conceptualisation of relapse focuses on patients' beliefs about the emergence of early warning signs. Thoughts such as 'I have no control' or 'I'll end up in hospital' might explain some of the emotional and behavioural symptoms observed during early relapse (Birchwood, 1995). Such beliefs are also associated with increased anxiety, demoralisation and the use of unhelpful coping strategies, such as avoidance, and may in themselves accelerate the speed of relapse. Similarly, Gumley et al. (2003) reported that increased risk of relapse was associated with negative beliefs about illness (particularly humiliation and loss), low self-esteem and safety behaviours such as avoidance. Cognitive techniques can be used to evaluate the accuracy of these negative beliefs.

Medication management

Many patients do not adhere to their medication regimen and non-compliance incurs substantial individual and social costs in terms of untreated morbidity and relapse. Patients cease taking their medication for various reasons: intolerance of side effects, lack of insight, fears about stigma or dependency, or the natural tendency to stop taking medication when feeling better. Purely psychoeducational approaches have limited effectiveness. Medication management is based on a combination of CBT and motivational interviewing (Rollnick et al., 1992). It has been evaluated by RCT, and leads to significant improvements in attitudes to medication, insight and compliance (Kemp et al., 1996). These advantages were maintained over an 18-month period, and social functioning and time to re-admission were increased (Kemp et al., 1998).

Dual diagnosis

A major difficulty in providing services is the issue of dual diagnosis of schizophrenia and substance abuse. The prevalence of substance abuse among psychotic patients is 30–50% (Mueser et al., 1990). Dual diagnosis leads to greater in-patient service use, poorer adherence to treatment, more frequent violent behaviour and to more severe clinical and social problems (Bartels et al., 1993; Scott et al., 1998). There was a major investment in attempts to help people with dual diagnosis in the USA during the 1990s (Osher et al., 1996). In the UK, a small RCT evaluated a combination of motivational interviewing, CBT and FI in the treatment of patients with both schizophrenia and substance abuse (Barrowclough et al., 2001), with positive results. A multi-site RCT is underway.

Evidence for efficacy

A number of RCTs in the UK have evaluated CBT for persistent symptoms in psychosis (recent reviews include: Gould et al., 2001; Pilling et al., 2002; Jones et al., 2004; Tarrier and Wykes, 2004; Turkington et al., 2004; Zimmerman et al., 2005). These trials have found that CBT is more effective than control treatments in improving symptoms, and that these benefits are maintained (and, in some cases, increased) at follow-up after therapy has ended. CBT has also been shown to be highly acceptable to patients (Miles et al., 2007) and to be cost effective. However, gains have tended to be greatest for delusions, with less improvement in other psychotic symptoms, depression or social functioning. The NICE (2003) meta-analysis included 13 RCTs ($n = 1,297$) and found good evidence that CBT reduced symptoms in people with schizophrenia at up to 1 year of follow-up. The evidence was stronger for those patients with persistent rather than acute symptoms.

EARLY INTERVENTION

Background

Evidence suggests that the longer the duration of untreated psychosis (DUP), the poorer the long-term outcome (McGlashan and Johannessen, 1996). In addition, secondary morbidity, including substance misuse and depression, are frequent at this stage of the illness (Addington et al., 1998; Cantwell et al., 1999) and the risk of suicide is at its highest (Power et al., 2003). EI is based on the rationale that effective intervention and good engagement with services at an early stage of illness may attenuate the medium and long-term consequences of psychosis and improve overall prognosis (see Birchwood et al., 2000b, for a guide to EI).

It is also possible to identify individuals who are particularly vulnerable to impending psychosis using a combination of genetic, personality and mental-state risk factors (Yung et al., 1998; Morrison et al., 2002). About one third of this high-risk group develop a first episode of psychosis within 12 months (Morrison et al., 2002; Yung et al., 2003, 2004). Detection of individuals with an 'at-risk mental state' (ARMS) paves the way for intervening before the onset of psychosis, with the chance of aborting or delaying a full psychotic episode. This approach is somewhat controversial due to the premature, and possibly unnecessary, labelling, stigma and treatment of young people (see *Schizophrenia Research*, 2001, vol. 51 for a discussion of the ethical issues).

Intervention

The key elements are early detection and treatment of the first psychotic episode, and interventions during the first few years of psychotic illness (the 'critical period'; Birchwood et al., 1998). Services for young people with an ARMS aim to improve current symptoms and functioning, prevent or delay transition to psychosis, and improve outcome for those who do become psychotic.

First-episode psychosis

EI services aim to reduce delays to treatment, optimise assessment and diagnosis, maximise recovery by providing integrated biopsychosocial treatment and prevent relapse. Specific psychological interventions are an important component of these services (Gleeson and McGorry, 2004). Targets for intervention include:

- making sense of experiences (both psychosis and hospitalisation)
- adaptation and recovery style, insight
- CBT for acute psychotic symptoms
- medication compliance
- co-morbid conditions, e.g. anxiety, post-traumatic stress
- depression, particularly hopelessness and suicide risk
- substance misuse, particularly cannabis
- relapse prevention
- CBT for persistent psychotic symptoms
- working with families.

At-risk mental states

Extrapolating from the treatments used in established psychosis, many clinical-research teams prescribe very low-dose antipsychotic medication to these individuals. This approach is under debate (see *Journal of Mental*

Health, 2003, vol. 12, issue 4). It has been argued that psychological intervention should be the treatment of choice for at-risk individuals, and that CBT may be particularly helpful for this client group (French and Morrison, 2004). As the cognitive models of psychosis (Garety et al., 2001; Morrison, 2001) emphasise the role of appraisals in the development of psychotic symptoms, CBT can target the interpretations of unusual experiences reported by clients before the clients develop fixed delusional explanations of these experiences.

Evidence

The impact of EI services has yet to be established by large-scale RCTs and prospective research studies. A few studies have evaluated specific psychological treatments in this group (Gleeson and McGorry, 2004), with mixed results. In one large ($n = 318$) RCT comparing CBT, supportive counselling and routine care for patients with a first or second episode of psychosis, patients received 15–20 hours of therapy over 5 weeks, with four later booster sessions, aimed at speeding recovery (Lewis et al., 2002). The results showed an overall improvement irrespective of treatment group, and a trend towards faster recovery of symptoms in the CBT group. No group differences were found in subsequent relapse or readmission rates (Tarrier et al., 2004).

There are two published RCTs so far on the prevention of psychosis in at-risk samples. McGorry et al. (2002) compared low-dose risperidone plus CBT with non-specific intervention. After 6 months of treatment, the transition rate to psychosis was 10% in the treatment arm compared to 36% in the control arm. However, this significant difference was not maintained at follow-up 6 months later. Morrison et al. (2004) compared CBT and monthly monitoring. At 12-month follow-up, 6% had become psychotic in the CBT group, compared with 22% in the control group. Both these trials have small samples and some methodological issues; further evaluations are currently in progress.

CONCLUSIONS

Recent years have seen a significant development in psychological interventions for established psychosis, together with increasing evidence of their efficacy. The recent NICE guidelines recommend that all patients with distressing psychotic symptoms should receive CBT and FI. However, services differ markedly in the degree of implementation of psychosocial approaches, and they are not yet routinely included in the care plan approach (CPA). There has been a more recent shift towards early intervention in psychosis and possible prevention, although the evidence for this approach is still preliminary.

REFERENCES

Addington, D., Addington, J. and Patten, S. (1998) Depression in people with first episode schizophrenia. *British Journal of Psychiatry*, 172, suppl 33, 90–92.

Anderson, C. M., Reiss, D. J. and Hogarty, G. E. (1986) *Schizophrenia and the Family*. New York: Guilford Press.

Barrowclough, C. and Tarrier, N. (1992) *Families of Schizophrenic Patients: Cognitive Behavioural Intervention*. London: Chapman and Hall.

Barrowclough, C., Haddock, G., Tarrier, N., Lewis, S. W., Moring, J., O'Brien, R. et al. (2001) Randomized controlled trial of motivational interviewing, cognitive behavior therapy, and family intervention for patients with comorbid schizophrenia and substance use disorders. *American Journal of Psychiatry*, 158, 1706–1713.

Bartels, S. J., Teague, G. B., Drake, R. E., Clark, R. E., Bush, P. W. and Noordsy, D. L. (1993) Substance abuse in schizophrenia: Service utilization and costs. *Journal of Nervous and Mental Disease*, 181, 227–232.

Beck, A. T., Rush, A. J., Shaw, B. F. and Emery, G. (1979) *Cognitive Therapy of Depression*. New York: Guilford Press.

Bellack, A. S., Gold, J. M. and Buchanan, R. W. (1999) Cognitive rehabilitation for schizophrenia: Problems, prospects and strategies. *Schizophrenia Bulletin*, 25, 257–274.

Bentall, R. P. (1990) The illusion of reality: A review and integration of psychological research on hallucinations. *Psychological Bulletin*, 107, 82–85.

Benton, M. K. and Schroeder, H. E. (1990) Social skills training with schizophrenics: A meta-analytic evaluation. *Journal of Consulting and Clinical Psychology*, 58, 741–747.

Birchwood, M. (1995) Early intervention in psychotic relapse: Cognitive approaches to detection and management. *Behaviour Change*, 12, 2–19.

Birchwood, M., Smith, J., McMillan, F., Hogg, B., Prasad, R., Harvey C. and Bering, S. (1989) Predicting relapse in schizophrenia: The development and implementation of an early signs monitoring system using patients and families as observers, a preliminary investigation. *Psychological Medicine*, 19, 649–656.

Birchwood, M., Todd, P. and Jackson, C. (1998) Early intervention in psychosis: The critical period hypothesis. *British Journal of Psychiatry*, 172, suppl 33, 53–59.

Birchwood, M., Meaden, A., Trower, P., Gilbert, P. and Plaistow, J. (2000a) The power and omnipotence of voices: Subordination and entrapment by voices and significant others. *Psychological Medicine*, 30, 337–344.

Birchwood, M., Fowler, D. and Jackson, C. (2000b) *Early Intervention in Psychosis. A Guide to Concepts, Evidence and Interventions*. Chichester: John Wiley.

Birchwood, M., Meaden, A., Trower, P. and Gilbert, P. (2002) Shame, humiliation, and entrapment in psychosis. A social rank theory approach to cognitive intervention with voices and delusions. In: A. P. Morrison (ed) *A Casebook of Cognitive Therapy for Psychosis*. Hove, UK: Brunner-Routledge.

Brenner, H., Roder, V., Hodel, B., Kienzle, N., Reed, D. and Liberman, R. (1994) *Integrated Psychological Therapy for Schizophrenia Patients*. Toronto: Hogrefe & Huber.

Brown, G. W. and Rutter, M. (1966) The measurement of family activities and relationships: A methodological study. *Human Relations*, 19, 241–263.

Byrne, S., Birchwood, M., Trower, P. and Meaden, A. (2005) *A Casebook of Cognitive Therapy for Command Hallucinations: A Social Rank Theory Approach*. London: Routledge.

Cantwell, R., Brewin, J., Glazebrook, C. et al. (1999) Prevalence of substance misuse in first episode psychosis. *British Journal of Psychiatry*, 174, 150–153.

Chadwick, P. (2003) Two chairs, self-schemata and a person based approach to psychosis. *Behavioural and Cognitive Psychotherapy*, 31, 439–449.

Chadwick, P. and Birchwood, M. (1994) The omnipotence of voices: A cognitive approach to auditory hallucinations. *British Journal of Psychiatry*, 164, 190–201.

Chadwick, P., Birchwood, M. and Trower, P. (1996) *Cognitive Therapy for Delusions, Voices and Paranoia*. Chichester: John Wiley.

Chadwick, P., Sambrooke, S., Rasch, S. and Davies, E. (2000) Challenging the omnipotence of voices: Group cognitive behavior therapy for voices. *Behaviour Research and Therapy*, 38, 993–1003.

Chadwick, P., Williams, C. and Mackenzie, J. (2003) Impact of case formulation in cognitive behaviour therapy for psychosis. *Behaviour Research and Therapy*, 41, 671–680.

Curson, D. A., Patel, M., Liddle, P. F. et al. (1988) Psychiatric morbidity of a long-stay hospital population with chronic schizophrenia and implications for future community care. *British Medical Journal*, 297, 819–822.

Delahunty, A. and Morice, R. (1993) *A Training Programme for the Remediation of Cognitive Deficits in Schizophrenia*. Albury, NSW: Department of Health.

Fadden, G., Bebbington, P. and Kuipers, L. (1987) Caring and its burden. *British Journal of Psychiatry*, 151, 660–667.

Falloon, I. R. H., Boyd, J. L. and McGill, C. W. (1984) *Family Care of Schizophrenia*. New York: Guilford Press.

Falzer, P. R., Stayner, D. A., and Davidson, L. (2004) Principles and strategies for developing psychosocial treatments for negative symptoms in early course psychosis. In: J. F. Gleeson and P. D. McGorry (eds) *Psychological Interventions in Early Psychosis: A Treatment Handbook*. Chichester: John Wiley.

Fowler, D. G., Garety, P. and Kuipers, E. (1995) *Cognitive Behaviour Therapy for Psychosis: Theory and Practice*. Chichester: John Wiley.

Fowler, D., Garety, P. and Kuipers, E. (1998) Cognitive therapy for psychosis: Formulation, treatment, effects and service implications. *Journal of Mental Health*, 7, 123–133.

Freeman, D., Garety, P., Fowler, D., Kuipers, E., Dunn, G., Bebbington, P. and Hadley, C. (1998) The London–East-Anglia randomised controlled trial of cognitive-behaviour therapy for psychosis. IV: Self esteem and persecutory delusions. *British Journal of Clinical Psychology*, 37, 415–430.

Freeman, D., Garety, P. A., Kuipers, E., Fowler, D. and Bebbington, P. E. (2002) A cognitive model of persecutory delusions. *British Journal of Clinical Psychology*, 41, 331–347.

Freeman, D. and Garety, P. A. (2003) Connecting neurosis and psychosis: The direct influence of emotion on delusions and hallucinations. *Behaviour Research and Therapy*, 41, 923–947.

Freeman, D., Garety, P. A., Fowler, D., Kuipers, E., Bebbington, P. E. and Dunn, G.

(2004) Why do people with delusions fail to choose more realistic explanations for their experiences? An empirical investigation. *Journal of Consulting and Clinical Psychology*, 72, 671–680.

French, P. and Morrison, A. P. (2004) *Early Detection and Cognitive Therapy for People at High Risk of Developing Psychosis. A Treatment Approach.* Chichester: John Wiley.

Frith, C. D. (1987) The positive and negative symptoms of schizophrenia reflect impairments in the perception and initiation of action. *Psychological Medicine*, 17, 631–648.

Garety, P. A. and Freeman, D. (1999) Cognitive approaches to delusions: A critical review of theories and evidence. *British Journal of Clinical Psychology*, 38, 113–154.

Garety, P., Kuipers, E., Fowler, D., Freeman, D. and Bebbington, P. (2001) A cognitive model of the positive symptoms of psychosis. *Psychological Medicine*, 31, 189–195.

Gleeson, J. F. M. and McGorry, P. D. (2004) *Psychological Interventions in Early Psychosis. A Treatment Handbook.* Chichester: John Wiley.

Gould, R. A., Mueser, K. T., Bolton, E., Mays, V. and Goff, D. (2001) Cognitive therapy for psychosis in schizophrenia: An effect size analysis. *Schizophrenia Research*, 48, 335–342.

Gumley, A., O'Grady, M., McNay, L., Reilly, J., Power, K. and Norrie, J. (2003) Early intervention for relapse in schizophrenia: Results of a 12-month randomized controlled trial of cognitive behavioural therapy. *Psychological Medicine*, 33, 419–431.

Haddock, H. and and Slade, P. (1996) *Cognitive Behavioural Interventions with Psychotic Disorders.* London: Routledge.

Haddock, G., Tarrier, N., Spaulding, W., Yusupoff, L., Kinney, C. and McCarthy, E. (1998) Individual cognitive-behavior therapy in the treatment of hallucinations and delusions: A review. *Clinical Psychology Review*, 18, 821–838.

Hall, P. L. and Tarrier, N. (2003) The cognitive-behavioural treatment to improve low self-esteem in psychotic patients: A pilot study. *Behaviour Research and Therapy*, 41, 317–332.

Hall, P. L. and Tarrier, N. (2004) Short-term durability of a cognitive behavioural intervention in psychosis: Effects from a pilot study. *Behavioural and Cognitive Psychotherapy*, 32, 117–121.

Herzog, T. (1992) Nurses, patients and relatives: A study of family patterns on psychiatric wards. In: C. L. Cazzullo and G. Invernizzi (eds) *Family Intervention in Schizophrenia: Experiences and Orientations in Europe.* Milan: ARS.

Hogarty, G. E. and Ulrich, R. F. (1998) The limitations of antipsychotic medication on schizophrenia relapse and adjustment and the contributions of psychosocial treatment. *Journal of Psychiatric Research*, 32, 243–250.

Johns, L. C., Sellwood, W., McGovern, J. and Haddock, G. (2002) Battling boredom: Group cognitive behaviour therapy for negative symptoms of schizophrenia. *Behavioural and Cognitive Psychotherapy*, 30, 341–346.

Jones, C., Cormac, I., Silveira da Mota Neto, J. and Campbell, C. (2004) CBT for schizophrenia. *Cochrane Database of Systematic Reviews* 2004, issue 4. Art. No. CD000524. DOI: 10.1002/14651858. CD000524 pub2.

Kapur, S. (2003) Psychosis as a state of aberrant salience: A framework linking biology, phenomenology, and pharmacology in schizophrenia. *American Journal of Psychiatry*, 160, 13–23.

Kemp, R., David, A. and Hayward, P. (1996) Compliance therapy: An intervention targeting insight and treatment adherence in psychotic patients. *Behavioural and Cognitive Psychotherapy*, 24, 331–350.

Kemp, R., Kirov, G., Everitt, B., Hayward, P. and David, A. (1998) Randomised controlled trial of compliance therapy: 18 months follow-up. *British Journal of Psychiatry*, 172, 413–419.

Kinderman, P. and Lobban, F. (2000) Evolving formulations: Sharing complex information with clients. *Behavioural and Cognitive Psychotherapy*, 28, 307–310.

Kingdon, D. and Turkington, D. (2002) *The Case Study Guide to Cognitive Behaviour Therapy of Psychosis*. Chichester: John Wiley.

Kingdon, D. and Turkington, D. (2005) *Cognitive Therapy of Schizophrenia*. New York: Guilford Press.

Krabbendam, L. and Aleman, A. (2003) Cognitive rehabilitation in schizophrenia: A quantitative analysis of controlled studies. *Psychopharmacology*, 169, 376–382.

Kuipers, E., Leff, J. and Lam, D. (2002) *Family Work for Schizophrenia: A Practical Guide*, 2nd edn. London: Guildford Press.

Lehman, A. F., Kreyenbuhl, J., Buchanan, R. W., Dickerson, F. B., Dixon, L. B., Goldberg, R. et al. (2004) The Schizophrenia Patient Outcomes Research Team (PORT): Updated treatment recommendations 2003. *Schizophrenia Bulletin*, 30, 193–217.

Lewis, S., Tarrier, N., Haddock, G., Bentall, R., Kinderman, R., Kingdon, D. et al. (2002) RCT of cognitive-behavioural therapy in early schizophrenia: Acute-phase outcomes. *British Journal of Psychiatry*, 181 (suppl 43), 91–97.

Liberman, R. P., Mueser, K. T. and Wallace, C. G. (1986) Social skills training for schizophrenic individuals at risk for relapse. *American Journal of Psychiatry*, 143, 523–526.

McGlashan, T. and Johannessen, J. (1996) Early detection and intervention with schizophrenia: Rationale. *Schizophrenia Bulletin*, 22, 201–222.

McGorry, P. D., Yung, A. R., Phillips, L. J., Yuen, H. P., Francey, S. et al. (2002) RCT of interventions designed to reduce the risk of progression to first-episode psychosis in a clinical sample with sub threshold symptoms. *Archives of General Psychiatry*, 59, 921–928.

Margo, A., Hemsley, D. R. and Slade, P. D. (1981) The effects of varying auditory input on schizophrenic hallucinations. *British Journal of Psychiatry*, 139, 122–127.

May, R. (2004) Making sense of psychotic experiences and working towards recovery. In: J. F. Gleeson and P. D. McGorry (eds) *Psychological Interventions in Early Psychosis: A Treatment Handbook*. Chichester: John Wiley.

Miles, H., Peters, E. R. and Kuipers, E. (2007) Service-user satisfaction with CBT for psychosis. *Behavioural and Cognitive Psychotherapy*, 35, 109–117.

Moore, E., Ball, R. and Kuipers, L. (1992). Expressed emotion in staff working with the long-term adult mentally ill. *British Journal of Psychiatry*, 161, 802–808.

Morrison, A. P. (2001) The interpretation of intrusions in psychosis: An integrative cognitive approach to hallucinations and delusions. *Behavioural and Cognitive Psychotherapy*, 29, 257–276.

Morrison, A. P. (2002) *A Casebook of Cognitive Therapy for Psychosis*. Hove, UK: Brunner-Routledge.

Morrison, A. P. and Renton, J. C. (2001) Cognitive therapy for auditory hallucinations: A theory-based approach. *Cognitive and Behavioral Practice*, 8, 147–160.

Morrison, A. P., Bentall, R. P., French, P., Walford, L., Kilcommons, A. et al. (2002) RCT of early detection and cognitive therapy for preventing transition to psychosis in high-risk individuals. Study design and interim analysis of transition rate and psychological risk factors. *British Journal of Psychiatry*, 181 (suppl 43), 78–84.

Morrison, A. P., Renton, J., Dunn, H., Williams, S. and Bentall, R. P. (2003) *Cognitive Therapy for Psychosis*. Hove, UK: Brunner-Routledge.

Morrison, A. P., French, P., Walford, L., Lewis, S. W., Kilcommons, A., Green, J. et al. (2004) Cognitive therapy for the prevention of psychosis in people at ultra-high risk: Randomised controlled trial. *British Journal of Psychiatry*, 185, 291–297.

Mueser, K. T., Yarnold, P. R., Levinson, D. F., Singh, H., Bellack, A. S., Kee, K. et al. (1990) Prevalence of substance abuse in schizophrenia: Demographic and clinical correlates. *Schizophrenia Bulletin*, 16, 31–56.

National Institute for Health and Clinical Excellence (NICE) (2003) *Schizophrenia; Full National Clinical Guideline on Core Interventions in Primary and Secondary Care*. London: Gaskell Press.

Nelson, H. (1997) *Cognitive Behavioural Therapy with Schizophrenia. A Practice Manual*. Cheltenham: Thornes Publishers.

Osher, F. C. and Drake, R. E. (1996) Reversing a history of unmet needs: Approaches to care for persons with co-occurring addictive and mental disorders. *American Journal of Orthopsychiatry*, 66, 4–11.

Padesky, C. (1994) Schema change processes in cognitive therapy. *Clinical Psychology and Psychotherapy*, 1, 267–278.

Penn, D. and Mueser, K. (1996). Research update on the psychosocial treatment of schizophrenia. *American Journal of Psychiatry*, 153, 607–617.

Pilling, S., Bebbington, P., Kuipers, E., Garety, P., Geddes, J., Orbach, G. and Morgan, C. (2002) Psychological treatments in schizophrenia. I: Meta-analysis of family intervention and cognitive behaviour therapy. *Psychological Medicine*, 32, 763–782.

Power, P. J. R., Bell, R. J., Mills, R., Herrman-Doig, T., Davern, M., Henry, L. et al. (2003) Suicide prevention in first episode psychosis. *Australian and New Zealand Journal of Psychiatry*, 37, 414–420.

Read, J., van Os, J., Morrison, A. P. and Ross, C. A. (2005) Childhood trauma, psychosis and schizophrenia: A literature review with theoretical and clinical implications. *Acta Psychiatrica Scandinavica*, 112, 330–350.

Rector, N. A., Seeman, M. V. and Segal, Z. V. (2003) Cognitive therapy of schizophrenia: A preliminary RCT. *Schizophrenia Research*, 63, 1–11.

Rollnick, S., Heather, N. and Bell, A. (1992) Negotiating behaviour change in medical settings: The development of brief motivational interviewing. *Journal of Mental Health*, 1, 25–37.

Romme, M. and Escher, A. (1989) Hearing voices. *Schizophrenia Bulletin*, 15, 209–216.

Scott, H., Johnson, S., Menezes, P., Thornicroft, G., Marshall, J. Bindman, J. et al. (1998) Substance abuse and risk of aggression and offending among the severely mentally ill. *British Journal of Psychiatry*, 172, 345–350.

Shergill, S. S., Murray, R. and McGuire, P. K. (1998) Auditory hallucinations: A review of psychological treatments. *Schizophrenia Research*, 32, 137–150.

Spaulding, W. D., Reed, D., Storzbach, D., Sullivan, M., Weiler, M. and Richardson,

C. (1998) The effects of a remediational approach to cognitive therapy for schizophrenia. In: T. Wykes, N. Tarrier and S. Lewis (eds.) *Outcome and Innovation in Psychological Treatment of Schizophrenia*. London: John Wiley.

Szmukler, G., Kuipers, E., Joyce, J., Harris, T., Leese, M., Maphosa, W. and Staples, E. (2003) An exploratory RCT of a support programme for carers of patients with a psychosis. *Social Psychiatry and Psychiatric Epidemiology*, 38, 411–418.

Tarrier, N. (2002) The use of coping strategies and self-regulation in the treatment of psychosis. In: A. P. Morrison (ed) *A Casebook of Cognitive Therapy for Psychosis*. Hove, UK: Brunner-Routledge.

Tarrier, N. and Barrowclough, C. (1995) Family interventions in schizophrenia and their long-term outcomes. *International Journal of Mental Health*, 24, 38–53.

Tarrier, N. and Wykes, T. (2004) Is there evidence that cognitive behaviour therapy is an effective treatment for schizophrenia? A cautious or cautionary tale? *Behaviour Research and Therapy*, 42, 1377–1401.

Tarrier, N., Harwood, S., Yusopoff, L., Beckett, R. and Baker, A. (1990) Coping Strategy Enhancement (CSE): A method of treating residual schizophrenic symptoms. *Behavioural Psychotherapy*, 18, 283–293.

Tarrier, N., Lowson, K. and Barrowclough, C. (1991) Some aspects of family interventions in schizophrenia. II: Financial considerations. *British Journal of Psychiatry*, 159, 481–484.

Tarrier, N., Lewis, S., Haddock, G., Bentall, R., Drake, R., Kinderman, R. et al. (2004) Cognitive-behavioural therapy in first-episode and early schizophrenia: 18-month follow-up of a randomised controlled trial. *British Journal of Psychiatry*, 184, 231–239.

Trower, P., Birchwood, M., Meaden, A., Byrne, S., Nelson, A. and Ross, K. (2004) Cognitive therapy for command hallucinations: Randomised controlled trial. *British Journal of Psychiatry*, 184, 312–320.

Turkington, D., Dudley, R., Warman, D. and Beck, A. (2004) CBT for schizophrenia: A review. *Journal of Psychiatric Practice*, 10, 5–16.

Wirshing, W. C., Marder, S. R., Eckman, T. et al. (1992) Acquisition and retention of skills training methods in chronic schizophrenic outpatients. *Psychopharmacological Bulletin*, 28, 241–245.

White, R., Bebbington, P., Pearson, J., Johnson, S. and Ellis, D. (2000) The social context of insight in schizophrenia. *Social Psychiatry and Psychiatric Epidemiology*, 35, 500–507.

Wykes, T. (1994) Predicting symptomatic and behavioural outcomes of community care. *British Journal of Psychiatry*, 165, 486–492.

Wykes, T. (2000) The rehabilitation of cognitive deficits. *Psychiatric Rehabilitation Skills*, 4, 234–248.

Wykes, T. and Reeder, C. (2005) *Cognitive Remediation Therapy for Schizophrenia: Theory and Practice*. Hove, UK: Routledge.

Wykes, T. and Van Der Gaag. (2001) Is it time to develop a new cognitive therapy for psychosis – cognitive remediation therapy (CRT)? *Clinical Psychology Review*, 21, 1227–1256.

Wykes, T., Parr, A. and Landau, S. (1999a) Group treatment of auditory hallucinations: Exploratory study of effectiveness. *British Journal of Psychiatry*, 175, 180–185.

Wykes, T., Reeder, C., Corner, J., Williams, C. and Everitt, B. (1999b) The effects of neurocognitive remediation on executive processing in patients with schizophrenia. *Schizophrenia Bulletin*, 25, 291–309.

Wykes, T., Reeder, C., Williams, C., Corner, J., Rice, C. and Everitt, B. (2003) Are the effects of CRT durable? Results from an exploratory trial in schizophrenia. *Schizophrenia Research*, 61, 163–174.

Yung, A. R., Phillips, L. J., McGorry, P. D., McFarlane, C. A., Francey, S., Harrigan, S. et al. (1998) Prediction of psychosis: A step towards indicated prevention of schizophrenia. *British Journal of Psychiatry*, 172 (suppl 33), 14–20.

Yung, A. R., Phillips, L. J., Yuen, H. P., Francey, S. M., McFarlane, C. A., Hallgren, M. and McGorry, P. D. (2003) Psychosis prediction: 12-month follow up of a high risk ('prodromal') group. *Schizophrenia Research*, 60, 21–32.

Yung, A. R., Phillips, L. J., Yuen, H. P. and and McGorry, P. D. (2004) Risk factors for psychosis in an ultra high-risk group: Psychopathology and clinical features. *Schizophrenia Research*, 67, 131–142.

Zimmermann, G., Favrod, J., Trieu, V. H. and Pomini, V. (2005) The effect of cognitive behavioural treatment on the positive symptoms of schizophrenia spectrum disorders: A meta-analysis. *Schizophrenia Research*, 77, 1–9.

Chapter 21

Personality disorder

Investigation

Peter Hayward and Julian Walker

INTRODUCTION

The philosopher Ludwig Wittgenstein wrote, 'Philosophy is a battle against the bewitchment of our intelligence by means of language' (1958, p. 47). By this he seems to have meant that the words we use for things can often confuse us about the nature of the things described. This is certainly true of the set of labels we give to certain problematic patterns of thought and behaviour, also known as systems of psychiatric diagnosis. One can believe in the reality of the phenomena described by such labels as 'schizophrenia' or 'alcoholism' without feeling that these particular labels provide the most appropriate descriptions of those phenomena. Nowhere is this more true than in the area of the so-called 'personality disorders'. Many psychiatric diagnoses are stigmatised but, unfortunately, even within the helping professions, the term 'personality disorder' carries overtones of malice, obstructiveness and untreatability (Lewis and Appleby, 1988).

As working clinicians, both of us feel that the use of this particular diagnosis can be unhelpful. At the same time, whatever one thinks about defining problems in this way, the concept of the personality disorders and the set of diagnoses that go with it are accepted psychiatric usage, and all professionals, including clinical psychologists, must know how to use them. Further, it is almost a statistical certainty that anyone working with adult clients will encounter patients either diagnosed or able to be diagnosed with these conditions. We hope in these chapters to offer a summary of useful information for the clinician as to how to understand and treat such clients.

WHY ASSESS PERSONALITIES AND PERSONALITY DISORDERS?

People naturally tend to categorise others based on their personalities; someone may be described as outgoing, reserved, generous or stingy. These traits can be moderate or excessive, helpful or harmful. Further, their effects are generally mediated by a social context; behaviour that would seem normal in a car salesman might seem abrasive in a vicar, while traits that produce a successful clinical psychologist would probably not produce a successful mercenary soldier. However, the two major systems of psychiatric diagnosis have developed categories describing particular personality types that were thought to be clinically important and worthy of special attention. The American *Diagnostic and Statistical Manual of Mental Disorders*, 4th edition (DSM-IV) says that each of these diagnoses represents 'an enduring pattern of inner experience and behaviour that deviates markedly from the expectations of the individual's culture,' and goes on to describe these patterns as inflexible, pervasive, and causing distress to either the patient or other people (American Psychiatric Association (APA), 1994, p 633). The European *International Statistical Classification of Diseases and Related Health Problems*, 10th edition (ICD-10) refers to 'deeply engrained and enduring behaviour patterns, manifesting themselves as inflexible responses to a broad range of personal and social situations' (World Health Organization (WHO), 1992, p. 200). Each of these general classes of diagnosis include a number of diverse conditions, which are described as 'personality disorders'; in the American diagnostic system these are set apart from other diagnoses by being placed on a separate diagnostic axis. As we shall see, there are certain conceptual and methodological problems about the current system for diagnosing personality disorders. However, many other psychiatric diagnoses have similar problems. What is more important is that the personality disorders have come to be seen by some professionals as difficult to deal with, or in some way as less deserving of treatment than other psychiatric conditions, as noted above.

For these reasons, we would like to suggest an alternative framework to bear in mind when dealing with patients with a diagnosis of personality disorder. We all have personalities, which are relatively stable, although certain traits may change gradually as one grows older. Further, these personalities are more or less adaptive depending on the social matrix in which we find ourselves, and any of us can strive, more or less successfully, to change our personalities and habits. Some people may have certain traits that are strong and maladaptive, which manifest themselves in a variety of situations and often lead to difficulties. Such strong traits might well interact with circumstances, or perhaps with some form of acute psychiatric disturbance or life stress, to bring their possessors into contact with the health-care and criminal justice systems. At that time, the person might or might not be diagnosed with a personality disorder. They might also receive therapeutic input aimed at modifying the maladaptive trait, and this could occur independent of diagnosis. If the trait is strong, well-established and pervasive in its effects, it is unlikely that it could be eliminated, but this does not mean that helpful therapeutic work could not be done.

We feel that the model represented in this brief outline is not merely a theoretical exercise but has important practical implications. Seeing personality disorders as an 'all-or-nothing' diagnosis encourages therapeutic nihilism. Instead, we should bear in mind that, for all of us, 'personality factors' influence everything we think, say and do. For this reason, personality factors can be important in dealing with any patient. At the same time, anyone practising in the mental health field should understand the current system for diagnosing personality disorders and should know what the implications of such diagnoses might be.

Having set out our general view, we would now like to turn to specific discussion of some of the research evidence bearing on the diagnosis and treatment of personality disorders. The subject is a huge one and we will only be able to skim the surface, but we hope to offer some useful guidelines about finding more information.

PERSONALITY DISORDERS: HISTORY AND SPECIFIC DIAGNOSES

Writers and thinkers have studied the human personality from as long ago as ancient Greece and today the study of the human personality forms an important part of psychological study (Pervin, 1990). At the same time, systems of psychiatric diagnosis were developed in the nineteenth and twentieth centuries to classify mental illness. Along with acute illness like the psychotic disorders and phobias, certain influential thinkers developed theories about specific maladaptive personality types or patterns, and some of these particular personality patterns were included in the evolving diagnostic systems, the DSM in the United States and the ICD in Europe; examples of this process can be seen in Cleckley's (1941) work on psychopathy or Kernberg's (1975) on Borderline Personality. In both systems, certain syndromes were grouped together as personality disorders. These were often described as associated with particular personality types and as being relatively stable over the lifespan. In ICD they were grouped together in one diagnostic category, while, starting with DSM-III, they were actually placed on a separate diagnostic axis, along with mental handicap. DSM-IV states that this use of a separate axis 'ensures that consideration will be given to the possible presence of Personality Disorders and Mental Retardation that might otherwise be overlooked when attention is directed to the usually more florid Axis I disorders' (APA, 1994, p. 26). In both diagnostic systems, they are described as being enduring and pervasive; this is the general rationale for their being grouped together. At the same time, DSM-IV notes that the fact that they are coded on a separate axis 'should not be taken to imply that their pathogenesis or range of appropriate treatment is fundamentally different from that for the disorders coded on Axis I' (APA, 1994, p. 26). Before we discuss the validity and utility of the current diagnostic system, we first offer a brief summary of the specific personality disorder diagnoses in the DSM-IV and the ICD-10.

The diagnoses in DSM-IV and, to a lesser extent, ICD-10, are polythetic, that is, a list of different diagnostic signs and symptoms is offered, and no one sign or symptom is either necessary or sufficient for a specific diagnosis. This is true of most psychiatric diagnoses and means that two patients with the same diagnosis may exhibit very different sets of behaviours. We offer a brief summary of each of the personality disorder diagnoses, following the order of diagnoses in DSM-IV, which is more commonly used for research. The diagnoses are divided into three clusters, labelled A, B and C. No description of the clusters is offered in DSM-IV, but they are often referred to as the 'Odd' cluster, the 'Impulsive' cluster and the 'Anxious' cluster, respectively.

Cluster A (the Odd cluster) begins with Paranoid Personality Disorder, which is characterised by suspiciousness, distrust of the motives of others, sensitivity to slights and jealousy in close relationships. The diagnosis specifies these suspicions do not occur in the context of a psychotic disorder; ICD-10 contains a similar diagnosis. Schizoid Personality Disorder describes a personality characterised by lack of emotional warmth and relatedness, few close relationships and a lack of pleasure and enjoyment in life; ICD-10 offers a similar diagnosis. Schizotypal Personality Disorder describes a person with many odd ideas and experiences, similar to but less intense than those experienced during psychotic illness, along with social difficulties and a lack of close relationships; ICD-10 offers a similar diagnosis but places it in the same category as the psychotic disorders.

Cluster B (the Impulsive cluster) begins with two disorders that have been the focus of much more research and thinking than most of the other personality disorder diagnoses. Antisocial Personality Disorder has much in common with the idea of psychopathy or sociopathy discussed in the writings of Cleckley (1941) and more recently Hare (1991), although the diagnosis does not correspond exactly to the personality type described in their works (Hare et al., 1991). DSM-IV notes that the diagnosis does not simply suggest criminal activity, carried out for personal benefit, but includes personality features such as impulsivity, irresponsibility and deceitfulness. It is sometimes noted that this diagnosis does not suggest the presence of personal distress; instead, those with this diagnosis are often said to cause distress to others; ICD-10 contains a similar diagnostic category, Dissocial Personality Disorder. The diagnosis of Borderline Personality Disorder was promoted in the works of Kernberg (1975) and Gunderson (2001), but patients with this diagnosis, or some aspects of it, are often seen in community mental health services. They are often described as lacking a firm sense of personal identity, being the victims of rapidly changing moods and impulsive actions and having unstable personal relationships. Patients who come into hospital following repeated suicide attempts or episodes of self-harm are often given this diagnosis; ICD-10 contains a similar diagnosis, Emotionally Unstable Personality Disorder, which has two subtypes: Impulsive type and Borderline type, the first being mainly characterised by lack of impulse control and the second being very similar to Borderine Personality Disorder. Patients with Histrionic Personality Disorder are described as emotionally shallow, loving attention and prone to manipulate and be sexually provocative with others; a similar diagnostic category appears in ICD-10. Finally, Narcissistic Personality Disorder probably owes its inclusion in DSM to the works of Kernberg (1975). Patients with this diagnosis are said to have an inflated, grandiose sense of their own self-esteem and self-importance, to have a great feeling of personal entitlement and to be exploitative; ICD-10 does not contain a similar diagnosis.

Cluster C (the Anxious cluster) begins with Avoidant Personality Disorder. Sufferers are characterised as avoiding a wide variety of stressors, predominantly of a social nature and including groups, friendships and intimate relationships; ICD-10 contains a similar diagnosis: Anxious (Avoidant) Personality Disorder. Sufferers from Dependant Personality Disorder are also described as avoiding stress, but in this disorder sufferers tend to rely to excess on a few trusted others, such as family, partners or close friends, and to avoid situations in which they will not be able to do this; a similar diagnosis with the same name appears in ICD-10. Finally, Obsessive-Compulsive Personality Disorder is characterised by inflexibility; excessive concentration on routines, structures and details; inability to be spontaneous; excessive thrift; stubbornness and a tendency to hoard worthless items. It is said to be often associated with obsessive-compulsive disorder; ICD-10 contains a similar diagnosis, referred to as Anankastic Personality Disorder.

It is worth mentioning, at this point, that the UK health service has recently been drawn by a government initiative into developing treatments for a group of people termed those with 'Dangerous and Severe Personality Disorder (DSPD)'. The Department of Health and Home Office are currently developing services to deal with such people. Below, we will comment on some problems in the use of such a concept. Here we would merely point out that, as those involved in this initiative themselves admit, DSPD is not diagnosis and does not correspond to any of the diagnostic categories discussed above. There is no evidence that most sufferers with either DSM-IV or ICD-10 personality disorder diagnoses are especially dangerous or in need of confinement. Even in the case of either Antisocial or Dissocial Personality Disorder, only a small subset of especially violent or dangerous people would fall into the DSPD category. This distinction is important to make because of the stigma often attached to the label of personality disorder (Lewis and Appleby, 1988).

METHODOLOGICAL ISSUES

As noted above, we have a number of methodological concerns about the current system of diagnosing personality disorders. We do not claim to be experts in this area or to have mastered all of the current research literature. Methodological questions continue to be raised about the most seemingly well established of diagnoses, such as schizophrenia. However, the research we have done for this chapter reinforces our belief that the current system of diagnosis is seriously flawed.

One striking area of difficulty is the high level of diagnostic overlap; that is, it is fairly common for patients to be diagnosed with several supposedly different personality disorders at the same time (Oldham et al., 1992). Many authors have suggested that this high level of overlap does not represent true co-morbidity (i.e. the co-occurrence of two disorders with independent causal mechanisms), but is instead due to overlap among diagnoses (Blais and Norman, 1997; Clark et al., 1997). Particular examples of this overlap result in difficulties in distinguishing Narcissistic and Histrionic Personality Disorders, as well as Avoidant and Dependent Personality Disorders (Blais and Norman, 1997). There are also a number of examples of diagnostic overlap between axis I and axis II disorders. One example is presented by the strikingly high co-occurrence of Antisocial Personality Disorder and substance abuse disorders (Widiger and Shea, 1991). High levels of substance abuse could be seen as an example of antisocial behaviour but, by the same token, heavy substance users are often impulsive, lacking in empathy and prone to commit crimes to obtain the money needed to obtain drugs or alcohol. An even more striking example is provided by social phobia and Avoidant Personality Disorder (Widiger, 1992; Reich, 2000). Both are described in DSM-IV as characterised by fear and avoidance of social and interpersonal situations. In fact, DSM-IV comments on the two diagnoses that, 'they may be alternative conceptualizations of the same or similar conditions' (APA, 1994, pp. 663–664). Some of the references cited above refer to earlier versions of DSM, but even in DSM-IV considerable diagnostic overlap remains.

A second issue involves the decision to group the personality disorders together, as the ICD system does, and even more so to place them on a separate axis, as in DSM. The presentation of many groups of disorders is similar; most anxiety disorders contain a strong element of fear, psychotic disorders include classes of abnormal experiences and substance-abuse disorders involve the taking in of various substances. The personality disorders constitute a heterogeneous group, including disorders that resemble diagnoses in other categories. The main argument for their being grouped together is that they are long-standing and pervasive. Yet we can point to many other diagnoses, such as schizophrenia or agoraphobia, that often last for many years and pervasively affect all areas of the sufferer's life. Shea and Yen (2003) note that the stability criterion is not a particular feature of personality disorders, with anxiety disorders, for example, being more stable. We also note disorders like Dysthymic Disorder, which is characterised by a long duration yet classified as a mood disorder, as well as the classification of schizotypal disorder as a psychotic disorder in ICD-10. The case seems strong to us that the placing of personality disorders on a separate axis, as Livesley says, was based '. . . on practical and conventional considerations rather than solid empirical or theoretical grounds . . .' (2001, p. 29).

Many authors have commented on these various problems and suggested that the most sensible solution would be to replace the current diagnostic system with dimensional ratings based on the basic dimensions of personality (Widiger and Sanderson, 1995; Cloninger, 2000; Livesley, 2001). This approach is based on the idea that normal personality has a number of dimensions, and that individuals who are unusually high or low on specific dimensions could have difficulties in dealing with normal social and interpersonal situations. Indeed, there is no evidence of natural 'points of rarity' in personality disorder diagnoses, that is, points that offer natural divisions between health and illness (Livesley et al., 1992). Examples of specific proposals to define personality disorder dimensionally are offered by Eysenck (1987), Cloninger (2000), and Costa and Widiger (1994), among others. This sort of approach seems eminently sensible to us, as it is in keeping with the model of human behaviour as lying on a continuum that has proved productive in so many areas of psychological thinking. If further research into the basis of personality could generate a reliable and easily measured set of personality traits applicable to everyone, then some day all patients could be rated on these basic dimensions, which could no doubt prove to be a very useful form of assessment. In the meantime, it has already been suggested that DSM-V should replace the current categorical system of diagnosis for personality disorder with a set of dimensions (Kendall, 2002), and ICD-11 may also be moving in this direction.

We feel we should also offer a brief comment on the concept of Dangerous and Severe Personality Disorder, mentioned above. Although those developing the DSPD programmes deny that the term is in fact a diagnosis, the use of the term 'disorder' would seem to imply that it is a condition or state that mental health professionals would be best equipped to identify. The category is meant to refer to those people who present with an especially high risk of repeated violence or sexual assault. Unfortunately, our current assessment tools can only identify such people at a level of better than chance with a considerable level of error (Dolan and Doyle, 2000). For example, Buchanan and Leese (2001) reviewed 21 studies of the use of clinical insight and statistical techniques to predict violent acts. Based on the sensitivity and specificity of the measures used, they calculated that six people would have to be detained for one violent act to be prevented. If such people are to be detained in hospital, an ethical issue also arises: involuntary detention has traditionally been justified as needed for the welfare of the patient, whereas detention in such cases would offer no benefit to the patient but is instead intended to protect society (Moran, 2002). We accept that some people may need to be detained to protect the public, and it is possible that mental health professionals may play some role in this, but this must be seen as something entirely separate from the normal health service task of assessment and treatment.

As noted above, we have offered only the briefest summary of the current methodological research and discussion going on with regards to personality disorder. We have also not alluded to some authors who have provided thoughtful and spirited defences of current diagnostic practices (e.g. Arntz, 1999). What we do feel very strongly is that the evidence discussed above undermines the case for treating those with a personality disorder diagnosis as somehow different from those diagnosed with other disorders. Our utopian view is that the separate category of 'personality disorder' should be abolished, and that those disorders that have proved their practical diagnostic usefulness should be grouped with related disorders (e.g. Schizotypal Personality Disorder with the psychotic disorders; Personality Disorder with Obsessive-Compulsive Disorder, etc.). In the mean time, clinicians should not view the diagnoses of a personality disorder as in any way different from any other diagnosis; our obligation as psychologists remains to assess, formulate and offer treatment as appropriate.

EPIDEMIOLOGY AND LIFE COURSE

De Girolamo and Reich (1993), Mattia and Zimmerman (2001) and Lyons and Jerskey (2002) all offer reviews of epidemiological studies of the personality disorders, although in all cases the reviews focus on DSM-III and DSM-III-R criteria, as studies using DSM-IV were not available to the authors, except for one study cited by Lyons and Jerskey (2002). The findings in different studies vary widely but all these reviews suggest that an overall rate of somewhere between 10% and 15% of the general public can be diagnosed as suffering from personality disorder, with much higher rates in medical, mental health and forensic settings. One more recent study, employing DSM-IV criteria, found an overall rate of 9% (Samuels et al., 2002). Those who are diagnosed with one disorder are often also diagnosed with two or three others; as noted above, the rate of co-morbidity (or diagnostic overlap) is high. The authors also point out the difficulties in such research: self-report measures may be inaccurate because of subjects concealing problems; the responses of informants may differ form those of subjects and different instruments may disagree (Perry, 1992). The unmarried and divorced seem to have higher rates of personality disorder diagnosis than those who are married, and there is some suggestion that a lower level of education may be correlated with such diagnoses (Torgersen et al., 2001). Of course, the cause and effect relationships can go both ways, as those with problems may find it harder to succeed in education and relationships, while supportive relationships and better opportunities also help people to cope better.

Personality disorders are thought to be stable over the life span, but some studies suggest that this is not always the case. At least some cases of both Antisocial and Borderline Personality Disorder get better with age, so that some subjects are no longer diagnosable after the passing of perhaps 10 to 20 years (Stone, 2001; Seivewright et al., 2002). Other recent studies also show decrease in the number of diagnosable cases as age increases (e.g. Kenen et al., 2000). One factor that may account for the improved functioning of some subjects is the fact that impulsivity, which seems to be an important trait in Cluster B disorders, tends to decrease with age (Stevenson et al., 2003). As clients with Borderline and Antisocial Personality diagnoses often come to the attention of the services, and are also often seen as presenting special difficulties, these findings are worth noting for the encouragement that they provide.

AETIOLOGY

If personality disorders are related to personality in general, then one would expect a biopsychosocial model to explain them; our personalities are generally thought to be formed by the interaction of genetic make-up, early experience and environmental factors. Paris (1996) offers a persuasive exposition of how such a model might be applied. The evidence suggests that genetic factors play a role, but it also seems clear that there are no specific genetic phenotypes underlying the specific disorders (McGuffin and Tharpar, 1992; Nigg and Goldsmith, 1994). Childhood attachment problems (Bartholomew et al., 2001) and adverse life events (Paris, 2001) probably also play a key causal role. Borderline Personality Disorder is one of the most studied of the personality disorders and adverse childhood events, including child sexual abuse, have often been held to play a causal role (Paris, 2001). It is also worth noting that some recent research suggests that early adverse events can produce permanent changes in physiological functioning (Heim and Nemeroff, 2001); this suggests one mechanism by which such events could alter personality functioning. However, many people suffer such abuse while not going on to develop Borderline Personality Disorder. In particular, early sexual abuse is '. . . neither necessary nor sufficient . . .' for the development of Borderline Disorder (Zanarini et al., 1997, p. 1101); some underlying biological vulnerability is probably also necessary. In addition, adverse life events often cluster together; a child who loses her father may also suffer poverty, neglect due to maternal depression, and sexual abuse by a step-parent or carer, creating a complex causal web. It is certainly our clinical experience that some patients seem to suffer a 'cascade' (Paris, 2001, p. 233) of negative life experiences, produced by a combination of poor circumstances, bad luck and poor coping skills. It is also worth noting that protective factors, such as intelligence, special abilities and personal attractiveness may help to mitigate adverse events (Stone, 2001; Helgeland and Torgersen,

2004). In addition, it has been suggested that social instability and the break-down of the family may also impact negatively on children with vulnerability factors, and so increase the likelihood of personality disorder diagnoses. We are clearly very far from understanding all the factors and interactions that contribute to creating either adaptive or a maladaptive personality traits.

FORMAL ASSESSMENT

A variety of tools now exists to formally assess personality disorders. These include structured interviews (First et al., 1997; Loranger, 1999), self-report instruments (Millon et al., 1994) and assessments that combine self-report with a separate instrument designed for use by an informant (Hyler, 1994). Some instruments are designed to diagnose the full spectrum of personality disorder diagnoses, whereas other instruments may focus on one particular trait, such as psychopathy (Hare, 1991) or Borderline pathology (Zanarini et al., 1989).

For those interested in research into personality disorders, there are comprehensive reviews of the available instruments (Kaye and Shea, 2000; Clark and Harrison, 2001). However, there are problems with both the convergent and discriminant validity of these instruments (Clark et al., 1997). In particular, there is a relatively low level of agreement between different instruments, so that findings based on one research instrument many well not apply to subjects who have been assessed with a different one. Some trait-based instruments may identify individuals held to be high in a certain personality trait, but who will not necessarily correspond to a particular diagnostic group. For example, Hare's Psychopathy Checklist (1991) is held to identify those who fit with Hare's model of psychopathic personality; such people have a high likelihood of re-offending, but many of those diagnosed with Antisocial Personality Disorder will not fulfil Hare's criteria for psychopathic personality (Hare et al., 1991). Other factors may also confuse the issue. For example, people diagnosed with personality disorders may present to services with another diagnosis, such as depression, and this may well affect the assessment of personality factors (Zimmerman, 1994). There may also be disagreements between assessments based on self-report and on the reports of informants, in that patients may have poor insight or may over- or under-emphasise, while informants might also confuse judgements of personality with the effects of acute illness (Zimmerman, 1994). As Clark and Harrison (2001) point out, problems with reliable and valid assessment may also reflect conceptual problems with diagnostic categories. It is also important to remember, as Zimmerman (1994) points out, that personality can change: perhaps a long-standing depressive illness might respond to treatment or remit, or perhaps a person might mature and modify his or her way of functioning. In sum, there are a number of ongoing problems and dilemmas in this area of research.

In general, research based on formal diagnosis is not directly relevant to the more clinically relevant area of assessment for treatment. There is one exception to this, and that is the field of forensic psychology and psychiatry. Here, various instruments, such as the Psychopathy Checklist – Revised (Hare, 1991), which we mentioned above, are used to help in the prediction of future offending. Some instruments, such as the Minnesota Multiphasic Personality Inventory (Hathaway and McKinley, 1989), are popular because they employ extra scales designed to detect deliberate deception in responding. Obviously, forensic assessment is a specialised field, and practitioners need to use all possible tools to increase the utility of their predictions. However, as we noted above, there are still considerable limits on the ability of any assessment instrument to predict who will re-offend and who will not. No instrument can be a substitute for clinical judgement, and all clinical judgements must be made in the light of the uncertainty that is inherent in any attempt to predict human behaviour.

As noted above, we have cited a number of useful summaries of assessment instruments in the Personality Disorder field. In Table 21.1, we offer some comments on a few selected instruments.

ASSESSMENT FOR TREATMENT

As noted above, the idea that 'personality disorder can't be treated' has a long history, and one that has provoked the recent Department of Health document entitled, *Personality Disorder: No Longer a Diagnosis of Exclusion* (National Institute for Mental Health in England (NIMHE), 2003). In fact, a key point that any assessment should address is, 'Is this particular patient amenable to treatment?' This question is relevant to all patients. However, although psychiatric and psychological treatments of depression and the anxiety disorders are well established, this does not mean that every patient with one of these disorders will be amenable to treatment. Tyrer et al. (2003) offer an interesting distinction between personality disorder patients who are 'type R', that is, rejecting of treatment, and those who are 'type S', that is, treatment seeking. They demonstrate that interviewing patient and informants can often provide a reasonable assessment of which group any patient falls into. In our experience, the CBT approach of initially offering a full assessment, perhaps four to six sessions, followed by a treatment contract, then reassessing and repeating the process, often offers a very fruitful way to distinguish those patients who are committed to treatment. If patients fail to attend or exhibit 'therapy interfering behaviours' (Allen, 1997), these issues can become the target of treatment. This method cannot resolve all dilemmas; in particular, it is important that the therapist also feels able to

Table 21.1 Measures of personality

Tool	Reference	Response format	Number of items	Subscales	Comments
Minnesota Multiphasic Personality Inventory (MMPI–2)	Hathaway and McKinley (1989)	True/False	542	Several reliability subscales; hypochondriasis; depression; conversion hysteria; psychopathic deviance; masculinity–femininity; paranoia; psychasthenia (neurosis); schizophrenia; hypomania; social introversion	One of the most well researched, recognised and used measures of personality. Common in forensic assessments of personality
Millon Clinical Multiaxial Inventory (MCMI-III)	Millon et al. (1994)	True/False	175	Several reliability subscales; schizoid; avoidant; dependent; histrionic; narcissistic; antisocial; aggressive/sadistic; compulsive; passive-aggressive; self-defeating; schizotypal; borderline; paranoid; anxiety; somatoform; bipolar–manic; dysthymia; alcohol dependence; drug dependence; thought disorder; major depression; delusional disorder	Well recognised measure conceptualised within a robust model, which fits with the DSM-IV diagnostic classification system for personality disorders

Personality Assessment Inventory (PAI)	Morey (1991)	4-point scale (false – very true)	344	Several reliability scales. *Clinical scales:* somatic complaints; anxiety; anxiety-related disorders; depression; mania; paranoia; schizophrenia; borderline features; anti-social features; alcohol problems; drug problems. *Treatment Scales:* aggression; suicide; stress; non-support; treatment. *Interpersonal Scales:* dominance; warmth	A measure of moderate length, with the advantages of reliability, clinical and therapy-relevant scales
Eysenck Personality Questionnaire – Revised (EPQ-R)	Eysenck and Eysenck (1991)	Yes/No	106	Psychoticism (toughmindedness); extraversion–introversion; neuroticism; lie scale (social desirability); addictions scale; criminality scale.	This measure has a strong theoretical and research basis. Psychoticism remains a good predictor of treatment outcome and criminality
Psychopathy Checklist Revised (PCL-R)	Hare et al. (1991)	3-point scale (0, 1, 2)	20	*Interpersonal Scale:* glibness/superficial charm; grandiosity; pathological lying; conning/manipulative; lack of remorse/guilt; shallow affect; callousness; failure to accept responsibility. *Behavioural Scale:* need for stimulation; parasitic lifestyle; poor behavioural controls; early behavioural problems; lack of long-term goals;	This is a highly specialised measure used in forensic assessments and should only be used on individuals with criminal convictions, it may be even less reliable outside this group, e.g. with mentally disordered offenders. The PCL-R is clinician administered using an interview, casenotes review and collateral information

Table 21.1 Continued

Tool	Reference	Response format	Number of items	Subscales	Comments
				impulsivity; irresponsibility; juvenile delinquency; revocation of licence. In addition: promiscuity; many short marital relationships; criminal versatility	
Schema Questionnaire	Young et al. (2003)	6-point Likert scale (completely untrue – perfectly true)	232 (short version also available)	No validity scales; emotional deprivation; abandonment; mistrust/abuse; social isolation; defectiveness; failure; dependence; vulnerability; enmeshment; subjugation; self-sacrifice; emotional inhibition; unrelenting standards; entitlement; insufficient self-control; approval seeking; negativity/pessimism; punitiveness.	This is a theoretically grounded questionnaire which works in conjunction with Schema Focussed Therapy for Personality Disorders using Young's model. A useful clinical tool in therapy both for assessment and monitoring purposes

Possible methods of assessing personality include: interview, self-report inventories, case-note assessment, third-party interview (e.g. relatives), semi-structured interview, observation and monitoring (e.g. by in-patient staff), neuropsychological testing and projective testing.

'commit' to treatment and strive to balance the needs of the patient with the capacity of the service. At the end of this chapter we offer some further comments on the issue of deciding whether or not to treat a challenging patient.

A further point concerns the diagnosis of the disorder being treated. Many so-called 'personality disordered' patients present with another diagnosis, such as depression or an anxiety disorder. A number of reviews and empirical studies have considered whether or not the presence of a personality disorder affects the success rate of psychological treatments for so-called axis I disorders. The results are mixed. Some authors (e.g. Dreessen and Arntz, 1998) suggest that axis II diagnoses have no effect on treatment success, whereas others (e.g. Reich, 2003) find that those with an axis II diagnosis have a somewhat lower success rate in treatment. But both these sets of findings suggest that axis I disorders can be treated in these circumstances; the presence of an axis II diagnosis clearly does not rule out treatment of a willing patient. A separate issue concerns the treatment of so-called personality disorders themselves. Chapter 22 reviews some of the literature on such treatments: suffice it to say here that evidence is beginning to accumulate that, again, some patients – and especially those who are motivated to engage in treatment – can certainly be helped to reduce their levels of distress and improve their long-term functioning.

Psychological approaches to treatment have also generated their own models of assessment; such assessments often form a productive opening phase to treatment. A key idea often seen in such assessments is that of 'schema', which is seen, especially in the CBT framework, as representing a long-term model of the self, rooted in childhood experiences and, in the case of those with personality problems, generating unhelpful and inflexible rules of thought and behaviour. Young (1994) was a pioneer in the CBT field and, more recently, Beck – the founder of cognitive therapy – has collaborated with others to develop treatment approaches to a variety of personality disorders (Beck et al., 1990). The schema model can be helpful in that the patient does not have to accept the label of personality disorder; if he or she finds a particular schema-based model helpful and relevant, it can well provide a basis for collaborative treatment. Instead of a focus on diagnosis, assessment can concentrate on describing particular patterns of thinking and behaviour that can then be addressed in treatment (Beck et al., 2003). This is not to imply that CBT is uniquely suited to the treatment of personality disorders: dialectical behavior therapy, cognitive analytic therapy and psychodynamic therapy have now all developed treatment approaches for the same sorts of problems. In all cases they offer the same advantage: instead of a stigmatising diagnosis they offer a model of the patient's difficulties and a treatment approach suited to that model.

CONCLUSIONS

Throughout this chapter, we have offered sceptical comments about the use of the term 'personality disorder' and about the specific diagnostic categories embraced by that term. This is not to say that we do not believe that such patients exist, that they do not seek or require help or that they are not often very difficult to treat. A pragmatic or operational definition of the 'personality disordered' patient is often of a person with many difficulties and few coping skills, one who has suffered from a variety of adverse life events and who may also have some rather rigid or maladaptive personality traits. We would like to stress that treatment decisions in such cases have to be taken in context. The working psychologist must first consider the needs and constraints of the setting in which he or she is working. Many professionals are expected to see a large number of patients and offer a relatively limited number of sessions; in such cases, one might well refer such a patient elsewhere or try to find a small but achievable goal to treatment. Equally, some patients, in particular those who engage in suicidal or self-harming behaviours and who have had multiple hospitalisations, can place a great strain on a whole service. In such a case, a therapist who can successfully engage with such patients and help them to manage their behaviour might provide a very great benefit; in such cases, long-term treatment might well seem a good and cost-effective option. Such factors must be weighed up when taking any referral for someone likely to challenge the capacity of services to offer helpful treatment, and obviously all treatment decisions need to be taken with input from other members of the clinical team.

Another point is equally important. To work with challenging clients, a therapist must have good supervision, a supportive work environment, and good liaison with other relevant professionals. Also, in our experience, such work can be personally stressful. Each worker should assess his or her own personal resources to cope with such behaviours as threats of suicide or self-harm and with possible histories of shocking and emotionally taxing misfortune and abuse. Each professional has the right to set limits on what he or she is willing to undertake; as Krawitz and Watson (2003) point out, limit-setting may be part of treatment but it is also a valid way for the therapist to protect his or her own quality of working life.

Having considered these issues, we urge therapeutic workers to be open to the idea of working with the so-called personality disorders. They are a highly varied group of people, too varied to be described by one category or set of categories. In our experience, such work can be taxing and frustrating. However, with realistic goals and appropriate support, it can also be very helpful to patients and rewarding to workers.

REFERENCES

Allen, D. M. (1997) Techniques for reducing therapy-interfering behavior in patients with Borderline Personality Disorder: similarities in four diverse treatment paradigms. *Journal of Psychotherapy Practice and Research*, 6, 25–35.

American Psychiatric Association (APA) (1994) *Diagnostic and Statistical Manual of Mental Disorders, 4th edn.* Washington, DC: APA.

Arntz, A. (1999) Do personality disorders exist? On the validity of the concept and its cognitive-behavioral formulation and treatment. *Behaviour Research and Therapy*, 37, S97–S134.

Bartholomew, K., Kwong, M. J. and Hart, S. D. (2001) Attachment. In: W. J. Livesley (ed) *Handbook of Personality Disorders: Theory, Research and Treatment*. London: Guildford Press.

Beck, A. T., Freeman, A. and associates (1990) *Cognitive Therapy of Personality Disorders*. New York: Guilford Press.

Beck, A. T., Butler, A. C., Brown, G. K., Dahlsgaard, K. K., Newman, C. F. and Beck, J. S. (2001) Dysfunctional beliefs discriminate personality disorders. *Behaviour Research and Therapy*, 39, 1213–1225.

Blais, M. A. and Norman, D. K. (1997) A psychometric evaluation of the DSM-IV Personality Disorder criteria. *Journal of Personality Disorders*, 11, 168–176.

Buchanan, A. and Leese, M. (2001) Detention of people with dangerous severe personality disorders: A systematic review. *Lancet*, 358, 1955–1959.

Clark, L. A. and Harrison, J. A. (2001) Assessment Instruments. In: W. J. Livesley (ed) *Handbook of Personality Disorders: Theory, Research and Treatment*. London: Guildford Press.

Clark, L. A., Livesley, W. J. and Morey, L. (1997) Personality disorder assessment: The challenge of construct validity. *Journal of Personality Disorders*, 11, 205–231.

Cleckley, H. (1941). *The Mask of Sanity*. St Louis: Mosby.

Cloninger, C. R. (2000) A practical way to diagnose personality disorder: A proposal. *Journal of Personality Disorders*, 14, 99–108.

Costa, P. T. and Widiger, T. A. (1994) *Personality Disorders and the Five Factor Model of Personality*. Washington, DC: American Psychiatric Association.

De Girolamo, G. and Reich, J. H. (1993) *Personality Disorders*. Geneva: World Health Organization.

Dolan, M. and Doyle, M. (2000) Violence risk prediction: Clinical and actuarial measures and the role of the Psychopathy Checklist. *British Journal of Psychiatry*, 177, 303–311.

Dreessen, L. and Arntz, A. (1998) The impact of personality disorders on treatment outcome of anxiety disorders: Best-evidence synthesis. *Behaviour Research and Therapy*, 36, 483–504.

Eysenck, H. J. (1987). The definition of personality disorders and the criteria appropriate to their definition. *Journal of Personality Disorders*, 1, 211–219.

Eysenck, H. J. and Eysenck, S. B. G. (1991) *Manual of the Eysenck Personality Scales (EPQ Adult)*. London: Hodder and Stoughton.

First, M., Gibbon, M., Spitzer, R. L., Williams, J. B. W. and Benjamin, L. S. (1997) *User's Guide for the Structured Clinical Interview for the DSM-IV Axis II Personality Disorders*. Washington, DC: American Psychiatric Association.

Gunderson, G. (2001). *Borderline Personality Disorder: A Clinical Guide*. Washington, DC: American Psychiatric Association.

Hare, R. D. (1991) *The Hare Psychopathy Checklist – Revised Manual*. New York: John Wiley.

Hare, R. D., Hart, S. D. and Harpur, T. J. (1991) Psychopathy and the DSM-IV criteria for Antisocial Personality Disorder. *Journal of Abnormal Psychology*, 100, 391–398.

Hathaway, S. R. and McKinley, J. C. (1989) *Minnesota Multiphasic Personality Inventory–2: Manual for Administration and Scoring*. Minneapolis, MN: University of Minnesota Press.

Heim, C. and Nemeroff, C. B. (2001) The role of childhood trauma in the neuro-biology of mood and anxiety disorders: Preclinical and clinical studies. *Biological Psychiatry*, 49, 1023–1039.

Helgeland, M. I. and Torgersen, S. (2004) Developmental antecedents of borderline personality disorder. *Comprehensive Psychiatry*, 45, 138–147.

Hyler, S. (1994) *Personality Diagnostic Questionnaire-IV (PDQ-IV)*. New York: New York State Psychiatric Institute.

Kaye, A. L. and Shea, T. M. (2000) Personality disorders, personality traits and defence mechanisms. In: A. J. Rush, H. A. Pincus and M. B. First (eds) *Handbook of Psychiatric Measures*. Washington, DC: American Psychiatric Association.

Kenan, M. M., Kendjelic, E. M., Molinari, V. A., Williams, W., Norris, M., and Kunik, M. E. (2000) Age-related differences in the frequency of personality disorders among inpatient veterans. *International Journal of Geriatric Psychiatry*, 15, 831–837.

Kendell, R. E. (2002) Author's reply. *British Journal of Psychiatry*, 181, 77–78.

Kernberg, O. F. (1975) *Borderline Conditions and Pathological Narcissism*. New York: Jason Aronson.

Krawitz, R. and Watson, G. (2003) *Borderline Personality Disorder: A Practical Guide to Treatment*. Oxford: Oxford University Press.

Lewis, G. and Appleby, L. (1988) Personality disorder: the patients psychiatrists dislike. *British Journal of Psychiatry*, 153, 44–49.

Livesley, W. J. (2001) Conceptual and taxonomic issues. In: W. J. Livesley (ed) *Handbook of Personality Disorders: Theory, Research and Treatment*. London: Guildford Press.

Livesley, W. J., Jackson, D. N. and Schroeder, M. L. (1992) Factorial structure of traits delineating personality disorders in clinical and general population samples. *Journal of Abnormal Psychology*, 101, 432–440.

Loranger, A. W. (1999) *International Personality Disorder Examination Manual: DSM-IV Module*. Washington, DC: American Psychiatric Association.

Lyons, M. J. and Jerskey, B. A. (2002) Personality disorders: Epidemiological findings, methods, and concepts. In: M. T. Tsuang and M. Tohen (eds) *Textbook in Psychiatric Epidemiology*. Chichester: John Wiley.

Mattia, J. I. and Zimmerman, M. (2001) Epidemiology. In: W. J. Livesley (ed) *Handbook of Personality Disorders: Theory, Research and Treatment*. London: Guildford Press.

McGuffin, P. and Tharpar, A. (1992) The genetics of personality disorder. *British Journal of Psychiatry*, 160, 12–23.

Millon, T., Davis, R. and Millon, C. (1994) *Manual for the Millon Clinical Multiaxial Inventory – III (MCMI-III)*. Minneapolis MN: National Computer Systems.

Moran, P. (2002) Dangerous severe personality disorder – bad tidings from the UK. *International Journal of Social Psychiatry*, 48, 6–10.

Morey, L. C. (1991) *Personality Assessment Inventory: Professional Manual.* Florida: Psychological Assessment Resources, Inc.

National Institute for Mental Health in England (NIMHE) (2003) *Personality Disorder: No Longer a Diagnosis of Exclusion.* London: Department of Health.

Nigg, J. T. and Goldsmith, H. H. (1994) Genetics of personality disorders: perspectives from personality and psychopathology research. *Psychological Bulletin*, 115, 346–380.

Oldham, J. M., Skodol, A. E., Kellman, H. D., Hyler, S. E., Rosnick, L. and Davies, M. (1992) Diagnosis of DSM-III-R personality disorders by two structured interviews: Patterns of comorbidity. *American Journal of Psychiatry*, 149, 213–220.

Paris, J. (1996) *Social Factors in Personality Disorder.* Cambridge: Cambridge University Press.

Paris, J. (2001) Psychosocial adversity. In: W. J. Livesley (ed) *Handbook of Personality Disorders: Theory, Research and Treatment.* London: Guildford Press.

Perry, J. C. (1992) Problems and considerations in the valid assessment of personality disorders. *American Journal of Psychiatry*, 149, 1645–1653.

Pervin, L. A. (1990) *Handbook of Personality: Theory and Research.* New York: Guilford Press.

Reich, J. (2000) The relationship of social phobia to avoidant personality disorder: A proposal to reclassify avoidant personality disorder based on clinical empirical findings. *European Psychiatry*, 15, 151–159.

Reich, J. (2003) The effect of Axis II disorders on the outcome of treatment of anxiety and unipolar depressive disorders: A review. *Journal of Personality Disorders*, 17, 387–405.

Samuels, J., Eaton, W. W., Bienvenu, O. J., Brown, C., Costa, P. T. and Nestadt, G. (2002). Prevalence and correlates of personality disorders in a community sample. *British Journal of Psychiatry*, 180, 536–542.

Seivewright, H., Tyrer, P. and Johnson, T. (2002) Change in personality status in neurotic disorders. *Lancet*, 359, 2253–2254.

Shea, M. T. and Yen, S. (2003) Stability as a distinction between Axis I and Axis II disorders. *Journal of Personality Disorders*, 17, 373–386.

Stevenson, J., Meares, R. and Comerford, A. (2003) Diminished impulsivity in older patients with borderline personality disorder. *American Journal of Psychiatry*, 160, 165–166.

Stone, M. H. (2001) Natural history and long-term outcome. In: J. W. Livesley (ed) *Handbook of Personality Disorders: Theory, Research, and Treatment.* New York: Guilford Press.

Torgersen, S., Kringlen, E. and Cramer, V. (2001) The prevalence of personality disorders in a community sample. *Archives of General Psychiatry*, 58, 590–596.

Tyrer, P., Mitchard, S., Methuen, C. and Ranger, M. (2003) Treatment rejecting and treatment seeking personality disorders: type R and type S. *Journal of Personality Disorders*, 17, 263–268.

Widiger, T. A. (1992). Generalized social phobia versus avoidant personality disorder: A commentary on three studies. *Journal of Abnormal Psychology*, 101, 340–343.

Widiger, T. A. and Sanderson, C. J. (1995) Toward a dimensional model of personality disorders. In: W. J. Livesley (ed) *The DSM-IV Personality Disorders: Diagnosis and Treatment of Mental Disorders*. New York: Guilford Press.

Widiger, T. A. and Shea, T. (1991) Differentiation of Axis I and Axis II disorders. *Journal of Abnormal Psychology*, 100, 399–406.

Wittgenstein, L. (1958) *Philosophical Investigations*. Oxford: Blackwell.

World Health Organization (WHO) (1992) *The ICD-10 Classification of Mental and Behavioural Disorders*. Geneva: WHO.

Young, J. (1994) *Cognitive Therapy for Personality Disorders: A Schema Focussed Approach*. Sarasota, FL: Professional Resources Exchange.

Young, J., Klosko, J. and Weishar, M. E. (2003) *Schema Therapy: A Practitioner's Guide*, London: Guildford Press.

Zanarini, M., Gunderson, J. G., Frankenburg, F. R., and Chauncey, D. L. (1989) The revised diagnostic interview for borderlines: Discriminating borderline personality disorder from other axis II disorders. *Journal of Personality Disorders*, 3, 10–18.

Zanarini, M. C., Williams, A. A., Lewis, R. E., Reich, R. B. et al. (1997) Reported pathological childhood experiences associated with the development of borderline personality disorder. *American Journal of Psychiatry*, 154, 1101–1106.

Zimmerman, M. (1994) Diagnosing personality disorder: A review of issues and research methods. *Archives of General Psychiatry*, 51, 225–245.

Chapter 22

Personality disorder

Treatment

Julian Walker and Peter Hayward

INTRODUCTION

One of the central issues surrounding the relationship between individuals with personality disorders and the mental health services (particularly psychiatric in-patient services) has been the issue of treatability. On the one hand, many clinicians have considered personality disorders to be untreatable, extremely difficult to treat or to involve problems that may consume an unjustifiable amount of health-service resources. On the other hand, such opinions do not stop people with personality disorders, problems or difficulties presenting to services in distress, wanting and needing help.

The term 'treatability' refers to that characteristic of a condition whereby its impact or presence may be reduced through treatment (for a review of 'treatability', see Adshead, 2001). Thus, treatability includes notions of cure – as in giving an antibiotic to 'cure' an infection – and notions of maintenance therapy, such as insulin therapy for diabetes, which does not cure the disorder in the long term but minimises the abnormalities created by the condition with the aim of improving the individual's physiology, functioning and quality of life. The ultimate treatment is prevention, and although something is now known about the aetiology of personality disorders, mental health services are years away from preventative treatments at the present time. The main focus of treatment is on working with the individual to understand or resolve problems, to minimise the negative effects and promote adaptive behaviour and skills.

At the most extreme end of the scale personality disorders are not only seen as untreatable but noxious (causing harm to self and others) and even deleterious to an individual's participation in treatment. For example, some studies show a deterioration following therapy in 'psychopaths' (Rice et al., 1992). It is not surprising that experts in the field have observed that 'psychopathy' is the only psychiatric diagnosis that results in the sufferer receiving less treatment rather than more (Gunn, 1999). The term 'psychopath' has become associated with negative outcomes in terms of risk to self and others, recidivism and treatment (Rice et al., 1992). However, a re-evaluation of treatment studies for even these most extreme individuals has shown less pessimistic results (Salekin, 2002).

Beck and Freeman's (1990) seminal text *Cognitive Therapy of Personality Disorders* has been in publication for over 16 years at the time of writing, has gone into a second edition (Beck, Freeman and Davis, 2003) and recent systematic reviews have shown hundreds of studies of treatment outcome (Home Office, 2003). It can no longer be concluded that the psychological technology for the treatment of personality disorders is unavailable, totally untested or completely ineffective. The current issue concerns the quality of the evidence for the effectiveness of treatments for personality disorder.

Treatability from a medical or psychiatric perspective has been associated with the clause in the United Kingdom's Mental Health Act (DoH, 1983) for those detained under the 'psychopathic disorder' classification that their condition should be treatable (see Davison, 2002). Treatment in this context is defined as an intervention that improves the condition or prevents further deterioration; from a practical point of view, the treatment must also be available at the hospital in which the person is detained. The simple fact is that such resources may vary or may not be available depending on where the person resides (National Institute for Mental Health in England (NIMHE), 2003). The United Kingdom's Department of Health paper *Personality Disorder: No Longer a Diagnosis of Exclusion* (NIMHE, 2003) suggested a broad variation in services, with 17% of NHS Trusts providing a dedicated service, 40% some level of service and 28% providing no identified service for patients with personality disorder (the remainder did not reply). The interpretation of this finding as suggested by the paper was that 'these Trusts do not see the provision of services for personality disorder as their core business' (p. 13). Although some Trusts recognised the inadequate nature of their provision, and the majority wanted to provide specialist services, a small minority of Trusts raised concern at 'medicalising' personality disorder and did not accept the need for providing services. This is important, because it suggests that the 'diagnosis of exclusion' problem referred to in the title of the paper may operate from the macro (Trusts) to the micro (individual professionals) level. Service-user views were enlightening on this point; they felt that the term 'personality disorder' carried greater stigma than any other mental health label, that they were the patients who were most disliked, seen as difficult and manipulative, and blamed for their condition. Patients surveyed also commented on experiences of patronising, belittling and the prejudiced views of staff; patients wanted choice and non-rejecting treatment (NIMHE, 2003).

A further issue that may increase the exclusion of individuals with personality disorder is the increase in the burden on services that such individuals may incur (Davison, 2002). When the problem is seen as untreatable, resources limited and the work as potentially difficult, distressing or dangerous, then inclusion criteria for the service are perhaps more likely to be structured so as to prevent the service becoming overwhelmed by the perceived demands. Interestingly, the cost benefits of relatively short treatments have been shown to be significant (Evans et al., 1999), as well as for longer treatment – twice weekly therapy for 1 year (Stevenson and Meares, 1999) – or even the most expensive – therapeutic communities (Dolan et al., 1996). All of these studies showed cost savings of thousands of pounds within 1 or 2 years of treatment.

Although the remit of this chapter is psychological approaches, it is important to extend a brief consideration to psychopharmacological approaches, which are likely to be part of any multi-disciplinary team intervention for individuals with personality disorder, either as an in-patient or out-patient. Again, there is relatively little evidence in this field, which is surprising, given that trials of medication are probably easier in some ways to control than therapy studies. Roy and Tyrer (2001) briefly review a number of drug treatments that have been tried for personality disorder, whilst noting that no drug is actually licensed for the treatment of personality disorder. They suggest that antipsychotics, antidepressants (both tricyclic and selective serotonin re-uptake inhibitors; SSRIs), and mood stabilisers (lithium, carbamazipine and sodium valproate) have all been used with various disorders, most notably Borderline Personality Disorder, with varying and equivocal degrees of success. Roy and Tyrer (2001) concluded that existing studies suggested that some 'personality disorders are responsive to drug treatment with SSRIs and sodium valproate' (p. 557) we presume by reducing symptoms without working on core psychological issues.

COMPULSION, COERCION OR COLLABORATION?

Towards the end of the last century and the beginning of the twenty-first century, the UK government made suggestions that individuals labelled as having 'Dangerous and Severe Personality Disorder' (DSPD) should be compelled, while incarcerated, to undertake therapy for their personality disorder and offending (see Feeney, 2003). Results have yet to be seen, but our contention is that any form of therapy requires some motivation and ownership on the part of the individual, hence 'collaboration' with the therapist may be coerced (as in prison settings) but difficult to compel.

The process of compulsory detention for treatment is based on mental illnesses such as psychosis, for which medication can be prescribed and administered involuntarily to a patient whose symptoms are active and who lacks insight. As the beneficial effects of treatment are realised, the treating team rely on the fact that patients will notice this benefit, gain insight, feel better and ultimately consent to treatment and even collaborate in their care. Compulsory psychological treatment is a contradiction in terms because the genuine collaboration of the patient is inherently required for any psychological treatment to work. Engagement, collaboration and thus ultimately treatment effectiveness is likely to be impaired by compulsion as the individual will lack ownership of the process. It is probably no coincidence that some of the most promising outcome studies for the treatment of personality disorder are from the USA, where patients 'opt in' for treatment and pay for their sessions.

OUTCOME: GENERAL ISSUES

For a full review of outcome studies there are several well-researched and well-written texts (Livesley, 2001a; Bateman and Tyrer, 2004) along with a number of commissioned reports (Home Office, 2003; Dolan and Coid, 1993). Suffice to say that good quality, controlled outcome studies are relatively rare. One of the difficulties relates to the uncertain conceptual basis of personality disorder (as discussed Chapter 21) and the broad population subsumed under the category; a second difficulty relates to the reliability of assessment measures and procedures. This is in contrast to other disorders, such as specific phobias, which may comprise a more homogenous and 'measureable' group of individuals. A third issue relates to the nature of personality itself and whether personality is stable, dynamic (or reactive), or both. For an interesting review of this issue, see Duggan (2003), who argues that not only is personality difficult to measure but that change is also difficult to measure and that different outcomes may give conflicting results. The view that personality is stable is clearly evident in the diagnostic and classification systems of personality disorders (DSM-IV (APA, 1994) and ICD-10 (WHO, 1992) (see Chapter 21), where the words 'enduring, pervasive and inflexible' are used), as well as being supported by evidence (Costa and McCrae, 1980; Caspi and Herbener, 1990). However, there is evidence from a small number of long-term follow-up studies of patients with Borderline Personality Disorder that this disorder shows natural partial remission over 10 years or more (McGlashan, 1986; Paris, Brown and Nowlis, 1987; Stone, 1990). This finding does not suggest complete remission, particularly in light of the figure that 10% of these patients committed suicide during the follow-up period.

The idea of personality being relatively stable but open to developmental, maturational and environmental influences provides a common-sense middle ground and is exemplified by Costa and McCrea's (1994) model, which suggests that 'basic tendencies', whilst relatively stable, can be influenced and activated by the environment, perhaps producing different behaviours in different settings. This approach has led to the conclusion that personality traits 'describe average and probable rather than invariant behaviour' (Blackburn, 1989).

The complexity of personality, its development, effects and outcomes, therefore demands a complex approach to both assessment and treatment, the central component of which is formulation. Formulation is a topic in itself and will not be reviewed here, but the authors suggest that personality factors should be understood not only in dimensional terms, but also through formulation. It could be argued that dispositional factors will have a place in any psychological formulation of a problem.

A final general outcome issue, before a consideration of therapeutic approaches to the treatment of personality disorder, is the effect of Axis II disorders on the outcome of Axis I disorders. A limited number of studies are available; however, some suggest that treatment efficacy of an Axis I disorder may be reduced by the presence of an Axis II disorder and some do not (Reich, 2003).

COGNITIVE BEHAVIOUR THERAPY

Cognitive behavioural therapy (CBT), based on Beck's (1976) original model for anxiety and depression, has been extended to personality by the same author (Beck et al., 1990; 2003). The model, based on the ideas of different 'levels' of thought structures and thinking errors with different constellations of these factors corresponding to different disorders, is maintained in the model for personality. Core beliefs, dysfunctional assumptions and coping strategies seem to be emphasised more strongly in the conceptualisation and treatment of Axis II compared to Axis I disorders. Beck et al. (1990) discuss the difference between the schemas relevant to Axis I and Axis II diagnoses (i.e. comparing depression, for example, with personality disorders). They note that:

> The extreme faulty beliefs and interpretations characteristic of the symptomatic disorders are relatively plastic – and, indeed, become more moderate as the depression subsides even without any therapeutic intervention. However, the more persistent dysfunctional beliefs of the personality disorder are 'structuralised'; that is, they are built into the 'normal' cognitive organisation.
>
> (Beck et al. 1990, p 58)

Beck et al. (1990) divide the general principles of cognitive therapy with personality disordered patients into two key areas:

1 *Conceptualisation of the case*, including the identification of schemas and the specification of underlying goals.
2 *Emphasis on the therapist–patient relationship*, including collaboration, guided discovery and the use of 'transference reactions'.

Beck et al. (1990) delineate several specialist techniques for working with personality-disordered patients within the cognitive therapy model, and emphasise flexibility and the 'art of therapy'. They go on to list ten core cognitive techniques, mainly taken from Beck et al. (1979), many of which are recognisable from the more general cognitive therapy literature:

1 guided discovery
2 searches for idiosyncratic meaning
3 labelling of inaccurate inferences and distortions
4 collaborative empiricism
5 examining explanations for other people's behaviour
6 scaling: translating extreme interpretations into dimensional terms to counteract typical dichotomous thinking
7 reattribution
8 deliberate exaggeration
9 examining the advantages and disadvantages of maintaining or changing beliefs or behaviours, and clarifying primary and secondary gains
10 decatastrophising.

They expand on the use of 'cognitive probes', initially to illicit automatic thoughts but also to uncover meaning and ultimately the salient core schemas at the basis of personality problems. Once schemas are uncovered, they are confronted and labelled using non-judgemental descriptions. Schematic re-structuring, modification and re-interpretation are explained as ways to transform or alter a patient's dysfunctional schemas. They warn of the anxiety likely to be aroused when schemas are changed, and suggest that patients should be prepared for this to prevent them relapsing into old dysfunctional ways of thinking. Table 22.1 shows the main core beliefs and personality profile for nine personality disorders (taken from Beck et al., 1990).

Freeman and Jackson (1998) add the following suggested emphases in cognitive therapy for people with personality disorder (p. 320):

- stability of the framework for treatment
- increased activity of the therapist
- the therapist's ability to tolerate negative transference
- establishing a connection between the patient's actions and feelings in the present
- making self-destructive behaviours ungratifying
- blocking acting-out behaviours
- focusing clarifications and interpretations on the here and now
- paying careful attention to counter-transference feelings (feelings in the therapist caused by the patient).

Reviews of this field suggest that very few controlled outcome studies of the effectiveness of cognitive therapy for personality disorders exist (Cottraux and Blackburn, 2001; Bateman and Tyrer, 2004). One controlled study by

Table 22.1 Personality profiles of personality disorders

Personality disorder	View of self	View of others	Main beliefs	Main Strategy
Avoidant	Vulnerable to depreciation, rejection Socially inept Incompetent	Critical Demeaning Superior	It's terrible to be rejected, put down If people *know* the real me, they will reject me Can't tolerate unpleasant feelings	Avoid evaluative situations Avoid unpleasant feelings or thoughts
Dependent	Needy Weak Helpless Incompetent	(Idealised) Nuturant Supportive Competent	Need people to survive, be happy Need for steady flow of support, encouragement	Cultivate dependent relationships
Passive-aggressive	Self-sufficient Vulnerable to control, interference	Intrusive Demanding Interfering Controlling Dominating	Others interfere with my freedom of action Control by other is intolerable Have to do things my own way	Passive resistance Surface submissiveness Evade, circumvent rules
Obsessive-compulsive	Responsible Accountable Fastidious Competent	Irresponsible Casual Incompetent Self-indulgent	I know what's best Details are crucial People *should* do better, try harder Apply rules	Apply rules Perfectionism Evaluate, control 'Shoulds'', criticise, punish
Paranoid	Righteous Innocent, noble Vulnerable	Interfering Malicious Discriminatory Abusive motives	Motives are suspect Be on guard Don't trust	Wary Look for hidden motives Accuse Counterattack

Continued overleaf

Table 22.1 Continued

Personality disorder	View of self	View of others	Main beliefs	Main Strategy
Antisocial	A loner Autonomous Strong	Vulnerable Exploitative	Entitled to *break* rules Others are patsies, wimps Others are exploitative	Attack, rob Deceive, manipulate

Narcissistic	Special, unique
	Deserve special rules,
	  superior
	Above the rules
		Inferior
		Admirers
			Since I'm special, I *deserve* special
			  rules
			I'm above the rules
			I'm better than others
				Use others
				Transient rules
				Manipulative
				Competitive

Histrionic	Glamorous
	Impressive
		Seducible
		Receptive
		Admirers
			People are there to serve or
			  admire me
			They have no right to deny me my
			  just deserts
			I can go by my feeling
				Use dramatics, charm,
				  temper tantrums,
				  crying, suicide gestures

Schizoid	Self-sufficient Loner	Intrusive	Others are unrewarding Relationships are messy, undesirable	Stay away

Source: Beck et al. (1990). Reproduced with permission of Guildford Press.

Woody et al. (1985) compared the treatment of 110 patients with drug addiction (with or with out depression and/or Antisocial Personality Disorder) in three treatment conditions: counselling, counselling plus cognitive therapy and counselling plus psychodynamic psychotherapy. They found that cognitive and psychodynamic therapy showed no difference in outcome, but gave improvements over counselling alone. Antisocial personality alone was a negative predictor of treatment but the presence of depression, a good therapeutic alliance and adherence to the therapeutic model (for cognitive or psychodynamic therapy) were related to better outcomes. A controlled study of 43 patients (with cluster B personality disorders; see Chapter 21) randomly allocated to manual-assisted cognitive therapy or treatment as usual, showed a significant benefit of brief cognitive therapy (six sessions, with elements of dialectical behaviour therapy) in terms of self-reported depressive symptoms and treatment cost, and a small benefit in terms of rate of suicidal acts (Evans et al., 1999). A meta-analysis on a limited number of studies (Leichsenring and Leibing, 2003) suggested large effect sizes, greater than 1.0 for both psychodynamic and cognitive behavioural therapy for personality disorder.

SCHEMA-FOCUSED THERAPY

Schema-focused therapy was developed as the natural next step on from Beck's earlier model of cognitive therapy (Beck et al., 1979) as cognitive therapists found themselves working with ever more complex and resistant problems and with patients described as having personality disorder. Young's (1994) work was based on the constructivist movement (Mahony, 1993), which focuses on the 'constructed' human systems, how they came about and the function they serve in protecting 'internal coherence'. Creative techniques and the use of imagery are common in such approaches, and schema-focused therapy makes use of these techniques with elements of interpersonal, experiential and psychodynamic therapies (Young et al., 2003). The appeal of schema-focused therapy to cognitive therapists is the overlap of nomenclature for mental operations, the emphasis on formulation and collaboration with the patient, and a recognition of the role of maintaining factors and developmental factors in the individual's presenting problems.

The model is a guiding theoretical framework that incorporates the use of the therapy relationship, exploration of childhood and patterns of thought and behaviour. These ideas may be seen as more psychodynamic in orientation, but the techniques use the concept of the schema (a broad and pervasive pattern of thoughts, feelings, emotions and memories regarding oneself and one's relationships) as a unifying element. Core beliefs comprise a central element of schemas, but the other elements are also emphasised. Schema modes represent the schemas, coping responses and reactions that are active at that particular point in time – a state rather than a trait. The theory proposes that each individual has a number of prevailing schema modes that become active in particular (internal and external) situations. People's presenting behaviour therefore represents the prevalent schema mode and the coping style that goes with it, rather than the maladaptive schema that underlies the schema mode.

The goal of therapy is to identify early maladaptive schemas and the schema modes developed from them, evaluate with the patient how these are maintained, avoided or compensated for and then attempt to challenge and change them. Techniques include a strong emphasis on imagery and 'partial reparenting' by the therapist (helping the patient to feel understood, cared about and contained). Particular constellations of maladaptive schemas and schema modes characterise the various personality disorders. Borderline personality disorder and narcissistic personality disorder have received particular emphasis by the originating author (Young and Behary, 1998).

At present, no outcome data are available on studies of schema-focused therapy for personality disorders. The originating author reports promising results among clinicians who have followed this approach to therapy (Young and Behary, 1998).

DIALECTICAL BEHAVIOUR THERAPY

Dialectical behaviour therapy (DBT) is a form of cognitive therapy developed by Linehan (1993) in response to the difficulty of applying the more rational perspective of CBT to personality problems, in particular, Borderline personality disorder characterised by emotional disregulation, interpersonal difficulties, suicidality and a negative, unstable, empty sense of self. DBT uses the principles of a holistic view, polarity and continuous change to explain the way therapist and patient respond to one another in therapy, the therapeutic goal being to bring a sense of balance to the emergent 'dialectics', offer behavioural coping strategies and support to decrease therapy-interfering behaviours and proceed with work on emotions and sense of self.

In practical terms, the therapist develops a validating environment in which the patient is helped to decrease dysfunctional behaviour (in particular, suicidal behaviour). Blaming of the patient is avoided, and patients are encouraged to take the risk of assuming responsibility for some self-efficacy. Any improvement is strongly reinforced by the therapist, and there is a strong emphasis on problem solving and skills training. Therapist characteristics and behaviour are regarded as paramount and, in common with other approaches, there is a nurturing approach to the patient. There is also considerable attention to the therapeutic relationship and an extended length of treatment (1 year) compared with traditional CBT.

Linehan et al. (1991) report one of the only controlled studies of DBT, comparing treatment as usual in the community with supportive or psychodynamic therapy with DBT (a combination of group and individual treatment as described by Linehan, 1993). Forty-four female patients were divided equally between the two groups, with the DBT group showing fewer drop-outs, less parasuicidal behaviour, less drug misuse and less abuse of medication. However, post treatment, the two groups did not differ on depression or other symptoms. Changes in the DBT group at post treatment were maintained 1 year later, and significant improvements in anger, parasuicidal behaviour, social adjustment and in-patient treatment were noted.

PSYCHOANALYSIS AND PSYCHODYNAMIC PSYCHOTHERAPY

The boundaries between psychoanalysis, psychoanalytic psychotherapy, psychodynamic psychotherapy and supportive psychotherapy may seem somewhat blurred to the uninitiated, but it is generally agreed that there are important differences in terms of frequency and length of therapy, and also in terms of the technical approach. At one extreme, psychoanalysis usually occurs four or five times a week, with the patient on the couch, and lasts for several years using a neutral and 'opaque' therapeutic stance. At the other end of the spectrum, psychotherapy is likely to be face to face, once a week, for up to 1 year and may be more supportive in style. Many psychoanalysts and psychotherapists would regard themselves as working almost exclusively with issues of personality and relatedness, particularly given the relative prevalence of referrals and the amenability of neurotic and psychotic disorders to psychopharmacological treatments and briefer forms of therapy.

As far back as some of Freud's (1908) original work, there was reference to character pathology, particularly in relation to what we may now understand as obsessional personality disorder, the traits of which (orderliness, miserliness and rigidity) Freud related to the anal psychosexual stage of development. More recently, Gabbard (2001) suggests that 'psychoanalytic understanding of character has broadened to view character traits as a series of compromise formations between wishes and defences that oppose those wishes on the one hand, and constellations of internal representations of the self and others, on the other' (p. 360). Psychoanalytic approaches use the relationship between the patient and therapist to explore the patterns of relatedness in the patient's internal and external worlds. Those patterns inevitably repeat in therapy because of the patient's own personality structures and patterns of behaviour. The therapist analyses these by making transference (the patient's unconscious feelings towards the therapist) and counter-transference (the therapist's feelings invoked towards the patient) reactions explicit to the patient. This insight-oriented approach is designed to give patients an understanding of their own patterns of thinking and behaviour with a view to them obtaining mastery, control and choice over how those patterns continue or change. Indeed, it is thought that, once explicit, many defences become less necessary.

The process of psychoanalysis and psychodynamic therapy involves close observation and abstraction of the patient's communications (verbal and non-verbal) in therapy, but also the containment of the patient through understanding his or her internal world. It has been argued that it is important for patients to first feel understood by the therapist before they can understand the therapist's interpretations (Steiner, 1993). Therapy proceeds in an experimental way whereby the therapist 'tries out' interpretations and observes the patient's response, adjusting the approach as therapy proceeds according to the patient's pathology, needs and progress. This approach is experienced by the patient as a new way of relating to another person (Cooper, 1989), which not only offers insight but also an alternative 'object' in the mind of the patient to relate to and on which to base or view other relationships. This description for the purposes of this chapter is necessarily an oversimplification of the process and is given in order to begin to describe the complexity of the patient–therapist interaction (see Gabbard, 2001, for a fuller review).

Bateman and Fonagy (1999) conducted one of the only randomised controlled studies of psychoanalytic psychotherapy, which involved 38 patients with Borderline personality disorder receiving 18 months of psychotherapy (also involving partial hospitalisation) versus routine care. The results were promising for the treatment group, who showed improvements in significant outcomes including in-patient hospitalisation, suicidality, self-harm and symptoms/functioning. An uncontrolled trial of psychoanalytic psychotherapy (Stevenson and Meares, 1992, 1999) showed significant improvements in self-harm, violence, hospitalisation and on other measures for 48 patients with Borderline personality disorder after 1 year of twice-weekly psychoanalytic psychotherapy (30 participants completed treatment). A cost–benefit analysis of this study showed an enormous saving of in-patient admission costs ($21,431 per patient) when the post-treatment costs per year were compared to the pre-treatment costs per year. Even though the therapeutic intervention was relatively expensive (twice-weekly therapy for a year), the cost of this was only $13,000 per patient, representing a net saving of $8,431 per patient in the first year. In a review of psychotherapeutic treatment for personality disorder, Bateman and Fonagy (2000) evaluated both in-patient and out-patient treatments and concluded that more effective treatments tend to be long term, integrated with other services, theoretically coherent and focused on compliance.

GROUP THERAPY

Interestingly, group therapy is the most widely used intervention for problematic interpersonal behaviour and offending in the UK prison system, where rates of personality disorder are typically several times the rate in the community (Singleton et al., 1998). Accredited prison programmes such as Enhanced Thinking Skills (ETS), Reasoning and Rehabilitation (R&R), the Cognitive Self Change Programme (CSCP) and the Controlling Anger and Learning to Manage it (CALM) programme are all primarily cognitive behavioural therapy based and often include a large didactic component as well as skills-based learning (see Towl, 2003, for a review of psychological treatments in prisons). The evidence for the effectiveness on prison inmates is equivocal, particularly for the main 'hard' outcome of reoffending (Falshaw et al., 2004). However, these groups are now being developed for use with mentally disordered offenders and within specialist personality disorder units (for a review, see Feeney, 2003).

Piper and Joyce (2001) outline the advantages of group therapy, which include: '(1) confronting resistant, ego-syntonic character traits that arise during group interactions; (2) fostering the integration of strong positive and negative affects; (3) providing *in vivo* demonstrations of maladaptive behaviours and a chance to experiment with new and adaptive ones; and (4) reducing the intensity of transference reactions that might occur in individual therapy' (p. 328). The additional benefits of a group experience may also include the validation, recognition and support of fellow sufferers, and the authenticity of challenges by fellow group members as opposed to a professional therapist.

As with many therapies, the evidence for effectiveness of group treatments for personality disorders is sparse (Piper and Joyce, 2001). However, for skills-based group work, such as social skills training, there is some evidence for the improvement in certain outcomes (target symptoms, work and general adjustment) following 10 weekly sessions with out-patients diagnosed with ('inadequate') personality disorder (Falloon et al., 1977). There were similar findings following 12 sessions of social skills training for out-patients with avoidant personality disorder (Stravynski et al., 1982). Bellack (1980) found psychodynamic therapy to be more effective for personality-disordered patients than didactic therapy.

THERAPEUTIC COMMUNITIES

Therapeutic communities use 'milieu' treatment in an in-patient setting to treat the underlying problems and symptom behaviours associated with personality disorder. The idea of a milieu treatment is that it simultaneously focuses on a range of issues that may be important in a safe and structured environment. There is a strong emphasis on voluntary participation and, if possible, the inclusion of the patient's family or significant others. The structure means that roles are clearly defined and a range of therapeutic approaches are used, including individual therapy, group therapy and rehabilitation. Examples of such units in the UK health service include the Henderson Hospital in Surrey, the Personality Disorder Unit at Arnold Lodge (Medium Secure Unit in Leicester) and HMP Grendon Underwood in Buckinghamshire.

Dolan and Coid (1993) suggest that therapeutic communities offer some of the best evidence for the successful treatment of personality disorders. Dolan et al., (1996) have shown that the high cost of therapeutic community treatment (£25,641 per year) is offset by the saving of £12,658 per year in psychiatric and prison service costs when pre- and post-treatment costs (£13,966 and £1,308 per year respectively) are compared. Thus, in this example, the costs of 1 year of treatment are recouped in 2 years and run at a saving thereafter.

THE PROBLEM OF PSYCHOPATHY

The term 'psychopathy' is not recognised by either of the classification systems (DSM-IV (APA, 1994) or ICD-10 (WHO, 1992)) as a separate type of personality disorder. However, it is often used as a diagnosis with strong implications for personality of the person so labelled. A set of criteria were devised originally by Cleckley (1941) and, later, in an attempt to operationalise the condition, by Hare (1991), who developed the Psychopathy Checklist Revised from some of Cleckley's original criteria as a way of measuring psychopathy. 'Psychopaths' in many ways represent our worst fears as clinicians and the term has become reified to represent the stereotype of all that is 'bad' in relation to personality disorder among offenders (Gunn, 1999). Psychopaths seem to possess all the features that are undesirable in personality disorders (deceitful, conning, manipulative) and all that is dangerous in offenders (violent, recidivist, callous). Some authors suggest that not only do psychopaths not do well in treatment, but that they may even be made worse by it (Rice et al., 1992). They are also reported to be more likely to engage in anti-social behaviour while in treatment and to terminate treatment prematurely (Harris et al., 1991). The measurement and labelling of psychopathy represents the antithesis of an individualised, meaningful and formulation-based approach, which aims to understand and destigmatise the more difficult psychological problems associated with offending.

However, therapeutic nihilism regarding psychopathy may have been circularly reinforced by other factors. First, 'Psychopathic Disorder' has remained the classification of choice under the Mental Health Act for individuals with personality disorder without mental illness who pose a risk to themselves and/or others and whose detention in hospital for treatment is likely to alleviate or prevent deterioration of their condition. In practice, the issue of treatability is the factor on which detention is hinged, and a binary decision must be made; this decision has been used to exclude patients from detention and other services (Davison, 2002). Of course, treatability is a dimensional and multi-faceted concept but, nevertheless, the decision must be made. Furthermore, as Adshead (2001) notes, nowhere else in medicine does 'treatable' equate with 'curable'. When this binary outcome problem is added to the fact that patients are detained by psychiatrists whose training is in the medical model, rather than by therapists or psychologists, it is not surprising when the 'untreatable' position is taken.

The second factor is the misunderstanding of the aetiological and psychological development of psychopathy. As Salekin (2002) points out, different individuals probably have different paths to their classification as a psychopath, and theoretical models are often surprisingly absent in the development of treatment programmes, particularly for psychopaths. Understanding the nature and development of different types of psychopathy is likely to lead to more successful treatment programmes and vice versa.

Salekin (2002) conducted a meta-analysis of 42 trials of therapy for psychopathic individuals; eight of these studies had control groups allowing for the calculation of a mean control group change score (20%) to which the other uncontrolled trials could be compared. The findings showed that the outcome for psychopaths became more positive when their outcome was compared with other untreated psychopaths rather than with other more successfully treated groups of patients. The majority of these studies (17) were psychoanalytic, with 88 participants taking part. Five used cognitive behaviour therapy (246 participants) and eight used therapeutic communities (371 participants). Interestingly, intensive individual psychotherapy (four times per week on average, for 1 year or more) showed the best outcome, with 91% of patients improving with therapy. Psychoanalytic treatment gave an average success rate of 59% improved and cognitive behavioural therapies achieved an average success rate of 62%; when group and individual therapy were combined, the percentage of patients who improved rose to 81%. Therapeutic communities, however, showed a success rate of 25%, similar to the control group figure of 20% who improved with no treatment. These findings have implications not only for the theoretical orientation of therapy but also for therapy format and the context of treatment delivery. Salekin (2002) concluded that 'psychopathy does not appear to be completely recalcitrant to treatment' (p. 105), that successful interventions were intensive, involved direct contact of the therapist with the patient, and a high degree of professional psychological input. When the reverse of these conditions was applied, the outcome was no change or even deterioration, with significant costs to the community in terms of violence (Rice et al., 1992).

Aside from the serious issue of psychopathy, many patients with personality disorder will be found in forensic services. Suffice it to say that in a forensic setting there are likely to be a range of issues to assess and work with. These include: immediate behaviour (including risk to self and others); illness symptoms (perhaps requiring psychopharmacological relief); broader clinical issues (probably including personality and interpersonal difficulties); substance misuse; socio-economic deprivation; deficits in cognitive abilities and skills; emotional difficulties; environmental issues (particularly in prison settings) and offending behaviour issues. It is likely that a multi-disciplinary, multiple model approach incorporating consideration of systemic issues will be necessary. Although prevalence estimates vary, the rate of personality disorder in the community (13%; Casey and Tyrer, 1990) is relatively low compared to the rate for male remand (78%), male sentenced (64%) or female prisoners (58%; Singleton et al., 1998). Similar or higher figures have been found in special hospitals (Blackburn et al., 1990).

CONCLUSIONS

Howells et al. (1997) state that well-founded psychological treatment programmes should include: an adequate theoretical basis, individual formulation, population needs analysis and targeting, a broad approach, cultural relevance, systematic integration and evaluation of outcomes. Added to these generic issues are those covered in this chapter, which apply more specifically to those with personality disorder. It appears that some of the more successful treatments do indeed have a strong theoretical basis, such as dialectical behaviour therapy for Borderline Personality Disorder or psycholanalytic psychotherapy for psychopathy. An individualised approach to treatment is exemplified by the psychoanalytic approach and strongly advocated by writers on CBT, along with an emphasis on individual formulation.

The length of therapy appears to be significant and extended compared to shorter treatments for Axis I disorders, the majority of approaches advocating more than 1 year. The addition of group therapy to individual therapy also seems beneficial. The co-morbidity of Axis I and Axis II disorders is also an important consideration because the personality disorder may make the depression, neurosis or psychosis more difficult to treat, but the Axis I disorder may also be amenable to intervention, whereas the underlying personality disorder may need longer to work with.

There is an interesting finding in relation to therapeutic communities, which are successful in the majority of cases of personality disorder but largely unsuccessful with severe personality pathology combined with criminality (psychopathy). Therapeutic nihilism for psychopaths cannot be justified when the evidence is evaluated appropriately. Again, the emphasis must be on theoretical understanding, intensity of input and cognisance of the treatment delivery setting.

For all therapy, the notion of compulsion seems to be at odds with the notion of voluntary participation, commitment and motivation by the patient. Indeed, how the therapy is delivered is likely to be as important as what is delivered. Common factors associated with improved outcome in psychotherapy regardless of orientation have been stated by Critelli and Neumann (1984), these include the use of suggestion and persuasion, treatment credibility, therapist attention, therapist belief, positive expectation of change, demand for improvement and therapeutic alliance. This last issue of therapeutic alliance is an intrinsic aspect of psychoanalytic and psychodynamic approaches, but is also recognised and prioritised in CBT approaches. Allen (1997, p. 34) suggests that 'successful' therapists with patients with Borderline Personality Disorder display a number of aspects to their therapy, being:

> . . . comfortable with their own limitations and unwilling to make unusual or risky interventions; unafraid of the patient's anger, neediness or anxiety; and unwilling to attack the patient in the face of provocation. They do not rush in to 'take care of' the patient in an infantilising manner . . . They are relentlessly respectful of the patient's suffering, abilities, and values. They communicate an expectation that the patient will be able to behave reasonably and cooperatively, and they play to the patients strengths.

We would add to these therapist attributes the importance of appropriate training and supervision for all staff working with people with personality disorder.

Livesley (2001b) presents a framework for an integrated approach to treatment of personality disorders and concludes that there are a number of promising approaches to the understanding and treatment of personality disorder and that a number of psychosocial and pharmacological treatments have been shown to be effective. Based on an extensive review of the literature, Livesley suggests that psychotherapy should be integrated, that is, the best interventions or combination of interventions should be selected when developing a treatment for an individual; this requires a knowledge of the literature and the evidence base. He recommends that theories should be integrated to provide a more integrated explanatory model of personality disorder, and moreover that the effectiveness of the common factors from different approaches should be maximised in any intervention. In particular he emphasises the importance of the therapeutic relationship (supportive and validating) and the opportunity for the patient to learn and develop new skills (Livesley, 2001b).

The theme of balance is essential for the realistic appraisal of treatments for personality disorder and more generally for the assessment and treatment of people with personality disorder. However, in reality there is very little evidence: a handful of controlled trials with small numbers. The difficulties for researchers are immense: how to assess and treat reliably with such a set of 'mixed bag' diagnoses, how to keep to a treatment protocol when individual approaches appear to be so helpful and when the signs are that the best treatments are lengthy and experimental, problems with the whole underlying theory (or theories) of personality and personality disorder and difficulties for the individual therapist in working with patients who may exhibit a range of severe and distressing symptoms and behaviour. However, this last point – the distress such patients suffer – means that this is an area worthy of study, despite the obvious difficulties and lack of evidence so far.

Neither therapeutic idealism nor nihilism is realistic or helpful. Idealism may be quickly demolished by difficult or intractable problems, and nihilism is unlikely to progress the field of discovery and mental health care for patients. Lack of evidence is not the same as 'untreatable', and our clinical experience is that such patients can be worked with and can improve the quality of their lives to some extent; there are clearly interventions that are more helpful and those that are unhelpful. We would emphasise the importance in all therapeutic modalities of training and supervision, an individual approach and formulation, extended treatment and looking at transference and counter-transference issues, which, are likely to play a bigger role with these patients than with many others.

ACKNOWLEDGMENTS

Thanks to Claire Blount and Gerrie Holloway for their helpful comments on this chapter.

REFERENCES

Adshead, G. (2001) Murmurs of discontent: treatment and treatability of personality disorder. *Advances in Psychiatric Treatment*, 7, 407–416.

Allen, D. M. (1997) Techniques for reducing therapy-interfering behaviour in patients with BPD. *Journal of Psychotherapy Practice and Research*, 6, 25–35.

American Psychiatric Association (APA) (1994) *Diagnostic and Statistical Manual of Mental Disorders, Fourth Edition*, Washington, DC: APA.

Bateman, A. W. and Fonagy, P. (1999) The effectiveness of partial hospitalisation in the treatment of borderline personality disorder – a randomised controlled trial. *American Journal of Personality Disorders*, 7, 232–240.

Bateman, A. W. and Fonagy, P. (2000) Effectiveness of psychotherapeutic treatment of personality disorder. *British Journal of Psychiatry*, 177, 138–143.

Bateman, A. W. and Tyrer, P. (2004) Psychological treatment for personality disorders. *Advances in Psychiatric Treatment*, 10, 378–388.

Beck, A. T. (1976) *Cognitive Therapy and the Emotional Disorders*. New York: Penguin.

Beck, A. T., Rush, A. J., Shaw, B. F. and Emery, G. (1979) *Cognitive Therapy of Depression.* New York: Guilford Press.

Beck, A. T., Freeman, A. and associates (1990) *Cognitive Therapy of Personality Disorders.* New York: Guilford Press.

Beck, A. T., Freeman, A. and Davis, D. (2003) *Cognitive Therapy of Personality Disorders* (2nd edn.). New York: Guilford Press.

Bellack, L. (1980) On some limitations of didactic psychotherapy and the role of group modalities. *International Journal of Group Psychotherapy*, 30, 7–21.

Blackburn, R. (1989) Psychopathy and personality disorder in relation to violence. In: K. Howells and C. R. Hollin (eds) *Clinical Approaches to Violence.* Chichester: John Wiley.

Blackburn, R., Crellin, M. C., Morgan, E. M. and Tullock, R. M. B. (1990) Prevalence of personality disorders in a special hospital population. *Journal of Forensic Psychiatry*, 1, 43–52.

Casey, P. R. and Tyrer, P. (1990) Personality disorder and psychiatric illness in general practice. *British Journal of Psychiatry*, 156, 261–265.

Caspi, A. and Herbener, E. S. (1990) Continuity and change: assortative marriage and the consistency of personality in adulthood. *Journal of Personality and Social Psychology*, 59, 250–258.

Cleckley, H. (1941) *The Mask of Sanity.* St Louis: Mosby.

Cooper, A. M. (1989) Concepts of therapeutic effectiveness in psychoanalysis: a historical review. *Psychoanalytic Inquiry*, 9, 4–25.

Costa, P. T. and McCrae, R. R. (1980) Still stable after all these years: personality as a key to some issues in aging. In: P. B. Baltes and O. G. Brim (eds) *Life-span Development and Behaviour.* San Diego, CA: Academic Press.

Costa, P. T. and McCrea, R. R. (1994) Set like plaster? Evidence for the stability of adult personality. In: T. F. Hetherton and J. L. Weinberger (eds) *Can Personality Change?* Washington, DC: American Psychological Association.

Cottraux, J. and Blackburn, I. M. (2001) Cognitive therapy. In: W. J. Livesley (ed) *Handbook of Personality Disorders: Theory, Research and Treatment.* London: Guildford Press.

Critelli, I. W. and Neumann, K. F. (1984) The placebo: a conceptual analysis of a construct in transition. *American Psychologist*, 39, 32–39.

Davison, S. E. (2002) Principles of managing patients with personality disorder. *Advances in Psychiatric Treatment*, 8, 1–9.

Department of Health (1983) *The Mental Health Act (1983).* London: HMSO.

Dolan, B. and Coid, J. (1993) *Psychopathic and Antisocial Personality Disorders: Treatment and Research Issues.* London: Gaskell.

Dolan, B., Warren, F., Menzies, D. and Norton, K. (1996) Cost-offset following specialist treatment of severe personality disorders. *Psychiatric Bulletin*, 20, 413–417.

Duggan, C. (2003) Does personality change and, if so, what changes? *Criminal Behaviour and Mental Health*, 14, 5–16.

Evans, K., Tyrer, P., Catalan, J., Schmidt, U., Davidson, K., Dent, J. et al. (1999) Manual-assisted cognitive-behaviour therapy (MACT): A randomised controlled trial of a brief intervention with bibliotherapy in the treatment of recurrent deliberate self-harm. *Psychological Medicine*, 21, 19–25.

Falloon, F. R. H., Lindley, P., MacDonald, R. and Marks, I. M. (1977) Social skills training of outpatient groups. *British Journal of Psychiatry*, 131, 599–609.

Falshaw, L., Friendship, C., Travers, R. and Nugent, F. (2004) Searching for 'what works': HM Prison Service accredited cognitive skills programmes. *British Journal of Forensic Practice*, 6(2), 3–13.

Feeney, A. (2003) Dangerous severe personality disorder. *Advances in Psychiatric Treatment*, 9, 349–358.

Freeman, A. and Jackson, J. T. (1998) Cognitive behavioural treatment of personality disorders. In: N. Tarrier, A. Wells and G. Haddock (eds) *Treating Complex Cases: the Cognitive Behavioural Therapy Approach*. Chichester: John Wiley.

Freud, S. (1908) Character and anal eroticism. In: J. Strachey (ed) (1959) *The Standard Edition of the Complete Psychological Works of Sigmund Freud*, Vol 9. London: Hogarth Press.

Gabbard, G. O. (2001) Psychoanalysis and psychoanalytic psychotherapy. In: W. J. Livesley (ed) *Handbook of Personality Disorders: Theory, Research and Treatment*. London: Guildford Press.

Gunn, J. (1999) Psychopathy: an elusive concept with moral overtones. In: T. Millon, E. Simonsen, M. Birket-Smith and R. D. Davis (eds) *Psychopathy: Antisocial, Criminal and Violent Behaviour*. New York: Guilford Press.

Hare, R. D. (1991) *The Hare Psychopathy Checklist – Revised Manual*. New York: John Wiley.

Harris, R. D., Rice, M. E. and Cormier, C. A. (1991) Psychopathy and violent recidivism. *Law and Human Behaviour*, 15, 625–637.

Home Office (2003) *Review of Treatments for Severe Personality Disorder*. London: HMSO.

Howells, K., Watt, B., Hall, G. and Baldwin, S. (1997) Developing programmes for violent offenders. *Legal and Criminological Psychology*, 2, 117–128.

Leichsenring, F. and Leibing, E. (2003) The effectiveness of psychodynamic therapy and cognitive behaviour therapy in the treatment of personality disorders: A meta-analysis. *American Journal of Psychiatry*, 160, 1223–1232.

Linehan, M. M. (1993) *Cognitive-Behavioural Treatment of Borderline Personality Disorder*. New York: Guilford Press.

Linehan, M. M., Armstrong, H. E., Suarez, A., Allmon, D. and Heard, H. L. (1991) Cognitive-behavioural treatment of chronically parasuicidal borderline patients. *Archives of General Psychiatry*, 48, 1060–1064.

Livesley, W. J. (2001) *Handbook of Personality Disorders: Theory, Research and Treatment*. London: Guildford Press.

Livesley, W. J. (2001) A framework for an integrated approach to treatment. In: W. J. Livesley (ed) *Handbook of Personality Disorders: Theory, Research and Treatment*. London: Guildford Press.

Mahoney, M. J. (1993) Introduction to special section: Theoretical developments in cognitive psychotherapies. *Journal of Consulting and Clinical Psychology*, 2, 187–193.

McGlashan, T. (1986) The Chestnut Lodge follow-up study III: Long-term outcome of borderline personalities. *Archives of General Psychiatry*, 43, 2–30.

National Institute for Mental Health in England (NIMHE) (2003) *Personality Disorder: No Longer a Diagnosis of Exclusion*. London: Department of Health.

Paris, J., Brown, R. and Nowlis, D. (1987) Long term follow up of borderline patients in a general hospital. *Comprehensive Psychiatry*, 28, 530–535.

Piper, W. E. and Joyce, A. S. (2001) Psychosocial treatment outcome. In: W. J. Livesley (ed) *Handbook of Personality Disorders: Theory, Research and Treatment*. London: Guildford Press.

Reich, J. (2003) The effect of Axis II disorders on the outcome of treatment of anxiety and unipolar depressive disorders: A review. *Journal of Personality Disorders*, 17, 387–405.

Rice, M., Harris, G. and Cormier, C. (1992) An evaluation of a maximum security community for psychopaths and other mentally disordered offenders. *Law and Human Behaviour*, 16, 399–412.

Roy, S. and Tyrer, P. (2001) Treatment of personality disorders. *Current Opinion in Psychiatry*, 14, 555–558.

Salekin, R. T. (2002) Psychopathy and therapeutic pessimism: Clinical lore or clinical reality? *Clinical Psychology Review*, 22, 79–112.

Singleton, N., Meltzer, H., Gatwood, R., Coid, J. and Deasy, D. (1998) *Psychiatric Morbidity Among Prisoners in England and Wales*. London: The Stationery Office.

Steiner, J. (1993). *Psychic Retreats*. London: Routledge.

Stevenson, J. and Meares, R. (1992) An outcome study of psychotherapy for patients with borderline personality disorder. *American Journal of Psychiatry*, 149, 358–362.

Stevenson, J. and Meares, R. (1999) Psychotherapy with borderline patients: II. A preliminary cost-benefit study. *Australian and New Zealand Journal of Psychiatry*, 33, 473–477.

Stone, M. N. (1990) *The Fate of Borderline Patients*. New York: Guilford Press.

Stravynski, A., Marks, I. M. and Yule, W. (1982) Social skills problems in neurotic outpatients: social skills training with and without cognitive modification. *Archives of General Psychiatry*, 39, 1378–1385.

Towl, G. (2003) *Psychology in Prisons*. Oxford: BPS/Blackwell.

Woody, G. E., McLellan, T., Luborsky, L. and O'Brien, C. P. (1985) Sociopathy and psychotherapy outcome. *Archives of General Psychiatry*, 179, 188–193.

World Health Organization (WHO) (1992) *The ICD-10 Classification of Mental and Behavioural Disorders*. Geneva: WHO.

Young, J. (1994) *Cognitive Therapy for Personality Disorders: A Schema-Focussed Approach*. Sarasota, FL: Professional Resources Exchange.

Young, J. and Behary, W. T. (1998) Schema-focused therapy for personality disorders. In: N. Tarrier, A. Wells and G. Haddock (eds) *Treating Complex Cases: The Cognitive Behavioural Therapy Approach*. Chichester: John Wiley.

Young, J., Klosko, J. and Weishar, M. E. (2003) *Schema Therapy: A Practitioner's Guide*. London: Guildford Press.

Chapter 23

Substance misuse disorders

Investigation

Michael Gossop

INTRODUCTION TO ASSESSMENT

The central purpose of clinical assessment is to obtain information that can be used to guide the processes of treatment. More specifically, assessment should be used to determine suitability for treatment, to evaluate patient needs and to devise a treatment plan. Assessment should not be seen as an impersonal and routine procedure to be completed as quickly as possible before moving on to the more interesting and important business of treatment: it is an important first stage of the therapeutic process.

Assessment has a *pragmatic* function. It should identify the nature and extent of the presenting problems, and the reasons why the person is making contact. This may be due to some objective or psychological crisis. Some of those seeking treatment may have needs that require immediate attention, for example, an acute medical illness, acute depression, or suicidal thoughts.

Assessment also has a *therapeutic* function. Assessment should be used to establish empathy and rapport and to form the basis for a working relationship. For stigmatised forms of behaviour such as the addictions, the offer of non-judgemental sympathy and concern can be helpful if patients are feeling hopeless, guilty or embarrassed about their behaviour. A patient may seek treatment because his or her substance misuse is a cause for concern to others, and ambivalence is often a characteristic of substance use from the earliest stages through to later addictive phases (Orford, 2001). Where the user may be ambivalent or resistant to change, assessment provides an opportunity for the application of motivational enhancement procedures to generate greater willingness for change. Where the user is more fully committed to change, assessment should clarify the goals, and move on to identify the barriers to change as well as actual or potential supportive factors.

Patients should be given a coherent account of the nature of their problem, a rationale and description of the type of therapy and of their own responsibilities for participating in treatment. For example, how many treatment sessions will there be? How long will they last? Where will treatment take place? Making these issues explicit can help to increase the agreement between the therapist and patient with regard to their expectations about treatment. This sort of structured and relevant information improves adherence rates (Dunbar and Stunkard, 1979) and can support and build motivation and strengthen commitment for change. If the patient and therapist have different expectations this can lead to subsequent problems, increasing the probability of treatment non-compliance and possibly leading to the patient dropping out of treatment.

The assessment of substance use problems can be made more difficult by the fact that those who seek treatment often present with generalised complaints linked to an undifferentiated array of difficulties. It is fairly typical, for example, for many people to present to treatment with the vague intentions of 'getting off' or 'getting myself sorted out'. This may be accompanied by generalised complaints of feeling that life is not worth living, getting no pleasure from any activity other than substance use (and often not even from that) and hopelessness.

The therapist should seek to clarify and differentiate the presenting problems so these can be made explicit and reduced to manageable proportions. The assessment can help to introduce some optimism by helping the patient to begin to see that change and recovery may be possible.

For all substance use problems that require treatment, the intervention should be tailored to the needs and circumstances of the individual. This apparently simple and uncontentious statement turns out to have complex and far-reaching implications for policy and services if it is seriously applied in clinical practice. There is not, nor can there be expected to be, any single best treatment for these problems. Both aetiology and outcome are influenced by a broad range of different factors. A thorough assessment should identify, for each individual case, the nature of the problem and appropriate and achievable goals for treatment. Also, assessment should identify as early as possible those particular factors (often outside the treatment setting) that will assist or hamper the achievement of the treatment goal(s).

Among the most basic issues that need to be explored are the following. What types of substances are being used, by which routes of administration and with what sorts of associated problems? What are the relevant contextual variables, both for substance use and for seeking treatment? Why has the person sought treatment? Why at this particular time? In what ways does the person feel better or different when he or she takes drugs? Many people have specific beliefs about how substance use improves their ability to function. How do they expect to feel when they have stopped using drugs? Do they want to give up all drugs? Or do they just want to stop taking one drug that is seen as causing particular problems? Many heroin addicts, for instance, do not see the use of either alcohol or cannabis as related to their difficulties and intend to continue using these substances after giving up heroin. Do they believe that they can learn how to regulate their problem drug use in future and that they can return to being a 'recreational' user?

Other important questions that need to be asked concern the obstacles to maintaining change once the person has stopped using drugs. The factors that assist or impede the initial stages of change (getting off) may be quite different to those that assist or impede the maintenance of change (staying off). The task of the therapist during assessment is to identify and understand the antecedents (environmental, emotional and cognitive) of episodes of addictive behaviour, and the consequences that maintain the behaviour (O'Leary and Wilson, 1975).

ASSESSMENT METHODS

The clinical interview is the main source of information during assessment. This is heavily reliant on the self-reported problems and behaviours of the patient, typically obtained during semi-structured interviews, which may or may not also include some use of structured instruments.

The apparently straightforward matter of determining the drug or alcohol usage of the patient can be complicated by the belief of some clinicians that drug misusers are unreliable informants. Although there are undoubtedly some occasions on which drug misusers may distort or conceal information (Morral et al., 2000), both drug addicts and alcoholics can be reliable informants with regard to a wide range of different types of information (DelBoca and Noll, 2000).

There are circumstances in which objective measures can be usefully applied to determine the presence or absence of one or more types of substances. Among the biochemical methods that can be used are analysis of blood, breath, saliva, urine, sweat and hair samples for direct metabolites of abused substances, or indirect evidence of biological changes related to prolonged use of drugs. The choice of screening method will be influenced by the pharmacokinetics of the drugs that are being investigated, and will depend also on the questions being asked (Wolff et al., 1999).

Biochemical tests can be of value when the consequences of error are potentially serious. The interpretation of laboratory findings should take place in conjunction with other contextual data. Self-report and laboratory tests can also be used interactively. Hamid et al. (1999) found that rates of agreement between self-reported drug use and urinalysis increased when urine was taken for testing prior to interview.

Weiss et al. (1998) found self-reported use to be consistent with urine screen results 95% of the time and, when the two sources of information did not agree, 89% of the time it was because subjects reported more substance use than was detected by urine analysis. Others have found that self-reported drug misuse can have high validity, which correlates well with objective measures such as urine analysis (Zanis et al., 1994) and hair analysis (Wolff and Strang, 1999). Weiss et al. (2000) also found a high level of agreement between self-reported drug use and collateral informant reports. Self-report remains an essential tool. In many circumstances it is the most practical way to obtain information, and in some circumstances it is the only possible way of obtaining information (as with internal states).

Although structured instruments are not widely used in routine clinical assessment, they may provide a useful means of collecting information and can help to avoid omitting questions about important behaviours and problems. Structured instruments can be particularly useful where there is a need for a systematic assessment of problems and of changes over time. Many such instruments are available but it is beyond the scope of this chapter to review them. Some of the more commonly used instruments are mentioned below.

The AUDIT is a short (10 item) questionnaire that provides a composite measure of alcohol consumption, problems and dependence during the previous year (Saunders et al., 1993). It was developed to identify hazardous drinkers before the onset of serious alcohol-related harm.

The Addiction Severity Index (ASI) is a standardised, structured clinical research interview that assesses drug and alcohol use, medical, legal, employment, family/social and psychiatric problems (McLellan et al. 1980, 1992). In each of these areas, the ASI assesses the number, frequency, intensity and duration of problems in the 30-day period preceding admission to treatment. ASI measures can also be taken for lifetime problems.

The Opiate Treatment Index (OTI; Darke et al., 1992) measures six domains: drug use, HIV risk-taking behaviour, social functioning, criminality, health status and psychological adjustment. Drug use is recorded on the last 3 days' use for 11 classes of drugs: heroin, other opiates (including illicit methadone), amphetamines, cocaine, tranquillisers, alcohol, cannabis, barbiturates, hallucinogens, inhalants and tobacco. A potential practical difficulty with the ASI and OTI is that they require a relatively lengthy completion time.

The Maudsley Addiction Profile (MAP) is a brief, interviewer-administered questionnaire that assesses substance use behaviours, health-risk behaviours and health problems, and various aspects of personal and social functioning. Like the ASI, the MAP assesses problems during the 30 days before treatment. For most users, the interview can be completed in about 12 minutes. It was designed to be easily incorporated within routine clinical practice and to be used as part of a modular approach in association with other assessment protocols (Marsden et al., 1998).

The Severity of Dependence Scale (SDS) provides a short, easily administered scale that assesses the psychological components of dependence and is primarily a measure of impaired behavioural control and compulsion to use (Gossop et al., 1995). These are essential ingredients of what we mean by an addictive behaviour. The SDS is easy to understand and can be completed within a matter of minutes. It can be readily adapted to measure dependence upon different types of substances.

ASSESSMENT IN THREE DIMENSIONS

Responsiveness to individual differences requires attention to specifics. These include issues such as what types of psychoactive substances are used, and for what purposes; whether the substance is taken orally, by smoking or intravenously; whether discontinuation will lead to a clinical withdrawal syndrome requiring medical treatment in its own right and whether the addiction is integrated within the user's personality and social lifestyle or whether it is seen as an isolated item of problem behaviour.

Many drug addicts have social and/or psychological problems that precede their drug dependence. These may include social behavioural problems from an early age, educational failure, literacy problems, family disintegration, lack of employment skills, or psychiatric disorders. Unless specific services are made available to deal with them, these problems may continue to cause difficulties for the individual and for his or her chances of recovery. For many addicts, recovery is not only a matter of giving up substance misuse but also involves tackling the social and behavioural problems that may have preceded the addiction and which have often been worsened by it. The treatment of substance misuse problems, therefore, may include interventions that extend beyond the focal point of drug or alcohol consumption and which tackle personal and social impairments.

A useful way of understanding the multi-faceted phenomena of substance misuse problems is to conceptualise them as being represented in terms of three dimensions. These are:

- consumption behaviours
- problems
- dependence.

These dimensions can be regarded as being conceptually distinct and separate. In reality, of course, they tend to be related (sometime closely) in a number of ways.

Assessment of consumption behaviour

The first dimension refers to the behavioural parameters of drug taking. The most immediately obvious features involve frequency and quantity of substance use. Misunderstandings often arise through a failure to distinguish between infrequent, frequent and regular patterns of use, or between low-dose and high-dose use. A thorough assessment requires information about types and quantities of drugs used, patterns of use, the social and psychological circumstances and consequences of drug use prior to treatment, throughout treatment, and during follow-up. Consumption behaviours have direct implications for the presence and severity of different types of risks and problems.

A minimum requirement for a substance use assessment should involve measurement of current or recent use, including measures of quantity and frequency of use, development and duration of use. In the case of alcohol, this is relatively straightforward.

For the assessment of drug consumption, which may involve a large number of different substances that can be used by different routes of administration, a commonly used assessment device is some sort of 'grid' (Table 23.1). This can be expanded to meet specific treatment needs. Extra measures (such as age of first use, main problem drug identified by the patient) can be added to the columns. The use of a grid of this sort provides a concise summary of a good deal of information within a single page. It also provides a reminder to the assessor of the information required. Frequency of consumption, for example, is often assessed for specified drugs during specified time periods (e.g. during the past 3 months), with the classification of drug use by pattern and history usually involving measures of the heaviest or most problematic level of use within a given period.

Routes of drug administration that are commonly used by drug misusers are:

- oral (tablets, liquids)
- intranasal/snorting/sniffing (e.g. cocaine powder, heroin powder)
- smoking (cannabis, opium)
- inhalation (chasing the dragon, volatile substances)
- injection (intravenous, intramuscular, subcutaneous/skin popping).

Table 23.1 Aid to assess drug consumption

Drug	Ever used	Age first used	Number of days used in last month	Typical amount used per day	Route of administration
Heroin					
Other opiates/opioids					
Crack cocaine					
Cocaine powder					
Amphetamines					
Benzodiazepines					
Cannabis					
Other drugs (specify)					

Route of administration is related to the effects of many illegal drugs, to dependence liability, to the risk of overdose and to the risk of infections and other health problems. Surprisingly, route of administration is often over-looked, and properties that are characteristics of the route of administration, or of an interaction between the drug and the route of administration, are sometimes attributed to the drug.

Patterns of drug taking can change with extreme rapidity. This was demon-strated at the national level by the rapid growth of crack cocaine misuse in the USA during the 1980s (Kleber, 1988) and the spread of heroin addiction in Pakistan during the 1980s (Gossop, 1989a). In the 1960s, all (or nearly all) heroin users in the UK injected it (Gardner and Connell, 1971). Today, the situation has changed considerably and virtually all heroin users in London start to use heroin by 'chasing the dragon' (Strang et al., 1992). Heroin chas-ing almost completely replaced injecting as an 'entry route' into heroin use in the years between 1970 and 1990.

Similar changes in routes of cocaine use occurred in many countries. The spread of crack cocaine in London during the 1980s was charted by Gossop et al. (1994). Those who first took cocaine before 1986 had mostly started to take the drug by snorting (65%) or injecting (30%), with only 6% having first used by smoking. After 1990, smoking became the most common route of first use.

The two predominant routes of heroin administration among regular users in the UK are injection and chasing the dragon. 'Chasing the dragon' involves placing heroin on a piece of tin-foil, heating until it liquefies and inhaling the fumes given off from the liquefied mixture (Gossop et al., 1991a). Griffiths et al. (1994) found that injecting was preferred as the main route of heroin administration by 54% and chasing by 44% of heroin users. Although some users reported having taken heroin by snorting, this is rarely used as a main route.

The progression from heroin chasing to injecting is not inevitable, and heroin chasing is not merely a first stage, or pre-injection phase, of heroin addiction (Gossop et al., 1988). Many heroin chasers do not switch to regular injecting despite using heroin in substantial doses for many years. Some chasers may also give up using heroin without ever moving on to injecting. However, there is a continuing risk of moving from chasing to injecting among those who continue to use heroin (Griffiths et al., 1994).

Patterns of drug taking are sensitive to social, environmental, and inter-personal influences, and there can be marked geographical differences in the types of drug being used, the amounts taken, or in routes of administration. Among drug users recruited from treatment services across England, Gossop et al. (2000a) found that rates of injecting varied between 5% and 58% according to the specific drugs being used. Rates of injecting were highest for heroin, and lowest for benzodiazepines (the second most frequently used drug).

Substance misusers who seek treatment rarely take just a single substance, and sometimes they use a wide range of drugs as part of a broad repertoire of multiple drug taking. It is commonplace to use shorthand terms such as 'heroin addict', 'cocaine user', 'problem drinker' or 'alcoholic', but these terms can be misleading. Most problem substance users take a range of substances.

Multiple drug use may involve the concurrent or sequential use of different substances. There may also be different reasons for multiple drug use. These include:

- *Drug enhancement*: several substances may be used at the same time to enhance the combined psychoactive effects. The combined use of opiates and benzodiazepines, for example, may be intended to increase the overall level of sedation.
- *Modification of effect*: different drugs may be combined to counteract the adverse or unwanted effects of one or more drugs. Cocaine and alcohol may be used together, with the alcohol taking away some of the unpleasant overstimulation and anxiety caused by the cocaine, or so that the stimulant offsets the sedation of the alcohol.
- *Substitution*: the user may take a substitute for his or her preferred drug if this is not available. Some heroin users may take alcohol in this way when heroin is not available. Substitute drugs may also sometimes be used to self-medicate withdrawal symptoms.
- *Social*: for some drug misusers, multiple substance use may be influenced by the social setting and the behaviour of other users. Sometimes this may be reflected in a generalised pattern of multiple drug abuse where a wide range of substances are taken in what appears to be an indiscriminate manner.

As part of the assessment, the patient should be asked about specific situations they have encountered that are associated with their use of drugs/alcohol. In what sorts of situation do they usually take their preferred drug(s)? What sorts of situation help them to stay off or to reduce their intake of drugs? They should be asked about physiological states, cognitions and interpersonal factors, as well as overt behaviour, and about how each of these groups of variables relates to the problem.

A properly directed assessment can have an educational role by helping to focus the patient's attention on internal and external variables that he or she may not previously have seen as being relevant to his or her problems. The identification and clarification of such functional relationships plays a crucial role in helping the addict to learn to take some control of his or her own drug taking behaviour.

Assesment of problems

The problems of drug misuse must be assessed in terms of risk as well as actual harm. Injecting drugs carries a number of serious risks. The most obvious of these is associated with the sharing of injecting equipment. A number of physical and psychological health problems, as well as the dangers of overdoses, are closely linked to route of drug administration, with injectors being at much higher risk. Because heroin chasing avoids the obvious dangers of injecting, many users, especially new and naïve users, see it as a safer way of taking drugs. However, regular heroin chasers and cocaine smokers may develop respiratory problems as a result of the inhalation of high temperature vapours. Heroin chasers are much less likely to take an overdose. In one study, only 2% of heroin chasers had overdosed compared to 31% of heroin injectors (Gossop et al., 1996). Heroin injectors are also at greater risk and are more likely to carry blood-borne infections, such as HIV and hepatitis C (Gossop et al., 1994).

Some problems arise, or are exacerbated, because of the illegality of drugs. The regular use of illicit drugs places an excessive economic burden on the user which, in most cases, cannot be met by normal means, and drug habits are often supported by crime, drug dealing and prostitution. High levels of criminal activity are often found among drug-misusing populations (Jarvis and Parker, 1989). In the UK, recent police estimates suggested that about half of all recorded crime may be drug-related, with costs to the criminal justice system alone of at least £1 billion per annum. However, crime among drug misusers may also be related to factors other than drug taking. Many drug misusers tend to have been involved in crime before they started taking drugs (Nurco et al., 1993), and crime and drug use often share common links with psychological and social lifestyle factors associated with social deviance (Hammersley et al., 1990). Crime and drug use also often coexist in economically disadvantaged and socially deprived neighbourhoods (Pearson and Gillman, 1994).

Acquisitive crimes involving theft are one of the most frequent ways of obtaining drugs, or of obtaining money for drugs (Jarvis and Parker, 1989; Stewart et al., 2000). Speckart and Anglin (1985) found that heroin addicts were charged with a higher number of property crimes than non-addict criminals. Crimes involving theft are common among heroin addicts. Shoplifting is one of the most common types of offence, both in terms of total number of crimes and in terms of percentage of drug users committing that offence (Gossop et al., 1998).

However, crime and addiction do not inevitably go together. In a study of drug dependent patients in UK treatment services, half of the patients had not committed any acquisitive crimes during the 3 months prior to admission and, of those who were involved in crime, the majority were relatively low-rate offenders. The vast majority of acquisitive crimes were committed by a small minority of the drug users, with 10% of them committing 76% of the crimes (Stewart et al., 2000). Those who were most heavily involved in crime were the drug users who were most severely dependent on heroin and cocaine. The onset of addictive drug use has been found to be associated with increased levels of criminal behaviour which continue during periods of addiction (Ball et al., 1983).

Goldstein (1979) found that between 30 and 70% of female drug addicts were also prostitutes, and that between 40 and 85% of prostitutes were also drug users. Some drug dependent men also support their habit through prostitution. In a non-clinical sample of heroin users in London, Gossop et al. (1993) found that 17% of the women and 6% of the men had been involved in some sort of prostitution. The more severely dependent heroin users were more likely to be involved in prostitution (Gossop et al., 1993). As unsafe drug injection and unprotected sex are two of the primary routes of HIV transmission, drug injectors and prostitutes are both potentially at great risk of contracting and transmitting HIV and other serious infections as a result of their behaviour. Prostitutes who also inject drugs are at especially high risk in this respect.

Prostitution may be used by some women as a means of financing their use of heroin or other drugs, and the primary link between addiction and prostitution may be economic necessity (Goldstein, 1979). Many women said that they only worked as a prostitute to fund their use of drugs (predominantly heroin), and that they would not continue working as a prostitute if they were not still using drugs. The more severely dependent on heroin they were, the more likely they were to report these links between heroin use and prostitution. However, prostitution may precede drug use and drug problems. Where this occurs, drugs or alcohol may be used in an instrumental manner to cope with the often stressful, anxiety-provoking and unpleasant demands of working as a prostitute.

Assessment of dependence

The majority of those who seek help from drug and alcohol treatment services have chronic and severe substance use problems. They tend to seek treatment as the result of pressures and selection processes, which may not be fully evident at the point of presentation. Typically, they have already made failed attempts (either on their own or with the support of others) to moderate or to give up substance use (Gossop et al., 1991b). Other people whose drug use is less problematic or less severely dependent, and those who have better resources to support behaviour change, may stop using drugs without help (Sobell and Sobell, 1998).

Dependence should be differentiated from other types of problematic drug taking. Edwards et al. (1981) suggested that these could include *unsanctioned use* – the use of a drug that is not approved by a society or by a powerful group within that society. Alternatively, the *hazardous use* of drugs represents another form of problematic use. This involves the use of a drug that could be expected to harmful consequences for the user (either to psychological dysfunction or to physical damage). It is possible to use illicit drugs, and even to use them by injection, without experiencing any actual harm, but it is known to be hazardous. Other forms of problematic use include *dysfunctional use* – use of a drug that leads to impaired psychological or social functioning (e.g. loss of job or marital problems) and *harmful use* – use of a drug by a person to whom it is known to have caused physical or psychological problems.

Each of these categories of drug problems may cause difficulties for the drug taker and each may require different sorts of intervention. The use of illegal drugs (unsanctioned use), particularly when it occurs among very young people, can cause enormous concern; it may lead to serious social sanctions, including being expelled from school, loss of job or imprisonment; and it may cause great anxiety among the family and friends of the user. However, it need not in itself be associated with clinical problems. Equally, drug taking may lead to many different types of problem. Acute intoxication often leads to hazardous behaviours and, not infrequently, to actual harm. This sort of behaviour may or may not be an appropriate reason for intervention by the addiction therapist.

The behaviours underlying 'addiction' or 'dependence' are the most frequent reasons for drug users seeking treatment, and dependence is a phenomenon that all therapists should fully understand. Addiction is a learned behaviour, a habit disorder, and is most often manifested, psychologically and behaviourally, in feelings of compulsion to use drugs or alcohol, and difficulty in resisting those urges.

Progression from occasional to dependent use of drugs is not inevitable. Nonetheless, many people who have started to use drugs find the effects rewarding and continue to do so, sometimes with increasing frequency and regularity, until they are taking drugs every day and several times a day. When this happens, the amount that they take usually also increases, and often they begin to run into many types of social, psychological and physical problems associated with their drug taking.

With the development of dependence, the relationship between the user and the drug is altered. The person becomes increasingly preoccupied by the drug and feels some degree of compulsion to use it. The initial reasons for drinking or taking drugs may or may not still be present, but new factors are added which complicate the picture and increase the likelihood, intensity and persistence of drug taking. Even when users want to cut down the amount or to give up using altogether, they experience great difficulty in giving up. They may have withdrawal reactions when they stop taking the drug, and they become preoccupied with thoughts about it. Despite their wishes to stop using, they frequently fail in their efforts to do so and go back to taking drugs again.

In practice, the assessment of dependence need not be complicated. In most clinical circumstances, the assessment of dependence typically involves the taking of a substance-use history, noting signs of intoxication or withdrawal and an examination for physical signs of drug injection (e.g. venopuncture marks and scarring). When conducted by experienced clinicians, this form of assessment probably provides the best and most practical method for assessing dependence and most other substance use problems.

For many years, the concepts of tolerance and withdrawal provided the twin pillars that supported the concept of addiction. Tolerance and withdrawal are typical of dependence on alcohol or heroin, but tolerance also occurs to drugs that are not physically addictive in the traditional sense, such as amphetamines and cannabis, and there may be withdrawal-like responses to the discontinuation of these drugs after regular use (Gossop et al., 1982). Whether or not one calls these responses 'withdrawal symptoms' could be regarded as a semantic rather than a scientific question. The phenomena of tolerance and withdrawal have been more precisely delineated as neuroadaptation (Edwards et al., 1981), and the physiological processes of neuroadaptation are just a part of the cluster of factors that may be associated with the dependence syndrome.

Although tolerance and withdrawal may no longer be regarded as essential defining features of dependence, their clinical significance should not be underestimated. The development of tolerance affects the requirements for any subsequent prescription of drugs, either as part of an addiction-treatment programme (e.g. methadone maintenance) or for the treatment of other medical conditions (e.g. for relief of pain). Drug withdrawal symptoms can also be a clinically important issue. For many physically dependent drug users, the prospect of withdrawal can provoke serious anxiety (Phillips et al., 1986). Fear of withdrawal may serve to perpetuate drug use to avoid onset of withdrawal symptoms, and it can be a barrier to entering treatment. If not properly treated, the discomfort of withdrawal may interfere with broader treatment plans and may lead the patient to drop out of treatment.

Where the assignment of a formal psychiatric diagnosis is required, this is done by reference to the criteria of one or other of the diagnostic systems (currently the *Diagnostic and Statistical Manual of Mental Disorders*, 4th edition (DSM-IV; APA, 1994) or the *International Statistical Classification of Diseases and Related Health Problems*, 10th edition (ICD-10; WHO, 1992)). DSM-IV distinguishes between two groups of disorders: *substance-use disorders* (substance dependence and substance abuse) and *substance-induced disorders* (intoxication, withdrawal and drug-induced psychosis).

The criteria for dependence as defined by both the American Psychiatric Association (APA) in DSM-IV and by the World Health Organization (WHO) in ICD-10 are very similar (Table 23.2). For a diagnosis of dependence, both systems require that three or more specified symptoms/behaviours should have occurred within a 12-month period.

Table 23.2 Dependence criteria as proposed by DSM-IV and ICD-10

Symptom	DSM-IV	ICD-10
Strong desire or compulsion to use	Yes	Yes
Difficulties in controlling use	Yes	Yes
Withdrawal	Yes	Yes
Tolerance	Yes	Yes
Increased dose or extended periods of use	Yes	Not specified
Neglect of other activities	Yes	Yes
Persistence despite problems	Yes	Yes

The two psychiatric classification systems make little reference to the notion of *severity* of dependence. Their view of dependence is as a categorical disorder, which conceptualises dependence as a state (is this person dependent/addicted?) and represents a contrasting approach to assessment to that which regards dependence as being distributed along a dimension (how severely dependent/addicted is this person?). The dimensional view is more in keeping with current psychological understanding of these disorders as learned behaviours.

If dependence is a learned behaviour, which develops over time and feeds on repeated exposure to the reinforcements of drug taking, it may be expected to exist in varying degrees of strength, and should be assessed as such. Where something can be assessed by means of a dimensional measurement system, this provides more useful information. Dependence may, therefore, be more appropriately assessed by using a dimensional formulation to determine not just whether there are signs of dependence but, more usefully, the degree of its development and its severity.

The psychiatric nosologies rely on multiple criteria for the identification of a dependence disorder. However, a strong case can be made for the centrality of the desire or compulsion to use drugs. The essence of dependence is the psychological desire for drugs. Gossop (1989b) noted that of these elements 'the sense of compulsion would seem to be an essential ingredient. It contradicts our understanding of what we mean by an "addiction" that someone could be said to be addicted to something but not experience a strong need for it.' In this respect, dependence must ultimately be regarded as a psychological phenomenon.

Relatively few studies have investigated multiple substance use with specific attention to severity of *dependence* on more than one substance (Gossop, 2001). Rawson et al. (1981) suggested that dually (drug and alcohol) dependent patients may have worse treatment outcomes than those who are not heavy drinkers, and codependence on alcohol among opiate users in methadone treatment programmes has been found to affect treatment response and treatment outcome (Chatham et al., 1997). Some recovering drug addicts turn to alcohol as a substitute (Simpson and Lloyd, 1977; Hunt et al., 1986; De Leon, 1987), though in a study of multiple substance dependencies, Gossop et al. (2002a) found no association (a zero correlation) between severity of dependence on alcohol and drugs.

INTERRELATIONSHIP OF THE THREE DIMENSIONS

The view that consumption behaviours, problems and dependence should be seen as separate dimensions serves as a useful device to emphasise the conceptual independence of these three aspects of substance misuse. In practice, however, they are often related. The regular and dependent use of drugs such as heroin and cocaine has been found to be strongly related to certain types of crime, psychiatric co-morbidity, impaired social functioning, accidents, physical health and deaths. Drummond (1992) found that alcohol-related problems and dependence were still correlated even after controlling for such consumption behaviours as quantity of consumption (but that there was no relationship between problems and consumption after controlling for dependence).

Psychiatric disorders and substance misuse can coexist with varying degrees of association or independence, and the presence of both substance use and psychiatric problems within the same individuals is increasingly recognised as among the more difficult issues to be tackled by psychiatry. Substance misusers with psychiatric problems have relatively high rates of contact with various sorts of health care services (Alterman et al., 1993). Anxiety and depressed mood are more prevalent among drug users in treatment than in the general population and many people who present to drug-use treatment services have these sorts of problem (Farrell et al., 1998).

Drug misuse can induce and perpetuate psychiatric disorders. Some psychological disorders may be due to chronic intoxication, or to acute or protracted withdrawal states. Cocaine, amphetamines and cannabis, for instance, may induce anxiety states or panic attacks during acute intoxication even among users without a previous history of panic disorder (Deas-Nesmith et al., 1998). Psychiatric disorders may also be secondary to psychosocial factors which are associated with addictive behaviour.

Where drug misusers with a psychiatric disorder present in an acutely disturbed state, it is good clinical practice to use a period of abstinence for observation and assessment before a diagnosis of a comorbid, non-substance-induced psychiatric disorder is made. The persistence or remission of psychological and psychiatric symptoms during periods of abstinence may help to clarify matters. Many depressive symptoms reported by heroin-dependent patients remit within the first week of methadone maintenance treatment and subsequent to abstinence from heroin (Strain et al., 1991). The course of depressive symptoms among opiate dependent patients was investigated over a 6-month period by Rounsaville et al. (1982). More than half (60%) reported depressive symptoms at intake, but only 11% after 6 months.

Problematic drug use and psychiatric disorders may also coexist by chance, as both disorders are relatively common. Nonetheless, even in these circumstances, psychiatric problems are likely to influence the course and outcome of drug misuse disorders, and may require a specially tailored treatment approach.

The presence of comorbid psychiatric disorders among drug misusers is generally associated with a poorer treatment prognosis (Rounsaville et al., 1986), as is the severity of psychiatric disorders (Moggi et al., 1999). The provision of appropriate treatment for underlying psychiatric or psychological disorders leads to improved treatment outcomes (McLellan et al., 1983). Some substance misusers approaching treatment services have suicidal thoughts and may require a special and immediate treatment response (Gossop et al., 1998).

One of the psychotic states that may be found among drug misusers is a direct consequence of drug use. Stimulant psychosis may occur after high dose and/or prolonged use of any of the stimulants, but is more often associated with amphetamines than cocaine because of the shorter duration of effect of cocaine and the greater difficulties of sustaining chronic, high levels of cocaine (King and Ellinwood, 1997). Stimulant psychosis typically starts with suspiciousness; this may be followed by beliefs about being watched or followed (Ellinwood, 1967). Stimulant psychosis has some similarities with an acute schizophrenic disorder but it differs in other ways. Schizophrenia tends to have a relatively slow onset, and to be accompanied by a stable, somewhat bland mood (Goodwin and Guze, 1988). The onset of a stimulant psychosis is rapid and is often accompanied by an agitated or manic mood state. One of the main differences is that the treatment of stimulant psychosis is relatively straightforward. When stimulant use is discontinued, a stimulant psychosis would be expected to clear within days, with the hallucinations disappearing first and the delusions later (Schuckit, 1989).

Severity of dependence has been found to be related to a range of different problems, including injecting risk and sexual risk behaviours for blood-borne infections (Gossop et al., 1993a, 1993b). The congruence of consumption behaviours, dependence and problems is well illustrated in the use of dangerous injection practices, such as attempts to inject into the femoral vein or the use of other inappropriate and dangerous injection sites. Drug users who present for treatment often have physical and psychological health problems in addition to their drug problems. Many dependent drug users have generally poor health associated with their lifestyles, and many physical health problems are closely directly associated with drug use. Intravenous drug users can develop respiratory complications after injecting insoluble adulterants

(Glassroth et al., 1986), and the inhalation of high temperature vapours, such as those of heroin or crack cocaine, can also cause respiratory disease or damage. Such associations can be important as the decision to seek treatment may be influenced more by the accumulation of health problems than by drug use *per se* (Ward, et al., 1998).

The shared use of injecting equipment gives rise to serious concern because of its role in the transmission of HIV and other blood-borne infections. Injecting drug use was rapidly identified as one of the principal factors implicated in the spread of HIV infection.

The appearance of HIV/AIDS had a dramatic impact on the behaviour of drug users. The urgent need to respond to the threat of HIV/AIDS also radically changed the addiction treatment agenda, produced many changes in national responses to drug problems and forced a rethinking of the nature of the problem and of the appropriateness and effectiveness of existing services.

For several years after its identification, concern about HIV tended to over-shadow other drug problems, including other serious blood-borne infections about which there is now an increased awareness, such as the viral hepatitis infections, and especially hepatitis C (HCV). These infections are not directly caused by drugs or by drug dependence. They are the result of drug consumption behaviours, specifically the use of injecting equipment that has been previously contaminated by infected blood.

Increasing concern has been voiced about hepatitis C infection and its extremely high prevalence among drug injectors (Crofts et al., 1997). A study of methadone maintenance patients in London found rates of seropositivity of 86% for HCV and 55% for HBV (Best et al., 1999): one of the strongest predictors of hepatitis status was the number of years of injecting drugs (Noble et al., 2000). The beliefs of drug injectors about their own viral status are frequently inaccurate. Best et al. (1999) found that addicts tended, mistakenly, to believe they were not infected with HBV or HCV when they were, in fact, seropositive for one or other of these infections. Clinicians should encourage testing in all injecting patients and use this as a catalyst for interventions.

Heavy drinking among HCV infected drug users is also a significant risk factor for mortality because of its adverse effects upon the physical health of the user. Heavy drinking is common among dependent drug users. More than one third of drug users seeking treatment in UK drug addiction services reported problematic or highly problematic patterns of alcohol consumption (Gossop et al., 2000b). For individuals chronically infected with HCV, heavy drinking is especially risky, but even low levels of alcohol consumption have been found to be associated with increased risk of viraemia and hepatic fibrosis (Pessione et al., 1998).

Deaths among drug users have many causes, including accidents, suicide, violence, AIDS, acute toxic reactions and various drug-related and other illnesses (Rivara et al., 1997; Hulse et al., 1999; Rossow and Lauritzen, 1999).

Drug overdoses continue to be one of the most frequent causes of death among dependent drug misusers (Ghodse et al., 1978; Hall and Darke, 1998; Powis et al., 1999). In a Scottish study, for instance, Frischer et al. (1993) found that more than 90% of deaths among drug misusers were due to drug overdose or suicide, and only 2% to HIV/AIDS.

Simpson and Sells (1983) found the death rates of drug users (predominantly heroin users) to be 3–14 times higher than those of their peers of the same age. The majority of deaths (68%) were associated with drug overdoses. Opiates were the drugs most commonly detected during post-mortem examinations. Mainly these showed the presence of heroin (in two-thirds of the overdose cases). Although fatal and non-fatal overdoses are commonly attributed to the use of opiates, the risk of overdose is strongly linked to, and increased by, polydrug use. Overdoses that are attributed to heroin are more likely to involve the combined use of opiates and alcohol or other sedatives (Gossop et al., 2002b).

CONCLUDING REMARKS

Few would disagree with the proposition that assessment should be thorough and comprehensive. What is more important than thoroughness, however, is relevance. The mere accumulation of information is no substitute for an effective and focused assessment. One of the most frequent errors of assessment is to become bogged down in an increasingly detailed, retrospective analysis of the presenting problem.

In general, the identification and setting of goals should occur as early as possible within the treatment process. The specification of goals and of the procedures required to reach those goals serves to identify, and to avoid or reduce problems of misunderstanding and failures of communication between therapist and patient. It may be more appropriate to think in terms of reaching mutual agreement (between the patient and therapist) about goals rather than simply setting goals. It is useful to discuss and agree the goals of treatment during the assessment phase. Specifying treatment goals, and negotiating the mutual agreement of these between therapist and patient, delineating treatment procedures, and providing feedback about progress are core features of effective treatments. Properly defined goals help both the therapist and the patient to be clear about the aims and purposes of treatment.

REFERENCES

Alterman, A., McLellan, A. and Shifman, R. (1993) Do substance abuse patients with more psychopathology receive more treatment? *Journal of Nervous and Mental Disease*, 181, 576–582.

American Psychiatric Association (APA) (1994) *Diagnostic and Statistical Manual of Mental Disorders, 4th edn*. Washington, DC: APA.

Ball, J., Shaffer, J. and Nurco, D. (1983) The day to day criminality of heroin addicts in Baltimore: a study in the continuity of offence rates. *Drug and Alcohol Dependence*, 12, 119–142.

Best, D., Noble, A., Finch, E., Gossop, M., Sidwell, C. and Strang, J. (1999). Accuracy of perceptions of hepatitis B and C status: Cross sectional investigation of opiate addicts in treatment. *British Medical Journal*, 319, 290–291.

Chatham, L. R., Rowan-Szal, G. A., Joe, G. W. and Simpson, D. D. (1997) Heavy drinking, alcohol dependent vs. nondependent methadone maintenance clients: A follow-up study. *Addictive Behaviours*, 22, 69–80.

Crofts, N., Nigro, L., Oman, K., Stevenson, E. and Sherman, J. (1997) Methadone maintenance and hepatitis C virus infection among injecting drug users. *Addiction*, 92, 999–1005.

Darke, S., Hall, W., Wodak, A., Heather, N. and Ward, J. (1992) Development and validation of a multi-dimensional instrument for assessing outcome of treatment among opiate users: The Opiate Treatment Index. *British Journal of Addiction*, 87, 733–742.

Deas-Nesmith, D., Brady, K. and Myrick, H. (1998) Drug abuse and anxiety disorders. In: H. Kranzler and B. Rousaville (eds) *Dual Diagnosis and Treatment*. New York: Marcel Dekker.

DelBoca, F. and Noll, J. (2000) Truth or consequences: The validity of self-report data in health services research on addictions. *Addiction*, 95, 347–360.

De Leon, G. (1987) Alcohol use among drug abusers: Treatment outcome in a therapeutic community. *Alcoholism*, 11, 430–436.

Drummond, D. C. (1992) Problems and dependence: Chalk and cheese or bread and butter? In: M. Lader, G. Edwards and D. C. Drummond (eds) *The Nature of Alcohol and Drug Related Problems*. Oxford: Oxford Medical Publications.

Dunbar, J. and Stunkard, A. (1979) Adherence to diet and drug regimen. In: R. Levy, B. Rifkind, B. Dennis and N. Ernst. *Nutrition, Lipids, Coronary Heart Disease*. New York: Raven.

Edwards, G., Arif, A. and Hodgson, R. (1981) Nomenclature and classification of drug- and alcohol-related problems: A WHO memorandum. *Bulletin of the World Health Organization*, 59(2), 225–242.

Ellinwood, E. H. (1967) Amphetamine psychosis. I. Description of the individuals and process. *Journal of Nervous and Mental Disease*, 144, 273.

Farrell, M., Howed, S., Taylor, C., Lewis, G., Jenkins, R., Bebbington, P. et al. (1998) Substance misuse and psychiatric comorbidity: An overview of the OPCS National Psychiatric Morbidity Survey. *Addictive Behaviors*, 23, 909–918.

Frischer, M., Bloor, M., Goldberg, D., Clark, J., Green, S. and McKeganey, N. (1993) Mortality among injecting drug users: A critical reappraisal. *Journal of Epidemiology and Community Health*, 47, 59–63.

Gardner, R. and Connell, PH, (1971) Opioid users attending a special drug dependence clinic 1968–1969. *Bulletin on Narcotics*, XXIII, 915.

Ghodse, A. H. (1978) The attitudes of casualty staff and ambulance personnel towards patients who take drug overdoses. *Social Science and Medicine*, 12, 341–346.

Glassroth, J. et al. (1986) The impact of substance abuse treatment on the respiratory system. *Chest*, 91, 596–602.

Goldstein, P. (1979) *Prostitution and Drugs*. Lexington: Lexington Books.

Goodwin, D. and Guze, S. (1988) *Psychiatric Diagnosis*. Oxford: Oxford University Press.

Gossop, M. (1989a) The detoxification of high dose heroin addicts in Pakistan. *Drug and Alcohol Dependence*, 24, 143–150.

Gossop, M. (1989b) *Relapse and Addictive Behaviour*. London: Routledge.

Gossop, M. (2001) A web of dependence. *Addiction*, 96, 677–678.

Gossop, M., Bradley, B. and Brewis, R. (1982) Amphetamine withdrawal and sleep disturbance. *Drug and Alcohol Dependence*, 10, 177–183.

Gossop, M., Griffiths, P. and Strang, J. (1988) Chasing the dragon: A comparison of heroin chasers and injectors seen by a London community drug team. *British Journal of Addiction*, 83, 1159–1162.

Gossop, M., Griffiths, P. and Strang, J. (1991a) Chasing the dragon. *Journal of Substance Abuse Treatment*, 8, 89–91.

Gossop, M., Battersby, M. and Strang, J. (1991b) Self-detoxification by opiate addicts: a preliminary investigation. *British Journal of Psychiatry*, 159, 208–212.

Gossop, M., Griffiths, P., Powis, B. and Strang, J. (1993a) Severity of heroin dependence and HIV risk: I. Sexual behaviour. *AIDS CARE*, 5, 149–157.

Gossop, M., Griffiths, P., Powis, B. and Strang, J. (1993b) Severity of heroin dependence and HIV risk: II. Sharing injecting equipment. *AIDS CARE*, 5, 159–168.

Gossop, M., Griffiths, P., Powis, B. and Strang, J. (1994) Cocaine: Patterns of use, route of administration, and severity of dependence. *British Journal of Psychiatry*, 164, 660–664.

Gossop, M., Darke, S., Griffiths, P., Hando, J., Powis, B., Hall, W. and Strang, J. (1995) The Severity of Dependence Scale (SDS): Psychometric properties of the SDS in English and Australian samples of heroin, cocaine and amphetamine users. *Addiction*, 90, 607–614.

Gossop, M., Griffiths, P., Powis, B., Williamson, S. and Strang, J. (1996) Frequency of non-fatal heroin overdose: Survey of heroin users recruited in non-clinical settings. *British Medical Journal*, 313, 402.

Gossop, M., Marsden, J., Stewart, D., Lehmann, P., Edwards, C., Wilson, A. and Segar, G. (1998) Substance use, health and social problems of clients at 54 drug treatment agencies: intake data from the National Treatment Outcome Research Study (NTORS). *British Journal of Psychiatry*, 173, 166–171.

Gossop, M., Marsden, J., Stewart, D. and Treacy, S. (2000a) Routes of drug administration and multiple drug misuse: Regional variations among clients seeking treatment at programmes throughout England. *Addiction*, 95, 1197–1206.

Gossop, M., Marsden, J., Stewart, D. and Rolfe, A. (2000b) Patterns of drinking and drinking outcomes among drug misusers: 1-year follow-up results. *Journal of Substance Abuse Treatment*, 19, 45–50.

Gossop, M., Marsden, J. and Stewart, D. (2002a) Dual dependence: Assessment of dependence upon alcohol and illicit drugs, and the relationship of alcohol dependence among drug misusers to patterns of drinking, illicit drug use, and health problems. *Addiction*, 97, 169–178.

Gossop, M., Marsden, J., Stewart, D. and Treacy, S. (2002b) A prospective study of mortality among drug misusers during a four year period after seeking treatment. *Addiction*, 97, 39–47.

Griffiths, P., Gossop, M., Powis, B. and Strang, J. (1994) Transitions in patterns of heroin administration: a study of heroin chasers and heroin injectors. *Addiction*, 89, 301–309.

Hall, W. and Darke, S. (1998) Trends in opiate overdose deaths in Australia 1979–1995. *Drug and Alcohol Dependence*, 52, 71–77.

Hamid, R., Deren, S., Beardsley, M. and Tortu, S. (1999) Agreement between urinalysis and self-reported drug use. *Substance Use and Misuse*, 34, 1585–1592.

Hammersley, R., Forsyth, A. and Lavelle, T. (1990) The criminality of new drug users in Glasgow. *British Journal of Addiction*, 85, 1583–1594.

Hulse, G. K., English, G. R., Milne, E. and Holman, C. D. J. (1999) The quantification of mortality resulting from the regular use of illicit opiates. *Addiction*, 94, 221–229.

Hunt, D., Lipton, D., Goldsmith, D. et al. (1986) 'It takes your heart': The image of methadone maintenance in the addict world and its effect on recruitment to treatment. *International Journal of the Addictions*, 20, 1751–1771.

Jarvis, G. and Parker, H. (1989) Young heroin users and crime. *British Journal of Criminology*, 29, 175–185.

King, G. R. and Ellinwood, E. H. (1997) Amphetamines and other stimulants. In: J. Lowinson, P. Ruiz, R. Millman, J. Langrod (eds) *Substance Abuse: A Comprehensive Textbook*. Baltimore: Williams and Wilkins.

Kleber, H. (1988) Epidemic cocaine abuse: America's present, Britain's future? *British Journal of Addiction*, 83, 1359–1371.

Marsden, J., Gossop, M., Stewart, D., Best, D., Farrell, M., Lehmann, P. et al. (1998) The Maudsley Addiction Profile (MAP): A brief instrument for assessing treatment outcome. *Addiction*, 93, 1857–1867.

McLellan, A. T., Luborsky, L., O'Brien, C. P. and Woody, G. E. (1980) An improved evaluation instrument for substance abuse patients: The Addiction Severity Index. *Journal of Nervous and Mental Disease*, 168, 26–33.

McLellan, A. T., Luborsky, L., Woody, G., Druley, K. and O'Brien, C. (1983) Predicting response to alcohol and drug abuse treatments: Role of psychiatric severity. *Archives of General Psychiatry*, 40, 620–625.

McLellan, A. T., Cacciola, J., Kushner, H., Peters, F., Smith, I. and Pettinati, H. (1992) The fifth edition of the Addiction Severity Index: Cautions, additions and normative data. *Journal of Substance Abuse Treatment*, 5, 312–316.

Moggi, F., Ouimette, P., Moos, R. and Finney, J. (1999) Dual diagnosis patients in substance abuse treatment: Relationship of general coping and substance specific coping to 1 year outcomes. *Addiction*, 94, 1805–1816.

Morral, A. R., McCaffrey, D. and Iguchi, M. (2000) Hardcore drug users claim to be occasional users: frequency underreporting. *Drug and Alcohol Dependence*, 57, 193–202.

Noble, A., Best, B., Finch, E., Gossop, M., Sidwell, C. and Strang, J. (2000) Injecting risk behaviour and year of first injection as predictors of hepatitis B and C status among methadone maintenance patients in south London. *Journal of Substance Use*, 5, 131–135.

Nurco, D., Kinlock, T. and Balter, M. (1993) The severity of pre-addiction criminal behaviour among urban, male narcotic addicts and two non addicted control groups. *Journal of Research in Crime and Delinquency*, 30(3), 293–316.

O'Leary, K. and Wilson, G. (1975) *Behavior Therapy: Application and Outcome*. Englewood Cliffs, NJ: Prentice Hall.

Orford, J. (2001) *Excessive Appetites: A Psychological View of Addictions*. Chichester: John Wiley.

Pearson, G. and Gillman, M. (1994) Local and regional variations in drug misuse: The British heroin epidemic of the 1980s. In: J. Strang and M. Gossop (eds) *Heroin Addiction and Drug Policy: The British System*. Oxford: Oxford University Press.

Pessione, F., Degos, F., Marcellin, P., Duchatelle, V., Njapoum, C., Martinot-Peignoux, M. et al. (1998) Effect of alcohol consumption on serum hepatitis C virus RNA and histological lesions in chronic hepatitis C. *Hepatology*, 27, 1717–1722.

Phillips, G., Gossop, M. and Bradley, B. (1986) The influence of psychological factors on the opiate withdrawal syndrome. *British Journal of Psychiatry*, 149, 235–238.

Powis, B., Strang, J., Griffiths, P., Taylor, C., Williamson, S., Fountain, J. and Gossop, M. (1999) Self-reported overdose among injecting drug users in London: Extent and nature of the problem. *Addiction*, 94, 471–478.

Rawson, R., Washton, A., Resnick, R. and Tennant, F. (1981) Clonidine hydrochloride detoxification from methadone treatment: The value of naltrexone aftercare. In: L. Harris (ed) *Problem of Drug Dependence 1980*. Research Monograph 34. Rockville, MD: National Institute on Drug Abuse.

Rivara, F. P., Mueller, B. A., Somes, G., Mendoza, C. T., Rushforth, N. B. and Kellerman, A. L. (1997) Alcohol and illicit drug use and the risk of violent death in the home. *Journal of the American Medical Association*, 278, 569–575.

Rossow, I. and Lauritzen, G. (1999) Balancing on the edge of death: Suicide attempts and life-threatening overdoses among drug addicts. *Addiction*, 94, 209–219.

Rounsaville, B. J., Weissman, M. M., Crits-Christoph, K., Wilber, C. and Kleber, H. (1982) Diagnosis and symptoms of depression in opiate addicts. *Archives of General Psychiatry*, 39, 151–156.

Rounsaville, B. J., Kosten, T., Weissman, M. and Kleber, H. (1986) Prognostic significance of psychopathology in treated opiate addicts. *Comprehensive Psychiatry*, 27, 480–498.

Royal College of Physicians (1987) *The Medical Consequences of Alcohol Abuse*. London: Tavistock.

Saunders, J., Aasland, O., Babor, T., De La Fuente, J. and Grant, M. (1993) Development of the Alcohol Use Disorders Identification Test (AUDIT): WHO collaborative project on early detection of persons with harmful alcohol consumption. *Addiction*, 88, 791–804.

Schuckit, M. A. (1989) *Drug and Alcohol Abuse: A Clinical Guide to Diagnosis and Treatment*. New York: Plenum.

Simpson, D. D. and Lloyd, M. R. (1977) *Alcohol and Illicit Drug Use: National Follow-up Study of Admissions to Drug Abuse Treatments in the DARP during 1969–1971*. Services Research Report. Rockville, MD: National Institute on Drug Abuse.

Simpson, D. and Sells, S. (1983) Effectiveness for treatment of drug abuse: An overview of the DARP research programme. *Advances in Alcohol and Substance Abuse*, 2(1), 7–29.

Sobell, M. and Sobell, L. (1998) Guiding self-change. In: W. Miller and N. Heather (eds) *Treating Addictive Behaviors*. New York: Plenum.

Speckart, G. and Anglin, M. D. (1985) Narcotics use and crime. An analysis of existing evidence for a causal relationship. *Behavioural Science and Law*, 3, 259–283.

Stewart, D., Gossop, M., Marsden, J. and Rolfe, A. (2000) Drug misuse and acquisitive crime among clients recruited to the National Treatment Outcome Research Study (NTORS). *Criminal Behaviour and Mental Health*, 10, 10–20.

Strain, E. C., Brooner, R. K. and Bigelow, G. E. (1991) Clustering of multiple substance use and psychiatric diagnoses in opiate addicts. *Drug andAlcohol Dependence*, 27, 127–134.

Strang, J., Griffiths, P. and Gossop, M. (1992) First use of heroin: Changes in route of administration over time. *British Medical Journal*, 304, 1222–1223.

Ward, J., Mattick, R. and Hall, W. (1998) *Methadone Maintenance Treatment and Other Opioid Replacement Therapies*. Australia: Harwood.

Weiss, R. D., Najavits, L. M., Greenfield, S. F., Soto, J. A., Shaw, S. R. and Wyner, D. (1998) Validity of substance use self-reports in dually diagnosed outpatients. *American Journal of Psychiatry*, 155, 127–128.

Weiss, R. D., Greenfield, S. F., Griffin, M. L., Najavits, L. M. and Fucinto, L. (2000) The use of collateral reports for patients with bipolar and substance use disorders. *American Journal of Drug and Alcohol Abuse*, 26, 369–378.

Wolff, K. and Strang, J. (1999) Therapeutic drug monitoring for methadone: Scanning the horizon. *European Addiction Research*, 5, 36–42.

Wolff, K., Farrell, M., Marsden, J., Monteiro, M., All, R., Welch, S. and Strang, J. (1999) A review of biological indicators of illicit drug use, practical considerations and clinical usefulness. *Addiction*, 94, 1279–1298.

World Health Organization (WHO) (1992) *The ICD-10 Classification of Mental and Behavioural Disorders*. Geneva: WHO.

Zanis, D., McLellan, A. T. and Randall, M. (1994) Can you trust patients' self-reports of drug use during treatment? *Drug and Alcohol Dependence*, 35, 127–132.

Chapter 24

Substance misuse disorders

Treatment

Michael Gossop

TREATMENT IN CONTEXT

A proper understanding of the treatment of drug or alcohol* problems is unlikely to follow from a mere listing of treatments with a description of their procedures. The interventions that occur during treatment are a part of a much wider range of factors that can influence outcome. Treatment is a complex, interactive and sometimes idiosyncratic process. In many cases, treatment may be neither the most important nor the most powerful influence on outcome. Treatment must be set in a much broader context.

Environmental supports and stressors can influence outcomes. Social factors such as peer and family relationships, unemployment and living arrangements, can have an important effect. An effective treatment programme can be undermined or neutralised by adverse social and environmental factors. Treatment is also influenced by individual psychological factors, including beliefs, attitudes and intentions. As in the rehabilitation of chronic illnesses such as multiple sclerosis or stroke, the treatment and rehabilitation of people with drug-dependence problems is, in many respects, more similar to education than to medical treatment with drugs or surgery.

To state this is not to demean or downplay the role of treatment. Treatment provides an important opportunity to intervene and interrupt the psychological, social and biological processes that act to confine the person within destructive patterns of addictive behaviour. Even where treatment factors do not act as direct determinants of change, treatment may still provide a facilitative setting in which behavioural improvements can take place.

For many years, the traditional view of addiction was pessimistic about outcome. Received wisdom suggested that people who become dependent on drugs or alcohol seldom gave up, and that treatment had little effect. An editorial in the first edition of the *International Journal of the Addictions*

---

* To avoid having to keep referring to drugs or alcohol, the chapter uses terms such as 'drugs', 'drug use' and 'substance use' to include both drugs and alcohol. Only where the text refers to specific drugs, including alcohol, are these mentioned by name.

stated that there was no relationship between treatment and outcome and that, regardless of the type of treatment provided, 'the great majority of addicts simply resume drug use' (Einstein, 1966). Similarly, an early review of treatment evaluation studies noted that 'the treatment of heroin addiction has been singularly unsuccessful' (Callahan, 1980). Addiction was seen in terms of inevitable and progressive deterioration.

The therapeutic landscape of addiction treatment has changed considerably since the 1960s. Promising treatment interventions and procedures have been developed. Different forms of psychological treatments have been developed. There are a range of pharmacological options where once there were very few. There is increasing evidence about the effectiveness of many treatment options. There is a clearer understanding of the importance of the social environment, behavioural functioning, cognitive processes and the use of active coping strategies during recovery. Nonetheless, the treatment and management of drug addiction continues to be characterised by changing perspectives and controversies of one kind or another.

Treatment is not always necessary for recovery. Not all drug users (not even all users of heroin or crack) go on to become addicted, and even among those who do, some will stop using drugs without formal treatment. There is a growing interest in the changes in drug use, including cessation, that occur without any formal treatment. Such changes may be more common than is usually believed.

Biernacki (1986) investigated a group of heroin addicts who had deliberately chosen not to become involved in treatment as a way of giving up. The majority believed either that there was no need for formal treatment because they could take care of themselves, or they thought that treatment would not help. Breaking away from addiction was often accomplished by moving away (geographically) from the location in which the drug taking patterns had been established. In other cases, the moving away was achieved by the person putting a 'social distance' between themselves and their previous drug using friends and environments.

Most heroin addicts make at least one self-detoxification attempt without treatment assistance and many make repeated attempts (Gossop et al., 1991; Noble et al., 2002). Some self-treatment episodes enable users to become drug-free for a time, the longer-term success rate, however, is rather poor.

It is not unusual for drug misusers to be ambivalent about treatment, and their commitment to change may fluctuate across time. Conflict and ambivalence are at the root of giving up an addiction. Individuals who are desperate for treatment prior to admission may be resistant to treatment and deny their presenting problems after admission. Ambivalence is common during the first days and weeks of treatment, and presents a challenge to clinicians. Ambivalence is different to denial. The ambivalence of the user toward treatment has several sources. It is always useful for treatment personnel to remember that whereas they may clearly see the problems, for the users, drugs are something that have, for many years, been a focal point for their lives and a source of repeated and intense positive reinforcement.

Also, in contrast to the easily obtained gratification of drug use, most addiction treatment programmes, especially if implemented according to best clinical practice, are rigorous and demanding, and require behavioural and psychological change. The difficulties of beginning and remaining committed to this sort of change should not be underestimated.

For many dependent drug misusers, neither external pressure from others nor internal motivation is sufficient to produce effective change (McLellan et al., 1997). The addiction may be sustained for many years, and they may require long-term treatment and support. It is not uncommon for drug careers to last for extended periods of time (sometimes for decades) and while dependent drug use continues, the costs to the individual, to those around them and to society are massive. Patients in the UK were found to have been using heroin for 9 years, on average, at the time of admission to treatment (Gossop et al., 1998). Hser et al. (1993), for example, assessed the outcome of 581 male heroin users over a 24-year period. At the final follow-up, about a quarter of them were still using opiates.

The evaluation of treatment effectiveness is a complicated matter. The apparently simple question 'Does addiction treatment work?' is too simple. Treatment involves different practices and procedures, which are used with different populations and which are designed to achieve different goals. Addiction treatments vary in content, duration, intensity, goal, setting, provider and target population. Also, different treatments may be required to tackle the initiation of change and the maintenance of change.

An important conclusion to be reached from the treatment evaluation literature is that no single type of treatment can be expected to be effective for everyone who has an addiction problem. Despite the widespread acceptance of these principles, current treatment provision at the programme level still tends to operate in a way that is more reflective of the view that 'one size fits all', with patients being expected to adjust to the programme being provided.

The pathways leading to recovery tend to be complicated with a variety of possible outcomes. People who are treated for drug addiction problems achieve a continuum of outcomes with respect to their drug taking behaviour and their drug-related problems. Different types of drug consumption and drug problems may increase or decrease following treatment, and the outcomes for different people will follow different time courses. After treatment, some people may show initial improvement with subsequent deterioration. Others may initially show little change but then gradually achieve a range of possibly substantial improvements. Others may oscillate between outcomes, with periods of abstinence alternating with periods of drug use.

TREATMENT INTERVENTIONS

In general, psychological treatments assume that addictive behaviours are substantially influenced by normal learning processes; that addictive behaviour is functional for the drug users and that, as a learned behaviour, addictive behaviour can be modified or 'unlearned'. Kazdin (1978) described five general characteristics which are common, if not universal, among these psychological treatments.

1   A focus on current rather than historical determinants of behaviour.
2   Reliance on psychological research as a source of hypotheses about treatment and therapy techniques.
3   Specificity in defining, measuring and treating the target problems.
4   Explicit description of treatment procedures in objective terms.
5   Emphasis on overt changes in behaviour as the main criterion for treatment effectiveness.

Conditioning treatments

Several attempts have been made to apply conditioning principles to the treatment of dependence disorders. These include: (1) attempts to reduce the strength of drug-related conditioned stimuli (CS) through classical extinction (repeated presentation of the CS not followed by drug administration); and (2) counter-conditioning of other responses to the drug-related CS.

Cue exposure and the treatment of craving

Cue exposure methods have been advocated as a treatment for addictive behaviours. The rationale most often cited for using cue exposure is based on a classical conditioning model, in which drugs are the unconditioned stimulus and drug effects are the unconditioned responses. The circumstances surrounding drug use become conditioned stimuli, which are capable of evoking conditioned responses that moderate or mediate drug seeking and consumption (Conklin and Tiffany, 2002).

Drug dependence is most often manifested, psychologically and behaviourally, in feelings of compulsion and difficulty in resisting those urges. Dependent users are confronted by various stimuli that have been conditioned to different aspects of their drug using behaviours. Relapse is often strongly cue and context specific (Drummond et al., 1995). When a user encounters drug-related cues, these can produce urges to use, withdrawal-like effects and drug seeking behaviour. Conditioned stimuli can elicit conditioned responses, which in turn are likely to lead to drug seeking/use, and which may be experienced by the individual as 'craving'. Cue exposure treatments have sometimes been seen specifically as treatments to reduce craving.

Typically, cue exposure treatments involve repeated unreinforced exposure to drug related stimuli in an attempt to extinguish conditioned responses to such cues. Exposure may be *in vivo* or may involve symbolic or cognitive cues (imagining being offered drugs, or looking at photographs or videotapes).

However, drug related cues do not reliably lead to conditioned responses. Rohsenow et al. (1992) found that one third of alcoholics did not report an increased urge to drink in a laboratory based, cue exposure situation. In another study, as many as 40–50% of alcoholics exhibited no elicited response to alcohol cues (Litt et al., 1990). Subjective and physiological reactivity to cues has been found to vary both within and across studies (Modesto-Lowe and Kranzler, 1999).

Another issue is whether cue reactivity predicts future substance-use behaviours. It is uncertain whether measures of craving taken prior to and after the cue exposure treatment are related to post-treatment outcomes. Drummond and Glautier (1994) found that cue exposure was more effective than relaxation training, not in preventing relapse but in reducing drinking after an initial lapse, and prolonging the time of progression to heavy drinking. Despite its sound theoretical base, the literature remains somewhat inconsistent both with regard to the extent to which cues elicit craving responses, and in the relationship of cue reactivity to subsequent substance use.

Aversion therapies

Some early attempts at behaviour therapy treatments for drug dependence that were based on counterconditioning involved aversive conditioning. Both chemical and electrical aversion therapies were used to treat dependent drinkers as early as the 1930s. Such treatments have seldom been used in standard clinical practice and they are extremely rare in current treatment programmes. Interest in aversion therapy declined, both for ethical reasons and because it proved to be ineffective (Rachman and Teasdale, 1969). An alternative form of aversion therapy involved covert conditioning or covert sensitisation, in which thoughts of the unwanted behaviour are paired in imagination with unpleasant stimuli. Again, despite some early enthusiasm, this approach is also of uncertain efficacy and is seldom used for the treatment of addiction.

Contingency management

The theoretical foundations for contingency management are based on operant conditioning principles in which addictive behaviour is maintained by environmental and other reinforcers and can be changed by altering the consequences.

Contingency management provides a system of incentives and disincentives, which are designed to make continued drug use less attractive and abstinence more attractive. As described by Stitzer et al. (1989), contingency management 'organizes treatment delivery, sets specific objective behavioural goals, and attempts to structure the environment in a manner that is conducive to change'.

Contingency management has been found to be useful for extinguishing negative or undesirable behaviours, such as continued drug use, or failure to comply with treatment requirements, and as a means of encouraging positive behaviours such as engagement with treatment services. Some contingency programmes have used positive reinforcement alone. Others have used mixed positive and negative reinforcement. Contingency management interventions have often been conducted with patients receiving methadone treatment because methadone (or factors such as dose level, dosing frequency or the take-home option) lend themselves readily for use as reinforcers. Contingency contracting has also been used to improve adherence to disulfiram treatment (Bigelow et al., 1976).

Robles et al. (1999) suggest that the key features of contingency management include:

- the target behaviour that treatment seeks to change (e.g. attending counselling sessions, producing alcohol-free urine specimens)
- the conditions (or antecedents) under which the target behaviours are to occur (e.g. attendance every Monday at a stated time with no reminders from programme staff)
- the reinforcer (e.g. one bus token)
- the contingency, which specifies the rules according to which re-inforcers are earned for producing the target behaviour (e.g. one bus token for each counselling session attended).

A persistent problem for addiction treatment services has involved those patients who do not comply with the requirements of treatment programmes or who do not get better as a result of their contact with treatment. Contingency management has been found to be particularly useful as a treatment intervention for 'non-responsive' patients.

Cognitive behavioural therapies and psychosocial treatments

Cognitive behavioural therapies are widely used in the treatment of addiction problems. Liese and Najavits (1997) suggested that cognitive-behavioural theories tended to make the following assumptions:

- Addiction is mediated both by cognitive and behavioural processes.
- Addiction and its associated cognitive behavioural processes are, to a large extent, learned.

- Addiction and associated cognitive behavioural processes can be modified.
- A major goal of cognitive behavioural treatment for addictive disorders is to facilitate the acquisition of coping skills for resisting substance use and for reducing related problems.
- Cognitive behavioural therapies require comprehensive and individualised case conceptualisations to select and guide specific cognitive-behavioural techniques.

Motivational interviewing

Motivational interviewing (MI) has been popular and clinically influential in recent years (Miller 1983; Miller and Rollnick, 1991). Motivation is conceptualised as the product of an interpersonal process in which the behaviour of the therapist has considerable influence on the subsequent attributions and behaviour of the patient. MI is used to help explore and resolve ambivalence about change. Its aim is to increase levels of cognitive dissonance until sufficient motivation is generated for the patient to consider the options and interventions for change. Motivational enhancement methods have often been closely linked to stages of change models (Prochaska and Diclemente, 1982; Prochaska et al., 1992).

MI is specifically concerned with the patient–therapist interaction and is seen primarily as a counselling *style* rather than a technique (Rollnick, 2001). Miller (1983) recommended that the therapist initially adopts an empathic stance and suggested using techniques similar to those operationalised by Carl Rogers. This process is, however, modified to selectively reinforce statements of concern and elicit self-motivational statements. The therapist is not just being reflective but subtly steers the patient towards change.

MI differs from some other treatment approaches in that it avoids trying to persuade or convince the patient to do something about his or her drug problems, but seeks to supervise a process of decision making in which the patient makes the decisions. MI has been found to be useful in many phases of treatment but it has been particularly useful in helping people who are still at an early stage of committing themselves to treatment or to changing their behaviour.

There has been considerable interest in the potential uses of brief interventions, often based on MI, to tackle substance abuse problems. Heather (2002) suggested that brief interventions *can* work but whether they actually work in day-to-day clinical practice depends on the manner in which they are provided. The effectiveness of such interventions is still somewhat uncertain. For example, although Wutzke et al. (2002) reported short-term changes among problem drinkers after brief interventions when compared to a no-treatment control group, there were no differences in long-term outcomes for the brief intervention and no-treatment groups. Also, it is not known to what extent such interventions are applicable or effective with people who are severely dependent, with co-dependence on other substances, or with serious medical and mental health problems. In this respect, the utility of brief interventions may be linked to the issue of patient/treatment matching.

One limitation of some addiction treatments is that they presume a prior commitment to change. MI assumes that the person in treatment is ambivalent about his or her substance use and sees itself as 'an approach designed to help clients build commitment and reach a decision to change' (Miller and Rollnick, 1991). MI challenges the idea of 'denial' as a characteristic of people with drug problems, and also challenges treatment interventions that use forms of aggressive confrontation. Denial, for example, is seen not as an attitude or personality characteristic of the drug user but as a product of the way in which the counsellor interacts with the patient. The strongest assertion of this view states that 'client resistance is a therapist problem' (Miller and Rollnick, 1991).

However, motives do not translate directly into outcomes, and motivation alone is unlikely to be sufficient for change or the maintenance of change among many of the long-term, severely dependent drug users who seek treatment in addiction services. The majority of these will already have committed themselves to change on repeated occasions, and will have made several serious attempts to change their behaviour. Nevertheless, the person's motivation to seek treatment is likely to influence his or her engagement with the treatment services offered, as well as the probability of remaining in treatment long enough to benefit from exposure to the therapeutic process.

Relapse prevention

An important distinction should be made between initial change and the maintenance of change. The factors and procedures that are most effective in inducing behaviour change may not be the most effective for producing generalisation and maintenance of treatment effects. The problem of relapse is an important characteristic of all of the addictive disorders. A large proportion of people who have been treated for such problems tend to return to those behaviours within a short time of leaving treatment.

Marlatt (1985) described Relapse Prevention (RP) as a self-control programme that combines behavioural skill training, cognitive interventions and lifestyle change procedures. RP seeks to teach those who are trying to change how to identify, anticipate, and cope with the pressures and problems that may lead towards a relapse. Two essential features are the identification of high risk situations that put the individual at increased risk of relapse, and the development and strengthening of effective coping responses.

Relapse Prevention typically includes:

- identification of high risk situations for relapse

- instruction and rehearsal of coping strategies
- self-monitoring and behavioural analysis of substance use
- planning for emergencies and lapses.

High Risk Situations may be situations, events, objects, cognitions or mood states that have become associated with drug use and/or relapse. Most lapses have been found to be related to negative emotional states, social pressure and interpersonal conflicts (Cummings et al., 1980). Antecedents to lapse may also include subjective experiences of 'urge' (sudden impulse to engage in an act) and 'craving' (subjective desire to experience effects of a given act); (Heather and Stallard, 1989). Risk factors often occur together, either in clusters or in sequence (Bradley et al., 1989) and they may operate in an additive or interactive manner (Shiffman, 1989).

RP requires an individualised assessment of high risk situations for relapse involving a microanalysis of each high risk drug taking situation for each patient in terms of his or her social and environmental circumstances, cognitive appraisal of those situations and expectations regarding the options for and effectiveness of coping behaviours that he or she could use in such situations. The effective delivery of RP requires a close interrelationship between assessment and treatment.

Patients are taught to recognise particular factors that increase their risk of returning to problematic behaviour(s), and to avoid or to cope with these factors. To support the maintenance of change, RP requires the development of specific coping strategies to deal with high risk situations. This may include skills training and the development or strengthening of more global coping strategies that address issues of lifestyle imbalance and antecedents of relapse. Assessment should take account of cognitive appraisals of past successes and failures in relation to these same drug taking situations (Annis, 1986).

RP procedures may help to anticipate and prevent the occurrence of a relapse after the initiation of a habit change attempt, and to help the individual recover from a 'slip' or lapse before it escalates into a full-blown relapse. In principle, RP procedures can be used regardless of the theoretical orientation of the therapist or the intervention methods applied during the initial treatment phase. Once a person has stopped using drugs, for example, RP can be used to support continued abstinence, regardless of the methods used to initiate abstinence (e.g. attending 12-step meetings, psychotherapy or voluntary cessation; Marlatt, 1985).

Marlatt and Gordon's (1985) relapse prevention model was the first major cognitive behavioural approach to be used in the treatment of substance use disorders, and it provides a straightforward conceptual model for understanding drug misuse problems. It identifies practical, flexible interventions that can be applied by clinicians with a range of backgrounds and skills; it has given direction and purpose to treatment in day-to-day clinical settings by showing how assessment should be targeted at key problem areas; and it can be adjunctively with other treatments.

RP methods have often been used, together with other elements (such as contingency management and social skills training) as part of community reinforcement treatment (Azrin, 1976; Kadden, 2001). However, despite its theoretical promise, community reinforcement interventions have not been widely implemented or evelauated, perhaps because of lack of the necessary community resources.

Narcotics Anonymous/Alcoholics Anonymous

For more than six decades, Alcoholics Anonymous (AA) has influenced the treatment of alcohol dependence and has gained increasing international popularity. It has been estimated to have as many as two million members world-wide (Makela, 1993). AA has been seen as the paradigm of the self-help movement for recovery from addiction, although many of the members tend to dislike the *self*-help label and prefer to see the fellowship as providing *mutual* support. Mutual support is seen as a key dynamic for change. It occurs both through the involvement of members of the fellowship, who share common problems, and through the specific support that can be offered by the sponsor (Brown et al., 2001).

Group meetings are one of the best known aspects of NA/AA. In groups, members are encouraged to share their experiences, achievements, fears and failures with peers who provide advice support and advice. When individuals join NA/AA, they are usually encouraged to attend more than one meeting a week, and a target of attending 90 meetings in 90 days is often set.

The programme consists of studying and following the Twelve Steps, which are the essential principles and ingredients of the recovery process (Emrick, 1999). The Steps emphasise two general themes:

1 *Spirituality*: belief in a 'higher power', which is defined by each individual and which represents faith and hope for recovery.
2 *Pragmatism*: belief in doing 'whatever works' for the individual, meaning doing whatever it takes to avoid taking the first drink.

NA/AA has sometimes been criticised for its 'religious' orientation. Six of the Steps make some reference to God, and prayer and meditation are seen as important for recovery. This can be a problem for non-religious people. Best et al. (2001) found many drug and alcohol dependent patients were reluctant to accept the Steps related to a 'higher power'. To deal with this, members of the fellowship are often encouraged to interpret the 'higher power' in a way that is based on their own personal understanding of a 'power greater than oneself'.

Apparently dissimilar treatment interventions such as Twelve-Step programmes and psychosocial treatments may share certain common underlying process factors. NA/AA offers a peer group, which can support efforts to achieve and maintain abstinence. Most people with drug problems have acquired a social network consisting of other users, and continuing involvement with this network greatly increases their risk of relapse. NA/AA provides a peer group that shares the same problems and that actively supports the learning of new, pro-social behaviours (Brown et al., 2001). Role modelling can be further assisted by the sponsor. NA/AA also provides a structure for the member's free time and evening meetings may provide a supportive activity during a high risk time of day.

NA/AA may also serve as an after care resource. Ouimette et al. (1998) investigated the impact of three types of after care (12-step groups only, out-patient treatment only and outpatient treatment plus 12-step groups). Substance misusing patients who received no after care had the poorest outcomes; patients who participated in outpatient treatment plus Twelve-Step groups achieved the best outcomes at follow-up. Similarly, in a study of alcoholics who received inpatient treatment, those who were frequent AA attenders after treatment had superior drinking outcomes to non-AA attenders and infrequent attenders (Gossop et al., 2003). This relationship was sustained after controlling for potential confounding variables.

A number of treatment services provide programmes based on Twelve-Step principles. Although these differ from NA/AA in certain respects, they also share many common features. One example is the Twelve-Step Facilitation (TSF) treatment programme within Project MATCH. This highly structured treatment was provided over a 12 week period in an outpatient treatment setting (Project MATCH Research Group, 1998). Although the TSF programme was based on the Twelve Steps of AA, it was a professionally delivered individual therapy, and in this respect it differed in an important way from the peer support system of normal AA meetings.

The main conclusions from Project MATCH were that TSF, cognitive behavioural therapy (CBT) and motivational enhancement therapy were all effective treatments. Those who received the TSF treatment had fewer drinking days than those who received either of the other treatments. For patients who were more severely dependent on alcohol, TSF led to greater improvement in drinking behaviour than CBT (Project MATCH Research Group, 1998).

Therapeutic communities and residential rehabilitation programmes

In many countries, residential rehabilitation programmes are one of the longest established forms of treatment and, in some countries, they remain one of the dominant treatment modalities. In the UK, two of the main types of residential alcohol dependence treatment programme are those which are largely based on the Twelve Steps and those based on the principles of therapeutic communities (TCs). Many TCs also use Twelve-Step principles.

Some residential programmes divide their treatment programme into the three main phases of induction/orientation, treatment and re-entry (Kennard, 1998). The induction/orientation phase may last for a few weeks or up to 2 months. The core, treatment delivery period involves the resident living, working and relating to others exclusively in the community, and progressing through the community hierarchy. This may often last for periods of about 12 months. In the re-entry phase, the resident has passes to go out while still living in the community. This enables the person to look for work and accommodation and may last for 6–12 months. Some agencies also operate 'half-way' houses with patients living in semi-independent houses after completing the main programme.

The essential element of the TC involves the community. TCs differ from other forms of addiction treatment intervention in that the continuing inter- action between the individual and the community is itself seen as the treat- ment process. The treatment ingredients are seen as the programme structure, the people in the TC, and the daily activities and social interactions in the TC. The primary staff members in many residential programmes are often recovering addicts who have themselves been rehabilitated in therapeutic communities.

The basic goal for residents in TCs in particular (but also in residential treatment programmes in general) involves a complete change in lifestyle involving abstinence from drugs, avoidance of antisocial behaviour, the devel- opment of prosocial skills and personal honesty (DeLeon and Rosenthal, 1979). The specific objective of the TCs has been described as to treat indi- vidual disorders, 'but their larger purpose is to transform lifestyles and personal identities' (De Leon, 2000).

Three important determinants of change within TCs are social role train- ing, vicarious learning and efficacy training (De Leon, 2000). The resident positions within the TC hierarchy provide experience of work roles and, as individuals learn their various social roles in the community, they undergo a wide range of social and psychological changes. The principle of vicarious learning is also seen as an important feature of community life, with peers and staff providing role models for appropriate behaviours and attitudes. Meeting community expectations in performance, responsibility, self-examination and autonomy leads to increased self-efficacy.

A system of privileges and sanctions is typically used to motivate and direct behaviour within residential programmes. Role modelling within the TC also includes a practising a broader range of behaviours and attitudes that reflect the values and expectations of the community. The residents' performance of various day-to-day jobs in the TC provides experience of the work roles that are required in the working environment of the outside world.

At one time, traditional TCs worked with planned durations of stay of

2–3 years. Recent changes in client population, and the realities of funding restrictions have led to modified residential TCs with shorter durations of stay. Modified TCs may work with a 6- to 9-month programme, and the short-term programmes with a 3- to 6-month programme (De Leon, 2000).

Another recent development has been the growth of relatively short-stay, residential 'chemical dependency' programmes (sometimes called 'Minnesota Model' or 'Hazelden' programmes), which are often based on the Twelve Steps and which are strongly focused on recovery through abstinence. These programmes typically provide a highly structured 3 to 6-week package of residential care involving an intensive programme of daily lectures and group meetings designed to implement a recovery plan.

In an evaluation of Twelve-Step, cognitive-behavioural, or combined Twelve-Step plus cognitive behavioural treatments provided in 3 to 4-week inpatient programmes, all three treatments appeared to be equally effective in reducing substance use and psychological symptoms, and in reducing post-treatment arrests and imprisonment (Ouimette et al., 1997; Moos et al., 1999). The casemix-adjusted outcomes showed that the patients who received Twelve-Step treatments were more likely to be abstinent, free of substance abuse problems and employed at 1 year follow-up. Moos et al. (1999) concluded that their findings provided evidence to support the effectiveness of Twelve-Step treatment.

Pharmacotherapies

Almost all countries that are confronted by a substantial opiate addiction problem have introduced methadone programmes for the treatment of opiate addicts. By the mid-1990s there were probably about 250,000 patients in methadone treatment worldwide.

Various rationales have been given for methadone maintenance, including preventing withdrawal, preventing craving and blocking the euphoric effects of heroin. The pragmatic rationale is that giving methadone in a clinical setting enables opiate addicts to be assessed and retained in treatment to tackle behavioural, social and health problems.

The provision of methadone treatments is rarely restricted merely to the provision of methadone pharmacotherapy (Strain and Stoller, 1999). The treatment also includes, and is a combination of, both pharmacological and non-pharmacological therapies. The latter may include cognitive-behaviour therapies, individual counselling, group therapy, couples counselling, urine testing, contingency contracting, HIV testing and counselling, primary medical care services, psychiatric assessments and treatment of co-morbid disorders. McLellan et al. (1983) found that the provision of additional counselling, medical and psychosocial services improved the efficacy of treatment compared to methadone alone.

Carroll et al. (1995) suggested that there may be advantages to using a combined therapy package of psychotherapy and pharmacotherapy in the treatment of drug dependence. Combined treatments may be useful with patients who present with complex mixtures of symptoms and problems. The offer of pharmacotherapy may also support treatment participation during the early stages of a programme where a developing therapeutic alliance may not be established, or until coping skills are mastered and integrated (Carroll, 1993).

Methadone treatments are extremely diverse and programmes differ in doses prescribed, provision of counselling services, treatment policies and in drug use outcomes (Gossop and Grant, 1990; Ball and Ross, 1991; Stewart et al., 2000). Methadone maintenance has been extensively studied over a period of four decades. In a meta-analysis of the treatment evaluation literature, Marsch (1998) reported consistent findings of reductions in illicit opiate use, HIV risk behaviours and crime.

Buprenorphine is a mixed agonist–antagonist, which is being increasingly used to treat opiate addiction. The drug may be at least as effective as methadone as a maintenance agent in terms of reducing illicit opioid use and retaining patients in treatment (Mattick et al., 1998).

One of the widely cited British treatment practices is believed to involve maintenance on medically prescribed heroin. However, except for a short period after the establishment of the clinic system in the late 1960s, heroin prescribing has not been widely used in the UK. By 1992, less than 1% of opiate dependents receiving a prescription in the UK were receiving injectable heroin, compared to about 98% who were receiving prescribed methadone (Strang et al., 1994). Interest in this practice has been revived in recent years as a result of the trials conducted in Switzerland and the Netherlands.

Disulfiram (Antabuse) was first introduced during the late 1940s and has been used widely used to treat alcohol dependence. Disulfiram blocks the breakdown of alcohol causing an unpleasant reaction, which starts within minutes of drinking and last several hours. The severity of the reaction varies from mild to very severe. Disulfiram is used for its deterrent action, and the rationale of the treatment is that as patients cannot drink while taking disulfiram, if they are willing to take the medication this helps to protect them from the temptation to drink. Disulfiram has been found to be effective when used as part of a comprehensive treatment package, for example with contingency reinforcement (Bigelow et al., 1976) or counselling (Chick et al., 1992). Despite the many years of disulfiram use, its appropriate role in the treatment of alcohol problems remains unclear (Edwards et al., 2003).

Naltrexone is a relatively pure opiate antagonist that selectively competes for opioid receptors, prevents reinforcement from opioids and prevents a return to regular use of opiates. It does not produce a 'high' and has little abuse potential. But, despite its promise, naltrexone has not lived up to early expectations, largely because the majority of opiate dependent patients are reluctant or resistant to take the drug. Greenstein et al. (1984) found that only

10–15% of opiate dependent patients were willing to accept treatment with a drug that 'keeps you from getting high'.

Naltrexone has been found to work well with highly motivated patients and when used under supervision (O'Brien, 1994). Opiate dependent patients with good social integration and social resources tend to respond well to treatment with naltrexone (Tennant et al., 1984).

Several studies have also suggested that naltrexone may reduce the euphoric effects of drinking and reduce craving for alcohol (Volpicelli et al., 1995; Monti et al., 1999) and, when used with psychosocial treatments, naltrexone has been found to reduce relapse rates in alcohol dependent patients (O'Malley et al., 1992; Volpicelli et al., 1992). However, other studies have failed to replicate this relapse prevention effect (Krystal et al., 2001).

Other interventions

The health risk behaviours of drug users have been the focus for various harm reduction activities. Dissemination of information about the transmission of HIV and other blood-borne infections is one of the least controversial prevention responses. This has been widely used and in some circumstances may be effective (Selwyn et al., 1987).

Needle and syringe exchange schemes have been more controversial, although these have now been established in many countries throughout the world (Stimson et al., 1990). Some critics have regarded the idea of providing needles and syringes to drug injectors as an unacceptable means of trying to prevent drug problems, and some countries (notably the USA) have shown great reluctance to implement such measures. Some countries have actively intervened to restrict the availability of injecting equipment.

In a study of London heroin users, Gossop et al. (1994) found that nearly a quarter of those who were injecting heroin (23%) had shared needles and/or syringes in the previous year. Although there are many reasons why people share syringes, it is often the result of a lack of availability of sterile equipment. Stimson et al. (1988) suggested that problems of restricted availability were reported by almost half of the injectors in their survey as a reason for sharing.

Syringes have been supplied to users in a number of ways. Some services provide needles and syringes (either free of charge or for sale) but make no requirement for the return of used equipment. In other services, needles and syringes are provided on an exchange basis (either on a one-for-one or some other agreed basis). All services make suitable and safe arrangements for the safe disposal of returned used needles and syringes.

The best known system involves the provision of needles and syringes to injectors on an exchange basis. This addresses public health concerns about used and possibly infected needles being left in public places, or otherwise disposed of in ways that may put others at risk. Exchange schemes were opened in the UK very swiftly after the identification of HIV among drug injectors. By the end of 1989, there were about 120 such schemes, and by the mid-1990s, there were over 300 dedicated syringe exchange schemes in England (Stimson, 1996). Needle exchanges in the UK are most often located in drug treatment agencies and in community pharmacies.

THE PROBLEM OF TREATMENT SELECTION

The US Institute of Medicine (1990) recommended that the simplistic question of whether a treatment works should be redefined as:

> Which kinds of individuals, with what kinds of . . . problems, are likely to respond to what kinds of treatments by achieving what kinds of goals when delivered by which kinds of practitioners?

> (p. 143)

To take account of the diversity among drug users, treatment interventions must be responsive to their differing problems and needs. The treatment or treatment setting that may be appropriate for a 35 year old heroin injector with a long history of dependence may be inappropriate or even contra-indicated for a 14 year old schoolboy sniffing glue. Similarly, the socially-integrated, 50 year old university lecturer who has become dependent on alcohol may require a different treatment intervention to the 20 year old, unemployed and socially alienated crack smoker.

If no single treatment can be universally effective for drug dependence, and a range of different interventions are required, this challenges many of the existing service delivery systems, which tend to offer a fixed package of treatment components. Despite widespread recognition of the importance of providing treatments that are appropriate to the diverse needs and problems of patients, many programmes offer only a single type of treatment. This Procrustean system expects patients to fit the services provided rather than making the adaptations and adjustments needed to identify and respond to the specific needs of the individual. In such situations, those patients who are a good fit for a given approach are more likely to remain in treatment, and those who are less well suited are more likely to drop out (Carroll, 1997).

The best known, as well as the largest and most costly ($27 million), comparative study of treatment effectiveness was Project MATCH. This compared three alcohol dependence treatments: Twelve-Step facilitation, cognitive behavioural therapy with relapse prevention, and motivational enhancement therapy. The assumption of Project MATCH was that the ran-domisation of patients to the treatment conditions would lead to some of them being 'correctly matched' and others being 'mis-matched'. It further assumed that correct matches ought to have a better outcome than mismatches (Drummond, 1999).

The study found improved drinking outcomes among patients in all treatment conditions, but little evidence of matching effects. However, Marlatt (1999) suggested that it is misleading to conclude that the study showed that treatment matching does not work, or that any one type of treatment works as well as any other. A major problem was that the study randomly assigned patients to the treatment conditions. Marlatt (1999) commented that:

> As a way of assigning patients to treatment, nothing could be more opposite than random assignment (assigning patients on a random basis similar to a coin toss) and treatment matching (assigning patients based on a professional therapist's knowledge and skills).

Glaser (1999) noted that whatever the merits and validity of the project's experimental design, a study of matching in which none of the patients was actually matched to a particular treatment lacked persuasiveness.

Different treatment settings may also be appropriate for different people. Inpatient hospital care may be most appropriate for those with coexisting acute medical or severe psychiatric problems. Residential care in a non-medical setting may be most appropriate for people who are socially unstable but who do not have coexisting acute medical or severe psychiatric problems. Out-patient care may be indicated for socially stable individuals who do not have co-existing acute medical or severe psychiatric problems. The differences in problems and in the individuals with these problems must be taken into account before an informed decision can be made about what type of treatment is likely to be most appropriate.

In 'stepped care' approaches, the recommended treatment is the one that is least intensive but likely to resolve the problem, with more intensive treatments being reserved for those with more severe problems (Sobell and Sobell, 1999). If the patient responds poorly to the initial treatment, further assessment takes place, with the decision about what to do next being based on the individual's case characteristics, what has been learned from the failure to respond to treatment, and what clinical judgement and research suggest as the most appropriate next phase of treatment and, if indicated, the next level of care.

The Patient Placement Criteria of the American Society of Addiction Medicine (ASAM, 2001) provided guidelines for matching patients to different treatment options. Six domains on which patients should be assessed and subsequently matched to an appropriate level of treatment were:

- acute intoxication and withdrawal
- biomedical condition
- emotional and behavioural problems

- acceptance of or resistance to treatment
- relapse potential
- recovery environment.

As with the random allocation procedures of some research trials, a major concern about these sorts of matching and placement procedures is that they differ in important respects from the 'consumer choice' paradigm in which drug users should be able, or even encouraged to assess the treatment options and then seek treatment from an agency of their choice. Attempts to impose a type of treatment or treatment method on the patient undoubtedly have an appeal for treatment planners and purchasers, but this may not be an especially efficient or productive way to achieve patient/treatment matching.

CONCLUSIONS AND IMPLICATIONS

There is broad agreement that many treatments and other factors may be related to outcome. Relatively little is known about what these factors are or how they affect outcome. An important question for clinicians and researchers, and one to which we currently have no satisfactory answer, is how can we identify and measure the impact of specific treatment process variables? The answer to this question may improve treatment effectiveness by helping to discriminate between 'active' and 'inert' components of treatment and enabling the elimination of the inert components (McLellan et al., 1997). It is probable that the important developments in addiction treatments during the next decades will occur not as a result of radical new discoveries but through the improvement of existing interventions and through improved provision of treatments.

REFERENCES

American Society of Addiction Medicine (ASAM) (2001) *ASAM Placement Criteria for the Treatment of Substance-Related Disorders*. Chevy Chase, MD: ASAM.

Annis, H. (1986) A relapse prevention model for the treatment of alcoholics. In: W. Miller and N. Heather (eds) *Treating Addictive Behaviors*. New York: Plenum.

Azrin, N. H. (1976) Improvements in the community reinforcement approach to alcoholism. *Behavior Research and Therapy*, 14, 339–348.

Ball, J. and Ross, A. (1991) *The Effectiveness of Methadone Maintenance Treatment*. New York: Springer-Verlag.

Best, D., Harris, J., Gossop, M., Manning, V., Man, L-H., Marshall, J. et al. (2001) Are the Twelve Steps more acceptable to drug users than to drinkers? A comparison of experiences of and attitudes to Alcoholics Anonymous (AA) and Narcotics Anonymous (NA) among 200 substance misusers attending inpatient detoxification. *European Addiction Research*, 7, 69–77.

Biernacki, P. (1986) *Pathways from Heroin Addiction: Recovery Without Treatment.* Philadelphia: Temple University Press.

Bigelow, G., Strickler, D., Liebson, I. and Griffiths, R. (1976) Maintaining disulfiram ingestion among outpatient alcoholics: A security-deposit contingency contracting procedure. *Behaviour Research and Therapy*, 14, 378–381.

Bradley, B., Phillips, G., Green, L. and Gossop, M. (1989) Circumstances surrounding the initial lapse to opiate use following detoxification. *British Journal of Psychiatry*, 154, 354–359.

Brown, B., Kinlock, T. and Nurco, D. (2001) Self-help initiatives to reduce the risk of relapse. In: F. Tims, C. Leukefeld and J. Platt (eds) *Relapse and Recovery in Addictions*. New Haven, CT: Yale University Press.

Callahan, E. (1980) Alternative strategies in the treatment of narcotic addiction: A review. In: W. Miller (ed) *The Addictive Behaviors*. Oxford: Pergamon.

Carroll, K. M. (1993) Psychotherapeutic treatment of cocaine abuse: Models for its evaluation alone and in combination with pharmacotherapy. In: F. Tims and C. Leukefeld (eds) *Cocaine Treatment: Research and Clinical Perspectives*. NIDA Research Monograph No. 135. Rockville, MD: National Institute on Drug Abuse.

Carroll, K. M. (1997) Enhancing retention in clinical trials of psychosocial treatments: Practical strategies. In: *Beyond the Therapeutic Alliance: Keeping the Drug-Dependent Individual in Treatment*. NIDA Research Monograph 165. Rockville, MD: National Institute on Drug Abuse.

Carroll, K. M., Rounsaville, B. J., Nich, C., Gordon, L. and Gawin, F. (1995) Integrating psychotherapy and pharmacotherapy for cocaine dependence: Results from a randomized clinical trial. In: L. Onken, J. Blaine and J. Boren (eds) *Integrating Behavioral Therapies with Medications in the Treatment of Drug Dependence*. NIDA Monograph No.150. Rockville, MD: National Institute on Drug Abuse.

Chick, J., Gough, K. and Falkowski, W. (1992) Disulfiram treatment of alcoholism. *British Journal of Psychiatry*, 161, 84–89.

Conklin, C. and Tiffany, S. (2002) Applying extinction research and theory to cue-exposure addiction treatments. *Addiction*, 97, 155–167.

Cummings, N., Gordon, J. and Marlatt, G. (1980) Relapse: Strategies of prevention and prediction. In: W. R. Miller (ed) *The Addictive Behaviors*. Oxford: Pergamon.

De Leon, G. (2000) *The Therapeutic Community: Theory, Model, and Method.* New York: Springer.

De Leon, G. and Rosenthal, M. S. (1979) Therapeutic communities. In: R. DuPont, A. Goldstein, and J. O'Donnell (eds) *Handbook on Drug Abuse* (pp. 39–48). Rockville, MD: National Institute on Drug Abuse.

Drummond, D. C. (1999) Treatment research in the wake of Project MATCH. *Addiction*, 94, 39–42.

Drummond, D. C. and Glautier, S. (1994) A controlled trial of cue exposure treatment in alcohol dependence. *Journal of Clinical and Consulting Psychology*, 41, 809–817.

Drummond, D. C., Tiffany, S., Glautier, S. and Remington, B. (1995) Cue exposure in understanding and treating addictive behaviour. In: D. C. Drummond, S. Tiffany, S. Glautier and B. Remington (eds) *Addictive Behaviours: Cue Exposure Theory and Practice*. London: John Wiley.

Edwards, G., Marshall, J. and Cook, C. (2003) *The Treatment of Drinking Problems.* Cambridge: Cambridge University Press.

Einstein, S. (1966) The narcotics dilemma: Who is listening to what? *International Journal of the Addictions*, 1, 1–6.

Emrick, C. D. (1999) Alcoholics Anonymous and other 12-step groups. In: M. Galanter and H. D. Kleber (eds) *The American Psychiatric Press Textbook of Substance Abuse Treatment, 2nd edn* (pp. 403–412). Washington, DC: American Psychiatric Press, Inc.

Glaser, F. (1999) The unsinkable Project MATCH. *Addiction*, 94, 34–36.

Gossop, M. and Grant, M. (1990) *The Content and Structure of Methadone Treatment Programmes: A Study in Six Countries* (WHO/PSA/90.3). Geneva: World Health Organization.

Gossop, M., Battersby, M. and Strang, J. (1991) Self-detoxification by opiate addicts: A preliminary investigation. *British Journal of Psychiatry*, 159, 208–212.

Gossop, M., Powis, B., Griffiths, P. and Strang, J. (1994) Multiple risks for HIV and hepatitis B infection among heroin users. *Drug and Alcohol Review*, 13, 293–300.

Gossop, M., Marsden, J., Stewart, D., Lehmann, P., Edwards, C., Wilson, A. and Segar, G. (1998) Substance use, health and social problems of clients at 54 drug treatment agencies: Intake data from the National Treatment Outcome Research Study (NTORS). *British Journal of Psychiatry*, 173, 166–171.

Gossop, M., Harris, J., Best, D., Man, L-H., Manning, V., Marshall, J. and Strang, J. (2003) Is attendance at Alcoholics Anonymous meetings after inpatient treatment related to improved outcomes? A six-month follow-up study. *Alcohol and Alcoholism*, 38, 421–426.

Greenstein, R. A., Arndt, J. C., McLellan, A. T., O'Brien, C. P. and Evans, B. (1984) Naltrexone: A clinical perspective. *Journal of Clinical Psychiatry*, 45, 25–28.

Heather, N. (2002) Effectiveness of brief interventions proved beyond reasonable doubt, *Addiction*, 97, 293–294.

Heather, N. and Stallard, A. (1989) Does the Marlatt model underestimate the importance of conditioned craving in the relapse process? In: M. Gossop (ed) *Relapse and Addictive Behaviour*. London: Routledge.

Hser, Y. I., Anglin, D. and Powers, K. (1993) A 24-year follow-up of California narcotics addicts. *Archives of General Psychiatry*, 50, 577–584.

Kadden, R. (2001) Behavioral and cognitive-behavioral treatments for alcoholism: Research opportunities. *Addictive Behaviors*, 26, 489–507.

Kazdin, A. (1978) *History of Behavior Modification*. Baltimore: University Park Press.

Kennard, D. (1998) *An Introduction to Therapeutic Communities*. London: Jessica Kingsley.

Krystal, J., Cramer, J., Krol, W., Kirk, G. and Rosenheck, R. (2001) Naltrexone in the treatment of alcohol dependence. *New England Journal of Medicine*, 345, 1734–1739.

Liese, B. and Najavits, L. (1997) Cognitive and behavioral therapies. In: J. Lowinson, P. Ruiz, R. Millman and J. Langrod (eds) *Substance Abuse: A Comprehensive Textbook*. Baltimore: Williams and Wilkins.

Litt, M., Cooney, N., Kadden, R. and Gaupp, L. (1990) Reactivity to alcohol cues and induced moods in alcoholics. *Addictive Behaviors*, 15, 137–146.

McLellan, A. T., Luborsky, L., Woody, G., O'Brien, C. and Druley, K. (1983) Increased effectiveness of substance abuse treatment: A prospective study of patient-treatment 'matching'. *Journal of Nervous and Mental Disease*, 171, 597–605.

McLellan, A. T., Wood, G. E., Metzger, D. S., McKay, J. and Alterman, A. I. (1997)

Evaluating the effectiveness of addiction treatments: Reasonable expectations, appropriate comparisons. In: J. A. Egerton, D. M. Fox, and A. I. Leshner (eds) *Treating Drug Abusers Effectively*. Oxford: Blackwell.

Makela, K. (1993) International comparisons of Alcoholics Anonymous. *Alcohol, Health, and Research World*, 17, 228–234.

Marlatt, G. A. (1985) Relapse prevention: Theoretical rationale and overview of the model. In: G. A. Marlatt, and J. R. Gordon (eds) *Relapse Prevention: Maintenance Strategies in the Treatment of Addictive Behavior*. New York: Guilford Press.

Marlatt, G. A. (1999) From hindsight to foresight: a commentary on Project MATCH. In: J. Tucker, D. Donovan and G. A. Marlatt (eds) *Changing Addictive Behavior*. New York: Guilford Press.

Marlatt, G. A. and Gordon, J. R. (1985) *Relapse Prevention: Maintenance Strategies in the Treatment of Addictive Behavior*. New York: Guilford Press.

Marsch, L. A. (1998) The efficacy of methadone maintenance interventions in reducing illicit opiate use, HIV risk behaviour and criminality: A meta-analysis. *Addiction*, 93, 515–532.

Mattick, R., Oliphant, D., Ward, J. and Hall, W. (1998) The effectiveness of other opioid replacement therapies: LAAM, heroin, buprenorphine, naltrexone and injectable maintenance. In: J. Ward, R. Mattick and W. Hall (eds) *Methadone Maintenance Treatment and Other Replacement Therapies*. Amsterdam: Harwood.

Miller, W. R. (1983) Motivational interviewing with problem drinkers. *Behavioural Psychotherapy*, 1, 147–172.

Miller, W. R. and Rollnick, S. (1991) *Motivational Interviewing*. New York: Guilford Press.

Modesto-Lowe, V. and Kranzler, H. (1999) Using cue reactivity to evaluate medications for treatment of cocaine dependence: A critical review. *Addiction*, 94, 1639–1651.

Monti, P. M., Rohsenow, D. J., Hutchison, K. E., Swift, R. M., Mueller, T. I., Colby, S. M. et al. (1999) Naltrexone's effect on cue-elicited craving among alcoholics in treatment. *Alcoholism, Clinical and Experimental Research*, 23, 1386–1394.

Moos, R. H., Finney, J. W., Ouimette, P. C. and Suchinsky, R. (1999) A comparative evaluation of substance abuse treatment: I. Treatment orientation, amount of care, and 1-year outcomes. *Alcoholism, Clinical and Experimental Research*, 23, 529–536.

Noble, A., Best, B., Man, L-H., Gossop, M., and Strang, J. (2002) Self-detoxification attempts among methadone maintenance patients: What methods and what success? *Addictive Behaviours*, 27, 575–584.

O'Brien, C. (1994) Opioids: Antagonists and partial antagonists. In: M. Galanter and H. Kleber (eds) *Textbook of Substance Abuse Treatment*. Washington, DC: American Psychiatric Press.

O'Malley, S., Jaffe, J., Chang, G., Schottenfield, R., Meyer, R. and Rousaville, B. (1992) Naltrexone and coping skills therapy for alcohol dependence: A controlled study. *Archives of General Psychiatry*, 49, 881–887.

Ouimette, P. C., Finney, J. W. and Moos, R. H. (1997) Twelve-step and cognitive-behavioral treatment for substance abuse: A comparison of treatment effectiveness. *Journal of Consulting and Clinical Psychology*, 65, 230–240.

Ouimette, P. C., Moos, R. H. and Finney, J. W. (1998) Influence of outpatient treatment and 12-step group involvement on one-year substance abuse treatment outcomes. *Journal of Studies on Alcohol*, 59, 513–522.

Prochaska, J. and DiClemente, C. (1982) Transtheoretical therapy: Towards a more integrative model of change. *Psychotherapy: Theory, Research and Practice*, 19, 276–288.

Prochaska, J., DiClemente, C. and Norcross, J. (1992) In search of how people change: Applications to the addictive behaviors. *American Psychologist*, 47, 1102–1114.

Project MATCH Research Group (1998) Matching alcoholism treatment to client heterogeneity: Project MATCH three year drinking outcomes. *Alcoholism: Clinical and Experimental Research*, 22, 1300–1311.

Rachman, S. and Teasdale, J. (1969) *Aversion Therapy and Behaviour Disorders*. Florida: University of Miami Press.

Robles, E., Silverman, K. and Stitzer, M. (1999) Contingency management therapies. In: E. Strain and M. Stitzer (eds) *Methadone Treatment for Opioid Dependence*. Baltimore: Johns Hopkins University Press.

Rohsenow, D., Monti, P., Abrams, D., Rubonis, A., Niaura, R., Sirota, A. and Colby, S. (1992) Cue elicited urge to drink and salivation in alcoholics: Relationship to individual differences. *Advances in Behavior Research and Therapy*, 14, 195–210.

Rollnick, S. (2001) Enthusiasm, quick fixes and premature controlled trials. *Addiction*, 96, 1769–1775.

Selwyn, P., Feiner, C., Cox, C., Lipshutz, C. and Cohen, R. (1987) Knowledge about AIDS and high-risk behavior among intravenous drug users in New York City. *AIDS*, 1, 247–254.

Shiffman, S. (1989) Conceptual issues in the study of relapse. In: M. Gossop (ed) *Relapse and Addictive Behaviour*. London: Routledge.

Sobell, M. and Sobell, L. (1999) Stepped care for alcohol problems: An efficient method for planning and delivering clinical services. In: J. Tucker, D. Donovan and G. A. Marlatt (eds) *Changing Addictive Behavior*. New York: Guilford Press.

Stewart, D., Gossop, M., Marsden, J. and Strang, J. (2000) Variation between and within drug treatment modalities: Data from the National Treatment Outcome Research Study (UK). *European Addiction Research*, 6, 106–114.

Stimson, G. (1996) Has the United Kingdom averted an epidemic of HIV-1 infection among drug injectors? *Addiction*, 91, 1085–1088.

Stimson, G., Alldritt, L., Dolan, K. and Donoghoe, M. (1988) Syringe exchange schemes for drug users in England and Scotland. *British Medical Journal*, 296, 1717.

Stimson, G., Donoghoe, M., Lart, R. and Dolan, K. (1990) Distributing sterile needles and syringes to people who inject drugs: the syringe-exchange experiment. In: J. Strang and G. Stimson (eds) *AIDS and Drug Misuse*. London: Routledge.

Stitzer, M., Bigelow, G. and Gross, J. (1989) Behavioral treatment of drug abuse. In: T. B. Karasu (ed) *Treatments of Psychiatric Disorders: A Task Force Report of the American Psychiatric Association, Vol. 2*. Washington, DC: American Psychiatric Association.

Strain, E. C. and Stoller, K. B. (1999) Introduction and historical overview. In: E. Strain and M. Stitzer (eds) *Methadone Treatment for Opioid Dependence*. Baltimore: Johns Hopkins University Press.

Strang, J., Ruben, S., Farrell, M. and Gossop, M. (1994) Prescribing heroin and other injectable drugs. In: J. Strang and M. Gossop (eds) *The British System*. London: Oxford University Press.

US Institute of Medicine (1990) *Broadening the Base of Treatment for Alcohol Problems*. Washington, DC: National Academy Press.

Volpicelli, J., Alterman, A., Hayashida, M. and O'Brien, C. (1992) Naltrexone in the treatment of alcohol dependence. *Archives of General Psychiatry*, 49, 876–880.

Wutzke, S., Conigrave, K., Saunders, J. and Hall, W. (2002) The long-term effectiveness of brief interventions for unsafe alcohol consumption: A 10-year follow-up. *Addiction*, 97, 665–675.

Chapter 25

Problems in later life

Investigation

Bob Woods

INTRODUCTION

Across the world, the proportion of older people continues to rise, resulting from factors such as longer life expectancy and lower birth rates. In developed countries, the particular challenge is the continued growth of the population over the age of 80. In this age group, there is a high prevalence of a wide range of health difficulties occurring in the context of a high risk of changes in the person's social support network. For clinical psychologists, this represents an important challenge: to develop methods that will contribute to the psychological well-being of older people and those who care for them.

It must be emphasised that old age is no more a disease than childhood – some would describe it rather as the penultimate stage of development. Not all older people require assessment or treatment; as with younger people, there must be a particular reason for psychological input. Although the dementias are much more common in older people than in younger people, over three-quarters of those over 80 do not have any degree of dementia (Woods, 1999a). Chronological age is an imperfect predictor of physical or mental health, so that all generalisations about older people are likely to be misleading and in need of qualification. There is huge variability in interests, abilities, opinions, experiences, health and lifestyle among older people; they have had longer to develop along different paths than younger people and 'later life' often covers an age span of 30 years.

Psychometric assessment was traditionally the major task of clinical psychologists with older people. Now, treatment and management of the problems of older people and those who care for them predominate. Assessment remains none the less important: any worthwhile treatment programme must be founded on a careful assessment and formulation, but it is psychological assessment in its widest sense that must be considered. Examples will be given of the tests, scales and procedures that may be used, but the ever-growing number of these means that a comprehensive account of each is not feasible. Clinical psychologists tend to have their own personal repertoire of measures which they use and with which they are familiar; the selection here includes some of the most widely used, but inevitably is incomplete. Morris and McKiernan (1994), Storandt and VandenBos (1994) and Clare (2004) provide detailed accounts of neuropsychological assessment, whilst Little and Doherty (1996) discuss other types of assessment fully.

PURPOSE OF ASSESSMENT

Formal psychological assessments have been used for a number of purposes:

- the measurement of the occurrence and extent of decline in cognitive functioning e.g. following a stroke or in Parkinson's disease
- the early detection of Alzheimer's disease and other dementias
- the characterisation and differentiation of the cognitive deficits in the various dementias
- monitoring change over time, e.g. describing the natural history of dementia
- evaluating the response of the person to a range of interventions (e.g. exercise, medication, psychological interventions) and examining side-effects (e.g. of antidepressants on memory)
- identification of patients suitable for particular treatments
- identification of the person's needs so that appropriate placements and services for the older person may be selected
- assessment of competence, e.g. to drive or to handle financial affairs
- provision of feedback to older people and/or their carers, regarding the person's strengths and weaknesses (including neuropsychological deficits) and possible compensatory strategies (Moniz-Cook and Woods, 1997)
- evaluating the effects of service provision, of various types, on the older person and his or her supporters.

Elsewhere, a distinction has been drawn between diagnostic assessment and descriptive assessment (Woods, 1999b). The former has the primary aim of discriminating, and eventually assigning the patient to some category or other. The latter aims to delineate the patient's profile of psychological functioning, the pattern of abilities and deficits, thus providing information potentially useful for a number of the above purposes. The purpose of an assessment must always be carefully clarified, as different strategies and procedures will be indicated for different objectives. The difficulties associated with assigning a diagnostic category simply from cognitive tests have been set out previously (Woods, 1999b). Diagnosis, say of a dementia, must also involve consideration of how the problems have developed, the person's physical health and the impact on everyday life, as reported by the person and others who know the person well. Dementia represents a change in cognitive function, and the clinical psychologist must use his or her skill in interpreting the person's profile of scores to judge whether the current pattern of performance represents a significant change, or may be attributed to the person's lifelong level of ability or perhaps to sensory problems. In the past there was an emphasis on distinguishing depression and dementia. To attempt this using only cognitive assessment is probably futile. Depression in older people is itself associated with a degree of cognitive impairment (Christensen et al., 1997); and, in any case, as many as a quarter of people with a dementia also have significant symptoms of depression (Ballard et al., 1996). It is important, of course, to assess depressed mood directly, and, where it is present, to consider appropriate treatment. Judgement about enduring cognitive impairment may have to be suspended until either the person's depression lifts or the progression of the cognitive impairment makes itself evident over time.

NORMAL AGEING

Making sense of a descriptive psychological assessment requires some knowledge of age-related changes in the normal older person. A good introduction to this topic is provided by Stuart Hamilton (2000) and Birren and Schaie's (2001) comprehensive text contains detailed reviews; here the central issues will be discussed.

Intelligence quotient

IQ is said to peak at about age 25 or 30, declining steadily to age 65 or so before decreasing more rapidly (Segal et al., 1998). These are age differences, obtained by the cross-sectional method of at one point in time assessing groups of subjects of all ages. The cohort of subjects born in, say, 1980 is compared with the cohort born in 1925. Subjects do not then differ simply in age but also in early medical care, nutrition, housing, education, occupational opportunities and so on. This cross-sectional approach underlies much of the literature on 'cognitive changes' and ageing. It can only, in fact, indicate age differences.

Longitudinal studies, following the same subjects over a number of years, should give a better indication of age changes. However, these are difficult to accomplish. Stability across much of the life-span appears to be the norm, rather than a decline from age 20. For example, Owens (1966) followed up subjects who had taken the Army Alpha Test at age 19. Thirty years later they had shown a general improvement and, by age 61, had shown little loss. Deary et al. (2000) assessed a sample of 101 people 66 years after they were assessed at age 11, using the identical IQ test. They found that scores increased over this time, but that a person's scores at age 11 and at age 77 were highly correlated.

Longitudinal results can also be misleading because of practice effects, both in terms of familiarity with the particular test and the test situation. Selective drop-out is also a problem. Subjects available for re-test have higher initial scores than those who drop out (Siegler and Botwinick, 1979). With every re-test there is an increasingly selected sample. Schaie (1996) and colleagues, in a series of classic studies, have succeeded in combining cross-sectional and longitudinal methods. Subjects from all age groups were assessed initially and then re-assessed after 7, 14 and 21 years. These four cross-sectional assessments were carried out both on the same subjects (longitudinal or repeated measures) and on fresh subjects (independent measures) in this 'cross-sequential' design. The longitudinal assessments showed least decline, the cross-sectional most, with independent measures intermediate. Decline appeared much later than typically thought: at age 50 on some functions, 60 or 70 on others. Groups of older people in longitudinal studies do show changes in cognition (Cullum et al., 2000), with increased variance reflecting probable variability in rates of individual change. The crucial point emerging is that cohort differences can be as large as age changes over much of the life-span. This emphasises the need for frequent re-standardisation of cognitive tests.

Multi-dimensional changes

Whatever the methodology used to measure them, different functions appear to decline at different rates. Verbal, well-learned and consolidated – 'crystallised' – abilities decline more slowly than 'fluid' abilities involving flexible reasoning in novel situations, although individual patterns of change are diverse (Schaie, 1990). Speed of processing seems particularly affected, at the level of central decision-making rather than simply of peripheral response. It is debatable whether this slowing is completely responsible for the early loss of performance abilities, where speed of performance is often emphasised, but it is widely regarded as a key factor (Salthouse, 2000).

It has been argued that current tests are based on predicting the educational and occupational attainment of children and adults. If abilities more relevant to cognitive demands on older people were assessed, an increase in ability might emerge in knowledge of practical information (Demming and Pressey, 1957) or in wisdom and integrative abilities (Baltes and Kunzmann, 2003).

Individual differences

There is a great variability in rate of change of intellectual abilities among older people. Schaie (1996) comments that in his large-scale longitudinal study assessing five areas of cognitive function, most people showed decline in one area by age 60, but that virtually no one had declined in all five areas even by age 88 (p. 355), suggesting that stability in at least some areas of cognition is normative, although the pattern of change probably differs considerably between individuals.

Cognitive decline with age is not a uniform or a universal phenomenon. Holland and Rabbitt (1991) illustrate, with data from a digit span test across different age groups, that whereas mean scores decrease with age, there is a marked increase in variance with age: while some are declining, others are maintaining or improving function. There are, then, differences between individuals as well as within the individual's profile of performance. It is now recognised that an individual may retain or develop further ability in a particular cognitive domain – perhaps through interest, experience or opportunity – while other areas show decline. This process has been described as encapsulation (Rybash et al., 1986). It finds parallels in the Selective Optimisation with Compensation (SOC) model (Baltes and Baltes, 1990). This can be applied to conceptualising the way in which many older people maintain good cognitive function, despite changes occurring at a neuro-physiological level. The suggests that older people ageing successfully select their goals carefully, focusing on the areas of most importance or interest to themselves; optimise goal-relevant means, perhaps by practising more or devoting more time and energy to a task than previously; and compensate for areas of lost function using substitute means. Thus, in particular domains – chess, bridge, an Open University degree, musical performance, wisdom – the person may maintain and develop function, despite experiencing age-related changes.

To talk in terms of a single ageing process is misleading: a number of other factors must also be taken into account in making sense of the lower mean scores of groups of older people on cognitive tests. Situational factors include fatigue (Furry and Baltes, 1973), cautiousness (Birkhill and Schaie, 1975) and older people evaluating their own performance more negatively (Bellucci and Hoyer, 1975). It is important to examine older people's strategies and approach to the task and their perception of what is expected from them, not just the level or speed of their performance (Rabbitt, 1982).

Among longer term factors related to reduced cognitive performance, physical health is crucial. For example, vascular disease has been shown in a large-scale study of older men (Elwood et al., 2002) to be related to the equivalent of 5 years of 'normal' age change. Diabetes (Holland and Rabbitt, 1991) and sensory problems have also been shown to be related to cognitive loss, with even mild hearing and visual impairment reducing performance (Rabbitt, 1988). Lifestyle may also have an influence, with those involved in activities that are complex and intellectually stimulating being said to show less decline (Schaie, 1996, p. 356). The person's physical activity level and medication (Curran et al., 2003) may also influence cognitive performance, and also have a relationship to physical health problems. Finally, the cognitive effects of psychiatric disorders, both organic and functional, are well established. A representative sample of older people could include up to 25% with a psychiatric disorder (depending on the definition of depression). Considerable individual variability is understandable given the variety of factors leading to cognitive loss in older people. Age *per se* is not a causal variable, merely a crude index of other events and processes occurring in time.

THE ASSESSMENT OF COGNITIVE ABILITIES

Intellectual function

Two major measures of global intellectual function have been used extensively. Raven's Progressive Matrices (Standard and Coloured) and the Mill Hill Vocabulary Scale (Raven, 1982) provide indications of performance and verbal intellectual levels, respectively; they are fairly simple and quick to administer. Limited old-age norms are available. The Coloured version is particularly useful with older patients, being briefer and less susceptible to floor effects in those with lower levels of function. The Matrices may be particularly useful with patients with limited verbal ability, e.g. following a dominant hemisphere cerebrovascular accident (CVA), and have been shown to predict outcome in this context (David and Skilbeck, 1984). Care should be taken, however, that results are not invalidated on this test through visual neglect or visual field deficits.

The Wechsler Adult Intelligence Scales (WAIS) are more time-consuming, requiring a highly trained tester, but tap a richer variety of skills and modalities. As they can only be used individually, the assessor is able to observe the patient's approach to the tasks and to consider alternative hypotheses for apparent deficits. The current version of the WAIS, the WAIS-III (Wechsler, 1997a) was standardised in the USA on a representative sample of adults up to age 89. The norms have been validated in the UK (up to age 80). The WAIS-III is a lengthy test for older people. The Wechsler Abbreviated Scale of Intelligence (Wechsler, 1999) provides a standardised short form, including the vocabulary, similarities, block design and matrix reasoning sub-tests, enabling good estimations of both verbal and performance IQ to be readily made, and again norms are available up to age 89.

In interpreting the current profile of cognitive performance, and indicating whether this represents a change in function, an estimate of the person's life-long level of function is helpful. Ideally, a comparison would be made with a measure of intellectual function administered during the person's middle years. Such an assessment is rarely, if ever, available. Alternatively, the current assessment is treated as a baseline, and then repeated after an appropriate time interval, to indicate whether any decline is ongoing. This latter approach will not detect a non-progressive change occurring before the first testing. In both instances some caution is required. Where possible, the same measure should be used on each occasion, as each test of intellectual function may produce slightly different IQ estimates. Practice effects and normal variability in cognitive function must be taken into account. These considerations can mean that quite a large change – of 15 IQ points, say – may have to be present for it to be considered clinically significant.

Some guide to lifelong function may be provided by demographic variables, such as occupation and level of education. Attempts have been made to draw up regression equations to make quantitative predictions using these variables, with limited success (Crawford et al., 1989). Particularly with the current generation of older people, where educational opportunities were less equitably available than today, these indices are likely to be unreliable in the individual case. They may be used in a positive sense, in that, for example, an older person who achieved well in higher education and/or in one of the professions might be safely assumed to be of above-average intellectual level; however, no assumptions could be made regarding someone who left school at 14 and worked as, say, a labourer.

A discrepancy between verbal and performance IQs is often considered to indicate cognitive decline (van den Broek and Bradshaw, 1990). However, a person may have a fairly large difference between verbal and performance IQs, greater than could be attributed to errors of measurement, without this being particularly unusual. In dementia, variability in patterns of change is common, between individuals and within the same person at different stages of the disorder. Thus, at first, performance abilities may well show more decline, but verbal abilities may decline more later, reducing the discrepancy, with performance levels showing a 'floor' effect.

Vocabulary test scores have similarly been evaluated as a possible indicator of pre-morbid intellectual levels and the comparison between the Mill Hill Vocabulary Scale and Raven's Progressive Matrices as an indication of decline is on this basis. Whilst vocabulary has been used in studies of normal ageing (Holland and Rabbitt, 1991) as a stable index of lifelong levels, it has been shown to decline in dementia (O'Carroll et al., 1987) and tests of word-reading ability are now thought to give a more accurate index of pre-morbid intellectual level (Nelson and McKenna, 1975). The National Adult Reading Test (NART; Nelson, 1982) consists of words unlikely to be read correctly unless the person is familiar with them. The Revised form (Nelson and Willison, 1991) was standardised against the WAIS-R and a similar test, the Wechsler Test of Adult Reading (WTAR; Wechsler, 2001) has been standardised against the WAIS-III. UK norms are available on this measure, which also enables demographic variables to be combined with word-reading performance to improve the prediction of lifelong IQ. The NART has been criticised for being over-long, and Beardsall and Brayne (1990) have shown the first 25 of the 50 items to give a good estimate of overall performance. Beardsall and Huppert (1994) have further modified the NART by placing each word in the context of a sentence, so that the words are not seen in isolation. It is suggested that this version, the Cambridge Contextual Reading Test (CCRT), may produce more accurate estimates of pre-morbid function (Beardsall, 1998).

Memory and learning

Deficits in these areas are well-established in both dementia and depression. The person with dementia shows a relatively mild reduction in primary memory but has a marked secondary-memory problem (Morris and Kopelman, 1986). The memory deficit in depression is less severe and less universally found, but has led to the use of the term 'pseudodementia', and is probably the major factor in the mis-diagnosis of depression as dementia (DesRosiers, 1992). Sahakian (1991) concludes that cognitive impairments in depression in older people do not disappear entirely when recovery from the depression occurs; there may well be at least a sub-group of older people with depression whose disorder is related to some degree of cerebral dysfunction, distinct from dementia. The pattern of memory impairment is in some ways similar to that found in early dementia; differences may lie in a greater tendency to random errors in dementia, and to automatic processing being less impaired in depression, with impairments tending to be in areas requiring effortful processes, or where speed of performance is important. People with dementia tend to have a wider range of impairments – aphasia, apraxia and agnosia, for example. However, in the early stages of dementia, when memory difficulties predominate, distinguishing the cognitive impairments associated with the two disorders may not be feasible in the clinical context.

Primary memory or working memory is typically assessed using the digit-span test from the WAIS-III and the spatial span from the Wechsler Memory Scale (WMS-III; Wechsler, 1997b). A number of measures of secondary memory are available, reflecting different memory modalities and, to an extent, different aspects of the memory process. Among memory tests currently available are the following:

Kendrick Object Learning Test (OLT; Kendrick and Watts, 1999): this test, involving free recall of a number of common objects presented pictorially, is acceptable to patients but would benefit from a recognition or cued-recall format. It does have two parallel forms and data on 6-week re-test aids its longitudinal use. The OLT Quotient should be calculated, giving a descriptive measure of the patient's performance in relation to his/her peer group.

Recognition Memory Tests (Warrington, 1984): this test uses a forced-choice recognition format, where the patient is required to indicate which of two stimuli he or she was shown previously. The test is in two parts, using single words and faces, with 50 items in each. The test enables an interesting comparison to be made between verbal and non-verbal aspects of memory.

Norms are available up to age 70. The recognition format tends to be more acceptable than free recall, but leads to a high chance level, with moderately impaired patients with dementia performing at chance levels. A briefer version is now available, complete with normative data on older people (The Camden Recognition Tests; Warrington, 1996).

The Rivermead Behavioural Memory Test (Wilson et al., 1985): designed to quickly and simply assess everyday memory and to reflect real-life performance more than conventional tests, this battery contains a useful variety of memory tests, including – unusually – tests of prospective memory, i.e. remembering to do something in the future, rather than some past event. The four parallel forms are especially useful for re-assessment purposes and a useful supplement to the test manual gives norms for 119 older adults, aged 70 to 94 (Cockburn and Smith, 1989). Ironically, some of the most useful sub-tests are very similar to conventional tests, e.g. prose recall, face recognition and orientation; the behavioural aspects play a relatively minor role. The scoring system does not allow detailed interpretation of performance on particular sub-tests in comparison with the standardisation sample.

Wechsler Memory Scale–III (Wechsler, 1997b): this revision has taken account of many of the criticisms of previous versions. Norms (validated in the UK) are available up to age 89, standardised in parallel with the WAIS-III and WTAR, so that valid score comparisons may readily be made. Although the scale is long, a number of useful indices relating to different aspects of memory are produced, and more of the materials appear meaningful.

The Doors and People Test (Baddeley et al., 1994) allows a direct comparison of verbal and non-verbal memory. For the non-verbal material, photographs of a huge variety of doors are preferred to faces, as it is thought the latter may be processed differently from other non-verbal stimuli. The test also incorporates both free recall and recognition components, with the person choosing from four options, so that chance scores are relatively low. There is a multiple trial, learning component for both verbal and non-verbal material, and a test of delayed recall in each modality. All in all, it provides a fairly comprehensive analysis of the person's memory and has reasonable norms for older people. As yet it has no parallel forms, so repeated testing may be a problem. For an older person with reasonable vision and hearing, without severe impairment, it is an acceptable test, which often captures the person's interest and attention.

The Benton Visual Retention Test (Benton, 1974) is a commonly used test of immediate visual memory (Crookes and McDonald, 1972). A series of ten line drawings of shapes of increasing complexity are shown to the patient for 10 seconds each; the patient draws them immediately each is removed. The copying version of the test (where the stimuli are not removed) provides a control for the effects of visuo-spatial, rather than memory difficulties. A detailed scoring system allows for analysis of the type of errors made. Norms for older people are available (Benton et al., 1981).

Speed

The Digit Copying Test, one of the Kendrick Assessment Scales (Kendrick and Watts, 1999) measures psycho-motor speed simply and acceptably. It is preferable to the WAIS Digit Symbol-Coding Test as it is less complex and relies less on memory and comprehension of instructions. The Digit Copying Quotient should be calculated to facilitate comparison with other aspects of the patient's abilities. Speed of performance may be impaired both in dementia and, to a lesser extent, in depression. Reaction time tests have been used in a number of research studies and would be an obvious method of assessing speed of information processing. However, these have usually been associated with the various computerised test batteries that have been developed (see below).

Language

Many aphasia batteries exist, but none specifically for older people. The Schuell Minnesota Aphasia Test is wide-ranging, has a useful short form (Powell et al., 1980) and has been standardised on normal older people (Walker, 1980). The Token Test (De Renzi and Vignolo, 1962; De Renzi and Faglioni, 1978) tests comprehension of instructions of increasing linguistic complexity, and is useful in delineating the extent of a receptive deficit. The Frenchay Aphasia Screening Test (FAST; Enderby et al., 1986), designed for use with stroke patients, may be useful as a brief, easily administered screening test for language problems.

Several naming tests are available; a specific test of nominal dysphasia – the Graded Naming Test – produced by McKenna and Warrington (1983) comprises 30 line drawings of increasing difficulty. Norms are available up to age 70. Williams et al. (1989) present data on a similar test – the Boston Naming Test – for patients with dementia and normal controls, and suggest a 30-item version of the original 60-item test. In dementia, the difficulty in naming is thought to also reflect difficulty in recognising the object, whereas with dysphasia the person may clearly recognise the object but still be unable to name it (Kirshner et al., 1984).

Verbal fluency may be assessed by asking the patient to name as many words as possible beginning with a certain letter in a particular time or name members of a particular set (e.g. animals). Normative data on verbal fluency measures are provided by Delis et al. (2001) and Lezak (1995).

Executive functioning

Problems in this area of assessment are usually thought of as reflecting dysfunction of frontal lobe pathways. The higher-level skills of planning, problem-solving and flexible thinking may be involved in many different tasks, and clues to such difficulties may be gathered from careful observation of the person's performance on a variety of tasks. Perseveration of response may be seen, or the person's attempt at a constructional task may be disorganised. The WAIS-III or WASI Similarities and Matrix Reasoning subtests may point to difficulties in abstract thinking. A wide range of tests is now available, tapping one or more aspects of executive function. Verbal fluency is a frequently used indicator of frontal lobe dysfunction and may also be seen as a measure of semantic memory (some of the tests available for initial letter and category fluency were described above, in the section on Language).

The Wisconsin Card Sorting Test is probably the best known test of executive function, requiring the patient to sort cards according to an undisclosed rule, which may reflect either the number or colour or the shape of symbols on the cards. The patient's task is to discern the correct rule from feedback given card by card; the rule is then changed, and the patient must discover the new rule. A short form is available (Nelson, 1976), as the full test would be extremely demanding for most older patients. Norms for older people are available (e.g. Axelrod et al., 1992).

The Weigl Colour Form Sorting Test provides a much simpler test of the person's ability to switch response set. The patient is given a number of different shapes of different colours and asked to sort them; having sorted them into piles of similar shape or colour, the patient is asked to sort them a different way. A patient with a severe dysexecutive difficulty will perseverate and sort them as previously, apparently being unable to perceive the second dimension on which they might be sorted. Colour tends to be the preferred sorting dimension for patients with dementia (Grewal et al., 1985, 1986).

The Trail Making Test, Part A, requires the patient to draw lines connecting in sequence numbers displayed on a page, and is a measure of psychomotor speed and perceptual organisation. Part B requires letters and numbers to be connected alternately, maintaining the sequence of each: A–1–B–2–C–3, etc. This additionally requires cognitive flexibility, and may give a guide to executive function. Norms for older adults are provided in Spreen and Strauss (1991). This source also provides older adult norms for the Stroop Test, where the person has to name the colour in which a word is printed, ignoring the word itself, which will be the name of a different colour. The person has to inhibit reading the colour word, and this slows performance in colour identification, a phenomenon particularly marked in patients with frontal lobe difficulties. Versions of these two tests are among a range of executive function tests included in the Delis–Kaplan Executive Function System (Delis et al., 2001), for which representative US norms up to 89 are provided.

Perceptual abilities

Perceptual difficulties may become apparent in a variety of tests; a difficulty in naming pictures of objects in a memory task, or an inability to carry out a simple psychomotor task such as the Digit Copying Test, for example. A test such as the Benton Visual Retention Test (described above) is useful in giving an indication of copying a design, as well as having a separate memory component. Other clinical tests of drawing ability, such as drawing a clock (Shulman et al., 1986; Sunderland et al., 1989; Bourke et al., 1995), or drawing a house (Moore and Wyke, 1984) can also be informative. Contrasting the person's ability to draw an object, such as a house, spontaneously with their ability to copy a given design, may indicate whether spatial relationships have become completely disorganised, or whether an external cue can assist in their expression. Sub-tests of the WAIS-III and WASI, especially Block Design, provide further evidence of the person's visuo-spatial abilities.

Most of the above tests involve a constructional element; the Visual Object and Space Perception Battery (VOSP; Warrington and James, 1991) includes a number of sub-tests that may be useful in addressing the perceptual element of perceptuo-motor skills more directly. However, older adult norms are limited. In particular, following a right hemisphere stroke, unilateral visual neglect is a common – but often unrecognised – feature. The person behaves as if no sensory input is being received from the contralateral side of visual space. Clock and other drawing tasks may reveal the problem, with the left-hand side of the drawing incomplete, but more systematic tests such as cancellation or line bisection tasks are more useful (Skilbeck, 1996). In the former, the patient with neglect will miss target letters, digits or symbols on the left hand side of the array; in the latter, the patient when asked to draw a cross in the middle of a line will typically respond with a cross in the right hand half of the line. Several of these tasks are included in the Behavioural Inattention Test (BIT; Wilson et al., 1987), as well as in other batteries (see Skilbeck, 1996).

Neuropsychological batteries

Such batteries have typically been developed for use with younger patients and should be used cautiously unless old-age norms are available. For example, normal old people show poor performance on some parts of the Halstead–Reitan Battery (Klisz, 1978) and on other neuropsychological tests (Benton et al., 1981). Generally, length and difficulty level make such batteries unsuitable for older people, although Blackburn and Tyrer (1985) report positively on the value of a shortened version of Luria's Neuropsychological Investigation in this context. More straightforward clinical testing will be informative with many older patients. Examples of such a clinical approach are provided by Holden and Woods (1995), Holden (1995) and Church and Wattis (1988).

It was hoped that automated testing would allow cognitive assessment of patients untestable conventionally (Miller, 1980). A number of reports of the development of such methods have appeared (Carr et al., 1986b; Sahakian, 1990; Simpson et al., 1991). The capabilities of microcomputers provide an excellent opportunity to devise a new generation of tests, emphasising success rather than failure, suitable for repeated use and taking into account information-processing models currently used in experimental psychology, including consideration of the strategies the patient adopts. Using response speed measures allows differentiation between patients even in error-free performance. Computer graphics can be used to increase the attractiveness and interest of the materials and the various studies have reported that such batteries are well received by older people, including those with dementia. There is some evidence that performance is enhanced through the use of a touch-sensitive screen, rather than through response buttons (Carr et al., 1986a). The CANTAB battery of tests (Sahakian, 1990) is now the best developed commercially available system in the UK. Considerable development work has taken place on normal samples and clinical groups, and a wide range of tests cover many cognitive functions, including memory and learning, attention, executive functions and visuo-spatial skills.

Brief cognitive assessment

By using brief cognitive tests clinicians can quantify clinical data in a structured and standardised form. Such tests should always have been given before patients are referred for detailed cognitive assessment as simple tests of information and orientation have often proved at least as valid as more detailed cognitive tests (Pattie and Gilleard, 1979). Many such tests exist; the 12-item Information/Orientation sub-test of the Clifton Assessment Procedures for the Elderly (CAPE) is widely available and has been extensively researched (Pattie, 1988). The CAPE also includes a concentration test and screening items for reading and writing, as well as a behaviour rating scale (see below). Other frequently used tests include Hodkinson's (1972) 10-item Abbreviated Mental Test (AMTS) and the rather longer Mini-Mental State Examination (MMSE; Folstein et al., 1975). The MMSE is a frequently used screening tool comprising 12 questions, which cover a variety of areas including memory and orientation.

Which of the various tests is used in practice will depend on the setting, how brief the test has to be and personal preference. The various measures have high inter-correlations (Orrell et al., 1992) and all are liable to be influenced by the patient's level of education; those with a below average education may score poorly on such tests, despite being unimpaired; those with a high level of education may maintain high scores despite actual cognitive decline. The MMSE has been shown to be particularly susceptible to this effect (Christensen and Jorm, 1992). The MMSE can also be criticised for combining a number of items tapping quite distinct areas of function (memory, concentration, praxis, etc.) into a single total score. Different patients may have identical scores but quite different patterns of performance on this test. Recommended cut-off points and score ranges on such tests should be treated with caution, as they are influenced by mood and health, as well as education (White et al., 2002). Very brief screening tools such as the 6CIT (Brooke and Bullock, 1999) may be useful in some circumstances but should be followed up with more detailed assessment.

Assessing other areas of function is important, for example, in describing the pattern of impairment (e.g. dementia with dysphasia or dementia of the frontal type). To achieve this, a profile is required rather than a single score. The Middlesex Elderly Assessment of Mental State (MEAMS; Golding, 1989) achieves just this, comprising 12 brief neuropsychological screening tests, including orientation, naming, drawing, arithmetic and perceptual tasks. It is brief, easy to administer and available in two parallel forms. Some clinical data is available. The Cambridge Examination for Mental Disorders of the Elderly (CAMDEX-Revised; Roth et al., 1998) is a psychiatric diagnosis scale for older people that includes CAMCOG-R, a screening test that covers a range of neuropsychological functions and in fact incorporates the MMSE and AMTS. Each area of function has relatively few items, but the examination is reported to show sufficient differentiation at higher levels of function to be of value in the detection of mild dementia (Huppert, 1991; Huppert et al., 1996). Excellent normative data for older people are available (Williams et al., 2003). Other brief assessments providing a profile of the person's function across different areas of cognition include the Dementia Rating Scale (Mattis et al., 2002) and the Repeatable Battery for the Assessment of Neuropsychological Status (RBANS; Randolph, 1998). All these scales need to be interpreted in the light of the best information regarding the person's pre-morbid intellectual and educational level. The same profile of scores would have a completely different interpretation for a retired head-teacher as for a person whose predicted lifelong intellectual level was in the below average range. For many purposes, the results from one of the measures giving a profile of performance will provide enough information, but if the findings are more ambiguous with more specific deficits, further assessment is usually indicated.

As one of the key issues in cognitive assessment relates to whether or not the person has shown an abnormal amount of cognitive decline, informant questionnaires have been developed to supplement cognitive tests. The best known of these is the Informant Questionnaire of Cognitive Decline in the Elderly (IQCODE; Jorm et al., 1989). This is now available as a 12-item scale, and appears to perform at least as well as the MMSE as a screening instrument (Stephens and Jorm, 1994).

Example of descriptive cognitive assessment

Referral

Mrs G, a 74-year-old retired primary school head-teacher was referred in view of occasional memory lapses; on several occasions she had become completely lost whilst driving, not knowing what town she was in, despite it being a place well-known to her. The referring physician commented that she had a history of hypertension.

Assessment

Mrs G was seen at home on two occasions, where she lives alone, with a sister living close by. As well as the problems with driving, she recounted how she would walk into a room and forget why she had gone there, and that she would occasionally forget appointments. She had begun to use memory aids, always making a shopping list and marking days off on the calendar. There was a hint of vagueness as she talked about her past life, with some of the details not being at all clear.

Results

National Adult Reading Test

Mrs G made four errors in reading the 50 irregular words on this test, giving an estimated lifelong IQ of 126, consistent with her educational and occupational history.

Rivermead Behavioural Memory Test

Mrs G's overall profile score on this test was 11 (maximum possible 24). The test manual supplement for older people suggests this score is below the 2.5th percentile for someone of Mrs G's age and estimated IQ level. The profile of performance on the various sub-tests is of interest. She scored maximum points on orientation, including being able to give the correct date. She performed well on the two recognition tasks, and was able to learn and remember a route around the room relatively well. However, her prospective memory was extremely poor, as was her free recall, especially after a delay. In recalling a brief memory passage, she was able immediately to give back the initial phrases of the passage, but then elaborated details not present in the original. After 20 minutes, although the story bore some tenuous relation to the original, there was no evidence of recall of the specific incident described.

WASI sub-tests

Mrs G did poorly on the Block Design and Similarities sub-tests of the WASI. Her T-scores were 33 and 37, respectively, both well below average (50) for her age, and representing a clear deficit in performance (more than 1 standard deviation below the mean; around standard deviations below her estimated life-long level from the NART). On the Block Design items, she placed the blocks in a line, and seemed to be unable to plan a strategy for tackling the task. On Similarities, she had some difficulty in abstract thinking. Both these deficits may be considered as reflecting frontal lobe dysfunction. Her Digit Span age-scaled score was 10, which although average for her age, might represent a change for someone of Mrs G's general intellectual level.

Digit Copying Test

On this test of psychomotor speed, her performance appeared unimpaired, with a test quotient of 112.

Verbal fluency

On being given 60 seconds each to produce words beginning with 'F', 'A' and 'S' respectively, Mrs G produced an average of 11 words per letter. She was able to name nine items that might be bought in a supermarket in a minute. All these scores are below average for someone of Mrs G's intellectual level and are supportive of the hypothesis of frontal lobe dysfunction.

Geriatric Depression Scale

Mrs G scored 2 on the 15-item short form of this scale. She said that she feels helpless when she is not able to find something she needs, but did not feel that she had more problems with memory than most people. There was no evidence for depressed mood.

Feedback

The results were discussed in detail with Mrs G together with her sister (with Mrs G's permission). Mrs G remembered clearly items from one testing session to the next (despite having had a holiday in the meantime), and had a good grasp of day-to-day events. Strengths as well as problem areas were discussed, in relation to the different tests used. Both had wondered about 'dementia', but were not entirely sure what this meant. Mrs G had had an aunt who at 90 had become very confused and been admitted to hospital. It was explained that the definition of dementia involved simply a loss from a previous level in some areas of function, but that there are many causes and types, which may have different implications. For Mrs G, the likelihood was of the changes relating to vascular damage in specific areas of the brain – possibly mini-strokes – and that medication, such as aspirin, aimed at preventing further strokes could be helpful to her. Mrs G found useful a diagram of the brain, indicating the relatively specific areas of possible dysfunction, e.g. frontal areas for verbal fluency, Block Design and Similarities; fronto-temporal in relation to recall difficulties. She found it reassuring that many aspects were still working normally and that her success in using memory aids showed that she could find ways of coping with her problems. Mrs G's sister commented that, earlier in life, Mrs G would readily become anxious over the smallest problem; now she felt she was more relaxed and accepting than ever before in her life, almost to the extent of a character change. This change may also relate to frontal lobe changes, and hopefully will make it easier for Mrs G to face the inevitability of giving up her car.

Conclusion

This assessment contributed to the diagnostic issues but went well beyond them in providing feedback that Mrs G and her sister found useful. Understanding the person's own thoughts and fears about diagnosis is essential before giving feedback; the person's image of ageing and memory, dementia or Alzheimer's will have been conditioned by personal experiences or media images. The good performance on orientation tests is quite common in frontal-type dementias, which may be missed if too much reliance is placed on screening measures having only items of this type.

PRACTICAL CONSIDERATIONS FOR COGNITIVE ASSESSMENT

Several practical points are important:

Sensory deficits are more common in older people. Care must be taken that the patient can see and hear adequately, with glasses or hearing aid if necessary. Large-print versions of some tests (e.g. the NART) are available; other tests have items that could be presented in enlarged versions if required. Ensure the testing room is quiet and free from distracting noises. If the sensory impairment is severe and uncorrectable, tests using only the unimpaired modalities will be needed. With deaf patients, written instructions can be useful for some tests. With practical tasks, check that painful joints or tremors are not making the test too difficult for the person, and note any effects on performance. Where the person's first language is not English, check whether interpretation is required; it is usually preferable to use a professional interpreter, with some prior knowledge of the tests, rather than a family member. Be cautious in interpreting the results of verbal tests, even where the person appears to understand and speak some English.

Older patients may take longer to adjust to the testing situation and often more time needs to be spent putting the patient at ease, establishing an atmosphere of cooperation and trust, and establishing with the person the purpose of the assessment and its benefits.

The patient is likely to be helped by supportive encouragement during testing. This usually has to be of a general nature; often it is useful to explain that everybody fails on some items because of the test design. Patients often under-estimate their performance level and realistic positive evaluations are often possible. Unrealistic praise where the patients' failure is blatantly evident is unhelpful.

The session should be paced gently: a rushed, pressured session will increase the apparent impairment level. Several short sessions are preferable to a lengthy one, to minimise the effects of fatigue. Ending each session on a note of success helps to maintain future cooperation.

The difficulty level of the tests used should be carefully reviewed so that the patient experiences as little overt failure as possible, particularly early in the session. Tests exposing the older patient to repeated overt failure are stressful, reduce co-operation and should be used with caution. It is sometimes suggested that tests should resemble 'real-life' situations as closely as possible, and this may have advantages in predicting the patient's function outside the test session. Paradoxically, tests that appear too similar to real-life tasks may increase the stress on the patient, whereas tests that are more in the form of a game may be more acceptable.

It is wise to commence the assessment with some brief, wide-ranging tests, to give an indication of possible areas of strength and weakness. If for any reason the assessment is cut short, there may still be some conclusions that can be drawn from a relatively brief contact.

When selecting tests, a wealth of possible is measures available. As well as difficulty level, consider whether the test in question has appropriate norms relevant to the person being assessed, and whether it has parallel forms, as reassessment is fairly common in work with older people.

ASSESSING MOOD AND WELL-BEING

Several self-report 'life-satisfaction' and 'morale' scales have been developed specifically for older people. Among those widely used have been the Philadelphia Geriatric Center Morale Scale (Lawton, 1975) and the Life Satisfaction Index (LSI) which is available in a number of forms (Twining, 1990), including the brief version described by Bigot (1974). This has eight items on two sub-scales 'acceptance-contentment' and 'achievement-fulfilment'. Gilleard et al. (1981) provide useful normative clinical data and suggest that the latter sub-scale reflects a more stable attitudinal component of morale, based on past life achievements and experiences.

The PGC Morale Scale and the LSI show considerable overlap with depression scales, although demoralisation and depression in the elderly are not necessarily identical constructs (Gurland, 1980). Gallagher et al. (1982) report normative and reliability data on the Beck Depression Inventory (BDI) with normal and depressed older people and conclude that it is an adequate clinical screening instrument. The Geriatric Depression Scale (Yesavage et al., 1983) has a simpler response format (Yes/No) than the BDI, and is now extensively used as a self-report measure for depression in older people. The original scale had 30 items but a 15-item short-form is more than adequate (Sheikh and Yesavage, 1986). O'Neill et al. (1992) suggest that this scale is more effectively administered by a rater, rather than being given to the older person to complete. An alternative is the SELFCARE (D) scale, which has been developed as a 12-item self-report measure for use in primary care settings (Bird et al., 1987). The Hospital Anxiety and Depression Scale (HADS; Kenn et al., 1987) allows a structured assessment of anxiety as well as depression, an aspect not addressed specifically by most of the available scales.

A number of observer-rated scales are available (see Montgomery, 1988), which may assist in overcoming some of the problems inherent in self-report measures with older people (such as visual acuity problems, inappropriateness of items, etc.). When assessing patients with cognitive impairment for mood disturbance – in whom self-report may be particularly unreliable – several observer-rated depression scales are available: the Depressive Signs Scale (Katona and Aldridge, 1985); the Cornell Scale for depression in dementia (Alexopoulos et al., 1988) and the Dementia Mood Assessment Scale (Sunderland et al., 1988). However, it is worth noting that in mild dementia it may be valid to use the self-report Geriatric Depression Scale (Ott and Fogel, 1992). The RAID is an observer-rated index of anxiety in dementia (Shankar et al., 1999).

There is increasing interest in the evaluation of health-related quality of life as a means of evaluating health-care interventions. A number of approaches are possible (see Bowling, 1997), including the SF–36, a brief questionnaire, which has been used in older populations (Hayes et al., 1995;

Murray et al., 1997). In recent years, it has been established that people with mild to moderate dementia are able to complete self-report quality-of-life scales (in an interview context), and several scales have been validated for this purpose: the Quality of Life in Alzheimer's Disease (QoL-AD; Logsdon et al., 2002; Thorgrimsen et al., 2003) and the Quality of Life Assessment Schedule (QOLAS; Selai and Trimble, 1999).

ASSESSMENT OF BEHAVIOUR

Often, particularly in dementia, a person's actual behaviour – level of function, excesses and deficits – is very important in finding a suitable placement or in monitoring change. Behaviour can be assessed in several ways.

Rating scales

Here, those familiar with the person's day-to-day behaviour (usually nurses, care workers or relatives) complete the scales from their uncontrolled, unsystematic observations of the person, perhaps over a specified time period. Many different scales are in use, differing in behavioural areas covered, range and depth of content, length and format. The purpose of the assessment should guide the choice of scale. Long scales are only likely to be completed conscientiously by busy care staff if the results are immediately relevant to patient management.

A number of scales indicate the person's general functional ability and degree of care needed (Little and Doherty, 1996). These scales include aspects of behaviour such as toileting, feeding, mobility and so on. Among the most frequently used are the Behaviour Rating Scale from the Clifton Assessment Procedures for the Elderly (CAPE; Pattie and Gilleard, 1979; Pattie, 1988); and the Behavioural Assessment Scale of Later Life (BASOLL; Brooker, 1998). These scales include items relating to behaviour problems as well as to self-care. Specific brief measures of basic self-care skills are provided by the Index of Activities of Daily Living (ADL; Katz et al., 1963) and the Physical Self Maintenance Scale (PSMS; Lawton and Brody, 1969). Higher level self-care skills (e.g. shopping, cooking, finances) are assessed by the Functional Activities Questionnaire (Pfeffer et al., 1982) and the Instrumental Activities of Daily Living Scale (Lawton and Brody, 1969).

Scales mixing self-care and problem behaviour items vary greatly in their breadth and depth of coverage, especially of challenging behaviour. Inter-rater reliabilities tend to be much lower for items such as aggression and social disturbance than for ratings of physical functioning, suggesting they are more difficult to define and rate objectively. The CAPE is probably most useful for general screening, whereas the BASOLL would be a useful basis for care-planning. Scales specifically designed for assessing challenging behaviour are now available, for example the Challenging Behaviour Scale (Moniz-Cook, 2001). Scales are being developed for specific behaviours such as aggression, for example the Rating of Aggressive Behaviour in the Elderly (RAGE; Patel and Hope, 1992) and agitated behaviour (Cohen-Mansfield et al., 1992).

Scales developed for use by professional staff in residential units have often not seemed ideally suited for assessment of an older person being cared for at home by a relative. The emotional involvement and 24-hour commitment of a relative mean that different behaviours from those emphasised in an institutional setting may affect the ability to cope. Greene et al.'s (1982) Behavioural and Mood Disturbance Scale is intended for completion by relatives. Gilleard's (1984) Problem Checklist has also been widely used in this context; Agar et al. (1997) provide a factor analysis of this scale, and indicate its potential utility. The Neuropsychiatric Inventory (Cummings, 1997) similarly gathers information on frequency and severity and resulting care-giver distress, but here the focus is on psychiatric symptoms (such as delusions, anxiety and irritability).

Structured observation

Here, in contrast, a person's performance is assessed in a structured situation. This approach may detect adaptive behaviour not prompted or encouraged in the person's usual environment: conventional rating scales are inevitably affected by the extent to which independence is reinforced and encouraged on a day-to-day basis. Conversely, under-functioning could occur if the patient is affected by the unfamiliarity of the structured situation, or has difficulty in understanding the instructions, or has test anxiety or motivation difficulties.

The ADL Situational Task was developed by Skurla et al. (1988); it aims to focus on tasks involving memory and reasoning. It has four tasks, with standardised equipment, materials and instructions and specified prompts. The tasks include making a cup of coffee and using money to purchase two items. Mahurin et al. (1991) have devised a longer measure on similar lines, the Structured Assessment of Independent Living Skills (SAILS).

Direct observation

This involves behaviour in the natural environment being systematically observed, usually using some kind of sampling procedure to keep the quantity of data collected manageable: perhaps only particular behaviours will be observed, or observations will be made at set time intervals. Direct observation requires considerable preparation, allowing time for adaptation to the observer's presence by both older people and staff/care-givers, and careful definition of behaviours and the settings in which they are to be observed.

Brooker (1995) provides a useful review of observational measures in dementia care. Some studies have looked at 'engagement' to assess the proportion of residents involved in some kind of activity, interacting with people or materials (Jenkins et al., 1977). The behavioural definitions can be extended to give a more detailed description of behaviour (e.g. Macdonald et al., 1985). Baltes et al. (1980) have used direct observation to assess the important sequential relationships in residents' and staff behaviour, and Lindesay et al. (1991) report its use in comparisons of long-term care settings for people with severe dementia. Bowie and Mountain (1993) describe the development of the Patient Behaviour Observation Instrument, where the observer uses a hand-held computer to record the occurrence of pre-defined categories of behaviour.

Increasingly, there is recognition that increasing the *quantity* of interactions is not enough; the *quality* of interactions is of crucial importance. An increase in low-quality or negative interactions is not likely to be helpful. This is reflected in the development of approaches such as Dementia Care Mapping (DCM; Kitwood and Bredin, 1992), which may be used to indicate the individual person's level of well-being, as well as giving an overall profile, reflecting the quality of the care environment (Ballard et al., 2001).

ASSESSING NEEDS

The recent emphasis on comprehensive assessment of needs to inform care-planning has revealed a dearth of standardised instruments in this area (Hamid et al., 1995). Most of the assessments previously described focus on specific areas and do not integrate the overall picture. Barrowclough and Fleming (1986a) use a constructional approach, assessing the whole situation and identifying the person's strengths as well as needs. Strengths are used in the care-plan to seek to meet the person's needs. The use of this approach in residential care has been validated (Barrowclough and Fleming, 1986b).

More recently, the Camberwell Assessment of Need (Slade et al., 1996), a scale developed for use with younger people with long-term psychiatric problems, has been adapted for use with older people (Reynolds et al., 2000; Orrell and Hancock, 2004). The Care Needs Assessment Pack for Dementia (Carenap-D; McWalter et al., 1998) has been developed specifically for people with dementia and their carers, and some reliability and validity data have been reported. These scales have the potential for identifying needs of the person or the carer that are not being met, and should assist in care-planning and, in aggregate, in service planning. However, it should be noted that the definition of 'need' is determined by the professional, not by the person or carer, and typically takes into account available resources and services. It does not necessarily map directly onto the person's wants or demands. The possibility – although this perhaps seems unlikely – of over-met needs should also be considered; it may be as detrimental as an unmet need. For example, a depressed older person who is provided with home help and meals on wheels might become dependent on these services and is reinforced in a passive role, which serves to maintain the depressed mood; or a person might be admitted to a residential home because he or she feels lonely at home alone, whereas radical and more specific ways of meeting needs should be the first step.

ASSESSMENT OF THE ENVIRONMENT

Methods of assessing institutional environments can assist in identifying features needing change and in monitoring intervention attempts. A comprehensive and detailed measure is the Multi-phasic Environmental Assessment Procedure (MEAP; Moos and Lemke, 1980), designed for and standardised on settings for older people. Physical and architectural features, resident and staff characteristics, the social climate and aspects of the setting's policies and regime are all covered. An example of its use is in comparing different types of care philosophy (Benjamin and Spector, 1992). More recently, Sloane et al. (2002) described an observational instrument for assessing the physical environment in institutions for people with dementia that has been used in a number of studies (e.g. in relating quality of care to quality of life; Zimmerman et al., 2005). Kitwood and Bredin (1992) have developed a direct observational method, Dementia Care Mapping, which focuses further on the quality dimension, evaluating the extent to which the environment and staff practices enhance, or detract from, the personhood of the dementia sufferer (see Brooker, 2005, for a review).

In community settings, it is of great importance to assess relatives' feelings of strain arising from, for example, looking after a person suffering from dementia. Some studies (e.g. Gilleard, 1984) have used non-specific measures of distress, such as the General Health Questionnaire (Goldberg, 1978) or the Beck Depression Inventory (see above). Other scales have been developed that more specifically assess strain arising directly from the relative's caregiving (e.g. Greene et al., 1982; Gilleard, 1984).

FUTURE DIRECTIONS

Considerable development in the psychological assessment of older people has occurred in recent years. The range of tests is now much greater, with many more measures having norms allowing their valid use with people in their 80s. Describing a person's profile of abilities is now much more feasible. However, it would perhaps be easy to gain the impression that a scale exists for anything a psychologist might wish to assess in relation to older people. It cannot be emphasised too strongly that a mechanistic approach to assessment is not appropriate. Well-developed psychological skills are needed, to identify the key questions to be addressed by any assessment, and to use appropriate tests and scales alongside other assessment skills such as interviewing and functional analysis.

The psychologist needs to be aware of the uses to which the assessment will be put, and be prepared to explain the purpose clearly to the patient in a manner he or she can understand. There is increasing awareness of the importance of the process of sharing the diagnosis with the patient and family – often judgementally described as 'breaking the bad news'. Good practice, however, demands that the process begins before any assessment, with pre-diagnostic assessment counselling. This is the time to begin to explore the patient's perception of the possible outcomes and to ensure that the patient is aware, say, that the assessment may result in advice about competence to drive. Feedback on a neuropsychological assessment cannot simply be fitted into a 5-minute slot at the end of the session; time must be allowed and further sessions scheduled as necessary.

A mechanistic approach in terms of the interpretation of test results is also not sustainable. Complex multiple pathologies befall older people and teasing out the differential effects of physical health changes, sensory losses and 'expected' age-related decline from a dementing process cannot be achieved by the application of cut-off scores in a one-off assessment. Uncertainty is common regarding aetiology; the psychologist is able, nonetheless, to helpfully describe functional strengths and weaknesses, and to indicate how this knowledge may inform and feed into plans of care. Assessment is not a goal in itself, but a means towards improving the quality of life for all concerned, through intervention (and sometimes inaction) that is planned and appropriate to the needs of the person and his or her supporters.

REFERENCES

Agar, S., Moniz-Cook, E., Orbell, S., Elston, C. and Wang, M. (1997) Measuring the outcome of psychosocial intervention for family caregivers of dementia sufferers: a factor analytic study. *Aging and Mental Health*, 1(2), 166–175.

Alexopoulos, G. S., Abrams, R. C., Young, R. C. and Shamoian, C. A. (1988) Cornell Scale for Depression in Dementia. *Biological Psychiatry*, 23, 271–284.

Axelrod, B. N. and Henry, R. R. (1992) Age-related performance on the Wisconsin Card Sorting, Similarities and Controlled Oral Word Association Tests. *Clinical Neuropsychologist*, 6, 16–26.

Baddeley, A., Emslie, H. and Nimmo-Smith, I. (1994) *Doors and People: A Test of Visual and Verbal Recall and Recognition*. Bury St Edmunds, UK: Thames Valley Test Company.

Ballard, C. G., Bannister, C. and Oyebode, F. (1996) Depression in dementia sufferers. *International Journal of Geriatric Psychiatry*, 11(6), 507–515.

Ballard, C., Fossey, J., Chithramohan, R., Howard, R., Burns, A., Thompson, P. et al. (2001) Quality of care in private sector and NHS facilities for people with dementia: Cross-sectional survey. *British Medical Journal*, 323, 426–427.

Baltes, P. B. and Baltes, M. M. (1990) Psychological perspectives on successful aging: The model of selective optimization with compensation. In P. B. Baltes and M. M. Baltes (eds) *Successful Aging: Perspectives from the Behavioral Sciences* (pp. 1–34). Cambridge: Cambridge University Press.

Baltes, P. B. and Kunzmann, U. (2003) Wisdom. *Psychologist*, 16(3), 131–133.

Baltes, M. M., Burgess, R. L. and Stewart, R. B. (1980) Independence and dependence in self-care behaviours in nursing home residents: An operant observational study. *International Journal of Behavioural Development*, 3, 489–500.

Barrowclough, C. and Fleming, I. (1986a) *Goal planning with elderly people*. Manchester: Manchester University Press.

Barrowclough, C. and Fleming, I. (1986b) Training direct care staff in goal-planning with elderly people. *Behavioural Psychotherapy*, 14, 192–209.

Beardsall, L. (1998) Development of the Cambridge Contextual Reading Test for improving the estimation of premorbid verbal intelligence in older persons with dementia. *British Journal of Clinical Psychology*, 37(2), 229–240.

Beardsall, L. and Brayne, C. (1990) Estimation of verbal intelligence in an elderly community; a prediction analysis using a shortened NART. *British Journal of Clinical Psychology*, 29, 83–90.

Beardsall, L. and Huppert, F. A. (1994) Improvement in NART word reading in demented and normal older persons using the Cambridge Contextual Reading Test. *Journal of Clinical & Experimental Neuropsychology*, 16, 232–242.

Bellucci, G. and Hoyer, W. J. (1975) Feedback effects on the performance and self-reinforcing behaviour of elderly and young adult women. *Journal of Gerontology*, 30, 456–460.

Benjamin, L. C. and Spector, J. (1992) Geriatric care on a ward without nurses. *International Journal of Geriatric Psychiatry*, 7, 743–750.

Benton, A. L. (1974) *The Revised Visual Retention Test*. New York: Psychological Corporation.

Benton, A. L., Eslinger, P. J. and Damasio, A. R. (1981) Normative observations on neuropsychological test performance in old age. *Journal of Clinical Neuropsychology*, 3, 33–42.

Bigot, A. (1974) The relevance of American life satisfaction indices for research on British subjects before and after retirement. *Age and Ageing*, 3, 113–121.

Bird, A. S., Macdonald, A. J. D., Mann, A. H. and Philpot, M. P. (1987) Preliminary experience with the SELFCARE (D): A self-rating depression questionnaire for use in elderly, non-institutionalized subjects. *International Journal of Geriatric Psychiatry*, 2, 31–38.

Birkhill, W. R. and Schaie, K. W. (1975) The effect of differential reinforcement of cautiousness in intellectual performance among the elderly. *Journal of Gerontology*, 30, 578–583.

Birren, J. E. and Schaie, K. W. (eds) (2001) *Handbook of the Psychology of Aging*, 5th edn. San Diego, CA: Academic Press.

Blackburn, I. M. and Tyrer, G. M. B. (1985) The value of Luria's neuropsychological investigation for the assessment of cognitive dysfunction in Alzheimer-type dementia. *British Journal of Clinical Psychology*, 24, 171–179.

Bourke, J., Castleden, M. C., Stephen, R. and Dennis, M. (1995) A comparison of clock and pentagon drawing in Alzheimer's disease. *International Journal of Geriatric Psychiatry*, 10(8), 703–705.

Bowie, P. and Mountain, G. (1993) Using direct observation to record the behaviour of long-stay patients with dementia. *International Journal of Geriatric Psychiatry*, 8, 857–864.

Bowling, A. (1997) *Measuring Health: A Review of Quality of Life Measurement Scales*, 2nd edn. Buckingham, UK: Open University Press.

Broek, M. D. V. D. and Bradshaw, C. M. (1990) Intellectual decline and the assessment of premorbid intelligence. In: J. R. Beech and L. Harding (eds) *Assessment of the Elderly* (pp. 13–28). Windsor, UK: NFER-Nelson.

Brooke, P. and Bullock, R. (1999) Validation of a 6-item cognitive impairment test with a view to primary care usage. *International Journal of Geriatric Psychiatry*, 14(11), 936–940.

Brooker, D. (1995) Looking at them, looking at me; A review of observational studies into the quality of institutional care for elderly people with dementia. *Journal of Mental Health*, 4, 145–156.

Brooker, D. (1998) *BASOLL – Behavioural Assessment Scale of Later Life*. Bicester, UK: Winslow.

Brooker, D. (2005) Dementia Care Mapping: A review of the research literature. *Gerontologist*, 45 (special issue 1), 11–18.

Carr, A. C., Woods, R. T. and Moore, B. J. (1986a) Automated cognitive assessment of elderly patients: A comparison of two types of response device. *British Journal of Clinical Psychology*, 25, 305–306.

Carr, A. C., Woods, R. T. and Moore, B. J. (1986b) Developing a microcomputer-based automated testing system for use with psychogeriatric patients. *Bulletin of the Royal College of Psychiatrists*, 10, 309–312.

Christensen, H. and Jorm, A. F. (1992) Short report: Effect of premorbid intelligence on the Mini-Mental State and IQCODE. *International Journal of Geriatric Psychiatry*, 7, 159–160.

Christensen, H., Griffiths, K., MacKinnon, A. and Jacomb, P. (1997) A quantitative review of cognitive deficits in depression and Alzheimer-type dementia. *Journal of International Neuropsychological Society*, 3, 631–651.

Church, M. and Wattis, J. P. (1988) Psychological approaches to the assessment and treatment of old people. In: J. P. Wattis and I. Hindmarch (eds) *Psychological Assessment of the Elderly* (pp. 151–179). Edinburgh: Churchill Livingstone.

Clare, L. (2004) Assessment and intervention in dementia of Alzheimer type. In: A. Baddeley, M. D. Kopelman and B. A. Wilson (eds) *The Essential Handbook of Memory Disorders for Clinicians* (pp. 255–283). Chichester: John Wiley.

Cockburn, J. and Smith, P. T. (1989) *The Rivermead Behavioural Memory Test; Supplement 3: Elderly People*. Titchfield, UK: Thames Valley Test Company.

Cohen-Mansfield, J., Werner, P. and Marx, M. S. (1992) The social environment of the agitated nursing home resident. *International Journal of Geriatric Psychiatry*, 7, 789–798.

Crawford, J. R., Stewart, L. E., Cochrane, R. H. B., Foulds, J. A., Besson, J. A. O. and Parker, D. M. (1989) Estimating premorbid IQ from demographic variables: regression equations derived from a UK sample. *British Journal of Clinical Psychology*, 28, 275–278.

Crookes, T. B. and McDonald, K. G. (1972) Benton's visual retention test in the differentiation of depression and early dementia. *British Journal of Social and Clinical Psychology*, 11, 66–69.

Cullum, S., Huppert, F., McGee, M., Dening, T., Ahmed, A., Paykel, E. S. and Brayne, C. (2000) Decline across different domains of cognitive function in normal ageing: results of a longitudinal population-based study using CAMCOG. *International Journal of Geriatric Psychiatry*, 15, 853–862.

Cummings, J. L. (1997) The Neuropsychiatric Inventory: Assessing psychopathology in dementia patients. *Neurology*, 48, S10–S16.

Curran, H. V., Collins, R., Fletcher, S., Kee, S. C. Y., Woods, B. and Iliffe, S. (2003) Older adults and withdrawal from benzodiazepine hypnotics in general practice: Effects on cognitive function, sleep, mood and quality of life. *Psychological Medicine*, 33, 1223–1237.

David, R. M. and Skilbeck, C. E. (1984) Raven's IQ and language recovery following stroke. *Journal of Clinical Neuropsychology*, 6, 302–308.

Deary, I., Whalley, L. J., Lemmon, H., Crawford, J. R. and Starr, J. M. (2000) The stability of individual differences in mental ability from childhood to old age: Follow-up of the 1932 Scottish Mental Survey. *Intelligence*, 28, 49–55.

Delis, D. C., Kaplan, E. and Kramer, J. (2001) *The Delis–Kaplan Executive Function System*. San Antonio, TX: Psychological Corporation.

Demming, J. A. and Pressey, S. L. (1957) Tests 'indigenous' to the adult and older years. *Journal of Counselling Psychology*, 4, 144–148.

DeRenzi, E. and Faglioni, P. (1978) Normative data and screening power of a shortened version of the token test. *Cortex*, 14, 41–49.

DeRenzi, E. and Vignolo, L. A. (1962) The token test: A sensitive test to detect receptive disturbances in aphasias. *Brain*, 85, 665–678.

DesRosiers, G. (1992) Primary or depressive dementia: Clinical features. *International Journal of Geriatric Psychiatry*, 7, 629–638.

Elwood, P. C., Pickering, J., Bayer, A. and Gallacher, J. E. J. (2002) Vascular disease and cognitive function in older men in the Caerphilly cohort. *Age and Ageing*, 31, 43–48.

Enderby, P. M., Wood, V. A., Wade, D. T. and Langton-Hewer, R. (1986) The Frenchay Aphasia Screening Test: A short, simple test for aphasia appropriate for non-specialists. *International Rehabilitation Medicine*, 8, 166–170.

Folstein, M. F., Folstein, S. E. and McHugh, P. R. (1975) 'Mini Mental State': A practical method for grading the cognitive state of patients for the clinician. *Journal of Psychiatric Research*, 12, 189–198.

Furry, C. A. and Baltes, P. B. (1973) The effect of age differences in ability – extraneous performance variables on the assessment of intelligence in children, adults and the elderly. *Journal of Gerontology*, 28, 73–80.

Gallagher, D., Nies, G. and Thompson, L. W. (1982) Reliability of the Beck Depression Inventory with older adults. *Journal of Consulting & Clinical Psychology*, 50, 152–153.

Gilleard, C. J. (1984) *Living with Dementia*. Beckenham, UK: Croom Helm.

Gilleard, C. J., Willmott, M. and Vaddadik, S. (1981) Self report measures of mood and morale in elderly depressives. *British Journal of Psychiatry*, 138, 230–235.

Goldberg, D. (1978) *Manual of the General Health Questionnaire*. Windsor, UK: NFER-Nelson.

Golding, E. (1989) *Middlesex Elderly Assessment of Mental State*. Titchfield, UK: Thames Valley Test Company.

Greene, J. G., Smith, R., Gardiner, M. and Timbury, G. C. (1982) Measuring behavioural disturbance of elderly demented patients in the community and its effect on relatives: A factor analytic study. *Age and Ageing*, 11, 121–126.

Grewal, B. S., Haward, L. R. and Davies, I. R. (1985) Colour and form stimulus values in a test of dementia. *IRCS Medical Science Psychology and Psychiatry*, 13, 703–704.

Grewal, B. S., Haward, L. R. and Davies, I. R. (1986) The role of colour discriminability in the Weigl test. *IRCS Medical Science Psychology and Psychiatry*, 14, 693–694.

Gurland, B. J. (1980) The assessment of the mental health status of older adults. In: J. E. Birren and R. B. Sloane (eds) *Handbook of Mental Health and Aging*. Englewood Cliffs, NJ: Prentice Hall.

Hamid, W. A., Howard, R. and Silverman, M. (1995) Needs assessment in old age psychiatry – a need for standardization. *International Journal of Geriatric Psychiatry*, 10, 533–540.

Hayes, V., Morris, J., Wolfe, C. and Morgan, M. (1995) The SF–36 health survey questionnaire: Is it suitable for use with older adults? *Age and Ageing*, 24, 120–125.

Hodkinson, H. M. (1972) Evaluation of a mental test score for assessment of mental impairment in the elderly. *Age & Ageing*, 1, 233–238.

Holden, U. (1995) *Ageing, Neuropsychology and the 'New' Dementias: Definitions, Explanations and Practical Approaches*. London: Chapman and Hall.

Holden, U. P. and Woods, R. T. (1995) *Positive Approaches to Dementia Care*, 3rd edn. Edinburgh: Churchill Livingstone.

Holland, C. A. and Rabbitt, P. (1991) The course and causes of cognitive change with advancing age. *Reviews in Clinical Gerontology*, 1, 81–96.

Huppert, F. A. (1991) Neuropsychological assessment of dementia. *Reviews in Clinical Gerontology*, 1, 159–169.

Huppert, F. A., Jorm, A. F., Brayne, C. and Girling, D. M. (1996) Psychometric properties of the CAMCOG and its efficacy in the diagnosis of dementia. *Aging, Neuropsychology and Cognition*, 3(3), 201–214.

Jenkins, J., Felce, D., Lunt, B. and Powell, E. (1977) Increasing engagement in activity of residents in old people's homes by providing recreational materials. *Behaviour Research and Therapy*, 15, 429–434.

Jorm, A. F., Scott, R. and Jacomb, P. (1989) Assessment of cognitive decline in dementia by informant questionnaire. *International Journal of Geriatric Psychiatry*, 4, 35–39.

Katona, C. L. E. and Aldridge, C. R. (1985) The dexamethasone suppression test and depressive signs in dementia. *Journal of Affective Disorders*, 8, 83–89.

Katz, S., Ford, A. B., Moskowitz, R. W., Jackson, R. A. and Jaffe, M. W. (1963) Studies of illness in the aged: The index of ADL. *Journal of American Medical Association*, 185, 914–919.

Kendrick, D. and Watts, G. (1999) *The Kendrick Assessment Scales for Cognitive Ageing*. Windsor, UK: NFER-Nelson.

Kenn, C., Wood, H., Kucyj, M., Wattis, J. P. and Cunane, J. (1987) Validation of the Hospital Anxiety and Depression Rating Scale (HADS) in an elderly psychiatric population. *International Journal of Geriatric Psychiatry*, 2, 189–193.

Kirshner, H. S., Webb, W. G. and Kelly, M. P. (1984) The naming disorder of dementia. *Neuropsychologia*, 22, 23–30.

Kitwood, T. and Bredin, K. (1992) A new approach to the evaluation of dementia care. *Journal of Advances in Health and Nursing Care*, 1, 41–60.

Klisz, D. (1978) Neuropsychological evaluation in older persons. In: M. Storandt, I. C. Siegler and M. F. Elias (eds) *The Clinical Psychology of Aging* (pp. 71–96). New York: Plenum Press.

Lawton, M. P. (1975) The Philadelphia Geriatric Center Morale scale: A revision. *Journal of Gerontology*, 30, 85–89.

Lawton, M. P. and Brody, E. (1969) Assessment of older people: Self-maintaining and instrumental activities of daily living. *Gerontologist*, 9, 179–186.

Lezak, M. (1995) *Neuropsychological Assessment*, 3rd edn. New York: Oxford University Press.

Lindesay, J., Briggs, K., Lawes, M., Macdonald, A. and Herzberg, J. (1991) The domus philosophy: A comparative evaluation of a new approach to residential care for the demented elderly. *International Journal of Geriatric Psychiatry*, 6, 727–736.

Little, A. and Doherty, B. (1996) Going beyond cognitive assessment: Assessment of adjustment, behaviour and the environment. In: R. T. Woods (ed) *Handbook of the Clinical Psychology of Ageing* (pp. 475–506). Chichester: John Wiley.

Logsdon, R. G., Gibbons, L. E., McCurry, S. M. and Teri, L. (2002) Assessing quality of life in older adults with cognitive impairment. *Psychosomatic Medicine*, 64, 510–519.

Macdonald, A. J. D., Craig, T. K. J. and Warner, L. A. R. (1985) The development of a short observational method for the study of the activity and contacts of old people in residential settings. *Psychological Medicine*, 15, 167–172.

Mahurin, R. K., DeBettignies, B. H. and Pirozzolo, F. J. (1991) Structured assessment of independent living skills: Preliminary report of a performance measure of functional abilities in dementia. *Journal of Gerontology*, 46, P58–P66.

Mattis, S., Jurica, P. and Leitten, C. (2002) *Dementia Rating Scale*, 2nd edn. San Antonio, TX: Psychological Corporation.

McKenna, P. and Warrington, E. K. (1983) *The Graded Naming Test*. Windsor, UK: NFER-Nelson.

McWalter, G., Toner, H., McWalter, A., Eastwood, J., Marshall, M. and Turvey, T. (1998) A community needs assessment: The Care Needs Assessment Pack for Dementia (Carenap-D) – its development, reliability and validity. *International Journal of Geriatric Psychiatry*, 13(1), 16–22.

Miller, E. (1980) Cognitive assessment of the older adult. In: J. Birren and R. Sloane (eds) *Handbook of Mental Health and Aging* (pp. 520–536). New York: Van Nostrand Reinhold.

Moniz-Cook, E., Woods, R., Gardiner, E., Silver, M. and Agar, S. (2001) The Challenging Behaviour Scale (CBS): Development of a scale for staff caring for older people in residential and nursing homes. *British Journal of Clinical Psychology*, 40(3), 309–322.

Moniz-Cook, E. and Woods, R. T. (1997) The role of memory clinics and psycho-social intervention in the early stages of dementia. *International Journal of Geriatric Psychiatry*, 12, 1143–1145.

Montgomery, S. A. (1988) Measuring mood. In: J. P. Wattis and I. Hindmarch (eds) *Psychological Assessment of the Elderly* (pp. 138–150). Edinburgh: Churchill Livingstone.

Moore, V. and Wyke, M. A. (1984) Drawing disability in patients with senile dementia. *Psychological Medicine*, 14, 97–105.

Moos, R. and Lemke, S. (1980) Assessing the physical and architectural features of sheltered care settings. *Journal of Gerontology*, 35, 571–583.

Morris, R. G. and Kopelman, M. D. (1986) The memory deficits in Alzheimer-type dementia: A review. *Quarterly Journal of Experimental Psychology*, 38A, 575–602.

Morris, R. G. and McKiernan, F. (1994) Neuropsychological investigation of dementia. In: A. Burns and R. Levy (eds) *Dementia* (pp. 327–354). London: Chapman and Hall.

Murray, M., Lefort, S. and Ribeiro, V. (1997) The SF–36: Reliable and valid for the institutionalized elderly? *Aging and Mental Health*, 2(1), 24–27.

Nelson, H. E. (1976) A modified card sorting test sensitive to frontal lobe deficits. *Cortex*, 12, 313–324.

Nelson, H. E. (1982) *The National Adult Reading Test*. Windsor, UK: NFER-Nelson.

Nelson, H. E. and McKenna, P. (1975) The use of current reading ability in the assessment of dementia. *British Journal of Social and Clinical Psychology*, 14, 259–267.

Nelson, H. E. and Willison, J. (1991) *National Adult Reading Test: Test Manual*. Windsor, UK: NFER-Nelson.

O'Carroll, R. E., Baikie, E. M. and Whittick, J. E. (1987) Does the National Adult Reading Test hold in dementia? *British Journal of Clinical Psychology*, 26, 315–316.

O'Neill, D., Rice, I., Blake, P., Walsh, J. B. and Coakley, D. (1992) The geriatric depression scale: Rater-administered or self-administered. *International Journal of Geriatric Psychiatry*, 7, 511–515.

Orrell, M. and Hancock, G. (eds) (2004) *CANE: Camberwell Assessment of Need for the Elderly*. London: Gaskell.

Orrell, M., Howard, R., Payne, A., Bergmann, K., Woods, R., Everitt, B. S. and Levy, R. (1992) Differentiation between organic and functional psychiatric illness in the elderly: An evaluation of four cognitive tests. *International Journal of Geriatric Psychiatry*, 7, 263–275.

Ott, B. R. and Fogel, B. S. (1992) Measurement of depression in dementia: Self versus clinician rating. *International Journal of Geriatric Psychiatry*, 7, 899–904.

Owens, W. (1966) Age and mental abilities: A second adult follow-up. *Journal of Educational Psychology*, 51, 311–325.

Patel, V. and Hope, R. A. (1992) A rating scale for aggressive behaviour in the elderly. *Psychological Medicine*, 22, 211–221.

Pattie, A. H. (1988) Measuring levels of disability – the Clifton Assessment Procedures for the Elderly. In: J. P. Wattis and I. Hindmarch (eds) *Psychological Assessment of the Elderly* (pp. 61–80). Edinburgh: Churchill Livingstone.

Pattie, A. H. and Gilleard, C. J. (1979) *Manual for the Clifton Assessment Procedures for the Elderly (CAPE)*. Sevenoaks, UK: Hodder & Stoughton Educational.

Pfeffer, R. I., Kurosaki, T. T., Harrah, C. H., Chance, J. M. and Filos, S. (1982) Measurement of functional activities in older adults in the community. *Journal of Gerontology*, 37, 323–329.

Powell, G. E., Bailey, S. and Clark, E. (1980) A very short version of the Minnesota Aphasia test. *British Journal of Social and Clinical Psychology*, 19, 189–194.

Rabbitt, P. (1982) How to assess the aged? An experimental psychologist's view:

Some comments on Dr Kendrick's paper. *British Journal of Clinical Psychology*, 21, 55–59.

Rabbitt, P. (1988) Social psychology, neurosciences and cognitive psychology need each other (and gerontology needs all three of them). *Psychologist*, 12, 500–506.

Randolph, C. (1998) *The Repeatable Battery for the Assessment of Neuropsychological Status*. Sidcup, UK: Psychological Corporation.

Raven, C. D. (1982) *Revised Manual for Raven's Progressive Matrices and Vocabulary Scale*. Windsor, UK: NFER-Nelson.

Reynolds, T., Thornicroft, G., Abas, M., Woods, B., Hoe, J., Leese, M. and Orrell, M. (2000) Camberwell Assessment of Need for the Elderly (CANE) – development, validity and reliability. *British Journal of Psychiatry*, 176, 444–452.

Roth, M., Huppert, F. A., Mountjoy, C. Q. and Tym, E. (1998) *CAMDEX-R: the Cambridge Examination for Mental Disorders of the Elderly – revised*. Cambridge: Cambridge University Press.

Rybash, J. M., Hoyer, W. J. and Roodin, P. A. (1986) *Adult Cognition and Aging: Developmental Changes in Processing, Knowing and Thinking*. New York: Pergamon.

Sahakian, B. J. (1990) Computerized assessment of neuropsychological function in Alzheimer's disease and Parkinson's disease. *International Journal of Geriatric Psychiatry*, 5, 211–213.

Sahakian, B. J. (1991) Depressive pseudodementia in the elderly. *International Journal of Geriatric Psychiatry*, 6, 453–458.

Salthouse, T. A. (2000) Steps toward the explanation of adult age differences in cognition. In: T. J. Perfect and E. A. Maylor (eds) *Models of Cognitive Aging* (pp. 19–49). Oxford: Oxford University Press.

Schaie, K. W. (1990) Intellectual development in adulthood. In: J. E. Birren and K. W. Schaie (eds) *Handbook of the Psychology of Aging*, 3rd edn (pp. 291–309). San Diego, CA: Academic Press.

Schaie, K. W. (1996) *Intellectual Development in Adulthood: The Seattle Longitudinal Study*. Canbridge: Cambridge University Press.

Segal, D. L., Coolidge, F. L. and Hersen, M. (1998) Psychological testing of older people. In: I. H. Nordhus, G. R. VandenBos, S. Berg and P. Fromholt (eds) *Clinical Geropsychology* (pp. 231–257). Washington, DC: American Psychological Association.

Selai, C. and Trimble, M. R. (1999) Assessing quality of life in dementia. *Aging and Mental Health*, 3(2), 101–111.

Shankar, K. K., Walker, M., Frost, D. and Orrell, M. W. (1999) The development of a valid and reliable scale for rating anxiety in dementia (RAID). *Aging and Mental Health*, 3(1), 39–49.

Sheikh, J. I. and Yesavage, J. A. (1986) Geriatric Depression Scale (GDS): Recent evidence and development of a shorter version. In: T. L. Brink (ed) *Clinical Gerontology: A Guide to Assessment and Intervention* (pp. 165–173). New York: Haworth Press.

Shulman, K. L., Shedletsky, R. and Silver, I. L. (1986) The challenge of time: Clock drawing and cognitive function in the elderly. *International Journal of Geriatric Psychiatry*, 1, 135–136.

Siegler, I. C. and Botwinick, J. (1979) A long term longitudinal study of the intellectual ability of older adults – the matter of selective subject attrition. *Journal of Gerontology*, 34, 242–248.

Simpson, P. M., Surmon, D. J., Wesnes, K. A. and Wilcock, G. K. (1991) The cognitive drug research computerized assessment system for demented patients: A validation study. *International Journal of Geriatric Psychiatry*, 6, 95–102.

Skilbeck, C. E. (1996) Psychological aspects of stroke. In: R. T. Woods (ed) *Handbook of the Clinical Psychology of Ageing* (pp. 283–301). Chichester: John Wiley.

Skurla, E., Rogers, J. C. and Sunderland, T. (1988) Direct assessment of activities of daily living in Alzheimer's disease: A controlled study. *Journal of American Geriatrics Society*, 36, 97–103.

Slade, M., Phelan, M., Thornicroft, G. and Parkman, S. (1996) The Camberwell Assessment of Need (CAN): Comparison of assessments by staff and patients of the needs of the severely mentally ill. *Social Psychiatry and Psychiatric Epidemiology*, 31, 109–113.

Sloane, P. D., Mitchell, C. M., Weisman, G., Zimmerman, S., Long, K. M. and Lynn, M. (2002) The Therapeutic Environment Screening Survey for Nursing Homes (TESS-NH): An observational instrument for assessing the physical environment of institutional settings for persons with dementia. *Journal of Gerontology: Social Sciences*, 57B, S69–S78.

Spreen, D. and Strauss, E. (1991) *A Compendium of Neuropsychological Tests*. New York: Oxford University Press.

Stephens, B. J. and Jorm, A. (1994) Validation of a short form of the Informant Questionnaire of Cognitive Decline in the Elderly (IQCODE). *International Journal of Geriatric Psychiatry*, 14, 235–238.

Storandt, M. and VandenBos, G. R. (eds) (1994) *Neuropsychological Assessment of Dementia and Depression in Older Adults: A Clinician's Guide*. Washington DC: American Psychological Association.

Stuart-Hamilton, I. (2000) *The Psychology of Ageing: An Introduction*, 3rd edn. London: Jessica Kingsley.

Sunderland, T., Alterman, I. S., Yount, D., Hill, J. L., Tariot, P. N., Newhouse, P. A. et al. (1988) A new scale for assessment of depressed mood in demented patients. *American Journal of Psychiatry*, 145, 955–959.

Sunderland, T., Hill, J. L., Mellow, A. M., Lawlor, B. A., Gundersheimer, J., Newhouse, P. A. and Grafman, J. H. (1989) Clock drawing in Alzheimer's disease: A novel measure of dementia severity. *Journal of American Geriatrics Society*, 37, 725–729.

Thorgrimsen, L., Selwood, A., Spector, A., Royan, L., de-Madariaga-Lopez, M., Woods, R. T. and Orrell, M. (2003) Whose quality of life is it anyway? The validity and reliability of the Quality of Life – Alzheimer's Disease (QoL-AD) Scale. *Alzheimer Disease and Associated Disorders*, 17(4), 201–208.

Twining, C. (1990) Assessment of personal adjustment. In: J. R. Beech and L. Harding (eds) *Assessment of the Elderly* (pp. 87–99). Windsor, UK: NFER-Nelson.

Walker, S. (1980) Application of a test for aphasia to normal old people. *Journal of Clinical and Experimental Gerontology*, 2, 185–198.

Warrington, E. (1984) *Recognition Memory Test Manual*. Windsor, UK: NFER-Nelson.

Warrington, E. (1996) *The Camden Memory Tests*. Hove, UK: Psychology Press.

Warrington, E. and James, M. (1991) *Visual Object and Space Perception Battery (VOSP)*. Bury St Edmunds, UK: Thames Valley Test Company.

Wechsler, D. (1997a) *Wechsler Adult Intelligence Scale – III*. New York: Psychological Corporation.

Wechsler, D. (1997b) *Wechsler Memory Scale – III*. New York: Psychological Corporation.

Wechsler, D. (1999) *The Wechsler Abbreviated Scale of Intelligence*. London: Harcourt Assessment.

Wechsler, D. (2001) *Wecshler Test of Adult Reading*. New York: Psychological Corporation.

White, N., Scott, A., Woods, R. T., Wenger, G. C., Keady, J. D. and Devakumar, M. (2002) The limited utility of the Mini-Mental State Examination in screening people over the age of 75 years for dementia in primary care. *British Journal of General Practice*, 52, 1002–1003.

Williams, B. W., Mack, W. and Henderson, V. W. (1989) Boston Naming Test in Alzheimer's disease. *Neuropsychologia*, 27, 1073–1079.

Williams, J. G., Huppert, F., Matthews, F. E., Nickson, J. and the MRC Cognitive Function and Ageing Study (2003) Performance and normative values of a concise neuropsychological test (CAMCOG) in an elderly population sample. *International Journal of Geriatric Psychiatry*, 18, 631–644.

Wilson, B. A., Cockburn, J. and Baddeley, A. D. (1985) *The Rivermead behavioural memory test*. Titchfield, UK: Thames Valley Test Company.

Wilson, B. A., Cockburn, J. and Halligan, P. (1987) *Behavioural Inattention Test (BIT)*. Bury St Edmunds, UK: Thames Valley Test Company.

Woods, R. T. (1999a) Mental health problems in late life. In: R. T. Woods (ed) *Psychological Problems of Ageing: Assessment, Treatment and Care* (pp. 73–110). Chichester: John Wiley.

Woods, R. T. (1999b) Psychological assessment of older people. In: R. T. Woods (ed) *Psychological Problems of Ageing: Assessment, Treatment and Care* (pp. 219–252). Chichester: John Wiley.

Yesavage, J. A., Brink, T. L. and Rose, T. L. (1983) Development and validation of a geriatric depression scale: A preliminary report. *Journal of Psychiatric Research*, 17, 37–49.

Zimmerman, S., Sloane, P. D., Williams, C. S., Reed, P. S., Preisser, J. S., Eckert, J. K. et al. (2005) Dementia care and quality of life in assisted living and nursing homes. *Gerontologist*, 45 (special issue 1), 133–146.

Chapter 26

Problems in later life

Treatment

Bob Woods

INTRODUCTION

The two most common mental health problems in later life are the dementias and depression (Woods, 1999b). Around 5% of people aged over 65 have a dementia condition; there is a sharp increase in prevalence in the over 80s, with perhaps 20% of a representative sample having this diagnosis when examined by a psychiatrist. Depression that would be rated as severe would be identified in 4% of over 65s. This would include those with psychotic features and those requiring in-patient hospital treatment; 13% would have a milder form of depression, primarily with lowered mood; around 3% would have a generalised anxiety disorder; 10% would have phobic disorders, mainly agoraphobia. Of the patients with a phobia, 40% would also be depressed (Lindesay et al., 1989). Readers are referred to Jacoby and Oppenheimer (2002) for a comprehensive account of psychiatric disorders in later life.

PSYCHOLOGICAL TREATMENT OF THE DEMENTIAS: INTRODUCTION

The natural history of the dementias has usually been considered to be of progressive deterioration in a range of cognitive abilities and self-care skills, often accompanied by changes in behaviour. The aim of treatment has not been to cure dementia but to improve the quality of life both of individuals with dementia and of their supporters. It is now widely acknowledged that these disorders have a great impact on the families involved, often associated with high levels of strain and depression (Zarit and Edwards, 1999). Interventions with the person with dementia may entail attempts to influence mood and particular aspects of behaviour, and to maintain function as much as possible, rather than to reverse the whole process. The evidence-base for psychological interventions in dementia has been reviewed by Woods and Roth (2005) and Woods (2002).

Historically, most approaches were developed in institutional settings, but recently more work has been undertaken with people in the earlier stages of dementia, living in the community, supported by relatives, friends, neighbours and formal support services. The developments in psychological approaches specifically geared to family care-givers will be discussed in a later section.

Person-centred care

If the quality of life of the person with dementia is to be maximised and an attempt made to meet psychological needs, then there are a number of implications for the care environment (Brooker, 2004):

First, the individual with dementia must be valued as a person, with full human value and status (King's Fund, 1986). Having a dementia may be a threat to personhood but it is the actions and attitudes of those around the person, which devalue, depersonalise and disempower, that result in its loss (Kitwood, 1997). Certainly the person may be disabled, perhaps severely, but he or she still has the right to be respected and not treated as an object, vegetable, doll or child. He or she has experienced adulthood and is attuned to the humiliation of public failure, being talked over and the other indignities so often seen in dementia care. The person's lack of insight or poor memory cannot be cited to imply that this does not matter. Apart from the humanitarian principle involved, it seems likely that people with dementia will function at their best in an environment that is structured so that individuals can experience some success and retain some independence, and not just know failure and indignity; where they can feel secure and not overstressed; where others care about them and they can care about others (Woods, 1999a). Kitwood, in a series of influential papers (Kitwood, 1990; Kitwood and Bredin, 1992) argues that what he describes as the 'malignant social psychology' around the person with dementia, which treats the person as less than a person, devaluing, invalidating and patronising, exacerbates and accelerates the neurological dysfunction. The essence of maintaining function then becomes person-centred care, which recognises and seeks out the personhood of the dementia sufferer.

Second, an implication of person-centred care is that care needs to be individualised. For example, activities, games, music and so on should be geared to individual tastes and preferences and there should be care plans that really are individually tailored to individual needs and choices (Holden and Woods, 1995).

Third, the care environment also needs to offer the person as much choice and control as possible, offered in such a way as to be within the person's range of abilities. The environment should elicit and encourage the person's remaining abilities, with the person being given sufficient time and support to feed or dress him- or herself, say, and not being fed or dressed for the sake of speed or to avoid disruption of a rigid routine. The environment should offer a rich choice of activities and materials that the person finds enjoyable and engaging.

Fourth, efforts must be made to ensure that the perspective of the person with dementia is sought and respected. It is a relatively recent development for people with dementia to have an active voice, usually through people in the early stages of the condition. However, structured interviews (e.g. Mozley et al., 1999) and observational methods (such as Dementia Care Mapping; Brooker, 2005) allow this perspective to emerge in moderate and severe dementia also.

Stimulation

Early attempts to 'treat' dementia psychologically aimed at stimulating patients in a variety of ways (see Holden and Woods, 1995). An analogy was drawn between the behaviour of the person with dementia and the cognitive and perceptual disturbances of young, healthy volunteers exposed to lengthy, extreme deprivation of sensory stimulation. The sensory deprivation of older people was attributed to a combination of loss of sensory acuity, the unstimulating environment of many institutions for older people and the person's own withdrawal from his or her environment. Sensory deprivation, it was argued, would be especially damaging to people with dementia as their impaired recent memory forces reliance on external stimulation to maintain appropriate environmental contact. Whether or not the analogy holds – and the evidence in favour is at best circumstantial – pioneering studies set the pattern for many subsequent efforts in attempting to change the physical environment and to introduce care regimes and group work encouraging more independence, socialisation and activity.

Types of stimulation currently used included music, hand massage, contact with pet animals and physical exercise (Woods, 1999c). For example, Goddaer and Abraham (1994) showed a 63.4% reduction in agitation during mealtimes in patients with moderate-severe dementia when relaxing music was played. Burns et al. (2002) have reviewed promising evidence from three trials for the impact of aromatherapy (using lemon balm or lavender oil) on agitation. Multi-sensory stimulation (often known as 'Snoezelen') comprising calming music, visual stimulation from fibre optics and lava lamps, tactile stimulation, aromatherapy, etc. has been shown in one study (Baker et al., 1997, 2001) to be associated with improvements in mood and behaviour and reduced behavioural disturbance; an activity group served as the control group. Physical exercise has been associated with cognitive changes, including increased alertness in a randomised controlled trial of 6 months of twice-weekly 'psychomotor activation' sessions (Hopman-Rock et al., 1999); little change on behavioural measures was reported.

Exposure to bright light also has some empirical support (see Burns et al., 2002); this would be expected to be most helpful with those patients who show clear 'sundowning', i.e. an increase in agitation and restlessness in the evening, which may be hypothesized to reflect a disturbed circadian rhythm. The exposure to bright light can be for 1–2 hours in the morning.

The individual nature of response to stimulation should be recognised: Brooker et al. (1997) evaluated hand massage and aromatherapy in four severely impaired patients. One patient showed a significant improvement in agitation in the hour following massage or aromatherapy, but two patients appeared to be more agitated following the interventions, possibly feeling confined by the intervention.

The care environment

There have been great changes in the quality of the care environment provided for people with dementia when they can no longer be supported in the community. In the UK, wards in converted workhouses and Victorian asylums have been largely replaced by provision in care homes. Individual bedrooms have replaced dormitories, and there is now much more scope for residents to have their own pictures and possessions around them. Day rooms are smaller and more 'homely' in style and furnishing. However, concerns regarding the overall quality of care remain (e.g. Ballard et al., 2001), particularly in relation to the lack of activity, engagement and interaction. Evaluative studies indicating the benefits of small living units (with a maximum of ten residents) and enhanced activity and interaction (Ritchie et al., 1992; Annerstedt et al., 1993; Dean et al., 1993; Skea and Lindesay, 1996) have had little influence on provision, with economies of scale making the development of smaller units more difficult.

Attempts to change the care environment have been reported: for example, Melin and Gotestam (1981) showed improved eating skills and social interaction in patients with dementia at meal-times by changing from a system with rigid time-limits, where slow patients were fed by staff, to one where unlimited time was given and the social character of the occasion was emphasised, allowing more choice and independence. In the same study, increases in social interaction and activity were noted when more choice and independence was allowed. Brane et al. (1989) described their regime as 'integrity promoting care'. It involved individualised care, choices being encouraged, a more home-like atmosphere, personalised clothes and possessions, and the prompting of activities whilst allowing patients to proceed at their own pace. After 3 months, a variety of improvements were noted in patients on this ward in comparison with a control group receiving traditional care. Mood, motor performance confusion, anxiety and distractibility were areas where benefits were reported.

Behavioural approaches

Three areas of behavioural intervention have been developed and evaluated, which differ in the target of intervention, focusing on mood, independent function and challenging behaviour respectively.

Mood

With increasing recognition of the prevalence of symptoms of anxiety and depression in people with dementia, have come attempts to apply psychological treatment techniques. Teri et al. (1997) taught family care-givers to use behavioural techniques with the person with dementia, including increasing participation in enjoyable activities and problem-solving techniques, and showed reduced depressed mood in both the people with dementia and their care-givers. There are also several reports of the feasibility of individual or group cognitive behaviour therapy with people in the early stages of dementia who are depressed (Scholey and Woods, 2003; Kipling et al., 1999). Finally, there have been several demonstrations that people with dementia can learn to use progressive muscle relaxation techniques, leading to reduction in anxiety symptoms (Suhr et al., 1999).

Enhancing independence

Dressing skills were targeted by Beck et al. (1997). In a large study of 90 nursing home residents with severe cognitive impairment, nursing assistants were trained to use simple behavioural and problem-solving techniques to increase the resident's degree of independence, with good results. Other studies have resulted in improved mobility (Burgio et al., 1986), increased skills in orientation (see the section Cognition-based approaches, below), greater social interaction and participation (Carstensen and Erickson, 1986) and greater participation in activities (Burton, 1980). Eliciting the desired behaviour through cueing or prompting, or providing a powerful discriminative stimulus for the behaviour, has often proved to be the key element of the programme, rather than the reinforcement schedule *per se*. For instance, progress in the Burgio et al. study, aimed at increasing mobility, was so rapid that the authors concluded that the opportunity to walk must have been an important component. Presumably, environmental contingencies in this nursing home setting had discouraged walking, with staff perhaps finding it more convenient to have residents in wheelchairs. This is a good example of the existence of 'excess disabilities', where the person functions at a worse level than that determined by his or her dementia, in response to the behaviour and attitudes of their care-givers, exemplifying Kitwood's concept of a 'malignant social psychology'.

There has been relatively little success in increasing continence. The 'prompted voiding procedure', described by Schnelle et al. (1989) and Burgio et al. (1988) has the aim of reducing incontinence but does not aim to encourage self-initiated toileting. Nursing home residents are simply asked on a regular schedule, say hourly, whether they wish to use the toilet, and continence is systematically reinforced. Results have been so dramatic that the intervention should be considered as a change in environmental contingency rather than a re-learning procedure. However, self-initiated toileting became less frequent in the latter study and, unfortunately, when the research team leave, staff seem to prefer to change residents when they become incontinent, rather than continue with this preventive approach (Schnelle et al., 1993), suggesting that contingencies for staff also need to be carefully considered (Burgio and Burgio, 1990). Continence requires a number of different skills – finding the toilet, recognising it, adjusting clothing and so on – and is affected in older people by a number of physical factors. Multi-modal approaches, tackling physical, psychological and environmental aspects, analysing the factors leading to incontinence in each case, and adapting toileting regimes to individual patterns of micturition, offer most help in this area.

Challenging behaviour

Woods and Bird (1999) argue that standard 'therapies' are not a promising response to challenging behaviour. Individualised approaches will always be required, in view of the complexity of the types and functions of behavioural problems encountered. Evidence for this view is provided by a number of single cases, using rigorous designs, tackling a variety of difficulties, including aggression, inappropriate urination, sexual disinhibition and wandering reported by Moniz-Cook et al. (2001, 2003), Bird et al. (1995) and Bird (2000).

Challenging behaviour is seen from a psychological perspective as an expression of unmet or poorly communicated need (Stokes, 1996). For example, aggression occurs most often during personal care, when the person is at greatest risk of feeling vulnerable or threatened; shouting and screaming may indicate physical pain or discomfort; wandering may reflect a search for something or someone familiar, in a place that seems frightening and unknown. Too often the behaviour is seen as a characteristic of the person with dementia, rather than the result of an interaction with the care environment. Thorough, individual assessment is required, including consideration of relevant medical, sensory and environmental factors, the person's life story, social relationships and coping styles. It is important to consider who the behaviour is a problem for: often, the person with dementia is not concerned but others are; sometimes it is the care-givers and their reaction and response that needs to be the target of the intervention. 'Aggression' or 'wandering' may include a variety of behaviours, which may arise for a wide range of reasons. Being specific and precise in describing the behaviour, its antecedents and consequences will be important in understanding why it is occurring and what factors are contributing to it.

Cognition-based approaches

There is a strong evidence-base in relation to cognitive stimulation approaches, including Reality Orientation (RO; Spector et al., 2000). For example, Spector et al. (2003) report a large trial of structured, small, cognitive stimulation group meetings with people with mild to moderate dementia living in care homes or attending day centres. A range of activities were used, encouraging cognitive activity in a social context (Spector et al., 2001). A total of 201 older people with dementia, drawn from 23 care homes and day centres, were randomised to standard care or to receive 14 bi-weekly sessions of the active intervention. There were significant improvements in cognitive function and in quality of life for those participating. The size of the effect on cognition proved comparable to those reported in published studies on the most frequently used medications for people with Alzheimer's disease (the acetylcholinesterase inhibitors). As well as small-group work, RO also aimed to have an impact on the care environment, with clear sign-posting and extensive use of memory aids. This aspect of RO has been the subject of fewer evaluations; improvements in spatial orientation (Reeve and Ivison, 1985) and significant cognitive and behavioural improvements (Williams et al., 1987) have been reported. There have been several studies, typically using single-case designs, demonstrating the efficacy of specific training sessions in helping disoriented patients find their way around the ward or home, often using signposting (Lam and Woods, 1986; McGilton et al., 2003).

Using training procedures to achieve specific, individualised cognitive or behavioural goals reflects a change of emphasis from cognitive stimulation towards cognitive rehabilitation (Clare and Woods, 2004). Learning techniques such as spaced retrieval or expanded rehearsal (Camp et al., 1996) have proved useful. This involves the learning of one item at a time, with the retrieval period being increased gradually each time the person correctly retrieves the item (Camp and Schaller, 1989; McKitrick et al., 1992). The active process of retrieval is thought to be important in consolidating the memory for the item. If the person is unable to retrieve the item, he or she is prompted and the retrieval interval is then reduced, before being built up once again. Camp et al. (1996) report the successful use of the spaced retrieval procedure to teach the person with dementia to make use of a memory aid (a calendar). Recently, attention has been drawn to the benefits of ensuring, as far as possible, that the learning proceeds without the person making errors; such errors often serve to interfere with effective learning, in that the person is likely to remember the error in competition with the correct response. Clare et al. (1999) describe the errorless learning procedure, where prompts are used to guide the person into giving the correct response, and guessing is discouraged. Procedural learning, where encoding proceeds through a motor act, or practice of a sequence of movements, has also been shown to be relatively intact (Bird and Kinsella, 1996), and has been applied to enhancing the performance of everyday skills in several studies (Zanetti et al., 1997).

Reminiscence therapy has been widely used with individuals and in small groups, and has proved a popular approach, although there has often been a lack of clarity regarding its aims (Woods and McKiernan, 1995). Photographs, music and archive recordings and items from the past are used to stimulate a variety of personal memories. Woods et al. (2005) carried out a Cochrane review and, although there were some positive indications of changes in cognition and mood, concluded that much more research was needed. Several studies have examined the immediate impact of involvement in a reminiscence group, with participants acting as their own controls. Head et al. (1990) found an increase in interaction in one group, compared with an alternative activity, but a group in another day centre failed to show a differential benefit from involvement in reminiscence activities. Brooker and Duce (2000) showed higher levels of well-being during reminiscence groups, compared with other activities and unstructured time, in people with dementia attending three day hospitals. Head et al. (1990) point out that the relative efficacy of reminiscence work will depend on the alternative activities on offer. Further studies are needed regarding the outcomes of different types of reminiscence work, in relation to aspects such as well-being and autobiographical memory, where it might be expected to have most impact.

Psychotherapeutic approaches

Validation therapy focuses on the emotional communication of the person with dementia, responding to feelings rather than facts (Feil, 1993). It was developed, at least in part, as a reaction to the insensitive application of cognition-based approaches, where too often the emphasis was on 'correcting' the person, rather than aiming to discern his or her meaning (Dietch et al., 1989). A validation group work approach has been developed, although the available evidence for its effects is mixed (Toseland et al., 1997). As a communication approach it has much to commend it, enabling those providing care to listen respectfully and sensitively to the feelings expressed. Responding to feelings rather than facts avoids unnecessary and distressing confrontations. Feil draws attention to unresolved conflicts and trauma emerging in the midst of the dementia in ways which are difficult to interpret. Knowledge of the person's life-story may help understanding; it helps to know that a patient who becomes angry and aggressive when he encounters a locked door was once a prisoner-of-war. The importance of providing a safe, containing environment where strong emotions can be expressed and validated cannot be over-emphasised. Feil suggests that universal needs and longings emerge in dementia: the need for safety, to feel loved, to have purposeful activity, to have others to love and care for. Miesen (1992, 1993) describes 'parent fixation', where the person is frequently searching for a parent, talking about them as if alive, in terms of the person's need for a safe, secure attachment figure, in the midst of the puzzling, perplexing world of dementia.

Earlier recognition and diagnosis is contributing to a sub-group of patients with dementia presenting who are clearly aware that something is wrong, that they are not able to function as they did previously, and who may have awareness of others (often their relatives) who have had dementia. Sharing the diagnosis with such individuals provides a therapeutic opportunity to assist with adjustment, discuss misconceptions and plan for the future (Husband, 1999). Cheston et al. (2003) describe a group psychotherapeutic approach, where participants discussed their memory difficulties and their concerns together, with some impact evident on mood.

Staff attitudes

Generally, evaluations of therapeutic approaches in dementia have concentrated on changes in the person with dementia, even though changing staff attitudes and behaviour may be equally important. For example, reminiscence may have a particular value in that it puts people with dementia in a position where they have something to give, by describing events and experiences to others, who have not shared these experiences. This enables staff to see the individual in the context of their whole life – work, relationships, interests and so on – which could help greatly in the individualisation of care. Indeed, in an evaluation of reminiscence in a care home (Baines et al., 1987), staff knowledge regarding residents' life stories increased for residents participating in reminiscence (and RO) groups. Other approaches may also lead to attitudinal change; Ingstad and Gotestam (1987) report positive changes in staff attitudes on a ward for patients with severe dementia following the changes to the environment described by Melin and Gotestam (1981). Lintern et al. (2002) report changes in person-centred and hopeful attitudes to people with dementia following training, which was associated with changes in the quality of staff behaviour with residents.

In any setting, it is important to make a careful analysis of staff attitudes and expectations and of the organisational framework, and to avoid rushing in with an 'off-the-shelf' treatment package. Usually, careful, persistent, patient work is needed with key staff, at all levels, if the intervention is to have any chance of being satisfactorily implemented. An individualised care-planning approach provides opportunities to focus on the individualisation of care, based on individual needs, assets and deficits, and for setting treatment goals in personalised care plans, identifying where the person is currently under-functioning. Barrowclough and Fleming (1986) show that staff in residential homes can be trained to effectively use this approach, which fits well with the integrative framework described by Holden and Woods (1995).

Care staff have a difficult task in coping with a disorder that has a natural history of progressive deterioration and which is physically and mentally demanding. Even reducing the rate of deterioration does not bring the reward of seeing the person improve. Staff need help to identify the more subtle, but potentially important, changes in quality of life that may be possible; mutual support and encouragement is vital in this stressful and taxing work. These aspects need consideration by psychologists as much as – if not more than – the details of the treatment packages to be implemented.

Interventions with family care-givers

The key role of family care-givers in supporting people with dementia at home is now well-recognised (see Zarit and Edwards, 1999). The emphasis in research has often been on carer burden, and it is important to respond to the increased risk of strain and depression in family carers. They find themselves having to cope with what appears to be the loss of the person as he or she was, as well as coping day by day with an unpredictably changing pattern of decline in the person's cognitive and self-care abilities, often accompanied by behavioural disturbances that are difficult to manage in a domestic setting. However, there is now also recognition of the remarkable degree to which carers do cope and manage the situation, and in many cases find positive aspects of the experience (Rapp and Chao, 2000).

At least three strategies for psychological interventions involving family care-givers have been described. The first is to teach the care-giver to use behavioural techniques to modify the behaviour of the person with dementia. The link between difficult behaviour and care-giver strain has often been made (Donaldson et al., 1997), and so reducing such behaviour could well reduce strain, perhaps also helping the care-giver feel a greater sense of control and less powerlessness. This was the basis of the Teri et al. (1997) study (discussed above) in which carers were successfully taught to reduce depression in the person with dementia, with an associated reduction in their own feelings of depression. Similarly, Hinchliffe et al. (1992, 1995) showed that carers who were taught to successfully use behavioural and other management techniques to reduce specific difficult behaviours reported significant reductions in strain.

The second strategy focuses specifically on the care-giver's feelings of stress or depression, using appropriate psychological approaches. For example, Gallagher-Thompson and Steffen (1994), compared cognitive-behavioural (CBT) and brief psychodynamic treatments in 66 clinically depressed family care-givers of frail older people (some but not all of whom had dementia). At post-treatment the two therapies were equally effective overall; 71% of patients no longer met clinical criteria for depression. However, there was an interaction between outcome and duration of care-giving. Those who had been caring for their relative for more than 3.5 years responded better to CBT, whereas those earlier in the care-giving career responded better to the brief psychodynamic approach, perhaps responding to the person's adjustment needs at that stage. Marriott et al. (2000) report a successful intervention approach described as a 'cognitive-behavioural family intervention', which appeared to include an educational component as well as problem-solving skills and relaxation, leading to reductions in psychological distress, in a group of carers selected in view of their high initial distress levels.

The third strategy is broadly educational and, in addition to elements of the first two approaches, also addresses cognitive aspects – the care-giver's perceptions of and attributions about the situation – and ways of maximising support from formal services and from family and friends. Brodaty et al. (2003) provide a helpful review of this literature and the mixed results that have been reported from studies of psychosocial interventions. In several studies, time to nursing home placement has been significantly extended following such an intervention. For example, Brodaty and Gresham (1989) brought both patient and carer into a special hospital unit, with carers receiving training in coping strategies while patients attended memory re-training sessions. Carers reported less strain at 12-month follow-up than a control group of carers, whose relative had been admitted for an equivalent period without them, so that they had received respite rather than training. The control patients tended to enter institutional care at an earlier stage than the relatives of carers who had received training, and this effect was still apparent at an 8-year follow-up (Brodaty et al., 1997). Debate continues regarding the advantages of individual counselling in relation to group approaches, with carers' support groups provided universally. Mittelman et al. (1995, 1996) report the use of family counselling sessions, backed up by encouragement to attend peer-support carer groups, with spouse care-givers of people with dementia. Carer depression improved significantly following this intervention and time to nursing home placement was increased.

TREATMENT OF AFFECTIVE DISORDERS

Introduction

Psychological treatment for depression seems to be offered less often to older people than to younger adults (Woods and Roth, 2005). Although effective pharmacological treatments are widely available, there are difficulties in their long-term use with some older people with particular physical health problems. Relapse rates are relatively high (Denihan et al., 2000) and a significant number of patients recover only partially, being left with disabling symptoms; some do not improve at all. Rates of suicide are high among older men

(Lindesay, 1991), reinforcing the serious nature of depression in later life. There is then certainly scope for psychological approaches to supplement physical treatments.

Generally, there are probably more similarities than differences between the treatment of younger and older patients. A number of special points are nonetheless worth considering.

Physical health

Depression is closely linked to ill-health in older people (Dent et al., 1999). Somatic symptoms are common in depressed older people and depression may present as a physical illness. Conversely, physical illnesses may present as, or precipitate, depression. Medication for various physical complaints may influence mood or interfere with treatment. A person's health may affect the range of achievable targets, or the energy he or she can devote to treatment. It is advisable to work closely with a medical colleague, so that treatment can be guided by the best available assessment of the patient's physical problems. Sensory impairments are also relevant. Loss of visual acuity may hamper the use of written materials in cognitive therapy, unless suitably modified. Hearing losses of even a mild degree may disrupt group work and can render the giving of relaxation instructions a taxing task! Portable voice amplifiers with headphones for the patient and microphone for the therapist have proved helpful for some patients with hearing loss. Although some health conditions, such as stroke and Parkinson's disease, are often associated with depression, Dent et al. (1999) suggest that the resulting disability is the key influence, rather than the particular condition. Health psychology interventions, e.g. self-management skills for people with chronic arthritis (Barlow et al., 1997) or increasing self-efficacy for fear of falling (Tennstedt et al., 1998), have a role to play in addressing directly the person's physical health problems, which may be leading to discomfort and functional limitations but which do not respond well to physical interventions.

Cognitive decline

Some writers (such as Church, 1986) have drawn attention to cognitive changes in older people, particularly in abstract ability, and have suggested these may make it more difficult to apply therapies involving abstract ideas. Cognitive therapy might then need to be more practically and behaviourally based. It is not clear to what extent actual age changes are occurring; generational differences are also likely to be operating. There are great individual differences between patients, and therapy needs to be carefully tailored to each person's intellectual capabilities. Many older patients find recording automatic thoughts quite difficult, for example; some, however, will be able to do this. The feasibility of CBT with people with early-stage dementia

(Scholey and Woods, 2003), suggests that mild cognitive changes are not an absolute limiting factor. There may need to be adaptations, such as additional summarising, ensuring the person has written details of homework tasks, etc., but these should fall within the usual individualisation of the approach.

Loss

Most older people have experienced a number of losses – work, health, sensory systems, family home, as well as loved ones. In assessing the depressed person, it is important to consider the impact of the various losses the person has experienced and the ways in which the person has attempted to cope with them. Parkes (1992), in a helpful review, suggests that anguish may be less extreme when an older person loses a spouse and that somatic symptoms are more pronounced. There may be a greater tendency towards withdrawal and, for them, in contrast to younger people, anticipatory grief may do more harm than good: having an opportunity to prepare for the person's death may be outweighed by the strain of caring for a terminally ill person, with its consequent social isolation.

Each grief reaction is different: much depends on the nature of the relationship with the person who dies. The components of grief identified with younger people can also help describe grief in older people, but no definite sequence should be assumed. Shock and disbelief are often the initial reactions: protest and yearning, searching for the dead person, disorganisation and despair, including features of anger and guilt, may occur later. Detachment and reorganisation are usually seen as the end point of the grief process.

One implication of these multiple losses is that the person may be undergoing real-life hardships. Therapy needs to help the person distinguish depressive hopelessness and helplessness from a realistic appraisal of his or her limitations. Cognitive distortions are harder to identify when the person does have a number of physical or social limitations with which to contend.

Chronicity of problems

The presenting problems may in some cases have been present for many years. As a result, the individual may have accepted the problems as part of his or her identity, e.g. 'I'm a depressive', or they may have a long history of previous interventions, perhaps with poor outcome. Taking a history of interventions, and the individual's view of these, becomes an important part of the assessment, as does identifying previously used ways of coping (successful or unsuccessful).

Expectations

Dysfunctional attitudes are not confined to patients! Therapists need to examine their own attitudes and beliefs about ageing and older people, to become aware of their own negative stereotypes (Knight, 1996). Frequent contact with healthy, coping older people is a valuable means of combating such attitudes. Therapists should be aware of local community resources and facilities, so that patients can be helped to make informed choices as they develop their problem-solving skills. Sometimes, a little practical help can be immensely helpful in relieving anxiety, but it is important to recognise that not all emotional problems have practical solutions; a patient may be just as unhappy in a new house as in the old one if the basic problem is one of making friendships, for example.

APPLICATIONS OF PSYCHOLOGICAL THERAPY WITH OLDER PEOPLE

Anxiety disorders

King and Barrowclough (1991) provide a useful clinical report describing the use of cognitive-behavioural interventions with ten out-patients (mean age 73) with anxiety disorders. In essence, the treatment involved assisting the person to re-interpret his or her anxiety symptoms. Rather than perceiving them as life-threatening or catastrophic they were encouraged to view them as non-threatening benign physical sensations. Techniques such as hyper-ventilation provocation tests and controlled breathing training were used to facilitate this process where appropriate. Nine of the ten patients showed a decrease in symptoms after treatment (an average of eight sessions) and this improvement was generally maintained at follow-up after 3–6 months.

A meta-analytic review by Nordhus and Pallesen (2003) identified six trials focusing on generalised anxiety disorder (GAD) and two on panic disorder, with promising results. In relation to GAD in older adults, Stanley et al. (2003) compared 15 weeks of group-based CBT with a minimal-contact (MC) condition (a weekly monitoring telephone call, offering a low level of support). There were 85 participants, all aged 60 and above (mean age 66.2), meeting DSM-IV criteria for GAD, but in this study not receiving any concurrent anxiolytic or antidepressant medication. During the treatment period, 45% of the CBT patients showed a clear response to treatment, compared with 8% of the MC group. At 1-year follow-up, only 19% of the CBT participants still met diagnostic criteria for GAD. Significant gains made by the CBT group during the treatment phase, in worry, anxiety, depression and quality of life, were maintained or enhanced over the follow-up period.

Barrowclough et al.'s (2001) study included patients with a range of anxiety disorders, and probably reflects better the spectrum of problems encountered in clinical practice, with all the participants having taken anti-depressant or anxiolytic medication (or both) for at least 3 months. This trial compared individual CBT with supportive counselling (SC), using a 6-week baseline phase, before the commencement of therapy, to give an indication of the impact of no treatment. There were 55 participants (mean age 72), meeting DSM-IV criteria for anxiety disorders; 51% had panic disorders and 19% had GAD. Therapy was usually conducted in the patient's home, as is common practice in the UK, with patients receiving 8–12 sessions over a 16-week period. The CBT approach used involved detailed assessment of the anxiety problems and a shared formulation; verbal and behavioural re-attribution techniques were used to challenge dysfunctional cognitions and maladaptive behaviours. No changes were evident over the baseline period. At the end of the treatment period, there were significant changes in favour of the CBT group on self-rated measures of anxiety and depression, although the SC group also improved. At 12-month follow-up, 71% of CBT patients met criteria for having responded to treatment, compared with 39% of the SC group. There was also a good treatment response for co-morbid depression, although the groups did not show a significant difference on this outcome.

Stanley et al. (2003) comment that, compared with published reports involving younger people, CBT appears to be less effective in studies of older adults with anxiety disorders. However, this study involved a group format, whereas studies on younger people typically involve individual treatment. Barrowclough et al.'s (2001) findings tend to support this position, although a comparative study would be required to confirm it. In addition, chronicity of anxiety symptoms is common in these studies (average of 20 years in Barrowclough et al.'s sample), which may reduce treatment effectiveness. Concurrent physical health problems are also relevant in influencing outcome; only 19% of Barrowclough's sample had no physical health problem.

Depression: treatment and maintenance

There is a significant literature on the use of cognitive therapy with depressed older people (see Laidlaw et al., 2003; Woods and Roth, 2005). The most systematic outcome data have been provided by Gallagher-Thompson and Thompson and their colleagues, with their clinical approach well described by Dick et al. (1999) and Laidlaw et al. (2003).

Thompson et al. (1987) report a comparative study where depressed out-patients were assigned to either cognitive or behavioural or insight-oriented psychotherapy for 16–20 individual sessions over 4 months. The behavioural therapy involved encouraging patients to increase their participation in activities they found pleasant, following Lewinsohn's (1975) model of depression. All three therapies seemed equally effective in reducing depression by the end of treatment, in comparison with a waiting-list control group. Although in an earlier study (Gallagher and Thompson, 1982), patients treated with insight-oriented therapy tended to be more depressed and to relapse more often during the 1-year follow-up period, in the later study no differences emerged between treatment approaches at 1- or 2-year follow-ups (Gallagher-Thompson et al., 1990). These and other studies provide evidence that cognitive therapy, suitably fitted to the individual's abilities and needs, is a viable and potentially effective treatment for depressed older people. However, there is as yet no indication that it is superior to other treatment modalities, and further work is clearly required to identify the most effective components of each.

Relapse prevention is a major concern, in view of the high rate of reoccurrence of depression in later life. An important study from the USA has established a potential role for psychological therapy in this regard (Reynolds et al., 1999). Initially, patients with recurrent depression were treated with a combination of antidepressant medication (nortriptyline) and weekly sessions of interpersonal psychotherapy (IPT). If and when patients' depression had lifted, they were randomised to one of four maintenance therapy conditions, receiving either nortriptyline or placebo, in combination with IPT or alone, over a period of up to 3 years. Only 20% of those receiving the combination of nortriptyline and monthly IPT sessions relapsed within 3 years, compared with 90% of those receiving the placebo alone. Slightly less relapsed with the medication alone than with IPT plus placebo (43% versus 64%). Lenze et al. (2002) indicated that the combined therapy is more likely to be associated with maintained social adjustment than either therapy alone. The greatest effect was in relation to interpersonal conflict/friction, which along with role transitions and abnormal grief is one of the three areas most commonly addressed in IPT in older depressed people.

Grief therapy

Few applications have been reported (see Fasey, 1990; Parkes, 1992; McKiernan, 1996). Parkes (1980) concludes that supportive counselling can reduce the risk of breakdown in a high-risk bereaved older person to that in a low-risk case. Risk factors include an unsupportive family (or no family), an ambivalent relationship with the deceased, a particularly traumatic loss and another concurrent major life crisis. Although it is difficult to establish exactly when a grief reaction becomes 'abnormal', behavioural analyses have identified at least two patterns (Gauthier and Marshall, 1977). The first is where the normal grief reaction is avoided. There may be a 'conspiracy of silence', with family and friends 'protecting' the bereaved person by not mentioning the loss, and perhaps advising them not to attend the funeral. The distressing emotional response is avoided, at the cost of never adjusting to the loss. The second pattern is where the grief reaction is extended, where family and friends continue to give attention to the person's grief, giving him or her special treatment because of it, at a point when the person could take up old activities again or follow new directions. In this case, therapy aims to help family and friends encourage this more appropriate behaviour, and to help the patient gradually start living once more. Where grief is avoided, guided mourning may be helpful (Hodgkinson, 1982). Here, the person is helped to go through the emotional reaction in a safe environment, using mementoes or images of the dead person to elicit the grief. Kavanagh (1990) has described a cognitive-behavioural approach to grief therapy. This incorporates the previously mentioned strategies of controlled exposure to bereavement cues and gradual increasing of activities and roles, with an additional emphasis on appraisal of excessively negative cognitions and increasing the availability of social support. It should be emphasised that not every older person who is bereaved requires treatment, and it is becoming clear that there are more individual differences in bereavement reactions than was acknowledged in the past (Wortman and Silver, 1989; Stroebe and Stroebe, 1991). A flexible, individualised approach is necessary, avoiding a dogmatic adherence to a particular notion of how and at what pace adjustment to bereavement should progress. A stage model may have utility as a guide to the range of grief phenomena, but should not be seen as a prescription.

Involving the family in treatment

Even where no relationship problems are immediately apparent, it is always worth, with the patient's permission, seeing family members or significant others. They may be able to assist in the treatment plan, or place the person's problems in a broader context. It may well be that the problem does have a relationship component, which would not emerge if only the patient were seen. Treating such problems involves sessions with the patient and family together, encouraging open communication of feelings, experiences and needs, joint problem solving and mutual re-inforcement. Where the relationship problem is long standing, goals may have to be limited. For example, it may be possible to encourage a couple to spend more time apart, even if no improvement in the quality of interaction is attainable. Some marital problems seem to arise from couples having to spend more time together following, say, the husband's retirement: this may upset a precarious equilibrium that had enabled the couple to tolerate each other previously.

With so many difficulties occurring in a family context, family therapy is increasingly being applied where the older person is the identified patient, based on systems theory approaches (Benbow et al., 1993; Roper-Hall, 1993; Gilleard, 1996). Even where it is not possible to convene family meetings, systemic thinking can help greatly in making sense of complex cases and presentations.

Sleep disorders

Reports of problems in sleeping increase markedly with age (Morgan, 1996), as does the rate of prescription of sleeping medications. Early morning waking may be an indicator of depression and should always be considered as a potential cause. However, in other cases, misattribution of normal ageing changes in sleep patterns (with more daytime naps and more broken sleep) as problematic may be a factor. Of particular concern is the continued high rate (over 10%) of benzodiazepine usage, in view of the widely recognised risk of dependence and the side effects, particularly on older people, such as increased risk of falls and impairment in memory function (Higgitt, 1992). Curran et al. (2003) report a study where older people receiving benzodiazepine prescriptions for sleep problems in primary care were offered the opportunity to withdraw; 60% had been on the medication for over 10 years, and 27% for over 20 years. In all, 57% accepted the offer and, with sleep hygiene advice and tapered withdrawal, 80% successfully withdrew completely. No negative impact on sleep quantity or quality was identified and there was some improvement in cognitive function. Martin et al. (2000) review psychological therapy for insomnia in older people. Successful therapeutic strategies include relaxation and stimulus control (where the aim is to strengthen the association between sleep and bed). Lichstein et al. (2001) describe sleep compression, where the person is encouraged to reduce his or her time in bed gradually until it reaches the level of actual sleep time recorded in a baseline sleep diary. This approach appears to work best with those not reporting daytime fatigue, who respond better to a relaxation approach, aimed at extending sleep duration.

CONCLUSIONS

There is tremendous scope for psychological therapy in the treatment of affective disorders in older people. Many questions remain but, in general, approaches used with younger clients are often applicable. The most important special consideration may prove to be that older people show great individual differences.

Treatment plans must then be carefully individually tailored; standard treatment 'packages' are of little general use given the diversity of people and problems encountered. This diversity leads to an attractive feature of work with older people. The psychologist working with older people can take on a great variety of roles: neuropsychological assessment, support of relatives, advising and training care staff in the management of patients with dementia and their problems, cognitive therapy, family therapy, grief therapy . . . The possibilities for improving the quality of life of older people and their supporters are challenging, and waiting to be grasped!

REFERENCES

Annerstedt, L., Gustafson, L. and Nilsson, K. (1993) Medical outcome of psychosocial intervention in demented patients: one-year clinical follow-up after relocation into group living units. *International Journal of Geriatric Psychiatry*, 8, 833–841.

Baines, S., Saxby, P. and Ehlert, K. (1987) Reality orientation and reminiscence therapy: A controlled cross-over study of elderly confused people. *British Journal of Psychiatry*, 151, 222–231.

Baker, R., Dowling, Z., Wareing, L. A., Dawson, J. and Assey, J. (1997) Snoezelen: Its long-term and short-term effects on older people with dementia. *British Journal of Occupational Therapy*, 60(5), 213–218.

Baker, R., Bell, S., Baker, E., Gibson, S., Holloway, J., Pearce, R. et al. (2001) A randomized controlled trial of the effects of multi-sensory stimulation (MSS) for people with dementia. *British Journal of Clinical Psychology*, 40, 81–96.

Ballard, C., Fossey, J., Chithramohan, R., Howard, R., Burns, A., Thompson, P. et al. (2001) Quality of care in private sector and NHS facilities for people with dementia: Cross-sectional survey. *British Medical Journal*, 323, 426–427.

Barlow, J. H., Williams, B. and Wright, C. C. (1997) Improving arthritis self-management among older adults: 'Just what the doctor didn't order'. *British Journal of Health Psychology*, 2(2), 175–186.

Barrowclough, C. and Fleming, I. (1986) Training direct care staff in goal-planning with elderly people. *Behavioural Psychotherapy*, 14, 192–209.

Barrowclough, C., King, P., Colville, J., Russell, E., Burns, A. and Tarrier, N. (2001) A randomized trial of the effectiveness of cognitive-behavioral therapy and supportive counseling for anxiety symptoms in older adults. *Journal of Consulting & Clinical Psychology*, 69, 756–762.

Beck, C. K., Heacock, P., Mercer, S. O., Walls, R., Rapp, C. G. and Vogelpohl, T. S. (1997) Improving dressing behavior in cognitively impaired nursing home residents. *Nursing Research*, 46(3), 126–132.

Benbow, S. M., Marriott, A., Morley, M. and Walsh, S. (1993) Family therapy and dementia: Review and clinical experience. *International Journal of Geriatric Psychiatry*, 8, 717–725.

Bird, M. (2000) Psychosocial rehabilitation for problems arising from cognitive deficits in dementia. In: R. D. Hill, L. Backman and A. S. Neely (eds) *Cognitive Rehabilitation in Old Age* (pp. 249–269). New York: Oxford University Press.

Bird, M. and Kinsella, G. (1996) Long-term cued recall of tasks in senile dementia. *Psychology and Aging*, 11, 45–56.

Bird, M., Alexopoulos, P. and Adamowicz, J. (1995) Success and failure in five case studies: Use of cued recall to ameliorate behaviour problems in senile dementia. *International Journal of Geriatric Psychiatry*, 10, 305–311.

Brane, G., Karlsson, I., Kihlgren, M. and Norberg, A. (1989) Integrity-promoting care of demented nursing home patients: Psychological and biochemical changes. *International Journal of Geriatric Psychiatry*, 4, 165–172.

Brodaty, H. and Gresham, M. (1989) Effect of a training programme to reduce stress in carers of patients with dementia. *British Medical Journal*, 299, 1375–1379.

Brodaty, H., Gresham, M. and Luscombe, G. (1997) The Prince Henry Hospital dementia caregivers' training programme. *International Journal of Geriatric Psychiatry*, 12, 183–192.

Brodaty, H., Green, A. and Koschera, A. (2003) Meta-analysis of psychosocial interventions for caregivers of people with dementia. *Journal of American Geriatrics Society*, 51, 657–664.

Brooker, D. (2004) What is person-centred care in dementia? *Reviews in Clinical Gerontology*, 13, 215–222.

Brooker, D. (2005) Dementia Care Mapping: A review of the research literature. *Gerontologist*, 45 (special issue 1), 11–18.

Brooker, D. and Duce, L. (2000) Wellbeing and activity in dementia: A comparison of group reminiscence therapy, structured goal-directed group activity and unstructured time. *Aging and Mental Health*, 4(4), 354–358.

Brooker, D. J. R., Snape, M., Johnson, E., Ward, D. and Payne, M. (1997) Single case evaluation of the effects of aromatherapy and massage on disturbed behaviour in severe dementia. *British Journal of Clinical Psychology*, 36(2), 287–296.

Burgio, L. D. and Burgio, K. L. (1990) Institutional staff training and management: A review of the literature and a model for geriatric, long-term care facilities. *International Journal of Aging and Human Development*, 30(4), 287–302.

Burgio, L. D., Burgio, K. L., Engel, B. T. and Tice, L. M. (1986) Increasing distance and independence of ambulation in elderly nursing home residents. *Journal of Applied Behavior Analysis*, 19, 357–366.

Burgio, L., Engel, B. T., McCormick, K., Hawkins, A. and Scheve, A. (1988) Behavioral treatment for urinary incontinence in elderly inpatients: Initial attempts to modify prompting and toileting procedures. *Behavior Therapy*, 19, 345–357.

Burns, A., Byrne, J., Ballard, C. and Holmes, C. (2002) Sensory stimulation in dementia. *British Medical Journal*, 325, 1312–1313.

Burton, M. (1980) Evaluation and change in a psychogeriatric ward through direct observation and feedback. *British Journal of Psychiatry*, 137, 566–571.

Camp, C. J. and Schaller, J. R. (1989) Epilogue: Spaced-retrieval memory training in an adult day-care center. *Educational Gerontology*, 15, 641–648.

Camp, C. J., Foss, J. W., O'Hanlon, A. M. and Stevens, A. B. (1996) Memory interventions for persons with dementia. *Applied Cognitive Psychology*, 10, 193–210.

Carstensen, L. L. and Erickson, R. (1986) Enhancing the social environments of elderly nursing home residents: Are high rates of interaction enough? *Journal of Applied Behavior Analysis*, 19, 349–355.

Cheston, R., Jones, K. and Gilliard, J. (2003) Group psychotherapy and people with dementia. *Aging and Mental Health*, 7, 452–461.

Church, M. (1986) Issues in psychological therapy with elderly people. In: I. G. Hanley and M. Gilhooly (eds) *Psychological Therapies for the Elderly* (pp. 1–21). London: Croom Helm.

Clare, L. and Woods, R. T. (2004) Cognitive training and cognitive rehabilitation for people with early-stage Alzheimer's disease: A review. *Neuropsychological Rehabilitation*, 14, 385–401.

Clare, L., Wilson, B. A., Breen, K. and Hodges, J. R. (1999) Errorless learning of face-name associations in early Alzheimer's disease. *Neurocase*, 5, 37–46.

Curran, H. V., Collins, R., Fletcher, S., Kee, S. C. Y., Woods, B. and Iliffe, S. (2003) Older adults and withdrawal from benzodiazepine hypnotics in general practice:

effects on cognitive function, sleep, mood and quality of life. *Psychological Medicine*, 33, 1223–1237.

Dean, R., Briggs, K. and Lindesay, J. (1993) The domus philosophy: A prospective evaluation of two residential units for the elderly mentally ill. *International Journal of Geriatric Psychiatry*, 8, 807–817.

Denihan, A., Kirby, M., Bruce, I., Cunningham, C., Coakley, D. and Lawlor, B. A. (2000) Three-year prognosis of depression in the community-dwelling elderly. *British Journal of Psychiatry*, 176, 453–457.

Dent, O. F., Waite, L. M., Bennett, H. P., Casey, B. J., Grayson, D. A., Cullen, J. S. et al. (1999) A longitudinal study of chronic disease and depressive symptoms in a community sample of older people. *Aging and Mental Health*, 3(4), 351–357.

Dick, L. P., Gallagher-Thompson, D. and Thompson, L. W. (1999) Cognitive-behavioural therapy. In: R. T. Woods (ed) *Psychological Problems of Ageing* (pp. 253–291). Chichester: John Wiley.

Dietch, J. T., Hewett, L. J. and Jones, S. (1989) Adverse effects of reality orientation. *Journal of American Geriatrics Society*, 37, 974–976.

Donaldson, C., Tarrier, N. and Burns, A. (1997) The impact of the symptoms of dementia on caregivers. *British Journal of Psychiatry*, 170, 62–68.

Fasey, C. N. (1990) Grief in old age: A review of the literature. *International Journal of Geriatric Psychiatry*, 5, 67–75.

Feil, N. (1993) *The Validation Breakthrough: Simple Techniques for Communicating with People with 'Alzheimer's Type Dementia'*. Baltimore: Health Professions Press.

Gallagher, D. and Thompson, L. (1982) Treatment of major depressive disorder in older adult outpatients with brief psychotherapies. *Psychotherapy: Theory, Research and Practice*, 19, 482–490.

Gallagher-Thompson, D. and Steffen, A. M. (1994) Comparative effects of cognitive-behavioral and brief psychodynamic psychotherapies for depressed family caregivers. *Journal of Consulting and Clinical Psychology*, 62, 543–549.

Gallagher-Thompson, D., Hanley-Peterson, P. and Thompson, L. (1990) Maintenance of gains versus relapse following brief psychotherapy for depression. *Journal of Consulting and Clinical Psychology*, 58, 371–374.

Gauthier, J. and Marshall, W. L. (1977) Grief: A cognitive-behavioural analysis. *Cognitive Therapy and Research*, 1, 39–44.

Gilleard, C. J. (1996) Family therapy with older clients. In: R. T. Woods (ed) *Handbook of the Clinical Psychology of Ageing* (pp. 561–573). Chichester: John Wiley.

Goddaer, J. and Abraham, I. L. (1994) Effects of relaxing music on agitation during meals among nursing home residents with severe cognitive impairment. *Archives of Psychiatric Nursing*, 8(3), 150–158.

Head, D., Portnoy, S. and Woods, R. T. (1990) The impact of reminiscence groups in two different settings. *International Journal of Geriatric Psychiatry*, 5, 295–302.

Higgitt, A. (1992) Dependency on prescribed drugs. *Reviews in Clinical Gerontology*, 2, 151–155.

Hinchliffe, A. C., Hyman, I., Blizard, B. and Livingston, G. (1992) The impact on carers of behavioural difficulties in dementia: A pilot study on management. *International Journal of Geriatric Psychiatry*, 7, 579–583.

Hinchliffe, A. C., Hyman, I. L., Blizard, B. and Livingston, G. (1995) Behavioural complications of dementia – can they be treated? *International Journal of Geriatric Psychiatry*, 10, 839–847.

Hodgkinson, P. E. (1982) Abnormal grief: The problem of therapy. *British Journal of Medical Psychology*, 55, 29–34.

Holden, U. P. and Woods, R. T. (1995) *Positive Approaches to Dementia Care*, 3rd edn. Edinburgh: Churchill Livingstone.

Hopman-Rock, M., Staats, P. G. M., Tak, E. C. P. M. and Droes, R. M. (1999) The effects of a psychomotor activation programme for use in groups of cognitively impaired people in homes for the elderly. *International Journal of Geriatric Psychiatry*, 14, 633–642.

Husband, H. J. (1999) The psychological consequences of learning a diagnosis of dementia: Three case examples. *Aging and Mental Health*, 3(2), 179–183.

Ingstad, P. J. and Gotestam, K. G. (1987) Staff attitude changes after environmental changes on a ward for psychogeriatric patients. *International Journal of Social Psychiatry*, 33, 237–244.

Jacoby, R. and Oppenheimer, C. (eds) (2002) *Psychiatry in the Elderly*, 3rd edn. Oxford: Oxford University Press.

Kavanagh, D. J. (1990) Towards a cognitive-behavioural intervention for adult grief reactions. *British Journal of Psychiatry*, 157, 373–383.

King, P. and Barrowclough, C. (1991) A clinical pilot study of cognitive-behavioural therapy for anxiety disorders in the elderly. *Behavioural Psychotherapy*, 19, 337–345.

King's Fund (1986) *Living Well into Old Age: Applying Principles of Good Practice to Services for People with Dementia*. Project Paper 63. London: King's Fund.

Kipling, T., Bailey, M. and Charlesworth, G. (1999) The feasibility of a cognitive behavioural therapy group for men with mild/moderate cognitive impairment. *Behavioural and Cognitive Psychotherapy*, 27, 189–193.

Kitwood, T. (1990) The dialectics of dementia: With particular reference to Alzheimer's disease. *Ageing and Society*, 10, 177–196.

Kitwood, T. (1997) *Dementia Reconsidered: The Person Comes First*. Buckingham, UK: Open University Press.

Kitwood, T. and Bredin, K. (1992) Towards a theory of dementia care: Personhood and well-being. *Ageing and Society*, 12, 269–287.

Knight, B. G. (1996) *Psychotherapy with the Older Adult*. Thousand Oaks, CA: Sage.

Laidlaw, K., Thompson, L. W., Dick-Siskin, L. and Gallagher-Thompson, D. (2003) *Cognitive Behaviour Therapy with Older People*. Chichester: John Wiley.

Lam, D. H. and Woods, R. T. (1986) Ward orientation training in dementia: A single-case study. *International Journal of Geriatric Psychiatry*, 1, 145–147.

Lenze, E. J., Dew, M. A., Mazumdar, S., Begley, A. E., Cornes, C., Miller, M. D. et al. (2002) Combined pharmacotherapy and psychotherapy as maintenance treatment for late-life depression: Effects on social adjustment. *American Journal of Psychiatry*, 159, 466–468.

Lewinsohn, P. M. (1975) The behavioural study and treatment of depression. In: M. Hersen, R. Eisler and B. Miller (eds) *Progress in Behavior Modification – 1*. London: Academic Press.

Lichstein, K. L., Riedel, B. W., Wilson, N. M., Lester, K. W. and Aguillard, R. N. (2001) Relaxation and sleep compression for late-life insomnia: A placebo-controlled trial. *Journal of Consulting and Clinical Psychology*, 69, 227–239.

Lindesay, J. (1991) Suicide in the elderly. *International Journal of Geriatric Psychiatry*, 6, 355–361.

Lindesay, J., Briggs, K. and Murphy, E. (1989) The Guys/Age Concern survey: Prevalence rates of cognitive impairment, depression and anxiety in an urban elderly community. *British Journal of Psychiatry*, 155, 317–329.

Lintern, T., Woods, B. and Phair, L. (2002) Before and after training: A case study of intervention. In: S. Benson (ed) *Dementia Topics for the Millennium and Beyond* (pp. 106–112). London: Hawker.

Marriott, A., Donaldson, C., Tarrier, N. and Burns, A. (2000) Effectiveness of cognitive-behavioural family intervention in reducing the burden of care in carers of patients with Alzheimer's disease. *British Journal of Psychiatry*, 176, 557–562.

Martin, J., Shochat, T. and Ancoli-Israel, S. (2000) Assessment and treatment of sleep disturbances in older adults. *Clinical Psychology Review*, 20, 783–805.

McGilton, K. S., Rivera, T. M. and Dawson, P. (2003) Can we help persons with dementia find their way in a new environment? *Aging and Mental Health*, 7(5), 363–371.

McKiernan, F. M. (1996) Bereavement and attitudes to death. In: R. T. Woods (ed) *Handbook of the Clinical Psychology of Ageing* (pp. 159–182). Chichester: John Wiley.

McKitrick, L. A., Camp, C. J. and Black, F. W. (1992) Prospective memory intervention in Alzheimer's disease. *Journal of Gerontology*, 47, P337–P343.

Melin, L. and Gotestam, K. (1981) The effects of rearranging ward routines on communication and eating behaviours of psychogeriatric patients. *Journal of Applied Behavior Analysis*, 14, 47–51.

Miesen, B. M. L. (1992) Attachment theory and dementia. In: G. Jones and B. M. L. Miesen (eds) *Care-giving in Dementia* (pp. 38–56). London: Routledge.

Miesen, B. M. L. (1993) Alzheimer's disease, the phenomenon of parent fixation and Bowlby's attachment theory. *International Journal of Geriatric Psychiatry*, 8, 147–153.

Mittelman, M. S., Ferris, S. H., Shulman, E., Steinberg, G., Ambinder, A., Mackell, J. A. and Cohen, J. (1995) A comprehensive support program: Effect on depression in spouse-caregivers of AD patients. *Gerontologist*, 35, 792–802.

Mittelman, M. S., Ferris, S. H., Shulman, E., Steinberg, G. and Levin, B. (1996) A family intervention to delay nursing home placement of patients with Alzheimer's disease: A randomized controlled trial. *Journal of American Medical Association*, 276(21), 1725–1731.

Moniz-Cook, E., Woods, R. T. and Richards, K. (2001) Functional analysis of challenging behaviour in dementia: The role of superstition. *International Journal of Geriatric Psychiatry*, 16(1), 45–56.

Moniz-Cook, E., Stokes, G. and Agar, S. (2003) Difficult behaviour and dementia in nursing homes: Five cases of psychosocial intervention. *Clinical Psychology and Psychotherapy*, 10(3), 197–208.

Morgan, K. (1996) Managing sleep and insomnia. In: R. T. Woods (ed) *Handbook of the Clinical Psychology of Ageing* (pp. 303–316). Chichester: John Wiley.

Mozley, C. G., Huxley, P., Sutcliffe, C., Bagley, H., Burns, A., Challis, D. and Cordingley, L. (1999) 'Not knowing where I am doesn't mean I don't know what I like': Cognitive impairment and quality of life responses in elderly people. *International Journal of Geriatric Psychiatry*, 14, 776–783.

Nordhus, I. H. and Pallesen, S. (2003) Psychological treatment of late-life anxiety: an empirical review. *Journal of Consulting and Clinical Psychology*, 71, 643–651.

Parkes, C. M. (1980) Bereavement counselling. *British Medical Journal*, 281, 3–6.

Parkes, C. M. (1992) Bereavement and mental health in the elderly. *Reviews in Clinical Gerontology*, 2, 45–51.

Rapp, S. R. and Chao, D. (2000) Appraisals of strain and gain: Effects on psychological well-being of caregivers of dementia patients. *Aging and Mental Health*, 4, 142–147.

Reeve, W. and Ivison, D. (1985) Use of environmental manipulation and classroom and modified informal reality orientation with institutionalized, confused elderly patients. *Age and Ageing*, 14, 119–121.

Reynolds, C. F., Frank, E., Perel, J. M., Imber, S. D., Cornes, C., Miller, M. D. et al. (1999) Nortriptyline and interpersonal psychotherapy as maintenance therapies for recurrent major depression: A randomized controlled trial in patients older than 59 years. *Journal of American Medical Association*, 281, 39–45.

Ritchie, K., Colvez, A., Ankri, J., Ledesert, B., Gardent, H. and Fontaine, A. (1992) The evaluation of long-term care for the dementing elderly: A comparative study of hospital and collective non-medical care in France. *International Journal of Geriatric Psychiatry*, 7, 549–557.

Roper-Hall, A. (1993) Developing family therapy services with older adults. In: J. Carpenter and A. Treacher (eds) *Using Family Therapy in the Nineties* (pp. 185–203). Oxford: Blackwell.

Schnelle, J. F., Traughber, B., Sowell, V. A., Newman, D. R., Petrilli, C. O. and Ory, M. (1989) Prompted voiding treatment of urinary incontinence in nursing home patients: A behavior management approach for nursing home staff. *Journal of American Geriatrics Society*, 37, 1051–1057.

Schnelle, J. F., Newman, D., White, M., Abbey, J., Wallston, K. A., Fogarty, T. and Ory, M. G. (1993) Maintaining continence in nursing home residents through the application of industrial quality control. *Gerontologist*, 33, 114–121.

Scholey, K. A. and Woods, B. T. (2003) A series of brief cognitive therapy interventions with people experiencing both dementia and depression: A description of techniques and common themes. *Clinical Psychology and Psychotherapy*, 10, 175–185.

Skea, D. and Lindesay, J. (1996) An evaluation of two models of long-term residential care for elderly people with dementia. *International Journal of Geriatric Psychiatry*, 11, 233–241.

Spector, A., Davies, S., Woods, B. and Orrell, M. (2000) Reality orientation for dementia: A systematic review of the evidence for its effectiveness. *Gerontologist*, 40(2), 206–212.

Spector, A., Orrell, M., Davies, S. and Woods, B. (2001) Can reality orientation be rehabilitated? Development and piloting of an evidence-based programme of cognition-based therapies for people with dementia. *Neuropsychological Rehabilitation*, 11(3/4), 377–397.

Spector, A., Thorgrimsen, L., Woods, B., Royan, L., Davies, S., Butterworth, M. and Orrell, M. (2003) Efficacy of an evidence-based cognitive stimulation therapy programme for people with dementia: Randomised controlled trial. *British Journal of Psychiatry*, 183, 248–254.

Stanley, M. A., Beck, J. G., Novy, D. M., Averill, P. M., Swann, A. C., Diefenbach, G. J. and Hopko, D. R. (2003) Cognitive-behavioral treatment of late-life generalized anxiety disorder. *Journal of Consulting & Clinical Psychology*, 71, 309–319.

Stokes, G. (1996) Challenging behaviour in dementia: A psychological approach. In: R. T. Woods (ed) *Handbook of the Clinical Psychology of Ageing* (pp. 601–628). Chichester: John Wiley.

Stroebe, M. and Stroebe, W. (1991) Does 'grief-work' work? *Journal of Consulting and Clinical Psychology*, 59, 479–482.

Suhr, J., Anderson, S. and Tranel, D. (1999) Progressive muscle relaxation in the management of behavioural disturbance in Alzheimer's disease. *Neuropsychological Rehabilitation*, 9, 31–44.

Tennstedt, S., Howland, J., Lachman, M., Peterson, E., Kasten, L. and Jette, A. (1998) A randomized, controlled trial of a group intervention to reduce fear of falling and associated activity restriction in older adults. *Journal of Gerontology*, 53B, P384–P392.

Teri, L., Logsdon, R. G., Uomoto, J. and McCurry, S. M. (1997) Behavioral treatment of depression in dementia patients: A controlled clinical trial. *Journal of Gerontology*, 52B, P159–P166.

Thompson, L. W., Gallagher, D. and Breckenridge, J. S. (1987) Comparative effectiveness of psychotherapies for depressed elders. *Journal of Consulting and Clinical Psychology*, 55, 385–390.

Toseland, R. W., Diehl, M., Freeman, K., Manzanares, T. and McCallion, P. (1997) The impact of validation group therapy on nursing home residents with dementia. *Journal of Applied Gerontology*, 16(1), 31–50.

Williams, R., Reeve, W., Ivison, D. and Kavanagh, D. (1987) Use of environmental manipulation and modified informal reality orientation with institutionalized confused elderly subjects: a replication. *Age and Ageing*, 16, 315–318.

Woods, R. T. (1999a) Institutional care. In: R. T. Woods (ed) *Psychological Problems of Ageing* (pp. 195–217). Chichester: John Wiley.

Woods, R. T. (1999b) Mental health problems in late life. In: R. T. Woods (ed) *Psychological Problems of Ageing: Assessment, Treatment and Care* (pp. 73–110). Chichester: John Wiley.

Woods, R. T. (1999c) Psychological 'therapies' in dementia. In: R. T. Woods (ed) *Psychological Problems of Ageing* (pp. 311–344). Chichester: John Wiley.

Woods, R. T. (2002) Non-pharmacological techniques. In: N. Qizilbash (ed) *Evidence-based Dementia Practice* (pp. 428–446). Oxford: Blackwell.

Woods, R. T. and Bird, M. (1999) Non-pharmacological approaches to treatment. In: G. Wilcock, K. Rockwood and R. Bucks (eds) *Diagnosis and Management of Dementia: A Manual for Memory Disorders Teams* (pp. 311–331). Oxford: Oxford University Press.

Woods, R. T. and McKiernan, F. (1995) Evaluating the impact of reminiscence on older people with dementia. In: B. K. Haight and J. Webster (eds) *The Art and Science of Reminiscing: Theory, Research, Methods and Applications* (pp. 233–242). Washington DC: Taylor & Francis.

Woods, R. and Roth, A. (2005) Effectiveness of psychological interventions with older people. In: A. Roth and P. Fonagy (eds) *What Works for Whom? A Critical Review of Psychotherapy Research*, 2nd edn. (pp. 425–446). New York: Guilford Press.

Woods, R. T., Spector, A., Jones, C., Orrell, M. and Davies, S. (2005) Reminiscence therapy for dementia. *The Cochrane Database of Systematic Reviews*, Issue 2. Chichester: John Wiley.

Wortman, C. B. and Silver, R. B. (1989) The myths of coping with loss. *Journal of Consulting and Clinical Psychology*, 57, 349–357.

Zanetti, O., Binetti, G., Magni, E., Rozzini, L., Bianchetti, A. and Trabucchi, M. (1997) Procedural memory stimulation in Alzheimer's disease: Impact of a training programme. *Acta Neurologica Scandinavica*, 95, 152–157.

Zarit, S. H. and Edwards, A. B. (1999) Family caregiving: Research and clinical intervention. In: R. T. Woods (ed) *Psychological Problems of Ageing* (pp. 153–193). Chichester: John Wiley.

Chapter 27

Psychosocial rehabilitation

Investigation

Nick Lake and Tony Lavender

INTRODUCTION

This chapter provides an overview of the key issues in the assessment of an individual's psychosocial needs, particularly for people suffering from severe and enduring mental health problems. It begins by introducing the term 'psychosocial rehabilitation', by outlining the UK policy context and by spelling-out the crucial role of psychosocial rehabilitation in helping individuals to overcome the negative impact of particular symptoms or problematic experiences (e.g. voices) and to take on valued roles in society. It then introduces a new framework for assessment that differentiates between an individual's capacities, competencies and capabilities to fulfil valued social roles. The rest of the chapter is devoted to reviewing how psychosocial assessment is conducted in practice and the psychometric assessment tools that are available.

What is psychosocial rehabilitation?

In general terms, psychosocial rehabilitation aims to help individuals to optimise their social performance in various social roles (e.g. work) in as valued a context as possible. A variety of interventions can contribute to this aim, and in psychosocial rehabilitation there is no sharp boundary between treatment practices and rehabilitation practices (Lavender and Watts, 1994). However, whereas much 'treatment' is concerned with reducing distress, disturbance or 'deviance' within an individual, psychosocial rehabilitation is characteristically concerned with achieving good social and emotional adjustment. It therefore places an emphasis on 'functioning'. In other words, while it recognises that people may suffer from long term and sometimes intractable symptoms, it places an emphasis not on the symptoms but on people's capacity to function at their optimal level.

Psychosocial rehabilitation particularly emphasises the interaction between a person's capacity, competence and capability, and his or her social environment. For example, if a person is to develop a valued working role then he or she must posses the physical and cognitive capacity to carry out the work task, the competence/capability to interact appropriately with work colleagues and to manage the emotional demands of the task/task setting, and the work environment must be able to accommodate the nature of a person's difficulties, or support them to overcome these.

There is considerable evidence that a person's ability to take on a particular social role is dependent on the type of environment in which the role is practised. The environment thus needs to be as important an object of assessment and intervention as an individual's capacity, competence and capability. When working with environments, this usually means avoiding the extremes of both overprotection and underprotection. Some clients may require some degree of 'shelter' from potential stresses, and need support in coping with them. Expectations of clients that take no account of these needs for shelter and support can be counter-productive and lead to an inherently unstable situation. However, providing an unnecessary sheltered environment gives people no opportunity to make the best use of their capabilities, and may indeed lead these to atrophy.

Changes in policy context

Traditionally, the aim of treatment for severe and enduring mental health problems (such as psychosis) has been to stabilise what are seen as a lifelong psychiatric conditions, primarily through the use of medication. This has often resulted in low expectations as far as psychosocial rehabilitation is concerned, and a set of attitudes that has emphasised dependence on services.

In contrast, there is now a growing mental health user and survivor movement that largely rejects this traditional view and instead emphasises the fact that people can 'recover' from severe mental illness to lead important and valued roles in society. This has lead to a 'recovery' model of mental illness (Warner, 2004) and a recognition that individuals may see themselves as 'recovered' even when they may still be suffering from symptoms. This has been accompanied (at least in clinical psychology, if not in services as a whole) by a shift towards a more symptom-focused (Bentall, 1990) or experience-focused approach (Bentall, 2004) to psychosis, with a rejection of labels such as schizophrenia (Boyle, 2002). This focus on individual symptoms or experiences, on the meaning people ascribe to them and on how to manage them differently, has encouraged services to develop treatments that enable service users to overcome the negative impact of particular symptoms or problematic psychosis-related experiences (e.g. voices). This aspect of psychological rehabilitation has helped to enhance an individual's capacity to take on valued roles that previously may have been seen as being beyond them.

Whilst many of these changes have yet to have a significant impact on mental health services in Britain, they are beginning to influence policy makers, and psychosocial rehabilitation is now at the forefront of the government's mental health agenda. This shift of emphasis is evident in the government's National Service Framework for Mental Health (Department of Health (DoH), 1999). Additionally, the government's Social Exclusion Unit published *Mental Health and Social Exclusion* (Office of the Deputy Prime Minister (ODPM), 2004), which highlights the difficulties faced by people with mental health problems in obtaining valued roles (e.g. work) and the enormous financial and social burden this places on society. It also sets out an ambitious agenda to tackle social exclusion in this population.

The social roles that are the focus of assessment and intervention

Although individuals occupy a variety of social roles, the valued social roles that are most often the focus of interventions in psychosocial rehabilitation are work and education, activities of daily living, family roles and friendship roles. Psychosocial rehabilitation is about both building a person's capability to take up these roles and the process of helping individuals find a social role they see as valued. Some of the difficulties individuals with severe and long-term mental health problems have in taking up these key social roles are highlighted in the following sections.

Work and education

Work plays a central role in defining our identity, purpose and social status, and in enabling us to access community resources through the salary received (Bell, 2003). It is also an important source of self-esteem, social relationships and friendships. Unfortunately, long-term mental health problems, such as psychosis, often begin in adolescence or early adulthood and this inevitably impacts on the development of a working role. Continuing disturbing experiences may then affect a person's motivation, capacity and opportunity to take on work.

Unemployment brings its own problems and studies from the general population suggest that unemployment can lead to reduced self-esteem, alienation and apathy, loss of social contacts, loss of financial resources and emotional and physical difficulties (Howarth et al., 1998; Dooley et al., 2000). Recent estimates indicate that unemployment for people with severe and enduring mental health problems ranges from 66% (O'Flynn, 2001) to over 90% (Perkins and Rinaldi, 2002). People with long-term mental health problems also benefit from meaningful employment. Mueser at al. (1997) and Bond et al. (2001) document a number of positive effects of working including symptom reduction, higher self-esteem and improved social functioning.

Educational opportunities can not only give a person a better chance of gaining employment, they can also give a person a sense of purpose and identity independent of work, and have a positive effect on self-esteem. In similar ways to work, people suffering from severe and enduring mental health problems may find themselves excluded from educational opportunities or there may be too little support to enable them to access it. The nature of the educational environment is also critical in enabling a person to successfully complete a course.

Daily living

Being able to engage in society and to master the tasks of everyday living is a particularly important goal for most people with mental health difficulties. The dignity, sense of self-respect and autonomy that comes from mastering these skills can have an immediate and positive impact on a person's mental health (Parry, 1991). Conversely, a failure to manage certain tasks (e.g. personal hygiene) can lead to social exclusion, and the inability to cope with the tasks and pressures of everyday living can contribute to the reoccurrence or exacerbation of psychological difficulties. The activities of daily living that are most often the focus of rehabilitation assessment and treatment packages are:

- self-care, including personal hygiene, grooming, washing (self and clothes), care of personal health, use of toilet and knowledge of basic first aid
- home management, including cooking, shopping, cleaning, sewing, budgeting, paying bills, carrying out simple house repairs and maintenance, use of appliances and household laundry
- use of community facilities, including public transport, social security, shops, entertainment and leisure facilities, financial services and health services.

Family roles

Whilst considerable research and much effort has gone into helping people with mental health problems gain meaningful employment, there is less research on supporting this group to take on family roles such as father, mother and partner. Yet these roles are central to cohesive family life, and arguably to the cohesion of society as a whole. There is also considerable evidence documenting the important role of the family as a protective factor in the maintenance of mental health (Brown et al., 1972; Tarrier et al., 1988). If a family is to function well, and be supportive, a person with severe and enduring mental health problems may need to be supported in maintaining positive relationships and in accomplishing his or her family role. This is especially important when children are involved. The family members may also need to be supported in managing their reactions to the individual's difficulties and in their attempts to support the individual. Finally, the family environment, and the patterns of communication within it (e.g. high expressed emotion, see the section Assessment of the family environment, below), can also have a significant impact on relapse and recovery, and this often needs to be the target of assessment and intervention.

Friendship roles

Friends offer support, are partners in shared leisure activities and form part of the social networks that are central to our sense of identity and self-esteem. There is also considerable evidence that individuals with mental health problems who have good social support (friendships) are likely to recover more quickly and be less vulnerable to relapse. For example, Jablensky et al. (1992), in their World Health Organization (WHO) research, found social support to be one of the main predictors of a positive outcome in psychosis.

Unfortunately, people with severe and enduring mental health problems sometimes lack the opportunity to form meaningful friendships and may struggle to master or maintain the social skills that are necessary to form and maintain them. This means that assistance in developing these friendship networks is particularly important and it can present difficult challenges.

ASSESSMENT

A comprehensive assessment is vital to the development of sensible and coherent psychosocial intervention programmes and it is a crucial component of case management systems and the care programme approach (Department of Health, 2000). Only by conducting a detailed assessment of all the factors that are relevant to a person's attempts to take on a particular social role, and by using this information to develop a comprehensive and psychologically sophisticated formulation, can a tailored programme be developed that takes into account both the individual and the environment.

It is important to introduce three key concepts that will be used throughout the chapter: capacity, competence and capability. To accomplish a particular role an individual must have the physical, cognitive, emotional and social *capacity* to take on the role, such as sufficient physical health, cognitive abilities, emotional stability, interpersonal understanding, and drive and motivation, to meet the demands of a role. Psychosocial interventions may work directly on these capacities.

At the next level, if an individual has the capacity to take on a role, they then need to acquire the *competencies* to carry out the tasks required of a particular role in particular settings. Whereas capacity refers to whether a person has the repertoire of essential core abilities that are needed to function in a particular social role, competence refers to whether people carry out tasks appropriately to attain a satisfactory level of functioning. To give an example, a client living alone may have it within his capacity to change his clothes and bed linen, which are relatively simple manual skills. However, when actually in a bed-sit, he may not perform these tasks adequately because he does not know how, because he lacks knowledge about how often they should be changed, or because he does not think it matters. So whilst he may have the *capacity* to change his clothes and bed linen, he may not be *competent* at the task.

At the final level, some psychosocial interventions aim to help individuals to develop an ability to generalise competencies across new and novel social environments. We refer to this as an individual's capability and this is important to the fulfilment of complex roles. Unfortunately, few psychosocial assessments and interventions focus on a person's capability, and professionals often fail to make a distinction between competence and capability. *Competence* can be assessed by observing a person attempting tasks in particular settings. However, it cannot be assumed that, because a person is competent at a particular task in a particular setting, he or she will be able to transfer this competence across contexts. Capability can only be assessed through observing a person attempting the tasks associated with particular social roles across a range of contexts. The failure to distinguish between competencies and capabilities partially explains why professionals can often be surprised when skills learnt in one setting (e.g. particular social skills) are not transferred or generalised to other settings. Psychosocial interventions often fail to give a sufficient focus to developing a client's capability to generalise competencies across settings.

Finally, the fulfilment of particular social roles is dependent on the environment (e.g. whether sufficient external support exists to support the individual). It is therefore vital to assess these environmental contexts to determine whether the opportunity to carry out the tasks associated with particular social roles exist. This is as important as the assessment of task competence.

The key areas of assessment, for each of the key valued social roles, are illustrated in Table 27.1.

ASSESSMENT OF CAPACITY

Motivation and personality

A key, but sometimes neglected, area in the literature on psychosocial rehabilitation is the need to gain an understanding of an individual's motivation and personality. Attempts to help a client reach his or her goals will fail if insufficient attention is given to the expectations, hopes, fears and temperament of the individual.

Table 27.1 A framework for assessment in psychosocial rehabilitation

	Social role			
	Daily living	Work and education	Family	Friendship
Assessment of capacity				
Motivation and personality: an assessment of an individual's desires, motivations and temperament				
Physical capacity: an assessment of an individual's physical abilities				
Cognitive capacity: an assessment of an individual's intellectual abilities				
Social capacity: an assessment of an individual's social awareness and social skills				
Emotional capacity: an assessment of an individual's emotional stability, self-esteem, symptoms and potentially abnormal experiences and beliefs				
Assessment of role				
Competence/capability: an assessment of whether an individual has the competence to carry out the task associated with particular social roles across the required range of settings				
Assessment of the environment				
An assessment of the environment and/or the opportunities/support to carry out the tasks associated with particular social roles				

An assessment of an individual's history

An assessment of an individual's history helps to provide an understanding of the context in which a person's personality has developed. This can be done through interviews, by talking to relatives or carers and through a thorough review of medical records. Exploring an individual's attachment history, relationship with parents and experience of parental expectations, early peer relationships, traumatic experiences, and developmental successes and failures, helps to inform an understanding of the developmental, family and cultural influences that impact on a particular individual and the expectations that he or she has for the future.

A thorough social history is also important, noting, for example, the variety of social roles that have been assumed over the years and what factors have led to these being successful. This may also include negative experiences that have served to reduce a client's expectations.

An assessment of an individual's hopes, aspirations and motivation

An individual's aspirations and motivations should not be regarded as stable personality traits, but things that change as that person's circumstances and experiences change. Hopes and aspirations will vary according to a variety of factors, including parental expectations, length and severity of mental health difficulties, previous success in a role, age, gender, social class, ethnicity, culture, the presence (or not) of supportive networks and a perceived opportunity to accomplish the social role.

When assessing motivation, it is helpful to identify the potential sources of satisfaction and dissatisfaction in particular social roles, and the gains and losses associated with taking them on. For some, the enhanced social status and self-esteem that might be gained will be a strong motivating factor. For others, the fear of being overwhelmed by the role, losing benefits, facing discrimination, or being rejected or ridiculed, will leave them with little motivation to take it on. Some people may be gaining conscious or unconscious secondary gains from their current difficulties (Van Egmond, 2003), such as safety or an identity as someone who is 'ill' and so does not have to carry the same responsibility as others. Care needs to be taken not to challenge these in a clumsy way through a professional's well-intentioned attempt to help a person move forward. This can lead to clients directly or indirectly sabotaging the rehabilitation programme. It is therefore as important to assess what might be lost as gained by taking on a particular social role.

An assessment of an individual's temperament and personality traits

A psychologist can also make good use of the personality assessments used in clinical practice. The information obtained from such tests can contribute to both a team's understanding of a client and what motivates them, as well as a clinical tool to help clients make sense of their feelings about work and friendships. Tests such as the Minnesota Multiphasic Personality Inventory – Version 2 (Butcher et al., 1990) and the Millon Clinical Multiaxial Inventory – Version 3 (Millon, 1994) have a long history of use in clinical practice.

Motivation, personality and work

It is vital to assess a person's aspirations and motivations when assessing his or her capacity to take on a working role or educational programme. Some individuals will not feel ready for work and may fear being overly stressed by the demands of it. There will be others who have received messages from family and society that they are incapable of working, and others who will have had negative previous experiences of working. These expectations need to be understood and addressed if a person is to change their expectations of what they can achieve.

Motivation, personality and daily living

The same is true for activities of daily living. Some clients may be frightened of the responsibilities that accompany increased participation in society and sometimes the result of learning to take on a particular task of daily living (e.g. living alone, doing the shopping, etc.) is a loss of social contact and support. Some clients may therefore be reluctant to leave the protected environment of a day centre or residential home and, if so, the reasons need to be understood and worked with.

Desired family roles and friendships

Conducting a detailed assessment of an individual's early family relation-ships and interpersonal history is particularly important when planning psychosocial interventions aimed at increasing an individual's capacity to take on family and friendship roles. An individual who has suffered early abusive relationships may be understandably reluctant to get close to others or to have much to do with their family. Also, not all forms of social support are beneficial to everyone and there is now convincing evidence that some forms are potentially harmful (Gibson, 1992). This may occur when certain types of support are not consistent with either a person's expectations or his or her coping style (Buchanan, 1995). For example, Wing (1978) argues that social withdrawal may actually be protective for some people with psychotic symptoms who have damaged social skills. Social isolation may assist them to maintain a balance between 'excessive and deficient social stimulation and prevent them being overwhelmed rather than supported by their connections' (Hirschberg, 1985).

Physical capacity

Physical health problems need to be considered in any comprehensive psychosocial assessment. The positive and negative symptoms of psychosis, the cognitive deficits that accompany some forms of mental health problems, and the financial hardship and social exclusion that people suffer, can often result in people taking less care of their physical health. Although this area is not traditionally the domain of clinical psychologists, many of the more basic physical health problems, such as poor eyesight or hearing, dental problems and weight problems can be screened for by any member of a mental health team, and then referrals made to the appropriate specialist. Psychologists may have a particular role in assessing the psychological impact of particular physical difficulties.

One valuable brief screening measure for assessing physical health is the Medical Outcomes Study 36-Item Short Form Health Survey (SF-36; Ware and Sherbourne, 1992). This measure assesses eight areas: physical functioning, role limitations because of physical health problems, bodily pain, social functioning, general mental health, role limitations because of emotional problems, vitality and general health perceptions.

A further important area of physical assessment concerns the various physical side effects that accompany psychotropic medication. There are a number of good rating scales, including the Abnormal Involuntary Movement Scale (AIMS; Munetz and Benjamin, 1988) and the Liverpool University Neuroleptic Side Effects Rating Scale (LUNSERS; Day et al., 1995).

Social capacity

Most valued social roles require individuals to interact socially with others. In fact, this can often be the most important factor in predicting whether an individual will be successful in particular social roles. For example, Watts (1978) showed that the quality of relationships with co-workers in an occupational rehabilitation unit was the best predictor of subsequent re-employment. In contrast, task performance failed to predict at all.

A careful assessment of an individual's history of social relationships can give important clues as to whether that person might have the capacity to manage the social relationships in particular social roles. This does, however, need to be supplemented by careful observation of current social functioning and by obtaining information from relatives and staff who know the client well. When interpreting observational data, it is important to keep in mind the conceptual difference between capacity and competence. Social capacity involves a complex set of cognitive, emotional and behavioural processes. These processes are evident in the individual's basic social abilities and include:

- an ability to express oneself coherently (e.g. using verbal and non-verbal signals)
- an ability to recognise and interpret social communication correctly
- an awareness of the social rules and conventions that govern relationships, such as the principle of reciprocity, turn-taking and an awareness of appropriate situation-specific behaviours, including appropriate interpersonal distance
- an ability to choose the appropriate social behaviour in particular circumstances, including an ability to relate immediate actions to long-term consequences
- the ability to reflect on the content of another's mind; this 'reflective-functioning' capacity is necessary if an individual is to discern other people's views and expectations.

Most general measures of social functioning (see the section Assessment of competence in social roles, below) assess a mix of capacity and competence using interviews and direct observation. In assessing social capacity it can also be useful to use role plays. The role play task of the Social Problem Solving Battery (Sayers et al., 1995) consists of six 3-minute role plays in which the client has to generate solutions to social problems.

If the above essential aspects of social capacity are poor, the task of rehabilitation is to help the individual develop the foundations of social competence.

Cognitive capacity

Cognitive difficulties (including those that accompany psychotic experiences) may limit an individual's capacity to take on more complex mental tasks. There is now a considerable body of evidence indicating that particular cognitive impairments either underlie or are caused by some forms of severe and enduring mental health problems (Nelson et al., 1990). In people given a diagnosis of schizophrenia, tests reveal mild impairments on overall intelligence and some perceptual tasks; moderate impairments in attention, delayed recall, working memory and verbal memory; and severe impairments in executive functioning, verbal fluency and motor skills (Wykes and Castle, 2003). Some of these cognitive difficulties appear to exist prior to the onset of the condition but they also worsen at onset (Addington et al., 2003). Some cognitive impairments remit on recovery, although memory difficulties can remain. In people suffering from severe depression, common cognitive impairments include attentional problems and memory difficulties, particularly for recent events.

Cognitive difficulties are a significant predictor of how much support a person requires in psychosocial rehabilitation programmes. They also are a strong predictor of social performance and success in vocational rehabilitation programmes. Bell and Bryson (2001) found that cognition rather than symptoms predicted improvement in work quality following a 6-month rehabilitation programme and Gold et al. (2001) found that the chance of gaining employment following a rehabilitation programme was affected by IQ, memory and speed of information processing.

A detailed cognitive assessment is vital to help to adapt psychosocial interventions to the cognitive abilities of clients. A person with significant difficulties in executive functioning is unlikely to thrive in a work placement requiring complex decision-making processes. Indeed, such a placement might well contribute to a deterioration in symptoms. Similarly, teaching someone how to budget using verbal teaching methods alone is unlikely to benefit someone with deficits in verbal memory.

In people suffering from severe and enduring mental health problems, tests of verbal memory, executive functioning, attention, motor skills and social cognition are particularly important. For example, poor verbal memory is significantly related to social skills impairments, poor functioning in the community and poor social problem-solving skills (e.g. Tollefson, 1996). Difficulties in executive functioning are also correlated with poor social and occupational adjustment (e.g. Penn et al., 1995).

It is beyond the scope of this chapter to provide a comprehensive description of the wide range of neuropsychological tests that are available to clinical psychologists. Some of the most commonly used are listed below:

General intellectual function

1 The Weschler Adult Intelligence Scale III (WAIS-III; Wechsler, 1997a)
2 The Standard Progressive Matrices (Raven, 1992)

Pre-morbid intellectual functioning

1 The National Adult Reading Test (NART; Nelson, 1982)
2 The Weschler Test of Adult Reading (Ginsberg, 2003)

Memory

1 The Logical Memory and Verbal Paired Associates subtests of the Wechsler Memory Scales – III (Wechsler, 1997b)
2 The Visual Reproduction, Faces and Family Pictures subtests of the Wechsler Memory Scales – III (Wechsler, 1997b)
3 The Story Recall and Figure Recall subtests of the Adult Memory and Information Processing Battery (AMIPB; Coughlan and Hollows, 1985)
4 The Rivermead Behavioural Memory Test (RBMT; Wilson et al., 1985)
5 The Recognition Memory Test (Warrington, 1984)

Attention

1   The Stroop Test (Jenson and Rohwer, 1966)
2   The Digit Symbol-Coding subtest of the WAIS-III (Wechsler, 1997a)
3   The Trail Making Test (TMT; Reitan 1958)

Motor skills

1   The Information Processing Tests of the AMIPB (Coughlan and Hollows, 1985)
2   The Trail Making Test (Reitan, 1958)

Executive functioning

1   Wisconsin Card Sorting Test (WCST; Heaton, 1981)
2   The Modified Wisconsin Card Sorting Test (MCST; Nelson, 1976)
3   Tower of Hanoi Task (Shallice, 1982)
4   Hayling Sentence Completion and Brixton Spatial Anticipation Test (Burgess and Shallice, 1996)

Emotional capacity

It is important to assess a person's emotional capacity and psychological health to determine its impact on his or her ability to carry out a particular social role. Such assessments will include assessments of general psychological health, self-esteem, the psychological difficulties that often accompany more severe forms of mental 'illness', as well as the symptoms of the 'illness' itself. The types of mood disorders that commonly accompany severe and enduring mental health problems like psychosis include anxiety and depression, anger and hostility, post-traumatic stress disorder and substance-use disorders.

The most common assessment method in assessing psychological health is the clinical interview. But there are also a number of other assessment tools that can complement the assessment process and some of these are outlined below.

General psychological health

1   The General Health Questionnaire (GHQ; Goldberg, 1972)
2   The Global Assessment Scale (GAS; Endicott et al., 1976)

Self-esteem

1   The Rosenberg Self-Esteem Questionnaire (Rosenberg, 1965)

General psychiatric screening questionnaires

1   The Symptom Checklist – 90 – R (Derogatis, 1994)
2   The Brief Symptom Inventory (Derogatis and Melisaratos, 1983)
3   Positive and Negative Syndrome Scale (Emsley et al., 2003)
4   The Health of the Nation Outcome Scales (Honos; Wing et al., 1996)

Accompanying mood disorders

1   The Beck Depression Inventory Version 2 (for depressive symptoms; Beck et al., 1996)
2   The Beck Anxiety Inventory Version 2 (for symptoms of anxiety; Beck and Steer, 1990)
3   The Revised Impact of Events Scale (for PTSD symptoms; Weiss and Marmar, 1997)

Psychotic symptoms

1   Scale for the Assessment of Negative Symptoms (SANS; Andreason, 1989)
2   Scale for the Assessment of Positive Symptoms (SAPS; Andreason, 1984)
3   Positive and Negative Syndrome Scale (PANSS; Kay et al., 1989)
4   Maudsley Assessment of Delusions Scale (MADS; Taylor et al., 1994)
5   Psychotic Symptom Rating Scale (PSYRATS; Haddock et al., 1999)
6   Belief About Voices Questionnaire (Chadwick and Birchwood, 1995)

Hopelessness

1   The Beck Hopelessnes Scale (Beck et al., 1974)
2   The Scale for Suicidal Ideation (Beck et al., 1979)

Anger

1   The Novaco Anger Inventory (Novaco, 1975)

Substance misuse

1   The Alcohol Use Disorders Identification Test (AUDIT; Saunders et al., 1993)
2   The Drug Abuse Screening Test (DAST; Gavin et al., 1989)

Quality of life

1   World Health Organization Quality of Life (WHO, 1998)

ROLE COMPETENCE AND CAPABILITY

The best way of determining whether an individual has the competence to perform the tasks required of a particular social role in a particular environment, or the capability to perform the tasks across different environments, is to observe the individual attempting the role in those environments. The closer this assessment setting is to the client's natural role setting, the more accurate this assessment will be. Although role competence is best assessed through observation, interviewing clients and carers can also provide important information when direct observation is unrealistic. Some of the assessment tools designed to assess the competencies required to fulfil the four major social roles are described below.

Assessments of work competence

In assessing work competence it is important to look at how well the person can accomplish the work task(s) over time, the quality of the person's work and how he or she actually goes about doing the work. Particularly important is his or her management of the changing work demands, the rules of the workplace, the social relationships that accompany the task, the support that might be available and the response to feedback. There are not many good, reliable scales to help in the assessment of work competence. One such scale is the Work Behaviour Inventory (Bryson et al., 1997). This scale combines behavioural observation and interview methods and generates ratings in five specific work domains as well as a total rating. Another is the Griffiths Scale (Griffiths, 1977), which measures five aspects of work behaviour. Other tools include the Minnesota Job Importance Questionnaire and the Minnesota Satisfaction Questionnaire (Lofquist and Dawis, 1975; Watts, 1991).

Assessment of competence in daily living skills

Formal assessments of daily living skills are not usually done by psychologists, despite their importance. They can be assessed using the self-report and informant versions of the Independent Living Skills Survey (Wallace et al., 2000). This includes information on areas such as self-care, care of personal possessions, money management and use of public transportation.

Assessment of competence in social roles (family and friendships)

Interviews with family and friends usually provide rich data when assessing competence in family and friendship roles. They can also promote engagement with family and friends that may subsequently be important in developing successful psychosocial rehabilitation programs. However, direct assessments are sometimes valuable, for example, in assessing parenting skills. An assessment of an individual's competence in each social role should include an assessment of his or her motivation to carry out the role, ability to do it effectively over time, other people's responses, the behaviours that impact negatively on his or her competence in the role, and the person's ability to accept his or her limitations and respond to feedback. It is also important to take a full history to determine how the quality of an individual's relationships may have varied over time. Some social difficulties may have been present before the onset of an individual's mental health difficulties, whereas others may have arisen as a consequence.

Interviews can be supplemented by specific assessment scales. Commonly used scales include:

- The Katz Adjustment Scale (KAS-R; Katz and Lyerly, 1963), which is used to obtain relatives' views of an individual's personal, interpersonal and social adjustment.
- The Work and Social Adjustment Scale, which examines the impact of an individual's mental health difficulties on work, home management, leisure activities, and ability to maintain close relationships (Mundt et al., 2002).
- The Social Behaviour Schedule (SBS; Wykes and Sturt, 1986), which is a schedule that is given by a trained interviewer to someone who knows the individual well. It measures 21 behavioural problems such as socially unacceptable habits, poor self-care and inappropriate social mixing.
- The Social Functioning Scale (SFS; Birchwood et al., 1990), which assesses seven areas of functioning and uses information provided by both the individual and other people who know the individual well.
- The Inventory of Interpersonal Problems (IIP; Horowitz et al., 1988), which is a 127-item questionnaire that assesses an individual's social problems in a variety of areas.

Other commonly used assessments include the Life Skills Profile (Rosen et al., 1989) and the Social Problem Solving Battery (Sayers et al., 1995).

Assessment of community participation

It is also important to conduct an assessment of how well an individual is able to utilise the community resources that are available. This can be done through direct observation or through interviewing clients and carers directly. For example, is the client able to use public transport, how good is he or she at handling money, can he or she shop effectively, does he or she have some enjoyable leisure activities and can he or she manage the social contact with others in the community?

ASSESSMENT OF OPPORTUNITIES AND THE ENVIRONMENT

The opportunities available for people to develop valued social roles can vary widely. A key factor is the kind of environments that are provided or that are available, and the effect this environment has in facilitating or hindering rehabilitation. A comprehensive psychosocial assessment will need to include a detailed assessment of the range of community facilities available to an individual and the nature of these facilities. The latter should include an assessment of the physical environment, the social relationships in the environment and the attitudes of people within it, the tasks that need to be managed within the environment, and the level and quality of support provided within it.

Assessments of the work environment

A number of important questions must be answered when assessing the work environment. At a basic level, an assessment must be made of the physical and cognitive demands of the work, and the environmental conditions (noise, lighting, etc.) in which the work takes place. There must be an assessment of the social demands that accompany the work and the level of support that might be available to overcome physical, cognitive or social difficulties. An assessment must also be made of the social desirability or social value of the work (noting status of work, pay, hours, holidays, etc.) and the extent to which it will promote social inclusion. A number of scales can facilitate the processes of assessing the quality of work environments, including the QUARTZ system developed by Leiper et al. (1992).

Assessment of the domestic environment

An assessment of the domestic environment must include an assessment of the environmental conditions. For example, where is the accommodation situated, how noisy is it, are there problematic neighbours, how close is it to community facilities, and how close it is to the individual's sources of social support? Similarly, what are the quality of the furnishings and decoration, is it clean, and is there enough room? An assessment of the equipment may also be necessary including its ease of use, the physical and cognitive abilities required to use it, and risk factors associated with it. This should be accompanied by an assessment of the domestic support available.

Assessment of the family environment

An assessment of the family environment is important to gain an understanding of how this impacts on the client, and whether the family environment can support the person in his or her attempts to take on particular family roles. As part of this, it will be important to assess the family's reaction to the client's mental health difficulties. Reactions can include feelings of loss and grief (Miller et al., 1990), stigma, shame, social isolation (Walsh and Harman, 1989) and economic hardship as family members take on a caring role. The style of relating in the family is also important. Considerable research has shown that a particular style of relating involving a combination of over-protective and/or hostile responses (known as 'high expressed emotion') has a negative impact on a person's capacity to recover from their symptoms and is strongly associated with relapse (Kavanagh, 1992).

Each of these factors can have a direct impact on how the family reacts to the client in their family roles and on the level of support provided. The family environment can be assessed through interviews with family members or through observing the family environment directly. Standardised interview schedules include:

- The Relatives Assessment Interview (Barrowclough and Tarrier, 1992): this interview schedule provides a useful guide for interviewing family relatives.
- The Family Interview and Questionnaire (Barrowclough and Tarrier, 1992): this interview schedule provides information on the level of a family member's distress and their coping strategies in relation to a checklist of problems experienced by people suffering from psychotic symptoms.
- The Knowledge about Schizophrenia Interview (Barrowclough and Tarrier, 1992): this enables the psychologist to assess a relative's views and knowledge about 'schizophrenia' and how they feel it should be managed.

Assessments of the social environment

Research suggests that people suffering from the symptoms of psychosis develop more limited networks that tend to be dependent on family or mental health services and relationships in which they are the recipients rather than providers of support (Sullivan and Poertner, 1989). Several studies have shown that the primary networks of a 'normal' sample consist of about 40 people who are seen regularly (Henderson et al., 1981). By contrast, people with psychotic symptoms have a social network of only four or five people who they see regularly and these are usually family members (McFarlane et al., 1981).

It is important to obtain an assessment of an individual's level of social inclusion, and the social support that is available to them. Although numbers of social contacts is informative, it is the nature and quality of these relationships that is particularly important. Social contact is not helpful if it leaves the person feeling stigmatised or overwhelmed by the demands of the relationship.

THE FORMULATION

One of the unique skills of psychologists lies in their ability to develop comprehensive psychosocial formulations that are informed by a broad empirical and theoretical information base. By drawing assessment information into such formulations, the psychologist can develop effective intervention plans that consider both the individual and their environment. The formulation also acts as a useful tool in communicating the outcome of the assessment to other staff and in enabling a coordinated plan to be developed across treatment agencies.

In bringing together the information from an assessment, and when considering where to target psychosocial rehabilitation programmes, it is useful to draw on the vulnerability model of mental illness, and psychosis in particular (Zubin and Spring, 1977). According to this model, an individual's likelihood of experiencing symptoms (e.g. psychosis) is dependent on a combination of vulnerability factors and environmental stressors. At the same time, personal protective factors, such as employment, financial independence and a positive home environment, can serve to reduce the likelihood of a person experiencing symptoms. It is therefore important to use the assessment of an individual's capacities and competencies, together with an assessment of the available environments, to design psychosocial intervention programmes that will maximise social inclusion without precipitating relapse, and enable the person to make the best use of their abilities in as valued a social context as possible.

REFERENCES

Addington, J., Brooks, B. L. and Addington, D. (2003) Cognitive functioning in first episode psychosis: Initial presentation. *Schizophrenia Research*, 62(1–2), 59–64.

Andreasen, N. C. (1984) *Scale for the Assessment of Positive Symptoms (SAPS)*. Iowa: Department of Psychiatry.

Andreasen, N. C. (1989) Scale for the assessment of negative symptoms (SANS). *British Journal of Psychiatry*, 155(7), 53–58.

Barrowclough, C. and Tarrier, N. (1992) *Families of Schizophrenic Patients: Cognitive Behavioural Intervention*. London: Chapman and Hall.

Beck, A. T. and Steer, R. A. (1990) *Manual for the Beck Anxiety Inventory*. San Antonio, TX: Psychological Corporation.

Beck, A. T., Weisman, A., Lester, D. and Trexler, L. (1974) The measurement of pessimism: The Hopelessness Scale. *Journal of Consulting and Clinical Psychology*, 47, 861–865.

Beck, A. T., Kovacs, M. and Weisman, A. (1979) Assessment of suicidal intention: The Scale for Suicide Ideation. *Journal of Consulting and Clinical Psychology*, 47, 343–352.

Beck, A. T., Steer, R. A. and Brown, G. K. (1996) *Beck Depression Inventory Manual, 2nd edn*. San Antonio, TX: Psychological Corporation.

Bell, M. D. (2003) Work and recovery in schizophrenia. In: D. Castle, D. L. Copolov and T. Wykes (eds) *Pharmacological and Psychosocial Treatments in Schizophrenia*. London: Martin Dunitz.

Bell, M. D. and Bryson, G. (2001) Work rehabilitation in schizophrenia: Does cognitive impairment limit performance? *Schizophrenia Bulletin*, 27(2), 269–279.

Bentall, R. (ed) (1990) *Reconstructing Schizophrenia*. London: Routledge.

Bentall, R. (2004) *Madness Explained: Psychosis and Human Nature*. London: Penguin.

Birchwood, M., Smith, J., Cochrane, R., Wetton, S. and Copestake, S. (1990) The Social Functioning Scale: The development and validation of a new scale of social adjustment for use in family intervention programmes with schizophrenic patients. *British Journal of Psychiatry*, 157, 853–859.

Bond, G. R., Resnick, S. G., Drake, R. E., Xie, H., McHugo, G. J. and Rebout, R. R. (2001) Does competitive employment improve nonvocational outcomes for people with severe mental illness? *Journal of Consulting and Clinical Psychology*, 6, 489–501.

Boyle, M. (2002) *Schizophrenia – A Scientific Delusion?* 2nd edn. London: Routledge.

Brown, G. W., Birley, J. L. T. and Wing, J. K. (1972) Influence of family life on the course of schizophrenic disorder: A replication. *British Journal of Psychiatry*, 121, 241–258.

Bryson, G., Morris, D. B., Lysaker, P. and Zito, W. (1997) The Work Behaviour Inventory: A scale for the assessment of work behaviour for people with severe mental illness. *Psychiatric Rehabilitation Journal*, 20(4), 47–54.

Buchanan, J. (1995) Social support and schizophrenia: A review of the literature. *Archives of Psychiatric Nursing*, 9(2), 68–76.

Burgess, P. W. and Shallice, T. (1996) Bizarre responses, rule detection and frontal lobe lesions. *Cortex*, 32, 241–259.

Butcher, J. N., Graham, J. R., Williams, C. L. and Ben-Porath, Y. S. (1990) *Development and Use of the MMPI-2 Content Scales*. Minneapolis, MN: University of Minnesota Press.

Chadwick, P. D. J. and Birchwood, M. (1995) The omnipotence of voices II: The beliefs about voices questionnaire. *British Journal of Psychology*, 165, 773–776.

Coughlan, A. K. and Hollows, S. E. (1985) *The Adult Memory and Information Processing Battery (AMIPB)*. Leeds: A. K. Coughlan.

Day, J. C., Wood, G., Dewey, M. and Bentall, R. P. (1995) A self-rating scale for measuring neuroleptic side-effects: Validation in a group of schizophrenic patients. *British Journal of Psychiatry*, 166(5), 650–653.

Department of Health (DoH) (1999) *National Service Framework for Mental Health.* London: The Stationery Office.

Department of Health (DoH) (2000) *Effective Care Co-ordination in Mental Health Services: Modernising the Care Programme Approach.* London: DoH.

Derogatis, L. N. (1994) SCL-90-R. *Administration, Scoring and Procedures Manual,* 3rd edn. Minneapolis, MN: National Computer Systems.

Derogatis, L. R. and Melisaratos, N. (1983) The Brief Symptom Inventory: An introductory report. *Psychological Medicine,* 13, 596–605.

Dooley, D., Prause, J. and Ham-Rowbottom, K. A. (2000) Underemployment and depression: Longitudinal relationships. *Journal of Health and Social Behaviour,* 41, 421–436.

Emsley, R., Rabinowitz, J. and Torreman, M. (2003) The factor structure for the Positive and Negative Syndrome Scale (PANSS) in recent onset psychosis. *Schizophrenia Research,* 61(1), 47–57.

Endicott, J., Spilz, R. L., Fless, J. L. and Cohen, J. (1976) The Global Assessment Scale. *Archives of General Psychiatry,* 33, 766–772.

Gavin, D. R., Ross, H. E. and Skinner, H. (1989) Diagnostic Validity of the Drug Abuse Screening Test in the assessment of DSM-III drug disorders. *British Journal of Addiction,* 84, 301–307.

Gibson, C. (1992) A revised conceptualisation of social support. *Journal of Clinical Nursing,* 1(5), 283–288.

Ginsberg, J. P. (2003) Wechsler Test of Adult Reading. *Applied Neuropsychology,* 10(3), 182–184.

Gold, J., Iannone, V., McMahon, R. and Buchanan, R. (2001) Cognitive correlates of competitive employment among patients with schizophrenia. *Schizophrenia Research,* 49, 134.

Goldberg, T. E. (1972) *The Detection of Psychiatric Illness by Questionnaire.* London: Oxford University Press.

Griffiths, R. D. P. (1977) The prediction of psychiatric patients' work adjustment in the community. *British Journal of Social and Clinical Psychology,* 16, 165–173.

Haddock, G., McCarron, J., Tarrier, N. and Faragher, E. D. (1999) Scales to assess dimensions of hallucinations and delusions: The Psychotic Symptom Rating Scales (PSYRATS). *Psychological Medicine,* 29(4), 879–889.

Heaton, R. K. (1981) *Wisconsin Card Sorting Test Manual.* Odessa, FL: Psychological Assessment Resources.

Henderson, S., Bryne, D. G. and Duncan-Jones, P. (1981) *Neurosis and the Social Environment.* Sydney: Academic Press.

Hirschberg, W. (1985) Social isolation among schizophrenic outpatients. *Social Psychiatry,* 20, 171–178.

Horowitz, L. M., Rosenberg, S. E., Baer, B. A., Ureno, G. and Villasenor, V. S. (1988) Inventory of Interpersonal Problems: Psychometric properties and clinical applications. *Journal of Consulting and Clinical Psychology,* 56, 885–892.

Howarth, C., Kenway, P., Palmer, G. and Street, C. (1998) *Monitoring Poverty and Social Exclusion: Labour's Inheritance.* York: Joseph Rowntree Foundation.

Jablensky, A., Sartorius, N., Ernberg, G., Anker, M., Korten, A., Cooper, J. E. et al. (1992) Schizophrenia: Manifestations, incidence and course in different cultures: A World Health Organisation ten-country study. *Psychological Medicine Monograph Supplementary,* 20, 1–97.

Jenson, A. R. and Rohwer, W. D. (1966) The Stroop Clour-Word Test: A review. *Acta Psychologica*, 25, 36–93.

Katz, M. M. and Lyerly, S. B. (1963) Methods for measuring adjustment and social behaviour in the community: 1. Rationale, description, discriminative validity and scale development. *Psychological Reports*, 13, 503–535.

Kavanagh, D. (1992) Recent developments in expressed emotion and schizophrenia. *British Journal of Psychiatry*, 160, 601–620.

Kay, S., Opler, L. and Lindenmayer, J. P. (1989) The positive and negative syndrome scale (PANSS): Rationale and standardisation. *British Journal of Psychiatry*, 155 (suppl 7), 59–65.

Lavender, A. and Watts, F. N. (1994) Rehabilitation: Investigation. In: S. J. E. Lindsay and G. E. Powell (eds) *The Handbook of Clinical Adult Psychology*, 2nd edn. London: Routledge.

Leiper, R., Pilling, S. and Lavender, A. (1992) *Implementing a Quality Review System: The QUARTZ Manuals*. Brighton: Pavilion.

Lofquist, L. H. and Dawis, R. V. (1975) Vocational needs, work reinforcers and job satisfaction. *Vocational Guidance Quarterly*, 24, 132–139.

McFarlane, A. H., Neale, K. A., Norman, G. R., Roy, R. G. and Strener, D. L. (1981) Methodological issues in developing a scale to measure social support. *Schizophrenia Bulletin*, 7, 90–100.

Miller, F., Dworkin, J., Ward, M. and Barone, D. (1990) A preliminary study of unresolved grief in families of seriously mentally ill patients. *Hospital and Community Psychiatry*, 41, 1321–1325.

Millon, T. (1994) *Millon Clinical Multiaxial Inventory – III (Manual)*. Minneapolis, MN: National Computer Systems.

Mueser, K. T., Becker, D. R., Torrey, W. C., Xie, H., Bond, G. R., Drake, R. E. and Bradley, J. D. (1997) Work and non-vocational domains of functioning in persons with severe mental illness: A longitudinal analysis. *Journal of Nervous and Mental Disease*, 185(7), 419–426.

Mundt, J. C., Marks, I. M., Shear, M. K. and Greist, J. M. (2002) The Work and Social Adjustment Scale: A simple measure of impairment in functioning. *British Journal of Psychiatry*, 180(5), 461–464.

Munetz, M. and Benjamin, S. (1988) How to examine patients using the abnormal involuntary movement scale. *Hospital and Community Psychiatry*, 39, 1172–1177.

Nelson, H. E. (1982) *The National Adult Reading Test (NART)*. Windsor, UK: NFER-Nelson.

Nelson, H. E. (1976) A modified card sorting test sensitive to frontal lobe deficits. *Cortex*, 12, 313–324.

Nelson, H. E., Pantelis, C., Carruthers, K., Speller, J. Baxendale, S. and Barnes, T. R. E. (1990) Cognitive functioning and symptomatology in chronic schizophrenia. *Psychological Medicine*, 20, 357–365.

Novaco, R. (1975) *Anger Control: The Development and Evaluation of an Experimental Treatment*. New York: Lexicon Books.

Office of the Deputy Prime Minister (ODPM) (2004) *Mental Health and Social Exclusion: Social Exclusion Unit Report*. London: Office of the Deputy Prime Minister.

O'Flynn, D. (2001) Approaching employment: Mental health, work projects, and the care program approach. *Psychiatric Bulletin*, 25, 169–171.

Parry, G. (1991) Domestic roles. In: F. N. Watts and D. H. Bennett (eds) *Theory and Practice of Psychiatric Rehabilitation*, 2nd edn. Chichester: John Wiley.

Penn, D. L., Mueser, K. M., Spaulding, W., Hope, D. A. and Reed, D. (1995) Information processing and social competence in chronic schizophrenia. *Schizophrenia Bulletin*, 21, 269–281.

Perkins, R. and Rinaldi, M. (2002) Unemployment rates among patients with long-term mental health problems: A decade of rising unemployment. *Psychiatric Bulletin*, 26(8), 295–298.

Raven, J. C. (1992) *Manual for Raven's Progressive Matrices and Mill Hill Vocabulary Scales*. Oxford: Oxford Psychologists Press.

Reitan, R. M. (1958) Validity of the Trail Making Test as an indicator of organic brain damage. *Perceptual and Motor Skills*, 8, 271–276.

Rosen, A., Hadzi-Pavlovic, D. and Parker, G. (1989) The Life Skills Profile: A measure assessing function and disability in schizophrenia. *Schizophrenia Bulletin*, 15, 325–337.

Rosenberg, M. (1965) *Society and the Adolescent Self Image*. Princeton, NJ: Princeton University Press.

Sayers, M. D., Bellack, A. S., Wade, J. H., Bennett, M. E. and Fong, P. (1995) An empirical method for assessing social problem solving in schizophrenia. *Behaviour Modification*, 19, 267–289.

Saunders, J. B., Aaasland, O. G., Babor, T. F., DeLaFuente, J. R. and Grant, M. (1993) Development of the Alcohol Use Disorders Identification Test (AUDIT): WHO collaborative project on early detection of persons with harmful alcohol consumption. *Addiction*, 88, 296–303.

Shallice, T. (1982) Specific impairments of planning. *Philosophical Transactions of the Royal Society of London. Series B. Biological Sciences*, 298, 199–209.

Sullivan, W. and Poertner, J. (1989) Social support and life stress: A mental health consumer's perspective. *Community Mental Health Journal*, 25(1), 21–32

Tarrier, N., Barrowclough, C., Vaughn, C., Bamrah, J. S. et al. (1988) The community management of schizophrenia: A controlled trial of behavioural intervention with families to reduce relapse. *British Journal of Psychiatry*, 153, 532–542.

Taylor, P. J., Garety, P., Buchanan, A., Reed, A., Wessely, S., Katarzyna, R. et al. (1994) In: J. Monahan and H. J. Steadman (eds) *Violence and Mental Disorder: Developments in Risk Assessment*. Chicago: University of Chicago Press.

Tollefson, G. D. (1996) Cognitive function in schizophrenic patients. *Journal of Clinical Psychiatry*, 57, 31–39.

Van Egmond, J. (2003) The multiple meanings of secondary gain. *American Journal of Psychoanalysis*, 63(2), 137–147.

Wallice, C. J., Liberman, R. P., Tauber, R. and Wallace, J. (2000) The Independent Living Skills Survey: A comprehensive measure of the community functioning of severely and persistently mentally ill individuals. *Schizophrenia Bulletin*, 26, 631–658.

Walsh, O. F. and Harman, C. P. (1989) Family views of stigma. *Schizophrenia Bulletin*, 15(1), 131–139.

Ware, J. E. and Sherbourne, C. D. (1992) The MOS 36-item short-form health survey (SF-36): I. Conceptual framework and item selection. *Medical Care*, 30(6), 473–483.

Warner, R. (2004) *Recovery from Schizophrenia: Psychiatry and Political Economy.* Hove, UK: Brunner-Routledge.

Warrington, E. K. (1984) *Recognition Memory Test.* Windsor, UK: NFER-Nelson.

Watts, F. N. (1978) A study of work behaviour in a psychiatric rehabilitation unit. *British Journal of Social and Clinical Psychology,* 17, 85–92.

Watts, F. N. (1991) Employment. In: F. N. Watts and D. H. Bennett (eds) *Theory and Practice of Psychiatric Rehabilitation.* Chichester: John Wiley.

Wechsler, D. (1997a) *Wechsler Adult Intelligence Scale,* 3rd edn. *Administration and Scoring Manual.* San Antonio, TX: Psychological Corporation.

Wechsler (1997b) *Wechsler Memory Scale,* 3rd edn. San Antonio, TX: Psychological Corporation.

Weiss, D. S. and Marmar, C. R. (1997) The Impact of Event Scale – Revised. In: J. P. Wilson and T. M. Keane (eds) *Assessing Psychological Trauma and PTSD.* New York: Guilford Press.

Wilson, B. A., Cockburn, J. and Baddley, A. (1985) *The Rivermead Behavioural Memory Test.* Reading, UK: Thames Valley Test Company.

Wing, J. K. (1978) Social influences on the course of schizophrenia. In: L. C. Wynne, R. L. Cromwell and S. Matthysse (eds) *The Nature of Schizophrenia: New Approaches to Research and Theory.* Chichester: John Wiley.

Wing, J. K., Curtis, R. H. and Beevor, A. S. (1996) *HONOS, Health of the Nation Outcome Scales: Report on Research and Development.* London: Research Unit, Royal College of Psychiatrists.

World Health Organization (WHO) (1998) *Quality of Life Questionnaire.* Geneva: WHO.

Wykes, T. and Castle, D. (2003) Cognitive dysfunction in schizophrenia. In: D. Castle, D. L. Copolov and T. Wykes (eds) *Pharmacological and Psychosocial Treatments in Schizophrenia.* London: Martin Dunitz.

Wykes, T. and Sturt, E. (1986) The measurement of social behaviour in psychiatric patients: An assessment of the reliability and validity of the S.S. schedule. *British Journal of Psychiatry,* 148, 1–11.

Zubin, J. and Spring, B. (1977) Vulnerability: A new view of schizophrenia. *Journal of Abnormal Psychology,* 86, 103–126.

Chapter 28

Psychosocial rehabilitation

Intervention

Nick Lake and Tony Lavender

INTRODUCTION

Psychological interventions in psychosocial rehabilitation need to be based on a thorough assessment of a client (see Chapter 27). This helps to ensure that: (1) the intervention is what the client wants; (2) the client has the physical, cognitive, emotional and social capacity to manage the demands of a particular role; (3) the environmental demands are not excessive and likely to make a client more vulnerable; (4) appropriate resources are available to support the client; and (5) resources are being targeted effectively.

In Chapter 27 we proposed that the objective of psychosocial rehabilitation is to enable people to make the best use of their abilities in as valued a social context as possible and we outlined a framework for assessment. This assessment information can be used to develop a psychological formulation and to plan interventions that aim to support and enable clients to function at their optimum level. This chapter reviews the range of interventions that are currently available to help individuals fulfil these aims. The interventions themselves may take place in a variety of service contexts, including acute in-patient wards, medium/long-term hostels, voluntary and social services residential and day-care facilities, and through work done by staff from community mental health teams, assertive outreach teams, early intervention teams and crisis resolution/home treatment teams (Department of Health (DoH), 1999; Lavender and Paxton, 2004).

In psychosocial treatment programmes, psychologists can intervene at a number of levels by: (1) working directly with individuals on improving their capacity to take on the physical, cognitive, emotional and social demands of a particular role; (2) working directly with individuals to help them to become more competent in taking on particular social roles in particular environments; (3) providing training and support for those who interact with the individual; and (4) altering or changing aspects of the environment itself.

Readers are encouraged to read Chapter 27 before this one, as it introduces a number of concepts, and a framework for assessment and intervention, that are drawn on further here. Much of the work reviewed below relates primarily to psychosocial interventions targeted at people suffering from psychotic experiences. This is partly because of the space limitations in this chapter, but it also reflects the relative lack of a broad research base into psychosocial interventions (rather than treatment) for some of the other more severe and enduring mental health problems. Research into psychosocial rehabilitation in individuals suffering from the symptoms of bipolar disorder is particularly underdeveloped although increasing (Craighead et al., 1998).

DIRECT WORK WITH THE INDIVIDUAL: IMPROVING CAPACITY

To accomplish a particular social role, an individual must have the physical, cognitive, emotional and social *capacity* to take on the role, such as sufficient physical health, cognitive abilities, emotional stability, interpersonal understanding and motivation, to meet the demands of a role. Psychosocial interventions that aim to address an individual's competencies and capabilities (i.e. his or her ability to actually carry out particular roles in different environmental contexts) are reviewed in subsequent sections (see Chapter 27 for definitions of capacity, competence and capability).

Understanding the client and developing the therapeutic alliance

For many years, the institutionalisation of individuals with severe and enduring mental health problems resulted in a significant emotional distance between 'patients' and 'staff'. This was reinforced by a very medical view of problems like psychosis, and a subsequent lack of interest in the desires, personality, views and feelings of individuals suffering from it (Repper, 2002; Bentall, 2004). There was also a common belief that talking to an individual about his or her experiences could worsen the 'illness'. Yet it is clear from research in other clinical populations that the quality of the therapeutic alliance is a central factor in predicting outcome. It is also central to the success of any psychosocial rehabilitation programme (Repper, 2002). This view is supported by the literature emerging from the increasingly powerful user movement.

As a service user (cited in Howe, 1993 p 16) puts it:

> First, I need to feel secure and I need to feel safe. My sense of security will be helped if I perceive you to be warm and friendly. And finally, you must accept me for what I am. You must acknowledge my thoughts and not deny my feelings, however bizarre or painful or perverse they might at first appear.

Developing a trusting relationship is not always easy when people are suffering from the serious positive and negative symptoms that can accompany severe and enduring mental health problems. But the building of rapport is critical and is helped by trying to really understand a client. This includes developing an understanding of the client's desires, views about his or her difficulties and about what 'recovery' means to him or her, his or her motivation, perceived strengths and weaknesses, and views on relationships. The professional must adopt an open, non-judgemental attitude that is sensitive to the client's values, beliefs and emotions, and while it is important to maintain a sense of optimism and to be clear about what a professional might offer, it is important that goals are set collaboratively and that the pace of change is realistic. Once rapport is established, it may begin to be possible for a psychologist to gently challenge some of the negative beliefs and attitudes that may be impacting on a client's motivation to take on more valued social roles, and to mutually explore alternatives to them.

Physical capacity and psychological adjustment to disability

To succeed in a psychosocial role, individuals must have the physical capacity to take on the role. Working with physical difficulties is usually the role of the medic or occupational therapist, the latter often adapting the environment to meet the needs of the individual. However, a clinical psychologist might help an individual to come to terms with a disability he or she has acquired through accident, illness or as a result of ageing. A person's psychological response to a physical difficulty can also result in a more severe disability than might be expected from the physical problem alone. Psychologists working with people with severe and enduring mental health problems have a broad literature in the area of health psychology to draw on (Camic and Knight, 2004).

Cognitive capacity and cognitive remediation

In Chapter 27 we outlined the evidence for the cognitive deficits that accompany many forms of more serious mental health difficulties, particularly psychosis, and explored how these can be assessed. Evidence suggests that cognitive performance is often the key predictor of success in a variety of psychosocial and vocational rehabilitation programmes (Twamley et al., 2003a). It is perhaps inevitable that clinical and research attention has therefore increasingly focused on programmes that directly aim to help individuals improve their cognitive capacity, or overcome their cognitive deficits on particular tasks.

In the area of severe and enduring mental health problems, a set of techniques known as cognitive remediation has received considerable research and clinical interest over recent years (Wykes and Van der Gaag, 2001). Although there are several different approaches, each shares the aim of improving cognitive performance by training individuals on particular tasks. Individuals usually direct their own learning efforts and the tasks come in various forms, including paper-and-pencil tasks and computer-based tasks. The tasks are carefully selected so that the individual can accomplish them but so that some learning and cognitive 'stretching' is required for the individual to be successful. The tasks should aim to bring about improvements in a specific task or one specific cognitive strategy (e.g. planning skills). The assumption is that, like physical training, cognitive remediation can identify weak areas of cognition and strengthen them through cognitive exercises (Spaulding et al., 1998).

There are too many cognitive remediation strategies from different research strands to be reviewed here. In their review of these strategies, Wykes and van der Gaag (2001) argue that three types of strategy, used across approaches, are likely to be particularly important in achieving positive outcomes. They named these strategies verbalising action criteria (in which the client verbalises the strategy and task description out loud in preparation for a task), errorless learning techniques (leading the client gradually through the different stages of a task at a pace where errors rarely occur) and scaffolding (providing learning support for tasks which only increase in difficulty very gradually over time).

Unfortunately, the evidence base for the effectiveness of such interventions has yet to be established. Although improvements are sometimes seen in experimental settings (e.g. an academic research institution) on specific and clearly defined cognitive tasks, it is not clear what causes the improvements on specific tests. Pilling et al. (2002a) conducted a meta-analytic review of five recent randomised controlled trails (RCTs) examining the effect of cognitive remediation in people suffering from psychosis. Unfortunately, the results indicated that cognitive remediation had no benefit on attention, verbal memory, visual memory, planning, cognitive flexibility or mental state. Other reviews have been more positive. For example, Twamley et al. (2003b), in their review of 17 RCTs, concluded that cognitive training (in various forms) 'held promise' for improving cognitive performance, symptoms and everyday functioning. However, they also criticised many studies for failing to look beyond changes on cognitive tests to changes in functioning in the real world, and there was no evidence that these effects would be generalisable to other contexts or sustainable.

Bellack et al. (1999) argue that cognitive remediation is unlikely to prove beneficial over the longer term and that clinicians should instead focus on environmental interventions aimed at supporting clients to take on valuable social roles with the cognitive deficits they have. The research programme being pursued by Wykes and colleagues (Wykes et al., 2003) seems more promising. The jury is still out, and it is not yet clear that, like social skills training, these cognitive remediation techniques have any real impact on improving cognitive performance beyond the specific task setting or over the longer term.

Emotional capacity and individual psychological therapy

Many therapeutic approaches aim to help individuals overcome emotional difficulties. All can be drawn on when helping an individual suffering from severe and enduring mental health problems to overcome the range of emotional difficulties that might be hindering that person in his or her attempts to take on valued roles in society. In recent years, a number of specific approaches have been developed to help with the particularly disabling psychotic experiences. These interventions can play a vital role in psychosocial rehabilitation programmes because these symptoms (e.g. the positive and negative symptoms of psychosis or the manic element of bipolar disorder) often interfere with a person's attempts to take on valued social roles, or with his or her belief that he or she can do so successfully. A brief description of these approaches are outlined below.

The treatment of hallucinations and delusions

Experiences such as voices and delusional beliefs can have an extremely negative impact on an individual's capacity to take on a social role, and can easily alienate other people in that environment. Evidence now points to the effectiveness of cognitive-behaviour therapy in helping to moderate these positive symptoms of psychosis (Pilling et al., 2002b) and this can include drug-resistant hallucinations and delusions (Tarrier et al., 1993; Sensky et al., 2000; National Institute for Health and Clinical Excellence (NICE), 2002). Much of the evidence comes from research in the UK, although the number of studies and the number of participants are still relatively small. The cognitive-behavioural approaches include the following.

Coping strategy enhancement

Coping strategy enhancement (CSE) provides specific strategies for helping a client identify and improve the coping strategies and resources he or she uses to manage his or her positive symptoms. These strategies include going for a run, blocking intrusive thoughts by listening to loud music, distracting oneself from one's symptoms and rationally challenging the accuracy of one's beliefs. Such an approach has proven effective in managing the positive symptoms of psychosis (Tarrier, 1987), although there are concerns that these gains may not be maintained or result in improved social functioning (Tarrier et al., 1993).

Cognitive-behaviour therapy and delusional experiences

Cognitive-behaviour therapy (CBT) for delusions involves working actively with a client to identify the range of possible explanations for the belief and examining the evidence for each explanation (Chadwick et al., 1994; Fowler et al., 1997). It is not about directly challenging a client's belief but instead involves a collaborative approach in which the therapist and client explore together how the belief developed, the client's level of conviction in the belief, the evidence for and against the client's belief, alternative explanations for the belief and the evidence for these, the identification of possible thinking errors, and an exploration of the consequences of thinking in particular ways (Everitt and Siddle, 2002).

Cognitive-behaviour therapy and hallucinations

CBT for hallucinations is similar to the above, and focuses on the client's beliefs about the voices or images that are experienced. Focusing techniques (Bentall et al., 1994) are also used to enable a client to become much more familiar with the properties of the voices in a way that enables a client to make links between these voices and his or her own thoughts, and thus help to challenge the belief that they come from forces outside the client. In addition, distraction techniques (Margo et al., 1981) are used to redirect a client's attention away from the hallucinations and thereby reduce the client's distress.

Summary

Research and developments into CBT for psychosis is still at an early stage of development. Initial findings suggest that it is useful in helping to reduce the frequency and intensity of hallucinations and delusions and the distress caused by them (NICE, 2002). It is not yet clear how this success might translate into improved social functioning, and into improved outcomes on psychosocial rehabilitation programmes. Fowler et al. (1997) provide an accessible practical guide to work with hallucinations and delusions.

The treatment of negative symptoms

The negative symptoms that can accompany psychosis and other severe mental health problems include alogia (impoverished thinking, including poverty of speech and thought blocking), anergia (a lack of energy or drive), anhedonia (a loss of interest in previously enjoyable activities) and emotional blunting (a difficulty in experiencing and demonstrating emotion). Each of these symptoms has a significant effect on an individual's capacity and motivation to carry out social roles, and can cause anger and resentment in people around the individual (Barrowclough and Tarrier, 1992). The assessment and treatment of these symptoms is therefore central to the success of any intervention programme.

The treatment of negative symptoms requires careful thought and patience. It is important not to place too many demands on the client too quickly, and shorter but more frequent meetings with a psychologist can be appropriate. The techniques used in the behavioural treatment of depression are usually the most effective. This includes graded task assignment (in which tasks are broken down into small manageable components) and activity scheduling (in which careful thought is given to the timing and demands of different activities in order to increase feelings of achievement and to avoid the sense of things 'hanging-over' the client). Cognitive restructuring techniques are also used, in which the therapist collaboratively identifies an individual's 'unhelpful' beliefs, identifies alternatives, and uses a variety of behavioural experiments to test out the reality of each.

There is little research into the effectiveness of cognitive-behavioural approaches in treating the negative symptoms of psychosis, although a study by Sensky et al. (2000) found improvements in negative symptoms and depressive symptoms at 9 months follow up.

The treatment of the symptoms of severe depression

All schools of psychological therapy offer treatments to individuals suffering from depressive symptoms, although the most thoroughly researched psychological intervention is Beck's cognitive-behaviour therapy (CBT) for depression (Beck et al., 1979). The techniques used are very similar to the approach taken for the negative symptoms of psychosis. The central components include cognitive restructuring, graded task assignment and activity scheduling. Evidence for its effectiveness in reducing symptoms is overwhelming (NICE, 2004). However, the evidence for its effectiveness in treating the symptoms of longstanding and severe depression, without the use of antidepressants, is less clear cut (Elkin et al., 1989) and there is a lack of evidence for the effects lasting beyond 2 years (Roth and Fonagy, 2004).

The other effective treatment for depression, with a clear research base, is interpersonal therapy (Elkin et al., 1989). This approach focuses primarily on the interpersonal problems that accompany (or possibly underlie) the depressive symptoms. The focus of such work is often on unresolved bereavement, interpersonal conflicts, social isolation, role transitions and interpersonal deficits. Again, the approach seems more beneficial in individuals with less severe symptoms and in individuals who have a higher level of pre-existing social functioning.

The treatment of the symptoms of bipolar disorder

Comparatively few research studies have examined the effectiveness of psychological treatments for bipolar disorder. There has been some success with psychoeducational interventions and cognitive-behavioural interventions aimed at improving medication compliance (Newman et al., 2001; Otto and Reilly-Harrington, 2002). Given that medication compliance has such an important role in preventing relapse of bipolar symptoms, and given the extremely negative impact of manic and depressive symptoms on work, finances, self-care, family relationships and friendships, it is important for psychosocial rehabilitation programmes to view medication compliance as a key part of their rehabilitative efforts for individuals vulnerable to the symptoms of bipolar disorder.

There is preliminary evidence that CBT is effective in enabling individuals to better manage the life stresses that can trigger bipolar symptoms, to recognise warning signs, and to develop coping strategies to manage their symptoms when they occur (e.g. Lam et al., 2000). The first stages of such cognitive-behavioural interventions focus on the treatment of depressive symptoms using psychoeducation and the techniques of cognitive restructuring and activity assignment. In subsequent stages, relapse prevention warning signs (or signatures) are identified for both the manic and depressive phases of the condition, and strategies are developed to help an individual to implement strategies for dealing with the emergence of symptoms when they occur.

Social capacity and social skills training

Given the vital role of social performance in most psychosocial roles, a great deal of effort has gone into designing and evaluating social skills training programmes for this client group. Most programmes draw on learning theory and involve working directly with clients to help them to acquire the social skills required in different social roles. Interventions include teaching an individual to pick up and correctly interpret social cues such as gestures, facial expression, tone of voice. Other interventions teach social problem solving skills or social cognition. Here, individuals must learn to correctly analyse social stimulus and plan appropriate responses.

As previously outlined, it is critical to conduct a detailed assessment of an individual's social skills deficits, and the contexts in which they need to apply the skills, to plan an effective intervention. Sometimes an individual may not have the appropriate social skills because cognitive or emotional difficulties interfered with peer relationships at school where these skills are initially learnt. Sometimes an individual may have these skills but fail to apply them in particular situations. This might be because of poor motivation, emotional difficulties (e.g. the negative symptoms of psychosis), or a lack of positive reinforcement in the environment for that behaviour.

Lauriello et al. (1999) identify three different forms of training that they call the 'basic model', the 'social problem-solving model' and the 'cognitive remediation model'.

The basic social skills model

This involves breaking down appropriate social behaviour into its constituent parts, assessing these constituent parts and then helping a client to improve his or her skill in each of these different elements through direct teaching of that skill, through therapist modelling, through repeated practice and homework, and through positive reinforcement. The basic social skills approach would focus on teaching a skill (e.g. turn-taking in conversation), initially in isolation, before integrating it with other social skills through role plays and eventually in external settings.

The social problem-solving model

This focuses on identifying and addressing the information-processing or cognitive deficits that are assumed to underlie difficulties in social performance. Complex social behaviours are again broken down into their constituent parts but particular focus in this model is paid to overcoming deficits in receptive learning, cognitive processing and social problem solving, and in responding skills (Lauriello et al., 1999). The aim is to help individuals to develop the cognitive skills to respond more flexibly to different social situations. There is a growing body of evidence to support the effectiveness of this model (Liberman et al., 1998).

Cognitive remediation and social skills training

Cognitive remediation aims to help individuals to address the cognitive deficits that underlie their difficulties in social performance. In this approach to social skills training, the enhancement of cognitive performance thus occurs as a precursor to training in specific social skills (see the section Cognitive capacity and cognitive remediation, above). One of the best examples is integrated psychological treatment (IPT; Brenner et al., 1994) for people experiencing symptoms of psychosis. In this approach, clients meet in groups three times a week and do three distinct sets of task. The first, the 'cognitive differentiation subprograms', use computer tasks that aim to address the specific cognitive impairments that underlie a person's social difficulties (e.g. to attend to the non-verbal cues in conversation). The second, the 'social perception and verbal communication subprograms', focus more on social perception. The third, the 'social skills and interpersonal problem solving subprograms', use techniques from more traditional social skill programmes. Whilst some support has been obtained for this approach, the same problems in generalising the skills learnt also apply to this approach (Wykes et al., 1999).

The evidence base

Reviews of social skills training research have generally reached positive conclusions about its effectiveness (e.g. Corrigan, 1991; Heinssen et al., 2000; Bellack, 2004). Overall, social skills training would appear to result in improvements in the specific social skills that are the focus of the intervention and clients report improved social confidence and general satisfaction with the outcome of such programmes.

One of the longstanding concerns has been the failure of social skills training to generalise to other settings. Studies that have included specific strategies designed to help generalisation or increase an individual's social capability (e.g. by including the use of community supports) have been more successful in achieving generalisation across settings (Tauber et al., 2000) and there is now a growing body of evidence documenting the success of combining social skills training with community case management (e.g. Glynn et al., 2002). This suggests that much more attention needs to be paid to the issue of generalisation of skills learnt, and that researchers should be careful to distinguish between the ability to perform social skills in particular settings (social competence) and the ability to generalise these skills across social contexts (social capability).

DEVELOPING COMPETENCIES IN SOCIAL ROLES THROUGH WORKING WITH THE INDIVIDUAL

Mental health services often pay too little attention to the psychosocial needs of clients, and this includes their education and employment needs. The Social Exclusion Unit (Office of the Deputy Prime Minister (ODPM), 2004), found that 35% of service user respondents thought that health and social services placed a low emphasis on employment. Only 6% thought that it was given a high priority. This is despite clear evidence that valued social roles can protect against relapse. In contrast, services tended to emphasise the health and psychiatric needs of clients.

Effective care co-ordination should take a broad perspective and include assessments of all of an individual's psychosocial needs. As outlined previously, it is vital to ensure that a psychosocial intervention programme for any social role is based on a comprehensive assessment, and is developed mutually between client and professional. This ensures that the interventions are not targeted inappropriately and that the intervention will not overwhelm the client.

Psychosocial interventions targeted at individuals' competencies and capabilities are reviewed below.

Work and educational roles

Despite the fact that the UK spends approximately £140 million pounds a year on vocational and day services for people with mental health problems (ODPM, 2004), we lag well behind the USA in supporting this group to obtain and maintain either meaningful employment, or education that might lead to meaningful employment. The gap is large; the Labour Force Survey (Office for National Statistics, 2003) concluded that only 24% of people with long-term mental health problems were in work in the UK, compared to up to 58% in the US (Crowther et al., 2004), although the government now requires all clients under enhanced community psychiatric assessment (CPA) to have active plans to help them develop suitable occupational activity (DOH, 1999).

A number of factors impact on an individual's ability to take on work and educational roles. These can include physical, cognitive, social and emotional difficulties. Difficulties can also result from low self-confidence, the danger of losing hard-won welfare benefits, and the lack of support in finding and maintaining a suitable job or educational opportunity. Low expectations of staff and trainers, and negative employer attitudes, can also be to blame (see the sections Changing the environment in mental health and social services settings and Community settings, below).

There are different models of vocational support for people suffering from severe and enduring mental health problems (ODPM, 2004). A longstanding approach is the sheltered workshop, where individuals are provided with employment opportunities in a protected setting. Unfortunately, there is typically a fairly high staff ratio in these settings that makes it expensive, the pay for service users is poor, service users often do not value the work, and this approach often fails to help users to move on to employment in the community. Part of the problem is that the work in these sheltered workshops often does not reflect what would be expected in the real world. Sheltered workshops therefore do little for social inclusion, although they are evidently valuable for some clients.

'Social firms' are a step forward from sheltered workshops in that they create employment in a supported setting but aim to trade their goods or services on the open market. There is therefore a sense of 'worthiness' to the work being done. 'Train and place' models provide another step forward in that they aim to enable a client to gain work skills in a sheltered setting but with the aim of eventually helping individuals to obtain work in the community.

Supported employment schemes are increasingly seen as the most effective way of helping individuals to obtain meaningful employment. Supported employment aims to help an individual to find immediate work in the community. The most influential, and the one with the clearest evidence base (Crowther et al., 2004), is the Individual Placement and Support (IPS) model. IPS aims to help individuals find immediate employment in a suitable post in the community, with support that includes ongoing advice and support from vocational workers, job-search support and a constant assessment of an individual's employment needs. Research from the USA clearly supports its effectiveness (Twamley et al., 2003a), with individuals having higher incomes and fewer symptoms than those in other models of employment. IPS is also preferred by service users (Torrey et al., 1995).

Psychologists have a role in their individual and group therapeutic work in supporting clients with the challenges faced in employment and education. This can include providing vocational guidance (taking into account capacity and interests), helping to deal with interpersonal difficulties faced in the educational environment and workplace, and using social skills training (especially role play) to help clients prepare for interviews, meeting with managers and other interpersonal challenges. Psychologists also need to encourage their teams to give more attention to the vocational and educational needs of their clients.

Domestic roles

Psychologists do not usually get involved in helping individuals to develop competencies in domestic skills such as cooking, washing and money management. The literature in this area will therefore not be reviewed here. It is important to note that psychologists are well placed to provide a detailed assessment of a client's capacity to become competent in different domestic roles (see Chapter 27). They are also well placed to offer advice and consultation on how to use operant conditioning principles so that successful domestic performance is accompanied by rewards that reinforce the behaviour.

Family roles

Whereas there has been considerable research into helping individuals to develop occupational roles, there has been considerably less research into supporting someone with their family roles. An individual's competency in the role of parent usually receives most attention from professionals. However, the role of partner is also important, as the breakdown of a relationship is one of the key stresses that can precipitate relapse.

A number of community resources are available to help mothers and fathers to develop the parenting skills required to care for their children (Reder and Lucey, 1995). However, people with mental health problems may face prejudice and discrimination in such contexts and there can sometimes be a role for setting up such classes in sheltered settings. Also, mental health professionals may sometimes have specific concerns. When these concerns are significant, the mental health professional should contact the appropriate statutory agencies; when the concerns are not so severe, a careful assessment of the specific skills and competencies required to be a good parent must be conducted to identify the areas in which the client needs support (Gopfert et al., 2004). It is also clear that becoming a parent is a significant life stressor and individuals who are vulnerable may need extra support to avoid relapse. This might include providing additional social care support, providing periods of respite care and identifying sources of support from the individual's wider family. Mental health professionals might also benefit from a knowledge of the self-help literature in this area so that they can make recommendations where appropriate (Gopfert et al. 2004).

In partnership roles, both partners have to work to maintain a relationship that is supportive and collaborative. When relationship difficulties occur, referrals should be made to specialists in relationship and family work where this is available. Whilst there are too many approaches to couple work to be reviewed here, it is important for any couple therapist to consider carefully the role that an individual's mental health difficulties may be having in the relationship. For example, at times an individual's mental health difficulties may be incorrectly targeted as the source of the marital difficulty. In other cases, an individual's symptoms might be being used by the couple as a way of masking other difficulties in the relationship. The impact of mental health difficulties may also change the nature of the relationship, from one based on mutual partnership to one of carer and 'cared for'. Following recovery, a couple may need support to enable them to re-establish more equal partnership roles.

Friendships

Friendships form a key part of our identity and are often central to our capacity to feel good about ourselves. However, evidence suggests that not all forms of social contact are useful or desirable for people suffering from severe and enduring mental health problems, and some forms can actually act as a stressor that can increase the risk of relapse. A comprehensive assessment of each individual's unique expectations for social relationships is therefore necessary. Once an assessment has identified the types of friendships that an individual desires, it is important to work collaboratively with that individual to explore how these relationships might be established in practice. It may be necessary to help an individual to overcome deficits in particular social skills (see the section Social capacity and social skills training, above) or to work through anxieties about interpersonal rejection or failure. Yet even if these difficulties are overcome, gaining and maintaining a valued set of relationships in the community can be a difficult task for individuals who sometimes suffer from unusual experiences, and this can be made worse by stigma and discrimination.

WORK WITH FAMILIES AND CARERS

There are mixed views about the role of families in causing psychosis. In Chapter 27 we explored the evidence that the family environment can have a significant role in shaping the expression of a person's psychotic experiences and in precipitating relapse. Other longer-term mental health problems can also be profoundly shaped by family relationships, including bipolar disorder (Miklowitz, 2002). This has led to a number of approaches to working directly with the families and carers of people suffering from longer-term mental health problems. Most of these approaches aim to help the family to reduce the likelihood of relapse in the individual suffering from psychosis or bipolar disorder. Much less attention has been paid to helping these individuals to take on or maintain valued roles within the family.

Perhaps the most well-researched approach is the Family Management model, which has proved to be particularly effective in reducing the likelihood of psychotic experiences returning (Lauriello et al., 1999). This is based on the research findings that individuals in families who exhibit a critical, hostile and over-involved interacting style (known as high expressed emotion) are more at risk of relapse (Leff, 1994). The approach aims to educate families or carers about the nature of psychosis and the need to support medication compliance, to help them to manage symptoms, to engage in less critical behaviours by improving their communication skills and to identify outside sources of support. Some interventions also teach family members and carers stress management techniques and problem solving skills.

A number of reviews have confirmed the benefits of this approach for individuals suffering from psychosis (Pilling et al., 2002b) although there have been too few studies to examine its effectiveness in individuals suffering from bipolar disorder (Craighead et al., 1998). The more recent tendency to treat families in groups, rather than individually, appears to be less effective (Pilling et al., 2002b). The evaluation studies tend not to assess the impact of these family interventions on the social adjustment and quality of life of individuals at risk (Lauriello et al., 1999). Hogarty et al. (1997) did look at the effect of family interventions on the client's social functioning but found no significant improvements between the experimental and control groups.

At times, it is important to work with a family containing a member with a longer-term mental health problem to help the family adjust to the impact of the onset of difficulties, to grieve for what might be lost as a result of it (e.g. financial security and family status), to adjust to changing roles in the family (e.g. who is the carer and provider of resources), to cope with the stigma and isolation they may feel and to help them to access community resources that might be available to help them feel better supported. With carers (family or otherwise) it may also be important to help them to set sufficient boundaries around their caring, or to identify other sources of support.

WORKING WITH THE ENVIRONMENT

Throughout, we have emphasised the central role of the environment in predicting the success of psychosocial rehabilitation programmes. The Social Desirability and Access model (Perkins and Repper, 1996) strongly argues that services need to think more about how to adapt the external environment to fit the needs of clients rather than necessarily expecting clients to accommodate to the environment. This focus on the environment requires a change in the patterns of work of mental health professionals and may be resisted by some who see it as less important than face-to-face work. Working with the external environment also requires careful thought if suggested changes are not to be seen as a criticism of what is already being done. It is therefore vital not to come in from an overly expert stance and to work jointly with those in the environment. In the following sections we give some examples of the type of work that psychologists might undertake to alter the environments of service users.

Changing the environment in mental health and social service settings

Mental health environments typically give insufficient attention to the psychosocial needs of clients and instead give more focus to acute physical and psychiatric difficulties. Staff can also have low expectations of success when it comes to helping individuals to find meaningful roles in society, and this can become a self-fulfilling prophesy. By encouraging staff to move away from a problem/symptom-focused approach towards a recovery-oriented model, psychologists can help to re-focus the attitudes of professionals towards the psychosocial needs of clients. This sometimes requires a cultural shift. The lack of psychosocial thinking and provision is particularly acute in in-patient settings and this has been a serious criticism in many recent government reports (e.g. Mental Health Act Commission and the Sainsbury Centre, 1997).

In-patient settings can actually be an extremely valuable setting for psychosocial rehabilitation because they provide the time to conduct a detailed assessment of a client's physical, cognitive, emotional and social capacity; they also often provide an opportunity to engage and work with the client's family, an opportunity to offer intensive input to clients, and they are settings where the perspective of many different professionals can be assimilated. Changing the culture of in-patient settings so that more focus is given to the psychosocial needs of clients often offers a significant challenge to psychologists and other staff. The psychologist may have to challenge the organisation of such settings, the allocation of staff time to different activities, the low morale and motivation of staff, and the lack of training in psychosocial rehabilitation (McKeown et al., 2002). Given the high levels of stress in acute in-patient settings and mental health teams, it is perhaps unsurprising that research has also shown that staff exhibit high levels of expressed emotion in such settings (Moore and Kuipers, 1992). Working with staff to help to reduce levels of expressed emotion is a valuable role for a psychologist given the research linking high levels of expressed emotion with an increased risk of relapse. There has not yet been research into the effectiveness of such an approach.

As with all organisations, when working to change the culture it is important for psychologists to remain aware of the barriers to organisational change, to work with process issues, and to think about appropriate strategies for managing the complex issues that organisational change raises (Schrin, 1988). Corrigan et al. (1997) and McKeown et al. (2000) document the approaches they have taken to bring about changes in the culture of care in in-patient settings. Both emphasise the need to work with the staff group rather than against it, and to synthesise the new approach with the expertise already held by staff.

Community settings

There is increasing recognition that psychologists can intervene effectively at a community level to reduce stigma and discrimination and to increase the community's knowledge of issues around mental health (Orford, 1992). Sometimes this involves working actively with particular parts of the community and with those who are planning community services. By forging links with local community centres, housing associations, higher and further education institutions, voluntary groups, the police and local churches, mental health professionals can help the community to better understand and respond to the needs of people with mental health problems.

Let us take the example of employment. It is increasingly being recognised that mental health services need to do more to help to create suitable employment opportunities for people suffering from serious mental health problems. Increased partnership working between Mental Health Trusts, the voluntary sector, potential employers and Jobcentre Plus offices, could help to ensure that each is working in a co-ordinated way to offer greater opportunities and to help overcome barriers to employment. Members of Community Mental Health Trusts also need to be encouraged to develop working relationships with potential employers so that suitable adjustments or 'accommodations' can be made to the working environment so that individuals can obtain and remain in employment.

Psychologists are in a good position to challenge the prejudice and misunderstanding that exists in the community regarding this group's capacity to work. Indeed, people suffering from severe and enduring mental health problems suffer from widespread job discrimination (Perkins and Repper, 1996). Psychologists need to draw on research evidence that highlights the prejudice that exists in society and in mental health services, and evaluates strategies for tackling this (see Droughton and Williams, 2002).

CONCLUSION

Effective psychosocial rehabilitation strategies need to be based on a comprehensive assessment of an individual's psychosocial needs. As long as these interventions are based on such assessments, and are developed in full collaboration with service users, then the evidence suggests that there is a great deal that we can do to help service users to obtain and maintain meaningful roles in society.

REFERENCES

Barrowclough, C. and Tarrier, N. (1992) *Families of Schizophrenic Patients: Cognitive Behavioural Intervention*. London: Chapman & Hall.

Beck, A. T., Rush, A. J., Shaw, B. F. and Emery, G. (1979) *Cognitive Therapy for Depression*. New York: Guilford Press.

Bellack, A. S. (2004) Skills training for people with severe mental illness. *Psychiatric Rehabilitation Journal*, 27(4), 375–390.

Bellack, A. S., Gold, J. M. and Buchanan, R. W. (1999) Cognitive rehabilitation for schizophrenia: Problems, prospects and strategies. *Schizophrenia Bulletin*, 25, 257–274.

Bentall, R. (2004) *Madness Explained: Psychosis and Human Nature*. London: Penguin.

Bentall, R. P., Haddock, G. and Slade, P. D. (1994) Cognitive behaviour therapy for persistent auditory hallucinations: From theory to therapy. *Behaviour Therapy*, 25, 51–66.

Brenner, H. D., Roder, V., Hodel, B. Kienzle, N., Reed, D. and Lieberman, R. P. (1994) *Integrated Psychological Therapy for Schizophrenic Patients (IPT)*. Goettingden: Hogrefe and Huber.

Camic, P. M. and Knight, S. J. (eds) (2004) *Clinical Handbook of Health Psychology: A Practical Guide to Effective Interventions*. Cambridge, MA: Hogrefe and Huber.

Chadwick, P., Lowe, C., Horne, P. and Higson, P. (1994) Modifying delusions: The role of empirical testing. *Behaviour Therapy*, 25, 35–49.

Corrigan, P. W. (1991) Social skills training in adult psychotic populations: A meta-analysis. *Behavioural Therapeutics and Experimental Psychology*, 22, 203–210.

Corrigan, P., McCracken, S., Edwards, M., Kommana, S. and Simpatico, T. (1997) Staff training to improve implementation and impact of behavioural rehabilitation programs. *Psychiatric Services*, 48, 1336–1338.

Craighead, W. E., Miklowitz, D. J., Vajk, F. C. and Frank, E. (1998) Psychosocial treatments for bipolar disorder. In: P. E. Nathan and J. M. Gorman (eds) *A Guide to Treatments that Work*. Oxford: Oxford University Press.

Crowther, R., Marshall, M., Bond, G. R. and Huxley, P. (2004) Vocational rehabilitation for people with severe mental illness. *The Cochrane Library*, Issue 1.

Department of Health (DoH) (1999) *National Service Framework for Mental Health*. London: The Stationery Office.

Droughton, J. and Williams, S. (2002) Working and schizophrenia. In: N. Harris, S. Williams and T. Bradshaw (eds) *Psychosocial Interventions for People with Schizophrenia*. Basingstoke, UK: Palgrave Macmillan.

Elkin, I., Shea, M. T., Watkins, J. T., Imber, S. D., Sotsky, S. M., Collins, J. F. et al. (1989) National Institute of Mental Health Treatment of Depression Collaborative Research Programme. *Archives of General Psychiatry*, 46, 971–982.

Everitt, J. and Siddle, R. (2002) Assessment and therapeutic interventions with positive psychotic symptoms. In: N. Harris, S. Williams and T. Bradshaw (eds) *Psychosocial Interventions for People with Schizophrenia*. Basingstoke, UK: Palgrave Macmillan.

Fowler, D., Garety, P. and Kuipers, E. (1997) *Cognitive Behaviour Therapy for Psychosis: Theory and Practice*. Chichester: John Wiley.

Glynn, S. M., Marder, S. R., Liberman, R. P., Blair, K., Wirshing, W. C., Wirshing, D. A. et al. (2002) Supplementing clinic-based skills training with manual-based community support sessions: Effects on social adjustment of patients with schizophrenia. *American Journal of Psychiatry*, 159, 829–837.

Gopfert, M., Webster, J. and Seeman, M. V. (eds) (2004) *Parental Psychiatric Disorder: Distressed Parents and their Families*. Cambridge: Cambridge University Press.

Heinssen, R. K., Liberman, R. P. and Kopelowitz, A. (2000) Psychosocial skills training for schizophrenia: Lessons from the laboratory. *Schizophrenia Bulletin*, 26, 21–46.

Hogarty, G. E., Greenwald, P., Ulrich, R. F., Kornblith, S. J., DiBarry, A. L., Cooley, S. et al. (1997) Three year trials of personal therapy with schizophrenics living with or independent of family. II: Effects on adjustment of patients. *American Journal of Psychiatry*, 154, 1514–1524.

Howe, D. (1993) *On Being a Client*. London: Sage.

Lam, D. H., Bright, J., Jones, S., Hayward, P., Schuck. N., Chisholm, D. and Sham, P. (2000) Cognitive therapy for bipolar disorder: A pilot study of relapse prevention. *Cognitive Therapy and Research*, 24, 503–520.

Lauriello, J., Bustillo, J. and Keith, S. J. (1999) A critical review of research on psychosocial treatment of schizophrenia. *Society of Biological Psychiatry*, 46, 1409–1417.

Lavender, T. and Paxton, R. (2004) *Estimating the Applied Psychology Demand in Adult Mental Health*. Leicester: Division of Clinical Psychology Workforce Planning Advisers, British Psychological Society.

Leff, J. (1994) Working with families of schizophrenic patients. *British Journal of Psychiatry*, 164(23), 71–76.

Liberman, R. P., Wallace, C. J., Blackwell, G., Kopelowitz, A. and Vaccaro, J. V. (1998) Skills training versus psychosocial occupational therapy for persons with persistent schizophrenia. *American Journal of Psychiatry*, 155, 1087–1091.

Margo, A., Hemsley, D. R. and Slade, P. D. (1981) The effects of varying auditory input on schizophrenic hallucinations. *British Journal of Psychiatry*, 139, 122–127.

McKeown, M., Mercer, D. and Finlayson, S. (2000) Targeting: The role of training. In: L. Cotterill and W. Barr (eds) *Targeting in Mental Health Services*. Aldershot, UK: Ashgate.

McKeown, M., McCann, G. and Forster, J. (2002) Psychosocial interventions in institutional settings. In: N. Harris, S. Williams and T. Bradshaw (eds) *Psychosocial Interventions for People with Schizophrenia*. Basingstoke, UK: Palgrave Macmillan.

Mental Health Act Commission and the Sainsbury Centre (1997) *The National Visit*. London: The Sainsbury Centre for Mental Health.

Miklowitz, D. J. (2002) Family-focused treatment for bipolar disorder. In: S. G. Hofmann and M. C. Tompson (eds) *Treating Chronic and Severe Mental Disorders: A Handbook of Empirically Supported Interventions*. London: Guilford Press.

Moore, E. and Kuuipers, E. (1992) Expressed emotion in staff working with the long-term adult mentally ill. *British Journal of Psychiatry*, 161, 802–808.

National Institute of Health and Clinical Excellence (NICE) (2004) *Depression: Management of Depression in Primary and Secondary Care (NICE Guidelines)*. London: NICE.

National Institute of Health and Clinical Excellence (NICE) (2002) *Schizophrenia: Core Interventions in the Treatment and Management of Schizophrenia in Primary and Secondary Care (NICE Guidelines)*. London: NICE.

Newman, C. F., Leahy, R. L., Beck, A. T., Reilly-Harrington, N. A. and Gyulai, L. (2001) *Bipolar Disorder: A Cognitive Therapy Approach*. Washington, DC: American Psychiatric Association.

Office for National Statistics (ONS) (2003) *Labour Force Survey*. London: ONS.

Office of the Deputy Prime Minister (ODPM) (2004) *Mental Health and Social Exclusion: Social Exclusion Unit Report*. London: ODPM.

Orford, J. (1992) *Community Psychology: Theory and Practice*. Chichester: John Wiley.

Otto, M. W. and Reilly-Harrington, N. (2002) Cognitive-behavioural therapy for the management of bipolar disorder. In: S. G. Hofmann and M. C. Tompson (eds) *Treating Chronic and Severe Mental Disorders: A Handbook of Empirically Supported Interventions*. London: Guilford Press.

Perkins, R. E. and Repper, J. M. (1996) *Working Alongside People with Long-Term Mental Health Problems*. London: Chapman and Hall.

Pilling, S., Bebbington, P., Kuipers, E., Garethy, P., Geddes, J., Martindale, B. et al. (2002a) Psychological treatments in schizophrenia: II. Meta-analyses of randomised controlled trials of social skills training and cognitive remediation. *Psychological Medicine*, 32, 783–791.

Pilling, S., Bebbington, P., Kuipers, P. G., Geddes, J., Orbach, G. and Morgan, C. (2002b) Psychological treatments in schizophrenia: I. Meta-analysis of family intervention and cognitive behaviour therapy. *Psychological Medicine*, 32, 763–782.

Reder, P. and Lucy, C. (eds) (1995) *Assessment of Parenting: Psychiatric and Psychological Contributions*. London: Routledge.

Repper, J. (2002) The helping relationship. In: N. Harris, S. Williams and T. Bradshaw (eds) *Psychosocial Interventions for People with Schizophrenia*. Basingstoke, UK: Palgrave Macmillan.

Roth, A. and Fonagy, P. (2004) *What Works for Whom? A Critical Review of Psychotherapy Research*. London: Guilford Press.

Schrin, H. (1988) *Process Consultation*. Reading, MA: Addison Wesley.

Sensky, T., Turkington, D., Kingdon, D., Scott, J., Siddle, R., O'Carroll, M. and Barnes, T. (2000) A randomised controlled trial of cognitive behaviour therapy for persistent symptoms in schizophrenia resistant to medication. *Archives of General Psychiatry*, 57, 165–172.

Spaulding, W., Reed, D., Stortzback, D., Sullivan, M., Weiler, M. and Richardson, C. (1998) The effects of a remediational approach to cognitive therapy for schizophrenia. In: Wykes, T., Tarrier, N. and Lewis, S. (eds) *Outcome and Innovation in Psychological Treatment of Schizophrenia*. Chichester: John Wiley.

Tarrier, N. (1987) An investigation of residual psychotic symptoms in discharged schizophrenic patients. *British Journal of Clinical Psychology*, 26, 141–143.

Tarrier, N., Beckett R., Harwood, S., Baker, A., Yusopoff, L. and Ugareburu, I. (1993) A trial of two cognitive-behavioural methods of treating drug-resistant psychotic symptoms in schizophrenic patients, I: Outcome. *British Journal of Psychiatry*, 162, 524–532.

Tauber, R., Wallace, C. J. and Lecompte, T. (2000) Enlisting indigenous community supporters in skills training programs for persons with severe mental illness. *Psychiatric Services*, 51, 1428–1432.

Torrey, W. C., Becker, D. R. and Drake, R. E. (1995) Rehabilitative day treatment vs. supported employment: II. Consumer, family and staff reactions to a program change. *Psychosocial Rehabilitation Journal*, 18(3), 67–75.

Twamley, E. W., Jeste, D. V. and Lehman, A. F. (2003a) Vocational rehabilitation in schizophrenia and other psychotic disorders: A literature review and meta-analysis of randomised controlled trials. *The Journal of Nervous and Mental Disease*, 191(8), 515–523.

Twanley, E. W., Jeste, D. V. and Bellack, A. S. (2003b) A review of cognitive training in schizophrenia. *Schizophrenia Bulletin*, 29, 359–382.

Wykes, T. and Van der Gaag, M. (2001) Is it time to develop a new cognitive therapy for psychosis – cognitive remediation therapy (CRT)? *Clinical Psychology Review*, 21, 1227–1256.

Wykes, T., Reeder, C., Corner, J., Williams, C. and Everitt, B. (1999) The effects of neurocognitive remediation on executive processing in patients with schizophrenia. *Schizophrenia Bulletin*, 25, 291–306.

Wykes, T., Reeder, C., Williams, C., Corner, J., Rice, C. and Everitt, B. (2003) Are the effects of cognitive remediation therapy (CRT) durable? Results from an exploratory trial in schizophrenia. *Schizophrenia Research*, 61, 163–174.

Chapter 29

Introduction to clinical health psychology

Jane Hutton

INTRODUCTION

Physical illness and its treatment can be very stressful. They often involve unpleasant and uncontrollable sensations, provoke fears about the future and require significant changes to activities, social roles and life goals. Hospitalisation presents further stresses in that privacy, independence and access to usual coping strategies are all reduced. Although most people adjust remarkably well, a significant proportion find it difficult to cope. Certain conditions are associated with high degrees of distress, notably those that are life-threatening or chronic, or involve the brain (Royal Colleges of Physicians and Psychiatrists, 2003). Between 20 and 25% of patients with chronic illness have clinically significant psychological symptoms (White, 2001). Response to illness depends on the patient's perception of it (Leventhal et al., 1992; Scharloo et al., 1998). Perception of illness as very threatening, or ability to cope with it as poor, increase vulnerability to anxiety and depression and impair ability to make beneficial lifestyle changes. Impact of illness is also influenced by individual differences. Anxiety can be greatly exacerbated by illness. Uncontrollable symptoms may be particularly distressing for people who seek ordered lives. People who have had little experience of coping with major difficulties or, conversely, have had their resources depleted by multiple stressors, may find it difficult to generate appropriate coping strategies. Personal or family history of illness can sensitise individuals to concerns about particular symptoms. Core beliefs related to a history of trauma, neglect or abuse may compromise readiness to trust health professionals, negatively influence perception of physically intrusive interventions and impair coping ability. More positive core beliefs about control and health may be challenged by illness, leading to great distress.

Clinical health psychologists work with people who are experiencing problems in living and coping with their illness, or for whom psychological issues have significant impact on their illness and treatment. These difficulties may or may not meet psychiatric diagnostic criteria. Major depression is twice as common in medical inpatients as in the general population, is under-diagnosed (Royal Colleges of Physicians and Psychiatrists, 2003) and predicts increased length of hospital stay, more outpatient visits, poorer quality of life (Koenig and Kuchibhatla, 1998) and greater disability (Pohjasvaara et al., 2001). Anxiety symptoms may be difficult to distinguish from symptoms of physical illness and may interfere with investigations or interventions (e.g. when they are associated with MRI scans or needles). Post-traumatic symptoms are common immediately after acute injury (Mayou and Bryant, 2001) and invasive interventions, as in ITU (Nickel et al., 2004).

Interpersonal factors and social support greatly influence both psychological response to illness and impact of illness on functioning (Singer and Lord, 1984; MacMahon and Lip, 2002). Relatives and carers may benefit from support, clear information and encouragement to allow the patient appropriate autonomy.

Thus, there are important roles for clinical psychologists in direct work with patients and families. They may specialise in particular medical problems or work more generically. However, the number of clinical health psychologists, although growing, remains small and so capacity for such work is limited. Also, the greatest benefit for patients is likely to be achieved by integrating psychological principles into medical and nursing care as fully as possible. Psychologists can contribute to this by offering teaching, training, modelling, advice and supervision to other professionals. This can be on various levels, from guidance with simple and specific interventions, such as behavioural programmes on wards, to courses and supervision for colleagues working towards a high level of psychological competence.

ROLES OF OTHER PROFESSIONALS

Liaison psychiatrists treat patients in physical healthcare settings. There is some overlap between their role and that of psychologists. They also have specialist expertise in prescribing appropriate medications and giving opinions on issues such as capacity for consent (Royal Colleges of Physicians and Psychiatrists, 2003). Some services employ counsellors to provide psychological support to patients and staff. Nurse therapists trained in cognitive-behavioural therapy (CBT) fulfil many of the roles of psychologists in some services.

PSYCHOLOGICAL ASPECTS OF MEDICAL CARE

A joint report by the Royal Colleges of Physicians and Psychiatrists (2003) makes detailed recommendations about psychological aspects of medical practice and promotes the ideal that all hospital staff should develop skills of good psychological care in the following domains.

Good communication is associated with patient satisfaction, decreased anxiety, understanding of and adherence to health advice, improved health outcome and fewer complaints (Michie et al., 2003). Accurate information, coupled with relaxation training, reduces the stressfulness of medical procedures (White, 2001). Information and advice should be given according to patients' existing knowledge and beliefs and what they want to know. However, this is seldom done (Maguire, 1999). Up to 50% of patients are critical of the communication they receive (Weinman, 2001) and, generally, want more information, but may be reluctant to ask due to fears of being seen as demanding or stupid. Understanding and recall are impaired if patients are anxious, information is detailed or complex, or lots of information is given at once (Ley, 1988). Information that is specific, structured and emphasised is more likely to be recalled and acted on. Primacy and recency effects should be taken into account. Special care is needed to present probabilistic information clearly. Written information may be a useful supplement. Patients' comprehension and recall should be checked and questions encouraged. This requires good communication skills, for example, positive verbal and non-verbal behaviour, such as asking open questions and clarifying concerns, and making eye contact.

Good communication between clinicians is also essential if patients are not to receive confusing messages. Stress impairs communication, which causes more stress, creating a vicious circle. Intervention is required at both individual and organisational levels (Michie, 2002). Training and support for clinicians can help them identify sources of stress and increase their coping resources. Employers can increase support and control over work available to clinicians and, where possible, make changes to particularly stressful situations.

Responses to bad news vary and clinicians should respond sensitively and allow patients control over how much information they receive. Not exploring concerns predicts later anxiety and depression (Maguire, 1985; Parle et al., 1996). Clinicians may avoid dealing with emotional aspects of bad news because they fear increasing patients' distress, and the impact on their own emotional well-being, particularly if they feel unsupported.

Adherence is the extent to which patients engage in medically recommended behaviours, including keeping appointments, taking medication and making lifestyle changes. Non-adherence may be due to practical barriers (e.g. cost), lack of understanding or beliefs incompatible with the treatment (Horne and Weinman, 1999). Clinicians should anticipate it, work with patients to tailor treatment to their needs and priorities and, where appropriate, involve colleagues and the patient's family. Most, but not all, patients prefer a collaborative approach. Offering choices of treatment reduces anxiety and depression (O'Connor and Pallas, 1998).

MODELS OF COPING AND SELF-MANAGEMENT

Coping with illness is a dynamic process, involving managing the emotional impact, constructing an understanding of the illness and the limitations it imposes, developing coping strategies and balancing the demands of illness and treatment with other responsibilities and life goals. The functions of coping have been described as reducing distress and impact on various domains of life and returning to active pursuit of pre-existing life goals (Spencer et al., 1998).

There is no single classification of coping strategies, but important distinctions are approach/avoidance and problem-/emotion-focused coping. Problem-focused coping includes seeking information and support, learning new skills, developing new activities and actively participating in treatment. Emotion-focused coping includes expressing feelings and concerns and using distraction to focus on other tasks. The same behaviour (e.g. telephoning a friend) might fall into either of these categories, depending on its function.

Folkman and Lazarus's (1988a) stress-coping model states that evaluation of stressors determines response to them. Perceived threat gives rise to anxiety and perceived loss to anger or grief. Appraisal of possible responses then follows. The model was later elaborated to include life events other than the index stressor, demographic, disease and treatment characteristics, emotional and cognitive responses, internal and external resources and psychological, social and physical consequences. Thus, careful individual formulation is emphasised. This will influence preferences for medical care. For example, people for whom a sense of control is important will benefit from detailed information about their illness and the treatment options.

Aldwin (1994) suggests that how well one copes is partly a matter of 'goodness of fit' between environmental demands and individual resources and preferences. Certain resources and responses are generally helpful (such as self-efficacy and extent of social network) but the relative usefulness of others will vary between situations. Most people have a repertoire of coping strategies, which they can employ flexibly, depending on the circumstances. Difficulties arise if an individual has a limited range of responses, which are affected by the illness. For example, someone who always deals with stress by exercising hard will struggle with any limitation on physical activity. Flexible coping (Cheng, 2001) and mindful action are likely to be more helpful than stereotyped reactions. Some degree of avoidance may be beneficial where the situation is time-limited, brief, uncontrollable and so intense that it might otherwise be overwhelming, and when psychological arousal may have adverse physiological effects, but not when lifestyle change or cognitive adjustment is needed. For example, a tendency towards denial predicts shorter stay in the coronary care unit and fewer signs of cardiac dysfunction during hospitalisation, but also poorer compliance with medical recommendations and more re-admissions during the following year (Levine et al., 1987).

There is an increasing emphasis in the NHS on empowering people with long-term conditions to be active partners in their care (Department of Health, 2001). This is likely to improve engagement with treatment and offer psychological benefits, such as increased confidence. Some aspects of it are illness specific, but the following are common: learning how to recognise and act on symptoms, dealing with acute attacks or exacerbations of the disease, accessing services, using treatments effectively, understanding advice, cost–benefit analysis of decisions, establishing a routine of sleep and rest, dealing with fatigue, managing work, accessing chosen leisure activities, developing practical coping strategies, dealing with psychological symptoms and coping with other people's responses. Much of this can be described in cognitive-behavioural terms. Although it could be described as adaptive coping, the term 'self-management' tends to be used. Benefits of this approach include reduced disability, improved social activity and perception of health, and reduced use of health services (Lorig et al., 1999).

MEDICALLY UNEXPLAINED SYMPTOMS

These are common in community samples (Escobar et al., 1987) but severity warranting psychiatric diagnosis is relatively rare (Bhui and Hotopf, 1996). About 25% of people seeing their GP (Gujere et al., 1998) and 40–50% of patients in hospital out-patient clinics have unexplained medical symptoms (Ninnuan et al., 2001). The more somatic symptoms reported, regardless of their nature, the greater the likelihood of associated psychiatric diagnosis (Russo et al., 1994).

In somatoform disorders, the principal problem is preoccupation with physical symptoms, causing significant distress or impairment. The symptoms are disproportionate to underlying organic disease, are not better accounted for by other psychiatric conditions and are precipitated and maintained by psychological factors. Specific functional syndromes are associated with symptom clusters in particular bodily systems. In somatisation disorder, symptoms are present in several parts of the body. These disorders can be contrasted with intentional production or feigning of symptoms, which is known as malingering, when there is an external (e.g. financial) motivation, or factitious disorder, when the sick role itself seems to be the motivator.

Vulnerability factors include particular illness beliefs (e.g. that bed-rest is necessary), tendencies to worry about illness and attend to bodily symptoms (Petrie et al., 2001), and lack of social support (which may increase physiological arousal and preoccupation with symptoms) or over-solicitous response of others to the symptoms. Financial gain may also be relevant, as may be childhood experience of illness, particularly when coupled with lack of parental care (Craig et al., 1990: McCauley et al., 1997). Children whose emotional needs are neglected may learn that physical illness elicits care and attention that they would not otherwise receive.

Physicians should avoid excessive investigation and intervention, which is likely to increase the patient's uncertainty and anxiety and reinforce their illness beliefs (Kouyanou et al., 1998). They should also enquire about psychological factors, such as life stressors and beliefs about symptoms, routinely and matter-of-factly, alongside physical factors throughout, not just when medical investigations have failed to find a cause. They should explain the symptoms in terms that the patient can understand, including physical, cognitive and behavioural factors. Reassurance should be focused on the patient's particular worries. It is important to offer a positive way forward, including symptom relief and improvement in functioning, rather than unrealistic ideas of cure. Patients with medically unexplained symptoms who receive clear information and advice on coping feel empowered (Salmon et al., 1999) and are more likely to accept advice and reassurance. Inviting a relative may be helpful, so that they are aware of the information and advice given. Physiotherapy can reduce secondary problems resulting from guarding and deconditioning. There is good evidence that patients with mild problems of recent onset respond to reassurance and information. Psychologists have a crucial role in supporting this and may offer direct intervention in more severe cases, although engagement can be very difficult. Intervention should be based on individual formulation and might include development of coping and relaxation strategies, work on unhelpful cognitions and helping family members to support the patient in ways consistent with improving function and well-being (Royal Colleges of Physicians and Psychiatrists, 2003).

ASSESSMENT

Careful assessment is required to develop a formulation incorporating physical and psychological factors. The starting point should be an interview covering symptoms, including time course, physical and psychological moderating factors, impact on life, responses of significant others, use of medical care and medication, sources of particular distress and attempts to cope. It should include a brief personal and psychiatric history, including any previous psychological therapy, and assessment of current mental state. Medical history should cover previous illnesses and how significant others responded to them, positive and negative experiences of medical care and family history of illness. The patient's tendency to attend to physical sensations, and his or her beliefs about the body, illness, treatment and ability to cope, should be assessed and key cognitions mediating emotional response to the situation identified. Social and cultural influences should be considered. There may be issues related to witnessing a relative's illness and treatment, or to parental responses to illness. Media coverage may also have effects. Psychologists should be aware of their own assumptions related to their experience of and beliefs about illness.

During the interview, any non-verbal responses to symptoms, such as grimaces or unusual postures, should be noted. Usually, supplementary information should be gathered from the referrer, GP or medical notes, taking account of confidentiality issues, to clarify what can be attributed to the person's medical condition. It may be difficult to tease out the relative contributions of physical and psychological factors to symptoms such as impaired sleep.

Customised diary forms may be helpful, particularly to explore variation of symptoms. The use of standardised self-report measures should also be considered. These may be generic or condition-specific. It is important to consider how relevant the available standardisation data are to the patient being assessed, and whether there are aspects of the illness or treatment that may interfere with validity or the physical process of completing the measure. A summary of key generic measures follows.

The Hospital Anxiety and Depression Scale (Zigmond and Snaith, 1983) is a brief and widely used measure that is relatively uninfluenced by physical symptoms.

Quality of life can be assessed using the SF-36 (Ware and Sherbourne, 1992; Garratt et al., 2002), which is widely used, well-standardised, responsive to change and relatively brief. It covers general health, physical and emotional functioning, pain and emotional distress.

A particularly useful measure is the revised Illness Perception Questionnaire (IPQ-R; Moss-Morris et al., 2002), which is well-standardised, based on Leventhal's self-regulation model and can be adapted for specific conditions. It measures five components of illness representation: identity, emotional representations, consequences, timeline, control and cause. It has good re-test reliability, discriminant validity and predictive validity with regard to psychological outcome.

The COPE inventory (Carver et al., 1989) measures responses to stressful situations in general and the Ways of Coping Questionnaire (Lazarus and Folkman, 1988b) measures responses to a specific stress.

The Measures in Health Psychology pack includes a number of other useful measures (Weinman et al., 1995).

GENERAL PRINCIPLES OF INTERVENTION

White (2001) provides an excellent introduction. Engagement is crucial. The psychologist should check the patient's understanding of the reasons for referral, and address any concerns that the patient might have about the referrer doubting his or her sanity or the validity of his or her symptoms. Suitability for CBT should be assessed, by considering the patient's ability to understand the model and report inner experience, and willingness to consider a psychological component to the problem and participate actively in therapy. However, problems in these areas are not absolute contra-indications. The possibility can be acknowledged that psychological factors are not relevant in this case and an initial trial offered to test this out and to work on engagement. The idea of coping with and adjusting to illness is often a useful starting point. A coping model is relatively non-stigmatising, non-pathologising and empowering. It supports attention to and development of individual strengths, coping resources and skills relevant to the current situation.

As always, specific and measurable goals should be set. Session structure and homework should be maintained as far as possible, although some flexibility may be required due to debilitating effects of illness and competing demands of medical appointments. Such barriers should be anticipated and discussed. It may be useful to have a medical update as a standing agenda item.

Standard techniques that are often relevant include graded exposure, relaxation training, activity scheduling, behavioural experiments, modelling and role play (of interactions with clinicians and relatives). The realism and usefulness of relevant cognitions must be considered. This may involve gathering medical information from colleagues. Meta-cognitions about thoughts should be considered and attentional control training (Wells, 2000) may be helpful.

Psychologists should have some knowledge of the conditions and interventions experienced by their clients and good skills in communicating with non-psychologist colleagues. Seeing a patient together may help both professionals to learn from how the other works. Careful feedback to referrers is another good way of communicating psychological ideas. Clinical evaluation and research is particularly important in this field, where the evidence base is still relatively limited.

OUTCOME VARIABLES

There is a need to consider multiple costs and benefits and to prioritise those variables most valued by the patient. Ultimate outcomes may be influenced directly or via intermediate variables, e.g. engagement with treatment. Outcome measures may be physiological (such as short-term physiological changes, long-term health changes, survival), psychological (such as cognitions, coping responses, general well-being and task performance), functional (impact on important life goals) or social (impact on relationships and roles).

SPECIFIC AREAS OF MEDICINE

Much work in clinical health psychology is driven by individual formulation rather than being specific to a particular medical problem. However, for most medical problems there is a specific, and sometimes large, psychological literature (see, for example, Chapter 30). It is impossible to provide even a brief overview in the space available here. Instead, I will concentrate on three areas of medicine, which are both important in themselves and illustrate broader psychological issues. The main focus will be on cognitive-behavioural interventions. Psychodynamic approaches are not covered.

In evaluating research findings, as well as the usual considerations of study design, it is important to consider inclusion and exclusion criteria, for example, nature, severity and stage of illness, any concurrent non-psychological treatments and the setting in which the study was carried out. Participants recruited from the community, from primary care and from secondary care are likely to differ in severity of medical problems and psychological distress and inclination to seek medical help.

Cancer

Cancer is a range of illnesses with different aetiologies, treatments and prognoses. Medical advances mean that more people can be cured, and that life expectancy is longer even for those who cannot. There is a very large relevant psychological literature, including many well-designed intervention studies. Psychological and social problems, and existential and spiritual doubts, are common. About 20% of patients have clinically significant psychological experiences (White, 2001; White and Macleod, 2002). There is some evidence that psychological stress is associated with increased mortality, as in Kojima et al.'s (2005) large-scale prospective study of colon cancer in women. Psychological distress is also common in relatives and health professionals.

Watson and Greer (1998) have defined five common coping styles in people with cancer: fighting spirit, avoidance, fatalism, anxious preoccupation and hopelessness. In their literature review, they found that fighting spirit and, less consistently, avoidance were associated with good disease outcome and the other styles with poorer disease outcome. More recently, psychological distress in women with breast cancer has been associated with cognitive avoidance at diagnosis (Hack and Degner, 2004) and emotional suppression combined with chronically high anxiety (Iwamitsu et al., 2005); in ovarian cancer, psychological distress is associated with lower perceived control and self-esteem (Norton et al., 2005). Many studies have investigated the links between psychological and physiological variables. For example, in McGregor et al.'s (2004) small randomised controlled trial (RCT), women with breast cancer who engaged in a cognitive-behavioural stress management intervention reported greater perceptions of benefit from their illness post-intervention and improved lymphocyte proliferation 3 months later, and the former predicted the latter.

Psychological measures specific to cancer include the Mental Adjustment to Cancer Scale (Watson et al., 1988) and the Cancer Behaviour Inventory (Merluzzi and Martinez-Sanchez, 1997), which measures coping.

Moorey and Greer (2002) describe a cognitive model of adjustment to cancer and adaptation of CBT for this population: adjunctive psychological therapy (APT). White (2001) provides guidelines for CBT, including working with thoughts about the meaning of cancer, increasing sense of control, finding ways of living with uncertainty, tackling avoidance and promoting re-engagement with social support. Simple behavioural interventions can help with conditioned nausea and vomiting related to chemotherapy.

It is difficult to combine the results of intervention studies to draw general conclusions because of the wide variety of kinds of cancer, disease stages, demographics, pre-intervention levels of psychological distress, interventions and outcome measures. However, there is good evidence for positive effects of psychosocial interventions. In a recent meta-analysis, Rehse and Pukrop (2003) consider 37 published, controlled studies. The overall effect size on quality of life was 0.3 and the most important moderating variable was duration of intervention. In a comparison of different interventions, Moorey et al. (1998) found APT superior to supportive counselling. The evidence for effects of psychosocial interventions on survival is less clear. Smedslund and Ringdal (2004) pooled data from 2,626 patients in 14 controlled intervention studies and found that no definite conclusion could be drawn.

Diabetes

Diabetes is a chronic disorder in which abnormal insulin production and utilisation leads to impaired glucose metabolism. Its prevalence is around 2.4% in white British people, but several times higher in some minority ethnic groups. Around 90% of cases are type 2 diabetes, in which some insulin is produced and treatment with diet and exercise may be sufficient. It is associated with older age, obesity and heredity. In type 1 diabetes, very little or no insulin is produced and insulin injections are always necessary. Heredity is more important and onset is generally earlier in this type of diabetes. However, type 2 diabetes is rapidly becoming more common in overweight younger people. Diabetes is incurable and carries the risk of severe (e.g. renal and visual) complications if it is not kept under control. Its treatment requires significant lifestyle changes. In diabetes and its care, physical and psychological issues are intertwined in striking and disease-specific ways. Some of the issues common to chronic disorders are also exemplified. There have been three excellent recent reviews of psychological issues in diabetes care, which also provide a good introduction to diabetes for the psychologist:

Gonder-Frederick et al. (2002), Musselman et al. (2003) and Rubin and Peyrot (2001).

There is an increasing emphasis, notably in the relevant National Service Framework (NSF) in the United Kingdom (Department of Health, 2001), on self-management of diabetes and developing care plans tailored to individual needs. Self-management has many components: monitoring of physical state, control of diet, smoking cessation, exercise, foot care and attending regular appointments. Patients must make choices on an ongoing basis to balance the risks of hyperglycaemia (which is associated with long-term complications) and hypoglycaemia (which acutely impairs cognition and can lead to unconsciousness if untreated), and in many situations there is no single best solution. The NSF notes that people who take more responsibility for their own diabetes management have better blood glucose control, higher quality of life and greater satisfaction with treatment.

The relationship between depression and diabetes exemplifies the interaction of physiological and psychological mechanisms in chronic illness. Depression is up to three times more common in people with diabetes than in the general population and controlling for shared risk factors does not remove this association. It is under-diagnosed. There is a bi-directional association with diabetic complications, which may induce low mood and helplessness but also be influenced by poorer self-care and physiological mechanisms. Depression and stress are associated with abnormal hormone release and action, glucose transport and immune function, which could contribute to insulin resistance or pancreatic dysfunction (Rubin and Peyrot, 2001).

There is less research on anxiety disorders but they are also more common than in the general population and may impact on diabetic control through physiological and behavioural mechanisms. For example, symptoms may be misattributed to hypoglycaemia, leading to unnecessary use of medication and risk of hyperglycaemia. Needle phobia also has an obvious impact. Eating disorders are particularly prevalent in young women with diabetes and are strong predictors of poor diabetic control and complications. The fact that diabetes treatment increases attention to food and weight is both a risk factor and a problem in diagnosis. As well as symptoms seen in the general population, a phenomenon exists specific to diabetes, in which patients take less insulin than they need, so that less glucose is stored as fat. This induces hyperglycaemia and is an example of a behaviour in which psychological factors lead to physical symptoms and medication being used in a way detrimental to health (Rubin and Peyrot, 2001).

The same authors discuss other problems in living with diabetes. They describe a tension between illness management and emotion-focused coping. The regimen is complex, demanding, unremitting and yet does not guarantee freedom from complications. Patients may well feel frustrated, fed up, overwhelmed, angry, guilty or fearful, all of which may impact on emotional well-being and practical self-care. Feelings of deprivation may lead to temptation to use food as a source of comfort and in an act of resistance to being 'told' what to eat. Seemingly irrelevant decisions (similar to those described in substance misuse) may lead to unhealthy behaviours. Blood glucose may be monitored less frequently than recommended, due to the discomfort and inconvenience of testing or fear of getting a high reading. Patients may resist beginning to take insulin due to what they perceive this to mean, for instance, that they have failed to control their diabetes or that their family will treat them differently. Some people with diabetes feel that their families offer too little support or harass them, or that health professionals do not understand or encourage them. Psychologists have an important role in helping people overcome such problems through direct intervention and offering guidance to colleagues. Training clinicians in patient empowerment improves satisfaction and emotional well-being in their patients (Gonder-Frederick et al., 2002) and more collaborative interventions are more effective (Norris et al., 2001). Patients are likely to benefit from clinicians supporting and encouraging them, helping them overcome barriers and build self-efficacy, reinforcing healthy behaviours, providing relevant information and addressing misconceptions.

Direct psychological intervention may relate to specific illness-related problems or broader issues, encompassing core cognitive structures. The former is more likely to produce change quickly, and so is preferable where it is possible. Social and cultural contexts must be considered. It should be remembered that the consequences of diabetes are not always negative and, in particular, coping well with the condition may bring a great sense of accomplishment (Rubin and Peyrot, 2001).

Bradley (1994) provides a comprehensive guide to psychological assessment. The Problem Areas in Diabetes Scale (Welch et al., 1997) is a useful measure that covers self-care and interactions with friends, family and professionals.

Snoek and Skinner (2002) review the literature on psychological intervention. They report one RCT (Lustman et al., 1998), in which individual CBT was added to diabetes education for people with type 2 diabetes and depression, with significant benefits in depression, blood glucose monitoring and subsequent blood glucose regulation. Mechanisms were not assessed and may have been physiological or related to treatment adherence. Two RCTs of group CBT for disordered eating (Kenardy et al., 2001; Olmsted et al., 1997) showed beneficial cognitive change and reduced binge eating. Glycaemic control was improved in an uncontrolled trial of brief group CBT, delivered jointly by a psychologist and diabetes nurse specialist (Snoek et al., 2001), and Fosbury et al. (1997) report a non-significant trend for CBT to improve glycaemic control to a greater degree than diabetes education. Clearly, group interventions maximise the number of people who can be reached by limited psychology resources. Snoek and Skinner (2002) suggest that CBT may be helpful in addressing specific anxieties, avoidance and self-destructive patterns (of chronic or periodically severe mismanagement), but that more evidence is needed for its efficacy. Psychology appointments may be an additional stressor, when added to an already complex regimen.

Gonder-Frederick et al. (2002) suggest that stress management, including relaxation training, may be beneficial through moderation of neurohormonal stress responses. They also note that both specific behavioural interventions and training in coping skills can improve glycaemic control, and that the latter can also increase psychological well-being. There is good evidence for lasting benefits of Cox et al.'s (e.g. 2001) blood-glucose awareness training in both domains. Rubin and Peyrot (2001) suggest that interpersonal psychotherapy may be helpful, due to the social components of self-management, but this has not been tested.

Dermatology

Psychological issues include the impact of psychological stress on the skin, through physiological and behavioural mechanisms and the impact of changed appearance on psychological well-being. Depression, somatoform disorders (Stangier et al., 2003), obsessive-compulsive disorder (OCD) (Fineberg et al., 2003) and body dysmorphic disorder (Uzun et al., 2003) are all more common than in the general population. Research from psoriasis has shown that, as in other areas of medicine, illness perceptions (Fortune et al., 2002) and maladaptive coping strategies, in this case venting emotions and mental disengagement (Hill and Kennedy, 2002) are important predictors of distress and disability. Strategies such as picking, scratching and using non-prescription remedies may be physically damaging. However, as with other medical problems, psychological consequences are not always negative. Fortune et al. (2005) found evidence for 'adversarial growth' or identification of benefits, in people with psoriasis, particularly those who were more psychologically minded and knowledgeable about the disease, and had developed it at an earlier age.

Self-reported stress is associated with exacerbations of lupus (Peralta-Ramirez et al., 2004). Many patients with psoriasis see stress as an important causal factors (O'Leary et al., 2004). However, Picardi et al. (2003a, 2003b) found no significant associations between stress and onset or exacerbation of psoriasis, although onset and exacerbation of vitiligo were associated with multiple uncontrollable stressors. Alexithymia, insecure attachment and poor social support increased susceptibility to vitiligo, possibly via poor emotional regulation or limited coping skills.

Pathological worry in psoriasis is common and associated with stronger beliefs in the condition having an emotional cause and serious consequences, but not with its clinical severity. Concerns tend to be focused on the social, rather than medical, consequences of the condition (Fortune et al., 2000). These authors later (2003) found evidence for preoccupation with psoriasis and its impact on the self in social situations, using modified Stroop task and recall paradigms.

Because skin problems affect physical appearance and are sometimes erroneously associated with contagion or poor hygiene, stigma is an issue. Wittkowski et al. (2004) found that skin-related perceptions of stigma strongly predicted of quality of life in atopic dermatitis. Kellett and Gilbert (2001) present a biopsychosocial model of acne and use an evolutionary analysis to suggest a role for body shame related to lower evaluations of attractiveness.

Dermatology-specific measures of quality of life and stigma exist (Wittkowski et al., 2004). Functional analysis of problematic behaviours, such as itching, is often useful.

White (2001) provides a useful introduction to intervention. In clinical health psychology, it is often important to acknowledge the compelling nature of physical sensations, and this is particularly the case for itching. Patients may have tried to use thought suppression to resist the urge to scratch, but this is likely to have been counter-productive. More helpful tactics include the use of imagery, behaviours incompatible with itching and graded reduction of itching, for example, progressing to gentle rubbing, then to resting a hand on the affected part. Interventions for social anxiety must be adapted to take account of the fact that others may well respond negatively to the patient's appearance. Fortune et al. (2004) provide evidence for specific changes in illness-related cognitions in response to psychological intervention. Patients undergoing a cognitive-behavioural symptom management programme showed significant reductions in illness identity, belief in severe consequences of their illness, and emotional causal attributions for their psoriasis, as measured by the IPQ. Training in mindfulness, or moment-to-moment non-judgemental awareness, during ultraviolet treatment for psoriasis was shown to speed response to that treatment in a randomised, blindly evaluated trial (Kabat-Zinn et al., 1998). Mindfulness-based interventions have also been shown to improve mental and physical well-being in pain, cancer and heart disease (Grossman et al., 2004; Tocon et al., 2003).

SUMMARY

Psychological issues are crucial to medical care and there are many opportunities for clinical psychologists to work both with patients and their families and with clinicians from other disciplines. Many psychological and physical benefits of psychological interventions and more psychologically informed care have been described, and many more opportunities exist for further developments into new areas of medicine.

REFERENCES

Aldwin, C. M. (1994) *Stress, Coping and Development: An Integrative Perspective.* New York: Guilford Press.

Bhui, K. and Hotopf, M. (1996) Somatization disorder. *British Journal of Hospital Medicine*, 171, 364–370.

Bradley, C. (1994). *Handbook of Psychology and Diabetes: A Guide to Psychological Measurement in Diabetes Research and Practice.* Langhorne, PA: Harwood Academic Publishers.

Carver, C. S., Scheier, M. F. and Weintraub, J. K. (1989) Assessing coping strategies: A theoretically based approach. *Journal of Personality and Social Psychology*, 56, 267–283.

Cheng, C. (2001) Assessing coping flexibility in real-life and laboratory settings: A multimethod approach. *Journal of Personality and Social Psychology*, 80, 814–833.

Cox, D. J., Gonder-Frederick, L. A., Polonsky, W. H., Schlundt, D. G., Kovatchev, B. P. and Clarke, W. L. (2001) Blood glucose awareness training (BGAT-II: Long-term benefits). *Diabetes Care*, 24, 637–642.

Craig, T. K. J., Drake, H., Mills, K. and Boardman, A. P. (1990) The South London Somatisation Study. I: Influence of stressful life events and secondary gain. *British Journal of Psychiatry*, 165, 248–258.

Department of Health (2001) *National Service Framework for Diabetes: Standards.* London: Department of Health.

Escobar, J. I., Burman M. A., Karno, M., Forsythe, A. and Golding, J. M. (1987) Somatization in the community. *Archives of General Psychiatry*, 44, 713–718.

Fineberg, N. A., O'Doherty, C., Rajagopal, S., Reddy, K., Banks, A. and Gale, T. M. (2003) How common is obsessive-compulsive disorder in a dermatology outpatient clinic? *Journal of Clinical Psychiatry*, 64, 152–155.

Folkman, S. and Lazarus, R. S. (1988a) The relationship between coping and emotion: Implications for theory and research. *Social Science & Medicine*, 26, 309–317.

Folkman, S. and Lazarus, R. S. (1988b) *Manual for the Ways of Coping Questionnaire.* Palo Alto, CA: Consulting Psychologist Press.

Fortune, D. G., Richards, H. L., Main, C. J. and Griffiths, C. E. M. (2000) Pathological worrying, illness perceptions and disease severity in patients with psoriasis. *British Journal of Health Psychology*, 5, 71–82.

Fortune, D. G., Richards, H. L., Griffiths, C. E. M. and Main, C. J. (2002) Psychological stress, distress and disability in patients with psoriasis: Consensus and variation in the contribution of illness perceptions, coping and alexithymia. *British Journal of Clinical Psychology*, 41, 157–174.

Fortune, D. G., Richards, H. L., Corrin, A., Taylor, R. J., Griffiths, C. E. M. and Main, C. J. (2003) Attentional bias for psoriasis-specific and psychosocial threat in patients with psoriasis. *Journal of Behavioral Medicine*, 26, 211–224.

Fortune, D. G., Richards, H. L., Griffiths, C. E. M. and Main, C. J. (2004) Targeting cognitive-behaviour therapy to patients' implicit model of psoriasis: Results from a patient preference controlled trial. *British Journal of Clinical Psychology*, 43, 65–82.

Fortune, D. G., Richards, H. L., Griffiths, C. E. M. and Main, C. J. (2005) Adversarial growth in patients undergoing treatment for psoriasis: A prospective study of the ability of patients to construe benefits from negative events. *Psychology, Health and Medicine*, 10, 44–56.

Fosbury, J. A., Bosley, C. M., Rye, A., Sonksen, P. H. and Judd, S. L. (1997) A trial of cognitive analytic therapy in poorly controlled type I patients. *Diabetes Care*, 20, 959–964.

Garratt, A., Schmidt, L., Mackintosh, A. and Fitzpatrick, M., (2002) Quality of life measurement: Bibliographic study of patient assessed health outcome measures. *British Medical Journal*, 324, 1417–1419.

Gonder-Frederick, L. A., Cox, D. J. and Ritterband, L. M. (2002) Diabetes and behavioural medicine: The second decade. *Journal of Consulting and Clinical Psychology*, 70, 611–625.

Grossman, P., Niemann, L., Schmidt, S. and Walach, H. (2004) Mindfulness-based stress reduction and health benefits: A meta-analysis. *Journal of Psychosomatic Research*, 57, 35–43.

Giyere, O., Von Korff, M., Simon, G., Gater, R. et al. (1998) Persistent pain and well-being. A World Health Organization study in primary care. *Journal of the American Medical Association*, 280, 147–151.

Hack, T. F. and Degner, L. F. (2004) Coping responses following breast cancer diagnosis predict psychological adjustment three years later. *Psycho-Oncology*, 13, 235–247.

Hill, L. and Kennedy, P. (2002) The role of coping strategies in mediating subjective disability in people who have psoriasis. *Psychology, Health and Medicine*, 7, 261–269.

Horne, R. and Weinman, J. (1999) Patients' beliefs about prescribed medicines and their role in adherence to treatment in chronic physical illness. *Journal of Psychosomatic Research*, 47, 555–567.

Iwamitsu, Y., Shimoda, K., Abe, H., Tani, T., Okawa, M. and Buck, R. (2005) Anxiety, emotional suppression, and psychological distress before and after breast cancer diagnosis. *Psychosomatics: Journal of Consultation Liaison Psychiatry*, 46, 19–24.

Kabat-Zinn, J., Wheeler, E., Light, T., Skillings, A., Scharf, M. J., Cropley, T. G. et al. (1998) Influence of a mindfulness meditation-based stress reduction intervention on rates of skin clearing in patients with moderate to severe psoriasis undergoing phototherapy (UVB) and photochemotherapy (PUVA). *Psychosomatic Medicine*, 60, 625–632.

Kellett, S. and Gilbert, P. (2001) Acne: A biopsychosocial and evolutionary perspective with a focus on shame. *British Journal of Health Psychology*, 6, 1–24.

Kenardy, J., Mensch, M., Bowen, K. and Dalton, M. (2001). Disordered eating in non-insulin dependent diabetes mellitus. *International Journal of Behavioural Medicine*, 7, A48.

Koenig H. G. and Kuchibhatla M. (1998) Use of health services by hospitalized medically ill depressed elderly patients. *American Journal of Psychiatry*, 155, 871–877.

Kojima, M., Wakai, K., Tokudome, S., Tamakoshi, K., Toyoshima, H., Watanabe, Y. et al. (2005) Perceived psychologic stress and colorectal cancer mortality: Findings from the Japan Collaborative Cohort Study. *Psychosomatic Medicine*, 167, 72–77.

Kouyanou, K., Pither, C. E., Rabe-Hesketh, S. and Wessely, S. (1998) A comparative study of iatrogenesis, medication abuse, and psychiatric morbidity in chronic pain patients with and without medically explained symptoms. *Pain*, 76, 417–426.

Leventhal, H., Leventhal, E. A. and Schaefer, P. M. (1992) Vigilant coping and health behaviour. In: M. G. Ory, R. P. Abeles and P. D. Lipman (eds) *Aging, Health, and Behavior*. Thousand Oaks, CA: Sage Publications.

Levine, J., Warrenburg, S., Kerns, R., Schwartz, G., Delaney, R., Fontana, A. et al. (1987) The role of denial in recovery from coronary heart disease. *Psychosomatic Medicine*, 49, 109–117.

Ley P. (1988) *Communication with Patients*. London: Croom-Helm.

Lorig, K. R., Sobel, D. S. and Stewart, A. L. (1999) Evidence suggesting that a chronic disease selfmanagement programme can improve health status while reducing hospitalisation. *Medical Care*, 37, 5–14.

Lustman, P. J., Griffith, L. S., Freedland, K. E., Kissel, S. S. and Clouse, R. E. (1998) Cognitive behaviour therapy for depression in type 2 diabetes mellitus: A randomized controlled trial. *Annals of Internal Medicine*, 129, 613–621.

Maguire, P. (1985) Barriers to psychological care of the dying. *British Medical Journal*, 291, 1711–1713.

Maguire, P. (1999) Improving communication with cancer patients. *European Journal of Cancer*, 35, 1415–1422.

Mayou, R. and Bryant, B. (2001) Outcome in consecutive emergency department attenders following a road traffic accident. *British Journal of Psychiatry*, 179, 528–534.

McGregor, B. A., Antoni, M. H., Boyers, A., Alferi, S. M., Blomberg, B. B. and Carver, C. S. (2004) Cognitive-behavioral stress management increases benefit finding and immune function among women with early-stage breast cancer. *Journal of Psychosomatic Research*, 56, 1–8.

McMahon, K. M. and Lip, G. Y. (2002) Psychological factors in heart failure: A review of the literature. *Archives of Internal Medicine*, 162, 509–516.

McCauley, J., Kern, D. E. and Kolodner, K. (1997) Clinical characteristics of women with a history of childhood abuse. *Journal of the American Medical Association*, 227, 1362–1368.

Merluzzi, T. V. and Martinez-Sanchez, M. A. M. (1997) Assessment of self-efficacy and coping with cancer: Development and validation of the cancer behaviour inventory. *Health Psychology*, 14, 101–108.

Michie, S. (2002) Causes and management of stress at work. *Occupational and Environmental Medicine*, 59, 67–72.

Michie, S., Miles, J. and Weinman, J. (2003) Patient-centredness in chronic illness: What is it and does it matter? *Patient Education and Counseling*, 51, 197–206.

Moss-Morris, R., Weinman, J., Petrie, K. J., Horne, R., Cameron, L. D. and Buick, D. (2002) The Revised Illness Perception Questionnaire (IPQ-R). *Psychology and Health*, 17, 1–16.

Moorey, S. and Greer, S. (2002) *Cognitive Behaviour Therapy for People with Cancer*. Oxford: Oxford University Press.

Moorey, S., Greer, S, Bliss, J. and Law, M. (1998) A comparison of adjuvant psychological therapy and supportive counselling in patients with cancer. *Psycho-Oncology*, 7, 218–228.

Musselman, D. L., Betan, E., Larsen, H. and Phillips, L. S. (2003) Relationship of depression to diabetes types 1 and 2: Epidemiology, biology and treatment. *Biological Psychiatry*, 54, 317–329.

Nickel, M., Leiebreich, P., Nickel, C., Tritt, K., Mitterlehner, F., Rother, W. and Loew, T. (2004) The occurrence of posttraumatic stress disorder in patients following intensive care treatment: A cross-sectional study in a random sample. *Journal of Intensive Care Medicine*, 19, 285–290.

Nimnuan, C., Hotopf, M. and Wessely, S. (2001) Medically unexplained symptoms: an epidemiological study in seven specialities. *Journal of Psychosomatic Research*, 51, 361–367.

Norris, S. L., Engelgau, M. M. and Narayn, K. M. (2001) Effectiveness of self-management training in type 2 diabetes: A systematic review of randomised controlled trials. *Diabetes Care*, 25, 561–587.

Norton, T. R., Manne, S. L., Rubin, S., Hernandez, E., Carlson, J., Bergman, C. and Rosenblum, N. (2005) Ovarian cancer patients' psychological distress: The role of physical impairment, perceived unsupportive family and friend behaviors, perceived control, and self-esteem. *Health Psychology*, 24, 143–152.

O'Connor, A. and Pallas, L. L. (1998) Decisional conflict. In: G. K. McFarlane and E. A. McFarlane (eds) *Nursing Diagnosis and Intervention*. Toronto: Mosby.

O'Leary, C. J., Creamer, D., Higgins, E. and Weinman, J. (2004) Perceived stress, stress attributions and psychological distress in psoriasis. *Journal of Psychosomatic Research*, 57, 465–471.

Olmsted, M. P., Rodin, G. M., Rydall, A. C., Lawson, M. L. and Daneman, D. (1997) Effect of psychoeducation on disordered eating attitudes and behaviours in young women with IDDM. *Diabetes*, 46, 88A.

Parle, M., Jones, B. and Maguire, P. (1996) Maladaptive coping and affective disorders in cancer patients. *Psychological Medicine*, 26, 736–744.

Peralta-Ramirez, M. I., Jimenez-Alonso, J., Godoy-Garcia, J. F. and Perez-Garcia, M. (2004) The effects of daily stress and stressful life events on the clinical symptomatology of patients with lupus erythematosus. *Psychosomatic Medicine*, 66, 788–794.

Petrie, K. J., Siverston, B., Hysing, M., Broadbent, E. et al. (2001) Thoroughly modern worries. The relationship of worries about modernity to reported symptoms, health and medical care utilization. *Journal of Psychosomatic Research*, 51, 395–401.

Peveler, R. C. and Fairburn, C. G. (1989) Anorexia nervosa in association with diabetes mellitus – a cognitive-behavioural approach to treatment. *Behaviour Research and Therapy*, 27, 95–99.

Picardi, A., Pasquini, P., Cattaruzza, M. S., Gaetano, P., Melchi, C. F., Baliva, G. et al. (2003a) Stressful life events, social support, attachment security and alexithymia in vitiligo: A case-control study. *Psychotherapy and Psychosomatics*, 72, 150–158.

Picardi, A., Pasquini, P., Cattaruzza, M. S., Gaetano, P., Baliva, G., Melchi, C. F. et al. (2003b) Only limited support for a role of psychosomatic factors in psoriasis: Results from a case-control study. *Journal of Psychosomatic Research*, 55, 189–196.

Pohjasvaara, T., Vataja, R., Leppavuori, A., Kaste, M. and Erkinjuntti, T. (2001) Depression is an independent predictor of poor long-term functional outcome post-stroke. *European Journal of Neurology*, 8. 315–319.

Rehse, B. and Pukrop, R. (2003) Effects of psychosocial interventions on quality of life in adult cancer patients: Meta analysis of 37 published controlled outcome studies. *Patient Education and Counseling*, 50, 179–186.

Royal College of Physicians / Royal College of Psychiatrists (2003) *The Psychological Care of Medical Patients: A Practical Guide*, 2nd edn. London: Royal College of Physicians / Royal College of Psychiatrists.

Rubin, R. R. and Peyrot, M. (2001) Psychological issues and treatments for people with diabetes. *Journal of Clinical Psychology*, 57, 457–478.

Russo, J., Katon, W., Sullivan, M., Clark, M. and Buchwald, D. (1994) Severity of somatisation and its relationship to psychiatric disorders and personality. *Psychosomatics*, 35, 546–556.

Salmon, P., Peters, S. and Stanley, I. (1999) Patients' perceptions of medical explanations for somatisation disorders: Qualitative analysis. *British Medical Journal*, 318, 372–376.

Scharloo, M., Kaptein A. A., Weinman J., Hazes J. M. et al. (1998) Illness perceptions, coping and functioning in patients with rheumatoid arthritis, chronic obstructive pulmonary disease and psoriasis. *Journal of Psychosomatic Research*, 44, 573–585.

Singer, J. E. and Lord, D. (1984) The role of social support in coping with chronic or life threatening illness. In: A. Baum, J. E. Singer and S. Taylor (eds) *Handbook of Psychology and Health*, Vol IV. Hillsdale, NJ: Lawrence Erlbaum Associates, Inc.

Smedslund, G. and Ringdal, G. I. (2004) Meta-analysis of the effects of psychosocial interventions on survival time in cancer patients. *Journal of Psychosomatic Research*, 57, 123–131.

Snoek, F. J. and Skinner, T. C. (2002) Psychological counselling in problematic diabetes: Does it help? *Diabetic Medicine*, 19, 265–273.

Snoek, F. J., van der Ven, N. C. W., Lubach, C. H. C., Chatrou, M., Ader, H. J., Heine, R. J. and Jacobson, A. M. (2001) Effects of cognitive behavioural group training (CBGT) in adult patients with poorly controlled insulin-dependent (type 1) diabetes: A pilot study. *Patient Education and Counseling*, 45, 143–148.

Spencer, S. M., Carver, C. S. and Price, A. A. (1998) Psychological and social factors in adaptation. In: J. C. Holland (ed) *Psycho-oncology*. New York: Oxford University Press.

Stangier, U., Kohnlein, B. and Gieler, U. (2003) Somatoform disorders in dermatological outpatients. *Psychotherapeutics*, 48, 321–328.

Tacon, A. M., McComb, J., Caldera, Y. and Randolph, P. (2003) Mindfulness meditation, anxiety reduction, and heart disease: A pilot study. *Family and Community Health*, 26, 25–33.

Uzun, O., Basoglu, C., Akar, A., Cansever, A., Vzsahin, A., Cetin, M. and Ebrinc, S. (2003) Body dysmorphic disorder in patients with acne. *Comprehensive Psychiatry*, 44, 415–419.

Ware, J. E., Jr and Sherbourne, C. D. (1992) The MOS 36-item short-form Health Survey (SF-36). Conceptual framework and item selection. *Medical Care*, 30, 473–483.

Watson, S, and Greer, M (1998) Personality and coping. In: J. C. Holland (ed) *Psycho-oncology*. New York: Oxford University Press.

Watson, L. M., Greer, S., Young, J., Inayat, Q., Burgess, C. and Robertson, B. (1988) Development of a questionnaire measure of adjustment to cancer: The MAC scale. *Psychological Medicine*, 18, 203–219.

Weinman, J. (2001). Health care. In: D. W. Johnston and M. Johnston (eds) *Health Psychology, Vol. 8: Introduction to Comprehensive Clinical Psychology*. Oxford: Elsevier Science.

Weinman, J., Wright, S. and Johnston, M. (1995) *Measures in Health Psychology: A Users Portfolio*. Windsor, UK: NFER-Nelson.

Welch, G. W., Jacobson, A. M. and Polonsky, W. H. (1997) The problem areas in diabetes scale: An evaluation of its clinical utility. *Diabetes Care*, 20, 760–766.

Wells, A. (2000) *Emotional Disorders and Meta Cognition: Innovative Cognitive Therapy*. Chichester: John Wiley.

White, C. A. (2001) *Cognitive Behaviour Therapy for Chronic Medical Problems: A Guide to Assessment and Treatment in Practice*. Chichester: John Wiley.

White, C. A. and Macleod, U. (2002) ABC of psychological medicine: Cancer. *British Medical Journal*, 325, 377–380.

Wittkowski, A., Richards, H. L., Griffiths, C. E. M. and Main, C. J. (2004) The impact of psychological and clinical factors on quality of life in individuals with atopic dermatitis. *Journal of Psychosomatic Research*, 57, 195–200.

Zigmond, A. S. and Snaith, R. P. (1983) The Hospital Anxiety Depression Scale. *Acta Psychiatrica Scandinavica*, 67(6), 361–370.

Chapter 30

Disorders of eating and weight

Investigation

Jane Wardle and Paul Chadwick

ASSESSMENT

Weight is important in our culture, especially for women. Obese people and anorexics, although they lie at opposite ends of the weight spectrum, may both pay the price of cultural expectations of thinness. The two weight disorders have been joined by a third eating disorder, bulimia nervosa, which is characterised by extreme dietary restriction alternating with voracious overeating in the context of intense fear of weight gain. Obesity, anorexia and bulimia are all associated with a variety of physical health hazards and reduced psychological well-being.

Research into the psychological processes that underlie these disorders points to some commonalities and some differences. A negative body image is found in all three groups, along with chronic, although not necessarily successful, dietary restraint. Eating and exercise patterns are often abnormal and, likewise, hunger, appetite and satiety may be disturbed. Anorexia and bulimia are much more common in women than men, and more women than men seek help for weight reduction. This sex difference is generally attributed to the fact that cultural pressures for thinness fall heavily on women, producing what has been described as 'the tyranny of slenderness' (Chernin, 1983). Few women escape these pressures, so a negative body image and attempts at weight control are common in the normal population (Serdula et al., 1999; Wardle and Johnson, 2002).

Clinical assessment in the area of weight and eating, as in other areas, consists of an attempt to produce a systematic and objective description of the biological, psychological and social factors contributing, in that individual, to the development and maintenance of the problem. Interviews with the patient and other informants are the basic method of data collection and other assessments essentially supplement this. Structured interviews or inventories such as the Eating Disorder Examination (Fairburn and Cooper, 1993), the Interview for Diagnosis of Eating Disorders (Williamson, 1990) or the Stanford Eating Disorders Questionnaire (Agras, 1987) can be used to gather systematic information. Standardised tests such as the Eating Disorders

Inventory (Garner, 1991), the Anorexic Cognitions Questionnaire (Mizes and Klesges, 1989), or the Bulimia Test (BULIT; Welch et al., 1993), have their place more obviously in research settings, but can contribute to data-gathering in a clinical setting. Finally, a medical examination is often necessary in conditions such as these, which have physical as well as psychological symptoms. These broader methods of enquiry will point to the specific areas that need detailed investigation with cognitive tests, rating scales and records of thoughts, feelings and behaviour.

INVESTIGATION OF OBESITY

The prevalence of obesity has increased dramatically over the past few decades and it is now recognised as one of the major unmet public health needs of Western societies. The definition of obesity as a body mass index (BMI) equal to or greater than 30 is somewhat arbitrary because body fatness is a continuous variable. But the label of obesity reflects the point at which excess weight becomes a threat to physical health; typically at around 20% overweight. In 2002, more than 60% of men and 50% of women were either overweight or obese in Britain (Health Survey for England, 2002). Obesity is related to increased risk of diabetes, coronary heart disease, arthritis and cancer (Calle et al., 1999; Must et al., 1999) and the most obese adults have been shown to have a 9-year lower life expectancy than normal weight adults (Fontaine et al., 2003). Obesity is more likely to occur in lower socio-economic groups in industrialised countries, and women are slightly more likely to be affected than men (Sobal and Stunkhard, 1989), although the gender gap appears to be narrowing. Most obese people are aware that their weight is too high, although overweight men are less likely than overweight women to recognise their weight as a problem (Wardle and Johnson 2002). The recognition of weight as a problem is not necessarily associated with attempts to lose weight, especially for men, who are much less likely than women of a similar weight to initiate weight control attempts (Wardle and Johnson, 2002).

Unfortunately, clinical psychologists are rarely directly involved in obesity management outside of specialist settings. However, given the prevalence of the disorder – currently 23% of women and 22% of men are obese in England (Health Survey for England, 2002) – the caseloads of most practitioners will contain several individuals for whom overweight is associated with significant physical and psychological consequences. The psychological impact of obesity and overweight is an issue over which there is some controversy. In clinical populations of obese adults, depression and low self-esteem are common, although there is less evidence for psychological adversity associated with obesity in community-based samples (Faith et al., 2002). However, poor body image appears to be a common concomitant of obesity and can lead to avoidance of social, sexual and physical activity. Obesity might therefore be implicated in the genesis of a wide range of problems routinely seen in primary care and adult mental health settings. Obesity may also be a factor influencing recovery from psychological disorder and physical health. The dramatic and sometimes irreversible weight gains produced by the anti-psychotic, antidepressant and antiviral drugs are one of the major determinants of non-adherence to these potentially life-saving medications (Green et al., 2000).

Obesity develops when more energy is taken in through the consumption of food than is expended in metabolic or physical activity. Even a small (2%) persistent discrepancy between daily intake and energy output will induce progressive and substantial weight gain over time. The fact that this small positive energy balance is not easily noticeable accounts for many obese people's perception that they do not eat more than others. Lay theories of obesity probably render the relationship between behaviour and body weight in over-simple terms; identifying the proximal cause (eating too much and exercising too little) without recognising the multiple genetic and environmental characteristics that make the individual susceptible to a positive energy balance. Obesity has a high heritability (Schousboe et al., 2003) and is reliably associated with a range of characteristics: higher maternal BMI in pregnancy (Eriksson et al., 2003a), birth weight (Eriksson et al., 2003a) and a faster rate of growth in early childhood [the so-called 'adiposity rebound' (Freedman et al., 2001)]. The significance of these aetiological factors for the treatment of obesity on an individual level are currently not well understood. It is easier to see their applicability for developing more sophisticated methods of prevention in high-risk children.

Exposure to childhood adversity had been associated with increased risk of obesity in later childhood and adulthood. One prospective study indicated that the experience of neglect in childhood is associated with a seven-fold increase in obesity during adulthood (Lissau and Sorensen, 1994), although there is currently no clear mechanism for the effect. Retrospective studies have identified the experience of all forms of abuse (physical, sexual, verbal and fear of abuse) during childhood as a risk factor for adult obesity (Williamson et al., 2002). The relevance of histories of adversity in childhood to the treatment of obesity in adulthood will depend on the treatment and setting. Obese people are a heterogeneous group, whilst most obesity treatment is homogeneous in that it is conducted in groups by non-psychologists. If group treatment is to be offered, it is advisable to have some form of screening procedure to ensure that the treatment is suitable for the clients' needs. Obese individuals presenting with substance misuse, relationship difficulties, eating dysregulation or who are morbidly obese, may require a more detailed approach to assessment that extends beyond weight and health concerns. In such cases, the targets of treatment should only be decided on after a detailed individualised case formulation has been constructed and shared with the client.

Assessment of body fat

The term 'obesity' refers to an excess of body fat, which itself is not easily measurable. Several techniques exist to estimate fatness, each of which has its drawbacks. The simplest is weight, which should be assessed on a lever- rather than spring-type balance. Weight, however, is not a direct measure of fatness, because lean body mass is also included, and some conversion must be performed. To take account of the expected difference in weights in adults of different heights, a simple index of weight-for-height has been devised as the body mass index (BMI). This is calculated as weight (kg)/height (m^2). The internationally accepted ranges of BMIs are: under-weight (< 18.5), normal weight (18.5–24.99), overweight (25.0–29.99), obesity (30.0–39.99) and extreme obesity (> 40) (World Health Organization (WHO), 1995).

Measurements of body circumference can also be used, of which waist circumference is particularly important because accumulation of abdominal fat has been shown to be reliably associated with increased risk of coronary heart disease. Men with a waist circumference at or above 94 cm are at increased risk of developing heart disease. At above 102 cm the risk is substantial. Waist circumferences of > 80 cm and > 88 cm for women represent increased and substantial risks, respectively (Lean et al., 1995).

Practitioners wanting to take such measurements themselves should seek training on the appropriate methods. Depending on the anticipated nature of the therapeutic endeavour, psychological practitioners should be mindful of the potential pitfalls of engaging in physical contact with clients. Support from an appropriately trained member of a multidisciplinary team may be useful in this area. As with anorexia and bulimia, weight and shape measurements may be emotive issues and should be dealt with sensitively.

Along with body fatness, it is also useful to collect information on the individual's weight history, which can be achieved simply by asking them if they were overweight compared to their peers at various times in life. Family history of obesity is also useful, as it may reveal a strong family pattern, which can help the individual client to understand the genetic contribution to the aetiology.

Assessment of eating behaviour

Obesity results from a persistent energy imbalance between energy input and energy output, but theoretical and therapeutic efforts have been devoted largely to the input side. No obvious 'eating style' differentiates the obese from their normal-weight counterparts, although there is some evidence for greater responsiveness to food cues and lower responsiveness to satiety cues (Koeppen-Schomerus et al., 2001). There is much evidence to suggest that the nutritional content of the diets of many obese people – as for the population as a whole – is both unhealthy and promotes weight gain (Hooper et al., 2001).

This means that assessment of dietary intake needs to look beyond the amount of energy consumed (typically calorie counting) to investigate the composition of the diet in relation to nutritional recommendations. It is also important to assess regularity of eating. Irregular eating could be unintentional but may also indicate swings from dietary restraint to disinhibition. Patterns of deliberate dietary restraint, as well as other common triggers to overeating, can be identified using the Dutch Eating Behaviour Questionnaire (Wardle, 1987) and the Three-factor Eating Questionnaire (Stunkard et al., 1985).

Assessment of food intake is typically achieved by a food diary, although there is increasing evidence that food records, particularly in the obese, underestimate energy intake and overestimate dietary quality. In the absence of a dietetic expertise to assess energy intake, the diary is most likely to be used to record progress towards specific goals of the client. The completion of food diaries can be seen as an arduous task for many people, who may need to be introduced to the process by stages. But monitoring of food intake has been linked with more successful weight control (Boutelle et al., 1998, 1999), so there is value to be gained from it. Most people eventually find the completion of a food diary a useful strategy and many continue to employ it following the termination of treatment.

Obesity and binge eating

Repeated episodes of binge eating without the compensatory behaviours seen in bulimia have now been given the label of binge eating disorder (BED). Estimates of the proportion of obese people with BED vary widely. Among those seeking treatment for obesity, BED prevalence rates range from 1 to 30% (Dingemans et al., 2002), while rates as high as 47% have been reported in patients presenting for bariatric surgery (Adami et al., 1995). Compared to obese people without BED, those with BED are more likely to have more severe obesity, become overweight and initiate dieting attempts at a younger age, and experience greater levels of depression, substance misuse and emotional difficulties (Spitzer et al., 1993).

Severe binge eating has been shown to respond well to structured cognitive-behavioural therapy programmes, most of which share the characteristics of treatment of bulimia nervosa (described in Chapter 31; Wifley et al., 1993). However, although such programmes tackle the eating pathology, they do not produce weight loss (Agras et al., 1997) and, depending on clinical need, most participants would benefit from structured weight-reducing programme that builds on skills learned in the binge-eating disorder treatment. Less severe forms of binge eating have been shown to respond well to conventional obesity treatment (Wardle et al., 2001). Assessment of binge-eating problems should follow the guidance described in section on bulimia (below).

Appetite

Hunger is often – and naturally – a stimulus for eating, but among those who are engaged in weight control, hunger cannot always be satisfied. Nonetheless, many episodes of overeating appear to occur in the absence of hunger and continuing to eat despite satiety can be part of the obese person's eating style. Ratings of hunger or satiety may therefore be useful in the therapeutic context, where a simple Likert-type scale should be adequate.

The inability to resist cravings for specific types of food is often a cause of overeating. Cravings can be defined as an intense desire for a particular food in the absence of physiological need and are distinguishable from hunger (Yanovski, 2003). Chocolate cravings are the most well known example of this type of appetitive behaviour. If cravings pose a threat to the weight-loss plan then they should be assessed using standard cognitive-behavioural assessment procedures. Cravings may serve the function of alleviating some other problematic circumstance, for example the amelioration of stress, anxiety or boredom. In suggesting that food may be a solution to non-food-related problem, care must be taken to not make the patient feel inadequate. It can help to point out the role played by the marketing industry in creating the specious desires and needs that their products are designed to fulfil.

Energy expenditure

By far the biggest proportion of energy expenditure is used for resting metabolic processes such as thermoregulation, with muscular activity accounting for less than one third in normal adults. It is a common fallacy that obese people have lower resting metabolic rates than their non-obese counterparts and that this difference accounts for weight gain. In fact, the resting metabolic levels of the obese tend to be higher than in the non-obese, because a greater amount of energy is required to maintain metabolic processes at heavier weights (Prentice et al., 1986). Age-related weight gain is likely to be the result of decreasing levels of physical activity with age (Prentice and Jebb, 1995). Whilst some research shows that the obese (adults and children) are less active than normal-weight people, one needs to be cautious about making an inference about causality from cross-sectional data. Recent data from children at risk of obesity (Wardle et al., 2002) give some support to this view, showing higher levels of sedentary activity in children of obese compared with non-obese families. However, there are likely to be multiple pathways, operating reciprocally, in the relationship between weight gain and physical activity.

In principle, assessment should cover all aspects of energy expenditure, but this is rarely practicable. Metabolic assessments are not routinely performed because the assessment techniques are highly specialised and metabolic activity is not yet an appropriate target of therapeutic intervention. Assessment of energy expenditure should be careful to distinguish between 'exercise' and 'physical activity'. Strict definitions of the two vary but a useful rule of thumb is that 'exercise' refers to periods of dedicated and strenuous physical activity conducted over a relatively discrete period, whereas 'physical activity' comprises behaviours that are performed as part of going about everyday life, such as walking or housework. Such behaviour is sometimes referred to as 'lifestyle activity' and is increasingly thought to be more important than exercise in the development of obesity. Many physically active individuals would not describe themselves as taking any form of exercise and some individuals who take regular exercise lead a sedentary existence outside their exercise sessions.

Like dietary assessment, measures of physical activity levels are necessarily crude. This need not be a problem. The purpose of measurement is rarely to gain a precise reading of the level of energy expenditure but rather to set targets for intervention and improve motivation for increased physical activity. Activity diaries and pedometers can be used to monitor progress over time.

People vary widely in the attitudes and emotional reactions they bring to the issue of increasing energy expenditure. Assessment should take account of the person's personal preferences, and elicit and correct any misinformation that may impede engagement with this aspect of the programme.

Body image

Western cultural ideals of beauty, especially for women and increasingly for men, demand a minimum of body fat. The obese are not only viewed as being physically unattractive, they are held to be personally responsible for their unattractiveness. Two widely held tenets of modern Western culture form the cornerstone of prejudicial attitudes towards the obese: (1) that it is bad to be fat; and (2) that body shape is infinitely malleable with sufficient effort. This concatenation of views legitimises the common understanding of obesity as the result of poor character and personal failure. This process of stigmatisation starts early, with children aged three viewing overweight peers as mean, ugly, stupid, unhappy, lazy and unpopular (Latner and Stunkard, 2003), and continues into adulthood (Puhl and Brownell, 2001). Such prejudicial attitudes result in discriminatory practices, which limit the social, intellectual and economic resources available to the obese person (Puhl and Brownell, 2003). Prejudices and discriminatory behaviours are also found in health-care settings, including psychologists and those specialising in the treatment of obesity (Teachman and Brownell, 2001). Not surprisingly, therefore, overweight people have been shown to have a negative body image (Stunkard and Wadden, 1992).

Body image is a complex multi-faceted construct resulting from the interaction of physical, perceptual, information-processing, emotional, behavioural and socio-cultural components (Slade, 1994). Assessment of body image should investigate all these factors using the appropriate combination of thought records, rating scales and psychometric instruments. Specific instruments for the assessment of body image in obesity and other conditions include the following: Body Image Avoidance Questionnaire (Rosen et al, 1991); Body Shape Questionnaire (Cooper et al., 1987); Body Satisfaction Scale (Slade et al., 1990).

INVESTIGATION OF BULIMIA NERVOSA

Bulimia nervosa is the only one of the three conditions discussed in this chapter that is essentially a disorder of eating rather than weight. The behavioural profile of the condition is characterised by episodes of binge eating, which are generally followed by some means of compensating for the energy intake. Compensatory methods can be divided into two types. Purging refers to activities that are designed to prevent the absorption of energy from the food, such as self-induced vomiting or the use of laxatives, diuretics and enemas. Non-purging methods of compensation refer to activities designed to use up the energy from the food, such as dietary restriction and excessive exercise.

Establishing rates of eating disorders within the community is difficult because of their low prevalence and the tendency for people with such disorders to conceal their problem and avoid professional help. Estimates of the prevalence of bulimia vary according to the criteria used to measure the disorder. Community-based studies based on the strict interpretation of DSM-IV place lifetime prevalence rates for women at 1.1%, with rates in males approximately one-tenth this figure (Garfinkel et al., 1995). When criteria are relaxed to include 'subclinical' cases, prevalence rates in young females can be as high as 5.4% (Whitehouse et al., 1992). It is likely that diagnostic approaches vastly underestimate the proportion of the population, particularly women, who engage at some level in binge-eating and compensatory behaviour (Halmi et al., 1981).

Development and maintenance of the bulimic behaviour

The development of bulimic behaviour needs to be understood within the context of a society that increasingly promotes a thin body as an aesthetic ideal and control over weight, body shape and appearance to be indicative of personal or moral strength. Individuals developing within such a culture will thus be exposed to socially sanctioned pressure to groom their bodies, usually through dietary restraint, so that it conforms to the cultural ideal. Empirical studies have repeatedly documented in women the presence of high levels of weight and shape concern. This has been shown in childhood (Sands and

Wardle, 2003) adolescence (Wardle and Marshland, 1990) and adulthood (Wardle et al., 1992). Weight and shape concern has also been documented for men. However, as men are exposed to pressures to conform to two contradictory body shapes, muscularity and leanness, the relationship between diet, body shape and weight may be more complex. Prospective studies indicate that dietary restraint, as measured by self-report, almost always precedes the onset of bulimic behaviour (Stice, 2001). Interestingly, this relationship has not been supported by the results of experimental manipulations, which have demonstrated that calorific deprivation leads to decreases in the level of bulimic behaviour (Presnell and Stice, 2003). Scales of dietary restraint may not be measuring actual caloric deprivation but some other variable that might present a risk factor for the development of bulimic behaviour. Subjective feelings of dietary restraint remains the most likely candidate. Further research is needed to establish the relationship between eating pattern, caloric intake and bulimic behaviour.

The restraint model asserts that dieting involves a shift in the mechanisms involved in the control of eating. During periods of restraint, physiological mechanisms of appetite are overridden by the cognitive system controlling eating. It is the characteristics of this cognitive system that determine whether this restriction is successful, as in anorexia, or breaks down, as in bulimia and binge eating. Cognitive control of eating involves the use of multiple, extreme and often arbitrary rules to help the person restrict his or her intake. When these rules are violated (e.g. eating a 'forbidden food') or the psychological processes supporting rule-governed behaviour are undermined (e.g. the experience of negative emotion), cognitive control of eating may break down, resulting in a binge. The tendency to evaluate self-worth in terms of the ability to control eating and maintain a thin body shape is thought to be central to the development and maintenance of a cognitive system that supports continued engagement in dietary restraint (Fairburn et al., 2003). The binge itself invokes a cathexis of thoughts and feelings, such as guilt and shame, and evaluations of self-failure, which lead to more intensive efforts at dietary restraint.

Compensatory behaviours (vomiting and purging) are learned from a number of sources, including the media, friends and family. They are facilitated by beliefs that engaging in such behaviour will 'undo' the damage done by the binge until dietary restraint can be re-established. Binges increase in size and frequency after the onset of purging behaviours. Vomiting carries a number of health risks as well as being, for most patients, a source of shame and anxiety (Pomeroy et al., 2002).

Assessment of bulimic behaviour

The goal of assessment in the treatment of bulimia is to explicate the factors that contribute to the maintenance of the vicious restraint–binge–purge cycle. Until recently, it was felt sufficient to restrict investigations to the thoughts and feelings that are associated directly with the behaviours of eating and compensation. In response to the intractability of some bulimic behaviour when dealt with in this way, workers are increasingly advocating the need to investigate more global cognitive, affective and social factors as potential maintaining mechanisms (Fairburn et al., 2003). Additional factors implicated in the maintenance of bulimia include core low self-esteem, which is independent of food and weight-related concerns, as well as a tendency to evaluate the self in terms of perfectionistic standards of achievement (Shafran et al., 2002). Hypothesised affective maintenance factors include the inability to cope appropriately with certain emotional states. According to this view, binge eating, self-induced vomiting and intense exercise serve the function of neutralising or removing from awareness of those factors triggering the intense mood state.

Assessment should therefore target descriptions of the factors, both internal and external, that triggers an episode of binge eating. This would importantly include a detailed food diary to assess dietary intake for the duration of the treatment. As binges vary considerably both within and between people it is important not to focus prematurely on a particular trigger as the 'key' precipitating factor. It will also be important to establish the range of compensatory behaviours and elucidate the cognitive and affective factors reinforcing their continued use. It may be useful to look for experiences within the personal history that might indicate that over-valuation of the self in terms of weight and shape are manifestations of more global dysfunctional assumptions about the self. It may also be instructive to find out how the individual has learned to deal with negative emotional states before the development of binge eating.

Social factors

The patient's interpersonal environment might also maintain bulimic behaviour in several ways. Dietary restraint can offer a potent sense of self-control within particular contexts, and certain interpersonal environments, such as peers, colleagues and families, can act to magnify concerns about eating and weight. Interpersonal difficulties are commonly reported as triggers of binge eating, which suggests that some individuals with bulimia struggle in social situations. In many cases the consequences of the disorder itself – for example, the need for secrecy and to adhere to strict dietary rules – can progressively undermine social confidence. For these reasons, assessment should always examine the social determinants of bulimic behaviour and the formulation should seek to understand the ways in which social factors contribute to its maintenance. This would usefully include the ways in which the behaviour is influenced by and influences the social environment (i.e. functional analysis) but also how it might contribute to other maintenance factors, for example, poor social skills or low self-esteem.

INVESTIGATION OF ANOREXIA NERVOSA

Individuals diagnosed with anorexia nervosa present with a constellation of symptoms. Core features include the refusal to maintain a minimally normal body weight, which is driven by an intense fear of gaining weight and distortions in the perception of body shape and size. Post-menarchal women with anorexia are typically amenorrheic. DSM-IV specifies that the individual should weigh less than 85% of a body weight that is considered normal for their age and height. As anorexia frequently has its onset in adolescence, the weight-related criterion may be a failure to gain an appropriate amount of weight as the individual grows. Identifying anorexia nervosa depends on ruling out the presence of any other medical or psychiatric conditions that might account for the symptoms, although it is increasingly recognised that anorexic-type presentations might be inextricably linked with some physical health problems, particularly neurological conditions (Ward et al., 2000). Individuals diagnosed with anorexia can have other concurrent psychological problems. Symptoms associated with depression and obsessive-compulsive disorder are common. When individuals with anorexia are significantly underweight, these symptoms may be a consequence of malnutrition, although some compulsive behaviour, particularly that relating to food, might be implicated in the maintenance of starvation. Individuals presenting with anorexia typically fall into one of two sub-types: (1) the 'restricting type', in which weight control is achieved almost exclusively by dietary restriction; and (2) the 'binge-eating/purging type', in which large quantities of food are eaten but the anticipated consequences of weight gain are avoided by vomiting or laxative abuse. It is now generally accepted that there are some areas of overlap between the binge-eating subtype of anorexia and bulimia nervosa. Distinguishing between these two conditions is primarily a matter of weight, with normal-weight women attracting the label of bulimia and very underweight women being labelled anorexic. The prevalence of anorexia in young females is reported to be 0.3%; there are no accurate data for men (Hoek and van Hoeken, 2003).

Anorexia is a complex disorder and most workers adhere to a multifactorial model in describing the onset and maintenance of this disturbing condition. Unlike the aetiological literature on bulimia and obesity, the understanding of anorexia is fragmented. Against the current vogue for cognitive-behavioural theories in clinical psychology, the contemporary literature on anorexia reflects the active contributions of many other therapeutic orientations, particularly systemic and psychodynamic approaches. This chapter focuses mainly on models derived from cognitive and behavioural theories.

Weight

Anorexia is primarily a disorder of weight and the regular assessment of this variable, whilst an essential component of treatment, poses a number of practical problems. Clients are likely to mislead the therapist by hiding heavy objects in their clothes to produce an apparent weight gain and this, and other methods, should be guarded against. Weighing is always an emotional matter for the patients and time should be set aside to discuss it.

Eating behaviour

There is no doubt that the nutritional intake of anorexic clients is abnormal, being not only low in calories but also specifically lacking in carbohydrate and fat. Eating style is usually also highly disordered. Many anorexics prefer to eat alone and will avoid family meals and other social occasions involving eating. Paradoxically, some individuals with anorexia have a great interest in preparing food and serving it to others. Assessment should therefore pay as much attention to the contexts of eating and non-eating episodes as to what is placed in the mouth. Such investigation should help the practitioner develop a functional analysis of those processes contributing to the maintenance of problematic eating. Investigation of food intake and eating behaviour is usually accomplished through the completion of food intake diaries. These might usefully be modified to include columns for recording potential compensatory behaviours such as vomiting, laxative abuse and exercise. The completion and veracity of such records will vary with the client's motivation for treatment. Strategies to improve motivation for this important component of intervention is likely itself to become a target of therapeutic efforts in the early stages of treatment (Vitousek et al., 1998).

Clients in in-patient settings may be more likely to present difficulties for the accurate assessment of eating behaviour. Self-report of food intake and compensatory behaviours may need to be supplemented by observational methods. As most in-patient treatment for anorexia is conducted within highly specialised settings, it is likely that staff will have developed their own methods of observation to deal with this issue. Sensitive handling of disparities between self-report and observational findings will be required to facilitate the desired behavioural change in this area.

Appetite

It was at one time assumed that the weight loss of anorexic patients reflected a loss of appetite, hence the name *anorexia*, which means absence of appetite. However, clinical research findings have indicated that appetite for food can be retained and the food restriction is an act of will (Garfinkel, 1974). Nevertheless, severe dietary restriction is likely to have an impact on appetite.

Evidence suggests that individuals with anorexia experience less hunger than normal-weight women (Codington and Bruch, 1970; Halmi et al., 1989) and have disordered satiety mechanisms (Wooley et al., 1975). For many anorexics, not eating is negatively reinforced by the experience of pain, bloating and weight gain commonly described after eating (Garfinkel, 1974). Assessment should therefore examine aspects of appetite such as hunger, urges to eat and food cravings. Understanding how these issues operate to maintain the problematic eating forms the basis of helping clients to learn how to bring their eating under physiological rather than cognitive control.

Activity and other physical anorectic methods

Excessive exercising is a common anorectic weight-loss device, and one that may be adopted by normal-weight men and women (Yates, 1991). Time spent engaging in vigorous exercising should be obtained by observational and/or self-report methods. In extreme cases, attention should be paid to less obvious ways of using physical activity to burn off energy. As with all targets of behavioural change, it may be important to assess the beliefs that are associated with engaging in such behaviours and the expected consequences of giving them up.

Body image

The contrast between the emaciated appearance of anorexic individuals and their statement that they are too fat is a striking feature of the condition. Early theories of anorexia suggested that states of emaciation arose from anorectic individuals' gross overestimation of their body size (Bruch, 1962; Slade and Russell, 1973). However, subsequent empirical work in this area showed that overestimation of body size operated to the same degree in non-eating-disordered women (Button et al., 1977). Nonetheless, it remains an important aspect of assessment and may provide a useful focus for discussions of body image.

Helping patients to recognise the tendency to overestimate their body size is an important step towards recovery for many anorexic individuals (Garner and Bemis, 1985). Facilitating this recognition can be used to help patients understand how cognitive processes contribute to the maintenance of their difficulties. The easiest technique to employ in a non-specialist clinical setting is described by Slade and Russell (1973). Individuals are asked to indicate their body width using two movable objects. Measurements are then taken on the individual's real body with using callipers or some other reliable device. Disparities between the two can then be highlighted and the experiment used to stimulate discussion about the processes contributing to overestimation of body size. Engaging with behavioural experiments of this nature are not without emotional costs for the patient. For some patients, these techniques can be seen as a challenge to their perception of reality and this can damage the therapeutic relationship. Careful attention needs to be paid to the setting-up of such experiments in the spirit of therapeutic collaboration.

Overestimation of body size is only one component of body image, which is increasingly recognised as a complex multi-factorial construct that is substantially influenced by socio-cultural factors (Slade, 1994). Evaluation by anorexic individuals of how their bodies look and feel, both to themselves and others, are consistently negative and this almost certainly contributes to the maintenance of extreme dietary restraint (Garner, 2002). Assessment should therefore assess behavioural, cognitive and affective aspects of the patients' experience of their shape. Information gained through thought records and behavioural experiments can be supplemented by the psychometric evaluations of body image discussed in the section Body image, above.

Weight-related self-schema

Theories of the maintenance of anorexia highlight the importance of a belief in which the core symptoms of the disorder are valued positively (Vitousek et al., 1998). This begs the question of why patients come to so value the often shocking results of such extreme dietary restraint. As with bulimia, the tendency to overemphasise the importance of weight and shape in evaluating self-worth provide the setting conditions for the gradual development of extreme dietary restraint. Thoughts and behaviours that are associated with the ability to maintain low body-weight are valued positively by the individual with anorexia, which makes them difficult to access and highly resistant to change. At least some individuals with anorexia hold global dysfunctional assumptions about the self, which predate the onset of the disorder (Tykra et al., 2002; Dobmyer and Stein, 2003) whereas for others experiences associated with becoming anorexic leads to negative self-evaluation.

Standard cognitive therapy techniques should be used to assess the influence of thoughts and feelings about weight and shape on patients' perception of themselves and others. Assessment should also look for more global negative evaluations of the self, although such content may be difficult to obtain during the early stages of therapy. Psychometric instruments can be used to investigate attitudes specific to weight, shape and eating – Eating Attitudes Test (Garner and Garfinkel, 1979), the Eating Disorder Inventory-2 (Garner, 1991) – as well as more global assumptions about the self and others (Young, 1994).

CONCLUSION

Throughout this chapter, the emphasis has been on the assessment of variables closely related to eating and weight. The process of careful assessment results in a descriptive account of the problem but also builds therapeutic rapport and helps patients gain insight into their difficulties. It is important that the emphasis on eating and weight should not be taken to imply that eating problems can be understood in isolation. In the clinical setting, the eating problem should always be placed in the context of a full psychological assessment.

REFERENCES

Agras, W. S. (1987) *Eating Disorders: Management of Obesity, Bulimia and Anorexia Nervosa.* New York: Pergamon.

Agras, W. S., Telch, C. F., Arnow, B., Eldredge, K. and Marnell, M. (1997) One-year follow-up of cognitive-behavioral therapy for obese individuals with binge eating disorder. *Journal of Consulting and Clinical Psychology*, 65, 343–347.

Boutelle, K. N. and Kirschenbaum, D. S. (1998) Further support for consistent self-monitoring as a vital component of successful weight control. *Obesity Research*, 6, 219–224.

Boutelle, K. N., Kirschenbaum, D. S., Baker, R. C. and Mitchell, M. E. (1999) How can obese weight controllers minimize weight gain during the high risk holiday season? By self-monitoring very consistently. *Health Psychology*, 18, 364–368.

Bruch, H. (1962) Perceptual and conceptual disturbances in anorexia nervosa. *Psychosomatic Medicine*, 24, 187–194.

Button, E. J., Fransella, F. and Slade, P. D. (1977) A reappraisal of body perception disturbance in anorexia nervosa. *Psychological Medicine*, 7, 235–243.

Calle, E. E., Thun, M. J., Petrelli, J. M., Rodriguez, C. and Heath, C. W., Jr. (1999) Body-mass index and mortality in a prospective cohort of U.S. adults. *New England Journal of Medicine*, 341, 1097–1105.

Chernin, K. (1983) *Women Size. The Tyranny of Slenderness.* London: The Womens Press.

Coddington, R. D. and Bruch, H. (1970) Gastric perceptivity in normal, obese and schizophrenic subjects. *Psychosomatics*, 11, 571–579.

Cooper, P. J., Taylor, M. J., Cooper, Z. and Fairburn, C. G. (1987) The development and validation of the Body Shape Questionnaire. *International Journal of Eating Disorders*, 6, 485–494.

Dingemans, A. E., Bruna, M. J. and van Furth, E. F. (2002) Binge eating disorder: A review. *International Journal of Obesity and Related Metabolic Disorders*, 26(3), 299–307.

Dobmeyer, A. C. and Stein, D. M. (2003) A prospective analysis of eating disorder risk factors: Drive for thinness, depressed mood, maladaptive cognitions, and ineffectiveness. *Eating Behaviour*, 4, 135–147.

Eriksson, J., Forsen, T., Osmond, C. and Barker, D. (2003a) Obesity from cradle to grave. *International Journal of Obesity and Related Metabolic Disorders*, 27, 722–727.

Eriksson, J. G., Forsen, T., Tuomilehto, J., Osmond, C. and Barker, D. J. (2003b) Early adiposity rebound in childhood and risk of Type 2 diabetes in adult life. *Diabetologia*, 46, 190–194.

Fairburn, C. G. and Cooper, Z. (1993) The Eating Disorder Examination, 12th edn. In: C. G. Fairburn and G. T. Wilson (eds) *Binge Eating: Nature, Assessment and Treatment* (pp. 317–360). New York: Guilford Press.

Fairburn, C. G., Cooper, Z. and Shafran, R. (2003) Cognitive behaviour therapy for eating disorders: A 'transdiagnostic' theory and treatment. *Behaviour Research and Therapeutics*, 41, 509–528.

Faith, M. S., Matz, P. E. and Jorge, M. A. (2002) Obesity-depression associations in the population. *Journal of Psychosomatic Research*, 53, 935–942.

Fontaine, K. R., Redden, D. T., Wang, C., Westfall, A. O. and Allison, D. B. (2003) Years of life lost due to obesity. *Journal of the American Medical Association*, 289, 187–193.

Freedman, D. S., Kettel-Khan L., Serdula, M. K., Srinivasan, S. R. and Berenson, G. S. (2001) BMI rebound, childhood height and obesity among adults: The Bogalusa Heart Study. *International Journal of Obesity and Related Metabolic Disorders*, 26(3), 299–307.

Garfinkel, P. E. (1974) Perception of hunger and satiety in anorexia nervosa. *Psychological Medicine*, 4, 309–315.

Garfinkel, P. E., Lin, E., Goering, P., Spegg, C., Goldbloom, D. S., Kennedy, S. et al. (1995) Bulimia nervosa in a Canadian community sample: prevalence and comparison of subgroups. *American Journal of Psychiatry*, 152, 1052–1058.

Garner, D. M. (1991) *Eating Disorder Inventory – 2 Manual*. Odessa, FL: Psychological Assessment Resources.

Garner, D. M. (2002) Body image and anorexia nervosa. In: T. F. Cash and T. Pruzinsky (eds). *Body Image: A Handbook of Theory, Research and Clinical Practice*. New York: Guilford Press.

Garner, D. M. and Bemis, K. M. (1985) Cognitive therapy for anorexia nervosa. In D. M. Garner and P. E. Garfinkel (eds) *Handbook of Psychotherapy for Anorexia and Bulimia*. New York: Guilford Press.

Garner, D. M. and Garfinkel, P. E. (1979) The eating attitudes test: An index of the symptoms of anorexia nervosa. *Psychological Medicine*, 9, 273–279.

Green, A. I., Patel, J. K., Goisman, R. M., Allison, D. B. and Blackburn, G. (2000) Weight gain from novel antipsychotic drugs: need for action. *General Hospital Psychiatry*, 22, 224–235.

Halmi, K. A., Falk, J. R. and Schwarts, E. (1981) Binge eating and vomiting: A survey of a college population. *Psychological Medicine*, 11, 697–706.

Halmi, K. A., Sunday, S., Puglisi, A. and Marchi, P. (1989) Hunger and satiety in anorexia and bulimia nervosa. *Annals of the New York Academy of Science*, 575, 431–445.

Health Survey for England (2002) London: HMSO.

Hoek, H. W. and van Hoeken, D. (2003) Review of the prevalence and incidence of eating disorders. *International Journal of Eating Disorders*, 34, 383–396.

Hooper, L., Summerbell, C. D., Higgins, J. P. T., Thompson, R. L., Capps., N. E., Davey Smith, G. et al. (2001) Dietary fat intake and prevention of cardiovascular disease: A systematic review. *British Medical Journal*, 322, 757–763.

Koeppen-Schomerus, G., Wardle, J. and Plomin, R. (2001) A genetic analysis of weight and overweight in 4-year-old twin pairs. *International Journal of Obesity and Related Metabolic Disorders*, 25, 838–844.

Latner, J. D. and Stunkard, A. J. (2003) Getting worse: the stigmatization of obese children. *Obesity Research*, 11, 452–456.

Lean, M. E., Han, T. S. and Morrison, C. E. (1995) Waist circumference as a measure for indicating need for weight management. *British Medical Journal*, 311, 158–161.

Lissau, I. and Sorensen, T. I. (1994) Parental neglect during childhood and increased risk of obesity in young adulthood. *Lancet*, 343, 324–327.

Mizes, J. S. and Klesges, R. C. (1989) Validity, reliability, and factor structure of the Anorectic Cognitions Questionnaire. *Addictive Behaviour*, 14, 589–594.

Must, A., Spadano, J., Coakley, E. H., Field, A. E., Colditz, G. and Dietz, W. H. (1999) The disease burden associated with overweight and obesity. *Journal of the American Medical Association*, 282, 1523–1529.

Pomeroy, C., Mitchell, J. E., Roerig, J. and Crow, S. (2002) *Medical Complications of Psychiatric Illness*. Washington, DC: American Psychiatric Association.

Prentice, A. M. and Jebb, S. A. (1995) Obesity in Britain: gluttony or sloth? *British Medical Journal*, 311, 437–439.

Prentice, A. M., Black, A. E., Coward, W. A., Davies, H. L., Goldberg, G. R., Murgatroyd, P. R. et al. (1986) High levels of energy expenditure in obese women. *British Medical Journal (Clinical Research edition)*, 292, 983–987.

Presnell, K. and Stice, E. (2003) An experimental test of the effect of weight-loss dieting on bulimic pathology: Tipping the scales in a different direction. *Journal of Abnormal Psychology*, 112, 166–170.

Puhl, R. and Brownell, K. D. (2001) Bias, discrimination, and obesity. *Obesity Research*, 9, 788–805.

Puhl, R. M and Brownell, K. D. (2003) Psychosocial origins of obesity stigma: Toward changing a powerful and pervasive bias, *Obesity Reviews*, 4(4), 213–227.

Rosen, J. C., Srebnik, D., Saltzberg, E. and Wendt, S. (1991) Development of a body image avoidance questionnaire. *Journal of Psychological Assessment*, 3, 32–37.

Sands, E. R. and Wardle, J. (2003) Internalization of ideal body shapes in 9–12-year-old girls. *International Journal of Eating Disorders*, 33, 193–204.

Schousboe, K., Willemsen, G., Kyvik, K. O., Mortensen, J., Boomsma, D. I., Cornes, B. K. et al. (2003) Sex differences in heritability of BMI: A comparative study of results from twin studies in eight countries. *Twin Research*, 6, 409–421.

Serdula, M. K., Mokdad, A. H., Williamson, D. F., Galuska, D. A., Mendlein, J. M. and Heath, G. W. (1999) Prevalence of attempting weight loss and strategies for controlling weight. *Journal of the American Medical Association*, 282, 1353–1358.

Shafran, R., Cooper, Z. and Fairburn, C. G. (2002) Clinical perfectionism: A cognitive-behavioural analysis. *Behaviour Research and Therapy*, 40, 773–791.

Slade, P. D. (1994). What is body image? *Behaviour Research and Therapy*, 32, 497–502.

Slade, P. D. and Russell, G. F. (1973) Experimental investigations of bodily perception in anorexia nervosa and obesity. *Psychotherapy and Psychosomatics*, 22, 359–363.

Slade, P. D., Dewey, M. E., Newton, T. and Brodie, D. A. (1990) Development and preliminary validation of the Body Satisfaction Scale (BSS). *Psychology and Health*, 4, 213–220.

Sobal, J. and Stunkard, A. J. (1989) Socioeconomic status and obesity: A review of the literature. *Psychological Bulletin*, 105, 260–275.

Spitzer, R. L., Yanovski, S., Wadden, T., Wing, R., Marcus, M. D., Stunkard, A. et al. (1993) Binge eating disorder: Its further validation in a multisite study. *International Journal of Eating Disorders*, 13, 137–153.

Stice, E. (2001) A prospective test of the dual-pathway model of bulimic pathology: Mediating effects of dieting and negative affect. *Journal of Abnormal Psychology*, 110, 124–135.

Stunkard, A. J. and Messick, S. (1985) The three factor eating questionnaire to measure dietary restraint, disinhibition and hunger. *Journal of Psychosomatic Research*, 29, 71–84.

Stunkard, A. J. and Wadden, T. A. (1992) Psychological aspects of severe obesity. *American Journal of Clinical Nutrition*, 55, 524S–532S.

Teachman, B. A. and Brownell, K. D. (2001) Implicit anti-fat bias among health professionals: is anyone immune? *International Journal of Obesity and Related Metabolic Disorders*, 25, 1525–1531.

Tyrka, A. R., Waldron, I., Graber, J. A. and Brooks-Gunn, J. (2002) Prospective predictors of the onset of anorexic and bulimic syndromes. *International Journal of Eating Disorders*, 32, 282–290.

Vitousek, K., Watson, S. and Wilson, G. T. (1998) Enhancing motivation for change in treatment-resistant eating disorders. *Clinical Psychological Review*, 18, 391–420.

Ward, A., Tiller, J., Treasure, J. and Russell, G. (2000) Eating disorders: Psyche or soma? *International Journal of Eating Disorders*, 27, 279–287.

Wardle, J. (1987) Eating style: A validation study of the Dutch Eating Behaviour Questionnaire in normal subjects and women with eating disorders. *Journal of Psychosomatic Research*, 31, 161–169.

Wardle, J. and Johnson, F. (2002) Weight and dieting: examining levels of weight concern in British adults. *International Journal of Obesity and Related Metabolic Disorders*, 26, 1144–1149.

Wardle, J. and Marsland, L. (1990) Adolescent concerns about weight and eating: A social-development perspective. *Journal of Psychosomatic Research*, 34, 377–391.

Wardle, J., Marsland, L., Sheikh, Y., Quinn, M., Fedoroff, I. and Ogden, J. (1992) Eating style and eating behaviour in adolescents. *Appetite*, 18, 167–183.

Wardle, J., Waller, J. and Rapoport, L. (2001) Body dissatisfaction and binge eating in obese women: the role of restraint and depression. *Obesity Research*, 9, 778–787.

Wardle, J., Waller, J. and Fox, E. (2002). Age of onset and body dissatisfaction in obesity. *Addictive Behaviour*, 27, 561–573.

Welch, G., Thompson, L. and Hall, A. (1993) The BULIT-R: Its reliability and clinical validity as a screening tool for DSM-III-R bulimia nervosa in a female tertiary education population. *International Journal of Eating Disorders*, 14, 95–105.

Whitehouse, A. M., Cooper, P. J., Vize, C. V., Hill, C. and Vogel, L. (1992) Prevalence of eating disorders in three Cambridge general practices: Hidden and conspicuous morbidity. *British Journal of General Practice*, 42, 57–60.

Wilfley, D. E., Agras, W. S., Telch, C. F., Rossiter, E. M., Schneider, J. A., Cole, A. G. et al. (1993) Group cognitive-behavioral therapy and group interpersonal psychotherapy for the nonpurging bulimic individual: A controlled comparison. *Journal of Consulting and Clinical Psychology*, 61, 296–305.

Williamson, D. A. (1990) *Assessment of Eating Disorders: Obesity, Anorexia and Bulimia Nervosa*. New York: Pergamon.

Williamson, D. F., Thompson, T. J., Anda, R. F., Dietz, W. H. and Felitti, V. (2002) Body weight and obesity in adults and self-reported abuse in childhood. *International Journal of Obesity Related Metabolic Disorders*, 26, 1075–1082.

Wooley, O. W., Wooley, S. C and Woods, W. A. (1975) Effect of calories on appetite for palatable food in obese and non-obese humans. *Journal of Comparative and Physiological Psychology*, 89, 619–625.

World Health Organization (WHO) (2002) *Obesity: Preventing and Managing the Global Epidemic. WHO Technical Report Series*, No. 894. WHO: Geneva.

Yanovski, S. (2003) Sugar and fat: Cravings and aversions. *Journal of Nutrition*, 133, 835S–837S.

Yates, A. (1991) *Compulsive Exercise and the Eating Disorder: Towards an Integrated Theory of Activity*. New York: Brunner/Mazel.

Young, J. E. (1994) *Cognitive Therapy for Personality Disorders: A Schema-Focussed Approach*, 2nd edn. Sarasota, FL: Professional Resource Press.

Chapter 31

Disorders of eating and weight

Treatment

Paul Chadwick and Jane Wardle

INTRODUCTION

Psychological treatments of the disorders of eating and weight have run a variable course. One the one hand, psychological approaches seem ideally suited to such abnormalities of behaviour as excessive eating, and some spectacular success have been achieved in uncontrolled case series (Stuart, 1967; Garfinkel et al., 1973). One the other hand, the disorders have not responded to treatment with the ease predicted by simple behavioural models. The prevailing view of the long-term impact of psychological treatments on obesity (Thomas, 1995), anorexia (Pike, 1998) and bulimia (Halmi et al., 2002) has lost its earlier optimism. In common with the treatments for other habit disorders, the real challenge is not the initial behavioural changes but long-term maintenance. It is now widely accepted that behaviour change is often short-lived, and that new treatments must demonstrate and respond to a realistic acceptance of this.

TREATMENT OF OBESITY

The 'problem' of obesity has attracted increasing attention in the Western world over the past few decades as levels grow to 'epidemic' proportions and research continues to document the health hazards of excess body weight. However, in the consciousness of overweight individuals, such health risks are usually secondary to the threat posed by fatness to achieving the hegemonic thin aesthetic preferred by Western culture. This potent combination of health and aesthetic concern has spawned a powerful and self-perpetuating commercial industry devoted to the generation of anxiety, overweight and body shape, and the sale of solutions. Given the scope of the problem, it is unlikely that limited NHS resources can tackle the problem effectively and active, responsible partnership from the commercial sector may be necessary to tackle this most recalcitrant of problems.

The early optimism engendered by the first reports of obesity management using behavioural principles (Stuart, 1967) has lost much of its shine; a large body of empirical data testifies to the grim reality that a significant and enduring reduction in body-weight is not necessarily available to the majority of overweight people. Outcomes of behavioural treatment of obesity have remained largely unchanged over the past 15 years and are best summarised as follows: 'those who complete weight loss programs lose approximately 10% of their body weight, only to regain two thirds of it back within a year and almost all of it back within five years' (Thomas, 1995). Nevertheless, this pattern of weight loss and maintenance needs to be set against the inexorable trend for untreated patients to continue gaining weight over time and the fact that modest weight losses of 10% are associated with substantial improvements in physical and psychological morbidity (Blackburn and Kanders, 1987; Goldstein, 1992, Knowler et al., 2002).

Psychological treatments for obesity generally fall into one of two types: behavioural treatments and non-dieting approaches. Behavioural treatment remains the most widely evaluated method of obesity management. Most programmes are procedural variations on the theme of learning to control food intake and increase activity levels to produce a consistent negative energy imbalance. Current expert opinion favours the initial use of a very-low-calorie diet, typically 1,200–1,500 kcal/day, to induce weight loss, followed by lifestyle modification to limit weight regain (Wadden et al., 2002). Larger initial weight losses are associated with better-sustained weight maintenance (Astrup and Rossner, 2000) and there has been much interest recently in the use of meal replacement plans to induce greater initial weight losses as means of improving outcomes (Look Ahead Group, 2003). Non-dieting approaches encourage clients to relinquish the cycle of dietary restraint and overeating by promoting size acceptance, boosting self-esteem and encouraging behaviours conducive to long-term health. Although such programmes rarely produce substantive weight loss, they are demonstrably successful at reducing levels of disordered eating and psychological morbidity while producing lasting improvements in health outcomes (Polivy and Herman, 1983; Ciliska, 1998; Bacon et al., 2002). Programmes that contain elements of both behavioural and non-dieting approaches are a welcome recent development in this field. These programmes aim to reduce obesity-related health risks by moderate weight loss, while improving the psychological morbidity associated with and contributing to the condition. Few controlled studies exist to demonstrate the efficacy of this 'third way', although those that have been conducted suggest that this approach can produce comparable results to traditional weight-oriented behavioural treatments (Rapoport et al., 2000) and, indeed, may be superior (Sbrocco et al., 1999).

Helping patients maintain a lower body weight following treatment cessation is the main challenge facing obesity management (Foreyt and Godrick, 1993). One attempt to meet this challenge has been to define obesity as a chronic condition requiring long-term care. A comprehensive series of studies by Perri and collegues demonstrate that a 10–15% weight loss can be maintained in the long term if individuals are offered continued behavioural care in the form of contact through the post or by telephone or clinic appointments (Perri et al., 1984, 1986, 1987, 1988, 1989, 1993, 1997, 2001). Interventions to harness social support also improve maintenance. Sadly, there seems to be a trade-off between the costs of offering continued intervention and the gains of treatment: longer-term interventions appear to delay rather than prevent weight regain Internet-based interventions may prove a promising cost-effective option for encouraging greater levels of maintenance (Tate et al., 2003).

Standard treatment of obesity in primary care, most commonly advice-giving masquerading as behavioural therapy, is demonstrably ineffective even with motivated patients (Moore et al., 2003). Self-help approaches to obesity management are increasingly popular, although, unless highly structured and based on behavioural principles, such treatments can actually induce weight gain (Latner, 2001). Commercial weight-loss programmes have been shown to be superior to standard NHS primary care in producing better weight loss and maintenance. Nevertheless, such programmes suffer from the same problems of poor compliance and weight regain as their professionally led behavioural counterparts (Heshka et al., 2003).

Most treatment programmes for obesity involve the following components: self-monitoring of behaviour, targeting of treatment goals, identification and modification of discriminating stimuli, reduction in energy intake, increase in activity level and the improvement of body-image. These are briefly described in the following sections.

Self-monitoring

Keeping records of food intake and activity levels is the mainstay of the assessment procedure, but also makes a therapeutic contribution. Recording the settings, timing and motivational states in which eating and activity takes place can be used to identify targets for change. Patients report that self-monitoring procedures can themselves produce change (Öst and Gottestam, 1976), and some studies have suggested that they can provide a weight loss comparable to more complex behavioural programmes (Romanczyk et al., 1973). The mechanism of the effect remains unclear, although it is assumed to lie in the increased opportunities for change that result from greater self-awareness. Continued monitoring of weight and eating has been shown to make a contribution to weight maintenance once formal treatment has ceased (Boutelle et al., 1999). Self-monitoring should be introduced to clients as something that is for their benefit and initial stages of treatment should teach clients the skills necessary to complete and interpret their diaries independently of the therapist. Written materials, such as treatment manuals, can be useful in this respect. The following manuals provide excellent materials for assisting the treatment of adult obesity: *Shape-Up* (Wardle et al., 2006), *The Learn Program for Weight Control* (Brownell, 1987), *Cognitive-Behavioural Treatment of Obesity* (Cooper et al., 2003).

Target setting

Two types of target need to be set in obesity management: the desired level of weight loss and the behavioural steps that will lead to this. The choice of target weight will depend on a number of factors, including the patient's desired weight, weight history, health considerations and the therapist's knowledge of what is generally achievable in the long term; typically 10% of initial body weight. Sub-goals of weekly weight loss are set fairly low (0.5–1 kg per week) both in order to minimise the effects of starvation and because there is some evidence that realistic goal setting is associated with better results. Studies of women entering weight-loss programmes show that participants want to lose 25% of their initial body-weight and would be disappointed to lose 17% (Foster et al., 1997a, 1997b). This desire to lose twice as much as the best pharmacological and behavioural treatments can produce persists even when subjects are repeatedly counselled about the benefits of modest weight loss. Thankfully, it does not seem to mitigate against participants being satisfied with the modest weight losses that are achieved (Wadden et al., 2003). Nevertheless, clients embarking on weight-management programmes should be counselled about the limitations of current treatments and the benefits of modest weight loss.

Stimulus control: identification and modification of discriminative stimuli

Ferster (1962) was the first to propose that eating behaviour is part of a behavioural chain under control of environmental cues and consequences, which, if manipulated appropriately, will result in the regulation of food intake without calling on 'will power'. Dietary records and interviews can be used to identify and modify antecedent conditions for unplanned eating. Stuart and Davis (1972) and Brownell (1987) list a number of common antecedent stimuli that can be modified to reduce caloric intake. These include: presence of desirable foods, situations that trigger excess intake and activities that take place during eating. Training in the techniques of problem solving can be used to help clients become skilled in formulating their own solutions to stimulus control dilemmas.

Reinforcement

Eating is assumed to have powerful and immediate positively reinforcing consequences, that is, eating is pleasurable. The adverse consequences of positive energy imbalance, such as fatness and reduced fitness, all lie in the future. Most behaviour therapy techniques are therefore set in the context of operant technologies and self- or external reinforcement paradigms are used to bridge the time before weight loss occurs. If possible, clients should be trained in the principles of reinforcement and encouraged to alter their life-style so that pleasant events are contingent on the performance of target behaviours or the achievement of goals relevant to the weight loss endeavour. Once clients have been trained in the basic principles of self-reinforcement, they are able to develop their own programmes of reinforcement independently of the therapist. Nonetheless, it is common to be met with initial scepticism about the power or necessity of formal reinforcement and behavioural experiments can be used to help clients experience the value of formal reinforcement.

Altering eating style

Although there was much early interest in the idea of an obesogenic eating style, research has failed to document a consistent pattern that differentiates the obese from normal-weight individuals (Mahoney, 1975). Interest in 'eating style' and obesity now centres on the contribution of binge- or 'emotional' eating (Wardle et al., 1992) to preventing the maintenance of a negative energy imbalance. Interventions to deal with emotionally driven eating follow much the same procedure as that described for bulimia. Standard cognitive therapy techniques can be used to identify and modify the thoughts and feelings driving the behaviour. At the same time, clients should be helped to develop skills in using more helpful methods of dealing with stress and distress. Attempts at weight reduction will not meet with success in individuals with extremely disordered eating unless this is first eliminated. For this reason, dealing with emotional distress itself may form the initial primary therapeutic target for a small subset of individuals presenting with binge eating and obesity. Elimination of binge eating in the absence of weight loss has been shown to improve psychological well-being in many individuals (Herman and Pilivy, 1982).

Altering food intake

Dietary change remains the mainstay of obesity treatment and is achieved through the application of behaviour-change principles. Obese individuals have little choice but to restrict their intake to induce a negative energy imbalance; the amount of time and effort required to induce weight loss by increasing physical activity alone is rarely practicable for most people. There is also growing evidence that poor diet contributes independently to the health risks associated with obesity. This suggests that calorie restriction within the context of a balanced diet is the most appropriate nutritional plan for weight reduction in obesity. Most clients will need systematic education about the principles of eating a balanced but reduced-energy diet, and this is best achieved by a dietician or nutritionist. Behavioural techniques of goal setting and reinforcement should be used to gradually change the client's existing diet to one that conforms to that suggested by the balance of good health (Hunt et al., 1995). The development of clients' skills to be able to select and prepare healthier choices should also be part of the programme. The manuals mentioned earlier contain comprehensive sections on nutrition and skill development.

Increasing energy output

Obesity treatment programmes should include interventions to increase physical activity for two reasons: (1) to increase the likelihood of obtaining a negative energy imbalance; and (2) to reduce the risk factors associated with physical inactivity. Most controlled trials have shown that the combination of diet plus exercise produces greater weight loss than diet alone (Skender et al., 1996) and continued exercise is consistently related to successful maintenance of weight lost (Pronk and Wing, 1994; Brownell, 1995, Wadden et al., 1998). Descriptive studies of individuals who maintain substantial weight losses indicate that such people engage in a very high level of physical activity, roughly 11,210 kJ per week, the equivalent of walking briskly for about 6.5 km a day. Such efforts are in addition to conscious restriction of food intake (Wing and Hill, 2001). Home-based physical activity, for example lifestyle activity and walking, is associated with better adherence and weight-loss maintenance than gym-based exercise (Perri et al., 1997). The question of how much physical activity is enough depends on what the individual is trying to achieve. Guidelines from the US Surgeon General recommend that people should accumulate, not necessarily in one period, up to 30 minutes of moderate to vigorous physical activity per day to reduce risk factors associated with inactivity (cited in Peters et al., 2002). Successful long-term weight maintainers have been found to perform more than twice the level of physical activity recommended for non-obese people by the US Surgeon General.

Pedometers and heart-rate monitors can be useful methods of monitoring and setting specific targets for increased physical activity. Regular attendance at exercise classes and having specific distances to swim, walk or run can also be useful ways of increasing activity. For most people, the most practicable approach is to engineer opportunities to walk into their daily routine. This can be achieved during lunchtime or on the journey to and from work. Exercise-on-prescription schemes are now routinely available within many primary care trusts and can help those clients whose physical health makes it difficult to engage in conventional exercise programmes. As with dietary change, all interventions to increase physical activity should be built with the principles of maintenance in mind.

Improving body image and self-esteem

Given the extreme and socially sanctioned stigma against excess weight, it is hardly surprising that the body image of obese people is generally poor and can be associated with much distress. Until recently, actual weight loss has been seen as the solution to body-image problems in the obese. Several factors militate against this view. As most individuals can expect to achieve only modest weight loss, the actual impact on their physical appearance may be minimal (Wadden et al., 2003). Furthermore, improvements in body image in obese women can be achieved without weight loss (Rosen, 1996), and weight reduction is not always associated with improvements in body image (Cash and Hicks, 1990). Clearly, weight loss is neither a necessary nor sufficient condition for improving body-image problems in the obese.

There are a number of reasons to promote better body image in the obese. Poor body image can be associated with a failure to engage in activities that might promote psychological and physical well-being in the absence of weight loss. Cognitions associated with poor body image have also been hypothesised to trigger episodes of binge eating (Fairburn et al., 2003). Specific programmes for improving body image have been developed and demonstrated to produce sustainable improvements in obese women (Rosen, 1996). These treatments share many of the characteristics for improving body image in anorexia and bulimia. Key strategies include: providing information to correct many of the myths associated with obesity (e.g. that the body is infinitely malleable); collaborative development of graded exposure programmes to overcome avoidance of body-related behaviours, thoughts and images; and the development of skills to identify and challenge thinking patterns that generate distress and maintain avoidance. Therapists should not shy away from engaging clients in debates about the influence of the media in the construction of stereotypes associated with obesity. Interventions to help clients deal constructively with the prejudice they encounter may also be a useful component of therapy. Puhl and Brownell (2003) describe some of the psychological theories relevant to helping people cope with the experience of stigma.

The therapeutic relationship

Therapists are not immune to prejudicial attitudes and most will share the wider society's preferences for thinness. It can be difficult for a thin, attractive psychologist who invests a great deal of time, money and effort in the pursuit of physical health and attractiveness to feel or demonstrate empathy with the psychological and physical state of an extremely overweight person. Given that stigma towards the obese is one of the last remaining socially sanctioned prejudices, therapists working with obese people need to be vigilant to the influence of their own attitudes towards weight and shape (Teachman and Brownell, 2001). The capacity for prejudice to affect the therapeutic alliance can happen regardless of one's own body weight or shape. It can help to think in advance about how one might respond sensitively and honestly to client's questions about one's own relationship with weight and food. Ideas from Vitousek et al. (1998) can be adapted to help manage therapeutic relationships with obese clients.

Conclusions

The treatment of choice for obesity is best described as nutritional counselling augmented by behavioural-change training. In recent years it has become commonplace to describe such treatments as cognitive-behavioural therapy because they contain elements to help clients recognise and challenge self-defeating thoughts. However, these approaches, usually conducted in group settings by professionals with only rudimentary training in psychological technologies, fall short of the individualised, maintenance-focused formulation-based CBT practised with anorexia and bulimia.

The issue of obesity is clearly complex and successful treatment requires lengthy, often multi-disciplinary input, across a number of areas. A satisfactory account of the onset and maintenance of this disorder must extend beyond psychology to include the influence of physiological realities and cultural pressures. The stigma associated with obesity can seduce even experienced practitioners into making the individual's character the inappropriate focus of both the problem and its solution. When working with clients who have this problem, the best adage might be – as with many other disorders – to help the client change that which can be changed and to accept that which cannot (Wilson, 1996).

THE TREATMENT OF ANOREXIA

The principal characteristics of anorexia involve abnormalities of food intake resulting in low weight and an abhorrence of weight gain. Approximately half of individuals with anorexia present with binge eating, vomiting and laxative abuse as part of their attempts to regulate weight. The medical consequences of anorexia can be very serious, and death from the complications of long-term starvation, vomiting and laxative abuse is frighteningly common. Treatment procedures for anorexia have tended towards a two-pronged approach. Nursing and medical efforts are directed towards immediate weight and metabolic restoration, often in an in-patient setting. Once some weight change has been achieved, psychological interventions are directed towards addressing the attitudes and beliefs that supposedly underlie the weight problem. Severe states of underweight significantly compromise physical health and psychological functioning (Pomeroy et al., 2002). Out-patient management in such cases is unlikely to be successful and in-patient management, often invoking compulsory detainment, may be necessary. Vandereycken and Beumont (1998) provide an overview of the ethical and legal aspects of eating disorder treatments, including perspectives from patients themselves.

Sequencing the therapeutic endeavour

Intervention with individuals presenting with anorexia is a complex undertaking. The tasks of therapy can be multiple, non-linear and will need continual renegotiation according to the balance of the patient's physical and emotional needs. In the early stages, treatment should be geared towards weight restoration, as severe emaciation affects emotional, cognitive and behavioural functioning. Weight restoration is commonly associated with significant improvement on all these dimensions, permitting the therapist to construct a more accurate formulation of the distal factors contributing to the development and maintenance of the disorder.

When constructing treatment goals, the therapist needs to be sensitive to the possibilities and constraints afforded by the client's familial and developmental contexts. A functional analysis of the role of the patient's non-eating is useful in this respect. Many aspects of the family environment can contribute to the maintenance of anorexic behaviour and may need to be modified using family-focused interventions (Eisler et al., 2000). The all-consuming nature of anorexia can induce a hiatus in the psychosocial development of some individuals. Thus, some anorexics may lack the confidence and skills necessary to pursue life beyond the disorder. Training in skills unrelated to weight management – encouraging confidence in social situations, for example – can address issues arising from arrested development. The long-term treatment of anorexia should therefore be driven by a process of ongoing reformulation of the client's difficulties as they move through the various stages of the disorder.

Motivation for change

Unlike those with obesity or bulimia, individuals with anorexia are usually highly resistant to treatment and are rarely brought for intervention of their own volition. The maintenance of the disorder, according to cognitive and behavioural formulations, depends on the individual holding positive beliefs about the core cognitive and behavioural manifestations of the condition, and the potential of such beliefs to generate positive reinforcement (Slade, 1982; Vitousek et al., 1998; Fairburn et al., 1999). Strategies to improve motivation for recovery are scattered throughout the various treatment components for anorexia. This includes the establishing of a therapeutic milieu as well as principles of positive reinforcement for weight gain. More recently, specific theories of motivational enhancement, particularly the transtheoretical model, have been applied to the domain of anorexia treatment (Blake et al., 1997; Jordan et al., 2003). Externalisation techniques have also been employed to facilitate recognition and discussion of the costs and benefits of the disorder (Serpell et al., 1999). Vitousek et al. (1998) offer a comprehensive guide to improving motivation for treatment engagement in this client group.

Weight management

Efforts to improve nutritional status are essential components of the treatment of anorexia nervosa. Operant procedures are well established in helping patients to develop eating patterns that facilitate weight gain (Bemis, 1987; Touyz and Beumont, 1997). A common operant procedure is to set a goal weight range and a target rate of regain that are acceptable to the patient. Rewards are agreed for the achievement of weight goals. The therapist and patient work together to generate ideas that will increase the likelihood of reaching the target weight gain. The nature of this support needs to evolve during treatment. Initially, patients are encouraged to eat according to a prescribed regimen of intake because the mechanisms of hunger and satiety are likely to be disturbed and therefore an unreliable guide to intake. As treatment progresses, the patient is encouraged to take increasing control of devising her or his own meal plans. Experiments to encourage generalisation of gains made in the therapeutic environment are crucial. *In vivo* exposure to the eating of avoided or forbidden foods is an important component of normalising eating behaviour. Such techniques can generate high affect and, when managed sensitively, can be a fertile ground for eliciting and challenging beliefs that maintain problematic eating. Nutritional education is also necessary. This might usefully include information on the physiological and psychological effects of starvation (see Keys et al., 1950).

Modification of body image

All individuals with anorexia exhibit intense body dissatisfaction. This can persist following an otherwise successful treatment of their eating problems (Deter and Herzog, 1994) and in such cases is a reliable predictor of relapse (Freeman et al., 1985; Fairburn et al., 1993). Interventions to improve body image aim to reduce the patient's distorted perception of body size and to improve body dissatisfaction by changing dysfunctional attitudes and behavioural disturbances. Directly changing body-size perceptions by itself plays a limited role in the treatment of anorexia; most patients have a long history of receiving feedback on this matter. Nevertheless, the use of mirrors as means of desensitising patients to their appearance has been shown to improve body satisfaction to a greater extent than other therapeutic procedures (Key et al., 2002). It is likely that the impact of this intervention derives from the use of *in vivo* exposure to generate awareness of the dysfunctional attitudes that maintain the negative body image. The capacity for such directive interventions to generate high levels of affect means that such work may only be appropriate for individuals undergoing treatment in a supported atmosphere. The literature currently gives no clear guidelines as to when the modification of body image should be introduced. Some programmes introduce body-image therapy once the patient has reached the target weight, although many patients may need to be supported through the difficult period as their weight increases.

Modifying beliefs about the self

Recent cognitive-behavioural models of anorexia suggest that the disorder develops when negative views about the self become associated with beliefs about weight and shape. This concordance supports the use of extreme dietary restriction as a means to maintain a positive self-concept: weight control becomes a way of dealing with the negative emotions generated by the presence of dysfunctional assumptions about the self and others (Cooper et al., 1998). Therapeutic efforts to dismantle this dysfunctional system of beliefs should be guided by an individualised cognitive case formulation and can encompass a wide range of cognitive therapy techniques. Clients should be helped to formulate their beliefs as testable hypotheses, which can be subject to the process of 'empirical' scrutiny. Cognitions relating to weight and shape may prove easier to elicit and manage than those relating to the self-schema. Modification of schema-level beliefs may involve the use of more directive strategies – for example, the mirror desensitisation process described above – and should only be attempted within the context of a strong therapeutic relationship.

Conclusions

Whereas short-term weight gain is achievable for most anorexic patients, the longer-term picture is discouraging. Rates of recovery vary widely across studies and higher rates cannot be consistently associated with any particular treatment modality (Pike, 1998). Following treatment cessation, significant proportions of treated anorexics continue to lose weight, engage in restrictive eating and experience disabling levels of co-morbid psychological disorders (Pike, 1997). Poorer outcomes are associated with several factors: lower body weight at time of referral, longer duration of illness, older age of onset and the persistence of negative attitudes regarding weight and shape following weight stabilisation (Pike, 1997).

The outcome literature on treatments for anorexia nervosa is sparse. Few randomised controlled trials for treatment have been conducted and those that have suggest no clear advantage for one modality of treatment over another (Dare et al., 2001). Most individuals with anorexia engage in a wide range of therapies in their efforts to recover from the condition and none of the long-term outcome studies control for specific treatment effects (Pike, 1997). Further research is clearly needed to further our understanding of this devastating disorder and its treatment.

TREATMENT OF BULIMIA

The last decade has seen a dramatic increase in the literature on the treatment of bulimia. Cognitive-behavioural therapy is now well-established as an effective treatment for the condition. Controlled outcome studies have shown that it is superior to the use of single antidepressant drugs and alternative psychological treatments (Wilson et al., 2002). Between 40 and 50% of individuals with bulimia who are treated with CBT cease binge eating and purging completely. However, this leaves 50–60% of individuals who show only partial improvement or derive no benefit at all. A substantial proportion of patients experience relapse following treatment cessation, even in cases where complete abstinence of binging and compensatory behaviour has been achieved. Factors predictive of relapse vary from study to study and include: shorter periods of abstinence for bingeing and purging (Halmi et al., 2002), low levels of self-esteem and higher degrees of attitudinal disturbance towards eating, weight and shape (Fairburn et al., 1993). The mechanisms via which such factors might contribute to relapse are not well understood and further research is needed to establish how intervention programmes could be adapted to prevent this. The search for predictive factors has generally been concerned with variables located within the individual as opposed to events and situations in the environment that could precipitate relapse.

The literature demonstrates a pronounced tendency towards the development and evaluation of treatment programmes for individuals. However, recent evidence suggests that individual cognitive-behavioural protocols can be adapted to a group setting and achieve comparable outcomes to individualised treatment (Chen et al., 2003). Participant reports of group treatment suggest that the group format is liked and provides much-valued additional support and motivation. In some cases, the need for careful development of an individualised treatment programme might override the advantages of group support.

Strategies used in the treatment of bulimia have much in common with those used to manage anorexia and obesity. The key elements of intervention are presented below.

Self-monitoring of food intake, compensation and pre-occupation with food

Initially, this is used as an assessment device but for most people it becomes a valued part of their system of control and allows a more objective evaluation of intake at times when anxiety prevents proper recall. Studies examining process factors in CBT find that 76% of the total improvement in the frequency of bingeing and 69% of total improvement in the frequency of vomiting were evident by the fifth session (Wilson et al., 2002). This relatively rapid improvement in symptomatology has been attributed to improvements in dietary restraint facilitated by the use of self-monitoring.

Modification of food intake

As dietary restraint almost certainly contributes to the maintenance of the binge–compensation cycle, a central feature of all therapy for bulima involves helping the patient to relinquish restraint and return to a normal pattern of eating. Some individuals can structure their food intake according to general guidelines, such as a daily food intake of approximately 2,000 calories in the form of three meals with two to three snacks. Others might require more detailed nutritional instruction, and consultation with a dietician may prove useful. Clients are likely to be emotionally attached to the practice of dietary restraint and modification of eating patterns may need to address the beliefs generating this attachment. Of particular importance to the maintenance of non-restrained eating is that the person should continue to eat with his or her planned eating pattern even if a binge has occurred. A 'normal' pattern of eating in treatment of bulimia refers not only to the *what* but also the *when* of food intake. The long-standing habits of bingeing and purging disrupt the links between appetite and subjective experience and patients need to relearn these by adopting regular eating habits.

Dismantling dietary rules

Individuals with bulimia have developed strict and idiosyncratic dietary rules as part of the cognitive system that controls their eating. Most commonly this is manifest as a division of foods into good and bad. The former are invariably low-calories foods, such as fruit and vegetables, and are consumed during non-binge periods, whereas the latter tend to be high-calorie foods, which are only consumed during a binge. The presence of banned or dangerous food is interpreted as a threat to dietary control and therefore invokes anxiety, which in turn increases the risk of binge eating. A key ingredient of treatment is therefore to dismantle these unhelpful dietary rules by a combination of cognitive and behavioural techniques. Timing is an important determinant of whether therapy succeeds in this task. Early stages of therapy are concerned with reducing binge frequency and this is most effectively achieved by helping the patient to use stimulus-control techniques to avoid binge triggers. Once the person has become skilled at coping with the anxiety that triggers binge eating, cue-exposure methods can be used to help the patient reintroduce forbidden foods into the diet. Cue exposure, distinct from the exposure and response prevention technique described in the next section, involves gradually exposing patients to forbidden foods in an attempt to extinguish the anxiety generated by that food and cues related to it. This method of cue exposure has not been studied extensively and is not routinely employed in the most common form of bulimia treatment. However, there is some evidence that it can be an effective stand-alone treatment for bulimic behaviour in people with high levels of motivation who have failed to respond to conventional CBT (Toro et al., 2003).

Reduction of compensatory behaviour

The nature of interventions to reduce compensatory behaviour is determined by their nature. Purging behaviours, vomiting and laxative abuse, are dealt with by educating the patient about the dangers of electrolyte imbalance (Johnson et al., 1987) as a way of helping them to become more motivated to change the behaviour. When sufficient motivation has been established, goal-setting and reward techniques can be used to reduce frequency of the target behaviours. Exposure and response prevention techniques, in which clients are asked to eat large amounts of food and prevented from engaging in the compensatory response, can be effective in extinguishing purging behaviour. However, this technique is logistically difficult to organise and has been found not to produce any additional benefits over comparable treatment programmes that omit it (Carter et al., 2003).

Coping with the urge to eat

Self-monitoring techniques can help people to identify the internal and external cues that precipitate binge eating. The most common triggers are: being alone, unoccupied and in the presence of 'bad' food. Although stimulus-control strategies are initially useful, they do not represent a feasible long-term solution. Individuals can be helped to develop a range of strategies that will help them to respond differently to binge-triggering stimuli. Such techniques may be cognitive – the rehearsal of positive coping statements, for example – or behavioural, such as engaging in an activity incompatible with eating.

Beyond weight and shape concern

Recent reformulations of the cognitive-behavioural model of bulimia have suggested that aspects of the cognitive-affective system responsible for global self-evaluation may be a cause of continued dysfunction in some individuals with this condition. Difficulties in regulating affect have also been hypothesised to account for the persistence of the disorder despite treatment (Fairburn et al., 1999). In such cases, cognitive therapy techniques directed to the elicitation and modification of core-belief and schema levels of representation may need to be employed. Fennell (1998) describes interventions with complex cases of low self-esteem, whereas Young (1994) provides an overview of the techniques of schema therapy.

Conclusions

Whereas a diagnosis of bulimia was once associated with a certain degree of therapeutic nihilism (Russell, 1979), the refinement of cognitive-behavioural approaches means that the prognosis for individuals with this condition is quite hopeful. Nevertheless, 50% of individuals remain symptomatic at the end of treatment and workers in the field continue to develop the cognitive model to incorporate both cognitive constructs, such as clinical perfectionism and low self-esteem, as well as difficulties within the domains of interpersonal relationships and affect regulation (Fairburn et al., 2003). The impact of such developments on treatment outcomes remains to be seen.

REFERENCES

Astrup, A. and Rossner, S. (2000) Lessons from obesity management programmes: greater initial weight loss improves long-term maintenance. *Obesity Review*, 1, 17–19.

Bacon, L., Keim, N. L., Van Loan, M. D., Derricote, M., Gale, B., Kazaks, A. et al. (2002) Evaluating a 'non-diet' wellness intervention for improvement of metabolic fitness, psychological well-being and eating and activity behaviors. *International Journal of Obesity and Related Metabolic Disorders*, 26, 854–865.

Bemis, K. M. (1987) The present status of operant conditioning for the treatment of anorexia nervosa. *Behaviour Modification*, 11, 432–463.

Blackburn, G. L. and Kanders, B. S. (1987) Medical evaluation and treatment of the obese patient with cardiovascular disease. *American Journal of Cardiology*, 60, 55G–58G.

Blake, W., Turnbull, S. and Treasure, J. L. (1997) Stages and processes of change in eating disorders. Implications for therapy. *Clinical Psychology and Psychotherapy*, 4, 186–191.

Boutelle, K. N., Kirschenbaum, D. S., Baker, R. C. and Mitchell, M. E. (1999) How can obese weight controllers minimize weight gain during the high risk holiday season? By self-monitoring very consistently. *Health Psychology*, 18, 364–368.

Brownell, K. D. (1995) Exercise and obesity treatment: Psychological aspects. *International Journal of Obesity and Related Metabolic Disorders*, 19 Suppl 4, S122–S125.

Brownell, K. D. (1987) *The Learn Program for Weight Control*. Philadelphia, PA: University of Pennsylvania School of Medicine.

Carter, F. A., McIntosh, V. V., Joyce, P. R., Sullivan, P. F. and Bulik, C. M. (2003) Role of exposure with response prevention in cognitive-behavioral therapy for bulimia nervosa: Three-year follow-up results. *International Journal of Eating Disorders*, 33, 127–135.

Cash, T. F. and Hicks, K. L (1990) Being fat versus thinking fat: Relationships with body image, eating behaviours, and well-being. *Cognitive Therapy and Research*, 14, 327–341.

Chen, E., Touyz, S. W., Beumont, P. J., Fairburn, C. G., Griffiths, R., Butow, P. et al. (2003) Comparison of group and individual cognitive-behavioral therapy for patients with bulimia nervosa. *International Journal of Eating Disorders*, 33, 241–254.

Ciliska, D. (1998). Evaluation of two nondieting interventions for obese women. *Western Journal of Nursing Research*, 20, 119–135.

Cooper, Z., Fairburn, C. G. and Hawker, D. N. (2003) *Cognitive-Behavioural Treatment of Obesity: A Clinician's Guide*. London: Guilford Press.

Cooper, M. J., Todd, G. and Wells, A. (1998) Content, origins and consequences of dysfunctional beliefs in anorexia nervosa and bulimia nervosa. *Journal of Cognitive Psychotherapy*, 12, 213–250.

Dare, C., Eisler, I., Russell, G., Treasure, J. and Dodge, L. (2001) Psychological therapies for adults with anorexia nervosa: Randomised controlled trial of out-patient treatments. *British Journal of Psychiatry*, 178, 216–221.

Deter, H. C. and Herzog, W. (1994) Anorexia nervosa in a long-term perspective: Results of the Heidelberg-Mannheim Study. *Psychosomatic Medicine*, 56, 20–27.

Eisler, I., Dare, C., Hodes, M., Russell, G., Dodge, E. and le Grange, D. (2000) Family therapy for adolescent anorexia nervosa: The results of a controlled comparison of two family interventions. *Journal of Child Psychology and Psychiatry*, 41, 727–736.

Fairburn, C. G., Peveler, R. C., Jones, R., Hope, R. A. and Doll, H. A. (1993) Predictors of 12-month outcome in bulimia nervosa and the influence of attitudes to shape and weight. *Journal of Consulting and Clinical Psychology*, 61, 696–698.

Fairburn, C. G., Shafran, R. and Cooper, Z. (1999) A cognitive behavioural theory of anorexia nervosa. *Behavior Research and Therapy*, 37, 1–13.

Fairburn, C. G., Cooper, Z. and Shafran, R. (2003) Cognitive behaviour therapy for eating disorders: a 'transdiagnostic' theory and treatment. *Behavior Research and Therapy*, 41, 509–528.

Fennell, M. (1998) Low self-esteem. In: N. Tarrier, A. Wells and G. Haddock (eds) *Treating Complex Cases: The Cognitive Behavioural Therapy Approach*. Chichester: Wiley.

Ferster, C. B., Nurnberger, J. I. and Levitt, E. B. (1962) The control of eating. *Journal of Mathematics*, 1, 87–109.

Foreyt, J. P. and Goodrick, G. K. (1993) Evidence for success of behavior modification in weight loss and control. *Annals of Internal Medicine*, 119, 698–701.

Foster, G. D., Sarwer, D. B. and Wadden, T. A. (1997a). Psychological effects of weight cycling in obese persons: a review and research agenda. *Obesity Research*, 5, 474–488.

Foster, G. D., Wadden, T. A., Vogt, R. A. and Brewer, G. (1997b). What is a reasonable weight loss? Patients' expectations and evaluations of obesity treatment outcomes. *Journal of Consulting and Clinical Psychology*, 65, 79–85.

Freeman, R. J., Beach, B., Davis, R. and Solyom, L. (1985) The prediction of relapse in bulimia nervosa. *Journal of Psychiatric Research*, 19, 349–353.

Garfinkel, P. E., Kline, S. A. and Stancer, H. C. (1973) Treatment of anorexia nervosa using operant conditioning techniques. *Journal of Nervous and Mental Disease*, 157, 428–433.

Goldstein, D. J. (1992) Beneficial health effects of modest weight loss. *International Journal of Obesity and Related Mental Disorders*, 16, 397–415.

Halmi, K. A. (2002) Eating disorders in females: Genetics, pathophysiology, and treatment. *Journal of Pediatric Endocrinology and Metabolism*, 15, Suppl 5, 1379–1386.

Halmi, K. A., Agras, W. S., Mitchell, J., Wilson, G. T., Crow, S., Bryson, S. W. et al. (2002) Relapse predictors of patients with bulimia nervosa who achieved abstinence through cognitive behavioral therapy. *Archives of General Psychiatry*, 59, 1105–1109.

Herman, C. P. and Pilivy, J. (1982) Weight change and dietary concern in the overweight: are they really independent? *Appetite*, 3(3), 280–281.

Heshka, S., Anderson, J. W., Atkinson, R. L., Greenway, F. L., Hill, J. O., Phinney, S. D. et al. (2003) Weight loss with self-help compared with a structured commercial program: A randomized trial. *Journal of the American Medical Association*, 289, 1792–1798.

Hunt, P., Rayner, M. and Gatenby, S. J. (1995) A national food guide for the UK? Background and development. *Journal of Human Nutrition and Dietetics*, 8, 315–322.

Johnson, C., Connors, M. E. and Tobin, D. L. (1987) Symptom management of bulimia. *Journal of Consulting and Clinical Psychology*, 55, 668–676.

Jordan, P. J., Redding, C. A., Troop, N. A., Treasure, J. and Serpell, L. (2003) Developing a stage of change measure for assessing recovery from anorexia nervosa. *Eating Behaviour*, 3, 365–385.

Key, A., George, C. L., Beattie, D., Stammers, K., Lacey, H. and Waller, G. (2002) Body image treatment within an inpatient program for anorexia nervosa: The role of mirror exposure in the desensitization process. *International Journal of Eating Disorders*, 31, 185–190.

Keys, A., Brozek, J., Henschel, A., Mikelson, O. and Taylor, H. L. (1950) *The Biology of Human Starvation*. Minneapolis: University of Minnesota Press.

Knowler, W. C., Barrett-Connor, E., Fowler, S. E., Hamman, R. F., Lachin, J. M., Walker, E. A. et al. (2002) Reduction in the incidence of type 2 diabetes with lifestyle intervention or metformin. *New England Journal of Medicine*, 346, 393–403.

Latner, J. D. (2001) Self-help in the long-term treatment of obesity. *Obesity Review*, 2, 87–97.

Latner, J. D., Wilson, G. T., Stunkard, A. J. and Jackson, M. L. (2002) Self-help and long-term behavior therapy for obesity. *Behavior Research and Therapy*, 40, 805–812.

Look AHEAD Research Group (2003) Look AHEAD (Action for Health in Diabetes): Design and methods for a clinical trial of weight loss for the prevention of cardiovascular disease in type 2 diabetes. *Control Clinical Trials*, 24(5), 610–628.

Mahoney, M. J. (1975) The obese eating style: bites, beliefs, and behavior modification. *Addictive Behaviour*, 1, 47–53.

Moore, H., Summerbell, C. D., Greenwood, D. C., Tovey, P., Griffiths, J., Henderson, M. et al. (2003) Improving management of obesity in primary care: cluster randomised trial. *British Medical Journal*, 327, 1085.

Öst, L.-G. and Gotestam, K. G. (1976) Behavioral and pharmacological treatments for obesity: An experimental comparison. *Addictive Behaviour*, 1, 331–338.

Perri, M. G., Shapiro, R. M., Ludwig, W. W., Twentyman, C. T. and McAdoo, W. G. (1984) Maintenance strategies for the treatment of obesity: An evaluation of relapse prevention training and posttreatment contact by mail and telephone. *Journal of Consulting and Clinical Psychology*, 52, 404–413.

Perri, M. G., McAdoo, W. G., McAllister, D. A., Lauer, J. B. and Yancey, D. Z. (1986) Enhancing the efficacy of behavior therapy for obesity: Effects of aerobic exercise and a multicomponent maintenance program. *Journal of Consulting and Clinical Psychology*, 54, 670–675.

Perri, M. G., McAdoo, W. G., McAllister, D. A., Lauer, J. B., Jordan, R. C., Yancey, D. Z. et al. (1987) Effects of peer support and therapist contact on long-term weight loss. *Journal of Consulting and Clinical Psychology*, 55, 615–617.

Perri, M. G., McAllister, D. A., Gange, J. J., Jordan, R. C., McAdoo, G. and Nezu, A. M. (1988) Effects of four maintenance programs on the long-term management of obesity. *Journal of Consulting and Clinical Psychology*, 56, 529–534.

Perri, M. G., Nezu, A. M., Patti, E. T. and McCann, K. L. (1989) Effect of length of treatment on weight loss. *Journal of Consulting and Clinical Psychology*, 57, 450–452.

Perri, M. G., Sears, S. F., Jr. and Clark, J. E. (1993) Strategies for improving maintenance of weight loss. Toward a continuous care model of obesity management. *Diabetes Care*, 16, 200–209.

Perri, M. G., Martin, A. D., Leermakers, E. A., Sears, S. F. and Notelovitz, M. (1997) Effects of group- versus home-based exercise in the treatment of obesity. *Journal of Consulting and Clinical Psychology*, 65, 278–285.

Perri, M. G., Nezu, A. M., McKelvey, W. F., Shermer, R. L., Renjilian, D. A. and Viegener, B. J. (2001) Relapse prevention training and problem-solving therapy in the long-term management of obesity. *Journal of Consulting and Clinical Psychology*, 69, 722–726.

Peters, J. C., Wyatt, H. R., Donahoo, W. T. and Hill, J. O. (2002) From instinct to intellect: The challenge of maintaining healthy weight in the modern world. *Obesity Review*, 3, 69–74.

Pike, K. M. (1998) Long-term course of anorexia nervosa: Response, relapse, remissions, and recovery. *Clinical Psychology Review*, 18(4), 447–475.

Polivy, J. and Herman, C. P. (1983) Undieting: A program to help people stop dieting. *International Journal of Eating Disorders*, 11, 261–268.

Pomeroy, C., Mitchell., J. E., Roerig, J. and Crow, S. (2002) *Medical Complications of Psychiatric Illness*. Washington, DC: American Psychiatric Association.

Pronk, N. P. and Wing, R. R. (1994). Physical activity and long-term maintenance of weight loss. *Obesity Research*, 2, 587–599.

Puhl, R. and Brownell, K. D. (2003) Ways of coping with obesity stigma: Review and conceptual analysis. *Eating Behaviour*, 4(1), 53–78.

Rapoport, L., Clark, M. and Wardle, J. (2000) Evaluation of a modified cognitive-behavioural programme for weight management. *International Journal of Obesity and Related Metabolic Disorders*, 24(12), 1726–1737.

Romanczyk, R. G., Tracey, D. A., Wilson, G. T. and Thorpe, G. L. (1973) Behavioral techniques in the treatment of obesity: A comparative analysis. *Behavior Research and Therapy*, 11, 629–640.

Rosen, J. C. (1996) Body image assessment and treatment in controlled studies of eating disorders. *International Journal of Eating Disorders*, 20, 331–343.

Russell, G. F. M. (1979) Bulimia nervosa: An ominous variant of anorexia nervosa. *Psychological Medicine*, 9, 429–448.

Ryan, D. H., Espeland, M. A., Foster, G. D., Haffner, S. M., Hubbard, V. S., Johnson, K. C. et al. (2003) Look AHEAD (Action for Health in Diabetes): Design and methods for a clinical trial of weight loss for the prevention of cardiovascular disease in type 2 diabetes. *Control Clinical Trials*, 24, 610–628.

Sbrocco, T., Nedegaard, R. C., Stone, J. M. and Lewis, E. L. (1999) Behavioral choice treatment promotes continuing weight loss: Preliminary results of a cognitive-behavioral decision-based treatment for obesity. *Journal of Consulting and Clinical Psychology*, 67, 260–266.

Serpell, L., Treasure, J., Teasdale, J. and Sullivan, V. (1999) Anorexia nervosa: Friend or foe? *International Journal of Eating Disorders*, 25, 177–186.

Skender, M. L., Goodrick, G. K., Del Junco, D. J., Reeves, R. S., Darnell, L., Gotto, A. M. et al. (1996) Comparison of 2-year weight loss trends in behavioral treatments of obesity: Diet, exercise, and combination interventions. *Journal of the American Dietetic Association*, 96, 342–346.

Slade, P. (1982). Towards a functional analysis of anorexia nervosa and bulimia nervosa. *British Journal of Clinical Psychology*, 21, 167–179.

Stuart, R. B. (1967) Behavioral control of overeating. *Behaviour Research and Therapy*, 5, 357–365.

Stuart, R. B. and Davis, B. (1972) *Slim Chance in a Fat World: Behavioural Control of Obesity*. Champaign, IL: Research Press.

Tate, D. F., Jackvony, E. H. and Wing, R. R. (2003) Effects of internet behavioral counseling on weight loss in adults at risk for type 2 diabetes: A randomized trial. *Journal of the American Medical Association*, 289, 1833–1836.

Teachman, B. A. and Brownell, K. D. (2001) Implicit anti-fat bias among health professionals: Is anyone immune? *International Journal of Obesity and Related Metabolic Research*, 25, 1525–1531.

Thomas, P. R. (ed) (1995) *Weighing the Options*. Washington, DC: National Academy Press.

Toro, J., Cervera, M., Feliu, M. H., Garriga, N., Jou, M., Martinez, E. et al. (2003) Cue exposure in the treatment of resistant bulimia nervosa. *International Journal of Eating Disorders*, 34, 227–234.

Touyz, S. W. and Beumont, P. (1997) Behavioural treatment to promote weight gain in anorexia nervosa. In: P. E. Garfinkel and D. M. Garner (eds) *Handbook of Treatment for Eating Disorders*, 2nd Edn. (pp 361–371). New York: Guilford Press.

Vandereycken, W. and Beumont, P. J. V. (eds) (1998) *Treating Eating Disorders: Ethical, Legal and Personal Issues* (pp. 1–29). London: The Athlone Press.

Vitousek, K., Watson, S. and Wilson, G. T. (1998) Enhancing motivation for change in treatment-resistant eating disorders. *Clinical and Psycholgical Review*, 18, 391–420.

Wadden, T. A., Vogt, R. A., Foster, G. D. and Anderson, D. A. (1998) Exercise and the maintenance of weight loss: 1-year follow-up of a controlled clinical trial. *Journal of Consulting and Clinical Psychology*, 66, 429–433.

Wadden, T. A., Brownell, K. D. and Foster, G. D. (2002) Obesity: Responding to the global epidemic. *Journal of Consulting and Clinical Psychology*, 70, 510–525.

Wadden, T. A., Womble, L. G., Sarwer, D. B., Berkowitz, R. I., Clark, V. L. and Foster, G. D. (2003) Great expectations: 'I'm losing 25% of my weight no matter what you say'. *Journal of Consulting and Clinical Psychology*, 71, 1084–1089.

Wardle, J., Marsland, L., Sheikh, Y., Quinn, M., Fedoroff, I. and Ogden, J. (1992) Eating style and eating behaviour in adolescents. *Appetite*, 18, 167–183.

Wardle, J., Liao, L. M., Rapoport, L., Hillsden, M., Edwards, C., Croker, H., Chipperfield, A. and Chadwick, P. (2006). *Shape-Up: A Lifestyle Programme to Manage Your Weight*. London: Weight Concern.

Wilson, G. T. (1996) Acceptance and change in the treatment of eating disorders and obesity. *Behavior Therapy*, 27, 417–439.

Wilson, G. T., Fairburn, C. C., Agras, W. S., Walsh, B. T. and Kraemer, H. (2002) Cognitive-behavioral therapy for bulimia nervosa: Time course and mechanisms of change. *Journal of Consulting and Clinical Psychology*, 70, 267–274.

Wing, R. R. and Hill, J. O. (2001) Successful weight loss maintenance. *Annual Review of Nutrition*, 21, 323–341.

Young, J. E. (1994) *Cognitive Therapy for Personality Disorders: A Schema-Focussed Approach*, 2nd edn. Sarasota, FL: Professional Resource Press.

Chapter 32

Disorders of sleep

Investigation

Matt Wild, Niall Broomfield and Colin Espie

INTRODUCTION

This chapter aims to equip clinicians with sufficient knowledge of sleep and its commonly related disorders to assess efficiently and to diagnose differentially the most common presentations. Sleep disorders will often present in adult mental health, as well as clinical health settings, and while not all presentations can be managed psychologically, most are treatable, providing there is a clear understanding of appropriate care options. An introduction to the functions of sleep and normal sleep physiology will be presented, before moving on to discuss core aspects of differential diagnosis and clinical sleep assessment.

NORMAL SLEEP PHYSIOLOGY

Although the exact function of sleep remains unknown, many theories have hypothesised why we need to sleep. These include evolutionary theories promoting the adaptive and protective qualities of sleep, and also regulatory and restorative theories extolling the importance of sleep in the maintenance of basic physiological processes necessary for good mental and physical health. For example, rapid eye movement (REM) sleep is thought to be vital in the consolidation of memories, the accommodation and assimilation of emotional conflicts, and stages 3 and 4 of non-REM sleep are associated with restoration of physical energy. Indeed, animal studies tell us that prolonged sleep deprivation will eventually lead to death (see Horne, 1990, for an extended discussion of sleep functions).

Sleep comprises discrete stages but can be divided into two distinct states: REM and non-REM (NREM). These states can be objectively identified using polysomnography (PSG), a technique that combines the measurement of electrical brain activity (electroencephalography; EEG), eye movements (electrooculography; EOG), muscle tone (electromyography; EMG), respiratory function, and cardiac function, using for example pulse oximetry and electrocardiography (ECG) respectively.

NREM sleep can be subdivided into four sleep stages through which an individual will initially progress (for further detail, see Guilleminault and Kreutzer, 2003). Figure 32.1 illustrates the wave forms and EEG features associated with identified sleep stages. From a state of drowsiness, an individual first advances to stage 1. This is defined by low-voltage, mixed-frequency EEG waves. Rapid eye movements are absent and muscle tone is preserved. Vertex sharp waves and slow, rolling eye movements may be observed. A transitional phase of sleep, stage 1 is light and of short duration, lasting generally between 1 and 7 minutes, and may be interrupted by periods of wakefulness. Once stage 1 has been consolidated, the individual will progress to NREM stage 2. This is associated with a steady increase in EEG voltage and reduced frequency through this and subsequent stages 3 and 4. Stage 2 will generally last for 10 to 25 minutes, and is identified when sleep spindles (i.e. groups of waves, with frequencies in the upper levels of alpha and lower levels of beta, which increase in amplitude initially then decrease slowly) and/or K complexes (i.e. large-amplitude delta-frequency waves, sometimes with a sharp apex, which occur during partial arousal from sleep) become apparent on EEG trace. Stages 3 and 4 are the deepest stages of sleep and last between 20 and 40 minutes in the first sleep cycle. Together these are referred to as slow-wave sleep (SWS), as they are associated with EEG delta waves, typified by slow-wave, high-amplitude activity. Following stage 4, the individual reverses through the NREM stages, prior to the initiation of the first REM sleep.

REM sleep is associated with a low-voltage, high-frequency EEG trace, the presence of rapid eye movements and postural relaxation. In REM sleep, core muscle tone is lost, and only interrupted by brief jerks. Our most vivid dreams also occur during periods of REM sleep. This has given rise to the characterisation of REM sleep as that of an awake brain in a paralysed body. The first REM period is typically brief, lasting between 4 and 8 minutes, after which a new sleep cycle will be initiated (Guilleminault and Kreutzer, 2003); REM sleep becomes more consolidated and longer in duration later in the night.

Periods of NREM and REM sleep then alternate throughout the night. In healthy, young adults 25% of sleep will be REM, while NREM periods constitute the remaining 75%. Of the NREM periods, stage 1 will represent 5%, stage 2 a further 50% and stage 3 and 4 SWS about 20%. Figure 32.2 illustrates the distribution of sleep stages across a night of sleep in a healthy adult.

These sleep patterns will vary on the basis of individual differences and circumstances, and also on the basis of other variables, particularly age. For example, SWS declines from a peak in childhood, throughout adulthood and reaches a low point in later life. In terms of REM sleep, this comprises more than 50% of a newborn child's sleep cycle, in comparison to 25% found in that of a young adult. A general deterioration in sleep quality is associated

Wakefulness; low voltage, fast activity

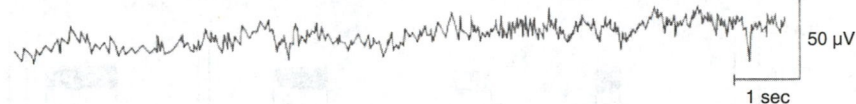

50 μV

1 sec

Sleepiness; alpha waves in the 8–12 Hertz range

Stage 1, theta waves in the 3–7 Hertz range

theta waves

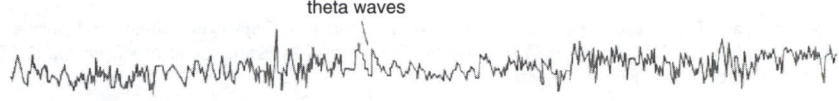

Stage 2, presence of 12 to 14 Hertz sleep spindles and K-comp

K complex

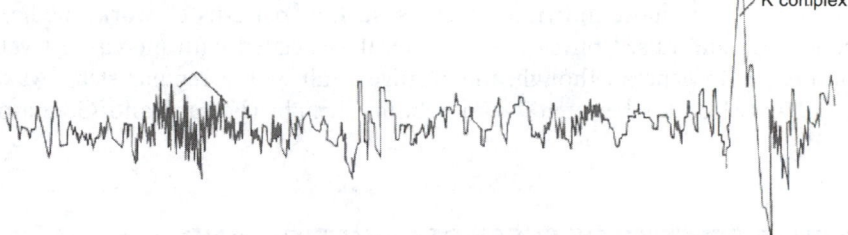

Stage 3 and 4, delta waves in the 0.5–2 Hertz range and of high amplitude (175 μ or greater)

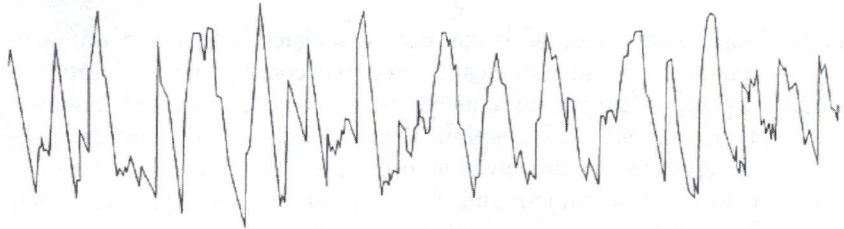

REM sleep; low voltage fast activity associated with saw-tooth waves

Saw-tooth waves

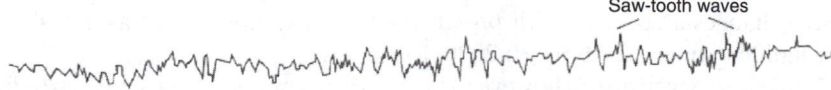

Figure 32.1 Sample electroencephalographic (EEG) traces obtained during relaxed wakefulness (eyes open and eyes closed), NREM sleep stages 1 to 4 and REM (from top to bottom).

Source: Guilleminault and Kreutzer (2003). Reproduced with kind permission of Springer Science and Business Media.

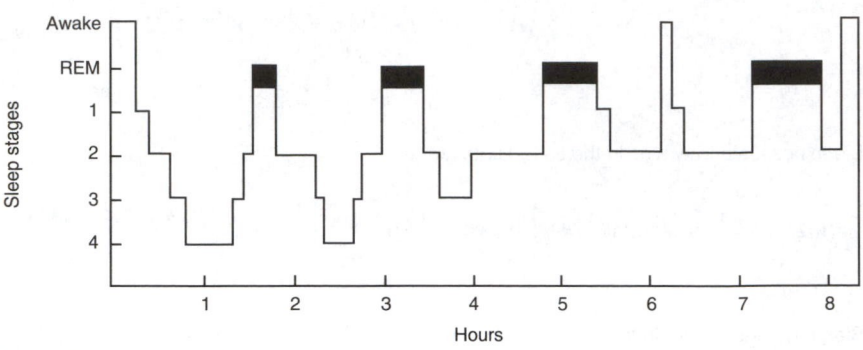

Figure 32.2 Healthy adult sleep histogram.

Source: Morin and Espie (2003). Reproduced with kind permission of Springer Science and Business Media. *Original source*: C.M. Morin (1993). *Insomnia: Psychological Assessment and Management*, p. 17. New York: Guilford Press. Reprinted with permission.

with increasing age, with many older adults consequently experiencing frequent and prolonged periods of wakefulness (Morgan, 2000). Sleep may also be disrupted by more individual factors, such as patterns of work, medical conditions and raised physiological arousal associated with increased levels of anxiety. In general, though, the average adult with a regular sleep–wake cycle will sleep for between 7 and 8 hours a night (Ferrara and Gennaro, 2001).

ACUTE EFFECTS OF SLEEP DEPRIVATION AND SLEEP DISRUPTION

As previously mentioned, sleep has been associated with the maintenance of good physical and mental health, and the consequences of total and partial sleep deprivation in humans has been widely investigated. Following two nights of total sleep deprivation, the individual will display irresistible micro-sleep episodes as homeostatic drive for sleep increases, with consequent lapses in wakefulness and attention. Other cognitive impairments have been reported, mostly associated with reduced vigilance and reaction times. Affective changes manifest after prolonged sleep loss. These include increased irritability and reduced motivation, and have also led to more severe changes associated with presentations of psychosis, such as delusions and hallucinations (see Bonnet, 2000, for review).

Total sleep deprivation, however, is rare. More commonly, sleep is partially disrupted, but this may reflect a chronic pattern, which has been linked to a number of threats to quality of life. Disorders that lead to chronic fragmentation of sleep, such as sleep apnoea and narcolepsy (see the section on Differential diagnosis, below, for a discussion of these disorders), may lead to severe daytime sleepiness. Similarly, painful medical conditions or shift work may lead to sufficient fragmentation to induce a state of chronic 'sleep debt'. In this state, there are serious consequences associated with reduced cognitive performance, quality of life and safety. For example, an increased frequency of road traffic accidents has been identified in sufferers of sleep apnoea due to excessive daytime sleepiness, impaired attention and vigilance, and falling asleep at the wheel (Barbe et al., 1998).

CHRONIC EFFECTS OF DISRUPTED SLEEP

Daytime sleepiness, although commonly reported, tends to be less severe in those who suffer from insomnia. Disrupted cognitive processes are also commonly reported. However, there has been some inconsistency in the literature regarding the association between subjective complaints and objective measurement of impairment (Vignola et al., 2000). This is also the case for subjectively and objectively measured sleep duration, with insomnia sufferers consistently overestimating their sleep onset latency and underestimating their total wakefulness. That said, insomnia has been reliably associated with psychological disturbance and impaired quality of life. It is understandably linked with fatigue, with consequent impact on levels of irritability and sense of helplessness in chronic cases. Long-term, untreated insomnia has also been found to be an independent risk factor for major depression (Ford and Kamerow, 1989; Riemann and Voderholzer, 2003).

Insomnia sufferers will commonly report physical problems associated with gastrointestinal and respiratory function. The sleep loss associated with insomnia has been linked with a variety of potential long-term threats to physical health (Alvarez and Ayas, 2004). Sleep loss has also been associated with the development of late-life depression (Cole and Dendukuri, 2003). Long-term threats to physical health have also been strongly linked to other sleep disorders such as sleep apnoea. Untreated sleep apnoea is associated with increased morbidity and mortality through cardiovascular disease, stroke, hypoxia and road traffic accidents (Fletcher, 2000a, 2000b; George, 2000). That said, excessive sleep (i.e. regularly > 8 hours per night) has also been reliably associated with increased mortality (Youngstedt and Kripke, 2004).

Overall, then, sleep disorders can be seen as common pathways to a variety of psychological, cognitive and physical symptoms and presentations, highlighting the importance of early identification and reaction to indicators of pathology. In addition, sleep problems and related symptoms have been found to be the most commonly reported mental health symptoms by people visiting their GP. Figure 32.3 shows that, in a UK sample of more than 8,000 adults, sleep problems were reported by 28% of the population, with fatigue being reported by 27% (Singleton et al., 2001).

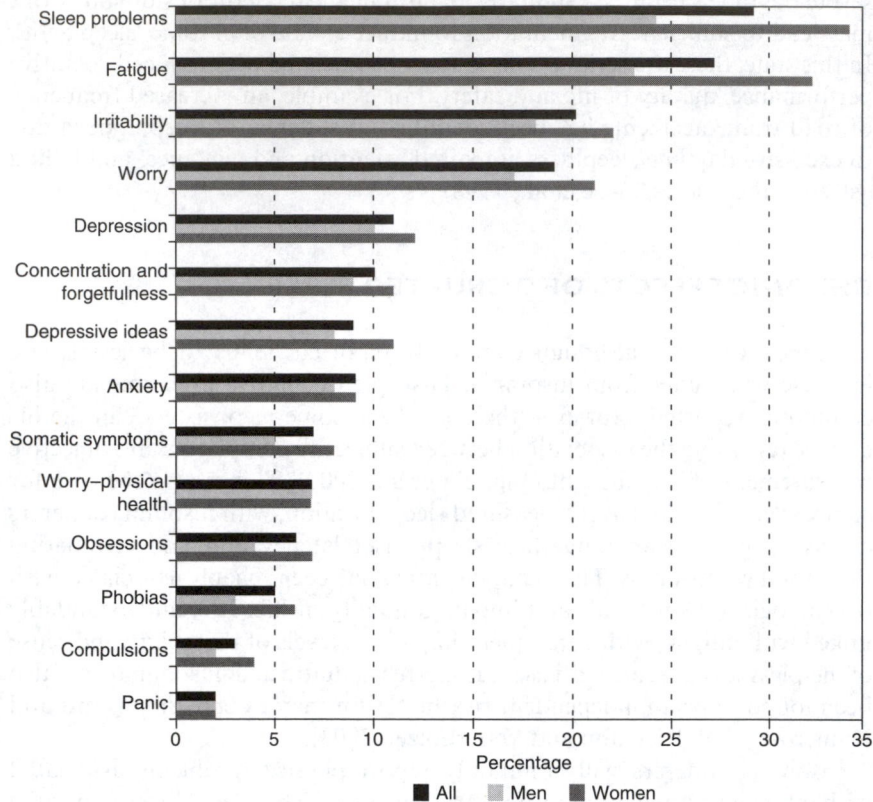

Figure 32.3 Most commonly reported symptoms in a survey of 8800 UK residents.

Source: National Statistics website (http//www.statistics.gov.uk). Crown copyright material is reproduced with the permission of the Controller of HMSO.

INSOMNIA

The most common sleep problem is insomnia. This section therefore focuses
on theories, assessment and diagnosis of insomnia. Insomnia is a subjective
complaint of persistent difficulty in initiating and/or maintaining sleep, or
non-restorative sleep, associated with marked distress and/or significant
impairments of social or occupational functioning. While it may manifest clinically in a variety of ways, insomnia complaints centrally reflect
dissatisfaction with the quality, duration, and/or continuity of sleep.

Alongside pain and fatigue, disturbed sleep is one of the symptoms most
commonly reported to GPs. Indeed, insomnia is by far the most common
mental health symptom in the UK adult community. Symptoms of anxiety
and depression are much less frequently reported (Singleton et al., 2001).

There is general agreement that insomnia can be a symptom of a wide range of disorders, or an independent sleep disorder. Primary or psychophysiologic insomnia (PI) is the most common insomnia sub-type, found in 12–15% of patients seen in sleep centres. Alongside paradoxical insomnia and insomnia due to mental disorder, it is amenable to cognitive-behaviour management.

The insomnias are often unpredictable and uncontrollable. Sufferers may be more prone to errors at work or whilst driving. The impact on personal, professional and social functioning can be considerable, with fatigue, cognitive impairment and poor motivation commonly reported. Research on the natural course of insomnia is lacking, although clinical indications are that untreated insomnia can last for tens of years, and may worsen. Fatigue, impaired functioning, mixed anxious and depressive symptoms and dysphoria may increase. Insomnia patients also report impaired cognitive performance in the domains of memory, attention, and concentration (Morin and Espie, 2003). Moreover, many insomnia patients show a cognitive distortion whereby time to fall asleep is overestimated relative to objective measures (e.g. actigraphy) and total sleep time underestimated.

Of particular note, failure to treat insomnia can lead to depression (Cole and Dendukuri, 2003). Although insomnia is a key symptom of depression, and an insomnia sub-type associated with mental disorder should be considered, insomnia is also a known, independent risk factor for depression (Riemann and Voderholzer, 2003). As insomnia can promote depression, failure to treat the primary sleep disturbance can put some patients at risk of major depressive disorder.

Failure to treat insomnia can also confer significant socio-economic costs, particularly as untreated PI persists and can worsen. Efforts to reduce prevalence and severity using effective psychological treatments will therefore have a substantial net economic, as well as health, benefit.

Models of insomnia

The insomnia literature is dominated by treatment research. Data confirming extant models is lacking. A detailed understanding of explanatory insomnia models is not essential but awareness of the interplay of cognitive and behavioural factors will facilitate formulation and treatment.

Acquisition Model

Spielman and Glovinsky (1991) provide a useful conceptualisation of insomnia development, comprising predisposing, precipitating and perpetuating factors. The model usefully informs the assessing clinician, and can be used to educate the patient to the clinical formulation.

Essentially, Spielman suggests predisposition may interact with precipitating factors to create temporary sleep disruption but that, in the absence of perpetuating factors, the plasticity of the sleep–wake schedule will drive toward homeostasis and re-establish good sleep. Both the *Diagnostic and Statistical Manual of Mental Disorders* (DSM-IV; American Psychiatric Association (APA), 1994) and the *International Classification of Sleep Disorders – Revised* (ICSD-R; American Academy of Sleep Medicine, 2001) report familial association with light, disrupted sleep, and ICSD-R reports anxious over-concern with health as predisposing. Indeed, insomniacs appear prone to introspection and worry. Elevated autonomic and metabolic rates also imply a vulnerability factor. However, predisposing factors alone are unlikely to create imbalance in sleep homeostasis or circadian timing, although they might impair sleep quality and, potentially, lead to sleep-state misperception. Studies investigating the onset of chronic insomnia have commonly found that stress or life change are key precipitating factors. According to Spielman, some other mechanism accounts for the persistence of a sleep problem.

Thus, whilst the clinician should examine potential predisposing and precipitating in assessment, a primary focus in assessment should be on hypothesised maintaining factors.

Maintenance: faulty conditioning model

Since first proposed by Bootzin (1972), the understanding of insomnia as the product of maladaptive sleep habits has had considerable appeal. Good sleep is seen as coming under the stimulus control of the bedroom environment, which acts as a discriminative stimulus for sleep. Difficulty falling asleep may result either from failure to establish discriminative stimuli for sleep or the presence of stimuli incompatible with sleep. Poor stimulus control, therefore, might compete with sleep drive by strengthening conditioned arousal, and with circadian timing by doing so at normal bedtime. The insomniac may also nap in an armchair and so strengthen further the associations between sleep and non-sleeping environments. Stimulus-control treatment instructions comprise lying down to sleep only when sleepy, avoiding using the bed for activities other than sleep (sexual activity excepted), getting up if unable to sleep quickly (within 15 minutes), repeating rising from bed as necessary throughout the night, getting up the same time every day and avoiding napping.

Maintenance: cognitive models

Poor sleepers typically complain of mental alertness more than physiological arousal. Mental events are usually central to the complaint (e.g. 'I can't switch off my thoughts), and research shows having an 'overactive mind' is the attribution rated most highly by people with psychophysiological insomnia. Supporting this, experimentally induced excessive pre-sleep thinking delays sleep onset in good sleepers. And there is evidence that cognitive processes mediate patient response to intervention (see Espie, 2002).

Accordingly, cognitive factors feature centrally within contemporary explanatory models of psychophysiological insomnia. Morin (1993) proposes an interacting sub-systems model, where hyperarousal interacts with dysfunctional cognitions, maladaptive habits and perceived consequences to promote and maintain psychophysiological insomnia. Morin suggests, just as in other mental health disorders, that patients with psychophysiological insomnia are characterised by dysfunctional thinking, believing, for example, that 'chronic insomnia will have serious consequences for my physical health'. Such dysfunctional appraisal of the insomnia and its consequences exacerbates sleep disturbance. This view led to the development of the Dysfunctional Beliefs and Attitudes about Sleep Scale (Morin 1994), which scale allows clinicians to identify dysfunctional thinking errors. Cognitive restructuring (see Chapter 33) can be used to challenge the patient's belief system, making use of behavioural experiments to test implicitly held beliefs about sleep and sleep loss.

Harvey (2002) also emphasises cognitive factors in the maintenance of psychophysiological insomnia. Harvey argues that individuals with psychophysiological insomnia tend to be overly worried about sleep and the consequences of poor sleep. This drives autonomic arousal and emotional distress, disturbing sleep and promoting selective attention orienting toward sleep-related threat cues. Just as individuals with generalised anxiety may selectively attend threat, so patients with psychophysiological insomnia selectively attend to time (clock watching), internal factors (e.g. body sensations consistent with falling asleep) and external factors (e.g. environmental noise). It is assumed this bias is relatively automatic, just as in the anxiety disorders. This automatic attention bias and its associated anxious state impairs sleep further and tricks the poor sleeper into overestimating the extent of his or her insomnia. Counterproductive safety behaviours initiated to ameliorate sleep loss, e.g. going to bed early, sleeping late, thought control, exacerbate the insomnia, as does excessive and escalating anxiety.

For the clinician, identification and reversal of sleep-related attention bias and counterproductive safety behaviours may improve the patient's sleep pattern. Evidence to support the Harvey model is converging. The Sleep Associated Monitoring Index (SAMI; Semler and Harvey, 2004) measures patient tendency to monitor sleep-related threat. This may prove to be a highly useful assessment/change measure for patients who present with this cognitive pattern.

Maintenance: psychobiological inhibition model

Espie's (2002) psychobiological inhibition model uniquely conceptualises psychophysiological insomnia as a difficulty with arousal down-regulation. Traditionally, insomnia has been considered an inability to initiate/maintain sleep: something is interfering with the 'sleep on' system. Espie (2002) suggests the converse: something is interfering with the 'wake off' system. Sleep homeostasis and circadian timing are recognised as the central controlling features of sleep continuity. Developing his previous position (Espie, 1991) about the importance of understanding normalcy, Espie (2002) emphasises that wake-offset and sleep-onset occur fairly unremarkably for good sleepers. Indeed, this lack of awareness and lack of personal agency is the hallmark of good sleep. In insomnia, however, this *automaticity* of function is impaired and 'sleep effort', incorporating its starting point in sleep-related attention bias, is framed as a central inhibitory force. Because good sleepers are essentially passive, internal and external cues act as automated setting conditions for sleep. Because insomnia patients show the opposite, i.e. heightened active effortful preoccupation with sleep, this inhibits natural de-arousal.

Sleep loss is threatening. It represents a risk to a fundamental life process. Thus, in our view, insomnia is highly likely to be anxiogenic, promoting attention bias and sleep effort (Broomfield et al., 2005). There is now converging evidence of attention bias for sleep-related words and objects as characterising insomnia patients (see Espie et al., 2006) and evidence that reducing 'sleep effort' improves sleep pattern (Broomfield and Espie, 2003). Clinical experience and the ICSD-R also reflect the importance of effort and attention bias as features of insomnia presentation. Patients with psychophysiological insomnia typically strive to control their sleep and are highly preoccupied with, and attentive to, sleep loss, whereas good sleepers, when asked what they do to fall asleep, usually appear bewildered and report not consciously delivering any behaviour. A study also demonstrated that the recently developed Glasgow Sleep Effort Scale (Broomfield and Espie, 2005) best distinguished depressed and non-depressed insomniacs from good sleepers (Kohn and Espie, 2005).

Stimulus-control and sleep-restriction therapies (see Chapter 33) probably act to increase natural sleep homeostatic function, thus restoring sleep automaticity within the Espie model, although research is needed on this. Indirect treatment methods, e.g. paradoxical intention, are also likely to impact on insomnia because they reduce effort, and focus attention away from sleep and sleep-related thoughts.

Maintenance: neurocognitive model

Perlis et al. (1997) offer an important counter-position to the more cognitively oriented models already outlined. Perlis extends the behavioural position on psychophysiological insomnia (Bootzin, 1972); the view that repeated episodes of sleep difficulty promote maladaptive coping strategies, e.g. staying in bed while awake, which in turn cause conditioned arousal – sudden alertness on entering the bedroom to sleep.

Perlis argues that whilst rumination and worry may extend wakefulness, they are *not* responsible for the inability to initiate sleep. That is, the individual is not awake because he or she is worrying. Rather, the individual is worrying because he or she is awake. Cortical arousal in the form of high-frequency beta and/or gamma EEG activity at or around sleep onset is seen as characteristic of insomnia. This leads to an increase in sensory processing (i.e. startle and orienting) and information processing (identification of stimuli). The former is thought to directly interfere with sleep; the latter makes it more likely that insomnia patients will be aware of, and respond to, interior and exteroceptive stimuli. The Perlis model therefore suggests that patients with insomnia maintain a level of information and memory processing not typically seen in good sleepers, which blurs the distinction between wakefulness and sleep. This model, in particular, might explain why individuals with paradoxical insomnia overreport sleep onset and underreport total sleep time relative to PSG. And also report being awake when PSG data defines them as asleep.

The core mechanism underpinning insomnia in the Perlis model is conditioned arousal. Stimulus-control therapy is designed to unwind this, and would be indicated in patients showing this pattern. Evidence for the efficacy of this treatment approach is good (Chesson et al., 1999), although the precise reasons it works to reduce arousal remain unknown.

Diagnostic issues in insomnia

Patients with insomnia disorder, whether psychophysiological, paradoxical or due to mental disorder (see later for a full description), and patients who present with inadequate sleep hygiene, all experience persistent difficulty initiating and/or maintaining sleep. There may be greater than 30 minutes of pre-sleep wakefulness (sleep-onset latency; SOL) on the majority of nights and/or intermittent wakefulness from sleep up to 30 minutes (wake-time after sleep onset; WASO). Sleep efficiency will be lower than 85%, meaning that the patient will be awake for more than 15% of time in bed. Early-morning awakening may be greater than 30 minutes before desired time, with an inability to get back to sleep, and before total sleep duration reaches 6.5 hours.

DSM-IV (APA, 1994) states that, for a positive diagnosis of insomnia disorder, these experiences will be consistent for more than three nights per week, and present for more than 1 month. The International Classification of Sleep Disorders (ICSD-R; AASM, 2001) suggests a period of 6 months as more reliable for research populations.

The importance of distinguishing between insomnia disorder subtypes for research purposes has recently been highlighted (Edinger et al., 2004). Knowledge of these subtypes is also important for the clinician however, as they present individual challenges with regard to formulation, and all are manageable using cognitive-behaviour therapy (CBT).

Psychophysiological insomnia

Psychophysiological insomnia is a stand-alone insomnia disorder representing the largest category of patients presenting with difficulty initiating and/or maintaining sleep. It occurs commonly in adults (Ford and Kamerow, 1989), particularly later in life (Foley et al., 1995), and is highly amenable to psychological intervention.

Psychophysiological insomnia is characterised by somatised tension and conditioned physiological arousal. High levels of anxiety, tension and effort to sleep impact on the individual's ability to initiate or sustain sleep. The sufferer may display excessive anxiety about sleep and be unable to fall asleep at night in the bedroom environment, but do so with relative ease during planned naps or when away from home. And there will be heightened intrusive cognitive activity in bed, alongside sustained, voluntary attempts to control sleep, which we refer to as 'sleep effort'.

Paradoxical insomnia

In psychophysiological insomnia, complaints of poor sleep are substantiated using polysomnography (PSG). This is not the case for paradoxical insomnia. Patients with this insomnia subtype report a chronic pattern of little or no sleep most nights, which is confirmed using diary assessment. However, there is a consistent mismatch between the subjective sleep complaint and objective findings on PSG. To some extent, all insomnia patients show such cognitive distortions whereby time to fall asleep is overestimated, relative to objective measures, and total sleep time is underestimated. However, in paradoxical insomnia, the subjective complaint of poor sleep is markedly out of proportion with any objective finding. Paradoxical insomnia has also been referred to as 'sleep-state misperception', and requires a quantitative evaluation of sleep duration (i.e. PSG) to confirm diagnosis. The condition is not the result of an underlying psychiatric condition or malingering, and remains poorly understood. It may represent a prodromal phase for more objectively verifiable insomnia.

Insomnia due to a mental disorder

Sleep disturbance features in a wide range of psychiatric disorders, most notably depression, although there is also an association with panic and generalised anxiety disorder. For insomnia due to a medical disorder to be diagnosed, there must be this association, typically reflected in the onset of the insomnia coinciding with the onset of the mental disorder, and/or the temporal course of the insomnia coinciding with the temporal course of the mental disorder.

The DSM-IV (APA, 1994) makes a distinction between 'primary' and 'secondary' insomnia. This can be a useful distinction for clinicians, which is of relevance to this insomnia subtype. Both psychophysiological and paradoxical insomnia are diagnosed in the absence of any known physical or mental illness aetiology, and thus may be considered 'primary' insomnias. Insomnia due to a mental disorder fits more closely the construct of secondary insomnia. However, in our view, the diagnostic criteria imply that insomnia is secondary when other problems predominate the overall clinical presentation. In many situations it might actually be more accurate to think of insomnia 'associated with' another disorder because both problems may merit clinical attention. It is also imperative for clinicians to remember that sleep disturbance is one of the most common early signs of the onset of depression, and may persist after depression lifts. Furthermore, there is emerging evidence of a similar pattern with respect to generalised anxiety disorder.

Despite some overlap between these insomnia subtypes, the above classification illustrates that insomnia does not always present as a single prototype. Rather, there are various insomnia profiles, with significant variations regarding the presenting complaints, its associated features, and the temporal course of the condition. These different subtypes may benefit from different treatment approaches, a point elaborated later in this chapter.

Inadequate sleep hygiene

In addition to the above insomnia types, inadequate sleep hygiene also has the potential to disrupt sleep onset and maintenance. The following factors should be considered in assessment.

Caffeine is a stimulant of the central nervous system (CNS). It is found in a variety of products other than tea and coffee, including cocoa, carbonated drinks (e.g. cola, lemonade) and non-prescription analgesics. As a stimulant, caffeine can significantly disrupt sleep architecture and, due to a long half-life, remains active in the body for many hours. Tobacco products contain nicotine, another CNS stimulant. While some patients report that on awakening they find it relaxing to have a cigarette, the overall effect is to raise physiological arousal, lessening the likelihood of sleep onset. Alcohol is a depressant, which increases the propensity for sleep onset, but it can also lead to sleep maintenance difficulties. As ethanol is metabolised by the body, withdrawal lightens sleep with increased numbers of arousals. Hunger can also cause awakenings, as can eating too much before going to bed. Those who are fit generally sleep better although, just as CNS stimulants wake the body up, so does exercise. Noise disrupts sleep. Some people habituate to regular noise disturbances. However, sleep may still be lighter. Extremes of temperature can also impact sleep quality and should be avoided.

OTHER FACTORS AND DISORDERS AFFECTING SLEEP

Normal ageing

Increasing age is naturally associated with changes in sleep structure, which impacts on the quality, continuity and depth of sleep (Morgan, 2000). By the age 60, many adults experience a decrease in the proportion of time spent in delta-wave sleep. However, the percentage of REM sleep remains relatively stable. Figure 32.4 contrasts the distribution of sleep stages across a night of sleep in a younger and older adult. While these natural changes are thought to be associated with physiological (e.g. reduced melatonin and growth hormone production) and lifestyle factors (e.g. decreasing structure and activity), a variety of medical problems associated with older adulthood (e.g. dementia, restless legs syndrome) must be ruled out. Also, despite expected changes in sleep architecture, primary insomnia can present in older adults as it does at younger ages. However, differentiating this from natural changes can be difficult and its diagnosis can only be made on the basis of clinical assessment. Evidence to consider in this context should include overall sleep structure, level of daytime sleepiness, and overall psychosocial functioning (e.g. mood, behaviour, interpersonal functioning) (Espie, 2000a).

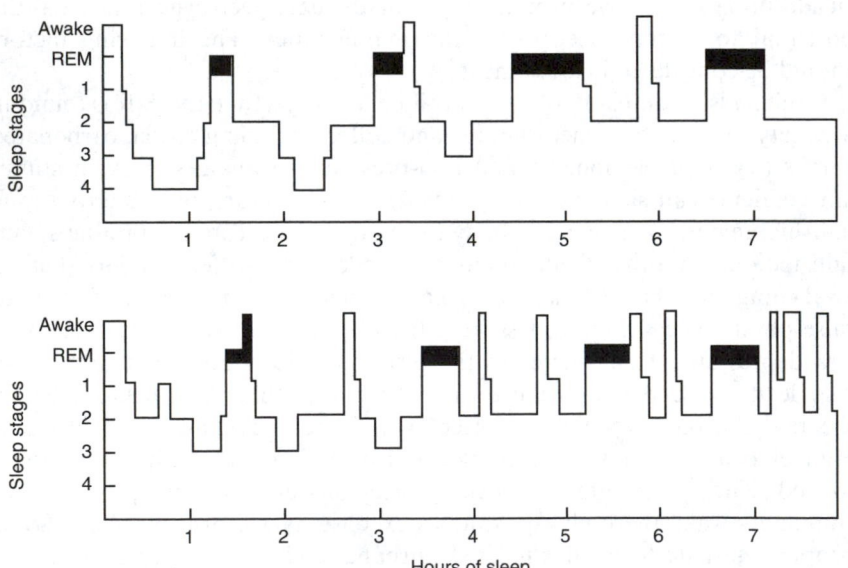

Figure 32.4 Typical sleep histograms for younger (top) and older (bottom) adults.

Source: Morgan (2000). Reproduced with kind permission of Sage Publications.

Sleep-related breathing disorders

This term refers to a group of disorders that seriously disrupt the patient's sleep pattern through impaired respiratory function (Krieger, 2003). In obstructive sleep apnoea, the upper airway collapses primarily during stages 1 and 2 of sleep, disrupting sleep and decreasing periods of stage 3 and 4, and REM. Breathing is disturbed through apnoeic (i.e. complete occlusions of the upper airway) and hypopnoea events (i.e. partial occlusions of the upper airway), which lead to disruption of sleep through micro-arousals. Sometimes patients are aware of waking suddenly short of breath. It is important to make the differential diagnosis with nocturnal panic. The most common day-time symptoms of a sleep-related breathing disorders (SBD) are excessive daytime sleepiness, impaired concentration and irritability. Daytime sleepiness in this population has been linked to an increased incidence of road traffic and industrial accidents (Goh and Lim, 2003). SBDs have also been associated with increased morbidity and mortality through hypoxic brain injury and cardiovascular disease (Gale and Hopkins, 2004; Hamilton et al., 2004).

While a clinical diagnosis can only be confirmed through PSG assessment, which indicates an Apnoea Hypopnoea Index (AHI) of > 15 events per hour and observable changes in ventilation or oxygen saturation, a number of indicators of SBD can be assessed at interview. By interviewing a partner, evidence of snoring and breathing pauses can be assessed. Other reliable indicators include a body mass index (BMI) of > 30, an Epworth Sleepiness Scale score (Johns, 1993) of > 11 and a shirt collar size of > 17 inches. SBDs are present in 2% of males between the ages of 30 and 65, and in 1% of females of the same age.

Periodic limb movement disorder and restless legs syndrome

Periodic limb movement disorder (PLMD) is associated with older age and involves muscle twitches in the extremities during sleep. It is often reported by those who suffer from sleep breathing disorders. These episodes disrupt sleep, causing arousals from sleep stages 1 and 2, and leading to complaints of day-time sleepiness and insomnia. However, some patients with frequent nocturnal limb movements remain asymptomatic for diurnal consequences. Diagnosis of PLMD, unlike restless legs syndrome (RLS), which can be confirmed on the basis of clinical observation, must be confirmed by PSG. The stereotypic leg movements associated with this disorder are accompanied by brief sleep arousals. Aetiology may be related to disturbance of circadian sleep–wake rhythms in older adults.

RLS is associated with periods of irresistible urges to move the legs. These are associated with unpleasant sensations in the legs, and occur mostly in the evening, potentially significantly delaying sleep onset. Episodes may occur at rest and also during sleep, leading to sleep fragmentation and arousals. That said, the extent to which RLS disturbs nocturnal sleep and leads to daytime sleepiness is yet to be established. RLS sufferers tend to be of middle or older age but, in one-third of cases, symptoms present before the age of 20 years. Aetiology is thought to be associated with changes in dopamine neurotransmission. RLS is also associated with pregnancy and end-stage renal disease.

Both disorders can impact significantly on occupational and interpersonal daytime functioning, thereby impacting negatively on quality of life. They are often also associated with SBDs, and many sufferers will experience episodes of RLS and PLMD. The Epworth Sleepiness Scale (Johns, 1993) will be a useful tool to employ in initial assessment, although, as mentioned above, PSG is required to confirm a diagnosis of PLMD. However, clinical interview with the patient's partner will help to identify whether periods of sleep disruption are present. See Stiasny et al. (2002) for review.

Circadian disorders

Age-related trends in circadian function have been reported. For example, sleep propensity in young adults is still high at 7 a.m., whereas this begins to decline from 5 a.m. in older adults. Older age is also associated with increases in sleepiness experienced between 7 p.m. and 9 p.m. These changes are thought to be central to the development of sleep problems such as delayed sleep phase syndrome (DSPS) and advanced sleep phase syndrome (ASPS) (Boivin and Santo, 2003). DSPS is therefore more often associated with younger age. This delayed phase disorder may present as insomnia, but central to complaints will be the inability to go to sleep at the desired time and the inability to wake up at the desired time. There will be little night-to-night variability and the affected patient will remain drowsy if woken at a normal hour, as the internal biological clock adjusts to signal wakefulness. Unlike insomnia, those with DSPS, if left to develop their own sleep schedule, will reflect normal sleep quality, duration and sleep-stage distribution. Onset may be reported proximally to events such as a change in shift work pattern, or a period of late night studying.

ASPS is associated with early morning wakening but should not be attributed to depression unless clear diagnostic criteria are fulfilled. Wakening will occur due to sleep-phase advance relative to clock time. Older age and its association with fragmented sleep may lead to daytime napping, thereby contributing to an already compromised circadian routine. The use of sleep diary and actigraphy (see the section Clinical assessment, below) will help to monitor the sleep–wake cycle and indicate consistent patterns of phase delay or advance.

Narcolepsy

Narcolepsy is a neurological disorder typified by daytime sleepiness and symptoms associated with abnormalities of REM sleep, including sleep paralysis (i.e. a period of inability to perform voluntary movements either at sleep onset or upon awakening), sleep attacks and excessive daytime sleepiness, hypnagogic or hypnopompic hallucinations (i.e. vivid, dreamlike experiences that occur around sleep onset or wakening) and cataplexy (i.e. attacks of flaccid muscle weakness triggered by extremes of emotion such as humour or anger; Billiard and Dauvilliers, 2003). Nocturnal sleep is therefore commonly disturbed. Diagnosis can only be determined through full polysomnographic (PSG) assessment and a multiple sleep latency test (MSLT), although clinical signs indicating the need for further investigation can be readily identified in the primary care setting. Genetic markers for this disorder have been identified, thereby improving the accuracy of diagnosis.

Parasomnias

Parasomnias comprise a group of disorders that intrude into the sleep process and create disruptive behavioural phenomena (Vecchierini, 2003). They are associated with disorders of arousal, partial arousal or of sleep-stage transition. Parasomnias commonly present in childhood and resolve naturally. However, they can also present or persist into adulthood, leading to considerable lifestyle disruption. The most common presentations of parasomnia include walking (i.e. somnambulism) or talking (i.e. somniloquy) while asleep, night terrors, and disorientation or confusion on wakening (i.e. confusional arousals). These constitute primary parasomnias, and are disorders of arousal.

Other primary parasomnias include REM sleep disorders, such as REM behaviour disorder (RBD), characterised by absence of the muscle atonia normally present during REM sleep. This means that the sufferer may be able to carry out complex and seemingly purposeful behaviour relating to his or her dreams, while remaining physiologically asleep. Primary parasomnias and their behavioural correlates may therefore lead to injury of the patient or bed partner, and have been associated with forensic events (Mahowald and Schenck, 2000).

REM sleep behaviour disorder is most common in middle age/older males, and is associated with a range of neurodegenerative diseases, e.g. Parkinsonian disorders, stroke. Certain medications, e.g. venlafaxine, may induce the disorders. Others can aggravate the disorder, e.g. the tricyclic antidepressants, selective serotonin re-uptake inhibitors.

The timing and presentation of these events is often crucial in determining the underlying disorder. For instance, sleep terrors occur as incomplete arousals out of stage 4 NREM sleep, often towards the end of the first or second phase of deep sleep, and will therefore commonly present in the first third of the night. Due to the associated phase of sleep there will rarely be any accurate recall of events, despite the sufferer crying out and sitting up in bed in a state of high physiological arousal. By contrast, nightmares occur during REM sleep, and therefore mostly occur in the second half of the night. Events will generally end with the sufferer waking up, becoming quickly lucid, and being unable to get back to sleep because of the associated anxiety. There will be narrative recall for the occurrence and content of these events.

Sleep problems associated with medical/psychiatric disorders

A large number of medical conditions are known to impact on the structure of sleep (McCrae and Lichstein, 2001). This may occur through indirect sequelae such as pain, or through more central physiological processes relating to cardiac, respiratory or neurological disease. Pharmacological treatment for a variety of these conditions may also have an adverse effect on the quality of sleep.

Almost all psychiatric disorders impact on sleep to some degree. Most commonly, depression is known to lead to symptoms of insomnia. However, anxiety disorders may also lead to similar difficulties. The close relationship between sleep and psychiatric disorder is further evidenced by the finding that sleep deprivation can reduce symptoms of depression in chronic cases, and contribute to episodes of mania in those with bipolar depression. Central to a presentation of insomnia and co-morbid psychiatric disorder is the issue of primary or secondary aetiology. Structured interview and the use of rating scales will help to discount possible psychopathology.

Although insomnia is a key symptom of depression, the clinician must bear in mind that insomnia is also a known, independent risk factor for depression (Riemann and Voderholzer, 2003). Insomnia may also persist following the successful treatment of a depressive condition.

Extrinsic sleep disorders

Difficulties with sleep onset and maintenance may be associated with the use of prescribed or non-prescribed substances. For example, CNS stimulants, beta-blockers, antihypertensives all impact negatively on the structure of sleep. Alcohol, a CNS depressant, and the most common form of self-medication, is known to impact negatively on sleep quality and quantity. Also, benzodiazapine hypnotics have been contraindicated for some time in the treatment of chronic insomnia, due to their association with the psychological and physiological effects of tolerance and withdrawal, the consequent adverse effects on sleep structure an increased risk of falls especially in older adults. For review see Roehrs (1993) and Roehrs and Roth (2000).

CLINICAL ASSESSMENT

This section addresses the process of sleep assessment in detail, first, by focusing on clinical interview parameters, and then by presenting and discussing other assessment methods and important clinical presentations to be considered. These comprise methods already familiar to clinical psychologists, including the use of self-report rating scales. However, more technologically advanced sleep assessment protocols will also be presented. A useful resource for further information regarding assessment is the website of the American Academy of Sleep Medicine (http://www.aasmnet.org), which gives links to their clinical practice parameters and to reviews regarding professional standards. The text by Morin and Espie (2003) is also a valuable source assessment information.

Clinical interview

As with any clinical assessment, the clinical interview will form the basis of assessment on which subsequent formulation of the presenting problem will be based. Taking a sleep history will enable the clinician to identify any predisposing, precipitating and perpetuating factors associated with the presenting problem, which may be amenable to psychological management. A considered, structured interview will also aid assessment of the nature, course and impact of the current difficulty.

A suggested semi-structured interview has been provided in Table 32.1. This will help to identify major features associated with the most common disorders of sleep described in the ICSD-R (American Academy of Sleep Medicine, 2001). This individual system of classification is divided into four main categories. Much like other diagnostic manuals used in adult mental health settings, such as the DSM-IV (APA, 1994), ICSD-R provides descriptions and diagnostic criteria for all sleep disorders. Severity and duration criteria are provided for many disorders, and a minimal diagnostic criteria threshold must be reached to establish a positive diagnosis.

As mentioned above, however, formulating a presenting sleep problem will be as important as diagnosing the presence of a specific disorder. It is only through the development of a clinical formulation, following a thorough assessment, that the presenting complaint can be appropriately managed.

As Table 32.1 suggests, to gain an overall perspective of the presenting sleep problem it will first be important to ask questions regarding sleep routines, onset, maintenance, duration and difficulties associated with any of

Table 32.1 Outline plan of clinical interview for assessment of sleep complaints

Content area	Initial assessment	Supplementary areas for assessment
Pattern of sleep complaint	Please describe your pattern of sleep on a typical night.	Time taken to fall asleep? Number and duration of awakenings? Time spent asleep? Nights per week reflecting this pattern?
Sleep quality	Please describe the quality of your sleep.	Refreshing? Enjoyable? Restless?
Daytime effects of complaint	In what way does your night's sleep affect you during the day?	Tired? Sleepy? Poor concentration? Irritable? Diurnal variation?
Development of complaint	Please describe how your difficulties with sleep first started.	Events and circumstances surrounding onset? Dates and times? Variance since then? Exacerbation factors? Alleviating factors? Degree of impact on life/intrusiveness?
Lifetime history of sleep complaint	Have you experienced these or other difficulties with your sleep in the past?	Sleep in childhood? Sleep in adulthood? Nature of past episodes? Dates and times? Resolution of past episodes?

General health status and medical history	Please describe your general state of health?	General medical history? Family medical history and history of sleep difficulties? Chronic medical problems? Dates and times? Recent changes in health?
Psychopathology and history of psychological functioning	How do you tend to cope with difficulties in your life?	General coping style/strategies? Evidence of cognitive/emotional suppression? Anxiety or depression? Dates and times?
Current and previous treatments	What have you tried in the past to address your problems with sleep?	Now and in the past? Who suggested this? Dates and times? What has worked? What have you tried yourself?
Sleep hygiene factors	Do you use any of the following substances? Alcohol, caffeine, tobacco, prescribed/non-prescribed or herbal substances? Please describe your bedtime routine. If you wake up in the night what do you tend to do?	History of use? Pattern of use? Variability? Promote physiological arousal? Lie in bed awake for extended periods?

these. This will suggest to the clinician whether, for instance, the difficulty might be associated with environmental factors, such as changing shift-work patterns, or whether psychophysiological factors may be impacting on the individual's ability to maintain sleep. Assessment of perceived sleep quality and the daytime effects of the presenting sleep problem will then help to quantify the impact this is having on the sufferer's quality of life and, importantly, the degree to which this is of concern to the individual. Chronological assessment regarding the development of the problem may provide vital information that will guide formulation. For example, sudden onset of a sleep difficulty may be suggestive of a secondary disorder initiated by a traumatic life event or organic process. More insidious onset, or reports of a relapsing and remitting course, may indicate a more cognitive-behavioural aetiological process. Similarly, a full medical history, incorporating assessment of previous periods of sleep disturbance in the index individual, and his or her wider family, will help to determine aetiological and maintaining factors. For example, some sleep disorders have a hereditary component (e.g. narcolepsy). This assessment will then highlight whether the difficulty seems to relate more specifically to individual differences, indicating the potential for psychological management. Relating to this, a full psychological assessment will indicate psychosocial factors that may be primary to, or maintaining of, the problem. Depression is known to impact on sleep quality and could be the primary cause of a presenting sleep disturbance. Assessment of the individual's history of adaptive and maladaptive coping, and interpersonal relations, may also indicate factors primary to the problem, which are amenable to psychological intervention.

In addition to these suggested assessment and diagnostic formats, other factors should be considered during assessment. For example, it is common among those who have problems relating to sleep that a variety of previous attempts will have been made to address the problem. These may range from self-help strategies to pharmacological intervention. Knowing what has been tried before will be vital when formulating treatment options, and is likely to provide insight into motivation, engagement and adherence factors associated with the presenting individual. It will often be important to interview a relative or partner of the individual with sleep problems. As some symptoms will occur during sleep, only observers will be able to reliably corroborate or report certain symptoms. For example, sleep apnoea sufferers will be unable to report the frequency and nature of their snoring, and those who experience night terrors will rarely be able to reliably report behaviours associated with such events. While these disorders may not be amenable to primary psychological intervention, it must be considered during the assessment phase whether aspects of the presentation can be appropriately managed with psychological techniques. For example, secondary adjustment reactions such as anxiety and depression may present in response to trauma associated with a primary sleep disorder (e.g. REM sleep behaviour disorder). Related to this, it has been recognised that certain sleep disorders may be primarily responsible for affective changes that may not necessarily be responsive to psychological or pharmacological intervention alone. Strong links exist between sleep apnoea and chronic low mood (Baran and Richert, 2003). Undiagnosed cases can present at primary care clinics as intractable depression, highlighting the need for clinicians to consider differential medical diagnoses when treating depression in these settings.

In addition to the clinical interview, a variety of other methods of assessment are available to the clinician to help with the identification of aetiological and maintaining processes affecting disordered sleep.

Sleep diary

The sleep diary, another self-report assessment method is essential in the assessment of sleep disorders. Figure 32.5 provides an example of a standard sleep diary. The use of such a diary over successive nights will provide considerable insight into an individual's sleep–wake cycle and sleep quality. A minimum of 2 weeks of data collection is recommended. Indicators of specific disorders will be provided by patterns of sleep onset latency, regularity of patterns of disturbed sleep maintenance, total sleep time, and patterns of time to bed and rising time. Although this method of data collection is subject to the usual biases associated with self-reported measures, it provides a reliable measure of actual level of complaint and disturbance as perceived by the patient. More objective measures of sleep quality and physiology are available should further investigation seem necessary.

Other self-report measures

Psychometric tools may be used to supplement the process of assessment (see Moul et al., 2004, for a comprehensive review). The Pittsburgh Sleep Quality Index (Buysse et al., 1989) is a short questionnaire (24 items) that was designed to measure sleep quality in clinical populations and to aid differential diagnosis. Assessed components include subjective sleep quality, sleep latency, sleep duration, habitual sleep efficiency, sleep disturbances, use of sleeping medication and daytime dysfunction. As a screening tool for other sleep disorders, the Epworth Sleepiness Scale (ESS; Johns, 1993), is a useful addition to the assessment process. This screens for the presence and severity of daytime sleepiness in the patient, potentially indicating the presence of disorders such as obstructive sleep apnoea.

Aetiological and maintaining cognitive factors have been associated with sleep disorders such as insomnia and delayed sleep phase syndrome (DSPS). The Dysfunctional Beliefs and Attitudes about Sleep Scale (DBAS; Morin, 1994) can be used to assess sleep-related cognitions. The Sleep Disturbance

Name _____

Week Beginning _____

MEASURING THE PATTERN OF YOUR SLEEP

	Day 1	Day 2	Day 3	Day 4	Day 5	Day 6	Day 7
1. What time did you rise from bed this morning?							
2. At what time did you go to bed last night?							
3. How long did it take you to fall asleep (minutes)?							
4. How many times did you wake up during the night?							
5. How long were you awake *during* the night (in total)?							
6. About how long did you sleep altogether (hours/mins)?							
7. How much alcohol did you take last night?							
8. How many sleeping pills did you take to help you sleep?							

MEASURING THE QUALITY OF YOUR SLEEP

1. How well do you feel this morning? 0 1 2 3 4 not at all moderately very							
2. How enjoyable was your sleep last night? 0 1 2 3 4 not at all moderately very							

Figure 32.5 Example of a sleep diary incorporating information on sleep pattern and sleep quality. Numerical information is entered for each measure based on the preceding night's sleep. Qualitative ratings can be personalised to suit the individual's own terminology regarding sleep.

Source: Morin and Espie (2003). Reproduced with kind permission of Springer Science and Business Media.

Questionnaire (SDQ; Espie et al., 2000b) assesses patient attributions regarding his or her inability to sleep. This measure considers physiological, behavioural and cognitive factors as possible pathways to insomnia. The Insomnia Severity Index (ISI; Bastien et al., 2001) targets the subjective symptoms and consequences of insomnia as well as the degree of concerns or distress caused by those difficulties, helping to quantify the degree to which the presenting problem is impacting on the patient's life. The Glasgow Content of Thoughts

Inventory (GCTI; Harvey and Espie, 2004) provides insight into pre-sleep intrusive thought content known to be incompatible with sleep. The Glasgow Sleep Effort Scale (Broomfield and Espie, 2005) is useful in the context of sleep-related performance effort; an important component of psychophysiological insomnia. The effort of trying to sleep is commonly found by those with insomnia to be an undermining experience and may perpetuate sleep disturbance. This tool will aid with the formulation of interventions based on paradoxical intention therapy (see Chapter 33).

It will also be important to screen for general psychopathology. A variety of screening tools are available. However, the Hospital Anxiety Depression Scale (HADS; Zigmond and Snaith, 1983) is commonly used. This has been developed for use with clinical populations, and will give the clinician an indication of potential presence and severity of symptoms relating to anxiety and depression.

Polysomnography

Polysomnography (PSG), as mentioned previously, combines the measurement of a variety of physiological domains regarding sleep function to provide what is considered the most objective and accurate diagnostic assessment procedure of disorders of sleeping and waking. Such assessments require specialist equipment and knowledge and are generally laboratory based. However, portable PSG units for home use are now available and have demonstrated comparable clinical accuracy to that of full laboratory-based assessment.

Although PSG is not required for a clinical diagnosis of insomnia, it is recommended for research diagnostic criteria in the study of insomnia (Edinger et al., 2004). PSG is vital, however, in the process of assessment and diagnosis of serious and complex presentations, such as narcolepsy, sleep apnoea and REM sleep behaviour disorder. These presentations can only be diagnosed with the aid of objective physiological measurement. PSG is also important in the monitoring of interventions such as continuous positive airway pressure (CPAP), the current treatment of choice for sleep apnoea.

Actigraphy

Body movement has been used over the past 30 years to study sleep, on the basis that absence of movement is a good indicator of sleep. Modern actigraphs are worn on the non-dominant wrist, are highly sensitive to movement and can be used over successive 24-hour periods to monitor activity and estimate periods of sleep. Data recorded by the actigraph can then be downloaded for analysis.

Figure 32.6 represents an example of an actigraphic trace. This 68-year-old

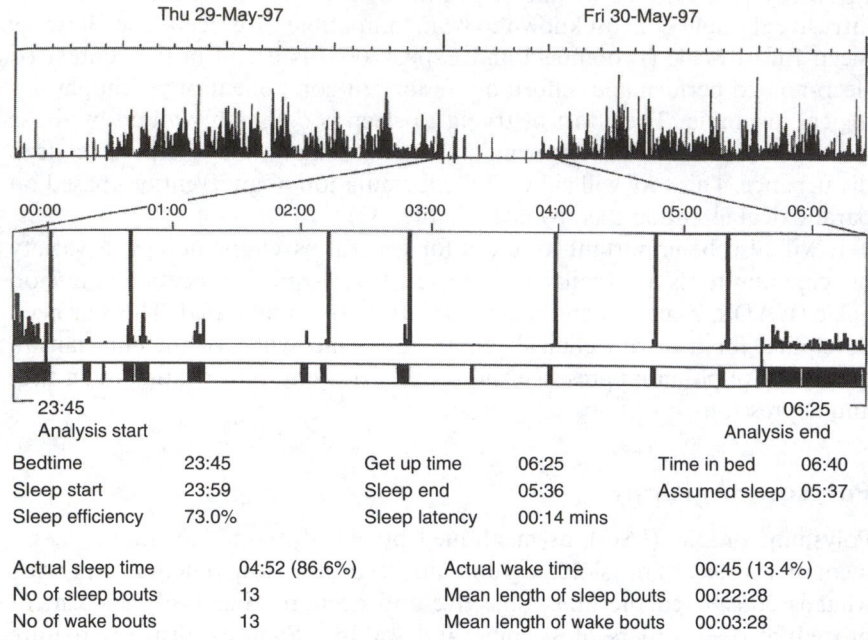

Bedtime	23:45	Get up time	06:25	Time in bed	06:40
Sleep start	23:59	Sleep end	05:36	Assumed sleep	05:37
Sleep efficiency	73.0%	Sleep latency	00:14 mins		

Actual sleep time	04:52 (86.6%)	Actual wake time	00:45 (13.4%)
No of sleep bouts	13	Mean length of sleep bouts	00:22:28
No of wake bouts	13	Mean length of wake bouts	00:03:28

Figure 32.6 Twenty four hour wrist actigraphic trace and sleep summary data from a 68-year-old woman with intermittent wakenings. Tall vertical lines represent perceived wakenings, entered by the subject depressing an event marker button on the actigraph.

Source: Morin and Espie (2003). Reproduced with kind permission of Springer Science and Business Media.

woman reported 'light sleep', intermittent arousals and unrestful, poor sleep quality. She did not experience problems in getting to sleep. Her sleep diary gave her bedtime as 11.45 p.m., and her rising time as 5.55 a.m. These parameters were used to set the 'window' for sleep analysis of actigraphic data. Inspection of the trace reveals severe awakenings from sleep, seven of which she identified by depressing an event marker on the actigraph. She had relatively short sleep (4 hours 52 minutes) and a score of 73% for sleep efficiency. This example illustrates the usefulness of the actigraph in confirming self-report information.

Actigraphy has been criticised, as gathered data are subject to certain biases. For example, not all movements necessarily indicate wakefulness. Similarly, absence of movement cannot be assumed to represent periods of sleep: patients may lie still but be awake at night. Actigraphy has also been found to correlate inconsistently with objective physiological measurements of sleep. However, recent evidence suggests that differences between PSG and actigraphic data are systematic, and can therefore be controlled for

(Tryon, 2004). Actigraphy remains supported as an important tool in the diagnosis of sleep disorders by the Standards of Practice Committee of the American Sleep Disorders Association (Standards of Practice Committee, 1995). It is particularly useful in the assessment of possible circadian disorders of sleep and the differentiation of these disorders from insomnia.

Daytime sleepiness

Daytime sleepiness and its cognitive and affective correlates can indicate the presence of several sleep disorders such as sleep apnoea, narcolepsy, idiopathic hypersomnia, circadian rhythm disorder and periodic limb movement disorder. Clinically excessive daytime sleepiness is associated with irresistible periods of sleep, with the potential for threats to personal and public safety. This should therefore be distinguished from feelings of fatigue, or tiredness, that are more often reported by those presenting with insomnia.

The Multiple Sleep Latency Test (MSLT) represents the 'gold standard' assessment of daytime sleepiness. This test uses PSG in a laboratory environment to assess an individual's sleep onset latency when given daytime nap opportunities. Such detailed assessment is not required in the context of insomnia and less technological, but reliable, tools are available for use in the adult mental health clinical setting. The Epworth Sleepiness Scale (ESS; Johns, 1993) is a self-report questionnaire commonly used in the assessment of sleep apnoea. A score of > 11 for men, and > 9 for women indicates the presence of excessive daytime sleepiness. This measure asks the individual to rate (on a 0–3 scale) how likely he or she is to fall asleep in a variety of everyday situations (e.g. sitting and reading, watching TV, in a car while stopped in traffic for a few minutes).

CONCLUSIONS

This chapter has discussed the primary assessment options for the common sleep disorders. Clinical psychologists may see such disorders in primary care. However, we are also increasingly involved in hospital settings where the acute and chronic effects of sleep disorders may lead to presentations in medical clinics such as respiratory medicine and neurology. Whether the problem presents in the context of primary or secondary care, liaison with, and support from, colleagues in neurology, respiratory medicine and psychiatry is important. This chapter emphasises the importance of considering all potential predisposing, precipitating and perpetuating factors when formulating a sleep-related complaint. Whether or not this indicates options for psychological management, it is only with a clear clinical formulation that the presenting problem can be appropriately identified and managed.

REFERENCES

Alvarez, G. G. and Ayas, N. T. (2004) The impact of daily sleep duration on health: a review of the literature. *Progress in Cardiovascular Nursing*, 19, 56–59.

American Academy of Sleep Medicine (AASM) (2001) *International Classification of Sleep Disorders, Revised (ICSD-R): Diagnostic and Coding Manual*, Rochester, MN: AASM. Online. Available: http//www.aasmnet.org

American Psychiatric Association (APA) (1994) *Diagnostic and Statistical Manual of Mental Disorders (DSM-IV)*. Washington, DC: APA.

Baran, A. S. and Richert, A. C. (2003) Obstructive sleep apnoea and depression. *CNS Spectrums*, 8, 128–134.

Barbe, F., Pericas, J., Munoz, A., Findley, L., Anto, J. M. and Agusti, A. G. (1998) Automobile accidents in patients with sleep apnoea syndrome: An epidemiological and mechanistic study. *American Journal of Respiratory and Critical Care Medicine*, 158, 18–22.

Bastien, C. H., Vallieres, A. and Morin, C. M. (2001) Validation of the Insomnia Severity Index as an outcome measure for insomnia research. *Sleep Medicine*, 2, 297–307.

Billiard, M. and Dauvilliers, Y. (2003) Narcolepsy. In: M. Billiard (ed) *Sleep: Physiology, Investigations and Medicine*. New York: Plenum.

Boivin, D. and Santo, J. (2003) Circadian rhythm sleep disorders related to an abnormal escape of the sleep-wake cycle. In: M. Billiard (ed) *Sleep: Physiology, Investigations and Medicine*. New York: Plenum.

Bonnet, M. H. (2000) Sleep deprivation. In: M. Kryger, T. Roth and W. Dement (eds) *Principles and Practice of Sleep Medicine, 3rd edn*. Philadelphia: W.B. Saunders.

Bootzin, R. R. (1972) A stimulus control treatment for insomnia. *Proceedings of the American Psychological Association*, 7, 395–396.

Broomfield, N. M. and Espie, C. A. (2003) Initial insomnia and paradoxical intention: An experimental investigation of putative mechanisms using subjective and actigraphic measurement of sleep. *Behavioural and Cognitive Psychotherapy*, 31, 313–324.

Broomfield, N. M. and Espie, C. A. (2005). Toward a valid, reliable measure of sleep effort. *Journal of Sleep Research*, 14, 1–7.

Broomfield, N. M., Gumley, A. I. and Espie, C. A. (2005) Candidate cognitive processes in psychophysiologic insomnia. *Journal of Cognitive Psychotherapy*, 19, 5–17.

Buysse, D. J., Reynolds, C. F., Monk, T. H., Berman, S. R. and Kupfer, D. J. (1989) The Pittsburgh Sleep Quality Index: A new instrument for psychiatric practice and research. *Psychiatry Research*, 28, 193–213.

Chesson, A. L., Anderson, W. M., Littner, M., Davila, D., Hartse, K., Johnson, S. et al. (1999) Practice parameters for the non-pharmacologic treatment of chronic insomnia. *Sleep*, 22(8), 1128–1133.

Cole, M. G. and Dendukuri, N. (2003) Risk factors for depression among elderly community subjects: A systematic review and meta-analysis. *American Journal of Psychiatry*, 160, 1147–1156.

Edinger, J. D., Bonnet, M. H., Bootzin, R. R., Doghramji, K., Dorsey, C. M., Espie, C. A. et al. (2004) Derivation of research diagnostic criteria for insomnia:

Report of an American Academy of Sleep Medicine work group. *Sleep*, 27, 1567–1596.

Espie, C. A. (1991) *The Psychological Treatment of Insomnia.* Chichester: John Wiley.

Espie, C. A. (2000a) Assessment and differential diagnosis. In: K. L. Lichstein and C. M. Morin (eds) *Treatment of Late-life Insomnia.* Thousand Oaks, CA: Sage Publications.

Espie, C. A. (2000b) Insomniacs' attributions: Psychometric properties of the Dysfunctional Beliefs and Attitudes about Sleep scale and the Sleep Disturbance Questionnaire. *Journal of Psychosomatic Research*, 48, 141–148.

Espie, C. A. (2002) Insomnia: Conceptual issues in the development, persistence, and treatment of sleep disorders in adults. *Annual Review of Psychology*, 53, 215–243.

Espie, C. A., Broomfield, N. M., MacMahon K. M. A. and MacPhee, L. M. (2006) The attention-intention-effort pathway in the development of psychophysiologic insomnia: A theoretical review. *Sleep Medicine Reviews*, 10, 215–245.

Ferrara, M. and Gennaro, L. (2001) How much sleep do we need ? *Sleep Medicine Reviews*, 5, 155–179.

Fletcher, E. C. (2000a) Cardiovascular consequences of obstructive sleep apnoea: experimental hypoxia and sympathetic activity. *Sleep*, 23, S127–S131.

Fletcher, E. C. (2000b) Cardiovascular effects of continuous positive airway pressure in obstructive sleep apnoea. *Sleep* 23, S154–S157.

Foley, D. J. et al. (1995) Sleep complaints among elderly persons: An epidimiologic study of three communities. *Sleep*, 10, 419–425.

Ford, D. E and Kamerow, D. B. (1989) Epidemiological study of sleep disturbances and psychiatric disorders: An opportunity for prevention? *Journal of the American Medical Association*, 262, 1479–1484.

Gale, S. D. and Hopkins, R. O. (2004) Effects of hypoxia on the brain: neuroimaging and neuropsychological findings following carbon monoxide poisoning and obstructive sleep apnoea. *Journal of the International Neuropsychological Society*, 10, 60–71.

George, C. F. P. (2000) Vigilance impairment: Assessment by driving simulators. *Sleep* 23, S115–S117.

Goh, Y. H. and Lim, K. A. (2003) The physiologic impact of sleep apnoea on wakefulness. *Otolaryngologic Clinics of North America*, 36, 423–435.

Guilleminault, C. and Kreutzer, M. L. (2003) Normal sleep. In: M. Billiard (ed) *Sleep: Physiology, Investigations and Medicine.* New York: Plenum.

Hamilton, G. S., Solin, P. and Naughton, M. T. (2004) Obstructive sleep apnoea and cardiovascular disease. *Internal Medicine Journal*, 34, 420–426.

Harvey A. G. (2002) A cognitive model of insomnia. *Behaviour Research and Therapy*, 40, 869–893.

Harvey, K. J. and Espie, C. A. (2004) Development and preliminary validation of the Glasgow Content of Thoughts Inventory (GCTI): A new measure for the assessment of pre-sleep cognitive activity. *British Journal of Clinical Psychology*, 43, 409–420.

Horne, J. (1990) *Why we Sleep: The Functions of Sleep in Humans and Other Animals.* New York: Oxford University Press.

Johns, M. W. (1993) Daytime sleepiness, snoring, and obstructive sleep apnoea: the Epworth Sleepiness Scale. *Chest*, 103, 30–36.

Kohn, L. and Espie, C. A. (2005) Sensitivity and specificity of the insomnia experience:

A comparative study of psychophysiologic insomnia, insomnia associated with mental disorder and good sleep. *Sleep*, 28, 104–112.

Krieger, J. (2003) Obstructive sleep apnoea-hypopnoea syndrome and upper airway resistance syndrome. In: M. Billiard (ed) *Sleep: Physiology, Investigations and Medicine*. New York: Plenum.

Mahowald, M. W. and Schenck, C. H. (2000) Parasomnias: sleepwalking and the law. *Sleep Medicine Reviews*, 4, 321–339.

McCrae, C. S. and Lichstein, K. L. (2001) Secondary insomnia: diagnostic challenges and intervention opportunities. *Sleep Medicine Reviews*, 5, 47–61.

Morin, C. M. (1993) *Insomnia: Psychological Assessment and Management*. New York: Guilford Press.

Morin, C. M. (1994) Dysfunctional beliefs and attitudes about sleep: Preliminary scale development and description. *The Behavior Therapist*, 17, 163–164.

Morin, C. M. and Espie, C. A. (2003) *Insomnia: A Clinical Guide to Assessment and Treatment*. New York: Plenum.

Morin, C. M., Stone, J., Trinkle, D., Mercer, J. and Remsberg, S. (1993) Dysfunctional beliefs and attitudes about sleep among older adults with and without insomnia complaints. *Psychology and Aging* 8, 463–467.

Morgan, K. (2000) Sleep and aging. In: K. L. Lichstein and C. M. Morin (eds) *Treatment of Late-life Insomnia*. Thousand Oaks, CA: Sage Publications.

Moul, D. E., Hall, M., Pilkonis, P. A. and Buysse, D. J. (2004) Self-report measures of insomnia in adults: Rationales, choices, and needs. *Sleep Medicine Reviews* 8:177–198.

Perlis, M. L., Giles, D. E., Mendelson, W. B., Bootzin, R. R. and Wyatt, J. K. (1997) Psychophysiological insomnia: The behavioural model and a neurocognitive perspective. *Journal of Sleep Research*, 6, 179–188.

Riemann, D. and Voderholzer, U. (2003) Primary insomnia: A risk factor to develop depression. *Journal of Affective Disorders*, 76, 255–259.

Roehrs, T. (1993) Alcohol. In: M. A. Carskadon, A. Rechtschaffen, G. Richardson, T. Roth and J Siegel (eds) *Encyclopaedia of Sleep and Dreaming*. New York: MacMillan.

Roehrs, T. and Roth, T. (2000) Hypnotics: Efficacy and adverse effects. In: M. Kryger, T. Roth and W Dement (eds) *Principles and Practice of Sleep Medicine, 3rd edn*. Philadelphia: W.B. Saunders.

Semler, C. and Harvey, A. G. (2004) Monitoring for sleep-related threat: A pilot study of the Sleep Associated Monitoring Index (SAMI). *Psychosomatic Medicine*, 66, 242–250.

Singleton, N., Bumpstead, R., OBrien, M., Lee, A. and Meltzer, H. (2001) *Psychiatric Morbidity Among Adults Living in Private Households, 2000*. London: Office for National Statistics.

Spielman, A. J. and Glovinsky, P. B. (1991) The varied nature of insomnia. In: P. Hauri (ed) *Case Studies in Insomnia* (pp. 1–15). New York: Plenum Press.

Standards of Practice Committee (1995) Practice parameters for the use of actigraphy in the clinical assessment of sleep disorders. *Sleep*, 18, 285–287.

Stiasny, K., Oertel, W. H. and Trenkwalder, C. (2002) Clinical symptomatology and treatment of restless legs syndrome and periodic limb movement disorder. *Sleep Medicine Reviews*, 6, 253–265.

Tryon, W. W. (2004) Issues of validity in actigraphic assessment. *Sleep*, 27, 158–165.

Vecchierini, M. F. (2003) Parasomnias. In: M. Billiard (ed) *Sleep: Physiology, Investigations and Medicine*, New York: Plenum.

Vignola, A., Lamoureux, C., Bastien, C. H. and Morin, C. M. (2000) Effects of chronic insomnia and use of benzodiazepines on daytime performance in older adults. *Journals of Gerontology. Series B, Psychological Sciences and Social Sciences*, 55, P54–P62.

Youngstedt, S. D. and Kripke, D. F. (2004) Long sleep and mortality: Rationale for sleep restriction. *Sleep Medicine Reviews*, 8, 159–174.

Zigmond, A. S. and Snaith, R. P. 1983 The Hospital Anxiety and Depression Scale. *Acta Psychiatrica et Neurologica Scandinavica*, 67, 361–370.

Chapter 33

Disorders of sleep

Treatment

Niall Broomfield, Matt Wild and Colin Espie

TREATMENT EVIDENCE FOR THE INSOMNIA DISORDERS

Drug therapy

Traditionally, insomnia is treated pharmacologically using benzodiazepine compounds. Controlled studies have demonstrated that a considerable number of benzodiazepines of short to intermediate half-life are effective hypnotic agents.

However, there are potential problems. Longer-acting hypnotics are prone to daytime carry-over effects, e.g. morning lethargy and sleepiness, and shorter-acting drugs to 'rebound insomnia' and elevated daytime anxiety; all part of a withdrawal syndrome. Tolerance can also develop, with frequent administration leading either to increased dosing or switching to alternative medication. Although benzodiazepines used for short periods or intermittently can maintain effectiveness, these are not the treatment of choice in chronic insomnia, and are contraindicated in older adults and where insomnia may involve sleep-related breathing disorder (National Institute of Health (NIH), 1984). A number of benzodiazepine compounds have been removed from the market in the UK, USA and elsewhere.

Nevertheless prescribing of hypnotic benzodiazepines (e.g. temazepam, nitazepam, lorazepam, oxazepam) remains high. In 1999, the NHS in England spent £33.6 million on anxiolytics and hypnotics. The current projected UK annual figure is at least £40 million (Department of Health, 1999). Trends in the duration of hypnotic use show a remarkably stable pattern. Long-term use is common. Such findings reflect the overwhelming demand for treatment and the limited progress made thus far in introducing non-pharmacological alternatives on a wide scale.

Three newer hypnotics (zolpidem, zopiclone and zaleplon) are not benzo-diazepines *per se*, but act on the same benzodiazepine and gamma ami-nobutryric acid-A ($GABA_A$) receptors. These newer drugs have more selective hypnotic effects but have not demonstrated greater treatment efficacy than benzodiazepines (National Institute for Health and Clinical Excellence

(NICE), 2003). Antidepressants with sedating properties (e.g. trazadone, amitriptiline, trimipramine and doxepin) are also commonly prescribed for insomnia, usually in small doses (e.g. 10–20 mg amitriptiline). Very few studies have examined the efficacy and safety of these agents when used as hypnotics with non-depressed insomniacs.

The active ingredient in most available over-the-counter preparations for insomnia (e.g. Sominex, Nytol, Sleep-Eze, Unisom) is an antihistamine such as diphenhydramine or doxylamine. These agents produce drowsiness. Again, despite widespread use, very few studies have evaluated safety and efficacy. The evidence suggests that diphenhydramine may be effective for mild insomnia, but there is no evidence of efficacy for chronic severe cases. Moreover, antihistamines can produce adverse (psychomotor and cognitive) and residual effects the next day (e.g. sleepiness). Some patients may also report agitation.

Hypnotic medications are effective for the acute and short-term management of insomnia. They produce quick relief on the first night of usage and benefits may last several nights, and in some cases up to a few weeks. There is currently little evidence of sustained benefit, all carry some risk of dependence, particularly with prolonged use, and their role in the clinical management of insomnia should always be as an adjunct to behavioural interventions (NIH, 1984, 1991, 1996). Typically, sleeping pills are recommended for only around 10 nights administration, although in practice patients often take them for years.

Psychological therapy

Psychological treatment has been investigated in over 50 controlled studies in the past 20 years, involving over 2,000 patients. These studies have mainly evaluated the efficacy of elements of cognitive-behavioural therapy (CBT) singly or in combination. Two meta-analyses have reported effect sizes of 0.87 for reductions in sleep latency, and significant effects have been found for number and duration of wakenings (0.53–0.65) and sleep quality (0.94) (Murtagh and Greenwood, 1995). Up to 70–80% of patients benefit from CBT (Morin et al., 1999a). CBT appears equally efficacious in older adults, although not for all sleep outcomes (Montgomery and Dennis, 2002a).

Recent clinical effectiveness research from Scotland also shows the beneficial effects of CBT in general practice. Two recent studies randomised 390 chronic insomniacs accessed via general practitioners to CBT or to treatment as usual (TAU) (Espie et al., 2001, 2004). Significant reductions in time awake in bed per night were observed following CBT. Severity of sleep disturbance and physical tension reduced significantly, and inaccurate beliefs about sleep were modified; these treatment effects hold at 6-months follow-up. The demonstration of durable effects is of critical importance – a feature notably lacking in the pharmacological literature on insomnia.

A number of strategies within the CBT model have strong empirical support. The American Academy of Sleep Medicine has published practice parameters for the assessment (Chesson et al., 2000) and non-pharmacological treatment (Chesson et al., 1999) of insomnia, the latter derived from systematic review (Morin et al., 1999b). Three meta-analyses have now been published demonstrating the efficacy of CBT for insomnia in adults (Morin et al., 1994; Murtagh and Greenwood, 1995; Smith et al., 2002) relative to pharmacotherapy. Another review came to similar conclusions (Edinger and Wohlgemuth, 1999), as did a recent examination of the merits of CBT in older patients (Irwin et al., 2006). The role of hypnotic medication has been debated, and there is little evidence of long-term efficacy of any drug. CBT, therefore, is the treatment of choice of insomnia.

As we have seen, insomnia does not always present as a single prototype. Various sub-types are possible. Although there is limited evidence for tailored treatment approaches, clinical experience would suggest patients with paradoxical insomnia may benefit from a more cognitive approach aimed to addressing misperceptions. We would strongly recommend that a combined CBT programme is delivered in full, whenever possible, for any case of psychophysiological insomnia. And for insomnias associated with known mental disorders, we would recommend that *both* the mental disorder and the insomnia be targeted in treatment.

Using cognitive-behavioural treatments

An excellent guide for the implementation of CBT for insomnia can be found in Morin and Espie (2003); we offer a summary here. Brief descriptions of effective management strategies are presented (Tables 33.1, 33.3 and 33.4). The text provides related explanation of underlying psychological models and further information on implementation.

Sleep education and sleep hygiene

The simple provision of information ameliorates the sense of being out of control. By understanding what sleep is, how common insomnia can be, sleep changes with age, good sleep hygiene practices and some facts about sleep loss, inaccurate attributions are challenged and misunderstandings corrected. Similarly, sleep hygiene provides patients with a starting point for self-management. Maximising bed comfort, exercise and minimising caffeine, nicotine, alcohol and noise are important behavioural/environment components (Table 33.1). These techniques are best construed as introductory and will not of themselves treat insomnia effectively.

Table 33.1 Summary description of sleep hygiene and education components for the treatment of chronic psychophysiological insomnia

Components of 'sleep education'
- The need for sleep and its functions
- Sleep patterns change across the lifespan
- Sleep is an active process with stages/phases
- Factors that adversely affect sleep (stress)
- The effects of sleep loss
- The concept of insomnia
- Measuring sleep and sleep problems (introduce sleep diary)

Components of 'sleep hygiene treatment'
- Ensure bedroom comfortable for sleep (temperature, air quality, bed)
- Encourage regular exercise and fitness, but avoid strenuous exercise before sleep
- Encourage a stable, appropriate diet. A light snack before bed aids sleep
- Remind patients of the undesirable effects of caffeine and nicotine
- Reduce alcohol consumption; even moderate alcohol disrupts sleep architecture

Stimulus-control treatment

Stimulus control increases the bedroom's cueing potential for sleep. For good sleepers, the pre-bedtime period and the stimulus environment are presumed to trigger positive associations of sleepiness and sleep. For the poor sleeper, however, the bedroom triggers associations with restlessness and lengthy nighttime wakening via a stimulus–response relationship, thereby continuing to promote wakefulness and arousal. The model is similar to phobic conditions where a conditioned stimulus precipitates an anxiety response.

Treatment involves removing from the bedroom all stimuli that are potentially sleep incompatible. Reading and watching television, for example, are confined to living rooms. Sleeping is excluded from living areas and from the daytime, and wakefulness is excluded from the bedroom. The individual is instructed to get up if not asleep within 15 minutes or if wakeful during the night. In our clinic we call this the 'quarter-of-an hour rule (QHR)'. While patients must rise from bed if still awake after 15 minutes, it is important the clinician does not encourage clock-watching on the part of the patients – this may increase frustration and worsen the insomnia. An estimate of time is advised.

Conceptually, stimulus control is a re-conditioning treatment that forces discrimination between daytime and sleeping environments. Stimulus control is an efficacious single-component treatment for psychophysiological insomnia according to American Psychiatric Association (APA) criteria (Morin et al., 1999a). Indeed, stimulus control is the only 'standard' non-pharmacological treatment for insomnia according to the American Academy of Sleep Medicine (AASM; Chesson et al., 1999).

Compliance is important to ensure a treatment effect, but ensuring this can be problematic. Communicating a clear treatment rationale is important. Lessening the discomfort of having to get up, using heating, lighting, music, hot drinks may also help. Further discussion on how to maximise compliance to CBT approaches is given below.

Sleep-restriction therapy

Often, stimulus-control instructions are combined with sleep-restriction therapy in what we refer to in our clinic as 'sleep scheduling' treatment. The essential components of a sleep scheduling protocol are outlined in Table 33.2.

Essentially, the sleep-restriction element restricts sleep to the length of time that the person is likely to sleep. This may be equivalent to promoting 'core sleep' at the expense of 'optional sleep'. Sleep restriction therefore aims to improve sleep efficiency. As sleep efficiency is the ratio of time asleep to time in bed, it can be improved either by increasing the numerator (time spent asleep) or by reducing the denominator (time spent in bed). Insomniacs generally seek the former, but this may not be necessary, either biologically or psychologically. Stimulus-control directives to minimise sleep-incompatible activities and to follow the QHR are then combined to form sleep scheduling.

Helping patients understand sleep-scheduling treatment will aid compliance. A useful sleep scheduling handout for patients is presented in Table 33.3. This includes stimulus-control aspects. The sleep-restriction component first involves getting patients to record their sleep in a sleep diary and to calculate their average nightly sleep duration. The aim, then, is to obtain this average each night. This is achieved by setting rising time as an 'anchor' each day and

Table 33.2 Summary description of stimulus control and sleep restriction therapy ('sleep scheduling') for the treatment of chronic insomnia

- Remove incompatible activity from bedroom environment (TV, reading, eating)
- Define individual sleep requirements using diary
- Establish parameters for bedtime period (threshold time and rising time) using diary
- Eliminate daytime napping
- Differentiate rest from sleep
- Schedule sleep periods with respect to needs
- Establish 7-day per week compliance
- Follow the QHR: rise from bed if wakeful for longer than 15 minutes
- Avoid recovery sleep as 'compensation'
- Establish stability from night to night
- Adjust the sleep period as sleep efficiency improves (15 minutes per week)

Table 33.3 Summary of 'sleep scheduling' treatment programme

1. Work out your current average sleep time and plan to spend that amount of time in bed
2. Decide on a set rising time to get up each morning and put that into practice
3. Establish a threshold time for going to bed by subtracting sleep time from rising time, and stay out of bed until your threshold time
4. Lie down, intending to go to sleep only when you feel sleepy at or after the threshold time
5. Follow this programme 7 days/nights per week
6. If you do not sleep within 15 minutes, get up and go into another room. Do something relaxing and go back to bed when you feel sleepy again. Repeat this if you still cannot sleep or if you waken in the night
7. Adjust the new schedule by a maximum of 15 minutes per week, depending on your sleep efficiency
8. Do not use your bed for anything except sleep and turn the light out when you go to bed
9. Do not nap during the day or evening

Source: Morin and Espie (2003).

delaying going to bed until a 'threshold time', which permits this designated amount of sleep. Thus the sleep period is compressed and sleep efficiency is likely to increase.

The AASM support sleep restriction as a 'guideline' intervention for insomnia (Chesson et al., 1999). This limited endorsement reflects the relatively small number of trials that have used sleep restriction alone as an intervention mode. In clinical practice, it is a core component of CBT packages.

Imagery and relaxation

There is a wide range of relaxation methods, including progressive relaxation, imagery training, biofeedback, meditation, hypnosis and autogenic training, but little evidence to indicate superiority of any one approach. Furthermore, there is also little evidence as yet to support the presumption that insomniacs are hyperaroused in physiological terms or that relaxation has its effect through autonomic change. At the cognitive level, these techniques may act through distraction and the promotion of mastery. During relaxation, the mind focuses on alternative themes, such as visualised images or physiological responses. In meditation, the focus is on a 'mantra' and in self-hypnosis on positive 'self' – statements. Relaxation may be effective for thought processes that are anxiety based, confused and which flit from topic to topic. Relaxation therapy is a moderately effective treatment strategy, particularly for initial insomnia, although there is little evidence to suggest differential efficacy across the range of methods available (Chesson et al., 1999; Morin et al., 1999a).

Cognitive control

This technique deals with thought material in advance of bedtime to reduce intrusive bedtime thinking. The insomnia patient sets aside 15 to 20 minutes in the early evening to rehearse the day and to plan ahead for tomorrow; thus putting the day to rest. This dealing with unfinished business may be most effective for rehearsal, planning and self-evaluative thoughts, which are important to the individual and that, if not dealt with, may intrude during the sleep-onset period.

Thought suppression

Thought-stopping and articulatory suppression are designed to interrupt the flow of thoughts. No attempt is made to deal with thought material *per se* but rather to attenuate thinking. With articulatory suppression the patient repeats, sub-vocally, the word 'the' every 3 seconds. This procedure is derived from the experimental psychology literature. Articulatory suppression is thought to occupy the short-term memory store used in information processing. The type of material most likely to respond is repetitive but non-affect-laden thoughts that are not powerful enough to demand attention. Additionally, this technique may be useful during the night to enable rapid return to sleep.

Cognitive restructuring

Cognitive restructuring challenges both the faulty beliefs that maintain wake-fulness and the helplessness reported by patients with psychophysiological insomnia. This treatment appears to work through appraisal by testing the validity of assumptions against evidence and real-life experience. As an evaluative technique, it may be effective with beliefs that are irrational but compelling. If such thoughts, e.g. 'I am going to be incapable at work tomor-row' are not challenged they will create high levels of preoccupation and anxiety and sleep is unlikely to occur. With cognitive restructuring, the insomnia patient learns alternative responses to replace inaccurate thinking. It is important with cognitive restructuring to help patients with insomnia, through dialogue and thought challenging, to keep more realistic expect-ations about sleep, and to revise their attributions about the causes of insomnia. A focus more on internal factors that the patient may change (irregular sleep scheduling, napping, spending excessive time in bed) will encourage more productive thinking. Patients must also be encouraged not to blame sleeplessness for all daytime impairments, not to catastrophise after a poor night's sleep, to place less emphasis on sleep in their lives and never to try to sleep (for detailed discussion see Morin and Espie, 2003).

Cognitive restructuring therapy has become an integral part of most multi-component protocols (Table 33.4). Thus it is not possible to determine

Table 33.4 Summary description of cognitive approaches for the treatment of chronic insomnia

- Identify thought patterns and content that intrude
- Address (mis-)attributions connecting sleep and waking life
- Establish rehearsal/planning time early evening
- Relaxation and imagery training
- Distraction and thought blocking
- Develop accurate beliefs/attributions about sleep and sleep loss
- Challenge negative and invalid thoughts
- Eliminate 'effort' to control sleep
- Motivate to maintain behaviour and cognitive change
- Utilise relapse prevention techniques

its specific contribution to overall outcome. Clinical experience would suggest it is very useful to distinguish normal age-related sleep changes from pathological insomnia, and to reduce emotional distress. Some preliminary evidence suggests it may play an important function in mediating and maintaining long-term outcome (Morin et al., 2002).

Insomnia patients often overestimate sleeplessness or sleep loss relative to objective measures. By highlighting such objective–subjective discrepancies with patients, for example using actigraphy, this cognitive distortion can be minimised. The approach may also reduce sleep-related anxiety and preoccupation (Tang and Harvey, 2004).

Meta-cognitive observation

This recently developed new approach to insomnia treatment encourages 'mindful observation' of cognitive and emotional processes in the pre-sleep phase. The technique would appear to promote sleep by interrupting worry, rumination and other sleep-interfering cognitive processes (Lundh and Hindmarsh, 2002). Further research using controlled studies to examine outcome and putative mechanisms is needed.

Paradoxical intention therapy

The technique of paradoxical intention is useful for individuals with psychophysiological insomnia where performance anxiety has developed, i.e. where the effort to produce a response inhibits that response itself. The paradoxical instruction is to allow sleep to occur naturally through passively attempting to remain quietly wakeful rather than attempting to fall asleep. Patients are instructed to lie gently awake, eyes open, at bedtime. Paradoxically, the likelihood of staying awake is reduced by encouragement to do so. Thus paradox may be regarded as a de-catastrophising technique because it appears to act on the ultimate anxious thought (of remaining awake indefinitely) initially by focusing on and enhancing this thought (a habituation model) and then subjecting it to appraisal through rationalisation and experience. By intending to remain awake, and failing so to do, the strength of the sleep drive is re-established and performance effort is reduced. Recent experimental evidence appears to confirm this (Broomfield and Espie, 2003). Paradoxical intention shows demonstrated efficacy in clinical trials, and reflects a 'moderate degree of clinical effectiveness' (Chesson et al., 1999)

Multi-component cognitive-behaviour therapy

Multi-component CBT typically combines several of the above interventions in a single treatment package (e.g. Morin et al., 1999a; Edinger et al., 2001; Espie et al., 2001, 2004; Morin and Espie, 2003). Cognitive restructuring may be, but is not always, an integral part of this multi-component therapy. The behavioural component usually involves therapies such as stimulus control, sleep restriction and progressive muscular relaxation. Evidence for multi-component therapy is still in evolution (Chesson et al., 1999).

Our CBT treatment package, summarised by Morin and Espie (2003) comprises five 1-hour treatment sessions and includes sleep education, relaxation, sleep scheduling and cognitive therapy. Recent data show the clinical effectiveness of this therapy when delivered in small groups by trained non-specialists in general practice settings (Espie et al., 2001, 2004). The clinical and cost effectiveness of this combined therapy in the general practice setting should be examined further.

Maximising patient compliance

The first strategy to ensure good patient compliance to CBT approaches for insomnia is to ensure your practice is best practice. The evidence is that CBT for insomnia works, if delivered faithfully. There is limited evidence for a tailored treatment approach at present – be cautious and err on the side of including components across the range outlined here. You should take the patient's problem seriously and establish a working relationship commensurate with the severity and intrusiveness of the problem. Work on problems in a focused, directed and organised manner and monitor and discuss readiness to implement change, at both the micro and macro level. Appraise progress collaboratively and be prepared to persist with interventions. Remember that stimulus control and sleep restriction, arguably the two most important components, are also the hardest to follow. Finally, be enthusiastic and provide encouragement (Morin and Espie, 2003)

The Good Sleep Guide

For poor sleepers, a useful summary handout on how best to regain, and maintain, a healthy sleep pattern is the *Good Sleep Guide* (National Medical Advisory Committee, 1993) (see Appendix 1, p 685). The guide is also available on the British Sleep Society website (http://www.sleeping.org.uk). It is a concise, easily understood handout summary of key cognitive-behavioural principles based on the extant insomnia treatment literature.

TREATMENT OF OTHER SLEEP DISORDERS

Sleep-related breathing disorder

The term 'sleep-related breathing disorder' (SBD) refers to a group of disorders that disrupt sleep pattern through impaired respiratory function. The treatment of choice is continuous positive airway pressure (CPAP). This comprises a mechanical pump, which delivers a stream of air through a mask during sleep, thus preventing upper airway collapse. CPAP efficacy has been well demonstrated, although it is not well tolerated; adherence is often poor. Psychological factors may improve CPAP acceptance and adherence (Engleman and Wild, 2003). Management of adherence is the most likely psychology role, alongside adjunct treatment of associated affective/anxiety disorder. Positional therapy to prevent the supine position, and weight loss therapy may also be beneficial, as are some surgical procedures in severe cases. Pharmacotherapy using Modafinil to reduce daytime sleepiness may also confer some benefit in mild/moderate cases (Cartwright, 2003).

Restless legs syndrome and periodic limb movement disorder

There are no known effective behavioural treatments for restless legs syndrome (RLS) and periodic limb movement disorder (PLMD). Both require sleep-laboratory assessment and are managed using pharmacotherapy. RLS is associated with restless, crawling sensations in the leg muscles, which are worst at night and only relieved with movement out of bed. Thus sleep onset is impaired. Dopamine agonists can impact RLS, as can sleep hypnotics. Iron supplements may also assist, as the condition may relate to iron deficiency (Allen and Earley, 2001). PLMD is associated with repeated, uncontrollable leg kicks, which cause brief arousals from stages 1 and 2 sleep, is often co-morbid with SDB and is particularly prevalent in later life. PLMD responds best to agents that act on dopamine receptor sites, which reduce PLM activity and improve sleep quality.

Circadian disorders

Circadian disorders involve difficulty falling asleep at the 'socially expected' time. In delayed sleep-phase syndrome (DSPS), sleep does not arrive until the early hours of the morning, with rising times subsequently delayed, often until midday or later. In advanced sleep-phase syndrome (ASPS), sleep arrives too early, with the sufferer struggling to stay wake in the early evening, but wide awake in the early hours of the morning. DSPS is more associated with younger age, ASPS with older age. Melatonin plays a central part in regulating bodily rhythms. Oral melatonin supplementation has been heralded as the treatment to improve sleep timing. At present, the available evidence supports this only to a limited degree (MacMahon et al., 2005); more research is needed. As endogenous melatonin levels drop off in later life, melatonin may have more impact in older adults with timing problems. Bright-light therapy may also ameliorate sleep-timing problems, particularly in older people (Montgomery and Dennis, 2002b). Psychological management, in combination with the above strategies, may focus on advancing or delaying sleep onset gradually, to re-establish a more appropriate phase of the sleep–wake cycle.

Narcolepsy

Narcolepsy is a neurological disorder typified by excessive daytime sleepiness and symptoms of REM sleep abnormality, including sleep paralysis, hypnagogic hallucinations and cataplexy. Disturbed nocturnal sleep is common also. Effective pharmacological treatments have been developed. These include Modafinil, a wake-promoting agent, and gamma hydroxybutyric acid, a sedative used for treating disturbed nocturnal sleep and cataplexy. However, whilst effective, these offer only symptomatic treatment of the presenting problems. Behavioural factors, such as maintaining a stable sleep pattern, avoiding sleep deprivation, scheduling daytime naps and not actively resisting daytime sleepiness, may also help. A combined pharmacological and behavioural approach may be optimal (Rogers and Mullington, 2003).

Parasomnias

Parasomnias involve undesirable phenomena during sleep. Sleepwalking and night terrors have been successfully treated in children with behavioural and other psychological methods. There is some evidence that psychological variables are associated with these presentations in adults, indicating the potential for psychological management (Crisp, 1996). Accurate diagnosis, information, education, reassurance and dealing with any triggering factors are important. Patients should avoid sleep deprivation and excessive use of alcohol. A risk assessment regarding potential injury or harm should be conducted particularly where the patient has a history of trying to leave the house.

CONCLUSION

This chapter summarises effective treatments for the three common insomnia disorders. Brief coverage is given to management options of the other more common sleep disorders. Our aim has been to inform clinicians how to recognise and practically manage these sleeping problems. As is hopefully clear, the insomnia disorders are amenable to psychological intervention using CBT. We strongly recommend a combined CBT programme be delivered in full whenever possible because there is only limited evidence supporting the tailoring of therapy (Morin and Espie, 2003). Detailed assessment and formulation will determine the precise choice of intervention, guided by extant explanatory models. Failure to diagnose and treat insomnia properly puts patients at risk of worsening sleep disturbance and depression. The core skills of assessment, differential diagnosis, formulation and intervention are ideally suited to identify and treat such cases.

APPENDIX I: THE GOOD SLEEP GUIDE

During the evening

1   Daily exercise is a good way to encourage sleep. Try some light exercise early in the evening, such as walking or swimming, as this will make your body ready for sleep later on.
2   Avoid drinking coffee or tea or eating chocolate in the evening because they all contain caffeine, which makes you more alert. A hot milky drink is a good alternative. Also, don't drink alcohol as a nightcap – it usually upsets sleep.
3   Wind down during the course of the evening. Try not to do anything that is mentally stimulating within 90 minutes of bedtime. Give yourself time to relax and prepare for sleep – try having a warm bath or listening to some soothing music.
4   Do not sleep or doze in the armchair because this can upset your night time sleeping patterns. Keep all your sleep for bedtime.
5   Feeling worried or anxious or just having an active mind can cause a sleepless night. Try to put the day to rest. Take time to think it through and write down any worries or concerns or loose ends in a notebook. Say goodbye to them before you go to bed – you can deal with them more effectively in the morning.

6   Make sure your bed and bedroom are comfortable for sleep. Your room should be well ventilated, not too cold or too warm.

At bedtime

1   Try to get up at the same time every day, even at weekends, use an alarm clock if you need to. This helps establish your sleep pattern to follow a regular routine.
2   Go to bed when you are 'sleepy tired' and not before. Try to notice when you are ready to sleep.
3   Try to avoid reading or watching TV in bed as this can stimulate the brain, sometimes making it difficult to relax. Keep these waking activities for another room.
4   Put the light out when you get into bed and try to ensure your room is as dark as possible. This helps signal to your body that it's time for sleep.
5   Let yourself relax. Tell yourself that 'sleep will come when it's ready'. Enjoy relaxing even if you don't at first fall asleep. If you are not good at relaxing, try to learn a relaxation method.
6   Do not try to fall asleep – let sleep find you. Sleep is not something you can switch on automatically. Trying too hard can switch sleep off.

If you have problems getting to sleep

1   Remember that sleep difficulties are quite common and are not as damaging as you might think. Most people cope quite well even after a disturbed night's sleep.
2   Try not to get upset or frustrated or to think about the next day. Avoid watching the clock, as this will only make the time pass more slowly.
3   Instead, if you are awake for more than 15 minutes, you just might not be ready for sleep. Try getting up, going into another room, and accepting it philosophically.
4   Do something relaxing while you are up, like listening to music or reading.
5   Go back to bed again when you feel 'sleepy tired'. Remember you may have to repeat this rising and returning to bed several times a night at first.
6   Whenever you experience difficulties sleeping, try to follow these tips. A good sleeping pattern may take a number of weeks to establish. Be confident that you will achieve this by working through 'The Good Sleep Guide'!

The Good Sleep Guide was prepared by Professor Colin A. Espie, Director of the University of Glasgow Sleep Research Laboratory, Southern General Hospital, Glasgow. The Good Sleep Guide is recommended by the British Sleep Society.

REFERENCES

Allen, R. P. and Earley, C. J. (2001) Restless legs syndrome: A review of clinical and pathophysiologic features *Journal of Clinical Neurophysiology*, 18, 128–147.

Broomfield, N. M. and Espie, C. A. (2003) Initial insomnia and paradoxical intention: An experimental investigation of putative mechanisms using subjective and actigraphic measurement of sleep. *Behavioural and Cognitive Psychotherapy*, 31, 313–324.

Cartwright, R. D. (2003). Sleep apnoea: A challenge for behavioural medicine. In: M. L. Perlis and K. L. Lichstein (eds) *Treating Sleep Disorders: Principles and Practice of Behavioural Sleep Medicine*. New Jersey: John Wiley.

Chesson, A. L., Anderson, W. M., Littner, M., Davila, D., Hartse, K., Johnson, S. et al. (1999) Practice parameters for the non-pharmacologic treatment of chronic insomnia. *Sleep*, 22(8), 1128–1133.

Chesson, A. L., Hartse, K., Anderson, W. M., Davila, D., Johnson, S., Littner, M. et al. (2000) Practice parameters for the evaluation of chronic insomnia. *Sleep*, 23, 237–241.

Crisp, A. H. (1996) The sleepwalking night terrors syndrome in adults. *Postgraduate Medicine*, 72, 599–604.

Department of Health (1999) Prescription cost analysis: England 1999. London: Department of Health.

Edinger, J. D. and Wohlgemuth, W. K. (1999) The significance and management of persistent primary insomnia: The past, present and future of behavioural insomnia therapies. *Sleep Medicine Review*, 3, 101–118.

Edinger, J. D., Wohlgemuth, W. K., Radke, R. A., Marsh G. R. and Quillan, R. E. (2001) Cognitive behaviour therapy for treatment of chronic primary insomnia: A randomised controlled trial. *Journal of the American Medical Association*, 285, 1856–1864.

Engleman, H. E. and Wild, M. R. (2003) Improving CPAP use in patients with the sleep apnoea/hypopnoea syndrome (SAHS). *Sleep Medicine Reviews*, 7, 81–99.

Espie, C. A., Inglis, S. J., Tessier, S. and Harvey, L. (2001) The clinical effectiveness of cognitive behaviour therapy for chronic insomnia: Implementation and evaluation of a sleep clinic in general medical practice. *Behaviour Research and Therapy*, 39, 45–60.

Espie, C. A., Broomfield, N. M., Kelly, H., MacMahon, K., McKinstry, B., Douglas, N. J. et al. (2004) Randomised intention to treat trial of nurse-administered cognitive behaviour therapy for insomnia in general practice. *Sleep*, 27, A269.

Irwin, M., Cole, J. C. and Nicassio, P. M. (2006) Comparative meta analysis of behavioural interventions for insomnia and their efficacy in adults and in older adults 55+ years.

Lundh, L. G. and Hindmarsh, H. (2002) Can metacognitive observation be used in the treatment of insomnia? A pilot study of a cognitive-emotional self-observation task. *Behavioural and Cognitive Psychotherapy*, 30, 233–236.

MacMahon, K., Broomfield, N. M. and Espie, C. A. (2005) A systematic review of the effectiveness of oral melatonin for adults (18 to 65 years) with delayed sleep phase syndrome and adults (18 to 65 years) with primary insomnia. *Current Psychiatry Reviews*, 1, 103–113.

Montgomery, P. and Dennis, J. (2002a) Cognitive behavioural interventions improve some sleep outcomes in older adults (Cochrane Review). *Cochrane Database Systematic Review, 2.*

Montgomery, P. and Dennis, J. (2002b) Bright light therapy for sleep problems in adults aged 60+ (Cochrane Review). *Cochrane Database Systematic Review, 4.*

Morin, C. M. and Espie, C. A. (2003) *Insomnia: A Clinical Guide to Assessment and Treatment.* New York: Plenum.

Morin, C. M., Culbert, J. P. and Schwartz, S. M. (1994) Nonpharmacological interventions for insomnia: A meta analysis of treatment efficacy. *American Journal of Psychiatry*, 151, 1172–1180.

Morin, C. M., Colecchi, C., Stone, J., Sood, R., and Brink, D. (1999a) Behavioral and pharmacological therapies for late-life insomnia: A randomized controlled trial. *Journal of the American Medical Association*, 281, 991–999.

Morin, C. M., Hauri, P. J., Espie, C. A., Spielman, A., Buysse, D. J. and Bootzin, R. (1999b) Nonpharmacologic treatment of chronic insomnia. *Sleep*, 22, 1–25.

Morin, C. M., Blais, F. and Savard, J. (2002) Are changes in beliefs and attitudes about sleep related to sleep improvements in the treatment of insomnia? *Behaviour Research and Therapy*, 40, 741–752.

Murtagh, D. R. R. and Greenwood, K. M. (1995) Identifying effective psychological treatments for insomnia. *Journal of Consulting and Clinical Psychology*, 63, 79–89.

National Institute for Health and Clinical Excellence (NICE) (2003) *Assessment Report: The Clinical and Cost Effectiveness of Zaleplom, Zolpidem and Zopliclone for the Management of Insomnia.* London: NICE.

National Institutes of Health (NIH) (1984) Drugs and insomnia: The use of medication to promote sleep. *Journal of the American Medical Association*, 18, 2410–2414.

National Institutes of Health (NIH) (1991) National Institutes of Health Consensus Development Conference Statement: the treatment of sleep disorders of older people. *Sleep*, 14, 169–177.

National Institutes of Health (NIH) (1996) NIH releases statement on behavioural and relaxation approaches for chronic pain and insomnia. *American Family Physician*, 53, 1877–1880.

National Medical Advisory Committee (1993) The good sleep guide. In: *Management of Anxiety and Insomnia.* London: HMSO.

Rogers, A. E. and Mullington, J. (2003) The symptomatic management of narcolepsy. In: M. L. Perlis and K. L. Lichstein (eds) *Treating Sleep Disorders: Principles and Practice of Behavioural Sleep Medicine.* New Jersey: John Wiley.

Smith, M. T., Perlis, M. L., Park, A., Smith, M. S., Pennington, J., Giles, D. E. et al. (2002) Comparative meta-analysis of pharmacotherapy and behaviour therapy for persistent insomnia. *American Journal of Psychiatry, 159,* 5–11.

Tang, N. K. Y. and Harvey, A. G. (2004) Correcting distorted perception of sleep in insomnia: a novel behavioural experiment? *Behaviour Research and Therapy*, 42, 27–39.

Chapter 34

Chronic pain

Investigation

Amanda C. de C. Williams

INTRODUCTION

Pain is defined as 'an unpleasant sensory and emotional experience associated with actual or potential tissue damage, or described in terms of such damage' (International Association for the Study of Pain, 1979). It is a subjective experience and, primarily, it is measured subjectively, not estimated by signs of damage or disease. Chronic or persistent pain is defined by timescale – pain that has lasted more than 6 months – and implicitly as beyond the time required for healing or resolution of lesions or pathology responsible for pain onset. Although cancer pain has some similarities with other persistent pain, the term 'chronic pain' is usually reserved for pain not attributable to a life-shortening or progressive disease. Pain also has a behavioural dimension, of relevance both for its measurement and for understanding the whole experience. It is not necessarily obvious where to draw the lines between the sensory, affective, cognitive and behavioural dimensions of pain and the associated cognitive, affective and behavioural events attributable to pain, as is evident from the mixed content of the categories under which assessment is organised below.

The main weaknesses in pain assessment arise from several factors. The first is the history of importing into pain psychological or, more often, psychopathological concepts and associated measures, without considering whether their meaning is the same in the presence of pain. The second, associated, factor is reification of measures as adequately representing whatever construct is named: disability, for instance, or depression. Such constructs may not even approximate the linear structure assumed by standard metrics (Michell, 1977) and there is poor understanding of the conventions guiding patients' responses, leading to the pathologising of certain responses (Schwarz, 1999). The third weakness, which is not unique to the study of pain, is the disregard of population differences and heterogeneity, and of basal rates of the variable of interest, when employing measures developed elsewhere. Fourth, threats to reliability from the influence of social desirability tend to be overestimated and those due to oversimplification underestimated (many medical measures are dichotomous, not without loss to meaning, but preferred by those who use the evidence as superior to continuously distributed psychological qualities). Finally, people with pain have rarely been consulted about choice or design of measures, whether to define outcomes or domains of importance, or to identify what is clinically significant improvement or worsening.

Any choice of assessment is necessarily a compromise, such as between brevity and inclusiveness. In clinical settings, it is useful to collect data with the purpose of assessment in mind, which largely falls into one or more of: diagnosis, decisions about treatment, evaluation of treatment effects or predicting response to treatment (Turk and Okifuji 2003). Fitzpatrick et al. (1998) listed the criteria for selection of any assessment tool as: fitness to purpose, reliability, validity, sensitivity to change, precision in making distinctions, interpretability, acceptability and feasibility. They deplored the fact that unsystematic testing and reporting made a league table of measures impossible. In addition, there is relatively little overlap between the measures used in studies of medical or physical treatments and of psychologically based treatments, although the situation is improving and there is a clear move to arrive at a common shortlist of satisfactory measures covering the necessary domains (see Turk et al., 2003). For any assessment, the domains that should be considered are: pain experience, cognition, emotion and mood, behaviour and activity across a range from physical performance to social roles, and use of health-care resources.

Reliability and validity coefficients are too often quoted as if they were universal properties of the measure, rather than of its performance in a particular context. For internal reliability, adjustments of content to reduce random effects may improve performance at the cost of losing clinically interesting coverage (see Dworkin and Sherman, 2001; Turk and Melzack, 2001a). Unfortunately, the construct may then acquire this narrowed meaning, despite clinical reality in which symptoms belonging to different measures and constructs commonly occur together: anxiety and depression are excellent examples of achieving consistency of diagnosis at the cost of distorting understanding of their phenomenology. Validation (Scientific Advisory Committee of the Medical Outcomes Trust, 2002; Terwee et al., 2003) is an even more perplexing exercise where there is no clear referent that does not also rely on self-report or on similar definitions of the problem. Those measures that are shown to predict observed behaviour inspire more confidence, provided they are not entirely proximal to that behaviour. However, without some attempt to crosscheck the meaning of the measure and of the implied construct, the exercise of trying to estimate what is clinically significant change is problematic: healthy norms may be available (often by implication: no disability or no pain), while obvious proportions of change, such as the 50% pain relief often targeted in drug trials, are rarely available (although they can be defined, for instance in performance of physical exercises or activities). Instead, many studies rely on statistical significance and, arguably, alternatives are underused in pain (Morley and Williams 2002) and non-pain settings (Hsu 1999; Jacobson et al., 1999; Kendall et al. 1999), including those using categorical outcomes and risk-based estimation (such as numbers needed to treat: see Sackett et al., 1991; Crombie and Davies, 1996).

While some measures are identified below, the reader is strongly recommended to consult the extensive handbooks on assessment by Turk and Melzack (2001b) and McDowell and Newell (1996).

ASSESSMENT OF PAIN EXPERIENCE

Pain is a multidimensional experience, and the simplest categorisation of dimensions is into those of sensory intensity, emotional and cognitive aspects and interference with everyday life (Holroyd et al., 1999; Price, 1999). Dimensions of pain co-vary somewhat loosely and predict different aspects of patients' function and psychological state (Clark and Yang, 2001; Jensen and Karoly, 2001). For these reasons, unidimensional pain ratings, as in various quality of life measures, are unsatisfactory. Rating is itself recursive, with emotional and motivational variables affecting the perceptual and memory processes activated (Kihlstrom et al., 1999; Price, 1999). There is, of course, no straightforward external referent for all pain, although attention and arousal appear to mediate the relationship between pain rating and an experimental pain stimulus (Donaldson et al., 2003). Given these measurement difficulties, there is surprisingly little interest in how patients arrive at a particular description of pain, and investigation reveals idiosyncratic decisions and the practice of quantifying chronic pain by reference to both function and mood (Williams et al., 2000). So the choice of dimensions, and the extent to which rating instructions anchor these dimensions in the pain experience, depends in part on the purpose of assessment.

Location of pain is another area of oversimplification, with often only the main site of pain (back, head, etc.) recorded. Yet the number of sites of pain appears to have implications for disability (Blyth et al., 2003) and the classification only by main site obscures site-specific aspects of disability. Temporal variation is also described only approximately, usually by the definition of pain used, which may require, for instance, that pain is constant over a year or that it is present on a majority of days over the last month. The existence of pain-free periods can have major implications for patients' activity. Beyond the first year or two, duration of pain since onset seems to have no consistent influence on function.

Other symptoms are often associated with persistent pains, such as fatigue, nausea and numbness, which are particularly common where the pain is due to chronic illness, such as cancer, or to adverse effects of treatment. Inherently unpleasant, these symptoms can have an additional negative impact on activity, mood and quality of life: they can be assessed using self-report scales similar to those used for pain; careful consideration of design is recommended (see Boynton and Greenhalgh, 2004).

Spatial, numerical and verbal scales

Each dimension can be measured in a variety of ways and at different points: intensity, for instance, can be described at its worst, least, average or at the moment of rating. Surprisingly, there is virtually no research on the effect of verbal anchors (e.g. 'worst pain', 'most intense pain imaginable' . . .) for the highest level of pain on numerical and visual analogue scales. The visual analogue scale remains one of the most popular measures, despite the slightly superior reliability and greater practicality of numerical rating scales, which can be given verbally as well as in writing (Jensen et al., 1999; Jensen and Karoly 2001; Turk and Okifuji, 2003; Williams et al., 2000). Any expression of pain is effectively an exercise in cross-modality matching, as of pain to spatial proportion in visual scales.

The numerical rating scale is often presented as 0–10 with half integers; 21 points appear to be as many as most respondents need or use (Williams et al., 2000). Jensen and Karoly (2001) discuss measurement of other important aspects of pain, including spatial aspects, such as locations and body systems where pain is felt; and temporal aspects, such as frequency, constancy, or pain-free periods. Verbal scales, although generally easy to administer and high in face validity, present problems for scaling and scoring, which may compromise their usefulness (Jensen and Karoly, 2001), as do additional aspects such as colour and expressive faces (faces alone, however, form reliable scales for use by children and people with cognitive impairment; Hadjistavropoulos et al., 2001). Another widely used verbal measure of pain is the McGill Pain Questionnaire (MPQ; Melzack, 1975; short form Melzack, 1987), developed partly for differential diagnosis but widely used in outcome evaluation. The derivation of sensory, affective and evaluative factors is generally supported, with some variation in factor structure and intercorrelation of factors (Melzack and Katz, 1999). The major strength of the MPQ in separately assessing pain dimensions is lost in the use of a single total, e.g. number of words chosen. There is surprisingly little use of patients' own descriptions of pain quantity, such as 'good/bad days'. The author found that two-thirds of the graduates of a pain management programme recorded an increase in 'good days' and a decrease in 'bad days', which were only in small part accounted for by decreased pain intensity and interference.

Given the complex interactions of pain, mood and memory, the use of averages of frequent recordings is recommended above single retrospective ratings of pain (Bolton, 1999; Jensen and Karoly, 2001; Haas et al., 2002; Stone et al., 2003). Contrary to expectations, reactivity does not seem to present a significant problem (Stone et al., 2003). Electronic diaries seem to achieve better adherence than pen and paper measures (Jamison et al., 2001; Stone et al., 2002), as well as allowing random sampling, which picks up possibly important variations in pain (Peters et al., 2000), and automatic data downloads, so that failure to respond can initiate a prompt (Stone et al., 2003).

Pain relief, the aim of many medical and physical interventions, is usually measured as a percentage; 50% pain relief is a common if arbitrary criterion for success of treatment. Ideally, pain relief would be titrated against an outcome, such as mobility. In one study of cancer inpatients, around 30% relief was sufficient for patients not to request additional analgesics (Farrar et al., 2000).

Behavioural expression of pain

Pain is often described as a private experience but it is also a public one, expressed behaviourally and, particularly, in the face (Craig et al., 2001; Williams, 2002). However, facial expression requires more detailed assessment than is usually practicable (Craig et al., 2001), a fact that results in a loss to our understanding of the communication of pain during clinical encounters, family interactions and in other social settings. Facial expression has often been measured only in composite constructs (e.g. 'grimacing') or combined with other non-verbal behaviours. Clinically, it is particularly important for assessing pain in people with compromised or underdeveloped communication capacities (Hadjistavropoulos et al., 2001). Other motor behaviours, particularly guarding, are of interest and can be assessed by observation (Keefe et al., 2001), for instance during routine physical examinations (Prkachin et al., 2002), and this seems preferable to self-reporting of those behaviours. For clinical settings, however, the significance of pain behaviour is in terms of what it communicates to those around the person in pain, intentionally or not, and it is important to recognise that it draws on different data and so is only somewhat related to self-report (Hadjistavropoulos and Craig, 2002; Labus et al., 2003).

PSYCHOLOGICAL CONTENT AND PROCESS

Concepts and measures in this area overlap and interact, and it cannot be assumed that any constructs coincide satisfactorily with actual processing of pain in the brain. Almost all are assessed by self-report, although some experimental methods identify non-conscious processes (see Eccleston and Crombez, 1999; Pincus and Morley, 2001).

In addition, the construct of coping, which has considerable face validity and is part of the patient and professional discourse on pain management, has been measured using tools that rely heavily on over-simple behavioural notions. Strategies used by patients can only really be classified as adaptive or not with reference to their context and to their short- and long-term outcomes (often different) in achieving the intended goals. However, it is simpler, and widespread practice, to classify them *a priori* as positive/negative or active/passive, without reference to their efficacy. Thus some strategies, such as using social support or analgesics, may be classified as adaptive in one questionnaire and maladaptive in another: it depends on how individuals use them to attain other functional gains. Coping checklists often combine behavioural and cognitive strategies in the same measure. This can present a problem if self-statements are assessed only by frequency, when occasion of use, or mood state at the time of use, may be far more important. In this light, it is impressive that several constructs have emerged from various studies and settings as predictive of behaviour and of pain in the longer term. The focus will be on these constructs.

Content of beliefs

Interestingly, the most commonly used measures in this field arise from clinical material, rather than from theory (e.g. Leventhal et al., 1984). The Illness Perception Questionnaire (IPQ), one of the most widely used measures of illness representation, developed outside pain (Weinman et al., 1996; revised IPQ-R; Moss-Morris et al., 2002; http://www.uib.no/ipq/), has been used in some pain studies. Few non-specific measures of beliefs have performed well in pain populations. Among the pain-specific instruments, some assume that patients should understand their pain, for instance that it is not necessarily equivalent to harm, although this may not have been explained and seems to contradict experience. More recently, misunderstandings have been reconceptualised in terms of fears about pain (Vlaeyen and Linton, 2000), and several instruments are proving useful (the Fear-Avoidance Beliefs Questionnaire (FABQ); Waddell et al., 1993; the Pain Symptoms Scale (PASS); McCracken et al., 1992; see Vlaeyen et al., 1995). Measures of locus of control have failed to illuminate patients' behaviour (see Skevington, 1995), whereas those of self-efficacy seem more promising and predictive (Asghari and Nicholas, 2001; for arthritis, see Lorig et al., 1989).

Cognitive processes

The most robust cognitive construct is that of catastrophising (Rosenstiel and Keefe 1983; Sullivan et al., 2001). Originally a subscale of a longer questionnaire (the Coping Strategies Questionnaire (CSQ); Rosenstiel and Keefe, 1983), it is now measured in its own right on the Pain Catastrophising Scale (PCS; Sullivan et al., 1995). This describes the tendency to attend to pain stimuli, to overestimate their threat value and to underestimate resources available to handle that threat (Sullivan et al., 2001) (cf. health anxiety; Salkovskis, 1996). Recently reconceptualised within a model of interpersonal communication (Sullivan et al., 2001; Thorn et al., 2003; but see Severeijns et al., 2004), it is associated with fears and anxiety about pain and with depressed mood and depressive thought content.

No other measure of appraisal or interpretation of internal or external events has proved as heuristic or explanatory. Measures in development include acceptance of chronic pain (McCracken, 1999), and cognitive processing is also sampled in measures of mood, emotion and cognitive content (for instance, frequency of hopeless self-statements); for a wider range of measures, see Turk and Melzack (2001a) and Williams (1999).

Mood and emotion

The predominant practice has been to use depression and anxiety questionnaires developed outside the field of pain mainly for diagnosis. This is problematic for several reasons: the dimensional rather than categorical approach is increasingly and appropriately taken to mood disorder (Widiger and Clark, 2000), the lack of re-standardisation in populations with illness or pain and the prevalence of somatic problems that Patients who are in pain can contribute disproportionately to a unidimensional total (see Pincus and Williams, 1999). Further, validation is particularly challenging when comparisons can only be made with subjective experience sampled in a different way (e.g. psychiatric interview) but using the same definitions (see Kendell and Jablensky, 2003).

The measures most commonly in use in pain studies for depression or depressed mood – the Beck Depression Inventory (BDI; Beck et al., 1961) and the Centre for Epidemiological Studies Depression Scale ((CES-D); Radloff, 1977) – despite their clinical value, are both subject to inflation of total score by somatic content. A commonly attempted solution (in the UK at least) is to use a scale free of somatic, but also of cognitive, content e.g. the Hospital Anxiety and Depression Scale (HADS); (Zigmond and Snaith, 1983; see also Dunbar et al., 2000). This is unsatisfactory because the concept of depression and depressed mood is poorly developed in chronic pain (Pincus and Williams, 1999): the Beck triad of negativity about self, world and future is not characteristic of many chronic pain patients (Morley et al., 2002).

As in depression, psychiatric categories and instruments imported from other patient populations may not describe pain patients' anxieties. The most relevant anxieties concern the meaning and implications of the pain, in part sampled by measures of cognitive content and described as fears. Anger is not well characterised; nor is it easy to see how situational features and coping options could be adequately addressed by the usual checklists of thought and behaviour frequency.

Two measures of depression and anxiety may offer better options for clinical and research studies: one includes a stress scale and is not distorted by its somatic content (Depression Anxiety Stress Scales (DASS); Lovibond and Lovibond, 1995; see also http://www.psy.unsw.edu.au/Groups/Dass/); the other was developed more recently to exclude somatic content (the Depression, Anxiety and Positive Outlook Scale (DAPOS); Pincus et al., 2004; http://www.dapos.org) and includes a scale of positive outlook, which is a neglected but clinically useful construct. The most commonly described emotional experience in persistent pain – that of frustration (Price, 1999) – is not the subject of current theorising or attempts at measurement. Most questionnaires in common use, which arise from personality or psychiatric models, make little reference to the meaning of emotional experience, whereas even a brief conversation with a person with persistent pain will involve frequent references to the impact of pain on mood, both directly and via interference with many facets of daily life.

MEASURES OF FUNCTION: FROM PHYSICAL PERFORMANCE TO QUALITY OF LIFE

This large category of assessment instruments ranges from direct measures of physical function or performance, some related to common clinical questions, through disability, impact or interference of pain, to quality-of-life measures with their broad sampling across social, psychological and other domains of activity. A significant shortcoming of most measures is that they draw largely on health professionals' definitions of what is normal or desirable (Bowling, 1997; Foster and Mash, 1999; Boynton et al., 2004). Some measures imply norms that do not apply to some patients (e.g. heterosexual relationships or adequate income).

The lack of underlying theory for much of this domain of measurement means that psychological influences are largely underrepresented, despite their powerful effect on both the development and progress of persistent pain and disability (Pincus et al., 2002). Self-report of activity levels and limitations is influenced both by mood and beliefs (Hyland, 1992; Mannion et al., 2001; Turk and Melzack, 2001a) and by interpretative biases differing for common and uncommon events (Menon and Yorkston, 1999). Better 'road testing' of questionnaires on the population of interest would identify problems due to these factors.

Impact of pain in terms of restriction of usual activity is increasingly included in epidemiological studies (Blyth et al., 2001; Reyes-Gibby et al., 2002; reviewed by Von Korff, 2001), where it may be assessed using a few carefully worded questions and a rating scale (such as the Chronic Pain Grade Scale; Von Korff et al., 1992); possibly even with a single pain rating (Jensen et al., 2004). Among longer questionnaires, some in common use are not specific to pain (for instance, the SF-36; Ware and Sherbourne 1992; Ware et al., 1993). These allow comparisons with healthy or with other disabled populations, but perform less well than pain-specific questionnaires. Other stakeholders in patients' health, well-being, or performance of particular social roles may be interested in third-party defined outcomes, such as work status or health-care use, even when these do not coincide with patients' goals: these are also briefly described. At the other end of the spectrum, attempts to create a subjective measure in goal attainment scaling will fail on comparability between patients, and make poor clinical sense in relation to treatment which brings about cognitive changes in expectations and therefore in the content and importance of goals (Schmitz et al., 1996; McCracken, 1998).

Physical performance

While not at first glance a domain of immediate interest to psychologists, physical performance data are associated with patients' fears, expectations and mood (Simmonds et al., 1998; Watson, 1999; Rudy et al., 2003). A patient who fears that lifting anything but the lightest weight will do lasting physical damage is unlikely to progress in strengthening exercises: authoritative and credible explanation that this is not the case can free the patient to proceed with the exercises. There is often a large confidence gap between ability to carry out exercises under supervision in a hospital setting and being able to carry them out at home, even more so to performing related activities. In this way, routine exercises tend to become disconnected from patient-specified goals. At the very least, the psychologist should be sceptical of physical performance measures as indices of impairment. Actimeters and pedometers are underused for cumulative measurements with more ecological validity.

Disability questionnaires

These focus on frequency or ease of activity, with the assumption (untested) that full performance of particular activities satisfactorily represents the overall domain of everyday activity for adults. This assumption may be acceptable, given the population under study, but should first be critically addressed before opting for it. One such questionnaire Roland and Morris Disability Questionnaire ((RMDQ); Roland and Morris, 1983) consists of items such as 'I walk more slowly than usual because of my back' with yes/no responses. (It is commonly reworded for pain in general.) Other questionnaires ask directly how much less the patient can do than he or she would normally do because of pain, or the comparison is implied by asking about impact of pain. The more time that has elapsed since the onset of disabling pain, and the more other relevant factors (such as income) have changed, the harder it can be for the patient to be able to compare. Two brief and fairly widely used questionnaires sampling impact of pain across diverse activities (the Wisconsin Brief Pain Questionnaire (BPQ); Daut et al., 1983; see also Tan et al., 2004; and the Pain Disability Index (PDI); Tait et al., 1987, 1990) fall into this category.

Quality of life

Notwithstanding the problems, described above, of lack of consultation with potential respondents, quality-of-life measures are an attempt to recognise respondents' subjectivity with an objective measure, and this paradox is never satisfactorily resolved (Stenner et al., 2003). The lack of theory and of research on what quality of life means compounds the problem (Bowling, 1997; Fitzpatrick et al., 1998; Gladis et al., 1999; Gagliese, 2001): the same overall construct, such as social support, may have very different meanings for people in different situations and with different options and preferences. For these reasons, among others, validation is a difficult procedure, as is the estimation of responsiveness to change (Terwee et al., 2003); the broader the content, the more users need to ask which aspects they expect to change as a result of treatment. Those questionnaires that take the broadest view of quality of life (including, for instance, feelings about the environment, and spirituality) may find these broader aspects harder to operationalise: the concept of a single numerical total is even harder to justify (Hyland, 1992). Content, even within domains (such as social activity or roles), varies considerably between questionnaires and, to be sufficiently sensitive, often requires supplementing with disease-specific items (Bowling, 1997; Fitzpatrick and Dawson, 1997). One cross-culturally developed questionnaire (World Health Organization Quality of Life Assessment (WHOQOL); WHOQOL Group, 1995; see also shorter versions: WHOQOL Group, 1998; http://www.who.int/msa/qol) has been tried in the pain field (Skevington et al., 2001). The most widely used quality-of-life measure in the pain field is the SF–36 (Ware and Sherbourne, 1992; Ware et al., 1993), although this is likely to lack sensitivity to change (Bowling, 1997) and is arguably more useful for comparison of pain patients with other ill and disabled populations than with the healthy norms available.

Work status

Return to work, often proposed as a primary outcome despite its obvious disadvantages in this population (Dionne et al., 1999), requires skills saleable in the job market, vacancies in suitable jobs and a lack of discrimination against people with a history of disability or illness. It also assumes that working is always better for the patient's overall psychological and social health than not working, but this may depend on the job, its demands and on pay and conditions. Work is usually defined as regular employment, ignoring casual or contract work, or the considerable contribution made by unpaid homemaking, caring and voluntary work. How, for instance, should the middle-aged woman, with disabling pain, the mortgage paid and children financially independent, answer the question 'Does your pain prevent you from working?'

Two recent studies show the extent to which quality of work and job prospects diminish with pain, even when the person retains his or her employment (Blyth et al., 2003), and the extent to which household income can fall because of pain in a wage-earner (Kemler and Furnee, 2002).

Health-care use

Given the emphasis in many treatment studies on the burden on the patient and on health-care services of unnecessary, ineffective or even damaging treatments, it is surprising that health-care use is not routinely assessed. Health records can provide valuable (although not perfect) data on patient consultations, investigations and treatments (such as drug prescriptions) initiated. More often, patients are asked to estimate or recall primary and secondary care consultations and treatments, and to report current drug intake, which may of course differ from what has been prescribed. Where drug intake is measured, the assumption is that less is better and none is best, while clinical experience recognises that some patients function better with judicious use of drugs and other aids. Unfortunately, there is little research to support the choice of targets identified by therapists.

A related issue is adherence to treatment methods, self-monitoring and other process measures. These are too often neglected in pain studies, despite well-established measures in trials of psychological therapy for depression and other psychological problems. Self-report of adherence is problematic but is usually the only source available, so careful wording and interpretation (Rand, 1999; Schwarz, 1999) are needed.

ASSESSMENT OF THE PATIENT BY A THIRD PARTY

It is not unusual to consider assessing patients' function, mood or other variables using a proxy respondent, such as someone close to the patient, recognising, of course, that this is no less subjective than the account from the patient. There are few well-developed measures (see review by Sharp and Nicholas, 2000); most are translations of existing self-report into the third person. An exception (the West Haven–Yale Multi-dimensional Pain Inventory (WHYMPI or MPI); Kerns et al., 1985; Kerns and Rosenberg, 1995) covers social support and significant other's responses to the patient; who the significant other is can affect reliability (Jacobs and Kerns, 2001).

SELECTION

The use of assessment measures for selection is usually supported by *post hoc* testing to show discrimination by the measure at baseline of better and worse outcomes, but any associations are likely to be specific to that population. In addition, the rate of false negatives and false positives should raise ethical questions for clinicians. A large study, with minimal exclusion criteria and randomisation to treatments, is required to provide reliable prediction of outcome. Further, it would be surprising if the processes underlying effective treatment could be represented in surface variables measured. Although the MPI has been subjected to prospective testing with encouraging results, the practice of *post hoc* 'prediction' generally owes much more to associations which may be unreplicable than to theory (see Morley and Williams, 2002).

CONCLUSIONS

There is a tension between older and newer assessment measures. Older ones were often developed with less attention to theoretical roots, to patient input, and to psychometric standards, but have acquired credibility, familiarity and a track record which helps interpretation. Newer measures, despite better sampling and psychometric testing, are often underpowered and conceptually disappointing; enthusiasm for the use of measurement models such as item response theory needs to be tempered with care over definitions and scaling (Cella and Chang, 2000; Hambleton, 2000). Choice of measure is always a compromise and *ad hoc* construction of questionnaires is more complicated than generally acknowledged (Boynton, 2004; Boynton and Greenhalgh, 2004).

Reification of assessment constructs remains a widespread problem. It obscures conceptual and content overlap between measures, whose relationship is addressed as if they were entirely independent. Disability checklists and coping questionnaires, for instance, often consist of similar questions about what the patient can and cannot do. Discovery of correlated scores should hardly be a surprise. Attention to the content of measures can largely obviate this problem.

Social and socio-economic measurement is also neglected, consistent with the individual focus of most treatment. This has also meant lack of attention to age, gender, cultural and other differences in relation to pain experience and psychological variance. Although pain is an individual experience, it can best be understood when the individual is recognised as a social being, and a more integrated approach to social variables in pain problems would provide a firmer foundation for addressing cultural and social differences.

REFERENCES

Asghari, A. and Nicholas, M. K. (2001) Pain self-efficacy beliefs and pain behaviour: A prospective study. *Pain*, 94, 85–100.

Beck, A. T., Ward, C. H., Mendelson, M., Mock, N. and Erbaugh, J. (1961) An inventory for measuring depression. *Archives of General Psychiatry*, 4, 561–571.

Blyth, F. M., March, L. M., Brnabic, A. J. M, Jorm, L. R., Williamson, M. and Cousins, M. J. (2001) Chronic pain in Australia: A prevalence study. *Pain*, 89, 127–134.

Blyth, F. M., March, L. M., Nicholas, M. K. and Cousins, M. J. (2003) Chronic pain, work performance and litigation. *Pain*, 103, 41–47.

Bolton, J. E. (1999) Accuracy of recall of usual pain intensity in back pain patients. *Pain*, 83, 533–539.

Bowling, A. (1997) *Measuring Health, 2nd edn*. Buckingham: Open University Press.

Boynton, P. M. (2004) Administering, analysing and reporting your questionnaire. *British Medical Journal*, 328 1372–1375.

Boynton, P. M. and Greenhalgh, T. (2004) Selecting, designing and developing your questionnaire. *British Medical Journal*, 328, 1312–1315.

Boynton, P. M., Wood, G. W. and Greenhalgh, T. (2004) Reaching beyond the white middle classes. *British Medical Journal*, 328, 1433–1434.

Cella, D. and Chang, C-H. (2000) A discussion of Item Response Theory and its applications to health status assessment. *Medical Care*, 38 (suppl. II), 66–72.

Clark, W. C. and Yang, J. C. (2001) Abstract: What do simple unidimensional pain scales really measure? *Journal of Pain*, 2 (suppl. 1), 6.

Craig, K. D., Prkachin, K. M. and Grunau, R. E. (2001) The facial expression of pain. In: D. C. Turk and R. Melzack (eds) *Handbook of Pain Assessment, 2nd edn*. (pp. 153–169). New York: Guilford Press.

Crombie, I. K. and Davies, H. T. O. (1996) *Research in Health Care: Design, Conduct and Interpretation of Health Services Research*. Chichester: John Wiley and Sons.

Daut, R. L., Cleeland, C. S. and Flaner, R. C. (1983) Development of the Wisconsin Brief Pain Questionnaire to assess pain in cancer and other diseases. *Pain*, 17, 197–210.

Dionne, C. E., Von Korff, M. and Koepsell, T. D. (1999) A comparison of pain, functional limitations and work status indices as outcome measures in back pain research. *Spine*, 24, 2339–2345.

Donaldson, G. W., Chapman, C. R., Nakamura, Y., Bradshaw, D. H., Jacobson, R. C. and Chapman, C. N. (2003) Pain and the defense response: Structural equation modeling reveals a coordinated psychophysiological response to increasing painful stimulation. *Pain*, 102, 97–108.

Dunbar, M., Ford, G., Hunt, K. and Der, G. (2000) A confirmatory factor analysis of the Hospital Anxiety and Depression scale: Comparing empirically and theoretically derived structures. *British Journal of Clinical Psychology*, 39, 79–94.

Dworkin, S. F. and Sherman, J. J. (2001) Relying on objective and subjective measures of chronic pain: Guidelines for use and interpretation. In: D. C. Turk and R. Melzack (eds) *Handbook of Pain Assessment, 2nd edn*. (pp. 619–638). New York: Guilford Press.

Eccleston, C. and Crombez, G. (1999) Pain demands attention: A cognitive-affective model of the interruptive function of pain. *Psychological Bulletin*, 125, 356–366.

Farrar, J. T., Portenoy, R. K., Berlin, J. A., Kinman, J. L. and Strom, J. (2000) Defining the clinically important difference in pain outcome measures. *Pain*, 88, 287–294.

Fitzpatrick, R. and Dawson, J. (1997) Health-related quality of life and the assessment of outcomes of total hip replacement surgery. *Psychology and Health*, 12, 793–803.

Fitzpatrick, R., Davey, C., Buxton, M. J. and Jones, D. R. (1998) Evaluating patient-based outcome measures for use in clinical trials. *Health Technology Assessment*, 2, 14.

Foster, S. L. and Mash, E. J. (1998) Assessing social validity in clinical treatment research: issues and procedures. *Journal of Consulting and Clinical Psychology*, 67, 308–319.

Gagliese, L. (2001) Assessment of pain in elderly people. In: D. C. Turk and R. Melzack (eds) *Handbook of Pain Assessment, 2nd edn.* (pp. 119–133). New York: Guilford Press.

Gladis, M. M., Gosch, E. A., Dishuk, N. M. and Crits-Cristoph, P. (1999) Quality of life: Expanding the scope of clinical significance. *Journal of Consulting and Clinical Psychology*, 67, 320–331.

Haas, M., Nyiendo, J. and Aickin, M. (2002) One-year trend in pain and disability relief in acute and chronic ambulatory low back pain patients. *Pain*, 95, 83–91.

Hadjistavropoulos, T. and Craig, K. D. (2002) A theoretical framework for understanding self-report and observational measures of pain: A communications model. *Behaviour Research and Therapy*, 40, 551–570.

Hadjistavropoulos, T., von Baeyer, C. and Craig, K. D. (2001) Pain assessment in persons with limited ability to communicate. In: D.C. Turk and R. Melzack (eds) *Handbook of Pain Assessment, 2nd edn.* (pp. 134–149). New York: Guilford Press.

Hambleton, R. K. (2000) Emergence of Item Response Modeling in instrument development and data analysis. *Medical Care*, 38 (suppl. II), 60–65.

Holroyd, K. A., Malinoski, P., Davis, M. K. and Lipchik, G. L. (1999) The three dimensions of headache impact: pain, disability and affective distress. *Pain*, 83, 571–578.

Hsu, L. M. (1999) Caveats concerning comparisons of change rates obtained with five methods of identifying significant client changes: comment on Speer and Greenbaum (1995). *Journal of Consulting and Clinical Psychology*, 67, 594–598.

Hyland, M. E. (1992) A reformulation of quality of life for medical science. *Quality of Life Research*, 1, 267–272.

International Association for the Study of Pain (IASP) (1979) Pain terms: A list with definitions and notes on usage. *Pain*, 6, 249–252.

Jacobs, M. C. and Kerns, R. D. (2001) Assessment of the psychosocial context of the experience of chronic pain. In: D. C. Turk and R. Melzack (eds) *Handbook of Pain Assessment, 2nd edn.* (pp. 362–384). New York: Guilford Press.

Jacobson, N. S., Roberts, L. J., Bems, S. B. and McGlinchey, J. B. (1999) Methods for defining and determining the clinical significance of treatment effects: Description, application and alternatives. *Journal of Consulting and Clinical Psychology*, 67, 300–307.

Jamison, R. N., Raymond, S. A., Levine, J. G., Slawsby, E. A., Nedeljkovic, S. S. and Katz, N. P. (2001) Electronic diaries for monitoring chronic pain: 1-year validation study. *Pain*, 91, 277–285.

Jensen, M. P. and Karoly, P. (2001) Self-report scales and procedures for assessing pain in adults. In: D. C. Turk and R. Melzack (eds) *Handbook of Pain Assessment, 2nd edn.* (pp. 15–34). New York: Guilford Press.

Jensen, M. P., Turner, J. A., Romano, J. M. and Fisher, L. D. (1999) Comparative reliability and validity of chronic pain intensity measures. *Pain*, 83, 157–162.

Jensen, M. K., Sjogren, P., Okholm, O., Rasmussen, N. K. and Eriksen, J. (2004) Identifying a long-term/chronic, non-cancer pain population using a one-dimensional verbal pain rating scale: An epidemiological study. *European Journal of Pain*, 8, 145–152.

Keefe, F. J., Williams, D. A. and Smith, S.J. (2001) Assessment of pain behaviors. In: D. C. Turk and R. Melzack, (eds) *Handbook of Pain Assessment, 2nd edn.* (pp. 170–187). New York, Guilford Press.

Kemler, M. A. and Furnee, C. A. (2002) The impact of chronic pain on life in the household. *Journal of Pain and Symptom Management*, 23, 433–441.

Kendall, P. C., Marrs-Garcia, A., Nath, S. R. and Sheldrick, R. C. (1999) Normative comparisons for the evaluation of clinical significance. *Journal of Consulting and Clinical Psychology*, 47, 285–299.

Kendell, R. and Jablensky, A. (2003) Distinguishing between the validity and utility of psychiatric diagnoses. *American Journal of Psychiatry*, 160, 4–12.

Kerns, R. D. and Rosenberg, R. (1995) Pain relevant responses from significant others: Development of a significant-other version of the WHYMPI scales. *Pain*, 61, 245–259.

Kerns, R. D., Turk, D. C. and Rudy, T. E. (1985) The West Haven–Yale Multidimensional Pain Inventory (WHYMPI). *Pain*, 23, 345–356.

Kihlstrom, J. F., Eich, E., Sandbrand, D. and Tobias, B. A. (1999) Emotion and memory: Implications for self-report. In: A. A. Stone, J. S. Turkkan, C. A. Bachrach, J. B. Jobe, H. S. Kirtzman and V. S. Cain (eds) *The Science of Self-report, Implications for Research and Practice* (pp. 81–99). Mahwah, NJ: Lawrence Erlbaum Associates, Inc.

Labus, J. S., Keefe, F. J. and Jensen, M. P. (2003) Self-reports of pain intensity and direct observations of pain behavior: when are they correlated? *Pain*, 102, 109–124.

Leventhal, H., Nerenz, D. R. and Steele, D. J. (1984). Illness representations and coping with health threats. In A. Baum, S. E. Taylor and J. E. Singer (eds) *Handbook of Psychology and Health, Vol. 4* (pp. 219–252). Hillsdale, NJ: Lawrence Erlbaum Associates, Inc.

Lorig, K., Chastain, R. L., Ung, E., Shoor, S. and Holman, H. R. (1989) Development and evaluation of a scale to measure perceived self-efficacy in people with arthritis. *Arthritis and Rheumatism*, 32, 37–44

Lovibond, P. F. and Lovibond, S. H. (1995) The structure of negative emotional states: Comparison of the depression anxiety stress scales (DASS) with the Beck depression and anxiety inventories. *Behaviour Research and Therapy*, 33, 335–343.

Mannion, A. F., Junge, A., Taimela, S., Müntener, M., Lorenzo, K. and Dvorak, J. (2001) Active therapy for chronic low back pain: Part 3. Factors influencing self-rated disability and its change following therapy. *Spine*, 26, 920–929.

McCracken, L. M. (1998) Learning to live with the pain: Acceptance of pain predicts adjustment in persons with chronic pain. *Pain*, 74, 21–27.

McCracken, L. M. (1999). Behavioral constituents of chronic pain acceptance: Results from factor analysis of the Chronic Pain Acceptance Questionnaire. *Journal of Back and Musculoskeletal Rehabilitation*, 13, 93–100.

McCracken, L. M., Zayfert, C. and Gross, R. T. (1992) The Pain Anxiety Symptoms Scale: Development and validation of a scale to measure fear of pain. *Pain*, 50, 67–73.

McDowell, I. and Newell, C. (1996) *Measuring Health: A Guide to Rating Scales and Questionnaires, 2nd edn.* New York: Oxford University Press.

Melzack, R. (1975) The McGill Pain Questionnaire: Major properties and scoring methods. *Pain*, 1, 277–299.

Melzack, R. (1987) The short-form McGill Pain Questionnaire. *Pain*, 30, 191–197.

Melzack, R. and Katz, J. (1999) Pain measurement in persons in pain. In: R. Melzack and P. D. Wall (eds) *Textbook of Pain, 4th edn.* (pp. 409–426). Edinburgh: Churchill Livingstone.

Menon, G. and Yorkston, E. A. (1999) The use of memory and contextual cues in the formation of behavioral frequency judgements. In: A. A. Stone, J. S. Turkkan, C. A. Bachrach, J. B. Jobe, H. S. Kirtzman, and V. S. Cain, (eds) *The Science of Self-report: Implications for Research and Practice* (pp. 63–79). Mahwah, NJ: Lawrence Erlbaum Associates, Inc.

Michell, J. (1977). Quantitative science and the definition of measurement in psychology. *British Journal of Psychology*, 88, 355–383.

Morley, S. and Williams, A. C. de C. (2002) Conducting and evaluating treatment outcome studies. In: D. C. Turk and R. Gatchel (eds) *Psychological Approaches to Pain Management: A Practitioners Handbook, 2nd edn.* (pp. 52–68). New York: Guilford Press.

Morley, S. J., Williams, A. C. de C. and Black, S. (2002) A confirmatory analysis of the Beck Depression Inventory in chronic pain. *Pain*, 99, 289–298.

Moss-Morris, R., Weinman, J., Petrie, K. J., Horne, R., Cameron, L. D. and Buick, D. (2002) The Revised Illness Perception Questionnaire (IPQ-R). *Psychology and Health*, 17, 1–16.

Peters, M. L., Sorbi, M. J., Kruise, D. A., Kerssens, J. J., Verhaak, P. F. M. and Bensing, J. M. (2000) Electronic diary assessment of pain, disability and psychological adaptation in patients differing in duration of pain. *Pain*, 84, 181–192.

Pincus, T. and Morley, S. (2001) Cognitive processing bias in chronic pain: A review and integration. *Psychological Bulletin*, 127, 599–617.

Pincus, T. and Williams, A. (1999) Models and measurements of depression in chronic pain. *Journal of Psychosomatic Research*, 47, 211–219.

Pincus, T., Burton, A. K., Vogel, S. and Field, A. P. (2002) A systematic review of psychological factors as predictors of chronicity/disability in prospective cohorts of low back pain. *Spine*, 27, E109–E120.

Pincus, T., Williams, A. C. de C., Vogel, S. and Field, A. (2004) The development and testing of the depression, anxiety and positive outlook scale (DAPOS). *Pain* 109, 181–188.

Price, D. D. (1999) *Psychological Mechanisms of Pain and Analgesia.* Seattle, WA: IASP Press.

Prkachin, K. M., Hughes, E., Schultz, I., Joy, P. and Hunt, D. (2002) Real-time assessment of pain behavior during clinical assessment of low back pain patients. *Pain*, 95, 23–30.

Radloff, L. S. (1977) The CES-D scale: A self-report depression scale for research in the general population. *Applied Psychological Measurement*, 1, 385–401

Rand, C. S. (1999) 'I took the medicine like you told me, doctor': Self-report of adherence with medical regimens. In: A. A. Stone, J. S. Turkkan, C. A. Bachrach, J. B. Jobe, H. S. Kirtzman and V. S. Cain (eds) *The Science of Self-report: Implications for Research and Practice* (pp. 257–276). Mahwah, NJ: Lawrence Erlbaum Associates, Inc.

Reyes-Gibby, C. C., Aday, L. and Cleeland, C. (2002) Impact of pain on self-rated health in the community-dwelling older adults. *Pain*, 95, 75–85.

Roland, M. and Morris, R. (1983) A study of the natural history of back pain. Part I. Development of a reliable and sensitive measure of disability in low-back pain. *Spine*, 8,141–144

Rosenstiel, A. K. and Keefe, F. J. (1983) The use of coping strategies in chronic low back pain patients: relationship to patient characteristics and current adjustment. *Pain*, 17, 33–44.

Rudy, T. E., Lieber, S. J., Boston, J. R., Gourley, L. M. and Baysal, E. (2003) Psychosocial predictors of physical performance in disabled individuals with chronic pain. *Clinical Journal of Pain*, 19, 18–30.

Sackett, D. L., Haynes, R. B., Guyatt, G. H. and Tugwell, P. (1991) *Clinical Epidemiology: A Basic Science for Clinical Medicine*. Boston, Little, Brown and Co.

Salkovskis, P. M. (1996). The cognitive approach to anxiety: Threat beliefs, safety-seeking behavior, and the special case of health anxiety and obsessions. In: P. M. Salkovskis (ed) *Frontiers of Cognitive Therapy* (pp. 48–74). New York: Guilford Press.

Schmitz, U., Saile, H. and Nilges, P. (1996) Coping with chronic pain: Flexible goal adjustment as an interactive buffer against pain-related distress. *Pain*, 67, 41–51.

Schwarz, N. (1999) Self-reports: How the questions shape the answer. *American Psychologist*, 54, 93–105.

Scientific Advisory Committee of the Medical Outcomes Trust (2002) Assessing health status and quality-of-life instruments: Attributes and review criteria. *Quality of Life Research*, 11, 193–205.

Severeijns, R., Vlaeyen, J. W. S. and van den Hout, M. A. (2004) Do we need a communal model of pain catastrophizing? An alternative explanation. *Pain*, 111, 236–239.

Sharp, T. J. and Nicholas, M. K. (2000) Assessing the significant others of chronic pain patients: the psychometric properties of significant other questionnaires. *Pain*, 88, 135–144.

Simmonds, M. J., Olson, S. L., Jones, S., Hussein, T., Lee, C. E., Novy, D. and Radwan, H. (1998) Psychometric characteristics and clinical usefulness of physical performance tests in patients with low back pain. *Spine*, 23, 2412–2421.

Skevington, S. M., Carse, M. S. and Williams, A. C. de C. (2001) Validation of the WHOQOL-100: Pain management improves quality of life for chronic pain patients. *Clinical Journal of Pain*, 17, 264–275.

Skevington, S. M. (1995) *Psychology of Pain*. Chichester: John Wiley.

Stenner, P. H. D., Cooper, D. and Skevington, S. M. (2003) Putting the Q into quality of life: The identification of subjective constructions of health-related quality of life using Q methodology. *Social Science and Medicine*, 57, 2161–2172.

Stone, A. A., Shiffman, S., Schwartz, J. E., Broderick, J. E. and Hufford, M. R. (2002) Patient non-compliance with paper diaries. *British Medical Journal*, 324, 1193–1194.

Stone, A. A., Broderick, J. E., Schwartz, J. E., Shiffman, S., Litcher-Kelly, L. and Calvanese, P. (2003) Intensive momentary reporting of pain with an electronic diary: reactivity, compliance and patient satisfaction. *Pain*, 104, 343–351.

Sullivan, M. J. L., Bishop, S. R. and Pivik, J. (1995) The Pain Catastrophizing Scale: Development and validation. *Psychological Assessment*, 7, 524–532.

Sullivan, M. J. L., Thorn, B., Haythornthwaite, J. A., Keefe, F. J., Martin, M., Bradley, L. A. and Lefebvre, J. C. (2001) Theoretical perspectives on the relation between catastrophizing and pain. *Clinical Journal of Pain*, 17, 52–64.

Tait, R. C., Pollard, C. A., Margolis, R. B., Duckro, P. N. and Krause, S. J. (1987) The Pain Disability Index: Psychometric and validity data. *Archives of Physical Medicine and Rehabilitation*, 68, 438–441.

Tait, R. C., Chibnall, J. T. and Krause, S. (1990) The Pain Disability Index: Psychometric properties. *Pain*, 40, 171–182.

Tan, G., Jensen, M. P., Thornby, J. I. and Shanti, B. F. (2004) Validation of the Brief Pain Inventory for chronic nonmalignant pain. *Journal of Pain*, 5, 133–137.

Terwee, C. B., Dekker, F. W. S., Wiersinga, W. M., Prummel, M. F. and Bossuyt, P. M. M. (2003) On assessing responsiveness of health-related quality of life instruments: Guidelines for instrument evaluation. *Quality of Life Research*, 12, 349–362.

Thorn, B. E., Ward, L. C., Sullivan, M. J. L. and Boothby, J. L. (2003) Communal coping model of catastrophising: Conceptual model building. *Pain*, 106, 1–2.

Turk, D. C. and Melzack, R. (2001a) The measurement of pain and the assessment of people experiencing pain. In: D. C. Turk and R. Melzack (eds) *Handbook of Pain Assessment, 2nd edn.* (pp. 3–11). New York, Guilford Press.

Turk, D. C. and Melzack, R. (eds) (2001b) *Handbook of Pain Assessment, 2nd edn.* New York: Guilford Press.

Turk, D. C. and Okifuji, A. (2003) Clinical assessment of the person with chronic pain. In: T. S. Jensen, P. R. Wilson and A. S. C. Rice (eds) *Clinical Pain Management: Chronic Pain* (pp. 89–100). London, Edward Arnold.

Turk, D. C., Dworkin, R. H., Allen, R. R., Bellamy, N., Brandenburg, N., Carr, D. B., Cleeland, C. et al. (2003) Core outcome domains for chronic pain clinical trials: IMMPACT recommendations. *Pain*, 106, 337–345.

Vlaeyen, J. W. S. and Linton, S. J. (2000) Fear-avoidance and its consequences in chronic musculoskeletal pain: A state of the art. *Pain*, 85, 317–332.

Vlaeyen, J. W. S., Kole-Snijders, A. M. J., Boeren, R. G. B. and van Eek, H. (1995) Fear of movement/(re)injury in chronic low back pain and its relation to behavioral performance. *Pain*, 62, 363–372.

Von Korff, M. (2001) Epidemiological and survey methods: Assessment of chronic pain. In: D. C. Turk and R. Melzack (eds) *Handbook of Pain Assessment, 2nd edn.* (pp. 603–618). New York: Guilford Press.

Von Korff, M., Ormel, J., Keefe, F. J. and Dworkin, S. F. (1992) Grading the severity of chronic pain. *Pain*, 50, 133–149.

Waddell, G., Newton, M., Henderson, I., Somerville, D. and Main, C. J. (1993) A Fear–Avoidance Beliefs Questionnaire (FABQ) and the role of fear-avoidance beliefs in chronic low back pain and disability. *Pain*, 52, 157–168.

Ware, J. E. and Sherbourne, C. D. (1992) The MOS 36-item short-form health survey (SF–36): I. Conceptual framework and item selection. *Medical Care*, 30, 473–483.

Ware, J. E., Snow, K. K., Kosinski, M. and Gandek, B. (1993) *SF–36 Health Survey:*

Manual and Interpretation Guide. Boston: Health Institute, New England Medical Center.

Watson, P. J. (1999) Non-physiological determinants of physical performance in musculoskeletal pain. In: M. Max (ed) *Pain 1999 – An Updated Review* (pp. 153–157). Seattle, WA: IASP Press.

Weinman, J., Petrie, K. J., Moss-Morris, R. and Horne, R. (1996) The Illness Perception Questionnaire: A new method for assessing the cognitive representations of illness. *Psychology and Health*, 11, 431–446.

WHOQOL Group (1995) The World Health Organization Quality of Life Assessment (WHOQOL): Position paper from the World Health Organization. *Social Science and Medicine*, 41, 1403–1409.

WHOQOL Group (1998) Development of the World Health Organization WHOQOL-BREF quality of life assessment. *Psychological Medicine*, 28, 551–558.

Widiger, T. A. and Clark, L. A. (2000) Toward DSM-V and the classification of psychopathology. *Psychological Bulletin*, 126, 946–963.

Williams, A. C. de C. (1999) Measures of function and psychology. In: R. Melzack and P. D. Wall (eds) *Textbook of Pain, 4th edn.* (pp. 427–444). Edinburgh: Churchill Livingstone.

Williams, A. C. de C. (2002) Facial expression of pain: An evolutionary account. *Behavioral and Brain Science*, 25, 439–488.

Williams, A. C. de C., Davies, H.T.O. and Chadury, Y. (2000) Simple pain rating scales hide complex idiosyncratic meanings. *Pain*, 85, 457–463.

Zigmond, A. S. and Snaith, R. P. (1983) The Hospital Anxiety and Depression Scale. *Acta Psychiatrica Scandinavica*, 67, 361–370.

Chapter 35

Chronic pain

Psychological approaches to management

Amanda C. de C. Williams

INTRODUCTION

Chronic or persistent pain is traditionally defined by duration, variously 12 or 6 months or less, and by its lack of response to treatment. This narrow description contrasts with the definition, 'an unpleasant sensory and emotional experience associated with actual or potential tissue damage or described in terms of such damage' (International Association for the Study of Pain (IASP), 1979). This emphasises the essential aversive nature of pain and specifies that it is not necessarily associated with tissue damage. Paradoxically, while pain is the patient's prime concern, its underlying cause is the focus of the medical system. And when a cause is not identified, the pain is often discounted.

Persistent pain is a feature of many long-term medical conditions, but also occurs without identifiable injury or pathology, or long after resolution. It also varies in severity and in its impact: what brings people with pain for treatment is the distress it causes and the interference with everyday life. Pain is surprisingly prevalent: a recent Scottish community survey found 14% of adults reporting intermittent or continuous pain for at least 3 months; for half of these, the pain severely limited activity (Elliott, 1999; Smith et al., 2001).

Understanding pain is a serious challenge for medical personnel. The patient's experience is hard to convey and medicine's aim has been to substantiate the subjective report by 'objective' findings. If these do not match clinicians' expectations of reasonable cause of pain, most reject the patient's account, with some turning to psychologists to explain the 'excessive' pain or pain-related behaviour. Psychologists, in turn, have redefined the agenda to address the inherent unpleasantness of the patient's pain, its destructive impact on his or her interactions with the outside world and on his or her emotional life, and how the patient might reduce these effects by methods that are under conscious control. To an extent, however, psychological concepts and treatments of pain have incorporated some of the dualistic thinking exemplified by the idea of 'excessive' pain, and have referred less to the patient than to medical or cultural norms. This is exemplified by DSM-IV and ICD classifications, which are poorly informed by current understanding of pain and of little clinical use.

THE NATURE OF PAIN

Pain is an essential survival mechanism: its aversiveness grabs attention and urges escape. It provides a powerful learning experience, not just for the individual who is injured but for those who observe the behaviour. After escape, or mitigation, pain keeps healing and recovery at the top of the organism's priorities, ahead of all but essential functions (Wall, 1999). However, such a sensitive and powerful system has evolved to produce false positives, rather than to miss signalling danger. Normal function is achieved by a fine balance of excitation and inhibition of pain transmission at each synapse. Information fed into the balance comes from the periphery, where much sensory information is collected; and from descending pathways from many cortical and subcortical areas that represent the individual's state of alertness and arousal; fears, hopes and expectations; memories and previous learning about painful events. The 'gate', as this synaptic balance was described by Melzack and Wall (1965), is a dynamic mechanism, responsive to all these inputs. Disturbance of the balance (reduced inhibition or enhanced activation and other mechanisms discovered since the 'gate control model') can lead to spontaneous pain signals, to amplification of background 'noise' to the level of a consistent pain message, to excessive firing to non-noxious stimuli or firing at a lower threshold, to transmission of touch or temperature information as pain, as far as changes in cortical representation of the painful area (Flor et al., 1997; Wall, 1999). Functional imaging of the brain has provided a further dimension to the study of pain processing (Price, 1999; Petrovic and Ingvar, 2002; Gracely et al., 2004), although so far mainly in experimental rather than clinical subjects.

It is clear, even from this oversimple description of pain mechanisms, that such changes in nervous system functioning will not be evident on structural investigation or haematological analysis, and may also fluctuate with mood, fears and stresses: hence the disparity between, for instance, imaging of discs and vertebral joints and the back pain reported by the patient (Breslau and Seidenwurm, 2000). However, there are still relatively few integrated models available – either within basic research, where animal models, peripheral lesions and very simple psychology predominate, or within psychology, which tends to use concepts at a level of abstraction that makes them hard to map onto known processes identified by clinical and basic research (Chapman and Gavrin, 1999; Price, 1999).

The mechanisms described are far better understood in acute pain and, in many cases of acute pain, management of anxiety by good care and information is sufficient psychological intervention, carried out by health-care personnel and by others around the patient. In chronic pain, the mechanisms are less understood and both the variance in problems and the size of the disparity between what distresses the patient and its putative cause are larger than in acute pain. Nevertheless, it is mainly psychosocial variables that predict who, among those with an acute injury or post-operative pain, will develop persistent pain and significant disability (Linton, 2002). The distinction between acute pain, accompanied over the early weeks by healing and recovery, and chronic pain, in which healing is complete but neither pain nor its interference with function has remitted, is unsurprisingly not appreciated by patients, who often interpret pain as failure of healing, if not of an undetected pathological process. Thinking along similar lines, health-care professionals continue to intervene as if healing has failed but their well-intentioned intervention may exacerbate the pain produced by an irritable and dysfunctional nervous system.

Meanwhile, the search for structural problems or pathology as a cause of pain, although appropriate to help formulate the pain problem, is likely to identify degeneration or 'wear and tear' (particularly in middle-aged or older adults), minor abnormalities or healed injuries. It is all too tempting to attribute pain to these (although many are as common in people with no pain), thereby supporting the patient's sense of being damaged. Pain clinics, while appreciating the complexity of pain, undertake investigations and attempt to modify or abolish pain by a range of techniques, some destructive, but most interfering with pain transmission by pharmacological or electrical methods. Some of these are effective in many patients, but at a cost in adverse effects that undermine long-term adherence (see *Bandolier*, 2003). In addition, in the mistaken belief that, with pain relief, the patient will recover physical function and psychological equanimity, little attention is given to patients' psychosocial needs until medical and physical treatments have been exhausted, although an integrated approach would have been preferable (Sullivan and Ferrell, 2005).

CONCEPTUAL ISSUES AND QUESTIONS

Persistent pain, then, is a complex set of interacting mechanisms, including information processing and behaviour. Most psychological interventions target beliefs, processing, behaviour and the wider social consequences of the pain *as* effects of pain and make little attempt to reduce the pain itself. For those that address the pain directly, largely through attention manipulation (including hypnotic methods), efficacy is far better demonstrated in acute (particularly expected, relatively short-lived and mild to moderate) pain than in persistent pain.

Regrettably, dualistic approaches persist in psychology, as in other areas of health care; when the patient's experience of pain is not substantiated by investigation, some mental health workers address pain as a transformation of distress, which will remit if and when the distress is resolved. This 'psychosomatic' model, in lay terms 'pain is all in the mind', is bewildering and disturbing to patients; its theoretical basis remains highly abstract and unrelated to pain mechanisms of pain, and it lacks supporting evidence (Sharpe and Williams, 2002). Of course, pain plays a function in the individual's life and relationships, a function of which he or she might not be aware, but to assume a causal role for this function goes beyond the evidence (Sharpe and Mayou, 2004).

TREATMENT

Treatment for pain, therefore, aims to modify unhelpful patterns of thinking and of behaviour; unhelpful in the sense that they are likely to perpetuate the pain or to reduce the patient's capacity to live a reasonably normal life despite pain. At a more abstract level, treatment aims to improve the patient's relationship with the pain, changing its meaning and its implications. The only treatment for which there is strong evidence of efficacy is cognitive-behavioural pain management (CBT), which is described in detail by Main and Spanswick (2000), Nicholas and colleagues (2003) and, for patients, by Berry (2001). Shorter guidelines are produced by the British Pain Society (2005) and European Guidelines Group (2004). Other treatment methods will not be described here (but see Erskine and Judd, 1994; Basler et al., 2002) because the evidence for efficacy is lacking (Raine et al., 2002): there is an urgent need for good quality trials of alternative psychological treatments.

CBT for persistent pain is usually delivered as a multi-component programme by a multi-disciplinary team working closely together: the aim is synergy between the components, integration of their use by patients, and repetition of key messages. Components are described separately below for clarity, not because this best represents practice. At the level of the meaning of pain, Morley and Eccleston (2004) describe the impact of persistent pain on the individual as a 'psychological cascade' from repeated interruption and disruption by pain of ongoing activity and thought; if these interruptions lead to ruminative distressing thoughts and images (Aldrich et al., 2000), pain thereby interferes with a range of activities, physical, intellectual and social; the result in the medium to long term is a serious loss of valued parts of the individual's identity (Harris et al., 2003). Successful treatment aims to enable the person with pain to remain calm in the face of that pain, to return to ongoing tasks after interruption, to negotiate with the pain a way to continue valued goals and activities, and to adjust identity realistically.

Education and information

Education covers pain phenomena and mechanisms, the characteristics of persistent pain that distinguish it from acute everyday pain, the purpose and limitations of investigations and treatments, and, based on those, the rationale of the various components of treatment. At best, expert knowledge and an interactive style provide patients with a chance to rewrite their medical history in a way that illuminates possibilities for significant improvements to their current state, and instils confidence in self-management. Patients' beliefs about their fragility and the inevitability of decline not infrequently originate in (perhaps misunderstood or misremembered) comments from health-care staff, including complementary practitioners, so that contradictory information needs to be delivered by someone perceived as equally or more authoritative.

Additionally, patients' lack of understanding of the repair mechanisms of bones, muscles and joints, and of the resilience of the human body, make it difficult to integrate accurate information. Beliefs such as that pain always implies damage (Rogers and Allison, 2004), that healing may fail to occur for years or even decades, and that physical demands and strain weaken the body, are common; a rational response to such a situation would be to rest, to avoid strain and to monitor pain as a sign of danger, as patients do. Repeated failure of remedies for acute pain, such as rest, cautious use of the painful part, and analgesics, increase the mystery and anxiety around the possible causes of pain. Visceral and head pains may be attributed to cancerous growths, which is rare in musculoskeletal pain where beliefs about damage are common.

Clinical trials of education alone are disappointing in persistent pain (European Guidelines, 2004), in contrast to efficacy in acute pain (Burton et al., 1999), but they are presumed to contribute to the resolution of unwarranted fears about movement and physical demands, and to underpin reactivation and recognition of the benefits of a more active lifestyle, as demonstrated in a recent trial (Moseley, 2004). Unexpectedly, a Belgian community sample showed that those with mild pain had fewer misconceptions about the implications of back pain and about suitable treatment than those without significant pain and than the few with disabling back pain (Goubert et al., 2004). The authors suggest that pain challenges common misconceptions, such as that pain is a sign of organic injury or disease, and that it necessitates avoidance of physical activity and medical attention. In addition, as in an American study (Roth and Geisser, 2002), these misconceptions mediated some of the consistent relationship between lower educational status and higher prevalence of low back pain.

Behavioural reactivation

Where valued or necessary activities have been abandoned because of the cost in pain, returning to them draws on both physical rehabilitation and behavioural techniques. A first step is careful goal-setting, aiming for a balance of self-care, routine and enjoyable social activities that are inherently satisfying or reinforcing and that promote maintenance. A common pattern for people with persistent pain is to attempt on 'good days' (less pain) to catch up with duties neglected on 'bad days', eventually exacerbating the pain, often incurring new muscular and joint pains from unaccustomed stresses, and abandoning the tasks or reckoning that the cost of the pain outweighs the satisfaction of completing the tasks undertaken. Planned levels of regular activity, increasing steadily and starting from a level compatible even with a 'bad day', enable patients to start to progress towards interim goals, such as going out independently, stopping using a walking aid, driving or using public transport, sitting long enough to share a meal with others. These in turn build towards longer-term goals, such as returning to work or retraining, taking part in social activities or going on holiday.

Reactivation is underpinned by work on fitness and stamina, stretch, flexibility, posture and movement, mainly directed by physiotherapists in a hands-off role. A mixture of routine exercises, building steadily by number or exertion, and specific remedial movements, is common. It is helpful if exercise routines are easily transferable outside hospital settings, and rewarding, and explicitly linked with goals. Exercise alone improves fitness but by rather small amounts (Hayden et al., 2005) and, as in the general population, is poorly maintained. All of these – exercises and building blocks of activity towards goals – are usually carried out according to a technique called 'pacing'. This has various elements: building by small increments, from a modest baseline, towards goal-related activity, by a quota (which is often time but can be number or effort). For instance, the individual aiming to walk without assistance will undertake to walk unassisted a little more each day, whether by time, number of steps, distance, speed or demand such as gradient. Regular breaks are another important element, possibly for rest but essentially for change of position or movement. Pacing is rarely clearly defined (but see Main and Spanswick, 2000; Nicholas et al., 2003) or tested, but it is commonly mentioned by treated patients as a crucial principle for remaining active.

However, physical shortcomings do not alone prevent goal attainment. The model of physical deconditioning, assumed to apply to patients who reported very restricted activity and frequent rest, appears to apply only to some (Verbunt et al., 2005a). A study of sub-acute back pain suggests that perceived decline may be more important than actual reduction in physical activity (Verbunt et al., 2005b). Fear of the consequences of movement or strain may be the major determinant of disability. It is these fears that are targeted in educational interventions, and in cognitive work, but behavioural experiment and graded exposure are also warranted (Vlaeyen et al., 2002). There is a risk of rigid instruction in 'correct' movements, or reliance on particular aids (such as adjustable office chairs or specially designed keyboards) as in much ergonomic practice, instituting unhelpful safety behaviours (Thwaites and Freeston, 2005) and even exacerbating fears of, for instance, prolonged sitting in normal chairs.

Some goals are highly complex: return to work after prolonged unemployment due to disability is a good example. Concerns about work demands, about the practicalities of pacing and about losing entitlement to hard-won welfare benefits are more immediate than the anticipated satisfactions of work, of earning and the social contact it brings (Marhold and Linton, 2002). Education about the benefits to mental health of work, including voluntary work (Thoits and Hewitt, 2001), may be helpful. Early initiatives to assist people who have been on long-term disability welfare to return to work, using individualised programmes and expertise on work placement, are proving effective.

Attention control and relaxation

Early behavioural work on persistent pain emphasised relaxation, on the basis that chronic muscle tension was thought to underlie much musculoskeletal pain. However, relaxation as an intervention for persistent pain is not supported by randomised controlled studies (Knost et al., 1999; *Bandolier*, 2003), although it may be useful in specific populations. The tension–pain model has not been systematically overhauled, although a variety of studies have shown that muscle tension is an issue of timing and co-ordination not normally under voluntary control in particular movements (Watson et al., 1997); that it arises in response to emotional stresses (Flor et al., 1992); and that the sense of control over musculature may be more important than the actual level of relaxation achieved. Nevertheless, relaxation can substantially increase patients' tolerances of positions and movements associated with pain and anxiety, and can help achieve more restful nights, even if not continuous sleep.

Relaxation is currently undergoing a resurrection, often combined with meditative methods and mindfulness; it is the baseline condition for the practice of attention control methods, from transformation of spontaneous imagery to a dispassionate focus on the pain (e.g. Nicholas et al., 2003).

Cognitive therapy

Cognitive therapy targets both the content of fearful and depressive thinking and the processing biases and tendencies that act on internal and external information and contribute to fears and depressed mood. A good psychological formulation will describe the pain in the context of patients' emotional and interpersonal lives, presenting many targets for cognitive therapy: this contrasts with the search for 'psychogenesis' and the neglect of pressing everyday problems. In persistent pain, anxiety or fear (specifically about pain and associated symptoms and their implications) and depressed mood are routinely assessed and addressed in treatment, although frustration over not being able to be normally active is the most common complaint of people with pain in treatment settings (Price, 1999). Currently, two particular targets of research activity and of treatment dominate: fears and related avoidance (Vlaeyen and Linton, 1999; Asmundson et al., 2004), and catastrophising, i.e. the tendency to be vigilant to threat, to overinterpret information as threatening and to underestimate coping resources (Sullivan et al., 2001).

The information given about pain mechanisms and the purpose of investigations and treatments enables patients and therapists to challenge erroneous beliefs about the dangers of pain, particularly when its intensity increases; about vulnerability to further damage and about the adequacy of medical care to date and the likely benefits and costs of pursuing pain relief further. Rather than labelling patients' beliefs as irrational, it is far more helpful to appreciate the extent to which their cautious behaviour makes sense to them. Common misapprehensions include that numbness, tingling or any diagnosis that suggests damage or threat to nerve pathways presages paralysis; that terms such as 'wear and tear' and 'degeneration', applied to discs and joints, indicate significant and inevitable deterioration in structure, strength and function; and that severe pain must originate in serious pathology, rather than in a dysfunction of the pain system. Given that humans are hard-wired to respond to pain as a threat, and that one of the functions of pain is to prioritise healing and recovery by resource conservation (Wall, 1999), it can be hard for patients to reconceptualise pain as unthreatening, although unpleasant, and more likely to be reduced by activity than by rest.

Many of the subjects for discussion and cognitive change arise from the requirements of treatment and of introducing the new behaviours into the patients' own environments. Pacing of activities requires suspension of long-held rules about completing tasks and maintaining standards. More importantly, the new behaviours can challenge others people's expectations of someone with pain. Because of the subjectivity of the pain problem, the patient may have found that others accommodated their needs only when they demonstrated their disability. Negotiating around changed behaviour requires clear explanations (which test the patient's recently acquired understanding) and assertions of need. All these can in turn disrupt the patient's identity: to avoid appearing to be weak, needy or defeated by pain, many people try instead to hide pain, to keep up with others' levels of activity when they can and to opt out in isolation when they cannot.

Direct discussion of depression and depressed mood is usually appropriate. People with pain are familiar with its being attributed to depression and usually feel misunderstood and diminished by this. Prescription of tricyclic antidepressants without adequate explanation, albeit in low doses, which can have analgesic properties, compounds the misunderstanding and patients often adhere rather poorly to courses of antidepressants, both because of their perception that they are inappropriate and because of intolerable unwanted effects.

The most widespread model of depression in chronic pain is that of Banks and Kerns (1996), who describe diathesis and stress, with chronic pain constituting the stress. However, this has not been subject to testing and, given the unsatisfactoriness of much measurement of depression and depressed mood in chronic pain (see Chapter 34), remains at a very general level. There are likely to be several variants of the relationship between persistent pain and depression (Pincus and Morley, 2001; Clyde and Williams, 2002). It is important to recognise that clinical depression, with a cognitive core of self-blame and global pessimism, cannot be diagnosed on the basis of a moderate score on a mixed questionnaire, as people with pain often score highly on somatic items but not on those assessing cognitive or affective depression (Pincus and Williams, 1999). Acknowledgement of the losses of roles, activities and social contacts suffered by people with pain, and of their longstanding uncertainties about the future, can open discussion to reveal cognitive biases of the sort that contribute to depressed mood or the maintenance of depression. Cognitive and behavioural work on depression is supported by progress in reactivation, as described above, and in turn feed into it.

The concept of acceptance and third-wave therapies is attracting increasing attention in pain management (Hayes et al., 1999, McCracken et al., 2004). It contrasts the stance of fighting pain and the thoughts and feelings associated with it, most often leading to frustration and sense of losing the fight, with one in which the pain and the content of pain-related thoughts are observed, dispassionately and with a sense of being able to choose not to let them determine action (or inaction) and feelings. Meaning in life is pursued according to the individual's key values rather than according to the vagaries of the pain. For some, it is practised with mindfulness, meditation and drawing on Buddhist philosophy (Kabat-Zinn et al., 1985, Segal et al., 2002); for others, it is a behavioural treatment supported by evidence (Ridson et al., 2003; McCracken and Eccleston, 2005).

Problem solving, contingency management, maintenance and application

Early behavioural management of pain (Fordyce, 1976) put considerable emphasis on contingency management, consistent with the model of pain behaviour as under operant control rather than related to moment-to-moment pain. Although this should certainly be considered as one explanation for the maintenance of unhelpful behaviour, careful observation has shown the assumptions of consistent social reinforcement for complaint, pain-related behaviour and avoidance of activity to be at best oversimplified. They were based largely on cross-sectional studies that showed an association of solicitous spouse behaviour with greater disability, but sequential study showed that either could precede the other (Romano et al., 1992, 1995). By contrast, classical conditioning of muscle tensions and habitual postures to pain-associated cues is probably underrecognised: keyboards for those with upper limb and neck pain, crowded and anonymous public places for the individual afraid of being bumped or falling. Careful observation can identify contingencies for unhelpful behaviours and allow the patient to take control and to change them; practice *in vivo* is desirable wherever possible.

As part of the new relationship with his or her pain, the person with pain frequently needs to revise actual or potential reliance on aids, drugs and consultations with medical and paramedical personnel. Although each of these can be helpful and improve function, all can undermine the individual's independence, constrain his or her options or bring unforeseen disadvantages. The use of walking aids commonly puts strain on the arms and neck, distorts the posture and can increase the likelihood of falls. Reliance on specially adapted chairs and beds may discourage the person with pain from moving far from them, ruling out most social and leisure activities. Analgesic and psychotropic drugs have adverse effects, may limit activities such as driving or drinking alcohol, and most people dislike the concept of using them indefinitely. Resort in a crisis to a medical or other health practitioner risks return to the cycle of investigation, attempts to diagnose and treat as if the pain were acute, when the crisis may be psychological or social in origin. On the other hand, it would be unreasonable to suggest that the individual managing his or her pain should never consult a general practitioner, take analgesics or use mobility aids. Helpful discussion of this area acknowledges the uncertainties inevitable in self-management of a health problem.

The skills acquired for long-term use by the person learning pain management have often been described in terms of coping, but it is unclear quite what this constitutes. Although the checklists would imply responses that are adaptive or maladaptive across cues and contexts, this makes poor psychological sense. A thoughtful review of the various models applied in pain (Lester et al., in press), including catastrophising, fear and avoidance, and acceptance, finds strengths in all of them. By contrast, a review of the concept of coping in various common chronic disorders is more critical of the field (de Ridder and Schreurs, 2001), particularly of the focus on response at the expense of appraisal and resources to bring to that response. They conclude that, although they have not been directly compared, emotion-focused and avoidance strategies seem to work less well than task-focused and confrontation strategies.

There is renewed interest in the involvement of partners in treatment (Kerns et al., 2002; Keefe et al., 2004), after early trials appeared to show no particular benefits. Even then, it may be mediated by the quality of the relationship, and by gender (Cano et al., 2004). There is also the beginning of some meeting ground between the intrapsychic cognitive factors and interpersonal ones in the proposal that catastrophising constitutes an attempt to obtain support rather than to attempt to minimise pain (Thorn et al., 2003; Sullivan et al., 2004). However, this is countered on the basis that conceptually catastrophising is an appraisal, and that many responses to pain communicate helplessness and thereby may elicit support (Severeijns et al., 2004). Beyond these, the psychological management of pain still remains predominantly asocial in its models and interventions.

In addition, although all can be delivered serially or in parallel to individuals, usual practice is to treat patients in groups, both for economy and to maximise opportunities to learn from one another (Keefe et al., 2002). Patients usually speak enthusiastically of the support of the group and the normalising effects of meeting others with pain and similar problems. It also minimises dependence on the treatment staff, consistent with the overall aims of enabling patients to be self-managing. A coherent programme requires that staff share models of pain and of appropriate interventions, implying training and ongoing supervision for psychologists and nonpsychologists alike.

OUTCOME

Evidence for efficacy of CBT for persistent pain, compared with no or minimal medical or physical treatment, is good, across outcomes of pain experience, cognitive coping, activity levels and mood (Morley et al., 1999; Guzmán et al., 2001; Raine et al., 2002). Other studies have shown reduced health care use (e.g. Williams et al., 1996, 1999) and costs compared to other treatments (Goossens and Evers, 1997; Okifuji et al., 1999). But there is considerable heterogeneity in trial in their populations, treatment components, outcomes and comparison conditions, such that the practitioner looking to these reviews for guidance on the best way to conduct CBT-based pain management would be disappointed. There has been a relative neglect of more focused single-component studies of mechanisms of change, or even of specification of theory that could generate such studies (Morley and Williams, 2002).

There is also confusion over delivery variables. Whereas longer interventions seem to achieve greater change (Guzmán et al., 2001; Williams et al., 1999), economic pressures and political currents engender shorter programmes and less staff expertise, risking dilution to the point of ineffectiveness, other than in producing short-term satisfaction in participants. Relatively little is understood about how changes occur during treatment (Morley, 2004) and the quality of the intervention – process variables such as staff skills, integration of programme components, therapeutic alliance between staff and patients – remains largely unaddressed, although it may account for a substantial amount of variance (Morley and Williams, 2002).

Another line of research has sought to identify patient variables that may predict treatment effectiveness. Atheoretical retrospective analyses of small populations have not yet provided consistently replicable findings and are unlikely to do so (McCracken and Turk, 2002; Morley and Williams, 2002). The development of classification systems appears to be more promising: the most advanced uses a multi-dimensional measure (the MPI) to identify three particular groups of patients for whom treatment is tailored (see Chapter 34; Turk, 2005) but evidence of differential benefits is so far elusive. Further, the application of the stages of change model, although highly problematic (West, 2005), has led to critical examination of the way potential patients are prepared for CBT programmes (Jensen et al., 2003).

Service organisation

Patients' initial search for explanation and advice about how to manage their pain and avoid worsening are often met with analgesic prescription and referral for investigation, on the assumption that this is what they want (Saunders et al., 1999; Salmon et al., 2004). Patients often receive physiotherapy at primary care level, and may also consult a range of practitioners of complementary medicine. From all of these, they may hear explanations and receive helpful advice, but there is a significant likelihood that this is not only inaccurate but potentially damaging. Recent studies sampling the beliefs of health-care professionals have illuminated the extent to which many hold incorrect beliefs about back pain that underpin unhelpful advice, such as restriction of activity and sick leave from work (Linton et al., 2002; Rainville et al., 2000). A qualitative study of physiotherapists and their patients, including observation of consultations (Daykin and Richardson, 2004), demonstrated gaps between the largely biomedical models held by physiotherapists, informing their explanations and treatment, along with stereotypes of 'good' and 'difficult' (psychologically needy) patients, and patients' beliefs about pain and limited understanding of the explanations given.

The last 10 years have seen the recognition of the need for earlier attention to psychological variables and there are now initiatives to prevent work loss, rather than addressing work only after the individual has long ago lost his or her job and become one of the long-term disabled population. The identification of psychosocial variables in the prediction of the development of persistent pain and disability has been particularly important in changing practice (Linton, 2002; Pincus et al., 2002), although early rehabilitation attempts, with psychological intervention delivered by minimally trained GPs or physiotherapists (UK BEAM, 2004; Jellema et al., 2005), have been somewhat disappointing (Main, 2005). There are several ways to try to integrate medical and psychological provision, from the stepped care promoted in the USA (Von Korff and Moore, 2001) to a system more focused on triage and selection (European Guidelines, 2004; Department of Health, 2005). It is possible that the negative contribution of health-care professionals in the development of persistent pain from the acute stage is being overlooked. Although pain report appears to represent cognitive and affective processing (Coghill et al., 2003), health-care practitioners remain sceptical about the reality or intensity of pain, and tend to discount it (Kappesser and Williams, 2002). Information and advice given by authoritative sources can be inaccurate, generating fears and avoidance of activity, or contributing to safety behaviours in the guise of 'coping' (Thwaites and Freeston, 2005). Further, many of the standard pain clinic medical and physical interventions produce disappointing results in the long term, particularly when evaluated on function and mood variables rather than pain relief alone (European Guidelines, 2004; e.g. Fairbank et al., 2005, *Bandolier*, 2003). Earlier attention to reversing the trend towards disability, depressed mood, social isolation and work loss is appropriate. Regrettably, one of the limitations on effective practice in this area is the shortage of clinical psychologists available to work in pain teams.

SUMMARY

Psychology has made substantial contributions to understanding and treating persistent pain and is making progress on prevention. An even greater contribution could emerge from the more widespread application to pain problems of the best of psychological theory and treatments: development of established theory, rigorous hypothesis testing, careful formulation of patients' problems and focused interventions based on those formulations.

REFERENCES

Aldrich, S., Eccleston, C. and Crombez, G. (2000) Worry about chronic pain: vigilance to threat and misdirected problem solving. *Behaviour Research and Therapy*, 38, 457–470.

Asmundson, G. J. G., Vlaeyen, J. W. S. and Crombez, G. (eds) (2004) *Understanding and Treating Fear of Pain*. Oxford: Oxford University Press.

Bandolier (2003) *Bandolier's Little Book of Pain*. Oxford, Oxford University Press. Online. Available: http://www.jr2.ox.oc.uk/bandolier/booth/painpag/index2.html

Banks, S. M. and Kerns, R. D. (1996) Explaining high rates of depression in chronic pain: A diathesis-stress framework. *Psychological Bulletin*, 199, 95–110.

Basler, S. C., Grzesiak, R. C. and Dworkin, R. H. (2002) Integrating relational psychodynamic and action-oriented psychotherapies: treating pain and suffering. In: D. C. Turk and R. J. Gatchel (eds) *Psychological Approaches to Pain Management*, 2nd edn. (pp. 94–127). New York: Guilford Press.

Berry, N. (2001) *Living with Chronic Pain*. Online. Available: http://www.chronicpain.org.uk

Breslau, J. and Seidenwurm, D. (2000) Socioeconomic aspects of spinal imaging:

impact of radiological diagnosis on lumbar spine-related disability. *Topics in Magnetic Resonance Imaging*, 11, 218–223.

British Pain Society (2005) *Recommended Guidelines for Pain Management Programmes*. Online. Available: http://www.britishpainsociety.org

Burton, K., Waddell, G., Tillotson, M. and Summerton, N. (1999) Information and advice to patients with back pain can have a positive effect. A randomized trial of a novel education booklet in primary care. *Spine*, 24, 2484–2491.

Cano, A., Johansen, A. B. and Geisser, M. (2004) Spousal congruence on disability, pain, and spouse responses to pain. *Pain*, 109, 258–265.

Chapman, C. R. and Gavrin, J. (1999) Suffering: the contributions of persistent pain. *Lancet*, 353, 2233–2237.

Clyde, Z. and Williams, A. C. de C. (2002) Depression and mood. In: S. J. Linton (ed), *New Avenues for the Prevention of Chronic Musculoskeletal Pain and Disability. Pain Research and Clinical Management*, Vol. 12 (pp. 105–121). Amsterdam: Elsevier Science.

Coghill, R. C., McHaffie, J. G. and Yen, Y-F. (2003) Neural correlates of interindividual differences in the subjective experience of pain. *Proceedings of the National Academy of Sciences*, 100, 8538–8542.

Daykin, A. R. and Richardson, B. (2004) Physiotherapists' pain beliefs and their influence on the management of patients with chronic low back pain. *Spine*, 29, 783–795.

Department of Health (2005) *Musculoskeletal Services Framework*. London: Department of Health.

Elliott, A. M. (1999) The epidemiology of chronic pain in the community. *Lancet*, 354, 1248.

Erskine, A. and Judd, D. (1994) *The Imaginative Body: Psychodynamic Therapy in Health Care*. Chichester: Whurr.

European Guidelines (2004) *European Guidelines for the Management of Non-specific Low Back Pain*. Online. Available: http://www.backpaineurope.org/web/files/WC2_Guidelines.pdf

Fairbank, J., Frost, H., Wilson-MacDonald, J., Yu, L-M., Barker, K. and Collins, R. for the Spine Stabilisation Trial Group (2005) Randomised controlled trial to compare surgical stabilisation of the lumbar spine with an intensive rehabilitation programme for patients with chronic low back pain: the MRC spine stabilisation trial. *British Medical Journal*, doi:10.1136/bmj.38441.620417.BF, 23 May.

Flor, H., Birbaumer, N., Schugens, M. M. and Lutzenberger, W. (1992) Symptom-specific psychophysiological responses in chronic pain patients. *Psychophysiology*, 29, 452–460.

Flor, H., Braun, C., Elbert, T. and Birbaumer, N. (1997) Extensive reorganization of primary somatosensory cortex in chronic back pain patients. *Neuroscience Letters*, 224, 5–8.

Fordyce, W. E. (1976) *Behavioral Methods for Chronic Pain and Illness*. St Louis: Mosby.

Goossens, M. E. J. B. and Evers, S. M. A. A. (1997). Economic evaluation of back pain interventions. *Journal of Occupational Rehabilitation*, 7, 15–32.

Goubert, L., Crombez, G. and De Bourdeaudhuij, I. (2004) Low back pain, disability and back pain myths in a community sample: prevalence and interrelationships. *European Journal of Pain*, 8, 385–394.

Gracely, R. H., Geisser, M. E., Giesecke, T., Grant, M. A. B., Petzke, F., Williams, D. A. and Clauw, D. J. (2004) Pain catastrophizing and neural responses to pain among persons with fibromyalgia. *Brain*, 127, 835–843.

Guzmán, J., Esmail, R., Karjalainen, K., Irvin, E. and Bombadier, C. (2001) Multidisciplinary rehabilitation for chronic low back pain: Systematic review. *British Medical Journal*, 322, 511–516.

Harris, S., Morley, S. and Barton, S. B. (2003) Role loss and emotional adjustment in chronic pain. *Pain*, 105, 363–370.

Hayden, J. A., van Tulder, M. W., Malmivaara, A. V. and Koes, B. W. (2005) Meta-analysis: exercise therapy for nonspecific low back pain. *Annals of Internal Medicine*, 142, 765–775.

Hayes, S. C., Strosahl, K. D. and Wilson, K. G. (1999) *Acceptance and Commitment Therapy: An Experiential Approach to Behavior Change*. New York: Guilford Press.

International Association for the Study of Pain (IASP) (1979) Pain terms: a list with definitions and notes on usage. *Pain*, 6, 249–252.

Jellema P., van der Windt, D. A. W. M., van der Horst, H. E., Twisk, J. W. R., Stalman, W. A. B. and Bouter, L. M. (2005) Should treatment of (sub)acute low back pain be aimed at psychosocial prognostic factors? Cluster randomised clinical trial in general practice. *British Medical Journal*, doi:10.1136/bmj.38495.686736.E0, 20 June.

Jensen, M. P., Nielson, W. R. and Kerns, R. D. (2003) Toward the development of a motivational model of pain self-management. *Journal of Pain*, 4, 477–492.

Kabat-Zinn, J., Lipworth, L. and Burney, R. (1985) The clinical use of mindfulness meditation for the self regulation of chronic pain. *Journal of Behavioral Medicine*, 8, 163–190.

Kappesser, J., and Williams, A. C. de C. (2002) Pain and negative emotions in the face: judgements by health professionals. *Pain*, 99, 197–206.

Keefe, F. J., Beaupré, P. M., Gil, K. M., Rumble, M. E. and Aspnes, A. K. (2002) Group therapy with patients with chronic pain. In: D. C. Turk and R. J. Gatchel (eds) *Psychological Approaches to Pain Management: A Practitioner's Handbook*, 2nd edn. (pp. 234–255). New York: Guilford Press.

Keefe, F. J., Rumble, M. E., Scipio, C. D., Giordano, L. A. and Perri, L. M. (2004). Psychological aspects of persistent pain: Current state of the science. *Journal of Pain*, 5, 195–211.

Kerns, R. D., Otis, J. D. and Wise, E. A. (2002) Treating families of chronic pain patients: Application of a cognitive-behavioral model. In: R. J. Gatchel and D. C. Turk (eds) *Psychosocial Factors in Pain*, 2nd edn. (pp. 256–275). New York: Guilford Press.

Knost, B., Flor, H., Birbaumer, N. and Schugens, M. M. (1999). Learned maintenance of pain: Muscle tension reduces central nervous system processing of painful stimulation in chronic and subchronic pain patients. *Psychophysiology*, 36, 755–764.

Lester, N., Keefe, F. J., Rumble, M. E. and Labban, J. D. (in press) Coping with chronic pain. In: S. Ayers, A. Baum, C. McManus, S. Newman, K. Wallston, J. Weinman and R. West (eds) *Cambridge Handbook of Psychology, Health and Medicine*, 2nd edn. Cambridge: Cambridge University Press.

Linton, S. J. (ed) (2002) *New Avenues for the Prevention of Chronic Musculoskeletal Pain and Disability*. Amsterdam: Elsevier.

Linton, S. J., Vlaeyen, J. and Ostelo, R. (2002) The back pain beliefs of health care providers: are we fear-avoidant? *Journal of Occupational Rehabilitation*, 12, 223–232.

Main, C. J. (2005) Commentary: Early psychosocial interventions for low back pain in primary care, *British Medical Journal*, doi:10.1136/bmj.38498.495000.ED 20 June.

Main, C. J. and Spanswick, C. C. (2000). *Pain Management: An Interdisciplinary Approach*. Edinburgh: Harcourt Publishers Limited.

McCracken, L. M. and Turk, D. C. (2002). Behavioral and cognitive behavioral treatment for chronic pain: Outcome, predictors of outcome, and treatment process. *Spine*, 27, 2564–2578.

McCracken, L. K. and Eccleston, C. (2005) A prospective study of acceptance of pain and patient functioning with chronic pain. *Pain*, 118, 164–169.

McCracken, L., Carson, J. W, Eccleston, C. and Keefe, F. J. (2004) Acceptance and change in the context of chronic pain. *Pain*, 109, 4–7.

Marhold, C. and Linton, S. J. (2002) Identification of obstacles for chronic pain patients to return to work: evaluation of a questionnaire. *Journal of Occupational Rehabilitation*, 12, 2–65.

Melzack, R. and Wall, P. (1965) Pain mechanisms: a new theory. *Science*, 150, 971–979

Morley, S. (2004) Editorial: Process and change in cognitive behaviour therapy. *Pain*, 109, 205–206.

Morley, S. and Eccleston, C. (2004) The object of fear in pain. In: G. J. G. Asmundson, J. W. S. Vlaeyen and G. Crombez (eds) *Understanding and Treating Fear of Pain* (pp. 163–188). New York: Oxford University Press.

Morley, S. and Williams, A. C. de C. (2002) Conducting and evaluating treatment outcome studies. In: R. J. Gatchel and D. C. Turk (eds) *Psychosocial Factors in Pain*, 2nd edn. (pp. 52–68). New York: Guilford Press.

Morley, S., Eccleston, C. and Williams, A. (1999) Systematic review and meta-analysis of randomized controlled trials of cognitive behaviour therapy and behaviour therapy for chronic pain in adults, excluding headache. *Pain*, 80, 1–13.

Moseley, G. L. (2004) Evidence for a direct relationship between cognitive and physical change during an education intervention in people with chronic low back pain. *European Journal of Pain*, 8, 39–45.

Nicholas, M., Molloy, A., Tonkin, L. and Beeston, L. (2003) *Manage Your Pain: Practical and Positive Ways of Adapting to Persistent Pain*, 2nd edn. London: Souvenir Press Limited.

Okifuji, A., Turk, D. C. and Kalauokalani, D. (1999) Clinical outcome and economic evaluation of multidisciplinary pain centers. In: A. R. Block, E. F. Kremer and E. Fernandez (eds) *Handbook of Pain Syndromes* (pp. 77–97). Mahwah, NJ: Lawrence Erlbaum Associates, Inc.

Petrovic, P. and Ingvar, M. (2002) Imaging cognitive modulation of pain processing. *Pain*, 95, 1–5.

Pincus, T. and Morley, S. (2001) Cognitive processing and bias in chronic pain: A review and integration. *Psychological Bulletin*, 127, 599–617.

Pincus, T. and Williams, A. (1999) Models and measurements of depression in chronic pain. *Journal of Psychosomatic Research*, 47, 211–219.

Pincus, T., Burton, A. K., Vogel, S. and Field, A. P. (2002) A systematic review of psychological factors as predictors of persistent pain/disability in prospective cohorts of low back pain. *Spine*, 27, 109–120.

Price, D. D. (1999) *Psychological Mechanisms of Pain and Analgesia.* Seattle, WA: IASP Press.

Raine, R., Haines, A., Sensky, T., Hutchings, A., Larkin, K. and Black, N. (2002) Systematic review of mental health interventions for patients with common somatic symptoms: Can research evidence from secondary care be extrapolated to primary care? *British Medical Journal,* 325, 1082–1093.

Rainville, J., Carlson, N., Polatin, P., Gatchel, R. J. and Indahl, A. (2000) Exploration of physicians' recommendations for activities in chronic low back pain. *Spine,* 25, 2210–2220.

de Ridder, D. and Schreurs, K. (2001) Developing interventions for chronically ill patients: Is coping a helpful concept? *Clinical Psychology Review,* 21, 205–210.

Ridson, A., Eccleston, C., Crombez, G. and McCracken, L. M. (2003) How can we learn to learn with pain? A Q-methodological analysis of the diverse understandings of acceptance of chronic pain. *Social Science and Medicine,* 56, 375–386.

Rogers, A. and Allison, T. (2004) What if my back breaks? Making sense of musculo-skeletal pain among South Asian and African-Caribbean people in the North West of England. *Journal of Psychosomatic Research,* 57, 79–87.

Romano, J. M., Turner, H. A., Friedman, L. S., Bulcroft, R. A., Jensen, M. P., Hops, H. et al. (1992) Sequential analysis of chronic pain behaviors and spouse responses. *Journal of Consulting and Clinical Psychology,* 60, 777–782.

Romano, J. M., Turner, J. A., Jensen, M. P., Friedman, L. S., Bulcroft, R. A., Hops, H. et al. (1995) Chronic pain patient–spouse behavioral interactions predict patient disability. *Pain,* 63, 353–360.

Roth, R. S. and Geisser, M. E. (2002) Educational achievement and chronic pain disability: mediating role of pain-related congitions. *Clinical Journal of Pain,* 18, 286–296.

Salmon, P., Dowrick, C. F., Ring, A. and Humphris, G. M. (2004) Voiced but unheard agendas. *British Journal of General Practice,* 54, 171–176.

Saunders, K. W., Von Korff, M., Pruitt, S. D. and Moore, J. E. (1999) Prediction of physician visits and prescription medicine use for back pain. *Pain,* 83, 369–377.

Segal, Z. V., Williams, J. M. G. and Teasdale, J. D. (2002) *Mindfulness-based Cognitive Therapy for Depression.* New York: Guilford Press.

Severeijns, R., Vlaeyen, J. W. S. and van den Hout, M. A. (2004) Do we need a communal model of pain catastrophizing? An alternative explanation. *Pain,* 111, 236–239.

Sharpe, M. and Mayou, R. (2004) Editorial. Somatoform disorders: a help or hindrance to good patient care? *British Journal of Psychiatry,* 184, 465–467.

Sharpe, M. and Williams, A. C. de C. (2002) Treating patients with somatoform pain disorder and hypochondriasis. In: D. C. Turk and R. Gatchel (eds) *Psychological Approaches to Pain Management: A Practitioners Handbook,* 2nd edn. (pp. 515–533). New York: Guilford Press.

Smith, B. H., Elliott, A. M., Chambers, W. A., Smith, W. C., Hannaford, P. C. and Penny, K. (2001) The impact of chronic pain in the community. *Family Practice,* 17, 292–299.

Sullivan, M. and Ferrell, B. (2005) Ethical challenges in the management of chronic nonmalignant pain: Negotiating through the cloud of doubt. *Journal of Pain,* 6, 1–9.

Sullivan, M. J. L., Thorn, B., Haythornthwaite, J. A., Keefe, F., Martin, M.,

Bradley, L. A. and Lefevre, J. C. (2001) Theoretical perspectives on the relation between catastrophising and pain. *Clinical Journal of Pain*, 17, 53–61.

Sullivan, M. J. L., Adams, H. and Sullivan, M. E. (2004) Communicative dimensions of pain catastrophising: Social cueing effects on pain behaviour and coping. *Pain*, 107, 230–236.

Thoits, P. A. and Hewitt, L. N. (2001) Volunteer work and well-being. *Journal of Health and Social Behavior*, 42, 115–131.

Thorn, B. E., Ward, L. C., Sullivan, M. J. L. and Boothby, J. L. (2003) Communal coping model of catastrophising: Conceptual model building. *Pain*, 106, 1–2.

Thwaites, R. and Freeston, M. (2005) Safety-seeking behaviours: Fact or fiction? How can we clinically differentiate between safety behaviours and adaptive coping strategies across anxiety disorders? *Behavioural and Cognitive Psychotherapy*, 33, 177–188.

Turk, D. C. (2005) The potential of treatment matching for subgroups of chronic pain patients: Lumping vs. splitting. *Clinical Journal of Pain*, 21, 44–55.

UK BEAM Trial Team (2004) United Kingdom back pain exercise and manipulation (UK BEAM) randomised trial: Effectiveness of physical treatments for back pain in primary care. *British Medical Journal*, doi:10.1136/bmj.38282.669225.AE. 19 November, 1–8.

Verbunt, J. A., Seelen, H. A., Vlaeyen, J. W., Bousema, E. J., van der Heijden, G. J., Heuts, P. H. and Knottnerus, J. A. (2005a) Pain-related factors contributing to muscle inhibition in patients with chronic low back pain: an experimental investigation based on superimposed electrical stimulation. *Clinical Journal of Pain*, 21, 232–240.

Verbunt, J. A., Sieben, J. M., Seelen, H. A. M., Vlaeyen, J. W. S., Bousema, E. J., van der Heijden, G. J. and Knottnerus, J. A. (2005b) Decline in physical activity, disability and pain-related fear in sub-acute low back pain. *European Journal of Pain*, 9, 417–425.

Vlaeyen, J. W. S. and Linton, S. J. (1999) Fear-avoidance and its consequences in chronic musculoskeletal pain: A state of the art. *Pain*, 85, 317–332.

Vlaeyen, J. W., de Jong, J., Geilen, M., Heuts, P. H. and van Breukelen, G. (2002) The treatment of fear of movement/(re)injury in chronic low back pain: Further evidence on the effectiveness of exposure *in vivo*. *Clinical Journal of Pain*, 18, 251–261.

Von Korff, M. and Moore, J. (2001) Stepped care for back pain: Activating approaches for primary care. *Annals of Internal Medicine*, 121, 187–195.

Wall, P. D. (1999) *Pain: The Science of Suffering*. London: Weidenfeld and Nicolson.

Watson, P. J., Booker, C. K., Main, C. J. and Chen, A. C. (1997) Surface electromyography in the identification of chronic low back pain patients: The development of the flexion relaxation ratio. *Clinical Biomechanics*, 11, 165–171.

West, R. J. (2005) Time for a change: Putting the Transtheoretical (Stages of Change) model to rest. *Addiction*, 100, 1036–1039.

Williams, A. C. de C., Richardson, P. H., Nicholas, M. K., Pither, C. E., Harding, V. R., Ridout, K. L. et al. (1996) Inpatient vs. outpatient pain management: results of a randomised controlled trial. *Pain*, 66, 13–22.

Williams, A. C. de C., Nicholas, M. K., Richardson, P. H., Pither, C. E. and Fernandes, J. (1999) Generalizing from a controlled trial: the effects of patient preference versus randomization on the outcome of inpatient versus outpatient chronic pain management. *Pain*, 83, 57–65.

Chapter 36

Introduction to neuropsychology and neuropsychological assessment

Graham Powell

INTRODUCTION

The purpose of this chapter is to introduce the topics of neuropsychology, neuropsychological assessment and assessment for neuropsychological rehabilitation. It will introduce the language of neurology and neuropsychology, describe the physical brain and its main components, outline the structure and function of the lobes, indicate what tasks and tests might be used to assess functions and detect dysfunctions of important regions, give classifications of the main neuropsychological disorders, and finally, deal with the process of interviewing, assessment and report writing.

TERMINOLOGY

A glossary of useful, high-frequency words is as follows.

Spatial orientation terminology

Anterior	front; towards the face
Caudal	towards the spinal cord
Central	on the plane dividing anterior from posterior
Contralateral	on the other side of the body
Distal	far
Dorsal	towards the back surface; towards the bottom of the brain in humans
Inferior	below
Ipsilateral	on the same side of the body
Lateral	on the side; away from the mid-line superior above
Medial	at or on the mid-line
Mesial	towards the mid-line
Mid-line	the line or plane dividing left and right hemispheres
Posterior	behind; towards the back of the head

Proximal	near
Rostral	away from the spinal cord
Ventral	towards the chest and abdominal surface; towards the top of the brain in humans

Anatomical terminology

Cortex	the grey matter covering the outside surface of the brain and tucked into the sulci
Grey matter	concentration of nerve-cell bodies
Gyrus	a bump or elevation on the surface of the brain
Lobe	an area of brain usually, but not always, marked off from the rest of the brain by prominent sulci
Lobule	a major feature within a lobe; one or two prominent gyri, say
Meninges	the above three layers taken together
Neuron	a nerve cell capable of transmitting an impulse
Pia mater, arachnoid, dura mater	the three tough layers or membranes between brain and skull
Sulcus	the groove or fissure between two gyri
Ventricle	space in the brain through which cerebro-spinal fluid (CSF) runs
White matter	concentration of nerve-cell projections (axons)

Lesion terminology

-oma	suffix indicating abnormal growth as in neuroma (tumour of the neurons), glioma (tumour of the glial cells that act as supportive structures of the brain) and meningioma (tumour of the meninges)
Aneurysm	abnormal swelling of a blood vessel
Angioma or arteriovenous malformation	(AVM) knot or tangle or growth of distended blood vessels
Brain injury	a slightly less imprecise term to screen out cases of only superficial damage to the face or head (eg screens out facial cuts and broken jaws); includes only those cases with damage to the CNS
Cerebro-vascular accident	(CVA) damage done by a spontaneous disruption of blood supply, usually attributable to degeneration of the arteries, as in old age, arteriosclerosis or certain diseases

Dementia	a general term for any disease causing progressive deterioration of the CNS, including many of the above but especially Alzheimer's disease (pre-senile dementia) and Pick's disease (senile dementia) or, inclusively, senile dementia Alzheimer's type (SDAT)
Demyelinating diseases	affecting the myelin sheaths of axons; includes multiple sclerosis
Diseases affecting the basal ganglia	includes Parkinsonism and Huntingdon's chorea
Embolism	the obstruction of blood flow, e.g. by a blood clot or air bubble
Haematoma	a collection of blood in one site
Haemorrhage	bleeding
Head injury	an imprecise term implying either a blow to the head or rapid acceleration/deceleration of it; or penetration by a foreign body or skull fragments
Infarct	localised area of damage due to an interrupted blood supply
Infectious diseases	those that affect the brain include bacterial meningitis, tuberculosis infection, brain abscess, neurosyphilis, leptospirosis (e.g. encephalitis and myelitis) and viral infections (e.g. meningitis, encephalitis, rabies, Creutzfeldt–Jakob disease (CJD) and new variant CJD)
Ischaemia	inadequate flow of blood
Lesion	any damage whatsoever to the brain
Neoplasm	any new growth of tissue (i.e. tumour)
Sclerosis	death of any brain tissue
Stroke	general term for the behavioural and cognitive effects of a cerebrovascular accident

Functional terminology

Afferent fibre	neuron conveying information into a specific area of brain; from the sense organs, for example
Association cortex	any cortex outside the primary zones
Coma	unconsciousness, usually for a prolonged period, of varying depth
Concussion	temporary disturbance of cognitive processing including confusion and minor memory upset after mild head injury
Dominance	as for localisation but with special reference to language functions

Efferent fibre	pathway conveying information from the brain to a given area; to the muscles, for example
Function	the specific job, or information-processing capacity, of a given area
Functional system	the linkage of several areas of brain (i.e. several functions) to subserve a complex task (e.g. walking, reading)
Lateralisation of function	the extent to which a given function is localised in one or other of the hemispheres
Localisation of function	the attempt to map a function on to one area of cortex, to map a functional system on to several connected areas
Minimally responsive/low awareness state	the person exhibits some interaction with the environment, e.g. responds to some simple concrete commands, but does not have the intellectual or cognitive ability to make decisions and to communicate, e.g. unable to indicate yes/no consistently
Neurotransmitter	the chemicals by which neurons communicate with each other at their synapses, especially acetylcholine, dopamine, noradrenaline, serotonin and gamma aminobutyric acid
Persistent vegetative state	the person appears to be awake but does not respond to the environment in any meaningful way and requires total physical care, such as feeding and toileting
Plasticity of function	the extent to which intact areas of brain can come to subserve a new function
Primary or nuclear zone	a 'projection' area of brain receiving or sending impulses to the periphery
Secondary zone	brain surrounding primary zones where information is decoded or encoded into a complex cognition
Tertiary zone	areas where secondary zones overlap, responsible for the most complex mental activity including cross-modal processing
Unconsciousness	the state in which the person exhibits a marked degree of reduced responsiveness to the environment after head injury; the eyes are closed

Terminology of investigations

Computerised transaxial tomography (CT)	computer-enhanced picture of the brain based on repeated low intensity X-rays taken from different angles

Electroencephalogram (EEG)	the changing electrical activity over different areas of the brain, usually recorded as a paper trace
Evoked potentials (EPs)	reaction of the EEG recording to sensory stimuli such as sounds, lights or tactile sensation, usually obtained by averaging over many trials
Functional imaging	any technique that visualises ongoing brain activity
Magnetic resonance imaging (MRI) and functional MRI (fMRI)	computer generated picture of the brain based upon radio waves given off by brain tissue as it relaxes after being in a strong magnetic field
Positron emission tomography (PET)	typically, radioactively labeled glucose or oxygen is taken up by the brain and the radioactivity that is detected is converted into a picture; often used to measure blood flow.
Regional cerebral blood flow (rCBF)	techniques visualising blood flow
Single photon emission computed tomography (SPECT)	similar to PET but uses single photons rather than X-rays
X-rays	simple X-rays or radiographs are still used in order to detect fractures of the skull; they are poor at visualising the soft tissues of the brain

OVERALL FEATURES OF THE BRAIN

Gross divisions of the brain

The cortex (or neocortex because of its recency in evolutionary terms) is grouped together with the most immediate subcortical structures (i.e. basal ganglia, limbic system, olfactory bulb, lateral ventricles and thalamus) to constitute the *fore brain*. The remaining structures (epithalamus, hypothalamus, third ventricle, tegmentum, cerebral aqueduct, cerebellum, pons, fourth ventricle and medulla oblongata) are less involved in complex sensory integration and more concerned with basic, primitive physiological functioning, such as the control of level of arousal; these structures are collectively known as the *brainstem*. Beneath the brainstem comes the *spinal cord*. The gross divisions of the brain are well presented by magnetic resonance images in Kolb and Whishaw (1990, pp. 854–860).

The gyri and lobes of the cortex

The cortex divides, to some extent arbitrarily, into four lobes – frontal, parietal, occipital and temporal – which are often divided at their boundaries by prominent gyri and sulci (Figures 36.1 and 36.2). The lobes refer simply to broad regions of brain and do not imply functional unity.

Cytoarchitectonic areas

The cortex can also be divided into areas with a similar structure of nerve cells. The cortex is 50–100 cells thick and arranged in six layers. Different layers predominate in different areas, which gives rise to Brodmann's well-known map of cortical structure, first published in 1909, which is depicted in a simplified fashion in Figure 36.3. Some areas have histologically distinct boundaries; other areas merge into each other.

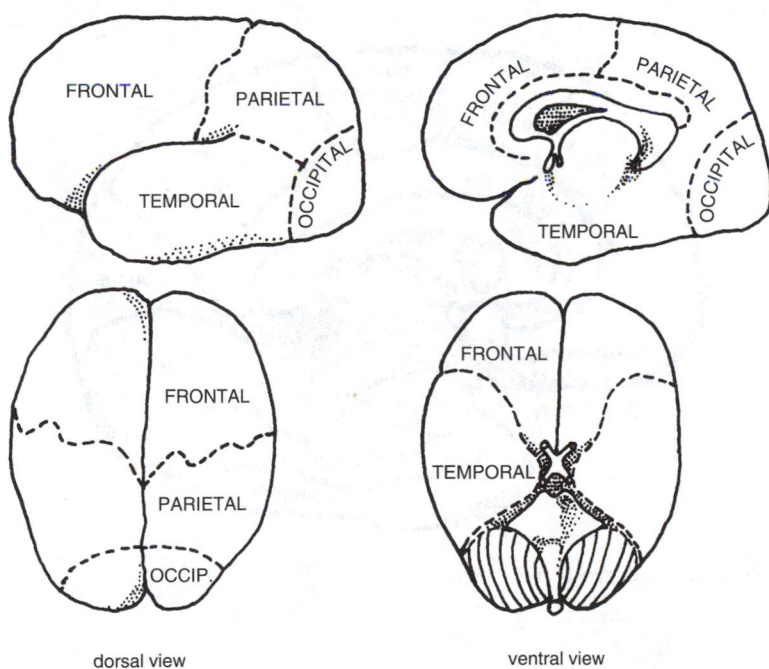

dorsal view   ventral view

Figure 36.1 The lobes of the brain.

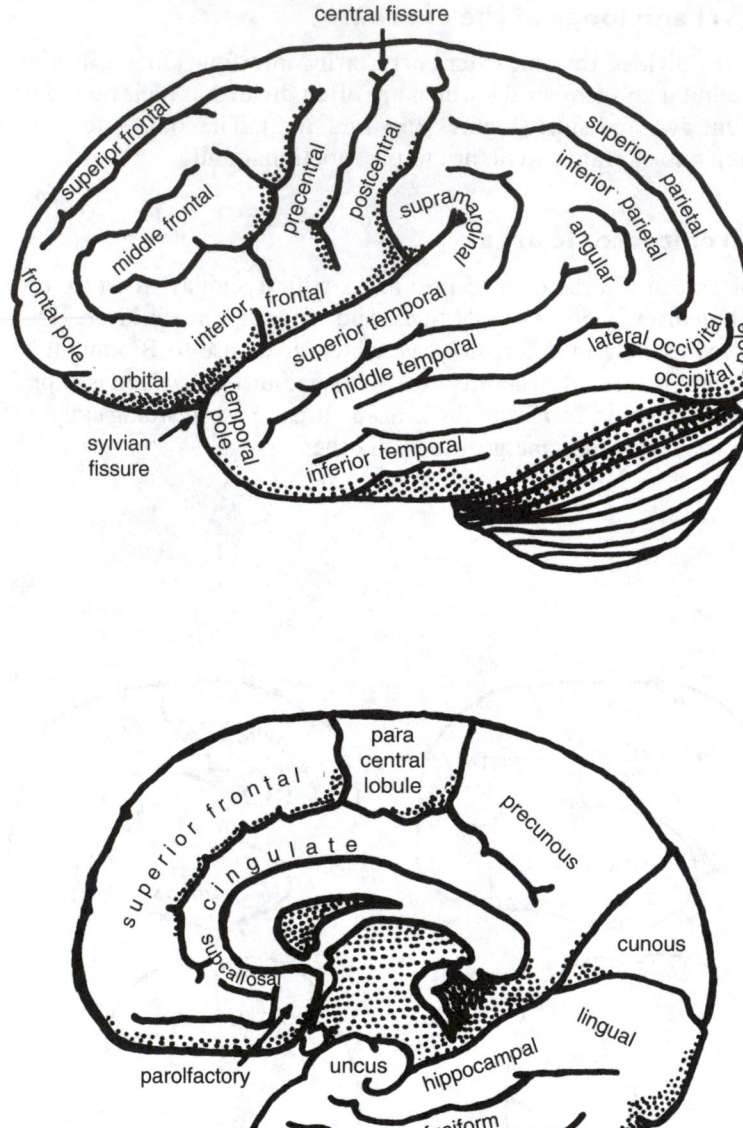

Figure 36.2 The main gyri of the brain.

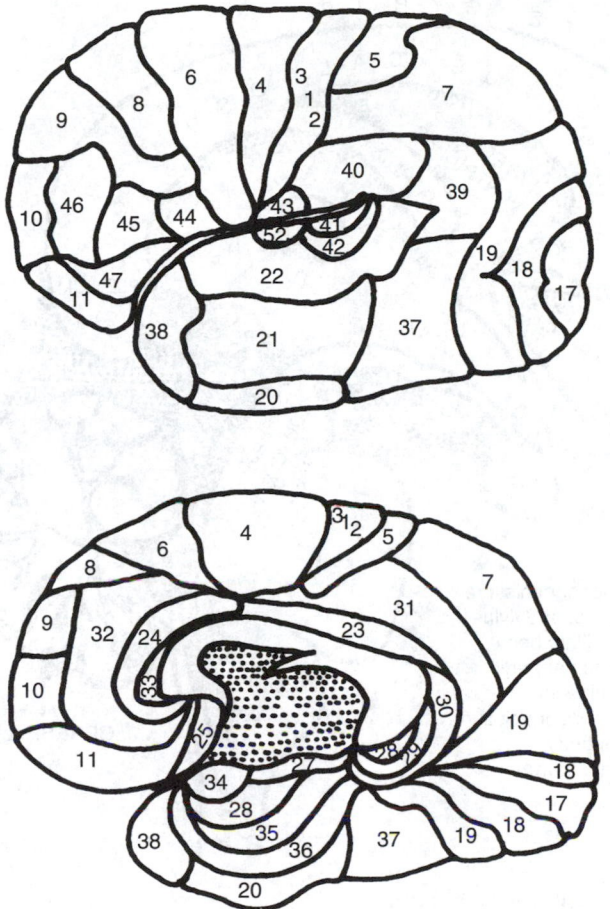

Figure 36.3 Simplified version of Brodmann's map.

Subcortical structures

These are detailed on pp 750–754, but for the moment the medial view of the brain in Figure 36.4 will orientate the reader to the location of some of the major structures.

The ventricles of the brain

The CSF-filled spaces in the brain used to be visualised by air encephalogram (AEG) but now this technique has been overtaken by CT and MRI images. A

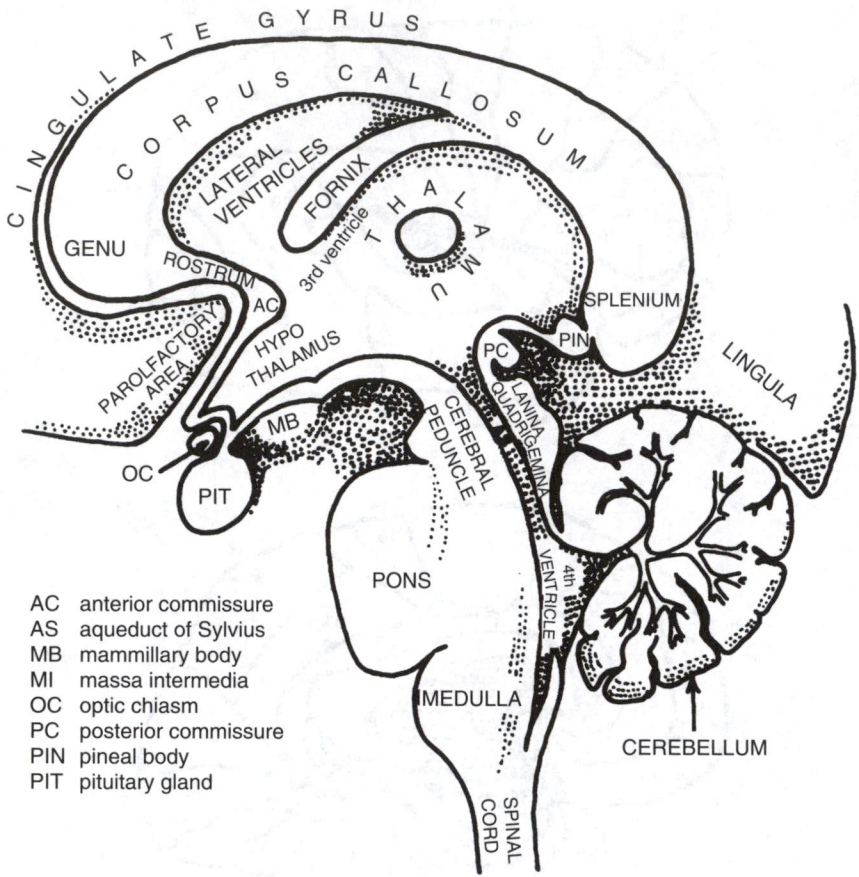

Figure 36.4 Medial view of the brain.

knowledge of their structure, given in Figure 36.5, is important because: (1) their damage can lead to a blockage of CSF flow, which can give rise to an increase in cranial pressure, crushing cortex against the skull or causing the head to swell if the skull is still malleable as in childhood hydrocephalus; and (2) distortions in their shape and size are a clue to the site and nature of space-occupying lesions. There are four ventricles. The first and second are the lateral ventricles, with anterior, posterior and inferior horns extending into the frontal, occipital and temporal lobes, respectively. The third ventricle is on the mid-line; one should note the 'hole' in the third ventricle, which is where the left thalamus joins the right thalamus (called the intermediate mass of the thalamus). The new student should firmly grasp this landmark as it accurately locates the thalamus and thence all remaining lower structures in

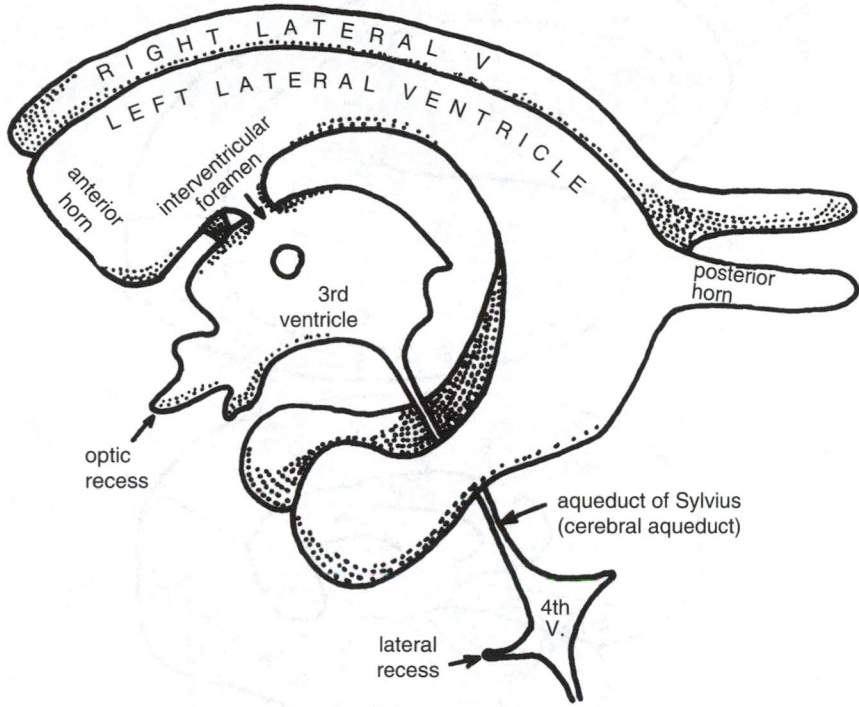

Figure 36.5 The ventricles of the brain.

relation to the cortex. The flow of CSF continues down a fine tube (cerebral aqueduct, aqueduct of Sylvius) to the fourth ventricle.

The blood supply

Arteries take oxygenated blood to the brain and veins drain deoxygenated blood away. Because damage and abnormalities of the blood supply (e.g. aneurysm, embolism, ischaemia) can impair cortical activity, it is necessary to know the three main cerebral arteries and the regions of cortex they fuel, as outlined in Figure 36.6.

The nerve supply

The brain is supplied with its sensory data and outputs motor commands via twelve cranial nerves entering at various points at the base. The nerves are: I olfactory (smells); II optic (vision); III oculomotor (reactions to light, lateral movement of eyes, eyelid movement); IV trochlear (vertical eye

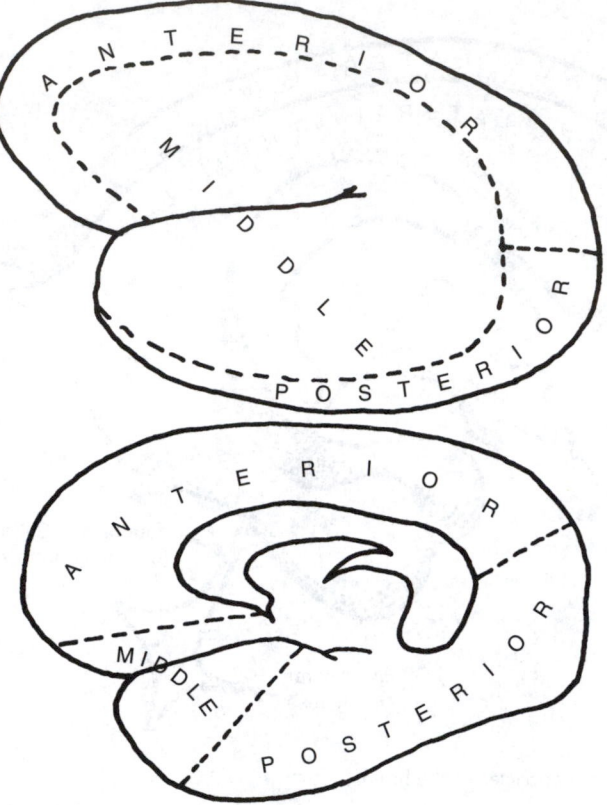

Figures 36.6 The areas of the cortex supplied by the anterior, middle and posterior cerebral arteries.

movement); V trigeminal (masticatory movements); VI abducens (lateral eye movement); VII facial (facial movements); VIII auditory vestibular (hearing); IX glossopharangeal (tongue and pharynx); X vagus; XI spinal accessory (neck muscles and viscera); XII hypoglossal (tongue muscles).

The projection zones of the cortex

Sensory data arrive at the cortex, via the cranial nerves, at a few well-defined points known as the 'nuclear' or 'primary' zones (Luria, 1966, 1973). The four primary zones (three sensory and one motor) are located as in Figure 36.7. A knowledge of these primary zones is the first step towards a functional topography of the cortex. The location of secondary and tertiary zones is also indicated, but it must be remembered that although primary and secondary zones are well demarcated, the boundaries between secondary and tertiary areas are somewhat hazy.

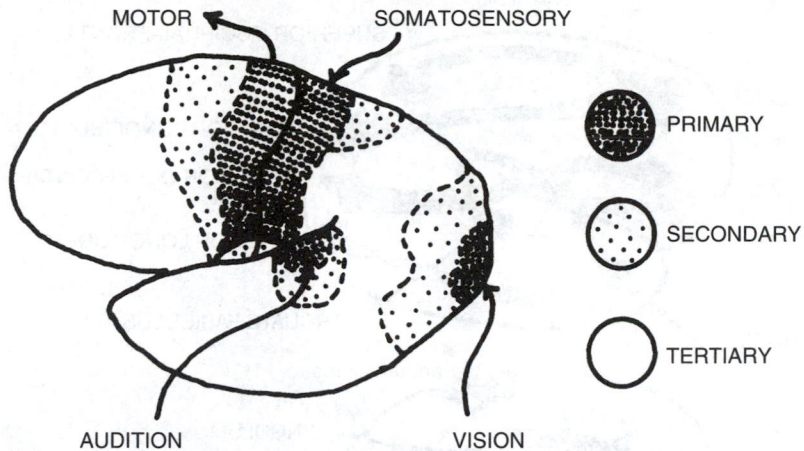

Figure 36.7 The functional zones of the cortex.

The primary, secondary and tertiary areas can be superimposed on Brodmann's cytoarchitectonic map as indicated in Table 36.1 (Kolb and Whishaw, 1980).

Main connections between regions of the cortex

There is naturally a flow of information between all the regions of the cortex. The flow from primary to secondary to tertiary has already been mentioned

Table 36.1 Functional areas of the cortex mapped onto Brodmann's system

Functional area	Brodmann's area
Vision	
primary	17
secondary	18, 19, 20, 21, 37
Audition	
primary	41
secondary	22, 42
Body senses	
primary	1, 2, 3
secondary	5, 7
Sensory, tertiary	7, 22, 37, 39, 40
Motor	
primary	4
secondary	6
eye movement	8
speech	44
Motor, tertiary	9, 10, 11, 45, 46, 47

Source of information: Kolb and Whishaw (1980, revised 1990).

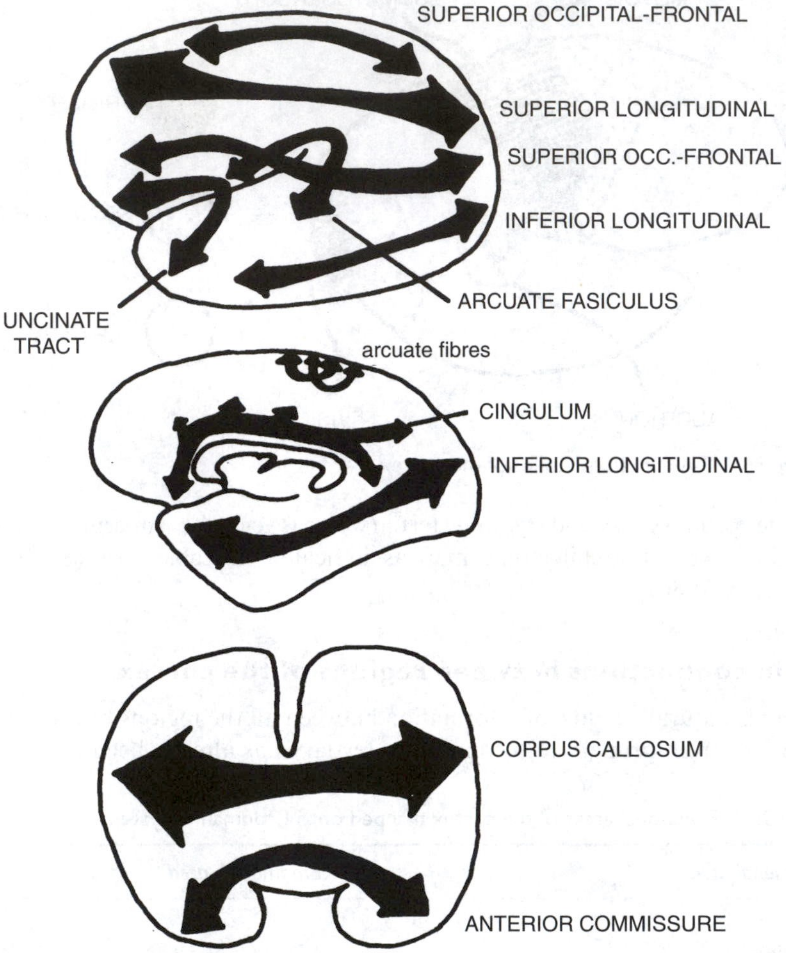

Figure 36.8 The main cortical pathways.

implicitly, and is part of a more general pattern of each neuron being connected to its neighbours, but there is also a flow of information between more
distal regions. Such a flow tends to occur along a few main pathways that are
represented in Figure 36.8. Note that the information exchange between one
hemisphere and the other occurs through two main bundles of fibres, the
corpus callosum and the anterior commisure, also indicated in Figure 36.8,
and also through the hippocampal commisure, shown in Figure 36.11 (p. 751).
Naturally the cortex is also linked to subcortical sites, via the projection
pathways, for example. The subcortical connections of the cortex will be dealt
with on p 750–754.

TEMPORAL LOBES

Summary of structure

The lateral surface comprises the superior, middle and inferior temporal gyri. The insular cortex, hidden from view within the Sylvian fissure, comprises three more gyri – the uncus, fusiform gyrus and parahippocampal gyrus – and are phylogenetically older and sometimes termed the archicortex. The archicortex also includes two subcortical or limbic structures, namely the amygdala and the hippocampus. The two cross-sections through the temporal lobe shown in Figure 36.9 make clear the external and internal structures of the temporal lobe.

Summary of connections

The sensory input to the temporal lobe is from the auditory pathways to the superior temporal gyrus at area 41, known as Herschl's gyrus.

As for cortico-cortical connections, the lateral cortex of the left temporal lobe is connected to that of the right via the corpus callosum, whilst the left and right archicortex is connected via the anterior commissure. Other distal connections are as given in Figure 36.8, to the frontal and occipital lobes.

Internally, the lateral temporal cortex is closely connected to the amygdala and hippocampus.

Functions and dysfunctions of the temporal lobes

It follows from the foregoing description of the structure and connections of the temporal lobe that its functioning is not unitary. There are four main functional areas to consider: auditory sensation and perception, language comprehension, long-term memory and personality or affect.

Auditory sensation is disturbed by lesions to the primary auditory projection areas of the left and right hemispheres, that is, Herschl's gyrus, or area 41. A bilateral lesion here could produce cortical deafness, but a unilateral lesion will not, instead merely raising the threshold for auditory sensation in the contralateral ear. Lesions to the secondary areas (22 and 42), especially on the right side, may lead to auditory agnosia; for example, amusia (tone deafness, melody deafness and poor perception of rhythm, tempo and prosody of music or speech) or agnosia for sounds (the inability to interpret the meaning of non-verbal sounds). Other higher-order deficits of auditory perception include deficits of selective attention on dichotic listening tasks (Schulhoff and Goodglass, 1969).

Language comprehension, too, is affected by unilateral lesions to the secondary zones (especially area 22) but this time on the left side in particular. Clinically, this is known as Wernicke's aphasia, but also termed sensory

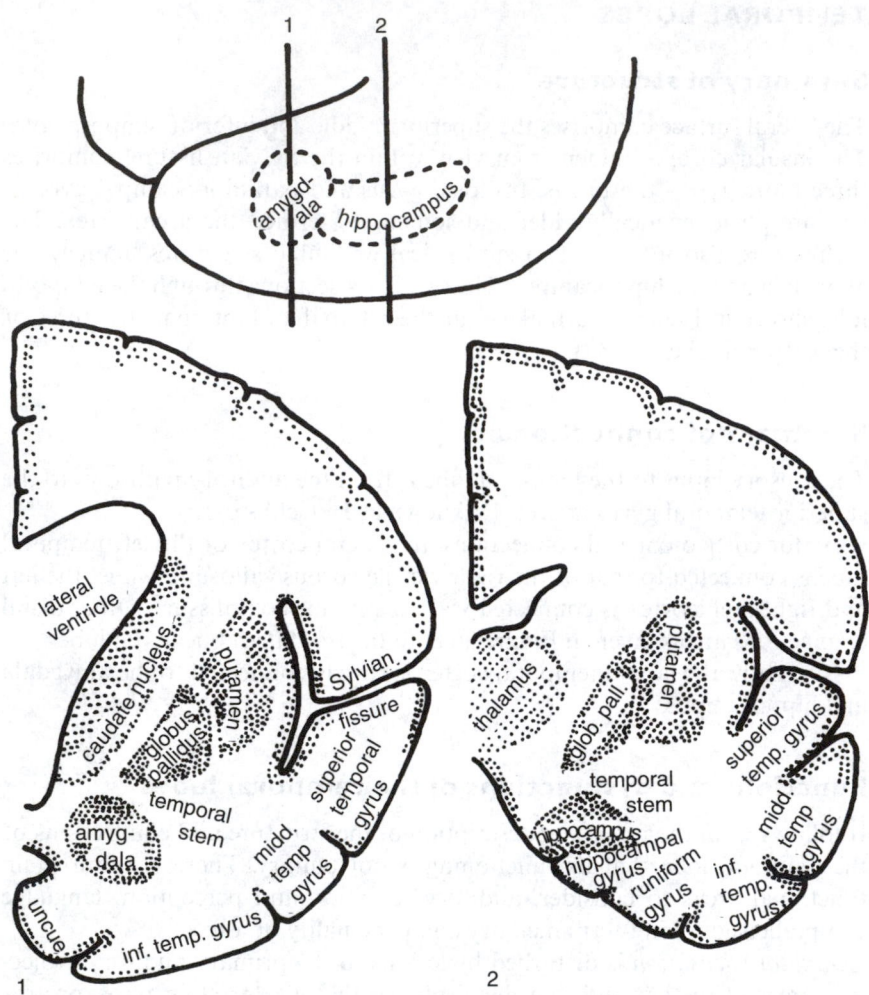

Figure 36.9 Cross-sections through the temporal lobe.

aphasia, acousticognostic aphasia, acoustico-mnestic aphasia or receptive aphasia. The precise symptoms vary according to how close the lesion is to the primary zone. Closer lesions will create disorders of the more elementary processes involved in decoding speech, whereas lesions more distant from the primary zone will create higher level semantic or symbolic processing problems. At the lowest level, there can be problems in perceiving and identifying phonemic characteristics; such patients might, for example, fail to discriminate between similar phonemes such as 'da–ta'. Further into the secondary area, the meanings of words might become obscure for patients, shown in the way they might fail to follow instructions adequately; there will be difficulties in naming objects (nominal aphasia); and recall of appropriate words can become difficult, patients often complaining of the tip-of-the-tongue phenomenon. There is naturally an effect on speech, which may become incoherent if words are used that fail to obey the rules of normal semantic relationships. There may be a more generalised deficit in the ability to organise material into meaningful classes or categories, which is related to some extent to a memory problem (Wilkins and Moscovitch, 1978).

Lesions to the posterior, tertiary portions of the temporal lobe around the angular gyrus cause special problems because the area overlaps with the tertiary zones of the occipital and parietal lobes. The understanding of single words may be perfect but there is a problem synthesising all the elements of a sentence, especially if it demands placing these elements into a logical or spatial schema (e.g. if Sam is taller than Bill and Tom is shorter than Sam, then who is the tallest?) Lesions here can also affect reading by disrupting cross-modal processing from the visual to auditory form (e.g. Luria, 1973, in his discussion of semantic aphasia).

Long-term memory is most profoundly affected when both temporal lobes are damaged in their medial or hippocampal aspects, as in bilateral temporal lobectomy for the relief of focal epilepsy (Falconer et al., 1955). The hippocampus or bitemporal syndrome is one of severe anterograde amnesia; that is, an almost complete inability to learn and retain new material. Unilateral damage to the anterior, medial or hippocampal aspects of the temporal lobe causes deficits dependent upon the site of damage. Left temporal lobectomies create a mild verbal learning and memory defect (Blakemore and Falconer, 1967; Rausch, 1981), which varies in severity in part according to the amount of hippocampus removed (Jones-Gotman and Milner, 1978). For example, patients are poor at remembering a prose passage across a delay of an hour or so, and are slow to learn lists of paired associates. Right temporal lobectomies, on the other hand, cause mild non-verbal or spatial memory defects, again varying in intensity according to the extent of hippocampal excision (Corkin, 1965; Milner, 1965). There may be difficulties in remembering faces, for example, or complex drawings or in learning routes or mazes.

Personality problems have long been associated with temporal lobe epilepsy and temporal lobe lesions. They include aggression (Falconer et al., 1955); alterations in sexual habits and desires, religiosity and paranoia (see Bear and Fedio, 1977, for a review); breakdown of a psychotic or thought disordered nature with a left site (Flor-Henry, 1969) and disturbances of emotion or emotional control with right sites (Lishman, 1968).

A general point that should be made at this juncture applies to the analysis and description of all the lobes and their functions. It is easy to talk in terms of syndromes (e.g. bi-temporal syndrome) or groups of symptoms (e.g. 'amnesia' or memory problems), and neurology and neuropsychology have made great progress by doing this. However, there is usually considerable controversy about whether syndromes exist or not and, if they do, what they comprise and what the underlying functional deficit is. An alternative to broad labels and group experiments is to analyse each case in fine detail and gradually to build a model of cognitive processes underlying observed deficits (Ellis and Young, 1988).

Tests of temporal lobe functioning

Clinical observations in the foregoing areas may all suggest the need for further neuropsychological (and psychiatric) assessment.

Dealing with memory testing: first some tests should be verbal in nature to detect left temporal involvement, such as:

- Recall of prose passages, as in the Wechsler Memory Scale-III (WMS-III; Wechsler, 1997b).
- Performance on list learning tasks, for example the Auditory-Verbal Learning Test (Schmidt, 1996) or the California Verbal Learning Test (Delis et al., 2000).
- Performance on paired associate learning tasks such as the paired associate sub-test of the WMS-III.

Conversely, some tests should be visual, spatial or non-verbal in nature to detect right temporal impairment, such as:

- Recall of a single complex design such as the Rey figure (Rey, 1959; Powell, 1979; Taylor, 1969; Corwin and Bylsma, 1993).
- Recall of progressively more complex figures such as the Visual Reproduction subtest of the WMS-III and the Benton Visual Retention Test (Benton, 1955).
- Performance on the Visual Spatial Learning Test (Malec et al., 1991).
- Memory for faces on the WMS-III or the Camden Memory Test (Warrington, 1986).

A good summary of episodic memory test is to be found in Bradley and Kapur (2003). For example, consideration should also be given to administering a behavioural memory test (e.g. Wilson et al., 2003), to asking questions that relate to autobiographical memory (Kopelman et al., 1990) or to using a self-report questionnaire (e.g. Crook and Larrabee, 1992).

There is a detailed review of language tests in Spreen and Risser (2003). They include:

- Aphasia test batteries, including the Boston Diagnostic Aphasia Examination (Goodglass et al., 2000).

- Individual naming tests, such as the Boston Naming Test (Goodglass and Kaplan, 2000) and the Graded Naming Test (Warrington, 1997).
- Variants of the Token Test in which subjects have to follow increasingly complex instructions (De Renzi and Vignolo, 1962; McNeil and Prescott, 1978).
- Reading and spelling tests, such as those included in the Wide Range Achievement Test (WRAT; Wilkinson, 1993).

THE PARIETAL LOBES

Summary of structure

From the lateral perspective, immediately behind the central fissure is the post-central gyrus (areas 1, 2, 3) followed by the superior parietal lobule (5, 7), the inferior parietal lobule (43, 40) and the angular gyrus. From a medial view, the parietal lobe comprises the posterior part of the paracentral lobule (1, 2, 3, 5) and the precuneus (7, 31).

Summary of connections

The anterior portion of the parietal lobe (areas 1, 2, 3, or the post-central gyrus) is the projection site for somatosensory information; a primary zone feeding information into the remaining parietal areas. The secondary and tertiary zones, having analysed and integrated this basic sensory data, project to the frontal and temporal cortex. Descending projections are to the basal ganglia and spinal cord.

Functions and dysfunctions of the parietal lobes

From the preceding description, it follows that the main functions of the parietal lobe are: (1) to receive and discriminate basic somatosensory data; (2) to analyse and 'perceive' such data; (3) to relate these data to auditory and visual information available from the temporal and occipital cortex; and (4) to help control bodily movements.

Somatosensory discrimination includes touch, sense of body position (kinaesthesis), pain, temperature and vibration. Increases in the threshold for these data occur only with lesions to the rolandic area in the post-central gyrus (Semmes et al., 1960; Corkin, 1964; Corkin et al., 1970), detectable on such tests as two-point discrimination, pressure sensitivity and point localisation.

Outside this primary zone, lesions produce a transient sensory loss, but disorders of tactile perception become common. The patient may display astereognosis, being the inability to identify the object manipulated in the hands whilst blindfolded (Brown, 1972; Hecaen and Albert, 1978).

With lesions to the tertiary zones, the patient can be deficient on cross-modal matching tasks (tactual–visual, visual–tactual, auditory–visual), as found by Butters and Brolly (1968), who confirmed that the ability to match auditory and visual signals is a prerequisite for reading. Finally, as for motor functions, the parietal lobe in areas 7 and 40 contributes to gross (not fine) limb movement. Therefore the apraxia (motor disorder) seen after parietal lobe lesioning tends to be confined to whole body or whole limb movements, not involving, say, fine finger or facial movements (Geschwind, 1975; Kimura, 1980). There is also a range of constructional disorders reflecting the underlying problem of understanding spatial relationships.

This four-way division of function by lobe, based on structure, does not quite do justice to the complexity of the parietal lobes, as lesions here can create a 'bewildering array' of symptoms. The common feature to this array tends to be that the task requires some kind of spatial analysis. This includes poor visual object recognition and a reduced ability to recognise objects from usual views (Warrington and Taylor, 1973). It is found rather more frequently in left than right cases (Warrington and Rabin, 1970). Other left-sided symptoms include disorders of reading or alexia; disorders of mental arithmetic, especially when problems require some spatial representation, as in the use of columns to add and subtract (Luria, 1973); and left–right orientation (Benton, 1959). Disturbances of spatial analysis also include problems of reaching and eye movement, as found in Balint's syndrome. Other signs of parietal lobe damage tend to indicate a right-sided focus, including contralateral neglect, in which the patient behaves and talks as if the left side of the body and of visual space does not exist (Battersby et al., 1956), and anosognosia (the failure to perceive illness or dysfunction). There may also be a general disturbance of body language.

Still other symptoms can be found with either left or right lesions, including the inability to draw or make up three-dimensional constructions out of sticks or cubes, termed constructional apraxia (Piercy et al., 1960). However, constructional apraxia may not be a single entity, and left and right lesion cases may fail the same constructional task but for rather different reasons (Benton, 1967): left cases because verbal analysis and motor control is deficient; right analysis because a 'spatial analysis' centre is deficient. Therefore one can conceive of an executive deficit versus a perceptual one.

Finally, the parietal lobes have a specific role to play in short-term memory, around the angular gyrus (areas 39 and 40) (Warrington and Weiskrantz, 1973).

Tests of parietal lobe function

Somatosensory perceptual function is routinely assessed by neurological examination (e.g. Strub and Black, 2000). Specific test such as the Tactile Form Recognition Test (Reitan and Wolfson, 2002) can also be used.

The ability to deal with spatial relationships can be assessed on a wide variety of tests including copying designs with blocks and doing jigsaws, as in the Block Design and Object Assembly subtests of the Wechsler Adult Intelligence Scale III (WAIS-III); copying a complex figure (Corwin and Bylsma, 1993); the copy version of the Benton Visual Retention Test (Sivan, 1992); and of course classic free drawing tasks such as asking someone to draw a person, bicycle, house, or clock face (see Lezak et al., 2004, for some scoring standardisations).

Tests of mathematical functions are included in the WAIS-III and WRAT.

Other characteristics of parietal lobe damage, such as apraxia, are more frequently detected through clinical observation and neurological examination than by any standardised tests, for example by asking the person to wave good-bye, show how to open a door with a key, stick out the tongue, blow out a match or make a sandwich (Heilman and Rothi, 2003).

THE OCCIPITAL LOBES

Summary of the structure

On the lateral surface, the occipital lobe comprises the lateral occipital gyrus and the occipital pole, merging indistinctly into the parietal and temporal lobes. On the medial surface are the cuneus and lingual gyrus, separated from the parietal lobe by the parieto-occipital fissure. The occipital lobe comprises areas 17, 18 and 19, arranged in an idiosyncratic concentric fashion (19 surrounding 18 in turn surrounding 17).

Summary of connections

Area 17 receives afferents direct from the retina along a route including the optic nerve, optic chiasm, optic tract and the lateral geniculate nucleus, and then geniculostriate radiations to the cortex. But it should be noted that visual information also reaches the tertiary visual cortex via a second pathway called the tectopulvinar system: optic nerve, superior colliculus, lateral posterior thalamus, pulvinar, areas 20 and 21. Connections radiate from the primary nucleus to the secondary area (18, or the parastriate region) and thence to the tertiary areas (19, or peristriate region). Distal connections are with the temporal lobes (inferior longitudinal tract) and frontal lobes (e.g. superior and inferior occipito-frontal tracts).

Functions of the occipital lobes

The geniculostriate system is mainly involved in the perception of form, colour and pattern, and the tectopulvinar system in locating a visual stimulus in space. Hence, the latter tends to locate objects to be analysed in detail by the former.

Lesions of any part of the geniculostriate system up to and including the primary cortical zones will produce visual field defects, such as hemianopia (blindness in the left or right visual fields) or scotomas (blind spots), which are sometimes coped with by constant tiny eye movements referred to as nystagmus.

Lesions in the secondary or tertiary areas cause higher level defects of which the visual agnosias are the most relevant here:

- Visual object agnosia: a deficit in naming, using or recognising objects presented visually in the absence of such a deficit when the same objects are presented tactually, most common after left lesions.
- Simultanagnosia (Balint's syndrome): when only one aspect of a stimulus can be perceived at any one time.
- Prosopagnosia: the inability to recognise faces, mainly found after right lesions.
- Colour agnosia and colour anomia: perhaps most related to left lesions.
- Colour imperception or achromatopsia: the inability to distinguish hues, especially after right-sided damage.
- Pure word blindness or agnosic alexia or alexia without agraphia: the inability to read words but with a retained ability to write them – a disconnection syndrome of the left hemisphere.
- Visual inattention: most commonly in the left visual field.

Tests of occipital lobe functioning

Visual field defects can be accurately mapped by a visual field analyser presenting points of light to different locations. Inattention can be picked up on tests such as the Behavioural Inattention Test (Halligan et al., 1991). The visual agnosias are usually detected by *ad hoc* tests and an analysis of performance on visual tasks in general (Damasio et al., 2000) or by inspection of performance on a battery of visual subtests, such as the Visual Object and Space Perception Battery (Warrington and James, 1991).

THE FRONTAL LOBES

Summary of structure

The frontal lobes make up one third of the mass of the cerebrum and are the newest part of the brain. The frontal lobe is divided from the parietal by the central fissure, and from the temporal lobe by the Sylvian fissure. On the lateral surface there are the superior, middle and inferior frontal gyri, which lie between the frontal pole anteriorly and the precentral gyrus posteriorly. On the medial surface is the cingulate gyrus, which follows the arched curve of the corpus callosum, and the parolfactory area surrounding the olfactory bulb. The cortex itself is often divided up into *granular* and *agranular* types, depending on whether cell layers II and IV are prominent or absent. Areas 4 and 6 and part of 8 and 44 are agranular and lie immediately anterior to the central fissure. The remaining areas are termed frontal granular cortex or pre-frontal cortex.

Summary of connections

The frontal lobes have no area receiving primary sense data, but the pre-frontal region does receive afferents from the visual, auditory and somatosensory areas, usually by way of the parietal lobe. The pre-frontal region also receives rich projections from subcortical structures, most especially the dorsomedial nucleus of the thalamus. Also importantly, the cingulate area receives afferents from the thalamus, specifically its anterior nucleus. On the efferent side, area 4 is a primary zone projecting ultimately to all muscular systems, and is hence known as the motor cortex. The pre-frontal region sends projections to parietal, temporal and cingulate cortex and to many subcortical structures, notably the basal ganglia, dorsomedial nucleus of the thalamus, amygdala, hippocampus and hypothalamus.

Functions of the frontal lobes

The broad functional divisions of the frontal lobes are shown in Figure 36.10, from the lateral perspective.

The motor strip controls movement, including, in the face area, all movements of the speech apparatus, such as the lips, tongue and pharynx, that is, a primary zone in Luria's terminology. The premotor zone, a secondary area, organises individual movement into ordered sequences (Kolb and Milner, 1981).

Lesions in and around the face area can, for example, cause dysarthria – the inability to speak rapidly and accurately or, on the reception side, to discriminate phonemes properly (Taylor, 1979). In a conceptually related manner, lesions to the frontal eye fields disrupt voluntary gaze, causing

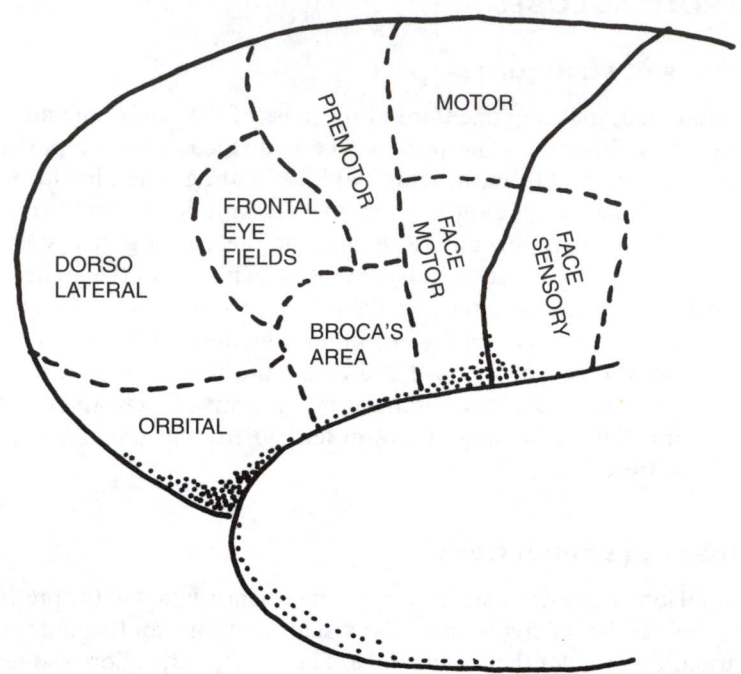

Figure 36.10 The broad functional divisions of the frontal lobes.

difficulties in the systematic searching of an array of shapes, for example (Teuber, 1964; Tyler, 1969, Guitton et al., 1982), or a disruption of the patient's scanning of a complex picture when trying to abstract the most important features (Luria, 1973). There can also be a general loss of fine movement (Kuypers, 1981) or strength (Leonard et al., 1988).

The remaining areas are tertiary, and lesion effects broadly (very broadly) fall into three categories: Broca's aphasia (44 on the left); changes in the highest of intellectual and cognitive functions (dorsolateral); and changes in personality (orbital and cingulate). In Broca's aphasia it is the expressive side of language that is most disrupted: patients can understand most words and sentences (unless they are extremely complex grammatically) but their speech is hesitant, dysfluent and ungrammatical; their writing follows suit. Repetition and reading aloud is also impaired, and in common with other aphasias, naming can be poor.

A variety of high-level intellectual and cognitive skills (i.e. executive functions) can be disrupted after dorsolateral frontal lesions, as shown in a range of classic early studies, including:

- Loss of abstract thinking or a tendency to think in a concrete fashion (Goldstein, 1944).

- Deficits in planning or problem solving, in which patients approach tasks in a haphazard trial-and-error manner (Crown, 1952) and show deficits in forming strategies (Shallice, 1982; Shallice and Evans, 1978).
- Rule breaking (Walsh, 1978; Miller, 1985).
- Poor visuo-constructional skills, related to poor planning, in which patients cannot spatially organise all the elements of the pattern to be reproduced (Luria and Tsvetkova, 1964).
- Poor error evaluation, as already suggested by poor rule-following, caused by a lack of self-monitoring or a failure of verbalisation to control action (Konow and Pribram, 1970).
- Inflexibility or rigidity, so that the patient cannot shift easily from one 'set' to another (Milner, 1964), and generally reduced spontaneity.
- Loss of verbal fluency (left-sided), where speech lacks spontaneity and is impoverished in content (adynamia or dynamic aphasia, but not a true aphasia).
- Loss of design fluency (right-sided), in which the drawing of nonsense shapes or 'doodles' is inhibited (Jones-Gotman and Milner, 1977).
- Disturbances to temporal memory (Smith and Milner, 1984; Freedman and Oscar-Berman, 1986).

Finally, as for lesions to the orbital and cingulate cortex, their effects on personality are fairly well established through studies of orbital (modified) leucotomy and cingulotomy (O'Callaghan and Carroll, 1982, provide a thorough summary; also Walsh, 1976). There is a significant reduction in the patient's appreciation of aversive emotional states, with reduced anxiety, depression and neuroticism. This can be understood by viewing the cingulate cortex as the primary cortical projection area for the 'emotional' circuits and processes of the limbic system. Naturally, if both orbital and dorsolateral cortex is destroyed, then more major personality changes occur – extreme inertia coupled with disinhibition or impulsivity is common, and this is why 'standard' leucotomy or lobotomy is no longer performed.

Tests of frontal lobe functioning

Clinical observation and neurological examination will reveal deficits in motor control. Expressive language deficits can be assessed formally on the appropriate sections of standard batteries, as set out above in the discussion of the temporal lobes. Otherwise, there is a range of broad approaches to the assessment of executive dysfunctions and the problems arising from them (Powell and Wood, 2001). The two main ones are the psychometric assessment of frontal systems and processes, and reports from self and others.

Psychometric tests include the assessment of fluency, e.g. verbal fluency on Controlled Oral Word Association (Spreen and Benton, 1977; Spreen and Strauss, 1998) or on the Word Fluency Test (Pendleton et al., 1982), or on

Design Fluency (Jones-Gotman, 1991); the ability to form rules and concepts and switch mental set, e.g. card sorting (Nelson, 1976), Rule Shift Cards Test (Wilson et al., 1996), rule attainment on the Brixton Test (Burgess and Shallice, 1997), switching between numbers and letters on the Trail Making Test (D'Eposito et al., 1996); the ability to make estimates, e.g. of various quantities on the Cognitive Estimates Test (Shallice and Evans, 1978; O'Carroll et al., 1994), of prices (Smith and Milner, 1984), and time on the Temporal Judgment Test (Wilson et al., 1996); the control of attention, e.g. the Test of Everyday Attention (Robertson et al., 1994), screening out distracting and competing information on the Stroop Test (Sachs et al., 1991), suppressing competing responses on the Hayling Test (Burgess and Shallice, 1997); and planning and organisation, e.g. using materials to achieve a given end on the Action Program Test (Wilson et al., 1996), to organise a route on the Zoo Mao Test (Wilson et al., 1996) or on the Route-Finding Task (Boyd and Sautter, 1993), to plan the order of tasks on the Six Elements Test (Wilson et al., 1996), and organising the Multiple Errands Task (Shallice and Burgess, 1991).

In addition, there is the battery of subtests comprising the Delis Kaplan Executive Function Scale (D-KEFS; Delis et al., 2001), which has subtests relating to most of the above areas, e.g. verbal fluency, design fluency and trail making.

Reports from self and others include ratings on the Dysexecutive Questionnaire (Wilson et al., 1996), the Executive Functions Scale (Coolidge and Griego, 1995) and the Frontal Systems Behaviour Scale (Grace and Malloy, 2001). In general, the standard personality, adjustment and coping scales can also be used to explore problems (e.g. Malia et al., 1995a, 1995b; Jackson et al., 1992; Kausar and Powell, 1996). Specific aspects of behaviour can also be assessed, e.g. using the Agitated Behaviour Scale (Corrigan and Bogner, 1994), the Overt Aggression Scale (Alderman et al., 1997), and the Family Assessment Device (Kreutzer et al., 1994a, 1994b).

SUBCORTICAL STRUCTURES

There are four main subcortical systems to consider: the limbic system, the basal ganglia, the thalamus and the hypothalamus.

The limbic system

The limbic system (limbic lobe or reptilian brain) is a collection of structures with a variety of functions. One of its main identifying features is the fornix, which arches underneath the corpus callosum and sweeps posteriorly round and underneath the thalamus (Figure 36.11). Papez's circuit (hippocampus to the mammillary bodies to the thalamus to the cingulate gyrus and back to the

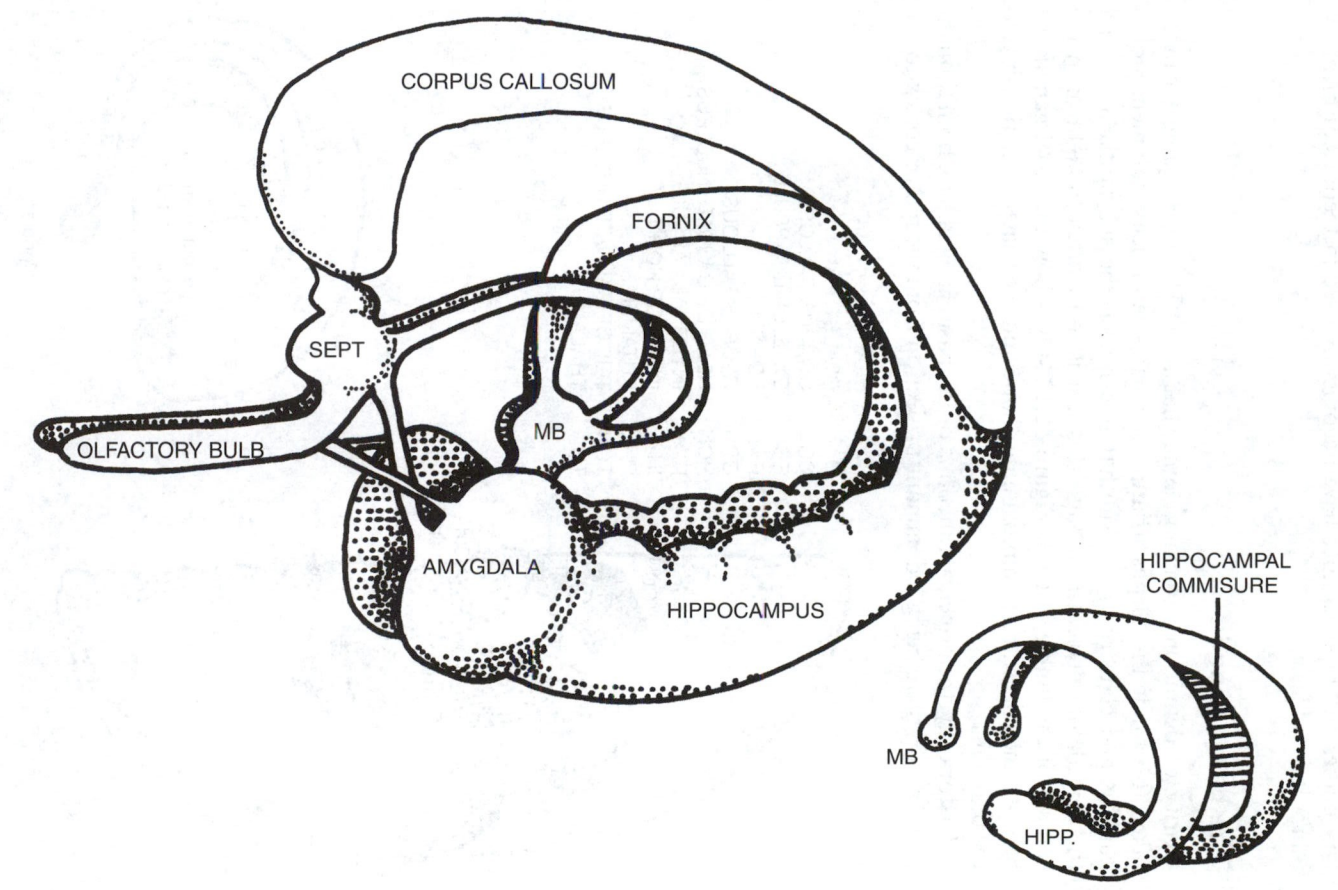

Figure 36.11 The limbic system.

hippocampus) is well known to be implicated in emotion, and the mammillary bodies and hippocampus have become involved in theories of memory, inhibition and learning.

The basal ganglia

Clarity of definition is lacking somewhat here. The basal ganglia can be taken to include the corpus striatum (i.e. caudate nucleus, putamen, globes pallidus and claustrum), the subthalamic nuclei, the substantia nigra and the amygdaloid nucleus (although this last is most often thought of in the context of the limbic system). Figure 36.12 shows how the basal ganglia lie beneath the cortex, their approximate shape and their lateral relationship to the thalamus.

Historically, the principal functions of the basal ganglia have been thought of as motor, there being a dominant projection from the motor cortex to the

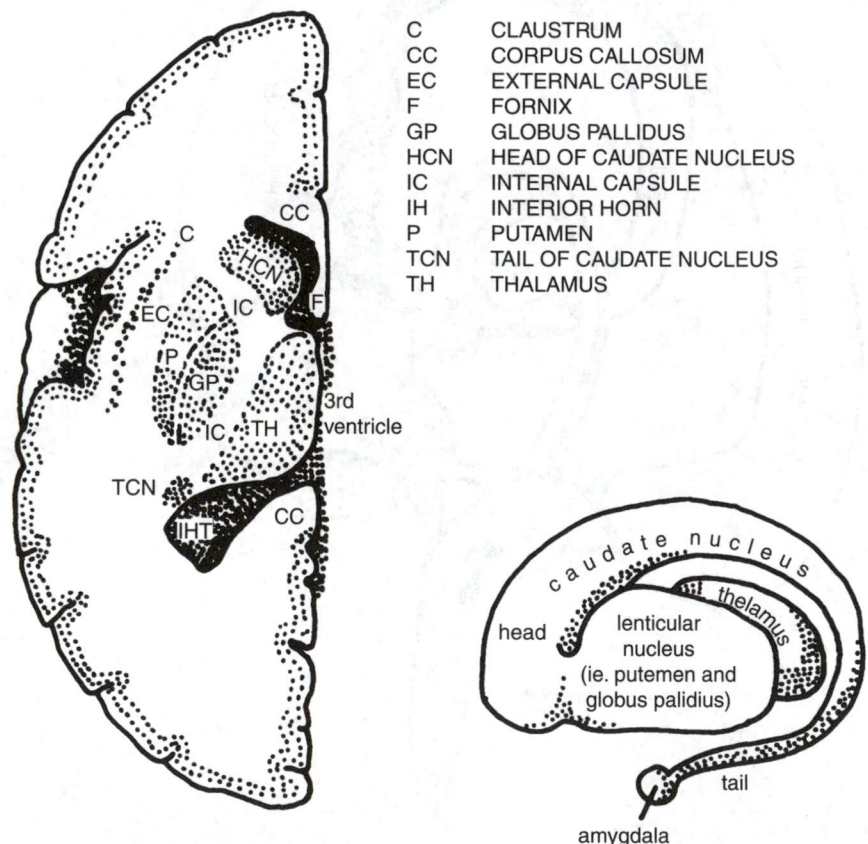

C	CLAUSTRUM
CC	CORPUS CALLOSUM
EC	EXTERNAL CAPSULE
F	FORNIX
GP	GLOBUS PALLIDUS
HCN	HEAD OF CAUDATE NUCLEUS
IC	INTERNAL CAPSULE
IH	INTERIOR HORN
P	PUTAMEN
TCN	TAIL OF CAUDATE NUCLEUS
TH	THALAMUS

Figure 36.12 The basal ganglia.

caudate nucleus and putamen. Hence, damage to the basal ganglia (as in Parkinsonism) produces changes in muscle tone and fine motor control. More recent research (Hassler, 1978) also relates these structures to sensory motor integration and motivation.

Thalamus

The thalamus, situated under the arch of the corpus callosum and fornix, lies on the medial surface of the hemispheres, its left and right portions joined by the intermediate mass. It is a massive relay station for sensory information radiating projections to all parts of the cortex as indicated in Figure 36.13.

Hypothalamus

The hypothalamus is a collection of nuclei at the base of the brain below the thalamus. It is intimately connected with the limbic system and, via the pituitary, the release of hormones. Thus it is the most important link between the neural and endocrine systems. It is divided into at least nine nuclei (pre-optic, paraventricular, anterior, supraoptic, lateral, dorsal, dorsomedial, ventromedial and posterior). Some of these nuclei and their position in the brain are indicated in Figure 36.14.

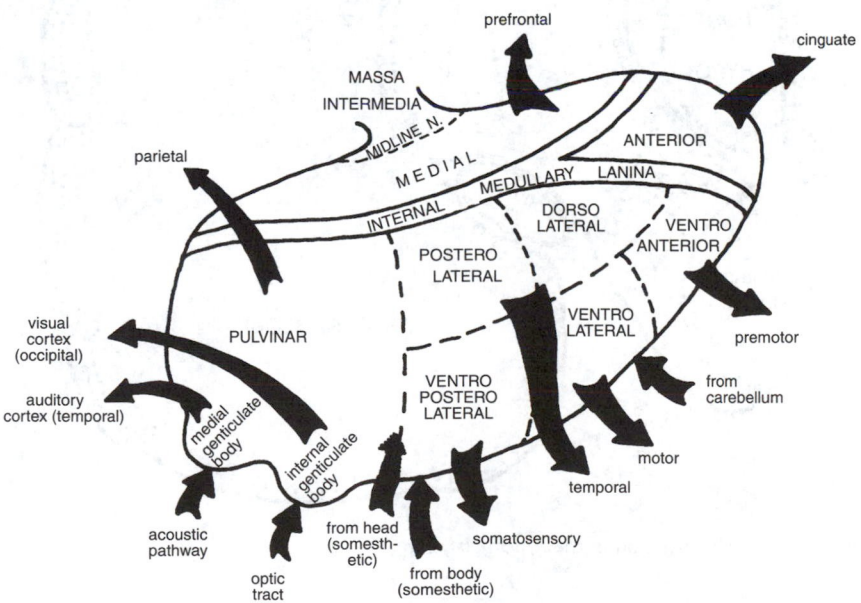

Figure 36.13 The main projections of the thalamus.

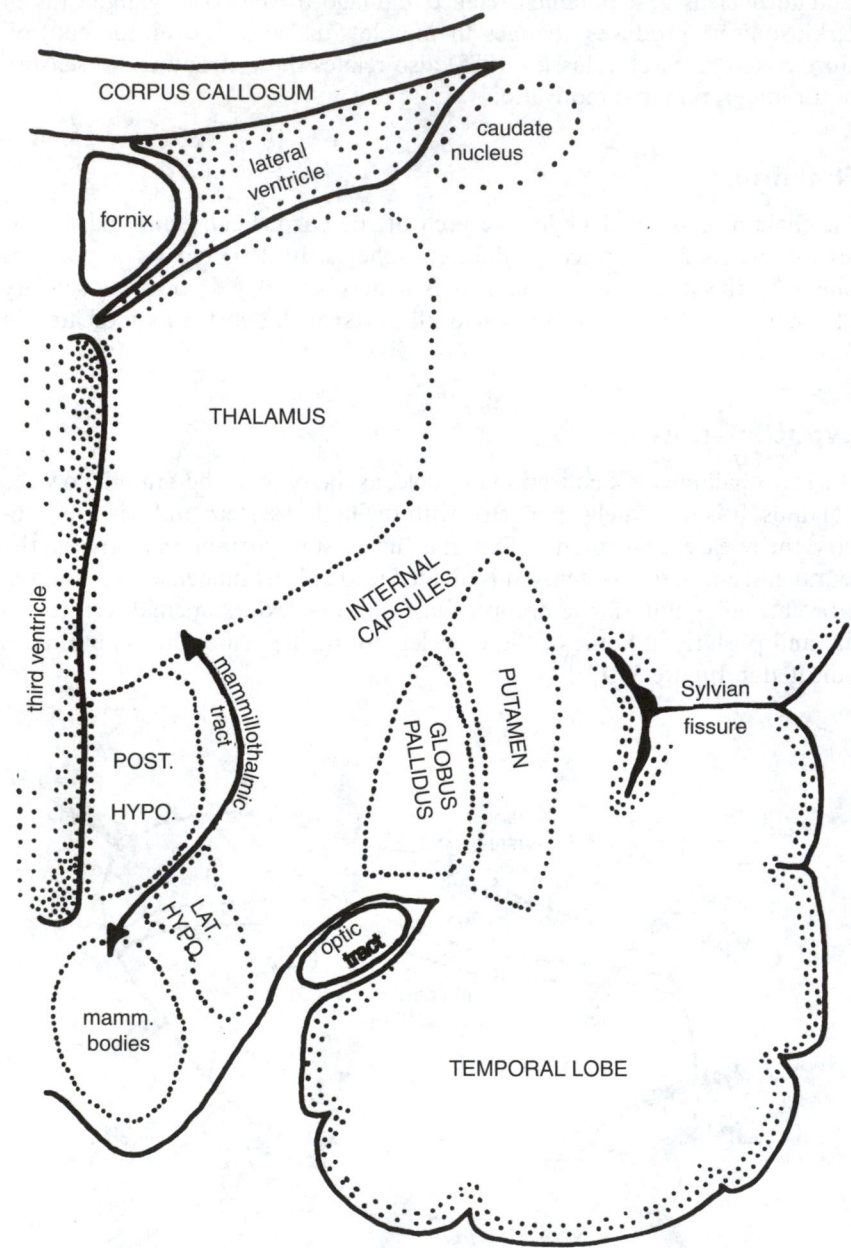

Figure 36.14 The position of the hypothalamus.

THE CLASSIFICATION OF DISORDERS

Many disorders have already been mentioned as the functions of the vertex have been described. The following subsections will complete the breakdown of functions into disorders, and terms that have not yet been introduced will be briefly described. These disorders may arise from a wide variety of aetiologies, including vascular problems (ischaemia, haemorrhage, aneurysms), head injury (closed, penetration, crushing injuries), epileptic foci, tumours (gliomas, meningioma, metastatic), infections such as meningitis and degenerative disorders such as multiple sclerosis, parkinsonism and Alzheimer's disease. The aetiology will not affect the nature of the disorder *per se*, but will relate to rate of onset, pattern of other associated symptoms and prognosis.

Disorders of movement

The general term for higher-order disorders of movement is *apraxia*: the inability to carry out purposeful movements on command in the absence of primary sensory or motor impairment. The apraxias include *ideomotor apraxia*, when the sequencing of a complex gesture is intact but each constituent element is performed badly; *ideational apraxia* when individual simple movements are intact but the sequence of a complex gesture is disordered; *constructional apraxia*, and *drawing apraxia*. Less common apraxies include melokinetic apraxia when involuntary movements of facial expression are intact but voluntary movement is impaired, *unilateral limb apraxia*, and *frontal apraxia*, the disorder involving a difficulty in initiating movements.

Lower-level movement disorders include ataxia, the failure of co-ordination or an irregularity of the flow of muscle action, often found after damage to the cerebellum; hemiplegia, the paralysis to one side of the body; paraplegia, the paralysis of the lower half of the body as after spinal cord injury; paralysis, the loss of movement or sensation in one part of the body and paresis, slight and incomplete paralysis. Abnormal movements are sometimes seen, including slow writhing movements (athetosis), involuntary jerks (chorea) and spasticity (increase in muscle tone) and intention tremor (e.g. Parkinsonism).

Disorders of language

The five basic syndromes are: Broca's aphasia, alternatively named motor, efferent motor, non-fluent, expressive or encoding aphasia; Wernicke's aphasia, sensory, acoustic-amnestic, decoding; conduction aphasia, in which it is hypothesised that the pathway between Wernicke's and Broca's area is severed to create a failure in the ability to repeat; transcortical aphasia (isolation syndrome), being the isolation of the speech circuit from remaining cortex, leading to a preserved ability to repeat but a low level of spontaneous speech and angular gyrus syndrome, in which a lesion in the parieto-occipito temporal area impairs reading and causes prominent anomic aphasic symptoms (although anomia is common in all syndromes). Global aphasia occurs when both receptive and expressive functions are affected. It should be noted that language can also be affected by subcortical lesions.

Some other terms that may be encountered are probably not true aphasias, such as dynamic aphasia (lack of spontaneous speech after pre-frontal lesions and really one aspect of a general behavioural inertia) and afferent motor aphasia (disturbed articulatory abilities caused by disrupted feedback from the speech apparatus due to a lesion in the postcentral gyrus). Language problems stemming from right or non-dominant lesions are gradually becoming recognised, including deficits of prosody and gesture (Benson, 1986).

Disorders of speech, such as oral dyspraxia (speech apraxia) and dysarthria, are discussed in Wallesch et al. (2003). Disorders of reading such as pure alexia, deep dyslexia and surface dyslexia are discussed in Hanley and Kay (2003).

The agnosias

These are disorders of higher cognitive understanding and integration in the absence of sensory loss. In the visual modality they include object agnosia, agnosia for drawings, prosopagnosia, colour agnosia, colour anomie, achromatopsia, visual–spatial agnosia and simultagnosia. In the auditory modality are amusia and agnosia for sounds. In the somatosensory mode are astereognosis, anosognosia, anosodiaphosia, autopognosia (failure to localise and name body parts), asymbolies for pain, finger agnosies, right–left disorientation and unilateral neglect.

Memory disorders

These are usually defined by aetiology or type or locus of damage. There is the bilateral hippocampal syndrome with profound anterograde amnesia across all modalities, although motor learning is rather better preserved; unilateral hippocampal (temporal) syndrome, as found after unilateral temporal lobectomy; Korsakoff syndrome resulting from severe vitamin B_1 deficiency, as found in chronic alcoholism, and consisting of an inability to lay down new memories, loss of some old memories, confabulation to 'make good' gaps in memory, meagre content in conversation and lack of insight and empathy; electroconvulsive shock syndrome when, for the treatment of severe depression, a 70–120-V AC current is passed through the temporal lobes for about 0.5 seconds, producing amnesia for the treatment and retrograde amnesia for events prior to the shock, and 2–3 weeks of anterograde amnesia, all of which can be reduced if the shock is administered unilaterally; transient global amnesia, which is temporary complete retro- and anterograde amnesia due, say, to a transient ischaemic attack; traumatic amnesia, consisting of a shrinking retrograde amnesia and a diminishing anterograde amnesia (post-traumatic amnesia; PTA); frontal amnesia, the failure of the intention to recall; dementing amnesia, the anterograde amnesia found in old age especially; and disassociative or hysterical amnesia, which is a motivated, temporary amnesia created by the secondary gain it accrues. Theories of memory and amnesia are covered by Baddeley (1990) and Baddeley et al. (2002).

The scientific literature (e.g. Mayes, 2000) also distinguishes between types of memory systems, in particular declarative or explicit memory versus non-declarative or implicit memory. Declarative memory is more open to conscious processing, such as semantic memory (memory for facts) and episodic memory (autobiographical memory). Nondeclarative memory is more unconscious in nature and includes item specific memories and procedural memory. There is also the broad distinction to be made between shorter term working memory and longer term retention processes, and between verbal memory and nonverbal/spatial memory (see Baddeley et al., 2002).

Disorders of intellect and related processing

Widespread diffuse lesions and lesions to the frontal lobe may well produce deficits that affect performance on tests of intelligence in fairly general or non-specific ways. Such deficits include slowed information processing (Gronwall, 1977; Spikman et al., 2000) and problems with attention, including difficulty focusing, dividing, switching, controlling or sustaining attention (Gentilini et al., 1989; Howieson and Lezak, 2002; van Zomeren and Spikman, 2003). Other specific deficits of reasoning have already been mentioned, e.g. disturbances to the ability to make abstractions, to organise responses, to plan solutions, to monitor one's own performance, to comprehend complex instructions, to retain appropriate amounts of material in mind while solving problems, and the complexity of problem solving that can be achieved.

Ability level is commonly classified by intelligence quotient (IQ) scores, as follows:

- Very superior   130+
- Superior   120–129
- High average   110–119
- Average   90–109
- Low average   80–89
- Borderline   70–79
- Retarded   ≤69

The use of broad IQ and index figures, e.g. IQs and indices from the

WAIS-III, can obscure specific underlying deficits, but IQ batteries can be useful in providing a range of tasks on which reasoning can be analysed and on which specific deficits can be observed, e.g. performance on verbal subtests can highlight language problems and performance on non-verbal tasks like Block Design subtest can reveal constructional problems. A knowledge of the profile across a range of subtests can also help clarify whether a low score in a particular area is due to a specific deficit as opposed to simply reflecting limited ability in general.

Ability level prior to brain injury can be estimated in a variety of ways with various advantages and disadvantages (Powell, 2000) but the common way is to use reading ability, e.g. the WTAR (Wechsler, 2001).

Disorders of emotional and related processing

It has been known for a long time that brain injury can cause changes to emotions, social behaviour and personality, in both animals and humans, but these changes have not been conveniently organised into 'syndromes' as has been achieved with language or memory disorders. As has already been mentioned, a pattern of inertia coupled with disinhibition and impulsivity is often linked with frontal injury (see the discussion of executive dysfunction, above; p 000), and a relationship between anger or aggression and temporal lesions and temporal lobe epilepsy is well known (Bear and Fedio, 1977). However, there are many more subtle emotional and related changes that are still poorly understood, including the perception of emotion in others (Tompkins and Mateer, 1985), the use of facial expression and gesture, the perception of social cues, the interpretation of social behaviour, and changes in humour (Birhle et al., 1986). In addition, the links between brain injury and frank psychiatric disorder, either of a schizophrenic/psychotic or affective/depressive in nature, are gradually being elucidated in the neuropsychiatry literature (Kopenen et al., 2002; O'Carroll, 2003).

Disorders of executive function

Executive functions are those high-level functions that enable a person to engage in purposive behaviour that helps to achieve independence and goals in life, in a controlled and self-regulated manner. There is no formal categorisation of types of dysfunction, but the various facets of the dysexecutive syndrome, impairment of executive functions (pp. 748–749), basically comprise the reduced control of cognitive processing, behaviour and emotions.

LOSS AND RECOVERY OF FUNCTION: THE EXAMPLE OF HEAD INJURY

Loss of function

Loss of function is due to several factors, including the lesion trauma itself, which halts the passage of the nerve impulse; retrograde degeneration of the axon between cell body and trauma; anterograde degeneration of the distal portion of the axon beyond the trauma site; transneuronal degeneration, being the degeneration of neurons to which the dying neuron is connected; the alteration of neurochemical pools, being an upset to nervous transmission over the whole brain; vascular disruption, such as haemorrhage; diaschisis, or the functional shock to a group of cells when they lose their afferents; oedema, or swelling of the brain, which can crush the brain against the skull; and finally raised CSF pressure or intracranial pressure, which also can compress the brain.

Recovery of function

Mechanisms of recovery of function fall into three categories, as shown in Table 36.2. A classic discussion of recovery is to be found in Finger et al. (1988).

Table 36.2 Mechanisms of recovery of function

Type of mechanism	Specific recovery mechanism
Physiological mechanisms	
Recovery from diaschisis	A diminution of the functional shock caused by deafferentation
Regeneration	Re-growth of previous connections, not seen in humans apart from random regenerative sprouting
Collateral sprouting	Neighbouring axons take over vacated synaptic sites
Re-routing	Axons seek new targets when previous ones are destroyed
Relatively ineffective/silent synapses	Pre-existing or dormant connections are innervated
Denervation supersensitivity	De-afferented tissue becomes hyper-responsive to residual connections
Nerve growth factor	Protein encouraging growth in damaged neurons and re-innervation
Structural mechanisms	
Redundancy	The same message is carried by more than one fibre

Continued

Table 36.2 Continued.

Type of mechanism	Specific recovery mechanism
Equipotentiality	The idea that (some) brain tissue is non-specific in its functions
Levels of representation	If higher level analysis is destroyed then lower level information still exists to be utilised
Substitution	The concept of a structural safety net comprising previously unused tissue
Vicaration	Substitution by adjacent area
Multiple control	Some functions are undertaken by more than one centre
Sparing	Those processes surviving damage in a specific area
Process mechanisms	
Simple functional substitution or behavioural compensation	Tasks are solved by an entirely different functional system
Re-routing	Reorganising the flow of processing to avoid a damaged area
Plasticity	An area of brain learns to perform a new task

Head injury

A good summary of neuropathology for neuropsychologists is to be found in Lezak et al. (2004), covering the effects of traumatic brain injury (TBI), vascular disorders, cortical dementias, subcortical dementias, progressive disorders of the CNS, toxic conditions, infectious processes, brain tumours, oxygen deprivation, metabolic disorders, and nutritional deficiencies.

Head injury requires a special mention: first, because it is the most common reason for loss of brain function in children and younger adults that the neuropsychologist will encounter; second, because it demonstrates very well the whole process of loss and recovery of function; and third, because it well illustrates the diversity of consequence arising from an injury to the brain.

The frequency of head injury varies considerably between countries, and estimates vary widely depending on the definitions and methodology used. In the USA it has been estimated at 300–450 per 100,000 per year overall (Kolb and Whishaw, 1990), although of these only 200–300 will be admitted to hospital (Jennett and Frankowski, 1990; Gronwall et al., 1990). The rate is about twice as high for men than for women (Kraus and Nourjah, 1989) and it peaks at more than 600 per 100,000 for young men, who are more likely to be involved in motor accidents, assaults and sporting injuries. The rate is, in general, elevated in childhood and again during old age, when falls are most likely. In total, 42% are due to road traffic accidents, 23% to falls, 14%

to assault, 6% to bicycle (not involving cars), 6% to sports and 6% to recreation activities; other causes account for 8% (Kraus and Nourjah, 1989 see also Jennett and Frankowski, 1990). Aetiology varies from centre to centre, depending on the availability of firearms, the socio-demographic characteristics of the community, the extent of alcohol abuse and so forth.

The mechanisms of head injury are well described by Stalhammar (1990) and Pang (1989). The primary injuries occur at the time of impact. In blunt injuries, there is an epidural haematoma at the site of impact, a brain contusion at the site of impact as the skull bends in and as the brain is accelerated, and brain contusions at the opposite side of the skull as the brain, having accelerated, hits and decelerates against the inside opposite surface. There are contusions as the brain is pulled over the bony protuberances and ridges on the base of the skull, causing particular damage to the poles of the frontal and temporal lobes. There are shearing and tensile strains within the white matter, as the brain rotates in relation to the head and as counter-rotational forces are set up between the two hemispheres, all causing the axons to snap or shear (diffuse axonal injury; DAI). Blood vessels also shear and bleed. There is a similar pathology in acceleration/deceleration injuries (whiplash) but without haematoma and contusion at an impact site. Severe DAI occurs in about 50% of cases of severe head injury without a mass lesion (Graham, 1996) and is often found in association with tiny (petechial) haemorrhages. In penetration injuries (Roy and Cooper, 1990), one has to distinguish between high-velocity military weapons, and civilian small-calibre, low-muzzle-velocity bullets, the former being 'incompatible with survival'. There is laceration and tearing along the track of both brain tissue and blood vessels and an instant rise in intracranial pressure as shock waves spread out, again causing contusion and haemorrhage at distal sites. The secondary effects of the brain injury can be due to lack of oxygen to the brain (hypoxic and ischaemic or hypotensive ischaemia) caused by damage to other organs, inadequate blood supply to the brain as blood pressure drops, raised intracranial pressure, brain swelling, the development of space-occupying lesions by way of haematomas, and the results of infection, especially in penetrating injuries. There are tertiary changes to metabolism and degenerative changes in the white matter.

The severity of the brain injury is often measured by the length of post-trauma amnesia (10 minutes = very mild; 10–60 minutes = mild; 1–24 hours = moderate, 1–7 days = severe, > 7 days = very severe, > 4 weeks = extremely severe). The depth of unconsciousness is often measured on the Glasgow Coma Scale (GCS; Teasdale and Jennett, 1974). The best eye opening is rated on a scale 1–4, the best motor response 1–6, and the best verbal response 1–5, which yields scores ranging from 3 to 15. In terms of severity, 3–5 is very severe, 6–8 severe, 9–12 moderate, and 13–15 is mild (this is the worst GCS score on the first day). Persons scoring 8 or below are considered to be unconscious.

Outcome, which is correlated negatively with initial severity, is often grossly measured by the Glasgow Outcome Scale (GOS; Jennett and Bond, 1975) in which 1 = death, 2 = persistent vegetative state, 3 = severe disability, i.e. relying on help at least once every 24 hours, 4 = moderate disability and 5 = good recovery and ability to return to work. As an example of outcome, after severe injury, 40% die, 5% are left in vegetative state, 10% have severe disability, 20% moderate disability and 25% make a good recovery (Levin et al., 1990). After moderate injury, 38% make a good recovery and 49% have a moderate disability. After mild injury, 78% make a good recovery and 22% have a moderate disability.

Many of the details of recovery and residual effects are given in Lezak et al. (1989). There are many subtle effects and repercussions even when an apparently good recovery has been made. For example, Brooks et al. (1986) found, in a 5-year follow-up, that 74% of patients who had had severe injury complain of some personality change, and 50% of mood change, irritability and temper; the reports of memory problems and fatigability are nearly as high. Even mild head injury has a pronounced effect. At 1 month after mild injury Dikmen et al. (1986) report that nearly 40% of patients are not yet working properly, over 50% have headaches, over 60% are fatigued, over 70% are irritable and over 50% have memory and anxiety problems. One has to be cautious, though, in interpreting results on the effects of mild head injury because this category contains a disproportionate number of those persons suspected of malingering after trivial head injury to achieve some sort of secondary benefit, e.g. financial gain, to avoid a return to a stressful situation or to gain attention. This is related to the general issue of why some people show or report persisting problems after a mild TBI, i.e. the post-concussion syndrome, which may reflect the search for secondary gain but may also reflect vulnerability factors (Richardson, 2000), or a complex interaction between these two factors (Halligan et al., 2003).

THE PROCESS OF NEUROPSYCHOLOGICAL ASSESSMENT

Purpose

Neuropsychological assessment aims to assess behaviour in its broadest sense, i.e. cognition (receptive functions, memory and learning, thinking, expressive functions), emotion and executive functions, so as to arrive ultimately at a robust and meaningful formulation, understanding, of the neurobehavioural disability (e.g. see Wood and McMillan, 2001). Neuropsychological testing is undertaken for a variety of reasons and the exact nature of the tests given will be dictated by the precise purpose. Such purposes include:

- to detect organic impairment

- to localise the site of organic lesioning
- to aid diagnosis
- to assess the current level of functioning so as to detect deterioration and to give a descriptive basis for rehabilitation
- to yield research data on the mechanisms of a dysfunction
- to give a baseline against which degree of recovery can be judged
- to make a prediction as to whether a particular surgical intervention, such as a temporal lobectomy, should take place.

Testing without a reasonable purpose is pointless, and it is up to the clinical neuropsychologist to decide what is reasonable. The history, principles and practice of neuropsychological assessment are well described in Spreen and Strauss (1998) and Lezak et al. (2004).

The basic procedure

Neuropsychological testing begins with a clear statement of purpose. Next come the screening observations, which include:

- reading the notes (Table 36.3)
- observing the client (Table 36.4)
- interviewing the client (Table 36.5)
- giving various psychometric tests, as have been described throughout this chapter (Table 36.6)
- obtaining information from others, e.g. reading statements, accounts of interviews with others, direct interviewing of others, questionnaires completed by family or significant others.

Psychometric tests and questionnaires will have been standardised to a greater or lesser degree, e.g. on an appropriate population, and with the derivation of its statistical properties such as the appropriate types of reliability and validity (Powell, 2000; Willmes, 2003).

Assessment for rehabilitation purposes

For rehabilitation purposes, the assessment as given in Table 36.7 must make a clear statement of the strengths and weaknesses of the person; not just what he or she cannot do, but what he or she can do. For example, there is little point in embarking on an image-mediated memory therapy programme if the individual's ability to form visual images is minimal; and there is little point in setting up a visual symbol system for an aphasic client if he or she also has spatial agnosia problems. The examination, then, of cognitive strengths and weaknesses will determine the gross strategy of the treatment.

Table 36.3 Checklist of background information to be collected from the client

Type of information	Examples
Purpose of the investigation	
Demographic variables	Age
	Sex
	Handedness
	Education
	Profession
	Previous brain injuries
	Brief medical history
Results of previous investigations	Neurological examination
	Previous psychology tests
	EEG and EPs
	AEG
	CAT
	MRI
	Functional imaging
	Angiogram
	X-rays
	Biochemical tests
	Previous diagnosis
History of the lesion	Site of trauma
	Age at which damage occurred
	Time since lesion occurred
	History of seizures
	History of anoxia
	Length of unconsciousness
	History of retrograde amnesia
	Post-traumatic amnesia
	Neurological signs
	Nature of lesion
	Reports from any operations
	History of any cognitive defects
	History of any emotional, behavioural, social changes
Factors affecting testing	Drug levels
	Recent seizure activity
	Mood and motivation
	Relevant deficits, such as visual or motor problems, that might interfere with other tests
	Effort
	Mental health status

Table 36.4 Checklist of observations to make on the client during general interaction and testing

Type of observation	Examples
Motor behaviour	Tics and mannerisms, limb weaknesses
	Awkward gaits and limps
	Tremor
	Awkwardness of movement (clumsiness, jerkiness, slowness)
	Writing ability
	Handedness
Language	Amount of speech
	Volume and prosody of speech
	Understanding of verbal instructions
	Unusual structure of speech (e.g. telegraphese and agrammatism)
	Unusual content of speech (word-finding difficulties, neologisms, paraphasia)
	Difficulties of pronunciation (oral apraxias, dysarthrias)
Memory	Orientation in time and place (e.g. age, date, hospital)
	Recall of instructions
	Recall of therapist's name
	Recall of what had occurred in the session
	Recall of recent history
Style of performance	Self-talk, self-instruction
	Haphazard vs. systematic performance
	Persistence
	Concentration
	Error checking
	Speed
	Concreteness in abstract tasks
	Perseveration
Spatial and visual awareness	Neglect of one side of body or environment
	Confusions of left or right orientation
	Attendance to only one side of tasks
	Whether glasses are used
	Viewing material from odd angles
	Holding material close to the eyes
	Failure to recognise objects
Personality	Activity level (lethargic or fatigued to overactive)
	Anxiety level
	Mood
	Extraversion (withdrawn versus friendly)
	Inappropriateness (e.g. over-familiarity)
	Overt psychiatric symptoms
	Impulsiveness
	Insight into deficits

Table 36.5 Examples of questions to ask the patient (and a close informant if possible)

Type of question	Examples
General questions to get the patient talking	How has the injury affected your life? How has it changed you? What problems have cropped up?
Work	How has it affected your employment? Do you find work more difficult? Do you become tired easily? Do you find it hard learning new things? Do you feel under pressure?
Social	What do you do in your spare time with friends? Do you have many friends? Do you meet new people? Do you find you have lost friends? Do you have any worries about people? Do you get anxious in company? about what?
Personality	Do you enjoy some things? Do you get really low sometimes? Do you lack energy? What sort of person are you? How do others see you?

Motor	Do you have any problems with:
	  walking?
	  moving?
	  co-ordinating?
	  clumsiness?

Language	Do you have to ask people to repeat things? Do you get stuck in conversations for something to say? Do you find words just won't come out? Do you stumble over pronouncing words?
Memory	What sort of things do you forget? How are you at learning things? Do you remember facts?
Spatial	Do you bump into things you didn't notice? Do you get confused looking at pictures? Do you get left and right mixed up? Do you get lost when going somewhere?
Executive	How do you cope when there are lots of things to do? How are you at deciding what to do and how to get things done? Are there any changes in the way you interact with people? Do you plan ahead in the same way that you used to?
Capacity to manage own affairs	Tell me about your financial situation Tell me about your income and expenditure How do you organise your budget When do you need advice and who do you seek it from? What plans have you got if you receive a lump sum of compensation?

Targets	Over the last month, what problems have you had to worry about?
	In the coming week or so, is there anything to do that you are worrying about?
	What are the most important things that you cannot do?
	Where shall we start?

Table 36.6 Typical protocol for a clinical neuropsychological assessment and report

Aspect of protocol	Examples
Aims	The purpose of the assessment, e.g. to describe deficits, monitor improvement, inform rehabilitation planning, address certain specific issues
Background of patient	Information relevant to the interpretation of test findings, e.g. language, handedness, age, educational history, occupational history, medical and psychiatric history
Nature of the brain injury	Time since injury, age at injury, mechanisms of injury, retrograde amnesia, loss of consciousness, post-traumatic amnesia, results of neurological examination, results of scans
Behaviour and mental state	Motivation, co-operation with procedures, anxiety, mood, mental health, medication any aspect that threatens reliability or validity, a clear statement as to whether or not reliability has been compromised
Intelligence	Verbal subtests as appropriate, non-verbal subtests as appropriate (overall IQ scores are not necessarily helpful), skills profile
Speed	Verbal, non-verbal, motor
Attention and concentration	Verbal/spatial tasks
	General behaviour
	Lapses on tests
Memory	Verbal/non-verbal
	Immediate/delayed recall
	Learning
Language	Reading
	Screening tests for dysphasia
	Aphasia battery if needed
Constructional skills	Refer to performance subtests
	Specific tests, e.g. copying a complex figure
Sensory deficits	Note gross deficits and subjective account
	Record problems noted on tests
	Refer to neurological examination
	Tests of spatial neglect
	Tests of visual agnosia

Continued

Table 36.6 Continued.

Aspect of protocol	Examples
Motor deficits	Note gross problems and subjective accounts Record problems noted on tests Refer to neurological examination Tests of apraxia Tests of manual dexterity as needed
Executive functions	Fluency, planning, estimation Personality/behaviour Record dysexecutive problems noted on other tests Self-report scales
Life situation	Way of life, typical day, leisure activities Nature and amount of any support Impact of deficits on everyday living Relationships Ability to manage own affairs
Interview with other informant	An observer's account of deficits, changes, coping, etc. Questionnaires filled in by significant others
Formulation	A coherent account of the injury and its repercussions, taking all information into account, focusing on the aims of the assessment

Next, the assessment should pinpoint specific targets for treatment; that is, translate the observed cognitive defect (e.g. 'a spatial memory problem') into real-life goals (e.g. the ability to remember the route to the toilets). This must of necessity involve forward planning; what type of environment will the client be moving to and what will be the most important requirements? Such forward planning must also take into account 'environmental' problems, such as shortages of suitable placements or restrictions of financial resources.

The issue of ecological validity i.e. the ability of psychometric tests to predict everyday or real life, is taken up by Lezak et al. (2004) and extensively by Sbordone and Long (1996). Lezak points out the strong relationship between psychometric test scores and diagnosis, imaging data, employability, treatment outcome and ability to perform activities of daily living.

Finally, the assessment must describe the client as a person: his or her aims, aspirations, personal difficulties, priorities, motivation and fears. It is the person being rehabilitated, not a collection of neuropsychological terms.

The report

Neuropsychological reports usually contain: a section on usual demographic variables; a statement of purpose including an outline of who the report is prepared for; details of the patient's educational record; details of the patient's occupational record; sources of information (e.g. interview and test of the

Table 36.7 Factors to be taken into account in regard to rehabilitation

Factor	Example
Areas of brain damaged	
Functions disrupted	
Probability of spontaneous recovery of these functions	
Areas of brain intact	
Functions intact	
Factors that might affect progress on a rehabilitation programme	Insight Motivation Social and interpersonal behaviour Neurotic and psychiatric disorder
Physical factors influencing the design of a rehabilitation programme	Ambulatory skills
Environmental factors influencing the outcome of a rehabilitation programme	Attitude of spouse Attitude of previous employer Local state of unemployment and jobs available Financial restrictions

patient, interview with relative, other reports available); a description of the accident/injury; a history of effects and treatment; a summary of previous tests; test-taking behaviour; present cognitive test results; personality; psychological state (e.g. the presence of associated or concurrent depression or post-traumatic stress disorder); comments and conclusions; prognosis or implications for treatment or management, for a return to work or productivity, and for regaining the capacity to manage financial and legal affairs if such capacity has been compromised.

REFERENCES

Alderman, N., Knight, C. and Morgan, C. (1997) Use of a modified version of the Overt Aggression Scale in the measurement and assessment of aggressive behaviour following brain injury. *Brain Injury*, 11, 503–523.

Baddeley, A. D. (1990) *Human Memory: Theory and Practice*. Hove, UK: Lawrence Erlbaum Associates.

Baddeley, A. D., Kopelman, M. D. and Wilson, B. A. (eds) (2002) *The Handbook of Memory Disorders*. Chichester: John Wiley.

Battersby, W. S., Ender, M. B., Pollack, M. and Kahn, R. L. (1956) Unilateral 'spatial agnosia' ('inattention') in patients with cerebral lesions. *Brain*, 79, 68–93.

Bear, D. M. and Fedio, P. (1977) Quantitative analysis of interictal behaviour in temporal lobe epilepsy. *Archives of Neurology*, 34, 454–467.

Benson, D. F. (1986) Aphasia and lateralization of language. *Cortex*, 22, 71–86.

Benton, A. L. (1955) *The Visual Retention Test*. New York: Psychological Corporation.

Benton, A. L. (1959) *Right–left Discrimination and Finger Localization*. New York: Hoeber Medical/Harper Row.

Benton, A. L. (1962) The visual retention test as a constructional praxis task. *Confina Neurologica*, 22, 141–155.

Benton, A. L. (1967) Constructional apraxia and the minor hemisphere. *Confina Neurologia*, 29, 1–16.

Benton, A. L. (1968) Differential behavioural effects in frontal lobe disease. *Neuropsychologia*, 6, 53–60.

Birhle, A., Brownell, H. H., Powellson, J. A and Gardner, H. (1986) Comprehension of humorous and non-humorous materials by left and right brain-damaged patients. *Brain and Cognition*, 5, 185–203.

Boyd, T. M. and Sautter, S. W. (1993) Route-finding, a measure of everyday executive functioning in the head-injured adult. *Applied Cognitive Psychology*, 7, 171–181.

Blakemore, C. B. and Falconer, M. A. (1967) Long-term effects of anterior temporal lobectomy on certain cognitive functions. *Journal of Neurology, Neurosurgery and Psychiatry*, 30, 364–367.

Bradley, V. and Kapur, N. (2003) Neuropsychological assessment of memory disorders. In: P. W. Halligan, U. Kischka and J. C. Marshall (eds) *Handbook of Clinical Neuropsychology*. Oxford: Oxford University Press.

Brooks, N., Campsie, L., Symington, C., Beanie, A. and McKinley, W. (1986) The five-year outcome of severe blunt head injury: a relative's view. *Journal of Neurology, Neurosurgery and Psychiatry*, 49, 764–770.

Brown, J. (1972) *Aphasia, Apraxia and Agnosia*. Springfield, IL: Charles C. Thomas.

Burgess, P. W. and Shallice, T. (1997) *The Hayling and Brixton Tests*. Bury St Edmunds, UK: Thames Valley Test Company Limited.

Butters, N, and Brolly, B. A. (1968) The role of the left parietal lobe in the mediation of intra-and cross-modal associations. *Cortex*, 4, 328–343.

Coolidge, F. L. and Griego, J. A. (1995) Executive function of the frontal lobes: psychometric properties of a self-rating scale. *Psychological Reports*, 77, 24–26.

Corkin, S. H. (1964) Somesthetic function after cerebral damage in man. Doctoral thesis, McGill University, Canada.

Corkin, S. (1965) Tactually-guided maze learning in man: effects of unilateral and bilateral hippocampal lesions. *Neuropsychologia*, 3, 339–351.

Corkin, S. B., Milner, B. and Rasmussen, T. (1970) Somatosensory thresholds. *Archives of Neurology*, 23, 41–58.

Corrigan, J. D. and Bogner, J. A. (1994) Factor Structure of the Agitated Behaviour Scale. *Journal of Clinical and Experimental Neuropsychology*, 16, 386–392.

Corwin, J. and Bylsma, F. W. (1993) Commentary on Rey and Osterrieth. *The Clinical Neuropsychologist*, 7, 15–21.

Crook, T. H. and Larrabee, G. J. (1992) Normative data on a self-rating scale for evaluating memory in everyday life. *Archives of Clinical Neuropsychology*, 7, 41–45.

Crown, S. (1952) An experimental study of psychological changes following prefrontal lobotomy. *Journal of General Psychology*, 47, 3–41.

Damasio, A. R., Tranel, D. and Rizzo, M. (2000) Disorders of complex visual processing. In: M-M. Mesulam (ed) *Principles of Behavioural and Cognitive Neurology, 2nd edn*. New York: Oxford University Press.

Delis, D. C., Kaplan, E., Kramer, J. H. and Ober, B. A. (2000) *California Verbal Learning Test, 2nd edn (CVLT-II) Manual,* San Antonio, TX: Psychological Corporation.

Delis, D. C., Kaplan, E. and Kramer, J. H. (2001) *Delis–Kaplan Executive Function Scale.* San Antonio, TX: Psychological Corporation.

De Renzi, E. and Vignolo, L. A. (1962) The token test: a sensitive test to detect receptive disturbances in aphasics. *Brain,* 85, 665–678.

D'Esposito, M., Alexander, M. P. and Fisher, R. (1996) Recovery of memory and executive function following anterior communicating artery aneurysm. *Journal of the International Neuropsychological Society,* 2, 565–570.

Dikmen, S., McLean, A. and Temkin, N. (1986) Neuropsychologies and psychological consequences of minor head injury. *Journal of Neurology, Neurosurgery and Psychiatry,* 49, 1227–1232.

Ellis, A. W. and Young, A. W. (1988) *Human Cognitive Neuropsychology.* Hove, UK: Lawrence Erlbaum Associates.

Falconer, M. A., Hill, D., Meyer, A., Mitchell, W. and Pond, D. A. (1955) Treatment of temporal-lobe epilepsy by temporal lobectomy: a survey of findings and results. *Lancet,* 1, 827–837.

Finger, S., LeVere, T. E., Almli, C. R. and Stein. D. G. (eds) (1988) *Brain Injury and Recovery: Theoretical and Controversial Issues.* New York: Plenum Press.

Flor-Henry, P. (1969) Psychosis and temporal lobe epilepsy: a controlled investigation. *Epilepsia,* 10, 363–388.

Freedman, M. and Oscar-Berman, M. (1986) Bilateral frontal lobe disease and selective delayed response deficits in humans. *Behavioural Neuroscience,* 100, 337–342.

Gentilini, M., Nichelli, P. and Schoenhuber, R. (1989) Assessment of attention in mild head injury. In: H. S. Levin, H. M. Eisenberg and A. L. Benton (eds) *Mild Head Injury.* New York: Oxford University Press.

Geschwind, N. (1975) The apraxias: neural mechanisms of disorders of learned movement. *American Scientist,* 63, 188–195.

Goldstein, K. (1944) Mental changes due to frontal lobe damage. *Journal of Psychology,* 17, 187–208.

Goodglass, H. and Kaplan, E. (1972) *The Assessment of Aphasia and Related Disorders.* Philadelphia: Lea and Febiger.

Goodglass, H. and Kaplan, E. (2000) *Boston Naming Test.* Philadelphia: Lippincott.

Goodglass, H., Kaplan, E. and Barresi, B. (2000) *The Boston Diagnostic Aphasia Examination.* Philadelphia: Lippincott.

Grace, J. and Malloy, P. F. (2001) *Frontal Systems Behaviour Scale.* Lutz, FL: Psychological Assessment Resources.

Graham, D. I. (1996) Neuropathology of head injury. In: R. K. Narayan (ed) *Neurotrauma.* New York: McGraw-Hill.

Gronwall, D. (1977) Paced auditory serial addition task: a measure of recovery from concussion. *Perceptual and Motor Skills,* 44, 367–373.

Gronwall, D., Wrighton, P. and Waddell, P. (1990) *Head injury: The Facts.* Oxford: Oxford University Press.

Guitton, D., Buchtal, H. A. and Douglas, R. M. (1982) Disturbances of voluntary saccadic eye-movement mechanisms following discrete unilateral frontal lobe removals. In: G. Lennerstrand, D. S. Lee and E. L. Kelley (eds) *Functional Basis of Ocular Motility Disorders*. Oxford: Pergamon Press.

Halligan, P. W., Cockburn, J. and Wilson, B. A. (1991) The behavioural assessment of visual neglect. *Neuropsychological Rehabilitation*, 1, 5–32.

Halligan, P. W., Bass, C. and Oakley, D. A. (eds) (2003) *Malingering and Illness Deception*. Oxford: Oxford University Press.

Hanley, J. R. and Kay, J. (2003) Neuropsychological assessment and treatment of disorders of reading. In: P. W. Halligan, U. Kischka and J. C. Marshall (eds) *Handbook of Clinical Neuropsychology*. Oxford: Oxford University Press.

Hassler, R. (1978) Striatal control of locomotion, intentional actions and integrating and perceptive activity. *Journal of Neurological Science*, 36, 187–224.

Hecaen, H. and Albert, M. L. (1978) *Human Neuropsychology*. New York: John Wiley.

Heilman, K. M. and Rothi, L. J. G. (2003) Apraxia. In: K. M. Heilman and E. Valenstein (eds) *Clinical Neuropsychology, 4th edn*. New York: Oxford University Press.

Howieson, D. B. and Lezak, M. D. (2002) Separating memory from other cognitive problems. In: A. Baddeley, M. D. Kopelman and B. A. Wilson (eds) *Handbook of Memory Disorders, 2nd edn*. Chichester: John Wiley.

Jackson, H. F., Hopewell, C. A. and Glass, C. A. (1992) The Katz Adjustment Scale: Modification for use with victims of traumatic brain and spinal injury. *Brain Injury*, 6, 109–127.

Jennett, B. and Bond, M. (1975) Assessment of outcome after severe brain damage. *Lancet:* 480–484.

Jennett, B. and Frankowski, R. F. (1990) The epidemiology of head injury. In: R. Braakman (ed) *Handbook of Clinical Neurology, Vol. 13(57): Head Injury*. Amsterdam: Elsevier Science Publishers.

Jones-Gotman, M. (1991) Localisation of lesions by neuropsychological testing. *Epilepsia*, 32, 541–552

Jones-Gotman, M. and Milner, B. (1977) Design fluency: the invention of nonsense drawings after focal cortical lesions. *Neuropsychologia*, 15, 653–674.

Jones-Gotman, M. and Milner, B. (1978) Right temporal lobe contribution to image mediated verbal teaming. *Neuropsychologia*, 16, 61–71.

Kausar, R. and Powell, G. E. (1996) Subjective burden on carers of patients with neurological problems as a consequence of precise objective symptoms (objective burden). *Clinical Rehabilitation*, 10, 159–165.

Kimura, D. (1980) Neuromotor mechanisms in the evolution of human communication. In: H. D. Steklis and M. J. Raleigh (eds) *Neurobiology of Social Communication in Primates: An Evolutionary Perspective*. New York: Academic Press.

Kolb, B. and Milner, B. (1981) Performance of complete earm and facial movements after focal brain lesions. *Neuropsychologie*, 19, 505–514.

Kolb, B. and Whishaw, I. Q. (1980) *Fundamentals of Human Neuropsychology*. San Francisco: W. H. Freeman.

Kolb, B. and Whishaw, I. Q. (1990) *Fundamentals of Human Neuropsychology, 3rd edn*. New York: Freeman and Company.

Konow, A. and Pribram, K. H. (1970) Error recognition and utilization produced by injury to the frontal cortex in man. *Neuropsychologia*, 8, 489–491.

Kopelman, M. D., Wilson, B. A. and Baddeley, A. D. (1990) *The Autobiographical Memory Interview*. Bury St Edmunds, UK: Thames Valley Test Company.

Kopenen, S., Taiminen, T. and Portin, R. (2002) Axis I and II psychiatric disorders after traumatic brain injury: A 30-year-follow up study. *American Journal of Psychiatry*, 159, 1315–1321.

Kraus, J. F. and Norjah, A. P. (1989) The epidemiology of mild head injury. In: H. S. Levin, H. M. Eisenberg and A. L. Benton (eds) *Mild Head Injury*. New York: Oxford University Press.

Kreutzer, J. S., Gervasio, A. M. and Camplair, P. S. (1994a) Patient correlates of caregivers' distress and family functioning after traumatic brain injury. *Brain Injury*, 8, 211–230.

Kreutzer, J. S., Gervasio, A. M. and Camplair, P. S. (1994b) Primary caregivers' psychological status and family functioning after traumatic brain injury. *Brain Injury*, 8, 197–210.

Kuypers, H. G. J. M. (1981) Anatomy of the descending pathways. In: V. B. Brooks (ed) *The Nervous System, Handbook of Physiology, Vol. 2*. Baltimore: Williams and Wilkins.

Leonard, G., Jones, L. and Milner, B. (1988) Residual impairment in handgrip strength after unilateral frontal-lobe lesions. *Neuropsychologia*, 26, 5554.

Levin, H. S., Hamilton, W. J. and Grossman, R. G. (1990) Outcome after head injury. In: R. Braakman (ed) *Handbook of Clinical Neurology, Vol. 13(57): Head Injury*. Amsterdam: Elsevier Science Publishers.

Lezak, M. (ed) (1989) *Assessment of the Behavioural Consequences of Head Trauma*. New York: Alan R. Liss Inc.

Lezak, M. D., Howieson, D. B. and Loring, D. W. (2004) *Neuropsychological Assessment, 4th edn*. Oxford: Oxford University Press.

Lishman, W. A. (1968) Brain damage in relation to psychiatric disability after head injury. *British Journal of Psychiatry*, 114, 37310.

Luria, A. R. (1966) *Higher Cortical Function in Man*. New York: Basic Books.

Luria, A. R. (1973) *The Working Brain*. London: Penguin.

Luria, A. R. and Tsvetkova, L. D. (1964) The programming of constructive activity in local brain injuries. *Neuropsychologia*, 2, 95–108.

Malec, J. F., Ivnik, R. J. and Hinkeldey, N. S. (1991) Visual Spatial Learning Test. *Psychological Assessment*, 3, 82–88.

Malia, K., Powell, G. E. and Torode, S. (1995a) Coping as psychosocial function after brain injury. *Brain Injury* 9, 607–618.

Malia, K., Powell, G. E. and Torode, S. (1995b) Personality and psychosocial function after brain injury. *Brain Injury*, 9, 697–712.

Mayes, A. R. (2000) The neuropsychology of memory. In: G. E. Berrios and J. R. Hodges (eds) *Memory Disorders in Psychiatric Practice*. Cambridge: Cambridge University Press.

McNeil, M. R. and Prescott, T. E. (1978) *Revised Token Test*. Baltimore: University Park Press.

Miller, L. (1985) Cognition risk taking after frontal or temporal lobectomy I. The synthesis of fragmented vial information. *Neuropsychologia*, 23, 359–369.

Milner, B. (1964) Some effects of frontal lobectomy in man. In: J. M. Warren and K. Akert (eds) *The Frontal Granular Cortex and Behaviour*. New York: McGraw-Hill.

Milner, B. (1965) Visually-guided maze learning in man: effects of bi-lateral hippocampal, bilateral frontal, and unilateral cerebral lesion. *Neuropsychologia*, 3, 317–338.

Nelson, H. E. (1976) A modified card sorting test sensitive to frontal lobe defects. *Cortex*, 12, 313–324.

O'Callaghan, M. A. J. and Carroll, D. (1982) *Psychosurgery: A Scientific Analysis.* Lancaster: MTP Press.

O'Carroll, R. (2003) The clinical presentation of neuropsychiatric disorders. In: P. W. Halligan, U. Kischka and J. C. Marshall (eds) *Handbook of Clinical Neuropsychology*. Oxford: Oxford University Press.

O'Carroll, R., Egan, V. and Mackenzie, D. M. (1994) Assessing cognitive estimation. *British Journal of Clinical Psychology*, 33, 193–197.

Pang, D. (1989) Physics and pathophysiology of closed head injury. In: M. Lezak (ed) *Assessment of the Behavioral Consequences of Head Trauma*. New York: Alan R. Liss, Inc.

Pendleton, M. G., Heaton, R. K., Lehmen, R. A. W. and Huliban, D. (1982) Diagnostic utility of the Thurstone Word Fluency Test in neuropsychological evaluations. *Journal of Clinical Neuropsychology*, 4, 307–317.

Piercy, M., Hecaen, H. and Ajuriaguerra, J. de (1960) Constructional apraxia associated with unilateral cerebral lesions – left and right sided cases compared. *Brain*, 83, 225–242.

Powell, G. E. (1979) The relationship between intelligence and verbal and spatial memory. *Journal of Clinical Psychology*, 35, 335–340.

Powell, G. E. (2000) Cognitive assessment. In: M. G. Gelder, J. J. Lopez-Ibor and N. C. Anderson (eds) *New Oxford Textbook of Psychiatry*. Oxford: Oxford University Press.

Powell, G. E. and Wood, R. Ll. (2001) Assessing the nature and extent of neurobehavioural disability. In: R Ll Wood and T M McMillan (eds) *Neurobehavioural Disability and Social Handicap*. Hove, UK: Psychology Press.

Rausch, R. (1977) Cognitive strategies in patients with unilateral temporal lobe excisions, *Neuropsychologia*, 15, 385–395.

Rausch, R. (1981) Lateralization of temporal lobe dysfunction and verbal encoding. *Brain and Language*, 12, 92–100.

Reitan, R. M. and Wolfson, D. (2002) Using the Tactile Form Recognition Test to differentiate persons with brain damage from control subjects. *Archives of Clinical Neuropsychology*, 17, 117–121.

Rey, A. (1959) *Le Teste de Copie de Figure Complexe*. Paris: Edition Centre de Psychologie Appliquée.

Richardson, J. T. E. (2000) *Clinical and Neuropsychological Aspects of Closed Head Injury, 2nd edn*. London: Taylor and Francis.

Robertson, I. H., Ward, T., Ridgeway, W. and Nimmo-Smith, I. (1994) *The Test of Everyday Attention*. Bury St Edmunds, UK: Thames Valley Test Company.

Roy, R. and Cooper, P. R. (1990) Penetrating injuries of the skull and brain. In: R. Braakman (ed) *Handbook of Clinical Neurology, Vol. 13(57): Head Injury*. Amsterdam: Elsevier Science Publishers.

Sachs, T. L., Clark, C. R., Pols, R. G. and Geffen, L. B. (1991) Comparability and stability of performance of six alternate forms of the Dodrill–Stroop Color–Word Tests. *The Clinical Neuropsychologist*, 5, 220–225.

Sbordone, R. J. and Long, C. J. (eds) (1996) *Ecological Validity of Neuropsychological Testing*. Florida: G R Press/St Lucia Press.

Schmidt, M. (1996) *Rey Auditory and Verbal Learning Test. A Handbook*. Los Angeles: Western Psychological Services.

Schulhoff, C. and Goodglass, H. (1969) Dichotic listening: side of brain injury and cerebral dominance. *Neuropsychologia*, 7, 149–160.

Semmes, J. S., Weinstein, S. and Teuber, H. L. (1960) *Somatosensory Changes after Penetrating Brain Wounds in Man*. Cambridge, MA: Harvard University Press.

Semmes, J., Weinstein, S., Ghent, L. and Teuber, H. L. (1963) Correlates of impaired orientation in personal and extra personal space. *Brain*, 86, 747–772.

Shallice, T. (1982) Specific impairments of planning. *Philosophical Transactions of the Royal Society London*, B298, 199–209.

Shallice, T. and Burgess, P. W. (1991) Deficits in strategy application following frontal lobe damage in man. *Brain*, 114, 727–741.

Shallice, T. and Evans, M. E. (1978) The involvement of the frontal lobes in cognitive estimation. *Cortex*, 14, 292–303.

Sivan, A. B. (1992) *Benton Visual Retention Test, 5th edn*. San Antonio, TX: Psychological Corporation.

Smith, M. L. and Milner, B. (1984) Differential effects of frontal-lobe lesions on cognitive estimation and spatial memory. *Neuropsychologia*, 22, 697–705.

Spikman, J. M., Deelman, B. G. and van Zomeren, A. H. (2000) Executive functioning, attention and frontal lesions in patients with chronic CHI. *Journal of Clinical and Experimental Neuropsychology*, 22, 325–338.

Spreen, O. and Benton, A. L. (1977) *Neurosensory Center Comprehensive Examination for Aphasia (NCCEA)*. Victoria, Canada: University of Victory Neuropsychology Laboratory.

Spreen, O. and Risser, A. (2003) *Assessment of Aphasia*. New York: Oxford University Press.

Spreen, O. and Strauss, E. (1998) *A Compendium of Neuropsychological Texts: Administration, Norms and Commentary, 2nd edn*. New York: Oxford University Press.

Stalhammer, D. A. (1990) The mechanisms of brain injury. In: R. Braakman (ed) *Handbook of Clinical Neurology, Vol. 13(57): Head Injury*. Amsterdam: Elsevier Science Publishers.

Strub, R. L. and Black, F. W. (2000) *The Mental State Examination in Neurology, 4th edn*. Philadelphia: Davis.

Taylor, L. B. (1969) Localization of cerebral lesions by psychological testing. *Clinical Neurosurgery*, 16, 269–287.

Taylor, L. (1979) Psychological assessment of neurosurgical patients. In: T. Rasmussen and R. Marino (eds) *Functional Neurosurgery*. New York: Raven Press.

Teasdale, A. and Jennett, B. (1974) The Glasgow Coma Scale. *Lancet*, 2, 81–84.

Teuber, H.-L. (1964) The riddle of frontal lobe function in man. In: J. M. Warren and K. Akert (eds) *The Frontal Granular Cortex and Behaviour*. New York: McGraw-Hill.

Tompkins, C. A. and Mateer, C. A. (1985) Right hemisphere appreciation of intonational and linguistic indications of affect. *Brain and Language*, 24, 185–203.

Tyler, H. R. (1969) Disorders of scanning with frontal lobe lesions. In: S. Locke (ed) *Modern Neurology*. London: Churchill.

van Zomeren, E. and Spikman, J. (2003) Assessment of Attention. In: P. W. Halligan, U. Kischka and J. C. Marshall (eds) *Handbook of Clinical Neuropsychology*. Oxford: Oxford University Press.

Walsh, K. W. (1976) Neuropsychological aspects of modified leucotomy. In: W. H. Sweet (ed) *Neurosurgical Treatment in Psychiatry, Pain and Epilepsy*. Baltimore: University Park Press.

Walsh, K. W. (1978) *Neuropsychology: A Clinical Approach*. Edinburgh: Churchill Livingstone.

Warrington, E. K. (1986) *The Camden Memory Tests*. Hove, UK: Psychology Press.

Warrington, E. K. (1997) The Graded Naming Test: a restandardization. *Neuropsychological Rehabilitation*, 7, 143–146.

Warrington, E. K. and James, M. (1991) *Visual Object and Space Perception Battery*, Bury St Edmunds, UK: Thames Valley Test Company.

Warrington, E. K. and Rabin, P. (1970) Perceptual matching in patients with cerebral lesions. *Neuropsychologia*, 8, 475–487.

Warrington, E. K. and Taylor, A. M. (1973) The contribution of the right parietal lobe to object recognition. *Cortex*, 9, 152–164.

Warrington, E. K. and Weiskrantz, L. (1973) An analysis of short-term and long-term memory defects in man. In: J. A. Deutsch (ed) *The Physiological Basis of Memory*. New York: Academic Press.

Wechsler, D. (1997a) *Wechsler Adult Intelligence Scale III*. San Antonio, TX: The Psychological Corporation.

Wechsler, D. (1997b) *Wechsler Memory Scale III*. San Antonio, TX: The Psychological Corporation.

Wechsler, D. (2001) *Wechsler Test of Adult Reading*. San Antonio, TX: The Psychological Corporation.

Wallesch, C-W., Johannsen-Horbach, H. and Blanken, G. (2003) Assessment of acquired spoken language disorders. In: P. W. Halligan, U. Kischka and J. C. Marshall (eds) *Handbook of Clinical Neuropsychology*. Oxford: Oxford University Press.

Wilkins, A. and Moscovitch, M. (1978) Selective impairment of semantic memory after temporal lobectomy. *Neuropsychologia*, 16, 73–79.

Wilkinson, G. S. (1993) *WRAT-3: The Wide Range Achievement Test*. Wilmington, DE: Wide Range.

Willmes, K. (2003) The methodological and statistical foundations of neuropsychological assessment. In: P. W. Halligan, U. Kischka and J. C. Marshall (eds) *Handbook of Clinical Neuropsychology*. Oxford: Oxford University Press.

Wilson, B. A., Alderman, N., Burgess, P. W., Ensie, H. and Evans, J. J. (1996) *Behavioural Assessment of the Dysexecutive Syndrome*, Bury St Edmunds, UK: Thames Valley Test Company.

Wilson, B. A., Cockburn, J. and Baddeley, A. D. (2003) *The Rivermead Behavioural Memory Test-II*. Bury St Edmunds, UK: Thames Valley Test Company.

Wood, R. Ll. and McMillan, T. M. (eds) (2001) *Neurobehavioural Disability and Social Handicap*. Hove, UK: Psychology Press.

Chapter 37

Neurological problems

Treatment and rehabilitation

Barbara Wilson

INTRODUCTION

Since the first edition of this book, clinical psychology has become an integral part of the treatment and rehabilitation of people with neurological problems. Clinical psychologists with expertise in this field are known as neuropsychologists. Although the Division of Neuropsychology (2003) quite rightly points out that 'clinical neuropsychologists design and advise on interventions to ameliorate problems with cognition and behaviour or personality change' (p. 3), it could be argued that this remains a rather narrow interpretation in the light of the fact that neuropsychologists are also heavily involved in the amelioration of emotional problems, and sometimes physical and sensory problems.

Patients or clients seen for treatment include those with: (1) progressive conditions, such as Alzheimer's disease and multiple sclerosis; (2) traumatic brain injury; (3) cerebrovascular disorders or strokes; (4) infections of the brain, in particular encephalitis; (5) hypoxic brain damage resulting from such causes as myocardial infarction, respiratory failure, carbon monoxide poisoning and anaesthetic accident; (6) epilepsy; (7) chronic alcohol abuse leading to Korsakoff's syndrome; (8) cerebral tumours; and (9) surgical procedures to relieve conditions affecting the brain. These conditions are not always mutually exclusive. For example, one patient referred for rehabilitation had a stroke while driving, as a result of which he crashed his car. As a result of the crash he stopped breathing and later developed a blood clot for which he needed surgery. Consequently, he had four sources of brain damage: the cerebrovascular accident, a head injury from the car crash, hypoxic damage from the shortage of oxygen and damage from the surgery to remove the clot.

The kinds of treatment and rehabilitation neuropsychologists can offer to these patients are varied and range from giving advice and teaching compensatory strategies to reduce cognitive difficulties to providing psychological support for emotional problems through to structured behaviour programmes. Sometimes patients are seen individually and sometimes in groups. As well as the involvement with patients and their families, neuropsychologists often work closely with occupational therapists, speech and language therapists, physiotherapists, nurses and members of the medical profession. Their role may be as partners in a treatment team or as advisors to these other professions in certain circumstances. Some examples of approaches to treatment and rehabilitation provided by clinical neuropsychologists are described in the remainder of this chapter.

ATTEMPTS TO RESTORE LOST FUNCTIONING IN PEOPLE WITH NEUROLOGICAL DEFICITS

Since the early days of rehabilitation one of the main questions faced by those working with neurologically impaired patients is whether to attempt to restore lost functioning or to compensate for problems these patients face in everyday life. In Robertson's words (2003) 'Should we try to treat the aphasia or teach an alternative communication system? Should we try to improve the hemiplegia or provide a wheelchair?' Some believe that restitution can only occur if there is sparing of a minimum proportion of cells or connections (Sabel, 1997; Robertson, 1999b). If more than the critical proportion of cells is destroyed then it is necessary to use compensatory strategies. This may depend, at least in part, on the function involved. Thus, for the restoration of language functions, the proportion of cells or connections spared may indeed be critical and there is some evidence that language might be more amenable to strategies aimed at the restoration of function than other cognitive areas (Kolb, 1995; Thomas et al., 1997). Robertson also believes that it is possible to restore the attention deficits underlying unilateral spatial neglect. Robertson et al. (1995) trained people with neglect to sustain their attention through a self-alerting procedure. Other studies with neglect patients have used a limb-activation procedure to reduce the neglect. This has established that people with neglect following right hemisphere stroke improve performance if they move their left arm or hand (Robertson et al., 1998). Later studies have shown that improvement occurs only if patients move the left limb in left space. Performance is not improved by moving the right hand in right space, the right hand in left space, the left hand in right space or *both* hands together. (This is also an example of how general stimulation, moving both hands together, can lead to poorer performance). Some would argue that self-alerting and limb activation are behavioural compensations but Robertson believes that they are remediating the basic underlying disorder.

Attempts were made to restore lost functioning in a young woman who sustained a severe head injury in a horse-riding accident. She lost the ability to read and to recognise objects. Over a period of several months she was taught to read again. This involved teaching her one letter of the alphabet at a time using a behavioural procedure of enhancing the discriminability between letters and positive reinforcement for successful identification of letters. Once she had learned the letters she was taught sound combinations ('igh', 'oa', etc.). Eventually, she learned to read again to the level of an average 12-year-old, although she did not read in the same way as she had before her accident. Instead, she sounded out the letters so she had become a letter-by-letter reader (Wilson, 1999). It could be argued, therefore, that partial restoration of function had taken place. Her object recognition difficulties were addressed through a rehearsal procedure whereby she was shown the objects she could not name and told the correct name. The new names were then rehearsed. Generalisation was ensured by showing the object in different orientations and then by showing different examples of the named object. Her object recognition improved over a period of years (Wilson and Davidoff, 1993), although she still had problems identifying animals. So, once again, restoration of function was incomplete. It is likely that this is the typical picture in brain injury rehabilitation, i.e. that some restitution can occur but this needs to be supplemented with compensatory approaches (to be addressed later).

Other cognitive functions, particularly memory, may be more resistant to restorative approaches (Schacter and Glisky, 1986; Wilson, 2003). The world's most famous amnesic patient, HM (Scoville and Milner, 1957) appears to have shown no recovery since his operation in 1957 (Freed et al., 1998). Another amnesic patient, CW, has shown no recovery over a 10-year period (Wilson et al., 1995). A recent review of cognitive rehabilitation (Robertson, 1999a) concluded that '. . . in the case of memory rehabilitation there is as yet no evidence for direct and lasting improvement of memory through restitution-oriented therapies. Hence, compensatory approaches to memory problems appear to be, for the time being at least, the treatment of choice' (p. 704). Even if attempts to restore lost memory functioning are likely to fail, there are a few reports of some memory-impaired people showing improvement or even recovery over time (Victor et al., 1989; Wilson, 1991; Wilson and Baddeley, 1993). Current approaches to the restoration of cognitive functioning include pharmacological treatments for people with Alzheimer's disease (Curran and Weingartner, 2002) and neural transplants for Huntington's disease (Barker and Dunnett, 1999). As far as the rehabilitation of memory impairments in people with non-progressive brain injury is concerned, some (and often considerable) recovery takes place in the first few months (Kapur and Graham, 2002). D'Esposito and Alexander (1995) say that the bilaterality and extent of the lesions determines prognosis. This would appear to indirectly support the view of Robertson (2003) that a minimum proportion of cells is required if recovery is to take place.

Natural recovery is often more or less complete before neuropsychological treatment begins. It is during this early stage that expectations for restoration of function are high both for cognitive recovery and for recovery of other functions. We try to teach people who cannot walk to walk again, and we try to teach those who have lost the ability to speak to speak again. If, however, restoration of function has not occurred by the end of the period of natural recovery, or when such recovery has slowed down considerably, then we tend to adjust our goals and work towards wheelchair independence, or alternative methods of communication, or teach the use of external memory aids. It is certainly true that the current focus of neuropsychological rehabilitation in most brain injury rehabilitation centres is less concerned with restoration of function and more with the identification of the practical problems faced by patients and their families and then finding ways to reduce or avoid these problems.

COMPENSATING FOR DEFICITS

Compensation is one of the major tools for enabling people with brain injury to cope in everyday life. Wilson and Watson (1996) described a framework for understanding compensatory behaviour in people with organic memory impairment. The framework was developed by Bäckman and Dixon (1992) and further modified by Dixon and Bäckman (1999). It distinguishes four stages in the evolution of compensatory behaviour: origins, mechanisms, forms and consequences. Wilson (2000) went on to use this framework to consider compensation for a variety of cognitive deficits. Evans et al. (2003) investigated factors that predict good use of compensations. The main predictors appear to be age (younger people compensate better), severity of impairment (very severely impaired people compensate less well), specificity of deficit (those with widespread cognitive deficits appear to compensate less well than those with more specific deficits) and pre-morbid use of strategies (those using some compensatory aids pre-morbidly appear to compensate better). This is an area where further work is required. If we can predict who is likely to compensate without too much difficulty, we can target our rehabilitation to help those who are less likely to compensate spontaneously.

Zangwill (1947) said compensation was the 're-organization of psychological function in order to minimize or circumvent a particular disability'. This re-organisation can be achieved in several ways. For example, one can arrange the environment to avoid the need for a particular function, one can try to achieve goals in a different way and one can try to help people make the most of their residual capacities.

Environmental modifications

People with severe physical disabilities can use environmental control systems to enable them to open and close doors, turn the pages of a book, answer the telephone and so forth. The ability to use one's limbs is no longer required in these circumstances as the environmental control systems can be manipulated by voice operated or mouth-control stick systems. Aggression in the workplace can be reduced by such environmental adaptations as improved lighting and escort services (Rei, 2002). Similarly, people with severe cognitive impairments can avoid the need to use a damaged cognitive function if the environment is structured in a certain way. Thus, someone with severe executive deficits may be able to function in a structured environment, with no distractions and where there is no need to problem solve as the task at hand is clear and unambiguous. Likewise, people with severe memory problems may not be handicapped in environments where there are no demands made on memory. Thus if doors, cupboards, drawers and storage jars are clearly labelled, if rooms are cleared of dangerous equipment, if someone appears to remind or accompany the memory-impaired person when it is time to go to the dentist or to eat dinner, the person may cope reasonably well. At a more sophisticated level there are 'smart houses' for people with dementia (Wilson and Evans, 2000). These attempt to 'disable the disabling environment' through the use of computers, video links and telephones, to remind people when to take medication, use bathrooms, turn electrical appliances on and off and ensure the water temperature is not too hot or too cold.

Functional adaptations

In addition to restructuring or modifying the environment, compensation can be achieved by teaching people to use strategies and techniques that enable them to reach their goals in other ways. For example, people who lose the ability to read because of damage to the brain can still enjoy 'talking books', people with speech problems can use a voice synthesiser and people with memory problems can use external memory aids to help them remember what they have to do each day. The principle here is to use an undamaged skill to overcome a damaged one. Luria et al. (1969) referred to this as 'functional adaptation' and, as early as 1947, Zangwill argued that this was one of the most important principles in rehabilitation (Zangwill, 1947).

Technological aids are increasingly used to help people compensate for cognitive deficits and a recent special issue of the journal *Neuropsychological Rehabilitation* (Gregor and Newell, 2004) is devoted to technology in cognitive rehabilitation and presents state of the art developments in this area.

Compensatory approaches to the treatment and rehabilitation of people with brain injury should target the functional consequences of any impairments, i.e. the everyday problems or disabilities rather than trying to remediate an underlying impairment (the restorative approaches do this). Compensatory aids for speech and language deficits are commonly encountered and there is a wide range of systems available to enable people to communicate with others. These include voice synthesisers, picture dictionaries and alternative communication systems such as Amerind (based on American Sign Language), Rebus (a pictorial communication system), Blissymbolics (a grammatical symbol system) and Makaton (based on British sign language) have all been used for people with neurological damage.

Bill became severely aphasic after a stroke at the age of 65 years. Five years after his stroke, Bill remained without any words, he had one sound – 'bah' – and his comprehension of single words was at the level of a 2-year-old (Wilson, 1999). At the age of 70 he was referred to the clinical psychology department to see if anything could be found to reduce the 'terrible rows at home'. The rows took the form of Bill shouting 'Bah, bah, bah' and becoming very distressed while his wife yelled in frustration because she could not communicate with her husband. The rows typically occurred when there was a change in Bill's routine that could not be communicated to him. Together with the speech and language therapist, the clinical psychologist devised a pictorial symbol system of line drawings for common nouns such as matches, newspaper and cup and abstract drawings for proper nouns such as Bill, Barbara and Anne. Bill was taught to use this through a modelling procedure. Real objects were placed on the table and one of us used the appropriate card to 'ask' for something, e.g. 'newspaper'; the other would respond and then we would show a card to Bill and gesture to him to select the right object. We then demonstrated the abstract cards so the symbol for 'Bill' was held in front of him, the symbol for 'Anne' held in front of her and so on. For absent people we used photographs and then paired the symbol with the photograph.

After three half-hour sessions each week for a period of 3 weeks, Bill had learned a sufficient number of symbols for useful comprehension. We could then explain changes in his routine such as 'no rehabilitation next week: stay in hospital for 3 days'. By now the symbol cards were kept in a photograph album that he could carry in his pocket. Any new words required or discovered were drawn to go into his album. Bill spent several days once trying to convey 'bird bath', we understood 'bird' as he drew a bird, we understood 'bath' once he had drawn it but we could not work out 'bird bath' for a long time until he showed us one in a book. As soon as we understood what he was trying to convey we made a picture symbol for it. Bill's wife was, by now, enthusiastic about the communication system and regularly added new symbols to the album. Not only had Bill and his wife found a way to communicate through this approach but the arguments at home had considerably reduced. Why did it take so long to devise this system? The main reason appears to be because Bill wasn't ready to use this for quite some time after his stroke. He wanted to regain his speech and language. By the time 5 years had passed it seemed that he accepted this was not going to happen. The frequent arguments may have also increased motivation to use a compensatory strategy.

Another left-hemisphere stroke patient who responded to a compensatory strategy was Ted, who had lost the ability to read the initial letters of words despite adequate eyesight and no evidence of unilateral neglect (Patterson and Wilson, 1990). Of several treatment strategies tried with Ted (Wilson, 1999), only one significantly reduced his errors: this was when he traced the initial letter with his finger first. From over 30% initial letter errors in a baseline period, his error rate went down to just under 10% with the tracing method.

Compensatory strategies for memory difficulties

One area where compensations are perhaps the main approach is in the treatment of memory problems. Although external memory aids are, arguably, the most efficient strategies for memory-impaired people to employ, it is not always easy for them to use such aids. Efficient use of external memory aids involves memory, so the people who need them most have the greatest difficulty in learning how to use them. People with memory problems forget to use aids, they may have difficulty programming them, they may use them in an unsystematic or disorganised way and they may be embarrassed by them. Ingenuity and patience are called for in teaching and enabling memory-impaired people to use external memory aids. Some people do learn to use compensatory strategies efficiently (Kime et al., 1996; Wilson et al., 1997a; Donaghy and Williams, 1998; Wilson, 1999). Why do some people use them well and others fail to use them at all? Two studies that attempted to answer this question (Wilson and Watson, 1996; Evans et al., 2003) suggested that factors such as age (younger people compensate better than older people), pre-morbid use of strategies, severity of memory impairment and fewer cognitive deficits in addition to memory were among the factors that predicted efficient use of compensations. In addition, those memory-impaired people who learn to compensate well through the use of external aids are far more likely to be independent (Wilson and Watson, 1996, Evans et al., 2003).

There are many different external memory aids, ranging from simple ones like lists of things to do, through pictorial aids for people who cannot read (Lincoln, 1989) to sophisticated electronic aids (Kapur et al., 2004). All have advantages and disadvantages. Wilson et al. (1997a) describe the natural history of the development of a compensatory memory system for a young man who became amnesic after a stroke. Kapur et al. (2004) and Gartland (2004) discuss factors to be considered when selecting aids for memory impaired people. One of the simplest electronic aids (at least as far as ease of use is concerned) is NeuroPage. This paging device has been the subject of several research studies.

NeuroPage is a simple and portable paging system with a screen that can be attached to a belt. The system uses an arrangement of microcomputers linked to a conventional computer memory and, by telephone, to a paging company. The scheduling of reminders for each individual is entered into the computer and from then on no further interfacing is necessary. On the appropriate date and time, NeuroPage accesses the user's data files, determines the reminder to be delivered and transmits the information.

A pilot study (Wilson et al., 1997b), two single-case studies (Evans et al., 1998; Wilson et al., 1999) and a randomised control study (Wilson et al., 2001a) demonstrated that NeuroPage significantly reduces the everyday memory and/or planning problems of people with brain injury. As a result of this research, a local health authority in the UK has set up a clinical service to provide this paging system to people throughout the country. A survey of the first 40 people to use this service (Wilson et al., 2003) showed that the most common messages to be sent were to do with medication (e.g. 'take your tablets'); 514 of these were sent each week. This was followed by messages to do with orientation (e.g. 'time to get up'); 380 of these were sent each week. Food messages (e.g. 'make lunch') came next (193 each week), with the least common messages being those about transport (e.g. 'wait for the taxi'; only eight of these being sent each week) and those to do with finance (e.g. 'check bank account'; of which only four were sent each week). Of the 40 patients, 32 were men, 13 (33%) had sustained a traumatic brain injury; 7 (17%) had had a stroke; 4 (10%) had sustained anoxic brain damage; 2 (5%) had survived encephalitis and the remainder had other conditions. The age range was 14–81 years Twenty six different health authorities referred clients and all clients were able to obtain funding.

NeuroPage is just one of a number of emerging technology-based compensatory aids for cognitive problems. It has several advantages over some other systems, simplicity of use and portability being its greatest advantages over other electronic aids. A limitation is that clients and carers do not have the flexibility to enter reminders directly; other systems exist that can do this. Wright et al. (2001), for example, describe palm-top computers and Kapur et al. (2002) discuss a range of electronic systems to help memory-impaired people cope with real-life, everyday problems. Nevertheless, for a large number of people NeuroPage seems a real support in the search for independent living.

Peter was 10 years old and had dyslexia and memory problems, which appeared to be getting worse as he got older. His mother saw a report about NeuroPage in a science programme on television and contacted the research team investigating NeuroPage. She felt that Peter's problems were restricting his independence and thought the pager might help. In particular, she said her son had poor concentration: he forgot to take things with him to school and to remember to bring things home at night; he did not remember where he had to go after school or where to catch the school bus; he forgot to do his homework and to feed his pets.

First, a screening test ensured that Peter could read messages on the screen and push the right button to retrieve and delete messages. A schedule was then designed and target behaviours selected. A 2-week baseline followed during which time the target behaviours were monitored. Peter was then given the pager with the messages programmed to be sent out about the target behaviours; different messages were sent out each day, depending on Peter's schedule. So on Monday, for example, Peter received the following messages:

7.00 a.m.   Hi, Peter, it's 7 o'clock on Monday
8.06 a.m.   Homework, PE kit, sandwiches bag
3.25 p.m.   Sandwich box
3.30 p.m.   Lee Centre, today. Wait at school to be picked up
7.30 p.m.   Feed fish and hamster.

The weekend messages were different, so on Saturday the following messages were sent:

7.30 a.m.   It's Saturday, up yet?
8.40 a.m.   Goggles, library books, swimming stuff
8.45 a.m.   Leave for swimming
7.30 p.m.   Have you done your homework yet?
7.55 p.m.   Feed fish and hamster

From the results, which can be seen in Figure 37.1, it is clear that Peter made a considerable improvement between the baseline and treatment periods. After 7 weeks with the pager, it was removed and the target behaviours were monitored as before. Peter maintained the level achieved during the treatment phase.

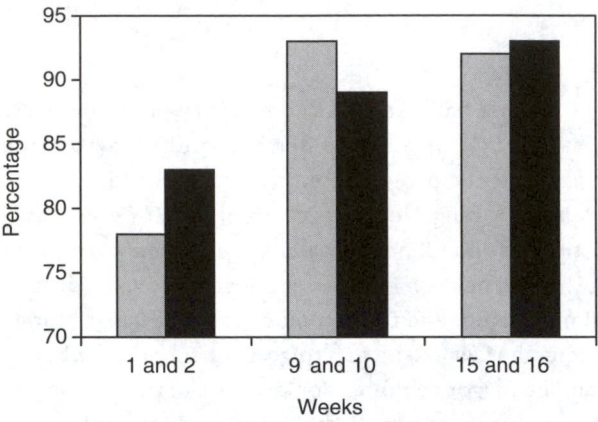

Figure 37.1 Peter's percentage success for targets.

Helping people to make better use of their residual abilities

Even the most densely amnesic person retains some memory functioning (Baddeley, 1992) so it is sometimes possible to use these remaining skills more efficiently through, for example, expending more time and effort (Bäckman and Dixon, 1992); or by encouraging a deeper level of processing (Craik and Lockhart, 1972); or by the use of spaced retrieval, i.e. gradually extending the retention interval (Camp, 1989; Landauer and Bjork, 1978) or through the use of mnemonics and rehearsal strategies (Wilson, 1987).

One of the most exciting recent developments in improving learning is a technique known as 'errorless learning', which was first described by Terrace (1963, 1966). In 1963, Terrace published his work on training pigeons using a technique he called 'errorless learning' or learning without making mistakes. He taught pigeons to discriminate a red key from a green key (apparently a hard discrimination for pigeons to make). Having trained the pigeons to peck reliably to one colour, he introduced a different colour when the birds were in a position where it was difficult to peck. Thus Terrace gradually faded in one colour in such a way that the pigeons learned the task while making no (or very few errors) *en route*. The principle of errorless learning was soon taken up by people working with children (and later adults) with developmental learning difficulties. Sidman and Stoddard (1967), for example, taught learning-disabled children to discriminate circles from ellipses, and Walsh and Lamberts (1979) used errorless learning principles to teach children to read. Errorless learning is used to this day in the teaching of children with developmental learning difficulties. As both this group and people with memory problems share a difficulty in new learning, it makes sense to investigate this method in memory rehabilitation.

Another theoretical impetus stimulating the use of errorless learning in cognitive rehabilitation came from studies of implicit memory and implicit learning in cognitive psychology and neuropsychology. It has been established for many years that people with the amnesic syndrome can learn some things normally or nearly normally (Brooks and Baddeley, 1976; Wilson et al., 1996). These are tasks where conscious recollection of the information to be remembered is not required. Learning is demonstrated through implicit means, i.e. without conscious recollection. Accuracy at tracking a visual stimulus on a screen, for example, typically improves with practice even in people with severe memory deficits who may not even remember having done the task earlier. Glisky and Schacter (1986) attempted to use the intact implicit learning abilities of people with amnesia to teach them new skills. Although they were successful in certain cases, learning typically required more effort than one normally expects in implicit learning tasks.

In some cases, anomalies are seen in implicit learning studies. When assessing amnesic patients on a perceptual priming (fragmented pictures) task, one may see the usual overall improvement (fragments are identified progressively earlier over trials) together with a few examples of no improvement over trials for certain items. If a fragmented picture of a hand is called a bicycle on trial one, it may be called a bicycle on trial after trial despite the amnesic person seeing the correct answer later in the sequence in every trial. These anomalies could be because errors injected into a system that has a very impoverished episodic memory may be difficult or impossible to eliminate (Baddeley and Wilson, 1994). To benefit from our mistakes, we need to remember the mistakes. As implicit memory is not good at error elimination, it may be that we should avoid errors for people with poor explicit and episodic memory.

To answer the question 'Do amnesic people learn better if prevented from making mistakes during the learning process?' an experiment was conducted (Baddeley and Wilson, 1994). Three groups of people were seen: group 1 comprised 16 people with a severe memory deficit as defined by zero delayed recall of a prose passage; group 2 comprised 16 young control subjects and group 3 comprised 16 older control subjects. All were administered a stem completion task under two conditions: errorless and errorful learning. In the errorless condition people were prevented from making mistakes – they were given a stem and told the correct answer immediately. In the errorful condition they were forced to make mistakes. They were given a stem and asked to guess what the word might be before being told the correct answer. Conditions and words were counterbalanced. After three learning trials, participants were tested by being given the two letter stems and asked for the correct word. Errorless learning was superior to errorful learning for all subjects but, in the case of the people with amnesia, every one of them showed better performance under the errorless learning condition. Obviously, the answer to the question was 'Yes, amnesic people do learn better if prevented from making mistakes during the learning process'. However, the purpose of rehabilitation is not to teach people stem completion tasks so it was necessary to demonstrate that errorless learning could also be applied to real-life tasks.

The first published study that applied errorless learning principles to the rehabilitation of memory impaired people seems to be that of Wilson et al. (1994). This reported several single case studies of people with non-progressive brain damage, including a man who had survived encephalitis, a stroke patient, a man with Korsakoff's syndrome and a man with head injury who was still in post-traumatic amnesia. In each case, two tasks were taught, one in an errorful way and one in an errorless way, the tasks were matched as far as possible for difficulty and number of subcomponents. Tasks included recognition of objects for a man with agnosia and amnesia, names of famous people, entering messages into an electronic organiser and orientation items. In each case, errorless learning was superior to errorful learning. Thus the effect had been demonstrated with people of different diagnostic groups and at different times post-insult.

Since then, errorless learning has been used by others. Wilson and Evans (1996), Squires et al. (1997) and Evans et al. (2000) have used it to teach a variety of tasks to people with non-progressive brain damage. Clare et al. (1999, 2000, 2001), in a series of studies, have used errorless learning in combination with other strategies for improving learning with people with Alzheimer's disease (AD). Fillingham et al. (2003) discuss the evidence for the effectiveness of errorless learning in the treatment of language disorders and Sage et al. (in press) use errorless learning in the treatment of a patient with acquired dyslexia).

Clare et al. (1999) published a report of a man who had been diagnosed with dementia of the Alzheimer type (DAT) 6 years earlier. He was seen at a memory clinic and invited to take part in a study investigating whether errorless learning was effective in helping people with AD to learn or relearn information. The man, VJ, agreed to take part. Following an assessment and a discussion with VJ and his sister, with whom he lived, it was decided to address a particular concern of VJ's, namely difficulty remembering the names of people at a social club he attended each week.

Fourteen of the man's friends were photographed at the club. VJ was then seen at home each week for several months. During baseline measures, it was clear that VJ could recall reliably three names of the people shown him on the photographs. These names were retained in the set so that VJ would always experience some success. The remaining 11 names were taught one at a time (one new name was introduced each week). A combination of errorless learning, spaced retrieval and vanishing cues was employed. The procedure was to present one photograph and say 'this is (e.g.) Caroline. Can you think of a way to remember her? Caroline was described as 'Caroline with the curls'. Other descriptors were used for other names/people. The name was then presented using vanishing cues so, for example 'Carolin_'; 'Caroli__'; 'Carol___', etc. VJ was required to complete the missing letters each time. Once he was able to write the entire name, a spaced retrieval method was employed in which VJ was asked to recall the name at gradually increasing intervals. The overriding principle was to ensure that no (or very few) errors were made during learning. The correct name was written on the back of each photograph: VJ was told never to guess and only say the name if he was sure. If he was not sure, he was asked to look at the name on the back. Following each weekly session, VJ's sister spent a few minutes a day practising the name. In addition, VJ attended the club each week so could practise there.

Once all 11 names had been learned, VJ was accompanied to the club, the photographs were given to him and he was required to look at each photograph, find the correct person and introduce this person by name to the psychologist. This was the generalisation stage and VJ's only error was with a woman who had dyed her hair and changed her hairstyle since the photograph was taken. Mean recall scores for the 11 names were 20% correct over the baseline sessions; 98% correct following intervention and 100% correct at the 3-month, 6-month and 9-month follow-up. Furthermore, VJ was very pleased with his relearning, saying that he had thought he would never learn anything new again and now he could greet everyone at the club by name. VJ was able to maintain this new learning with short daily practices despite the fact that his disease was progressing.

In 2001, Clare et al. published a 3-year follow-up of VJ. After the 9-month follow-up period, VJ and his sister were asked to stop the daily practice sessions and the photographs were removed. His only practice, therefore, was during his weekly visits to the club. He was regularly assessed on the set of faces, including the three he had always known without any training, but was given no feedback on whether or not these were correct. VJ was monitored for a further 2 years. His performance remained stable for the first year and then showed a modest decline over the second year, although it remained well above baseline levels. Potentially, this is a highly important clinical finding. If people with AD can be taught useful everyday information and hold on to this information in the face of neurological and neuropsychological decline, it could reduce the stress on carers and postpone admission to long-term care.

Dealing with the emotional consequences of brain injury

Over the past few years there has been an increasing recognition that rehabilitation should deal with the emotional consequences of brain injury as well as the cognitive sequelae (Williams et al., 2003b). Such disorders are common in survivors of brain injury (Williams et al., 2003a). Prigatano (1991) suggests that rehabilitation is likely to fail if we do not deal with emotional issues. Consequently, an understanding of theories and models of emotion is crucial to successful rehabilitation. Social isolation, anxiety and depression are common in survivors of brain injury (Wilson, 2004). McKinlay et al. (1981) thought that about two-thirds of people surviving traumatic brain injury (TBI) experience anxiety and depression. Evans and Wilson (1992) found that anxiety was common in people attending a memory group. Kopelman and Crawford (1996) found that 40% of 200 consecutive referrals to a memory clinic were suffering from clinical depression. Bowen et al. (1998) found that 38% of survivors of TBI experienced mood disorders. Williams et al. (2002) found that investigations into the prevalence of post-traumatic stress disorder (PTSD) following TBI ranges from 3% to 27%. In their own study they found 18% of 66 community-living survivors of TBI experienced PTSD.

Judd (2003) suggests that there are three components to the emotions of a person with brain injury: first, the patient's pre-morbid personality; second, the emotional reactions to the person's disabilities; and third, the organic changes in emotional functioning due to the brain damage. This is similar to Gainotti's (1993) classification, which distinguishes three main factors causing emotional and psychosocial problems after brain injury. First, there are emotional problems resulting from neurological factors, for example, someone with brainstem damage might exhibit the so-called 'catastrophic reaction' in which swings from tears to laughter may follow in rapid succession. Second, are those emotional problems arising from psychological or psychodynamic factors, for example, someone with language deficits might show loss of self-esteem together with depression because of an inability to communicate normally. Third, are those emotional problems arising from psychosocial factors, for example, someone who loses all his or her friends and colleagues following a brain injury, and is thus very socially isolated, could suffer from low mood and anxiety. PTSD would also fit into this section. Fear of what might happen in the future, panic because one cannot remember what has happened in the last few minutes, grief at loss of functioning and reduced self-esteem because of changes in physical appearance may all contribute to emotional changes. One aspect not covered by Gainotti is the influence of pre-morbid personality. This is discussed by Moore and Stambrook (1995) and Williams et al. (1999).

Other models and theories that need to be taken into account are those of pre-morbid personality and neurological, physical and biochemical models such as those described by Robinson and Starkstein (1989). This addresses the issue of why emotional problems arise following an insult to the brain but does not offer much help in understanding the psychodynamic and psychosocial causes of emotional and mood disorders. Perhaps the most helpful models come from cognitive-behavioural therapy (CBT).

Ever since Beck's highly influential book *Cognitive Therapy and Emotional Disorders* appeared in 1976, CBT has become one of the most important and best validated psychotherapeutic procedures (Salkovskis, 1996). An update of Beck's model appeared in 1996. One of its major strengths has been the development of clinically relevant theories. There are several theories not only for depression and anxiety but also for panic, obsessive-compulsive disorders and phobias.

Analytic psychotherapy is also used in rehabilitation, particularly in the USA. Perhaps the best known proponent of this for the treatment of people surviving TBI is Prigatano. He describes his approach (based on the milieu therapy approach of Ben-Yishay) in his book *Principles of Neuropsychological Rehabilitation* (Prigatano, 1999).

> Kate contracted encephalitis in 1997 at the age of 26. She was reported to be in a vegetative state for almost 6 months. Even though less than 10% of such patients regain consciousness (and extremely few show significant recovery), Kate achieved a considerable degree of cognitive recovery and emotional adjustment despite being unresponsive for several months. During this period of unresponsiveness Kate received a PET scan (Menon et al., 1998), which showed that she was able to differentially respond to photographs of her family, demonstrating she could perceive and process visual stimuli despite showing no behavioural signs of awareness. Two years later she was referred for an assessment of her cognitive functioning. Despite being severely physically handicapped, tube fed, with a tracheostomy tube and communicating with a letter board, Kate's test scores were almost all within the normal range (Wilson et al., 2001b). She was very angry and distressed at her earlier treatment and the loss of so many things in her life.

Kate's psychological reaction to her illness was considerable. Pre-morbidly, Kate was reported by her family to have been very bright and kind, She had been successful academically, was in a professional job and in a long-term relationship with her boyfriend: they had just bought a house together and had plans to marry. Kate was a young woman who had been thinking about her future and who had a happy life. Following her illness, Kate's relationships, employment, social existence and identity had all altered. At a stage when she had been thinking about marriage and a family, her illness appeared to have changed everything. Not surprisingly, Kate was experiencing low mood, anger and anxiety reactions that reflected the shocking change in her circumstances.

During her time in rehabilitation Kate was withdrawn and depressed, prone to screaming, especially during physiotherapy, and was known to bite other people, often when they were helping with her personal care. Later, this behaviour was thought to be an attempt to communicate to those providing her care that she was frightened and in pain. Kate's difficulties with communication and her reliance on a communication board often led to misunderstandings, and this resulted in frustration both for Kate and her carers.

Kate's anger became a dominant theme in her discussion of what had happened to her and lasted for a number of years. From a cognitive-behavioural perspective, Kate's depression could be seen to involve suicidal ideation, a sense of worthlessness and a pattern of negative thinking, feeling, behaviour and physical sensation.

It was clear that Kate's insight into the changes in her life was increasing and with it the realisation that she had lost a great deal. The enormous task of beginning to recognise the changes in her life now and in the future was beginning to become clear to Kate at the point at which she began therapy. A therapeutic alliance was established between Kate and the clinical psychology trainees who worked with her over the years. Formulation of her history and current situation was used as the basis of intervention (see MacNiven et al., 2003, for a detailed discussion). On the grounds that rehabilitation should have a broad theoretical base, a number of different theoretical models were used in treatment.

The formulation suggested that environmental factors, i.e. Kate's dependence on her carers, and internal factors, i.e. her pattern of negative thinking, kept Kate focused on the past and what she had lost. It was as if she was enmeshed in the trauma she had experienced and over-whelmed with the loss of normality. In addition, she had very low self-esteem and frequently said, 'I'm stupid and useless'. These ideas were explored with Kate.

Personal Construct Theory (Kelly, 1955) was used to help her to see herself in the present rather than living in the past. This particular approach enables the individual to create her own ways of seeing the world and reduces the feeling of being a passive recipient of imposed ideas or perspectives. 'Constructs' are templates about the world that the individual holds and adapts as life's realities are experienced. Therapy using these ideas encourages individuals to develop new ideas about themselves in the world (Blowers and O'Connor, 1995).

Anger management techniques (Demark and Gemeinhardt, 2002) combined with cognitive therapy (Segal et al., 2002) allowed Kate to focus on specific patterns of thinking while also clarifying her present identity. Interpersonal problem-solving work (Malia et al., 1995) focused on developing Kate's ability to empathise with others, especially her carers, with whom there had been some difficulties. This potentially challenging work was possible mainly because of the quality of the therapeutic alliance between Kate and her therapist.

Using ideas from narrative therapy (Nicholson, 1995) and mindfulness techniques (Segal et al., 2002), again combined with cognitive work, enabled Kate to focus more on the present and to think realistically and optimistically about her future. Further problem-solving work looking at specific 'problem situations' enabled Kate to interact more successfully with carers. Kate reported, 'I can't believe how much I have changed. I now want to be alive and I am looking forward to the future . . . I can now keep myself occupied and busy, instead of sitting on my own doing nothing . . .' Kate continues to improve and even her physical status is starting to change 7 years post-insult. For an up-to-date account of the assessment and rehabilitation of vegetative and minimally conscious patients, see Coleman (2005).

A HOLISTIC APPROACH TO THE TREATMENT AND REHABILITATION OF PEOPLE WITH BRAIN INJURY

The holistic approach to rehabilitation is, perhaps, the most likely approach to succeed in enabling patients to return to their own most appropriate environments. The person most responsible for setting up holistic programmes is Yehuda Ben-Yishay. The Israeli government asked Ben-Yishay to set up a programme for Israeli soldiers who had survived injuries to the brain during the Six-Day War. He set up a programme called 'milieu therapy', which was the forerunner of later holistic programmes. Proponents of the holistic approach regard it as futile to separate the cognitive sequelae of brain injury from the emotional, social and functional sequelae. After all, how we think, remember, communicate and solve problems affects how we feel emotionally and how we behave, and vice versa. Most holistic programmes are concerned with increasing a client's awareness, alleviating cognitive deficits, developing compensatory skills and providing vocational counselling. All such programmes provide a mixture of individual and group therapy. 'Although there is as yet no irrefutable evidence of the success of the holistic programs, they appear to have been subjected to more research on efficacy than other approaches' (Diller, 1994). Furthermore, Cope (1994) argues that there is reasonably convincing evidence that comprehensive rehabilitation does make a substantial difference in the reduction of handicap for brain injured patients.

Cognitive rehabilitation, then, is carried out in a number of ways (discussed in more detail by Wilson, 1997). Combining the strengths of these approaches is probably the best way forward. Clinically, the holistic approach is probably the best for the majority of brain injured people. However, this approach, as advanced by Prigatano and Ben Yishay, could perhaps be improved by: (1) incorporating ideas and practical applications from learning theory, such as task analysis, baseline recording, monitoring and the implementation of single-case experimental designs to individual treatment programmes; and (2) by referring to cognitive neuropsychological models to identify cognitive strengths and weaknesses in more detail, to explain observed phenomena and make predictions about cognitive functioning.

CONCLUSIONS

This chapter is based on the assumption that clinical neuropsychologists have a crucial part to play in the treatment of people with brain injury. Several different approaches to treatment are described and discussed. Attempts to restore lost functioning have a part to play particularly in the early days following brain injury. It is possible that certain functions, for example, attention, respond better to restorative approaches than other functions, such as memory. One of the main approaches to treatment, however, is to help people compensate for their deficits. Consideration is given to three ways in which this might be done: environmental modifications, functional adaptations (learning to do things in a different way) and helping people make better use of their residual skills. It is now recognised that the emotional consequences of brain injury are important and that dealing with these is an integral part of neuropsychological rehabilitation. Holistic programmes are, perhaps, the best model we have at present to increase the likelihood of independence and promote success in real-life settings. The main characteristics of these programmes are provided. Rehabilitation for people with brain injury makes clinical and economic sense and no brain-injured person should be considered unsuitable for rehabilitation.

REFERENCES

Bäckman, L. and Dixon, R. A. (1992) Psychological compensation: A theoretical framework. *Psychological Bulletin*, 112, 259–283.

Baddeley, A. D. (1992) Memory theory and memory therapy. In: B. A. Wilson and N. Moffat (eds) *Clinical Management of Memory Problems*, 2nd edn. London: Chapman & Hall.

Baddeley, A. D. and Wilson, B. A. (1994) When implicit learning fails: Amnesia and the problem of error elimination. *Neuropsychologia*, 32, 53–68.

Barker, R. A. and Dunnett, S. B. (1999) *Neural Repair, Transplantation and Rehabilitation*. Hove, UK: Psychology Press.

Beck, A. T. (1976) *Cognitive Therapy and Emotional Disorders*. New York: International Universities Press.

Blowers, G. H. and O'Connor, K. P. (1995) Construing contexts: Problems and prospects of George Kelly's personal construct psychology. *British Journal of Clinical Psychology*, 34, 1–16.

Bowen, A., Neumann, V., Conner, M., Tennant, A. and Chamberlain, M. A. (1998) Mood disorders following traumatic brain injury: Identifying the extent of the problem and the people at risk. *Brain Injury*, 12, 177–190.

Brooks, D. N. and Baddeley, A. D. (1976) What can amnesic patients learn? *Neuropsychologia*, 14, 111–122.

Camp, C. J. (1989) Facilitation of new learning in Alzheimer's disease. In G. Gilmore, P. Whitehouse and M. Wykle (eds) *Memory and Aging: Theory, Research and Practice*. New York: Springer.

Clare, L., Wilson, B. A., Breen, E. K. and Hodges, J. R. (1999) Errorless learning of face–name associations in early Alzheimer's disease. *Neurocase*, 5, 37–46.

Clare, L., Wilson, B. A., Carter, G., Breen, E. K., Gosses, A. and Hodges, J. R. (2000) Intervening with everyday memory problems in dementia of Alzheimer type: An errorless learning approach. *Journal of Clinical and Experimental Neuropsychology*, 22, 132–146.

Clare, L., Wilson, B. A., Carter, G., Hodges, J. R. and Adams, M. (2001) Long-term maintenance of treatment gains following a cognitive rehabilitation intervention in early dementia of Alzheimer type: A single case study. *Neuropsychological Rehabilitation*, 11, 477–494.

Coleman, M. R. (ed) (2005) *The Assessment and Rehabilitation of Vegetative and Minimally Conscious Patients*. Hove, UK: Psychology Press.

Cope, N. (1994) Traumatic brain injury rehabilitation outcome studies in the United States. In: A-L. Christensen and B. P. Uzzell (eds) *Brain Injury and Neuropsychological Rehabilitation: International Perspectives*. Hillsdale, NJ: Lawrence Erlbaum Associates, Inc.

Craik, F. I. M. and Lockhart, R. S. (1972) Levels of processing: A framework for memory research. *Journal of Verbal Learning and Verbal Behavior*, 11, 671–684.

Curran, V. and Weingartner, H. (2002) The psychopharmacology of memory. In:

A. Baddeley, M. Kopelman and B. A. Wilson (eds) *Handbook of Memory Disorders*, 2nd edn. Chichester: John Wiley.

Demark, J. and Gemeinhardt, M. (2002) Anger and its management for survivors of acquired brain injury. *Brain Injury*, 16, 91–108.

D'Esposito, M. and Alexander, M. P. (1995) Subcortical aphasia: Distinct profiles following left putaminal hemorrhage. *Neurology*, 45, 38–41.

Diller, L. (1994) Changes in rehabilitation over the past 5 years. In: A-L. Christensen and B. P. Uzzell (eds) *Brain Injury and Neuropsychological Rehabilitation: International Perspectives*. Hillsdale, NJ: Lawrence Erlbaum Associates, Inc.

Dixon, R. A. and Bäckman, L. (1999) Principles of compensation in cognitive neurorehabilitation. In: D. T. Stuss, G. Winocur and I. H. Robertson (eds) *Cognitive Neurorehabilitation: A Comprehensive Approach*. New York: Cambridge University Press.

Division of Neuropsychology (2003) *Commissioning Clinical Neuropsychology Services*. Leicester: The British Psychological Society.

Donaghy, S. and Williams, W. (1998) A new protocol for training severely impaired patients in the usage of memory journals. *Brain Injury*, 12, 1061–1076.

Evans, J. J. and Wilson, B. A. (1992) A memory group for individuals with brain injury. *Clinical Rehabilitation*, 6, 75–81.

Evans, J. J., Emslie, H. and Wilson, B. A. (1998) External cueing systems in the rehabilitation of executive impairments of action. *Journal of the International Neuropsychological Society*, 4, 399–408.

Evans, J. J., Wilson, B. A., Schuri, U., Andrade, J., Baddeley, A., Bruna, O. et al. (2000) A comparison of 'errorless' and 'trial-and-error' learning methods for teaching individuals with acquired memory deficits. *Neuropsychological Rehabilitation*, 10, 67–101.

Evans, J. J., Wilson, B., Needham, P. and Brentnall, S. (2003) Who makes good use of memory aids? Results of a survey of people with acquired brain injury. *Journal of the International Neuropsychological Society*, 9, 925–935.

Fillingham, J. K., Hodgson, C., Sage, K. and Ralph, M. A. L. (2003) The application of errorless learning to aphasic disorders: A review of theory and practice. *Neuropsychological Rehabilitation*, 13(3), 337–363.

Freed, D. M., Corkin, S. and Cohen, N. J. (1998) Forgetting in HM: A second look. *Neuropsychologia*, 25, 461–471.

Gainotti, G. (1993) Emotional and psychosocial problems after brain injury. *Neuropsychological Rehabilitation*, 3, 259–277.

Gartland, D. (2004) Considerations in the selection and use of technology with people who have cognitive deficits following acquired brain injury. *Neuropsychological Rehabilitation*, 14, 61–75.

Glisky, E. L. and Schacter, D. L. (1986) Long-term retention of computer learning by patients with memory disorders. *Neuropsychologia*, 26, 173–178.

Gregor, P. and Newell, A. (eds) (2004) *Neuropsychological Rehabilitation. Special Issue on Technology in Cognitive Rehabilitation*. Hove, UK: Psychology Press.

Judd, T. (2003). Rehabilitation of the emotional problems of brain disorders in developing countries. *Neuropsychological Rehabilitation*, 13, 307–325.

Kapur, N. and Graham, K. S. (2002) Recovery of memory function in neurological disease. In: A. D. Baddeley, M. D. Kopelman and B. A. Wilson (eds) *Handbook of Memory Disorders*, 2nd edn. Chichester: John Wiley.

Kapur, N., Glisky, E. L. and Wilson, B. A. (2002) External memory aids and computers in memory rehabilitation. In: A. D. Baddeley, M. D. Kopelman and B. A. Wilson (eds) *Handbook of Memory Disorders*, 2nd edn. Chichester: John Wiley.

Kapur, N., Glisky, E. L. and Wilson, B. A. (2004) External memory aids and computers in memory rehabilitation. In: A. D. Baddeley, M. D. Kopelman and B. A. Wilson (eds) *The Essential Handbook of Memory Disorders for Clinicians*. Chichester: John Wiley.

Kelly, G. (1955) *The psychology of personal constructs*. New York: W. W. Norton.

Kime, S. K., Lamb, D. G. and Wilson, B. A. (1996) Use of a comprehensive program of external cuing to enhance procedural memory in a patient with dense amnesia. *Brain Injury*, 10, 17–25.

Kolb, B. (1995) *Brain Plasticity and Behavior*. Mahwah, NJ: Lawrence Erlbaum Associates, Inc.

Kopelman, M. and Crawford, S. (1996) Not all memory clinics are dementia clinics. *Neuropsychological Rehabilitation*, 6, 187–202.

Landauer, T. K. and Bjork, R. A. (1978) Optimum rehearsal patterns and name learning. In: M. M. Gruneberg, P. E. Morris and R. N. Sykes (eds) *Practical Aspects of Memory*. London: Academic Press.

Lincoln, N. B. (1989) Management of memory problems in a hospital setting. In: L. W. Poon, D. C. Rubin and B. A. Wilson (eds) *Everyday Cognition in Adulthood and Late Life*. Cambridge: Cambridge University Press.

Luria, A. R., Naydin, V. L., Tsvetkova, L. S. and Vinarskaya, E. N. (1969) Restoration of higher cortical functions following local brain damage. In: P. J. Vinken and G. W. Bruyn (eds) *Handbook of Clinical Neurology*. New York: Elsevier.

MacNiven, J. A., Poz, R., Bainbridge, K., Gracey, F. and Wilson, B. A. (2003) Emotional adjustment following cognitive recovery from 'persistent vegetative state': psychological and personal perspectives. *Brain Injury*, 17, 525–533.

Malia, K., Powell, G. and Torode, S. (1995) Personality and psychosocial function after brain injury. *Brain Injury*, 9, 697–712.

McKinlay, W. W., Brooks, D. N., Bond, M. R., Martinage, D. P. and Marshall, M. M. (1981) The short-term outcome of severe blunt head injury as reported by relatives of the injured persons. *Journal of Neurology, Neurosurgery and Psychiatry*, 44, 527–533.

Menon, D. K., Owen, A. M., Williams, E. J., Minhas, P. S., Allen, C. M. C., Boniface, S. J. et al. (1998) Cortical processing in persistent vegetative state. *Lancet*, 352, 220.

Moore, A. D. and Stambrook, M. (1995) Cognitive moderators of outcome following traumatic brain injury: A conceptual model and implications for rehabilitation. *Brain Injury*, 9, 109–130.

Nicholson, S. (1995) The narrative dance – A practice map for White's therapy. *Australian and New Zealand Journal of Family Therapy*, 16, 23–28.

Patterson, K. E. and Wilson, B. A. (1990) A ROSE is a ROSE or a NOSE: A deficit in initial letter identification. *Cognitive Neuropsychology*, 7, 447–477.

Prigatano, G. P. (1991) Disordered mind, wounded soul. The emerging role of psychotherapy in rehabilitation after brain damage. *Journal of Head Trauma Rehabilitation*, 6, 1–10.

Prigatano, G. P. (1999) *Principles of Neuropsychological Rehabilitation*. New York: Oxford University Press.

Rei, S. (2002) Preventing workplace aggression and violence: A role for occupational therapy. *Work*, 18, 15–22.

Robertson, I. H. (1999a) Setting goals for cognitive rehabilitation. *Current Opinion in Neurology*, 12, 703–708.

Robertson, I. H. (1999b) Theory-driven neuropsychological rehabilitation: The role of attention and competition in recovery of function after brain damage. In: D. Gopher and A. Koriat (eds) *Attention and Performance XVII. Cognitive Regulation of Performance: Interaction of Theory and Application*. Cambridge, MA: The MIT Press.

Robertson, I. H. (2003) *The Mind's Eye: An Essential Guide to Boosting Your Mental Power*. London: Bantam.

Robertson, I. H., Tegnér, R., Tham, K., Lo, A. and Nimmo-Smith, I. (1995) Sustained attention training for unilateral neglect: Theoretical and rehabilitation implications. *Journal of Clinical and Experimental Neuropsychology*, 17, 416–430.

Robertson, I. H., Hogg, K. and McMillan, T. M. (1998) Rehabilitation of unilateral neglect: Improving function by contralesional limb activation. *Neuropsychological Rehabilitation*, 8, 19–29.

Robinson, R. G. and Starkstein, S. E. (1989) Mood disorders following stroke: New findings and future directions. *Journal of Geriatric Psychiatry*, 22, 1–15.

Sabel, B. A. (1997) Unrecognized potential of surviving neurons: Within-systems plasticity, recovery of function and the hypothesis of minimal residual structure. *The Neuroscientist*, 3, 366–370.

Sage, K., Hesketh, A. and Lambon-Ralph, M. A. (in press) Using errorless learning to treat letter-by-letter reading: Contrasting word versus letter-based therapy. *Neuropsychological Rehabilitation*.

Salkovskis, P. M. (ed) (1996) *Frontiers of Cognitive Therapy*. New York: Guilford Press.

Schacter, D. L. and Glisky, E. L. (1986) Memory remediation: Restoration, alleviation, and the acquisition of domain-specific knowledge. In: B. Uzzell and Y. Gross (eds) *Clinical Neuropsychology of Intervention*. Boston: Martinus Nijhoff.

Scoville, W. B. and Milner, B. (1957) Loss of recent memory after bilateral hippocampal lesions. *Journal of Neurology, Neurosurgery and Psychiatry*, 20, 11–21.

Segal, Z. V., Williams, J. M. G. and Teasdale, J. D. (2002) *Mindfulness-based Cognitive Therapy for Depression: A New Approach to Preventing Relapse*. London: Guilford Press.

Sidman, M. and Stoddard, L. T. (1967) The effectiveness of fading in programming simultaneous form discrimination for retarded children. *Journal of Experimental Analysis of Behavior*, 10, 3–15.

Squires, E. J., Hunkin, N. M. and Parkin, A. J. (1997) Errorless learning of novel associations in amnesia. *Neuropsychologia*, 35, 1103–1111.

Terrace, H. S. (1963) Discrimination learning with and without 'errors'. *Journal of Experimental Analysis of Behavior*, 6, 1–27.

Terrace, H. S. (1966) Stimulus control. In: W. K. Honig (ed) *Operant Behavior: Areas of Research and Application*. New York: Appleton-Century-Crofts.

Thomas, C., Altenmuller, E., Marckmann, G., Kahrs, J. and Dichgans, J. (1997) Language processing in aphasia: Changes in lateralisation recovery patterns reflect cerebral plasticity in adults. *Electroencephalography and Clinical Neurophysiology*, 102, 86–97.

Victor, M., Adams, R. D. and Collins, G. H. (1989) *The Wernicke–Korsakoff Syndrome and Related Neurological Disorders due to Alcoholism and Malnutrition.* Philadelphia: F. A. Davis Company.

Walsh, B. F. and Lamberts, F. (1979) Errorless discrimination and fading as techniques for teaching sight words to TMR students. *American Journal of Mental Deficiency*, 83, 473–479.

Williams, W. H., Evans, J. J. and Wilson, B. A. (1999) Outcome measures for survivors of acquired brain injury in day and outpatient neurorehabilitation programmes. *Neuropsychological Rehabilitation*, 9, 421–436.

Williams, W. H., Evans, J. J., Wilson, B. A. and Needham, P. (2002) Prevalence of post-traumatic stress disorder symptoms after severe traumatic brain injury in a representative community sample. *Brain Injury*, 16, 673–679.

Williams, W. H., Evans, J. J. and Fleminger, S. (2003a) Neurorehabilitation and cognitive-behaviour therapy of anxiety disorders after brain injury: An overview and a case illustration of obsessive-compulsive disorder. *Neuropsychological Rehabilitation*, 13, 133–148.

Williams, W. H., Evans, J. J. and Wilson, B. A. (2003b) Neurorehabilitation for two cases of post-traumatic stress disorder following traumatic brain injury. *Cognitive Neuropsychiatry*, 8, 1–18.

Wilson, B. A. (1987) *Rehabilitation of memory.* New York: Guilford Press.

Wilson, B. A. (1991) Long term prognosis of patients with severe memory disorders. *Neuropsychological Rehabilitation*, 1, 117–134.

Wilson, B. A. (1997) Cognitive rehabilitation: How it is and how it might be. *Journal of the International Neuropsychological Society*, 3, 487–496.

Wilson, B. A. (1999) *Case studies in neuropsychological rehabilitation.* New York: Oxford University Press.

Wilson, B. A. (2000) Compensating for cognitive deficits following brain injury. *Neuropsychology Review*, 10, 233–243.

Wilson, B. A. (2003) Treatment and recovery from brain damage. In: L. Nadel (ed) *Encyclopedia of Cognitive Science.* London: Nature Publishing Group.

Wilson, B. A. (2004) Theoretical approaches to cognitive rehabilitation. In: L. H. Goldstein and J. McNeil (eds) *Clinical Neuropsychology: A Guide to Assessment and Management for Clinicians.* Chichester: John Wiley.

Wilson, B. A. and Baddeley, A. D. (1993) Spontaneous recovery of impaired memory span: Does comprehension recover? *Cortex*, 29, 153–159.

Wilson, B. A. and Davidoff, J. (1993) Partial recovery from visual object agnosia. *Cortex*, 29, 529–542.

Wilson, B. A. and Evans, J. J. (1996) Error free learning in the rehabilitation of individuals with memory impairments. *Journal of Head Trauma Rehabilitation*, 11, 54–64.

Wilson, B. A. and Evans, J. J. (2000) Practical management of memory problems. In: G. E. Berrios and J. R. Hodges (eds) *Memory Disorders in Psychiatric Practice.* Cambridge: Cambridge University Press.

Wilson, B. A. and Watson, P. C. (1996) A practical framework for understanding compensatory behaviour in people with organic memory impairment. *Memory*, 4, 465–486.

Wilson, B. A., Baddeley, A. D., Evans, J. J. and Shiel, A. (1994) Errorless learning in the rehabilitation of memory impaired people. *Neuropsychological Rehabilitation*, 4, 307–326.

Wilson, B. A., Baddeley, A. D. and Kapur, N. (1995) Dense amnesia in a professional musician following herpes simplex virus encephalitis. *Journal of Clinical and Experimental Psychology*, 17, 668–681.

Wilson, B. A., Green, R., Teasdale, T., Beckers, K., Della Sala, S., Kaschel, R. et al. (1996) Implicit learning in amnesic subjects: A comparison with a large group of normal control subjects. *The Clinical Neuropsychologist*, 10, 279–292.

Wilson, B. A., J. C. and Hughes, E. (1997a) Coping with amnesia: The natural history of a compensatory memory system. *Neuropsychological Rehabilitation*, 7, 43–56.

Wilson, B. A., Evans, J. J., Emslie, H. and Malinek, V. (1997b) Evaluation of NeuroPage: A new memory aid. *Journal of Neurology, Neurosurgery and Psychiatry*, 63, 113–115.

Wilson, B. A., Emslie, H., Quirk, K. and Evans, J. (1999) George: Learning to live independently with NeuroPage®. *Rehabilitation Psychology*, 44, 284–296.

Wilson, B. A., Emslie, H. C., Quirk, K. and Evans, J. J. (2001a) Reducing everyday memory and planning problems by means of a paging system: A randomised control crossover study. *Journal of Neurology, Neurosurgery and Psychiatry*, 70, 477–482.

Wilson, B. A., Gracey, F. and Bainbridge, K. (2001b) Cognitive recovery from 'persistent vegetative state': psychological and personal perspectives. *Brain Injury*, 15, 1083–1092.

Wilson, B. A., Scott, H., Evans, J. J. and Emslie, H. (2003) Preliminary report of a NeuroPage Service within a health care system. *Neurorehabilitation*, 18, 3–8.

Wright, P., Rogers, N., Hall, C., Wilson, B. A., Evans, J. J., Emslie, H. and Bartram, C. (2001) Comparison of pocket-computer aids for people with brain injury. *Brain Injury*, 15, 787–800.

Zangwill, O. L. (1947) Psychological aspects of rehabilitation in cases of brain injury. *British Journal of Psychology*, 37, 60–69.

Chapter 38

Psychological evidence in court

Gisli Gudjonsson

INTRODUCTION

The word 'forensic' is derived from the Latin *forensis*, which specifically refers to the Roman forum. Therefore, the use of the term 'forensic' is most appropriately restricted to evidence pertaining to the court. In line with this correct use of the term, Haward defines forensic psychology as 'that branch of applied psychology which is concerned with the collection, examination and presentation of evidence for judicial purposes' (Haward, 1981, p 21). The term 'forensic psychology' is used more broadly by some American (e.g. Weiner and Hess, 1987; O'Donohue and Levensky, 2004) and English writers (Adler, 2004) and by the Division of Forensic Psychology of the British Psychological Society (BPS), which views this specialty as any professional practice and research endeavour where psychology and the law interact (Gudjonsson and Haward, 1998). Reviewing the range of definitions, Blackburn (1996) argues that the central element of a definition of forensic psychology encompasses 'the provision of psychological information for the purpose of facilitating a legal definition' (p 8).

This chapter deals specifically with psychological evidence in court; therefore Haward's definition of forensic psychology is ideal, because it focuses on the two main features of forensic psychology. These are: (1) the collection and examination of evidence (e.g. by assessing suspects, victims and witnesses, and by studying documents); and (2) the presentation of evidence, written or oral, in judicial proceedings.

The chapter highlights some of the unique contributions that psychologists can make and the types of problem that may arise when they prepare court reports and present evidence in court. Those readers who are interested in the history of forensic psychology as it developed in Great Britain during the second part of the twentieth century, and how that links to current practice, should read Gudjonsson and Haward (1998). Lionel Haward was the first 'forensic psychologist' in Great Britain, and did much to shape the roles of forensic psychology and bring its unique contributions to the attention of the judiciary. His groundbreaking efforts, which stimulated the 'new' generation of forensic psychologists, including the present author, were fundamental in subsequently bringing expert psychological testimony before the Court of Appeal (Criminal Division) and the House of Lords in landmark judgements (Heaton-Armstrong, 2005).

The contributions that psychologists can make to judicial proceedings are influenced, to a large extent, by the legal framework within which they have to work. Individual legal systems have their own 'law of evidence' or 'roles of evidence' that govern the admissibility and presentation of evidence before the court (Gudjonsson, 2003a). Therefore, any discussion about psychological evidence in court must address the legal constraints within which such evidence is going to be allowed. I shall accordingly discuss briefly the English legal system and the significant changes that have taken place in recent years with regard to the admissibility of psychological evidence.

It is now over a century since psychologists began to provide the courts with psychological evidence (Gudjonsson and Haward, 1998). In that time, the scope of forensic psychology has grown immensely. This has resulted in increased demand for psychological services, with psychologists functioning more independently than ever before in judicial proceedings (Sigurdsson and Gudjonsson, 2004). The growth in the demand for court reports has occurred in both civil and criminal proceedings (Gudjonsson and Haward, 1998). In civil cases the demand for a clinical evaluation is typically in relation to head injuries, post-traumatic stress disorder and child-care proceedings, whereas in criminal cases the focus is on sentencing, mitigation, disputed confessions and fitness to plead and stand trial issues.

THE LEGAL FRAMEWORK

Within the English and Scottish legal systems, cases can be divided into civil and criminal proceedings. Criminal cases are generally brought against defendants by the Crown Prosecution Service in England and Wales or the Procurator Fiscal in Scotland, who are acting on behalf of the State. A civil proceeding involves all those cases brought before the court which are not criminal. Action is typically brought against another individual or company with the intention of seeking financial compensation for such matters as a breach of contract or personal injury. Civil cases may also involve family issues (e.g. child-care proceedings, divorce) and property disputes. Gudjonsson and Haward (1998) provide a detailed description of the English legal framework in relation to both civil and legal cases.

Broadly speaking, two main types of legal system exist; these are typically referred to as 'inquisitorial' and 'adversarial', respectively. The former system, which is favoured in other European countries, is based on the foundation that justice is best served by the court itself searching for the facts in the case by listening to witnesses and examining available material surrounding the case. Further police investigations are ordered if the judge considers it necessary. Under this system, it would be the responsibility of the court to commission psychological and psychiatric reports, and all reports would be made available to the judge.

The 'adversarial' system, on the other hand, which is used in English law, is based on the assumption that justice is best derived from direct confrontation by the defence and prosecution sides rather than from an inquiry.

The main advantage for psychologists working within an inquisitorial system is that expert witnesses have access to all the salient documents and far more background information about the case than when instructed within an adversarial system (Gudjonsson and Haward, 1998). Furthermore, their findings are suppressed when deemed to be unfavourable to one side, which is often the case in England (Gudjonsson, 2003a). The main disadvantage for psychologists working within an inquisitorial system is that their role is rather limited, with psychiatric evaluations dominating (Gudjonsson and Haward, 1998).

The main reason for this seems to be that the inquisitorial approach to issues is less inclined to stimulate the development of new ideas than the adversarial approach. However, it is worth remembering that until the 1970s the role of British psychologists in forensic evaluations was typically restricted to referrals coming from psychiatrists rather than the police, the prosecution or the legal profession (Gudjonsson and Haward, 1998).

From the point of view of an expert witness, there are some distinct advantages with the adversarial system. First, psychologists are more likely to be instructed to address specific issues rather than being required to give a general psychological profile of the defendant (i.e. the instructions tend to be more focused). Second, psychologists working within an adversarial system are more likely to be required to give oral evidence in court, which means that their testimony is potentially open to rigorous cross-examination. This has the advantage of making expert witnesses more careful in their examination of defendants and overcomes some of the dangers of unsubstantiated opinions being uncritically accepted by the court. Indeed, I would argue that the adversarial system makes psychologists more aware of the strengths and limitations of their evidence and encourages them to look for improved methods and techniques, thereby stimulating empirical research (Gudjonsson, 2003b).

Most civil litigation is dealt with by the County Court. However, the Magistrates' Courts, which deal with up to 98% of all criminal cases, also process some civil cases, such as domestic disputes and child-care proceedings. The Crown Court deals with the most serious criminal cases and provides defendants with a trial by jury in contested cases. The Crown Court also deals with cases committed for sentence from the Magistrates' Court. When defendants wish to appeal against the decision of magistrates, this is heard in the Crown Court. Further appeals are heard in the Court of Appeal, which is divided into civil and criminal divisions. Final domestic appeals, which are generally on points of law and of general public importance, are heard in the House of Lords. When domestic appeals fail, cases involving contentious issues can be taken to the European Court of Human Rights.

Clinical psychologists sometimes give evidence in the Magistrates' Court, particularly in juvenile and domestic cases (Gudjonsson and Haward, 1998). In the Crown Court they tend to be instructed in the most serious cases, such as those involving sexual offences and violence, including murder. The role of clinical psychologists in such cases is very varied (Cooke, 1980; Haward, 1981; Blau, 1984; Weiner and Hess, 1987; Lloyd-Bostock, 1988; Gudjonsson and Haward, 1998; O'Donohue and Levenskey, 2004).

THE ROLE OF THE FORENSIC PSYCHOLOGIST

The different roles of psychologists in judicial proceedings have been described in detail by Haward (1981, 1990), who identifies four main roles and describes the types of court where psychologists may find themselves giving evidence. These roles are referred to by Haward as 'experimental', 'clinical', 'actuarial' and 'advisory'.

In the *experimental role*, psychologists perform a unique function that is generally outside the expertise of forensic psychiatrists. In this role, human behaviour is studied by experimentation rather than by a clinical interview, and it requires the ability and knowledge to apply psychological principles and techniques to unique forensic problems. On occasions it involves devising ingenious experiments, both in civil and criminal cases (Haward, 1981, 1990).

For example, Gudjonsson and Sartory (1983) used an experimental procedure involving a polygraph as an aid to the diagnosis of blood-injury phobia, which resulted in the overturning on appeal of a defendant's conviction for failing to provide a specimen of blood in a suspected drunken driving case. The case involved a young man who had been stopped by the police for suspected drunken driving. The man was breathalysed by the police. After failing two breathalyser tests, he was asked to provide a specimen of blood for analysis, which he refused to do on the basis that he was mentally unable to do so. The man was subsequently convicted in the Magistrates' Court for failing to give a specimen. He appealed against his conviction on the basis that he was a genuine blood phobic and therefore had a reasonable excuse for failing to provide a specimen of blood. The man was referred to the present author for an assessment of the genuineness of his alleged blood-injury phobia. At the time, it was known in the clinical psychology literature

(Sartory et al., 1977) that genuine blood-injury phobia was associated with unique cardiac reactions (lowering of heart rate and blood pressure), which could be monitored physiologically by a polygraph (Gudjonsson, 1992). A polygraph examination of the man's heart rate to blood-related and neutral items clearly indicated that he exhibited cardiac reactions typical of blood-injury phobia (Gudjonsson and Sartory, 1983). This evidence was presented by the present author at the man's appeal and his conviction was overturned by the judges.

In another case, an experimental procedure was applied to a case of alleged rape of a person with severe learning disability in order to differentiate between areas of the victim's reliable and unreliable testimony (Gudjonsson and Gunn, 1982). The victim's testimony was the main prosecution evidence against six defendants. In view of the victim's learning disability, the prosecution was concerned about the likely reliability of her evidence against the defendants and how she would be able to cope with cross-examination in court. A detailed psychological examination indicated that she was able to distinguish between facts and fantasy when the facts were clear to her, but when she was unsure of the facts she became readily suggestible to questioning. Most importantly, those of her statements that had no objective basis could be easily altered under pressure, whereas those answers that were correct could not be altered. The psychological findings were presented to the jury at the Old Bailey in order to provide them with guidelines by which they could discriminate between the reliable and unreliable evidence as pertaining to the case being tried. Five of the six defendants were convicted.

This case, which subsequently stimulated the development of the Gudjonsson Suggestibility Scales (Gudjonsson, 1997, 2003a), demonstrated how a highly suggestible person with learning disability was capable of giving reliable testimony pertaining to basic facts she clearly remembered.

Haward (1981) highlights the forensic importance of experiments into perception and memory. This kind of evidence falls into two distinct categories. First is general evidence about scientific findings concerning the limitations of human memory and its fallibility, particularly in relation to eyewitness identification evidence (Loftus, 1979). This kind of expert evidence, which is commonly presented in the courts in the USA, is not admissible in Britain (Davies, 1983). This relates to the fact that British courts are reluctant to admit evidence of a general nature, which does not directly focus on abnormality in the personality or mental state of the defendant.

The second type of scientific evidence that is admissible in the British courts, relates to experiments directly relevant to the individual case. For example, in one case described by Haward (1981), four motorcyclists had been involved in a collision with a sports car. Three of them were charged with dangerous driving on the basis that a police officer claimed to have seen them earlier in the day travelling at a dangerously high speed. The basis of the police officer's identification of the motorcyclists was that he had been able to memorise their registration numbers when he had seen them earlier in the day. Haward carried out an experiment on a sample of 100 normal subjects and demonstrated that the police officer would have been extremely unlikely to be able to record the registration numbers as he had claimed (i.e. the findings indicated that none of the 100 subjects had been able to replicate the police officer's claimed perceptual efficiency under experimental conditions).

The *clinical role* is most appropriately fulfilled by chartered clinical psychologists. This is the most common role among psychologists who have been instructed to prepare a court report (Gudjonsson and Haward, 1998) and overlaps with the role fulfilled by forensic psychiatrists. Here, the psychologist interviews a client and carries out the required assessment, which may include extensive psychometric testing (e.g. the administration of tests of intelligence, neuropsychological functioning, personality and mental state) and behavioural data. The nature of the assessment will, of course, depend on the instruction of the referral agent and the type of problem being assessed. Clients may need to be assessed on more than one occasion. In addition, whenever possible and appropriate, informants should be consulted for providing further information. Previous reports, including school reports and psychological and psychiatric assessments, should be obtained whenever they are likely to be relevant to the present assessment.

The *actuarial role* refers to the application of statistical probabilities to events and behaviour. This role is not confined to psychologists and is commonly used by statisticians and other scientists when interpreting observational and behavioural data. The type of probabilities and observational data analysed by psychologists may include estimating the probability that a person with a given psychological deficit could earn a living or live independently in the community (Haward, 1981).

The *advisory role* generally consists of psychologists advising counsel about what questions to ask when cross-examining psychologists who are testifying for the other side. For example, the prosecuting counsel may request that a psychologist sits behind him in court and advises him how to cross-examine the defence psychologist. Reports by psychologists are increasingly being subjected to peer review by an expert for the other side. That expert may have carefully studied the psychological report and, in addition, may have carried out an assessment of the defendant.

Having another psychologist in court evaluating one's testimony has been reported to increase the stress experienced when psychologists testify (Gudjonsson, 1985). Sometimes there is considerable disagreement between the opinions of psychology experts and this may result in lengthy and stressful cross-examination (Tunstall et al., 1982). When preparing a court report, psychologists should always assume that their report will be subjected to a careful peer review by the other side. Even if it is not, lawyers are becoming increasingly familiar with psychological testimony and are able to ask some very searching questions. The psychologist must be thoroughly familiar with the development and validation of the instruments and tests used.

PSYCHOLOGISTS' CONTRIBUTIONS TO CRIMINAL PROCEEDINGS

In most legal systems, there are three distinct stages to criminal proceedings: pre-trial, trial and sentencing. The nature and contribution of the psychological assessment will be influenced by the relevant legal issues. It is therefore essential that psychologists who are preparing court reports are familiar with the relevant legal concepts at each stage of the criminal proceedings, as well as being full briefed about the legal issues in the case they are assessing.

Pre-trial issues

At the pre-trial stage, the defendant's fitness to plead and fitness to stand trial may be questioned by the defence (Grubin, 1996). This happens when the defendant's physical or mental state at the time of the trial is such that proceeding with the case is thought to interfere with due process of the law (that is, the defendant may not have a fair trial if the case proceeds). The ability of the defendant to give adequate instructions to his or her lawyers, to understand the charge against him or her, to distinguish between a plea of guilty and not guilty, to testify, and to follow the proceedings in court are the main legal issues to be decided upon at the pre-trial stage. In England, fitness to plead and stand trial is generally raised only in serious cases because of their legal and clinical significance (Grubin, 1996).

The main problem for the forensic psychiatrist and psychologist, which applies equally to British and American expert witnesses, is that the legal constructs of fitness criteria are defined and described too inadequately in case law to enable the expert to evaluate satisfactorily the defendant's psychiatric and psychological vulnerabilities within the context of the legal criteria. This often means that the psychiatric evaluation is only going to be peripherally related to the legal criteria.

In the USA, clinical psychologists are actively involved in this area of the criminal proceedings, where their role overlaps considerably with that of psychiatrists (Cooke, 1980; Blau, 1984; Weiner and Hess, 1987). Special psychological instruments, commonly referred to as 'competency tests', have been developed by American psychologists to assess objectively the psychological deficits that are relevant to the legal issues (Blau, 1984). Recent factor analytic studies into competency tests have raised concern about the lack of stable factor structure across different subject samples (Bagby et al., 1992). Bagby et al. (1992) recommend that what is needed is a further development of empirical measures that better match the legal construct of competency to stand trial.

In the UK, psychiatrists are mainly involved at this stage of the proceedings, and psychologists become involved only occasionally. In recent years, however, psychologists are being increasingly requested by defence lawyers to carry out a psychological assessment on these cases, because it provides the court with an objective and standardised assessment of the defendant's strengths and weaknesses. This may involve an assessment of the defendant's intellectual and neuropsychological status, as well as an assessment of problems related to anxiety and depression.

For example, in one case referred to the present author, a middle-aged man was charged with very serious criminal offences connected with the laundering of millions of pounds in proceeds from a robbery. He had been assessed by a number of psychiatrists, who were concerned about the defendant's fitness to stand trial because of a depressive illness, which appeared to impair his ability to brief counsel and follow the proceedings in court. The case involved complicated international financial dealings where the defendant had to be able to cope with a lengthy trial and taxing cross-examination. The present author was asked to conduct a psychological investigation on the defendant, with a view to establishing whether or not he was fit to stand trial. The psychological assessment indicated that the defendant was severely depressed, which was accompanied by impaired intellectual functioning. In particular, he had serious attentional problems and slowness in cognitive processing, which would have made it impossible for him to follow adequately the court proceedings, considering the complexity of the case. For example, he found it very difficult to concentrate on questions and tasks during the psychological assessment and it took him a long time to grasp instructions and complete simple tasks. This resulted in his failing to earn points on many of the timed subtests of the WAIS-R.

All the experts testified in court about the defendant's mental condition. The defendant was found unfit to stand trial and was provided with psychiatric treatment for his depression. Two years later he was considered by psychiatrists to be fit to stand trial and was convicted and given a substantial prison sentence.

Adverse inferences for failure to testify

In the great majority of cases where a defendant is physically or mentally unable to testify, he or she would also be considered unable to plead and stand trial (e.g. *R. v. Billy-Joe Friend*, [2004], EWCA Crim 2661). An issue that is of growing importance in criminal trials is whether or not a defendant chooses to testify at trial. This is due to recent changes in the law. The Criminal Justice and Public Order Act 1994 (Wasik and Taylor, 1995) makes it possible for the court to draw adverse inferences from the accused's silence, whether at the police station (Section 34) or from failure to give evidence at trial (Section 35). Section 35 applies to defendants who are 14 years or older. However, according to Subsection 1(b) no adverse inferences should be drawn if:

> . . . it appears to the court that the physical or mental condition of the accused makes it undesirable for him to give evidence.

Until recently, the legal precedent used regarding issue of 'undesirability' to go into the witness box due to mental factors was that in the case of *R. v. Billy-Joe Friend* ([1997], Cr. App. R. 231). The case involved a 15-year-old youth who was charged with murder. Shortly before trial, I had assessed the defendant for the defence and found him to have an IQ score of 63. He did not prove to be suggestible on testing and, unusually, his verbal comprehension on the WAIS-III fell in the average range. I testified at the Central Criminal Court during a *voir dire* and stated that in spite of his low intelligence the defendant could give a clear account in an interview if allowed time to express himself and if care was taken that he understood. However, I expressed great concern about the defendant's attentional problems and distractibility, which would be exacerbated if he were to go in the witness box. The defence counsel submitted that on the basis of my evidence the jury should not be invited to draw an adverse inference from his failure to give evidence:

> . . . because his mental condition made it undesirable to do so in light of Section 35(1)(b). The judge declined so to rule and referred to the fact that children as young as eight years old gave evidence in Crown Court trials. In his summing-up he directed the jury that it was open to them to draw an adverse inference from the appellant's failure to give evidence. The appellant was convicted of murder.

> (p. 231)

In October 2004, the Court of Appeal, due to new evidence that showed that at the time of trial in 1996 Billy-Joe was suffering from undiagnosed attention deficit hyperactivity disorder (ADHD) and could not have effectively participated in his own trial, quashed his conviction. In their ruling, the Court of

Appeal relied on the written evidence of Dr Susan Young, an expert on ADHD, who concluded:

> In his evidence Professor Gudjonsson highlighted Billy Joe Friend's general intellectual impairment as well as his relative intellectual strengths. He drew attention to the fact that that Billy Joe Friend 'was disadvantaged overall to a significant degree with those specific strengths that he has'. He stated that his main concern was Billy Joe Friend's distractibility, however Professor Gudjonsson was unaware at the time of the full extent of Billy Joe Friend's impairment in attention and response inhibition. Billy Joe Friend was suffering with Attention Deficit Hyperactivity Disorder and his cognitive deficits were secondary to his primary problem, ADHD, which was not diagnosed at the time . . . due to his ADHD (and cognitive deficits being exacerbated by anxiety) and combined with verbal deficits, it was undesirable for Billy Joe Friend to give evidence
>
> (*R.* v. *Billy-Joe Friend*, [2004], EWCA Crim 2661;
> Gudjonsson and Young, 2006, p. 214).

The word 'undesirable' means something less than unfit to plead (*R.* v. *Barry George*, Central Criminal Court, 15 June 2001). In the Jill Dando murder case, the defendant, Barry George, who had a history of epilepsy and significant neuropsychological deficits, was considered fit to plead and stand trial by three defence expert witnesses (Professor Gisli Gudjonsson, Professor Michael Kopelman and Dr Susan Young). Nevertheless, the experts considered that serious problems might arise during his testimony, which made it potentially undesirable for him to go into the witness box. The judge agreed and advised the jury that no adverse inferences should be drawn about Mr George's failure to go into the witness box.

The Jill Dando case set an important legal precedent relevant to fitness to plead and stand trial. At the beginning of the 10-week trial, the judge ruled that a social worker would stay with Mr George in the dock to provide him with emotional and practical support and, in addition to that, a clinical psychologist, Dr Susan Young, was commissioned by the judge to sit in Court throughout the trial, observe Mr George's demeanour and provide him in the breaks with the clinical psychology service required to help him cope with the trial. It was only by this provision that Mr George was fit to stand trial and the case proceeded without any further problems and delays. During lengthy legal arguments, at the beginning of the trial, Mr George had developed a psychogenic blindness, which lasted 5 days and was overcome by my successfully providing him with a brief session of hypnosis.

Trial issues

In English law, a criminal offence consists of a number of different elements. These fall into two main categories and are referred to as *actus reus* and *mens rea* (see Leng, 1990, for a detailed review). The former comprises elements relevant to the criminal act itself, whereas the latter generally, but not exclusively, focuses on the mental state of the defendant. During the *actus reus* stage, the prosecution has to prove: (1) that a criminal offence was committed; and (2) that the defendant committed it. Issues related to *mens rea* focus on the state of mind of the accused at the time of the alleged offence and its blameworthiness (e.g. whether the offence was committed either intentionally or recklessly).

The criteria for establishing *mens rea* depend on the nature of the offence. The reason for this is that each offence is defined separately in law and there are no standard criteria for defining *mens rea* across different offences, even among related offences. Some offences do not require an element of *mens rea* for the defendant to be convicted (that is, they are offences of 'strict liability' and the prosecution only has to prove *actus reus*). However, in such cases, a mental condition relevant to *mens rea* can be used as mitigation at the sentencing stage.

Psychologists in England are commonly asked to prepare court reports that are relevant to both *actus reus* and *mens rea* issues and their involvement in such cases is expanding rapidly (Gudjonsson and Haward, 1998). The contribution of clinical psychologists to *mens rea* issues complements that of their psychiatrist colleagues (Sigurdsson and Gudjonsson, 2004). This may include dealing with issues relevant to 'abnormality of mind' and diminished responsibility in cases of homicide and the question of intent in cases of alleged shoplifting.

Sentencing issues

Sentencing is the final stage in the criminal proceedings and takes place after the defendant has been found guilty of the charged offence. If the defendant is acquitted by the jury or magistrates, then he or she is free to go. Where the defendant pleads guilty or is convicted, the judge or the magistrates have to pass a sentence. Various sentencing options are available, depending on the nature of the offence and the circumstances of the case (Eysenck and Gudjonsson, 1989). These include a prison sentence, a financial penalty, probation and community service orders. In the case of minor offences, a fine is the most common sentence. In more serious cases, depending on the nature of any aggravating features (e.g. domestic burglaries carried out at night with the occupants in the house asleep), the defendant may be sentenced to prison or given up to 240 hours of community service (i.e. given some tasks to do in the local community under close supervision).

Psychologists are less involved at the sentencing stage than their psychiatrist colleagues, but increasingly they are providing court reports about factors that are relevant to mitigation and sentencing (Gudjonsson and Haward, 1998). This includes offering an opinion about treatment options and likely prognosis. The advice given may involve offering treatment to persons convicted of sexual offences, compulsive shoplifting (Gudjonsson, 1987) or car theft (Brown, 1985).

PSYCHOLOGICAL TESTING

There is very little information available about the extent to which psychological tests are used in forensic assessment. Forensic psychiatrists almost invariably base their assessment on a clinical interview and they do not, on the whole, have the necessary training or expertise for administering psychological tests. Clinical psychologists, on the other hand, have the advantage of being able to use standardised psychological tests for measuring functional skills and deficits, personality and mental status (Blau, 1984; Grisso, 1986; Heilbrun, 1992). This means that their evidence is generally more factually based than the evidence of psychiatrists, who rely almost exclusively on an opinion.

Blackburn (1996) discusses the utility of forensic psychology and emphasizes the 'need for assessment procedures which are responsive for forensic issues' (p. 14), but argues that few important contributions have been made in this area, the exceptions being instruments developed for assessing legal criteria or competence in the USA (Grisso, 1987) and the development of the Gudjonsson Suggestibility Scales in the UK (Gudjonsson, 1992).

Gudjonsson (1996), in his survey of members of the British Psychological Society, found that 96% of the psychologists studied said they generally used psychological tests when carrying out a forensic assessment. The most common tests used were those that focused on functional strengths and deficits, such as the WAIS and various neuropsychological tests. A small minority (9%) said that they most commonly used personality tests, including the MMPI and the EPQ. In spite of the large proportion of psychologists who generally used psychological tests in their forensic assessment, most also relied on behavioural assessment and interview data. Therefore, although psychological tests are commonly applied when conducting a forensic assessment, they typically form a part of the overall assessment.

The extent to which psychological tests are used in a forensic assessment will depend on the practice and orientation of the individual psychologist concerned. However, it also depends on the instruction received from the referral agent and the nature of the problem to be assessed. For example, subjects referred specifically for assessment of intellectual functioning or neuropsychological status would invariably need to be tested, whereas in child custody cases the psychological assessment is typically heavily dependent on information obtained by interviews and observations (Keilin and Bloom, 1986). Where the instruction given by the referral agent is not clear, the psychologist will need to clarify the purpose of the assessment verbally or in writing. It is often useful to know the legal issues involved in a given case, so that the psychological assessment can be planned accordingly.

Heilbrun (1992) provides useful guidelines for the use of psychological testing in forensic assessment. These include:

- The test used should be adequately documented and reviewed in the scientific literature and need to contain a manual describing the test's development, psychometric properties and procedure.
- The reliability of the test chosen should be considered carefully.
- The test chosen must be relevant to (i.e. valid for) the legal issue addressed, or the psychological construct underlying the legal issue. Preferably, relevance should be supported by published validation research, although on occasions justification for using a particular test may be made on theoretical grounds.
- The standard administration recommended in the test's manual should be used, which normally requires a quiet and distraction-free testing environment.
- The findings from a particular test should not be applied towards a purpose for which the test was not developed (e.g. making inferences about psychopathology, suggestibility or confabulation from the results of IQ tests). Interpretation of the results should be guided by population and situation specificity; that is, the closer the individual 'fits' the population and situation of those described in the validation studies, the greater the confidence one can express in the applicability of the results. Many tests used in forensic practice were standardised on non-forensic populations, which may make generalisability of the results difficult.
- There is considerable controversy in the literature about clinical versus statistical predictions (e.g. Meehl, 1954). Using a combination of results from objective tests and actuarial data is preferable. Of course, very much depends on the type of assessment that is being carried out, and the circumstances under which the test is administered. For example, many clinical judgements of intellectual skills and suggestibility traits are often grossly wrong (Gudjonsson, 1992a), and objective measurements would give more reliable information than clinical judgements. Conversely, a clinical interview is often essential for assessing the person's current or past mental state, and this may be supplemented by objective tests, such as the General Health Questionnaire (GHQ) and the Beck Depression Inventory (BDI).
- When interpreting the results from tests it is important that the 'forensic'

psychologist is sensitive to behaviours ('response style') that have a bearing on the validity of the results (e.g. defensiveness, evasiveness, denial and malingering).

One of the most important points that Heilbrun makes is that psychological testing should be viewed as a part of hypothesis testing Thus:

> Psychological testing can serve as one source of information that can both formulate and confirm or disconfirm hypotheses about psychological constructs relevant to legal issues, but there are others as well: history, medical testing, interview data, and third-party observations of behaviour can all be used for these purposes'
>
> (Heilbrun, 1992, p. 268).

Once the hypotheses have been formulated they need to be tested out by objective means.

ASSESSMENT IN CASES OF RETRACTED CONFESSION

Prior to the early 1980s, most cases involving retracted or disputed confession were referred to psychiatrists, who were typically ill-equipped to assess the relevant psychological issues (Gudjonsson, 2003a). Following the present author's research activities in the area of suggestibility and false confession (Gudjonsson, 2003a), and his involvement in a number of notable cases in the Court of Appeal (Gudjonsson, 2002, 2003b), clinical psychologists are increasingly being referred cases where confession evidence is disputed, including psychologists in the USA (DeClue, 2005). Legal precedents have been created in over 20 cases in the Court of Appeal since 1989, when the 'Guildford Four' were released. The landmark case in relation to psychological evidence in cases of disputed confessions is that of Engin Raghip, whose conviction was quashed by the Court of Appeal in December 1991 on the basis of expert psychological evidence. In this case, known as the 'Tottenham Three', the criteria for admissibility of expert psychological evidence were broadened and separated from medical/psychiatric evidence. The admissibility of psychological evidence could now be admitted in its own right rather than falling under the umbrella of general medical evidence of mental disorder. According to the judgement, the crucial question for the judge to decide with regard to the admissibility of expert psychological evidence is as follows:

> Is the mental condition of the defendant such that the jury would be assisted by expert help in assessing it?

In this context, the term 'mental condition' refers not only to intellectual functions and mental state, but also to personality traits, such as suggestibility (see Gudjonsson, 2003a, pp 455–468). Subsequent to this judgement, other Court of Appeal judgements have expanded on the nature of psychological evidence to include such vulnerabilities as compliance, acquiescence, confabulation, high trait anxiety, and personality disorder (Gudjonsson, 2002). Undoubtedly, the most important judgement is that in the case of *R. v. Pendleton in the House of Lords* (13 December 2001, UKHL 66). In June 2000 I had testified in the Court of Appeal in relation to Mr Pendleton's psychological vulnerabilities (e.g. abnormal suggestibility, compliance, acquiescence and anxiety proneness), stating that I had 'severe reservations' about the confession to murder that Mr Pendleton had made to the police. Even though my testimony was not disputed, the Lordship found 'it inconceivable that his [the defendant's] accounts were imagined or invented' and upheld the conviction (Gudjonsson, 2003a). The defence appealed to the House of Lords on the basis that the Court of Appeal should not have acted as jury in the case and the conviction should have been quashed on the basis of the psychological evidence. The House of Lords agreed and stated:

> In light of these uncertainties and this fresh psychological evidence it is impossible to be sure that this conviction is safe, and that is so whether the members of the House ask whether they themselves have reason to doubt the safety of the conviction or whether they ask whether the jury might have reached a different conclusion.
>
> (13 December 2001, UKHL 66, p. 22)

The English criminal courts have now become more accepting of psychological evidence. This has resulted in solicitors referring many more cases to psychologists for evaluation concerning psychological constructs relevant to the assessment of the reliability of confession evidence. The specific legal issues addressed in the assessment of these cases and the type of psychological examination that needs to be conducted are discussed in detail by Gudjonsson (2003a). For a comprehensive assessment, Gudjonsson (2003a) recommends four groups of factors to be assessed:

1   Characteristics of the defendant (e.g. age, knowledge of legal rights, intelligence, memory capacity, personality).
2   The circumstances of the arrest and custody.
3   The defendant's physical and mental state during custody and interrogation.
4   Interrogative factors (e.g. the length and type of interrogation).

Most commonly, solicitors ask for an assessment of intellectual functioning and suggestibility. The type of suggestibility directly relevant to the assessment is 'interrogative suggestibility', which refers to the tendency of the individual to yield to leading questions and to give in to interrogative pressure (Gudjonsson and Clark, 1986; Gudjonsson, 1992). This type of suggestibility, which differs in many ways from other types of suggestibility (e.g. hypnotic suggestibility), can be measured objectively (Gudjonsson, 1997). The findings from the psychological testing may need to be interpreted within the context of the overall case, especially if the psychologist testifies in court. It is therefore important that the psychologist has access to all the relevant documents in the case before interviewing the defendant, including the tape-recorded interviews and a copy of the custody record.

PRESENTING PSYCHOLOGICAL EVIDENCE

The purpose of the psychological evidence is to present information that is outside the knowledge of the judge and juror in order to assist them with their decision-making. Poor psychological evidence is that which either *fails to inform* or *misleads* the judge and jury (Gudjonsson, 1993).

Most of the time, psychologists will not be required to give evidence in person in court, often because the opposing side accepts the psychological report and does not need to cross-examine the psychologist on it. In the event of the findings being unfavourable, the defence would normally not forward a copy of the report to the prosecution and the psychologist would not be required to give evidence. If the psychologist has been commissioned by the prosecution, then the report will invariably be forwarded to the defence, irrespective of whether or not the findings are favourable to the prosecution. Normally, if the defence decides to rely on the psychological report, then the report has to be served on the prosecution well in advance of the trial, and they may instruct their own expert to evaluate the report.

A psychological report sometimes contains both favourable and unfavourable findings. For example, a defendant may prove to possess poor intellectual abilities, but score low on tests of suggestibility, which by implication means that he or she may be able to cope reasonably well with interrogation in spite of limited cognitive abilities. Similarly, the psychologist may recommend treatment as an alternative to a custodial sentence, but he or she may also express reservations about the defendant's motivation or about the prognosis. When this happens, solicitors may request the psychologist to delete the unfavourable findings from the report or to alter the report in such a way as to make it look more favourable to the court. No psychologist should ever be tempted to comply with the solicitors' wishes to alter the report in such a way that it could mislead the court, but unfortunately on occasions they do (Gudjonsson, 1996). The only time psychologists should consider altering the report is when the findings or terms used need to be clarified, or when a mistake has been made that needs to be corrected (Gudjonsson and Haward, 1998).

The way psychological findings are presented in a report is often of major importance to the court's understanding and appraisal of the report. The psychologist's findings must be presented clearly and succinctly. The conclusions and opinions drawn should be substantiated and made relevant to the issues addressed. When the findings are presented clearly, and are relevant to the legal issues, the report may be accepted by the respective legal advocates without the psychologist's having to give oral evidence. This commonly happens. In some instances the prosecution may withdraw the charges after considering the psychological findings, particularly in cases of learning disability and mental illness. According to the 1995 BPS Survey (Gudjonsson, 1996), in only about one fifth of criminal cases does the psychologist have to give oral evidence in court, sometimes both during the *voir dire* and the trial proper (Gudjonsson, 2003a). The great majority of civil cases involving compensation are settled out of court, so psychologists very infrequently have to testify in person. In contrast, psychologists in compensation cases testify in no more than 2% of case; this figure rises to 10% in family, youth and matrimonial proceedings.

Gudjonsson and Haward (1998) provide psychologists with useful information about how to present themselves and their findings when testifying in court. This includes knowing the difference between 'expert' and other witnesses. The former can, with the permission of the legal advocates, sit in court and listen to other witnesses giving evidence before testifying themselves. This is often useful because it provides the psychologist with a certain familiarity with the court's layout and the approach and strategy of the legal advocates. Another difference between expert witnesses and other witnesses is that the former are allowed to give opinions as well as factual (real) evidence. Ordinary witnesses are only allowed to give factual evidence. However, expert witnesses are well advised to concentrate on factual evidence and limit their opinions to evidence that can be substantiated by empirical testing (Carson, 1990).

Psychologists must be aware that courts are formal settings where certain rituals and conventions must be followed. For example, the expert witness should be formally dressed and speak slowly, clearly and confidently, and, even when asked questions by different legal advocates, the psychologist should address his or her answers to the judge. The psychologist first provides evidence in chief, and he or she will then be cross-examined about the evidence, after which there may be re-examination of various matters raised during the cross-examination. When giving evidence, the psychologist can be asked probing and challenging questions by the legal advocates and the judge. The psychologist should always be fully prepared by knowing the basic facts of the case and being intimately familiar with the tests used in the assessment, and any relevant documents or tapes. Notes of the interviews with the client and the findings of any psychological test that they bring into court may be closely inspected. Psychologists should think carefully before answering questions. If they consider the question asked as being unreasonable or impossible to answer, which is often the case with hypothetical questions (Tunstall et al., 1982), they should not hesitate to say so.

Giving evidence in court is a stressful experience for most expert witnesses. Attending court and listening to court proceedings before giving evidence is often helpful. The stress will be exacerbated when the psychologist is poorly prepared, has not carried out a thorough or competent evaluation or does not feel confident in the witness box. In one recent high-profile terrorist case an experienced clinical psychologist had been commissioned by the Crown Prosecution Service to challenge my evidence in court. In 1999 I had prepared a report at the request for the Criminal Cases Review Commission (CCRC) that resulted in the case being referred to the in the Court of Appeal. I then testified on behalf of the defence, after which the Crown expert went into the witness box. After about 10 minutes I could see sweat running down his neck and soon thereafter he requested a break, stating that he was about to faint. The Lordship adjourned for a short break, after which the expert collapsed in the witness box and was unconscious for a few minutes. An ambulance was called and he was taken to causality for an examination, where it was found that his condition had been brought about by stress. This expert, who had previous experience of court work, had in this case taken on a job that was beyond him, and suffered the added humiliation of having to withdraw from the case.

In addition to satisfactory training and experience, the most important factors for the 'forensic psychologist' are integrity, open-mindedness, a thorough assessment, good preparation, and clear presentation of the evidence.

CONCLUSIONS

Clinical psychologists are becoming independent of psychiatrists and they now typically receive instruction directly from solicitors rather than depending on referrals from their medical colleagues. Indeed, psychologists should always insist on being instructed directly by solicitors or other referrers (e.g. police, prosecution, social services). The demand for the services and expertise of psychologists is growing rapidly both in civil and criminal cases. The landmark Court of Appeal judgement in the case of R. v. *Raghip* in 1991, followed 10 years later by an influential decision in the House of Lords in R. v. *Pendledon*, demonstrates the increased acceptability of psychological evidence among legal advocates and the highest courts in Britain (Gudjonsson, 2003a, 2006). This transition from the hostile attitude towards psychology in the early 1980s and apparent lack of credibility in court, was largely the consequence of a combination of innovative applied research in forensic psychology, teaching to lawyers and judges, and persistence in the courtroom (Gudjonsson, 2003b).

REFERENCES

Adler, J. R. (ed) (2004) *Forensic Psychology. Concepts, Debates and Practice.* Devon: Willan Publishing.

Bagby, R. M., Nicholson, R. A., Rogers, R. and Nussbaum, D. (1992) Domains of competency to stand trial. A factor analytic study. *Law and Human Behavior,* 16, 491–507.

Bartol, C. R. and Bartol, A. M. (1987) History of forensic psychology. In: I. B. Weiner and A. K. Hess (eds) *Handbook of Forensic Psychology.* New York: John Wiley and Sons.

Blackburn, R. (1996) What is forensic psychology? *Legal and Criminological Psychology,* 1, 3–16.

Blau, T. H. (1984) *The Psychologist as an Expert Witness.* New York: John Wiley and Sons.

Brown, B. (1985) The involvement of psychologists in sentencing. *Bulletin of the British Psychological Society,* 38, 180–182.

Carson, D. (ed) (1990) *Professionals and the Courts. A Handbook for Expert Witnesses. Psychological Evidence in Court, Issues in Criminological and Legal Psychology II* (pp. 58–64). Leicester: British Psychological Society.

Cooke, G. (ed) (1980) *The Role of the Forensic Psychologist.* Springfield, IL: Charles C. Thomas.

Davies, G. M. (1983) The legal importance of psychological research in eyewitness testimony. British and American experiences. *Journal of the Forensic Science Society,* 24, 165–75.

DeClue, G. (2005) *Interrogations and Disputed Confessions. A Manual for Forensic Psychological Practice.* Florida: Professional Resources Press.

Eysenck, H. J. and Gudjonsson, G. H. (1989) *The Causes and Cures of Criminality.* New York: Plenum Press.

Grisso, T. (1986) *Evaluating Competencies. Forensic Assessments and Instruments.* New York: Plenum Press.

Grisso, T. (1987). The economic and scientific future of forensic psychological assessments. *American Psychologist,* 42, 821–839.

Grubin, D. (1996) *Fitness to Plead in England and Wales.* Hove, UK: Psychology Press.

Gudjonsson, G. H. (1985) Psychological evidence in court: Results from the BPS surgery *Bulletin of the British Psychological Society,* 38, 327–330.

Gudjonsson, G. H. (1987) The significance of depression in the mechanism of compulsive shoplifting. *Medicine, Science and the Law,* 27, 171–176.

Gudjonsson, G. H. (1992) *The Psychology of Interrogation, Confessions and Testimony.* Chichester: John Wiley and Sons.

Gudjonsson, G. H. (1993) The implications of poor psychological evidence in court. *Expert Evidence,* 2, 120–124.

Gudjonsson, G. H. (1996). Psychological evidence in Court. Results from the 1995 survey. *The Psychologist,* 5, 213–217.

Gudjonsson, G. H. (1997) *The Gudjonsson Suggestibility Scales Manual.* Hove, UK: Psychology Press.

Gudjonsson, G. H. (2002) Unreliable confessions and miscarriages of justice in Britain. *International Journal of Police Science and Management,* 4, 332–343.

Gudjonsson, G. H. (2003a) *The Psychology of Interrogations and Confessions. A Handbook.* Chichester: John Wiley & Sons.

Gudjonsson, G. H. (2003b). Psychology brings justice. The science of forensic psychology. *Criminal Behaviour and Mental Health*, 13, 159–167.

Gudjonsson, G. H. (2006) Disputed confessions and miscarriages of justice in Britain: expert psychological and psychiatric evidence in Court of Appeal. *The Manitoba Law Journal*, 31, 489–521.

Gudjonsson, G. H. and Clark, N. K. (1986) Suggestibility in police interrogation: a social psychological model. *Social Behaviour*, 1, 83–104.

Gudjonsson, G. H. and Haward, L. R. C. (1998) *Forensic Psychology: A Guide to Practice*. London: Routledge.

Gudjonsson, G. H. and Gunn, J. (1982) The competence and reliability of a witness in a criminal court. *British Journal of Psychiatry*, 141, 624–627.

Gudjonsson, G. H. and Sartory, G. (1983) Blood-injury phobia: a 'reasonable excuse' for failing to give a specimen in a case of suspected drunken driving. *Journal of the Forensic Science Society*, 23, 197–201.

Gudjonsson, G. H. and Young, S. (2006). An overlooked vulnerability in a defendant: Attention deficit hyperactivity disorder and a miscarriage of justice. *Legal and Criminological Psychology*, 11, 211–218.

Haward, L. R. C. (1981) *Forensic Psychology*. London: Batsford.

Haward, L. R. C. (1990) *A Dictionary of Forensic Psychology*, Chichester: Barry Rose.

Heaton-Armstrong, A. (2005) A book review of 'The Psychology of Interrogations and Confessions: A Handbook'. *Criminal Law Review*, 672–674.

Heilbrun, K. (1992) The role of psychological testing in forensic assessment. *Law and Human Behavior*, 16, 257–272.

Keilin, W. G. and Bloom, L. J. (1986) Child custody evaluation practices: A survey of experienced professionals. *Professional Psychology: Research and Practice*, 17, 33–46.

Leng, R. (1990) *Mens rea* and the defences to a criminal charge. In: R. Bluglass and P. Bowden (eds) *Principles and Practice of Forensic Psychiatry* (pp. 237–250). London: Churchill Livingstone.

Lloyd-Bostock, S. M. A. (1988) *Law in Practice. Applications of Psychology to Legal Decision Making and Legal Skills*. Leicester: British Psychological Society.

Loftus, E. (1979) *Eyewitness Testimony*. London: Harvard University Press.

Meehl, P. E. (1954) *Clinical versus Statistical Predictions*. Minneapolis: University of Minnesota Press.

O'Donohue, W. and Levensky, E. (eds) (2004) *Handbook of Forensic Psychology. Resource for Mental Health and Legal Professionals*. London: Elsevier.

Sartory, G., Rachman, S. and Grey, S. J. (1977) An investigation of the relation between reported fear and heart rate. *Behaviour Research and Therapy*, 15, 435–438.

Sigurdsson, J. F. and Gudjonsson, G. H. (2004). Forensic psychology in Iceland. A survey of members of the Icelandic Psychological Society. *Scandinavian Journal of Psychology*, 45, 325–329.

Tunstall, O., Gudjonsson, G., Eysenck, H. and Haward, L. (1982) Professional issues arising from psychological evidence presented in Court. *Bulletin of the British Psychological Society*, 35, 329–331.

Wasik, M. and Taylor, R. (1995) *Blackstone's Guide to the Criminal Justice and Public Order Act 1984*. Blackstone Press: London.

Weiner, I. B. and Hess, A. K. (1987) *Handbook of Forensic Psychology*. New York: John Wiley and Sons.

Chapter 39

Single-case methodology in psychological therapy

Stephen Morley

This chapter is dedicated with thanks and affection to the memory of Monte Shapiro: a superb teacher and compassionate clinician

INTRODUCTION

Single-case designs can be used for a number of purposes. It is possible to incorporate aspects of single-case designs into daily clinical work, e.g. assessment of a client on standardised measures at critical junctures (pre- and post-treatment). In such instances, simple experimental designs can be used to build up informative case series. Single-case designs are valuable tools to investigate unusual problems or monitor the development of new treatments (Johnson and Pennypacker, 1980; Vlaeyen et al., 2001; Wells and Sembi, 2004). Single-case methods can be combined with elements of traditional group designs to elucidate clinical problems (McKnight et al., 1984). Finally, single-case methods play an important part in the training of clinical psychologists and other health-care professionals. Understanding the basis of single-case research can give students an insight into clinical research issues and may facilitate their clinical development and their ability to think strategically and scientifically about clients. This chapter has been written primarily with clinical psychology students in mind: it provides a basic introduction to the intricacies of single-case studies, but it may also be a refresher for experienced psychologists and other health-care professionals.

Single-case methods are well established in clinical psychology. They were highly influential in the development of behaviour therapy. Shapiro (1963, 1966) advocated the use of single-subject research methods as the method of choice for investigating clinical phenomena, but it was the development of applied behaviour analysis in North America that led to a set of formal experimental designs (Baer et al., 1968). Subsequently, single-case methods have been elaborated and refined; experimental designs have been developed, a range of statistical analyses for the data have been considered, and the methods have been applied in medicine with some success (Jenicek, 2001).

Anyone who considers using single-case methods extensively should consult one of the standard texts (Johnson and Pennypacker, 1980; Kazdin, 1982; Barlow and Hersen, 1984; Barlow et al., 1984; Kratochwill and Levin, 1992; Franklin et al., 1997; Haynes and O'Brien, 2000). There are also many instances of single-case methods being used in non-behavioural psychotherapies (Parry et al., 1986; Fonagy and Moran, 1990; Elliott, 2002).

VALIDITY OF EXPERIMENTS

Experimental methods have been developed to eliminate plausible rival hypotheses, and to enable the investigator to make valid inferences about the available data. Campbell and colleagues (Campbell and Stanley, 1966; Cook and Campbell, 1979) provided an anatomy of experimental and quasi-experimental design, and this anatomy can be extended to experiments with single cases. Campbell separates threats to the valid interpretation of experiments into four groups:

1   *Internal validity*: these are factors concerned with the design and execution of a particular study that may provide a plausible alternative account for the pattern of the results. They prevent one from concluding that the intervention was responsible for the change. The major threats will be introduced in this chapter in discussing how single-case research can help a clinician answer six general questions about a case.

2   *External validity*: this is concerned with how far the results obtained in the particular study may be extended to other subjects, therapists and settings. External validity is not usually an issue for many users of single cases. It is an issue if the researcher wishes to make an argument for the effectiveness of a new therapy. In this situation, the first step to establishing external validity is to replicate the effect over a series of clients (Wells and Sembi, 2004).

3   *Statistical conclusion validity*: this refers to whether the statistical analysis applied to the data is appropriate and has been carried out competently. Statistical conclusion validity has been a source of some debate within single-case research where much of the data is technically difficult to analyse because of the small sample size and almost certain violation of important statistical assumptions about the structure of errors. Some (Baer, 1977; Parsonson and Baer, 1992) eschew statistical analysis in favour of visual inspection of a data plot. Although this is a valid method under some circumstances, there are occasions when visual analysis can draw the wrong conclusions (Franklin et al., 1997; Fisher et al., 2003). It might be more appropriate to call this threat to validity *analytic conclusion validity* so that it covers all aspects of data analysis and inference.

4   *Construct validity*: construct validity concerns the theoretical interpretations that may be placed on the data. In many group-based studies, researchers are interested in the relationship between two constructs, e.g. health status and exercise. These cannot usually be indexed by a single measure and it is usual to take multiple measures. In the majority of single-case studies, clinicians and researchers are interested in criterion variables, such as the number of panic attacks and frequency of self-mutilation, and the 'causal' variables are directly manipulated and measured. However, a common aspect of studies where the effects of therapy are being considered is that we may wish to make a statement about treatment effects. This is problematic unless we have a measure of therapy *per se*, e.g. the extent to which the therapist has adhered to a treatment protocol and delivered it competently (Waltz et al., 1993). Even if we were satisfied that the therapist were competent there may be other explanations for the effectiveness of therapy, e.g. non-specific alliance factors. These issues have been problematic for many years (Wampold, 2001). Issues of construct validity are not often discussed in single-case reports, but careful conceptual analysis of the measures and intervention should always be made (see Youell and McCullough, 1975, for an example).

To these threats to the validity of interpretations, we might add two other considerations:

1   *Standard contextual alternatives*: in any field of study there are well-known alternative hypotheses that can be put forward to explain data. In the case of psychological treatments, two such alternatives are 'expectation of therapeutic gain' and the general placebo effect. There are recognised procedures for designing outcome studies to take these explanations into account.
2   *Non-standard alternatives*: these are the alternative explanations in which the researcher is ultimately interested. They involve comparison between two competing theories. For example, Teasdale and Fennell (1982) tested whether change in beliefs were attributable to cognitive-behavioural therapy (CBT) 'thought change strategies' or to mere exploration of thoughts. They used a replicated single case method to show that greater changes in belief occurred after the thought change intervention.

FEATURES OF SINGLE-CASE EXPERIMENTS

Formal single-case experimental methods were developed by behaviourists working in the operant learning tradition (Sidman, 1960). A notable feature of this approach is that single-case experiments can be 'data driven'. The design of the experiment may be constructed in response to the data as it is collected and analysed. There are, of course, penalties to be paid for such an approach, e.g. the potential loss of experimental control, and one has to pay careful attention to reasons for implementing changes at each point (Morley, 1996).

The second feature of single-case methods is that they are closely tied to idiographic measures. Group-based studies frequently use assessments based on the shared variance of a measure. For example, questionnaire measures are developed through factor analyses that eliminate variance specific to the individual. Thus a questionnaire designed to measure anger or anxiety will include only items that are shared by a sufficient number of people in the sample and may eliminate items that are important to individuals. By contrast, single-case methods allow the investigator to use measures that are of particular relevance to the individual subject. These may include personal questionnaire assessments of subjective state (Philips, 1986), frequency counts of a specific problem behaviour (Cone, 2001) or measures of physiological functioning, e.g. electromyographic recordings. Many common psychometrically validated measures, such as the Beck Depression Inventory (BDI), were not designed to be repeatedly administered over short periods of time. Their length and psychometric characteristics make them quite unsuitable for this purpose. They can, however, be used to track the resolution of a problem over longer periods of time. Other measures, such as personal questionnaires and short adjective checklists, are more suitable for frequent repeated applications. Morley (1996) has outlined an assessment–evaluation funnel as a strategy for measurement with single cases (Figure 39.1).

Third, single-case methods explicitly acknowledge variability within an individual, whereas group-based methods often obscure this and 'wash out' fluctuations in individual states by pooling the data. Single-case methods offer a way of investigating fluctuations and the effect of treatment is judged against the fluctuations. This focus on variability is problematic in some aspects. In a clinical setting, variability in the patient's problem provides clues about factors that control and moderate it. Clinical problems that appear static and immune from influences are often difficult to formulate and understand. As Johnson and Pennypacker (1980, p. 70) note, variability is the 'window through which to observe the workings of basic controlling relationships'. However, single-case data are much more easily evaluated when there is little variability within different experimental phases of the study. In laboratory conditions, and artificially contrived field settings, investigators take considerable pains to ensure that the environment remains as constant as possible and that there are no uncontrolled extraneous influences. In many clinical settings this is not possible, and investigators must analyse variability through graphical or statistical means.

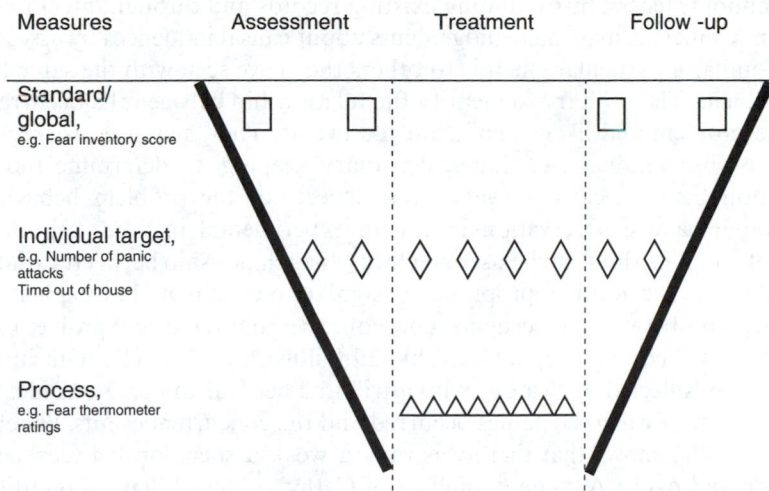

Figure 39.1 Assessment-evaluation funnel (after Morley, 1996). The figure illustrates a general strategy for selecting measures for single-case studies and experiments. *Standard/global* measures are those that have been developed on known populations and for which there are appropriate psychometric data. These include assessments such as the Beck Depression Inventory and the SCL-90R. Ideally, there should be norms for different clinical groups. In general, these measures should be given only two or three times, during the assessment phase, at the end of treatment and at follow up. *Individual target* measures are those measures that index the client's complaint. They are normally idiographic and developed for a particular client. Typical examples are: frequency counts of target behaviour and personal questionnaire measures and ratings of subjective states. These measures should be taken frequently during base-line and treatment conditions. Psychometric characteristics are usually those concerned with the inter-rater reliability and internal consistency of the measures. *Process* measures are taken more frequently than individual target measures. They may be used by investigators to track changes within a single session. For example, a therapist may track the intensity of pain while a client is engaged in imagery exercises. It is quite usual for process measures to be 'quick and dirty'. Reproduced, with permission, from Morley (1996).

SIX QUESTIONS FOR THE PRACTISING CLINICIAN

1. Questions about case formulation

Therapeutic intervention should always be preceded by a clinical formulation of the case. Most schools of psychotherapy require that the individual should be understood in terms of his or her developmental history and that the influence of the current social environment on the individual's behaviour is known. Much of the relevant data are obtained through interviews with the client, his or her family and others involved with the individual's well-being, e.g. school teachers, by examining existing records and through direct observation. Clinicians may make judgements about causal influences by assessing how similar a particular client is to others they have seen with the same type of problem. They will try to identify the relationship between the occurrence of the problem and likely significant life events. They may use prospective, passive observational techniques, e.g. diary keeping, to determine the co-variation between current events and aspects of the problem behaviour. Although passive observation is not an experimental method, aspects of experimental method can be used to clarify the relationship between variables of interest. The most appropriate 'design' is one that makes explicit the co-variation between antecedents, consequences and the target problem in a simple 2×2 contingency table. Table 39.1 illustrates this. The data in this table were collected by 'Cathy', who attributed her fear to being outside. She kept a diary of when the panics occurred and the concurrent events. Panel (a) of Table 39.1 shows that there was only a weak association between being outside and panic. A content analysis of Cathy's detailed diary showed that the important trigger event seemed to be certain types of assertive social interaction (panel b) and that assertive responses were as likely to be demanded at home and were not just associated with being outside (panel c).

Table 39.1 Assessing co-variation between panic attacks and other events. Panel (a) shows the association (lack of) between location and the occurrence of panic attacks. Panel (b) shows the association between the demands of the social situation and the occurrence of panic attacks. In Panel (c) the frequency of panic attacks is tallied by location and the demands of the social situation. It is clear that panics occur when assertion is demanded rather than when Cathy was out of her home.

Panel (a)	Location	
Panic attacks	*At home*	*Outside*
Panic attack	8	14
No panic attack	29	29

Panel (b)	Social situation	
Panic attacks	*Assertion required*	*No assertion required*
Panic attack	19	3
No panic attack	0	58

Panel (c)	Social situation	
Location	*Assertion required*	*Assertion not required*
At home	8	0
Outside	11	3

Mace and Lalli (1991) provide an example of how a descriptive analysis based on passive observation of a problem may be enhanced by a subsequent experimental analysis. Experimental analyses have two important features. First, the order of the treatments is planned so that they are balanced across such features as the time of day and the number of times in which they precede and succeed each other. Second, they are applied independently of the individual's behaviour, subject to ethical considerations.

In Mace and Lalli's report, Mitch, a 46-year-old man with moderate learning difficulties living in a community facility, made frequent bizarre statements. Initial observations suggested two hypotheses: (1) that Mitch's talk was positively reinforced by the staff paying attention to him; or (2) that the bizarre talk was negatively reinforced by the staff discontinuing instructing Mitch in independent living skills or by Mitch withdrawing from the currently assigned task. Mace and Lalli tested these hypotheses by arranging four conditions that systematically varied the task demands and consequences of social interaction. The analysis of these data led to the development of two interventions, one in which Mitch was scheduled to receive attention on a variable-time schedule irrespective of his behaviour, and a second one in which Mitch was trained to initiate and maintain conversations and social interactions with others. These successfully reduced Mitch's bizarre speech and increased the frequency with which he initiated conversations.

2. Simple questions about the outcome of treatment: 'Has the client improved?'

The minimal requirements for determining whether improvement has occurred are 'pre-' and 'post'-intervention measures. However, any change in the measure could be attributable to a number of factors other than genuine change (internal validity).

Testing

This is the general name given to effects that can occur with repeated measurement. Different measures are likely to show different specific effects of testing. For example, intelligence and memory tests are likely to show practice effects, whereas people may learn to fake 'good' or 'bad' on personality tests and symptom checklists. Measurement may also be *reactive* so that the very act of measurement provokes a significant change in the subject's behaviour. Reactivity usually, but not always, declines over time, so that changes between two occasions may not be due to a 'true' change but merely to a decrease in reactivity. Reactivity is a significant feature in behavioural observation but it can countered by using unobtrusive recording measures.

Instrumentation

This refers to a change in the calibration of the instrument itself. An example of this is 'observer drift', found when observers change their criteria for detecting or recording behaviour during the study. Consistent scoring can be maintained by repeated checking of the observers by independent judges (Cone, 2001). Self-report measures of symptom intensity are also subject to instrumentation effects. The differential sensitivity across the scale may lead to problems, including 'ceiling' or 'floor' effects.

Statistical regression

If an investigator uses a test of less than perfect reliability any score will only be an estimate of the true score. On repeating the test the person's score will change; if he or she initially scored at one extreme of the scale, the second score will tend towards the middle of the scale for purely statistical reasons. When standardised questionnaires are used in pre-test-post-test designs, the effect of repeated measurement can be estimated if a test-retest reliability co-efficient is part of the standardisation. An example of how to do this is given later (see p 836).

3. Is the treatment effective?

The simple pre-test–post-test design does not enable us to infer that the change produced is due to therapy. Even if the testing, reactivity, instrumentation and regression threats have been eliminated the observed change may be due to effects. *Maturation* refers to changes occurring within the individual over a given period that produce changes in the target variable irrespective of treatment. Studies that involve children's acquisition of language and other skills are obviously prone to this effect. By contrast, *history* denotes the possible impact of extra-treatment events mimicking a therapeutic effect on the target problem. For example, the resolution of a contested divorce settlement or a change in medication may improve a client's anxiety independently of any therapeutic activity. A number of experimental designs have been suggested to control for these alternative hypotheses:

The AB or interrupted time-series design (Figure 39.2, panel A)

In this design, A and B represent series of repeated observations under two conditions, baseline (A) and treatment (B). By taking repeated measurements testing, reactivity, regression and maturation may be assessed and controlled. Each of these threats would be expected to produce a systematic trend in the baseline data. The effectiveness of the treatment is judged by the extent to which the data-points shift when the intervention is introduced, and by whether this change is sustained throughout the intervention. This design can also control for the effects of history. If the client's problem is reasonably stable during baseline and treatment phases, despite the documented presence of various extraneous events, it is not unreasonable to infer that any major change occurring at the time of introducing treatment is due to the treatment.

The AB design is not a true experiment because the treatment is not systematically manipulated and it is impossible to rule out all the threats due to internal validity, but it is a considerable advance on single observations obtained at pre- and post-treatment. Despite the advantages gained with repeated measures, two other general threats to validity must be considered. First, one must be explicit about the factors determining the decision to change from baseline to treatment phases. There are three common issues:

1   Clinicians may decide to introduce a treatment as soon as possible to reassure the client. This is not necessarily good practice, as the baseline may be too short to enable the study to be evaluated. It is also often not desirable on clinical grounds if a clinical formulation has not been developed.
2   Treatments may be applied as soon as the therapist is convinced that an adequate formulation of the case has been achieved. While this is a good clinical criterion, it is possible that a less than adequate number of baseline points have been obtained.
3   A *reactive intervention* might occur. Glass et al. (1975) noted that it is possible for clinicians and experimenters to introduce a treatment in response to deterioration in the baseline, perhaps brought about by a crisis. Although this is ethically understandable, it is quite usual for crises to dissipate quickly and, if treatment had been withheld, the client's score would returned to a less extreme level. Extreme scores are also likely to be associated with significant personal or environmental events. These may provide important information about the factors controlling the target problem.

The second issue to consider concerns the problem of detecting a change in the client's behaviour due to treatment when there is variability in the data. Repeated measurements during the baseline often reveal considerable variability and one might wrongly attribute changes to treatment when they are attributable to natural variation. This problem can be ameliorated if longer baseline and treatment phases are used when the extent of the variability can be taken into account when evaluating the interventions. The presence of

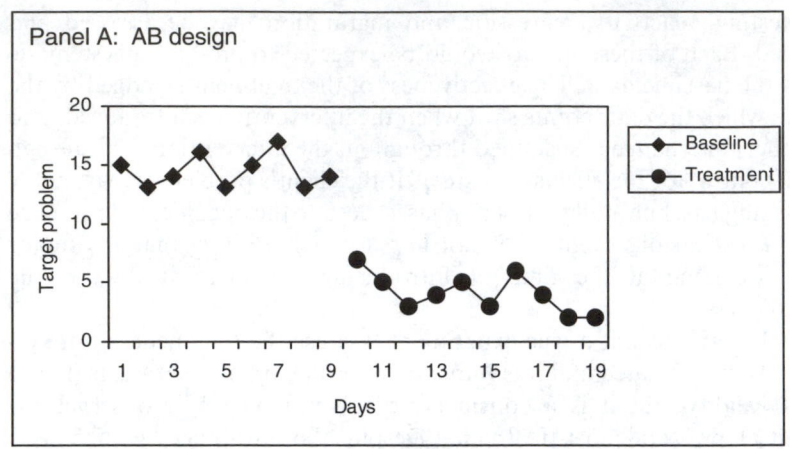

Panel A: AB design

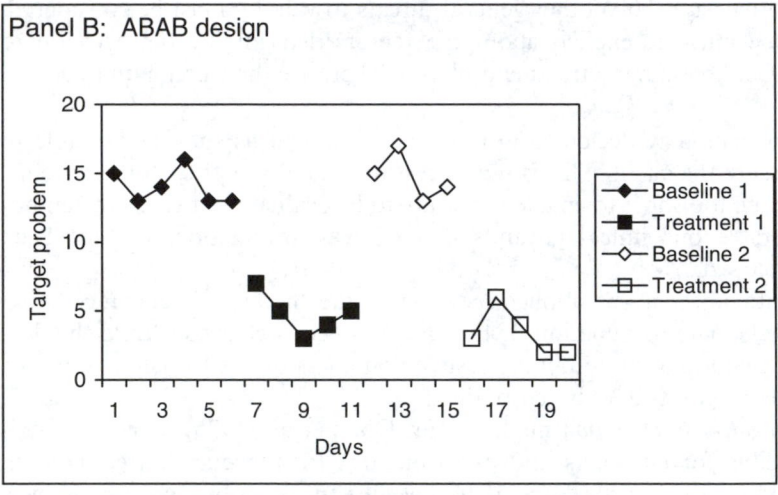

Panel B: ABAB design

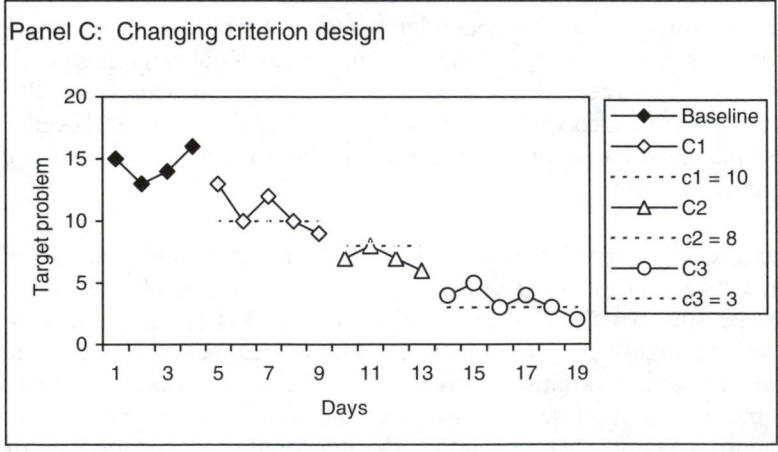

Panel C: Changing criterion design

large variability in the baseline should lead the clinician to explore its sources. Plotting the data may reveal systematic cycles (Morley and Adams, 1991) that may relate to regular biological or environmental events, and attempts should be made to correlate environmental changes with change in the target variable. This will often lead to a refined formulation.

The AB design is widely used in clinical practice. Its overriding advantage is that it fits in naturally with the requirements of investigators and clients alike. A combination of sufficient data points, careful documentation of treatment and extra-treatment events, and systematic and cautious analyses of variability and change, justifies its continued use. Elliott (2002) provides a stimulating consideration of how this basic design, supplemented by other measures and methods can be used as a clinical research tool.

ABAB or the reversal design (Figure 39.2, panel B)

In this design, the baseline (A) and intervention (B) phases are alternated. Increased control over the threats of history is achieved if the treatment is withdrawn and the client's behaviour reverses to the original baseline. Ashbaugh and Peck (1998) used fading and response cost methods to help the parents of a 2-year-old girl, Alicia, get her to sleep at a reasonable time. If Alicia fell asleep within 15 minutes of the target bedtime then her scheduled time was advanced by 30 minutes the next night (fading). If Alicia had not gone to sleep within 15 minutes, her parents kept her awake by playing with her for 30 minutes and her bedtime was delayed by 30 minutes the following night (response cost). During the first treatment phase, the number of 15-minute intervals with disturbed sleep fell markedly over eight 24-hour periods. At that point, the baseline was reinstated, i.e. no intervention, and Alicia immediately reverted to her prior pattern of sleep disturbance. The treatment was reinstituted and Alicia's sleep disturbance returned to minimal values very quickly. By increasing the number of treatment-baseline reversals, this design strengthens the case against history as a plausible rival hypothesis.

Figure 39.2 Three basic single-case designs. *Panel A* shows the AB design: the baseline period (no-treatment) is followed by a treatment period. In the figure this is show by a break in the line joining the data points. In this example treatment results in an almost immediate reduction in the frequency of the target problem. *Panel B* shows the changing criterion design. The baseline period – shown by the solid data points – is followed by three treatment phases. Each treatment phase (C1 to C3) is shown by different-shaped data points and the three different criteria and their values (c1 to c3) are shown by dotted lines. In this figure it is clear that the frequency of the target problem decreases each time the criterion is made more stringent. *Panel C* shows the ABAB design, with each baseline and treatment shown by a different code. The impact of the treatment is evident from the increase in the target problem in the second baseline period and the subsequent reduction when treatment is reintroduced.

There may be clinical and ethical reasons against using any design that entails a degree of reversal. Clinicians and clients may be reluctant to reverse treatments that are seen to be effective. This can be partly circumvented by using brief probes that return the patient to baseline conditions. It may also be impossible to reverse certain behaviour that has been learned and brought under the client's internal control.

Changing criterion design (Figure 39.2, panel C)

This design circumvents some of the problems raised by the ABAB design. Baseline observations are followed by a series of treatment phases, each of which uses the same treatment applied to successively prescribed changes (criteria) in the target behaviour. Allen and Evans (2001) used a changing criterion design to help Amy, a 15-year-old with insulin-dependent diabetes, reduce excessive checking of her blood glucose levels, (between 80 to 95 times a day). The reduction was achieved by limiting Amy's access to the test strips. Initially, the number was set to 60 per day, which, was reduced to 12 per day (the interim steps were 60, 40, 20, 18, 16 and 14). This treatment was essentially a graded exposure to an anxiety-provoking situation (not being able to check blood glucose level).

Hartmann and Hall (1976), note that successive baselines should be long enough to rule out history, maturation and measurement threats to internal validity. Phases should also be of unequal length to ensure that the step-like changes in the criterion are not in synchrony with any natural changes in the target behaviour. This design can also be extended to probe performance under criteria that have not yet been instituted (Horner and Baer, 1978).

Multiple baseine designs (Figure 39.3)

The fundamental idea behind multiple baseline designs is the introduction of control variables (problems). The logic of the design involves two assumptions. First, treatment is introduced to one variable at a time on the assumption that if only this problem changes then the effects of a coincidental event (history) may be eliminated. The second assumption is that if an extra-treatment event is responsible for the change in the target problem then also it will also influence control problems. There is an inconsistency in this argument (Kazdin and Kopel, 1975) in that it is assumed that treatments will have specific effects but that extra-treatment factors will have general effects. In practice, this means that the interpretation of the design is dependent on the outcome. If specific changes occur with the treatment of each variable, then one might reasonably rule out history and maturation effects, but if untreated variables change with the introduction of a specific treatment, it is unclear whether this is due to a generalised treatment effect, or to history or maturation. Nevertheless, this design does force clinicians to take note of more than

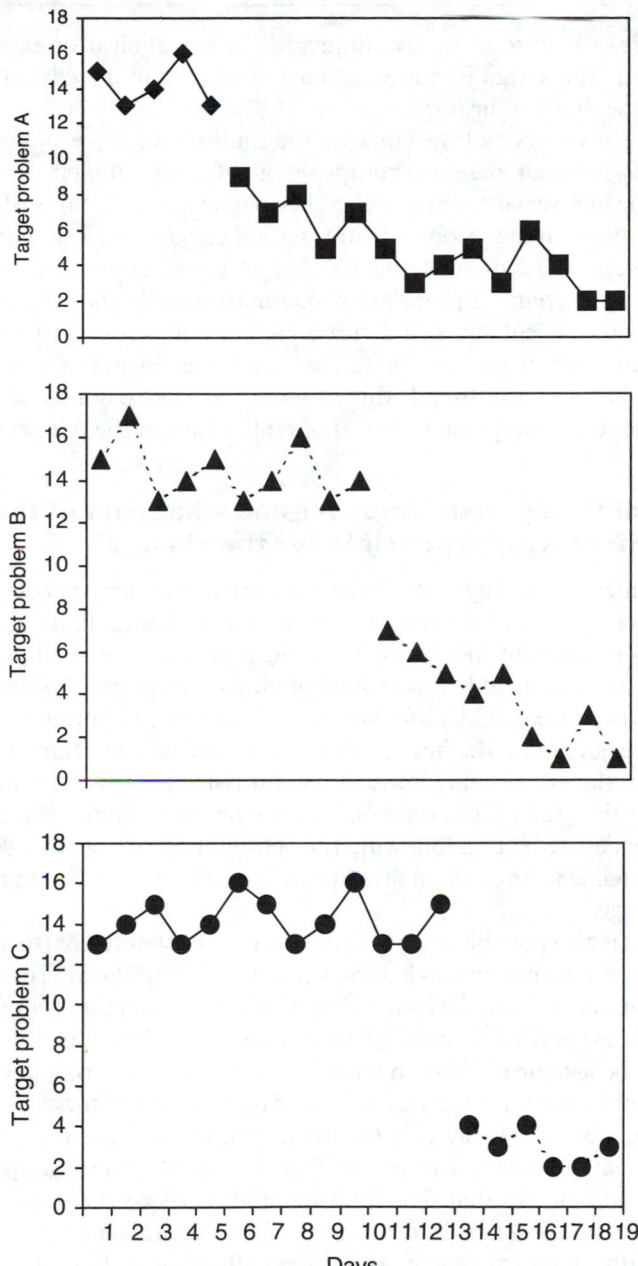

Figure 39.3 The multiple baseline design. This figure shows a multiple baseline design for one subject with three target problems. Baseline data is collected for each problem and the intervention is introduced for each problem after successively longer baseline periods. The step-like pattern of the data plot is typical of successful treatment in multiple baseline designs.

one variable, a feature to be recommended in any clinical or experimental investigation. The design is, however, much weaker than the ABAB design in ruling out the threat of history.

There are a number of variants of the multiple baseline design. In the original design, each baseline comprises a different problem for a single client. In the first variant, one problem behaviour in one client is observed in different settings. In the second variant, several clients with a similar problem are treated and the length of the baseline is varied across each client. To implement this variant appropriately, one must assume that the problem is functionally equivalent across individuals and it is also necessary to treat the clients concurrently in time period to ensure that treatment is not confounded with general effects of history. If this cannot be achieved, it might be wiser to consider the study comprising a series of replications of the AB design.

4. Why did the patient improve and what part of the treatment was responsible for the change?

Any experimental investigation of why a treatment works (a process question) involves a comparison between two or more conditions. Three designs are particularly suitable for this type of investigation. First, the multiple baseline design can be used if individuals have multiple symptoms. Each symptom (variable) can be treated by different methods and simple comparisons made between the methods. Rachman (1974) described a condition of primary obsessional slowness, characterised by excessively slow and meticulous self-care, in the absence of common obsessional symptoms, such as ruminations or anxiety reduction following the behaviour. Clark et al. (1982) used a multiple baseline method in an attempt to separate the effective components in the package.

Second, it is also possible to investigate the impact of different treatments, or treatment components on single target problems using the alternating treatments design (Barlow and Hersen, 1984). Ollendick et al. (1981) compared the relative effectiveness of positive practice and physical restraint in reducing stereotypic behaviour in children with learning difficulties. Baseline observations were obtained for three sessions per day, and each of these sessions was allocated in a balanced way to a treatment condition, During the treatment phase, the treatments were delivered so that they were balanced across the time of the day, and also so that they followed and preceded the others in a systematic fashion. The relative effectiveness of each treatment could be assessed independently of any extraneous and potentially confounding variables.

There are a number of constraints in using this design. It is necessary to use interventions that have a rapid and powerful effect within each session, so that there is a minimum 'warm-up' necessary. There should be little carry-over effect, i.e. the effect of one treatment should not continue into the next session. The target behaviour should not be too close to the floor or ceiling of the observation range. One feature of the alternating treatments design is that it is possible to designate one of the treatments as a no-treatment control. Ollendick et al. (1981) did this and were able to demonstrate that stereotypic behaviour changed only when treatments were applied. This procedure helps to rule out the threats of history and maturation.

The third approach to investigating differential treatment effects in single cases is to extend the AB design by adding on successive phases in which treatment conditions are systematically related. Mace and Lalli (1991) provide an example of this approach in their treatment of Mitch. This approach can be used when the impact of the treatment is expected to be gradual, and when prolonged periods of observation and data collection are possible.

5. Will this treatment be of any use to other clients and clinicians?

This question concerns the external validity or generalisation of findings from an experiment; it can only be answered empirically. Several authors (Campbell and Stanley, 1966; Cook and Campbell, 1979; Kratochwill and Levin, 1992) provide excellent discussions of the relevant issues. It is useful to consider three domains to which one might wish to generalise the findings of a case study:

1 *Population validity*: to which members of which populations is this procedure useful or applicable?
2 *Ecological validity*: how far can the findings be replicated with different experimenters, settings and measurement procedures?

Answering both of these questions is essentially a matter of replication by many investigators across different populations. And:

3 *Manipulation or construct validity*: will a conceptually similar intervention have the same effect? For example, it is tacitly assumed that many events will serve as punishment reinforcers, yet these events may not be interchangeable. An example of this is the differential effectiveness of shock and time-out in their capacity to suppress self-mutilation in Lesch-Nyhan syndrome (Anderson et al., 1978). These investigators conducted a series of single-case studies demonstrating that shock was not an effective punisher, whereas time-out from social reinforcement was effective and did suppress self-mutilation.

6. Questions pertaining to theory testing

We encountered the idea of theory testing in Question 1, where the theories were hypotheses about particular patients. It is possible to use single cases to test well-articulated general theories about therapeutic processes and this enables the clinician to contribute to research without recourse to generally expensive group studies.

EVALUATING SINGLE-CASE DATA: ANALYTIC CONCLUSION VALIDITY

The analysis of pre-treatment–post-treatment changes

Arguably, data on pre-treatment and post-treatment functioning should be collected in all clinical cases as part of routine clinical audit. When measurement uses well-standardised tools, this information can be used to determine two things (Jacobson and Revenstorf, 1988; Jacobson and Truax, 1991). First, if the client has made a statistically reliable change on the selected measure, that is, whether the change observed is greater that that might be expected with the known reliability of the measure. (Note that it is also possible to determine whether a client has made a significant deterioration in functioning, thus raising the possibility that the intervention has resulted in harm.) To establish a statistically reliable change, one needs two pieces of information about the test, its reliability (r) and its standard deviation (SD), to compute the standard error of measurement (SE_m) and the standard error of a difference score (SE_{diff}). To compute the reliable change index (RCI), find the difference between the pre-treatment (X_1) and post-treatment (X_2) scores and divide this by SE_{diff}. If the result is greater than 1.96 then a statistically reliable change has occurred. Table 39.2 provides a worked example of this.

Table 39.2 Calculating the reliable change index (RCI)

Step	Theory	Example
I.	Required data SD of population on the test Reliability of the test (r) Pre- and post-treatment scores of client X_1 and X_2	SD = 10 r = 0.8 Pre-treatment score = 70 Post-treatment score = 50
2.	Compute standard error of the mean (SE_m) $SE_m = SD \times \sqrt{1 - r}$	$= 10 \times \sqrt{1 - 0.8}$ $= 4.47$
3.	Compute the standard error of the difference (SE_{diff}) $SE_{diff} = \sqrt{(2 \times SE_m^2)}$	$= \sqrt{(2 \times 4.47^2)}$ $= 6.32$
4.	Compute reliable change index (RCI) $RCI = (X_1 - X_2) / SE_{diff}$	$= (70 - 50) / 6.32$ $= 2.37$, which is greater than the critical value of 1.96

If the client has made a statistically reliable change, we can then ask the second question; has he or she made a clinically significant gain? Jacobson and colleagues have suggested that the statistically normative properties of the measurement tool can be used to set three criteria for clinical change. What is required is the distribution of scores from either or both a non-clinical (non-dysfunctional) and a clinical (dysfunctional) population. The different criteria, called a, b and c by Jacobson, use different combinations of the norms. For criterion a, the level of functioning after therapy should fall outside the range of the dysfunctional population (defined as more than 2 standard deviations from the mean of the dysfunctional group in the direction of the normal reference group). For criterion b, the level of functioning should fall within the range of the non-dysfunctional group (within 2 standard deviation units of the mean of the non-dysfunctional group). For criterion c, the level of functioning should place the client closer to the mean of the functional group than the mean of the dysfunctional group. A graphic representation of these is shown in Figure 39.4. The use of these statistical criteria is dependent on the availability of appropriate normative data. For some clients groups it is questionable whether norms derived from fully functional samples can be meaningfully applied, e.g. it may be inappropriate to apply such norms to people with schizophrenia.

Statistical methods for analysing single-case designs

When single-case designs were introduced (Baer et al., 1968), analysis of the data was entirely dependent on inspection of graphical displays and the application of statistical techniques was eschewed (Baer, 1977). Applied behaviour analysts paid attention to two features that made this possible. First, they established 'steady state' baseline conditions, i.e. the mean level was constant and there was little variability during the course of the baseline. Second, they employed interventions that had rapid, large-magnitude effects, producing changes in the target variable within the first few sessions (often within the first session). Under these conditions, data can be easily evaluated by plotting the data points against time.

As single-case methods became more widely used, the data became less amenable to analysis by visual inspection and statistical approaches to ana-lysing the data were advocated. One suggestion was to apply conventional parametric t and F tests to the data. These tests are generally not appropriate for time-series data because, for them to be valid, they assume that the error in measurement is uncorrelated. Furthermore, t and F tests are only sensitive to the changes in mean (repeated measures analyses of variance can assess trend) and would not be able to detect a change in the trend of the data. In general, these tests are not recommended.

A second approach to the statistical analysis of single-case data has been to use the statistical approach known as time-series analysis (Franklin et al.,

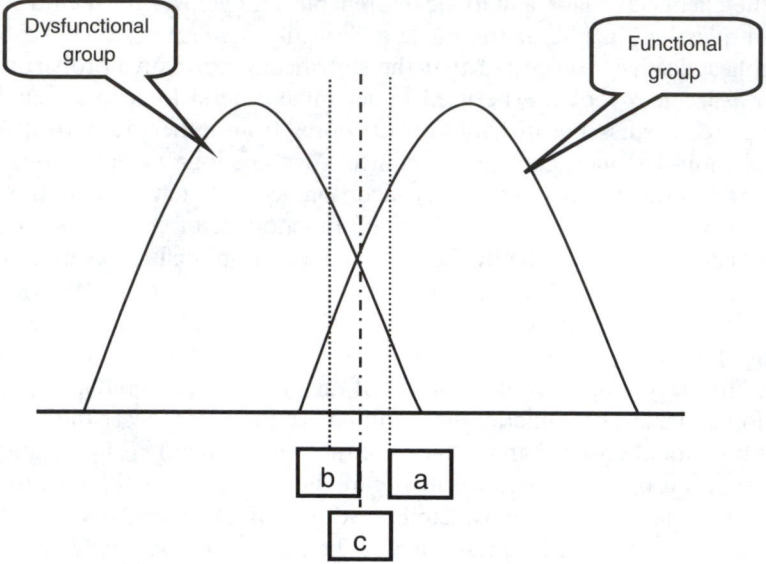

(A) Overlapping distributions

Dysfunctional group

Functional group

b | a

c

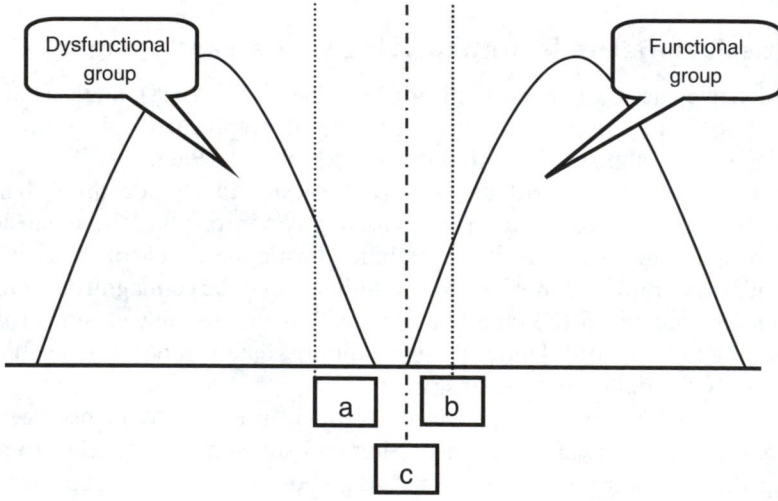

(B) Non-overlapping distributions

Dysfunctional group

Functional group

a | b

c

Figure 39.4 Clinically significant change. Diagrammatic representation of Jacobson's three definitions of significant clinical change. a = score falling outside the range of the dysfunctional group; b = score falling within the range of the functional group; c = score closer to the mean of the functional group. Jacobson suggests that when norms are available, criteria b and c are preferable; if the groups overlap then c is preferable; when they do not overlap, b should be adopted. If norms for a functional group are not available then a is the only criterion available. The figure shows the effect of adopting different criteria for overlapping (A) and non-overlapping (B) distributions.

1997). The method involves making a statistical model of the baseline phase and testing whether data from the intervention phase fit this model. They provide an elegant and powerful solution to the problems raised by conventional tests. There are two practical problems in applying these tests. First, they require a considerable number of data points (at least 50 in each phase) to identify the statistical model of the data with any reliability. Second, they require a degree of statistical 'know how' that is often beyond that which clinicians are willing to obtain. They are not recommended for use without considerable expertise (Huitema and McKean, 2000).

One other approach to the statistical analysis of intervention effects can be used with relatively small sample sizes (20 or so data points) and the analysis does not require the investigator to make assumptions about the distribution of the data. Randomisation tests use only the available data (Edgington, 1996). The basic strategy of the test is to determine the exact probability with which the observed data, or a more extreme pattern of data, would occur. The major requirement of the test is that the scheduling of the intervention(s) shall be decided at random before the beginning of the study. Randomisation tests are relatively easy to conduct and can be adapted to test a range of hypotheses about the means, and trend in single case data (Onghena and Edgington, 2005).

Statistics can also be used to describe the data and to carry out analyses of whether segments of the data contain trends or other features. Morley and Adams (1989) have summarised a set of easily computable, non-parametric tests that can be used to explore the characteristics of single-case data, either as a prelude to further analysis or to supplement visual inspection.

Graphical methods for analysing single-case designs

It is probable that most clinicians will rely on graphs and 'visual analysis' to draw conclusions. Indeed, even if statistical analyses are to be used, the data should be inspected and manipulated to highlight a variety of features. Parsonson and Baer (1992) have outlined the basics of preparing visual displays for single-case data and Morley and Adams (1991) have compiled a set of methods that enable an investigator to explore the data in some depth. Visual analysis has also been subjected to investigation in its own right (Parsonson and Baer, 1992; Franklin et al., 1997; Fisher et al., 2003) and it is clear that visual displays can be misinterpreted, especially when the data contain trends and variability.

CONCLUSIONS

Single-case methods have a long history in psychology and have been applied to clinical problems in a systematic manner for 40 years. A range of formal designs has been developed to circumvent threats to the valid interpretation of the data. Variations on the designs appear with regularity as inventive clinicians and researchers face new problems, issues of interpretation and design continue to be debated and new approaches to the analysis of data are considered. Single-case methods provide a useful set of tools for research-minded clinicians and researchers alike. In the age of evidence-based practice, the offer a way of both auditing the evidence in clinical settings and providing an input from practice-based evidence.

RESOURCES

Journals

Several journals regularly publish single-case studies, and provide up-to-date examples of many of the designs and measurement issues discussed in this chapter.

The *Journal of Applied Behavior Analysis* is the leading journal for operant behavioural studies. It publishes single-case studies almost exclusively. The studies are sophisticated and some knowledge of operant theory is useful. The journal's website (http://seab.envmed.rochester.edu/jaba/) provides free access to a limited number of papers. *Behavioural and Cognitive Psychotherapy* and *Clinical Psychology and Psychotherapy* are primarily cognitive-behavioural in orientation. *Psychotherapy Research* publishes studies from psychodynamic psychotherapy and CBT. Many of the papers report sophisticated studies of psychotherapy processes. Reading the literature will provide insight into the area and should stimulate one to reflect on ones own practice.

Websites

Robert Elliott's experiential psychotherapy website has good resources for those interested in process issues (http://experiential-researchers.org/).

A version of Shapiro's personal questionnaire suitable for use in the clinic is available from the author's website (http://www.leeds.ac.uk/medicine/divisions/psychiatry/staff/morley.htm).

Several websites will compute statistically reliable change and show the clinical change criteria as suggested by Jacobson (http://www.psyctc.org/stats/rcsc.htm).

Software for graphing and statistics

All single-case data should be graphed and the graphing utility available in Microsoft's Word and Excel programmes will generally suffice. Carr and

Burkholder (1998) give a detailed set of instruction of how to draw the basic types of graph in Excel.

Most statistical packages (SPSS, SAS) will perform time series analyses but I strongly recommend against their use without large data-sets and some statistical expertise. Although randomisation tests can be computed by hand, Onghena has written a set of programs for analysing randomisation tests. The software runs under the old DOS environment, but will also run in a Microsoft Windows environment.

REFERENCES

Allen, K. D. and Evans, J. H. (2001) Exposure-based treatment to control excessive blood glucose monitoring. *Journal of Applied Behavior Analysis*, 34, 497–500.

Anderson, L., Dancis, J. and Alpert, M. (1978) Behavioral contingencies and self-mutilation in Lesch-Nyhan disease. *Journal of Consulting and Clinical Psychology*, 46, 529–536.

Ashbaugh, R. and Peck, S. M. (1998). Treatment of sleep problems in a toddler: A replication of the faded bedtime with response cost procedure. *Journal of Applied Behavior Analysis*, 31, 127–129.

Baer, D. M. (1977). Perhaps it would be better not to know everything. *Journal of Applied Behavior Analysis*, 10(1), 167–172.

Baer, D. M., Wolf, M. M. and Risley, T. R. (1968). Some current dimensions of applied behavior analysis. *Journal of Applied Behavior Analysis*, 1(1), 91–97.

Barlow, D. H. and Hersen, M. (1984). *Single Case Experimental Designs: Strategies for Studying Behavioral Change* (2nd edn). New York: Pergamon Press.

Barlow, D. H., Hayes, S. C. and Nelson, R. O. (1984). *The Scientist Practitioner: Research and Accountability in Clinical and Educational Settings*. Boston: Alleyn and Bacon.

Campbell, D. T. and Stanley, J. C. (1966). *Experimental and Quasi-experimental Designs for Research*. Chicago: Rand McNally.

Carr, J. E. and Burkholder, E. O. (1998). Creating single-subject design graphs with Microsoft Excel(™). *Journal of Applied Behavior Analysis*, 31, 245–251.

Clark, D. A., Sugrim, I. and Bolton, D. (1982) Primary obsessional slowness: A nursing treatment programme with a 13 year old. *Behaviour Research and Therapy*, 20, 289–292.

Cone, J. D. (2001). *Evaluating Outcomes: Empirical Tools for Effective Practice* (1st edn). Washington, D. C.: American Psychological Association.

Cook, T. D. and Campbell, D. T. (1979) *Quasi-Experimentation: Design and Analysis Issues for Field Settings*. Chicago: Rand McNally.

Edgington, E. S. (1996) Randomized single-subject experimental designs. *Behaviour Research and Therapy*, 34(7), 567–574.

Elliott, R. (2002) Hermeneutic single-case efficacy design. *Psychotherapy Research*, 12, 1–21.

Fisher, W. W., Kelley, M. E. and Lomas, J. E. (2003) Visual aids and structured criteria for improving visual inspection and interpretation of single-case designs. *Journal of Applied Behavior Analysis*, 36, 387–406.

Fonagy, P. and Moran, G. S. (1990) Studies on the efficacy of child psychoanalysis. *Journal of Consulting and Clinical Psychology*, 58, 684–695.

Franklin, R. D., Allison, D. B. and Gorman, B. S. (eds) (1997) *Design and Analysis of Single-case Research*. Mahwah, N.J: Lawrence Erlbaum Associates, Inc.

Glass, G. V., Willson, V. L. and Gottman, J. M. (1975) *Design and Analysis of Time Series Experiments*. Boulder, CO: Colorado University Press.

Hartmann, D. P. and Hall, R. V. (1976) The changing criterion design. *Journal of Applied Behavior Analysis*, 9, 527.

Haynes, S. N. and O'Brien, W. H. (2000) *Principles and Practice of Behavioral Assessment*. New York: Kluwer Academic.

Horner, R. D. and Baer, D. M. (1978) Multiple probe technique: a variation of the multiple baseline. *Journal of Applied Behavior Analysis*, 11, 189–196.

Huitema, B. E. and McKean, J. W. (2000) Design specification issues in time-series intervention models. *Educational and Psychological Measurement*, 60(1), 38–58.

Jacobson, N. S. and Revenstorf, D. (1988) Statistics for assessing the clinical significance of psychotherapy techniques: issues, problems and new developments. *Behavioral Assessment*, 10, 133–145.

Jacobson, N. S. and Truax, P. (1991) Clinical significance: a statistical approach to defining meaningful change in psychotherapy. *Journal of Consulting and Clinical Psychology*, 59, 12–19.

Jenicek, M. (2001) *Clinical Case Reporting in Evidence-based Medicine* (2nd edn). London: Edward Arnold.

Johnson, J. M. and Pennypacker, H. S. (1980) *Strategies and Tactics in Human Behavioural Research*. Hillsdale, NJ: Lawrence Erlbaum Associates, Inc.

Kazdin, A. E. (1982) *Single Case Research Designs: Methods for Clinical and Applied Settings*. New York: Oxford University Press.

Kazdin, A. E. and Kopel, S. A. (1975) On resolving ambiguities in the multiple-baseline design: Problems and recommendations. *Behavior Therapy*, 6, 601–608.

Kratochwill, J. R. and Levin, J. R. (eds) (1992) *Single-case Research Designs and Analysis*. Hove, UK: Lawrence Erlbaum Associates.

Mace, F. C. and Lalli, J. S. (1991) Linking descriptive and experimental analyses in the treatment of speech. *Journal of Applied Behavior Analysis*, 24(3), 553–562.

McKnight, D. L., Nelson, R. O., Hayes, S. C. and Jarrett, R. B. (1984) Importance of treating individually assessed response classes in the amelioration of depression. *Behavior Therapy*, 15, 315–335.

Morley, S. (1996) Single case research. In: G. Parry and F. N. Watts (eds) *Behavioural and Mental Health Research: A Handbook of Skills and Methods* (2nd edn) (pp. 277–314). Hove, UK: Lawrence Erlbaum Associates.

Morley, S. and Adams, M. (1989) Some simple statistical tests for exploring single-case time-series data. *British Journal of Clinical Psychology*, 28(1), 1–18.

Morley, S. and Adams, M. (1991) Graphical analysis of single-case time series data. *British Journal of Clinical Psychology*, 30(Pt 2), 97–115.

Ollendick, T. H., Shapiro, E. S. and Barrett, R. P. (1981) Reducing stereotypic behaviors: an analysis of treatment procedures utilizing an alternating treatments design. *Behavior Therapy*, 12, 570–577.

Onghena, P. and Edgington, E. S. (2005) Customisation of pain treatments: Single-case design and analysis. *Clinical Journal of Pain*, 21(1), 56–68.

Parry, G., Shapiro, D. A. and Firth, J. (1986) The case of the anxious executive:

A study from the research clinic. *British Journal of Medical Psychology*, 59, 221–233.

Parsonson, B. S. and Baer, D. M. (1992) The visual analysis of data, and current research into the stimuli controlling it. In: T. R. Kratochwill and J. R. Levin (eds) *Single-case Research Design and Analysis: New Directions for Psychology and Education* (pp 15–40). Hillsdale, NJ: Lawrence Erlbaum Associates, Inc.

Philips, J. P. N. (1986) Shapiro personal questionnaire techniques: a repeated measures individualised outcome measurement. In: L. S. Greenberg and W. M. Pinsof (eds) *The Psychotherapeutic Process: A Research Handbook*. New York: Guilford Press.

Rachman, S. (1974) Primary obsessional slowness. *Behaviour Research and Therapy*, 12, 9–18.

Shapiro, M. B. (1963) A clinical approach to fundamental research with special reference to the study of the single patient. In: P. Sainsbury and N. Kreitman (eds) *Basic Research Techniques in Psychiatry*. Oxford: Oxford University Press.

Shapiro, M. B. (1966) The single case in clinical psychological research. *Journal of General Psychology*, 74, 3–23.

Sidman, M. (1960) *The Tactics of Scientific Research*. New York: Basic Books.

Teasdale, J. D. and Fennell, M. J. V. (1982) Immediate effects on depression of cognitive therapy interviews. *Cognitive Therapy and Research*, 6, 343–353.

Vlaeyen, J. W. S., de Jong, J., Geilen, M., Heuts, P. H. T. G. and van Breukelen, G. (2001) Graded exposure in vivo in the treatment of pain-related fear: A replicated single-case experimental design in four patients with chronic low back pain. *Behaviour Research and Therapy*, 39(2), 151–166.

Waltz, J., Addis, M. E., Koerner, K., and Jacobson, N. S. (1993) Testing the integrity of a psychotherapy protocol: assessment of adherence and competence. *Journal of Consulting and Clinical Psychology*, 61(4), 620–630.

Wampold, B. E. (2001) *The Great Psychotherapy Debate: Models, Methods, and Findings*. Mahwah, N. J.: Lawrence Erlbaum Associates, Inc.

Wells, A. and Sembi, S. (2004) Metacognitive therapy for PTSD: a preliminary investigation of a new brief treatment. *Journal of Behavior Therapy and Experimental Psychiatry*, 35(4), 307–318.

Youell, K. J. and McCullough, J. P. (1975) Behavioural treatment of mucous colitis. *Journal of Consulting and Clinical Psychology*, 43, 740–745.

Chapter 40

Single-case methodology in clinical neuropsychology

Lidia Yágüez and Tony Canavan

INTRODUCTION

The aim of this chapter is to provide an introduction to the kind of investigation that could be carried out following a standard clinical neuropsychological assessment. This type of thorough neuropsychological single-case study is indicated when the results of a standard assessment are not easy to interpret. They not only provide valuable clinical information for the understanding of the deficits (i.e. poor test performance) that a patient presents, but they are also essential for developing optimal individualised neuropsychological treatment plans. In addition, the results of neuropsychological single-case investigations can help the patient and carers understand in more detail the cognitive problems and difficulties that the patient encounters. Neuropsychological single-case evaluations also play an essential role in certain semi-invasive investigations, such as the sodium amytal test, in which each hemisphere is in turn anaesthetised to allow the assessment of the other hemisphere's function – in isolation – to determine whether the removal of an epileptic focus would be indicated (Powell et al., 1987).

Single-case studies also have an important value for understanding the relationship between brain and behaviour. Indeed, most of the information regarding brain function was originally derived from single-case studies of brain-damaged patients (Luria, 1968). Traditionally, single-case studies were concerned with the anatomical localisation of functions. However, in more recent times, single-case studies of patients with brain lesions have been directed more to what Shallice (1979) called '. . . providing information relevant to theories of functional organisation of the systems underlying human cognition'.

There is still some controversy relating to the use of single-case studies as a basis of research. Caramazza (1984, 1986), in an extreme position, argued that only single cases can supply the data needed for testing different brain processing models, because it is not adequate to average the performance of different patients (as is the case in group methodology) as it is not possible, *a priori*, to ensure that the brain damage sustained by each patient in the group is equivalent. However, Kolb and Whishaw (1980) state: '. . . studies of single cases are not a legitimate basis for neuropsychological theory'. It is obvious that single-case studies should not replace group studies as the only method of investigation in neuropsychology, because the generalisation from a single instance is a very risky undertaking. However, certain syndromes, or specific lesions, are so rare that the probability of employing a group design is very low. Therefore, the choice of which methodology to apply in neuro-psychological research would be dependent on the type of patients to be studied. When the research is focused on describing the cognitive profile and specific deficits of particular neurological diseases, then a group methodology is indicated. For instance, specific cognitive impairments have been described for diseases such as Parkinson's disease (Lees and Smith, 1983), multiple sclerosis (Grant et al., 1984), Alzheimer's disease and other degenerative dementias (Haxby et al., 1990), just to mention a few.

As stated above, the single-case methodology would be applied in cases of specific lesions or syndromes. This type of methodology can be considered as theory driven and is of fundamental importance in the study of the organ-isation of cerebral functions, and especially in the understanding of normal cognitive functioning (Cipolotti and Warrington, 1995). Nevertheless, neuro-psychological single-case studies pose several difficulties, which are discussed later.

Another topic discussed in this chapter is the use of functional imaging techniques for the neuropsychological single-case approach. In the past three decades, functional imaging has generated considerable evidence about the relationship between the structure and the function of the human brain. Functional imaging has some advantages but also several disadvantages: among others, the fact that the data acquired are critically dependent on the designs and baselines used. Hence the neuropsychological perspective is still very useful. Functional neuroimaging should rather be seen as comple-mentary to the neuropsychological single-case, or lesion-based, method. Indeed, the two approaches can provide converging evidence of functional organisation of the systems underlying human cognition.

PERFORMING A NEUROPSYCHOLOGICAL SINGLE-CASE STUDY

The type of neurological single-case study described in this chapter relies strongly on experimental quantitative methodology. As pointed out above, this kind of study should be performed when the nature of the underlying dysfunction that a patient displays needs to be determined. This is the case when the results of a standard assessment reveal that a patient has one or more specific deficits that are not easy to interpret. For instance, reporting that a patient performs poorly on the Block Design sub-test of the Wechsler scales does not give any further information about the reasons for that impaired performance. Thus, to investigate possible causes for that deficit, it is necessary to apply the single-case methodology and this, as is discribed later, would be hypothesis driven.

Preliminary and background data

Frequently, the starting point for a neuropsychological evaluation would be a significant discrepancy between the summarised scores of the Wechsler scales (i.e. the intelligence quotient (IQ) measures). It is obvious that, in order to establish whether such a discrepancy actually reflects a 'real' deficit, it is important to have information about the pre-morbid level of functioning. For instance, most of the verbal sub-tests of the Wechsler Intelligence Scales rely heavily on the level of education achieved by the subject. Thus, if, for instance, the verbal IQ achieved by a patient is significantly lower than his or her performance IQ, it would be incorrect to conclude, without having data about the educational and cultural background, that this patient has a verbal impairment. However, the information about the educational background alone is in itself not sufficient to establish the pre-morbid optimal level of functioning. For instance, a patient, despite not having completed many years of formal education, may have continued to educate him- or herself and thus a poor verbal performance may indeed indicate a true dysfunction. It cannot be emphasised too highly that it is essential to present a clear report of the patient's educational and occupational background, special interests and disinterests, pre-morbid existing difficulties (for instance, pre-morbid dyslexia, a learning difficulty), current motivational level and so forth.

Furthermore, it is essential that background testing should be exhaustive, as the delineation of a specific deficit (or syndrome) may be achieved only by ruling out all other possible deficits. Thus, for instance, a description of a 'specific' verbal memory deficit without the background data regarding language functions in general would be unconvincing, as would be the description of a 'specific' visual memory impairment without the assessment data regarding visuospatial perception abilities. Therefore, according to Shallice (1988), reports of single-case studies should include the results of standard clinical psychometric tests, such as the Wechsler Adult Intelligence Scale (WAIS), the Boston Aphasia Battery (Goodglass and Kaplan, 1972), memory batteries (for instance the Wechsler Memory Scale or other equivalent batteries). The results of these tests are not only important for ruling out possible deficits, without such results it is very difficult for others to gain a global impression of the patient's level of cognitive performance. This is also of major importance for comparing the results of different patients.

Finally, the background data should include the results of all physical investigations. In particular, the results of computerised tomography (CT) scans, magnetic resonance imaging (MRI), electroencephalogram (EEG) investigations and any other relevant information. These data are not only important for determining the localisation and extent of the lesion, but also for excluding longstanding abnormalities (e.g. enlarged ventricles, areas of calcification or atrophy, or displaced cortical or subcortical structures) other than the lesion in question.

One classic example of how theories of anatomical localisation of function in single-case observations can fail when the extent of the lesion is not taken into account, is the description by Broca, in 1861, of a patient who had lost his speech (Joynt, 1964). Broca indicated that the third convolution of the left frontal lobe was the focus of the subject's lesion. However, Mohr et al. (1978) pointed out that Broca's patient had sustained a massive lesion encompassing the left insula, frontal, central and parietal operculum, and extending even into the adjacent inferior parietal region posterior to the Sylvian fissure. Broca was aware of this, and yet attributed the patient's dysphasia to only that small portion of the lesion, which has since become known as 'Broca's area'. In fact, the syndrome described by Broca arises only from the large amount of damage actually present in Broca's original case (Mohr, 1976), whereas lesions of Broca's area alone typically produce little persisting deficit in articulation, and frequently no persisting disturbance in language function at all.

Locus, extent and type of lesion, as well as age at injury and time since it occurred, all play a role in interpreting the test performance of the individual patient and are important for the single-case study. Patients with lesions restricted to small areas of cortex or to particular subcortical areas tend to have very specific deficits that are not always detectable or explained with standardised test batteries. For example, Miller et al. (2003) reported a single-case study of a patient who presented an unusual autobiographical memory loss, which initially led the authors to suspect a possible psychogenic amnesia. Further investigations revealed that the patient had suffered a medial thalamic infarction.

Ad hoc testing

Once all the background tests have been performed, specification of the syndrome can proceed to *ad hoc* testing. The background data may have revealed a single deficit or a pattern of deficits, but will not necessary have sufficiently explained the nature of the dysfunction underlying such deficits. From this point on, the single-case study adopts an experimental methodology, involving the formation of hypotheses and devising experimental critical tests or tasks to test such hypotheses.

According to Shallice (1988), the best methodological approach in single-case studies to provide conclusions about the organisation of the cognitive system is the dissociation-fractionation approach. Dissociation is a classical concept in neuropsychology (Teuber, 1955). Dissociation occurs when a patient performs poorly in a task, preferably in the impaired range, but performs better or at the normal level in another task. What is crucial is that the two tasks in question assess the same domain of functions. For instance, single-case studies of selective impairments of visual recognition have shown that different classes of stimuli can be dissociated. Thus, patients can show selective impairments in face recognition but not in place recognition, and vice versa (Hecaen, 1980; Ladis et al., 1986; Farah, 1996; Moscovitch et al., 1997; Maguire and Cipolotti, 1998; Nunn et al., 2001). Such results imply that faces and places are recognised in specific ways not employed in other types of visual recognition and thus that specific brain regions process each class of stimuli.

Fractionation, according to Shallice (1979), refers to the case when a patient presents with less than the defining number of deficits for a syndrome. That is, if the patient shows that certain of the associated impairments that define the syndrome dissociate, then the previous observed functional syndrome has fractionated in specific syndromes (Shallice, 1988). Such fractionation would be of theoretical interest because it demonstrates the manner in which a functional system may be organised.

In any case, the first step when designing the tasks needed to test dissociation and fractionation of the pattern of deficits observed in the preliminary assessment will be hypothesis driven. A number of sources for the generation of hypotheses can be identified and the next sections are intended to help the researcher in going on about this task

Hypotheses derived from the test material itself

A consideration of the properties of the particular psychometric test, or tests, that first elicited the deficit is a good starting point for a single-case study. To take the Wechsler Block Design sub-test as an example. This task involves arranging, within a set time, either four or nine red and white blocks into patterns according to a model presented either by the examiner demonstrating the solution or in the form of a two-dimensional picture on a card, without demonstration. If a patient fails in this test, there are a few possible hypotheses for it.

The task is composed of several variables: number of blocks, time limit, presence or absence of demonstration. These variables can be systematically explored using items additional to those presented in the original test. Such parametric variation will determine the circumstances under which the patient succeeds or fails and will generate further hypotheses and further tasks to narrow the specific impairment. For example, the variable of time limit can be changed such that the patient has unlimited time to complete the task. A patient who is slow or particularly sensitive to time demands may be able to complete the task, whereas a patient with a serious perceptual or visual-constructive deficit, or apraxia, will not benefit from being allowed extra time. Indeed, such patients often produce erroneous solutions quite quickly. In the case of the first patient, the next step could be to define whether the slowness is for instance generalised or specific to certain tasks, or is a consequence of other variables, such as performance anxiety, etc. In the second case, again, further visuo-constructive tasks can be devised to narrow and specify the deficit.

Again, exploring the variable as to whether or not the correct solution is first modelled by the examiner could lead to hypotheses concerning planning ability on the part of the patient. If the patient always succeeds when the solution is first modelled but otherwise fails, then further experiments could be devised to assess the patient's ability to formulate strategies and carry them out.

Psychometric variation of test properties, then, is in itself a beginning to the process of hypotheses generation and testing that forms the basis of the neuropsychological single-case study.

Hypotheses derived from a consideration of functions underlying test performance

Determining the precise cognitive functions underlying neuropsychological tests presents some problems. Most of the employed tests do not assess 'pure' cognitive functions. For instance, with the Block Design described above, most researchers would agree that it assesses some kind of visuospatial constructive ability, with elements of panning and perceptual matching. This is hardly an operational definition, open to experimental investigation. Indeed, most standardised tests available measure some mixture of poorly defined cognitive abilities. Nevertheless, this shortcoming can prove a good source of hypotheses for the single-case study.

For example, verbal paired associative learning is usually employed as a verbal memory task, and on the anatomical level is it supposed to implicate left temporal lobe function. These tests usually contain 'easy' pairs, such as *fruit–apple*, or *iron–metal* and 'difficult' pairs, such as *obey–inch*, or *cabbage–pen*. The former pairs tend to be learned quite well, even by patients who have undergone left temporal lobectomy (Goldstein et al., 1988). The difficult pairs, however, pose a severe problem to such patients.

These kind of data, even from a single case, would be a convincing pointer to the anatomical location of the ability to form difficult verbal association. They also provide a clue to why total loss of either verbal or visuosparial memory functions is rarely seen after unilateral temporal lesions. At least two possible explanations are raised, which can be regarded as hypotheses that could be tested in single-case studies.

First hypothesis: clinical neuropsychological memory tests are rarely 'pure' verbal or 'pure' visual, or visuospatial. That is, tests considered to be verbal are in fact contaminated with visuospatial properties, while tests considered to be visuospatial in nature can in fact be verbalised. For instance, it might be argued that the easy pairs cited above could be visualised, utilising the functions of the right hemisphere, while this would not be the case in the difficult pairs. If this were so, the effect of the left temporal lobectomy would be to abolish performance on the difficult pairs but not on the easy pairs.

Second hypothesis: the easy pairs are extremely common, and are therefore over-learned pairs, and occur in everyday life, whereas the probability for the patient to have encountered the difficult pairs prior to the lesion or operation is minimal. In this kind of test, recall is prompted by the presentation of the first word in a pair, for example, by saying either *fruit?* or *obey?* in the example given before. If it is assumed that each of these words will generate a list of 'free' or 'logical' associations, it is likely that the list generated by *fruit?* will include *apple!* whereas the list generated by the prompt *obey?* is unlikely to include *inch!* Thus, while the 'difficult' pairs constitute a recall task, the 'easy' may, in contrast, represent a recognition task. Therefore, the data cited above could be interpreted as evidence that left temporal lobectomy results in a dysfunction of verbal recall but not of verbal recognition.

These two hypotheses could then be investigated with a single-case study applying the dissociation method. For example, if recognition memory were intact, other recognition memory tasks should be performed equally well. Finally, paired associations derived from a knowledge of the patient's lifelong occupations or hobbies, but non-visualisable and not usually associated outside that occupation or hobby, could form items for a further task in this case study.

That is, considering the possible functions underlying task performance can in itself lead to the development of testable hypotheses in a case study. As this often requires the development of new tasks, especially designed to test a specific hypothesis, appropriate control groups, as will be discussed further on, would be necessary.

Hypotheses derived from a consideration of the effects of the lesion

As pointed out before, the localisation of the lesions, as well as the extent and type of the lesion, are relevant when interpreting the test performance on an individual patient. The knowledge about what kind of functions are typically disturbed by larger lesions in a particular region could be a source of hypotheses generation and would also determine the choice of tasks to be used.

Large lesions of the occipital cortex, for instance, produce extensive anopia (loss of vision). Therefore, the hypothesis can be generated that small lesions or epileptic foci in this area will produce scotomas (small blind spots in the visual field). These may not be subjectively noticeable by the patient, but may be of clinical relevance. Another example could be lesions in the left temporal lobe or in the frontal lobes. Patients with lesions in that region may not show any motor deficits or any gross dysphasia, dyslexia or dysgraphia, but further testing may reveal subtle language deficits, for example, an inability to name specific classes of words, such as colour names (colour anomia) or specific executive functions deficits. Thus, knowledge of the functions of the affected brain region is a good source of hypothesis generation.

Another factor to be considered for interpreting the effects of brain damage – and, accordingly, for developing hypotheses to be tested in single-case studies – is the type of lesion. Different types of lesion can have different effects on brain functions. To mention just a few:

- *Tumours*: for example, gliomas tend to affect only the regions they infiltrate, whereas meningiomas may exert pressure on widespread parts of the brain. Slow-growing tumours may not be as devastating in their effects as fast-growing tumours.
- *Closed-head injuries*: these lesions are likely to have widespread effects, but in particular *contrecoup* effects, i.e. damage to areas exactly opposite to the site of external injury.
- *Vascular lesions*: are also likely to have widespread effects, with anoxia affecting all regions supplied by the vessel affected. These may also include subcortical structures, which might be adversely affected by such lesions. For instance, a lesion of the anterior communicating or cerebral arteries will affect orbital and medial frontal cortex, but it may also affect limbic functioning, as these arteries also supply the cingulate gyrus and the anterior columns of the fornix. Such a lesion may also affect the functioning of the neostriatum. These types of vascular lesion can have profound effects not only on cognitive abilities but also on motivational and motor mechanisms. Therefore, a case study investigating the effects of the lesion on cognitive abilities must take into account that performance deficits can be affected from disruption of motivational or motor mechanisms.
- *Surgical resections*: these types of lesion are in principle the most precise and circumscribed lesions to be found in the clinic. However, it must be remembered that surgery is never carried out on a healthy brain. Thus, the nature of the pathology requiring surgical intervention needs to be taken into account. For example, removal of a meningioma may be carried out with minimal damage to the underlying tissue. However, the widespread effects of pressure from this space-occupying tumour may still be observed post-surgery. In this instance, a single-case study could also be employed to follow up the recovery process. Such case studies could be of value for elucidating different courses of recovery in patients with differing clinical pictures.

Two further factors that have to be taken into account when performing a single-case study are age at injury and time since it occurred. These two factors can also serve as sources for hypotheses that can be tested in such studies.

In 1975, Teuber demonstrated that recovery of various motor, somatosensory, visual and language functions is better in the 17–20 age group than in the 21–25 age group, which is better than in patients over the age of 26. Therefore, the pattern of deficits observed in a patient following a specific lesion may differ from the pattern of deficits observed in another patient with the same lesion depending on the age at the time of injury. This situation poses a strong argument for single-case studies and against group studies in which patients of varying ages and stages of recovery are mixed together.

Time elapsed since the lesion or surgery took place is also an important factor to consider when performing a single-case study. For instance, Geshwind (1974) pointed out that the brains of patients who have undergone frontal lobectomies (for the removal of epileptic foci, for example) show marked and continuous shrinkage from the time of surgery onwards, and thus they can show cognitive deficits years later that were not present immediately after surgery (Hamlin, 1970).

Short-term changes also need to be taken into account in single-case studies. Immediately after surgery, oedemas can appear and thus the performance of a patient can deteriorate drastically. Such oedemas may be noticeable 3 days after surgery and disappear about 3 weeks later (Geschwind, 1974). Tests results observed at this time will be unreliable, as areas of brain far removed from the surgical resection site may be only temporarily affected; the same applies to vascular lesions. Immediately after lesion, the performance of the patient can be much more impaired than weeks and months after the event, when some degree of recovery has taken place. Shallice (1988) states that a single-case study is of no value unless the quantitative procedures are employed during a period when the patient's clinical condition is at least qualitatively static. Clearly, the difficulty in defining unstable syndromes poses a major problem in single-case studies, but it is often at this time that some of the most intriguing neurological symptoms occur, for instance, unilateral neglect or ideomotor apraxia, which tend to recover in most patients. Nevertheless, observations and single-case studies of such transient symptoms are also the source of some of the theories about attention (Weintraub and Mesulam, 1987; Haeske-Dewick et al., 1996) and functions of the motor system (Heilman et al., 1975; Alexander et al., 1992).

Control groups

As in all experiments in which new tasks are developed, the single-case design requires the use of a control group. The size of the control group would depend on the task in question. For instance, if the variance in the performance of the controls is very small or even zero, which will be the case when the task in question is performed at ceiling level by healthy subjects, the size of the control group does not need to be very large. However, in other tasks, in particular when reaction times are measured, the variance in performance can be very large. In these cases, the sample needs to be large enough to define the normal range of performance in that task, thus power calculations are necessary.

The composition of the control group is a matter of some debate. There is a general agreement that the control subjects should match the patient in age, gender and scores on all tests other than the particular test in question. There is, nevertheless, less agreement as to how this matching should be achieved. Shallice (1979) recommends that matching should be carried out with respect to the pre-morbid IQ. However, in most cases, pre-morbid IQ can only be estimated after the lesion by means of educational and occupational background, which, as mentioned before, poses some difficulties. Another possibility of estimating pre-morbid IQ is using reading tests, which inevitably would be dependent on the educational level. In addition, these types of reading test would be limited to patients who had not suffered any lesion affecting their language abilities, including reading and even specific perceptual abilities.

Problems with single-case studies

At this point it should be apparent that findings obtained on a single patient are not enough for developing theories about the brain functions. However, conclusions drawn from single-case studies may provide hypotheses for further examination with a group study. However, while single cases may well form an insecure basis from which to develop theories, it is often true that a single instance is all that is necessary to reject a hypothesis.

One of the main problems encountered with single-case studies is the fact that most patients seen in the clinic will have rather diffuse lesions, which do not respect any particular anatomical boundaries, and, in these cases, very little can be inferred about localisation of function. Nevertheless, the use of imaging techniques and the use of more refined experimental procedures drawn from cognitive psychology can help overcome these difficulties.

Furthermore, there is a growing acceptance that functions tend to be organised in systems rather than as separate entities, and that a large number of systems exist that display fairly non-specific functions. This implies that even small lesions at any level in a serially organised system can have quite devastating effects on the system as a whole, and that many different lesions can have seemingly similar effects, albeit for different reasons. For example, the substantia nigra supplies the neoestriatum (caudate nucleus and putamen), the tegmentum and the whole of the frontal cortex with dopamine. Damage confined to this relatively tiny structure has as a consequence disruption of multiple functions. This is in fact the case in Parkinson's disease, and the similarities and differences between the Parkinsonian syndrome and the 'frontal lobe syndrome' have been subject of much intensive investigation (Gotham et al., 1988; Canavan et al., 1989a, 1989b; Linden et al., 1990).

Another problem relates to single-case studies after surgical resections. As pointed out before, the study of surgical removals in human beings is confounded by the fact that such interventions are carried out only on abnormal brains, and thus data gathered from such cases are more likely to reflect the underlying pathology than the intervention itself. In such cases, findings from experimental and comparative psychology, in particular animal studies, can prove a valuable source for developing hypotheses and provide information on healthy brain functions. It is also quite possible that studies of patients who have suffered missile wounds (see, for example, Newcome, 1969), where there can be relatively little suspicion of previous pathology, are among the most valuable of the studies to be performed in the clinic.

In addition, as pointed out before, the age at when the injury occurred in a patient may determine the pattern of deficits, which could differ from another patient with the same lesion but of a different age. This draws attention to a severe limitation in generalising the results of single-case studies, namely, that no one case can fully describe the pattern of deficits to be expected from a particular lesion.

AN EXAMPLE OF SINGLE-CASE STUDIES

A case of cerebral akinetopsia: LM

The study of patient LM, who suffered a specific loss of visual motion perception (akinetopsia) due to extrastriate cortical damage (Zihl et al., 1983) is an example of an intensively investigated single case. Apart from the original report, LM has been further described by Hess et al. (1989), Baker et al. (1991) and Zihl et al. (1991) and, together, these studies provide a classic lesson in how a specific deficit may be painstakingly defined in order to reveal the underlying dysfunction.

The first study employed a battery of neuropsychological tests to document LM's poor performance on motion-related visual tasks, and normal performance on other perceptual tasks not involving motion, such as Snellen and Vernier acuity, temporal resolution, stereopsis, colour discrimination and saccadic localisation. Later studies used forced-choice discrimination psychophysics and sine-wave grating or random-dot stimuli to confirm the specificity of the akinetopsia. They could show that the dysfunction lay in the judgement of stimulus motion attributes, rather than in reduced sensitivity to moving stimuli. These results led to the conclusion that extrastriate cortex (the area damaged bilaterally in LM) might be particularly involved in the processing of stimuli with low signal-to-noise ratio. They also suggested that the akinetopsia might have arisen from a reduction in the number of neurons processing directional information, rather than from a total loss of a discrete brain area responsible for a specific function.

In summary, this particular case study followed a course in which an already seemingly specific deficit in motion vision was ever more narrowly defined, with residual function being carefully documented, to the point where the nature of the underlying dysfunction could be clearly formulated. The result, therefore, not surprisingly took an important place in the neuroscience literature (see Zeki, 1991) even though it was based on only a single case.

FUNCTIONAL NEUROIMAGING OF SINGLE CASES

Posner and Raiche (1994) wrote:

> A remarkable thing happened in the mid-1980s. For the first time we could actually look at pictures of the human brain while people thought. The pictures were areas of increased blood flow caused by enhanced neural activity during mental effort.

Indeed, since 1980, functional neuroimaging has produced significant evidence about its value in unravelling relationships between the structure and function of the normal human brain. Since the emergence of this technique, considerable advances have been made that allow better image resolution. In particular, functional magnetic resonance imaging (fMRI) has proved to be the method of choice in recent times. It is beyond the scope of the present chapter to discuss the different neuroimaging techniques (see Van Heertum and Tikofsky, 2000, Jezzard et al., 2001; Toga et al., 2002 for an overview). Nevertheless, the validity of the results obtained with this technique relies heavily on the task employed, as well as on the baseline. Therefore, knowledge about cognitive neuropsychology is fundamental to be able to design tasks that can with some level of certainty measure specific cognitive functions. Functional neuroimaging allows testing empirically hypotheses derived from neuropsychological single-case studies and cognitive psychology.

However, a main constraint of the use of these techniques with patients is, according to Price and Frison (2002), that interpretations of abnormal neuronal responses in patients can be made only when patients are able to perform the tasks to a level similar to normal subjects. For instance, if a patient cannot produce speech, the corresponding neuronal area will not be significantly activated. One possible explanation could be that reduced activation compared with normal subjects is the physiological cause for the impairment. However, reduced activation could also be caused because unimpaired processes (e.g. semantic and perceptual, attention) are not employed when the task cannot be performed. Another possible finding could be that the patient activates an area that does not appear in normal subjects when performing the same task. One intuitive explanation could be that this area is compensating for the damaged area. This explanation could have some validity if the patient were able to perform the task. To test this, it would be necessary to carry out further experiments to observe the brain activity of the patient while actually performing the task.

Although this approach may seem counter-intuitive from a neuro-psychological perspective, which mainly focuses on detecting tasks that the patient cannot perform, it has to be argued that normal task performance, i.e correct answers, does not always mean normal neurological responses, in particular with patients that have neurological damage (Price and Frison, 2002).

The following sections discuss the possible uses of functional neuroimaging with patients.

Characterisation of the brain damage

Functional imaging of patients can provide information about residual activity in the areas damaged, as well as abnormal activity in other undamaged areas. These findings can contribute to further understanding normal functional anatomy, connectivity and functional integration of brain regions (Price and Frison, 2002) and thus provide empirical evidence for the functional organisation of the systems underlying human cognition.

Residual activity within the damaged area indicates that some level of functionality may still be preserved in the affected area. This finding is of importance for the patient, as it could be helpful for understanding how some degree of task performance can be maintained and recovered after brain damage (Heiss et al., 1997; Warburton et al., 1999).

Abnormal activity in other non-damaged areas refers to under- or over-activation in comparison to normal subjects (Mummery et al., 1999). This abnormal activity could be caused by the effects of the lesion on other parts of the system. This distant effect of the lesion is known as 'diaschisis'. That is, diaschisis refers to specific decreases in metabolic rate at sites that are distant, but connected, to the damaged area (Price and Friston, 2002). A classic example is 'crossed cerebellar diaschisis', in which lesions within the motor cortex produce abnormalities of cerebellar metabolism (Feeney and Baron, 1986). Another possibility of diaschisis is what Price et al. (2001) called 'dynamic diaschisis', which refers to the elicited responses of a non-damaged cortical region dependent on the task being performed. That is, when a specific task requires that an undamaged area interacts with the damaged area, the undamaged area can show abnormal responses. However, the same area can show normal responses when this interaction is not required. For example, Price et al. (2001) studied a patient with left frontal damage. This patient showed normal activation of the left posterior temporal cortex during a semantic task, but the activity was abnormal during a reading task. The authors concluded that the activity on the left posterior temporal area relied on the interaction with the damaged area for the reading task, while the damaged area was not involved in the semantic task.

Structure–functional relationships

In some cases, a patient may retain the ability to perform a task despite damage to the system that is normally associated with the task. For instance, neuropsychological studies have shown that familiar, regularly spelled words can be read using at least two mechanisms: (1) by spelling to sound relationships; or (2) by lexical-semantic routes (e.g. Marshall and Newcome, 1973; Seidenberg and MacClelland, 1989). Therefore, the ability to read regularly spelled words may be preserved following damage to areas mediating only one of these mechanisms. Or for instance, objects can be recognised by their global shape or from the recognition of distinguishing features (Humphreys and Riddoch, 1984).

Thus, when a patient shows the capability to perform a specific task even after damage to the system thought to be responsible for that task, functional neuroimaging can help determine whether task performance is maintained by residual activation within the damaged area, by the activation of a subset of undamaged areas or by the activation of areas that are not observed in normal subjects. The latter could indicate that those areas were either inhibited or untrained in normal subjects, but nevertheless contribute to the performance of the task. The activation in a subset of areas could suggest that the damaged areas were not essential for the task or were part of another related system. For instance, in a reaction time (RT) task of naming facial expressions, Morris et al. (1998) showed that face-naming elicited emotional responses that did not affect the RT but that nevertheless changed the distribution of the haemodynamic responses. According to Price and Frison (2002), the effect of facial expression was 'not necessary' for the task of naming the expression but is evoked 'implicitly' by the stimulus. In another experiment with a patient with blind-sight, Morris et al. (2001) reported that although the patient was not aware of fearful faces being presented, nevertheless, discriminatory responses were detected in the amygdala with functional imaging. This study replicates classic single-case studies of patients with blind-sight (Weiskrantz et al., 1974; Weiskrantz, 1986; Cowey and Stoering, 1991), which showed that some level of residual function was present even when patients were nor aware of 'seeing'.

Therefore, the combination of neuropsychological single-case studies with functional neuroimaging of patients can contribute to the understanding of neuronal mechanisms that permit task performance to be maintained or recovered following damage to the normal system. The observations in one patient would thus generate hypotheses that could be tested empirically with functional imaging experiments of other patients with different lesions.

Design considerations in functional imaging studies with patients

As discussed above, functional imaging of patients can be useful for two purposes: (1) to better understand the patient's deficits; and (2) to investigate normal functional anatomy. Accordingly, the choice of task and design would be determined by the deficits found during the neuropsychological assessment. It is obvious that the number of experiments that can be performed at one time with one patient is limited with functional imaging. Therefore, a preliminary exhaustive neuropsychological investigation can provide the relevant hypothesis and tasks to be tested in the scanner. The results of this type of experiment should provide answers to questions such as whether significant activation of a different set of regions, related to normal subjects, are observed in the patient during task performance; whether is it possible to detect residual activation within the damaged region; how does the activity of undamaged areas in the patient compare to that of the normal subjects and so forth.

CONCLUSION

Neuropsychological single-case studies provide valuable clinical information for understanding specific deficits in patients; they can also be very useful for developing optimal individualised neuropsychological treatment plans. In addition, this methodology is useful for further understanding the relationship between brain and behaviour, and for providing data relevant to theories of the functional organisation of brain systems implicated in human cognition. Hypotheses worth testing in such studies can be drawn from a number of sources, varying from a consideration of the properties of the test material itself to speculation about likely effects of the lesion. Functional neuroimaging can be seen as a complementary technique for the single-case study that allows empirical testing of such hypotheses.

REFERENCES

Alexander, M. P., Baker, E., Naeser, M. A., Kaplan, E. and Palumbo, C. (1992) Neuropsychological and neuroanatomical dimensions of ideomotor apraxia. *Brain*, 115, 87–107.

Baker, C. L., Hess, R. F. and Zihl, J. (1991) Residual motion perception in a 'motion-blind' patient, assessed with limited-lifetime random dot stimuli. *Journal of Neuroscience*, 11, 545–561.

Canavan, A. G. M., Passingham, R. E., Marsden, C. D., Quinn, N., Wyke, M. and Polkey, C. E. (1989a) The performance on learning tasks of patients in the early stages of Parkinson's disease. *Neuropsychologia*, 27, 141–156.

Canavan, A. G. M., Passingham, R. E., Marsden, C. D., Quinn, N., Wyke, M. and Polkey, C. E. (1989b) Sequencing ability in Parkinsonians, patients with frontal lobe lesions and patients who have undergone unilateral temporal lobectomies. *Neuropsychlogia*, 27, 787–798.

Caramazza, A. (1984) The logic of neuropsychological research and the problem of patient classification in aphasia. *Brain and Language*, 21, 9–20.

Caramazza, A. (1986) On drawing inferences about the structure of normal cognitive systems from the analysis of patterns of impaired performance: The case for single-patient studies. *Brain and Cognition*, 5, 41–66.

Cipolotti, L. and Warrington, E. K. (1995) Neuropsychological assessment. *Journal of Neurology, Neurosurgery and Psychiatry*, 4, 272–277.

Cowey, A. and Stoering, P. (1991) Neurobiology of blindsight. *Trends in the Neurosciences*, 14, 140–145.

Farah, M. (1996) Is face recognition 'special'? Evidence from neurpsychology. *Behavioural Brain Research*, 76, 181–189.

Feeney, D. M. and Baron, J. C. (1986) Diaschisis. *Stroke*, 17, 317–377.

Geshwind, N. (1974) Late changes in the nervous system: An overview. In: D. G. Steib, J. J. Rosen and N. Butters (eds) *Plasticity and Recovery of Function in the Central Nervous System*. New York: Academic Press.

Goldstein, L. H., Canavan, A. G. M and Polkey, C. E. (1988) Verbal and abstract designs paired associate learning after unilateral temporal lobectomy. *Cortex*, 24, 41–52.

Goodglass, H. and Kaplan, D. (1972) *The Assessment of Aphasia and Related Disorders*. Philadelphia: Lea and Febiger.

Gotham, A. M., Brown, R. G., and Marsden, C. D. (1988) 'Frontal' cognitive functions in patients with Parkinson's disease 'on' and 'off' levodopa. *Brain*, 111, 299–321.

Grant, I., McDonald, W. I., Trimble, M. R., Smith, E. and Reed, R. (1984) Deficient learning and memory in early and middle phases of multiple sclerosis. *Journal of Neurology, Neurosurgery and Psychiatry*, 47, 250–255.

Haeske-Dewick, H. C., Canavan, A. G. M., and Hoemberg, V. (1996) New developments in the understanding and treatment of hemispatial neglect syndrome. In W. H. Zangemeister, H. S. Stiehl and C. Freksa (eds) *Visual Attention and Cognition* (pp. 115–123). New York: Elsevier.

Hamlin, R. M. (1970) Intellectual functions fourteen years after frontal lobe surgery. *Cortex*, 6, 299–307.

Haxby, J., Grady, C., Koss, E., Horwitz, B., Heston, L., Schapiro, M., Friedland, R. P. and Rapoport, S. I. (1990) Longitudinal study of cerebral metabolic asymmetries and associated neuropsychological patterns in early dementia of the Alzheimer-type. *Archives of Neurology*, 47, 753–760.

Hecaen, H., Tzortzis, C. and Rondot, P. (1980). Loss of topographic memory with learning deficits. *Cortex*, 16, 525–542.

Heilman, K., Schwartz, H. D. and Geschwind, N. (1975) Defective motor learning in ideomotor apraxia. *Neurology*, 25, 1018–1020.

Heiss, W. D., Karber, H., Weber-Luxenburger, G., Herholz, K., Kessler, J., Pietrzyk, U. and Pawlik G. (1997) Speech-induced cerebral metabolic activation reflects recovery from aphasia. *Journal of the Neurological Sciences*, 145, 213–217.

Hess, R. F., Baker, C. L. and Zihl. J. (1989) The 'motion blind' patient: Low-level spatial and temporal filters. *Journal of Neuroscience*, 9, 1628–1640.

Humphreys, G. W. and Riddoch, M. I. (1984) Routes to object constancy. Implications from neurological impairments in object constancy. *Quarterly Journal of Experimental Psychology*, 36A, 385–415.

Jezzard, P., Matthews, P. M. and Smith S. M. (2001) *Functional MRI: An Introduction to Methods*. Oxford: Oxford University Press.

Joynt, R. (1964) Paul Pierre Broca: his contribution to the knowledge of aphasia. *Cortex*, 1, 206–213.

Kolb B. and Whishaw, I. Q. (1980) *Fundamentals of Human Neuropsychology*. San Francisco: Freeman.

Ladis, T., Cummings, J. L., Benson, D. F., and Palmer, E. P. (1986) Loss of topographic familiarity: an environmental agnosia. *Archives of Neurology*, 43, 132–136.

Lees, A. J. and Smith, E. (1983) Cognitive deficits in early stages of Parkinson's disease. *Brain*, 106, 257–270.

Linden, A., Bracke-Tolkmitt, R., Lutzenberger, W., Canavan, A. G. M., Scholz, E., Diener, H. C. and Birbaumer, N. (1990) Slow cortical potentials in Parkinsonian patients during the course of an associative learning test. *Journal of Psychophysiology*, 4, 145–162.

Luria, A. R. (1968) *Mind of a Mnemonist*. New York: Basic Books.

Maguire, E. and Cipolotti, L. (1998) Selective sparing of topographical memory. *Journal of Neurology, Neurosurgery, and Psychiatry*, 65, 903–909.

Marshall, J. C. and Newcome, F. (1973). Pattern of paralexia: A psycholinguistic approach. *Journal of Psycholinguistic Research*, 2, 175–199.

Miller, L. A., Caine, D. and Watson, J. D. G. (2003) A role for the thalamus in memory for unique entities. *Neurocase*, 9, 504–514.

Mohr, J. P. (1976) Broca's area and Broca's aphasia. In: H. Avakian-Whitaker and H. A. Whitaker (eds) *Studies in Neurolinguistics*, 1, (pp. 202–235). New York: Academic Press.

Mohr J. P., Pessin, M. S., Finkelstein, S., Funkenstein, H. H., Duncan, G. W. and Davis, K. R. (1978) Broca aphasia: pathologic and clinical. *Neurology*, 28, 311–324.

Morris, J. S., Ohman, A. and Doland, R. I. (1998), Conscious and unconscious emotional learning in the human amygdala. *Nature*, 393, 467–470.

Morris, J. S., DeGelder, B., Weiskrantz, L. and Dolan, R. J. (2001) Differential extregeniculostriate and amygdala responses to blind field presentation of emotional faces. *Brain*, 124, 1241–1252.

Moscovitch, M., Winocur, G. and Behmann, M. (1997) What is special about face recognition? Nineteen experiments on a person with visual objects agnosia and dyslexia but normal face recognition. *Journal of Cognitive Neuroscience*, 9, 555–604.

Mummery, C. I., Patterson, K., Wise, R., Vandenberghe, R., Price, C. L. and

Hodges, J. (1999) Disrupted temporal lobe connections in semantic dementia. *Brain*, 122, 61–73.

Newcome, F. (1969) *Missile Wounds of the Brain. A Study of Psychological Deficits.* Oxford: Oxford University Press.

Nunn, J. A. Postma, R. and Pearson, R. (2001) Developmental prosopagnosia: Should it be taken at face value? *Neurocase*, 7, 15–27.

Posner, M. and Raiche, M. (1994) *Images of Mind.* New York: Scientific American Library.

Powell, G. E., Polkey, C. E. and Canavan, A. G. M. (1987) Lateralisation of memory functions in epileptic patients by the use of sodium amytal (Wada) technique. *Journal of Neurology, Neurosurgery and Psychiatry*, 50, 665–672.

Price, C. J. and Friston, K. J. (2002) Functional imaging studies of neuropsychological patients: applications and limitations. *Neurocase*, 8, 345–354.

Price, C. J., Warburton E. A., Moore, CI., Frackowiak, R. S. I. and Frison, K. J. (2001) Dynamic diaschisis: context sensitive human brain lesions. *Journal of Cognitive Neuroscience*, 13, 419–429.

Seidenberg, M. S. and MacClelland, J. L. (1989) A distributed developmental model of word recognition and naming. *Psychological Reviews*, 96, 523–568.

Shallice, T. (1979) Case study approach in neuropsychological research. *Journal of Clinical Neuropsychology*, 1, 183–211.

Shallice, T. (1988) *From Neuropsychology to Mental Structure.* Cambridge: Cambridge University Press.

Teuber H. L. (1955) Physiological psychology. *Annual Review of Psychology*, 6, 267–296.

Teuber, H. L. (1975) Recovery of functions after brain injury in man. *Ciba Foundation Symposium 34.* Amsterdam: Elsevier.

Toga, A. W., Mazziotta, J. C. and Frackowiak, R. S. J. (2002) *Brain Mapping: The Trilogy.* New York: Academic Press.

Van Heertum, R. and Tikofsky, R. S. (2000) *Functional Cerebral SPECT and PET Imaging.* Philadelphia: Lippincott Williams and Wilkins.

Warburton, E. A., Price, C. I., Swinburn, K. and Wise, R. J. S. (1999) Mechanisms of recovery from aphasia: evidence from positron emission tomography studies. *Journal of Neurology, Neurosurgery and Psychiatry*, 66, 155–161.

Weintraub, S. and Mesulam, M. M. (1987) Right cerebral dominance in spatial attention. Further evidence based on ipsilateral neglect. *Archives of Neurology*, 44, 621–625.

Weiskrantz, L. (1986) *Blindsight. A Case Study and Implications.* Oxford: Oxford University Press.

Weiskrantz, L., Warrington E. K., Sanders, M. D. and Marshall, J. (1974) Visual capacity in the hemianoptic field following a restricted occipital ablation. *Brain*, 97, 709–728.

Zeki, S. (1991) Cerebral akinetopsia (visual motion blindness). A review. *Brain*, 114, 811–824.

Zihl, J., von Cramon, D. and Mai, N. (1983) Selective disturbance of movement vision after bilateral brain damage. *Brain*, 106, 313–340.

Zihl, J., von Cramon, D., Mai, N. and Schmidt, C. (1991) Disturbance of movement vision after bilateral posterior brain damage. Further evidence and follow-up observations. *Brain*, 114, 2234–2252.

Chapter 41

Professional issues in the new century

New demands, new skills

Catherine Dooley

INTRODUCTION

The chapter on professional issues in the second edition of this book considered the impact of a societal shift on the position of all professions within the UK. This represented a change from professionals being accepted as self-regulating 'monopoly' providers of an area of expertise, into a requirement for more formal accountability to the wider service system and society.

In the last 10 years, the position of all professions has continued to evolve, to the extent that there is questioning of the very status of professions as a distinct body of expert practitioners (Allsop and Saks, 2002). The United Kingdom government paper '*Working Together: Securing a Quality Workforce for the NHS*' (Department of Health, 1999c) identified as a strategic aim the need to have a 'quality workforce in the right numbers, with the right skills and diversity, organised in the right way', and saw this as requiring major organisational change. The focus is on delineating the underpinning competencies and skills required for the delivery of expertise with an expectation that these could be provided by a wider range of staff with different training and experiences than has traditionally been the case.

For all professions, there is considerable unease that this will lead to a loss of that specialist expertise that comes from intense study and experience. For clinical psychologists, the implications of considering how psychological expertise can be delivered within the NHS, rather than the provision of clinical psychologists, creates a particular challenge. Psychology is a general subject whose theories and models and (to some extent) therapeutic techniques are available to a very wide range of people; this can be seen as creating new opportunities for psychologists to influence the systemic delivery of health care through enhancing the level of psychological knowledge and skills of the workforce; or it can be viewed as a threat that will reduce the numbers of psychologists employed and water down the expertise to the lowest common denominator.

This chapter considers the factors that have shaped the current situation

– both those acting at a general level within the UK and those acting more directly within mental health services. The particular impact of these on clinical psychology practice will be covered later. Because the rate of introduction of new structures and ideas is currently very rapid, the stress is on major directions and themes that seem likely to be relevant in the future. The focus will be predominantly on England in terms of legislation and government policy; Wales, Northern Ireland and Scotland have different health structures and policy frameworks but the general direction of developments is, however, broadly similar.

WHAT IS DRIVING THE CHANGES?

A number of trends have radically affected the direction and style of delivery of health services. These are epitomised in the UK by *The NHS Plan* (Department of Health, 2000), which has been followed by a series of further government publications, such as *The NHS Improvement Plan* (Department of Health, 2004b). These trends include:

- The continual rising cost of health care: with a recognition that demand will always outstrip capacity unless a different approach is developed.
- Changing disease patterns: now that the need to focus resources on treating infectious diseases is reduced (due to the impact of antibiotics) this allows a focus on chronic disease management (Plumridge, 2004), which includes mental health.
- Better information about the aetiology of disorders: so that it is possible to develop a strategic approach to health promotion and prevention.
- Shortage of all staffing, but particularly within skilled professions.

Public issues

The general public is considerably more knowledgeable and interested in self-management of health, and far less willing to place blind trust in 'experts' (Klein, 1995), than in the past. This is due to various factors:

- The internet: this has led to easy access to knowledge of health matters. For instance, guidelines produced by the National Institute for Health and Clinical Excellence (NICE) are openly available on its website (http://www.nice.nhs.uk); NHS Direct posts information and advice about health matters, including mental health, on its website.
- The continued rise of the consumer society: with heightened awareness of rights, higher expectations and less tolerance of poor standards of service. The European Convention on Human Rights was incorporated into UK law in 1998 and has raised expectations on those delivering

services and provided a means for recipients of services to challenge decisions that appear to breach the Act.

- The impact of scandals within medicine, the law and other professions: this has led to a distrust of professions' ability to police themselves and supported the drive for greater external accountability. In particular the Alder Hey and Bristol scandals resulted in widespread review of consent within clinical practice and research (Royal Liverpool Hospital Enquiry, 2001) and the communication skills of doctors (Kennedy, 2001).

These factors have resulted in a formal policy to make patient involvement and public participation a reality (Department of Health, 2005a). The particular results of these within mental health has been the recognition of the need for effective advocacy for the individual client, but also an emphasis (identified within policy and monitored as part of local targets) on the formalisation of users' and carers' roles within the ongoing management and development of services (NHS Modernisation Agency, 2001; Rose, 2001).

GOVERNMENT POLICY

The dilemma for all governments is how to control costs within the NHS (especially labour costs) and also how to maintain an accountability framework to allow monitoring and review of the use of resources in health care. Both the Conservative government in the early 1990s and the present Labour administration have struggled with this dilemma, although with different policy approaches. The following sections illustrate some of the main features.

The public health agenda

The public health agenda has been developed as a strategic attempt to reduce the causes of ill health as a main thrust of the *NHS Improvement Plan*. This has led to a shift towards promoting health generally within society, the result being more policies that reflect 'joined up thinking' across the environment, social services, education, etc.; the recent Sainsbury Centre policy paper *The Future of Mental Health: a Vision for 2015* (Sainsbury Centre, 2005) epitomises this. As part of this there has been a focus on diversity issues as a means of ensuring genuine equality of access to health provision, across all social groups. Within mental health there has been recognition of the effects of social exclusion generally, as well as concerns over the increased vulnerability of minority non-white groups to mental health problems and issues of engagement with services (Sainsbury Centre for Mental Health, 2002; Social Exclusion Unit, 2004).

Evidence-based practice

There has been a marked emphasis on using evidence-based practice to justify the use of resources – a shift from just enhancing efficiency towards demonstrating the clinical effectiveness of services. This is most obviously shown in the role of NICE, which promulgates explicit expectations and standards for the delivery of a range of health services. The British Psychological Society (BPS) Centre for Outcomes Research and Effectiveness (CORE) (http://www.core.org.uk) and the Royal College of Psychiatrists' Research Unit are joint partners in the Mental Health Collaborating Centre, the body that is funded by NICE to produce its mental health guidance. Recent guidance has covered schizophrenia, eating disorders, deliberate self-harm, generalised anxiety, post-traumatic stress disorder (PTSD), obsessive-compulsive disorder (OCD), bipolar disorders, depression and computerised cognitive-behaviour therapy (CBT).

Standards and targets

There has also been a shift to targets and objective setting as a means for central government to determine how priorities are met within the NHS. The most obvious of these has been the production of National Service Frameworks (NSFs), for instance those for cancer, coronary heart disease, diabetes and older people. The NSF for the mental health for adults of working age (Department of Health, 1999b) laid out explicit expectations for the level of service provision and the style of delivery. For psychologists, this has been of mixed benefit. The role of clinical psychologists has been formally recognised; however, it has clearly demonstrated the quandary of a small profession's ability to expand rapidly and the need for a wider pool of psychology expertise to be available, either through other staff (such as community psychiatric nurses; CPNs) or the development of new types of worker, such as graduate mental health workers in primary care.

Another concern for psychologists working in adult community mental health teams (CMHTs) has been that the NSF has specified that the role of such teams be for those with severe and enduring mental health problems. Whilst this is recognised as needed to ensure that scarce resources are focused on those most in need, it can produce problems for job satisfaction and in maintaining core clinical skills.

Government policies have promoted the development of mental health trusts, partly as a means of ensuring adequate resources and specialisms. This has led to the establishment of large trusts – often combining four or more trusts and psychology departments. This has been an interesting phenomenon and, as with other developments, has had both positive and negative effects. On the positive side, it has produced psychology departments (and specialties, such as adult mental health) of a considerable size and weight, which allows a stronger influence within a trust (thus fulfilling the predictions of the Manpower Planning Advisory Group (MPAG), 1990). On the down side, this can be seen as drawing psychology into the sphere of, and control by, mental health and the loss of the breadth of activity and flexibility of roles.

Local commissioning and accountability

At the same time as the NSFs have set out clear parameters for services, there has been a parallel move away from central control to more local commissioning and accountability (Department of Health, 2001a). There has been flattening of the levels within the NHS, with the abolition of regions and the institution of Strategic Health Authorities as the only tier between national government and local commissioners and trusts. The continued shift towards primary care trusts (PCTs) as having the prime role in the commissioning of health services, based on local conditions and needs, could lead to different relationships between primary and secondary care services for mental health, with the general practioners' priorities and agendas increasingly having a central position (NHS Confederation, 2003).

Modernisation of delivery

Another strand has been the emphasis on the modernisation of delivery of services generally, and within mental health (Department of Health, 2005b). The aim of modernisation is to improve capacity and capability through enhancing the quality of the services delivered, increasing the capacity within organisations, equipping the workforce with improved skills and supporting innovation and new ways of working. This has been demonstrated in the shift towards commissioning of whole services and/or teams with a more flexible, locally driven skill mix. The focus on multi-agency working is reflected in the establishment of Health and Social Care Trusts, where there is impetus for creating integrated teams between health and social services.

Acceptance of the role of the private sector in the delivery of health services has continued under both Conservative and Labour administrations. The use of private finance in the building of new hospitals is now accepted (whether or not approved) and recent policies to use private facilities, or even overseas services, for operations have been introduced. However, if anything, within mental health services the opposite trend has been apparent, with pressure on local services to be self-sufficient rather than purchase from the private sector, except in selected areas, such as for personality disorders or forensic services. There is evidence from Canada that 'not-for-profit' psychiatric services are better for patients, as their social focus outweighs the financial incentives of private providers (Deber, 2003). However, it is possible, as foundation hospitals develop their role, that they may wish to expand into mental health, perhaps jointly with a private provider. Perhaps most significantly, the new GP contracts allow more scope for direct employment of therapists or contracting with a diverse range of providers.

Modernisation of the workforce

In parallel with the drive to modernise the methods of delivery has been the drive to modernisation of the workforce – a shift towards identifying the capabilities and competencies required to deliver health care (reflected in the titles of recent government publications, such as *A Workforce of all the Talents* and *Skills for Health*) and identify new and flexible ways of delivering this. This has been driven partly through the problems of training, recruiting and retaining staff in the NHS; it has partly been driven by more ideological views, such as distrust of the paternalistic and elitist position of some professions (doctors in particular (Saks,1995)) and more radical views about the nature of clinical expertise. A report, jointly from the National Institute of Mental Health for England (NIMHE) and the Royal College of Psychiatrists, reviews and makes recommendations for changes to the role of consultant psychiatrists and thence to the roles of other staff within the multidisciplinary team (Department of Health, 2005c); it makes it clear that professions must overcome resistance to change in order to provide effective care.

Another result has been the development of occupational standards for mental health, applicable across all professional groups, following on from the Sainsbury's Centre *Capable Practioner* report (Sainsbury Centre for Mental Health, 2001). This identified values, skills and priorities for mental health services and those staff working in it.

Agenda for Change (Department of Health, 1999a) is currently being introduced within the NHS and provides a framework for the range and level of skills within all (non-medical) areas of health care to allow a coherent and explicit comparison of expertise. In the long term, the Knowledge and Skills Framework (Department of Health, 2003c) is likely, if fully implemented, to have a significant impact. This provides a descriptive and structured framework to delineate types of and levels of competencies and may be used eventually as the basis of person specifications and for career progression within appraisals. The effect would be that the individual's training, professional qualifications and experience would only be relevant inasmuch as it relates to the person specification; this opens up the possibility that the professional title 'clinical' psychologist may not be able to be used to exclude those with related qualifications, such as counselling psychologists.

Monitoring and regulation

In parallel with government initiatives, a wide range of bodies monitor whether targets are being met by Trusts and services. For example, the

Healthcare Commission for England and Wales encompasses the work of the defunct Commission for Health Improvement, the Mental Health Commission and the Audit Commission.

There has been increased direct regulation of professions by the State, partly as a result of the perceived failure of professions to regulate themselves. The government has initiated the Health Professions Council (Department of Health, 2003a), which has taken over many of the regulatory powers that many health professions, such as occupational therapy and physiotherapy, previously held. This establishes clear links between fitness to practice and explicit external standards such as training, continuing professional development (CPD) and supervision.

THE MENTAL HEALTH NATIONAL SERVICE FRAMEWORK (ADULTS OF WORKING AGE)

The Adult Mental Health NSF built on an earlier government publication, *Modernising Mental Health Services* (Department of Health, 1999b), and represented for the first time a shared national prioritisation of mental health, setting out guiding principles that services will:

- involve service users and their carers in planning and delivery of care
- deliver high-quality treatment and care that is known to be effective and acceptable
- be well suited to those who use them, and be non-discriminatory
- be accessible, so that help can be obtained when and where it is needed
- promote users' safety and that of their carers, staff and the wider public
- offer choices that promote independence
- be well co-ordinated between all staff and agencies
- deliver continuity of care for as long as this is needed
- empower and support their staff
- be properly accountable to the public, service users and carers.

National Service Frameworks identify national standards and service models, establish local programmes for delivery and identify and monitor milestones and performance indicators for implementation. The Adult NSF covered health promotion, assessment and diagnosis, treatment, rehabilitation and care, and encompassed primary and specialist care and the roles of partner agencies. It also touched on the needs of children and young people, highlighting areas where services for children and adults interact, for example, the interface between services for 16-18-year-olds, and the needs of children with a mentally ill parent.

The Department of Health established a standard-based planning framework for the period 2005/06 to 2007/08. This moved away from national targets and gave more scope for addressing local priorities. This is likely to strengthen the position of PCTs in negotiating for services shaped to their local population, and is likely to require the large, multi-borough Health and Social Care Trusts to become less centralised and shaped more to local needs and preferences.

CLINICAL PSYCHOLOGY

It should be clear from the previous sections that clinical psychologists have now been drawn into a wide process of change within the health service. Mental health has been the focus of substantial government attention and initiatives (and more financial investment) and is now subject to greater scrutiny and regulation. This section will summarise the ways in which these factors are impacting on clinical psychology.

Professional regulation and guidance

There is now increased internal regulation of the profession. This is evidenced through the increased activity (and speed of response) of the BPS Division of Clinical Psychology (DCP) in providing guidance and advice to its members in recent years, such as guidelines for services (DCP, 1998c), CPD (DCP, 2001a), policy and guidelines for supervision (DCP, 2003d) and a range of information leaflets (DCP, 2003a).

Involvement with government

The DCP is now working closely in collaboration with the Department of Health and NIMHE at a national level and is working towards a document on new ways of working for applied psychologists. Clinical psychologists have had a considerable involvement in the re-drafting of the revised Mental Health Bills, in both England and Scotland, and are increasingly being invited on to government working groups. The DCP is considering how to enable there to be more local influence on Strategic Health Authorities and Trusts. It is also envisaging changes in its structures and organisation to take account of devolution, and the rapid changes in the organisation of the NHS.

The family of psychology

Counselling psychologists (who represent 3% of the workforce; Division of Clinical Psychology, 2003b), health and forensic psychologists are beginning to challenge the near monopoly held by clinical psychologists within the NHS (both in training and jobs) and it is clear that there is a very high overlap of expertise, at least at a general level, as evidenced in the work on competencies following on from the Occupational Standards in Applied Psychology (British Psychological Society, 2001). The effect of the Knowledge and Skills Framework is likely to remove the use of professional titles, as inclusion criteria for posts. European Community Directives also impact on this situation as they work to homogenise qualifications across the member states (Lunt, 2004).

The DCP's response to this has been to develop the notion of the 'Family of Psychology', reflecting the view that there are shared interests and concerns within applied psychology that need to be addressed internally within the profession.

Agenda for Change

The implications of Agenda for Change is that clinical psychology at every level will be relatively more expensive than before and in comparison with other staff, such as CPNs, due to the very high loading given to academic qualifications. The view is that this will require a much stronger case to be made for what clinical psychology can offer within the NHS, in particular an elaboration of the higher-level skills, such as supervision, consultancy and training, service development and research. Some consideration is being given to the possibility that clinical psychology might develop more of a consulting and supervisory role rather than in direct service provision.

Increased demand for psychologists and psychological therapies

There appears to be significant increased demand for psychology from NSFs and other reports.

The NSF for mental health identified a clear need for clinical psychologists within CMHTs. In addition, other areas were identified, many of these leading to specialist posts within crisis resolution and early intervention, acute in-patient care, assertive outreach, continuing care and rehabilitation and services for people with dual diagnosis or personality disorders. Specialties such as substance misuse and forensic are also growing. The need for access to psychological therapies were also described within NICE guidelines for mental health problems, with an emphasis on CBT as the preferred model. Psychologists are working in PTSD services, and with refugees and asylum seekers (which raises difficulties in providing assessment and therapy through interpreters). More recently, the Layard Report (Layard, 2004) has recommended widening access to psychological therapies in primary care, partly to reduce the proportion of individuals on incapacity benefit.

BPS publications have in recent years focused on providing guidance for assessment and intervention in a range of clinical areas and/or client groups:

severe and enduring mental illness (DCP, 2002a), psychotic experiences (DCP, 2000), substance misuse (DCP, 1998b), HIV and sexual health (DCP, 2002b) and general areas – primary care (DCP, 1999), and for black and minority ethnic people (DCP, 1998a). There have also been publications on measuring outcomes in clinical practice (Sperlinger, 2001, 2003)

The increased focus on evidence-based practice has resulted in recognition of the value of CBT and this is seen as the treatment of choice for a range of conditions (anxiety, depression, etc.) (Department of Health, 2001b). This can therefore be viewed as the default therapeutic approach by commissioners and team managers and thus requires the local psychologist to be able to argue coherently for other approaches if they seem more appropriate for the individual client. Within the profession there has also been concern that the enthusiasm for CBT is based on an overemphasis on its time-limited nature and a simplistic view of its application, given that there is considerable evidence that the basis of CBT is culturally bound, and of less obvious efficacy when used with clients with socio-economic deprivation and more severe conditions (Maloney and Kelly, 2004, provide a review).

In primary care, the work has continued to develop, albeit piece-meal, with psychologists promoting a formal model of delivery that includes clear criteria, risk assessment and audit of outcomes (e.g. Ryan-Morgan et al., 2004) and can include broader advice, such as on nutrition (Baker et al., 2002) and self-help literature (Papworth, 2000); a focus on group work and more psychoeducational models is also evident (O'Loughlin et al., 2004).

There has been an increase in psychology applied to physical health conditions and medical settings, partly supported by NSFs. This work covers areas such as cardiac rehabilitation, diabetes, asthma, oncology and palliative care, HIV and sexual health and intensive care. The Faculty of Clinical Health Psychology was instituted in 2003.

In-patient mental health wards used to be the neglected area of adult mental health (Sainsbury Centre for Mental Health,1998; Campling et al., 2004). The recent focus on these in government policy and priorities (Department of Health, 2002a) has placed new demands on psychologists but also raised opportunities to make a more systemic impact on the culture of care (Holmes, 2002). Psychologists can work at all three levels outlined in the 1990 MPAG report: therapist, consultant and strategic change agent (Hall and Parry, 1988).

Psychological interventions for personality disorders have been developing in recent years, with Dialectical Behaviour Therapy (Linehan, 1993) having the clearest evidence base. There is now a recognition that there should be access to therapy services for people with this diagnosis (NIMHE, 2003). Within CMHTs there is some ambivalence as to whether people with personality disorders meet the criteria for access. However, it is likely that with the shift in commissioning to more of a primary-care focus there will be stronger demand for such services. Commissioning that recognises that certain client groups need substantially longer (over several years) and intense (once or twice weekly) therapy would be welcomed by the profession but would require an investment in training and staff to achieve; it would also require an investment in research to evaluate the efficacy of available therapeutic interventions.

The Department of Health (2001b) published guidelines for psychological therapies and counselling using the available evidence base. In 2004, a government report *Organising and Delivering Psychological Therapies* (Department of Health, 2004a) took this further and described their essential role within health care, the range of providers and the lack of adequate provision as 'patchy, uncoordinated, idiosyncratic, potentially unsafe and not fully integrated' (p. 1). A number of actions were identified, including improving access, promoting choice and developing care pathways and awareness of the needs of different groups. Recommendations for training, management and leadership and accountability were also made. This could, if implemented, have a significant impact both on the provision and quality of psychological therapies and on the position of psychologists within its organisation and delivery.

Workforce issues: numbers and skill mix

Although the last 10 years have seen a steady increase in the number of psychologists trained and practising within the UK, the numbers do not match the increased demand within adult mental health, let alone the other specialisms that clinical psychology work in – CAMHS (Child and Adolescent Mental Health Service), older people, general health, etc., as indicated by the *English Survey of Applied Psychology* (DCP, 2004a). There is also a high vacancy rate across all specialties (over 17%; Gray and Kate, unpublished data). A number of approaches are addressing this:

- The move to competency-based training (DCP, 2001b) was introduced for a number of reasons, partly ideological (given the significance of occupational standards) but also pragmatic, given the restrictions in expansion due to lack of placement availability.
- There has also been recognition that a diversity of routes can be used to expand the workforce; the Statement of Equivalence route has been used for many years to allow overseas-trained clinical psychologists to practise in the UK; they currently make up 7–8% of the total annual output from training courses (DCP, 2004a). Recently, there have been moves to make their passage through the accreditation process faster and more efficient, with a move towards delegating the examination role to local courses and to provide financial support for candidates and employers (Whittington et al., 2004).
- Skill mix is also being addressed. The employment of psychology

assistants has been common within adult mental health and they can provide substantial support in clinical areas, such as assessment, behavioural interventions and running groups, as well as carrying out audits and service evaluation.

- The role of the graduate mental health worker has just been established (Department of Health, 2003b). Their role is to support PCTs in implementing proposals in the National Plan and to improve the quality of, and access to, mental health services.

- Some thought has been given within the DCP to developing 'associate psychologists', who would be trained to Masters level and work in one speciality. Their role would be to deliver specific techniques, delineated by protocols (level 2), under the supervision of people with level 3 systemic/ consultancy skills (Management Advisory Service, 1989). A feasibility project was commissioned (Management Advisory Service, 2003) and this is currently being piloted, with mixed views within the profession as to the need for and viability of such a scheme.

There are implications for expanding the numbers of unqualified staff, as this inevitably requires qualified staff to take on the supervisory role and thus leads to a subsequent reduction in their direct clinical activity.

Diversity

There is a strong thrust within the NHS to promote diversity within the workforce of the NHS. Clinical psychology is not exempt from this and in recent years there have been studies of the workforce and of the factors that lead to a predominantly white workforce. A publication by Turpin (DCP, 2004b) has shown that the barrier occurs before selection for clinical psychology training, which does not markedly discriminate; that is, the barriers arise earlier in the process of gaining education and work experience to fit the criteria for selection.

The development of the Special Interest Group (SIG) in Race and Culture reflects the increased awareness that the profession needs to increase its awareness of the issue and to ensure that staff are equipped to address this; the SIG has been empowered by the DCP in developing awareness training for the profession.

Management and accountability

There are major implications of the stronger organisational pressures, expectations and standards and for psychologists' freedom and autonomy. Within CMHTs, many psychologists will now be managed by the team manager while being professionally managed by another psychologist, although the managers' SIG has proposed a 'win–win' model that address both the professionals' and service managers' concerns (Hewson and White, 2004). This can mean that decisions about use of time, clinical priorities and clinical decisions (such as length of treatment) may be determined largely with reference to the commissioner's team and service needs, rather than professional judgement (DCP, 2001d).

One particular issue is the question of whether psychologists should take on generic team roles, such as generic team assessments, generic care co-ordinator roles or manning the duty desk. Interestingly, the Agenda for Change process may mitigate against this, given that psychologists will be an increasing expensive resource compared to others within the team.

However, for many, if not most, CMHT psychologists, working within a team is seen as a positive experience and a natural means of delivering their expertise in conjunction with others. A challenge for the profession over the next years may be to develop a recognised position within teams and services as holding the expertise in psychological models and applications in a systemic fashion, much as psychiatrists are viewed in relation to diagnosis and medication.

Regulation

The increased regulation of professions means that, increasingly, they are bound by policies from a national level, or from their employing Trust or local team or service. Nationally, there is now a requirement to report concerns about possible child abuse and the new Mental Health Act (currently draft) will establish the role of clinical supervisor, which psychologists may be required to undertake and that may or may not be voluntary (Pilgrim, 2005). Psychologists may also be able to take formal positions within assessment and management of mental capacity. Local policies on confidentiality, risk assessment and management, abuse of vulnerable adults and even some of the conflicts within a team can create ethical dilemmas for individual psychologists and can raise a concern that their relationship with and responsibility for the individual patients is not prime but subsumed by the organisational demands.

This is not unique to the profession of clinical psychology but there are some particular issues given that clinical psychologists enter therapeutic roles with clients, which do require careful agreement about confidentiality and boundaries. In particular, it can be an issue if the psychologist is also asked to be the care co-ordinator within a CMHT.

IMPLICATIONS FOR THE FUTURE FOR PSYCHOLOGY PRACTICE AND SKILLS

Expertise

This will be increasingly internally owned and held by the individual with the requirements by the BPS, under the Knowledge and Skills Framework and under the Health Professions Council (HPC) (if the BPS decides to enter), being to keep a record of training, CPD and other professional activity and to formally use such evidence within career progression (Department of Health, 2003c).

The profession will offer a very wide range of therapeutic approaches, from brief interventions to specialist CBT for complex problems and more systemic work. This has implications for post-qualification training, as it is likely that this will require additional training towards specialist skills.

There will be a focus on the unique contribution of psychologists to health care. The DCP (2001c) identified four core skills of the professions: assessment, formulation, intervention and evaluation, but Kinderman (2001) has emphasised the importance of formulation, arguing that this gives clinical psychologists their special position within health provision. This may be important as the implications of Agenda for Change work through, because it is likely that it is within the clinical management of complex clients that these skills will be most in evidence.

The delivery of psychological expertise will need to be shaped much more around authentic user involvement and collaboration. User involvement can be conceptualised as a demand from the organisation (such as to copy correspondence to all clients) or it can be seen as a way of addressing, at a more fundamental level, the power differential between professionals and service users. This has been addressed by psychologists from a social constructionist standpoint (Soffe, 2004) and those with a community psychology perspective (Smail, 1995), but is only just being implemented within the profession and individual Trusts.

The role of qualified psychologists will be to support other staff's use of psychological skills – assistant and associates and others – so they will need to accept more of a supervisory and consultancy role. This does have implications for job satisfaction, as well as indicate a need for training in order to develop these skills.

The position of psychologists within teams is likely to alter, with a recognition of a more specialist role and higher expectations for delivery of such roles. Senior posts will increasingly be viewed as consultant 'level 3' posts, as envisaged by the MAS report.

Training

As it produces trained graduates, the competency model could lead to a more individualised profile of competencies at the end of training, and highlight the need for further specialist training. There will be an integration of pre- and post-qualification training and development of more formal courses (e.g. the Diploma in Clinical Neuropsychology). It may be, for instance, that training in supervision skills is a pre-requisite for re-grading.

The profession will become much more diverse in its make up, with psychology departments representing the 'family of psychology' (counselling, health, forensic), a broader range of staff and broader skills mix. This has implications for quality control, within supervision, appraisal and CPD.

Development of 'higher order' skills will be a priority to equip staff with the ability to carry out, describe and disseminate their expertise – through supervision, consultancy, training, research and service development skills. Currently, training is not well organised for this area for psychologists and this may be a focus for CPD initiatives, possibly across the Strategic Health Authority and funded by the Workforce Development Confederation, as happens in the North of England for newly qualified psychologists (Wisely, 2004).

There will be pressure for all training to be multi-disciplinary at all levels, from pre- to post-qualification levels, and especially so when training is funded by external bodies.

Research activity

Agenda for Change gave high factor loading for psychology posts in research, although there is a recognition within the profession that NHS psychologists do not use this as part of usual clinical activities (Jones, 1994).

Research and development is now part of the clinical governance agenda within the NHS (Department of Health, 2002b) and increasing research activity is being monitored and regulated within Trusts, largely to ensure that such work is relevant, well conducted and completed.

An important development is the focus on inter-professional and inter-agency research, and the priority is now towards multi-centre studies where the benefits of scale give more statistical power to results. An important recent innovation, especially for mental health, has been the Mental Health Research Network established under NIMHE to allow access to cohorts of patients and staff in mental health across the country (Fielding, 2004).

For psychologists, this clearly opens up opportunities to engage product-ively in research that is supported and constructive; however, it requires a collaborative approach and an integration with others' timescales.

Regulation

The implication of applied psychology coming under the HPC has been recognised (Lindsay, 2004); the BPS decided against entry in 2005. Much of the regulatory activities undertaken by the BPS might be handed over to this body, although the BPS will remain as the professional body responsible for establishing standards and for training. For the individual practitioner, renewal of the practising certificate each year will depend on satisfactory evidence of completion of professional activities, such as training, CPD, supervision and appraisal.

There has been an extension within the NHS of statutory responsibility in a number of areas; child protection has been one such area. Within mental health, the new (currently draft) Mental Health Act could impose additional responsibilities for psychologists. Within mental capacity legislation, which is currently passing through Parliament, similar responsibilities in assessment and management are likely. Although these may not be compulsory for all applied psychologists, the fact that they could be within the range of expected duties concerns those psychologists who see their prime role as being to ally with the individual client and who have concerns about being drawn into coercive relationships.

In Trusts, there are now requirements to establish clinical governance arrangements that are inspected by national bodies and require the production of evidence and reports (Department of Health, 2004c); psychologists are part of this, either as individual practitioners or through their teams/services.

Detailed professional guidance from the DCP was published in 2003 (DCP, 2003c) to guide individual practitioners and departments both to reflect on and to enhance individual practice, and also to contribute to the quality agenda of their Trust. This emphasised two principles: (1) that improvements to the experience of the service user are the touchstone of effective clinical governance, and so need to be demonstrated; and (2) that systems thinking is necessary to achieve this.

These standards include managers/professional advisers and the individual practitioner, involvement of service users and links with other systems of governance. The document also sets explicit standards, for instance in CPD time and supervisor training.

Ethics

It can seem hard to identify the role of ethics within professional activity, and particularly individual, profession-specific ethical codes.

In the past, a professional ethical code might have been the sole source of guidance to the individual practitioner; monitoring was primarily by the individual, with the professional body in the background to deal with complaints. Now there is a plethora of guidance from government and local management, with an array of monitoring mechanisms, including clinical governance. Much of these are based on principles (such as service-user involvement) that the profession would fully support.

Standards and expectations are increasingly high and it is more likely that unprofessional behaviour would lead to disciplinary proceedings from the BPS or employer, with the potential for sanctions. The BPS has an ethical code and code of conduct for all psychologists (BPS, 2000). Its regulatory affairs team deals with enquiries about professional and ethical matters. The reports of the BPS's disciplinary committee into complaints against individual psychologists, published in *The Psychologist*, also indicate the expectations of standards of practise and so are of value to the individual practitioner.

The HPC has generic standards of conduct, performance and ethics for all registered professions.

It is probably easier to think of these different codes as working as spheres of influence on the individual, rather than in a hierarchical way. However, the implication is that individuals will have to incorporate these into their practice and to be aware of the varied accountability they represent.

CONCLUSION

This chapter has attempted to capture some of the factors that are leading to rapid shifts in the context, and expectations of, adult clinical psychology. The real challenge for the profession is to make the changes in attitude, presentation and expertise required by these forces, whilst maintaining a principled and informed stance that allows psychology be used to enhance the well-being of service users, both directly and indirectly.

ACKNOWLEDGMENT

Grateful thanks are due to John Cape, who assisted in the conceptualisation of this chapter and gave valuable feedback and advice throughout.

REFERENCES

Allsop, J. and Saks, M. (eds) (2002) *Regulating the Health Professions*. London: Sage.
Baker, J., Cunnane, B., Godfery, J., McCulloch, A., Mills, N., Ryan-Morgan, T. and Thornton, G. (2002) Integrating nutrition and exercise into brief psychotherapy. *Clinical Psychology*, 19, 22–27.
British Psychological Society (BPS) (2000) *A Code of Conduct for Psychologists*. Leicester: BPS.

British Psychological Society (BPS) (2001) *A General Introduction to the Review of National Occupational Standards for Applied Psychology.* Leicester: BPS.

Campling, P., Davies, S. and Farquhason, G. (eds) (2004) *From 'Toxic Institutions to Therapeutic Environments.* London: Gaskell/Royal College of Psychiatrists.

Deber, R. B. (2003) *Delivering Health Care Services: Public, Not-for-profit or Private?* Ottawa: Commission on the Future of Health Care in Canada.

Department of Health (1999a) *Modernising the NHS Pay System.* London: Department of Health.

Department of Health (1999b) *National Service Framework for Mental Health.* London: Department of Health.

Department of Health (1999c) *Working Together: Securing a Quality Workforce for the NHS.* London: Department of Health.

Department of Health (2000) *The NHS Plan.* London: Department of Health.

Department of Health (2001a) *Shifting the Balance of Power.* London: Department of Health.

Department of Health (2001b) *Treatment Choice in Psychological Therapies and Counselling.* London: Department of Health.

Department of Health (2002a) *Mental Health Policy Implementation Guide: Adult Acute Inpatient Care.* London: Department of Health.

Department of Health (2002b) *NHS R & D Aims and Objectives.* London: Department of Health.

Department of Health (2003a) *Establishing the New Health Professions Council.* London: Department of Health.

Department of Health (2003b) *Fast-forwarding Primary Care Mental Health.* London: Department of Health.

Department of Health (2003c) *Knowledge and Skills and Development Review: Working Draft – Version 6.* London: Department of Health.

Department of Health (2004a) *Organising and Delivering Psychological Therapies.* London: Department of Health.

Department of Health (2004b) *The NHS Improvement Plan: Putting People at the Heart of Public Services.* London: Department of Health.

Department of Health (2004c) *Standards for Better Health.* London: Department of Health.

Department of Health (2005a) *Creating a Patient-led NHS – Delivering the NHS Improvement Plan.* London: Department of Health

Department of Health (2005b) *Health Reform in England: Update and Next Steps.* Leeds: Department of Health.

Department of Health (2005c) *New Ways of Working for Psychiatrists: Enhancing Effective, Person-centred Services Through New Ways of Working in Multidisciplinary and Multiagency Working.* London: Department of Health.

Division of Clinical Psychology (DCP) (1998a) *Briefing Paper 16: Services to Black and Minority Ethnic People.* Leicester: British Psychological Society.

Division of Clinical Psychology (DCP) (1998b) *Briefing Paper 14: Clinical Psychology in Substance Misuse Services.* Leicester: British Psychological Society.

Division of Clinical Psychology (DCP) (1998c) *Guidelines for Clinical Psychology Services.* Leicester: British Psychological Society.

Division of Clinical Psychology (DCP) (1999) *Briefing Paper 15: Clinical Psychology in Primary Care.* Leicester: British Psychological Society.

Division of Clinical Psychology (DCP) (2000) *Recent Advances in Understanding Mental Illness and Psychotic Experience*. Leicester: British Psychological Society.

Division of Clinical Psychology (DCP) (2001a) *DCP Guidelines for CPD*. Leicester: British Psychological Society.

Division of Clinical Psychology (DCP) (2001b) *Expanding Clinical Psychology Training to Achieve the National Plan Workforce Requirements: Options for Innovation and Development*. Leicester: British Psychological Society.

Division of Clinical Psychology (DCP) (2001c) *The Core Purpose and Philosophy of the Profession*. Leicester: British Psychological Society.

Division of Clinical Psychology (DCP) (2001d) *Working in Teams*. Leicester: British Psychological Society.

Division of Clinical Psychology (DCP) (2002a) *Briefing Paper 18: Clinical Psychology in Services for People with Severe and Enduring Mental Illness*. Leicester: British Psychological Society.

Division of Clinical Psychology (DCP) (2002b) *Briefing Paper 17: Clinical Psychology Services in HIV and Sexual Health*. Leicester: British Psychological Society.

Division of Clinical Psychology (DCP) (2003a) *A Guide to DCP Publications*. Leicester: British Psychological Society.

Division of Clinical Psychology (DCP) (2003b) *DCP Managers Faculty: Skill Mix Survey 2002 and 2003*. Leicester: British Psychological Society.

Division of Clinical Psychology (DCP) (2003c) *Guidance for NHS Psychologists on Clinical Governance*. Leicester: British Psychological Society.

Division of Clinical Psychology (DCP) (2003d) *Policy and Guidelines on Supervision in the Practice of Clinical Psychology*. Leicester: British Psychological Society.

Division of Clinical Psychology (DCP) (2004a) *The English Survey of Applied Psychology*. Leicester: British Psychological Society.

Division of Clinical Psychology (DCP) (2004b) *Widening Access Within Undergraduate Education and its Implication for Professional Psychology: Gender, Disability and Ethnic Diversity*. Leicester: British Psychological Society.

Fielding, D. (2004) Widening our research base. *The Psychologist*, 17(5), 272–273.

Hall, J. and Parry, G. (1988) *Key Tasks of Clinical Psychology Services, Manpower Planning Group Project on Clinical Psychology Services, Manpower and Training Issues*. Leicester: British Psychological Society.

Hewson, S. and White, R. (2004) Win–win organisation for psychology services: why service managers really need the professional group. *Clinical Psychology Forum*, 34, 11–14.

Holmes, J. (2002) Creating a psycho-therapeutic culture in acute psychiatric wards. *Psychiatric Bulletin*, 26, 383–385.

Jones, A. (1994) Research in clinical psychology: one trial aversion learning. *Clinical Psychology Forum*, 66, 13–15.

Kennedy, I. (2001) *Learning from Bristol: The Report of the Public Inquiry into Children's' Heart Surgery at the Bristol Royal Infirmary 1984–1995* (CM 5207).

Kinderman, P. (2001) The future of clinical psychology. *Clinical Psychology*, 8, 6–10.

Klein, R. (1995) *The New Politics of the NHS*, 3rd edn. London: Longman.

Layard, R. (2004) Mental Health: Britain's Biggest Social Problem? Online. Available: http://www.strategy.gov.uk/downloads/files/mh_layard.pdf

Lindsay, G. (2004) Public consultation begins. *The Psychologist*, 17(7), 372.

Linehan, M. M. (1993) *Cognitive-behavioural Treatment of Borderline Personality Disorders*. New York: Guilford Press.

Lunt, I. (2004) *The Implications of Developments in Mainland Europe for Education and Training Practice*. Paper presented at BPS Professional Practice Board Conference 'Shaping the Future of Applied Psychology', 27th February: London.

Maloney, P. and Kelly, P. (2004). Beck never lived in Birmingham: why CBT may be a less useful treatment for psychological distress than is often supposed. *Clinical Psychology Forum*, 34, 4–10.

Management Advisory Service (MAS) (1989) *Review of Clinical Psychology Services*. Cheltenham: MAS.

Management Advisory Service (MAS) (2003) *The Development of a Role of Associate Clinical Psychologist: A Feasibility Study*. Cheltenham: MAS.

Manpower Planning Advisory Group (MPAG) (1990) *Clinical Psychology Project: Summary Report*. London: Department of Health.

National Institute for Mental Health (England) (NIMHE) (2003) *Personality Disorder: No Longer a Diagnosis of Exclusion*. London: NIMHE.

NHS Confederation (2003) *New GMS Contract 2003. Investing in General Practice*. London: The NHS Confederation.

NHS Modernisation Agency (2001) *Improvement Leaders Guide to Involving Patients and Carers*. London: Department of Health.

O'Loughlin, S., Evans, J. and Sherwood, J. (2004) Providing an anger management service through psycho-educational classes – and avoiding therapy. *Clinical Psychology*, 33, 17–20.

Papworth, M. A. (2000) Primary care psychology: towards a model of service delivery. *Clinical Psychology Forum*, 142, 22–26.

Pilgrim, D. (2005) A case for psychologists becoming clinical supervisors. *Clinical Psychology Forum*, 155, 4–7.

Plumridge, N. (2004) Acute little idea. *Health Services Journal*, 8th July, p 27.

Rose, D. (2001) *Users' Voices: The Perspective of Mental Health Service Users on Community and Hospital Care*. London: Sainsbury Centre for Mental Health.

Royal Liverpool Hospital Enquiry (2001) *The Report of the Royal Liverpool Children's Enquiry*. Liverpool: Department of Health.

Ryan-Morgan, T., Scott-Lawson, A., Godfrey, J. and Thornton, G. (2004) The establishment and audit of a brief intervention service in primary care. *Clinical Psychology Forum*, 37, 19–22.

Sainsbury Centre for Mental Health (SCMH) (1998) *Acute Problems: A Survey of the Quality of Care on Acute Psychiatric Wards*. London: SCMH.

Sainsbury Centre for Mental Health (SCMH) (2001) *Capable Practitioner Framework*. London: SCMH.

Sainsbury Centre for Mental Health (SCMH) (2002) *Breaking the Circles of Fear (Briefing 17)*. London: SCMH.

Sainsbury Centre for Mental Health (SCMH) (2005) *The Future of Mental Health: A Vision for 2015*. London: SCMH.

Saks, M. (1995) *Professions and the Public Interest: Medical Power, Altruism and Alternative Medicine*. London: Routledge.

Smail, D. (1995) Power and the origins of unhappiness: Working with individuals. *Journal of Community and Applied Social Psychology*, 5, 347–356.

Social Exclusion Unit (2004) *Report: Mental Health and Social Exclusion*. London: Office of the Deputy Prime Minister.

Soffe, J. (2004) Clinical psychology and service user involvement: Our business? *Clinical Psychology Forum*, 37, 15–18.

Sperlinger, D. (2001) *Paper 1. Outcome Assessment in Routine Clinical Practice in Psychosocial Services*. Leicester: British Psychological Society.

Sperlinger, D. (2003). *Paper 2. Measuring Treatment Outcomes with Drug Misuse Clients*. Leicester: British Psychological Society.

Whittington, A., Golding, L., Fraise, J. and Geraghty, R. (2004) The statement of equivalence in clinical psychology: problems and proposals. *Clinical Psychology Forum*, 41, 10–16.

Wisely, J. (2004). CONTACT: Meeting the professional development needs of recently qualified clinical psychologists in the North West of England. *Clinical Psychology*, 36, 32–34.

Index

The term cognitive behavioural therapy is denoted by the abbreviation CBT
Page references to figures and tables appear in **bold type**
Page entries for headings which also have subheadings refer only to general aspects of that topic

THE PAPERS OF

THOMAS JEFFERSON

JAMES P. McCLURE, EDITOR

ELAINE WEBER PASCU, SENIOR ASSOCIATE EDITOR

TOM DOWNEY, MARTHA J. KING &

W. BLAND WHITLEY, ASSOCIATE EDITORS

ANDREW J. B. FAGAL & MERRY ELLEN SCOFIELD, ASSISTANT EDITORS

LINDA MONACO, EDITORIAL ASSISTANT

JOHN E. LITTLE, RESEARCH ASSOCIATE

42

November 1803 to March 1804

PRINCETON UNIVERSITY PRESS

THE PAPERS OF
Thomas Jefferson
VOLUME 42
16 November 1803–10 March 1804

EDITED BY JAMES P. MCCLURE

Confessing that he may be acting "with more boldness than wisdom," Jefferson in November 1803 drafts a bill to create Orleans Territory. Cautioning "never let any person know that I have put pen to paper on the subject," he entrusts the bill to John Breckinridge for introduction in the Senate. The administration prepares and sends stock certificates to France in payment for Louisiana. Relieved that affairs in the Mediterranean have improved with the evaporation of a threat of war with Morocco, the president does not know yet that Tripoli has captured the frigate *Philadelphia* with its officers and crew. He deals with never-ending issues of appointment to office and quarreling within his own party, while hearing that some Federalists are "as Bitter as wormwood." He shares seeds of the Venus flytrap with Elizabeth Leathes Merry, the wife of the British minister. She and her husband, however, create a diplomatic storm over seating arrangements at dinner parties. Having reached St. Louis, Meriwether Lewis reports on the progress of the western expedition. Congress passes the Twelfth Amendment, which if ratified by the states will provide for the separate election of president and vice president. In detailed notes made after Aaron Burr calls on him in January, Jefferson records his longstanding distrust of the New Yorker. Less than a month later, a congressional caucus nominates Jefferson for a second term, with George Clinton to replace Burr as vice president. Jefferson makes his first trials of the "double penned writing box" called the polygraph.

James P. McClure, senior research historian at Princeton University, is general editor of The Papers of Thomas Jefferson.